Fodor's 97

Italy

" "When it comes to information on regional history, what to see and do, and shopping, these guides are exhaustive."

—*USAir Magazine*

"Usable, sophisticated restaurant coverage, with an emphasis on good value."

—Andy Birsh, *Gourmet Magazine* columnist

"Valuable because of their comprehensiveness."

—*Minneapolis Star-Tribune*

"Fodor's always delivers high quality...thoughtfully presented...thorough."

—*Houston Post*

"An excellent choice for those who want everything under one cover."

—*Washington Post* "

AT & T

Italy 172 1011

France 0800 99 0011

Fodor's Travel Publications, Inc.
New York • Toronto • London • Sydney • Auckland
http://www.fodors.com/

Fodor's Italy '97

Editor: Fionn Davenport

Editorial Contributors: Steven Amsterdam, Robert Andrews, Barbara Walsh Angelillo, Barbara Lazear Ascher, Judy Blumenberg, Sheila Brownlee, Giuliano Davenport, Roderick Conway Morris, Mary Ellen Schultz, M. T. Schwartzman, Dinah Spritzer, George Sullivan

Creative Director: Fabrizio La Rocca

Associate Art Director: Guido Caroti

Photo Researcher: Jolie Novak

Cartographer: David Lindroth

Cover Photograph: Peter Gutman

Text Design: Between the Covers

Copyright

Special Sales

Fodor's Travel Publications are available at special discounts for bulk purchases for sales promotions or premiums. Special editions, including personalized covers, excerpts of existing guides, and corporate imprints, can be created in large quantities for special needs. For more information, contact your local bookseller or write to Special Markets, Fodor's Travel Publications, 201 E. 50th Street, New York, NY 10022. Inquiries from Canada should be directed to your local Canadian bookseller or sent to Random House of Canada, Ltd., Marketing Department, 1265 Aerowood Drive, Mississauga, Ontario L4W 1B9. Inquiries from the United Kingdom should be sent to Fodor's Travel Publications, 20 Vauxhall Bridge Road, London SW1V 2SA, England.

PRINTED IN THE UNITED STATES OF AMERICA

10 9 8 7 6 5 4 3 2 1

CONTENTS

Maps

ON THE ROAD WITH FODOR'S

WE'RE ALWAYS THRILLED to get letters from readers, especially one like this:

It took us an hour to decide what book to buy and we now know we picked the best one. Your book was wonderful, easy to follow, very accurate, and good on pointing out eating places, informal as well as formal. When we saw other people using your book, we would look at each other and smile.

Our editors and writers are deeply committed to making every Fodor's guide "the best one"—not only accurate but always charming, brimming with sound recommendations and solid ideas, right on the mark in describing restaurants and hotels, and full of fascinating facts that make you view what you've traveled to see in a rich new light.

About Our Writers

Amid the shops along Rome's Via Condotti, inside the trattorias of Trieste, and at the latest art exhibitions in Venice, you'll find Barbara Walsh Angelillo, Robert Andrews, and Giuliano Davenport studying the sights and looking for all the world like undercover agents. They won't be searching for signs of foul play, but rather for signs of excellence, innovation, and expertise. Their purpose: To track down the best of Italy—and eliminate the worst—to help our readers enjoy the trip of a lifetime.

The first time that **Barbara Walsh Angelillo** arrived in Rome, she was traveling on a tight schedule; still, she had time to fall in love with both the city and a dark-eyed Italian—simultaneously. Well aware that this was one of the hazards of touring Italy, she kept to her schedule and left Rome after only three days. Within a year, however, Barbara said *arrivederci* to her native New York City to settle, marry, and raise three children in Italy. As a freelance travel writer and editor, she loves to share her expertise about Italy with readers, and she has been doing so—mostly covering the regions of Rome, Florence, Tuscany, Liguria, and Piedmont—for Fodor's for more than 30 years. She also

is associate editor of the glossy, bimonthly, English-language magazine, *Italy Italy*, which is published in Rome and distributed in the United States and elsewhere. To unwind, Barbara vacations in what she calls "two of Italy's most special places," Umbria and the Amalfi Coast.

The history, art, and architecture of European cities have been freelance writer **George Sullivan's** favorite subject since he spent a college summer in London many years ago. Having authored our exploring tour of Florence, he is currently working on an architectural guidebook on Rome. He now knows the city so well he's on a first-name basis with its entire population of stray cats.

Robert Andrews has familial roots in Sicily and has been wedded to Italy (the south of the country in particular) for most of his life. Though based in Bristol, England, where he pursues a parallel career as an anthologist of quotations, Robert visits the old boot annually and leaves ever more perplexed and exhilarated. In addition to covering Emilia–Romagna Umbria, Campania, Apulia, Sicily, and Sardinia for us, he has written for many publications and coauthored books on Sardinia and Sicily.

Although he was born in Ireland, **Giuliano Davenport** gives away his Italian roots at the mere mention of his name. From his base in Dublin (where he works as a tour guide and is training to be an architect), he has covered much of the north for us—Venice, The Venetian Arc, The Dolomites, and Milan, Lombardy, and the Lakes—all the while visiting friends and family that are scattered throughout the peninsula.

Editor **Fionn Davenport** has, like his brother Giuliano, mixed Irish–Italian roots. His love affair with Italy has been a lifelong passion, and from his small apartment on New York's Lower East Side he dreams of owning a rustic cottage on a hill overlooking the sun-warmed vineyards and olive groves of the Tuscan countryside. Art and architecture *do* make Italy beautiful, but he reserves his greatest affections for the Italians themselves: In the words of E.M.

Forster, Fionn advises travelers not to "go with that awful idea that Italy's only a museum of antiquities and art. Love and understand the Italians, for the people are more marvelous than the land."

New This Year

A New Design

This year we've reformatted our guides to make them easier to use. Each chapter of *Italy '97* begins with brand-new recommended itineraries to help you decide what to see in the time you have; a section called When to Tour points out the optimal time of day, day of the week, and season for your journey. You may also notice our fresh graphics, new in 1996. More readable and more helpful than ever? We think so—and we hope you do, too.

On the Web

Also check out Fodor's Web site (http://www.fodors.com), where you'll find travel information on major destinations around the world and an ever-changing rray of travel-savvy interactive features.

How to Use This Book

Organization

Up front is the **Gold Guide.** Its first section, **Important Contacts A to Z,** gives addresses and telephone numbers of organizations and companies that offer destination-related services and detailed information and publications. **Smart Travel Tips A to Z,** the Gold Guide's second section, gives specific information on how to accomplish what you need to in Italy as well as tips on savvy traveling. Both sections are in alphabetical order by topic.

Chapters in *Italy '97* are arranged in order of tourist interest. Rome, the hub of all visits to Italy, comes first, followed by Italy's other quintessential crowd-puller, Florence. Venice, perhaps the most beautiful city in the world, follows after Tuscany, Florence's pastoral hinterland. Each city chapter begins with an Exploring section, which is subdivided by neighborhood; each subsection recommends a walking or driving tour and lists sights in alphabetical order. Each regional chapter is divided by geographical area; within each area, towns are covered in logical geographical order, and attractive stretches of road and

minor points of interest between them are indicated by the designation *En Route.* Throughout, Off the Beaten Path sights appear after the places from which they are most easily accessible. And within town sections, all restaurants and lodgings are grouped together.

To help you decide what to visit in the time you have, all chapters begin with recommended itineraries; you can mix and match those from several chapters to create a complete vacation. The A to Z section that ends all chapters covers getting there, getting around, and helpful contacts and resources.

Icons and Symbols

★   Our special recommendations

✕   Restaurant

🏨   Lodging establishment

✕🏨   Lodging establishment whose restaurant warrants a detour

🐤   Rubber duckie (good for kids)

☞   Sends you to another section of the guide for more info

✉   Address

☎   Telephone number

FAX   Fax number

🕐   Opening and closing times

💷   Admission prices (those we give apply only to adults; substantially reduced fees are almost always available for children, students, and senior citizens)

Numbers in white and black circles—② and ❷, for example—that appear on the maps, in the margins, and within the tours correspond to one another.

Dining and Lodging

The restaurants and lodgings we list are the cream of the crop in each price range. Price charts appear in the Pleasures and Pastimes section that follows each chapter introduction.

Hotel Facilities

We always list the facilities that are available—but we don't specify whether they cost extra: When pricing accommodations, always ask what's included.

Assume that hotels operate on the **European Plan** (EP, with no meals) unless we note that they use the **Full American Plan** (FAP, with all meals), the **Modified American Plan** (MAP, with breakfast and dinner daily), or the **Continental Plan** (CP, with a Continental breakfast daily).

Restaurant Reservations and Dress Codes

Reservations are always a good idea; we note only when they're essential or when they are not accepted. Book as far ahead as you can, and reconfirm when you get to town. Unless otherwise noted, the restaurants listed are open daily for lunch and dinner. We mention dress only when men are required to wear a jacket or a jacket and tie. Look for an overview of local habits under Dining in Smart Travel Tips A to Z and in the Pleasures and Pastimes section that follows each chapter introduction.

Credit Cards

The following abbreviations are used: **AE**, American Express; **DC**, Diners Club; **MC**, MasterCard; and **V**, Visa.

Don't Forget to Write

You can use this book in the confidence that all prices and opening times are based on information supplied to us at press time; Fodor's cannot accept responsibility for any errors. Time inevitably brings changes, so always confirm information when it matters—especially if you're making a detour to visit a specific place. In addition, when making reservations be sure to mention if you have a disability or are traveling with children, if you prefer a private bath or a certain type of bed, or if you have specific dietary needs or any other concerns.

Were the restaurants we recommended as described? Did our hotel picks exceed your expectations? Did you find a museum we recommended a waste of time? If you have complaints, we'll look into them and revise our entries when the facts warrant it. If you've discovered a special place that we haven't included, we'll pass the information along to our correspondents and have them check it out. So send your feedback, positive *and* negative, to the Italy Editor at 201 East 50th Street, New York, New York 10022—and have a wonderful trip!

Karen Cure

Karen Cure
Editorial Director

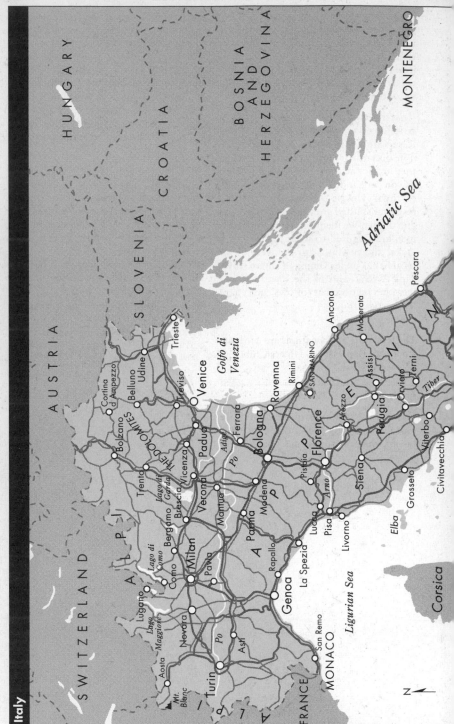

Italy

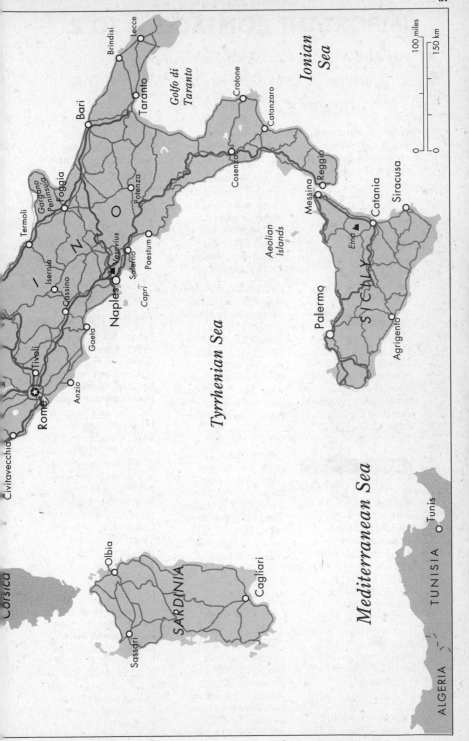

IMPORTANT CONTACTS A TO Z

An Alphabetical Listing of Publications, Organizations, & Companies that Will Help You Before, During, & After Your Trip

THE GOLD GUIDE / IMPORTANT CONTACTS

No single travel resource can give you every detail about every topic that might interest or concern you at the various stages of your journey—when you're planning your trip, while you're on the road, and after you get back home. The following organizations, books, and brochures will supplement the information in Fodor's *Italy '97.* For related information, including both basic tips on visiting Italy and background information on many of the topics below, study the second section of the gold pages, Smart Travel Tips A to Z.

A

AIR TRAVEL

The major gateways to Italy include Rome's **Leonardo da Vinci Airport,** better known as Fiumicino after its location (☎ 011–39–6/659–53640), and Milan's **Malpensa Airport** (☎ 011–39–2/380–11172). Flying time is 8½ hours from New York, 10–11 hours from Chicago, and 12–13 hours from Los Angeles.

CARRIERS

Carriers serving Italy include **Alitalia** (☎ 800/223–5730), **American Airlines** (800/624–6262), **Continental** (☎ 800/525–0280), **Delta** (☎ 800/241–4141),

TWA (☎ 800/892–4141), and **United** (☎ 800/241–6652).

Flying into **Rome** are Alitalia, Continental, Delta, and TWA; for flights to **Milan,** call Alitalia, Continental, Delta, TWA, and United. Into **Venice,** contact Alitalia.

FROM THE U.K.➤ Direct service from Heathrow is provided by **Alitalia** (☎ 0171/602–7111; outside London, 0345/212–121) and **British Airways** (☎ 0181/897–4000; outside London, 0345/222–111). Flying time to Rome is two hours. Service is also available to Milan, Venice, Pisa, Turin, Genoa, Bologna, Florence, and Naples. From Manchester there are one or two direct flights daily to Rome and Milan. **Meridiana** (☎ 0171/839–2222) has direct flights between London and Olbia in Sardinia on Friday and Saturday during summer.

COMPLAINTS

To register complaints about charter and scheduled airlines, contact the U.S. Department of Transportation's **Aviation Consumer Protection Division** (✉ C-75, Washington, DC 20590, ☎ 202/366–2220). Complaints about lost baggage or ticketing problems and safety concerns may

also be lodged with the **Federal Aviation Administration (FAA) Consumer Hotline** (☎ 800/322–7873).

CONSOLIDATORS

For services that will help you find the lowest airfares, *see* Discounts, *below.*

DISCOUNT PASSES

See Discounts, *below.*

PUBLICATIONS

For general information about charter carriers, ask for the Department of Transportation's free brochure **"Plane Talk: Public Charter Flights"** (✉ Aviation Consumer Protection Division, C-75, Washington, DC 20590, ☎ 202/366–2220). The Department of Transportation also publishes a 58-page booklet, **"Fly Rights,"** available from the Consumer Information Center (✉ Supt. of Documents, Dept. 136C, Pueblo, CO 81009; $1.75).

For other tips and hints, consult the Consumers Union's monthly **"Consumer Reports Travel Letter"** (✉ Box 53629, Boulder, CO 80322, ☎ 800/234–1970; $39 1st year) and the newsletter **"Travel Smart"** (✉ 40 Beechdale Rd., Dobbs Ferry, NY 10522, ☎ 800/327–3633; $37 per year).

Some worthwhile publications on the subject are **The Official**

Frequent Flyer Guidebook, by Randy Petersen (✉ Airpress, 4715-C Town Center Dr., Colorado Springs, CO 80916, ☎ 719/597–8899 or 800/487–8893; $14.99 plus $3 shipping); *Airfare Secrets Exposed,* by Sharon Tyler and Matthew Wunder (✉ Studio 4 Productions, Box 280400, Northridge, CA 91328, ☎ 818/700–2522 or 800/408–7369; $16.95 plus $2.50 shipping); *202 Tips Even the Best Business Travelers May Not Know,* by Christopher McGinnis (✉ Irwin Professional Publishing, 1333 Burr Ridge Pkwy., Burr Ridge, IL 60521, ☎ 800/634–3966; $11 plus $3.25 shipping); and *Travel Rights,* by Charles Leocha (✉ World Leisure Corporation, 177 Paris St., Boston, MA 02128, ☎ 800/444–2524; $7.95 plus $3.95 shipping).

For information on how to avoid jet lag, there are two publications: *Jet Lag, A Pocket Guide to Modern Treatment* by Peter Casano M.D. (✉ MedEd Publications, Box 12415, Columbus, OH 43212, ☎ 614/488–9457; $5.95) and *How to Beat Jet Lag* (✉ Henry Holt, 115 W. 18th St., New York, NY 10011, ☎ 800/288-2131; $14.95).

Travelers who experience motion sickness or ear problems in flight should get the brochures **"Ears, Altitude, and Airplane Travel"** and **"What You Can Do for Dizziness & Motion Sickness"** from the American Academy of Otolaryngology (✉ 1 Prince St., Alexandria, VA 22314, ☎ 703/836–4444, FAX 703/683–5100, TTY 703/519–1585).

WITHIN ITALY

Alitalia (main Rome office, ☎ 06/65621 or 06/65628246; main Milan office, ☎ 02/62811) and its domestic affiliate **ATI,** in addition to smaller, privately run companies such as **Meridiana** (main Olbia office, ☎ 0789/4745057), complete an extensive network of internal flights in Italy. Ask your domestic or Italian travel agent about discounts, which include a 50% family reduction and up to 30% off certain night flights.

B

BETTER BUSINESS BUREAU

For local contacts in the hometown of a tour operator you may be considering, consult the **Council of Better Business Bureaus** (✉ 4200 Wilson Blvd., Suite 800, Arlington, VA 22203, ☎ 703/276–0100, FAX 703/525–8277).

BOAT TRAVEL

Ferries connect the mainland with all major islands. Car ferries operate to Sicily, Sardinia, Elba, Ponza, Capri Ischia, and other islands. **Tirrenia** (☎ 06/481–4779) operates ferries to Sicily and Sardinia. **Lauro** (☎ 081/552–2838) has hydrofoils and car ferries to Capri and Ischia. **Adriatica** (☎ 06/481–8341) connects Italy with Greece.

BUS TRAVEL

FROM THE U.K.

Eurolines (✉ 52 Grosvenor Gardens, London SW1W 0AU, ☎ 0171/730–8235 or 0171/730–3499; or contact any National Express agent) runs a weekly bus service to Rome that increases to three times a week between June and September.

WITHIN ITALY

Among the major Italian long-distance bus companies are **SITA** (✉ Viale Cadorna 105, Florence, ☎ 055/278611), which operates throughout the country; **Autostradale** (✉ Piazzale Castello 1, Milan, ☎ 02/801161), which serves much of northern Italy; and **Lazzi** (✉ Via Mercadante 2, Florence, ☎ 055/363041), which operates in Tuscany and central Italy. Bus information is available at local tourist offices and travel agencies.

C

CAR RENTAL

The major car-rental companies represented in Italy are **Avis** (☎ 800/331–1084; in Canada, 800/879–2847), **Budget** (☎ 800/527–0700; in the U.K., 0800/181181), **Hertz** (☎ 800/654–3001; in Canada, 800/263–0600; in the U.K., 0345/555888), and **National InterRent** (sometimes known as Europcar InterRent outside North America; ☎ 800/227–3876; in the U.K., 01345/222–525). **Maggiore** is one of Italy's largest car-rental companies (☎ 06/229–

1530). Rates in Rome begin at $54 a day and $237 a week for an economy car with unlimited mileage. This does not include tax on car rentals, which is 19%. Note that recent Italian legislation now permits certain rental wholesalers, such as Auto Europe (☞ *below*), to drop the VAT tax. Many companies impose mandatory theft insurance on all rentals. Coverage costs $10–$15 a day.

RENTAL WHOLESALERS

Contact **Auto Europe** (☎ 207/828–2525 or 800/223–5555), **Europe by Car** (☎ 800/223–1516; in CA, 800/252–9401), or the **Kemwel Group** (☎ 914/835–5555 or 800/678–0678).

THE CHANNEL TUNNEL

For information, contact **Le Shuttle** (in the U.S., ☎ 800/388–3876; in the U.K., 0990/353535), which transports cars, or **Eurostar** (in the U.S., ☎ 800/942–4866; in the U.K., 0345/881881), the high-speed train service between London (Waterloo) and Paris (Gare du Nord). Eurostar tickets are available in the U.K. through **Inter-City Europe,** the international wing of BritRail (⊠ Victoria Station, London, ☎ 0171/834–2345 or 0171/828–0892 for credit-card bookings), and in the United States through **Rail Europe** (☎ 800/942–4866) and **BritRail Travel** (☎ 800/677–8585).

CHILDREN & TRAVEL

FLYING

Look into **"Flying with Baby"** (⊠ Third Street Press, Box 261250, Littleton, CO 80163, ☎ 303/595–5959; $4.95 includes shipping), cowritten by a flight attendant. **"Kids and Teens in Flight,"** free from the U.S. Department of Transportation (⊠ Aviation Consumer Protection Division, C-75, Washington, DC 20590, ☎ 202/366–2220), offers tips on children flying alone. Every two years the February issue of *Family Travel Times* (☞ Know-How, *below*) details children's services on three dozen airlines. **"Flying Alone, Handy Advice for Kids Traveling Solo"** is available free from the American Automobile Association (AAA); send a stamped, self-addressed, legal-size envelope (⊠ Flying Alone, Mail Stop 800, 1000 AAA Dr., Heathrow, FL 32746).

GAMES

Milton Bradley has games to help keep little (and not so little) children from fidgeting while in planes, trains, and automobiles. Try packing the Travel Battleship sea-battle game ($7); Travel Connect Four, a vertical strategy game ($8); the Travel Yahtzee dice game ($6); the Travel Trouble dice and board game ($7); and the Travel Guess Who mystery game ($8). Parker Brothers has travel versions of Clue!, Sorry, and Monopoly.

KNOW-HOW

Family Travel Times, published quarterly by Travel with Your Children (⊠ TWYCH, 40 5th Ave., New York, NY 10011, ☎ 212/477–5524; $40 per year), covers destinations, types of vacations, and modes of travel.

The *Family Travel Guides* catalog (⊠ Carousel Press, Box 6061, Albany, CA 94706, ☎ 510/527–5849; $1 postage) lists about 200 books and articles on traveling with children. Also check *Take Your Baby and Go! A Guide for Traveling with Babies, Toddlers and Young Children,* by Sheri Andrews, Judy Bordeaux, and Vivian Vasquez (⊠ Bear Creek Publications, 2507 Minor Ave. E, Seattle, WA 98102, ☎ 206/322–7604 or 800/326–6566; $5.95 plus $1.50 shipping).

LODGING

The Luxury Collection of **ITT-Sheraton Hotels** (☎ 800/221–2340) has more than 20 properties in Italy, all of which welcome families. Notable are the two on the Lido in Venice, which are right on the beach and have a park-like area for children to enjoy. **Club Med** (⊠ 40 W. 57th St., New York, NY 10019, ☎ 800/258–2633) has a "Mini Club" (for ages 4–9) and a "Kids Club" (for ages 10 and 11) at its ski village in Sestriere; there are also kids' programs at summer resort villages in Metaponto (Basilicata) and on the islands of

Sicily and Sardinia, marketed mainly to Europeans. Some of the **Valtur** vacation villages (⊠ Via Milano 42, Rome, ☎ 06/482–1000, ℻ 06/470–6334) also have special facilities and activities for children.

TOUR OPERATORS

Contact **Grandtravel** (⊠ 6900 Wisconsin Ave., Suite 706, Chevy Chase, MD 20815, ☎ 301/986–0790 or 800/247–7651), which has tours for people traveling with grandchildren ages 7–17; or **Families Welcome!** (⊠ 4711 Hope Valley Rd., Durham, NC 27707, ☎ 919/489–2555 or 800/326–0724).

If you're outdoorsy, look into family-oriented programs run by the **American Museum of Natural History** (⊠ 79th St. and Central Park West, New York, NY 10024, ☎ 212/769–5700 or 800/462–8687).

CUSTOMS

IN THE U.S.

The **U.S. Customs Service** (⊠ Box 7407, Washington, DC 20044, ☎ 202/927–6724) can answer questions on duty-free limits and publishes a helpful brochure, **"Know Before You Go."** For information on registering foreign-made articles, call 202/927–0540.

COMPLAINTS➤ Note the inspector's badge number and write to the commissioner's office (⊠ 1301 Constitution Ave. NW, Washington, DC 20229).

CANADIANS

Contact **Revenue Canada** (⊠ 2265 St. Laurent Blvd. S, Ottawa, Ontario K1G 4K3, ☎ 613/993–0534) for a copy of the free brochure **"I Declare/Je Déclare"** and for details on duty-free limits. For recorded information (within Canada only), call 800/461–9999.

U.K. CITIZENS

HM Customs and Excise (⊠ Dorset House, Stamford St., London SE1 9NG, ☎ 0171/202–4227) can answer questions about U.K. customs regulations and publishes a free pamphlet, **"A Guide for Travellers,"** detailing standard procedures and import rules.

D
DISABILITIES & ACCESSIBILITY

COMPLAINTS

To register complaints under the provisions of the Americans with Disabilities Act, contact the U.S. Department of Justice's **Disability Rights Section** (⊠ Box 66738, Washington, DC 20035, ☎ 202/514–0301 or 800/514–0301, ℻ 202/307–1198, TTY 202/514–0383 or 800/514–0383). For airline-related problems, contact the U.S. Department of Transportation's **Aviation Consumer Protection Division** (☞ Air Travel, *above*). For complaints about surface transportation, contact the Department of Transportation's **Civil Rights Office** (☎ 202/366–4648).

LOCAL INFORMATION

The Italian Government Travel Office (ENIT; ☞ Visitor Information, *below*) can provide a list of accessible hotels and with the addresses of Italian associations for travelers with disabilities.

ORGANIZATIONS

TRAVELERS WITH HEARING IMPAIRMENTS➤ The **American Academy of Otolaryngology** (⊠ 1 Prince St., Alexandria, VA 22314, ☎ 703/836–4444, ℻ 703/683–5100, TTY 703/519–1585) publishes a brochure, **"Travel Tips for Hearing Impaired People."**

TRAVELERS WITH MOBILITY IMPAIRMENTS➤ Contact the **Information Center for Individuals with Disabilities** (⊠ Box 256, Boston, MA 02117, ☎ 617/450–9888; in MA, 800/462–5015; TTY 617/424–6855); **Mobility International USA** (⊠ Box 10767, Eugene, OR 97440, ☎ and TTY 541/343–1284, ℻ 541/343–6812), the U.S. branch of a Belgium-based organization (☞ *below*) with affiliates in 30 countries; **MossRehab Hospital Travel Information Service** (☎ 215/456–9600, TTY 215/456–9602), a telephone information resource for travelers with physical disabilities; the **Society for the Advancement of Travel for the Handicapped** (⊠ 347 5th Ave., Suite 610, New York, NY 10016, ☎ 212/447–7284, ℻ 212/725–8253; membership $45); and **Travelin' Talk** (⊠ Box

THE GOLD GUIDE / IMPORTANT CONTACTS

3534, Clarksville, TN 37043, ☎ 615/552–6670, FAX 615/552–1182) which provides local contacts worldwide for travelers with disabilities.

TRAVELERS WITH VISION IMPAIRMENTS➤ Contact the **American Council of the Blind** (⊠ 1155 15th St. NW, Suite 720, Washington, DC 20005, ☎ 202/467–5081, FAX 202/467–5085) for a list of travelers' resources or the **American Foundation for the Blind** (⊠ 11 Penn Plaza, Suite 300, New York, NY 10001, ☎ 212/502–7600 or 800/232–5463, TTY 212/502–7662), which provides general advice and publishes **"Access to Art"** ($19.95), a directory of museums that accommodate travelers with vision impairments.

IN THE U.K.

Contact the **Royal Association for Disability and Rehabilitation** (⊠ RADAR, 12 City Forum, 250 City Rd., London EC1V 8AF, ☎ 0171/250–3222) or **Mobility International** (⊠ rue de Manchester 25, B-1080 Brussels, Belgium, ☎ 00–322–410–6297, FAX 00–322–410–6874), an international travel-information clearinghouse for people with disabilities.

PUBLICATIONS

Several publications for travelers with disabilities are available from the **Consumer Information Center** (⊠ Box 100, Pueblo, CO 81009, ☎ 719/948–3334). Call or write for its free catalog of current titles. The

Society for the Advancement of Travel for the Handicapped (☞ Organizations, *above*) publishes the quarterly magazine **"Access to Travel"** ($13 for 1-year subscription).

The 500-page *Travelin' Talk Directory* (⊠ Box 3534, Clarksville, TN 37043, ☎ 615/552–6670, FAX 615/552–1182; $35) lists people and organizations who help travelers with disabilities. For travel agents worldwide, consult the *Directory of Travel Agencies for the Disabled* (⊠ Twin Peaks Press, Box 129, Vancouver, WA 98666, ☎ 360/694–2462 or 800/637–2256, FAX 360/696–3210; $19.95 plus $3 shipping).

TRAVEL AGENCIES & TOUR OPERATORS

The Americans with Disabilities Act requires that all travel firms serve the needs of all travelers. That said, you should note that some agencies and operators specialize in making travel arrangements for individuals and groups with disabilities, among them **Access Adventures** (⊠ 206 Chestnut Ridge Rd., Rochester, NY 14624, ☎ 716/889–9096), run by a former physical-rehab counselor.

TRAVELERS WITH MOBILITY IMPAIRMENTS➤ Contact **Flying Wheels Travel** (⊠ 143 W. Bridge St., Box 382, Owatonna, MN 55060, ☎ 507/451–5005 or 800/535–6790), a travel agency specializing in European cruises and tours; **Hinsdale**

Travel Service (⊠ 201 E. Ogden Ave., Suite 100, Hinsdale, IL 60521, ☎ 708/325–1335), a travel agency that benefits from the advice of wheelchair traveler Janice Perkins; and **Wheelchair Journeys** (⊠ 16979 Redmond Way, Redmond, WA 98052, ☎ 206/885–2210 or 800/313–4751), which can handle arrangements worldwide.

TRAVELERS WITH DEVELOPMENTAL DISABILITIES➤ Contact the nonprofit **New Directions** (⊠ 5276 Hollister Ave., Suite 207, Santa Barbara, CA 93111, ☎ 805/967–2841).

TRAVEL GEAR

The **Magellan's** catalog (☎ 800/962–4943, FAX 805/568–5406), includes a range of products designed for travelers with disabilities.

DISCOUNTS & DEALS

AIRFARES

For the lowest airfares to Italy, call 800/FLY–4–LESS.

CLUBS

Contact **Entertainment Travel Editions** (⊠ Box 1068, Trumbull, CT 06611, ☎ 800/445–4137; $28–$53, depending on destination), **Great American Traveler** (⊠ Box 27965, Salt Lake City, UT 84127, ☎ 800/548–2812; $49.95 per year), **Moment's Notice Discount Travel Club** (⊠ 7301 New Utrecht Ave., Brooklyn, NY 11204, ☎ 718/234–6295; $25 per year, single or family), **Privilege Card** (⊠ 3391 Peachtree Rd.

NE, Suite 110, Atlanta, GA 30326, ☎ 404/262–0222 or 800/236–9732; $74.95 per year), **Travelers Advantage** (✉ CUC Travel Service, 49 Music Sq. W, Nashville, TN 37203, ☎ 800/548–1116 or 800/648–4037; $49 per year, single or family), or **Worldwide Discount Travel Club** (✉ 1674 Meridian Ave., Miami Beach, FL 33139, ☎ 305/534–2082; $50 per year for family, $40 single).

HOTEL ROOMS

For hotel room rates guaranteed in U.S. dollars, call **Steigenberger Reservation Service** (☎ 800/223–5652).

PASSES

See Train Travel, *below.*

PUBLICATIONS

Consult *The Frugal Globetrotter,* by Bruce Northam (✉ Fulcrum Publishing, 350 Indiana St., Suite 350, Golden, CO 80401, ☎ 800/992–2908; $15.95). For publications that tell how to find the lowest prices on plane tickets, *see* Air Travel, *above.*

STUDENTS

Members of Hostelling International–American Youth Hostels (☞ Students, *below*) are eligible for discounts on car rentals, admissions to attractions, and other selected travel expenses.

DRIVING

AUTO CLUBS

The main organization is the **Automobile Club of Italy** (✉ ACI, Via Marsala 8, 00185 Rome, ☎ 06/499–82389, FAX 06/499–

8234 with offices in cities throughout Italy).

To become a member of the AAA, call 800/564–6222. In the United Kingdom, contact the Automobile Association (AA) or the Royal Automobile Club (RAC).

BREAKDOWNS

ACI Emergency Service (✉ Servizio Soccorso Stradale, Via Solferino 32, 00185 Rome, ☎ 06/44595) offers 24-hour road service. Dial 116 from any phone, 24 hours a day, to reach the nearest ACI service station.

E
EMERGENCIES

Important emergency numbers in Italy are 112 for 24-hour access to Carabinieri (military police); 113 for Police; 115 for Fire; 116 for the Italian Automobile Club; 118 for medical emergency and ambulance (this number is not yet operational in all areas; alternatively call 113).

G
GAY & LESBIAN TRAVEL

ORGANIZATIONS

The national gay and lesbian association in Italy is **ARCIGAY** (✉ Via Acciaresi 7, 00157 Rome, ☎ 06/417–30752), which will provide information on events of interest to gays and lesbians.

The **International Gay Travel Association** (✉ Box 4974, Key West, FL 33041, ☎ 800/448–8550, FAX 305/296–6633), a consortium of

more than 1,000 travel companies, can supply names of gay-friendly travel agents, tour operators, and accommodations.

PUBLICATIONS

The 16-page monthly **"Out & About"** (☎ 212/645–6922 or 800/929–2268, FAX 800/929–2215; $49 for 10 issues and quarterly calendar) covers gay-friendly resorts, hotels, cruise lines, and airlines.

TOUR OPERATORS

Cruises and resort vacations for gays are handled by **R.S.V.P. Travel Productions** (✉ 2800 University Ave. SE, Minneapolis, MN 55414, ☎ 612/379–4697 or 800/328–7787). **Olivia** (✉ 4400 Market St., Oakland, CA 94608, ☎ 510/655–0364 or 800/631–6277) specializes in such bookings for lesbians. For mixed gay and lesbian travel, contact **Toto Tours** (✉ 1326 W. Albion Ave., Suite 3W, Chicago, IL 60626, ☎ 312/274–8686 or 800/565–1241, FAX 312/274–8695) which offers group tours to worldwide destinations.

TRAVEL AGENCIES

The largest agencies serving gay travelers are **Advance Travel** (✉ 10700 Northwest Fwy., Suite 160, Houston, TX 77092, ☎ 713/682–2002 or 800/292–0500), **Islanders/Kennedy Travel** (✉ 183 W. 10th St., New York, NY 10014, ☎ 212/242–3222 or 800/988–1181), **Now Voyager** (✉ 4406 18th St., San Francisco, CA 94114, ☎ 415/626–1169 or

THE GOLD GUIDE / IMPORTANT CONTACTS

800/255–6951), and **Yellowbrick Road** (✉ 1500 W. Balmoral Ave., Chicago, IL 60640, ☎ 312/561–1800 or 800/642–2488). **Skylink Women's Travel** (✉ 2460 W. 3rd St., Suite 215, Santa Rosa, CA 95401, ☎ 707/570–0105 or 800/225–5759) serves lesbian travelers.

H
HEALTH ISSUES

FINDING A DOCTOR

For its members, the **International Association for Medical Assistance to Travellers** (✉ IAMAT, membership free; 417 Center St., Lewiston, NY 14092, ☎ 716/754–4883; ✉ 40 Regal Rd., Guelph, Ontario N1K 1B5, ☎ 519/836–0102; ✉ 1287 St. Clair Ave., Toronto, Ontario M6E 1B8, ☎ 416/652–0137; ✉ 57 Voirets, 1212 Grand-Lancy, Geneva, Switzerland, no phone) publishes a worldwide directory of English-speaking physicians meeting IAMAT standards.

MEDICAL ASSISTANCE COMPANIES

The following companies are concerned primarily with emergency medical assistance, although they may provide some insurance as part of their coverage. For a list of full-service travel insurance companies, *see* Insurance, *below.*

Contact **International SOS Assistance** (✉ Box 11568, Philadelphia, PA 19116, ☎ 215/244–1500 or 800/523–

8930; ✉ Box 466, Pl. Bonaventure, Montréal, Québec H5A 1C1, ☎ 514/874–7674 or 800/363–0263; ✉ 7 Old Lodge Pl., St. Margarets, Twickenham TW1 1RQ, England, ☎ 0181/744–0033), **Medex Assistance Corporation** (✉ Box 5375, Timonium, MD 21094-5375, ☎ 410/453–6300 or 800/537–2029), **Traveler's Emergency Network** (✉ 3100 Tower Blvd., Suite 3100A, Durham, NC 27702, ☎ 919/490–6065 or 800/275–4836, FAX 919/493–8262), **TravMed** (✉ Box 5375, Timonium, MD 21094, ☎ 410/453–6380 or 800/732–5309), or **Worldwide Assistance Services** (✉ 1133 15th St. NW, Suite 400, Washington, DC 20005, ☎ 202/331–1609 or 800/821–2828, FAX 202/828–5896).

I
INSURANCE

IN CANADA

Contact **Mutual of Omaha** (✉ Travel Division, 500 University Ave., Toronto, Ontario M5G 1V8, ☎ 800/465–0267 (in Canada) or 416/598-4083).

IN THE U.S.

Travel insurance covering baggage, health, and trip cancellation or interruptions is available from **Access America** (✉ 6600 W. Broad St., Richmond, VA 23230, ☎ 804/285–3300 or 800/334–7525), **Carefree Travel Insurance** (✉ Box 9366, 100 Garden City Plaza, Garden City, NY 11530, ☎ 516/294–0220 or

800/323–3149), **Near Travel Services** (✉ Box 1339, Calumet City, IL 60409, ☎ 708/868–6700 or 800/654–6700), **Tele-Trip** (✉ Mutual of Omaha Plaza, Box 31716, Omaha, NE 68131, ☎ 800/228–9792), **Travel Guard International** (✉ 1145 Clark St., Stevens Point, WI 54481, ☎ 715/345–0505 or 800/826–1300), **Travel Insured International** (✉ Box 280568, East Hartford, CT 06128, ☎ 203/528–7663 or 800/243–3174), and **Wallach & Company** (✉ 107 W. Federal St., Box 480, Middleburg, VA 22117, ☎ 540/687–3166 or 800/237–6615).

IN THE U.K.

The **Association of British Insurers** (✉ 51 Gresham St., London EC2V 7HQ, England, ☎ 0171/600–3333) gives advice by phone and publishes the free pamphlet **"Holiday Insurance,"** which sets out typical policy provisions and costs.

L
LODGING

Options are numerous, from hotels to camping grounds to short-term rentals in city or country. Rural accommodations in the Agritourism category are increasingly popular with both Italians and tourists.

For information on hotel consolidators, *see* Discounts, *above.*

APARTMENT & VILLA RENTAL

Cuendet USA (✉ 165 Chestnut St., Allendale, NJ 07041, ☎ 201/327–2333; ✉ Suzanne T. Pidduck, c/o Rentals in

Italy, 1742 Calle Corva, Camarillo, CA 93010, ☎ 800/726–6702), the American representative of Cuendet of Italy, is one of the largest agencies offering apartment and villa rentals. Their color catalogue features myriad listings of farmhouses, villas, castles, and apartments in Tuscany, Umbria, and the Veneto. Another agency specializing in Italy is **Vacanze in Italia** (✉ 22 Railroad St., Great Barrington, MA 01230, ☎ 413/528–6610 or 800/533–5405).

Other companies to contact are **At Home Abroad** (✉ 405 E. 56th St., Suite 6H, New York, NY 10022, ☎ 212/421–9165, FAX 212/752–1591), **Europa-Let** (✉ 92 N. Main St., Ashland, OR 97520, ☎ 541/482–5806 or 800/462–4486, FAX 541/482–0660), **Hometours International** (✉ Box 11503, Knoxville, TN 37939, ☎ 423/588–8722 or 800/367–4668), **Interhome** (✉ 124 Little Falls Rd., Fairfield, NJ 07004, ☎ 201/882–6864, FAX 201/808–1742), **Property Rentals International** (✉ 1008 Mansfield Crossing Rd., Richmond, VA 23236, ☎ 804/378–6054 or 800/220–3332, FAX 804/379–2073), **Rental Directories International** (✉ 2044 Rittenhouse Sq., Philadelphia, PA 19103, ☎ 215/985–4001, FAX 215/985–0323), **Rent-a-Home International** (✉ 7200 34th Ave. NW, Seattle, WA 98117, ☎ 206/789–9377 or 800/488–7368, FAX 206/789–9379, hmari@aol.com),

Vacation Home Rentals Worldwide (✉ 235 Kensington Ave., Norwood, NJ 07648, ☎ 201/767–9393 or 800/633–3284, FAX 201/767–5510), **Villas and Apartments Abroad** (✉ 420 Madison Ave., Suite 1003, New York, NY 10017, ☎ 212/759–1025 or 800/433–3020, FAX 212/755–8316), or **Villas International** (✉ 605 Market St., Suite 510, San Francisco, CA 94105, ☎ 415/281–0910 or 800/221–2260, FAX 415/281–0919). Members of the travel club **Hideaways International** (✉ 767 Islington St., Portsmouth, NH 03801, ☎ 603/430–4433 or 800/843–4433, FAX 603/430–4444, info@hideaways.com; $99 per year) receive two annual guides plus quarterly newsletters and arrange rentals among themselves.

In the United Kingdom, book through **CV Travel** (✉ 43 Cadogan St., London SW3 2PR, England, ☎ 0171/581–0851) and **Magic of Italy** (✉ 227 Shepherds Bush Rd., London W6 7AS, England, ☎ 0181/748–7575).

CAMPING

You can obtain a directory of campgrounds in Italy by writing to the **Federazione Italiana del Campeggio e del Caravanning** (✉ Federcampeggio, Casella Postale 23, 50041 Calenzano, Florence, FAX 055/882–5918) and requesting *Campeggiare in Italia*; send three international reply coupons to cover mailing. (This directory is also available through

the ENIT office in the United States and at tourist information offices in Italy; ☞ Visitor Information, *below*). Camper rental agencies operate throughout Italy: Contact your travel agent for details.

FARM HOLIDAYS AND AGRITOURISM

Contact **Italy Farm Holidays** (✉ 547 Martling Ave., Tarrytown, NY 10591, ☎ 914/631–7880, FAX 914/631–8831). For information on Agritourism accommodations, contact **Agriturismo** (✉ Corso Vittorio 101, 00186 Rome, ☎ 06/68521), **Terra Nostra** (✉ Via XXIV Maggio 43, 00187 Rome, ☎ 06/46821), or **Turismo Verde** (✉ Via degli Scialoja 6, 00196 Rome, ☎ 06/320–03356).

HOME EXCHANGE

Some of the principal clearinghouses are **HomeLink International/Vacation Exchange Club** (✉ Box 650, Key West, FL 33041, ☎ 305/294–1448 or 800/638–3841, FAX 305/294–1148; $70 per year), which sends members three annual directories, with a listing in one, plus updates; and **Intervac International** (✉ Box 590504, San Francisco, CA 94159, ☎ 415/435–3497, FAX 415/435–7440; $65 per year), which publishes four annual directories.

HOTELS

Among the best-known chains operating in Italy are **ITT-Sheraton/The Luxury Collection** (✉ 745 5th Ave., New York, NY 10151, ☎

THE GOLD GUIDE / IMPORTANT CONTACTS

800/221–2340, FAX 212/421–5929), which has more than 20 Italian properties, almost all five-star deluxe; **Jolly** (⊠ 800/247–1277 in New York state, 800/221–2626 elsewhere, 800/237–0319 in Canada), with 32 four-star hotels in Italy; **Atahotels** (⊠ Via Lampedusa 11/A, 20141 Milano, ☎ 02/895261 or toll-free in Italy 1678/23013, FAX 02/8465568; some bookable through E&M Associates, ☎ 212/599–8280 or 800/223–9832), with 20 mostly four- and five-star hotels; and **Starhotels** (⊠ Via Belfiore 27, 50144 Florence, ☎ 055/36921, FAX 055/36924, or book through 800/448–8355), with 14 mainly four-star hotels. **Space Hotels** (toll-free in Italy ☎ 1678/13013; or book through Supranational, ☎ 416/927–1133 or 800/843–3311) has about 50 independently owned four- and five-star (some three-star) hotels. **Italhotels** (toll-free in Italy ☎ 1678/01004) also has about 50 independently owned four- and five-star hotels.

AGIP Motels (☎ 06/444–0183 reservations in Italy) is a chain of about 50, mostly four-star motels on main highways; the motels are commercial, functional digs for traveling salesmen and tourists needing forty winks, but they—and the Jolly hotels—can be the best choice in many out-of-the-way places). **The Forte** group has taken over some top-of-the-

line AGIP properties throughout Italy. **Best Western,** an international association of independently owned hotels, has some 75 mainly three- and four-star hotels in Italy (☎ 800/528–1234 for reservations or to request the *Europe and Middle East Atlas* that lists them).

Family Hotels (⊠ Via Faenza 77, 50123 Florence, Italy, ☎ 055/217975, FAX 055/238–1905), grouping about 75 independently owned, family-run two- and three-star hotels (some one-star), offers good value. For information in Italy, contact the address above (it's not a central booking service, however). A spin-off of this group, the **Sun Rays Pool** comprises three- and four-star hotels (information and reservations ☎ 055/462–0080).

Major cities have hotel-reservation service booths in train stations.

M
MONEY MATTERS

ATMS

For specific foreign **Cirrus** locations, call 800/424–7787; for foreign **Plus** locations, consult the Plus directory at your local bank.

CURRENCY EXCHANGE

If your bank doesn't exchange currency, contact **Thomas Cook Currency Services** (☎ 800/287–7362 for locations). **Ruesch International** (☎ 800/424–2923 for locations) can also provide you with foreign bank-

notes before you leave home and publishes a number of useful brochures, including a "Foreign Currency Guide" and "Foreign Exchange Tips."

WIRING FUNDS

Funds can be wired via **MoneyGram** (for locations and information in the U.S. and Canada, ☎ 800/926–9400) or **Western Union** (for agent locations or to send money using MasterCard or Visa, ☎ 800/325–6000; in Canada, 800/321–2923; in the U.K., 0800/833833; or visit the Western Union office at the nearest major post office).

P
PACKING

For strategies on packing light, get a copy of *The Packing Book,* by Judith Gilford (⊠ Ten Speed Press, Box 7123, Berkeley, CA 94707, ☎ 510/559–1600 or 800/841–2665, FAX 510/524–4588; $7.95).

PASSPORTS & VISAS

IN THE U.S.

For fees, documentation requirements, and other information, call the State Department's **Office of Passport Services** information line (☎ 202/647–0518).

CANADIANS

For fees, documentation requirements, and other information, call the Ministry of Foreign Affairs and International Trade's **Passport Office** (☎ 819/994–3500 or 800/567–6868).

U.K. CITIZENS

For fees, documentation requirements, and to request an emergency passport, call the **London Passport Office** (☎ 0990/210410).

The **Kodak Information Center** (☎ 800/242–2424) answers consumer questions about film and photography. The **Kodak Guide to Shooting Great Travel Pictures** (available in bookstores; or contact Fodor's Travel Publications, ☎ 800/533–6478; $16.50) explains how to take expert travel photographs.

S

"Trouble-Free Travel," from the AAA, is a booklet of tips for protecting yourself and your belongings when away from home. Send a stamped, self-addressed, legal-size envelope to Flying Alone (✉ Mail Stop 75, 1000 AAA Dr., Heathrow, FL 32746).

EDUCATIONAL TRAVEL

The nonprofit **Elderhostel** (✉ 75 Federal St., 3rd Floor, Boston, MA 02110, ☎ 617/426–7788), for people 60 and older, has offered inexpensive study programs since 1975. Courses cover everything from marine science to Greek mythology and cowboy poetry. Costs for two- to three-week international trips—including room, board, and transportation from the United States—range from $1,800 to $4,500.

For people 50 and over and their children and grandchildren, **Interhostel** (✉ University of New Hampshire, 6 Garrison Ave., Durham, NH 03824, ☎ 603/862–1147 or 800/733–9753) runs 10-day summer programs that feature lectures, field trips, and sightseeing. Most last two weeks and cost $2,125–$3,100, including airfare.

ORGANIZATIONS

Contact the **American Association of Retired Persons** (✉ AARP, 601 E St. NW, Washington, DC 20049, ☎ 202/434–2277; annual dues $8 per person or couple). Its Purchase Privilege Program secures discounts for members on lodging, car rentals, and sightseeing.

Additional sources for discounts on lodgings, car rentals, and other travel expenses, as well as helpful magazines and newsletters, are the **National Council of Senior Citizens** (✉ 1331 F St. NW, Washington, DC 20004, ☎ 202/347–8800; annual membership $12) and Sears's **Mature Outlook** (✉ Box 10448, Des Moines, IA 50306, ☎ 800/336–6330; annual membership $9.95).

PUBLICATIONS

The 50+ Traveler's Guidebook: Where to Go, Where to Stay, What to Do, by Anita Williams and Merrimac Dillon (✉ St. Martin's Press, 175 5th Ave., New York, NY 10010, ☎ 212/674–5151 or 800/288–2131; $13.95), offers many useful tips. **"The Mature Traveler"** (✉ Box 50400, Reno, NV 89513, ☎ 702/786–7419; $29.95), a monthly newsletter, covers all sorts of travel deals.

Cunard Line (555 5th Ave., New York, NY 10017, ☎ 212/880–7545 or 800/221–4770) operates the *Queen Elizabeth II (QE2)*, the only ocean liner that makes regular transatlantic crossings (Apr.–Dec., between New York City, NY, and Southampton, England). Other cruise lines whose ships are in Europe for the summer and the Caribbean for the winter make repositioning crossings (eastbound in spring and westbound in fall). Check the travel section of your newspaper or contact a travel agent for lines and sailing dates.

Italians are sports lovers, and there are several daily newspapers devoted solely to sports. The climate makes it almost impossible to resist the temptation to try a cannonball serve on the red-clay tennis courts, sink a birdie putt on a scenic green, or just hike up a hill to savor the fresh air and views. Winters, of course, see ski enthusiasts trying their luck on the slopes of the Apennines and the Alps (see regional chapters for recommended resorts).

BASKETBALL

Many Americans play on Italian pro teams, and basketball is gaining a big following around the country. For information, contact the **Federazione Italiana Pallacanestro** (✉ Via Fogliano 15, 00199 Rome, ☎ 06/886–3071).

CANOEING

The swift rivers rushing down the slopes of the Alps and the Apennines make for exciting canoeing. Kayak races are held in the Dolomites and on the Aniene River near Subiaco in Lazio. For information, get in touch with the **Federazione Italiana Canoa e Kayak** (✉ Viale Tiziano 70, 00196 Rome, ☎ 06/368–58525).

GOLF

Relatively new to Italy, golf is catching on. Contact the **Federazione Italiana Golf** (✉ Viale Tiziano 74, 00196 Rome, ☎ 06/36851).

HORSEBACK RIDING

For information on equestrian excursions, contact the **Associazione Nazionale per il Turismo Equestre** (✉ Via A. Borelli 5, 00161 Rome, ☎ 06/444–1179).

SAILING

It is especially popular on the major lakes, off the Ligurian Riviera, off northern Sardinia, and the coasts of Tuscany and Lazio. Contact the **Federazione Italiana Vela** (✉ Viale Brigata Bisagno 2, 16129 Genoa, ☎ 010/589431). Windsurfers should head for Lake Garda.

SOCCER

Calcio (soccer) is the most popular spectator sport in Italy. All major cities, and most smaller ones, have teams in one league or another. Big-league games are played on Sunday afternoons from September through May. Inquire locally or write to the **Federazione Italiana Giuoco Calcio** (✉ Via Gregorio Allegri 14, 00198 Rome, ☎ 06/84911).

TENNIS

A major international Grand Prix tennis tournament is held in Rome in May. Tennis court facilities are being added at a constant rate to Italian cities and towns; inquire when booking your hotel.

STUDENTS

GROUPS

The major tour operators specializing in student travel are **Contiki Holidays** (✉ 300 Plaza Alicante, Suite 900, Garden Grove, CA 92640, ☎ 714/740–0808 or 800/266–8454) and **AESU Travel** (✉ 2 Hamill Rd., Suite 248, Baltimore, MD 21210-1807, ☎ 410/323–4416 or 800/638–7640).

HOSTELING

In the United States, contact **Hostelling International–American Youth Hostels** (✉ 733 15th St. NW, Suite 840, Washington, DC 20005, ☎ 202/783–6161 or 800/444–6111 for reservations at selected hostels, FAX 202/783–6171); in Canada, **Hostelling International–Canada** (✉ 205 Catherine St., Suite 400, Ottawa, Ontario K2P 1C3, ☎ 613/237–7884); and in the United Kingdom, the **Youth Hostel Association of England and Wales** (✉ Trevelyan House, 8 St. Stephen's Hill, St. Albans, Hertfordshire AL1 2DY, ☎ 01727/855215 or 01727/845047). Membership (in the U.S., $25; in Canada, C$26.75; in the U.K., £9.30) gives you access to 5,000 hostels in 77 countries that charge $5–$30 per person per night.

I.D. CARDS

To be eligible for discounts on transportation and admissions, get either the **International Student Identity Card,** if you're a bona fide student, or the **GO 25: International Youth Travel Card,** if you're not a student but under age 26. Each includes basic travel-accident and illness coverage, plus a toll-free travel hot line. In the United States, either card costs $18; apply through the Council on International Educational Exchange (☞ Organizations, *below*). In Canada, cards are available for $15 each ($16 by mail) from Travel Cuts (☞ Organizations, *below*), and in the United Kingdom for £5 each at student unions and student travel companies.

ORGANIZATIONS

The **Centro Turistico Studentesco** (CTS) is a student and youth travel agency with offices in major Italian cities; CTS helps its clients find low-cost accommodations and bargain fares for travel in Italy and elsewhere and also serves as a meeting place for young people of all nations. The main Rome office is at Via Genova 16, near the railroad station (☎ 06/467–9271). CTS is also the Rome representative for **EuroTrain International.**

A major contact is the **Council on International Educational Exchange** (✉ mail orders only: CIEE, 205 E. 42nd St., 16th Floor, New York, NY 10017, ☎ 212/822–2600, info@ciee.org). The **Educational Travel Centre** (✉ 438 N. Frances St., Madison, WI 53703, ☎ 608/256–5551 or 800/747–5551, FAX 608/256–2042) offers rail passes and low-cost airline tickets, mostly for flights that depart from Chicago.

In Canada, also contact **Travel Cuts** (✉ 187 College St., Toronto, Ontario M5T 1P7, ☎ 416/979–2406 or 800/667–2887).

PUBLICATIONS

Check out the *Berkeley Guide to Italy* (available in bookstores; or contact Fodor's Travel Publications, ☎ 800/533–6478; $16.95).

T

TELEPHONE MATTERS

The country code for Italy is 39. For local access numbers abroad, contact **AT&T** USADirect (☎ 800/874–4000), **MCI** Call USA (☎ 800/444–4444), or **Sprint** Express (☎ 800/793–1153).

TOUR OPERATORS

Among the companies that sell tours and packages to Italy, the following are nationally known, have a proven reputation, and offer plenty of options.

GROUP TOURS

SUPER-DELUXE➤ **Abercrombie & Kent** (✉ 1520 Kensington Rd., Oak Brook, IL 60521-2141, ☎ 708/954–2944 or 800/323–7308, FAX 708/954–3324) and **Travcoa** (✉ Box 2630, 2350 S.E. Bristol St., Newport Beach, CA 92660, ☎ 714/476–2800 or 800/992–2003, FAX 714/476–2538).

DELUXE➤ **Globus** (✉ 5301 S. Federal Circle, Littleton, CO 80123-2980, ☎ 303/797–2800 or 800/221–0090, FAX 303/795–0962), **Maupintour** (✉ Box 807, 1515 St. Andrews Dr., Lawrence, KS 66047, ☎ 913/843–1211 or 800/255–4266, FAX 913/843–8351), and **Tauck Tours** (✉ Box 5027, 276 Post Rd. W, Westport, CT 06881, ☎ 203/226–6911 or 800/468–2825, FAX 203/221–6828). Specialists in Italy include **Central Holiday Tours** (✉ 206 Central Ave., Jersey City, NJ 07307, ☎ 201/798–5777 or 800/935–5000), **Donna Franca Tours** (✉ 470 Commonwealth Ave., Boston, MA 02215, ☎ 617/375–9400 or 800/225–6290, and **Perillo Tours** (✉ 577 Chestnut Ridge Rd., Woodcliff Lake, NJ 07675, ☎ 201/307–1234 or 800/431–1515).

FIRST CLASS➤ Try **Brendan Tours** (✉ 15137 Califa St., Van Nuys, CA 91411, ☎ 818/785–9696 or 800/421–8446, FAX 818/902–9876), **Caravan Tours** (✉ 401 N. Michigan Ave., Chicago, IL 60611, ☎ 312/321–9800 or 800/227–2826), **Collette Tours** (✉ 162 Middle St., Pawtucket, RI 02860, ☎ 401/728–3805 or 800/832–4656, FAX 401/728–1380), **Gadabout Tours** (✉ 700 E. Tahquitz Canyon Way, Palm Springs, CA 92262, ☎ 619/325–5556 or 800/952–5068), **Insight International Tours** (✉ 745 Atlantic Ave., #720, Boston, MA 02111, ☎ 617/482-2000 or 800/582–8380, FAX 617/482–2884 or 800/622–5015), and **Trafalgar Tours** (✉ 11 E. 26th St., New York, NY 10010, ☎ 212/689–8977 or 800/854–0103, FAX 800/457–6644).

BUDGET➤ **Cosmos** (☞ Globus, *above*).

PACKAGES

Independent vacation packages are available from **American Airlines Fly AAway Vacations** (☎ 800/321–2121), **Delta Dream Vacations** (☎ 800/872–7786), and **United Vacations** (☎ 800/328–6877). Many tour operators also sell independent packages to Italy. Contact **DER Tours** (✉ 11933 Wilshire Blvd., Los Angeles, CA 90025, ☎ 310/479–4140 or 800/782–2424), **4th Dimension Tours** (✉ 7101 S.W. 99th Ave., #105, Miami, FL 33173, ☎ 305/279–0014 or 800/877–1525, FAX 305/273–9777, http://www.4thdimension.com), and **Jet Vacations** (✉ 1775 Broadway, New York, NY 10019, ☎ 212/

474–8740 or 800/538–2762). **Funjet Vacations,** based in Milwaukee, Wisconsin, and **Gogo Tours,** based in Ramsey, New Jersey, sell packages only through travel agents.

FROM THE U.K.➤ **Italian Escapades** (✉ 227 Shepherds Bush Rd., London W6 7AS, ☎ 0181/748–2661) and **Page and Moy Holidays** (✉ 136–140 London Rd., Leicester LE2 1EN, England, ☎ 0116/250–7676) offer tours of historical sights. **Carefree Italy** (✉ 44 Central Parade, New Addington, Surrey CR0 0JD, England, ☎ 01689/841–900) offers accommodations in apartments, castles, and farmhouses.

THEME TRIPS

Travel Contacts (✉ Box 173, Camberley GU15 1YE, England, ☎ 011/44/1/27667–7217, FAX 011/44/1/2766–3477), which represents 150 tour operators, can satisfy virtually any special interest in Italy.

ADVENTURE➤ Contact **Adventure Center** (✉ 1311 63rd St., #200, Emeryville, CA 94608, ☎ 510/654–1879 or 800/227–8747, FAX 510/654–4200), **Himalayan Travel** (✉ 112 Prospect St., Stamford, CT 06901, ☎ 203/359–3711 or 800/225–2380, FAX 203/359–3669), **Mountain Travel-Sobek** (✉ 6420 Fairmount Ave., El Cerrito, CA 94530, ☎ 510/527–8100 or 800/227–2384, FAX 510/525–7710, Info@MTSobek.com, http://www.MTSobek.com), and **Uniquely Europe** (✉ 2819 1st Ave., #280, Seattle, WA

98121-1113, ☎ 206/441–8682 or 800/426–3615, FAX 206/441–8862).

ART AND ARCHITECTURE➤ For tours of southern Italy and Sicily, contact **Amelia Tours International** (✉ 260 N. Broadway, Hicksville, NY 11801, ☎ 516/433–0696 or 800/742–4591, FAX 516/579–1562) and **Archaeological Tours** (✉ 271 Madison Ave., New York, NY 10016, ☎ 212/986–3054). **Endless Beginnings Tours** (✉ 9825 Dowdy Dr., #105, San Diego, CA 92126, ☎ 619/566–4166 or 800/822–7855, FAX 619/549–9655) explores the art, culture, and natural environment of Italy.

BALLOONING➤ Contact **Buddy Bombard European Balloon Adventures** (✉ 855 Donald Ross Rd., Juno Beach, FL 33408, ☎ 407/775–0039 or 800/862–8537, FAX 407/775–7008).

BICYCLING➤ **Ciclismo Classico** (✉ 13 Marathon St., Arlington, MA 02174, ☎ 617/646–3377 or 800/866–7314, FAX 617/641–1512, info@ciclismoclassico.com) specializes in bicycle tours of Italy. Also try **Backroads** (✉ 1516 5th St., Berkeley, CA 94710-1740, ☎ 510/577–1555 or 800/462–2848, FAX 510/527–1444, goactive@Backroads.com), **Bike Riders** (✉ Box 254, Boston, MA 02113, ☎ 617/723–2354 or 800/473–7040), FAX 617/723–2355, bikeride@tiac.net, http://www.tiac.net/users/bikeride), **Butterfield & Robinson** (✉ 70 Bond St., Toronto, Ontario,

Canada M5B 1X3, ☎ 416/864–1354 or 800/678–1147, FAX 416/864–0541, info@butterfield.com), **Euro-Bike Tours** (✉ Box 990, De Kalb, IL 60115, ☎ 800/321–6060, FAX 815/758–8851), **Rocky Mountain Worldwide Cycle Tours** (✉ Box 1978, Canmore, Alberta, Canada TOL OMO, ☎ 403/678–6770 or 800/661–2453, FAX 403/678–4451, RMCT@CIA.COM, http://www.worldweb.com/rmct), and **Uniquely Europe** (✉ 2819 1st Ave., #280, Seattle, WA 98121-1113, ☎ 206/441–8682 or 800/426–3615, FAX 206/441–8862).

CRUISES➤ For all types and sizes of ships, call **EuroCruises** (✉ 303 W. 13th St., New York, NY 10014, ☎ 212/691–2099 or 800/688–3876).

FOOD AND WINE➤ For wine tours of Sicily, contact **Amelia Tours** (☞ Art and Architecture, *above*). For a culinary adventure, try **Annemarie Victory Organization** (✉ 136 E. 64th St., New York, NY 10021, ☎ 212/486–0353, FAX 212/751–3149, CuisineInt@aol.com). **Cuisine International** (✉ Box 25228, Dallas, TX 75225, ☎ 214/373–1161, FAX 214/373–1162) has weeklong Italian cooking programs hosted by expert chefs in Tuscany, Amalfi, Positano, Venice, Puglia, Sicily, and Umbria. **Donna Franca Tours** (☞ Group Tours, *above*) has a cooking program in Venice. **Hazan Classicas** (✉ Box 285, Circleville,

NY 10919, ☎ 914/692-7104, FAX 914/692-2659) offers master classes in Italian food and wine, which are held at a 16th-century Venetian palazzo.

GOLF➤ **ITC Golf Tours** (✉ 4134 Atlantic Ave., #205, Long Beach, CA 90807, ☎ 310/595-6905 or 800/257-4981) arranges customized itineraries.

HISTORY➤ History buffs should look into **Herodot Travel** (✉ 775 E. Blithedale, Box 234, Mill Valley, CA 94941, ☎ FAX 415/381-4031) for 10- to 22-day tours.

HOMES AND GARDENS➤ **Coopersmith's England** (✉ 6441 Valley View Rd., Oakland, CA 94611, ☎ 510/339-2499) spends an "Enchanted June" visiting the floral delights of Venice and the lake region. **Endless Beginnings Tours** (☞ Art and Architecture, *above*) visits gardens and villas around Rome and Tuscany. **Esplanade Tours** (✉ 581 Boylston St., Boston, MA 02116, ☎ 617/266-7465 or 800/426-5492, FAX 617/262-9829) visits gardens in the lake region.

HORSEBACK RIDING➤ **FITS Equestrian** (✉ 685 Lateen Rd., Solvang, CA 93463, ☎ 805/688-9494 or 800/666-3487, FAX 805/688-2943) has tours for every level of rider.

LEARNING➤ **Earthwatch** (✉ Box 403, 680 Mount Auburn St., Watertown, MA 02272, ☎ 617/926-8200 or 800/776-0188, FAX 617/926-8532,

info@earthwatch.org, http://www.earthwatch.org) recruits volunteers to serve in its Earth-Corps as short-term assistants to scientists on research expeditions. **Smithsonian Study Tours and Seminars** (✉ 1100 Jefferson Dr. SW, Room 3045, MRC 702, Washington, DC 20560, ☎ 202/357-4700, FAX 202/633-9250) focuses on art and culture.

MOTORCYCLE➤ **Beach's Motorcycle Adventures** (✉ 2763 W. River Pkwy., Grand Island, NY 14072-2053, ☎ 716/773-4960, FAX 716/773-5227, robbeach@buffnet.net) can take you on motorcycle adventures on Italy's back roads.

MUSIC➤ **Dailey-Thorp Travel** (✉ 330 W. 58th St., #610, New York, NY 10019-1817, ☎ 212/307-1555 or 800/998-4677, FAX 212/974-1420) specializes in classical music and opera programs throughout Europe.

PILGRIMAGES➤ **Pilgrimage Tours and Travel** (✉ 39 Beechwood Ave., Manhasset, NY 11030, ☎ 516/627-2636 or 800/669-0757) arranges pilgrimages to the shrines of Rome, Lanciano, Loreto, Assisi, and San Giovani.

SPAS➤ **Spa-Finders** (✉ 91 5th Ave., #301, New York, NY 10003-3039, ☎ 212/924-6800 or 800/255-7727) represents several spas in Italy.

TENNIS➤ **Championship Tennis Tours** (✉ 7350 E. Stetson Dr., #106, Scottsdale, AZ 85251, ☎ 602/990-8760 or 800/468-3664,

FAX 602/990-8744, mike@tennistours.com, http://www.tennistours.com) has packages to the Italian Open.

VILLA RENTALS➤ **Rentals in Italy** (✉ 1742 Calle Corva, Camarillo, CA 93010-8428, ☎ 805/987-5278 or 800/726-6702, FAX 805/482-7976) represents Cuendet, the largest villa-rental company in Italy. Cottages and villas can also be rented through **Eurovillas** (✉ 1398 55th St., Emeryville, CA 94608, ☎ FAX 707/648-0266) or **Villas International** (✉ 605 Market St., San Francisco, CA 94105, ☎ 415/281-0910 or 800/221-2260, FAX 415/281-0919). Castle stays with balloon trips can be arranged by **B&V Associates** (✉ 140 E. 56th St., #4C, New York, NY 10022, ☎ 800/546-4777, FAX 212/688-9467.

WALKING/HIKING➤ For long strolls in the countryside, try **Abercrombie & Kent** (☞ Group Tours, *above*); **Above the Clouds Trekking** (✉ Box 398, Worcester, MA 01602, ☎ 508/799-4499 or 800/233-4499, FAX 508/797-4779); **Backroads** (☞ Bicycling, *above*); **Butterfield & Robinson** (☞ Adventure, *above*); **Country Walkers** (✉ Box 180, Waterbury, VT 05676-0180, ☎ 802/244-1387 or 800/464-9255, FAX 802/244-5661); **Euro-Bike Tours** (☞ Bicycling, *above*); **Uniquely Europe** (☞ Bicycling, *above*); and **Wilderness Travel** (✉ 801 Allston Way, Berkeley, CA 94710,

THE GOLD GUIDE / IMPORTANT CONTACTS

☎ 510/548–0420 or 800/368–2794, FAX 510/548–0347, info@ wildernesstravel.com).

YACHT CHARTERS➤ **Huntley Yacht Vacations** (✉ 210 Preston Rd., Wernersville, PA 19565, ☎ 610/678–2628 or 800/322–9224, FAX 610/670–1767, yachts4u@enter.net), **Lynn Jachney Charters** (✉ Box 302, Marblehead, MA 01945, ☎ 617/639–0787 or 800/223–2050, FAX 617/639–0216), **Ocean Voyages** (✉ 1709 Bridgeway, Sausalito, CA 94965, ☎ 415/ 332–4681, FAX 415/ 332–7460).

ORGANIZATIONS

The **National Tour Association** (✉ NTA, 546 E. Main St., Lexington, KY 40508, ☎ 606/226–4444 or 800/755–8687) and the **United States Tour Operators Association** (✉ USTOA, 211 E. 51st St., Suite 12B, New York, NY 10022, ☎ 212/750–7371) can provide lists of members and information on booking tours.

PUBLICATIONS

Contact the USTOA (☞ *above*) for its **"Smart Traveler's Planning Kit."** Pamphlets in the kit include the "Worldwide Tour and Vacation Package Finder," "How to Select a Tour or Vacation Package," and information on the organization's consumer protection plan. Also get copy of the Better Business Bureau's **"Tips on Travel Packages"** (✉ Publication 24-195, 4200 Wilson Blvd., Arlington, VA 22203; $2).

TRAIN TRAVEL

From the United Kingdom, travelers have several options for getting to Italy by rail. Trains leave from London's Charing Cross and Victoria stations and from Calais. For schedules contact **British Rail** (☎ 0171/834–2345) and **French Railways** (☎ 0891/515–477; calls charged at 49p a minute peak rate, 39p all other times). Also *see* The Channel Tunnel, *above*.

DISCOUNT PASSES

Eurail and EuroPasses are available through travel agents and **Rail Europe** (✉ 226-230 Westchester Ave., White Plains, NY 10604, ☎ 914/682–5172 or 800/438–7245; 2087 Dundas E., Suite 105, Mississauga, Ontario L4X 1M2, ☎ 416/602–4195, **DER Tours** (✉ Box 1606, Des Plaines, IL 60017, ☎ 800/782–2424, FAX 800/282–7474), or **CIT Tours Corp.** (✉ 342 Madison Ave., Suite 207, New York, NY 10173, ☎ 212/ 697–2100 or 800/248–8687 or 800/248–7245 in western U.S.). Italian rail passes can be purchased through DER Tours or CIT Tours as well.

TRAVEL GEAR

For travel apparel, appliances, personal-care items, and other travel necessities, get a free catalog from **Magellan's** (☎ 800/ 962–4943, FAX 805/ 568–5406), **Orvis Travel** (☎ 800/541–3541, FAX 703/343–7053), or **TravelSmith** (☎ 800/950–1600, FAX 415/455–0554).

ELECTRICAL CONVERTERS

Send a self-addressed, stamped envelope to the **Franzus Company** (✉ Customer Service, Dept. B50, Murtha Industrial Park, Box 142, Beacon Falls, CT 06403, ☎ 203/723–6664) for a copy of the free brochure "Foreign Electricity Is No Deep, Dark Secret."

TRAVEL AGENCIES

For names of reputable agencies in your area, contact the **American Society of Travel Agents** (✉ ASTA, 1101 King St., Suite 200, Alexandria, VA 22314, ☎ 703/739–2782), the **Association of Canadian Travel Agents** (✉ Suite 201, 1729 Bank St., Ottawa, Ontario K1V 7Z5, ☎ 613/521–0474, FAX 613/521–0805) or the **Association of British Travel Agents** (✉ 55-57 Newman St., London W1P 4AH, ☎ 0171/637–2444, FAX 0171/637–0713).

U

U.S.

GOVERNMENT

TRAVEL BRIEFINGS

The U.S. Department of State's American Citizens Services office (✉ Room 4811, Washington, DC 20520; enclose SASE) issues **Consular Information Sheets** on all foreign countries. These cover issues such as crime, security, political climate, and health risks as well as listing embassy locations, entry requirements, currency regulations, and providing other useful information. For the latest information, stop in at any U.S. passport office, consulate, or embassy; call the interactive hot line (☎ 202/647–5225, FAX 202/647–3000); or, with your PC's modem, tap into the department's computer bulletin board (☎ 202/647–9225).

VISITOR INFORMATION

IN THE U.S.

Contact the **Italian Government Travel Office** (✉ IGTO, 630 5th Avenue, Suite 1565, New York, NY 10111, ☎ 212/245–4822, FAX 212/586–9249; 500 N. Michigan Avenue, Chicago, IL 60611,

☎ 312/644–0990, FAX 312/644–3019; 12400 Wilshire Boulevard., Suite 550, Los Angeles, CA 90025, ☎ 310/820–0098, FAX 310/820–6357).

IN CANADA

Contact IGTO (✉ 1 Place Ville Marie, Montréal, Québec H3B 3M9, ☎ 514/866–7667).

IN THE U.K.

Contact IGTO (✉ 1 Princes St., London W1R 8AY, ☎ 0171/408–1254).

WEATHER

For current conditions and forecasts, plus the local time and helpful travel tips, call the **Weather Channel Connection** (☎ 900/932–8437; 95¢ per minute) from a Touch-Tone phone.

The *International Traveler's Weather Guide* (✉ Weather Press, Box 660606, Sacramento, CA 95866, ☎ 916/974–0201 or 800/972–0201; $10.95 includes shipping), written by two meteorologists, provides month-by-month information on temperature, humidity, and precipitation in more than 175 cities worldwide.

SMART TRAVEL TIPS A TO Z

Basic Information on Traveling in Italy & Savvy Tips to Make Your Trip a Breeze

The more you travel, the more you know about how to make trips run like clockwork. To help make your travels hassle-free, Fodor's editors have rounded up dozens of tips from our contributors and from travel experts all over the world, as well as basic information on visiting Italy. For names of organizations to contact and publications that can give you more information, *see* Important Contacts A to Z, *above*.

A

AIR TRAVEL

If time is an issue, **always look for nonstop flights,** which require no change of plane. If possible, **avoid connecting flights,** which stop at least once and can involve a change of plane, even though the flight number remains the same; if the first leg is late, the second waits.

For better service, **fly smaller or regional carriers,** which often have higher passenger satisfaction ratings. Sometimes they have such in-flight amenities as leather seats or greater legroom and they often have better food.

CUTTING COSTS

The Sunday travel section of most newspapers is a good place to look for deals.

MAJOR AIRLINES➢ The least-expensive airfares from the major airlines are priced for round-trip travel and are subject to restrictions. Usually, you must **book in advance and buy the ticket within 24 hours** to get cheaper fares, and you may have to **stay over a Saturday night.** The lowest fare is subject to availability, and only a small percentage of the plane's total seats is sold at that price. It's smart to **call a number of airlines, and when you are quoted a good price, book it on the spot**—the same fare may not be available on the same flight the next day. Airlines generally allow you to change your return date for a $25 to $50 fee. If you don't use your ticket, you can apply the cost toward the purchase of a new ticket, again for a small charge. However, most low-fare tickets are nonrefundable. To get the lowest airfare, **check different routings.** If your destination has more than one gateway, **compare prices to different airports.**

FROM THE U.K.➢ To save money on flights, **look into an APEX or Super-Pex ticket.** APEX tickets must be booked in advance and have certain restrictions. Super-PEX tickets can be purchased right at the airport.

CONSOLIDATORS➢ Consolidators buy tickets for scheduled flights at reduced rates from the airlines, then sell them at prices below the lowest available from the airlines directly—usually without advance restrictions. Sometimes you can even get your money back if you need to return the ticket. Carefully read the fine print detailing penalties for changes and cancellations. If you doubt the reliability of a consolidator, **confirm your reservation with the airline.**

CHARTER FLIGHTS➢ Charters usually have the lowest fares and most restrictions. Departures are infrequent and seldom on time, and you can lose all or most of your money if you cancel. (The closer to departure you cancel, the more you lose, although sometimes you can pay only a small fee if you supply a substitute passenger.) The flight may be canceled for any reason up to 10 days before departure (after that, only if it is physically impossible to operate). The charterer may also revise the itinerary or increase the price after you have bought the ticket, but only if the new arrangement constitutes a "major change" do you have the right to a refund. Before buying a charter ticket, **read the fine print** regarding the company's refund policies. Money for charter flights is usually paid into a bank escrow account, the name of which should be on the contract, and if you don't pay by credit card, **make your check payable to the carrier's escrow account** (unless you're dealing with a travel agent, in which case his or her check should be made payable to the escrow account). The U.S. Department of Transportation's Aviation Consumer Protection Division has jurisdiction over charters.

Charter operators may offer flights alone or with ground arrangements that constitute a charter package. Normally, you must book charters through a travel agent.

ALOFT

AIRLINE FOOD➤ If you hate airline food, **ask for special meals when booking.** These can be vegetarian, low-cholesterol, or kosher, for example; commonly prepared to order in smaller quantities than standard fare, they can be tastier.

JET LAG➤ To avoid this syndrome, which occurs when travel disrupts your body's natural cycles, try to maintain a normal routine. At night, **get some sleep.** By day, move about the cabin to **stretch your legs, eat light meals, and drink water—not alcohol.**

SMOKING➤ Smoking is banned on all flights of less than six hours' duration within the United States and on all Canadian flights; the ban also applies to domestic segments of international flights aboard U.S. and foreign

carriers. Delta has banned smoking system-wide. On U.S. carriers flying to Italy and other destinations abroad, a seat in a no-smoking section must be provided for every passenger who requests one, and the section must be enlarged to accommodate such passengers as long as they have complied with the airline's deadline for check-in and seat assignment. If smoking bothers you, request a seat far from the smoking section.

Foreign airlines are exempt from these rules but do provide no-smoking sections. British Airways has banned smoking; some nations, including Italy, have banned smoking on all domestic flights, and others may not allow smoking on some flights. Talks continue on the feasibility of broadening no-smoking policies.

B

BEACHES

Italy isn't the place for an exclusively "beach" holiday. With the exception of Sardinia, you'll find cleaner water and better beaches at lower prices in other parts of the world. The waters that are least polluted and best for swimming are in Sardinia (except around Cagliari, Arbatax, and Porto Torres); off portions of the coasts of Calabria and Apulia; and off the islands of Elba, Capri, Ischia, Ustica, the Aeolian group, and western Sicily. Topless bathing is widespread, except for a few staid

family-type beaches near large cities. Nudism is discreetly practiced on out-of-the-way beaches, mainly on the islands and on deserted stretches of the mainland coast. Singles will find the liveliest resorts on the Adriatic Coast and on the coasts of Tuscany and Calabria.

BUS TRAVEL

If you're traveling by bus from the United Kingdom, **bring a few French francs to spend en route.** And be sure to consider the train, as bus fares are quite high, especially when you consider the long and tiring overnight journey.

WITHIN ITALY

Italy's bus network is extensive, although not as attractive as those in other European countries, partly because of the low cost of train travel. Schedules are often drawn up with commuters and students in mind and may be sketchy on weekends. Regional bus companies often provide the only means of getting to out-of-the-way places. Even when this is not the case, buses can be faster and more direct than local trains, so it's a good idea to compare bus and train schedules.

Local bus companies operate in many regions (☞ Getting Around, By Bus *in* most chapters). In the hillier parts of Italy, particularly in the Alpine north, they take over when the gradients become too steep for train travel. A village shop or café will sometimes double as the ticket office and bus stop for these. You should have your ticket before you board.

Most of the major cities have urban bus services, usually operating on a system involving the purchase of tickets before you board (from a machine, a newsstand, or a tobacco store) and stamping the ticket in the machine on the bus. These buses are inexpensive, but they can become unbearably jammed at rush hours. Remember that there are also lunchtime rush hours in the hotter periods, particularly in the south, when people go home for a siesta.

BUSINESS HOURS

Banks are open weekdays 8:30–1:30 and 2:45–3:45.

Most **churches** are open from early morning until noon or 12:30, when they close for two hours or more; they open again in the afternoon, closing about 7 PM or later. Major cathedrals and basilicas, such as St. Peter's, are open all day. Note that sightseeing in churches during religious rites is usually discouraged. Be sure to have a fistful of 100-lire coins handy for the *luce* (light) machines that illuminate the works of art in the perpetual dusk of ecclesiastical interiors. A pair of binoculars will help you get a good look at painted ceilings and domes.

Museum hours vary and may change with the seasons. Many important national museums are closed one day a week, often on Monday. Always check locally.

Most **shops** are open 9:30–1 and 3:30 or

4–7 or 7:30. In all but resorts and small towns, shops close on Sunday and one half-day during the week. Some tourist-oriented shops in places such as Rome and Venice are open all day, also on Sunday, as are some department stores and supermarkets.

Post offices are open 8–2; central and main district post offices stay open until 8 or 9 PM for some operations. The main post office in major cities is open on Sunday 8:30–7.

Barbers and hair-dressers, with some exceptions, are closed Sunday and Monday.

NATIONAL HOLIDAYS

January 1 (New Year's Day); January 6 (Epiphany); March 30, 31, (Easter Sunday and Monday); April 25 (Liberation Day); May 1 (Labor Day or May Day); August 15 (Assumption of Mary, also known as Ferragosto); November 1 (All Saints' Day); December 8 (Immaculate Conception); December 25, 26 (Christmas Day and Boxing Day).

The feast days of patron saints are also holidays, observed locally. Many businesses and shops may be closed in Florence, Genoa, and Turin on June 24 (St. John the Baptist); in Rome on June 29 (Sts. Peter and Paul); in Palermo on July 15 (Santa Rosalia); in Naples on September 19 (San Gennaro); in Bologna on October 4 (San Petronio); in Trieste on November 3 (San Giusto); and in Milan on December 7

(St. Ambrose). Venice's feast of St. Mark is April 25, the same as Liberation Day.

C
CAMERAS, CAMCORDERS, & COMPUTERS

LAPTOPS

Before you depart, **check your portable computer's battery;** at security you may be asked to turn on the computer to prove that it is what it appears to be. At the airport, you may prefer to **request a manual inspection,** although security X-rays do not harm hard-disk or floppy-disk storage. Also, **register your foreign-made laptop with U.S. Customs.** If your laptop is U.S.-made, call the consulate of the country you'll be visiting to find out whether it should be registered with local customs upon arrival. You may want to **find out about repair facilities at your destination** in case of problems.

PHOTOGRAPHY

If your camera is new or if you haven't used it for a while, **shoot and develop a few rolls of film** before you leave. Always **store film in a cool, dry place**—never in your car's glove compartment or on the shelf under the rear window.

Select the right film for your purpose—**use print film if you plan to frame or display your pictures,** but **use slide film if you hope to publish your shots.** Also, **consider black-and-white film** for different and dramatic images. For best results, **use a custom lab** for processing; use a one-hour lab only if time is a factor.

The chances of your film growing cloudy increase with each pass through an X-ray machine. To protect against this, carry it in a clear plastic bag and **ask for hand inspection at security.** Such requests are virtually always honored at U.S. airports, and are usually accommodated abroad. Don't depend on a lead-lined bag to protect film in checked luggage—the airline may increase the radiation to see what's inside.

Keep a skylight or haze filter on your camera at all times to protect the expensive (and delicate) lens glass from scratches. Better yet, **use an 81B warming filter,** which—unlike skylight or haze filters—really works in overcast conditions and will pump up those sunrises and sunsets.

VIDEO

Before your trip, **test your camcorder, invest in a skylight filter to protect the lens, and charge the batteries.** (Airport security personnel may ask you to turn on the camcorder to prove that it's what it appears to be.) The batteries of most newer camcorders can be recharged with a universal or worldwide AC adapter-charger (or multivoltage converter), whether the voltage is 110 or 220. All that's needed is the appropriate plug.

Videotape is not damaged by X-rays, but it may be harmed by the magnetic field of a walk-through metal detector, so **ask that videotapes be hand-checked.** Prerecorded videotape sold in Italy is based on the PAL standard, which will not play back in the United States. Blank tapes bought in Italy can be used for camcorder taping, but they are pricey. Some U.S. audiovisual shops convert foreign tapes to U.S. standards; contact an electronics dealer to find the nearest.

CAR RENTAL

CUTTING COSTS

To get the best deal, **book through a travel agent who is willing to shop around.** Ask your agent to **look for fly-drive packages,** which also save you money, and **ask if local taxes are included** in the rental or fly-drive price. These can be as high as 20% in some destinations. Don't forget to find out about required deposits, cancellation penalties, drop-off charges, and the cost of any required insurance coverage.

Also **ask your travel agent about a company's customer-service record.** How has it responded to late plane arrivals and vehicle mishaps? Are there often lines at the rental counter, and—if you're traveling during a holiday period—does a confirmed reservation guarantee you a car?

Always **find out what equipment is standard** at your destination

before specifying what you want; automatic transmission and air-conditioning are usually optional—and very expensive.

Be sure to **look into wholesalers**—companies that do not own their own fleets but rent in bulk from those that do and often offer better rates than traditional car-rental operations. Prices are best during off-peak periods; rentals booked through wholesalers must be paid for before you leave the United States.

INSURANCE

When driving a rented car, you are generally responsible for any damage to or loss of the rental vehicle. Before you rent, **see what coverage you already have** under the terms of your personal auto insurance policy and credit cards.

If you do not have auto insurance or an umbrella insurance policy that covers damage to third parties, purchasing CDW or LDW is highly recommended.

Collision policies that car-rental companies sell for European rentals typically do not cover stolen vehicles. Before you buy additional coverage for theft, find out if your credit card or personal auto insurance will cover the loss. All car-rental companies operating in Italy mandate the purchase of theft-protection policies.

LICENSE REQUIREMENTS

In Italy your own driver's license is ac-

SMART TRAVEL TIPS / THE GOLD GUIDE

ceptable. An International Driver's Permit is a good idea; it's available from the American or Canadian automobile associations, or, in the United Kingdom, from the AA or RAC.

SURCHARGES

Before you pick up a car in one city and leave it in another, **ask about drop-off charges or one-way service fees,** which can be substantial. Note, too, that some rental agencies charge extra if you return the car before the time specified on your contract. To avoid a hefty refueling fee, **fill the tank just before you turn in the car**—but be aware that gas stations near the rental outlet may overcharge.

THE CHANNEL TUNNEL

The "Chunnel" is the fastest way to cross the English Channel short of flying—35 minutes from Folkestone to Calais, 60 minutes from motorway to motorway, or 3 hours from Waterloo, London, to Paris's Gare du Nord. It consists of two large 50-kilometer- (31-mile-) long train tunnels, and a smaller service tunnel running between them.

CHILDREN & TRAVEL

Although Italians love children and are generally very tolerant and patient with them, they provide few amenities for them. In restaurants and trattorias you may find a high chair or a cushion for the child to sit on, but rarely do they offer a children's menu. Order a *mezza porzione*

(half-portion) of any dish, or ask the waiter for a *porzione da bambino* (child's portion).

Discounts do exist. Always ask about a *sconto-bambino* (child's discount) before purchasing tickets. Children under six or under a certain height ride free on municipal buses and trams. Children under 18 are admitted free to state-run museums and galleries, and there are similar privileges in many municipal or private museums.

When traveling with children, **plan ahead** and **involve your youngsters** as you outline your trip. When packing, **include a supply of things to keep them busy** en route (☞ Children & Travel *in* Important Contacts A to Z). On sightseeing days, try to **schedule activities of special interest to your children,** like a trip to a zoo or a playground. If you **plan your itinerary around seasonal festivals,** you'll never lack for things to do. In addition, **check local newspapers for special events** mounted by public libraries, museums, and parks.

BABY-SITTING

For recommended local sitters, **check with your hotel desk.**

DRIVING

If you are renting a car, don't forget to **arrange for a car seat when you reserve.** Sometimes they're free.

FLYING

Always **ask about discounted children's fares.** On international flights, infants under 2

not occupying a seat generally travel free or for 10% of the accompanying adult's fare; the fare for children ages 2–11 is usually half to two-thirds of the adult fare. On domestic flights, children under 2 not occupying a seat travel free, and older children are charged at the lowest applicable adult rate.

BAGGAGE➤ In general, the adult baggage allowance applies to children paying half or more of the adult fare. If you are traveling with an infant, **ask about carry-on allowances** before departure. In general, for infants charged 10% of the adult fare you are allowed one carry-on bag and a collapsible stroller; you may be limited to less if the flight is full.

SAFETY SEATS➤ According to the FAA, it's a good idea to **use safety seats aloft** for children weighing less than 40 pounds. Airline policies vary. U.S. carriers allow FAA-approved models but usually require that you buy a ticket, even if your child would otherwise ride free, since the seats must be strapped into regular seats. Foreign carriers may not allow infant seats, may charge a child rather than an infant fare for their use, or may require you to hold your baby during takeoff and landing—defeating the seat's purpose.

FACILITIES➤ When making your reservation, **request for children's meals or freestanding bassinets** if you need them; the latter are available only to those seated at the bulkhead, where there's enough legroom. If you don't need a bassinet, **think twice before requesting bulkhead seats**—the only storage space for in-flight necessities is in inconveniently distant overhead bins.

LODGING

Most hotels allow children under a certain age to stay in their parents' room at no extra charge; others charge them as extra adults. Be sure to **ask about the cutoff age.**

CUSTOMS & DUTIES

IN ITALY

Of goods obtained anywhere outside the EU or goods purchased in a duty-free shop within an EU country, the allowances are: (1) 200 cigarettes or 100 cigarillos or 50 cigars or 250 grams of tobacco; (2) 2 liters of still table wine or 1 liter of spirits over 22% volume or 2 liters of spirits under 22% volume or 2 liters of fortified and sparkling wines; and (3) 50 milliliters of perfume and 250 milliliters of toilet water.

Of goods obtained (duty and tax paid) within another EU country, the allowances are: (1) 800 cigarettes or 400 cigarillos or 400 cigars or 1 kilogram of tobacco; (2) 90 liters of still table wine plus (3) 10 liters of spirits over 22% volume plus 20 liters of spirits under 22% volume plus 60 liters of sparkling wines plus 110 liters of beer.

IN THE U.S.

You may bring home $400 worth of foreign goods duty-free if you've been out of the country for at least 48 hours and haven't already used the $400 allowance, or any part of it, in the past 30 days.

Travelers 21 or older may bring back 1 liter of alcohol duty-free, provided the beverage laws of the state through which they reenter the United States allow it. In addition, regardless of their age, they are allowed 100 non-Cuban cigars and 200 cigarettes. Antiques and works of art more than 100 years old are duty-free.

Duty-free, travelers may mail packages valued at up to $200 to themselves and up to $100 to others, with a limit of one parcel per addressee per day (and no alcohol or tobacco products or perfume valued at more than $5); on the outside, the package should be labeled as being either for personal use or an unsolicited gift, and a list of its contents and their retail value should be attached. Mailed items do not affect your duty-free allowance on your return.

IN CANADA

If you've been out of Canada for at least seven days, you may bring in C$500 worth of goods duty-free. If you've been away for fewer than seven days but for more than 48 hours, the duty-free allowance drops to C$200; if your trip lasts between 24 and 48 hours, the allowance is C$50. You cannot pool allowances with family members. Goods claimed under the C$500 exemption may follow you by mail; those claimed under the lesser exemptions must accompany you.

Alcohol and tobacco products may be included in the seven-day and 48-hour exemptions but not in the 24-hour exemption. If you meet the age requirements of the province or territory through which you reenter Canada, you may bring in, duty-free, 1.14 liters (40 imperial ounces) of wine or liquor or 24 12-ounce cans or bottles of beer or ale. If you are 16 or older, you may bring in, duty-free, 200 cigarettes, 50 cigars or cigarillos, and 400 tobacco sticks or 400 grams of manufactured tobacco. Alcohol and tobacco must accompany you on your return.

An unlimited number of gifts with a value of up to C$60 each may be mailed to Canada duty-free. These do not affect your duty-free allowance on your return. Label the package "Unsolicited Gift—Value Under $60." Alcohol and tobacco are excluded.

IN THE U.K.

If your journey was wholly within European Union (EU) countries, you no longer need to pass through customs when you return to the United Kingdom. If you plan to bring back large quantities of alcohol or tobacco, check in advance on EU limits.

D

DISABILITIES & ACCESSIBILITY

Italy has only recently begun to provide facilities such as ramps, telephones, and rest rooms for people with disabilities; such things are still the exception, not the rule. Travelers' wheelchairs must be transported free of charge, according to Italian law, but the logistics of getting a wheelchair on and off trains and buses can make this requirement irrelevant. Seats are reserved for people with disabilities on public transportation, but few buses have lifts for wheelchairs. High, narrow steps for boarding trains create additional problems. In many monuments and museums, even in some hotels and restaurants, architectural barriers make it difficult, if not impossible, for those with disabilities to gain access. In Rome, however, St. Peter's, the Sistine Chapel, and the Vatican Museums are all accessible by wheelchair, as is the Uffizi in Florence.

Bringing a Seeing Eye dog into Italy requires an import license, a current certificate detailing the dog's inoculations, and a letter from your veterinarian certifying the dog's health. Contact the nearest Italian consulate for particulars.

When discussing accessibility with an operator or reservationist, **ask hard questions.** Are there any stairs, inside *or* out? Are there grab bars next to the toilet *and* in the shower/tub? How wide is the doorway to the room? To the bathroom? For the most extensive facilities, meeting the latest legal specifications, **opt for newer accommodations,** which more often have been designed with access in mind. Older properties or ships must usually be retrofitted and may offer more limited facilities as a result. Be sure to **discuss your needs before booking.**

DISCOUNTS & DEALS

Always inquire about discount rates for plane and train travel within Italy, which may be available for students, senior citizens, family groups or other groups traveling together and for travel on weekends or to particular destinations at certain times.

You shouldn't have to pay for a discount. In fact, you may already be eligible for all kinds of savings. Here are some time-honored strategies for getting the best deal.

LOOK IN YOUR WALLET

When you **use your credit card to make travel purchases,** you may get free travel-accident insurance, collision damage insurance, medical or legal assistance, depending on the card and bank that issued it. Visa and MasterCard provide one or more of these services, so **get a copy of your card's travel benefits.** If you are a member of the AAA or an oil-company-sponsored road-assistance plan, always **ask hotel or car-rental reservationists for auto-club discounts.** Some clubs offer additional discounts on tours, cruises, or admission to attractions. And don't forget that auto-club membership entitles you to free maps and trip-planning services.

SENIORS CITIZENS & STUDENTS

As a senior-citizen traveler, you may be eligible for special rates, but you should mention your senior-citizen status up front. If you're a student or under 26 you can also get discounts, especially if you have an official ID card (☞ Senior-Citizen Discounts *and* Students on the Road, *below*).

DIAL FOR DOLLARS

To save money, **look into "1-800" discount reservations services,** which often have lower rates. These services use their buying power to get a better price on hotels, airline tickets, and sometimes even car rentals. When booking a room, always **call the hotel's local toll-free number** (if one is available) rather than the central reservations number—you'll often get a better price. Ask the reservationist about special packages or corporate rates, which are usually available even if you're not traveling on business.

JOIN A CLUB?

Discount clubs can be a legitimate source of savings, but you must use the participating hotels and visit the participating attractions in order to realize any benefits. Remember, too, that you have to pay a fee to join, so **determine if you'll save enough to warrant your membership fee.** Before booking with a club, **make sure the hotel or other supplier isn't offering a better deal.**

GET A GUARANTEE

When shopping for the best deal on hotels and car rentals, **look for guaranteed exchange rates,** which protect you against a falling dollar. With your rate locked in, you won't pay more even if the price goes up in the local currency.

DRIVING

There is an extensive network of *autostradas* (toll highways), complemented by equally well-maintained but free *superstrade* (expressways). All are clearly signposted and numbered. The ticket you are issued upon entering an autostrada must be returned when you exit and pay the toll; on some shorter autostradas, mainly connecting highways, the toll is paid upon entering. Viacard cards, on sale at many autostrada locations, make paying tolls easier and faster. A *raccordo* is a connecting expressway. *Strade statali* (state highways, denoted by *S* or *SS* numbers) may be single-lane roads, as are all secondary roads; directions and turnoffs are not always clearly marked.

FUEL AVAILABILITY AND COSTS

Only a few gas stations are open on Sunday, and most close for a couple of hours at lunchtime and at 7 PM for the night. Self-service pumps may be few and far between outside major cities. Gas stations on autostradas are open 24 hours.

PARKING

In most cities, parking space is at a premium; historic town centers are closed to most traffic, and peripheral parking areas are usually full. Parking in an area signposted ZONA DISCO is allowed for limited periods (30 minutes to 2 hours or more—the limit is posted); if you don't have the cardboard disk to show what time you parked, you can use a piece of paper. It's advisable to leave your car only in guarded parking areas. Unofficial parking attendants can help you find a space but offer no guarantees. In major cities your car may be towed away if illegally parked.

RULES OF THE ROAD

Driving is on the right, as in the United States. Regulations are largely as in Britain and the United States, except that the police have the power to levy on-the-spot fines. In most Italian towns the use of the horn is forbidden in certain, if not all, areas; a large sign, ZONA DI SILENZIO, indicates where. Speed limits are 130 kph (80 mph) on autostradas and 110 kph (70 mph) on state

and provincial roads, unless otherwise marked. Fines for driving after drinking are heavy, with the additional possibility of six months' imprisonment, but testing is not routine.

H
HEALTH
CONCERNS

The Centers for Disease Control and Prevention (CDC) in Atlanta caution that most of Southern Europe is in the "intermediate" range for risk of contacting traveler's diarrhea. Part of this risk may be attributed to an increased consumption of olive oil and wine, which can have a laxative effect on stomachs used to a different diet. The CDC also advises all international travelers to swim only in chlorinated swimming pools, unless they are absolutely certain the local beaches and freshwater lakes are not contaminated.

I
INSURANCE

Travel insurance can protect your monetary investment, replace your luggage and its contents, or provide for medical coverage should you fall ill during your trip. Most tour operators, travel agents, and insurance agents sell specialized health-and-accident, flight, trip-cancellation, and luggage insurance as well as comprehensive policies with some or all of these coverages. Comprehensive policies may also reim-

THE GOLD GUIDE / SMART TRAVEL TIPS

burse you for delays due to weather—an important consideration if you're traveling during the winter months. Some health-insurance policies do not cover preexisting conditions, but waivers may be available in specific cases. Coverage is sold by the companies listed in Important Contacts A to Z; these companies act as the policy's administrators. The actual insurance is usually underwritten by a well-known name, such as The Travelers or Continental Insurance.

Before you make any purchase, **review your existing health and homeowner's policies** to find out whether they cover expenses incurred while traveling.

BAGGAGE

Airline liability for baggage is limited to $1,250 per person on domestic flights. On international flights, it amounts to $9.07 per pound or $20 per kilogram for checked baggage (roughly $640 per 70-pound bag) and $400 per passenger for unchecked baggage. Insurance for losses exceeding the terms of your airline ticket can be bought directly from the airline at check-in for about $10 per $1,000 of coverage; note that it excludes a rather extensive list of items, shown on your airline ticket.

COMPREHENSIVE

Comprehensive insurance policies include all the coverages described above plus some that may not be available in more specific policies. If

you have purchased an expensive vacation, especially one that involves travel abroad, comprehensive insurance is a must; **look for policies that include trip delay insurance,** which will protect you in the event that weather problems cause you to miss your flight, tour, or cruise. A few insurers will also sell you a waiver for preexisting medical conditions. Some of the companies that offer both these features are Access America, Carefree Travel, Travel Insured International, and TravelGuard (☞ Important Contacts A to Z).

FLIGHT

You should **think twice before buying flight insurance.** Often purchased as a last-minute impulse at the airport, it pays a lump sum when a plane crashes, either to a beneficiary if the insured dies or sometimes to a surviving passenger who loses his or her eyesight or a limb. Supplementing the airlines' coverage described in the limits-of-liability paragraphs on your ticket, it's expensive and basically unnecessary. Charging an airline ticket to a major credit card often automatically provides you with coverage that may also extend to travel by bus, train, and ship.

HEALTH

Medicare generally does not cover health care costs outside the United States; nor do many privately issued policies. If your own health insurance policy does not cover you outside

the United States, **consider buying supplemental medical coverage.** It can reimburse you for $1,000–$150,000 worth of medical and/or dental expenses incurred as a result of an accident or illness during a trip. These policies also may include a personal-accident, or death-and-dismemberment, provision, which pays a lump sum ranging from $15,000 to $500,000 to your beneficiaries if you die or to you if you lose one or more limbs or your eyesight, and a medical-assistance provision, which may either reimburse you for the cost of referrals, evacuation, or repatriation and other services, or automatically enroll you as a member of a particular medical-assistance company. (☞ Health Issues *in* Important Contacts A to Z.)

U.K. TRAVELERS

You can buy an annual travel insurance policy valid for most vacations during the year in which it's purchased. If you are pregnant or have a preexisting medical condition make sure you're covered before buying such a policy.

TRIP

Without insurance, you will lose all or most of your money if you cancel your trip regardless of the reason. Especially if your airline ticket, cruise, or package tour is nonrefundable and cannot be changed, it's essential that you **buy trip-cancellation-and-interruption insurance.** When considering how much coverage you need, look for a policy that will cover the cost of your trip plus the nondiscounted price of a one-way airline ticket should you need to return home early. Read the fine print carefully, especially sections that define "family member" and "preexisting medical conditions." Also **consider default or bankruptcy insurance,** which protects you against a supplier's failure to deliver. Be aware, however, that if you buy such a policy from a travel agency, tour operator, airline, or cruise line, it may not cover default by the firm in question.

L
LANGUAGE

In the main tourist cities, language is no problem. You can always find someone who speaks at least a little English, albeit with a heavy accent; remember that the Italian language is pronounced exactly as it is written (many Italians try to speak English as it is written, with disconcerting results). You may run into a language barrier in the countryside, but a phrase book and close attention to the Italians' astonishing use of pantomime and expressive gestures will go a long way.

Try to master a few phrases for daily use, and familiarize yourself with the terms you'll need to decipher signs and museum labels. To get the most out of museums, you'll need English-language guidebooks to exhibits; look for them in bookstores

and on newsstands, as those sold at the museums are not necessarily the best.

LODGING

Italy offers a good choice of accommodations, especially in the main tourist capitals of Rome, Florence, and Venice. It is becoming more difficult to find satisfactory accommodations in the lower categories in these cities, however, as more and more hotels are being refurbished and upgraded.

APARTMENT & VILLA RENTAL

If you want a home base that's roomy enough for a family and comes with cooking facilities, **consider taking a furnished rental.** This can also save you money, but not always—some rentals are luxury properties (economical only when your party is large). Home-exchange directories list rentals—often second homes owned by prospective house swappers—and some services search for a house or apartment for you (even a castle if that's your fancy) and handle the paperwork. Some send an illustrated catalog; others send photographs only of specific properties, sometimes at a charge; up-front registration fees may apply.

CAMPING

Camping is a good way to find accommodations in otherwise overcrowded resorts. Make sure you **stay only on authorized campsites** (camping on private land is frowned

upon), and **get an international camping carnet (permit)** from your local camping association before you leave home. The Touring Club Italiano publishes a multilingual *Guida Camping d'Italia* (campsite directory), available in bookstores in Italy for about 30,000 lire, with more detailed information on sites. Camp rates for two people, with car and tent, average about 45,000 lire a day.

HOME EXCHANGE

If you would like to find a house, an apartment, or some other type of vacation property to exchange for your own while on holiday, **become a member of a home-exchange organization,** which will send you its updated listings of available exchanges for a year, and will include your own listing in at least one of them. Arrangements for the actual exchange are made by the two parties involved, not by the organization.

HOTELS

Italian hotels are classified from five-star (deluxe) to one-star (very basic hotels and small inns). Stars are assigned according to standards set by regional boards (there are 20 in Italy), but rates are set by each hotel. During slack periods, or when a hotel is not full, it is often possible to negotiate a discounted rate. In the major cities, room rates are on a par with other European capitals: Deluxe and four-star rates can be downright extravagant.

In those categories, **ask for one of the better rooms,** since less desirable rooms—and there usually are some—don't give you what you're paying for. Except in deluxe and some four-star hotels, rooms may be very small compared to U.S; standards.

In all hotels there is a rate card inside the door of your room, or inside the closet door; it tells you exactly what you will pay for that particular room (rates in the same hotel may vary according to the location and type of room). On this card, breakfast and any other optionals must be listed separately. Any discrepancy between the basic room rate and that charged on your bill is cause for complaint to the manager and to the local tourist office.

Although, by law, breakfast is supposed to be optional, most hotels quote room rates including breakfast. When you book a room, specifically **ask whether the rate includes breakfast** (*colazione*). You are under no obligation to take breakfast at your hotel, but in practice most hotels expect you to do so. It is encouraging to note that many of the hotels we recommend are offering generous buffet breakfasts instead of simple, even skimpy "continental breakfasts." Remember, if the latter is the case, you can **eat for less at the nearest coffee bar.**

Hotels that we list as ($$) and ($)—moderate to inexpensively priced accommodations—may charge extra for optional air-conditioning. In older hotels the quality of the rooms may be very uneven; if you don't like the room you're given, request another. This applies to noise, too. Front rooms may be larger and have a view, but they also may have a lot of street noise. **If you're a light sleeper, request a quiet room when making reservations.** Specify whether you care about having either a bath or shower, since not all rooms have both.

Major cities, such as Rome and Milan, have no official off-season as far as hotel rates go, though some hotels will reduce rates during the slack season upon request. Always inquire about special rates. You can save considerably on hotel rooms in Venice and Florence and in such resorts as Sorrento and Capri during their off-seasons.

M
MAIL

Airmail letters (lightweight stationery) to the United States and Canada cost 1,250 lire for the first 19 grams and an additional 400 lire for every additional unit of 20 grams. Airmail postcards cost 1,000 lire if the message is limited to a few words and a signature; otherwise, you pay the letter rate. Airmail letters to the United Kingdom cost 750 lire; postcards, 600 lire. You can buy stamps at tobacconists.

RECEIVING MAIL

Mail service is generally slow; allow up to 10 days for mail from Britain, 15 days from North America. Correspondence can be addressed to you care of the Italian post office. Letters should be addressed to your name, "c/o Ufficio Postale Centrale," followed by "Fermo Posta" on the next line, and the name of the city (preceded by its postal code) on the next. You can collect it at the central post office by showing your passport or photo-bearing ID and paying a small fee. American Express also has a general-delivery service. There's no charge for cardholders, holders of American Express Traveler's checks, or anyone who booked a vacation with American Express.

MEDICAL ASSISTANCE

No one plans to get sick while traveling, but it happens, so **consider signing up with a medical assistance company.** These outfits provide referrals, emergency evacuation or repatriation, 24-hour telephone hot lines for medical consultation, cash for emergencies, and other personal and legal assistance. They also dispatch medical personnel and arrange for the relay of medical records.

MONEY & EXPENSES

The unit of currency in Italy is the lira. There are bills of 100,000, 50,000, 10,000, 5,000, 2,000, and 1,000 lire. Coins are 500, 200, 100 and 50 lire. At press time, the exchange rate was about 1,595 lire to the U.S. dollar, 1,157 lire to the Canadian dollar, and 2,402 lire to the pound sterling.

Italy's prices are in line with those in the rest of Europe, with costs in its main cities comparable to those in other major capitals, such as Paris and London. The days when the country's high-quality attractions came with a comparatively low Mediterranean price tag are long gone. With the cost of labor and social benefits rising and an economy weighed down by the public debt, Italy is therefore not a bargain, but there is an effort to hold the line on hotel and restaurant prices that had become inordinately expensive by U.S. standards. Depending on season and occupancy, you may be able to obtain unadvertised lower rates in hotels; always inquire. Among major cities, Venice and Milan are the most expensive; resorts such as the Costa Smeralda, Portofino, and Cortina d'Ampezzo cater to the rich and famous and charge top prices. Though Capri is generally considered a millionaire's playground, it can accommodate the less affluent. Everywhere in Italy, if you want the luxury of four- and five-star hotels, be prepared to pay top rates.

As in most countries, prices vary from region to region and are a bit lower in the countryside than in the cities. Good value for the money can be had in the scenic Trentino–Alto Adige region and in the Dolomites, in Umbria and the Marches, and on the Amalfi Coast. With a few exceptions, southern Italy, Sicily, and Sardinia also offer good values, but hotels are not always up to par.

When you make hotel reservations, ask explicitly whether breakfast is included in the rate. By law, breakfast is optional, but some hotels pressure guests to eat breakfast on the premises—and then charge a whopping amount for it. Find out what breakfast will cost at the time you book, or at least when you check in, and if it seems high, avoid misunderstanding by clearly stating that you want a room without breakfast.

ATMS

CASH ADVANCES➤ Cirrus, Plus, and many other networks that connect automated teller machines operate internationally. Chances are that you can **use your bank card, Master-Card, or Visa at ATMs** to withdraw money from an account or get a cash advance. Before leaving home, **check on frequency limits** for withdrawals and cash advances. Also **ask whether your card's PIN must be reprogrammed** for use in Italy. Four-digit numbers are commonly used overseas. Note that Discover is accepted mostly in the United States.

TRANSACTION FEES➤ On credit-card cash advances you are charged interest from the day you receive the money, whether from a teller or an ATM. Although fees charged for ATM transactions may be higher abroad than at home, Cirrus and Plus exchange rates are excellent, because they are based on wholesale rates offered only by major banks.

COSTS

Admission to the Vatican Museums is 15,000 lire; to the Uffizi Gallery, 12,000 lire. The cheapest seat at Rome's Opera House runs 25,000 lire; a movie ticket is 12,000 lire. Going to a Milan disco will set you back about 35,000 lire. A daily English-language newspaper is 2,400 lire.

A Rome taxi ride (1 mile) costs 10,000 lire. An inexpensive hotel room for two, including breakfast, in Rome is about 170,000 lire; an inexpensive Rome dinner is 38,000 lire, and a ½ liter carafe of house wine, 4,000 lire. A simple pasta item on the menu runs about 12,000 lire, a cup of coffee 1,200–1,400 lire, and a Rosticerria lunch, about 14,000 lire. A McDonald's Big Mac is 4,800 lire, and a Coke (standing) at a café is 2,200 lire, and a pint of beer in a pub is 7,000 lire.

EXCHANGING CURRENCY

For the most favorable rates, **change money at banks** (unless the lines are too long; it may not be worth wasting precious time to gain a few hundred lire). You won't do as well at exchange booths in airports or rail and bus stations, in hotels, in restaurants, or in stores, although you may find their hours more convenient. Exchange agencies in tourist cities may be competitive with the banks. To avoid lines at airport exchange booths, **get a small amount of the local currency before you leave home.**

TAXES

HOTEL➤ The service charge and the 9% IVA, or VAT tax, are included in the rate except in five-star deluxe hotels, where the IVA (13% on luxury hotels) may be a separate item added to the bill at departure.

RESTAURANT➤ A service charge of approximately 15% is added to all restaurant bills; in some cases the menu may state that the service charge is already included in the menu prices.

VAT➤ Value-added tax (IVA), is 12% on clothing, 19% on luxuries. On most consumer goods, it is already included in the amount shown on the price tag, whereas on services, it may not be.

To get an IVA refund, when you are leaving Italy take the goods and the invoice to the customs office at the airport or other point of departure and have the invoice stamped. (If you return to the United States or Canada directly from Italy, go through the procedure at Italian customs; if your return is, say, via Britain, take the Italian goods and invoice to British customs.) Under Italy's IVA-refund

system, a non-EU resident can obtain a refund of tax paid after spending a total of 300,000 lire in one store (before tax—and note that price tags and prices quoted, unless otherwise stated, include IVA). Shop with your passport and ask the store for an invoice itemizing the article(s), price(s), and the amount of tax. Once back home—and within 90 days of the date of purchase—mail the stamped invoice to the store, which will forward the IVA rebate to you. A growing number of stores in Italy (and Europe) are members of the Tax-Free Shopping System, which expedites things by providing an invoice that is actually a Tax-Free Cheque in the amount of the refund. Once stamped, it can be cashed at the Tax-Free Cash refund window at major airports and border crossings.

TRAVELER'S CHECKS

Whether or not to buy traveler's checks depends on where you are headed; **take cash to rural areas and small towns, traveler's checks to cities.** The most widely recognized checks are issued by American Express, Citicorp, Thomas Cook, and Visa. These are sold by major commercial banks for 1%–3% of the checks' face value—it pays to **shop around.** Both American Express and Thomas Cook issue checks that can be countersigned and used by either you or your traveling companion. So you won't be left with

excess foreign currency, **buy a few checks in small denominations** to cash toward the end of your trip. Before leaving home, **contact your issuer for information on where to cash your checks** without a incurring a transaction fee. Record the numbers of all your checks, and keep this listing in a separate place, crossing off the numbers of checks you have cashed.

WIRING MONEY

For a fee of 3%–10%, depending on the amount of the transaction, you can have money sent to you from home through MoneyGram℠ or Western Union (☞ Money Matters *in* Important Contacts A to Z). The transferred funds and the service fee can be charged to a MasterCard or Visa account.

P
PACKING FOR
ITALY

The weather is considerably milder in Italy than in the north and central United States or Great Britain. In summer, stick with clothing that's as light as possible, although a sweater may be necessary in the cool of the evening, especially in the mountains and even during the hot months. Brief summer afternoon thunderstorms are common in Rome and inland cities, so carry an umbrella. During the winter bring a medium-weight coat and a raincoat for Rome and farther south; northern Italy calls for heavier clothes, gloves, hats, and boots. Even in Rome and other milder areas, central heating may not be up to your standards, and interiors can be cold and damp; take wools or flannel rather than sheer fabrics. Bring sturdy shoes for winter, and comfortable walking shoes in any season.

Italians dress well and are not sloppy. They do not usually wear shorts in the city, unless longish Bermudas happen to be in fashion. Men aren't required to wear ties or jackets anywhere, except in some of the grander hotel dining rooms and top-level restaurants, but are expected to look reasonably sharp. Formal wear is the exception rather than the rule at the opera nowadays, though people in expensive seats usually do get dressed up.

Dress codes are strict for visits to churches—especially St. Peter's in Rome and St. Mark's in Venice—and to the Vatican Museums. Women must cover bare shoulders and arms—a shawl will do—but no longer need cover their heads. Shorts are taboo for both men and women. For the huge general papal audiences, no rules of dress apply other than those of common sense. For other types of audience, the Vatican Information Office will give requirements.

Take your own soap if you stay in budget hotels, as many do not provide it or else give guests only one tiny bar per room. Bring an extra pair of eyeglasses or contact lenses in your carry-on luggage, and if you have a health problem, **pack enough medication** to last the trip or have your doctor write you a prescription using the drug's generic name, because brand names vary from country to country (you'll then need a duplicate prescription from a local doctor). It's important that you **don't put prescription drugs or valuables in luggage to be checked,** for it could go astray. To avoid problems with customs officials, carry medications in the original packaging. Also, don't forget the addresses of offices that handle refunds of lost traveler's checks.

ELECTRICITY

To use your U.S.-purchased electric-powered equipment, **bring a converter and an adapter.** The electrical current in Italy is 220 volts, 50 cycles alternating current (AC); wall outlets take plugs with two round prongs.

If your appliances are dual-voltage, you'll need only an adapter. Hotels sometimes have 110-volt outlets for low-wattage appliances near the sink, marked FOR SHAVERS ONLY; don't use them for high-wattage appliances like blow-dryers. If your laptop computer is older, carry a converter; new laptops operate equally well on 110 and 220 volts, so you need only an adapter.

LUGGAGE

Airline baggage allowances depend on the airline, the route, and the class of your ticket; ask in advance. In general, on domestic flights and on international flights between the United States and foreign destinations, you are entitled to check two bags. A third piece may be brought on board, but it must fit easily under the seat in front of you or in the overhead compartment. In the United States, the FAA gives airlines broad latitude regarding carry-on allowances, and they tend to tailor them to different aircraft and operational conditions. Charges for excess, oversize, or overweight pieces vary.

If you are flying between two foreign destinations, note that baggage allowances may be determined not by piece but by weight—generally 88 pounds (40 kilograms) in first class, 66 pounds (30 kilograms) in business class, and 44 pounds (20 kilograms) in economy. If your flight between two cities abroad *connects* with your transatlantic or transpacific flight, the piece method still applies.

SAFEGUARDING YOUR LUGGAGE➤ Before leaving home, **itemize your bags' contents** and their worth, and label them with your name, address, and phone number. (If you use your home address, cover it so that potential thieves can't see it readily.) Inside each bag, **pack a copy of your itinerary.** At check-in, **make sure that each bag is correctly tagged** with the destination airport's three-letter code. If your bags arrive damaged—or fail to arrive at all—file a written report with the airline before leaving the airport.

PASSPORTS & VISAS

If you don't already have one, **get a passport.** It is advisable that you **leave one photocopy of your passport's data page** with someone at home and keep another with you, separated from your passport, while traveling. If you lose your passport, promptly call the nearest embassy or consulate and the local police; having the data page information can speed replacement.

IN THE U.S.

All U.S. citizens, even infants, need only a valid passport to enter Italy for stays of up to 90 days. Application forms for both first-time and renewal passports are available at any of the 13 U.S. Passport Agency offices and at some post offices and courthouses. Passports are usually mailed within four weeks; allow five weeks or more in spring and summer.

CANADIANS

You need only a valid passport to enter Italy for stays of up to 90 days. Passport application forms are available at 28 regional passport offices, as well as post offices and travel agencies. Whether for a first or a renewal passport, you must apply in person. Children under

16 may be included on a parent's passport but must have their own to travel alone. Passports are valid for five years and are usually mailed within two to three weeks of application.

U.K. CITIZENS

Citizens of the United Kingdom need only a valid passport to enter Italy for stays of up to 90 days. Applications for new and renewal passports are available from main post offices and at the passport offices in Belfast, Glasgow, Liverpool, London, Newport, and Peterborough. You may apply in person at all passport offices, or by mail to all except the London office. Children under 16 may travel on an accompanying parent's passport. All passports are valid for 10 years. Allow a month for processing.

PERSONAL SECURITY & COMFORT

The best way to protect yourself against purse snatchers and pickpockets is to wear a money belt. If you carry a bag or camera, make sure it has straps that you can sling across your body bandolier-style. Beware of pickpockets in big-city buses and subways and when making your way through the corridors of crowded trains.

S

SENIOR-CITIZEN DISCOUNTS

EU citizens over 60 are entitled to free admission to state museums, as well as to many other museums—always ask

at the ticket office. Older travelers may be eligible for special fares on Alitalia. When renting a car, **ask about promotional car-rental discounts**—they can net lower costs than your senior-citizen discount.

To qualify for age-related discounts, **mention your senior-citizen status up front** when booking hotel reservations, not when checking out, and before you're seated in restaurants, not when paying the bill. Note that discounts may be limited to certain menus, days, or hours. When renting a car, **ask about promotional car-rental discounts**—they can net even lower costs than your senior-citizen discount.

SHOPPING

The notice PREZZI FISSI (fixed prices) means just that; in shops displaying this sign it's a waste of time to bargain unless you're buying a sizable quantity of goods or a particularly costly object. Always bargain, however, at outdoor markets (except food markets) and when buying from street vendors. For a comprehensive introduction to the joys of shopping, Italian-style, (☞ Pleasures & Pastimes *in* Chapter 1).

STUDENTS ON THE ROAD

To save money, **look into deals available through student-oriented travel agencies.** To qualify, you'll need to have a bona fide student ID card. Members of international student groups are also eligible (☞ Students *in* Important Contacts A to Z).

T
TELEPHONES

LONG-DISTANCE

Since hotels tend to overcharge, sometimes exorbitantly, for long-distance and international calls, it is best to make such calls from Telefoni offices, where operators will assign you a booth, help you place your call, and collect payment when you have finished, at no extra charge. There are Telefoni offices, designated TELECOM), in all cities and towns, usually in major train stations and in the center business districts. **You can make collect calls from any phone by dialing 172-1011, which will get you an English-speaking operator.** Rates to the United States are lowest round the clock on Sunday and 11 PM–8 AM, Italian time, on weekdays.

From major Italian cities, you can place a direct call to the United States by reversing the charges or using your phone credit card number. When calling from pay telephones, insert a 200-lire coin which will be returned upon completion of your call). You automatically reach an operator in the country of destination and thereby avoid all language difficulties.

The long-distance services of AT&T, MCI, and Sprint make calling home relatively convenient, but in many hotels you may find it

impossible to dial the access number. The hotel operator may also refuse to make the connection. Instead, the hotel will charge you a premium rate—as much as 400% more than a calling card—for calls placed from your hotel room. To avoid such price gouging, travel with more than one company's long-distance calling card—a hotel may block Sprint but not MCI. If the hotel operator claims that you cannot use any phone card, ask to be connected to an international operator, who will help you to access your phone card. You can also dial the international operator yourself. If none of this works, try calling your phone company collect in the United States. If collect calls are also blocked, call from a pay phone in the hotel lobby. Before you go, **find out the local access codes** for your destinations.

The following are the **area codes for the major cities**: Bologna, 051; Brindisi, 0831; Florence, 055; Genoa, 010; Milan, 02; Naples, 081; Palermo, 091; Perugia, 075; Pisa, 050; Rome, 06; Siena, 0577; Turin, 011; Venice, 041; Verona, 045. When calling from abroad, the 0 should be left out. Example: a call from New York City to Rome would be dialed as follows: 011 + 39 + 6 + phone number.

OPERATORS AND INFORMATION

For general information in English, dial 176. To place calls from one European country to

another via operator-assisted service, dial 15. **To place intercontinental telephone calls** via operator-assisted service (or for intercontinental information), dial 170 or long-distance access numbers (☞ Telephone Matters *in* Important Contacts, *above*).

PAY PHONES

Pay phones take either a 200-lire coin, two 100-lire coins, a 500-lire coin, or a *carta telefonica* (prepaid calling card). Scheda phones are becoming common everywhere. You buy the card (values vary—5,000 lire, 10,000 lire, etc.) at Telefoni offices, post offices, and tobacconists. Tear off the corner of the card, and insert it in the slot. When you dial, its value appears in the window. After you hang up, the card is returned so you can use it until its value runs out.

TIPPING

Tipping practices vary, depending on where you are. The following guidelines apply in major cities, but Italians tip smaller amounts in smaller cities and towns. Tips may not be expected in cafés and taxis north of Rome.

In restaurants a service charge of about 15% usually appears as a separate item on your check. A few restaurants state on the menu that cover and service charge are included. Either way, it's customary to leave an additional 5%–10% tip for the waiter, depending on the service. Tip checkroom attendants 500 lire per person, rest room attendants 200 lire; in both cases tip more in expensive hotels and restaurants. Tip 100 lire for whatever you drink standing up at a coffee bar, 500 lire or more for table service in a smart café, and less in neighborhood cafés. At a hotel bar tip 1,000 lire and up for a round or two of cocktails.

Taxi drivers are usually happy with 5%–10% of the meter amount. Railway and airport porters charge a fixed rate per bag. Tip an additional 500 lire per person, but more if the porter is very helpful. Theater ushers expect 500 lire per person, but more for very expensive seats. Give a barber 2,000–3,000 lire and a hairdresser's assistant 3,000–8,000 lire for a shampoo or cut, depending on the type of establishment.

On sightseeing tours, tip guides about 2,000 lire per person for a half-day group tour, more if they are very good. In museums and other places of interest where admission is free, a contribution is expected; give anything from 500 to 1,000 lire for one or two persons, more if the guardian has been especially helpful. Service station attendants are tipped only for special services.

In hotels, give the *portiere* (concierge) about 15% of his bill for services, or 5,000–10,000 lire if he has been generally helpful. For two people in a double room, leave the chambermaid about 1,000 lire per day, or

about 4,000–5,000 a week, in a moderately priced hotel; tip a minimum of 1,000 lire for valet or room service. Increase these amounts by one-half in an expensive hotel, and double them in a very expensive hotel. In very expensive hotels, tip doormen 1,000 lire for calling a cab and 2,000 lire for carrying bags to the check-in desk, bellhops 3,000–5,000 lire for carrying your bags to the room and 3,000–5,000 lire for room service. One-third to one-half of these amounts is acceptable in moderately priced hotels.

TOUR OPERATORS

A package or tour to Italy can make your vacation less expensive and more hassle-free. Firms that sell tours and packages reserve airline seats, hotel rooms, and rental cars in bulk and pass some of the savings on to you. In addition, the best operators have local representatives available to help you at your destination.

A GOOD DEAL?

The more your package or tour includes, the better you can predict the ultimate cost of your vacation. Make sure you know exactly what is covered, and **beware of hidden costs.** Are taxes, tips, and service charges included? Transfers and baggage handling? Entertainment and excursions? These can add up.

Most packages and tours are rated deluxe, first-class superior, first class, tourist, or budget.

The key difference is usually accommodations. If the package or tour you are considering is priced lower than in your wildest dreams, **be skeptical.** Also, **make sure your travel agent knows the accommodations** and other services. Ask about the hotel's location, room size, beds, and whether it has a pool, room service, or programs for children, if you care about these. Has your agent been there in person or sent others you can contact?

BUYER BEWARE

Each year a number of consumers are stranded or lose their money when operators—even very large ones with excellent reputations— go out of business. To avoid becoming one of them, take the time to **check out the operator**— find out how long the company has been in business and ask several agents about its reputation. Next, **don't book unless the firm has a consumer-protection program.** Members of the USTOA and the NTA are required to set aside funds for the sole purpose of covering your payments and travel arrangements in case of default. Nonmember operators may instead carry insurance; look for the details in the operator's brochure—and for the name of an underwriter with a solid reputation. Note: When it comes to tour operators, **don't trust escrow accounts.** Although there are laws governing those of charter-flight operators, no governmental body prevents tour operators from raiding the till.

Next, **contact your local Better Business Bureau and the attorney general's offices** in both your own state and the operator's; have any complaints been filed? Finally, **pay with a major credit card.** Then you can cancel payment, provided that you can document your complaint. Always **consider trip-cancellation insurance** (☞ Insurance, *above*).

BIG VS. SMALL➤ Operators that handle several hundred thousand travelers per year can use their purchasing power to give you a good price. Their high volume may also indicate financial stability. But some small companies provide more personalized service; because they tend to specialize, they may also be more knowledgeable about a given area.

USING AN AGENT

Travel agents are excellent resources. In fact, large operators accept bookings made only through travel agents. But it's good to **collect brochures from several agencies** because some agents' suggestions may be skewed by promotional relationships with tour and package firms that reward them for volume sales. If you have a special interest, **find an agent with expertise in that area**; ASTA can provide leads in the United States. (Don't rely solely on your agent, though; agents may be unaware of small-niche operators, and some special-interest travel companies only sell direct.)

SINGLE TRAVELERS

Prices are usually quoted per person, based on two sharing a room. If traveling solo, you may be required to pay the full double-occupancy rate. Some operators eliminate this surcharge if you agree to be matched up with a roommate of the same sex, even if one is not found by departure time.

TRAIN TRAVEL

All Italian trains have first and second classes. On local trains the higher first-class fare gets you little more than a clean doily on the headrest of your seat, but on long-distance trains you get wider seats and more legroom and better ventilation and lighting. At peak travel times, first-class train travel is worth the difference. Remember to always make seat reservations in advance, for either class.

The fastest trains on the Ferrovie dello Stato (FS), the Italian State Railways, are the Pendolino Eurostar (ETR 460 trains), operating on several main lines, including Rome–Milan, via Florence and Bologna; seat reservations and supplement are included in the fare; Next fastest trains are the Intercity (IC) trains, for which you pay a supplement and for which seat reservations may be required and are always advisable. *Interregionale* trains usually make more stops and are a little slower. *Regionale* and *locale* trains are the slowest; many serve commuters.

To avoid long lines at station windows, **buy tickets and make seat reservations up to two months in advance** at travel agencies displaying the FS emblem. Agencies cannot make same-day seat reservations, but can sell tickets for the same day. If you have to reserve at the last minute, reservation offices at the station accept reservations up to three hours before departure. You may be able to get a seat assignment just before boarding the train; look for the conductor on the platform. Trains can be very crowded on weekends and during holiday and vacation seasons; reserve seats in advance or, if the train originates where you get on, get to the station early to find a seat. A card just outside the compartment or over the seat indicates whether it has been reserved. Carry compact bags for easy overhead storage. All tickets must be date-stamped in the small yellow or red machines near the tracks before you board. Once stamped, your ticket is valid for six hours if your destination is within 200 kilometers, for 24 hours for destinations beyond that. You can get on and off at will for the duration of the ticket's validity. If you don't stamp your ticket in the machine, you must actively seek out a conductor to validate the ticket on the train, paying 10,000 lire extra for the service. If you merely wait in your seat for him to collect your ticket, you must pay a 30,000 lire fine in addition. You also pay a hefty penalty if you purchase your ticket on board the train. You can buy train tickets for destinations within a 100-kilometer (62-mile) range at tobacconists and at ticket machines in stations.

Note that in some Italian cities (including Milan, Turin, Genoa, Naples, and Rome) there are two or more main-line stations, although one is usually the principal terminal or through-station. Be sure of the name of the station at which your train will arrive, or from which it will depart.

There is refreshment service on all long-distance trains, with mobile carts and a cafeteria or dining car. Tap water on trains is not drinkable.

DISCOUNT PASSES

If Italy is your only destination in Europe, **consider purchasing an Italian Railpass,** which allows unlimited travel on the entire Italian Rail network. Prices begin at $132 for four days of travel in second class within a one-month period and $194 in first class. Passes which good for longer periods of time are also available, as are flexi-passes, which allow a limited amount of train travel within a certain period.

Once in Italy, **inquire about the Carta Verde if you're under 26** (40,000 lire for one

year), which entitles the holder to a 20% discount on all first- and second-class tickets. Those under 26 should also inquire about discount travel fares under the Billet International Jeune (BIJ) scheme. The special one-trip tickets are sold by EuroTrain International at its offices in various European cities and by travel agents, mainline rail stations, and youth travel specialists.

You can **purchase the Carta d'Argento if you're over 60** (40,000 lire for one year), good for a 30% discount on all first- and second-class tickets, except for travel June 26–August 14 and December 18–28.

Italy is one of 17 countries in which you can **use EurailPasses,** which provide unlimited first-class rail travel, in all of the participating countries, for the duration of the pass. If you plan to rack up the miles, get a standard pass. These are available for 15 days ($522), 21 days ($678), one month ($838), two months ($1,148), and 3 months ($1,468). If your plans call for only limited train travel, **look into a Europass,** which costs less money than a EurailPass. Unlike EurailPasses, however, you get a limited number of travel days, in a limited number of countries, during a specified time period. For example, a two month pass ($316) allows between five and fifteen days of rail travel, but costs $200 less than the least

expensive EurailPass. Keep in mind, however, that the Europass is good only in France, Germany, Italy, Spain, and Switzerland, and the number of countries you can visit is further limited by the type of pass you buy. For example, the basic two-month pass allows you to visit only three of the five participating countries.

In addition to standard EurailPasses, **ask about special rail-pass plans.** Among these are the Eurail Youthpass (for those under age 26), the Eurail Saverpass (which gives a discount for two or more people traveling together), a Eurail Flexipass (which allows a certain number of travel days within a set period), the Euraildrive Pass and the Europass Drive (which combines travel by train and rental car).

Whichever pass you choose, remember that you must **purchase your EurailPass or EuroPass before you leave** for Europe.

Many travelers assume that rail passes guarantee them seats on the trains they wish to ride. Not so. You need to **book seats ahead even if you are using a rail pass;** seat reservations are required on some European trains, particularly high-speed trains, and are a good idea on trains that may be crowded—particularly in summer on popular routes. You will also need a reservation if you purchase sleeping accommodations.

For those planning to travel through Italy by

rail, a unique guide is *Italy by Train* by Tim Jepson (Fodor's Travel Publications, 800/533–6478 or from bookstores; $16).

TRAVEL GEAR

Travel catalogs specialize in useful items that can **save space when packing** and make life on the road more convenient. Compact alarm clocks, travel irons, travel wallets, and personal-care kits are among the most common items you'll find. They also carry dual-voltage appliances, currency converters and foreign-language phrase books. Some catalogs even carry miniature coffeemakers and water purifiers.

U
UNITED KINGDOM TO ITALY—VIA CAR AND TRAIN

BY CAR

The distance from London to Rome is 1,810 kilometers (1,125 miles) via Calais/Boulogne/Dunkirk and 1,745 kilometers (1,085 miles) via Oostende/Zeebrugge (excluding sea crossings). Milan is about 575 kilometers (360 miles) closer. The drive from the Continental ports takes about 24 hours; the total trip takes about three days. The shortest, quickest channel crossings are via Dover or Folkestone to one of the French ports (Calais or Boulogne); the ferry takes around 75 minutes and the Hovercraft just 35 minutes. Crossings from Dover to the Belgian ports take about four hours, but Oostende and

Zeebrugge have good road connections. The longer crossing from Hull to Zeebrugge is useful for travelers from the north of England. The Sheerness-Vlissingen (Holland) route makes a comfortable overnight crossing; it takes about nine hours.

Fares on the cross-channel ferries vary considerably from season to season. Until the end of June and from early September onward, savings can be made by traveling midweek. Don't forget to budget for the cost of gas and road tolls, plus a couple of nights' accommodations.

The Channel Tunnel opened officially in May 1994 and provides the fastest route across the channel—25 minutes from Folkestone to Calais, or 60 minutes from motorway to motorway. For more information, *see* The Channel Tunnel *in* Smart Travel Tips, *above.*

Roads from the channel ports to Italy are mostly toll-free. The exceptions are French autoroutes, the road crossing the Ardennes, the Swiss superhighway network (for which a special tax sticker must be bought at the frontier or in advance), the St. Gotthard Tunnel, and the road between the tunnel and the Italian superhighway system. The reduced-price petrol coupons once offered by the Italian government have been discontinued, but it won't hurt to check with the AA or RAC before departure to be sure

they haven't become available again.

If these distances seem too great to drive, there's always the Motorail from the channel ports. However, no car/sleeper expresses run beyond Milan, 575 kilometers (360 miles) north of Rome, during the winter. From June/July–September there is car/sleeper service between Calais and Bologna, Livorno and Rome.

BY TRAIN

Visitors traveling to Italy by train have several options. You can leave London's Victoria Station at 9:25 AM for the Folkestone–Boulogne Seacat catamaran service; from Boulogne Maritime, you take the train to Gare du Nord in Paris (arrival time 4:15 PM) and then a taxi or metro across town to Gare de Lyons. From there, you pick up the 8:56 PM "Napoli Express" for Rome. There are first-and second-class sleeping cars and second-class couchettes (bed bunks) for the overnight run to Italy. From Paris to Dijon there's a refreshment service, and a buffet car is attached in the morning. The train reaches Turin at 6:10 AM the next day and Rome at 2:19 PM. Construction of a high-speed train line between France and Italy should be under way in 1997.

Alternatively, the 8:55 AM Victoria service catches the Dover–Calais ferry crossing; arrival time in Paris is 5:20 PM. The "Palatino" leaves Paris at Gare de Lyons and travels via Chambéry and the Mont Cenis tunnel to Turin, arriving about 2:50. You reach Rome by 9:35 AM. The train has first- and second-class sleepers and second-class couchettes, but no ordinary day cars for sitting up overnight. There's a buffet car from Paris to Chambéry and from Genoa to Rome.

A year-round service leaves Victoria at 1:25 PM, catching the Jetfoil for Oostende in plenty of time to take the 8:53 PM train to Brig, Switzerland, arriving at about 9 AM. Change there for the 10:31 AM Milan train. At Milan there's a 12:55 PM departure for Bologna, Florence, and Rome, arriving in Rome at 5:50 PM.

Since the Channel Tunnel opened, train journeys between London Waterloo to Paris Gare du Nord take only three hours, or 3¼ hours to Brussels. Departures are hourly from 6:30 AM to 8 PM: Check-in about 20 minutes before departure time. Call (☎ 0181/784–1333) for more information. For further information, *see* The Channel Tunnel *in* Smart Travel Tips, *above.*

W
WHEN TO GO

The main tourist season runs from April to mid-October. It follows that for serious sightseers the best months are from fall to early spring. The so-called low season may be cooler and inevitably rainier, but it has its rewards: less time waiting on lines and closer-up, unhurried views of what you want to see. Weatherwise, the best months for sightseeing are April, May, June, September, and October, generally pleasant and not too hot. The hottest months are July and August, when brief afternoon thunderstorms are common in inland areas. Winters are relatively mild in most places on the main tourist circuit but always include some rainy spells. In general, the northern half of the peninsula and the entire Adriatic Coast, with the exception of Apulia, are rainier than the rest of Italy.

Foreign tourists crowd the major art cities at Easter, when Italians flock to resorts and to the country. From March through May, bus loads of eager schoolchildren on excursions take cities of artistic and historical interest by storm.

If you can avoid it, don't travel at all in Italy in August, when much of the population is on the move, especially around Ferragosto, the August 15 national holiday, when cities such as Rome and Milan are deserted and many restaurants and shops are closed. (Of course, with residents away on vacation, this makes crowds less of a bother for tourists.) Except for a few year-round resorts, such as Taormina and some towns on the Italian Riviera, coastal resorts usually close up tight from October or November to April; they're at their best in June and September, when everything is open but uncrowded.

CLIMATE

The following are average daily maximum and minimum temperatures for Italy.

Climate in Italy

MILAN

Jan.	40F	5C	May	74F	23C	Sept.	75F	24C
	32	0		57	14		61	16
Feb.	46F	8C	June	80F	27C	Oct.	63F	17C
	35	2		63	17		52	11
Mar.	56F	13C	July	84F	29C	Nov.	51F	10C
	43	6		67	20		43	6
Apr.	65F	18C	Aug.	82F	28C	Dec.	43F	6C
	49	10		66	19		35	2

ROME

Jan.	52F	11C	May	74F	23C	Sept.	79F	26C
	40	5		56	13		62	17
Feb.	55F	13C	June	82F	28C	Oct.	71F	22C
	42	6		63	17		55	13
Mar.	59F	15C	July	87F	30C	Nov.	61F	16C
	45	7		67	20		49	10
Apr.	66F	19C	Aug.	86F	30C	Dec.	55F	13C
	50	10		67	20		44	6

VENICE

Jan.	42F	6C	May	70F	21C	Sept.	75F	24C
	33	1		56	13		61	16
Feb.	46F	8C	June	76F	25C	Oct.	65F	19C
	35	2		63	17		53	12
Mar.	53F	12C	July	81F	27C	Nov.	53F	12C
	41	5		66	19		44	7
Apr.	62F	17C	Aug.	80F	27C	Dec.	46F	8C
	49	10		65	19		37	3

THE GOLD GUIDE / SMART TRAVEL TIPS

1 Destination: Italy

UNDER THE SPELL OF ITALY

THEY CAME FOR THE LIGHT, they came for culture, they came for inspiration. Above all, they came to discover something that was missing in themselves. Passion, perhaps. A heightened sense of awareness. They came not simply to find themselves but to become their best selves.

Keats, Shelley, Byron, James, Goethe, Wagner, Prendergast, Renoir, Monet, and centuries of tourists who did not record their inspiration for the ages, but who, like Miss Lavish in E. M. Forster's *Room with a View,* knew that "one doesn't come to Italy for niceness . . . one comes for life."

And how is this life delivered unto one? If you ask the traveler of this decade, the answers will be various. For some it is the layers of history, physically present to walk upon, the reassuring sense of place and continuity that comes from a casual coexistence with antiquity. Twentieth-century businessmen and women stroll through the Roman Forum, swinging their briefcases and chatting of today's deals as they pass between the 5th-century-BC Corinthian columns of the Temple of Castor and Pollux.

It is as if one could hold out a hand and feel the touch of Pliny the Elder, Livy, or Catullus. A young woman, fresh from college Latin, made the mistake of visiting the Forum at high noon in August, suffered heat stroke, and was certain she heard Cicero speak before she fainted. There are those who would tell you that it wasn't the heat—Cicero *had* spoken.

Another woman, seven months pregnant when she and her husband traveled to Ravenna, swears that as she beheld the dazzling gold and lapis lazuli of San Vitale's 5th-century mosaics her unborn child leapt for joy. There is no guarding against it; life will fill you to brimming as Italy has its way with you.

For the sybarite, the palate is awakened by the clear, true flavors of wine and food that taste faintly of the earth and sea from which they came. Buckwheat pasta in Bormio; polenta, black with squid ink, in

Venice; creamy gelato at Giolitti in Rome; or the perfectly comforting bowl of risotto in Siena, served by a family in their nameless restaurant. You will hear, on the other side of the Atlantic, the longings of travelers returned home, who, as the light begins to change in early September, yearn for *gamberetti,* Venetian shrimp the size of a baby's fingertip. Summer causes them to recall the simple delight of sitting beneath large shade trees on the banks of Lake Como, drinking cool wine from earthenware pitchers. Winter's winds bring memories of Alpine chills chased by a fiery draft of grappa.

It is the dream that takes you back, just as it was the dream that enveloped you while you were there. You will notice that those who travel in Italy seem to do so in a state of reverie. Perhaps it is the diaphanous gauze of light that softens physical outlines and blurs the distinction between past and present. A light conducive to daydreams. A light that both intensifies life and makes it gentler to the touch.

Of course, there are those who have been rudely awakened from the dream by a revved-up 1990s state-of-the-art motorcycle outside their 19th-century Roman hotel. They will grumpily tell of the shocking presence of 20th-century blight in a land that seemed impervious to such intrusion. In the heat of disillusion, they will complain of the "real" Italy, of Roman traffic jams, thefts in Naples, Venice as Disneyland, a highway system around Milan as attractive as the New Jersey Turnpike. They will warn that you, a woman, must not be persuaded by the charms of an Italian gentleman who commits his heart and future within a three-minute walk across a piazza.

There is truth in what they say, but the generosity of the Italians and the striking physical beauty of their land make it possible to live in the dream alongside the blight. You cannot arrive in Venice without driving through the gray air of Mestre, polluted by oil refineries. But once your water taxi is negotiating the Grand Canal, you lose yourself in time and space. And that is what Italy is about . . . losing and finding yourself in time and space. By morning, as the rudely awakened dreamer stands on the Palatine Hill and smells the wild fennel just as Horace did, all is forgiven.

I**T IS THE NATURAL** as well as the man-made wonders that entrance. In the Valtellina Valley you will sit in grottoes where the Caesars sat to soak in hot mineral springs, and you will feel the curing effects of waters that were said to ease the pain of gout, arthritis, and politics. You can indulge in the mindless delights of the Amalfi Coast exactly as 19th-century English travelers did when they came to rest their minds, weary from the obligatory acquisition of culture in the north. Here, where rocky cliffs are caught in a perpetual dive to the sea, nothing seems more important than tonight's dinner or lovemaking.

Italy may be the most sensual of countries. Perhaps it is the basic simplicity that returns one to the simplest human emotions: the organic nature of all that surrounds you, each century seeming to grow from the land. Or perhaps it is the heightened sense of romance that comes from the constant reminders of the very best of that which people are capable—the serenity of Bellini's altarpiece in San Zaccaria, the compassion of Michelangelo's *Pietà* in St. Peter's, the symmetry of a Palladian villa rising from the earth of the Veneto. Or it could be living among people for whom life's pleasures are celebrated rather than guiltily indulged.

Whatever it is, to experience Italy one needs time, not necessarily in days but in solitude. It is in the silent times that Italy will be revealed to you. Early morning, watching the light shine on the Pantheon, while strong Italian coffee wakens your senses. Dawn on the Grand Canal as dark green water is sprayed with gold and the only sound is a gondolier's oar breaking the silent surface. Midnight in the Forum, Daisy Miller's undoing and Byron's inspiration. Sunrise in Stelvio National Park, where eagles soar overhead and you are knee-deep in wildflowers.

And one must believe in that elusive commodity, happiness. This is a country that, through the ages, in fact and fiction, has promised that possibility. Goethe, having fled the restrictive court life of Weimar, wrote from Rome in September 1788: "I can honestly say I have never been so happy in my life as now." And in *Room with a View,* Forster observed that when his young provincial heroine, Lucy, finally dared forfeit her Baedeker for experience, "then the pernicious charm of Italy worked on her, and, instead of acquiring information, she began to be happy."

You, too, should relinquish this book from time to time and observe with an uninstructed eye, drift into the dream, and allow yourself to be charmed.

—*By Barbara Lazear Ascher*

A frequent writer about Italy for the New York Times, *Barbara Lazear Ascher is also the author of a collection of essays,* Playing After Dark.

WHAT'S WHERE

Like a Santa Claus stocking, the boot of Italy overflows with unsurpassable sights—from top to toe. Here is a sampling of the infinite variety of the country's many regions and attractions.

Rome

Antique, Renaissance, Baroque—and always papal—the city that is the "Mother of Us All" continues to enthrall visitors, just as she has since time immemorial. This is where Nero fiddled, Mark Antony came to praise Caesar, and Charlemagne was crowned. The wonder is that you can still walk around where Nero played, visit the Forum in which the Romans crowded to hear Mark Antony's eulogy, and lunch in the vicinity of Charlemagne's coronation site. Begin by discovering the grandeur that was Rome: the Colosseum, the Forum, and the Pantheon. Then explore early Christian Rome via the Catacombs; tour the closest thing to heaven on earth for many people—the Vatican—and take in such Baroque marvels as the Piazza Navona and the glorious Trevi Fountain. Arrive refreshed—thanks to an espresso at the Caffè Greco—at the foot of the Spanish Steps, where the picturesque world of the classic grand tour—the 19th-century world of John Keats and Tosca—

awaits you. Rome is a veritable Grand Canyon of culture, built up with stratified layers of pagan, medieval, and modern. To help you catch your historic breath, Rome provides delightful ways to relax: a walk through the cobblestone alleys of Trastevere—Rome's Greenwich Village; a *Campari* break in a café facing a timeless piazza; an hour stolen alongside a splashing fountain, under the balm of Roman sunshine. A visit to the Eternal City will live up to its name in memory.

Florence

Florence, the "Athens of Italy" and the key to the Renaissance, hugs the banks of the Arno River where it lies folded in the emerald green hills of north-central Tuscany. Elegant and somewhat aloof, as if set apart by its past greatness, this historic center of European civilization still shares with Rome the honor of first place among Italian cities for the abundance and importance of its artistic works. Every street, square, and *vicolo* (alley) functions as a display window of Romanesque, Gothic, or Renaissance architecture in churches, palaces, and towers. Gaze at Michelangelo's towering *David*. Explore the Uffizi—shrine of the Renaissance—where you'll find Botticelli's and Raphael's most reverential Madonnas. Marvel at the magnificent chapels and homes (particularly the Palazzo Medici-Riccardi) of the Medici family, whose art patronage rocketed Florence to the forefront of the Renaissance. Impressive piazzas and an incomparable 15th-century skyline make outdoor sightseeing in Florence particularly rewarding. World-class stores and restaurants make shopping and dining memorable as well: perhaps you'll discover a gold necklace fashioned from a 19th-century watch, enjoy the famous *bistecca alla Fiorentina* (Florentine steak), or take a twilight stroll along the Arno. Such experiences can make up the stock of some of your most precious memories.

Tuscany

Without a doubt, Nature outdid herself in Tuscany. Punctuated by thickly wooded hills, snowcapped peaks, sun-warmed vineyards, olive groves, and dramatic hill towns, Tuscany's milk-and-honey vistas have changed little since Renaissance artists first beheld them. Not surprisingly, you'll find some of Italy's greatest art treasures here, including the 13th-century Leaning Tower of Pisa and Piero della Francesca's *Legend of the True Cross* frescoes in Arezzo. The time traveler will love Siena, "the Pompeii of the Middle Ages" (as it was called by the philosopher Taine). One of the best-preserved medieval towns, it is known both for its Gothic school of art and for the eponymous hue that tints its buildings. Every July and August, the city explodes in a frenzy of excitement at the historic Corsa del Palio (Parade of the Banner)—an all-day festival that culminates in the dizzying horse race at Piazza del Campo.

Escape to a celebrated Tuscan hill town—perched dramatically above a fertile valley—such as San Gimignano (with its Manhattan-like skyline of medieval towers) and experience the Who–turned-back-the-clock? sensation of Mark Twain's Connecticut Yankee when he arrived in King Arthur's court. With a glass of Vernaccia di San Gimignano in hand, you'll feel like lingering long.

Venice

Rising from the waters of the Venetian lagoons like a mirage, the city of canals is unlike any other. A romantic maze of alleys, waterways, and tiny squares and bridges playing hide-and-seek with each other, Venice rarely fails to engage the imagination. In this city of Marco Polo, Titian, and Vivaldi, start your tour with a *vaporetto* ride down the Grand Canal and savor Venice's most sumptuous palaces—the Ca' Rezzonico, the Palazzo Pésaro, and the Ca' d'Oro—mirrored in the waters of Venice's own Fifth Avenue. Head for the city's heart, the Piazza San Marco, where you'll find even the pigeons pressed for space. Climb the Campanile for a ravishing bird's-eye view. "Venice is like eating an entire box of chocolate liqueurs in one go," Truman Capote once remarked, and he's right: As you walk (or, more preferably, glide) from one sight to another, gallery gout can easily set in. So, after touring the city's museums, churches, and landmarks—stuffed with the most spectacular Bellini, Veronese, and Tiepolo paintings—ferry out to the peaceful lagoon island of Torcello for a bracing restorative. The best time to catch Venice is during the Historic Regatta (the first week of September) when the 18th-century canvases of Canaletto seem to come to life.

The Venetian Arc

The green plains of the mainland beyond the Venetian lagoon are studded with some of Italy's smaller art cities. The individual artistic variations on the overall Venetian theme make each town distinctly charming. Elegant Vicenza, which bears the signature of the great 16th-century architect Andrea Palladio, blends rustic beauty with a jigger of 18th-century Venetian chic. Here, the wealthy citizenry devised ways to make la vita all the more dolce at noble villas (many of which are now museums): Palladio's La Rotonda, the hauntingly beautiful La Malcontenta (along the idyllic Brenta Canal), and the Villa Barbaro in Maser. Further west, Verona is famed for the Tombs of the Scaligeri, the romantic settings associated with Shakespeare's *Romeo and Juliet,* and an ancient Roman arena (still packing in the crowds for thrilling opera performances). Art lovers head for Padua to catch Giotto's Scrovegni Chapel and Donatello's powerful statue of the *condottiere* (mercenary general) Gattamelata. To truly unwind, head for Asolo, the City with a Hundred Horizons: it's a magical hill town replete with villas and gardens, but there's not a single souvenir shop or espresso bar.

The Italian Rivieras

The Italians perfected *il dolce far niente*—the sweet art of idleness—and they must have done it right here in Liguria, site of the Italian rivieras. Called "the island," the province is enclosed by mountain ranges that create an ideal climate for the narrow coastal strip (you can sip coffee outdoors in winter and linger under palm trees at Christmastime). Here, in jet-set resorts and quaint fishing villages, tourists recover from vacation overload. The Riviera di Ponente (Western Riviera) runs from the French border to Genoa and is best known for San Remo, Monte Carlo's less expensive cousin. The eastern counterpart, the Riviera di Levante, is made up of Camogli, Rapallo, Levanto, Cinque Terre, Portovenere, San Fruttuoso, glowing like pearls on a string. Of these, Portofino—the Palm Beach of Italy—is the beauty-contest winner. The Crusaders, who once used Portofino for its refueling resources, have been replaced by today's top-of-the-heap who arrive in their yachts to sun and soak. In a region of lavish natural beauty, man has tried to go nature one better: Every restaurant and café delights with rainbow sun blinds and pastel terraces. When doing nothing becomes too exhausting, there is always Genoa—the region's thriving metropolis—for stimulation.

Piedmont/Val d'Aosta

Piedmont and the magnificent Val d'Aosta in the northwest corner of Italy come as delightful surprises in a land of continuous natural splendor. The characteristics of neighboring France and Switzerland blend harmoniously with the region's Italian heritage. Geographically, the area combines the lure of the highest Alpine peaks—such as Mont Blanc and Mont Cervino (the Matterhorn)—in ranges that fan out along the south, west, and north boundaries and the broad flatlands of the plain. Here, at Breuil-Cervinia, Courmayeur, and Sestriere, skiing is at its best. Alpine valleys harboring 14th and 15th-century castles—witnesses to turbulent days of old—are anchored by Turin, the "Italian Detroit," home of the Fiat empire. The city's other well-known imports—Borsalino hats, vermouth, and Asti Spumante—mark it as a great cosmopolitan center.

Milan, Lombardy, and the Lakes

Lombardy stretches south from the Alps to the River Po, and not far from the modern metropolis of Milan are the dreamlike resort lakes of Como, Maggiore, and Garda, whose 19th-century summer palaces, exotic formal gardens, and Alpine vistas give them some of the most achingly beautiful settings in Italy. Milan's cultural identity is as diverse as its changeable weather: international fashion capital, industrial and banking center, crucible of modern design. The must-see's here include La Scala—the equivalent of paradise to opera performers and fans; the gigantic Gothic Duomo; the Brera and Poldi Pezzoli museums; Leonardo da Vinci's *Last Supper;* and, of course, stopping and shopping at Versace, Valentino, and Armani. Farther south, tour the great Renaissance cities of the plain: Pavia, Cremona, and Mantua, home to the palaces of the Gonzaga. On the edge of the Alps, Bergamo awaits with its hilltop *città alta,* a charming medieval center. For those who believe holidays are fantasies (or should be!), the apricot-color villages, palaces, and gardens of the lakes region cannot be bettered. Lake Como has gorgeous villas, many around the beguiling town of Bellagio; along Lake Garda is the Brescian Riviera, and on Lake Maggiore you'll find the storybook Borromean Islands and glowing Stresa. Here you may not find great art treasures or encounter the long-lost pagan past, but, if you are in search of it, you will certainly find peace.

The Dolomites

Northwest Italy's Dolomite Mountains— Nature's skyscrapers—draw scenery-hungry tourists by the thousands. Many come in hot pursuit of the charming meadows and valleys; the crystal clear lakes; the stupifying cliffs, curiously shaped peaks, and splintered crags whose resplendent hues range from pale rose at dawn to declamatory purple at dusk. (Leonardo da Vinci depicted these peaks in the haunting background of his *Mona Lisa*.) For other visitors this region is the ultimate year-round sports playground—with the seeing just as important as the skiing in jet-set Cortina d'Ampezzo. Take the Strada del Vino (Wine Route) from Bolzano to Trento, where there is a famous cathedral and the moated Castello del Buonconsiglio; enjoy the "grape cure" at Merano; zip along the 48 hairpin turns of the Stelvio Pass; absorb the vistas of the Grande Strada delle Dolomiti (Great Dolomites Road); and top it all off with a skydiving stop at the historic town of Bressanone, where Gothic and Baroque art blend harmoniously.

Emilia-Romagna

Gourmets the world over argue that Emilia-Romagna's greatest contribution to mankind has been gastronomic. Birthplace of fettucine, prosciutto, tortellini, and lasagna, you need never worry about any of the restaurants you walk into. The area also contains an abundance of cultural riches—the legacies of the Farnese family in Piacenza and Parma, the Este family in Modena and Ferrara, the Malatesta in Rimini, and the Bentivoglio in Bologna. Bologna—*dotta e grassa* (learned and fat)—is home to Italy's oldest university as well as to the spirits of Copernicus, Galileo, and Dante. The area between Piacenza and Parma is opera country—Verdi's villa of Sant'Agata is in Bussetto. The polished city of Parma nourished two

of Italy's greatest painters, Parmigianino and Correggio. For a breather, head along the Adriatic coast to the principal summer resort of Rimini and the Byzantine beauty of mosaic-rich Ravenna, glittering as brightly as it did 1,500 years ago.

Umbria and the Marches

Legends linger here in the evergreen land of the saints, the birthplace of St. Francis and St. Claire (Assisi), St. Benedict (Norcia), and St. Rita (Cascia). The strange, bluish haze that tints the landscape has inspired writers to characterize the region as mystical and ethereal. Here, medieval enclaves wear their ancient histories lightly, and majestic valleys refuse to pose for tourists' cameras. Umbria's rich artistic inheritance includes the frescoes of Giotto and Pietro Lorenzetti in Assisi's Basilica of St. Francis, the brooding Palazzo dei Consoli in Gubbio, and the Gothic glory of Orvieto's cathedral. For a "deep, delicious bath of medievalism," as Henry James wrote, a visit to Assisi is an imperative; the spirit of St. Francis gently permeates the hillside town. For more urbane pleasures, head for Spoleto's celebrated Festival of Two Worlds or Perugia's popular jazz concerts. Eastward, in the off-the-beaten-track region of the Marches, is Urbino, where the Renaissance first came to full flower. It is full of treasures by such illustrious artists as Bramante, Raphael, and Piero della Francesca. A visit to its Ducal Palace reveals more about the wealth and artistic energy of the Renaissance than a shelf of history books.

Campania

Magnetic, magical, and magnificent, Campania is the Italy many travelers dream about. Emperors and kings, popes and artists, musicians and writers have made its sea-wreathed resorts and starlit isles their homes for more than 2,000 years—and well they might, for this is a compressed realm of undiluted beauty. Naples—the most operatic of cities—rules over the unequaled panorama of its bay. Once ancient Romans led the carefree life at nearby Pompeii; today, travelers soak up the 24-karat sun on Capri—a pint-size island paradise that is as intoxicating as its delicious wines. Down the shoreline along Amalfi Drive is shockingly beautiful Ravello, where just about the bluest view on tap takes in the Gulf of Salerno. From here, take a day trip to Paestum's ancient temples. Head back to Sorrento, Positano, and Amalfi, famed as places of play and pleasure. Locals dare you to conjure up towns that are as lovely, even in your imagination.

Apulia

Misguided tourists think that after a visit to Naples and a drive around the Amalfi coast to Salerno (maybe as far afield as Paestum) they have seen Italy's south. The truth is they have barely entered the gate. Italy's far south is composed of the ancient provinces of Apulia (Puglia), Lucania (the Basilicata), and Calabria—the heel, instep, and arch, respectively, of Italy's boot. Often overlooked Apulia is steeped in ancient history and rich with tantalizing sights that are only now coming to the surface. The region invites aimless exploration: Seek out its whitewashed ports, imposing castles, and strange igloo-shape dwellings called *trulli*. The cities of Brindisi, Bari, and Lecce hold many fascinations, and the coastline is full of seductions—unspoiled coves, bougainvillea-draped vistas, and seas that shimmer like sheets of turquoise.

Sicily

On this fabled island, you may ski down a snow-muffled volcano, walk through palm and orange groves, and swim within sight of flowering almond trees—all in the same day. Many visitors first head for Taormina, a town whose natural beauties are so great that even the overdevelopment of the past 50 years has not spoiled its grandeur. The city's views of the sea and Mt. Etna come close to panoramic perfection. In summer, Taormina hosts an arts festival, with many of its events held in its spectacular 3rd-century bc Greek Theater. Sicily's main metropolis, Palermo, has always been at the crossroads of civilization: Phoenician colony, Carthaginian town, capital of an Arab emirate, commercial hub of Europe and Asia under Norman rule, center of learning under Frederick II. Nearby is Sicily's most important art treasure, the cathedral of Monreale, with its magnificent medieval mosaics. On the western coast lies Agrigento, where antiquity-focused visitors can fulfill their greatest expectations at the Valley of the Temples. Almost 100 ancient Greek buildings are here (the Temple of Concord being the best preserved in the world after that of Theseus in Athens).

Sardinia

Too distant from imperial and papal Rome to be influenced by the character of the mainland, Sardinia is as unique as its weather-worn landscape. Visitors arrive at this jewel-in-the-rough landscape by air or sea at Cagliari in the south, Olbia in the northeast, or Alghero in the northwest. Although the indigenous culture is one of Italy's most interesting, many travelers opt to explore the high-profile Costa Smeralda. This chic resort was developed by the Aga Khan, who discovered its charms when his yacht took shelter from a storm. "Secret paradise" of tycoons and actresses in years past, the Costa is now an open, upscale vacationland. Sardinia's most expensive hotels are here, and the current scions of the House of Savoy—modern Italy's one royal dynasty—return annually in their yachts. Intrepid travelers head for the *nuraghe,* cyclopean stones that are among prehistory's enigmas. Severely beautiful Sardinia remains a prime destination for those in search of a vacation forgetaway.

PLEASURES AND PASTIMES

The Art of Enjoying Art

Travel veterans will tell you that the endless series of masterpieces in Italy's churches, palaces, and museums can cause first-time visitors—eyes glazed over from a heavy downpour of images, dates, and names—to lean, Pisa-like, on their companions for support. After a surfeit of Botticellis and Bronzinos and the 14th Raphael, even the miracle of the High Renaissance may begin to pall. The secret, of course, is to act like a turtle—not a hare—and take your sweet time. Instead of trotting after briskly efficient tour guides, allow the splendors of the age to unfold—slowly. Get out and explore the actual settings—medieval chapels, Rococo palaces, and Romanesque town squares—for which these marvelous examples of Italy's art and sculpture were conceived centuries ago and where many of them may still be seen in situ.

Musems are only the most obvious places to view art; there are always the trompe l'oeil renderings of Assumptions that float across Baroque church ceilings and piazza scenes that might be Renaissance paintings brought to life. Instead of studying a Gothic statue in Florence's Bargello, spend an hour in the medieval cloisters of the nearby convent of San Marco; by all means, take in Michelangelo's *Slaves* in Florence's Accademia, but then meander down the 15th-century street, a short bus ride away, where he was born. You'll find that after three days traipsing through museums, a walk through a quiet neighborhood will act as a much-needed restorative of perspective. You'll even discover more artistic treasures along the streets of Italy than in many a museum back home.

To truly enjoy art, it also helps to know some basic vocabulary. Of course, there may be many art treasures that will not quicken your pulse, but one morning you may see a Caravaggio so perfect, so beautiful, that your knees will buckle.

Il Dolce Far Niente

When Italians work, they work harder than anyone—and when they play, they do that harder than anyone, too. After all, the idea of vacation was probably invented by some hardworking Roman emperor and, ever since, the Italians have been finetuning what they call il dolce far niente—the sweet art of idleness. Today, even relaxing can feel like a chore, but thanks to Italy's opulent villas, picture-perfect coastal resorts, and dreamy hill towns, you can idle here more successfully than anywhere else. Tourists could learn from the natives who just breathe in the beauty and relax. But it takes more than trading in a silk tie for a T-shirt; you have to adjust to the deeper, subtler rhythms of leisure, Italian-style. Unclocked hours spent over a Campari in a sun-splashed café; days spent soaking up the sun on the Amalfi coast; an afternoon spent painting a watercolor on the shores of Lake Como: You may be pleasantly surprised to find that such pursuits prove more beneficial than forced marches through the obligatory sights. Remember—the luxury is often in the lingering.

Dining

In Italy, cookery is civilization. In the days of the Roman legions, pundits used to say, *"Ubi Roma ibi allium"* (Where there are Romans, there is garlic). Ever since the days of the Caesars—when emperors quickly learned the wisdom of *"Stomaco pieno, anima consolata"* (Full stomach, satisfied soul)—Italian chefs have taken one of life's sensory pleasures and made it into an art, and today travelers can feast on an incredible array of culinary delights. Of course, Italian food has come a long way since the days when Horace, the great poet of ancient Rome, feasted on lamprey boiled in five-year-old wine, the liver of a goose fattened on figs, and apples picked by the light of the waning moon. But you can still enter restaurants in Bologna, enjoy a dish of tortellini, and be told, *"Anche Dante le ha mangiato cósi"* (Dante also ate them this way). In fact, the newest trend in Italian cooking is to serve up the old—the simple, rustic, time-honored forms of cucina *simpatica, rustica,* and *trattoria*—with a nouvelle flair.

Among Italian chefs, there is concern that membership in the European Union will affect the country's unique regional cooking. The use of processed ingredients and nonorganically grown vegetables is taking its toll. Happily, food critics rejoice that much of Italian cooking remains *puro* and *sincero*—true to the country's culinary traditions.

Dining is a marvelous part of the total Italian experience, a chance to enjoy authentic specialties and ingredients. Visitors have a choice of eating places, ranging from a *ristorante* (restaurant) to a trattoria, *tavola calda,* or *rosticceria*. A trattoria is usually a family-run place, simpler in decor, menu, and service than a ristorante, and slightly less expensive. Some rustic-looking spots call themselves *osterie* but are really restaurants. (A true *osteria* is a wineshop—a basic, down-to-earth tavern.) The countless fast-food places opening everywhere are variations of the older Italian institutions of the tavola calda or rosticceria, which offer a selection of hot and cold dishes to be taken out or eaten on the premises. At either a tavola calda or rosticceria some items are priced by the portion, others by weight. You usually select your food, find out how much it costs, and then pay the cashier, who gives you a stub that you hand to the man at the counter when you pick up the food.

None of the above eateries serves breakfast; in the morning you go to a coffee bar, which is where you can also find sandwiches, pastries, and other snacks that are perfect for later in the day. Tell the cashier what you want, pay for it, and then take the stub to the counter, where you order. Remember that table service is extra; don't sit at a table unless you want to be served. On the other hand, if you do sit down, you'll be allowed to linger as long as you like.

In eating places of all kinds the menu is posted in the window or just inside the door so you can see what you're getting into (in a snack bar or tavola calda the price list is usually displayed near the cashier). In all but the simplest places there's a *coperto* (cover charge) and usually also a *servizio* (service charge) of 10%–15%, only part of which goes to the waiter. A *menù turistico* (tourist menu) includes taxes and service, but beverages are usually extra.

Generally, a typical meal in a restaurant or trattoria consists of at least two courses: a first course of pasta, risotto, or soup; and a second course of meat or fish. Side dishes such as vegetables and salads cost extra, as do desserts. There is no such thing as a side dish of pasta; pasta is a course in itself and Italians would never think of serving a salad with it; the salad comes later. Years ago, pasta dishes were inexpensive because restaurateurs made their profit on the total of the first and second courses. Now, tourists and even some diet-conscious Italians tend to order only one course—usually a pasta, perhaps followed by a salad or vegetables—so hosts have jacked up the price of first courses. Now, about antipasto: Many a misunderstanding arises over a lavish offering of antipasto, which literally means "before the meal." No matter how generous and varied the antipasto, the host expects those who have one to order at least one other course. Pizza is in a category by itself and is a one-dish meal, even for the Italians. But some replace the starter course of pasta with a small pizza.

Tap water is safe almost everywhere unless labeled *"non potabile."* Most people order bottled *acqua minerale* (mineral water), either *gassata* (carbonated), or *naturale,* or *non gassata* (without bubbles). In a restaurant you order it by the *litro* (liter) or *mezzo litro* (half-liter); often the waiter will bring it without being asked, so if you don't like it, or want to keep your check down, make a point of ordering *acqua semplice* (tap water). You can also order *un bicchiere di acqua minerale* (a glass of mineral water) at any bar. If you are on a low-sodium diet, ask for everything (within reason) *senza sale* (without salt).

Lunch is served in Rome from 1 to 3, dinner from 8 to 10, or later in some restaurants. Service begins and ends a half hour earlier in Florence and Venice, an hour earlier in smaller towns in the north, and a half hour to one hour later in the south. Almost all eating places close one day a week and for vacations in summer and/or winter. *Buon appetito!*

Shopping

"Made in Italy" has become synonymous with style, quality, and craftsmanship whether it refers to high fashion or Maserati automobiles. The best buys are leather goods of all kinds—from gloves to bags to jackets—silk goods, knitwear, gold jewelry, ceramics, and local handicrafts. The most important thing to keep in mind when shopping in Italy is that every region has its specialties. Venice is known for glassware, lace, and velvet; Milan and Como for silk; the Dolomites and the mountainous regions of Calabria and Sicily for hand-carved wooden objects; Florence for straw goods, gold jewelry, leather, and paper products; Naples for coral and cameos; Assisi for embroidery; and Deruta, Gubbio, Vietri, and many towns in Apulia and Sicily for ceramics.

In general, the idea that bargaining is the rule in Italy is mistaken. There is no universal policy, but for the most part prices are fixed in the better shops. Where you see the sign PREZZI FISSI (fixed prices) you can be sure that there is no bargaining to be done. However, you can bargain to your heart's delight at outdoor markets and when buying from street vendors.

Unless your purchases are too bulky, avoid having them shipped home; if the shop seems extremely reliable about shipping, get a written statement of what will be sent, when, and how. (*See* Shopping *in* individual chapters for details.)

Spas

Thanks to its location in the Mediterranean region—one of the world's most active volcano belts—Italy is rich in thermo-mineral springs. Consequently, the Italians have developed a special attitude about what we call spas since the ancient Romans advanced the idea of *"mens sana in corpore sano"* (a sound mind in a healthy body). Perhaps old-fashioned today, taking the waters remains a unique part of Italian culture; it is state-supported and medically supervised. Never mind Greco-Roman worship of the body in templelike baths, choices now range from antiaging cures to American-style aerobic workouts to fangotherapy (medicinal mud therapy). Today, more and more travelers are taking vacations from their vacations by visiting one of Italy's sybaritic spas.

But don't say spa (in Italian, s.p.a. denotes a business corporation). Forget the Roman origins: the term in Italy is *terme* (baths). A peek into a typical Italian health resort can present an image worthy of Dante: a host of monkishly clad and mud-caked figures moving through mists of steam; these are health- and beauty-conscious aficionados enjoying a dizzying range of curative techniques. At over 200 of these centers, drinking and bathing cures are based on naturally produced thermal mineral waters, with mornings devoted to sipping and strolling as well as occasional forays into espresso bars. Then come hot mud packs, muscle massage, anticellulite treatments, and sinus-targeted steam inhalations.

Cura means "treatment," not miracle(s). After the obligatory evaluation by a staff doctor, a regimen is designed which allows plenty of time for sightseeing, jogging, and post-lunch shopping. If staying at a *terme* in places like Abano and Montecatini, you can add outings to nearby Etruscan ruins, country inns, and wineries.

Health Italian-style comes in a variety of health, beauty, and antistress packages. Many of the new offerings at terme are based on old methods. Among them: therapeutic skin-care treatments using natural ingredients—flowers, fruits, muds, herbs, honey—in sophisticated salons devoted to *"benessere e bellezza"* (health and beauty); acupuncture, reflexology, shiatsu, facials, and colonic irrigations; longevity cures; and for *la buona figura* (healthy body), *dietetico* meals—based on light but delicious regional cuisine.

Increasingly, travelers to Italy are finding a visit to a thermal spa the best antidote for tourist fatigue, with many repeat visitors swearing by the benefits of particular waters (i.e. Terme Stabiane has 28 different springs). The pleasures at some are delightfully varied: you can sample the local acqua minerale while walking through a spa's park or garden accompanied by the strains of Puccini or Verdi. Heading from north to south, here are some of the best of Italy's healthy escapes.

LOMBARDY➤ Milanese socialites shed pounds at state-of-the-art Stresa Wellness Centre on Lake Maggiore. Weeklong programs include a personal diet consultation, a medical checkup, and deluxe accommodations at the Grand Hotel des Iles Borromees (Corso Umberto I, 67, 28049 Stresa, ☎ 039/23282, FAX 039/32405). Bilingual Merano/Meran in the Alpine arc at the foot of the Dolomites offers hikes, skiing, and thermal waters. Steeped in Tyroleian charm, with medieval porticoed streets, old-world palaces, and neoclassic bathhouses, it's a good base for exploring the Alto Adige. A leading hotel is the Kurhotel Palace (✉ Via Cavour 2, 39012 Merano, ☎ 039/34734, FAX 039/237200). Sip at the source of San Pellegrino near Bergamo, and admire Art Nouveau villas and the casino.

THE VENETO➤ When you've had enough tours of Palladian villas, the Venetian Arc region can provide respite and easy access to the splendors of Venice. Fangotherapy at Abano Terme—one of Italy's leading spa towns—in the Euganean hills near Padua and Verona is an art form in mud body wraps, followed by bathing and swimming in mineral waters. More than 100 hotels in the area mix thermal water with fine high-mineral clay for fango treatments (instead of offering drinking cures). Among the best spas: Hotel Trieste & Victoria (✉ Via Pietro d'Abano 1, 35031 Abano Terme, ☎ 039/669101, FAX 039/669779), with grand gardens in the center of town, indoor/outdoor pools, a café, and private treatment rooms; Hotel Bristol Buja (✉ Via Monteortone 2, 35031 Abana Terme, ☎ 039/669390, FAX 039/667910) with Old World–style mud/massage rooms on each floor and a beauty/well-being center with yoga, pools, and aerobics; and Hotel Augustus (✉ Viale Stazione 150, 35036 Montegrotto

Terme, ☎ 039/793200, FAX 039/793518), with hillside views and a quiet location as well as comprehensive fangotherapy.

TUSCANY➤ Vineyards surround hillside terme where Tuscan food and wine can restore your spirits just in case the waters don't. Diversions range from golf to horse races, but hiking the unspoiled country-side—dotted with castles and Roman ruins—is the best way to discover the region's riches.

There is a wide range of spas from which to choose. Spadeus (⊠ Via le Piane 35, 53042 Chianciano Terme, ☎ 39/63232, FAX 39/64329) offers workouts with American fitness trainers and attracts people from all walks of life to Christina Newburgh's four-star hotel and Centro Benessere (Health Center). On site, you'll find an indoor Olympic-size pool, hydrotherapy, and medical services. With daily outings to ancient hill towns such as Montepulciano or Bagno Vignoni, you might forget to take the waters (closed mid-Dec.–Mar. 1). Grotta Giusti Terme (⊠ Via Grotta Giusti, 171, 51015 Monsummano, ☎ 39/51007) allows you to descend, dressed in a monklike robe, to vapor caves that conjure up Dante's Inferno. Set in a vast park outside of Florence, the stone-arched villa has modern hydromassage, facials, and swimming pools. Here, the season runs from April to November.

The town of Montecatini Terme—Italy's most famous spa town—has it all: grand hotels and pensions, nightlife, sports, skin care, as well as traditional balneotherapy baths, fangotherapy, and drinking cures. Preventative and detoxicating treatments supervised by medical staff are optional, but don't miss the morning promenade at Tettuccio, one of the town's nine watering places and Italy's grandest temple of health. Perhaps the best place to stay is the five-star Grand Hotel e la Pace (⊠ Viale Delle Toretta 1, 51016, ☎ 39/75801, FAX 39/78451; closed November to March), where you can step back to a gilded age of princes and movie stars. Terme de Saturnia (⊠ 58050 Saturnia, ☎ 39/601061, FAX 39/601266) is set in a valley threaded with warm sulfuric waters. Here, aquarelaxation is combined with antistress programs; there are also new cosmetic treatments researched by staff scientists to ease the ravages of time. Thermal swimming pools and waterfalls, a gymnasium,

and horseback excursions enhance this private retreat.

ROME AND LATIUM➤ Michelangelo flushed his kidney stone at the springs of Fiuggi, a fashionable summer resort since the 1200s. Buy a one-day ticket and a souvenir cup at the public park, then stroll the town's pleasant shopping center in the shadow of the Ernici Mountains, 90 minutes south of Rome. The best places to stay are the modern, centrally located Silva Hotel Splendid (⊠ Corso Nuovo Italia 18, 03014 Fiuggi, ☎ 039/5791, FAX 039/506546), which has in-house treatment facilities, and the Grand Hotel Palazzo della Fonte, (⊠ Via Dei Villini, 03014 Fiuggi, ☎ 039/5081, FAX 039/506752; closed mid-Dec.–Jan.), which allows guests to linger in Belle Epoque luxury while working off pounds at its new health club. Located in a private park overlooking the town, the resort—restored by Trusthouse Forte—features indoor and outdoor swimming pools, steam baths, and tennis courts.

CAMPANIA➤ Absorbing the sights in Pompeii may not let you think happily of mud and fiery steam, but spa treatments within view of Mt. Vesuvius and the Bay of Naples can be excellent. Castellemare di Stabia, heir to the ancient Roman resort of Stabiae, between Sorrento and Naples, has numerous hotels near the sea, and waters from 28 springs are prescribed at the health center. Centrally located is the four-star Hotel Dei Congressi (⊠ Viale Delle Nuove Terme 49, Castellammare di Stabia, ☎ 039/8722277, FAX 039/8722277).

Among sybaritic resorts in the Tyrhennian Sea off the coast of Naples, the islands of Capri and Ischia lure weary travelers with spas that offer comprehensive beauty and health programs. On Capri, head for the Capri Beauty Farm at the first-class Europa Palace Hotel (⊠ Via Capodimonte 2, 80071 Anacapri, ☎ 039/8373800, FAX 039/8373191). After taking in Capri's celebrated Blue Grotto and chic marina scene, let this full-service spa relax you with a variety of physiotherapy and cosmetic treatments. The season is from April to November.

Ischia has numerous sulfurous springs and thermal mud baths that you can enjoy at the Poseidon Gardens, a day spa and beach club, where you can relax amid 12 hot springs with massage, sand baths, and a wide range of treatments. For pampering and luxe accommodations, there are two standout hotels nearby: the Regina Isabella e Royal Sporting (⊠ Piazza S. Restituta, 80076 Lacca Ameno, ☎ 039/994322, FAX 039/900190; closed mid-October–mid-Apr.), where you can bathe in thermal waters or take a heated sand dip at the hotel's Santa Restituta Thermal/Health Spa, and the Hotel San Montano, (⊠ Via Montevico, 800 Lacco Ameno, ☎ 039/994033, FAX 039/980242; closed mid-Oct.–Apr.), a hilltop resort with breathtaking views, peace and quiet, and a full-service beauty farm.

Prior to leaving home, be sure to consult your physician, as heat treatments usually are not advised for people with high blood pressure or sensitive skin. Bring medical records if a cure program is planned. Treatments are scheduled daily except Sunday and holidays. Some hotels close during the winter season; check to be sure your reservations are confirmed. Two travel agencies that specialize in Italian terme trips are Custom Spa Vacations (⊠ 1318 Beacon St., Brookline, MA 02146, ☎ 617/566–5144) and Spa Trek/Spas Plus (⊠ 475 Park Ave. S, New York, NY 10016, ☎ 212/779–3480).

—Bernard Burt

Longtime spa buff, Bernard Burt is the author of Healthy Escapes: 240 Resorts and Retreats Where You Can Get Fit, Feel Good, Find Yourself and Get Away From It All *(Fodor's).*

NEW AND NOTEWORTHY

There's good news for those who plan to travel by rail or plane in Italy. FS, the Italian state railway, now provides **high-speed trains** for more destinations at reasonable rates. The ETR 460 Pendolino trains now serve Rome, Florence, Milan, Venice, and other major cities, with additional destinations due to be added in 1997. The trains are fast and the fares are competitive; the Milan-Rome route, for instance, offers a shorter travel time and more affordable fares than traveling by plane. In the air, Alitalia's former monopoly on domestic travel has been shattered by some new and aggressively marketed airlines such as **Air One** and **Meridiana.** As a result, passengers are finding a wider range of bargain fares to choose from.

In 1997 **Rome** will be in the throes of constructing new viaducts, a new subway line, and various other infrastructural repairs to get ready for the **Jubilee** celebrations in the year 2000. The main inconveniences to visitors will probably be traffic snarls around the Vatican, as construction of an underpass will be underway to eliminate a bottleneck at Castel Sant'Angelo.

Restoration work on the **Colosseum** will continue into 1997, and if Rome's superintendent of monuments has his way, visitors will have to pay to get inside the magnificent arena. He has proposed a prepaid pass for admission to the city's numerous classical attractions; the idea is being considered for nationwide adoption.

Structural renovations of the **Galleria Borghese** in Rome should be largely completed by the beginning of 1997, and it is expected that the refurbished main floor will be fully reopened at that time. This may mean that the temporary entrance, some distance from the main entrance to the estate, may no longer be used.

Also in Rome, it has finally become possible to buy a new pair of socks, or some milk and crackers at 2 AM. Several versions of what the Italians call a "drugstore" opened in Rome in 1996. Actually convenience stores, they are stocked with food and a range of other basic articles; they are the first stores in Italy to open 20 hours a day. One is located in Termini train station and another will soon open in Tiburtina Station. No prescriptions or over-the-counter medicines sold here, though; you can find those at all-night pharmacies.

In **Florence,** the **Torre dei Pulci,** the 15th-century tower adjacent to the Uffizi that was gutted by a terrorist bomb in 1993, has been almost completely restored, and by 1997 it will once again house the headquarters of that historic cultural institution, the Accademia dei Georgofili. If you go to Florence, take a look at the tower, on a side street of Piazza degli Uffizi: Demolition work revealed that the exterior was originally painted to look like brickwork; restorers have reproduced the original effect.

The 1997-8 season at **Milan's La Scala** will be operagoers' last chance to attend performances in the splendid theater at the heart of the city before it is temporarily closed for restoration. In the fall of 1998, La Scala will move to a modern, 2,300-seat concert hall in Bicocca-Tecnocity, in the postindustrial outskirts of Milan. The restoration project, which includes a brand-new stage and a refurbishing of the theater's interior, should be complete by 2000. In the meantime, the increased capacity of the Tecnocity hall and a fuller program will mean that it may be a little easier to get tickets for the famous opera company's productions.

The **Excelsior Hotel** in **Naples,** formerly a CIGA hotel, is being refurbished by a consortium of local hoteliers who purchased it from ITT-Sheraton under a franchise agreement. When the three-year restoration project has been completed, the Excelsior will join Sheraton's exclusive Luxury Collection of world-class hotels.

Naples will continue to offer **special packages** and **tours** as part of its highly-successful efforts to attract tourists. Capodimonte Museum has reopened after restoration, and many more of the city's historic churches and palaces are being opened on a regular basis. The May Monuments program, an intensively scheduled opening of rarely seen churches, palaces, and other sites, has attracted so much attention that long lines may discourage foreign visitors. Most of these sights are open only on weekends during the event, which will probably be extended into June 1997.

The most popular after-dinner drink in 1997 will almost surely be the lemon-flavored liqueur called *limoncello,* available under many brand names in varying degrees of sweetness. Unknown to most until about a year ago, it is now the rage. The best comes from the Capri–Sorrento–Amalfi area, where it was originally made. It should be served ice-cold, and it supposedly aids digestion. In any case, it is delicious.

FODOR'S CHOICE

No two people agree on what makes a perfect vacation, but it's fun and helpful to know what others think. Here's a compendium drawn from the must-see lists of hundreds of Italian tourists. For detailed information about these memories-in-the-making, refer to the appropriate chapters in this book.

Quintessential Italy

★**Bellagio, Lake Como.** Once called "Italy's prettiest town," it still seems to be more of an operetta set than a resort. Surrounded by sumptuous villas and gardens, the town has long played host to honeymooners, kings, and celebrated visitors who love its faded millionaires' gentility. Across the lake, on its own elm-graced promontory, you'll find Villa Balbaniello: Could this enchanted abode—now a museum—be the most beautiful spot in Italy?

★**Florence, Piazza della Signoria.** A Renaissance painting come to life, this piazza symbolizes all the grace, refinement, and power of the Renaissance. Nearby, discover Michelangelo's old neighborhood.

★**Positano, on the Amalfi Drive.** Strong calves and a healthy set of lungs are essential for anyone spending time in Positano, possibly the only resort you're likely to leave in better shape than when you arrived.

★**San Gimignano, Tuscany.** Stand on the steps of the Collegiata church at sunset as the swallows swoop in and out of the famous medieval towers, twittering softly as they coast on the air.

★**Venice, Piazza San Marco.** If you get up at dawn to catch this square *senza popolo*—without people—it will look like a three-dimensional Canaletto painting.

Lodging and Dining Gems

★**L'Albereta, Erbusco, on Lago d'Iseo.** At the countryside domain of Italy's most famous chef, Gualtiero Marchesi—founder of the cooking style known as *la cucina nuova*—try the *ravioli aperti* (open ravioli), *fazzoletto* (handkerchief pasta), or turbot salt-baked in the Chinese style. His kitchen adds a Far East touch to great Italian cooking, resulting in one of the 15 greatest restaurants in the world. *$$$$*

★**I Carracci, in the Grand Hotel Baglioni, Bologna.** One of the finest restaurants in the capital of Italian food is imposingly decorated with frescoes attributed to the famed 17th-century Carracci. With so many gourmet delights on the menu, you might simply tell the waiter, "*Un pranzo alla Bolognese*" (A Bolognese luncheon, please). $$$$

★**Grand Hotel Villa Serbelloni, Bellagio.** Enjoying a stay at this romantic old-world villa (often overshadowed by its more showy neighbor, the Villa d'Este Hotel) is like stepping into a 19th-century canvas. Visitors—among them Winston Churchill and John F. Kennedy—have come here to Lake Como not so much to escape, as to return; not so much to get away from it all, but to enjoy a sweetness of life rarely found today. $$$$

★**Il Pitosoforo, Portofino.** Enjoy 10 of the most relentlessly romantic minutes in Italy here when the restaurant lights are turned off for an interlude so that diners can drink in the harborside view. $$$$

★**La Scalinatella, Capri.** At breakfast, contemplate the blue of the sky from this hotel's terrace—then spend the rest of the morning gazing at the water 30 feet below; it's full of kaleidoscopic hues of turquoise, lavender, and aquamarine. $$$

★**Il Troia, Florence.** Florence has the best steaks in Italy and here you'll find the best bistecca alla Fiorentina. $$

★**La Tazza d'Oro, Rome.** Those who claim that the national coffee habit is the key to the Italian disposition find conclusive proof here in Italy's best cup of coffee. Do as the Romans do: Order a glass of water as a chaser. $

Special Memories

★**Corso del Palio (Parade of the Banner), Siena.** Medieval pageantry and passion explode every July 2 and August 16 in this perfectly preserved city, when its historic Piazza del Campo becomes a racecourse for 17 horses.

★**Gondola Ride Down the Grand Canal, Venice.** For the most *felicissima notte* (beautiful night), this treat can't be beat— to enhance the magic, join one of the flotillas of gondolas that glide down the canal en masse.

★**The Passegiata, Rome.** For perfect people-watching, head for the Corso at dusk (usually between 7 and 9 pm to watch Romans promenade by the thousands on their evening *passegiata*. It's one of Italy's most delightful spectacles.

★**Procession of San Efisio, Caligari.** Tradition isn't just a cliché in Sardinia's tourist-trade lexicon, and none of the island's other time-honored festivals has the exuberance of Caligari's annual binge.

Where Art Comes First

★**I Frari, Venice.** In this great Venetian Gothic church, you'll find two of Titian's most spectacular altarpieces; their blazing colors and luminosity cast 20th-century electricity into shadow.

★**House of the Mysteries, Pompeii.** Enter this private house—adorned with the most famous frescoes surviving from antiquity—and the days of the Caesars won't seem that remote.

★**Riace Bronzes, Reggio di Calabria.** Handsome, refined, philosophical—the ancient Riace Bronzes exude these qualities. People once sweltered in long lines for a turn at them—now that the fuss has died down, a pleasant ride across the Straits of Messina allows you to contemplate them at leisure.

★**La Rotonda, Vicenza.** Italy's most famous Palladian villa, La Rotonda, was the inspiration for Thomas Jefferson's Monticello. If you run into the delightfully friendly owner, Count Ludovico di Valmarana, he'll direct you to the unequaled Tiepolo frescoes at his family's Villa of the Dwarfs down the road.

★**Sistine Chapel, The Vatican.** The world's most famous frescoed ceiling has come vibrantly alive through a restoration that has brought out the glowing bright colors of Michelangelo's masterpiece.

★**Accademia, Florence.** Compare the perfection of Michelangelo's *David* with the rough-hewn power of his struggling *Slaves*.

★**Valley of the Temples, Agrigento, Sicily.** More than 20 centuries of silence and solitude greet you at this famous archeological site, where more than 100 structures built "before the year 1" have been preserved.

FESTIVALS AND SEASONAL EVENTS

Italy's top seasonal events are listed below, and any one of them could provide the stuff of lasting memories. Contact the **Italian Government Travel Office** for exact dates and further information.

EARLY DEC.➤ The **Feast of St. Ambrose,** in Milan, officially opens La Scala's opera season.

DEC.–JUNE➤ The **Opera Season** is in full swing at La Scala in Milan and elsewhere, notably in Turin, Rome, Naples, Parma, Venice, and Genoa.

DEC. 31➤ Rome stages a rousing **New Year's Eve** celebration, with fireworks, in Piazza del Popolo.

JAN. 5–6➤ **Epiphany Celebrations.** Roman Catholic Epiphany celebrations and decorations are evident throughout Italy. Notable is the Epiphany Fair at Piazza Navona in Rome.

EARLY FEB.➤ **Almond Blossom Festival** in Agrigento. A week of folk music and dancing, with groups from many countries, in the Valley of the Temples.

FEB. 2–12.➤ **Carnival in Venice.** A big do in the 18th century, revived in the last half of the 20th century, this includes plays, masked balls, fireworks, and indoor and outdoor happenings of every sort. **Carnival in**

Viareggio. Masked pageants, fireworks, a flower show, and parades are among the festivities along the Tuscan Riviera.

FEB.➤ **Carnival in Ivrea,** near Turin. Three days of folklore, costumes, and parades, culminating in the Battle of the Oranges, with real fruit flying through the air.

MAR. 28➤ In Rome, a torchlit nighttime **Good Friday Procession** led by the pope winds from the Colosseum past the Forum and up the Palatine Hill.

MAR. 30➤ The Easter Sunday **Scoppio del Carro,** or "Explosion of the Cart," in Florence, is the eruption of a cartful of fireworks in the Cathedral Square, set off by a mechanical dove released from the altar during High Mass.

LATE APR.–EARLY JULY➤ The **Florence May Music Festival** is the oldest and most prestigious Italian festival of the performing arts.

MAY 1➤ The **Feast of Sant'Efisio** in Cagliari sees a procession of marchers and others in splendid Sardinian costume.

MID-MAY➤ **Race of the Candles.** This procession of bearers, in local costume, carrying towering wooden pillars, leads to the top of Mt. Ingino in Gubbio.

MAY 20➤ **Sardinian Cavalcade.** A traditional procession of more than 3,000 people in Sardinian costumes makes its way through Sassari.

LATE MAY➤ The **Palio of the Archers** is a medieval crossbow contest in Gubbio.

EARLY JUNE➤ The **Battle of the Bridge,** in Pisa, is a medieval parade and contest.

The **Flower Festival,** in Genzano (Rome), is a religious procession along streets carpeted with flowers in magnificent designs.

The **Regatta of the Great Maritime Republics** sees keen competition among the four former maritime republics—Amalfi, Genoa, Pisa, and Venice.

LATE JUNE➤ **Soccer Games in 16th-Century Costume,** in Florence, commemorate a match played in 1530. Festivities include fireworks displays.

LATE JUNE–EARLY JULY➤ The **Festival of Two Worlds,** in Spoleto, is a famous performing-arts festival.

JUNE AND JULY➤ The **Summer Operetta Festival** is held in Trieste.

EARLY JULY AND MID-AUG.➤ The **Palio Horse Race,** in Siena, is a colorful bareback horse race with participants competing for the *palio* (banner).

MID-JULY➤ The **Feast of the Redeemer** is a procession of gondolas and other craft, commemorating the end of the epidemic of 1575 in Venice. The fireworks over the lagoon are spectacular.

EARLY JULY–LATE AUG.➤ The **Arena of Verona Outdoor Opera Season** heralds spectacular productions in the 22,000-seat Roman amphitheater of Verona.

EARLY AUG.➤ The **Joust of the Quintana** is a historical pageant in Ascoli Piceno.

LATE AUG.–EARLY SEPT.➤ The **Siena Music Week** features opera, concerts, and chamber music.

The **Venice Film Festival,** oldest of the international film festivals, takes place mostly on the Lido.

LATE AUG.–MID-SEPT.➤ The **Stresa Musical Weeks** comprise a series of concerts and recitals in Stresa.

AUTUMN

EARLY SEPT.➤ The **Historic Regatta** includes a traditional competition between two-oar gondolas in Venice.

The **Joust of the Saracen** is a tilting contest with knights in 13th-century armor in Arezzo.

MID-SEPT.➤ The **Joust of the Quintana** is a 17th-century-style joust and historical procession in Foligno.

EARLY OCT.➤ Alba's **100 Towers Tournament** features costumes and races and is held simultaneously with the **Truffle Fair,** a food fair centered on the white truffle.

OCT. 4➤ The **Feast of St. Francis** is celebrated in Assisi, his birthplace.

2 Rome

The city to which all roads lead, Mamma Roma enthralls visitors today as she has since time immemorial. Here is where Nero fiddled, where Mark Antony praised Caesar, and where Charlemagne was crowned—and the wonder is that you can walk precisely where these events occurred. Hallowed by golden light and thick with treasures, Rome has more masterpieces per square foot than any other place on earth. Nowhere else will you find such a heady mix of eternity, elegance, earthiness, and energy.

Updated by
Barbara Walsh
Angelillo

COMING OFF THE AUTOSTRADA at Roma Nord or Roma Sud, you can tell by the traffic that you are entering a grand nexus: All roads lead to Rome. And then the interminable suburbs, the railroad crossings, the intersections—no wonder they call it the Eternal City. As you enter the city proper, features that match your expectations begin to take shape: a bridge with heroic statues along its parapets; a towering cake of frothy marble decorated with allegorical figures in extravagant poses; a piazza and an obelisk under an umbrella of pine trees. Then you spot what looks like a multistory parking lot; with a gasp, you realize it is the fabled Colosseum.

The excitement of arriving in Rome jolts the senses and sharpens expectations. More than Florence, more than Venice, Rome is Italy's treasure storehouse, packed as it is with masterpieces from more than two millennia of artistic achievement. Here, the ancient Romans made us heirs-in-law to what we call Western civilization; here, Michelangelo painted the Sistine Ceiling; here, at Cinecitta Studios, Federico Fellini filmed *La Dolce Vita* and *8½*. Little wonder that for centuries Rome has been challenging visitors to produce a better superlative than "the greatest," a term travelers who become intimate with the city find totally inadequate.

History is ever present here, knit into the fabric of everyday life. Popes, Vandals, the Borgias and Napoléon, Gianlorenzo Bernini, Mussolini, and the ancient Romans themselves all left their physical and spiritual marks on the city. Students walk dogs in the park that used to be the mausoleum of the family of the Emperor Augustus; Raphaelesque madonnas line up for buses on every corner. Modern Rome has one foot in the past, one in the present—a delightful stance that allows you to have coffee in a square designed by Bernini, then take a subway home to a flat in a renovated Renaissance palace. "When you first come here you assume that you must burrow about in ruins and prowl in museums to get back to the days of Numa Pompilius or Mark Anthony," Maud Howe observes in her book, *Roma Beata*. "It is not necessary; you only have to live, and the common happenings of daily life—yes, even the trolley car and your bicycle—carry you back in turn to the Dark Ages, to the early Christians, even to prehistoric Rome."

Rome is often regarded by tourists as merely an introduction or a farewell: They arrive at Rome's airport, stay a night or two, then depart for a tour of Italy. But there are too many Romes—Early Christian, Ancient, Baroque, Etruscan, Neoclassical, Papal—to treat the city as just a jumping-off point. Whether your Roman visit turns out to be a short or long one, keep your sightseeing schedule flexible. Plan your day to take into account the wide diversity of opening times—which usually means mixing classical and Baroque, museums and parks, the center and the environs. No one will fault you for choosing a lazy ramble through a picturesque quarter of Old Rome over a deadly earnest trek through marbled miles of museum corridors.

Remember, *"Bisogna vivere a Roma coi costumi di Roma"* (When in Rome, do as Rome does). Don't feel intimidated by the press of art and culture. Instead, contemplate the grandeur from a table at a sun-drenched café on Piazza Navona; let Rome's colorful life flow around you without feeling guilty because you haven't seen everything. It can't be done, anyway. There's just so much here that you will have to come back again, so be sure to throw a coin in the Trevi Fountain. It works.

Pleasures and Pastimes

Dining

Eating is the Romans' main preoccupation, aside from their families and perhaps their cars. Dining out is all the nightlife most Romans need, and a summer evening's meal alfresco can be one of the city's most pleasant experiences. There was a time when you could predict the clientele and prices of a Roman eating establishment by whether it was called a *ristorante*(restaurant), a trattoria, or an *osteria* (tavern). Now these names are interchangeable. A rustic-looking spot that calls itself an osteria may turn out to be chic and expensive. Generally speaking, however, a trattoria is a family-run place, simpler in decor, menu, and service—and slightly less expensive—than a ristorante. A true osteria is a wineshop, very basic and down-to-earth, where the only function of the food is to keep the customers sober.

Lodging

Rome has the range of accommodations you would expect of any great city, from the squalid *pensioni* (boardinghouses) around the railway station to the grand monuments to luxury and elegance on Via Vittorio Veneto. Appearances can be misleading here: many crumbling stucco facades may promise little from the outside, but they often hide interiors of considerable elegance.

EXPLORING ROME

With more masterpieces per square foot than any other city in the world, Rome presents a particular challenge for visitors: Just as they begin to feel hopelessly smitten by the spell of the city, they realize they don't have the time—let alone the stamina—to see more than a fraction of its treasures. It's wise to start out knowing this, and to have a focused itinerary. These 10 tours of clustered sightseeing encapsulate quintessential Rome while allowing roamers to make minidiscoveries of their own not found in the guidebooks.

We begin where Rome itself began—amid the ancient ruins of the Roman Forum—and then follow up with a look at St. Peter's and the Vatican. Combined with strolls around central Rome—the *centro storico* (historic center) and its indescribably sumptuous Baroque artworks—these itineraries introduce you to the sights highest on practically everyone's list of priorities. The first itinerary is an introduction to "The grandeur that was Rome": the Capitoline Hill, the Roman Forum, and the Colosseum. The second and third itineraries take you through the incomparable sights of St. Peter's Basilica, the Sistine Chapel, and the Vatican Museums. Next we cover Baroque Rome— jewel-encrusted churches, Caravaggio paintings, and urban showstoppers such as Piazza Navona (plus the Pantheon). The fifth itinerary goes deep into Rome's postcard-country of the Spanish Steps and the Trevi Fountain. The next itinerary brings you to three of Rome's most historic churches (and Michelangelo's *Moses*). The following itinerary is a journey thick with Baroque treasures, including the Palazzo Colonna—Rome's most splendorous palace—and several of Bernini's best sculptures. The eighth walking itinerary ranges from the palatial 17th-century Galleria Borghese to the Villa Medici, home to the city's most poetic gardens. The ninth walk explores the Ghetto and Trastevere, Rome's own "Greenwich Village." Finally we take you from the atmosphere-rich Catacombs to the Appian Way.

Its natives are fond of reminding visitors that Rome wasn't built in a day. Neither can it be seen in a day, or even two or three. Perhaps vis-

itors should be Nero-esque in their rambles—and fiddle while they roam:
People who occasionally stop for a cappuccino get more out of these
breaks than those who breathlessly try to make every second count.
After all, there is no way to see everything. The Italian author Silvio
Negro said it best: *"Roma, non basta una vita"* (Rome, a lifetime is
not enough).

Great Itineraries

IF YOU HAVE 3 DAYS

Begin your first day at Piazza Venezia and see the Capitoline Hill, the
Roman Forum, Palatine Hill and Colosseum to get an idea of "The
Grandeur that was Rome". In the afternoon, visit St. Peter's and the
Sistine Chapel. The following morning, walk through Baroque Rome
to see jewel-encrusted churches such as the Gesù, Caravaggio paintings in Santa Maria del Popolo and San Luigi dei Francesci, and urban
showstoppers such as Piazza Navona and the Pantheon, one of the
world's most beautiful buildings. After lunch, combine sightseeing
with shopping and make your way through the picture-postcard neighborhood around the Spanish Steps and Trevi Fountain. Your third morning should be devoted to spending some time in one of the museums
that interest you the most and then relax at a café and watch the passing parade until it is time for lunch. Spend your final afternoon and
evening exploring the picturesque Ghetto and Trastevere neighborhoods.

IF YOU HAVE 5 DAYS

If you have an extra couple of days, spend your first three exploring
the sights covered above, but on the morning of the fourth day wander through Villa Borghese and see the Canova and Bernini sculptures
in the Galleria Borghese. On the fifth day, make an excursion either
to the Appian Way or to Ostia Antica, an ancient city comparable to
Pompeii for interest and atmosphere. In the afternoon, see some of
Rome's most historic churches and Michelangelo's *Moses*.

IF YOU HAVE 7 DAYS

Devote more time to the museums and galleries mentioned above that
interest you most. Explore one of the neighborhoods you liked best,
allowing plenty of time for poking into odd corners and courtyards
and churches, and for café-sitting. Make a couple of excursions outside Rome.

Ancient Rome: Glories of the Caesars

This walk takes you through the very core of Roman antiquity, through
what was once the epicenter of the known world, the Roman Forum,
and gives you a look at how Michelangelo transformed the Capitoline
Hill—the seat of ancient Rome's government—into a Renaissance
showcase. The rubblescape of marble fragments scattered over the area
of the Forum makes all but students of archeology ask: Is this the
grandeur that was Rome? Just consider that much of the history fed
to students the world over happened right here. This square—once an
enormous banquet hall where the entire population of a city could be
simultaneously entertained (as our times have observed thanks to such
Hollywood epics as *Quo Vadis, Ben-Hur,* and *Cleopatra*)—was the birthplace for much of Western civilization. Roman law and powerful
armies were created here, banishing the barbarian world for a millennium. Here, all Rome shouted as one, "Caesar has been murdered,"
and crowded to hear Mark Antony's eulogy for the fallen leader. Legend has it that St. Paul traversed the Forum en route to his audience
with Nero. After a more than 27-century-long parade of pageantry, it
is not surprising that Shelley and Gibbon had their dreams of *Sic transit gloria mundi* on these same grounds.

A Good Walk

Numbers in the text correspond to numbers in the margin and on the Rome and Old Rome: The Historic Center maps.

Rome, as everyone knows, was built on seven hills. Begin your walk at the **Capitoline Hill** ①—the site of Michelangelo's spectacular piazza and Rome's City Hall, **Palazzo Senatorio,** which was built over the Tabularium, the ancient hall of records. Flanking the palazzo are both halves of Rome's most noteworthy museum complex, the **Musei Capitolini** ②, made up of the **Museo Capitolino** and the **Palazzo dei Conservatori,** which contain works of art gathered by Pope Sixtus V, one of the earliest papal patrons of the arts. Off to the side of the Capitoline, at the head of its formidable flight of steep steps, stands the ancient redbrick church of **Santa Maria d'Aracoeli** ③. Below the gardens to the left of the Palazzo Senatorio are **Caesar's Forum** and the forum named after the Emperor Trajan, separated by Via dei Fori Imperiali; the latter contains the ruins of **Trajan's Column** ④. Descend Via San Pietro in Carcere, actually a flight of stairs, to the gloomy **Mamertine Prison** ⑤ and the **Roman Forum** ⑥, continuing along Via dei Fori Imperiali where, on the right, you will come across the **Palatine Hill** ⑦, site of Rome's earliest settlement. Leaving the Palatine by way of the San Gregorio exit, you'll come upon the imposing **Arch of Constantine** ⑧ and, beyond it, the **Colosseum** ⑨, one of antiquity's most famous monuments. Don't forget to check out the ruins of Nero's **Domus Aurea** ⑩, his sumptuous palace, behind the Colosseum.

TIMING

It takes about 30 minutes to walk the route, plus two hours to visit the Capitoline Museums, two to three hours to explore the Roman Forum and Palatine, and 20 minutes to an hour to see the Colosseum.

Sights to See

Numbers in the margin correspond to points of interest on the Rome map.

❽ **Arch of Constantine.** This imposing arch was erected in AD 315 to celebrate Constantine's victory over Maxentius. Not only is it the best preserved of Rome's triumphal arches, it is also the largest (69 feet high, 85 feet wide, and 23 feet deep) and one of the last great monuments of ancient Rome. It once stood at the head of the Via Sacra, but now stands in glorious isolation alongside the Colosseum (☞ *below*).

OFF THE BEATEN PATH

PROTESTANT CEMETERY – About 20 minutes' walk south from the Arch of Constantine along Viale Aventino, behind the Piramide, a stone pyramid built in 12 BC at the order of the Roman *praetor* (senior magistrate) who was buried there, is a cemetery reminiscent of a country churchyard. Among the headstones you'll find Keats's tomb and the place where Shelley's heart was buried. ⊠ *Via Caio Cestio 6,* ☎ *06/574-1141 (ring bell for custodian).* ⊡ *Offering of 500 lire–1,000 lire.* ☉ *Daily 8–11:30 and 3:20–5:30.*

Caesar's Forum. This is the oldest of the Imperial Fora, those built by the emperors as opposed to those built during the earlier, Republican period (6th–1st centuries BC) as part of the original Roman Forum.

★ ❶ **Capitoline Hill.** Though most of the buildings on Michelangelo's piazza date from the Renaissance, the hill was once the epicenter of the Roman Empire, the place where the city's first and holiest temples stood, including its most sacred, the Temple of Jupiter. The city's archives were kept in the Tabularium (hall of records), the tall, gray-stone structure that forms the foundation of today's city hall, **Palazzo Senatorio.** By

the Middle Ages, the Campidoglio, as the hill was already called then, had fallen into ruin. In 1537, Pope Paul III decided to restore its grandeur for the triumphal entry into the city of Charles V, the Holy Roman Emperor, and called upon Michelangelo to create the staircase ramp; the buildings on three sides of the Campidoglio Square; the slightly convex pavement and its decoration; and the pedestal for the bronze equestrian statue of Marcus Aurelius. A work from the 2nd century AD, the statue stood here from the 16th century until 1981. The statue—the most celebrated equestrian bronze to survive from classical antiquity—was mistakenly believed to represent the Christian emperor Constantine rather than the pagan Marcus Aurelius, hence its survival through the centuries. A legend foretells that some day the statue's original gold patina will return, heralding the end of the world. To forestall destiny, the city fathers had it restored and placed in Palazzo dei Conservatori (☞ *below*), saving not only what was left of the gold, but also the statue's bronze, once seriously menaced by air pollution. A copy of the statue may be set up outdoors by 1997, installed on the original pedestal. As Michelangelo's preeminent urban set piece, the piazza sums up all the majesty of High-Renaissance Rome.

★ ❾ **Colosseum.** Massive and majestic, ancient Rome's most famous monument was begun by the Flavian emperor Vespasian in AD 72, and inaugurated eight years later with a program of games and shows lasting 100 days. More than 50,000 spectators could sit within the arena's 573-yard circumference, which was faced with marble, accented with hundreds of statues, and had the velarium—an ingenious system of sail-like awnings rigged on ropes manned by sailors culled from imperial warships—to protect the audience from the sun and rain. Before the imperial box, gladiators would salute the emperor and cry, *"Ave, imperator, morituri te salutant"* (Hail, emperor, men soon to die salute thee); it is said that when one day they heard the emperor Claudius respond, "or maybe not," they became so offended that they called a strike. Although originally known as the Flavian Amphitheater, it was called the Colosseum by later Romans, as reported by the Venerable Bede in 730, after a truly colossal gilded bronze statue of Nero in the vicinity that stood until the end of the 6th century. The arena later served as a quarry from which materials were filched to build Renaissance-era churches and palaces. Finally, it was declared sacred by the Vatican in memory of the many Christians believed martyred there (scholars now maintain that no Christians met their death in the Colosseum, but rather in Rome's imperial circuses). During the 19th century, romantic poets lauded the glories of the amphitheater when viewed by moonlight. Now its arches glow at night with mellow golden spotlights, less romantic, perhaps, but still unforgettable. Portions of the arena will be closed during ongoing restoration. ⊠ *Piazza del Colosseo,* ☎ *06/700–4261.* ⊡ *General admission free, upper levels 8,000 lire.* ☉ *Apr.–Sept., Mon., Tues., Thurs.–Sat. 9–7, Wed. and Sun. 9–1; Oct.–Mar., Mon., Tues., Thurs.–Sat 9–3, Wed. and Sun. 9–1.*

NEED A   About half a block from the Colosseum is **Pasqualino** (⊠ Via Santi Quattro
BREAK?   66), a reasonably priced neighborhood trattoria with a few sidewalk ta-
           bles providing a view of the arena's marble arches. The restaurant is
           closed Monday. For delicious ice cream try **Ristoro della Salute** (⊠ Piazza
           del Colosseo 2a), one of Rome's best *gelaterie* (ice-cream parlors).

---

❿ **Domus Aurea.** On the Colle Oppio (Oppian Hill), a ridge of the Esquiline Hill, is what's left of Nero's sumptuous palace—later buried under Trajan's Baths—which was built after the great fire of AD 64 destroyed much of the city. (Incidentally, historians now believe Nero to be blameless in this event.) Also known as the Golden House, it was a structure so huge it evoked the complaint, "All Rome has become a villa."

⑤ Mamertine Prison. This series of gloomy, subterranean cells is where Rome's vanquished enemies were finished off. Some historians believe that St. Peter was held prisoner here, and legend has it that he miraculously brought forth a spring of water with which to baptize his jailers. ▨ *Donation requested.* ⏺ *Daily 9–12:30 and 2–7:30.*

② Musei Capitolini. The collections in the twin Museo Capitolino and Palazzo dei Conservatori were assembled in the 15th century by Pope Sixtus V, one of the earliest of the great papal patrons of the arts. Although parts of the collection may excite only archaeologists and art historians, others contain some of the most famous—and not to be missed—pieces of classical sculpture, such as the poignant *Dying Gaul,* the regal *Capitoline Venus* (recently identified as another Mediterranean beauty, Cleopatra herself), and the delicate *Marble Faun* that inspired 19th-century novelist Nathaniel Hawthorne's novel of the same name. Remember that many of the works here and in Rome's other museums were copied from Greek originals. For hundreds of years, craftsmen of ancient Rome prospered by producing copies of Greek statues, using a process called "pointing," by which exact replicas could be created to order.

Portraiture, however, was one area in which the Romans outstripped the Greeks. The hundreds of Roman portrait busts in the Sala degli Imperatori and Sala dei Filosofi of the **Museo Capitolino** constitute an ancient *Who's Who.* Within these serried ranks are 48 of the Roman emperors, ranging from Augustus (died AD 14) to Theodosius (died 395). Many of them were eminently forgettable, but some were men of genius; a few added nothing to the Roman way of life except new ways of dying. On one console, you'll see the handsomely austere Augustus, who "found Rome a city of brick and left it one of marble." On another rests Claudius "the stutterer," an indefatigable builder brought vividly to life in Robert Graves's *I, Claudius.* In this company is also Nero, most notorious of the emperors—though by no means the worst—who built for himself the fabled Domus Aurea (☞ *above*). And, of course, the baddies: cruel Caligula and Caracalla, and the dissolute, eerily modern boy-emperor, Heliogabalus.

Unlike the Greeks, whose portraits are idealized and usually beautiful, the Romans belonged to the "warts and all" school of representation. Many of the busts that have come down to us, seen clearly in that of Commodus, the emperor-gladiator (found in a gallery on the upper level of the museum), are nearly savage in the relentlessness of their portrayals. As you leave the museum, be sure to stop in the courtyard at the gigantic, reclining figure of Oceanus, found in the Roman Forum and later dubbed Marforio, one of Rome's famous "talking statues" to which citizens from the 1500s up to the 20th century affixed anonymous notes of political protest and satirical verses.

The **Palazzo dei Conservatori** is a trove of ancient and Baroque treasures. Lining the courtyard are the colossal fragments of a head, leg, foot, and hand, all that remains of the famous statue of the emperor Constantine the Great, who believed that Rome's future in the 3rd century AD lay with Christianity; these immense effigies were much in vogue in the later days of the Roman empire. The resplendent Salone dei Orazi e Curiazi on the first floor is a ceremonial hall with a magnificent gilt ceiling, carved wooden doors, and 16th-century frescoes. At either end of the hall reign statues of the Baroque Age's most charismatic popes, Bernini's marble effigy of Urban VIII and his rival Algardi's bronze statue of Innocent X. World-renowned symbol of Rome, the *Capitoline Wolf*, a 6th-century-BC Etruscan bronze, has a place of honor in the museum; the suckling twins were added during the Renaissance to adapt the statue to the legend of Romulus and Remus. ⊠ *Museo Capitolino and Palazzo dei Conservatori, Piazza del Campidoglio,* ☎ *06/671–002475.* ✍ *10,000 lire, free last Sun. of month.* ☉ *May–Sept., Tues. 9–1:30 and 5–8, Wed.–Fri. 9–1:30, Sat. 9–1:30 and 8–11, Sun. 9–1; Oct.–Apr., Tues. and Sat. 9–1:30 and 5–8, Wed.–Fri. 9–1:30, Sun. 9–1.*

❼ Palatine Hill. The Clivus Palatinus (as it was known in Latin), whose worn paving stones were once trod by emperors and their slaves, is where historians point to Rome's earliest settlement. About a century ago, Rome's greatest archaeologist, Rodolfo Lanciani, excavated a site on the Palatine Hill—and found evidence testifying to Romulus's historical presence, thereby contradicting early critics who deemed Romulus to be a myth. The story goes that the twins Romulus and Remus were abandoned as infants but were suckled by a she wolf on the banks of the Tiber and adopted by a shepherd. Encouraged by the gods to build a city, the twins chose a site in 735 BC, fortifying it with a wall that Lanciani identified by digging on the Palatine. During the building of the city, the brothers quarreled, and in a fit of anger Romulus killed Remus.

Despite its location overlooking the Forum with its extreme traffic congestion and attendant noise, the Palatine was the most coveted address for ancient Rome's rich and famous. More than a few of the 12 Caesars called the Palatine home—including Caligula, who met his premature end in the still-standing and unnerving—even today—tunnel, the Cryptoporticus. The palace of Tiberius was the first to be built here; others followed, most notably the gigantic extravaganza constructed for emperor Domitian.

In the **Circus Maximus,** the giant arena laid out between the Palatine and Aventine hills, more than 300,000 spectators watched chariot races while the emperor surveyed the scene from his palace on the Palatine Hill.

❻ Roman Forum. In what was once a marshy valley between the Capitoline and Palatine hills, this was the civic heart of Republican Rome, the austere enclave that preceded the hedonistic society that grew up under the emperors in the 1st to the 4th century AD. Today it seems no more than a baffling series of ruins, marble fragments, isolated columns, a few worn arches, and occasional paving stones. Yet it once was filled with stately and extravagant buildings—temples, palaces, shops—and crowded with people from all corners of the world. What you see today are the ruins not of one period, but of almost 900 years, from about 500 BC to AD 400. Making sense of these scarred and pitted stones is not easy; you may want just to wander along, letting your imagination dwell on Cicero, Julius Caesar, and Mark Antony, who delivered the funeral address in Caesar's honor from the rostrum just left of the **Arch of Septimius Severus.**

In addition to this arch—one of the grandest of all antiquity, it was built in AD 203 to celebrate the emperor Severus's victory over the Parthians, and was topped by a bronze equestrian statuary group with no fewer than six horses—most visitors explore the large brick senate hall, the **Curia,** which survives as it was in the era of Diocletian in the late 3rd century AD; the three Corinthian columns (a favorite of 19th-century poets)—all that remains of the **Temple of Vespasian;** the circular **Temple of Vesta,** where the highly privileged vestal virgins kept the sacred flame alive; and the **Arch of Titus,** which stands in a slightly ele-

vated position on a spur of the Palatine Hill. The view of the Colosseum from the arch is superb, and reminds us that it was the emperor
Titus who helped finish the vast amphitheater, begun earlier by his father,
Vespasian. Now cleaned and restored, the arch was erected in AD 81
to celebrate the sack of Jerusalem 10 years earlier, after the great Jewish revolt. A famous relief shows the captured contents of Herod's Temple—including its huge seven-branched menorah—being carried in
triumph down Rome's Via Sacra. ⊠ *Entrances on Via dei Fori Imperiali, Piazza Santa Maria Nova, and Via di San Gregorio,* ☎ *06/699–
0110.* 🎫 *12,000 lire.* ⊘ *Apr.–Sept., Mon.–Sat. 9–6, Sun. 9–1;
Oct.–Mar., Mon.–Sat. 9–3, Sun. 9–1.*

❸ **Santa Maria d'Aracoeli.** This stark, redbrick church is one of the first
Christian churches in Rome. Legend recounts that it was on this spot
that the Sybil predicted to Augustus the coming of a Redeemer. The
emperor responded by erecting the Ara Coeli—the Altar of Heaven.
The Aracoeli is best known for Pinturicchio's 15th-century frescoes in
the first chapel on the right and for the **Santa Bambino,** a much-
revered wooden figure of the Christ Child (today a copy of the 15th-
century original). During the Christmas season, children recite poems
from a miniature pulpit here. ⊠ *Piazza d'Aracoeli.*⊘ *Oct. 1–May 31,
daily 7–12 and 4–6; June 1-Sept., 30 daily 7–12 and 4–6:30.*

❹ **Trajan's Column,** in the base of which emperor Trajan's ashes were buried,
stands in what was once **Trajan's Forum,** with its huge semicircular
market building, adjacent to the ruins of the **Forum of Augustus.**

The Vatican: Rome of the Popes

The Vatican is a place where some people go to find a work of art—
Michelangelo's frescoes, rare archaeological marbles, or Bernini's statues. Others go to find their souls. In between these two extremes lies
an awe-inspiring landscape that offers a famous sight for every taste
and inclination. Rooms decorated by Raphael, antique sculptures like
the *Apollo Belvedere* and the *Laocoön,* walls daubed by Fra Angelico,
famous paintings by Giotto and Leonardo, and chief among revered
non plus ultras, the ceiling of the Sistine Chapel: For the lover of
beauty, few places are as historically important as this epitome of faith
and grandeur. What gave all this impetus was a new force that emerged
as the emperors of ancient Rome presided over their declining empire:
Christianity came to Rome, and the seat of the popes was established
over the tomb of St. Peter, thereby making the Vatican the spiritual core
of the Roman Catholic Church. Today, there are two principal reasons
for seeing the Vatican. One is to visit St. Peter's, the largest church in
the world and the most overwhelming architectural achievement of the
Renaissance; the other is to visit the Vatican Museums, which contain
collections of staggering richness and diversity.

A Good Walk

Start your walk at the **Castel Sant'Angelo** ⑪, the fortress that once
guarded the Vatican, and take in the angel-studded beauty of the **Ponte
Sant'Angelo** before turning right onto Via della Conciliazione (or taking a more picturesque route along Borgo Pio) to the Vatican. Once inside **Piazza San Pietro** ⑫ you are inside Vatican territory, and a feast of
artistic delights awaits you: **St. Peter's Basilica** ⑬, the largest church in
Christendom. To the right as you enter you'll find Michelangelo's stunning *Pietà;* of the many treasures to be seen, be sure not to miss the Historical Museum in the Sacristy, the excavations below the church, the
Vatican gardens, and the Vatican Grottoes, the last repose of the popes.

Finally, the Vatican is where millions of Catholics (and, indeed, many non-Catholics) come in hope of a **papal audience**; the chance to see the pope in person is for many the highlight of a trip to Rome.

TIMING

Allow two hours for a visit to Castel Sant'Angelo. The walk from Castel Sant'Angelo to St. Peter's takes about 30 minutes. You'll need an hour to see St. Peter's, plus 30 minutes for the Historical Museum, 15 minutes for the Vatican Grottoes, 30 minutes to visit the roof, and an hour to climb to the lantern. To avoid the crowds, get to St. Peter's early in the morning, at lunchtime, or in the late afternoon.

Sights to See

⑪ Castel Sant'Angelo. For hundreds of years this fortress guarded the Vatican, to which it is linked by the Passetto, an arcaded passageway. Anyone harboring doubts as to the almost unimaginable wealth and power of ancient Rome's emperors will have them dashed here: Though it may look like a stronghold, Castel Sant'Angelo was in fact built as a tomb for the emperor Hadrian in AD 135. By the 6th century, it had been transformed into a fortress, and it remained a refuge for the popes for almost 1,000 years. It has dungeons, battlements, cannons and cannonballs, and a collection of antique weaponry and armor.

One of Rome's most beautiful bridges, **Ponte Sant'Angelo** spans the Tiber in front of the fortress and is studded with graceful angels designed by Giovanni Lorenzo Bernini (1598–1680).

According to legend, the Castel Sant'Angelo got its name during the plague of 590, when Pope Gregory the Great, passing by in a religious procession, had a vision of an angel sheathing its sword atop the stone ramparts. The lower levels formed the base of Hadrian's mausoleum; ancient ramps and narrow staircases climb through the castle's core to courtyards and frescoed halls and rooms holding a collection of antique arms and armor. Off the loggia is a café. The upper terrace, below the massive bronze angel commemorating Gregory's vision, evokes memories of Tosca, Puccini's poignant heroine in the opera of the same name, who threw herself off these ramparts with the cry, *"Scarpia, avanti a Dio!"* ("Scarpia, we meet before God!"). ⊠ *Lungotevere Castello 50,* ☎ *06/687–5036.* ▣ *8,000 lire.* ◷ *Mon.–Sat. 9–2, Sun. 9–noon; closed 2nd and 4th Tues. of month.*

⑫ Piazza San Pietro (St. Peter's Square). As you enter the square you are entering Vatican territory. This square (actually an oval) is one of Bernini's most spectacular masterpieces. Completed in 1667, after 11 years' work—a relatively short time in those days, considering the vastness of the task—the square can hold 400,000 people. It is surrounded by a curving pair of quadruple colonnades, which are topped by a balustrade and statues of 140 saints. Look for the two stone disks set into the pavement on each side of the obelisk. If you stand on one disk, a trick of perspective makes the colonnades seem to consist of a single row of columns. Bernini had an even grander visual effect in mind when he designed the square. By opening up this immense, airy and luminous space in a neighborhood of narrow, shadowy streets, he created a contrast that would surprise and impress anyone who emerged from the darkness into the light, in a characteristically Baroque metaphor. But in the 1930's, Mussolini ruined it all. To celebrate the "conciliation" between the Vatican and the Italian government under the Lateran Pact of 1929, he conceived of Via della Conciliazione, the broad, rather soulless avenue that now forms the main approach to St. Peter's and gives the eye time to adjust to the enormous dimensions of the square and church, ruining Bernini's grand Baroque effect.

★ ⑬ **St. Peter's Basilica.** Most viewers find this, the largest church of Christendom, to be one of Rome's most impressive sights. The physical statistics are imposing: It covers about 18,100 square yards, runs 212 yards in length, and carries a dome that rises 435 feet and measures 138 feet across its base. Its history is equally impressive: No fewer than five of Italy's greatest artists—Bramante, Raphael, Peruzzi, Antonio Sangallo the Younger, and Michelangelo—died while striving to erect this new St. Peter's. The history of the original St. Peter's goes back to the year AD 319, when the emperor Constantine built a basilica over the site of the tomb of St. Peter. This early church stood for more than 1,000 years, undergoing a number of restorations, until it was on the verge of collapse. Reconstruction began in 1452, but was abandoned due to a lack of funds. In 1506 Pope Julius II instructed the architect Donato Bramante (1444–1514) to raze the existing structure and build a new and greater basilica, but it wasn't until 1626 that the new church was completed and dedicated. In 1546 Pope Paul III persuaded the aging Michelangelo to take on the job of completing the building. Returning to Bramante's ground plan, Michelangelo designed the dome to cover the crossing, but his plans, too, were modified after his death. The cupola, one of the most beautiful in the world, was completed by Della Porta and Fontana. Under the portico, Filarete's 15th-century bronze doors, salvaged from the old basilica, are in the central portal. Ushers at the entrance will not allow persons wearing shorts, miniskirts, sleeveless T-shirts, or other revealing clothing (it's advisable for women to carry a scarf to cover bare shoulders and upper arms) into St. Peter's church. Off the entry portico, Bernini's famous *Scala Regia,* the ceremonial entryway to the Vatican Palace—the residence of the pope—and one of the most magnificent staircases in the world, is graced with Bernini's dramatic statue of Constantine the Great.

The cherubs over the holy water fonts will give you an idea of just how huge St. Peter's is: the sole of the cherub's foot is as long as the distance from your fingers to your elbow. It is because the proportions of this giant building are in such perfect harmony that its vastness may escape you at first. But in its megascale—inspired by the spatial volumes of ancient Roman ruins—it reflects Roman *grandiosità* in all its majesty.

Over an altar in a side chapel is Michelangelo's *Pietà.* It is difficult to determine whether this moving work, sculpted when he was only 22, owes more to the man's art than to his faith. As we contemplate this masterpiece we are able to understand a little better that art and faith sometimes partake of the same impulse.

Four massive piers support the dome at the crossing, where the mighty Bernini *baldacchino* (canopy) rises high above the papal altar. "What the barbarians didn't do, the Barberini did," 17th-century wags quipped when Barberini Pope Urban VIII had the bronze stripped from the Pantheon's portico and melted down to make the baldacchino (using what was left over for cannonballs). The pope celebrates mass here, over the grottoes holding the tombs of many of his predecessors. Also here, deep in the excavations under the foundations of the original basilica, is what is believed to be the tomb of St. Peter. The bronze throne above the main altar in the apse, the Cathedra Petri, is Bernini's work (1656) and it covers a wooden and ivory chair that St. Peter himself is said to have used. However, scholars tell us that this throne probably dates only to the Middle Ages. We come to these contradictions often. Faith, in the end, outweighs authenticity when it is a question of sacred objects. See how the adoration of a million lips has completely worn down the bronze on the right foot of the statue of St. Peter near the crossing.

The scale of the aisles and decoration and the vast sweep of the dome over the ceremonial entrance to the crypt, which is surrounded by votive lamps, bring home the point that St. Peter's is much more than a church; it was intended to function as the glorious setting for all the pomp and panoply of ecclesiastical ceremony. Indeed, only when it serves as the brightly lit background for a great gathering do its vast dimensions find their full expression.

A small but rich collection of Vatican treasures is housed in the **Historical Museum** in the Sacristy, among them precious antique chalices and the massive 15th-century sculptured bronze tomb of Pope Sixtus V by Antonio Pollaiuolo (1429–98). ✉ *3,000 lire.* ☉ *Apr.–Sept., daily 9–6:30; Oct.–Mar., daily 9–5:30.*

The entrance to the **Vatican Grottoes,** which hold the tombs of many popes, is at the crossing. The only exit from the grottoes leads outside St. Peter's, to the courtyard that holds the entrance to the roof and dome. ✉ *Free.* ☉ *Apr.–Sept., daily 7–6; Oct.–Mar., daily 7–5.*

The **roof** of the church, reached by elevator or stairs, is an interesting landscape of domes and towers. A short interior staircase leads to the base of the dome for a dove's-eye view of the interior of the church. Only if you are stout of heart and sound of lung should you attempt the very taxing and claustrophobic climb up the narrow stairs—there's no turning back!—to the balcony of the lantern, where the view embraces the Vatican gardens as well as all of Rome. ✉ *Elevator 6,000 lire, stairs 5,000 lire.* ☉ *Apr.–Sept., daily 8–6; Oct.–Mar., daily 8–5.*

OFF THE BEATEN PATH

EXCAVATIONS – Visit these under St. Peter's for a fascinating glimpse of the underpinnings of the great basilica, which was built over the cemetery where archaeologists say they have found St. Peter's tomb. Apply a few days in advance (or try in the morning for the same day) to Ufficio Scavi (Excavations Office), on the right beyond the Arco delle Campane entrance to Vatican, which is left of the basilica. Tell the Swiss guard you want the Ufficio Scavi, and he will let you by. ☎ *06/6988-5318.* ✉ *Guide 10,000 lire, audiotape tour 6,000 lire.* ☉ *Ufficio Scavi Mon.–Sat. 9–5.*

NEED A BREAK?

Borgo Pio, a street a block or two from St. Peter's Square, has several trattorias offering economical tourist menus. For about 20,000 lire you can have a simple meal at **Il Pozzetto** (✉ Borgo Pio 167). The restaurant is closed Monday. The tiny **Dolceborgo** pastry shop (✉ Borgo Pio 162) is the place to go for cookies and creamy concoctions.

Papal Audience. For many, this is a highlight of a trip to Rome. John Paul II, 264th Pope of the Roman Catholic Church, holds mass audiences on Wednesday mornings at 11, in a large modern audience hall or in St. Peter's Square in summer, if it's not too hot. You must apply for tickets in advance; there are several sources (☞ *below*), but if you are pressed for time it may be easier to arrange for them through a travel agency. Of course, you can avoid the formalities by seeing the pope when he makes his weekly appearance at the window of the Vatican Palace, every Sunday at noon when he is in Rome, to address the crowd and give a blessing. On summer Sundays he may give the blessing at his summer residence at Castel Gandolfo. For audience tickets apply in writing well in advance to Prefettura della Casa Pontificia (✉ 00120 Vatican City), indicating the date you prefer, the language you speak, and the hotel where you will be staying. Or go to the prefecture (☎ 06/6982), through the bronze door in right-hand colonnade; the office is open Monday and Tuesday 9–1 for the Wednesday audience, although last-minute tickets may be available. You can also pick up free tickets at North American College (⊠ Via dell'Umiltà 30, ☎ 06/678–9184) and through Santa Susanna American Church (⊠ Piazza San Bernardo, ☎ 06/482–7510). For a fee, travel agencies make arrangements that include transportation (☞ Guided Tours *in* Rome A to Z, *below*).

The **Vatican gardens** tour offers a two-hour jaunt through the pope's backyard, half by bus and half on foot, with a guide. Tickets are available at the Vatican Information Office (⊠ Piazza San Pietro, ☎ 06/6988–4466). Make reservations two or three days in advance. ☒ *16,000 lire.* ☉ *Sat. at 10.*

The Vatican Museums: More than Just the Sistine Ceiling

The Vatican Palace has been the residence of Popes since 1377. Actually, it represents a collection of buildings that cover more than 13 acres, containing an estimated (no one has bothered to count them) 1,400 rooms, chapels, and galleries. Other than the Pope and his papal court, the occupants are some of the most famous art masterpieces in the world. The main entrance to the museums, on Viale Vaticano, is a long walk from Piazza San Pietro, but there is bus service between the St. Peter's Square information office and a secondary museum entrance. The bus goes through the Vatican gardens and costs 2,000 lire, and although it deposits you at a side entrance, it saves a lot of walking and allows a glimpse of some of Vatican City that would be off-limits otherwise. Some city buses stop near the museums' main entrance on Viale Vaticano: Bus 49 from Piazza Cavour stops right in front; Bus 80 and Tram 19 stop at Piazza Risorgimento, halfway between St. Peter's and the museums. The Ottaviano stop on Metro A also is in the vicinity.

A Good Walk

For many, the highlight of any visit to the **Vatican Museums** ⑭ is the Sistine Chapel. Not to be overlooked, however, are the recently rearranged **Egyptian Museum** and the **Chiaramonti** and **Pio Clementino Museums**, which are given over to classical sculptures (among them some of the best-known statues in the world—the *Laocoön,* the *Belvedere Torso,* and the *Apollo Belvedere*—works that, with their vibrant humanism, had a tremendous impact on Renaissance art), and the **Etruscan Museum** and three other sections of special interest. Finally, you should make sure to visit the **Candelabra Gallery** and the **Tapestry Gallery,** which is hung with magnificent tapestries executed from Raphael's designs.

TIMING

The shortest itinerary takes approximately 90 minutes; others take three hours and 3½ hours, and the longest takes 4½ hours. To avoid the crowds, get there before opening time, or go at lunch time or in the last few hours before closing.

Sights to See

⑭ **Vatican Museums.** The immense collections housed here are so rich that unless you are an art history fan, you will probably want to just skim the surface, concentrating on pieces that strike your fancy. The Sistine Chapel is a must, of course, and that's why you may have to wait on line to see it; after all, every tourist in Rome has the same idea. Pick up a leaflet at the main entrance to the museums in order to see the overall layout. Special posters at the entrance and throughout the museums plot a choice of four color-coded itineraries. The Sistine Chapel is at the far end of the complex, and the leaflet charts two abbreviated itineraries through other collections to reach it. You can rent a taped commentary in English explaining the Sistine Chapel and the Raphael Rooms. Below, we give some of the highlights, whether or not you follow the itineraries suggested by the curators.

The **Gallery of Maps** is intriguing; the **Apartment of Pius V**, a little less so. The **Stanze di Raffaello** (the Raphael Rooms), are second only to the Sistine Chapel in artistic interest. In 1508, Pope Julius II employed Raphael Sanzio, on the recommendation of Bramante, to decorate the rooms with biblical scenes. The result was a Renaissance masterpiece. Of the four rooms, the second and third were decorated mainly by Raphael; here are his exceptional *Transfiguration, Coronation,* and *Foligno Madonna.* The others were decorated by Giulio Romano and other assistants of Raphael; the first room is known as the Incendio Room, with frescoes painted by Romano. It's hard to overstate the importance of the **Segnatura Room** (the Room of the Signature); here papal bulls were signed. When people talk about the High Renaissance—thought by many to be the pinnacle of Western art—these frescoes often come to mind. The theme of the room—which may broadly be said to be "enlightenment"—reflects the fact that this was Julius's private library. Theology triumphs in the fresco known as the *Disputa,* or *Debate on the Holy Sacrament.* The *School of Athens* glorifies some of philosophy's greatest exponents, including Plato and Socrates at the fresco's center. The pensive figure on the stairs is sometimes thought to be modelled on Michelangelo, who was painting the Sistine Ceiling at the same time Raphael was working here. All the revolutionary characteristics of High Renaissance paintings are here: naturalism (Raphael's figures lack the awkwardness that pictures painted only a few years earlier still contained); humanism (the idea that man is the most noble and admirable of God's creatures); and a profound interest in the ancient world, the result of the 15th-century rediscovery of archaeology and classical antiquity. There's a tendency to go into something of a stupor when confronted with "great art" of this kind. The fact remains that the frescoes in this room virtually dared its occupants to aspire to the highest ideas of law and learning—an amazing feat for an artist not yet 30.

The tiny **Chapel of Nicholas V** is aglow with frescoes by Fra Angelico (1387–1455), the Florentine monk whose sensitive paintings were guiding lights for the Renaissance. The **Borgia Apartments** are worth seeing for their elaborately painted ceilings, designed and partially executed by Pinturicchio (1454–1513), but the rooms have been given over to the Vatican's large, but not particularly interesting, collection of modern religious art.

★ In 1508, while Raphael was put to work on his series of rooms, the redoubtable Pope Julius II commissioned Michelangelo to fresco the more than 10,000 square feet of the **Sistine Chapel** ceiling singlehandedly. The task took four years of mental and physical anguish. It's said that for years afterward Michelangelo couldn't read anything without holding it up over his head. The result, however, was the masterpiece that you can now see, its colors cool and brilliant after recent restoration. Bring a pair of binoculars to get a better look at this incredible work (unfortunately, you're not allowed to lie down on the floor to study the frescoes above, the viewing position of choice in decades past; by the time you leave the chapel, your neck may feel like Michelangelo's, so you may also want to study it—to take a cue from 19th-century visitors—with the aid of a pocket mirror). The ceiling is literally a painted Bible: Michelangelo's subject was the story of humanity before the coming of Christ, seen through Augustinian tenets of faith popular in early 16th-century theological circles. While some of the frescoed panels are veritable stews of figures, others—especially the depiction of God's outstretched hand giving Adam the spark of life in the *Creation of Adam*—are majestically simple, revealing how much art Michelangelo brought to the field of painting from the discipline of sculpture. In 1541, some 30 years after completing the ceiling, Michelangelo was commissioned to paint the *Last Judgment* on the wall over the altar. If the artist's ceiling may be taken as an expression of the optimism of the High Renaissance, the *Last Judgment,* by contrast, is a veritable guided tour through Hell. Not surprisingly, since in the intervening years Rome had been sacked and pillaged by the French (who, in fact, had used the Sistine Chapel to stable their horses).

In the interim, the grim Counter Reformation movement had been adopted by the Church, and the papal court was now so offended by the nakedness of Michelangelo's *Last Judgment* figures that they hired artist Daniele da Volterra—forever after known as *il braghettone* (the breeches-maker)— to paint loincloths over the offending parts. The aged and embittered artist painted his own face on the wrinkled human skin in the hand of St. Bartholomew, below and to the right of the figure of Christ, which he clearly modeled on the *Apollo Belvedere* (now on exhibit in the Vatican galleries). Like the ceiling, the *Last Judgment* has been cleaned, surprising viewers with its clarity and color after restorers unveiled their work in April 1994. Was Michelangelo a master of vibrant color? Or is the "new" Sistine a travesty of Michelangelo's intentions? Opinions remain divided, but most art historians believe the restoration is true to Michelangelo's original vision.

The exhibition halls of the **Vatican Library** are bright with frescoes and contain a sampling of the library's rich collections of precious manuscripts. Room X, Room of the Aldobrandini Marriage, holds a beautiful Roman fresco of a nuptial rite. More classical statues are on view in the new wing. At the Quattro Cancelli, a cafeteria offers a well-earned break. The **Pinacoteca** (Picture Gallery) displays mainly religious paintings by such artists as Giotto, Fra Angelico, and Filippo Lippi.

In the **Pagan Antiquities Museum,** modern display techniques enhance another collection of Greek and Roman sculptures. The **Christian Antiquities Museum** has Early Christian and medieval art (its most famous piece is the 3rd-century AD statue, the *Good Shepherd*). The **Ethnological Museum** shows art and artifacts from exotic places throughout the world. The complete itinerary ends with the **Historical Museum,** whose collection of carriages, uniforms, and arms can be opened by a custodian on request.

In all, the Vatican Museums offer a staggering excursion into the realms of art and history. It's foolhardy to try to see all the collections in one day, and it's doubtful that anyone could be interested in everything on display. Simply aim for an overall impression of the collections' artistic and cultural riches. If you want to delve deeper, you can come back another day. ⊠ *Viale Vaticano,* ☎ *06/698–3333.* ⊠ *13,000 lire; free last Sun. of month.* ☉ *Easter wk and July–Sept., weekdays 8:45–5 (last admission at 4), Sat. 8:45–2; Oct.–June (except Easter), Mon.–Sat. 9–2 (last admission at 1); religious holidays (Jan. 1 and 6, Feb. 11, Mar. 19, Easter Sun. and Mon., May 1, Ascension Thurs., Corpus Christi, June 29, Aug. 15 and 16, Nov. 1, Dec. 8, Dec. 25 and 26) and last Sun. of every month 9–2.*

NEED A
BREAK?

Neighborhood trattorias that are far better and far less popular with tourists than those opposite the Vatican Museum entrance include **Hostaria Dino e Toni** (⊠ Via Leone IV 60)—where you can dine on typical Roman fare at moderate, even inexpensive, prices—and **La Caravella** (⊠ Via degli Scipioni 32 at Via Vespasiano, off Piazza

Risorgimento), which serves Roman specialties and has pizza on the lunch menu. La Caravella is closed Thursday.

Old Rome: Gold and Grandeur

The neighborhood known as Vecchia Roma (Old Rome) is one of Rome's most beautiful districts, thick with narrow streets with curious names, airy Baroque piazzas, and picturesque courtyards. Occupying the horn of land that pushes the Tiber westward toward the Vatican, it has been an integral part of the city since ancient times, and its position between the Vatican and the Lateran palaces, both seats of papal rule, puts it in the mainstream of Rome's development from the Middle Ages onward. It includes such world-famous sights as the Pantheon—ancient Rome's most perfectly preserved building—but it is mainly an excursion into the 16th and 17th centuries, when Baroque art triumphed in Rome. Today, it boasts some of Rome's most coveted residential addresses.

The most important clue to the Romans is their Baroque art—not its artistic technicalities, but its spirit. When you understand that, you will no longer be a stranger in Rome. Flagrantly emotional, heavily expressive, and sensuously visual, the 17th-century artistic movement known as the Baroque was born in Rome, the creation of three geniuses, the sculptor and architect Gianlorenzo Bernini and the painters Annibale Caracci and Caravaggio. Ranging from the austere drama found in Caravaggio's painted altarpieces to the jewel-encrusted, gold-on-gold decoration of 17th-century Roman palace decoration, the Baroque sought to both shock and delight by upsetting the placid, "correct" rules of the Renaissance masters. By appealing to the emotions, it became a powerful weapon in the hands of the Counter Reformation.

A Good Walk

Numbers in the text correspond to numbers in the margin and on the Old Rome, the Historic Center map.

Start on Via del Plebiscito, near Piazza Venezia, at the huge church of **Il Gesù** ①, the grandmother of all Baroque churches. Move on to Piazza della Minerva, where in the church of **Santa Maria sopra Minerva** ② you will find the tomb of Fra Angelico. Turn down Via della Minerva to reach the **Pantheon** ③. From Piazza della Rotonda in front of the Pantheon, take Via Giustiniani onto Via della Dogana Vecchia to the church of **San Luigi dei Francesi** ④, a pilgrimage spot for art lovers everywhere. Move on to the church of **Sant'Agostino** ⑤ in the eponymous piazza and the historic **Palazzo Altemps** ⑥, off Piazza Sant'–Apollinaire, before arriving at **Piazza Navona** ⑦, one of Rome's showpiece piazzas, home to Bernini's **Fountain of the Four Rivers** and the church of **Sant'Agnese in Agone**, the quintessence of Baroque architecture. Take Via Tor Millini over to Via della Pace and follow it to Piazza della Pace, where a semicircular portico stands in front of the 15th-century church of **Santa Maria della Pace** ⑧. Explore the byways on that side of Corso Vittorio before crossing over one of Rome's great thoroughfares and making a loop along aristocratic **Via Giulia** to **Palazzo Falconieri** ⑨, and, just ahead, **Palazzo Farnese** ⑩, perhaps the most beautiful Renaissance palace in Rome. On your way back to Corso Vittorio Emanuele, visit the **Campo dei Fiori** ⑪, site of a colorful market, before coming to the **Baracco Museum** ⑫. Across the way, note one of the outstanding architectural monuments of Renaissance Rome, the **Palazzo Massimo alle Colonne** ⑬, and, several blocks along the bustling street, the huge, 17th-century church of **Sant'Andrea della Valle** ⑭. Finally, head down the Corso del Rinascimento to No. 40, the church of **Sant'Ivo alla Sapienza** ⑮, with a golden dome in the shape of a spiral.

TIMING

Allow about three hours for this walk, plus 10 or 15 minutes for each church visited along the way.

Sights to See

⑫ **Baracco Museum.** Housed in a charming little Renaissance town house, this museum features a varied collection of sculptures from ancient Mediterranean civilizations. ⊠ *Via dei Baullari 1,* ☎ *06/688–06848.* 🖃 *3,750 lire.* ⊙ *Wed., Fri., and Sat. 9–1:30; Tues. and Thurs. 9–1:30 and 5–8, Sun. 9–1.*

⑪ **Campo dei Fiori.** The best time to visit this square—whose name translates as the Field of Flowers—is on weekday mornings, when the outdoor market fills the square with color and bustle. It was once the scene of public executions (including that of philosopher-monk Giordano Bruno, whose statue broods in the center). ⊙ *Mon.–Sat. 7–1:30.*

❶ **Il Gesù.** Grandmother of all Baroque churches, this huge structure was designed by Vignola in about 1650. The church is the tangible symbol of the power of the Jesuits, who were a major force in the Counter Reformation in Europe. It remained undecorated for about 100 years, but when it finally was decorated, no expense was spared. Its interior drips with gold and lapis lazuli, gold and precious marbles, gold and more gold, all covered by a fantastically painted ceiling by Baciccia that seems to swirl down to merge with the painted stucco figures at its base. ⊠ *Piazza del Gesù.*

❻ **Palazzo Altemps.** Those interested in ancient sculpture should not miss one of Rome's greatest collections of classical antiquities, housed in this historic building. Opened in 1996, it houses the collections of ancient Roman (and Egyptian) sculpture of the Museo Nazionale Romano. Look for the *Galata,* a poignant work portraying a barbarian warrior who chooses death for himself and his wife rather than humiliation by the enemy, in the famed Ludovisi collection. The palace's stunning early 16th-century courtyard and gorgeously frescoed ceilings make an impressive setting for the sculptures. ⊠ *Via Sant'Apollinare 8,* ☎ *06/683–3759.* 🖃 *12,000 lire (includes admission to Museo Nazionale delle Terme).*

❾ **Palazzo Falconieri.** Borromini's masterful work of architecture houses nothing of interest to the visitor, but the building itself makes one of Rome's most elegant attractions. In order to get a good look at this gracefully imposing building, go around the block and view it from along the Tiber embankment. ⊠ *Via Giulia 1.*

❿ **Palazzo Farnese.** Michelangelo had a hand in building what is now the French Embassy and perhaps the most beautiful Renaissance palace in Rome. Within is the Galleria vault painted by Annibale Carracci between 1597 and 1604—the second-greatest ceiling in Rome; write in advance to the embassy (⊠ Ambassador, French Embassy, Piazza Farnese 64, 00186 Rome) for special permission to view it. The Carracci gallery depicts the loves of the gods, a supremely pagan theme that the artist painted in a swirling style which announced the birth of Baroque. It's said that Carracci was so dismayed at the miserly fee he received—the Farnese family was extravagantly rich even by the standards of 15th- and 16th-century Rome's extravagantly rich—that he took to drink and died shortly thereafter. Those who sympathize with the poor man's fate will be further dismayed to learn that the French government pays

Old Rome: The Historic Center

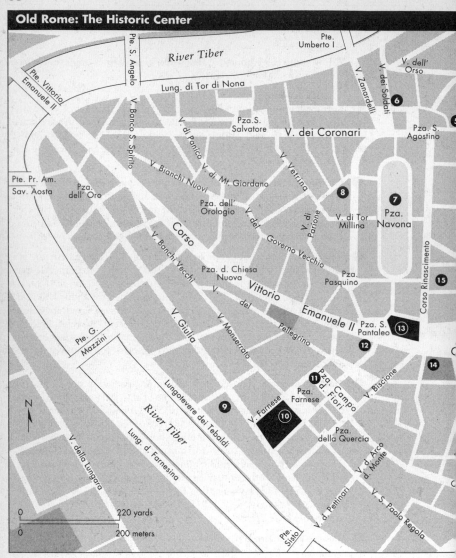

Pte. Umberto I

River Tiber

Pte. S. Angelo

Lung. di Tor di Nona

Pte. Vittorio Emanuele II

V. Zanardelli

V. dei Soldati

V. dell' Orso

Pza. S. Salvatore

V. dei Coronari

6

Pza. S. Agostino

5

V. di Panico

V. di Mt. Giordano

V. Vetrina

V. Bianco S. Spirito

Pte. Pr. Am. Sav. Aosta

Pza. dell' Oro

V. Bianchi Nuovi

Pza. dell' Orologio

V. del

V. di Parione

V. di Tor Millina

8

7

Pza. Navona

Corso

V. Banchi Vecchi

Governo Vecchio

Pza. d. Chiesa Nuova

Vittorio

Pza. Pasquino

Corso Rinascimento

15

V. Giulia

V. del

Emanuele II

Pza. S. Pantaleo

13

Pte. G. Mazzini

V. Monserrato

Pellegrino

12

14

N

11 Pza. Campo d. Fiori

Pza. Farnese

9

V. Farnese

10

V. Biscione

River Tiber

Lungotevere dei Tebaldi

Pza. della Quercia

V. d. Arco d. Monte

Lung. d. Farnesina

V. della Lungara

V. d. Pettinari

V. S. Paolo Regola

Pte. Sisto

| 0 | 220 yards |
| 0 | 200 meters |

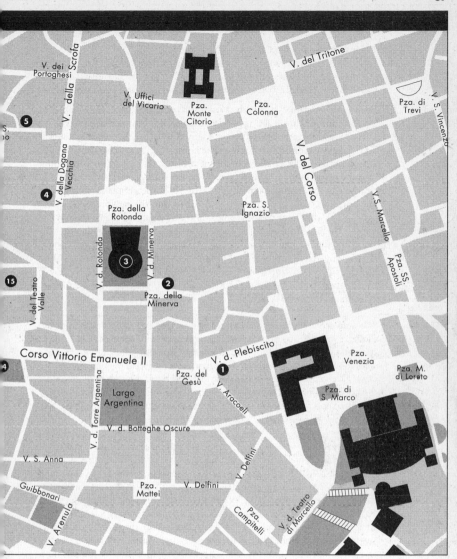

V. dei Portoghesi

V. della Scrofa

V. del Tritone

V. Uffici del Vicario

Pza. Monte Citorio

Pza. Colonna

Pza. di Trevi

V. S. Vincenzo

S.

V. della Dogana Vecchia

V. del Corso

Pza. della Rotonda

Pza. S. Ignazio

V. S. Marcello

V. d. Rotonda

V. d. Minerva

Pza. SS. Apostoli

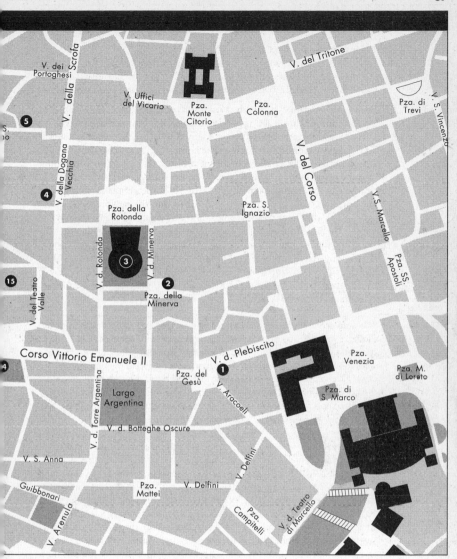

Pza. della Minerva

V. del Teatro Valle

Corso Vittorio Emanuele II

V. d. Plebiscito

Pza. Venezia

Pza. M. di Loreto

Pza. del Gesù

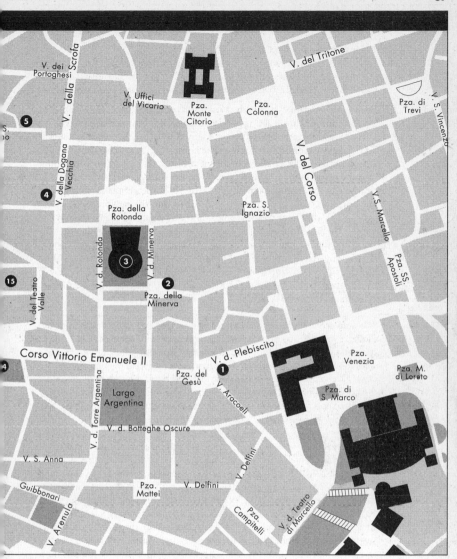

V. Aracoeli

Pza. di S. Marco

V. d. Torre Argentina

Largo Argentina

V. d. Botteghe Oscure

V. S. Anna

V. Delfini

Pza. Mattei

V. Delfini

Guibbonari

V. Arenula

Pza. Campitelli

V. d. Teatro di Marcello

one lira every 99 years as rent for their sumptuous embassy. ⊠ *Piazza Farnese.*

⑬ Palazzo Massimo alle Colonne. A graceful columned portico marks this inconspicuous but seminal architectural monument of Renaissance Rome, built by Baldassare Peruzzi in 1527. Via del Paradiso, around the corner, affords a better view. ⊠ *Corso Vittorio Emanuele 141.*

❸ Pantheon. Paradoxically, this is one of Rome's most perfect, best-preserved, and perhaps least-appreciated ancient monuments. Built on the site of an earlier pantheon erected in 27 BC by Augustus's general Agrippa, it was entirely rebuilt by the emperor Hadrian around AD 120. It was actually designed by Hadrian himself. The most striking thing about the Pantheon is not its size, immense though it is (until 1960 the dome was the largest ever built); rather it is the remarkable unity of the building. You don't have to look far to find the reason for this harmony: The diameter of the dome is exactly equal to the height of the walls. The hole in the ceiling is intentional: The oculus at the apex of the dome signifies the "all-seeing eye of heaven." Note the original bronze doors: They have survived more than 1,800 years, centuries more than the interior's rich gold ornamentation, long since plundered by popes and emperors. ⊠ *Piazza della Rotonda,* ☎ *06/6830–0230.* ⊠ *Free.* ☺ *Mon.–Sat. 9–4:30, Sun. 9–1.*

NEED A BREAK? The café scene in the square in front of the Pantheon rivals that of nearby Piazza Navona. The area is ice-cream heaven, with some of Rome's best *gelaterie* within a few steps of one another. Romans consider nearby **Giolitti** (⊠ Via Uffizi del Vicario 40) superlative and take the counter by storm. Remember to pay the cashier first and hand the stub to the man at the counter when you order your cone. Giolitti has a good snack counter, too. The shop is closed Monday. If you're a cappuccino addict, head for the nearby **Tazza d'Oro** (⊠ Via degli Orfani 84).

★ ☙ ❼ Piazza Navona. This famed 17th-century piazza, which traces the oval form of Emperor Domitian's stadium, is one of Rome's showpiece attractions. It still has the carefree air of the days when it was the scene of Roman circus games, medieval jousts, and 17th-century carnivals. Today, this ravishing setting often attracts fashion photographers and Romans out for their evening *passeggiata* (promenade). The Christmas fair held in the piazza from early December through January 6 is lively and fun for children, with rides, games, Santa Claus and the Befana (the ugly but good witch who brings candy and toys to Italian children on the Epiphany). Bernini's splashing **Fountain of the Four Rivers,** with an enormous rock squared off by statues representing the four corners of the world, makes a fitting centerpiece. Behind the fountain stands the church of **Sant'Agnese in Agone,** the absolute quintessence of Baroque architecture, built by the Pamphili Pope Innocent X and still owned by his descendants, the Princes Doria-Pamphili. The facade—a wonderfully rich melange of bell towers, concave spaces, and dovetailed stone and marble—is by Carlo Rainaldi and Francesco Borromini (1599–1667), a contemporary and sometime rival of Bernini. One story has it that the Bernini statue nearest the church is hiding its head because it can't bear to look upon the "inferior" Borromini facade; in fact, the facade was built after the fountain, and the statue hides its head because it represents the Nile River, whose source was unknown until relatively recently.

NEED A BREAK? The sidewalk tables of the **Tre Scalini** (⊠ Piazza Navona 30) café offer a grandstand view of the piazza. This is the place that invented the *tartufo,* a luscious chocolate-covered ice-cream specialty. Note that it costs twice as much if you eat it outside as inside. The café is closed Wednesday. For a salad or a light lunch, go to **Cul de Sac** (⊠ Piazza Pasquino 73 off Piazza Navona) or to **Insalata Ricca** (⊠ Via del Paradiso next to church of Sant'Andrea della Valle). Both are informal and inexpensive.

❹ San Luigi dei Francesi. Art lovers will want to make a pilgrimage to this church. In the last chapel on the left are three stunningly dramatic works by Caravaggio (1571–1610), the master of the heightened approach to light and dark. The inevitable coin machine will light up his *Calling of St. Matthew, Matthew and the Angel,* and *Matthew's Martyrdom,* seen from left to right, and Caravaggio's mastery of light takes it from there. Time has fully vindicated the artist's patron, Cardinal Francesco del Monte, who commissioned these works and stoutly defended their worth from the consternation of the clergy of San Luigi, who didn't appreciate the artist's roistering and unruly lifestyle; they are now acknowledged as among the world's greatest paintings. ⊠ *Piazza San Luigi dei Francesi.* ⊙ *Fri.–Wed. 7:30–12:30 and 3:30–7, Thurs. 7:30–12:30.*

❺ Sant'Agostino. Caravaggio's celebrated *Madonna of the Pilgrims*—which scandalized all Rome because it pictured pilgrims with dirt on the soles of their feet—can be found in this small church, over the first altar on the left. ⊠ *Piazza di Sant'Agostino.*

⓮ Sant'Andrea della Valle. This huge, 17th-century church looms mightily over a busy intersection. Puccini set the first act of his opera *Tosca* here. Puccini lovers have been known to hire a horse-drawn carriage at night for an evocative journey that traces the course of the opera (from Sant'Andrea up Via Giulia to Palazzo Farnese—Scarpia's headquarters—to the locale of the opera's climax, Castel Sant'Angelo, landmarks that define this part of Rome). ⊠ *Piazza Vidoni 6.*

⓯ Sant'Ivo alla Sapienza. Borromini's inspirational church has what must surely be the most fascinating dome in all Rome—a golden spiral said to have been inspired by a bee's stinger. ⊠ *Corso Rinascimento 40.*

❿ Santa Maria della Pace. Hidden away in a corner of Old Rome, gracing Piazza Santa Maria della Pace, are a semicircular portico and 15th-century church. In 1656, Pietro da Cortona was commissioned by Pope Alexander VII to enlarge its tiny piazza (to accommodate the carriages of the church's wealthy parishioners), and the result was one of Rome's most delightful little architectural stage sets, complete with bijou-size palaces. Within the church are two great Renaissance treasures: Raphael's frescoes of the Sibyls (above the first altar on the right near the front door) and the cloister designed by Bramante, the very first expression of High Renaissance style in Rome. Santa Maria della Pace is rarely open but if you take the alleylike Vicolo along the left-hand side of the church and ring the bell at the first entryway on the right, the nuns will usually permit you to enter.

❷ Santa Maria sopra Minerva. Practically the only Gothic-style church in Rome, the attractions are Michelangelo's *Risen Christ* and the tomb of the gentle 15th-century artist Fra Angelico. Have some coins handy for the *luce* (light) boxes that illuminate the **Carafa Chapel** in the right transept, where exquisite 15th-century frescoes by Filippo Lippi (circa 1457–1504) are well worth the small investment (Lippi's most famous student was Botticelli). In front of the church, Bernini's charming elephant bearing an Egyptian obelisk has an inscription on the base stating something to the effect that it takes a strong mind to sustain solid wisdom. ⊠ *Piazza della Minerva.*

Via Giulia was named after its builder, Pope Julius II (of Sistine Ceiling fame), and it has functioned for more than four centuries as the "salon of Rome," address of choice for Roman aristocrats. It is lined with elegant palaces, including Palazzo Falconieri (☞ *above*), and old churches (one, San Eligio, reputedly designed by Raphael himself). The area around Via Giulia is a wonderful section to wander through and get the feel of daily life as carried on in a centuries-old setting; this experience is enhanced by the dozens of antiques shops in the neighborhood.

Vistas and Views: From the Spanish Steps to the Trevi Fountain

Though it has a bustling commercial air, this part of the city also holds some great scenic attractions. The most extravagant of all is the elaborate marble confection that is the monument to Vittorio Emanuele II. Among the things to look for are stately palaces, Baroque ballrooms, and the greatest example of portraiture in Rome, Velazquez's incomparable *Innocent X*. Those with a taste for the sumptuous theatricality of Roman ecclesiastical architecture, and in particular for heroic illusionistic ceiling painting, will find this a rewarding area. But for most, the highlights are the Trevi Fountain and the Spanish Steps, 18th-century Rome's most famous example of city planning.

A Good Walk
Numbers in the text correspond to numbers in the margin and on the Rome map.

Start at the flamboyant **Vittorio Emanuele Monument** ⑮ in Piazza Venezia, home of the **Tomb of the Unknown Soldier.** As you look up the Corso bearing the king's name, to your left is **Palazzo Venezia** ⑯, an art-laden Renaissance palace where Mussolini once addressed the crowds. On Saturdays, you can visit the picture gallery known as **Galleria Colonna,** in the **Palazzo Colonna** ⑰, home to Rome's most patrician family. Along Via del Corso, one of the busiest shopping streets in the city, is the **Palazzo Doria Pamphili** ⑱. A detour to the left will bring you to the sumptuous 17th-century church of **Sant'Ignazio** ⑲. If you continue straight along the Corso you will reach Piazza Colonna and the ancient **Column of Marcus Aurelius** ⑳. Take a left onto chic Via Condotti, which gives you a head-on view of the Piazza di Spagna and the **Spanish Steps** ㉑; on the right of the steps, at No. 26, is the **Keats and Shelley Memorial House** ㉒, in which the English Romantic poet Keats lived. Don't forget to debouch slightly onto Via Gregoriana to discover the **Palazzetto Zuccari** ㉓, designed to look like a grimacing monster. From the narrow end of the piazza, take Via Propaganda Fide to Sant'Andrea delle Fratte, swerving onto Via del Nazareno, then crossing busy Via del Tritone to Via della Stamperia. This street leads to the **Trevi Fountain** ㉔, one of Rome's most familiar landmarks.

TIMING
The walk takes approximately two to three hours. In the morning the air is cleaner and car and pedestrian traffic is lighter.

Sights to See
Numbers in the margin correspond to points of interest on the Rome map.

⓴ **Column of Marcus Aurelius.** This ancient column is an extraordinary stone history-book. Its marvelously detailed reliefs spiraling up to the top relate the emperor's victorious campaigns against the barbarians. ⊠ *Piazza Colonna.*

NEED A
BREAK?

The **Antico Caffè Greco,** a 200-year-old institution, ever a haunt of artists and literati, has tiny, marble-top tables and velour settees; it's a beautifully preserved place. Goethe, Byron, and Liszt were habitués; Buffalo Bill stopped in when his Wild West road show hit Rome. It's still a haven for writers and artists, and for ladies carrying Versace shopping bags. You pay a premium for table service. ⊠ *Via Condotti 86. Closed Sun.*

㉒ Keats and Shelley Memorial House. English Romantic poet Keats lived next to the Spanish Steps in what is now a museum dedicated to himself and his great contemporary and friend, Shelley. You can visit his tiny rooms, which have been poignantly preserved as they were when he died here in 1821. ⊠ *Piazza di Spagna 26,* ☎ *06/678–4235.* 🖾 *5,000 lire.* ☉ *June–Sept., weekdays 9–1 and 3–6; Oct.–May, weekdays 9–1 and 2:30–5:30.*

㊨ **㉓ Palazzetto Zuccari.** Near the top of the Spanish Steps (☞ *below*) stands what many consider the most amusing house in all of Italy, at Via Gregoriana 30, designed to look like a grimacing stone monster. The entrance is through the monster's mouth; the eyes are the house's windows. It was designed in 1591 by the Mannerist painter Federico Zuccari (1540–1609), whose home this was. Zuccari sank all his money into this bizarre creation, dying in debt before his curious memorial, as it turned out to be, was completed. It is now the property of the **Biblioteca Hertziana,** Rome's prestigious fine arts library. ⊠ *Via Gregoriana 30.*

⑰ Palazzo Colonna. Rome's most patrician family opens up its fabulous home to the public once a week, and the invitation is irresistible to anyone who ever wondered what a palace looks like inside. The entrance to the picture gallery, Galleria Colonna, which is open only on Saturday mornings, is a secondary one, behind a plain, obscure-seeming door. The old masters are lackluster, but the gallery should be on your mustdo list because the Sala Grande is truly the grandest 17th-century room in Rome. More than 300 feet long, and decorated with a bedazzlement of chandeliers, colored marble, and enormous paintings, it is best known today as the site where Audrey Hepburn met the press in *Roman Holiday.* ⊠ *Via della Pilotta 17,* ☎ *06/679–4362.* 🖾 *10,000 lire.* ☉ *Sept.–July, Sat. 9–1.*

⑱ Palazzo Doria Pamphili. The graceful 18th-century facade of this palazzo on Via del Corso is only a small part of a bona-fide patrician palace, still the residence of a princely family, who rent out many of the palazzo's 1,000 rooms. You shouldn't miss seeing the family's incredibly rich art collection, open to the public a few mornings a week. Pride of place is given to the famous (and pitiless) 17th-century Velazquez portrait of the Pamphili Pope Innocent X, but don't overlook Caravaggio's poignant *Rest on the Flight to Egypt*—and, time permitting, catch the guided tour of the state apartments, which gives a discreet glimpse of an aristocratic lifestyle. Pundits say most Roman palazzi consist of one bathroom, two bedrooms, and 40 ballrooms, and after this tour, you can understand why. ⊠ *Piazza del Collegio Romano 1/a,* ☎ *06/679–7323.* 🖾 *Picture gallery 10,000 lire, private-apartments tour 5,000 lire.* ☉ *Mon., Tues., and Fri.–Sun. 10–1.*

⑯ Palazzo Venezia. This building is a blend of medieval solidity and Renaissance grace. It offers a unique chance to see what a Renaissance palace really looked like and contains a good collection of paintings, sculptures, and objets d'art in grand salons, some of which Mussolini used as his offices. Notice the balcony over the main portal, from which ㊨ Il Duce addressed huge crowds in the eponymouse **Piazza Venezia** below. Nowadays, the square's most imposing figure is the policeman directing traffic from his little podium in the middle, whose almost comical display of orchestration is a constant source of amusement to passersby. ✉ *Via del Plebiscito 118,* ☎ *06/679–8865.* ✉ *8,000 lire.* ☉ *Tues.–Sat. 9–1:30, Sun. 9–12:30.*

⑲ Sant'Ignazio. The false interior dome in this sumptuous 17th-century church is an oddity among the lavishly frescoed domes of the Eternal City. To get the full effect of the marvelous illusionistic ceiling painted by Andrea del Pozzo, stand on the small disk set into the floor of the nave to view his *Glory of St. Ignatius Loyola.* The church contains some of Rome's most splendorous, jewel-encrusted altars. If you're lucky, you might be able to catch one of the evening concerts offered here. The church is the focus of Raguzzini's 18th-century Rococo piazza, where the buildings are arranged almost as in a stage set, reminding us that theatricality was a key element of almost all the best Baroque and Rococo art. ✉ *Piazza Sant'Ignazio.*

★ **㉑ Spanish Steps.** Both the steps and the **Piazza di Spagna,** from which the steps emerge, get their names from the Spanish Embassy to the Holy See (the Vatican), opposite the American Express office, though the staircase was built with French funds in 1723. In an allusion to the Church of Trinità dei Monti at the top of the hill, the staircase is divided by three landings (beautifully banked with blooming azaleas from mid-April to mid-May). For centuries, the Scalinata (as natives refer to the steps) has been the place to see and be seen. This area has always welcomed tourists: 18th-century dukes and duchesses on their Grand Tour, 19th-century artists and writers in search of inspiration—among them, Stendhal, Balzac, Thackeray, and Byron—and today's enthusiastic hordes. Bernini's **Fountain of the Barcaccia** (Old Boat) is near the center of the piazza.

NEED A BREAK?   **Babington's Tea Rooms** (✉ Piazza di Spagna 23), at the foot of the Spanish Steps, has catered to the refined cravings of Anglo-Saxon travelers since its establishment by two genteel English ladies in 1896, but it's definitely not a budgeter's cup of tea. At weekday lunches you're likely to find yourself next to a Bulgari, Fendi, or Agnelli. The restaurant is closed Monday.

★ **㉔ Trevi Fountain.** The Colosseum's rival as the sight everyone wants to see in Rome, after St. Peter's, is tucked away off Via del Tritone. The fountain, all the more effective for its cramped setting in a tiny piazza, is a spectacular fantasy of mythical sea creatures amidst cascades of splashing waters. It was featured in the 1954 film *Three Coins in the Fountain* and, of course, was the scene of Anita Ekberg's aquatic frolic in Fellini's *La Dolce Vita.* The fountain is the world's most spectacular wishing well: Legend has it that you can ensure your return to Rome by tossing a coin into the fountain. At night, the spotlit piazza takes on the festive air of a crowded outdoor party.

⑮ Vittorio Emanuele Monument. The huge bronze sculpture group atop this vast marble monument is visible from many parts of the city, making this modern Rome's most flamboyant landmark. It was erected in the late 19th century to honor Italy's first king, Vittorio Emanuele II, and the unification of Italy. Sometimes said to resemble a typewriter in the Victorian mode, it houses the **Tomb of the Unknown Soldier,** with its eternal flame. Although the monument has been closed to the public for many years, plans are in the works to reopen it; the views from the top of the steps are among Rome's best, because for one thing, the monument isn't in it. Opposite the monument, note the enclosed wooden veranda fronting the palace on the corner of Via del Plebiscito and the Corso. For the many years that she lived in Rome, Napoléon's mother had a fine view from here of the local goings-on. ⊠ *Piazza Venezia.*

Historic Churches: Heavenly Monuments of Faith

It is hard not to be impressed by the historic and architectural grandeur of Rome's major churches. Three churches are the highlights of this walk, two of them major basilicas with roots in the early centuries of Christianity.

A Good Walk

Not far from Piazza Venezia and the Roman Forum, off Via Cavour is the church of **San Pietro in Vincoli** ㉕. Look for Via San Francesco da Paola, a street staircase that passes under the old Borgia palace and leads to the church. Via Cavour leads to **Santa Maria Maggiore** ㉖, and from there Via Merulana leads straight to **San Giovanni in Laterano** ㉗. The adjoining **Lateran Palace** houses the Vatican Historical Museum; across the street, a small building houses the **Scala Santa** ㉘, or Holy Stairs, supposedly from Pilate's Jerusalem palace. Circle the palace to see the 6th-century octagonal **Baptistery of San Giovanni,** forerunner of many such buildings throughout Italy.

TIMING

The walk alone takes approximately 90 minutes, plus 15–20 minutes in the churches. Allow at least an hour to explore San Clemente. The visit to the Vatican Historical Museum takes about 45 minutes.

Sights to See

㉗ **San Giovanni in Laterano.** Many are surprised when they discover that the cathderal of Rome is not St. Peter's but this church. Dominating the piazza whose name it shares, this immense building was where the early popes once lived and where the present pope still officiates in his capacity as Rome's bishop. The towering facade and Borromini's cool Baroque interior emphasize the majesty of its proportions.

The adjoining **Lateran Palace,** once the popes' official residence and still technically part of the Vatican, now houses the offices of the Rome Diocese and the Vatican Historical Museum. ⌧ *6,000 lire.* ☉ *museum Sat. and the first Sun. of each month 8:45–1.*

OFF THE BEATEN PATH

SAN CLEMENTE – The remains of ancient Roman dwellings and a 4th-century church below the upper church of San Clemente are among Rome's most intriguing subterranean sights. ⊠ *Via San Giovanni in Laterano,* ☎ *06/704-51018.* ⌧ *Donation requested.* ☉ *Mon.–Sat. 9–noon and 3:30–6, Sun. 10–noon.*

SANTI QUATTRO CORONATI – This 12th-century church, part of a fortified abbey that provided refuge to early popes and emperors, is in one of the most unusual corners of Rome, a quiet island that has resisted the tide of time and traffic flowing beneath its ramparts. Few places in Rome are as redolent of the Middle Ages. Don't miss the cloister with its well-tended gardens and 12th-century fountain. The entrance is the door in the left nave; ring if it's not open. You can also ring at the adjacent convent for the key to the Oratory of San Silvestro, with charming 13th-century frescoes.

㉖ **Santa Maria Maggiore.** One of the oldest and most spacious churches in Rome, it was built on the spot where a 3rd-century pope witnessed a miraculous midsummer snowfall. It is resplendent with gleaming mosaics—those on the arch in front of the main altar date from the 5th century; the apse mosaic dates from the 13th century—and an opulently carved wood ceiling believed to have been gilded with the first gold brought from the New World. ⊠ *Piazza Santa Maria Maggiore off Via Cavour.*

㉕ The church of **San Pietro in Vincoli** houses St. Peter's chains (under the altar) and Michelangelo's *Moses,* a powerful statue almost as famed as his frescoes in the Sistine Chapel. The *Moses* was destined for the tomb of Julius II, but Michelangelo was driven to distraction by the interference of Pope Julius and his successors, and the tomb was never finished. The statue is a remarkable sculpture but the church is usually jammed with tour groups, and the monument itself fronts a large, ugly souvenir shop. ⊠ *Piazza San Pietro in Vincoli off Via Cavour.*

㉘ **Scala Santa.** A small building opposite the Lateran Palace (☞ *above*) houses the so-called Holy Stairs, claimed to be the staircase from Pilate's palace in Jerusalem. Behind the palace is the 6th-century octagonal **Baptistery of San Giovanni,** forerunner of many similar buildings throughout Italy, and Rome's oldest and tallest obelisk, brought from Thebes and dating from the 15th century BC.

From the Quirinale to the Piazza della Repubblica: Princely Palaces and Romantic Fountains

Although this walk takes you from ancient Roman sculptures to early Christian churches, it's mainly an excursion into the 16th and 17th centuries, when Baroque art—and Bernini—triumphed in Rome.

A Good Walk

Begin at the **Quirinal** ㉙ the highest of Rome's seven hills. Here you'll find the Palazzo del Quirinale, official residence of the president of Italy. Also of note is the **Palazzo Pallavicini-Rospigliosi** ㉚, a 17th-century palace with some exquisite examples of Baroque art. Along Via del Quirinal (which becomes Via XX Settembre) is the church of **Sant'Andrea** ㉛, considered by many to be Bernini's finest work, and, at the Quattro Fontane (Four Fountains) crossroads, the church of **San Carlo alle Quattro Fontane** ㉜, designed by Bernini's rival Borromini. Turn left down Via delle Quattro Fontane to reach the imposing Palazzo Barberini, home of the **Galleria Nazionale** ㉝, home to splendid masterpieces by Raphael and Caravaggio. Down the hill is Piazza Barberini and the **Tritone Fountain** ㉞, another Bernini design. Cross the piazza and begin your gradual climb up Via Veneto, curving past the U.S. Embassy and turning off onto Via Bissolati. On the corner of Piazza San Bernardo is to the church of **Santa Maria della Vittoria** ㊱, known for Bernini's Baroque decoration. It's not far to **Piazza della Repubblica** ㊲, where you will find the pretty **Fountain of the Naiads.** On one side of the square is an ancient Roman brick facade, which marks the church of Santa Maria degli Angeli. On the opposite side of the square is the last stop on this walk, the **Museo Nazionale Romano** ㊳, where there are plentiful examples of the fine mosaics and masterful paintings that decorated ancient Rome's villas and palaces.

TIMING

The walk takes approximately 90 minutes, plus 10–15 minutes for each church visited, and two hours each for visits to the Galleria Nazionale in Palazzo Barberini and the Museo Nazionale Romano.

Sights to See

㉝ **Galleria Nazionale.** Along with architect Carlo Maderno, Borromini helped make the splendid 17th-century Palazzo Barberini a residence worthy of Rome's leading art patron, Pope Urban VIII, who began this palazzo for his family in 1625. Inside, the gallery offers some fine works by Raphael (the *Fornarina*) and by Caravaggio. The palazzo boasts Rome's biggest ballroom, which has a ceiling painted by Pietro da Cortona; this shows Immortality bestowing a crown upon Divine Providence escorted by—"a bomber squadron," to quote Sir Michael Levey—of mutant bees (bees featured prominently in the heraldic device of the Barberini). ✉ *Via delle Quattro Fontane 13,* ☎ *06/481–4591.* 🎟 *8,000 lire.* ⊙ *Tues.–Sat. 9–2, Sun. 9–1.*

㊳ Museo Nazionale Romano. Palazzo Massimo alle Terme holds a major part of the collections of the National Museum. Here you can see extraordinary examples of the fine mosaics and masterful paintings that decorated ancient Rome's palaces and villas, as well as some of antiquity's most fabled sculptures, including the *Ludovisi Throne,* the *Lancellotti Discus Thrower,* and the *Castelporziano Discus Thrower.* Don't miss the fresco—depicting a lush garden in bloom—which came from the villa that Livia, wife of Emperor Augustus, owned outside Rome. ✉ *Largo Villa Peretti 2,* ☎ *06/489–03501.* 🎟 *12,000 lire (includes Terme di Diocleziano museum).* ⊙ *Tues.–Sat. 9–2, Sun. 9–1.*

㉚ Palazzo Pallavicini-Rospigliosi. This palace was built in 1605 for Cardinal Scipione Borghese; on the first day of each month, visitors can view Guido Reni's fresco of *Aurora*—a landmark in Baroque painting—in the palace's park pavilion. It is just off the square. ✉ *Via XXIV Maggio 43,* ☎ *06/482–7224.* 🎟 *Free.* ⊙ *1st day of month 10–noon and 3–5.*

㊲ Piazza della Repubblica. has a characteristic 19th-century layout, but the curving porticoes echo the plan of those portions of the immense ancient **Baths of Diocletian,** which once stood here. Built in the 4th century AD, they were the largest and most impressive of the baths of ancient Rome, and their vast halls, pools, and gardens could accommodate 3,000 people at a time. Also part of the great baths was an **Octagonal Hall** which now holds a sampling of ancient sculptures found there, including two beautiful bronzes. ✉ *Via Romita.* 🎟 *Free.* ⊙ *Daily 9–1 and 3–6.*

Another part of the Baths of Diocletian was later transformed into a monastery and then into the **Terme di Diocleziano Museum,** holding the Museo Nazionale Romano's collection of ancient inscriptions on stone, interesting to the average visitor mainly as a chance to see the lovely cloister, with bits and pieces of ancient Rome lining the garden paths. ✉ *Viale E. De Nicola 79,* ☎ *06/488–0530.* 🎟 *12,000 lire (includes Palazzo Massimo alle Terme).* ⊙ *Tues.–Sat. 9–2, Sun. 9–1.*

The pretty **Fountain of the Naiads,** a turn-of-the-century addition to the piazza, features voluptuous bronze ladies wrestling happily with marine monsters. The curving ancient Roman brick facade on one side of the piazza marks the church of **Santa Maria degli Angeli,** adapted by Michelangelo from the vast central chamber of the colossal baths. The scale of the church's interior gives you an idea of the grandeur of the ancient building.

㉙ Quirinal. This is the highest of ancient Rome's seven hills (the others are the Capitoline, Palatine, Esquiline, Viminal, Celian, and Aventine) and the one where ancient Romans and, later, the popes built their residences in order to escape the deadly miasmas and the malaria of the low-lying area around the Forum. Every day at 4 PM the ceremony of the changing of the guards at the portal includes a sprightly miniparade, complete with band. The fountain in the square boasts ancient statues of Castor and Pollux reining in their unruly steeds, and a basin salvaged from the Roman Forum. The **Palazzo del Quirinale,** the largest on the Quirinal square, belonged first to the popes, then to Italy's kings, and is now the official residence of the nation's president.

㉜ San Carlo alle Quattro Fontane. Borromini's church at the Quattro Fontane (Four Fountains) crossroads is an architectural gem. In a space no larger than the base of one of the piers of St. Peter's, Borromini created a church that is an intricate exercise in geometric perfection. Characteristically, the architect chose a subdued white stucco for the interior decoration, so as not to distract from the form. The exterior of the church is Borromini at his bizarre best, all curves and rippling movement. Outside, four charming fountains frame views in four directions.

㉟ Santa Maria della Concezione. One of the most bizarre sights in Rome is the crypt of this Capuchin church, where you can see—if you like that sort of thing—the skeletons and assorted bones of 4,000 dead monks artistically arranged in four macabre chapels. ⊠ *Via Veneto 27,* ☎ *06/ 487–1185.* 🖾 *Donation requested.* ☉ *Daily 9–noon and 3–6.*

㊱ Santa Maria della Vittoria. This church in Via XX Settembre is known for Bernini's Baroque decoration of the Cornaro Chapel, an exceptional fusion of architecture, painting, and sculpture, in which the *Ecstasy of St. Teresa* is the focal point. Bernini's audacious conceit was to model the chapel as a theater: Members of the Cornaro family—sculpted in colored marble—watch from theater boxes as, center stage, St. Teresa, in the throes of mystical rapture, is pierced by a gilded arrow held by an angel. To quote one 18th-century observer, President de Brosses: "If that is divine love, I know what it is." No matter what your reaction may be, you'll have to admit it's great theater.

㉛ Sant'Andrea. This is a small but imposing Baroque church designed and decorated by Bernini, who considered it one of his finest works and liked to come here occasionally just to sit and enjoy it. ⊠ *Via del Quirinale.*

㉞ Tritone Fountain. Centerpiece of Piazza Barberini is Bernini's graceful fountain, designed in 1637 for the sculptor's munificent patron, Pope Urban VIII, whose Barberini coat of arms, featuring bees once again, is at the base of the large shell.

NEED A BREAK? Next to a movie house, **La Piazza** (⊠ Via Barberini 19) offers the Italian version of fast food, tasty and inexpensive. The restaurant is closed Sunday.

Amid Sylvan Glades: From the Villa Borghese to the Ara Pacis

Beautiful masterpieces are as common as bricks on this walk, which offers more visual excitement than most cities possess in their entire environs. Along the way, Villa Borghese, Rome's largest park, can prevent gallery gout by offering an oasis in which to enjoy an espresso at the Casino Valadier or picnic under the ilex trees. Just be sure to pick up your foodstuffs in advance, whether ready-to-go from the snack bars or do-it-yourself from *alimentari* (grocery stores), as you'll find only fast-food carts within the park itself.

A Good Walk

Start at **Porta Pinciana** ㊴, one of the entrances to Rome's largest park, Villa Borghese. Taking a looping route through the park you will come upon the **Galleria Borghese** ㊵ and its fabulous sculpture collection. Enjoy the view of Rome from the **Pincio** ㊶ terrace, in the southwest corner of the park, before descending the ramps to **Piazza del Popolo** ㊷. At the north end of the piazza, next to the 400-year-old city gate, the Porta del Popolo, is the church of **Santa Maria del Popolo** ㊸, with one of the richest art collections of any church in the city. Stroll along Via Ripetta to the Augusteum, built by Caesar Augustus; next to it is the **Ara Pacis** ④, built in 13 BC.

TIMING

The walk takes approximately two hours; allow an additional hour for the Galleria Borghese and 20–30 minutes for the Augusteum.

Sights to See

④ Ara Pacis (Altar of Augustan Peace). This altar, sheltered in an unattractive modern edifice on the northwest corner of Piazza Augusto Imperatore, was erected in 13 BC to celebrate the era of peace ushered in by Augustus's military victories. The reliefs showing the procession of the Roman imperial family are magnificent and moving. Notice the poignant presence of several forlorn children; historians now believe they attest to the ambition of Augustus's wife, the Empress Livia, who succeeded in having her son, Tiberius, ascend to the throne by dispatching his family rivals with poison. Next to it is the imposing bulk of the marble-clad **mausoleum** Augustus built for himself and his family. ⊠ *Mausoleum: Via Ripetta,* ☎ *06/671–0271.* ☎ *3,750 lire.* ☉ *May–Sept., Wed.–Fri. 9–1:30; Tues., Thurs., and Sat. 9–1:30 and 4–7; Sun. 9–1. Oct.–Apr., Tues.–Sat. 9–1:30, Sun. 9–1.*

④ Galleria Borghese was a pleasure palace created by Cardinal Scipione Borghese in 1613 as a showcase for his fabulous antiquities collection and elegant fetes. Today, it's a monument to Roman 18th-century interior decoration at its most extravagant: room after room opulently adorned with porphyry and alabaster. Throughout the grand salons are statues of various deities, including one officially known as Venus Vincitrix, but there has never been any doubt as to its real subject: Pauline Bonaparte, Napoléon's sister, who married Prince Camillo Borghese in one of the storied matches of the 19th century. Sculpted by Canova, the princess reclines on a chaise longue, bare-bosomed, her hips swathed in classical drapery, the very model of haughty detachment and sly come-hither. Pauline is known to have been shocked that her husband took pleasure in showing off the work to his guests. This coyness seems all the more curious given the reply she is supposed to have made to a lady who asked her how she could have posed for the work: "Oh, but the studio was heated." But then it was exactly the combination of aristocratic disdain and naïveté that is said to have made her irresistible in the first place. Other rooms at the Galleria Borghese hold important sculptures by Bernini, including the *David* and *Apollo and Daphne.* The gallery's renowned picture collection has been moved to the large San Francesco a Ripa complex in Trastevere; it will probably be there through 1997 (☞ Across the Tiber, *below*). ⊠ *During renovation, use Galleria Borghese entrance off Via Raimondi,* ☎ *06/854–8577.* ☎ *4,000 lire.* ☉ *May–Sept., Tues.–Sat. 9–7, Sun. 9–1; Oct.–Apr., Tues.–Sun. 9–1.*

④ Piazza del Popolo For many years this beautifully proportioned square functioned as an exceptionally attractive parking lot which happened to have a 3,000-year-old obelisk in the middle (now traffic and parking are limited). The often-photographed bookend Baroque churches at the southern end of the piazza are not, first appearances to the contrary, twins. At one end of the square is the 400-year-old **Porta del Popolo,** Rome's northern city gate.

| NEED A BREAK? | **Rosati** (⊠ Piazza del Popolo 4) is a café that has never gone out of style, forever a rendezvous of literati, artists, and actors. Its sidewalk tables, tearoom, and upstairs dining room can revive you with an espresso, snack, lunch, or dinner—all with a hefty price tag. |

㊶ **Pincio.** The southwestern corner of Villa Borghese is taken up by the Pincian Hill, one of the seven hills of ancient Rome. It was laid out by the early 19th-century architect Valadier as part of his overall plan for Piazza del Popolo. Back then, counts and countesses liked to take their evening passeggiata here in the hopes of meeting Pius IX, the last Pope to go about Rome on foot. Here you'll find the pricey Casina Valadier restaurant, where you can enjoy the views from the terrace café—the prettiest place in Rome to have a cappuccino.

㊴ The **Porta Pinciana** (Pincian Gate) is one of the historic city gates in the Aurelian Walls surrounding Rome. The Porta itself was built in the 6th century AD, about three centuries after the walls were built to keep out the barbarians. These days it is one of the entrances to **Villa Borghese,** Rome's peaceful 17th-century park, built as the pleasure gardens of the powerful Borghese family.

㊸ **Santa Maria del Popolo.** This church next to the Porta del Popolo (☞ *above*) goes almost unnoticed, but it has one of the richest collections of art of any church in Rome. Here you'll find Raphael's High Renaissance masterpiece, the Chigi Chapel, as well as two stunning Caravaggios in the Cerasi Chapel, which definitively prove just how modern 17th-century art can be. Elsewhere in the church, the great names—Bramante, Bernini, Pinturicchio, Sansovino, Caracci—resound in the silence. ✉ *Piazza del Popolo.*

Across the Tiber: The Ghetto, Tiber Island, and Trastevere

For the authentic atmosphere of old Rome, the areas covered in this walk are unbeatable. It takes you through separate communities, each staunchly resisting the tides of change, including the Jewish ghetto; and the Trastevere, a picturesque neighborhood, where you will find "the Romans of Rome": blunt, uninhibited, sharp-eyed, friendly, sincere, often beautiful, and seldom varnished. Despite rampant gentrification, Trastevere remains about the most tightly knit community in Rome, its inhabitants proudly proclaiming their descent—whether real or imagined—from the ancient Romans.

A Good Walk

Begin in the old ghetto, on Via del Teatro Marcello. Turn into Piazza Campitelli and make your way to Piazza Mattei, where one of Rome's loveliest fountains, the 16th-century **Fontana delle Tartarughe** ㊺, is tucked away. Take Via della Reginella into **Via Portico d'Ottavia,** heart of the Jewish ghetto. On the Tiber is a **synagogue.** The **Teatro di Marcello** ㊻, behind the **Portico d'Ottavio,** was originally a theater designed to hold 20,000 people. Follow Via di Teatro di Marcello, passing the ruins of two small temples: the **Temple of Fortuna Virilis** ㊼ and the circular **Temple of Vesta** ㊽. From there, follow the Tiber to **Piazza Bocca della Verità** ㊾, home to the marble "mouth of truth" set into the entry portico of the 12th-century **Santa Maria in Cosmedin.** Retracing your steps, cross **Tiberina Island** ㊿, and then head into **Trastevere.** Begin your exploration of the neighborhood at **Piazza in Piscinula** (you will need a good street map to make your way around this intricate maze of winding side streets), take Via dell'Arco dei Tolomei, cross Via dei Salumi, and turn left into Via dei Genovesi and then right to the piazza in front of **Santa Cecilia in Trastevere** (51). Aficionados of the Baroque will want to walk several blocks down Via Anicia to **San Francesco a Ripa** (52), another Bernini creation. Follow Via San Francesco a Ripa to the very heart of the *rione,* or district, of Trastevere, to the lovely **Piazza di Santa Maria in Trastevere** (53), site of the lovely 12th-century church of **Santa Maria in Trastevere.** With the help of a map, find your way through the narrow byways to Piazza Sant'Egidio and Via della Scala, continuing on

On the road with **Fodor's**

Amalfi Coast, Positano, Italy
Photo © 1987 Peter Gutman,
author of Fodor's *Nights to Imagine*

Fodor's is a registered trademark of Fodor's Travel Publications, Inc.

to Via della Lungara, where you'll find **Villa Farnesina** ⑤④, which includes frescoes by Raphael. From Trastevere, climb Via Garibaldi to the Janiculum Hill, which offers views spanning the whole city, and where you'll find the church of **San Pietro in Montorio** ⑤⑤, built in 1481.

TIMING

The walk takes approximately 3 hours, plus 10–15 minutes for each church visited, and about 30 minutes for a visit to Villa Farnesina.

Sights to See

④⑤ **Fontana della Tartarughe.** The 16th-century "Fountain of the Turtles" in Piazza Mattei is one of Rome's loveliest. Designed by Giacomo della Porta in 1581 and sculpted by Taddeo Landini, the piece revolves around four bronze boys, each grasping a dolphin that jets water into marble shells, and several bronze tortoises each held in the boys' hands and drinking from the fountain's upper basin. The tortoises are the fountain's most brilliant feature, a 17th-century addition by, inevitably, Bernini. The piazza is named for the Mattei family, which built **Palazzo Mattei** on Via Caetani, worth a peek for its sculpture-rich courtyard and staircase.

Palazzo Corsini. This elegant palace holds a collection of large, dark, and dull paintings, but stop in to climb the extraordinary 17th-century stone staircase, itself a drama of architectural shadows and sculptural voids. ✉ *Via della Lungara 10.*

⑪⑨ **Piazza Bocca della Verità**—the Square of the Mouth of Truth— is on the site of the Forum Boarium, ancient Rome's cattle market, later used for public executions. Its sinister name is derived from the marble mouth—actually part of an ancient drain cover—set into the entry portico of the 12th-century church of **Santa Maria in Cosmedin**. In the Middle Ages anyone accused of lying would be forced to put his hand into the mouth and warned that if he didn't tell the truth the mouth would close and cut off his hand.

OFF THE
BEATEN PATH

AVENTINE HILL – One of the seven hills of ancient Rome, it is now a quiet residential neighborhood that most tourists don't see. It has several of the city's oldest and least-visited churches, and some surprises: the view from the keyhole in the gate to the garden of the Knights of Malta (✉ Piazza Cavalieri di Malta) and another, unusual view of Rome from the walled park off Via Santa Sabina.

⑤③ **Piazza di Santa Maria in Trastevere,** with its elegant raised fountain and sidewalk cafés, is a sort of outdoor living room, open to all comers. The showpiece is the 12th-century church of **Santa Maria in Trastevere**. The mosaics on the church's facade—which add light and color to the piazza, especially at night when they are spotlit—are believed to represent the Wise and Foolish Virgins. The interior often produces involuntary gasps from unsuspecting visitors: an enormous nave bathed in a mellow glow from medieval mosaics and overhead gilding, the whole framed by a processional of two rows of gigantic columns. There are larger naves in Rome, but none quite so majestic. Indeed, although it was completed in the 12th century, it approximates—as well as any structure could—the over-the-top splendor of an ancient Roman basilica hall.

⑤② **San Francesco a Ripa.** This church in Piazza San Francesco d'Assisi is a must for fans of the Baroque. It holds one of Bernini's most hallucinatory sculptures, a dramatically lighted statue of the Blessed Ludovica Albertoni, ecstatic at the prospect of entering heaven as she expires on her deathbed.

55 **San Pietro in Montorio.** One of the key Renaissance buildings in Rome stands in the cloister of this church, built by order of Ferdinand and Isabella of Spain in 1481 over the spot where tradition says St. Peter was crucified. The **Tempietto**, Bramante's little temple, is an architectural gem, and was one of the earliest and most successful attempts to produce an entirely classical building. ✉ *Via Garibaldi Gianicolo.* ⊘ *Daily 9–12 and 4–6.*

51 **Santa Cecilia in Trastevere.** Mothers and children love to wander in the delightful little garden in front of this church in Piazza Santa Cecilia, and there's no reason why you shouldn't join them for a bit before you duck inside for a look at the very grand 18th-century interior and the languid statue of St. Cecilia under the altar.

Synagogue. The large, bronze-roofed synagogue on the Tiber is a Roman landmark. It contains an interesting museum of precious ritual objects and fabrics and other exhibits documenting the history of the Jewish community in Rome. ✉ *Lungotevere Cenci,* ☎ *06/686–4648.* ⚑ *8,000 lire.* ⊘ *Mon.–Thurs. 9:30–1:30 and 2–5, Fri. 9:30–2, Sun. 9:30–12:30.*

46 **Teatro di Marcello.** The Teatro is hardly recognizable as a theater today, but originally it was a huge place, designed to hold 20,000 spectators. It was begun by Julius Caesar; today, the apartments carved out in its remains have become one of Rome's most prestigious residential addresses. ✉ *Via del Teatro di Marcello.* ⊘ *Only for concerts.*

47 **Temple of Fortuna Virilis.** This rectangular temple dates from the 2nd century BC and is built in the Greek style, as was the norm in the early years of Rome. For its age, it is remarkably well-preserved, in part due to its subsequent consecration as a Christian church. ✉ *Piazza Bocca della Verità*

48 **Temple of Vesta.** One of Rome's most evocative little ruins, all but one of its 20 original Corinthian columns remain intact. Like the Temple of Fortuna Virilis (☞ *above*), it was built in the 2nd century BC, considerably before the ruins you see in the Roman Forum. ✉ *Piazza Bocca dell Verità*

50 **Tiberina Island.** Ancient Ponte Fabricio links the ghetto neighborhood of Trastevere (☞ *below*) to this island, where a city hospital stands on a site that has been dedicated to healing ever since a temple to Aesculapius was erected here in 291 BC. If you have time, and if the river's not too high, walk down the stairs for a different perspective on the island and the Tiber.

Trastevere. This area consists of a maze of narrow streets that is still, despite evident gentrification, one of the city's most authentically Roman neighborhoods. Literally translated, Trastevere means "across the Tiber," and indeed the Trasteverini, a breed apart, have always been proud and combative, chagrined at the reputation their quarter has acquired for purse snatching (but it happens; don't carry a purse and keep your camera out of sight). Among self-consciously picturesque trattorias and trendy tearooms, you also find old shops and dusty artisans' workshops in alleys festooned with laundry hung out to dry. One of the most unaffected parts of Trastevere lies around **Piazza in Piscinula,** where the tiny **San Benedetto,** the smallest medieval church in the city, is opposite the restored medieval Casa dei Mattei. Via dell'Arco dei Tolomei and Via dei Salumi are interesting old streets.

Via Portico d'Ottavia. Along this street at the heart of the Jewish ghetto are buildings where medieval inscriptions, ancient friezes, and half-buried classical monuments attest to the venerable history of this neighborhood. The old **Church of Sant'Angelo in Pescheria** was built right into the ruins of the Portico d'Ottavia, which served as a kind of foyer for the Teatro di Marcello (☞ *above*).

54 **Villa Farnesina.** Money was no object to extravagant host Agostino Chigi, a banker from Siena who financed many a papal project. His munificence is evident in this elegant villa, built for him about 1511. When Raphael could steal some precious time from his work on the Vatican Stanze and from his wooing of the Fornarina, he came over to execute some of the frescoes, notably a luminous *Galatea*. Chigi delighted in impressing guests by having his servants clear the table by casting precious dinnerware into the Tiber. Naturally, the guests did not know of the nets he had stretched under the waterline to catch everything. ⊠ *Via della Lungara 230,* ☎ *06/654–0565.* ☺ *Free.* ☺ *Mon.–Sat. 9–1.*

Quo Vadis? The Catacombs and the Appian Way

The legendary beginnings of Christianity in Rome are the focus of this tour. Although it offers a respite from museums, the itinerary is no easier on the feet. Do it on a sunny day and take along a picnic or have lunch at one of the pleasant restaurants near the catacombs. The Rome EPT office offers a free, informative pamphlet on this itinerary.

A Good Walk

Resist any temptation to undertake the 1½ km walk between Porta San Sebastiano and the catacombs; it is a dull and tiring hike on a heavily trafficked, cobblestone road, with stone walls the only scenery. Instead, hop on Bus 218 from San Giovanni in Laterano or Bus 660 from the Colli Albani Metro stop on Line A to the **Via Appia Antica** ⑤⑥ Stay on the bus until you reach the catacombs; the most interesting and scenic walk along the ancient road lies beyond them.

TIMING

One hour, plus one hour for visit to catacombs.

Sights to See

56 **Via Appia Antica.** This is "the Queen of Roads", completed in 312 BC by Appius Claudius, who also built Rome's first aqueduct. One of the two important catacombs on Via Appia Antica is that of **San Callisto**, one of the best preserved of these underground cemeteries. A friar will guide you through its crypts and galleries. ⊠ *Via Appia Antica 110,* ☎ *06/513–6725.* ☺ *8,000 lire.* ☺ *Apr.–Sept., Thurs.–Tues. 8:30–noon and 2:30–5:30; Oct.–Mar., Thurs.–Tues. 8:30–noon and 2:30–5.*

The 4th-century catacomb of **San Sebastiano** was named for the saint who was buried here. It burrows underground on four levels. The only one of the catacombs to remain accessible during the Middle Ages, it is the origin of the term "catacomb," for it was in a spot where the road dips into a hollow, a place the Romans called *catacumbas* (near the hollow). Eventually, the Christian cemetery that had existed here since the 2nd century came to be known by the same name, which was applied to all underground cemeteries discovered in Rome in later centuries. ⊠ *Via Appia Antica 136,* ☎ *06/788–7035.* ☺ *8,000 lire.* ☺ *Apr.–Sept., Fri.–Wed. 9–noon and 2:30–7:30; Oct.–Mar., Fri.–Wed. 9–noon and 2:30–5.*

On the east side of Via Appia Antica are the ruins of the **Circus of Maxentius**, where the obelisk now in Piazza Navona once stood.

The circular **Tomb of Cecilia Metella**, mausoleum of a Roman noblewoman who lived at the time of Julius Caesar, was transformed into a fortress in the 14th century. It marks the beginning of the most interesting and evocative stretch of Via Appia Antica, lined with tombs and fragments of statuary. Cypresses and umbrella pines stand guard over the ruined sepulchers, and the occasional tracts of ancient paving stones are the same ones trod by triumphant Roman legions.

DINING

As the pace of Roman life quickens, more fast-food outlets are opening, offering tourists a wider choice of light meals. There are variations of the older Italian institutions of the *tavola calda* (hot table) and the *rosticceria* (roast meats), both of which offer hot and cold dishes to be taken out or eaten on the premises, some sold by the portion, others by weight. You usually select your food and pay for it at the cashier, who gives you a stub to give to the counter person when you pick up the food. Newer snack bars are cropping up, and pizza *rustica* (rustic-style) outlets selling slices of various kinds of pizza seem to have sprouted on every block.

Despite these changes, many Romans stick to the tradition of having their main meal at lunch, from 1 to 3, although you won't be turned away if hunger strikes shortly after noon. Dinner is served from 8 or 8:30 until about 10:30 or 11. Some restaurants stay open much later, especially in summer, when patrons linger at sidewalk tables to enjoy the *ponentino* (cool breeze). Almost all restaurants close one day a week (it's usually safest to call ahead to reserve) and for at least two weeks in August, when it can sometimes seem impossible to find sustenance in the deserted city. This is not a bad time to picnic. You can buy provisions in neighborhood *alimentari* that aren't closed for vacation.

The typical Roman pasta is fettuccine, golden egg noodles that are at their classic best when freshly made and laced with *ragù*, a thick, rich tomato and meat sauce. Carbonara-style pasta is usually made with spaghetti or thicker, spaghettilike *bucatini*; the cooked pasta is tossed with raw egg, chunks of fried *guanciale* (unsmoked bacon), and lots of freshly ground black pepper. Spaghetti *all'amatriciana* has a piquant sauce of tomato, guanciale, and hot red pepper. Gnocchi, a Roman favorite for Thursday dinner, are tiny dumplings of flour and potatoes and are served with a tomato sauce and a sprinkling of grated cheese.

Abbacchio, baby lamb, is at its best in the spring; a summer favorite is *pollo coi peperoni,* stewed chicken with peppers. *Fritto misto* usually includes morsels of zucchini, artichokes, and *baccalà* (codfish) fried in batter. *Carciofi* (artichokes) are served *alla romana* (sautéed whole with garlic and mint), or *alla giudia* (fried whole, with each petal crisp and light enough to melt in your mouth). Tender peas are sautéed with prosciutto to make *piselli al* prosciutto.

Local cheeses are mild *caciotta* and sharp pecorino. Fresh ricotta is also used in a number of dishes. Typical wines of Rome are those of the Castelli Romani: Frascati, Colli Albani, Marino, and Velletri.

Acqua semplice (tap water) is safe everywhere in Rome, so if you're on a budget, order it rather than *acqua minerale* (mineral water). The automatically applied *pane e coperto* (bread and cover charge) has been eliminated in many restaurants but you may be charged extra for bread, anyway. And a *servizio* (service charge) of 10%–12% still appears on many checks; remember that in the end your waiter will see only a small part of that sum, so another 5% is welcome. A fixed-price *menù turistico* (tourist menu) includes taxes and services, but usually not drinks.

CATEGORY	COST*
$$$$	over 120,000 lire
$$$	70,000–120,000 lire
$$	40,000–70,000 lire
$	under 40,000 lire

per person, for a three-course meal, including house wine and taxes

Central Rome

$$$$ ✕ **El Toulà.** Take a byway off Piazza Nicosia in Old Rome to find this prestigious restaurant, one of a number in Italy of the same name; all are spin-offs of a renowned restaurant in Treviso in northern Italy. Rome's El Toulà has the warm, welcoming atmosphere of a 19th-century country house, with white walls, antique furniture in dark wood, heavy silver serving dishes, and spectacular arrangements of fruits and flowers. There's a cozy bar off the entrance, where you can sip a *prosecco* (Venetian semisparkling white wine), the aperitif best suited to the chef's Venetian specialties, which include risotto with artichokes and *fegato alla veneziana* (liver with onions). ⊠ *Via della Lupa 29/b,* ☎ *06/687–3750. Reservations essential. Jacket and tie. AE, DC, MC, V. No lunch Sat. Closed Sun., Aug., and Dec. 24–26.*

$$$$ ✕ **La Pergola.** A grand view. A grand restaurant. The conjunction is
★ not automatic—but in this case, both elements are imposingly present. From this elegant rooftop restaurant of the Cavalieri Hilton—built on Monte Mario, one of the highest of the hills overlooking the city—a fabulous view of Rome whets your appetite for imaginatively prepared cuisine. Wraparound windows and mirrors ensure that everyone gets a panoramic view of the city's skyline. And if you can take your eyes off the vista you will find a distinctively Italian ambience, with frescoes and a Tuscan garden theme featuring lattice-work and potted lemon trees. The menu changes with the seasons, and might include pasta with shrimp and arugula or breast of guinea hen on a red wine-and-onion confit. Order à la carte or from three special menus, priced at 85,000, 105,000, and 135,000 lire. Then have an after-dinner drink in the adjacent bar and try to spot the constellations in the Roman sky. You may dine outdoors in fair weather. ⊠ *Via Cadlolo 101,* ☎ *06/35091. Jacket and tie. AE, DC, MC, V. No lunch. Closed Sun. and Mon.*

$$$$ ✕ **Le Jardin.** Located in the Parioli residential district, this restaurant is famous for its chichi crowd. It's in the exclusive Lord Byron hotel, itself a triumph of studied interior decoration. The imaginative menu is a tempting compendium of seasonal specialties served with newer-than-now nouvelle style. If they are on the menu, try the risotto with seafood and vegetable sauce or the fillet of beef with morels. ⊠ *Hotel Lord Byron, Via Giuseppe De Notaris 5,* ☎ *06/322–0404. Reservations essential. Jacket and tie. AE, DC, MC, V. Closed Sun. and Aug.*

$$$$ ✕ **Les Etoiles.** If you're looking for an ascension-into-heaven moment
★ when dining in Rome, just book a window table at this restaurant. As candles flicker at your side, enjoy the *nuova cucina* (the Italian variation of nouvelle cuisine) specials and sit back and watch the blue fade out of the dome of St. Peter's. The rooftop restaurant of the Atlante Star hotel, in the Prati section of Rome, has big window walls to frame the breathtaking view of the Vatican, which is especially magical later in the evening when the cupola's graceful curves are illuminated. The menu varies, depending on what the chef chooses at the market. There are interesting pasta dishes with porcini mushrooms or seasonal vegetables, classic or creative risotto (for two), fresh seafood, and choice grilled meats. When you reserve, ask for a table with a view of St. Peter's. ⊠ *Hotel Atlante Star, Via dei Bastioni 1,* ☎ *06/689–3434. Reservations essential. Jacket and tie. AE, DC, MC, V.*

54

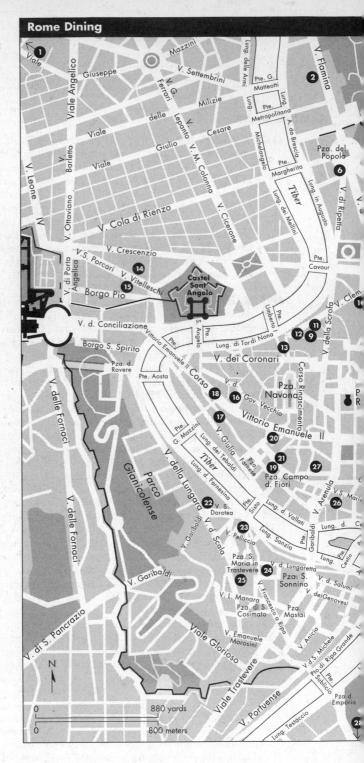

Rome Dining

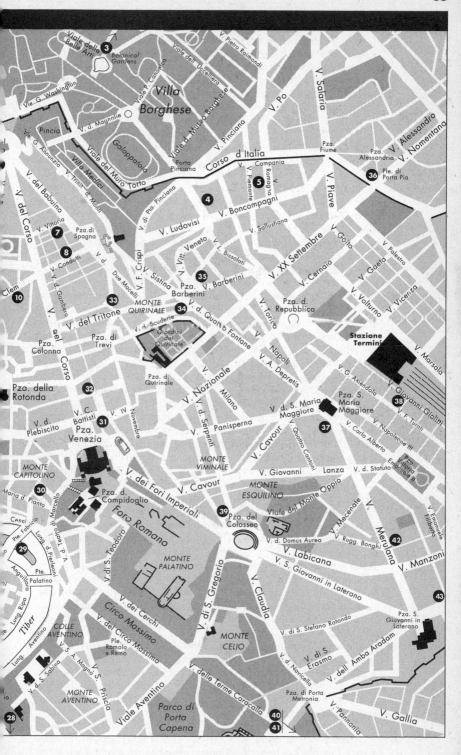

$$$$ ✕ **Sans Souci.** All the glitz and glamour of the dolce vita days of Rome in the 1950s lives on in this overdecorated but superb downstairs sanctuary of gourmet delights. Service is literally fit for a king—and the Sans Souci has had a few among its customers, along with Hollywood biggies and business magnates. It is the only restaurant in Rome with a doorman, but don't let that intimidate you, for the staff is courteous and attentive. The menu presents both French and Italian dishes, among them truffled terrine de foie gras and *agnello al timo* (roast lamb with thyme). ✉ *Via Sicilia 20,* ☎ *06/482–1814. Reservations essential. Jacket and tie. AE, DC, MC, V. No lunch. Closed Mon. and mid-Aug.–Sept. 6.*

$$$ ✕ **Coriolano.** The only tourists who find their way to this classic restaurant near Porta Pia are likely to be gourmets looking for quintessential Italian food, and that means light homemade pastas, choice olive oil, and market-fresh ingredients, especially seafood. The small dining room is decorated with antiques, and tables are set with immaculate white linen, sparkling crystal, and silver. Although seafood dishes vary, *tagliolini all'aragosta* (thin noodles with lobster sauce) is usually on the menu, as are porcini mushrooms in season (cooked according to a secret recipe). The wine list is predominantly Italian, but includes some French and California wines, too. ✉ *Via Ancona 14,* ☎ *06/442–49863. Jacket and tie. AE, DC, MC, V. Closed Sun.; Sat. in July; and Aug. 1–25.*

$$$ ✕ **Corsetti—Il Galeone.** Located on a market square in Trastevere, this spot is decorated like an old galleon, lined with well-seasoned wood and laded with nautical accessories. Seafood is the specialty, but you will also find an ample selection of typical Roman pastas and meat dishes, as well as the famous carciofi alla romana. ✉ *Piazza San Cosimato 27,* ☎ *06/581–6311. AE, DC, MC, V. Closed Wed.*

$$$ ✕ **Da Checco er Carrettiere.** You'll find Da Checco tucked away behind Piazza Trilussa in Trastevere. It has the look of a country inn, with hanging braids of garlic and an antipasto table that features some unusual specialties, such as a well-seasoned mashed potato-and-tomato mixture. Among the hearty pasta offerings are spaghetti *alla carrettiera* (with black pepper, sharp cheese, and olive oil), and linguine with scampi. Seafood (which can be expensive) is the main feature on the menu, but traditional Roman meat dishes are offered, too. This is a great place to soak up genuine Trastevere color and hospitality. ✉ *Via Benedetta 10,* ☎ *06/581–7018. Reservations essential. AE, DC, MC, V. No dinner Sun. Closed Mon. and Aug. 10–Sept. 10.*

$$$ ✕ **Il Convivio.** Don't be intimidated by the opaque glass, closed door, and doorbell at the entrance. This, as its name suggests, is a convivial little restaurant, and it is earning a reputation as one of Rome's best. Reservations are essential, for it accommodates only 30 diners. The food is what it's all about: classic Italian (and Roman) dishes prepared with flair and a brilliant use of herbs, as in shellfish with tarragon and lamb with thyme. The *menù degustazione* (tasting menu) is good value. ✉ *Via dell'Orso 44,* ☎ *06/686–9432. Reservations essential. AE, DC, MC, V. Closed Sun.*

$$$ ✕ **Passetto.** Benefiting from a choice location near Piazza Navona, Passetto has been a favorite with Italians and tourists for many years: It's a place you can rely on for classic Italian food and courteous service. If you can, eat on the terrace—it's especially memorable at night; the mirrored dining room is more staid. Roman specialties, such as cannelloni and abbacchio, are featured. ✉ *Via Zanardelli 14,* ☎ *06/654–0569. Jacket and tie. AE, DC, MC, V. No lunch Mon. Closed Sun.*

$$$ ✕ **Piperno.** A favorite, in the old Jewish ghetto next to historic Palazzo Cenci, Piperno has been in business for more than a century. It is *the* place to go for Rome's extraordinary carciofi alla giudia. You eat in three small wood-paneled dining rooms or at one of a handful of tables outdoors. Try *filetti di* baccalà (fillet of cod), pasta *e ceci* (a thick soup of pasta tubes and chickpeas), *fiori di zucca* (stuffed zucchini flowers), and artichokes. ⊠ *Monte dei Cenci 9,* ☎ *06/654–2772. AE, DC, MC, V. No dinner Sun. Closed Mon., Dec. 25, Easter, and Aug.*

$$$ ✕ **Ranieri.** Walk down a quiet street off fashionable Via Condotti, near
★ the Spanish Steps, to find this historic restaurant, founded by a onetime chef of Queen Victoria. Ranieri remains a favorite for its traditional atmosphere and decor, with damask-covered walls, velvet banquettes, crystal chandeliers, and old paintings. The Italian-French cuisine is excellent: Portions are abundant, and checks remain comfortably in the low end of this price category. Among the many specialties on the vast menu are *gnocchetti alla parigina* (feather-light dumplings with cheese sauce) and *mignonettes alla Regina Vittoria* (veal with pâté and an eight-cheese sauce). ⊠ *Via Mario dei Fiori 26,* ☎ *06/678–6505. Reservations essential. AE, DC, MC, V. Closed Sun.*

$$$ ✕ **Vecchia Roma.** It's everything a Roman restaurant should be. Two
★ decades ago, discerning American travelers realized that Vecchia Roma was too special to be left to the Romans—so they've made it their own. Exceptional cuisine, beautiful setting, gracious service— it all adds up to a deliciously sublime evening. Tucked away on a frozen-in-time piazza near the Campidoglio, Vecchia Roma has an airy and polished interior of beige walls and frescoed accents. It is a decor that is quintessentially Roman—a testament to rich simplicity and unpretentious nobility. The same can be said of the food. Together with classic Roman specialties, it features a range of main-course salads in summer and a wide choice of sauces served with polenta in the winter. Romans in the know always choose the seasonal specialties—such as porcini, mushrooms that taste just like filet mignon— which can be extraordinary. During fine weather, dining at one of the tables set up on the piazza will lend a very special flavor to your meal. As Vecchia Roma's fame has spread, it has maintained its high standards: Let's hope this will continue to be the case. ⊠ *Piazza Campitelli 18,* ☎ *06/686–4604. Reservations essential. AE, DC. Closed Wed. and mid-Aug.*

$$ ✕ **Cannavota.** On the square next to San Giovanni in Laterano, Cannavota has a large and faithful following and has fed generations of neighborhood families over the years. Seafood dominates, but carnivores are catered to, also. Try one of the pastas with seafood sauce— fettuccine with shrimp scampi is a good choice—and then go on to grilled fish or meat. The cheerful atmosphere and rustic decor make for an authentically Roman experience. ⊠ *Piazza San Giovanni in Laterano 20,* ☎ *06/772–05007. AE, DC, MC, V. Closed Wed. and Aug. 1–20.*

$$ ✕ **Colline Emiliane.** Not far from Piazza Barberini this unassuming trattoria offers exceptionally good food. Behind an opaque glass facade are a couple of plain dining rooms, where you are served light homemade pastas, a special chicken broth, and meats ranging from boiled beef to *giambonetto di vitella* (roast veal) and *cotoletta alla bolognese* (veal cutlet with cheese and tomato sauce). Family-run, it's quiet and soothing—a good place to rest after a sightseeing stint. Service is cordial and discreet. ⊠ *Via degli Avignonesi 22,* ☎ *06/481–7538. No credit cards. Closed Fri. and Aug.*

$$ ✕ **Costanza.** In Rome, one man's archaeological site can be another man's eatery. As its ancient Roman brickwork reveals, this fashionable trattoria occupies a small part of the Theater of Pompey, where Julius Caesar met his end. Serious gourmands rave about this spot, which has become a meeting place for artists, actors, and politicos. The mixed hot and cold antipasto is a specialty, as are crepes with mushrooms

and risotto with zucchini flowers. ⊠ *Piazza del Paradiso 65,* ☎ *06/ 686–1717. AE, DC, MC, V. Closed Sun. and Aug.*

$$ ✕ **Dal Bolognese.** Long a favorite with the art crowd, this classic restaurant on Piazza del Popolo is a trendy choice for a leisurely lunch between sightseeing and shopping. While dining, feast your eyes on an extensive array of contemporary paintings and check out the clientele, many of whom are wearing the latest Fendi turnout. As the name of the restaurant promises, the cooking here adheres to the hearty tradition of Bologna, with homemade pastas in creamy sauces and steaming trays of boiled meats. For dessert, there's *dolce della mamma* (a concoction of ice cream, zabaglione, and chocolate sauce). ⊠ *Piazza del Popolo 1,* ☎ *06/361–1426. DC, V. Closed Mon. and Aug. 7–22.*

$$ ✕ **La Campana.** This inconspicuous trattoria off Via della Scrofa has a venerable history: There has been an inn on this spot since the 15th century, and the two plain dining rooms occupy what were once stables. It's a homey place, with friendly waiters, snowy white linens on close-set tables, and good Roman food at reasonable prices. The menu offers specialties like *vignarola* (sautéed fava beans, peas, and artichokes), rigatoni with prosciutto and tomato sauce, and *olivette di vitello con purée* (tiny veal rolls with mashed potatoes). ⊠ *Vicolo della Campana 18,* ☎ *06/686–7820. AE, DC, MC, V. Closed Mon. and Aug.*

$$ ✕ **Le Maschere.** For a taste of southern Italian (Calabrian) fare, look for this cellar restaurant hidden away between Largo Argentina and Piazza Campo dei Fiori. A couple of planters, with a few outdoor tables in summer, mark this informal spot. Downstairs you pass an impressive antipasto buffet, and a pizza oven glows in a corner of the dining room. Dark rustic walls are hung with everything from paper garlands to old utensils; there are pottery wine jugs and rush-bottom chairs. Order spicy Calabria salami to start and then go on to pizza or southern favorites such as pasta with broccoli or with tomato and eggplant sauce. Grilled meat and seafood make up the list of second courses. Music on weekends and efficient service make for a pleasant evening. ⊠ *Via Monte della Farina 29,* ☎ *06/687–9444. AE, DC, MC, V. No lunch. Closed Mon. and mid-Aug.–mid-Sept.*

$$ ✕ **Mariano.** Near Via Veneto, Mariano (who is actually Tonino, Mariano's son-in-law and successor) is an exponent of quality and tradition. Since he leaves flights of culinary fancy to others, you can be sure of finding authentic Roman and central-Italian cuisine here, including delicate egg pastas, game, and abbacchio in season. ⊠ *Via Piemonte 79,* ☎ *06/474–5256. AE, DE, MC, V. No lunch Sat. Closed Sun.*

$$ ✕ **Orso 80.** This bright and bustling trattoria is in Old Rome, on a street famed for artisans' workshops. It has both a Roman and an international following, and is known, above all, for a fabulous antipasto table. Try the homemade egg pasta or the bucatini all'amatriciana; there's plenty of seafood on the menu, too. For dessert, the ricotta cake, a genuine Roman specialty, is always good. ⊠ *Via dell'Orso 33,* ☎ *06/686–4904. AE, DC, MC, V. Closed Mon. and Aug. 10–20.*

$$ ✕ **Osteria da Nerone.** Between the Colosseum and the church of San Pietro in Vincoli, this family-run trattoria features a tempting antipasto table and fresh pastas. The specialty is fettuccine *al Nerone* (with peas, salami, and mushrooms), but the homemade ravioli are good, too. In fair weather you eat outdoors with a view of the Colosseum. ⊠ *Via Terme di Tito 96,* ☎ *06/474–5207. Closed Sun. and mid-Aug.*

$$ ✕ **Otello alla Concordia.** The clientele in this popular spot—it's off a shopping street near Piazza di Spagna—is about evenly divided between tourists and workers from shops and offices in the area. The former like to sit outdoors in the courtyard in any weather; the latter have their regular tables in one of the inside dining rooms. The menu offers classic Roman and Italian dishes, and service is friendly and efficient.

Since every tourist in Rome knows about it, and since the regulars won't relinquish their niches, you may have to wait for a table; go early. ✉ *Via della Croce 81,* ☎ *06/678–1454. Reservations not accepted. AE, DC. Closed Sun. and Dec. 25.*

$$ ✕ **Paris.** On a small square just off Piazza Santa Maria in Trastevere, Paris (named after a former owner, not the city) has a reassuring, understated ambience, without the hokey, folky flamboyance of so many eating places in this gentrified neighborhood. It also has a menu featuring the best of classic Roman cuisine: homemade fettuccine, delicate fritto misto and, of course, baccalà. In fair weather opt for tables on the little piazza. ✉ *Piazza San Callisto 7/a,* ☎ *06/581–5378. AE, DC, MC, V. No dinner Sun. Closed Mon. and 3 wks in Aug.*

$$ ✕ **Pierluigi.** Pierluigi, in the heart of Old Rome, is a longtime favorite with foreign residents of Rome and Italians in the entertainment field. On busy evenings it's almost impossible to find a table, so make sure you reserve well in advance. Seafood dominates (if you're in the mood to splurge, try the lobster), but traditional Roman dishes are offered, too, including *orecchiette* (ear-shape pasta) con broccoli and simple spaghetti. Eat in the pretty piazza in summer. ✉ *Piazza dei Ricci 144,* ☎ *06/686–8717. AE, V. Closed Mon. and 2 wks in Aug.*

$$ ✕ **Romolo.** Nowhere else do the lingering rays of the setting Roman
★ sun seem more inviting than from the tavern garden of this charming Trastevere haunt—reputedly the onetime home of Raphael's lady love, the Fornarina. Generations of Romans and tourists have enjoyed its romantic courtyard and historic dining room, where, in the evening, strolling musicians serenade diners. The cuisine is appropriately Roman; specialties include mozzarella *alla fornarina* (deep-fried, with ham and anchovies) and *braciolette d'abbacchio scottadito* (grilled baby lamb chops). Alternatively, try one of the new vegetarian pastas featuring carciofi or radicchio. Meats are charcoal-grilled; there's also a wood-burning oven. ✉ *Via di Porta Settimiana 8,* ☎ *06/581–8284. AE, DC, V. Closed Mon. and Aug. 2–23.*

$$ ✕ **Sora Lella.** What was once a simple trattoria ensconced on the Tiberina Island is now a monument to the late foundress herself, beloved example of true Roman warmth and personality. And although prices are much higher than when Sora Lella presided over the cash desk, the cooking is still 100% Roman. Rigatoni all'amatriciana and *seppie con piselli* (cuttlefish stewed with tomatoes and peas) are usually on the menu, but leave room for the quintessential Roman ricotta cake. ✉ *Via Ponte Quattro Capi 16,* ☎ *06/686–1601. AE, MC, V. Closed Sun. and Aug.*

$$ ✕ **Tana del Grillo.** Near Santa Maria Maggiore, this family-run restaurant features the specialties of one of Italy's least-known regional cuisines—that of Ferrara. Sausages and salami of various types, gnocchi and lasagna or *pasticcio di maccheroni* (pasta casserole) are typical dishes, but the pièce de résistance is the *bollito,* a steaming cart laded with several types of boiled meat, which the waiter will carve to your order. ✉ *Via Alfieri 4,* ☎ *06/704–53517. AE, DC, MC, V. No lunch Mon. Closed Sun.*

$$ ✕ **Tullio.** This Tuscan trattoria off Via Veneto and Piazza Barberini opened in the dolce vita days of the 1950s, when this area was the center of Roman chic and bohemian life. It soon acquired a faithful clientele of politicians, journalists, and artists, and it has changed little over the years. Decor and menu are simple. The latter offers typically Tuscan pasta *e fagioli* (with beans), grilled steaks and chops, and fagioli *all'uccelletto* (with tomato and sage). ✉ *Via San Nicolò da Tolentino 26,* ☎ *06/481–8564. Reservations essential. AE, DC, MC, V. Closed Sun. and Aug.*

$ ✕ Abruzzi. Here's a simple trattoria off Piazza Santi Apostoli near Piazza Venezia that specializes in the regional cooking of the mountainous Abruzzo region, southeast of Rome. *Tonnarelli* (square pasta) is served with mushrooms, peas, and ham or with a meat sauce. Baby lamb is another classic regional dish. ✉ *Via del Vaccaro 1,* ☎ *06/679–3897. V. Closed Sat. and Aug.*

$ ✕ Baffetto. The emphasis here is on good old-fashioned value: Baffetto is Rome's best-known inexpensive pizza restaurant, plainly decorated and very popular. You'll probably have to wait in line outside on the cobblestones and then share your table once inside. The interior is mostly given over to the ovens, the tiny cash desk, and the simple, paper-covered tables. *Bruschetta* (toast) and *crostini* (mozzarella toast) are the only variations on the pizza theme. Turnover is fast: This is not the place to linger over your meal. ✉ *Via del Governo Vecchio 114,* ☎ *06/686–1617. Reservations not accepted. No credit cards. No lunch. Closed Sun. and Aug.*

$ ✕ Birreria Tempera. This old-fashioned beer hall is very busy at
★ lunchtime, when it's invaded by businesspeople and students from the Piazza Venezia area. There's a good selection of salads and cold cuts, as well as pasta and daily specials. Bavarian-style specialties such as goulash and wurst and sauerkraut prevail in the evening, when light and dark Italian beers flow freely. ✉ *Via San Marcello 19,* ☎ *06/678–6203. Reservations not accepted. No credit cards. Closed Sun. and Aug.*

$ ✕ Cottini. For lunch or supper, this cafeteria on the corner of Piazza Santa Maria Maggiore is reliable; the food counter and tables are in the back, beyond the large coffee bar and pastry counters. Salads, hot pastas, and main courses are always fresh, and they are served with a smile. The in-house bakery provides such tempting desserts as crème caramel and chocolate cake. ✉ *Via Merulana 287,* ☎ *06/474–0768. Reservations not accepted. No credit cards. Closed Mon.*

$ ✕ Fagianetto. Massive wooden beams on high are as solid as the reputation of this family-run trattoria near Termini Station. It has a regular neighborhood clientele, but also satisfies tourists' appetites with a special menu for about 20,000 lire. But you may well be tempted by à la carte offerings such as rigatoni *alla norcina* (with a sauce of crumbled sausage and cream) or osso buco *con funghi* (with mushrooms). Service is swift and courteous. ✉ *Via Filippo Turati 21,* ☎ *06/446–7306. AE, DC, MC, V. Closed Mon.*

$ ✕ Fratelli Menghi. Neighborhood regulars frequent this trattoria that has been in the same family for as long as anyone can remember (a portrait of Pop is on the wall in one dining room) and produces typical Roman fare. There's usually a thick hearty soup such as minestrone, and other standbys, including *involtini* (meat roulades). ✉ *Via Flaminia 57,* ☎ *06/320–0803. Reservations not accepted. No credit cards. Closed Sun.*

$ ✕ Grappolo d'Oro. This centrally located trattoria off Campo dei Fiori
★ has been a favorite for decades with locals and foreign residents, one of whom wrote it up in the *New Yorker* some years ago. This measure of notoriety has not induced the graying, courteous owners to change their two half-paneled dining rooms or menu, which features pasta all'amatriciana and scaloppine any way you want them. Inquire about the day's special. ✉ *Piazza della Cancelleria 80,* ☎ *06/686–4118. AE, MC, V. Closed Sun.*

$ ✕ Perilli. A bastion of authentic Roman cooking and trattoria atmosphere since 1913, this is the place to go to try rigatoni *con pagliata* (with baby lamb's intestines)—if you're into that sort of thing. Otherwise the all'amatriciana and carbonara sauces are classics. The house wine is a golden nectar from the Castelli Romani. ✉ *Via Marmorata 39,* ☎ *06/574–2415. No credit cards. Closed Wed.*

$ ✕ **Polese.** It's best to come here in good weather, when you can sit out-doors under trees and look out on the charming square off Corso Vit-torio Emanuele in Old Rome. Like most centrally located inexpensive eateries in Rome, it is crowded on weekends and weekday evenings in the summer. Straightforward Roman specialties include fettuccine *alla Polese* (with cream and mushrooms) and *vitello alla fornara* (roast brisket of veal with potatoes). ✉ *Piazza Sforza Cesarini 40,* ☎ *06/686–1709. AE, DC, MC, V. Closed Tues., 15 days in Aug., and 15 days in Dec.*

$ ✕ **Pollarola.** This typical Roman trattoria, near Piazza Navona and Campo dei Fiori, has artificial flowers on the tables but—as a special feature—it also has an ancient, authentic Roman column embedded in the rear wall. You can eat outdoors in fair weather. Try a pasta spe-cialty such as fettuccine with creamy gorgonzola sauce and a mixed plate from the array of fresh antipasti. The house wines, white or red, are good. ✉ *Piazza della Pollarola 24 (Campo dei Fiori),* ☎ *06/6880– 1654. AE, V. Closed Sun.*

$ **Tavernetta.** The central location—between the Trevi Fountain and the Spanish Steps—and the good-value tourist menu make this a reliable bet for a simple but filling meal. The menu features Sicilian and Abruzzese specialties; try the pasta with eggplant or the *porchetta* (roast suckling pig). Both the red and the white house wines are good. ✉ *Via del Nazareno 3,* ☎ *06/679–3124. Reservations essential. AE, DC, MC, V. Closed Mon. and Aug.*

$ **Tre Pupazzi.** The "three puppets" after which the trattoria is named are the worn stone figures on a fragment of an ancient sarcophagus that embellishes a building on this byway near the Vatican. The tav-ern, founded in 1625, wears its centuries lightly, upholding a tradition of good food, courteous service, and reasonable prices. The menu of-fers classic Roman/Abruzzese trattoria fare, including fettuccine and abbacchio, plus pizzas at lunchtime (a rarity in Rome) and well past midnight. ✉ *Via dei Tre Pupazzi at Borgo Pio,* ☎ *06/686–8371. AE, MC, V. Closed Sun.*

Along Via Appia Antica

$$ ✕ **Cecilia Metella.** From the entrance on Via Appia Antica, practically opposite the catacombs, you walk uphill to a low-lying but sprawling construction designed for wedding feasts and banquets. There's a large terrace shaded by vines for outdoor dining. Although obviously geared to larger groups, Cecilia Metella also gives couples and small groups full attention, good service, and fine Roman-style cuisine. The specialties are the searing-hot *crespelle* (crepes), served in individual casseroles, and *pollo al Nerone* (chicken à la Nero; flambéed, of course). ✉ *Via Appia Antica 125,* ☎ *06/513–6743. AE, MC, V. Closed Mon. and last 2 wks in Aug.*

$$ **L'Archeologia.** In this farmhouse just beyond the catacombs, you dine indoors beside the fireplace in cool weather or in the garden under age-old vines in the summer. The atmosphere is friendly and intimate, and specialties include homemade pastas, abbacchio scottadito, seafood and some Greek dishes. ✉ *Via Appia Antica 139,* ☎ *06/788–0494. AE, MC, V. Closed Thurs.*

LODGING

The wide range of Roman accommodations are graded according to regional standards, from five stars down to one. Palatial surroundings, luxurious comfort, and high standards of service can be taken for granted in the city's five-star ($$$$) establishments, but in other cat-egories, especially $$ and $, standards vary considerably. Fortunately for tourists, many Rome hotels have upgraded their facilities, readjusting their rates only slightly. In general, Fodor's hotel choices for Rome have been made with an eye to good value and convenient location. The old-fashioned Roman pensione no longer exists as an official category, but, although now graded as inexpensive hotels, some preserve the homey atmosphere that makes visitors prefer them, especially for longer stays.

There are distinct advantages to staying in a hotel within easy walking distance of the main sights, particularly now that so much of downtown Rome is closed to daytime traffic. You can leave your car at a garage and explore by foot. One disadvantage, however, is noise, because the Romans are a voluble people—with or without cars to add to the racket. Ask for an inside room if you are a light sleeper, but don't be disappointed if it faces a dark courtyard.

Because Rome's religious importance makes it a year-round tourist destination, there is never a period when hotels are predictably empty, so you should always try to make reservations, even if only a few days in advance, by phone or fax. Always inquire about special low rates, often available in both winter and summer if occupancy is low. If you do arrive without reservations, try one of the following: **HR,** Hotel Reservation service (☎ 06/699–1000), with desks at Leonardo da Vinci Airport (more commonly referred to as Fiumicino Airport) and Termini Station (an English-speaking operator is available daily 7 AM–10 PM); **EPT** information offices: Via Parigi 5 (☎ 06/4889–9253), Termini Station (☎ 06/487–1270), Leonardo da Vinci Airport (☎ 06/6595–6074); municipal tourist information booths at Largo Goldoni (✉ Via del Corso), Via dei Fori Imperiali, and Via Nazionale. All can help with accommodations, and there is no charge. Avoid official-looking men who approach tourists at Termini Station: They tout for the less desirable hotels around the train station. **CTS,** a student travel agency, can help find rooms; the main office is at Via Genova 16 (☎ 06/46791, 10 minutes' walk from the station).

Room rates in Rome are on a par with, or even higher than, those in most other European capitals, but a favorable exchange rate can make them more attractive. Ask whether the room rate includes breakfast. An extra charge, anything from 7,000 to 27,000 lire depending on the category of hotel, may be added for this, but remember that you're not obliged to take breakfast in the hotel. If you don't want to, make this clear when you check in. Air-conditioning in lower-priced hotels may cost extra; in more expensive hotels it will be included in the price. All hotels have rate cards on the room doors or inside the closet. These specify exactly what you have to pay and detail any extras. If business is slack, hotels in all categories may give you a discount rate. Ask for *la tariffa scontata* (the discount rate).

CATEGORY	COST*
$$$$	over 450,000 lire
$$$	300,000–450,000 lire
$$	220,000–300,000 lire
$	under 220,000 lire

*All prices are for a standard double room for two, including tax and service.

$$$$ 🏨 **Cavalieri Hilton.** Though the Cavalieri is outside the imaginary confines of the city's center, distance has its advantages, one of them being the magnificent view from the hotel's hilltop site (ask for a room facing the city). This hotel is an oasis of quiet and comfort. Good taste and a distinctive Italian flair keynoted extensive renovations and redecorating in 1994. If you can tear yourself away from your balcony, the terraces, gardens, and swimming pool, you will find a courtesy shuttle bus leaving for Piazza Barberini in the center of Rome every 30 minutes. ✉ *Via Cadlolo 101,* ☎ *06/35091,* ꜰᴀx *06/3509–2241. 376 rooms and suites with bath. 2 restaurants, bar, pool, health club. AE, DC, MC, V.*

$$$$ ⊞ **Eden.** A hotel for whispered superlatives in praise of its dashing el-
★ egance and stunning vistas of Rome, the Eden was once the preferred haunt of Hemingway, Ingrid Bergman, and Fellini, and of many celebrities before them. It was totally renovated and reopened in 1994 under the aegis of the Forte group. Precious antiques, sumptuous Italian fabrics, linen sheets, and marble baths create an atmosphere of understated elegance. The views from the rooftop bar and restaurant will take your breath away, and the cuisine merits raves, too. ✉ *Via Ludovisi 49,* ☎ *06/474–3551,* ꜰᴀx *06/482–1584. 112 rooms and suites with bath. Restaurant, bar, exercise room, parking. AE, DC, MC, V.*

$$$$ ⊞ **Excelsior.** To Romans and many others, the white Victorian cupola of the Excelsior is a symbol of Rome at its most cosmopolitan. The hotel's porte cochere has sheltered Europe's aristocrats and Hollywood's royalty as they alighted from their Rollses and Ferraris. They entered the polished doors that still open onto a world of luxury lavished with mirrors, carved moldings, Oriental rugs, crystal chandeliers, and huge, baroque floral arrangements. The theme of gracious living prevails throughout the hotel in splendidly appointed rooms and marble baths. ✉ *Via Veneto 125,* ☎ *06/4708,* ꜰᴀx *06/482–6205. 377 rooms and suites with bath. Restaurant, bar, barbershop, beauty salon, parking. AE, DC, MC, V.*

$$$$ ⊞ **Grand.** A 100-year-old establishment of class and style, this hotel caters to an elite international clientele. It's only a few minutes from Via Veneto. Off the richly decorated, split-level main salon—where afternoon tea is served every day—there are a smaller, intimate bar and a buffet restaurant. The spacious bedrooms are decorated in gracious empire style, with smooth fabrics and thick carpets in tones of blue and pale gold. Crystal chandeliers and marble baths add a luxurious note. The Grand also offers one of Italy's most beautiful dining rooms, called simply Le Restaurant. ✉ *Via Vittorio Emanuele Orlando 3,* ☎ *06/4709,* ꜰᴀx *06/474–7307. 170 rooms and suites with bath. 2 restaurants, bar, beauty salon, sauna, parking. AE, DC, MC, V.*

$$$$ ⊞ **Hassler.** Located at the top of the Spanish Steps, the Hassler boasts
★ sweeping views of Rome from its front rooms and penthouse restaurant; other rooms overlook the gardens of Villa Medici. The hotel is run by the distinguished Wirth family of hoteliers, which assures a cordial atmosphere and magnificent service from the well-trained staff. The public rooms have an extravagant 1950s elegance—especially the first-floor bar, a chic rendezvous, and the glass-roofed lounge, with gold marble walls and a hand-painted tile floor. The comfortable guest rooms are decorated in a variety of classic styles, some with frescoed walls. The penthouse suite has a mirrored ceiling in the bedroom and a huge terrace. ✉ *Piazza Trinità dei Monti 6,* ☎ *06/678–2651,* ꜰᴀx *06/678–9991. 101 rooms and suites with bath. Restaurant, bar. AE, DC, MC, V.*

$$$$ ⊞ **Majestic.** In the 19th-century tradition of grand hotels, this establishment on Via Veneto offers sumptuous furnishings and spacious rooms, with up-to-date accessories such as CNN-TV, minibars, strongboxes, and white marble bathrooms. There are authentic antiques in the public rooms, and the excellent restaurant looks like a Victorian conservatory. The Ninfa grill/café on street level is an intimate venue for light meals and drinks. ✉ *Via Veneto 50,* ☎ *06/486841,* ꜰᴀx *06/488–0984. 95 rooms and suites with bath, many with whirlpool baths. Restaurant, bar, parking. AE, DC, MC, V.*

Rome Lodging

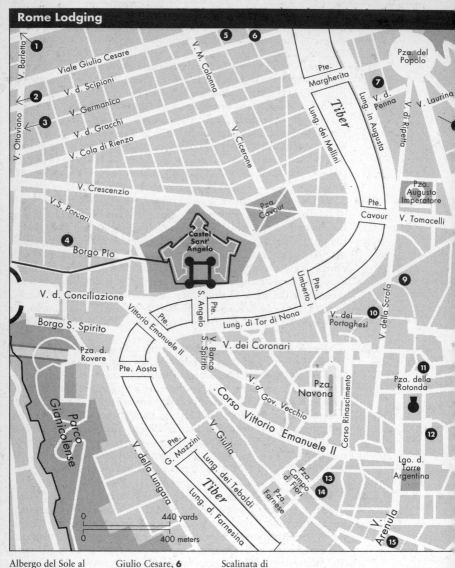

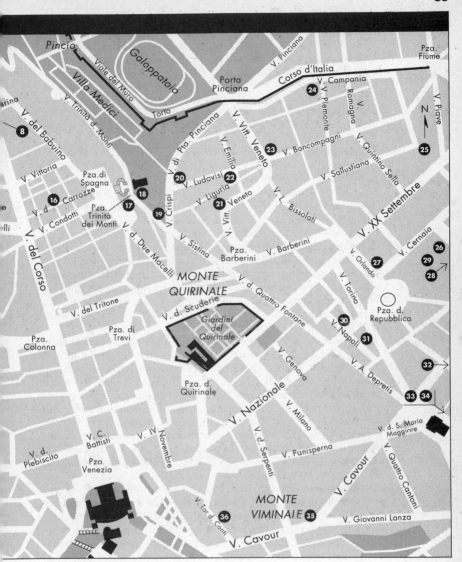

$$$$ 🖬 **Minerva.** The Holiday Inn Crowne Plaza Minerva is the very stylish reincarnation of the hostelry that occupied this 17th-century palazzo for centuries, hosting literati from Stendhal to Sartre and de Beauvoir. Entirely redone, with a stunning new stained-glass lobby ceiling designed by renowned architect Paolo Portoghesi, the Minerva has everything a guest could want in the way of comfort, all in an absolutely central location. And from the roof terrace you can almost touch the immense, flattened dome of Hadrian's Pantheon. ✉ *Piazza della Minerva 69,* ☎ *06/6994–1888,* 🖷 *06/679–4165. 134 rooms with bath. Restaurant, bar. AE, DC, MC, V.*

$$$ 🖬 **Albergo del Sole al Pantheon.** This small hotel has been in its central location opposite the Pantheon since the 15th century. It was entirely renovated in 1989 and has been tastefully decorated with a blend of modern and antique furnishings. Ceilings are high, floors are tiled in terra-cotta, and there is a charming courtyard for alfresco breakfast in good weather. ✉ *Piazza della Rotonda 63,* ☎ *06/678–0441,* 🖷 *06/684–0689. 26 rooms with bath. Bar. AE, DC, MC, V.*

$$$ 🖬 **Farnese.** A turn-of-the-century mansion, totally renovated in 1991,
★   the Farnese is near the Metro and within walking distance of St. Peter's. Furnished with great attention to detail in art deco style, it has dazzling modern baths and charming fresco decorations. Room rates are low for the category and include a banquet-size breakfast. ✉ *Via Alessandro Farnese 30,* ☎ *06/321–2553,* 🖷 *06/321–5129. 24 rooms with bath. Bar, parking, roof garden. AE, DC, MC, V.*

$$$ 🖬 **Forum.** A centuries-old palace converted into a fine hotel, the Forum
★   is on a quiet street within shouting distance of the Roman Forum and Piazza Venezia. Although it seems tucked away out of the mainstream, it's actually handy to all the main sights. The wood-paneled lobby and street-level bar are warm and welcoming. The smallish bedrooms are furnished in rich pink and beige fabrics; the bathrooms are ample, with either tub or shower. What's really special, though, is the rooftop restaurant and bar: The view toward the Colosseum is superb. Breakfast or a nightcap up here can be memorable. ✉ *Via Tor dei Conti 25,* ☎ *06/679–2446,* 🖷 *06/678–6479. 76 rooms with bath. Restaurant, bar. AE, DC, MC, V.*

$$$ 🖬 **Giulio Cesare.** An aristocratic town house in the residential, but central, Prati district, the Giulio Cesare is a 10-minute walk across the Tiber from Piazza del Popolo. It's beautifully run, with a friendly staff and a quietly luxurious air. The rooms are elegantly furnished, with chandeliers, thick rugs, floor-length drapes, and rich damasks in soft colors. Public rooms have Oriental carpets, old prints and paintings, marble fireplaces, and a grand piano. ✉ *Via degli Scipioni 287,* ☎ *06/321–0751,* 🖷 *06/321–1736. 90 rooms with bath. Bar, garden. AE, DC, MC, V.*

$$$ 🖬 **Victoria.** A 1950s luxury in the public rooms, solid comfort throughout, and impeccable management are the main features of this hotel near Via Veneto. Oriental rugs, oil paintings, welcoming armchairs, and fresh flowers add charm to the public spaces, and the rooms are well furnished with armchairs and other amenities ignored by many modern decorators. American businessmen, who prize the hotel's personalized service and restful atmosphere, are frequent guests. Some upper rooms and the roof terrace overlook the majestic pines of Villa Borghese. ✉ *Via Campania 41,* ☎ *06/473931,* 🖷 *06/487–1890. 110 rooms with bath. Restaurant, bar. AE, DC, MC, V.*

$$ ▦ **Art Deco.** This hotel's name tells all about its glamorous decor, attuned to the elegance and fancy of the 1920s, with whimsical accents in Deco paintings and antiques. Underlying the style is reassuring technology: a fail-safe electrical system, key cards, air-conditioning, and whirlpool baths. You can breakfast on the roof terrace. The hotel is in a residential neighborhood 10 minutes from Termini Station and handy to public transport. Book through Best Western for the best rates. ⊠ *Via Palestro 19,* ☎ *06/445–7588,* FAX *06/444–1483. 49 rooms with bath. Restaurant, bar. AE, DC, MC, V.*

$$ ▦ **Britannia.** This fine small hotel is a very special place, offering su-
★ perior quality at moderate rates. Its quiet but central location is one attraction; a caring management is another. Guests are coddled with English-language dailies and local weather reports delivered to their rooms each morning, and with sybaritic marble bathrooms and well-furnished rooms. Even if you don't choose one of the top-floor terrace rooms, you can still enjoy the splendid Roman panorama, actually a marvelous wraparaound painting, which lights up the breakfast room and its ample buffet. ⊠ *Via Napoli 64,* ☎ *06/488–3153,* FAX *06/488–2343. 32 rooms with bath. 2 bars. AE, DC, MC, V.*

$$ ▦ **Carriage.** The Carriage's location is what makes it special: It's just two blocks away from the Spanish Steps, in the heart of Rome. The stylish decor uses subdued Baroque accents and antique reproductions to give the hotel a touch of elegance. Though some of the rooms are pint-size, and a couple open onto an air shaft, several have little terraces, and all guests can avail of the roof garden. ⊠ *Via delle Carrozze 36,* ☎ *06/679–3312,* FAX *06/678–8279. 27 rooms and suites with bath. AE, DC, MC, V.*

$$ ▦ **D'Este.** Within hailing distance of Santa Maria Maggiore and close to Termini Station (you can arrange to be picked up there by the hotel car), this is in a solidly renovated and distinguished 19th-century building. The fresh-looking decor evokes turn-of-the-century comfort, with brass bedsteads and lamps and dark wood period furniture. Rooms are quiet, light, and spacious; many can accommodate family groups. The attentive owner-manager likes to have fresh flowers in the halls and sees that everything works. He encourages inquiries about special rates, particularly during the slack summer months. ⊠ *Via Carlo Alberto 4/b,* ☎ *06/446–5607,* FAX *06/446–5601. 37 rooms with bath. Bar. AE, DC, MC, V.*

$$ ▦ **Duca d'Alba.** In the Suburra, a neighborhood near the Colosseum and the Roman Forum and rich in genuine Roman atmosphere, this elegant hotel has made a stylish contribution to the area's ongoing gentrification. The tasteful neo-classic decor is in character with ancient Roman motifs, custom-designed furnishings and marble bathrooms. All rooms are entirely soundproofed; a few have tiny terraces. The four-bed suite with kitchenette is an excellent money-saving option for a family or a group of friends. This well-run establishment offers exceptionally good value: Rates are a the lowest rung in the category. The attentive staff is another plus. ⊠ *Via Leonina 14,* ☎ *06/484471,* FAX *06/488–4840. 24 rooms with bath or shower. AE, DC, MC, V.*

$$ ▦ **Internazionale.** It has an excellent location near the top of the Spanish Steps. In a totally renovated building on desirable Via Sistina, it has double-glazed windows to ensure peace and quiet. Rooms on the fourth floor have terraces; the fourth-floor suite has a private terrace and a frescoed ceiling. The decor throughout is in soothing pastel tones, with some antique pieces, mirrors, and chandeliers. Guests relax in small, homey lounges downstairs and begin the day in the pretty breakfast room. ⊠ *Via Sistina 79,* ☎ *06/699–41823,* FAX *06/678–4764. 40 rooms with bath. AE, MC, V.*

$$ 🏨 **La Residenza.** In a converted town house near Via Veneto, this
★ hotel offers first-class comfort and atmosphere at reasonable rates. The canopied entrance, spacious well-furnished lounges, and the bar and terrace are of the type you would expect to find in a deluxe lodging. Rooms, decorated in aquamarine and beige with bentwood furniture, have large closets, color TV, fridge-bar, and air-conditioning; bathrooms have heated towel racks. The clientele is mostly American. Rates include a generous American-style buffet breakfast. ⊠ *Via Emilia 22,* ☎ *06/488–0789,* FAX *06/485721. 27 rooms with bath or shower. Bar, parking. MC, V.*

$$ 🏨 **Locarno.** The central location off Piazza del Popolo helps keep the Locarno a favorite among the art crowd, which also goes for its intimate mood, though some of Locarno's fine fin de siècle character has been lost in renovations. An attempt has been made to retain the hotel's original charm, however, while modernizing the rooms with such additions as electronic safes and air-conditioning. The decor features coordinated prints in wallpaper and fabrics, lacquered wrought-iron beds, and some antiques. ⊠ *Via della Penna 22,* ☎ *06/361–0841,* FAX *06/321–5249. 38 rooms with bath. Bar, lobby lounge. AE, V.*

$$ 🏨 **Marcella.** Known to connoisseurs as one of Rome's best midsize ho-
★ tels, with the feel of a smaller, more intimate establishment, it is 10 minutes from Via Veneto or Termini Station. Here you can do your sightseeing from the roof terrace, taking in the view while you breakfast. Many rooms also have good views, and they are all furnished with flair, showing a tasteful use of color, floral prints, and mirrored walls, echoing the elegant winter-garden decor of the lounges and bar. The spacious and flexible suites are ideal for families. ⊠ *Via Flavia 106,* ☎ *06/474–6451,* FAX *06/481–5832. 75 rooms with bath. Bar, parking. AE, DC, MC, V.*

$$ 🏨 **Morgana.** An elegantly conceived hotel, the Morgana offers excel-
★ lent value in a convenient location near Termini Station. From a dashingly marbled lobby to the antique accents in fully carpeted halls and soundproofed rooms decorated with fine fabrics, this hotel shows the management's attention to comfort and detail. The atmosphere is cordial and the rates are low in this category. ⊠ *Via Filippo Turati 33,* ☎ *06/446–7230,* FAX *06/446–9142. 70 rooms with bath. Bar, airport shuttle. AE, DC, MC, V.*

$$ 🏨 **Portoghesi.** In the heart of Old Rome, the Portoghesi is a small hotel with considerable atmosphere. From a tiny lobby, an equally tiny elevator takes you to the quiet bedrooms, all decorated with floral prints and reproduction antique furniture. There's a breakfast room but no restaurant. ⊠ *Via dei Portoghesi 1,* ☎ *06/686–4231,* FAX *06/687–6976. 27 rooms with bath or shower. MC, V.*

$$ 🏨 **Sant'Anna.** An example of the gentrification of the picturesque old Borgo neighborhood in the shadow of St. Peter's, this fashionable small hotel has ample, air-conditioned bedrooms in deco style. The frescoes in the breakfast room and fountain in the courtyard are typically Roman touches. There is no elevator to take you up to the top floors but it's worth the climb to stay in one of the spacious attic rooms, each with a little terrace. ⊠ *Borgo Pio 134,* ☎ *06/688–01602,* FAX *06/683–08717. 20 rooms with bath. AE, DC, MC, V.*

$$ 🏨 **Scalinata di Spagna.** An old-fashioned pension loved by generations of romantics, this tiny hotel is booked solid for months—even years—ahead. The location at the top of the Spanish Steps, the inconspicuous little entrance, the quaint mixtures of styles in the old furniture, and the view from the terrace where you breakfast bring home the privilege of having gained a place in a very special and exclusive inn. And that's why rates for some rooms go over the top of this category. ✉ *Piazza Trinità dei Monti 17,* ☎ *06/679–3006,* FAX *06/684–0598. 15 rooms with bath. MC, V.*

$$ 🏨 **Siviglia.** You are transported back to a more opulent era in this freshly renovated 19th-century mansion in the quieter residential fringe of the Termini Station area. Like the several embassies in the neighborhood, it, too, has bright flags flying at the entrance. Inside, Venetian glass chandeliers and antique reproduction furniture give the lounges considerable character; rooms are simpler, with a light, airy touch. ✉ *Via Gaeta 12,* ☎ *06/444–1196,* FAX *06/444–1195. 42 rooms with bath. Bar. AE, MC, V.*

$$ 🏨 **Teatro di Pompeo.** Where else can you breakfast under the ancient stone vaults of Pompey's Theater, historic site of Julius Caesar's assassination? At this intimate and refined little hotel in the heart of Old Rome you are part of that history; at night, guests sleep under restored beamed ceilings that date from the days of Michelangelo. The tastefully furnished rooms offer comfort as well as charm. Book well in advance. ✉ *Largo del Pallaro 8,* ☎ *06/687–2812,* FAX *06/688–15531. 13 rooms with bath. AE, DC, MC, V.*

$ 🏨 **Alimandi.** On a side street only a block from the Vatican Museums, ★ this family-operated hotel offers excellent value in a neighborhood with moderately priced shops and restaurants. A spiffy lobby and ample lounges, a tavern for night owls, terraces, and roof gardens are some of the perks here. Rooms are spacious, airy, and well-furnished; many can accommodate extra beds. The few rooms without bath are real bargains. ✉ *Via Tunisi 8,* ☎ *06/397–23948,* FAX *06/397–23943. 32 rooms, 26 with bath. Parking (fee). AE, MC, V.*

$ 🏨 **Amalia.** Handy to the Vatican and the Cola di Rienzo shopping district, this small former pensione is owned and operated by the Consoli family—Amalia and her brothers. On several floors of a 19th-century building, it has large rooms with functional furnishings, TV sets, direct-dial telephones, pictures of angels on the walls, and gleaming marble bathrooms (hair dryers included). The Ottaviano stop of Metro A is a block away. ✉ *Via Germanico 66,* ☎ *06/397–23354,* FAX *06/397–23365. 25 rooms, 21 with bath or shower. Bar. AE, MC, V.*

$ 🏨 **Arenula.** In a four-story building on an age-worn byway off central Via Arenula, on the edge of the picturesque Ghetto neighborhood, this hotel is one of Rome's best values for the price. The all-white interior is luminous and cheerful. Rooms have pale wood furnishings and gleaming new bathrooms, as well as double-glazed windows and air-conditioning. Several have space for extra beds. Breakfast is optional, so the room rate is free and clear of extras. But nobody is perfect, and the catch at the Arenula is that the graceful oval staircase of white marble and wrought iron is the only way up. There is no elevator, so if you're short-winded ask for a room on the first (second by American standards) floor. ✉ *Via Santa Maria dei Calderari 47 (Via Arenula),* ☎ *06/687–9454,* FAX *06/689–6188. 50 rooms with bath. MC, V.*

$ 🏨 **Campo dei Fiori.** Frescoes, exposed brickwork, and picturesque effects throughout this little hotel in Old Rome could well be the work of a set designer. There's an aura of fantasy and romanticism in the decoration, with the layout cleverly designed to make the most of limited space (with a few rooms so compact as to be claustrophobic). Others rooms are larger, and all have an unusual decorative feature of some kind to remind you that you are in the heart of Rome. There is no elevator, but the climb to the roof terrace rewards you with a marvelous view and a place to relax in pleasant weather. Rates for the best rooms exceed the parameters this price category. ⊠ *Via del Biscione 6,* ☎ *06/688–06865,* FAX *06/68–6003. 27 rooms, 14 with bath. MC, V.*

$ ⊡ **Marcus.** The location, down the street from the Spanish Steps, is the premier feature of this small, homelike hotel occupying a large apartment on one floor of an 18th-century cardinal's palazzo. Many rooms have graceful antique fireplaces; otherwise they are furnished in a rather dowdy, old-fashioned style, as seen in the main living room, which has comfortable armchairs and a crystal chandelier. Double-glazed windows keep out most of the noise of central Rome. ⊠ *Via Clementina 94,* ☎ *06/683–00320,* FAX *06/683–00312. 15 rooms with bath. AE, MC, V.*

$ ⊡ **Margutta.** This small hotel is centrally located on a quiet side street
★ between the Spanish Steps and Piazza del Popolo. Lobby and halls are unassuming, but rooms are a pleasant surprise, with a clean and airy look, attractive wrought-iron bedsteads, and modern baths. Though it's in an old building, there is an elevator. ⊠ *Via Laurina 34,* ☎ *06/322–3674. 21 rooms with bath or shower. AE, DC, MC, V.*

$ ⊡ **Miami.** Its location in a dignified 19th-century building on Rome's important Via Nazionale puts this hotel in a strategic spot for sightseeing, shopping, and getting around in general; it is on main bus lines and near Termini Station and the Metro. The marble floors, chrome trim, and dark colors are brightened by the friendly family-style management. Rooms on the courtyard are quieter. High-season rates are slightly higher than category guidelines. ⊠ *Via Nazionale 230,* ☎ *06/481–7180,* FAX *06/484562. 22 rooms with bath. AE, DC, MC, V.*

$ ⊡ **Montreal.** This is a compact hotel on a central avenue across the square from Santa Maria Maggiore, only three blocks from Termini Station, with bus and subway lines close by. On two floors of an older building, it has been totally renovated and offers fresh-looking rooms. The owner-managers are pleasant and helpful, and the neighborhood has plenty of reasonably priced eating places, plus one of Rome's largest outdoor markets. ⊠ *Via Carlo Alberto 4,* ☎ *06/446–5522,* FAX *06/445–7797. 16 rooms with bath or shower. MC, V.*

$ ⊡ **Romae.** In the better part of the Termini Station neighborhood, the Romae has the advantages of a strategic location (within walking distance of many sights, and handy to bus and subway lines), a very friendly and helpful management, and good-size rooms that are clean and airy. The vivid pictures of Rome in the small lobby and breakfast room, the luminous white walls and light wood furniture in the bedrooms, and the bright little baths all have a fresh look. Amenities such as satellite TV and a hair dryer in every room, and breakfast included in the room rate, make this hotel a very good value. Families benefit from special rates and services. ⊠ *Via Palestro 49,* ☎ *06/446–3554,* FAX *06/446–3914. 20 rooms with bath. AE, MC, V.*

NIGHTLIFE AND THE ARTS

The Arts

Rome offers a vast selection of music, dance, opera, and film. Schedules of events are published in daily newspapers; in *Trovaroma,* the weekly entertainment guide published every Thursday as a supplement to the daily *La Repubblica;* in the *Guest in Rome* booklet distributed free at hotel desks; and in flyers available at EPT and city tourist information offices. An English-language periodical, *Wanted in Rome* (1,000 lire), is available at centrally located newsstands and has good listings of events. There are listings in English in the back of the weekly *Romac'è* booklet, with handy bus information for each listing.

Concerts

Rome has long hosted a wide variety of classical music concerts, although it is a common complaint that the city does not have adequate concert halls; a new concert hall is currently under construction. Depending on the location, concert tickets can cost from 15,000 to 50,000 lire. The principal concert series are those of the **Accademia di Santa Cecilia** (⊠ Concert hall and box office: Via della Conciliazione 4, ☎ 06/6880–1044), the **Accademia Filarmonica Romana** (⊠ Teatro Olimpico, Via Gentile da Fabriano 17, ☎ 06/320–1752), the **Istituzione Universitaria dei Concerti** (⊠ San Leone Magno auditorium, Via Bolzano 38, ☎ 06/361–0051), and the **RAI** Italian Radio-TV series at Foro Italico (☎ 06/368–65625). There is also the internationally respected **Gonfalone** series, which concentrates on Baroque music (⊠ Via del Gonfalone 32, ☎ 06/687–5952). The **Associazione Musicale Romana** (☎ 06/656–8441) and **Il Tempietto** (☎ 06/481–4800) organize music festivals and concerts throughout the year. There are also many small concert groups. Many concerts are free, including all those performed in Catholic churches, where a special ruling permits only concerts of religious music. Look for posters outside churches announcing free concerts. The Church of Sant'Ignazio often hosts concerts in its spectacular nave setting.

Rock, pop, and jazz concerts are frequent, especially in summer, although even performances by big-name stars may not be well advertised. Tickets for these performances are usually handled by **Orbis** (⊠ Piazza Esquilino 37, ☎ 06/474–4776) and the **Ricordi** music store (⊠ Via del Corso 506, ☎ 06/361–2331; ⊠ Viale Giulio Cesare 88, ☎ 06/372–0216).

Dance

The **Rome Opera Ballet** gives regular performances at the Teatro dell' Opera (☞ Opera, *below*), often with leading international guest stars. Rome is regularly visited by classical ballet companies from Russia, the United States, and Europe; performances are at the Teatro dell'Opera, Teatro Olimpico, or at one of the open-air venues in summer. Small classical and modern dance companies from Italy and abroad give performances in various places; check concert listings for information.

Film

Rome has dozens of movie houses, but the only one to show exclusively English-language films is the **Pasquino** (⊠ Vicolo del Piede off Piazza Santa Maria in Trastevere, ☎ 06/580–3622). Films here are not dubbed, but are shown in English, sometimes with Italian subtitles. Several movie theaters show films in the original language on certain days of the week; the listings in *Romac'è* are reliable. Pick up a weekly schedule at the theater or consult the daily papers.

Opera

The opera season runs from November to May, and performances are staged in the **Teatro dell'Opera** (⊠ Piazza Beniamino Gigli, ☎ 06/481–7003). Tickets go on sale two days before a performance, and the box office is open 10–5. Prices range from 26,000 to 142,000 lire for regular performances; they can go much higher for an opening night or an appearance by an internationally acclaimed guest singer. Standards may not always measure up to those set by Milan's fabled La Scala, but, despite strikes and shortages of funds, most performances are respectable.

The summer opera season has been evicted from the ruins of the ancient **Baths of Caracalla.** By 1997, however, a new open-air venue should be ready, probably in Villa Pepoli, a parklike area adjacent to the ruins of the Baths.

Nightlife

Although Rome is not one of the world's most exciting cities for nightlife (despite the popular image of the city as the birthplace of *La Dolce Vita*), discos, live-music spots, and quiet late-night bars have proliferated in recent years. This has been true in the streets of the old city and in far-flung parts of town. The "flavor of the month" factor works here, too, and many places fade into oblivion after a brief moment of popularity. The best sources for an up-to-date list of late-night spots are the "Night Scene" section of *Romac'è* and *Metropolitan,* an English-language biweekly sold at many newsstands.

Bars

Rome has a range of bars offering drinks and background music. Jacket and tie are in order in the elegant **Blue Bar** of the Hostaria dell'-Orso (✉ Via dei Soldati 25, ☎ 06/686–4250) and in **Le Bar** of the Grand hotel (✉ Via Vittorio Emanuele Orlando 3, ☎ 06/482931). **Jazz Club** (✉ Via Zanardelli 12, ☎ 06/686–1990), near Piazza Navona, is a classic watering hole with seating at the bar or in leather-upholstered booths. Light meals are available, and there's live music a few nights a week. It's open from 9:30 PM to 2:30 AM and on Sunday from noon to 4 for brunch. **Flann O'Brien** (✉ Via Napoli 29, ☎ 06/448–0418) has the look and atmosphere of an upscale Irish pub, but it is open all day, also functioning as an Italian coffee bar.

Attendance at **Antico Caffè della Pace** (✉ Via della Pace 3, ☎ 06/686–1216), near Piazza Navona, ranges from coffeehouse intellectuals to showier types. **Bar del Fico** (✉ Piazza del Fico 26, ☎ 06/686–5205), is a down-to-earth, authentically Roman alternative to the more sophisticated bars in the Piazza Navona area. **Le Cornacchie** (✉ Piazza Rondanini 53, ☎ 06/686–4485), near the Pantheon, has an oversize (for Rome) bar, serves meals and is open until 2 AM.

Beer halls and a plethora of new pubs are popular with young Italians. **Birreria Marconi** (✉ Via di Santa Prassede 9/c, ☎ 06/486636), near Santa Maria Maggiore, is also a pizzeria. It is closed Sunday. **Birreria Santi Apostoli** (✉ Piazza Santi Apostoli 52, ☎ 06/678–8285) is open every day until 2 AM. Among the pubs, **Fiddler's Elbow** (✉ Via dell'-Olmata 43, ☎ 06/487–2110) is open 5 PM–midnight and encourages singing. **Four Green Fields** (✉ Via Costantino Morin 42, off Via della Giuliana, ☎ 06/359–5091) features live music and is open daily from 8:30 PM to 2 AM. **Fonclea** (✉ Via Crescenzio 82/a, ☎ 06/689–6302), near Castel Sant'Angelo, has a pub atmosphere and live music ranging from jazz to Latin American to rhythm-and-blues, depending on who's in town. The kitchen serves Mexican and Italian food.

WINE BARS

Informal wine bars are popular with Romans who like to stay up late but don't dig disco music. Near the Pantheon is **Spiriti** (✉ Via Sant'-Eustachio 5, ☎ 06/689–2499), which also serves light lunches at midday and is open until 1:30 AM. **Enoteca Roffi** (✉ Via della Croce 76/a, ☎ 06/679–0896) is near the Spanish Steps. **Cavour 313** (✉ Via Cavour 313, ☎ 06/678–5496), near the Roman Forum, offers snacks and cheese plates to accompany the wine of your choice. **Trimani Wine Bar,** between Piazza della Repubblica and Porta Pia (✉ Via Cernaia 37/b, ☎ 06/446–9630), is the family-run annex of one of Rome's most esteemed wine shops. You can sample some great wines at the counter or with a light, fixed-price meal at an upstairs table. The bar is open Monday–Saturday noon–3:30 and 6–midnight. At **Cul de Sac** (✉ Piazza Pasquino 73, ☎ 06/688–01094), near Piazza Navona, you find good wines and snacks in cramped quarters.

Discos and Nightclubs

Most discos open about 10:30 PM and charge an entrance fee of around 30,000–35,000 lire, which may include the first drink. Subsequent drinks cost about 10,000–15,000 lire. Some discos also open on Saturday and Sunday afternoons for patrons under 16.

There's a full range of disco music at **Smile** (⊠ Via Schiaparelli 29–30, ☎ 06/322–1251) for the under-30 crowd, which sometimes includes young actors. Special events, such as beauty pageants, fashion shows, and theme parties, are featured. It is closed from Sunday to Tuesday. An annex is around the corner. **Tatum** (⊠ Via Luciani 52) has deafening disco music for the underage. The club is open Thursday–Saturday.

Jackie O' (⊠ Via Boncompagni 11, ☎ 06/488–5754) is an upscale favorite with the rich and famous for dinner and/or disco dancing. Roman yuppies mingle with a trendy and sophisticated crowd while dancing to disco music at **Spago** (⊠ Via di Monte Testaccio, ☎ 06/574–4999). The club is hard to find, so take a taxi.

Gilda (⊠ Via Mario dei Fiori 97, near Piazza di Spagna, ☎ 06/678–4838) is the place to spot famous Italian actors and politicians. This hot nightspot has a piano bar, as well as a restaurant, dance floors, and live music. Jackets are required. It's closed Monday. **Palladium** (⊠ Piazza B. Romano 8, Ostiense district, ☎ 06/511–0203) is out of the way but has the excitement of innovation in rock, rap, and funky music, whether live or recorded. Closing day varies. The **New Open Gate** (⊠ Via San Nicola da Tolentino 4, ☎ 06/482–4464) has changed mood and is now the trendiest disco in town.

One of Rome's first discos, **The Piper** (⊠ Via Tagliamento 9, ☎ 06/841–4459) keeps up with the times and is still a magnet for energetic young adults. It has disco music, live groups, and pop videos. Occasionally, there's ballroom dancing for an older crowd, and Sunday afternoons is for teenagers. It is open from 10 PM until 5 AM and is closed Monday and Tuesday. **Gossip Café** (⊠ Via Romagnosi 11, ☎ 06/361–1348) is a disco where sophisticated under-25s let loose. **Follia** (⊠ Via Ovidio 17, ☎ 06/683–08435) attracts celebrities and a sophisticated young crowd with disco music and a piano bar.

Music Clubs

Jazz, folk, pop, and Latin music clubs are flourishing in Rome, particularly in the picturesque Trastevere and Testaccio neighborhoods. Jazz clubs are especially popular, and talented local groups may be joined by visiting musicians from other countries. As admission, many clubs require that you buy a membership card for about 10,000–20,000 lire.

In the Trionfale district near the Vatican, **Alexanderplatz** (⊠ Via Ostia 9, ☎ 06/372–9398) has both a bar and a restaurant, and features nightly live programs of jazz and blues played by Italian and foreign musicians. For the best live music, including jazz, blues, rhythm and blues, African, and rock, go to **Big Mama** (⊠ Vicolo San Francesco a Ripa 18, ☎ 06/581–2551). There is also a bar and snack food. Latin rhythms are the specialty at **El Charango** (⊠ Via di Sant'Onofrio 28, ☎ 06/687–9908), near Ponte Amedeo d'Aosta, a live music club.

In the trendy Testaccio neighborhood, **Caffè Latino** (⊠ Via di Monte Testaccio 96, ☎ 06/574–4020) attracts a thirtysomething crowd with concerts (mainly jazz) in one room and a separate video room and bar for socializing. **Music Inn** (⊠ Largo dei Fiorentini 3, ☎ 06/688–02220) is Rome's top jazz club and features some of the biggest names on the international scene. It also has a restaurant, which is closed Monday.

Live performances of jazz, soul, and funk by leading musicians draw celebrities to **St. Louis Music City** (⊠ Via del Cardello 13/a, ☎ 06/474–5076). There is also a restaurant. The club is closed Sunday.

For Singles

Locals and foreigners of all nations and ages gather at Rome's cafés on **Piazza della Rotonda** in front of the Pantheon and in the vicinity of **Piazza Navona,** or in **Piazza Santa Maria in Trastevere,** as well as at the host of English, Scottish and Irish pubs that have opened throughout the city. The cafés on **Via Veneto** and the bars of the big hotels draw mainly tourists and are good places to meet other travelers in the over-30 age group. In fair weather, those under 30 will find crowds of contemporaries on the **Spanish Steps,** where it's easy to strike up a conversation.

OUTDOOR ACTIVITIES AND SPORTS

Beaches

The beaches nearest Rome are at **Ostia,** a busy urban center in its own right; **Castelfusano,** nearby; **Fregene,** a villa colony; and **Castelporziano,** a public beach area maintained by the city. At Ostia and Fregene, you pay for changing cabins, cabanas, umbrellas, and such, and for the fact that the sand is kept clean and combed. Some establishments, such as **Kursaal** (⊠ Lungomare Catullo 36, at Castelfusano, ☎ 06/562–1303) have swimming pools, strongly recommended as alternatives to the notoriously polluted waters of this part of the Mediterranean. You can reach Ostia by train from Ostiense Station, Castelfusano and Castelporziano by bus from Ostia, and Fregene by COTRAL bus from Via Lepanto stop of Metro A in Rome. All beaches are crowded during July and August.

For cleaner water and more of a resort atmosphere, you have to go farther afield. To the north of Rome, **Santa Marinella** and **Santa Severa** offer shoals, sand, and attractive surroundings. To the south, **Sabaudia** is known for miles of sandy beaches, **San Felice Circeo** is a classy resort, and **Sperlonga** is a picturesque old town flanked by beaches and pretty coves.

Participant Sports

Biking

You can rent a bike at **I Bike Rome** (⊠ Underground parking lot at Villa Borghese, ☎ 06/322–5240) and at **St. Peter Motor Rent** (⊠ Via di Porta Castello 43, ☎ 06/687–5714; ⊠ Piazza Navona 69). There are rental concessions at the Piazza di Spagna and Piazza del Popolo metro stops, at Largo San Silvestro, Largo Argentina, Viale della Pineta in Villa Borghese, and at Viale del Bambino on the Pincio.

Bowling

There's a large American-style bowling center, **Bowling Brunswick** (⊠ Lungotevere Acqua Acetosa, ☎ 06/808–6147), and a smaller one, **Bowling Roma** (⊠ Viale Regina Margherita 181, ☎ 06/855–1184).

Fitness Facilities

The **Cavalieri Hilton** (⊠ Via Cadlolo 101, ☎ 06/35091) has a jogging path on its grounds as well as an outdoor pool, two clay tennis courts, an exercise area, a sauna, and a steam room. The **Sheraton Roma** (⊠ Viale del Pattinaggio, ☎ 06/5453) has a heated outdoor pool, a tennis court, two squash courts, and a sauna, but no gym. The **Sheraton Golf** (⊠ Viale Parco de' Medici 22, ☎ 06/659788) has a fitness center and golf course. The **St. Peter's Holiday Inn** (✉ Via Aurelia Antica 415, ☎ 06/6642) has two tennis courts on the hotel grounds. It also has a 75-foot outdoor pool.

The **Roman Sport Center** (✉ Via del Galoppatoio 33, ☎ 06/320–1667) is a full-fledged sports center occupying vast premises next to the underground parking lot in Villa Borghese; it has two swimming pools, a gym, aerobic workout areas, squash courts, and saunas. It is affiliated with the **American Health Club** (✉ Largo Somalia 60, ☎ 06/862–12411).

Golf

The oldest and most prestigious golf club in Rome is the **Circolo del Golf Roma** (✉ Via Acqua Santa 3, ☎ 06/784–3079). The newest are the **Golf Club Parco de' Medici** course (✉ Viale Parco de' Medici 22, ☎ 06/655–3477) and the **Country Club Castel Gandolfo** (✉ Via Santo Spirito 13, Castel Gandolfo, ☎ 06/931–2301). The **Golf Club Fioranello** (✉ Viale della Repubblica, ☎ 06/713–8212) is at Santa Maria delle Mole, off Via Appia Antica. There is an 18-hole course at the **Olgiata Golf Club** (✉ Largo Olgiata 15, Via Cassia, ☎ 06/3088–9141). Nonmembers are welcome in these clubs but must show the membership cards of their home golf or country clubs.

Horseback Riding

There are several riding clubs in Rome. The most central is the **Associazione Sportiva Villa Borghese** (✉ Via del Galoppatoio 23, ☎ 06/360–6797). You can also ride at the **Società Ippica Romana** (✉ Via Monti della Farnesina 18, ☎ 06/324–0592) and at the **Circolo Ippico Olgiata** (✉ Largo Olgiata 15, ☎ 06/3088–8792), outside the city on Via Cassia.

Jogging

The best bet for jogging in the inner city is the **Villa Borghese,** which offers a circuit of the Pincio, among the marble statuary, running about ⅔ kilometers (½ mile). A longer run in the park itself might include a loop around **Piazza di Siena,** a grass horse track. Although most traffic is barred from Villa Borghese, government and police cars sometimes speed through. Be careful to stick to the sides of the roads. For a long run away from all traffic, try **Villa Ada** and **Villa Doria Pamphili** on the Janiculum. On the other hand, if you really love history, jog at the old **Circus Maximus,** or along Via delle Terme di Caracalla, which is flanked by a park (☞ Cavalieri Hilton *in* Fitness Facilities, *above*).

Swimming

The outdoor pools of the **Cavalieri Hilton** (✉ Via Cadlolo 101, ☎ 06/35091) and the **Hotel Aldovrandi** (✉ Via Ulisse Aldovrandi 15, ☎ 06/322–3993) are lush summer oases open to nonguests. The **Roman Sport Center** (✉ Via del Galoppatoio 33, ☎ 06/320–1667) has two swimming pools, and there's another one at the **American Health Club** (✉ Largo Somalia 60, ☎ 06/862–12411).

Tennis

Increasingly popular with Italians, tennis is played in private clubs and on many public courts that can be rented by the hour. Your hotel *portiere* (concierge) will direct you to the nearest courts and can book for you. A prestigious Roman club is the **Tennis Club Parioli** (✉ Largo de Morpurgo 2, Via Salaria, ☎ 06/862–00882).

Spectator Sports

Basketball

Basketball continues to grow in popularity in Italy, with many American pros now playing on Italian teams. In Rome, games are played at the **Palazzo dello Sport** in the EUR district (✉ Piazzale dello Sport, ☎ 06/592–5107).

Horse Racing

There's flat racing at the lovely century-old **Capannelle** track (✉ Via Appia Nuova 1255, ☎ 06/718–3143), frequented by a chic crowd on big race days. The trotters meet at the **Tor di Valle** track (✉ Via del Mare, ☎ 06/529–0269).

Horseback Riding

The **International Riding Show,** held in May, draws a stylish crowd to the amphitheater of Piazza di Siena in Villa Borghese. The competition is stiff, and the program features a cavalry charge staged by the dashing mounted corps of the carabinieri. For information, call the **Italian Federation of Equestrian Sports** (✉ Viale Tiziano 74, ☎ 06/3685–8528).

Soccer

Italy's favorite spectator sport stirs passionate enthusiasm among partisans. Games are usually held on Sunday afternoon throughout the fall–spring season. Two teams—Roma and Lazio—play their home games in the Olympic Stadium at **Foro Italico.** Tickets are on sale at the box office before the games; your hotel portiere may be able to help you get tickets in advance. The Olympic Stadium is on Viale dei Gladiatori, in the extensive Foro Italico sports complex built by Mussolini on the banks of the Tiber (☎ 06/333–6316).

Tennis

A top-level international tournament is held at the Tennis Stadium at **Foro Italico** in May. For information, call the **Italian Tennis Federation** (✉ Viale Tiziano 70, ☎ 06/368–58510).

SHOPPING

Shopping in Rome is part of the fun, no matter what your budget. You're sure to find something that suits your fancy *and* your pocketbook, but don't expect to get bargains on Italian brands, such as Benetton, that are exported to the United States; prices are about the same on both sides of the Atlantic.

Shops are open from 9 or 9:30 to 1 and from 3:30 or 4 to 7 or 7:30. There's a tendency in Rome for shops in central districts to stay open all day, and hours are generally becoming more flexible throughout the city. Department stores and centrally located UPIM and Standa stores are open all day. Remember that most stores are closed Sunday, though this is changing, too. Generally, with the exception of food and technical-supply stores, most stores also close on Monday mornings from September to June and Saturday afternoons in July and August. Most Italian sizes are not uniform, so always try on clothing before you buy, or measure gift items. Glove sizes are universal. In any case, remember that Italian stores generally will *not* refund your purchases and that they often cannot exchange goods because of limited stock. *Always* take your purchases with you; having them shipped home from the shop can cause hassles. If circumstances are such that you can't take your goods with you, and if the shop seems reliable about shipping, get a firm written statement of *when* and *how* your purchase will be sent.

Prezzi fissi means that prices are fixed, and it's a waste of time bargaining unless you're buying a sizable quantity of goods or a particularly costly object. Most stores have a fixed-price policy, and most honor a variety of credit cards. They will also accept foreign money at the current exchange rate, give or take a few lire. Ask for a receipt for your purchases; you may need it at customs on your return home. Bargaining is still an art at Porta Portese flea market and is routine when purchasing anything from a street vendor.

It's possible to obtain a refund on the VAT tax, which is included in the selling price. To be eligible, you must spend at least 300,000 lire in one store. For more information, *see* Smart Travel Tips.

Bargains

You can often find good buys in knitwear and silk scarves at stands on the fringes of outdoor food markets. These vendors move to another market each day, so finding one is question of luck. On **Via Cola di Rienzo** there is usually a stand with a range of blown-glass items. The market at **Via Sannio** (San Giovanni in Laterano) features job lots of designer shoes and ranks of stalls selling new and used clothing at bargain prices. It is open weekdays 10–1, Saturday 10–6. The morning market in the piazza at the center of the **Testaccio** neighborhood also is known for stands selling designer shoes. For boutique fashions at discount prices, bargain hunters will love **Labels-for-Less** (⊠ Via Viminale 35, in the vicinity of Termini Station), and **Vesti a Stock** (⊠ Via Germanico 170).

Department Stores

Rome has only a handful of department stores. **Rinascente,** near Piazza Colonna, sells clothing and accessories only. Another Rinascente, at Piazza Fiume, has the same stock, plus furniture and housewares. **Coin,** on Piazzale Appio, near San Giovanni in Laterano, has fashions for men and women and housewares. There is another Coin store in the U.S.-style shopping mall at CinecittàDue (☞ Shopping Malls, *below*). The **UPIM** and **Standa** chains offer low to moderately priced goods. They're the place to go for a pair of slippers, a sweater, a bathing suit, or such to see you through until you get home. In addition, they carry all kinds of toiletries and first-aid needs. Most Standa and UPIM stores have invaluable while-you-wait shoe-repair service counters.

Food and Flea Markets

Rome's biggest and most colorful outdoor food markets are at **Campo dei Fiori** (south of Piazza Navona), **Via Andrea Doria** (about a five-minute walk north of the entrance to the Vatican museums), and **Piazza Vittorio** (down Via Carlo Alberto from the church of Santa Maria Maggiore). There's a flea market on Sunday morning at **Porta Portese;** it now offers mainly new or secondhand clothing, but there are still a few dealers in old furniture and intriguing junk. Bargaining is the rule here, as are pickpockets; beware. To reach Porta Portese, take Via Ippolito Nievo, off Viale Trastevere. All outdoor markets are open from early morning to about 2, except Saturday, when they may stay open all day.

Shopping Districts

The most elegant and expensive shops are concentrated in the **Piazza di Spagna** area especially along **Via Condotti** and **Via Borgognona. Via Margutta** is known for art galleries. **Via del Babuino** is the place to go for antiques. There are several high-fashion designer establishments on **Via Gregoriana** and **Via Sistina.** Bordering this top-price shopping district is **Via del Corso,** which—along with **Via Frattina** and **Via del Gambero**—is lined with shops and boutiques of all kinds where prices and goods are competitive.

Rome Shopping

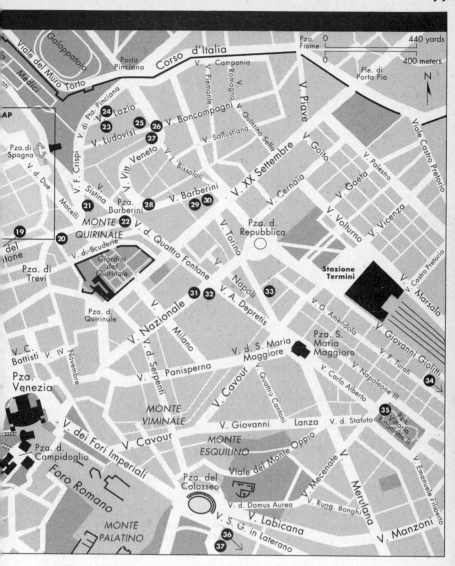

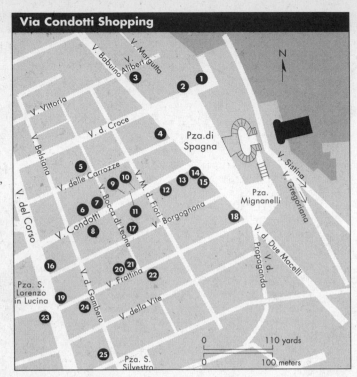

Via del Tritone, leading up from Piazza Colonna off Via del Corso, has some medium-priced, and a few expensive, shops selling everything from fashion fabrics to trendy furniture. On **Via Veneto** you'll find more high-priced boutiques and shoe stores, as well as newsstands selling English-language newspapers, magazines, and paperback books. **Via Nazionale** features shoe stores, moderately priced boutiques, and shops selling men's and women's fashions. **Via Cola di Rienzo** offers high-quality goods of all types; it's a good alternative to the Piazza di Spagna area.

In Old Rome, **Via dei Coronari** has antiques and designer home accessories. **Via Giulia** and **Via Monserrato** also feature antiques dealers galore, plus a few art galleries. In the **Pantheon** area there are many shops selling liturgical objects and vestments. But the place to go for religious souvenirs is, obviously, the area around St. Peter's, especially **Via della Conciliazione** and **Via di Porta Angelica**.

Shopping Malls
The **Cinecittà Due** mall was the first of several megamalls now catering to Roman consumers, and it is the handiest—just take Metro A to the Subaugusta stop. The mall has 100 shops, including a **Coin** department store branch, a big supermarket, snack bars, and cafés (⌧ Piazza di Cinecittà, Viale Palmiro Togliatti, ☎ 06/722–0902).

Specialty Stores
ANTIQUES AND PRINTS
For old prints and antiques, the **Tanca** shop (⌧ Salita dei Crescenzi 10, near Pantheon) is a good hunting ground. Early photographs of Rome and views of Italy from the archives of **Alinari** (⌧ Via Aliberti 16/a) make interesting souvenirs. **Nardecchia** (⌧ Piazza Navona 25) is reliable for prints. Stands in Piazza della Fontanella Borghese sell prints and old books.

CLOTHING BOUTIQUES

All the big names in Italian fashion—Versace, Ferre, Valentino, Armani, Missoni—are represented in the Piazza di Spagna area. **Sorelle Fontane** (⊠ Salita San Sebastianello 6), one of the first houses to put Italy on the fashion map, has a large boutique with an extensive line of ready-to-wear clothing and accessories. **Carlo Palazzi** (⊠ Via Borgognona 7) has elegant men's fashions and accessories. **Mariselaine** (⊠ Via Condotti 70) is a top-quality women's fashion boutique. **Le Tartarughe** (⊠ Via Piè di Marmo 17) has understated, versatile, and easy-to-wear fashions, including packable knits and jerseys. **Camomilla** (⊠ Piazza di Spagna 85) has trendy styles for women.

HANDICRAFTS

For pottery, handwoven textiles, and other handicrafts, **Myricae** (⊠ Via Frattina 36; ⊠ Piazza del Parlamento 38) has a good selection. **La Galleria** (⊠ Via della Pelliccia 29) in Trastevere is off the beaten track but well worth a visit; it has a wealth of handicrafts, beautifully displayed in a rustic setting. A bottle of liqueur, jar of marmalade, or bar of chocolate handmade by Cistercian monks in several monasteries in Italy makes an unusual gift to take home; they are all for sale at **Ai Monasteri** (⊠ Piazza Cinque Lune 2).

HOUSEHOLD LINENS AND EMBROIDERY

Frette (⊠ Piazza di Spagna 11) is a Roman institution for fabulous trousseaux. **Cesari** (⊠ Via Babuino 195) is another; it also has less-expensive gift items, such as aprons, beach towels, and place mats. **Lavori Artigianali Femminili** (⊠ Via Capo le Case 6) offers exquisitely embroidered household linens, infants' and children's clothing, and blouses. **Jesurum** (⊠ Via Barberini 23) has a good stock of embroidered linens and fine lace.

JEWELRY

Bulgari (⊠ Via Condotti 10) is to Rome what Cartier is to Paris; the shop's elegant display windows hint at what's beyond the guard at the door. **Buccellati** (⊠ Via Condotti 31) is a tradition-rich Florentine jewelry house famous for its silver work; it ranks with Bulgari for quality and reliability. **Fornari** (⊠ Via Frattina 71) and **Frugoni** (⊠ Via Arenula 83) have tempting selections of small silver objects. **Bozart** (⊠ Via Bocca di Leone 4) features dazzling costume jewelry geared to the latest fashions.

KNITWEAR

Luisa Spagnoli (⊠ Via Frattina 116; ⊠ Via Veneto 130) is always reliable for good quality at the right price and styles to suit American tastes. **Miranda** (⊠ Via Bocca di Leone 28) is a treasure trove of warm jackets, skirts, and shawls, handwoven in gorgeous colors of wool or mohair, or in lighter yarns for summer. **Albertina** (⊠ Via Lazio 20) elevates knitwear to the level of high fashion, imparting line and substance to creations that never go out of style.

LEATHER GOODS

Gucci (⊠ Via Condotti 8 and 77) is the most famous of Rome's leather shops. It has a full assortment of accessories on the first floor; a fashion boutique for men and women and a scarf department on the second floor; and many Japanese customers, who line up to get in on busy days. **Roland's** (⊠ Piazza di Spagna 74) has an extensive stock of good-quality leather fashions and accessories, as well as stylish casual wear in wool and silk. **Ceresa** (⊠ Via del Tritone 118) has more reasonably priced fine-leather goods, including many handbags and leather fashions. **Volterra** (⊠ Via Barberini 102) is well stocked and offers a wide selection of handbags at moderate prices. **Sermoneta** (⊠ Piazza di Spagna 61) shows a varied range of gloves in its windows, and there are many more inside.

Di Cori, a few steps away, also has a good selection of gloves; there's another Di Cori store at Via Nazionale 183. **Merola** (⊠ Via del Corso 143) carries a line of expensive top-quality gloves and scarves.

Nickol's (⊠ Via Barberini 21) is in the moderate price range and is one of the few stores in Rome that stocks shoes in American widths. **Ferragamo** (⊠ Via Condotti 73) is one of Rome's best stores for fine shoes and leather accessories, and its silk scarves are splendid; you pay for quality here, but you can get great buys during the periodic sales. **Mario Valentino** (⊠ Via Frattina 58) is a top name for stylish shoes and leather fashions. In the dolce vita days, Hollywood stars bought their shoes at **Albanesi** (⊠ Via Lazio 21), still a center of fashion in footwear. **Magli** (⊠ Via del Gambero 1; ⊠ Via Veneto 70) is known for well-made shoes and matching handbags at high to moderate prices. **Campanile** (⊠ Via Condotti 58) has four floors of shoes in the latest, as well as classic, styles, and other leather goods.

SILKS AND FABRICS

Galtrucco (⊠ Via del Tritone 18) and **Meconi** (⊠ Via Cola di Rienzo 305) have the best selections of world-famous Italian silks and fashion fabrics. You can find some real bargains when *scampoli* (remnants) are on sale.

SIDE TRIPS

Ostia Antica

One of the easiest excursions from the capital takes you west to the sea, where tall pines stand among the well-preserved ruins of Ostia Antica, the main port of ancient Rome. Founded around the 4th century BC, Ostia Antica conveys the same impression as Pompeii, but on a smaller scale and in a prettier, parklike setting. It makes for a fascinating visit and a welcome change from museums and churches. Fair weather and good walking shoes are requisites. On hot days, be there when the gates open, or go late in the afternoon.

Ostia Antica is about 12 kilometers (7½ miles) from Rome. If you decide to go by car, follow Via del Mare, which leads directly from Rome Ostia (a 30- to 40-minute trip). There is regular train service to the Ostia Antica station from Ostiense train station, near Porta San Paolo; the ride takes about 30 minutes. A long walkway links Ostiense station with the Piramide stop on Metro B; save steps by making connections with the train from Ostiense at the Magliana stop on Metro B. Trains from Ostiense run every half hour. A visit to the excavations takes two to three hours, including 15–20 minutes for the museum.

Numbers in the margin correspond to points of interest on the Rome Environs map.

❶ Ostia Antica was inhabited by a cosmopolitan population of rich businessmen, wily merchants, sailors and slaves. The great *horrea* (warehouses) were built in the 2nd century AD to handle huge shipments of grain from Africa; the *insulae* (forerunners of the modern apartment building) provided housing for the growing population. Under the combined assaults of the barbarians and the anopheles mosquito, and after the Tiber changed course, the port was eventually abandoned. Tidal mud and windblown sand covered the city, which lay buried until the beginning of this century. Now it has been extensively excavated and is well maintained. **Porta Romana,** one of the city's three gates, opens onto the **Decumanus Maximus,** the main thoroughfare crossing the city from end to end.

Rome Environs

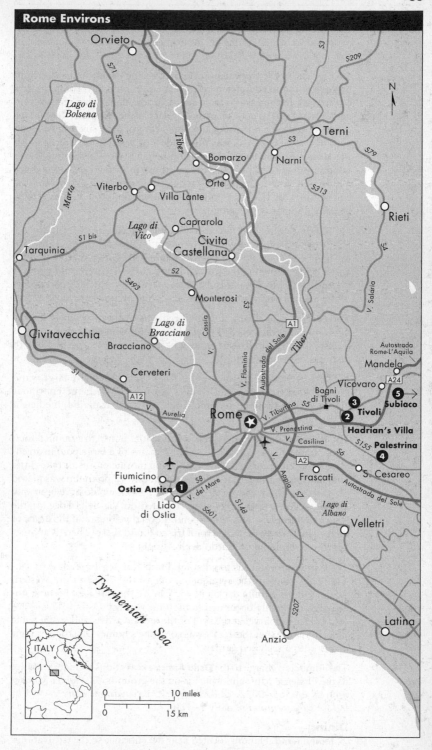

N

Orvieto

S71

Lago di
Bolsena

S2

Tiber

S3

S209

Terni

Narni

S79

Bomarzo

Orte

Viterbo

Villa Lante

Caprarola

Civita
Castellana

S313

Rieti

S4

Maria

S1 bis

Lago di
Vico

S493

S2

Monterosi

S3

A1

V. Salaria

Tarquinia

Civitavecchia

Lago di
Bracciano

Bracciano

Cassia

V.

V. Fiaminia

Autostrada del Sole

Tiber

Autostrada
Rome-L'Aquila

Mandela

S1

Cerveteri

A12

V.

Aurelia

Rome ★

V. Tiburtino

Bagni
di Tivoli

S5

Vicovaro

A24

Subiaco **5**

Tivoli **2**

3

Hadrian's Villa

✈

V. Pronestina

V. Casilina

S155

Palestrina **4**

Fiumicino

Ostia Antica **1**

A2

S8

V. del Mare

Frascati

Appia

S6

S7

Autostrada del Sole

S. Cesareo

Lido
di Ostia

S601

S148

Lago di
Albano

Velletri

Tyrrhenian
Sea

ITALY

S207

Anzio

Latina

0 ———— 10 miles

0 ———— 15 km

Black-and-white mosaic pavements representing Neptune and Amphitrite decorate the **Terme di Nettuno** (Baths of Neptune). Directly behind the baths is the barracks of the fire department, which played an important role in a town with warehouses full of valuable goods and foodstuffs.

On one side of the Decumanus Maximus is the beautiful **theater,** built by Augustus and completely restored by Septimius Severus in the 2nd century AD. In the vast Piazzale delle Corporazioni, where trade organizations similar to guilds had their offices, is the **Temple of Ceres:** This is appropriate for a town dealing in grain imports, since Ceres, who gave her name to cereal, was the goddess of agriculture. You can visit the **House of Apuleius,** built in Pompeiian style—containing fewer windows than, and built lower than those in Ostia. Next to it is the **Mithraeum,** with balconies and a hall decorated with symbols of the cult of Mithras. This men-only religion, imported from Persia, was especially popular with legionnaires.

On Via dei Molini you can see a mill, where grain for the warehouses next door was ground with the stones that are still there. Along Via di Diana you come upon a *thermopolium* (bar) with a marble counter and a fresco depicting the fruit and foodstuffs that were sold here. At the end of Via dei Dipinti is the **Museo Ostiense,** which displays some of the ancient sculptures and mosaics found among the ruins.

The **Forum** holds the monumental remains of the city's most important temple, dedicated to Jupiter, Juno, and Minerva; other ruins of baths; a basilica (in Roman times a basilica served as a secular hall of justice); and smaller temples.

Via Epagathiana leads toward the Tiber, where there are large warehouses, erected in the 2nd century AD to deal with the enormous amounts of grain imported into Rome during that period, the height of the Empire.

The **House of Cupid and Psyche,** a residential house, was named for a statue found there; you can see what remains of a large pool in an enclosed garden decorated with marble and mosaic motifs. It takes little imagination to notice that even in ancient times a premium was placed on water views: The house faces the shore, which would have been only about ⅓ kilometer (¼ mile) away. Located on Via della Foce are the **House of Serapis,** a 2nd-century multilevel dwelling, and the **Baths of the Seven Wise Men,** named for a fresco found there. There is another apartment building on Cardo degli Aurighi.

The **Porta Marina** leads to what used to be the seashore. In the vicinity are the ruins of the **synagogue,** one of the oldest in the Western world. On Via Semita dei Cippi you can see the **House of Fortuna Annonaria,** the richly decorated house of a wealthy Ostian. This is another place to marvel at the skill of the mosaic artists and, at the same time, to realize that this really was someone's home. One of the rooms opens onto a secluded garden.

The admission charge to the **Ostia Antica** excavations includes entrance to the Ostiense Museum, which is on the grounds. ⊠ *Via dei Romagnoli,* ☎ *06/565–0022.* ⊠ *8,000 lire.* ☉ *Excavations daily 9* AM*–1 hr before sunset, museum daily 9–1:30.*

Dining

$$ ✕ **Monumento.** Handily located near the entrance to the excavations, this attractive trattoria serves Roman specialties and seafood. ⊠ *Piazza Umberto I,* ☎ *06/565–0021. AE, DC, MC, V. Closed Mon. and Aug. 20–Sept. 7.*

$$ ✕ **Sbarco di Enea.** Also near the excavations, this restaurant is heavy on ancient-Roman atmosphere, with Pompeiian-style frescoes and chariots in the garden. On summer evenings you dine outdoors by torchlight, served by waiters in Roman costume. You'll probably come for lunch, when you can enjoy *farfalle con granchio* (bow-tie pasta with crab sauce) or linguine with lobster sauce and other seafood specialties, without all the hoopla. ✉ *Via dei Romagnoli 675,* ☎ *06/565–0034. AE, MC. Closed Mon. and Feb.*

Tivoli, Palestrina, and Subiaco

East of Rome lie some of the region's star attractions, which could be combined along a route that loops through the hills where ancient Romans built their summer resorts. The biggest attraction is Tivoli, which could be seen on a half-day excursion from Rome. But if you continue eastward to Palestrina, you can see a vast sanctuary famous in ancient times. And you could also fit in a visit to the site on which St. Benedict founded the hermitage that gave rise to Western monasticism. The monastery of St. Benedict is in Subiaco—not easy to get to unless you have a car, but you may want to make the effort to gain an insight into medieval mysticism.

This itinerary takes you to two of the Rome area's most attractive sights: Hadrian's Villa and the Villa d'Este in Tivoli, though the road east from Rome to Tivoli passes through some unattractive industrial areas and burgeoning suburbs. You'll know you're close when you see vast quarries of travertine marble and smell the sulphurous vapors of the little spa, Bagni di Tivoli. The was once green countryside; now it's ugly and overbuilt. The Villa d'Este is a popular destination; fewer people go to Hadrian's Villa. Both are outdoor sights, sights that entail a lot of walking, and in the case of the Villa D'Este, stair climbing. That also means that good weather is a virtual prerequisite for enjoying the itinerary.

Hadrian's Villa is about 3 kilometers (2 miles) below Tivoli. Visit Hadrian's Villa first, especially in summer, to take advantage of the cool of the morning. The visit can take from 90 minutes to three hours. The visit to Villa d'Este takes about an hour. (*See* Tivoli, Palestrina, and Subiaco A to Z, *below,* for how to get to all of the sites from Rome.)

❷ **Hadrian's Villa** was an emperor's theme park, an exclusive retreat where the marvels of the classical world were reproduced for a ruler's pleasure. Hadrian, who succeeded Trajan as emperor in AD 117, was a man of genius and intellectual curiosity. Fascinated by the accomplishments of the Hellenistic world, he decided to re-create it for his own enjoyment by building this villa over a vast tract of land below the ancient settlement of Tibur. From AD 118 to 130, architects, laborers, and artists worked on the villa, periodically spurred on by the emperor himself, as he returned from another voyage full of ideas for even more daring constructions. After his death in AD 138, the fortunes of his villa declined. It was sacked by barbarians and Romans alike; by the Renaissance, many of his statues and decorations had ended up in the Villa d'Este. Still, it is an impressive complex.

The exhibits in the visitors' center at the entrance and the scale model in the building adjacent to the bar will increase your enjoyment of the villa by helping you make sense out of what can otherwise be a maze of ruins. It's not the single elements, but the peaceful and harmonious effect of the whole, that makes Hadrian's Villa such a treat. Oleanders, pines, and cypresses growing among the ruins heighten the visual impact. ⊠ *Villa Adriana.* ▩ *8,000 lire.* ⊙ *Daily 9 AM–90 min before sunset.*

The **Adriano** restaurant, at the entrance to Hadrian's Villa, is a handy place to have lunch and to rest before heading up the hill to the Villa d'Este. The food is good, the cost moderate, and the atmosphere relaxing. It's closed Monday.

❸ **Villa d'Este** is the main attraction in the town of **Tivoli.** Ippolito d'Este was an active figure in the political intrigues of mid-16th-century Italy. He was also a cardinal, thanks to his grandfather, Alexander VI, the infamous Borgia pope. To console himself at a time when he saw his political star in decline, Ippolito tore down part of a Franciscan monastery that occupied the site he had chosen for his villa. Then the determined prelate diverted the Aniene River into a channel to run under the town and provide water for the Villa d'Este's fountains. Big, small, noisy, quiet, rushing, and running, the fountains create a late-Renaissance playground. Though time is beginning to take its toll, and the fountains and gardens aren't as well kept as in the cardinal's day, it is easy to see why many travelers of the past considered Villa d'Este one of the most beautiful spots in Italy. ⊠ *Villa d'Este, Tivoli.* ▩ *5,000 lire.* ⊙ *Daily 9 AM–90 min before sunset.*

❹ Only 27 kilometers (17 miles) south of Tivoli on S636 and 37 kilometers (23 miles) outside Rome along Via Prenestina, **Palestrina** is set on the slopes of Mt. Ginestro, from which it commands a sweeping view of the green plain and distant mountains. It is surprisingly little known outside Italy, except to students of ancient history and music lovers. Its most famous native son, Giovanni Pierluigi da Palestrina, born here in 1525, was the renowned composer of 105 masses, as well as madrigals, magnificats, and motets. But the town was celebrated long before the composer's lifetime.

Ancient Praeneste, modern Palestrina, was founded much earlier than Rome. It was the site of the Temple of Fortuna Primigenia, which dates from the beginning of the 2nd century BC. This was one of the biggest, richest, and most frequented temple complexes in all antiquity. People came from far and wide to consult its famous oracle, yet in modern times, no one had any idea of the extent of the complex until World War II bombings exposed ancient foundations that stretched way out into the plain below the town. It has since become clear that the temple area was larger than the town of Palestrina is today. Now you can make out the four superimposed terraces that formed the main part of the temple; they were built up on great arches and were linked by broad flights of stairs. The whole town sits on top of what was once the main part of the temple.

Large arches and terraces scale the hillside up to the **Palazzo Barberini,** built in the 17th century along the semicircular lines of the original temple. It's now a museum containing material found on the site, some dating back to the 4th century BC. The collection of splendid engraved bronze urns was plundered by thieves in 1991, but they couldn't carry off the chief attraction, a 1st-century-BC mosaic representing the Nile in flood. This delightful work—a large-scale composition in which form, color, and innumerable details captivate the eye—is alone worth the trip to Palestrina. But there's more: a model of the temple as it was in ancient times, which will help you appreciate the immensity of the original construction. ⊠ *Museo Nazionale Archeologico, Palazzo Barberini, Palestrina,* ☎ *06/953–8100.* ▩ *6,000 lire.*

🕐 *spring and fall, Tues.–Sun. 9–6; summer, Tues.–Sun. 9–7:30; winter, Tues.–Sun. 9–4.*

❺ If you are driving or if you don't mind setting out on a roundabout route by local bus, you could continue on to **Subiaco,** tucked away in the mountains above Tivoli and Palestrina. Take S155 east for about 40 kilometers (25 miles) before turning left onto S411 for the remaining 25 kilometers (15 miles) to Subiaco. Its inaccessibility was undoubtedly a point in its favor for St. Benedict. This excursion is best made by car because it's nearly a 3-kilometer (2-mile) walk from Subiaco to Santa Scolastica, and another half hour by footpath up to San Benedetto. If you don't have a car, inquire in Subiaco about a local bus to get you at least part of the way.

What draws travelers to Subiaco is the 6th-century **monastery of St. Benedict,** a landmark of Western monasticism. Located between the town and St. Benedict's hermitage on the mountainside is the **convent of Santa Scolastica,** the only one of the hermitages founded by St. Benedict to have survived the Lombard invasion of Italy in the 9th century. It has three cloisters; the oldest dates from the 13th century. The library, which is not open to visitors, contains some precious volumes; this was the site of the first print shop in Italy, set up in 1474. 🎟 *Free.* 🕐 *Daily 9–12:30 and 4–7.*

The monastery of St. Benedict was built over the grotto where the saint lived and meditated. Clinging to the cliff on nine great arches, it has resisted the assaults of humans for almost 800 years. Over the little wooden veranda at the entrance a Latin inscription augurs PEACE TO THOSE WHO ENTER. Every inch of the upper church is covered with frescoes by Umbrian and Sienese artists of the 14th century. In front of the main altar, a stairway leads down to the lower church, carved out of the rock, with yet another stairway down to the grotto where Benedict lived as a hermit for three years. The frescoes here are even earlier than those above; look for the portrait of St. Francis of Assisi, painted from life in 1210, in the Chapel of St. Gregory, and for the oldest fresco in the monastery, in the Shepherd's Grotto. 🎟 *Free.* 🕐 *Daily 9–12:30 and 3–6.*

In the town of Subiaco, the 14th-century **church of San Francesco** is decorated with frescoes by Il Sodoma. Ring the bell for admission.

Dining
PALESTRINA
$$ ✕ **Stella Coccia.** In this dining room of a small, centrally located hotel
★ in Palestrina's public garden, you'll find simple decor, a cordial welcome, local dishes, such as light and freshly made fettuccine served with a choice of sauces, and more unusual items, such as pasta e fagioli *con frutti di mare* (with shellfish). ✉ *Hotel Stella, Piazzale Liberazione,* ☎ *06/953–8172. AE, DC, MC, V.*
SUBIACO
$ ✕ **Belvedere.** This small hotel on the road between the town and the monasteries is equipped to serve crowds of skiers from the slopes of nearby Mt. Livata, as well as pilgrims on their way to St. Benedict's hermitage. The atmosphere is homey and cordial. Specialties include homemade fettuccine with a tasty ragù sauce and grilled meats and sausages. ✉ *Via dei Monasteri 33,* ☎ *0774/85531. Reservations not accepted. No credit cards.*
$ ✕ **Mariuccia.** This modern barnlike restaurant, close to the monasteries, caters to wedding parties and other groups but is calm enough on weekdays. There's a large garden and a good view from the picture windows. House specialties are homemade fettuccine with porcini

mushrooms and *scaloppe al* tartufo (truffled veal scallops). In the summer you dine outdoors under bright umbrellas. ⊠ *Via Sublacense,* ☎ *0774/84851. No credit cards. Closed Mon. and Nov.*

TIVOLI

\$ ✕ **Del Falcone.** A central location—on the main street leading off Largo Garibaldi—means that this restaurant is popular and often crowded. In the ample and rustic dining rooms, you can try homemade fettuccine and cannelloni. Country-style grilled meats are excellent. ⊠ *Via Trevio 34,* ☎ *0774/22358. No credit cards. Closed Mon.*

Tivoli, Palestrina, and Subiaco A to Z

GETTING AROUND

By Car: For Tivoli, take Via Tiburtina or the Rome–L'Aquila autostrada (A24). From Tivoli to Palestrina, follow signs for Via Prenestina and Palestrina. To get to Palestrina directly from Rome, take either Via Prenestina or Via Casilina or take the Autostrada del Sole (A2) to the San Cesareo exit and follow signs for Palestrina; this trip takes about one hour. To get to Subiaco from either Tivoli or Palestrina or directly from Rome, take the autostrada for L'Aquila (A24) to the Vicovaro–Mandela exit, then follow the local road to Subiaco; from Rome, the ride takes about one hour.

By Train: The FS train from Termini Station to Palestrina takes about 40 minutes; you can then board a bus from the train station to the center of town.

By Bus: COTRAL buses leave for Tivoli every 15 minutes from the terminal at the Rebibbia stop on Metro B, but not all take the route that passes near Hadrian's Villa. Inquire which bus passes closest to Villa Adriana and tell the driver to let you off there. The ride takes about 60 minutes. For Palestrina, take the COTRAL bus from the Anagnina stop on Metro A. There is local bus service between Tivoli and Palestrina, but check schedules locally. From Rome to Subiaco, take the COTRAL bus from the Rebibbia stop on Metro B; buses leave every 40 minutes and those that take the autostrada make the trip in 70 minutes, as opposed to one hour and 45 minutes by another route.

GUIDED TOURS

American Express (☎ 06/67641) and **CIT** (☎ 06/47941) have half-day excursions to Villa d'Este in Tivoli. **Appian Line** (☎ 06/488–4151) and **Carrani Tours** (☎ 06/482–4194) have morning tours that include Hadrian's Villa.

VISITOR INFORMATION

Tivoli (⊠ Largo Garibaldi, ☎ 0774/21249). **Subiaco** (⊠ Via Cadorna 59, ☎ 0774/822013).

ROME A TO Z

Arriving and Departing

By Bus

There is no central bus terminal in Rome. COTRAL (☎ 06/591–5551) is the suburban bus company that connects Rome with outlying areas and other cities in the Lazio region. Long-distance and suburban buses terminate either near Tiburtina Station or near outlying Metro stops such as Rebbibia and Anagnina. The COTRAL terminal at the Lepanto Metro station, for buses to Civitavecchia and towns along the coast northwest of Rome, will be relocated when the new leg of Metro A is completed. For COTRAL bus information call weekdays 7:45 AM–4:40 PM, Saturday 7:45 AM–2 PM.

By Car

The main access routes from the north are A1 (Autostrada del Sole) from Milan and Florence or the A12/E80 highway from Genoa. The principal route to or from points south, including Naples, is the A2. All highways connect with the GRA, which channels traffic into the center. Markings on the GRA are confusing: Take time to study the route you need.

By Plane

Most international flights and all domestic flights arrive at **Leonardo da Vinci Airport,** also known as **Fiumicino,** 30 kilometers (19 miles) outside the city. Some international and charter flights land at **Ciampino,** a civil and military airport on Via Appia Nuova, 15 kilometers (9 miles) from the center of Rome. For airport and flight information for Fiumicino (☎ 06/659–53640); for Ciampino (☎ 06/794941).

BETWEEN LEONARDO DA VINCI (FIUMICINO) AIRPORT
AND DOWNTOWN

By Car: Follow the signs for Rome on the expressway from the airport, which links with the Grande Raccordo Anulare (GRA), the beltway around Rome. The direction you take on the GRA depends on where your hotel is, so get directions from the car-rental people at the airport.

By Taxi: A taxi from the airport to the center of town costs about 65,000 lire, including supplements for airport service and luggage, and the ride takes 30–40 minutes, depending on traffic. Private limousines can be hired at booths in the arrivals hall; they charge a little more than taxis but can take more passengers. Ignore gypsy drivers; stick to yellow or white cabs. A booth inside the arrivals hall provides taxi information.

By Train: To get to downtown Rome from Fiumicino Airport you have a choice of two trains. Inquire at the airport (at EPT or train information counters) as to which takes you closest to your hotel. The nonstop Airport-Termini express (marked FS and run by the state railway) takes you directly to Track 22 at Termini station, Rome's main train station, well served by taxis and the hub of Metro and bus lines. The ride to Termini takes 30 minutes; departures are hourly, beginning at 7:50 AM from the airport, with a final departure at 10:05 PM. Tickets cost 13,000 lire. The other airport train (FM1) runs from the airport to Rome and beyond, with its terminal in Monterotondo, a suburban town to the east. The main stops in Rome are at Trastevere, Ostiense, and Tiburtina stations; at each you can find taxis and bus and/or metro connections to other parts of Rome. This train runs from Fiumicino from 6:15 AM to 12:15 AM, with departures every 20 minutes, a little less frequent in off-hours. The ride to Tiburtina takes 40 minutes. Tickets cost 7,000 lire. For either train you buy your ticket at automatic vending machines (you need Italian currency). There are ticket counters at some stations (✉ Termini Track 22, Trastevere, Tiburtina).

By Train

Termini Station is Rome's main train terminal; the Tiburtina and Ostiense stations serve some long-distance trains, many commuter trains, and the FM1 line to Fiumicino Airport. Some trains for Pisa and Genoa leave Rome from, or pass through, the Trastevere Station. For train information, call 06/4775, 7 AM–10:30 PM. You can find English-speaking staff at the information office at Termini Station, or ask for information at travel agencies. You can purchase tickets up to two months in advance either at the main stations or at travel agencies bearing the FS (Ferrovie dello Stato) emblem (☞ Rail Travel *in* Smart Travel Tips). Lines at station ticket windows may be very long, but you can save time by buying your ticket at a travel agency. However, remember that you can reserve a seat up to one day in advance at a travel agency, or up to three hours in advance at a train station. Tickets for train rides within a radius of 100 kilometers (161 miles) of Rome can be purchased at tobacco shops as well as at ticket machines on the main concourse. Like all train tickets, they must be date-stamped before you board, at the machine near the track.

Getting Around

Although most of Rome's sights are in a relatively circumscribed area, the city is too large to be seen solely on foot. Take the Metro (subway), a bus, or a taxi to the area you plan to visit, and expect to do a lot of walking once you're there. Wear a pair of comfortable, sturdy shoes, preferably with rubber or crepe soles to cushion the impact of the *sampietrini* (cobblestones). Heed our advice on security and get away from the noise and polluted air of heavily trafficked streets by taking parallel streets whenever possible. You can buy transportation-route maps at newsstands, and ATAC (Rome's public transit authority) information and ticket booths may have free maps, which can also be obtained from the municipal information booths. The free city map distributed by Rome EPT offices is good; it also shows Metro and bus routes, although bus routes are not always marked clearly.

Rome's integrated **Metrebus** transportation system includes buses and trams (ATAC), Metro and suburban trains and buses (COTRAL), and some other suburban trains (FS) run by the state railways. A ticket valid for 75 minutes on any combination of buses and trams and one entrance to the Metro costs 1,500 lire. You are supposed to date-stamp your ticket when you board the first vehicle, stamping it again when boarding for the last time within 75 minutes. Tickets are sold at tobacconists, newsstands, some coffee bars, automatic ticket machines positioned in Metro stations and some bus stops, and at ATAC and ACOTRAL ticket booths (in some Metro stations, on the lower concourse at Termini station, and at a few main bus terminals). A BIG tourist ticket, valid for one day on all public transport, costs 6,000 lire. A weekly ticket (Settimanale, also known as CIS) costs 24,000 lire and can be purchased only at ATAC booths. Try to avoid the rush hours (8–9, 1–2:30, 7–8), and beware of pickpockets, especially when boarding and getting off vehicles, particularly on the Metro and on Buses 64 (Termini–Vatican) and 218 and 660 (Catacombs). When purchasing tickets for excursions outside Rome on COTRAL buses or trains, buy a return ticket, too, to save time at the other end.

By Bicycle

Pedaling through Villa Borghese, along the Tiber, and through the center of the city when traffic is light is a pleasant way to see the sights, but remember: Rome is hilly. (For information on bicycle rentals, *see* Outdoor Activities and Sports, *above*.) **Secret Walks** (⊠ Viale Medaglie d'Oro 127, 00136 Rome, ☎ 06/397–28728) organizes all-day bike tours of Rome covering major sights and some hidden ones; summer tours include a stop for a swim. The same tours are available by moped.

By Bus

Orange ATAC city buses and tram lines run from about 6 AM to about midnight, with night buses (indicated N) on some lines. *Remember to board at the back and exit at the middle.* The compact electric buses of Line 119 take a handy route through the center of Rome that can save lots of steps. For ATAC information call 06/469–54444.

By Horse-Drawn Carriage

A ride in a horse-drawn carriage can be fun when traffic is light, especially on a Sunday or holiday or during the summer. Come to terms with the driver before starting out. City-regulated rates are about 50,000 lire for a 30-minute ride, and about 85,000 for an hour. Refuse to pay more. You can find carriages at Piazza di Spagna, Piazza Venezia and on Via del Corso near the Hotel Plaza.

By Metro

This is the easiest and fastest way to get around and there are stops near most of the main tourist attractions. The Metro opens at 5:30 AM, and the last trains leave the farthest station at 11:30 PM. There are two lines—A and B—which intersect at Termini Station.

By Scooter

You can rent a moped or scooter and mandatory helmet at **Scoot-a-Long** (✉ Via Cavour 302, ☎ 06/678–0206), **St. Peter's Moto** (✉ Via di Porta Castello 43, ☎ 06/687–5714) or **Happy Rent** (✉ Piazza Esquilino 8/h, ☎ 06/481–8185).

By Taxi

Taxis in Rome do not cruise, but if empty they will stop if you flag them down. Taxis wait at stands and can also be called by phone, in which case you're charged a small supplement. The meter starts at 6,400 lire, a fixed rate for the first 3 kilometers (2 miles); there are supplements for night service (10 PM–7 AM) and on Sundays and holidays, as well as for each piece of baggage. Avoid unmarked, unauthorized, unmetered gypsy cabs (numerous at airports and train stations), whose drivers actively solicit your trade and may demand astronomical fares. Use only licensed, metered yellow or white cabs, identified by a numbered shield on the side, an illuminated taxi sign on the roof, and a plaque next to the license plate reading SERVIZIO PUBBLICO. To call a cab, dial 3875, 3570, 4994, or 88177. **Radio Taxi** (☎ 06/3875) accepts American Express and Diners Club credit cards, but you must specify when calling that you will pay that way.

Contacts and Resources

Being Streetwise in Rome

A (repeat) word of caution: Gypsy children, present around sights popular with tourists throughout Europe, are rife in Rome and are adept pickpockets. One modus operandi is to approach a tourist and proffer a piece of cardboard with writing on it. While the unsuspecting victim attempts to read the message *on* it, the Gypsy children's hands are busy *under* it, trying to make off with purses or valuables. If you see such a group (recognizable by their unkempt appearance), do not even allow them near you—they are quick and know more tricks than you do. Also be aware of persons, usually young men, who ride by on motorbikes, grab the shoulder strap of your bag or camera, and step on the gas. Keep your bag well under your arm, especially if you're walking on the street edge of the sidewalk, or, best of all, wear a money belt. Don't carry more money than you need, and don't carry your passport unless you need it to exchange money. A useful expression to ward off panhandlers is *"Vai via!"* (Go away!).

Car Rentals

Avis (☎ 06/4282–4728), **Budget** (☎ 06/482–0966), **Eurodollar** (☎ 06/1670–18668), **Hertz** (☎ 06/167–808016), **Maggiore** (☎ 06/1678–67067).

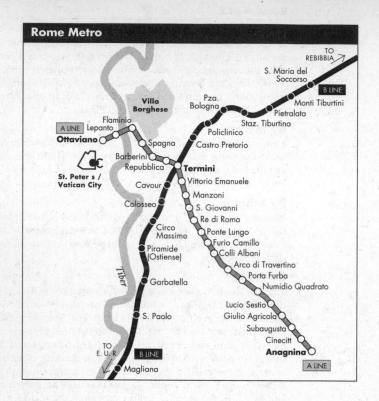

Rome Metro

Consulates

U.S. Consulate (✉ Via Veneto 121, ☎ 06/46741), **Canadian Consulate** (✉ Via Zara 30, ☎ 06/445981), **U.K. Consulate** (✉ Via Venti Settembre 80A, ☎ 06/482–5441).

Doctors and Dentists

Call your consulate or the private Salvator Mundi Hospital (☎ 06/588961) or Rome American Hospital (☎ 06/22551), which have English-speaking staff, for recommendations.

Emergencies

Police (☎ 06/4686).

Ambulance (Red Cross), (☎ 06/5510).

English-Language Bookstores

English-language paperback books and magazines are available at newsstands in the center of Rome, especially on Via Veneto. For all types of books in English, visit the **Economy Book and Video Center** (✉ Via Torino 136, ☎ 06/474–6877), the **Anglo-American Bookstore** (✉ Via della Vite 102, ☎ 06/679–5222), the **Lion Bookshop** (✉ Via del Babuino 181, ☎ 06/322–5837), or, in Trastevere, the **Open Door** (✉ Via della Lungaretta 25, ☎ 06/589–6478) and the **Corner Bookstore** (✉ Via del Moro 48, ☎ 06/583–6942).

Guided Tours

ORIENTATION

American Express (☎ 06/67641), **CIT** (☎ 06/47941), **Appian Line** (☎ 06/488–4151), and other operators offer three-hour tours in air-conditioned 60-passenger buses with English-speaking guides. There are four standard itineraries: "Ancient Rome" (including the Roman Forum and Colosseum), "Classic Rome" (including St. Peter's Basilica, Trevi Fountain, and the Janiculum Hill), "Christian Rome" (some major churches and the Catacombs), and "The Vatican Museums and Sistine Chapel." Most cost about 53,000 lire, but the Vatican Museums tour costs about 60,000 lire. American Express tours depart from Piazza di Spagna, and CIT from Piazza della Repubblica, both with some hotel pickups; Appian Line picks you up at your hotel.

American Express and other operators can provide a luxury car for up to three people, a limousine for up to seven, and a minibus for up to nine—all with English-speaking driver—but guide service is extra. Almost all operators offer "Rome by Night" tours, with or without pizza or dinner and entertainment. You can book tours through travel agents.

The **Rome Trolley Tour,** with a recorded tour broadcast, operates continuously on a circle route, making 11 stops along the way at important sights, among them Piazza del Popolo, the Vatican Museums and the catacombs on Via Appia Antica. You can get on and off at will. Tickets cost 26,000 lire and are valid 24 hours. The bus operates daily 9:30–6.

The least-expensive organized sightseeing tour of Rome is run by **ATAC,** the municipal bus company. Bus 110 tours leave from Piazza dei Cinquecento, in front of Termini Station, last about three hours, and cost about 15,000 lire. The driver provides a commentary, and you're given an illustrated guide with additional information. Buy tickets at the ATAC information booth in front of Termini Station; there is at least one tour daily, departing at 2:30 (3:30 in summer).

The least-expensive sightseeing "tours" of Rome are the routes of certain buses and trams which pass major sights. Time your ride to avoid rush hours. The small electric Bus 119 scoots through the heart of Old Rome, with stops near the Pantheon, the Spanish Steps, and Piazza del Popolo, among other sights. Several buses have long routes crossing Piazza Venezia, heart of the city. They are Bus 56 from Via Po and Via Veneto to Trastevere; Bus 62 from Porta Pia to the Vatican walls; Bus 81 from San Giovanni in Laterano to the Vatican walls; Bus 492 from Tiburtina station to the Vatican walls; Bus 90 from the Baths of Caracalla to Foro Italico. Trams 13 and 19 offer views of many neighborhoods. The fare for 75 minutes of sightseeing is a bargain 1,500 lire.

PERSONAL GUIDES

You can arrange for a personal guide through **American Express** (☎ 06/67641), **CIT** (☎ 06/47941), or the main **EPT Tourist Information Office** (☎ 06/4889–9253).

SPECIAL-INTEREST

You can make your own arrangements (at no cost) to attend a public papal audience in the Vatican or at the pope's summer residence at Castel Gandolfo. Or you can book through **CIT** (☎ 06/47941), **Appian Line** (✉ Via Barberini 109, ☎ 06/488–4151), or **Carrani Tours** (✉ Via Vittorio Emanuele Orlando 95, ☎ 06/488–0510). These agencies take you by bus to the Vatican for the audience, showing you some sights along the way and returning you to or near your hotel, for about 40,000 lire. The excursion for the pope's noon blessing on summer Sundays at Castel Gandolfo costs about 45,000 lire (☞ Walking, *below*).

WALKING

Secret Walks (✉ Viale Medaglie d'Oro 127, 00136 Rome, ☎ 06/397–28728) has a repertory of 30 theme walks for small groups conducted in English by connoisseurs of the city who give an insider's view of Rome's major sights as well as its hidden corners. They also offer full-day walks, evening strolls, full-day bike tours, a tour for the physically disabled, and a three-day comprehensive tour of the city that costs about 120,000 lire. Most walks last 2½ hours and cost about 20,000 lire.

If you have a reasonable knowledge of Italian, you can take advantage of the free guided visits and walking tours organized by Rome's cultural associations and the city council for museums and monuments. These usually take place on Sunday mornings. Programs are announced in the daily newspapers.

Late-Night Pharmacies

You will find American and British products—or their equivalents—and English-speaking staff at **Farmacia Internazionale Capranica** (✉ Piazza Capranica 96, ☎ 056/679–4680), **Farmacia Internazionale Barberini** (✉ Piazza Barberini 49, ☎ 06/482–5456), and **Farmacia Cola di Rienzo** (✉ Via Cola di Rienzo 213, ☎ 06/324–3130), among others. Most are open 8:30–1, 4–8; some are open all night. Pharmacies take turns opening on Sunday. A schedule is posted in each pharmacy.

Travel Agencies

American Express (✉ Piazza di Spagna 38, ☎ 06/67641), **CIT** (✉ Piazza della Repubblica 64, ☎ 06/482–7052). **CTS** (✉ Via Genova 16, ☎ 06/46791 or 06/467–9271) specializes in youth and budget travel and discount fares.

Visitor Information

EPT (✉ Via Parigi 5, ☎ 06/4889–9253; ☉ Mon.–Fri. 8:15–7:15 and Sat. 8:15–1:15); offices also at Termini Station (near Track 4) and Leonardo da Vinci Airport. Municipal tourist-information booths are at Largo Goldoni (✉ at the corner of Via Condotti and Via del Corso in the Spanish Steps area), Via dei Fori Imperiali (✉ at the corner of Via Cavour and across the street from the entrance to the Roman Forum), and Via Nazionale (✉ in front of the Palazzo delle Esposizioni). They are open Tuesday–Saturday 10–6, Sunday 10–1. All will help you find a hotel room (☞ Lodging, *above*).

You can find helpful information, including museum hours and listings of what's going on in Rome in the English language biweekly *Wanted in Rome,* and in the English pages of the weekly *Romac'è,* both available on newsstands. Many hotels distribute the free booklet *"Un Ospite a Roma"* ("A Guest in Rome"), with selected listings.

3 Florence

Birthplace of the Renaissance, Florence has been a mecca for travelers since the 19th century, when English ladies flocked here to stay in charming pensiones and paint romantic watercolors. They were captivated by a wistful Botticelli smile, impressed by the graceful dignity of Donatello's bronze David, *and moved by Michelangelo's provocative* Slaves *twisting restlessly in their marble prisons. Since then, millions have followed in their footsteps.*

FLORENCE IS ONE OF THE PREEMINENT TREASURES of Europe, and it is a time-honored mecca for sightseers from all over the world. But as a city, it can be surprisingly forbidding—at first glance. Its architecture is predominantly Early Renaissance and retains many of the implacable, fortresslike features of pre-Renaissance palazzi, whose facades were mostly meant to keep intruders out rather than to invite sightseers in. With the exception of a very few buildings, the classical dignity of the High Renaissance and the exuberant invention of the Baroque are not to be found here. The typical Florentine exterior gives nothing away, as if obsessively guarding secret treasures within.

The treasures, of course, are very real. And far from being a secret, they are famous the world over. The city is an artistic treasure trove of unique and incomparable proportions. A single historical fact explains the phenomenon: Florence gave birth to the Renaissance. In the early 15th century the study of antiquity—of the glory that was Greece and the grandeur that was Rome—became a Florentine passion, and with it came a new respect for learning and a new creativity in art and architecture. In Florence, that remarkable creativity is everywhere in evidence.

Though there had been a town here since Roman times, it wasn't until the 11th and 12th centuries that Florence started to make its mark. At this time Florentine cloth began to do particularly well in foreign markets, the various trades organized themselves in powerful unions (or *arti*), and the Florentines took over as the most important bankers in Europe thanks to their florin-based currency. They were perpetually at loggerheads with other Tuscan towns, such as Pisa and Siena, and this is why Florence has such a defensive air, and why its cathedral—the town's symbol—is so huge: It had to be bigger and more splendid than anyone else's. They kept expanding, despite periodic devastating plagues, and equally destructive civil strife. (One of the victims of the internal rift was the great poet Dante, author of the *Divine Comedy,* who happened to be on the losing side; he died in exile, cursing his native town.)

Meanwhile the banking families became more and more powerful, and in the early 15th century one of them, the Medici, began to outstrip all others. The most famous of them, Lorenzo de' Medici, was not only an astute politician, he was also a highly educated man and a great patron of the arts. He gathered around him, in the late 15th century, a court of poets, artists, philosophers, architects, and musicians, and organized all kinds of cultural events, festivals, and tournaments. It was Florence's golden period of creativity, when art made great leaps toward a new naturalism through the study of perspective and anatomy, when architects forged a new style based on the techniques used by the ancient Romans. The Renaissance man was born, a man who, like Leonardo da Vinci, could design a canal, paint a fresco, or solve a mathematical problem with equal ease.

Things changed with Lorenzo's death in 1492. First, his successor handed over most of Florence's key territories to the invading French king, Charles VIII, and then the city was sacked by the French army. A "republic" was set up, and one of its most vocal citizens was a charismatic, hellfire-preaching Dominican monk, Savonarola, who activated a moral cleanup operation to which the Florentines took with fanatical enthusiasm. He himself was accused of heresy and burned at the stake. After a decade or so of internal unrest, the Republic fell and the Medici were recalled to power. But even with the Medici back, Florence never regained its former prestige. By the 1530s all the major artistic talent had left the city—Michelangelo, for one, had settled in Rome. The now ineffectual Medici, calling themselves grand dukes, remained nominally in power until the line died out in 1737, and thereafter Florence passed from the Austrians to the French and back again, until the mid-19th-century unification of Italy, when for seven years it became the capital of Italy under King Vittorio Emanuele II.

Florence—Firenze in Italian—was "discovered" in the 19th century by the first art historians. It became a mecca for travelers, particularly the Romantics, including Keats and Shelley, who were inspired by the grandeur of its classicism and the elegance of its child, the Renaissance. It was also the favorite city of those English ladies of the *Room-with-a-View* type, who flocked here to stay in charming pensiones and paint romantic watercolors of the surrounding countryside. For them, the allure of Florence lay in its artistic treasures: They were captivated by a wistful Botticelli smile, impressed by the graceful dignity of Donatello's bronze *David,* and moved by Michelangelo's provocative Slaves twisting restlessly in their marble prisons. Today, millions of modern visitors follow in their footsteps. As the sun sets over the Arno and, as Mark Twain described it, "overwhelms Florence with tides of color that make all the sharp lines dim and faint and turn the solid city to a city of dreams," it's hard not to fall under the city's magic spell.

Pleasures and Pastimes

Art
No city in Italy can match Florence's astounding artistic wealth. Important paintings and sculptures are everywhere, and art scholars and connoisseurs have been investigating the subtleties and complexities of these works for hundreds of years. But what makes the art of Florence a revelation to the ordinary sightseer is a simple fact that scholarship often ignores: An astounding percentage of Florence's art is just plain beautiful. Nowhere in Italy—perhaps in all of Europe—is the act of looking at art more rewarding.

Dining
Florentines are justifiably proud of their robust food, claiming that it became the basis for French cuisine when Catherine de' Medici took a battery of Florentine chefs with her when she reluctantly relocated to become Queen of France in the 16th century. You can sample such specialties as *fagioli al fiasco* (slow-cooked beans) and *ribollita* (a thick soup of white beans, bread, cabbage, and onions) in bustling trattorias where you share long wooden tables set with paper place mats. The casual, convivial atmosphere in these places puts you in the Florentine mode. Like the Florentines, take a break at a wineshop during the day and discover some little-known but excellent types of Chianti.

Lodging
Whether you are in a five-star hotel or a more modest establishment you may have one of the greatest pleasures of all: a room with a view. Florence has so many famous landmarks that it's not hard to find lodgings with a vista to remember. And the equivalent of the genteel pensiones of yesteryear still exist, though they are now officially classified as hotels. Usually small and intimate, they often have a quaint appeal that fortunately does not preclude modern plumbing.

Shopping
Since the days of the medieval guilds, Florence has been synonymous with fine craftsmanship and good business. Such time-honored Florentine specialties as antiques (and reproductions), bookbinding, jewelry, lace,

leather goods, silk, and straw attest to that. More recently, the Pitti fashion shows and the burgeoning textile industry in nearby Prato have added fine clothing to the long list of merchandise available in the shops of Florence.

Another medieval feature is the distinct feel of the different shopping areas, a throwback to the days when each district supplied a different product. Florence's most elegant shops are concentrated in the center of town, with Via Tornabuoni and the Galleria Tornabuoni, the world's chicest shopping mall, leading the list for designer clothing. Borgo Ognissanti and Via Maggio across the river have the city's largest concentration of antiques shops, and the Ponte Vecchio houses the city's jewelers, as it has since the 16th century. Boutiques abound on Via della Vigna Nuova and in the trendy area around the church of Santa Croce, heart of the leather merchants' district. In the less-specialized, more residential area near the Duomo and in Florence's trendiest area, the Oltrarno, just about everything goes on sale.

Those with a tight budget or a sense of adventure may want to take a look at the souvenir stands under the loggia of the Mercato Nuovo, the stalls that line the streets between the church of San Lorenzo and the Mercato Centrale, the Flea Market on Piazza dei Ciompi, or the open-air market that takes place in the Cascine park every Tuesday morning. A crafts fair is held in Piazza Santo Spirito on the first Sunday of the month.

EXPLORING FLORENCE

Sightseeing in Florence is space-intensive. Everything that you probably want to see is concentrated in a relatively small district in the historic core of the city. But there is so much packed into the area that you may find yourself slogging from one mind-boggling sight to another until your perception numbs and you become oblivious to beauty. A few words of warning are in order here. For some years now, Florentine psychiatrists have recognized a peculiar local malady to which foreign tourists are particularly susceptible. It's called "Stendhal's syndrome," after the 19th-century French novelist, who was the first to describe it in print. The symptoms can be severe: confusion, dizziness, disorientation, depression, and sometimes persecution anxiety and loss of identity. Some victims immediately suspect food poisoning, but the true diagnosis is far more outlandish. They are suffering from art poisoning, brought on by overexposure to so-called Important Works of High Culture. Consciously or unconsciously, they seem to view Florentine art as an exam (Aesthetics 101, 10 hours per day, self-taught, pass/fail), and they are terrified of flunking.

Obviously, the art of Florence should not be a test. So if you are not an inveterate museumgoer or church collector with established habits and methods, take it easy. Don't try to absorb every painting or fresco that comes into view. There is second-rate art even in the Uffizi and the Pitti (*especially* the Pitti), so find some favorites and enjoy them at your leisure. Getting to know a few paintings well will be far more enjoyable than seeing a vast number on the run.

And when fatigue begins to set in, stop. Take time off, and pay some attention to the city itself. Too many first-time visitors trudge dutifully from one museum to the next without really seeing what is in between. They fail to notice that Florence is a living, breathing phenomenon: a bustling metropolis that has managed to preserve its predominantly medieval street plan and predominantly Renaissance infrastructure while successfully adapting to the insistent demands of 20th-century life. The resulting marriage between the very old and the very new is not always tranquil, but it is always fascinating. Florence the city can be chaotic, frenetic, and full of uniquely Italian noise, but it is alive in a way that Florence the museum, however beautiful, is not. Do not miss the forest for the trees. And, speaking of forests, during the Guelph–Ghibelline conflict of the 13th and 14th centuries, Florence was a forest of towers—more than 200 of them, if the smaller three- and four-story towers are included. Today only a handful survive, but if you look closely you'll find them as you explore the city's core.

Great Itineraries

You can see most of Florence's outstanding sights in three days. Plan your day around the opening hours of museums and churches; to gain a length on the tour groups in high season, go very early in the morning or toward closing time. If you can, allow a day to explore each of the neighborhoods indicated in this chapter.

IF YOU HAVE 3 DAYS
Start from the Duomo, magnificent monument to Florentine pride, and pause at the Battistero doors in which Michelangelo saw Paradise, before heading for the Museo dell'Opera del Duomo for a look at some of the art that once graced the cathedral, including one of Michelangelo's three *Pietás*. Then head for Palazzo della Signoria and Palazzo Vecchio, seat of civic power in Florence since the Middle Ages. From there it's just a few steps to the Uffizi and its world-class collections of Renaissance art. Walk across the Ponte Vecchio and back again to the Mercato Nuovo for some shopping. On the second day, get an early start, because the Medici Chapels and the Museo di San Marco close at 2. Visit San Lorenzo and see Michelangelo's sculptures in the Cappelle Medicee (Medici Chapels) before making your way through the San Lorenzo outdoor market (you can come back later; the stalls are open in the afternoon) to Palazzo Medici-Riccardi, where you can admire the small but lavishly frescoed Cappella dei Magi (Chapel of Magi). Then head for the Museo di San Marco and Fra Angelico's delightful paintings of Madonnas, saints, and angels. By that time, the tour groups should have thinned out at the Accademia, giving you an uncluttered view of Michelangelo's *David*. This leaves you much of the afternoon for another walk, perhaps to Santa Croce, or Santa Maria Novella. On the third day, cross the Arno on Ponte Vecchio and explore the Oltrarno district, starting with Pitti Palace and the Boboli Gardens and taking in the Brunelleschi-designed church of Santo Spirito and Masaccio's frescoes in the church of Santa Maria del Carmine, along with a lot of the local color of the trendy but unspoiled Oltrarno. In the afternoon visit either Santa Croce or Santa Maria Novella.

IF YOU HAVE 5 DAYS
Break down the above itineraries into shorter ones, adding a few of the optionals, such as Piazzale Michelangelo—where the picture-postcard view of the city is yours to savor—and San Miniato, or the Cenacolo di Sant'Apollonia. When visiting the Duomo, climb Giotto's Campanile, which also affords breathtaking views of the city. Take a bus to Fiesole. Spend more time in the Uffizi and Bargello or one of the smaller museums such as the Museo dell'Opificio delle Pietre Dure and the Museo di Santa Maria Novella.

IF YOU HAVE 8 DAYS
Follow the five-day itinerary, but add an all-day excursion to Siena or a couple of half-day trips to the Medici villas around Florence. Visit more of Florence's interesting smaller churches, including Santa Maria Maddalena dei Pazzi and the Cenacolo di Sant'Appollonia.

The Historic Heart of Florence: From the Duomo to the Boboli Gardens

To say that Florence's historic center, stretching from the Piazza del Duomo in the north to the Boboli Gardens across the Arno to the south, is beautiful, could be misconstrued as an understatement. Indeed, this relatively small area is home to some of the most important artistic treasures in the world. This smorgasbord of churches, medieval towers, Renaissance *palazzi* (palaces), and world-class museums and galleries is not a static testimony to the artistic and architectural genius of the past millenium, but a living, breathing shrine to some of the most outstanding aesthetic achievements of Western history, challenging both the mind and the heart to come away untouched. Believe us, it cannot be done.

A Good Walk

Numbers in the text correspond to numbers in the margin and on the Florence map.

Start at the **Duomo** ① and **Battistero** ②, climbing the **Campanile** ③ if you wish, then visit the **Museo dell'Opera del Duomo** ④, behind the Duomo. You can go directly to the Piazza della Signoria by way of Via Calzaiuoli, passing **Orsanmichele** ⑤, or make a detour along Via del Proconsolo to the **Bargello** ⑥ (opposite the ancient Badia Fiorentina, built in 1285), before discovering the architectural splendors of the **Piazza della Signoria** ⑦, including the Loggia dei Lanzi and the **Palazzo Vecchio** ⑧. The **Palazzo degli Uffizi** ⑨, Italy's most important art gallery, is just off the piazza. Leave the piazza from the southwest corner along Via Vaccereccia. At the corner with Via Por Santa Maria (which is lined with stores) is the **Mercato Nuovo** ⑩, whose stalls are packed with typical Florentine wares. Follow Via Por Santa Maria to the river and Florence's most famous bridge, the **Ponte Vecchio** ⑪.

TIMING

Before much of the historic heart of Florence was closed to traffic, you had to keep dodging passing cars and mopeds as you walked the narrow streets. Now you have to elbow your way through moving masses of fellow-tourists, especially in the neighborhood delimited by the Duomo, Piazza Signoria, Uffizi, and Ponte Vecchio. It takes about 40 minutes to walk the route, with 45 minutes to one hour each for the Museo dell'Opera del Duomo and for Palazzo della Signoria; one to 1½ hours for the Bargello and a minimum of two hours for the Uffizi. To avoid the crowds, you may want to make this walk in the afternoon, when all the sights and museums (except the Bargello) are open.

A special museum ticket valid for six months at seven city museums, including the Palazzo Vecchio, the Museum of Firenze Com'Era (Museum of Florentine History), and the Museum of Santa Maria Novella, costs 10,000 lire and is a good buy if you're planning to do some of these museums. Inquire at any city museum.

Sights to See

Badia Fiorentina. This ancient church was built in 1285; its graceful bell tower (best seen from the interior courtyard) is one of the most beautiful in Florence. The interior of the church proper was half-heartedly remodeled in the Baroque style during the 17th century; its best-known work of art is Filippino Lippi's delicate *Apparition of the Virgin to St. Bernard* (1486), on the left as you enter. The painting—one of Lippi's finest—is in superb condition and is worth exploring in detail. The Virgin's hands are perhaps the most beautiful in the city. (To illuminate, drop a coin in the box near the floor to the painting's right). ⊠ *Via del Proconsolo.*

★ ❻ **Bargello.** During the Renaissance this building was used as a prison, and the exterior served as a "most-wanted" billboard: Effigies of notorious criminals and Medici enemies were painted on its walls. Today, it houses the **Museo Nazionale,** home to what is probably the finest collection of Renaissance sculpture in Italy. Michelangelo, Donatello, and Benvenuto Cellini are the preeminent masters here, and the concentration of masterworks is remarkable, though they stand among an eclectic array of arms, ceramics, and enamels. For Renaissance art lovers, the Bargello is to sculpture what the Uffizi is to painting.

One particular display—easily overlooked—should not be missed. In 1402 Filippo Brunelleschi and Lorenzo Ghiberti competed to earn the most prestigious commission of the day: the decoration of the north doors of the baptistery in Piazza del Duomo. For the competition, each designed a bronze bas-relief panel on the theme of the Sacrifice of Isaac; both panels are on display, side by side, in the room devoted to the sculpture of Donatello on the upper floor. The judges chose Ghiberti for the commission; you can decide for yourself whether or not they were right. ✉ *Via del Proconsolo 4,* ☎ *055/238–8606.* ✇ *8,000 lire.* ⊙ *Tues.–Sun. 9–2.*

★ ❷ **Battistero.** The octagonal baptistery is one of the supreme monuments of the Italian Romanesque. The Baptistery is one of the oldest buildings in Florence, and local legend has that it was once a Roman temple of Mars; modern excavations, however, suggest its foundation was laid in the 6th or 7th century AD, well after the collapse of the Roman Empire. The round-arched Romanesque decoration on the exterior probably dates from the 11th or 12th century. The interior ceiling mosaics (finished in 1297) are justly famous, but—glitteringly beautiful as they are—they could never outshine the building's most renowned feature: its bronze Renaissance doors decorated with panels crafted by Lorenzo Ghiberti (1378–1455). The doors, on which Ghiberti spent most of his adult life (from 1403 to 1452), are on the north and east sides of the baptistery—at least copies of them are—while the south door panels, in the Gothic style, were designed by Andrea Pisano in 1330. The originals of the Ghiberti doors were removed to protect them from the effects of pollution and acid rain and have been beautifully restored; some of the panels are now on display in the Cathedral Museum (☞ Museo dell'Opera del Duomo, *below*). The copy of the east doors now installed on the Baptistery does not do Ghiberti's work justice.

Ghiberti's north doors depict scenes from the life of Christ; his later east doors, facing the Duomo facade, depict scenes from the Old Testament. They are worth a close examination, for they are very different in style and illustrate with great clarity the artistic changes that marked the beginning of the Renaissance. Look, for instance, at the far right panel of the middle row on the earlier north doors (*Jesus Calming the Waters*). Ghiberti here captured the chaos of a storm at sea with great skill and economy, but the artistic conventions he used are basically pre-Renaissance: Jesus is the most important figure, so he is the largest; the disciples are next in size, being next in importance; the ship on which they founder is a mere toy. But you can sense Ghiberti's impatience with these artificial spatial conventions. The Cathedral Works Committee made him retain the decorative quatrefoil borders of the south doors for his panels here, and in this scene Ghiberti's storm seems to want to burst the bounds of its frame.

On the east doors, the decorative borders are gone. The panels are larger, more expansive, more sweeping, and more convincing. Look, for example, at the middle panel on the left-hand door. It tells the story of Jacob and Esau, and the various episodes of the story (the selling of

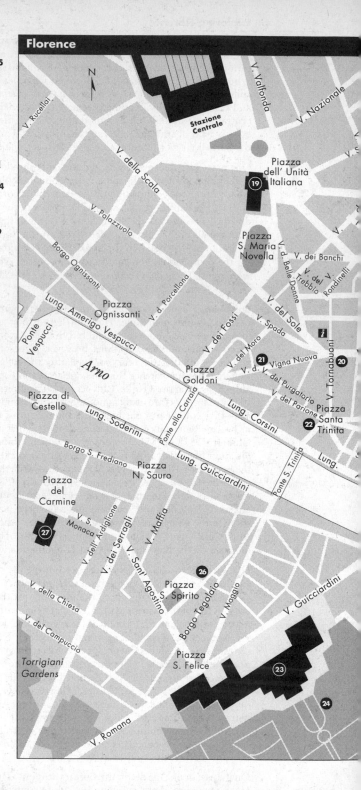

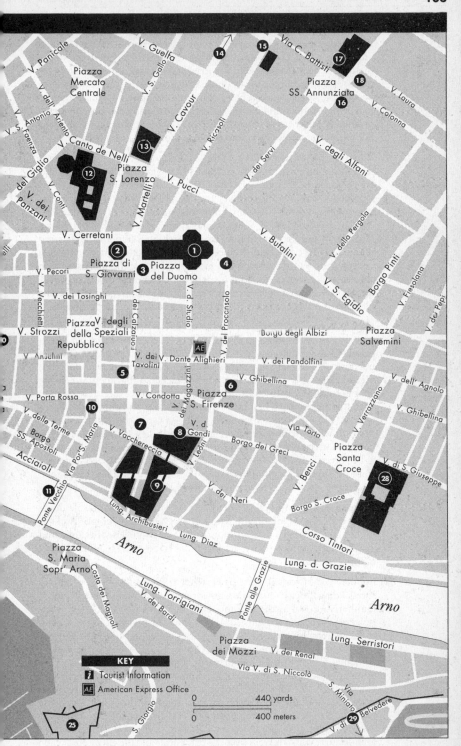

V. Panicale

Piazza
Mercato
Centrale

V. Guelfa

V. dell' Ariento

V. S. Antonio

V. Faenza

V. S. Gallo

V. Canto de Nelli

V. Cavour

V. Ricasoli

Via C. Battisti

Piazza
SS. Annunziata

V. Laura

V. Colonna

V. degli Alfani

V. dei Servi

V. della Pergola

del Giglio

V. Conti

V. dei
Panzani

12

13

Piazza
S. Lorenzo

V. Pucci

V. Martelli

V. Bufalini

Borgo Pinti

V. Fiesolana

V. Cerretani

2

1

3

4

Piazza di
S. Giovanni

Piazza
del Duomo

V. S. Egidio

V. dei Pepi

V. Pecori

V. dei Tosinghi

Piazza
Salvemini

V. Vecchietti

Piazza
della Speziali
Repubblica

V. degli
Speziali

V. d. Studio

V. del Proconsolo

Borgo degli Albizi

V. Strozzi

V. Anselmi

AE

V. dei
Tavolini

V. Dante Alighieri

V. dei Pandolfini

V. Ghibellina

V. dell' Agnolo

V. Calzaiuoli

5

V. dei Magazzini

6

V. Condotta

Piazza
S. Firenze

V. dell'Agnolo

V. Ghibellina

V. Porta Rossa

10

V. delle Terme

V. Vacchereccia

V. Leoni

7

8

V. d.
Gondi

Via Torta

V. Verrazzano

Borgo
SS. Apostoli

Via Por S. Maria

Borgo dei Greci

Piazza
Santa
Croce

V. di S. Giuseppe

Acciaioli

9

V. dei Neri

V. Benci

28

11

Ponte Vecchio

Lung. Archibusieri

Lung. Diaz

Borgo S. Croce

Corso Tintori

Piazza
S. Maria
Sopr' Arno

Arno

Costa dei Magnoli

Lung. Torrigiani

V. dei Bardi

Ponte alle Grazie

Lung. d. Grazie

Arno

Piazza
dei Mozzi

V. dei Renai

Lung. Serristori

Via V. di S. Niccolò

Via S. Miniato

S. Giorgio

KEY

i Tourist Information

AE American Express Office

0 ———— 440 yards

0 ———— 400 meters

25

Belvedere

V. di

29

the birthright, Isaac ordering Esau to go hunting, the blessing of Jacob, and so forth) have been merged into a single beautifully realized street scene. A perspective grid is employed to suggest depth, the background architecture looks far more convincing than on the north door panels, the figures in the foreground are grouped realistically, and the naturalism and grace of the poses (look at Esau's left leg) have nothing to do with the sacred message being conveyed. Although the religious content remains, man and his place in the natural world are given new prominence and are portrayed with a realism not seen in art since the fall of the Roman Empire, more than a thousand years before.

When Ghiberti was working on these panels, three of his artist friends were bringing the same new humanistic focus to their own very different work. In sculpture, Donato di Niccolò Betto Bardi, known as Donatello, was creating statuary for churches all over town; in painting, Tommaso di Ser Giovanni, known as Masaccio, was executing frescoes at the churches of Santa Maria del Carmine and Santa Maria Novella; in architecture, Filippo Brunelleschi was building the Duomo dome, the Ospedale degli Innocenti, and the church interiors of San Lorenzo and Santo Spirito. They are the fathers of the Renaissance in art and architecture—the four great geniuses who created a new artistic vision—and among them they began a revolution that was to make Florence the artistic capital of Italy for more than a hundred years.

As a footnote to Ghiberti's panels, one small detail of the east doors is worth a special look. Just to the lower left of the Jacob and Esau panel, Ghiberti placed a tiny self-portrait bust. From either side, the portrait is extremely appealing—Ghiberti looks like everyone's favorite uncle—but the bust is carefully placed so that there is a single spot in front of the doors from which you can make direct eye contact with the tiny head. When that contact is made, the impression of intelligent life—of *modern* intelligent life—is astonishing. It is no wonder that when these doors were completed, they received one of the most famous compliments in the history of art, from a competitor known to be notoriously stingy with praise: Michelangelo himself declared them so beautiful that they could serve as the Gates to Paradise. ⌧ *Free to Baptistery interior.* ☾ *Mon.–Sat. 1:30–6, Sun. 9–1:30.*

❸ **Campanile.** Giotto's bell tower is a shaft of multicolor marble decorated with reliefs now in the Museo dell'Opera del Duomo. A climb of 414 steps rewards you with a close-up of Brunelleschi's dome and a sweeping view of the city. ⌧ *8,000 lire* ☾ *Apr.–Oct., Mon–Sat. 9–6:30; Nov.–Mar. 9–4:20.*

★ ❶ **Duomo.** The historical heart of Florence is Piazza Duomo, the square surrounding the city's majestic Cathedral of Santa Maria del Fiore, more familiarly known as the Duomo. Don't be surprised if you feel overpowered on seeing the cathedral: it's the fourth largest in the world. In 1296 Arnolfo di Cambio was commissioned to build "the loftiest, most sumptuous edifice human invention could devise" in the newest Romanesque style on the site of the old church of Santa Reparata. The immense Duomo was not completed until 1436, the year when it was consecrated. The imposing facade dates only from the 19th century; it was added in the neo-Gothic style to complement Giotto's genuine Gothic (14th-century) campanile. The real glory of the Duomo, however, is Filippo Brunelleschi's dome, herald of the new Renaissance in architecture, which hovers over the cathedral (and the entire city, when seen from afar) with a dignity and grace that few domes, even to this day, can match. It was the first of its kind in the world, and for many people it is still the best.

Brunelleschi's **dome** was epoch-making as an engineering feat, as well. The space to be enclosed by the dome was so large and so high above the ground that traditional methods of dome construction—wooden centering and scaffolding—were of no use whatever. So Brunelleschi developed entirely new building methods, which he implemented with equipment of his own devising (including the modern crane). Beginning work in 1420, he built not one dome but two, one inside the other, and connected them with common ribbing that stretched across the intervening empty space, thereby considerably lessening the crushing weight of the structure. He also employed a new method of bricklaying, based on an ancient Roman herringbone pattern, interlocking each new course of bricks with the course below in a way that made the growing structure self-supporting. The result was one of the great engineering breakthroughs of all time: Most of Europe's great domes, including St. Peter's in Rome, were built employing Brunelleschi's methods, and today the Duomo has come to symbolize Florence in the same way that the Eiffel Tower symbolizes Paris. The Florentines are justly proud, and to this day the Florentine phrase for "homesick" is *nostalgia del cupolone* (homesick for the dome).

The interior is a fine example of Italian Gothic, although anyone who has seen the Gothic cathedrals of France will be disappointed by its lack of dramatic verticality. Italian architecture, even at the height of the Gothic era, never broke entirely free of the influence of Classical Rome, and its architects never learned (perhaps never wanted to learn) how to make their interiors soar like the cathedrals in the cities around Paris.

Much of the cathedral's best-known art has been moved to the nearby **Cathedral Museum** (☞ *below*). Notable among the works that remain, however, are two equestrian frescoes honoring famous soldiers: Andrea del Castagno's *Niccolò da Tolentino,* painted in 1456, and Paolo Uccello's *Sir John Hawkwood,* painted 20 years earlier; both are on the left-hand wall of the nave. *Niccolò da Tolentino* is particularly impressive: He rides his fine horse with military pride and wears his even finer hat—surely the best in town—with panache. It took restorers more than a decade from 1983 to 1995 to restore the structure of Brunelleschi's dome and clean the vast and crowded fresco of the *Last Judgment*—painted by Vasari and Zuccaro—on its interior. Originally, Brunelleschi wanted mosaics to cover the interior of the great ribbed cupola, but by the time the Florentines got around to commissioning the decoration, 150 years later, tastes had changed.

If time permits, you may want to explore the upper and lower reaches of the cathedral, as well. Ancient remains have been excavated beneath the nave; the stairway down is near the first pier on the right. The climb to the top of the dome (463 steps) is not for the fainthearted, but once there the view is superb; the entrance is on the left wall just before the crossing. ✉ *Piazza del Duomo,* ☎ *055/230–2885. Duomo* ⊙ *Weekdays 9–6, Sat. 8:30–5 (first Sat. of month 8:30–3:20).* 🎟 *Excavation: 3,000 lire.* ⊙ *Mon.–Sat. 10–5.* 🎟 *Ascent to dome: 8,000 lire.* ⊙ *Weekdays 9:30–5:30, Sat. 9:30–5 (first Sat. of month 9:30–3:20).*

⑩ **Mercato Nuovo (New Market).** This open-air loggia was new in 1551. Today it harbors mostly souvenir stands; its main attraction is Pietro Tacca's bronze *Porcellino* (Piglet) fountain on the south side, dating from around 1612 and copied from an earlier Roman work now in the Uffizi. Rubbing its drooling snout is a Florentine tradition—it is said to bring good luck. ✉ *Corner of Via Por San Maria and Via Porta Rossa.*

★ ④ **Museo dell'Opera del Duomo (Cathedral Museum).** The major attractions here—other than the originals of the Ghiberti door panels mentioned earlier and the *cantorie* (choir loft) reliefs by Donatello and Luca della Robbia—are two: Donatello's *Mary Magdalen* and Michelangelo's *Pietà* (not to be confused with his more famous *Pietà* in St. Peter's, in Rome). The High Renaissance in sculpture is in part defined by its revolutionary realism, but Donatello's *Magdalen* goes beyond realism: It is suffering incarnate. Michelangelo's heart-wrenching *Pietà* was unfinished at his death; the female figure supporting the body of Christ on the left was added by one Tiberio Calcagni, and never has the difference between competence and genius been manifested so clearly. ⊠ *Piazza del Duomo 9,* ☎ *055/230–2885.* ⊞ *8,000 lire.* ⊙ *Mar.–Oct., Mon.–Sat. 9–6:50; Nov.–Feb., Mon.–Sat. 9–5:20.*

❺ Orsanmichele. This church, containing a beautifully detailed 14th-century Gothic tabernacle by Andrea Orcagna, was originally a granary. The building was transformed in 1336 into a church with 14 exterior niches. Each of the major Florentine trade guilds was assigned its own niche and paid for the sculpture the niche was to contain. The niches soon held works by Florence's most talented sculptors. Unfortunately, the best have been removed and replaced with copies. The originals will eventually be placed in a museum, perhaps even in Orsanmichele. Even so, all the statues are worth examining. One of those removed—Andrea del Verrocchio's *Doubting Thomas* (circa 1470)—was particularly deserving of scrutiny. Were the niche not empty, you would see Christ, like the building's other figures, entirely framed within the niche, and St. Thomas standing on its bottom ledge, with his right foot outside the niche frame. This one detail, the positioning of a single foot, brought the whole composition to life. It is particularly appropriate that this is the only niche to be topped with a Renaissance pediment, for it is the revolutionary vitality of sculpture like this that gave the Renaissance its name. ⊞ *Free.* ⊙ *Daily, 9–12, 4–6.*

★ ❾ Palazzo degli Uffizi. The Galleria degli Uffizi occupies the top floor of this U-shape building fronting on the Arno, designed by Vasari in 1559 to hold the administrative offices of Medici duke Cosimo I—*"uffizi"* means "offices" in Italian. And here later Medicis installed their art collections, creating what was Europe's first modern museum, open to the public (at first only by request, of course) since 1591. Today the palazzo houses the finest collection of paintings in Italy. Hard-core museumgoers will want to pick up a complete guide to the collections, sold in bookshops and on newsstands, before they go.

The collection's highlights include Paolo Uccello's *Battle of San Romano* (its brutal chaos of lances is one of the finest visual metaphors for warfare ever committed to paint); Fra Filippino Lippi's *Madonna and Child with Two Angels* (the foreground angel's bold, impudent eye contact would have been unthinkable prior to the Renaissance); Sandro Botticelli's *Primavera* (its nonrealistic fairy-tale charm exhibits the painter's idiosyncratic genius at its zenith); Leonardo da Vinci's *Adoration of the Magi* (unfinished and perhaps the best opportunity in Europe to investigate the methods of a great artist at work); Raphael's *Madonna of the Goldfinch* (darkened by time, but the tenderness with which the figures in the painting touch each other is undimmed); Michelangelo's *Holy Family* (one of the very few easel works in oil he ever painted, clearly reflecting his stated belief that draftsmanship is a necessary ingredient of great painting); Rembrandt's *Self-Portrait as an Old Man* (which proves that even Michelangelo could, on occasion, be wrong); Titian's *Venus of Urbino* and Caravaggio's *Bacchus* (two very great paintings whose attitudes toward myth and sexuality are—to put it mildly—diametrically opposed); and many, many more. If panic sets in at the prospect of absorbing all this art at one go, bear in mind that the Uffizi is, except on Sunday, open late and isn't usually crowded in the late afternoon. The coffee bar inside the Uffizi has a terrace with a fine close-up view of Palazzo Vecchio. ⊠ *Piazzale degli Uffizi 6,* ☎ *055/23885.* 🖭 *12,000 lire.* ⊘ *Tues.–Sat. 9–7, Sun. 9–2.*

⑧ Palazzo Vecchio. Looming over Piazza della Signoria is Florence's forbidding, fortresslike city hall. The palazzo was begun in 1299 and designed (probably) by Arnolfo di Cambio, and its massive bulk and towering campanile dominate the piazza. It was built as a meeting place for the heads of the seven major guilds that governed the city at the time; over the centuries it has served lesser purposes, but today it is once again the City Hall of Florence. The interior courtyard is a good deal less severe, having been remodeled by Michelozzo in 1453; the copy of Verrocchio's bronze *puttino,* topping the central fountain, softens the effect considerably.

Although most of the interior public rooms are well worth exploring, the main attraction is on the second floor: two adjoining rooms that supply one of the most startling contrasts in Florence. The first is the vast **Sala dei Cinquecento** (Room of the Five Hundred), named for the 500-member Great Council, the people's assembly established by Savonarola, which met here. The Sala was decorated by Giorgio Vasari, around 1570, with huge frescoes celebrating Florentine history; depictions of battles with neighboring cities predominate. Continuing the martial theme, the Sala also contains Michelangelo's *Victory* group, intended for the never-completed tomb of Pope Julius II, plus others' miscellaneous sculptures of decidedly lesser quality.

The second room is the little **Studiolo,** entered to the right of the Sala's entrance. The study of Cosimo de' Medici's son, the melancholy Francesco I, it was designed by Vasari and decorated by Vasari and Agnolo Bronzino. It is intimate, civilized, and filled with complex, questioning, allegorical art. It makes the vainglorious proclamations next door ring more than a little hollow. ⊠ *Piazza della Signoria,* ☎ *055/276–8465.* 🖭 *10,000 lire.* ⊘ *Mon.–Wed., Fri.–Sat. 9–7, Sun. 8–1.*

Piazza della Repubblica. This square marks the site of the ancient forum that was the core of the original Roman settlement The street plan in the area around the piazza still reflects the carefully plotted orthogonal grid of the Roman military encampment. The Mercato Vecchio (Old Market), located here since the Middle Ages, was demolished at the end of the last century, and the current piazza was constructed between 1890 and 1917 as a neoclassical showpiece. Nominally the center of town, it has yet to earn the love of most Florentines.

★ ⑦ Piazza della Signoria. This is by far the most striking square in Florence. It was here, in 1497, that the famous "bonfire of the vanities" took place, when the fanatical monk Savonarola induced his followers to hurl their worldly goods into the flames; it was also here, a year later, that he was hanged as a heretic and, ironically, burned. A bronze plaque in the piazza pavement marks the exact spot of his execution.

The statues in the square and in the 14th-century **Loggia dei Lanzi** on the south side vary in quality. Cellini's famous bronze *Perseus Holding the Head of Medusa* is his masterpiece; even the pedestal is superbly executed. Other works in the loggia include *The Rape of the Sabine Women* and *Hercules and the Centaur,* both late–16th-century works by Giambologna, and, in the back, a row of sober matrons that date from Roman times. When the loggia underwent a lengthy structural restoration a few years ago, many of the statues were replaced by copies.

In the square, Bartolomeo Ammannati's Neptune Fountain, dating from 1565, takes something of a booby prize. Even Ammannati himself considered it a failure, and the Florentines call it *Il Biancone,* which may be translated as "the big white man" or "the big white lump," depending on your point of view. Giambologna's equestrian statue, to the left of the fountain, pays tribute to the Medici Grand Duke Cosimo I. Occupying the steps of the Palazzo Vecchio are a copy of Donatello's proud heraldic lion of Florence, known as the *Marzocco* (the original is now in the Bargello); a copy of Donatello's *Judith and Holofernes* (the original is inside the Palazzo Vecchio); a copy of Michelangelo's *David* (the original is now in the Accademia); and Baccio Bandinelli's *Hercules* (1534).

NEED A   At the west end of Piazza della Signoria, facing the statuary on the
BREAK?   steps of the Palazzo Vecchio, is **Rivoire,** a café famous for its chocolate
             (both packaged and hot). Its outdoor tables and somewhat less expen-
             sive indoor counter are stylish, if pricey, places from which to observe
             the busy piazza.

★ ⑪ **Ponte Vecchio (Old Bridge).** This elegant bridge is to Florence what Tower Bridge is to London. It was built in 1345 to replace an earlier bridge that was swept away by flood, and its shops housed first butchers, then grocers, blacksmiths, and other merchants. But in 1593 the Medici Grand Duke Ferdinando I, whose private corridor linking the Medici palace (the Palazzo Pitti) with the Medici offices (the Uffizi) crossed the bridge atop the shops, decided that all this plebeian commerce under his feet was unseemly. So he threw out all the butchers and blacksmiths and installed 41 goldsmiths and eight jewelers. The bridge has been devoted solely to these two trades ever since.

In the middle of the bridge, take a moment to study the **Ponte Santa Trinitá,** the next bridge downriver. It was designed by Bartolomeo Ammannati in 1567 (possibly from sketches by Michelangelo), blown up by the retreating Germans during World War II, and painstakingly reconstructed after the war ended. Florentines like to claim it is the most beautiful bridge in the world. Given its simplicity, this may sound like idle Tuscan boasting. But if you commit its graceful arc and delicate curves to memory and then begin to compare these characteristics with those of other bridges encountered in your travels, you may well conclude that the boast is justified. The Ponte Santa Trinita is a beautiful piece of architecture.

Michelangelo Country: From San Lorenzo to the Accademia

Poet, painter, sculptor, and architect, Michelangelo was a consummate genius. His prodigious energy and virtuoso technique overcame the political and artistic vicissitudes of almost a century to produce some of the greatest sculpture of his—or any—age. This itinerary takes us to some of his most important creations, from the Biblioteca Laurenziana, perhaps his most intuitive work of architecture; to the Cappelle Medicee, whose magnificent sculptures are a key to understanding Michelangelo's genius; and to the Galleria dell'Accademia, home to his most recognized work (including even the Sistine Chapel), the towering and beautiful *David.*

A Good Walk

Start at the church of **San Lorenzo** ⑫, visiting the **Biblioteca Laurenziana** and its famous anteroom, before circling the church and making your way through the San Lorenzo outdoor market on Via del Canto de' Nelli to the entrance of the **Cappelle Medicee** to see the tombs Michelangelo sculpted for his Medici patrons. Retrace your steps through the market and take Via dei Gori to Via Cavour and the **Palazzo Medici-Riccardi** ⑬, home to Florence's most important family throughout the Renaissance. Follow Via Cavour two blocks north to Piazza San Marco and the church of the same name, attached to which is the **Museo San Marco** ⑭, a memorial to the pious and exceptionally talented painter-monk, Fra Angelico. From Piazza San Marco, take a short detour a half-block down Via Ricasoli (which runs back toward the Duomo) to the **Galleria dell'Accademia** ⑮, where Michelangelo's most recognizable masterpiece, *David,* looks down on the admiring crowds. If you have time to make a detour, return to Piazza San Marco and take Via Cesare Battisti into Piazza della Santissima Annunziata, one of Florence's prettiest squares, site of the **Ospedale degli Innocenti** ⑯ and, at the north end of the square, the church of **Santissima Annunziata** ⑰. One block southeast of the entrance to Santissima Annunziata, through the arch and on the left side of Via della Colonna, is the **Museo Archeologico** ⑱.

TIMING

The walk alone takes about one hour, plus 45 minutes for the Cappelle Medicee, 20 minutes for the Palazzo Medici-Riccardi, 40 minutes for the Museo di San Marco, 30 minutes for the Accademia (*David*), and 40 minutes for the Museo Archeologico. After visiting San Lorenzo, resist the temptation to explore the clothes' market that surrounds the church before going to the Palazzo Medici-Riccardi; you can always come back later, when the churches and museums have closed; the market is open until 7 PM.

Sights to See

Biblioteca Laurenziana. The Laurentian Library and its famous anteroom, adjacent to the church of San Lorenzo, were designed by Michelangelo. The entrance to the library is to the left of the church facade. Michelangelo the architect was every bit as original as Michelangelo the sculptor. Unlike Brunelleschi (the architect of San Lorenzo), however, he was not interested in expressing the ordered harmony of the spheres in his architecture. He was interested in experimentation and invention and in expressing a personal vision that was at times highly idiosyncratic.

It was never more idiosyncratic than here. This strangely shaped anteroom has had scholars scratching their heads for centuries. In a space more than two stories high, why did Michelangelo limit his use of columns and pilasters to the upper two-thirds of the wall? Why didn't he rest them on strong pedestals instead of on huge, decorative curlicue scrolls, which rob them of all visual support? Why did he recess them into the wall, which makes them look weaker still? The architectural elements here do not stand firm and strong and tall, as inside the church next door; instead, they seem to be pressed into the wall as if into putty, giving the room a soft, rubbery look that is one of the strangest effects ever achieved by Classical architecture. It is almost as if Michelangelo purposely set out to defy his predecessors—intentionally to flout the conventions of the High Renaissance in order to see what kind of bizarre, mannered effect might result. His innovations were tremendously influential and produced a period of architectural experimentation—the Mannerist era in architecture—that eventually evolved into the Baroque. As his contemporary Giorgio Vasari (the first art historian) put it, "Artisans have been infinitely and perpetually indebted to him because he broke the bonds and chains of a way of working that had become habitual by common usage."

Many critics have thought the anteroom a failure and have complained that Michelangelo's experiment here was willful and perverse. But nobody has ever complained about the room's staircase (best viewed head-on), which emerges from the library with the visual force of an unstoppable flow of lava. In its highly sculptural conception and execution, it is quite simply one of the most original and beautiful staircases in the world. ▨ *Free.* ⊘ *Mon.–Sat. 9–1.*

★ **Cappelle Medicee.** This magnificent complex includes the **Cappella dei Principi,** the Medici chapel and mausoleum that was begun in 1605 and kept marble workers busy for several hundred years, and the **New Sacristy,** designed by Michelangelo, so called to distinguish it from Brunelleschi's Old Sacristy. Both are part of the San Lorenzo complex.

Michelangelo received the commission for the New Sacristy in 1520 from Cardinal Giulio de' Medici, who later became Pope Clement VII and who wanted a new burial chapel for his father, Giuliano, his uncle Lorenzo the Magnificent, and two recently deceased cousins. The result was a tour de force of architecture and sculpture. Architecturally, Michelangelo was as original and inventive here as ever, but it is—quite properly—the powerful sculptural compositions of the side wall tombs that dominate the room. The scheme is allegorical: On the wall tomb to the right are figures representing day and night, and on the wall tomb to the left are figures representing dawn and dusk; above them are idealized portraits of the two cousins, usually interpreted to represent the active life and the contemplative life. But the allegorical meanings are secondary; what is most important is the intense presence of the sculptural figures, the force with which they hit the viewer. Michelangelo's contemporaries were so awed by the impact of this force (in his sculpture here and elsewhere) that they invented an entirely new word to describe the phenomenon: *terribilità* (dreadfulness). To this day it is used only when describing his work, and it is in evidence here at the peak of its power. ⊠ *Piazza di Madonna degli Aldobrandini,* ☏ *055/213206.* ▨ *10,000 lire.* ⊘ *Tues.–Sun. 9–2.*

★ ⑮ **Galleria dell'Accademia.** This is the home of the statue that everyone comes to Florence to see. The museum contains a notable collection of Florentine paintings dating from the 13th to the 18th centuries, but it is most famous for its collection of statues by Michelangelo, including the unfinished *Slaves*—which were meant for the tomb of Michelangelo's patron and nemesis Pope Julius II (and which seem to be fighting their way out of the marble)—and the original *David,* which was moved here from Piazza della Signoria in 1873. The *David* was commissioned in 1501 by the Opera del Duomo (Cathedral Works Committee), which gave the 26-year-old sculptor a leftover block of marble that had been ruined by another artist. Michelangelo's success with the defective block was so dramatic that the city showered him with honors, and the Opera del Duomo voted to build him a house and a studio in which to live and work.

Today the *David* is beset not by Goliath but by tourists, and seeing the statue at all—much less really studying it—can be a trial. After a 1991 attack upon it by a hammer-wielding frustrated artist who, luckily, inflicted only a few minor nicks on the toes, the sculpture is surrounded by a plexiglass barrier. But a close look is worth the effort it takes to combat the crowd. The statue is not quite what it seems. It is so poised and graceful and alert—so miraculously *alive*—that it is often considered the definitive embodiment of the ideals of the High Renaissance in sculpture. But its true place in the history of art is a bit more complicated.

As Michelangelo well knew, the Renaissance painting and sculpture that preceded his work were deeply concerned with ideal form. Perfection of proportion was the ever-sought Holy Grail; during the Renaissance, ideal proportion was equated with ideal beauty, and ideal beauty was equated with spiritual perfection. In painting, Raphael's tender Madonnas are perhaps the preeminent expression of this philosophy: They are meant to embody a perfect beauty that is at once physical and spiritual.

But Michelangelo's *David,* despite its supremely calm and dignified pose, departs from these ideals. As a moment's study will show, Michelangelo did not give the statue ideal proportions. The head is slightly too large for the body, the arms are slightly too large for the torso, and the hands are dramatically too large for the arms. By High Renaissance standards these are defects, but the impact and beauty of the *David* are such that it is the *standards* that must be called into question, not the statue. Michelangelo was a revolutionary artist (and the first Mannerist) because he brought a new expressiveness to art: He created the "defects" of the *David* intentionally. He knew exactly what he was doing, calculating that the perspective of the viewer would be such that, in order for the statue to appear proportioned, the upper body, head, and arms would have to be bigger as they are further away from the viewer's line of vision. But he also did it in order to express and embody, as powerfully as possible in a single figure, an entire biblical story. David's hands *are* too big, but so was Goliath, and these are the hands that slew him. ⊠ *Via Ricasoli 60,* ☎ *055/214375.* ✎ *12,000 lire.* ☉ *Tues.–Sat. 9–7, Sun. 9–2.*

OFF THE
BEATEN PATH

MUSEO DELL'OPIFICIO DELLE PIETRE DURE – This is one of Florence's many fascinating small museums. It is attached to an Opificio, or workshop, which was established in 1588 by Ferdinando I de' Medici to train craftsmen in the art of working with precious and semiprecious stones and marble, with an eye to the future decoration of the Cappella dei Principi. The institute is now known internationally, especially as a center for the restoration of mosaics and inlays in semiprecious stones. The informative exhibits include some magnificent antique examples of this highly specialized craft. ⊠ *Via degli Alfani 78.* ✎ *4,000 lire.* ☉ *Tues.–Sat. 9–7, Sun. 9–2.*

⑱ Museo Archeologico This interesting museum contains Etruscan, Egyptian, and Greco-Roman antiquities; guidebooks in English are available. The Etruscan collection is particularly notable—the largest in northern Italy—and includes the famous bronze *Chimera,* which was discovered (without the tail, which is a reconstruction) in the 16th century. ⊠ *Via della Colonna 36,* ☎ *055/247–8641.* ✎ *8,000 lire.* ☉ *Tues.–Sat. 9–2, Sun. 9–1.*

OFF THE
BEATEN PATH

SANTA MARIA MADDALENA DEI PAZZI – One of Florence's hidden treasures, Perugino's cool and composed *Crucifixion,* is in the chapter hall of the monastery adjacent to this church. ⊠ *Borgo Pinti 58.* ✎ *Donation requested.* ☉ *Daily 9–12, 5–7.*

TORRE DEI CORBIZI – The tower at the south end of the small Piazza San Pier Maggiore (from the Museo Archeologico, follow Via della Colonna east to Borgo Pinti and turn right, following Borgo Pinti through the arch of San Piero into the piazza) dates from the Middle Ages, when, during the Guelph–Ghibelline conflict of the 13th and 14th centuries, Florence was awash with such towers—more than 200 of them. Today only a handful survive. ⊠ *Piazza San Pier Maggiore.*

⑭ Museo San Marco. A former Dominican monastery adjacent to the church of San Marco now houses this museum, which—in fact, the entire monastery—is a memorial to Fra Angelico, the Dominican monk who, when he was alive, was as famous for his piety as for his painting. When the monastery was built in 1437, he decorated it with his frescoes, which were meant to spur religious contemplation; when the building was turned into a museum, other works of his from all over the city were brought here for display. His paintings are simple and direct and furnish a compelling contrast to the Palazzo Medici-Riccardi chapel (☞ *below*. Fra Angelico probably would have considered the glitter of Gozzoli's work there worldly and blasphemous). The entire monastery is worth exploring, for Fra Angelico's paintings are everywhere, including the Chapter House, at the top of the stairs leading to the upper floor (the famous *Annunciation*), in the upper-floor monks' cells (each monk was given a different religious subject for contemplation), and in the gallery just off the cloister as you enter. The latter room contains, among many other works, his beautiful *Last Judgment;* as usual with Last Judgments, the tortures of the damned are far more inventive than the pleasures of the redeemed. ⊠ *Piazza San Marco 1,* ☎ *055/238–8608.* 🎫 *8,000 lire.* ⊘ *Tues.–Sun. 9–2.*

OFF THE
BEATEN PATH   **CENACOLO DI SANT'APOLLONIA** – This refectory of a former Benedictine monastery is worth a visit for the frescoes painted in sinewy style on its wall by Andrea del Castagno, a follower of Masaccio. The *Last Supper* is a powerful version of this typical refectory theme. From the Cenacolo entrance, walk around the corner to Via San Gallo 25 and take a peek at the lovely 15th-century cloister which belonged to the same monastery but is now part of the University of Florence. ⊠ *Via XXVII Aprile 1,* 🎫 *Free.* ⊘ *Tues.–Sun. 9–2.*

---

⑯ Ospedale degli Innocenti. Built by Brunelleschi in 1419 to serve as a foundling hospital, it takes the historical prize as the very first Renaissance building. Brunelleschi designed the building's portico with his usual rigor, building it out of the two shapes he considered mathematically (and therefore philosophically and aesthetically) perfect: the square and the circle. Below the level of the arches, the portico encloses a row of perfect cubes; above the level of the arches, the portico encloses a row of intersecting hemispheres. The whole geometric scheme is articulated with Corinthian columns, capitals, and arches borrowed directly from antiquity. At the time he designed the portico, Brunelleschi was also designing the interior of San Lorenzo, using the same basic ideas. But since the portico was finished before San Lorenzo, the Ospedale degli Innocenti can claim the honor of ushering in Renaissance architecture. The 10 ceramic medallions depicting swaddled infants that decorate the portico are by Andrea della Robbia, done approximately in 1487.

★ ⑬ Palazzo Medici-Riccardi. The main attraction of this palace, begun in 1444 by Michelozzo for Cosimo de' Medici, is the interior chapel, the so-called **Capella dei Magi** on the upper floor. Painted on its walls is Benozzo Gozzoli's famous Procession of the Magi, finished in 1460 and celebrating both the birth of Christ and the greatness of the Medici family, whose portraits it contains. Like his contemporary Ghirlandaio, Gozzoli was not a revolutionary painter and is today considered less than first rate because of his technique, old-fashioned even for his day. Gozzoli's gift, however, was for entrancing the eye, not challenging the mind, and on those terms his success here is beyond question. The paintings are full of activity yet somehow frozen in time in a way that fails utterly as realism, but succeeds triumphantly as soon as the demand for realism is set aside. Entering the chapel is like walking into the middle of a magnificently illustrated child's storybook, and the beauty of the illustrations makes this one of the most unpretentiously enjoyable rooms in the entire city. ⊠ *Via Cavour 1,* ☎ *055/276–0340.* ⊠ *6,000 lire.* ☉ *Mon., Tues., Thurs.–Sat. 9–1 and 3–6; Sun. 9–1.*

⑫ San Lorenzo. The facade of this church was never finished. Like Santo Spirito on the other side of the Arno, the interior of San Lorenzo was designed by Filippo Brunelleschi in the early 15th century. The two church interiors are similar in design and effect and proclaim with ringing clarity the beginning of the Renaissance in architecture. You may want to read the entry on Santo Spirito now; it describes the nature of Brunelleschi's architectural breakthrough, and its main points apply equally well here (☞ The Pitti Palace, Boboli, and Oltrarno, *below*). San Lorenzo possesses one feature that Santo Spirito lacks, however, which considerably heightens the dramatic effect of the interior: the grid of dark, inlaid marble lines on the floor. The grid makes the rigorous regularity with which the interior was designed immediately visible and offers an illuminating lesson on the laws of perspective. If you stand in the middle of the nave at the church entrance, on the line that stretches to the high altar, every element in the church—the grid, the nave columns, the side aisles, the coffered nave ceiling—seems to march inexorably toward a hypothetical vanishing point beyond the high altar, exactly as in a single-point-perspective painting. Brunelleschi's **Old Sacristy** has stucco decorations by Donatello; the entrance is at the end of the left transept.

OFF THE
BEATEN PATH

MERCATO CENTRALE – Florence's busy main food market is a reminder that Florence is more than just a museum. In this huge, two-story market hall, food is everywhere, some of it remarkably exotic, and many of the displays verge on the magnificent. At the Mercato Nuovo, near the Ponte Vecchio, you will see tourists petting the snout of the bronze piglet for good luck; here you will see Florentines petting the snout of a real one, very recently deceased and available for tonight's dinner. The Mercato Centrale has a number of small coffee bars scattered about; there is even one upstairs among the mountains of vegetables. The square, too, has a full complement of cafés and down-to-earth trattorias. Have a coffee, watch the activity, and enjoy the fact that for once there is not a painting in sight.

⑰ Santissima Annunziata. This church was designed in 1447 by Michelozzo, who gave it an uncommon (and lovely) entrance cloister. The interior is an extreme rarity for Florence: a sumptuous example of the Baroque. But it is not really a fair example, since it is merely 17th-century Baroque decoration applied willy-nilly to an earlier structure— exactly the sort of violent remodeling exercise that has given the Baroque a bad name ever since. The **Tabernacle of the Annunziata,** immediately inside the entrance to the left, illustrates the point. The lower half, with its stately Corinthian columns and carved frieze bearing the Medici arms, was built at the same time as the church; the upper half, with its erupting curves and impish sculpted cherubs, was added 200 years later. Each is effective in its own way, but together they serve only to prove that dignity is rarely comfortable wearing a party hat.

Around Santa Maria Novella

Piazza Santa Maria Novella is near the train station, and like the train stations of most other European cities, it is an area pervaded by a certain squalor, especially at night. Nevertheless, the streets in and around the piazza are an architectural treaure-trove, lined with some of Florence's most elegant palazzi. This walk ends at Santa Trinità, home of Ghirlandaio's fresco cycle.

A Good Walk

Start in the Piazza Santa Maria Novella, dominated by the church of **Santa Maria Novella** ⑲ on the north side, then take Via delle Belle Donne, which leads to a minuscule square, at the center of which a curious shrine, known as the Croce al Trebbio, stands. Take Via del Trebbio and turn right onto **Via Tornabuoni**, Florence's finest shopping street. At the intersection of Via Tornabuoni and Via Strozzi is the classical **Palazzo Strozzi** ⑳. One block west, down Via della Vigna Nuova, is Alberti's High Renaissance-style **Palazzo Rucellai** ㉑. Follow the narrow street opposite the palazzo (Via del Purgatorio) almost to its end, then zigzag right and left to reach Piazza di Santa Trinita, where, in the middle, stands the **Colonna della Giustizia**, erected by Cosimo de' Medici in 1537. Halfway down the block to the right (toward the Arno) is the church of **Santa Trinita** ㉒, home to Ghirlandaio's glowing frescoes. Then follow Borgo Santi Apostoli, a typical medieval street flanked by tower-houses, to Via Por Santa Maria. Alternatively, from Piazza Santa Trinita you can cross Ponte Santa Trinita and head into the Oltrarno neighborhood.

TIMING

The walk takes about 30 minutes, plus 30 minutes for Santa Maria Novella and 15 minutes for Santa Trinita. A visit to the Santa Maria Novella museum and cloister takes about 30 minutes. Allow 30 minutes for the museum.

Sights to See

Croce al Trebbio. This roofed crucifix was erected in 1308 by the Dominican friars (nearby Santa Maria Novella is a Dominican church) to commemorate a victory famous locally: It was here that they defeated their avowed enemies, the Patarene heretics, in a bloody street brawl. ⊠ *Via del Trebbio.*

㉑ **Palazzo Rucellai.** Architect Leon Battista Alberti designed perhaps the very first private residence done in High Renaissance style—which goes a step further than the Palazzo Strozzi. A comparison between the two is illuminating. Evident on the facade of the Palazzo Rucellai is the ordered arrangement of windows and rusticated stonework seen on the Palazzo Strozzi, but Alberti's facade is far less forbidding. Alberti devoted a far larger proportion of his wall space to windows, which soften the facade's appearance, and filled in the remainder with rigorously ordered classical elements borrowed from antiquity. The end result, though still severe, is less fortresslike, and Alberti strove for this effect purposely (he is on record as stating that only tyrants need fortresses). Ironically, the Palazzo Rucellai was built some 30 years *before* the Palazzo Strozzi. Alberti's civilizing ideas here, it turned out, had little influence on the Florentine palazzi that followed. To the Renaissance Florentines, power—in architecture, as in life—was just as impressive as beauty. ⊠ *Via della Vigna Nuova.* ☉ *Mon., Tues., Thurs., and Sun. 10–7:30, Fri.–Sat. 10–11:30 PM.*

⑳ **Palazzo Strozzi.** This is the most imposing palazzo on Via Tornabuoni. Designed (probably) by Giuliano da Sangallo around 1489 and modeled after Michelozzo's earlier Palazzo Medici-Riccardi (☞ Michelangelo Country, *above*), the exterior of the palazzo is simple and severe; it is not the use of classical detail but the regularity of its features, the stately march of its windows, that marks it as a product of the early Renaissance. The interior courtyard (entered from the rear of the palazzo) is another matter altogether. It is here that the classical vocabulary—columns, capitals, pilasters, arches, and cornices—is given uninhibited and powerful expression. Unfortunately, the courtyard's effectiveness is all but destroyed by the addition of a brutal metal fire escape. Its introduction here is one of the most disgraceful acts of 20th-century vandalism in the entire city. ⊠ *Via Tornabuoni.*

⑲ Santa Maria Novella. The facade of this church looks distinctly clumsy by later Renaissance standards, and with good reason: It is an architectural hybrid. The lower half of the facade was completed mostly in the 14th century; its pointed-arch niches and decorative marble patterns reflect the Gothic style of the day. About a hundred years later (around 1456), architect Leon Battista Alberti was called in to complete the job. The marble decoration of his upper story clearly defers to the already existing work below, but the architectural features he added evince an entirely different style. The central doorway, the four ground-floor half-columns with Corinthian capitals, the triangular pediment atop the second story, the inscribed frieze immediately below the pediment—these are classical features borrowed from antiquity, and they reflect the new Renaissance era in architecture, born some 35 years earlier at the Ospedale degli Innocenti (☞ *Michelangelo Country, above*). Alberti's most important addition, however, the S-curve scrolls that surmount the decorative circles on either side of the upper story, had no precedent whatever in antiquity. The problem was to soften the abrupt transition between wide ground floor and narrow upper story. Alberti's solution turned out to be definitive. Once you start to look for them, you will find scrolls such as these (or sculptural variations of them) on churches all over Italy, and every one of them derives from Alberti's example here.

The architecture of the interior is, like the Duomo, a dignified but somber example of Italian Gothic. Exploration is essential, however, because the church's store of art treasures is remarkable. Highlights include the 14th-century stained-glass rose window depicting *The Coronation of the Virgin* (above the central entrance door); the Filippo Strozzi Chapel (to the right of the altar), containing late–15th-century frescoes and stained glass by Filippino Lippi; the chancel (the area around the altar), containing frescoes by Domenico Ghirlandaio (1485); and the Gondi Chapel (to the left of the altar), containing Filippo Brunelleschi's famous wooden crucifix, carved around 1410 and said to have so stunned the great Donatello when he first saw it that he dropped a basket of eggs.

One other work in the church is worth special attention, for it possesses great historical importance as well as beauty. It is Masaccio's *Holy Trinity with Two Donors,* on the left-hand wall, almost halfway down the nave. Painted around 1425 (at the same time Masaccio was working on his frescoes in Santa Maria del Carmine, ☞ *The Pitti Palace, Boboli, and Oltrarno, below*), it unequivocally announced the arrival of the Renaissance era. The realism of the figure of Christ was revolutionary in itself, but what was probably even more startling to contemporary Florentines was the coffered ceiling in the background. The mathematical rules for employing perspective in painting had just been discovered (probably by Brunelleschi), and this was one of the first paintings to employ them with utterly convincing success. As art historian E. H. Gombrich expressed it, "We can imagine how amazed the Florentines must have been when this wall-painting was unveiled and seemed to have made a hole in the wall through which they could look into a new burial chapel in Brunelleschi's modern style." ⊠ *Piazza Santa Maria Novella.* ▤ *5,000 lire.* ☉ *Sat.–Thurs. 9–2, Sun. 8–1.*

OFF THE BEATEN PATH **MUSEO DI SANTA MARIA NOVELLA** – This museum, entered to the left of the church, includes the church's cloisters, interesting for the faded fresco cycle by Paolo Uccello depicting tales from Genesis, with a dramatic vision of the Deluge. There are more, earlier and better preserved frescoes, painted by Andrea di Firenze in the 1360s in the chapter hall, or Cappella degli Spagnoli, off the cloisters. ⊠ *The church of Santa Maria Novella.*

㉒ **Santa Trinita.** Originally built in the Romanesque style, the church underwent a Gothic remodeling during the 14th century (remains of the Romanesque construction are visible on the interior front wall). Its major artistic attraction is the cycle of frescoes and the altarpiece in the Sassetti Chapel, the second to the altar's right, painted by Domenico Ghirlandaio, around 1485. Ghirlandaio was a conservative painter for his day, and generally his paintings exhibit little interest in the investigations into the laws of perspective that had been going on in Florentine painting for more than 50 years. But his work here possesses such graceful decorative appeal that his lack of interest in rigorous perspective hardly seems to matter. The wall frescoes illustrate the life of St. Francis, and the altarpiece, *The Adoration of the Shepherds,* seems to stop just short of glowing.

In the center of Piazza Santa Trinita is a column from the Baths of Caracalla, in Rome, given to the Medici Grand Duke Cosimo I by Pope Pius IV in 1560. The column was raised here by Cosimo in 1565, to mark the spot where he heard the news, in 1537, that his exiled Ghibelline enemies had been defeated at Montemurlo, near Prato; the victory made his power in Florence unchallengeable and all but absolute. The column is called, with typical Medici self-assurance, the **Colonna della Giustizia,** the Column of Justice.

Via Tornabuoni. For those who can afford it, this is probably Florence's finest shopping street, and it supplies an interesting contrast to the nearby Piazza della Repubblica (☞ The Historic Heart of Florence, *above*). There, at the turn of the century, the old was leveled to make way for the new; here, past and present cohabit easily and efficiently, with the oldest buildings housing the newest shops. Ironically, the "modern" Piazza della Repubblica now looks dated and more than a little dowdy, and it is the unrenewed Via Tornabuoni, lined with Renaissance buildings, bustling with activity, that seems up-to-the-minute.

NEED A BREAK?

For a midmorning pickup in the company of stylish Florentines, try **Giacosa,** at No. 83 Via Tornabuoni, for excellent coffee, cappuccino, and pastries, or **Procacci,** at No. 64, for finger sandwiches and cold drinks. (Both closed Mon.)

The Pitti Palace, Boboli, and Oltrarno

This walk takes in two very different aspects of Florence: the splendor of the Medicis, manifest in the riches of mammoth Pitti Palace and the gracious Boboli gardens; and the charm of the Oltrarno, literally, "beyond the Arno," a now-gentrified neighborhood of artisans and antique shops.

A Good Walk

Numbers in the text correspond to numbers in the margin and on the Florence map.

If you start from Santa Trinita, cross the Arno over Ponte Santa Trinita and continue down Via Maggio until you reach the crossroads of Sdrucciolo dei Pitti (on the left) and the short Via Michelozzi (on the right). Turn left onto the Sdrucciolo dei Pitti. **Palazzo Pitti** ㉓, Florence's largest architectural set piece, lies before you as you emerge onto Piazza Pitti. Behind the palace are the **Boboli Gardens** ㉔. If you have time, walk uphill in the gardens all the way to the **Belvedere Fortress** ㉕, which is worth it for the view. Return to Via Maggio from the Pitti, take Via Michelozzi to Piazza Santo Spirito, dominated at its north end by the unassuming facade of the church of **Santo Spirito** ㉖. After your visit to perhaps Italy's most important architectural interior, take Via Sant'Agostino, diagonally across the square from the church entrance, and follow it to Via dei Serragli. Cross and follow Via Santa Monaca through the heart of Florence's working-class and fiercely proud Oltrarno neighborhood—the equivalent of Rome's Trastevere—to Piazza del Carmine and the church of **Santa Maria del Carmine** ㉗, where, in the attached Brancacci Chapel, is the Masaccio cycle that is famous throughout the world. Go to the far end of Piazza del Carmine and turn right onto Borgo San Frediano, then follow Via di Santo Spirito and Borgo San Jacopo to reach the Ponte Vecchio.

TIMING

The walk alone takes about 45 minutes; allow one hour to visit the Galleria Palatina in the Pitti Palace, or more if you visit the other galleries. Spend at least 30 minutes to an hour savoring the graceful elegance of the Boboli gardens. When you reach the crossroads of the Sdrucciolo dei Pitti and Via Michelozzi, you have a choice. If the noon hour approaches, you may want to postpone the next stop temporarily to see the churches of Santo Spirito and Santa Maria del Carmine before they close for the afternoon. Otherwise, proceed to the Palazzo Pitti, where you should bank on spending at least 30 minutes visiting the palace. The churches of Santo Spirito and Santa Maria del Carmine can be visited in 15 minutes each, but we strongly recommend that if you have the time, linger a while in either church to soak up the sheer historical and artistic grandeur that is the essence of Florence's beauty.

㉕ **Belvedere Fortress.** This imposing structure was built in 1429 to help defend the city against siege. But time has effected an ironic transformation, and what was once a first-rate fortification is now a first-rate picnic ground. Buses carry view-seeking tourists farther up the hill to the Piazzale Michelangelo, but, as the natives know, the best views of Florence are right here. To the north, all the city's monuments are spread out in a breathtaking cinemascopic panorama, framed by the rolling Tuscan hills beyond: the squat dome of Santa Maria Novella, Giotto's proud campanile, the soaring dome of the Duomo, the forbidding medieval tower of the Palazzo Vecchio, the delicate Gothic spire of the Badia, and the crenellated tower of the Bargello. It is one of the best city views in Italy. To the south the nearby hills furnish a complementary rural view, in its way equally memorable. If time and weather permit, a picnic lunch here on the last day of your stay is the perfect way to review the city's splendors and fix them forever in your memory. The fortress, occasionally used as a setting for art exhibitions, is adjacent to the top of the Boboli Gardens and is connected with the gardens by a secondary entrance. ⌑ *Free.* ☉ *Daily 9–sunset.*

㉔ **Boboli Gardens.** The main entrance to these landscaped gardens is in the right wing of the Pitti Palace. The gardens began to take shape in 1549, when the Pitti family sold the palazzo to Eleanor of Toledo, wife of the Medici Grand Duke Cosimo I. The initial landscaping plans were laid out by Niccolò Pericoli Tribolo. After his death in 1550 development was continued by Bernardo Buontalenti, Giulio, and Alfonso Parigi, and, over the years, many others, who produced the most spectacular backyard in Florence. The Italian gift for landscaping—less formal than the French but still full of sweeping drama—is displayed here at its best. A description of the gardens' beauties would fill a page but would be self-defeating, for the best way to enjoy a pleasure garden is to wander about, discovering its pleasures for yourself. One small fountain deserves special note, however: the famous *Bacchino,* near the main entrance. It is a copy of the original, showing Pietro Barbino, Cosimo's favorite dwarf, astride a particularly unhappy tortoise. It seems to be illustrating—very graphically, indeed—the perils of too much pasta. At the top of the gardens, a gate gives access to the Belvedere Fortress. ✉ 4,000 lire. ☉ *Daily, except first and last Mon. of each month, 9–1 hr before sunset.*

㉓ **Palazzo Pitti.** This enormous palace is one of Florence's largest—if not one of its best—architectural set pieces. The original palazzo, built for the Pitti family around 1460, comprised only the middle cube (the width of the middle seven windows on the upper floors) of the present building. In 1549 the property was sold to the Medicis, and Bartolomeo Ammannati was called in to make substantial additions. Although he apparently operated on the principle that more is better, he succeeded only in producing proof that more is just that, more.

Today the immense building houses several museums: the former **Royal Apartments,** containing furnishings from a remodeling done in the 19th century; the **Museo degli Argenti,** containing a vast collection of Medici household treasures; the **Galleria del Costume,** a showcase of the fashions of the past 300 years; the **Galleria d'Arte Moderna,** containing a collection of 19th- and 20th-century paintings, mostly Tuscan; and, most famous of all, the **Galleria Palatina,** containing a broad collection of 16th- and 17th-century paintings. The rooms of the latter remain much as the Medici family left them, but, as Mary McCarthy pointed out, the Florentines invented modern bad taste, and many art lovers view the floor-to-ceiling painting displays here as Italy's most egregious exercise in conspicuous consumption, aesthetic overkill, and trumpery. Still, the collection possesses high points that are very high indeed, including a number of portraits by Titian and an unparalleled collection of paintings by Raphael, among them the famous *Madonna of the Chair.* ✉ *Piazza Pitti,* ☎ *055/210323.* ✉ *Royal Apartments: 8,000 lire; Museo degli Argenti and Galleria del Costume: 8,000 lire (valid for both); Galleria d'Arte Moderna: 4,000 lire; Galleria Palatina: 12,000 lire.* ☉ *Tues.–Sun. 9–2.*

㉗ **Santa Maria del Carmine.** The **Brancacci Chapel,** at the end of the right transept of this church, a masterpiece of Renaissance painting: a fresco cycle that changed the course of art forever. Fire almost destroyed the church in the 18th century; miraculously, the Brancacci Chapel survived almost intact.

The cycle is the work of three artists: Masaccio and Masolino, who began it in 1423, and Filippino Lippi, who finished it, after a long interruption during which the sponsoring Brancacci family was exiled, some 50 years later. It was Masaccio's work that opened a new frontier for painting; tragically, he did not live to experience the revolution his innovations caused, as he died in 1428 at the age of 27.

Masaccio collaborated with Masolino on several of the paintings, but by himself he painted *The Tribute Money* on the upper-left wall; *Peter Baptizing the Neophytes* on the upper altar wall; *The Distribution of the Goods of the Church* on the lower altar wall; and, most famous, *The Expulsion of Adam and Eve* on the chapel's upper-left entrance pier. If you look closely at the latter painting and compare it with some of the chapel's other works, you will see a pronounced difference. The figures of Adam and Eve possess a startling presence, a presence primarily due to the dramatic way in which their bodies seem to reflect light. Masaccio here shaded his figures consistently, so as to suggest emphatically a single, strong source of light within the world of the painting but outside its frame. In so doing, he succeeded in imitating with paint the real-world effect of light on mass, and he thereby imparted to his figures a sculptural reality unprecedented in its day. To contemporary Florentines his Adam and Eve must have seemed surrounded by light and air in a way that was almost magical. All the painters of Florence came to look.

These matters have to do with technique, but with *The Expulsion of Adam and Eve*, his skill went beyond technical innovation, and if you look hard at the faces of Adam and Eve, you will see more than just finely modeled figures. You will see terrible shame and terrible suffering, and you will see them depicted with a humanity rarely achieved in art. ⊠ *Brancacci Chapel.* ⊞ *5,000 lire.* ☉ *Mon. and Wed.–Sat. 10–5, Sun. 1–5.*

NEED A BREAK? A popular spot for lunch on Piazza del Carmine is **Carmine,** a moderately priced restaurant with outdoor tables during the warmer months. It is at the end of the piazza's northern extension. ⊠ *Piazza del Carmine. Closed Sun.*

❷❻ **Santo Spirito.** The plain, unfinished facade gives nothing away, but, in fact, the interior, although it appears chilly (cold, even) compared with later churches, is one of the most important pieces of architecture in all Italy. One of a pair of Florentine church interiors designed by Filippo Brunelleschi in the early 15th century (the other is San Lorenzo, ☞ Michelangelo Country, *above*) it was here that Brunelleschi supplied definitive solutions to the two main problems of interior Renaissance church design: how to build a cross-shaped interior using classical architectural elements borrowed from antiquity and how to reflect in that interior the order and regularity that Renaissance scientists (of which Brunelleschi was one) were at the time discovering in the natural world around them.

Brunelleschi's solution to the first problem was brilliantly simple: Turn a Greek temple inside out. To see this clearly, look at one of the stately arch-topped arcades that separate the side aisles from the central nave. Whereas the ancient Greek temples were walled buildings surrounded by classical colonnades, Brunelleschi's churches were classical arcades surrounded by walled buildings. This was perhaps the single most brilliant architectural idea of the early Renaissance, and its brilliance overthrew the previous era's religious taboo against pagan architecture once and for all, triumphantly reclaiming that architecture for Christian use.

Brunelleschi's solution to the second problem—making the entire interior orderly and regular—was mathematically precise: He designed the ground plan of the church so that all its parts are proportionally related. The transepts and nave have exactly the same width; the side aisles are exactly half as wide as the nave; the little chapels off the side aisles are exactly half as deep as the side aisles; the chancel and transepts are exactly one-eighth the depth of the nave; and so on, with dizzying exactitude. For Brunelleschi, such a design technique would have been far more than a convenience; it would have been a matter of passionate conviction. Like most theoreticians of his day, he believed that mathematical regularity and aesthetic beauty were opposite sides of the same coin, that one was not possible without the other. The conviction stood unchallenged for a hundred years, until Michelangelo turned his hand to architecture and designed the Medici Chapel and the Biblioteca Laurenziana in San Lorenzo across town (☞ Michelangelo Country, *above*), and thereby unleashed a revolution of his own that spelled the end of the Renaissance in architecture and the beginning of the Baroque. ⊠ *Piazza Santo Spirito.* ☉ *Thurs.–Tues. 8–12, 4–6; Wed. 8–12*

From Santa Croce to San Miniato

The Santa Croce neighborhood, on the southwest fringe of the historic center of Florence, was built up in the Middle Ages just outside the medieval city walls. The centerpiece of the neighborhood was the church of Santa Croce, which could hold great numbers of worshipers and accommodate the overflow in the vast piazza, which also served as a fairground and playing field for traditional, no-holds-barred football games. A center of leather-working since the Middle Ages, the neighborhood is still packed with leather craftsmen and shops selling leather goods.

A Good Walk
Numbers in the text correspond to numbers in the margin and on the Florence map.

Begin your walk at the church of **Santa Croce** ㉘, take Via de' Benci and cross the Arno over Ponte alle Grazie. Turn left onto Lungarno Serristori and continue to Piazza Poggi, where a series of ramps and stairs climbs to **Piazzale Michelangelo,** where the city lies before you like a painting. From Piazzale Michelangelo, climb the stairs to the church of San Salvatore al Monte, and follow the lane to the stairs that climb to **San Miniato al Monte** ㉙, cutting through the fortifications hurriedly built by Michelangelo in 1529 when Florence was threatened by Emperor Charles V's troops. If you prefer, you can avoid the long walk by taking Bus 12 or 13 at the west end of Ponte alle Grazie and get off at the stop after Piazzale Michelangelo. You still have to climb the monumental stairs to San Miniato, but then the rest of your itinerary will be downhill. From San Miniato descend to San Salvatore al Monte and then to Piazzale Michelangelo, where you can get a bus back to the center of town.

TIMING
The walk alone takes about 1½ hours one way, plus 30 minutes in Santa Croce, 30 minutes in the Museo di Santa Croce, and 30 minutes in San Miniato. Depending on the amount of time you have, you can limit your sightseeing to Santa Croce or continue on to Piazzale Michelangelo. The walk to Piazzale Michelangelo is a long uphill hike, with the prospect of another climb to San Miniato from there. If you decide to take a bus, remember to buy your ticket before you board. Finally, since you go to Piazzale Michelangelo for the view, skip that stop on the itinerary if it's a hazy day.

Sights to See
Piazzale Michelangelo. From this lookout, you have a marvelous view of Florence and the hills around it, rivaling the vista from the Belvedere Fortress (☞ The Pitti Palace, Boboli, and Oltrarno, *above*). It has a copy of Michelangelo's *David* and outdoor cafés that are packed with tourists during the day and with Florentines in the evening. In May, the Iris Garden off the piazza is abloom with more than 2,500 varieties of the flower that has been Florence's symbol since 1251, and it is open to the public. The Rose Garden on the terraces below the piazza is also open in May and June.

NEED A
BREAK?   After seeing the light of the setting sun cast a glow on Florence's domes and towers from a vantage point on Piazzale Michelangelo, have supper or a snack at the **Antico Vineria** on Via San Nicolò, off Piazza Poggi at the foot of the hill. It's a busy wineshop-trattoria with atmosphere. ☒ *Via San Nicolò 60/r. Closed Sun.*

㉙ **San Miniato al Monte.** This church, like the Baptistery (☞ The Historic Heart of Florence, *above*), is a fine example of Romanesque architecture and is one of the oldest churches in Florence, dating from the 11th century. The lively green and white marble facade has a 12th-century mosaic topped by a gilded bronze eagle, emblem of San Miniato's sponsors, the Calimala (Wool Merchant's Guild). Inside are a 13th-century inlaid marble floor and apse mosaic. Artist Spinello Aretino covered the walls of the Sacristy with frescoes of the life of St. Benedict. The adjacent Chapel of the Portuguese Cardinal is one of the richest Renaissance works in Florence. Built to hold the tomb of a Portuguese cardinal, Prince James of Lusitania, who died young in Florence in 1459, it has a glorious ceiling by Luca della Robbia, a sculptured tomb by Antonio Rossellini and inlaid pavement in multicolored marble.

★ ㉘ **Santa Croce.** Like the Duomo, this church is Gothic, but (also like the Duomo) its facade dates only from the 19th century. The interior is most famous for its art and its tombs. As a burial place, the church is a Florentine pantheon and probably contains a larger number of important skeletons than any church in Italy. Among others, the tomb of Michelangelo is immediately to the right as you enter (he is said to have chosen this spot so that the first thing he would see on Judgment Day, when the graves of the dead fly open, would be Brunelleschi's Duomo dome through Santa Croce's open doors); the tomb of Galileo Galilei, who produced evidence that the earth is not the center of the universe (and who was not granted a Christian burial until 100 years after his death because of it), is on the left wall, opposite Michelangelo; the tomb of Niccolò Machiavelli, the Renaissance political theoretician whose brutally pragmatic philosophy so influenced the Medici, is halfway down the nave on the right; the grave of Lorenzo Ghiberti, creator of the Gates of Paradise doors to the Baptistery, is halfway down the nave on the left; the tomb of composer Gioacchino Rossini, of "William Tell Overture" fame, is at the end of the nave on the right. The monument to Dante Alighieri, the greatest Italian poet, is a memorial rather than a tomb (he is actually buried in Ravenna); it is on the right wall near the tomb of Michelangelo.

The collection of art within the church and church complex is by far the most important of that in any church in Florence. Historically, the most significant works are probably the Giotto frescoes in the two adjacent chapels immediately to the right of the altar. They illustrate scenes from the lives of St. John the Evangelist and St. John the Baptist (in the right-hand chapel) and scenes from the life of St. Francis (in the left-hand chapel). Time has not been kind to them; over the centuries, wall tombs were introduced into the middle of them, whitewash and plaster covered them, and in the 19th century they underwent a clumsy restoration. But the reality that Giotto introduced into painting can still be seen. He did not paint beautifully stylized symbols of religion, as the Byzantine style that preceded him prescribed; he instead painted drama—St. Francis surrounded by grieving monks at the very moment of his death. This was a radical shift in emphasis, and it changed the course of art. Before him, the role of painting was to symbolize the attributes of God; after him, it was to imitate life. The style of his work is indeed primitive, compared with later painting, but in the proto-Renaissance of the early 14th century, it caused a sensation that was not equalled for another 100 years. He was, for his time, the equal of both Masaccio and Michelangelo.

Among the church's other highlights are Donatello's *Annunciation,* one of the most tender and eloquent expressions of surprise ever sculpted (on the right wall two-thirds of the way down the nave); Taddeo Gaddi's 14th-century frescoes illustrating the life of the Virgin, clearly showing the influence of Giotto (in the chapel at the end of the right transept); and Donatello's *Crucifix*, criticized by Brunelleschi for making Christ look like a peasant (in the chapel at the end of the left transept). Outside the church proper, in the **Museo dell'Opera di Santa Croce** off the cloister, is Giovanni Cimabue's 13th-century *Triumphal Cross*, badly damaged by the flood of 1966. The **Pazzi Chapel**, yet another of Brunelleschi's crisp exercises in architectural geometry, is at the end of the cloister. ✉ *Piazza Santa Croce 16*, ☎ *055/244619. Church:* ⊙ *Apr.–Sept., Mon.–Sat. 8–6:30, Sun. 8–12:30, 3–6:30; Oct.–Mar., Mon.–Sat. 8–12:30, 3–6:30, Sun. 3–6. Church cloister and museum:* 🎟 *3,000 lire.* ⊙ *Apr.–Sept., Thurs.–Tues. 10–12:30, 2:30–6:30; Oct.–Mar., Thurs.–Tues. 10–12:30, 3–5.*

NEED A
BREAK?

The Santa Croce neighborhood has some sweet surprises hidden among its byways: **Vivoli** (✉ Via Isola delle Stinche 7/r, off Via dell'Anguillara, one of the streets opposite the facade of Santa Croce) is Florence's most famous *gelateria* (ice-cream parlor). If you're homesick for brownies and chocolate-chip cookies, find your way to **Carlie's American Bakery.** ✉ *Via della Brache, also known as Via dei Legnaioli 12/r, a narrow street off Via dei Neri between Via dei Benci and Via dei Rustici; open 10–1:30 and 3:30–7:30.*

DINING

A typical Tuscan repast starts with an antipasto of *crostini* (toasted bread spread with a chicken liver pâté) or cured meats such as prosciutto *crudo* (a salty prosciutto), *finocchiona* (salami seasoned with fennel), and *salsiccia di cinghiale* (sausage made from wild boar). This is the time to start right in on the local wine—Chianti, *naturalmente*. Don't be surprised if the waiter brings an entire flask to the table. Customers are charged only for what they consume (*al consumo*, the arrangement is called), but it's wise to ask for a flask or bottle to be opened then and there, since leftover wines are often mixed together.

Primi piatti (first courses) can consist of excellent local versions of risotto or pasta dishes available throughout Italy. Peculiar to Florence, however, are the vegetable-and-bread soups such as *pappa al pomodoro* (tomatoes, bread, olive oil, onions, and basil), ribollita, or, in the summer, a salad called *panzanella* (tomatoes, onions, vinegar, oil, and bread). Before they are eaten, these are often christened with *un "C" d'olio*, a generous C-shape drizzle of the excellent local olive oil from the ever-present tabletop cruet.

Second to none among the *secondi piatti* (main courses) is *bistecca alla fiorentina*—a thick slab of local Chianina beef, grilled over charcoal, seasoned with olive oil, salt, and pepper, and served rare. *Trippa alla fiorentina* (tripe stewed with tomatoes in a meat sauce) and *arista* (roast loin of pork seasoned with rosemary) are also regional specialties, as are many other roasted meats that go especially well with the Chianti. These are usually served with a *contorno* (side dish) of white beans, sautéed greens, or artichokes in season, all of which can be drizzled with more of that wonderful olive oil.

Tuscan desserts are typically spartan. The cheese is the hard pecorino, and locals like to go for the even tougher *biscottini di Prato*, a caramelized cookie, which provide an excuse to dunk them in the potent, sweet dessert wine called *vin santo*, made of dried grapes, which they say will bring the dead back to life!

Remember that dining hours are earlier here than in Rome, starting at 12:30 for the midday meal and at 7:30 for dinner. Many of Florence's restaurants are small, so reservations are a must. Note that the *r* in some of the following addresses indicates the red numbering system used for Florentine businesses, which differs from the black numbers used for residences.

CATEGORY	COST*
$$$$	over 110,000 lire
$$$	80,000–110,000 lire
$$	35,000–80,000 lire
$	under 35,000 lire

per person, for a three-course meal, including house wine and taxes

$$$$ ✕ **Enoteca Pinchiorri.** A sumptuous Renaissance palace with high, fres-
★ coed ceilings and bouquets in silver vases is the setting for this restaurant, one of the most expensive in Italy, and also considered one of the
best (though it has been known to have its off days). The "enoteca"
part of the name comes from its former incarnation as a wineshop under
owner Giorgio Pinchiorri, who still keeps a stock of vintage bottles in
the cellar. Wife Annie Feolde has added her refined interpretations of
Tuscan cuisine—*triglie alla viareggina* (mullet with tomato sauce) and
arrosto di coniglio (roast rabbit)—to a nouvelle menu that includes *can-
nelloni di astice* (pasta stuffed with lobster), *filetto d'agnello con melanzane e pomodori canditi* (filet of lamb with eggplant and candied
tomatoes). ✉ *Via Ghibellina 87,* ☎ *055/242777. Reservations essential. Jacket and tie. AE, MC, V. Closed Sun., Mon., Aug., and 1 wk in
Dec. No lunch Wed.*

$$$ ✕ **Harry's Bar.** Americans love it, and it *is* the only place in town to
get a perfect martini or a hamburger or a club sandwich, but it offers
two typical Tuscan dishes every day. The small menu also has well-pre-
pared international offerings, and the bar is open until midnight. ✉
Lungarno Vespucci 22/r, ☎ *055/239–6700. Reservations essential. AE,
MC, V. Closed Sun. and Dec. 15–Jan. 8.*

$$$ ✕ **Il Cestello.** Across the Arno from the church of San Frediano in Ces-
tello, the restaurant is part of the Excelsior hotel and moves to the roof
during the warmer months to enjoy a stupendous view of the city. The
Tuscan-based menu features delicious risotto and pasta dishes, including an exemplary pasta *e fagioli* (with beans), a rare selection of
seafood, and an ever-changing sampling of whatever is fresh from the
market. ✉ *Hotel Excelsior, Piazza Ognissanti 3,* ☎ *055/264201.
Jacket and tie. AE, DC, MC, V.*

$$$ ✕ **Il Verrocchio.** In an elegant 18th-century villa, now a deluxe hotel,
the restaurant is about 20 minutes from downtown Florence by car or
taxi, and well worth the ride. The dining room has a huge fireplace,
columns, and a high, vaulted ceiling. Outdoors you dine on a terrace
overlooking the Arno. The menu changes with the seasons but can be
described as Tuscan-creative, with such offerings as *agnello con salsa
di albicocche* (lamb with apricot sauce) and delicate, fresh pasta dishes.
✉ *Villa La Massa, Via La Massa 6, Candeli,* ☎ *055/651–0101. Jacket
and tie. AE, DC, MC, V. Closed Mon. and Tues. Nov.–Mar.*

$$$ ✕ **La Capannina di Sante.** Florence's best fish restaurant is situated,
★ not surprisingly, along a quiet stretch of the Arno, with indoor tables
in an ample, unpretentious trattoria setting and tables outdoors on the
terrace during the warmer months. Risotto and various types of pasta
are combined with seafood, and the *grigliata mista di pesce* (mixed grill
of fish) is among the standouts. ✉ *Piazza Ravenna,* ☎ *055/688345.
AE, DC, MC, V. Closed Sun., 10 days in Aug., Dec. 23–30. No lunch.*

$$$ ✕ **La Loggia.** The view of Florence from the glassed-in veranda or din-
ing terrace of a century-old mansion on Piazzale Michelangelo is what
you and all the other tourists come for, but the relatively new man-
agement wants you to remember the food, too. Along with Florentine

124

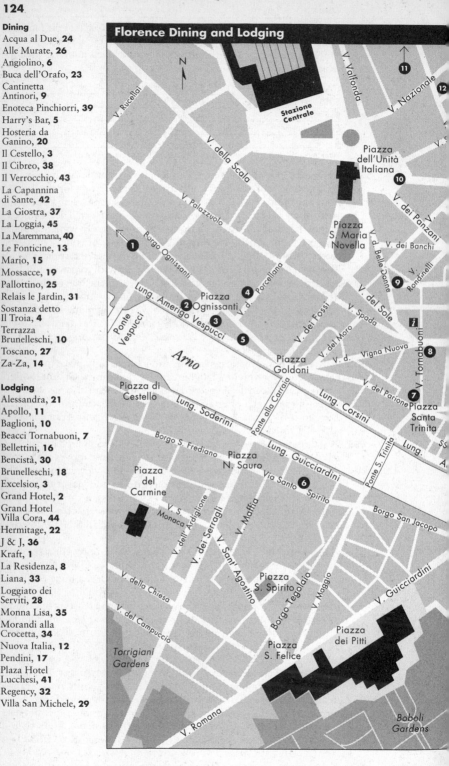

Florence Dining and Lodging

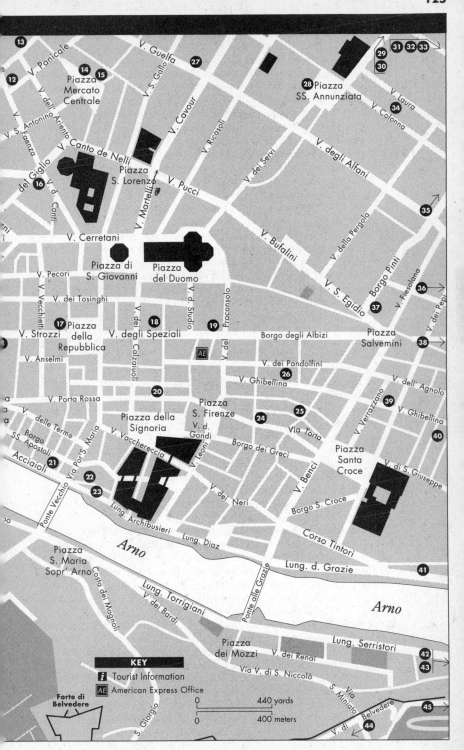

KEY

ℹ️ Tourist Information

AE American Express Office

0   440 yards

0   400 meters

classics, host Gaetano offers seafood and southern Italian dishes, using produce from his farm in Impruneta. ⊠ *Piazzale Michelangelo 1,* ☏ *055/234–2832. Jacket and tie. AE, DC, MC, V. Closed Wed.*

$$$ ✕ **Relais le Jardin.** Another hotel restaurant, this one with a turn-of-the-century, stained-glass-and-wood-paneling setting, stands on its own. This is gourmet cooking at its most refined, including such dishes as *fagottino di vitello* (veal roulade), stuffed with eggplant and cheese in wine sauce, or *calamari farciti* (shrimp-stuffed cuttlefish) with seafood sauce. ⊠ *Hotel Regency, Piazza Massimo D'Azeglio 3,* ☏ *055/245247. Reservations essential. Jacket and tie. AE, DC, MC, V. Closed Sun.*

$$$ ✕ **Terrazza Brunelleschi.** The rooftop restaurant of the Hotel Baglioni
★ has the best view in town. The dining room, decorated in pale blue and creamy tones, has wraparound picture windows framing a close-up of Brunelleschi's dome. The summer terrace outside is charming, with tables placed under arbors and with turrets for guests to climb to get an even better view. The menu offers some traditional Tuscan dishes, such as pappa al pomodoro and *tagliata* (sliced Tuscan steak garnished with arugula and aromatic olive oil). If you order carefully, your check may be in the $$ category. ⊠ *Hotel Baglioni, Piazza Unità Italiana 6,* ☏ *055/215642. Jacket and tie. AE, DC, MC, V.*

$$ ✕ **Acqua al Due.** You'll find this tiny restaurant near the Bargello. It serves an array of Florentine specialties in a lively, very casual setting. Acqua al Due is popular with young Florentines, partly because it's air-conditioned in the summer and always open late. It's known for pastas and salads, even if some customers find its clubby atmosphere downright frosty. ⊠ *Via della Vigna Vecchia 40/r,* ☏ *055/284170. Reservations not accepted. AE, MC, V. Closed Mon. and Aug.*

$$ ✕ **Alle Murate.** Situated between the Duomo and Santa Croce, this is a sophisticated but informal restaurant. The menu features creative versions of classic Tuscan dishes—*anatra alle erbe* (duck with herb and orange sauce)—but also southern Italian specialties such as *cavatelli con broccoli* (homemade pasta with broccoli and cheese). The main dining room has an elegant, uncluttered look, with warm wood floors and paneling and soft lights. In a smaller adjacent room called the *vineria,* table settings are simpler and the menu more limited. Since the Murate is known for its wine list, this is the place to splurge on a good vintage. ⊠ *Via Ghibellina 52/r,* ☏ *055/240618. No credit cards. Closed Mon. No lunch.*

$$ ✕ **Angiolino.** This bustling little trattoria in the Oltrarno district is pop-
★ ular with locals and visitors. It has a real charcoal grill and an old wood-burning stove to keep customers warm on nippy days. The menu offers Tuscan specialties such as ribollita and a classic bistecca alla fiorentina. The bistecca can push the check up, as you pay by weight (order one for two people). ⊠ *Via Santo Spirito 36/r,* ☏ *055/239–8976. AE, DC, MC, V. Closed Mon. and last 3 wks in July. No dinner Sun.*

$$ ✕ **Buca dell'Orafo.** One of the best of the Florentine *buca,* meaning hole-in-the-wall, restaurants, Buca dell'Orafo is set in the cellar of a former goldsmith's shop near the Ponte Vecchio. It offers all the Florentine specialties and prides itself on its bistecca. ⊠ *Via dei Girolami 28,* ☏ *055/213619. No credit cards. Closed Sun., Mon., and Aug.*

$$ ✕ **Cantinetta Antinori.** Set on the ground floor of a Renaissance palace, this is an elegant place for lunch after shopping in nearby Via Tornabuoni. The Antinori family is best known as wine producers, and their wares may be sampled with light salads, bread, sausage, and cheese snacks or more complete meals. ⊠ *Piazza Antinori 3,* ☏ *055/292234. AE, DC, MC, V. Closed Sat., Sun., and Aug.*

$$ ✕ **Hosteria da Ganino.** On a side street between the Duomo and Palazzo Vecchio, this trattoria is informal, rustic, and cheerful. The menu features homemade pasta, and the fettuccine

with porcini mushrooms is a specialty. Main courses uphold Florentine tradition, with grilled steak and chops and bean dishes. Get there early: It seats only about 35; double that number in good weather at outside tables. ⊠ *Piazza dei Cimatori 4/r,* ☎ *055/214125. AE, DC, V. Closed Sun. and Aug. 15–25.*

$$ ✕ Il Cibreo. Trendsetter that he is, chef Fabrio Picchi has made Cibreo
★ into Florence's newest pilgrimage spot for gourmands. His menu of Tuscan country dishes relies less on his memories than on his lively imagination, which has created updated versions of Florentine classics, such as pappa al pomodoro, presented as a thick red dollop on a sparkling white Ginori plate, and *anatra farcita di pinoli e uvetta* (duck stuffed with pine nuts and raisins). Don't miss the yellow-pepper soup—made, thanks to the restaurant's location near the Sant'-Ambrogio market, with the freshest ingredients available. You'll dine in an upscale trattoria-style dining room or, during warmer weather, in a piazza overlooking the market. A café annex across the street serves drinks and snacks all day. There is also a small, inconspicuous, and inexpensive tavern annex around the corner. ⊠ *Via dei Macci 118/r,* ☎ *055/234–1100. Reservations essential. AE, DC, MC, V. Closed Sun., Mon., July 25–Sept. 5, and Dec. 31–Jan. 7.*

$$ ✕ La Giostra. Only about five minutes from the cathedral or from Santa Croce, the Giostra has the typically unpretentious look of a trattoria, but with a difference: the gourmet touch of the courteous owner-chef. Try his fusilli *del Boboli* (with fresh vegetables and mozzarella cheese). Like the menu, the wine list offers good value. Service is informal, and the restaurant is open until midnight, a rarity in Florence. ⊠ *Borgo Pinti 10/r,* ☎ *055/241341. AE, DC, MC, V.*

✓ **$$ ✕ Le Fonticine.** Owner Silvano Bruci is from Tuscany, wife Gianna
★ from Emilia-Romagna, and the restaurant combines the best of both
☺ worlds in a setting liberally hung with their extensive collection of paintings. Emilia-Romagna specialties such as tortellini ready the taste buds for Tuscan grilled porcini mushrooms so meaty they provide serious competition for the bistecca alla fiorentina. ⊠ *Via Nazionale 79/r,* ☎ *055/282106. AE, DC, MC, V. Closed Sun., Mon, and July 25–Aug. 25.*

$$ ✕ Pallottino. Pallottino has the look of a typical Florentine trattoria, with dark wood tables and benches and copper utensils and old photos on the walls, but here the decor is somehow improved. The menu features traditional fare, from bread or bean soup to spaghetti *alla fiaccheraia* (with piquant fresh tomato sauce). Meat courses are varied; try *involtini alla pallottino* (beef roulades with a creamy sauce). Prices are at the low end of this category. For dessert go down the street for ice cream at Vivoli. ⊠ *Via Isola delle Stinche 1/r,* ☎ *055/289573. AE, DC, MC, V. Closed Mon. and Aug. 1–20.*

$$ ✕ Sostanza (a.k.a. Il Troia). Il Troia is Florence's oldest restaurant,
★ founded in 1869. Travelers usually love it, in spite of, or perhaps because of, the no-frills decor and the brusque service. Why? Along with a quintessential bistecca alla fiorentina with a hefty price tag, within this small room you'll be sure to find an entire world of Florence aficionados. The waiters may be surly but the new friends you'll make at the communal tables—chances are you'll sit next to an art historian from Vassar or a bookstore owner from London—will more than make up for it. ⊠ *Via del Porcellana 25/r,* ☎ *055/212691. No credit cards. Closed Sun. and Aug. No dinner Sat.*

$$ ✕ Toscano. A small table attractively set in a show window identifies this restaurant, located about five minutes from Palazzo Medici-Riccardi. It lives up to its name in ambience and cuisine. The cold-cuts counter at the entrance, terra-cotta tile floors, and beamed ceilings typify a Tuscan trattoria, but the pink tablecloths, arty photos on the walls, and a touch of creative cuisine take it out of the ordinary. The kitchen prides itself on top-quality meat; this is the place to try tagliata or *spezzatino peposo* (beef stew with lots of black pepper and a wine sauce). The fixed-price menu is a good value, at about 35,000 lire. ⊠ *Via Guelfa 70/r,* ☏ *055/215475. AE, DC, MC, V. Closed Tues. and Aug.*

$ ✕ **La Maremmana.** A display of garden-fresh vegetables and fruit catches your eye as you enter this popular trattoria near Santa Croce. Authentic Tuscan cuisine is offered in the dining room, which has the usual wood paneling and long tables that you will probably be asked to share. The fixed-price menu offers generous servings and good value, and it may include ribollita and *stracotto* (beef stew). ⊠ *Via dei Macci 77/r,* ☏ *055/241226. DC, MC, V. Closed Sun. and Aug.*

$ ✕ **Mario.** Clean and classic, this family-run trattoria on the corner of Piazza del Mercato near San Lorenzo offers genuine Florentine atmosphere and cooking, with no frills. Open for lunch only, it's just around the corner from Za-Za (☞ *below*). ⊠ *Via Rosina 2/r (Piazza del Mercato Centrale),* ☏ *055/218550. Reservations not accepted. No credit cards. Closed Sun. No dinner.*

$ ✕ **Mossacce.** You share a heavy wooden trattoria table here and watch the cook in the glassed-in kitchen prepare your order, chosen from a menu of Florentine classics. ⊠ *Via del Proconsolo 55/r,* ☏ *055/294361. Reservations not accepted. AE, MC, V. Closed weekends and Aug.*

$ ✕ **Za-Za.** Slightly more upscale than neighboring trattorias, Za-Za attracts white-collar workers and theater people. Posters of movie stars hang on wood-paneled walls, but you couldn't ask for a more typically Florentine dining experience, with traditional atmosphere and food. ⊠ *Piazza Mercato Centrale 16/r,* ☏ *055/215411. AE, DC, MC, V. Closed Sun.*

Wineshops

Don't have time for a trattoria? Head for one of Florence's wine bars for a fast focaccia, sandwich or snack, and a glass of Chianti Classico. Of these, **Le Cantine** (⊠ Via dei Pucci) is stylish and popular, as is **Cantinone del Gallo Nero** (⊠ Via Santo Spirito 6), which also serves meals in a brick-vaulted wine cellar; **Le Volpi e l'Uva** (⊠ Piazza de' Rossi 1), and—the city's best, although a 15-minute walk from the center of town—**Fuori Porta** (⊠ Via dei Monte all Croci 10). More modest are **Borgioli** (⊠ Piazza dell'Olio), **Fiaschetteria** (⊠ Via dei Neri 2, corner of Via dei Benci), **Fratellini** (⊠ Via dei Cimatori), **Nicolino** (⊠ Volta dei Mercanti), and **Piccolo Vinaio** (⊠ Via Castellani).

LODGING

Florence's importance not only as a tourist city but as a convention center and the site of the Pitti fashion collections throughout the year has guaranteed a variety of accommodations, many in former villas and palazzos. However, these very factors mean that, except during the winter, reservations are a must.

Near the A1 autostrada exits, drivers will find the **Sheraton Firenze** (☏ 055/64901, ℻ 055/680747, $$$$), the **Holiday Inn** (☏ 055/653–1841, ℻ 055/653–1806, $$$), and the **Forte Agip** (☏ 055/420–5081, ℻ 055/421–9015, $$$).

If you do find yourself in Florence with no reservations, go to the **Consorzio ITA** office in the train station. It's open every day from 8:20 AM to 9 PM. If the office is shut, your best bet is to try some of the inexpensive (but clean) accommodations at a one- or two-star hotel; many are on **Via Nazionale** (which leads east from Piazza Stazione) and on **Via Faenza,** the second left off Via Nazionale.

CATEGORY	COST*
$$$$	over 450,000 lire
$$$	280,000–450,000 lire
$$	190,000–280,000 lire
$	under 190,000 lire

All prices are for a double room for two, including tax and service.

$$$$ ★ ▦ **Excelsior.** Traditional Old World charm finds a regal setting at the Excelsior, a neo-Renaissance palace complete with painted wooden ceilings, stained glass, and acres of Oriental carpets strewn over marble floors in the public rooms. The rooms are furnished with the opulence of 19th-century Florentine antiques and sumptuous fabrics, set off by charming old prints of the city and long mirrors of the Empire style. Plush touches include wall-to-wall carpeting in the rooms and thick terry-cloth towels on heated racks in the bathrooms. Try to get a room facing the Piazza Ognissanti. The Il Cestello restaurant serves excellent food, and in summer moves up to the roof for a wonderful view. ⊠ *Piazza Ognissanti 3,* ☎ *055/264201,* 𝐅𝐀𝐗 *055/210278. 177 rooms with bath. Restaurant, piano bar. AE, DC, MC, V.*

$$$$ ▦ **Grand Hotel.** Across the piazza from the Excelsior, this Florentine classic, also owned by the CIGA chain, provides all the luxurious amenities of its sister. Most rooms and public areas are decorated in sumptuous Renaissance style, many with frescoes. Baths are in marble. Some rooms have balconies overlooking the Arno. ⊠ *Piazza Ognissanti 1,* ☎ *055/288781,* 𝐅𝐀𝐗 *055/217400. 107 rooms with bath. Restaurant, bar, parking (fee). AE, DC, MC, V.*

$$$$ ▦ **Grand Hotel Villa Cora.** Built near the Boboli Gardens and Piazzale Michelangelo in 1750, the Villa Cora retains the opulence of the 18th and 19th centuries. The decor of its remarkable public and private rooms runs the gamut from neoclassical to rococo and even Moorish, and reflects the splendor of such former guests as the Empress Eugénie, wife of Napoléon III, and Madame Von Meck, Tchaikovsky's mysterious benefactress. ⊠ *Viale Machiavelli 18,* ☎ *055/229–8451,* 𝐅𝐀𝐗 *055/229–086. 48 rooms with bath. Restaurant, piano bar, pool. AE, DC, MC, V.*

$$$$ ▦ **Regency.** In this stylish hotel in a respectable residential district near the synagogue, the noise and crowds of Florence seem far away, though you are less than 10 minutes away from the Accademia and Michelangelo's *David*. The rooms are decorated in richly colored and tasteful fabrics and antique-style furniture faithful to the hotel's 19th-century origins as a private mansion. It has one of Florence's best hotel restaurants (☞ *above*). ⊠ *Piazza Massimo D'Azeglio 3,* ☎ *055/245247,* 𝐅𝐀𝐗 *055/234–6735. 34 rooms with bath. Restaurant, parking (fee). AE, DC, MC, V.*

$$$$ ▦ **Villa San Michele.** The setting for this hideaway is so romantic—nestled in the hills of nearby Fiesole—that it once attracted Brigitte Bardot for her honeymoon. The villa was originally a monastery whose facade and loggia have been attributed to Michelangelo. Many of the rooms now contain sumptuous statuary, paintings, and whirlpool baths. Many have a panoramic view of Florence, while others look onto the former cloister. A luxuriant garden surrounds the whole affair. The restaurant is excellent. This is one of Italy's costliest hotels. ⊠ *Via Doccia 4, Fiesole,* ☎ *055/59451,* 𝐅𝐀𝐗 *055/598734. 36 rooms with bath. Restaurant, piano bar, pool. AE, DC, MC, V. Closed Dec.–mid-Mar.*

$$$ ▦ **Baglioni.** This large turn-of-the-century building was conceived in the European tradition of grand hotels; it's between the train station and the cathedral. The charming roof terrace has the best view in Florence and is home to the Terrazza Brunelleschi restaurant. The hotel has well-proportioned rooms, some decorated in antique Florentine style, and many with leaded-glass windows. Most rooms have been done in pastel tones harmonizing with the carpeting or mellow parquet. There

is a full range of conference facilities, which makes it a favorite of businesspeople. ⊠ *Piazza dell'Unità Italiana 6,* ☎ *055/23580,* 🖷 *055/235–8895. 195 rooms with bath. Restaurant. AE, DC, MC, V.*

$$$ 🖬 **Beacci Tornabuoni.** This is perhaps *the* classic Florentine pensione (although by law all lodgings have been reclassified as hotels of various categories). Set in a 14th-century palazzo, it has old-fashioned style and just enough modern comfort to keep today's guests happy. Half board is required, but the food is good and can also be served in the rooms, most of which have views of the red-tile roofs in the neighboring downtown area. ⊠ *Via Tornabuoni 3,* ☎ *055/212645,* 🖷 *055/283594. 30 rooms with bath. Restaurant, bar. AE, DC, MC, V.*

$$$ 🖬 **Brunelleschi.** Architects united a Byzantine tower, a medieval church,
★   and a later building in a stunning structure in the very heart of Renaissance Florence to make this the city's most unique hotel. This remarkable place even has its own museum displaying the ancient Roman foundations and pottery shards found during restoration. Medieval stone walls and brick arches contrast pleasingly with the plush, contemporary decor. The comfortable, soundproof bedrooms, many with good views, are done in coordinated patterns and soft colors; the ample bathrooms feature beige travertine marble. Brunelleschi ranks high for atmosphere, interest, and comfort. ⊠ *Piazza Sant'Elisabetta (Via dei Calzaiuoli),* ☎ *055/562068,* 🖷 *055/219653. 96 rooms with bath, 7 junior suites. Restaurant, bar, meeting rooms. AE, DC, MC, V.*

$$$ 🖬 **J&J.** Away from the crowds, on a quiet street within walking distance of the sights, this unusual hotel is a converted 16th-century monastery. Its large, suitelike rooms are ideal for honeymooners, families, and small groups of friends traveling together. Some rooms are on two levels, and all are imaginatively arranged around a central courtyard and decorated with flair. There are also smaller, more intimate rooms, some opening onto their own little courtyard. The gracious owners chat with guests in the elegant lounge; breakfast is served in a glassed-in Renaissance loggia or in the central courtyard. ⊠ *Via di Mezzo 20,* ☎ *055/234–5005,* 🖷 *055/240282. 20 rooms with bath. Bar. AE, DC, MC, V.*

$$$ 🖬 **Kraft.** The efficient and comfortable Kraft is modern, but it has many period-style rooms, some with balconies, and a rooftop terrace café. Its location near the Teatro Comunale (it is also next to the U.S. consulate) gives it a clientele from the music world. ⊠ *Via Solferino 2,* ☎ *055/284273,* 🖷 *055/239–8267. 78 rooms with bath. Pool. AE, DC, MC, V.*

$$$ 🖬 **Monna Lisa.** Housed in a Renaissance palazzo, the hotel retains its
★   original marble staircase, terra-cotta floors, and painted ceilings. Its rooms still have a rather homey quality, and though on the small side, many have contemplative views of a lovely garden. The ground-floor lounges give you the feel of living in an aristocratic town house. ⊠ *Borgo Pinti 27,* ☎ *055/247–9751,* 🖷 *055/247–9755. 30 rooms with bath. Bar. AE, DC, MC, V.*

$$$ 🖬 **Plaza Hotel Lucchesi.** Elegant without being ostentatious, this hotel
★   is right on the Arno near Santa Croce. Front bedrooms have views of the river and hills beyond; rear rooms on the top floor have balconies and knockout views of Santa Croce. Spacious, quiet bedrooms (double glazing throughout) are furnished comfortably in mahogany and pastel fabrics against creamy white walls. The roomy, welcoming lounges and piano bar are favorite meeting places for Florentines. ⊠ *Lungarno della Zecca Vecchia 38,* ☎ *055/26236,* 🖷 *055/248–0921. 97 rooms with bath. Restaurant, piano bar, parking (fee). AE, DC, MC, V.*

$$ 🖬 **Bencistà.** Below the luxurious Villa San Michele in Fiesole, this hotel has the same tranquil setting and is even two centuries older. The rooms are furnished with antiques, and half board is required. ⊠ *Via Benedetto da Maiano 4, Fiesole,* ☎ *055/59163,* 🖷 *055/59163. 40 rooms, 30 with bath. No credit cards.*

$$ ⊞ **Hermitage.** Comfortable and charming are suitable adjectives for this hotel occupying the top two floors of a palazzo next to Ponte Vecchio and the Uffizi. Inviting living rooms overlooking the Arno, bright breakfast rooms, flowered roof terrace, and well-lighted bedrooms have the decor and atmosphere of a well-kept Florentine home. Double glazing, air-conditioning, and attentive maintenance sustain the relaxing ambience. (The hotel has an elevator at the top of a short flight of stairs from the street.) ⊠ *Vicolo Marzio 1 (Piazza del Pesce, Ponte Vecchio),* ☎ *055/287216,* Ⅲ *055/212208. 29 rooms with bath. MC, V.*

$$ ⊞ **La Residenza.** Centrally located on Florence's most elegant shopping street, on the upper floors of a restored 15th-century building, La Residenza has character and comfort. The roof garden and adjacent sitting room are added attractions. Paintings and etchings add interest to the room decor, while soundproofing and satellite TV help guests to relax. ⊠ *Via Tornabuoni 8,* ☎ *055/218684,* ⅢX *055/284197. 24 rooms, 20 with bath. Restaurant, parking (fee). AE, DC, MC, V.*

$$ ⊞ **Loggiato dei Serviti.** This hotel was not designed by Brunelleschi,
★ Florence's architectural genius, but it might as well have been. A mirror image of the architect's famous Ospedale degli Innocenti across the way, the Loggiato is tucked away on one of the city's quietest and loveliest squares. Occupying a 16th-century former monastery, the building was originally a refuge for traveling priests. Vaulted ceilings and tasteful furnishings, some of them antiques, make this a place for those who want to get the feel of Florence in a spare, Renaissance building while enjoying modern creature comforts. The hotel has no restaurant. ⊠ *Piazza Santissima Annunziata 3,* ☎ *055/289592,* ⅢX *055/289595. 29 rooms with bath. AE, DC, MC, V.*

$$ ⊞ **Morandi alla Crocetta.** Near Piazza Santissima Annunziata, this is
★ a charming and distinguished residence in which guests are made to feel like privileged friends of the family. It is close to the sights but very quiet, in a former monastery, and is furnished comfortably in the classic style of a gracious Florentine home. The Morandi is not only an exceptional hotel but also a good value. Very small, it is worth booking well in advance. ⊠ *Via Laura 50,* ☎ *055/234–4747,* ⅢX *055/248–0954. 10 rooms with bath. AE, DC, MC, V.*

$$ ⊞ **Pendini.** The atmosphere of an old-fashioned Florentine pensione is intact here, though most bedrooms have been freshly renovated. Public rooms are delightful; furnishings throughout are early 19th-century antiques or reproductions. Most bedrooms have brass or walnut beds, pretty floral wallpaper, and pastel carpeting; baths are modern. Many rooms can accommodate extra beds. The location is central, and rates are low for the category. Off season rates are a real bargain. ⊠ *Via Strozzi 2,* ☎ *055/211170,* ⅢX *055/281807. 42 rooms with bath. AE, DC, MC, V.*

$ ⊞ **Alessandra.** The location, a block from the Ponte Vecchio, and clean, ample rooms make this a good choice. The English-speaking staff is friendly and helpful. ⊠ *Borgo Santi Apostoli 17,* ☎ *055/283438. 25 rooms, 18 with bath. AE, MC, V.*

$ ⊞ **Apollo.** A friendly Italian-Canadian couple owns and manages this conveniently located hotel near the station, offering good value in spacious rooms decorated in Florentine style. The gleaming new bathrooms, though compact, have such amenities as hair dryers. The staff is helpful and attentive to guests' needs. ⊠ *Via Faenza 77,* ☎ *055/284119,* ⅢX *055/210101. 15 rooms with bath. Parking (fee). AE, DC, MC, V.*

$ ⊞ **Bellettini.** You couldn't ask for anything more central; this small hotel
★ is on three floors (the top floor has two nice rooms with a view) of a palazzo near the Duomo. The cordial family management takes good care of guests, providing a relaxed atmosphere and attractive public rooms with a scattering of antiques. Breakfast, with homemade cakes, and air-conditioning are included in the low room rate. The good-size

rooms have Venetian or Tuscan provincial decor; bathrooms are bright and modern. ✉ *Via dei Conti 7,* ☎ *055/213561,* FAX *055/283551. 28 rooms with bath. Bar, parking (fee). AE, DC, MC, V.*

$ 🏨 Liana. This small hotel near the English Cemetery is in a quiet 19th-century villa that formerly housed the British Embassy. Its clean and pleasant rooms all face a stately garden. ✉ *Via Vittorio Alfieri 18,* ☎ *055/245303,* FAX *055/234–4596. 17 rooms with bath or shower. AE, MC, V.*

$ 🏨 Nuova Italia. Near the train station and within walking distance of the sights, this hotel is run by a genial English-speaking family. It has a homey atmosphere; rooms are clean and simply furnished, bright with pictures and posters, and all with private baths. Some rooms can accommodate extra beds. Low bargain rates include breakfast. ✉ *Via Faenza 26,* ☎ *055/268430,* FAX *055/210941. 20 rooms with bath. AE, DC, MC, V.*

NIGHTLIFE AND THE ARTS

The Arts

Concerts

The **Maggio Musicale Fiorentina** series of internationally acclaimed concerts and recitals is held in the Teatro Comunale (✉ Corso Italia 16, ☎ 055/277–9236) from late April through June. From December to early June, there is a concert season of the **Orchestra Regionale Toscana** in the church of Santo Stefano al Ponte Vecchio (☎ 055/210804). **Amici della Musica** organizes concerts at the Teatro della Pergola (✉ Box office, Via della Pergola 10/r, ☎ 055/247–9652).

Opera

Operas are performed in the Teatro Comunale from December through February.

Film

English-language films are shown at the **Cinema Astro** on Piazza San Simone near Santa Croce. There are two shows every evening, Tuesday through Sunday (closed in July).

Festival del Popolo. This festival, held each December, is devoted to documentaries and is held in the Fortezza da Basso.

Florence Film Festival. An international panel of judges gathers in late spring at the Forte di Belvedere to preside over a wide selection of new releases.

Nightlife

Unlike the Romans and Milanese, the frugal and reserved Florentines do not have a reputation for an active nightlife; however, the following places attract a mixed crowd of Florentines and visitors.

Piano Bars

Many of the more expensive hotels have their own piano bars, where nonguests are welcome to come for an *aperitivo* or an after-dinner drink. The best view is from the bar at the **Excelsior** (✉ Piazza Ognissanti 3, ☎ 055/264201), on a roof garden overlooking the Arno. The accent is on Brazil at **Caffè Voltaire** (✉ Via della Scala 9/r, ☎ 055/218255), where there's Latin food and music. Music is on tape at the **Champagneria** (✉ Via Lambruschini 15/r, ☎ 055/490804), a bistro-type watering hole (closed Sun.).

Nightclub

River Club (✉ Lungarno Corsini 8, ☎ 055/282465) has winter-garden decor and a large dance floor (closed Sun.).

Discos

The two largest discos, with the youngest crowds, are **Yab** (✉ Via Sassetti 5r, ☎ 055/282018) and **Space Electronic** (✉ Via Palazzuolo 37, ☎ 055/239–3082). Less frenetic alternatives are **Jackie O'** (✉ Via Erta Canina 24, ☎ 055/234–4904) and **Full Up** (✉ Via della Vigna Vecchia 21/r, ☎ 055/293006). **Meccanò** (✉ Viale degli Olmi 1, in Cascine Park, ☎ 055/331371) is a multimedia experience in a high-tech disco with a late-night restaurant (closed Mon.).

OUTDOOR ACTIVITIES AND SPORTS

Participant Sports

Bicycling

Bikes are a good way of getting out into the hills, but the scope for biking is limited in the center of town. *See* Getting Around *in* Florence A to Z, *below,* for information on where to rent bicycles.

Canoeing

Those who get the urge to paddle on the Arno can try **Società Canottieri Firenze** (✉ Lungarno dei Medici 8, ☎ 055/282130) near the Uffizi.

Golf

Golf Club Ugolino (✉ Via Chiantigiana 3, Impruneta, ☎ 055/230–1009) is a hilly 18-hole course in the heart of Chianti country just outside town. It is open to the public.

Jogging

Don't even think of jogging on city streets, where tour buses and triple-parked Alfa Romeos leave precious little space for pedestrians. Instead, head for the **Cascine,** the park along the Arno at the western end of the city. You can jog to the Cascine along the Lungarno (stay on the sidewalk), or take Bus 17 from the Duomo. A cinder track lies on the hillside just below **Piazzale Michelangelo,** across the Arno from the city center. The views of the Florence skyline are inspirational, but the locker rooms are reserved for members, so come ready to run.

Swimming

There are a number of pools open to foreigners who want to beat the Florentine heat, among them **Bellariva** (✉ Lungarno Colombo 6, ☎ 055/677521), **Circolo Tennis alle Cascine** (✉ Viale Visarno 1, ☎ 055/356651), **Costoli** (Viale Paoli, ☎ 055/675–744), and **Le Pavoniere** (✉ Viale degli Olmi, ☎ 055/367506).

Tennis

The best spot for an open court is **Circolo Tennis alle Cascine** (✉ Viale Visarno 1, ☎ 055/356651). Other centers include **Tennis Club Rifredi** (✉ Via Facibeni, ☎ 055/432552) and **Il Poggetto** (✉ Via Mercati 24/b, ☎ 055/460127).

Spectator Sports

Horse Racing

You can make your bets at the **Ippodromo Visarno** (✉ Piazzale delle Cascine, ☎ 055/360056). Check the local papers to see when they're running.

Soccer

Calcio (soccer) is a passion with the Italians, and the Florentines are no exception; indeed, *tifosi* (fans) of the Fiorentina team are renowned for their passionate support. The team plays its home games at the Stadio Comunale (Municipal Stadium) at the top of Viale Manfredo Fanti. Tickets for all games (which are played on Sunday afternoons) except those against their biggest rivals, Juventus of Turin and A. C. Milan, are difficult but not impossible to come by; try the Chiosco degli Sportivi, a ticket booth on the north side of Piazza della Repubblica. The season runs from about late August to May. A medieval version of the game is played in costume each year on or around June 24, feast day of St. John the Baptist.

SHOPPING

Shops in Florence are generally open from 9 to 1 and 3:30 to 7:30 and closed Sundays and Monday mornings most of the year. During the summer the hours are usually 9 to 1 and 4 to 8, with closings on Saturday afternoons but not Monday mornings. When locating the stores, remember that the addresses with *r* in them, which stands for *rosso* (red), and indicates a commercial address, follow a separate numbering system from the black residential addresses. A rule of thumb for shopping in Florence is that if it *looks* expensive, it will more than likely be *more* expensive than you had anticipated. Most shops take major credit cards and will ship purchases, though it's wiser to take your purchases with you.

Borgo Ognissanti

Alberto Pierini (⊠ Borgo Ognissanti 22/r). The rustic Tuscan furniture here is all antique, and much of it dates back to the days of the Medici.
Fallani Best (⊠ Borgo Ognissanti 15/r). The eclectic collection of antiques, although it concentrates on 18th- and 19th-century Italian paintings, has enough variety to appeal to an international clientele.
Giotti (⊠ Piazza Ognissanti 3/r). The largest selection of Bottega Veneta's woven-leather bags are stocked at this shop, which carries a full line of the firm's other leather goods, as well as its own leather clothing.
Loretta Caponi (⊠ Borgo Ognissanti 12/r). Signora Caponi is synonymous with Florentine embroidery, and her luxury lace, linens, and lingerie have earned her a worldwide reputation.
Paolo Ventura (⊠ Borgo Ognissanti 16/r). Specialties here are antique ceramics from all periods and places of origin. As with the other shops, the rule of thumb is that the Italian goods are best.
Pratesi (⊠ Lungarno Amerigo Vespucci 8/r). The name Pratesi is a byword for luxury, in this case linens that have lined the beds of the rich and famous, with an emphasis on the former.

Duomo

Bartolini (⊠ Via dei Servi 30/r). For housewares, nothing beats this shop, which has a wide selection of well-designed, practical items.
Calamai (⊠ Via Cavour 78/r). One of Florence's largest gift shops, Calamai carries everything from inexpensive stationery to housewares in bright, bold colors and designs in its largest of three stores.
Casa dello Sport (⊠ Via dei Tosinghi 8/r). Here you'll find casual wear for the entire family—sporty clothes by some of Italy's most famous manufacturers.
Emilio Pucci (⊠ Via dei Pucci 6/r). A member of an aristocratic Italian family, the Marchese di Barsento was a household name in Florence, and until his death in 1992, he presided over the opening of the Renaissance *Calcio in Costume* festivities each year. He became an in-

ternational name during the early 1960s, when the stretch ski clothes
he designed for himself caught on with the dolce vita crowd. His prints
and "palazzo pajamas" then became the rage. The shop in the family
palazzo still sells the celebrated Pucci prints, along with a line of wines
from the family estate in Chianti.

Pineider (⊠ Piazza della Signoria 14/r and Via Tornabuoni 76/r). Pineider now has shops throughout the world, but it began in Florence and
still does all its printing here. Personalized stationery and business cards
are its main business, but the stores also sell fine desk accessories.

Ponte Vecchio

Della Loggia (⊠ Via Por Santa Maria 29/r). For a contemporary look,
try this store, which combines precious and semiprecious stones in settings made of precious and nonprecious metals, such as the gold and
steel pieces usually on display in its windows.

Gherardi (⊠ Ponte Vecchio 5). The king of coral in Florence has the
city's largest selection of finely crafted and encased specimens, as well
as other precious materials such as cultured pearls, jade, and turquoise.

Melli (⊠ Ponte Vecchio 44/r). Antique jewelry is the specialty here; it
is displayed alongside period porcelains, clocks, and other museum-
quality objects.

Piccini (⊠ Ponte Vecchio 23/r). This venerable shop has literally been
crowning the heads of Europe for almost a century, and combines its
taste for the antique with contemporary jewelry.

Oltrarno

Centro Di (Piazza dei Mozzi 1). Its name stands for Centro di Docu-
mentazione Internazionale, and it publishes art books and exhibition
catalogues for some of the most important organizations in Europe.
Centro Di stocks its own publications along with many others.

Galleria Luigi Bellini (⊠ Lungarno Soderini 5). The Galleria claims to
be Italy's oldest antiques dealer, which may be true, since father Mario
Bellini was responsible for instituting Florence's international antiques
biennial. At any rate, what matters is that the merchandise is genuine.

Giannini (⊠ Piazza Pitti 37/r). One of Florence's oldest paper-goods
stores, Giannini is *the* place to buy the marbleized versions, which come
in a variety of forms, from flat sheets to boxes and even pencils.

Santa Croce

I Maschereri (⊠ Borgo Pinti 18/r). Spurred on by the revival of Carnival in recent years, I Maschereri has begun to produce fanciful masks
in commedia dell'arte and contemporary styles.

Leather Guild (⊠ Piazza Santa Croce 20/r). This is one of many such
shops throughout the area that produce inexpensive, antique-looking
leather goods of mass appeal, but here you can see the craftspersons
at work, a reassuring experience.

Salimbeni (⊠ Via Matteo Palmieri 14/r). Long one of Florence's best
art bookshops, Salimbeni specializes in publications on Tuscany; it publishes many itself.

Sbigoli Terrecotte (⊠ Via Sant'Egidio 4/r). This crafts shop carries a
wide selection of terra-cotta and ceramic vases, pots, cups, and saucers.

Via Maggio

Giovanni Pratesi (⊠ Via Maggio 13/r). This shop specializes in Italian
antiques, in this case furniture, with some fine paintings, sculpture, and
decorative objects turning up from time to time.

Guido Bartolozzi (⊠ Via Maggio 18/r). Vying with Luigi Bellini as one
of Florence's oldest antiques dealers, Bartolozzi's collection of pre-
dominately Florentine objects from all periods is as highly selected as
it is priced.

Paolo Paoletti (⌧ Via Maggio 30/r). Look for Florentine antiques, with an emphasis on Medici-era objects from the 15th and 16th centuries.
Soluzioni (⌧ Via Maggio 82/r). This offbeat store displays some of the most unusual items on this staid street, ranging from clocks to compacts, all selected with an eye for the eccentric.

Via della Vigna Nuova

Alinari (⌧ Via della Vigna Nuova 46/r). This outlet is one of Florence's oldest and most prestigious photographers, and in this store, next to its museum, prints of its historic photographs are sold along with books and posters.
Antico Setificio Fiorentino (⌧ Via della Vigna Nuova 97/r). This fabric outlet really *is* antique, as it has produced antique fabrics for over half a millennium. Swaths of handmade material of every style and description are for sale, and the decorative tassels make lovely typically Florentine presents as well.
Et Cetera (⌧ Via della Vigna Nuova 82/r). In a city of papermakers, this store has some of the most unusual such items, most of which are handmade and some of which have made it into the design collection of New York's Museum of Modern Art.
Filpucci (⌧ Via della Vigna Nuova 14/r). This is Italy's largest manufacturer of yarns. Nearby factories produce skeins of the stuff for Italy's top designers, and the extensive stock of its retail outlet in Florence encourages the talented to create their own designs.
Il Bisonte (⌧ Via del Parione 31/r). The street address is just off Via della Vigna Nuova; Il Bisonte is known for its natural-look leather goods, all stamped with the store's bison symbol.
Laurèl (⌧ Via della Vigna Nuova 67/r). An elegant boutique, Laurèl has a reputation for the quality and understatement that is the hallmark of Florentine women's fashions.

Via Tornabuoni

Casadei (⌧ Via Tornabuoni 33/r). The ultimate fine leathers are crafted into classic shapes here, winding up as women's shoes and bags.
Ferragamo (⌧ Via Tornabuoni 16/r). Born near Naples, the late Salvatore Ferragamo made his fortune custom-making exotic shoes for famous feet, especially Hollywood stars, and so this establishment knows about less-than-delicate shoe sizes. His palace at the end of the street has since passed on to his wife, Wanda, and displays designer clothing, but elegant footwear still underlies the Ferragamo success.
Gucci (⌧ Via Tornabuoni 73/r). The Gucci family is practically single-handedly responsible for making designers' initials (in this case the two interlocking Gs) a status symbol. This Florence store is the one that started it all, and prices on the clothing and leather goods are slightly better here than elsewhere.
Settepassi-Faraone (⌧ Via Tornabuoni 25/r). One of Florence's oldest jewelers, Settepassi-Faraone has supplied Italian (and other) royalty with finely crafted gems for centuries. Its selection of antique-looking classics has been updated with a choice of contemporary silver.
Ugolini (⌧ Via Tornabuoni 20/r). This shop once made gloves for the Italian royal family, but now anyone who can afford it can have the luxury of its exotic leathers, as well as silk and cashmere ties and scarves.

SIDE TRIPS

Fiesole

An excursion to the ancient Roman town of **Fiesole,** set in the hills 8 kilometers (5 miles) above Florence, gives you a respite from museums and breaks up the inevitable monotony of city sightseeing. Fiesole began life as an ancient Etruscan and later Roman village that held some power until it succumbed to the barbarian invasions and eventually gave up its independence in exchange for Florence's protection. The medieval cathedral, some other old churches, the ancient Roman amphitheater, and lovely old villas behind garden walls are clustered on a series of hilltops. Fiesole is a place for walking and admiring the views; a nice half-day jaunt in fair weather.

The ride from Florence by car or bus takes about 20 minutes. A walk around Fiesole can take from one to two or three hours, depending on how far you stroll from the main piazza.

Take city Bus 7 from the Santa Maria Novella train station, Piazza San Marco, or the Duomo to Fiesole. The cathedral and other old buildings are on the main piazza, and the Roman amphitheater is about 30 yards away. Climb the hill to the church of San Francesco to get to the terrace for a good view of Florence and the plain below. The air is usually clearest early in the morning or late in the afternoon. If you really want to stretch your legs, walk along Via Vecchia Fiesolana, a narrow lane, to the church of San Domenico and the Badia Fiesolana, Fiesole's cathedral, 4 kilometers (2½ miles) southwest of Fiesole.

The **Duomo** has a stark medieval interior. In the raised presbytery, the Salutati Chapel was frescoed by 15th-century artist Cosimo Rosselli, but it was his contemporary, sculptor Mino da Fiesole, who put the town on the artistic map. The Madonna on the altarpiece and the tomb of Bishop Salutati are his work.

Nightlife and the Arts

Estate Fiesolana. From June through August, this festival of theater, music, dance, and film takes place in the churches and the archaeological area of Fiesole (✉ Teatro Romano, Fiesole, ☎ 055/599931).

FLORENCE A TO Z

Arriving and Departing

By Bus

Long-distance buses run by **SITA** (✉ Via Santa Caterina da Siena 15/r, ☎ 055/483651 weekdays, 211487 on weekends) and **Lazzi Eurolines** (✉ Via Mercadante 2, ☎ 055/215154) offer inexpensive if somewhat claustrophobic service between Florence and other cities in Italy and Europe.

By Car

Florence is connected to the north and south of Italy by the Autostrada del Sole (A1). It is about an hour's scenic drive from Bologna (although heavy truck traffic over the Apennines often makes for slower going) and about three hours from Rome. The Tyrrhenian coast is an hour away on A11 West. In the city, abandon all hope of using a car, since most of the downtown area is a pedestrian zone. For traffic information in Florence, call 055/577–777.

By Plane

The A. Vespucci Airport, called **Peretola** (☎ 055/333–498), is 10 kilometers (6 miles) northwest of Florence. Although it accommodates flights from Milan, Rome, and some European cities, it is still a relatively minor airport. **Galileo Galilei Airport** in Pisa (☎ 050/500–707) is 80 kilometers (50 miles) west of Florence and is used by most international carriers; for flight information, call the Florence Air Terminal at Santa Maria Novella train station (☎ 055/216–073) or Galilei airport information.

International travelers flying on Alitalia to Rome's **Leonardo da Vinci Airport** and headed directly for Florence can make connections at the airport for a flight to Florence, but if the layover is a long one, consider taking the FS airport train to Termini station in Rome, where fast trains for Florence are frequent during the day.

BETWEEN THE AIRPORTS AND DOWNTOWN

By Bus. There is no direct bus service from Pisa's airport to Florence. Buses do go to Pisa itself, but then you have to change to a slow train service. There is a local bus service from Peretola to Florence.

By Car. From Peretola take autostrada A11 directly into the city. Driving from the airport in Pisa, take S67, a direct route to Florence.

By Train. A scheduled service connects the station at Pisa's Galileo Galilei Airport with Santa Maria Novella Station in Florence, roughly a one-hour trip. Trains start running about 7 AM from the airport, 6 AM from Florence, and continue service every hour until about 11:30 PM from the airport, 8 PM from Florence. You can check in for departing flights at the air terminal at Track 5 of the train station (☎ 055/216–073).

By Train

Florence is on the principal Italian train route between most European capitals and Rome and within Italy is served quite frequently from Milan, Venice, and Rome by nonstop Intercity (IC) trains. The **Santa Maria Novella Station** is near the downtown area; avoid trains that stop only at the Campo di Marte Station in an inconvenient location on the east side of the city. For train information in Florence, call 055/288–785.

Getting Around

By Bicycle

Brave souls (cycling in Florence is difficult, at best) may rent bicycles at easy-to-spot locations at Fortezza da Basso, the Santa Maria Novella train station, and Piazza Pitti, from **Alinari** (⊠ Via San Zanobi 9/r, ☎ 055/490–113) or **Motorent** (⊠ Via Guelfa 85/r, ☎ 055/280–500), or from **Ciao e Basta** (⊠ Lungarno Pecori Girardi 1, ☎ 055/234–2726).

By Bus

Maps and timetables are available for a small fee at the **ATAF** booth next to the train station or at the office at Piazza del Duomo 57/r, or for free at visitor information offices (☞ Contacts and Resources, *below*). Tickets must be bought in advance and can be purchased at tobacco stores, newsstands, from automatic ticket machines near main stops, or at ATAF booths (next to the station and at strategic locations throughout the city). The ticket must be canceled in the small validation machine immediately upon boarding. Two types of tickets are available, both valid for one or more rides on all lines. One costs 1,400 lire and is valid for 60 minutes from the time it is first canceled; the other costs 1,900 lire and is valid for 120 minutes. A multiple ticket—four tickets each valid for 60 minutes—costs 5,400 lire. A 24-hour tourist ticket costs 5,000 lire. Long-term visitors or frequent users of the bus should consider a monthly pass, which is sold at the ATAF office.

By Moped

Those who want to go native and rent a noisy Vespa (Italian for "wasp") or other make of motorcycle or moped may do so at **Motorent** or **Alinari** (☞ By Bicycle, *above*). Helmets are mandatory and can be rented at either place.

By Taxi

Taxis usually wait at stands throughout the city (such as in front of the train station and in Piazza della Repubblica), or they can be called (☎ 055/4390 or 055/4798). The meter starts at 4,000 lire.

Contacts and Resources

Consulates

U.S. Consulate. (⊠ Lungarno Vespucci 38, ☎ 055/239–8276. ☉ Weekdays 8:30–noon and 2–4). **U.K. Consulate.** (⊠ Lungarno Corsini 2, ☎ 055/284133. ☉ Weekdays 9:30–12:30 and 2:30–4:30). **Canadians** should contact their embassy in Rome.

Doctors and Dentists

For English-speaking doctors and dentists, get a list from the U.S. consulate, or contact **Tourist Medical Service** (⊠ Viale Lorenzo Il Magnifico, ☎ 055/475411).

Emergencies

Police: (☎ 113); main police station (⊠ Via Zara 2, near Piazza della Libertà). **Ambulance:** (☎ 118), or Misericordia (⊠ Piazza del Duomo 20, ☎ 055/212222). If you need hospital treatment—and an interpreter—you can call AVO, a group of volunteer interpreters who offer their services free (☎ 055/403126; Mon., Wed., Fri. 4–6 PM, ☎ 055/234–4567).

English-Language Bookstores

Paperback Exchange (⊠ Via Fiesolana 31/r, ☎ 055/247–8154) will do just that, besides selling books outright. **BM Bookshop** (⊠ Borgo Ognissanti 4/r, ☎ 055/294575) has a fine selection of books on Florence. **Seeber** (⊠ Via Tornabuoni 68, ☎ 055/215697) has English-language books alongside the other titles. ☉ *All are open 9–1 and 3:30–7:30. Closed Sun. and Mon. morning.*

Guided Tours

EXCURSIONS

Contact bus operators (☞ Arriving and Departing, *above*) a day in advance, if possible, because excursions are popular. Comfortable buses with English-speaking guides make full-day trips from Florence to Siena and San Gimignano (departure 9 AM, return 6 PM, lunch not included) and afternoon excursions to Pisa (departure 2 PM, return 7 PM), with pickup and return from the main hotels. The Siena excursion costs about 68,000 lire, the Pisa excursion about 48,000 lire. Good bus and train connections make it easy for you to do these on your own, however.

ORIENTATION TOURS

Visitors who have a limited amount of time in Florence may find guided tours an efficient way of covering the city's major sights. The major bus operators (☞ Arriving and Departing, *above*) offer half-day itineraries, all of which generally follow the same plan, using comfortable buses staffed with English-speaking guides. Morning tours begin at 9, when buses pick visitors up at the main hotels. Stops include the cathedral complex, the Accademia, Piazzale Michalangelo, and the Pitti Palace (or, on Mondays, the Museo dell'Opera del Duomo). Afternoon tours stop at the main hotels at 2 PM and take in Piazza della Signoria, the Uffizi Gallery (or the Palazzo Vecchio on Monday, when the Uffizi is closed), the nearby town of Fiesole, and, on the return, the church of Santa Croce. A half-day tour costs about 48,000 lire, including museum admissions.

Late-Night Pharmacies

The following are open 24 hours a day, seven days a week. (For others, ☎ 055/110.)

Comunale No. 13 (✉ Santa Maria Novella Station, ☎ 055/289435). **Molteni** (✉ Via Calzaiuoli 7/r, ☎ 055/289490). **Taverna** (✉ Piazza San Giovanni 20/r, ☎ 055/284013).

Travel Agencies

American Express (✉ Via Guicciardini 49/r, near Piazza Pitti, ☎ 055/288751; ✉ Via Dante Alighiere 20/r, ☎ 055/50981) is also represented by **Universalturismo** (✉ Via Speziali 7/r, off Piazza della Repubblica, ☎ 055/217241). **CIT** (✉ Via Cavour 56, ☎ 055/294306; ✉ Piazza Stazione 51, ☎ 055/239–6963). **Thomas Cook** is represented by **World Vision** (✉ Via Cavour 154/r, ☎ 055/579294). All agencies are open weekdays 9–12:30 and 3:30–7:30, Saturday 9–noon.

Visitor Information

The city information office is open from 8:30 to 7 Via Cavour 1/r (✉ next to Palazzo Medici–Riccardi, ☎ 055/290–832). Another municipal information office is next to the train station (☎ 055/212245; closed after 2 PM in winter). There is another information office near Piazza della Signoria (✉ Chiasso dei Baroncelli 17/r, ☎ 055/230–2124).

The **APT** (tourist office) is just off Piazza Beccaria (✉ Via Manzoni 16, ☎ 055/234–6284. ☉ Mon.–Sat. 8:30–1:30).

4 **Tuscany**

Lucca, Siena, and the Hill Towns

Without a doubt, Nature outdid herself in Tuscany. Punctuated by thickly wooded hills, snowcapped peaks, sun-warmed vineyards, olive groves, and dramatic hill towns, Tuscany's milk-and-honey vistas have changed little since Renaissance artists first beheld them.

ROME MAY BE THE CAPITAL OF ITALY, but Tuscany is its heart. Stretching from the Apennines to the sea, midway between Milan and Rome, the region is quintessentially Italian, in both its appearance and its history. Its scenic variety is unmatched in Italy; its past has been ignoble (it produced the Guelph–Ghibelline conflict of the Middle Ages) and glorious (it gave birth to the Renaissance). Its towns are justly famous for their wealth of fine architecture and art, but visitors often go home even more enthusiastic about Tuscany's unspoiled hilly landscapes, about the delicious Chianti wines produced by vineyards on those hills, and about the robust and flavorful Tuscan cooking. Be sure to allot some portion of your time here for leisurely strolls, unhurried meals, and aimless wandering around this peerless countryside, where the true soul of Tuscany is to be found.

Tuscany also produced the Italian language. Thanks to the eminence of their writings, it was the Tuscan dialect of Dante, Petrarch, and Boccaccio, all native sons, that grew to be the national tongue, a fact of which the Tuscans are rightly proud. Today the purest Italian is said to be spoken in the area between Siena and Arezzo, and even visitors with limited textbook Italian can often hear the difference. As they enter the region, the language suddenly becomes much easier to understand and takes on a bell-like clarity and mellifluous beauty unequaled throughout the rest of Italy.

It also takes on a notorious wit. As a common proverb has it, "Tuscans have Paradise in their eyes and the Inferno in their mouths" (a wry reference to Dante), and the sting of their wit is as famous throughout Italy as is the beauty of their speech. Happily, the Tuscans usually reserve their wit for each other and treat visitors with complete and sincere courtesy.

For a long time, the Tuscan hill towns were notorious as well. Even their earliest civilized settlers, the Etruscans, chose their city-sites for defensive purposes (the fortress-town of Fiesole, above Florence, is a fine surviving example). With the end of the Roman Empire, the region fell into disunity, and by the 11th century, Tuscany had evolved into a collection of independent city-states, each city seeking to dominate, and sometimes forcibly overpower, its neighbors. The region then became embroiled in an apparently endless international quarrel between a long succession of popes and Holy Roman Emperors. By the 13th century, Tuscany had become a battleground: The infamous conflict between the Guelphs and the Ghibellines had begun.

The Guelphs and the Ghibellines are the bane of Italian schoolchildren; their infinitely complicated, bloody history is to Italy what the Wars of the Roses are to England. To oversimplify grossly, the Ghibellines were mostly allied with both the Holy Roman Emperor (headquartered over the Alps in Germany) and the local aristocracy (dominated by feudal lords); the Guelphs were mostly allied with both the pope (headquartered in Rome) and the emerging middle class (dominated by the new trade guilds). Florence, flourishing as a trade center, was (most of the time) Guelph; its neighboring city-states Pisa and Siena were (most of the time) Ghibelline. But the bitter struggles that resulted were so byzantine in their complexity, so full of factional disputes and treachery, that a dizzying series of conflicts within conflicts resulted. (Dante, for instance, was banished from Florence not for being a Ghibelline but for being the wrong brand of Guelph.)

Eventually the Florentine Guelphs emerged victorious, and in the 15th century the region was united to become the Grand Duchy of Tuscany, controlled from Florence by the Medici grand dukes. Today the hill towns are no longer fierce, although they retain a uniquely medieval air, and in most of them the citizens walk the same narrow streets and inhabit the same houses that their ancestors did 600 years ago.

Tuscan art, to most people, means Florence, and understandably so. The city is unique and incomparable, and an astonishing percentage of the great artists of the Renaissance lived and worked there. But there is art elsewhere in Tuscany, and too often it is overlooked in favor of another trip to the Uffizi. Siena, particularly, possesses its own style of architecture and art quite different from the Florentine variety; the contrast is both surprising and illuminating. And even the smallest of the hill towns can possess hidden treasures, for the artists of the Middle Ages and the Renaissance took their work where they could find it. Piero della Francesca's fresco cycle in the church of San Francesco in Arezzo is perhaps the preeminent hidden treasure. Tucked away in a small church in a small town, and, sadly, faded, the frescoes are artistically the equal of almost everything Florence has to offer and are all the more appealing for their uncrowded setting.

Pleasures and Pastimes

Dining

Though Florentine cuisine now predominates throughout Tuscany, the Etruscan influence on regional food still persists after more than three millennia. Just as the ancient Etruscans were responsible for the introduction of the cypress to the Tuscan landscape, so they are also credited with the use of herbs in cooking. Basic ingredients such as tarragon, sage, rosemary, and thyme appear frequently, happily coupled with game, Chianina beef, or even seafood. Each region has its own specialties, usually based on simple ingredients, and Tuscans are disparagingly called *mangiafagioli,* or bean eaters, by other Italians. However, Tuscan chefs have recently discovered the rest of the world, and for better or worse, an "international cuisine" has been gradually making its appearance throughout the region.

Fortunately, Tuscany's wines remain unaltered. Grapes have been cultivated here since Etruscan times, and Chianti still rules the roost (almost literally when selected by the Gallo Nero Black Rooster label, a symbol of one of the region's most powerful wine-growing consortiums; the other is a putto, or cherub). The robust red wine is still a staple on most tables, and the discerning can select from a multitude of other varieties, including such reds as Brunello di Montalcino and Vino Nobile di Montepulciano, and whites such as Valdinievole and Vergine della Valdichiana. The dessert wine *vin santo* is produced throughout the region and is often enjoyed with *biscottini di Prato,* (caramelized cookies which are perfect for dunking)

CATEGORY	COST*
$$$$	over 110,000 lire
$$$	60,000 lire–110,000 lire
$$	35,000 lire–60,000 lire
$	under 35,000 lire

*per person, for a three-course meal, including house wine and taxes

Lodging

Tuscany is not an inexpensive place to stay, especially the main towns and tourist centers. But the selection of options includes some wonderful properties, including some fine Renaissance hotels and even medieval palazzi where you'll feel more like Lorenzo de Medici than a 20th-century tourist. To keep costs down, stick to less-visited towns and farmhouse lodgings.

CATEGORY	COST*
$$$$	over 300,000 lire
$$$	220,000 lire–300,000 lire
$$	100,000 lire–220,000 lire
$	under 100,000 lire

All prices are for a double room for two, including tax and service.

Exploring Tuscany

Tuscany has two basic geographical regions—the area immediately to the south of Florence, which contains the famous Tuscan hill towns, and the area immediately to the west, a string of cities that were historically the enemies of Florence, which fought to control them in order to have access to the sea. We describe each of these regions in its own section, below.

Great Itineraries

Numbers in the text correspond to numbers in the margin and on the maps.

Although Tuscany is relatively small—no sight of importance is more than a few hours' drive from Florence—the desire to linger is strong: Can anyone ever really get enough of sitting on a hillside *terrazza* (terraces) with a good espresso or a robust chianti and watch the evening settle over a landscape of soft-edged hills, proud medieval towns, quiet villages, and cypress-ringed villas?

It only takes a few days for the region to leave an indelible mark on the memory and, for many, the soul. Ten days would allow for leisurely explorations of the main towns and for meandering along country roads to rustic-elegant estates and wineries. If you have five days, you can see the most interesting towns, but you'll need to stick to the main sights and move briskly between destinations. In three days, you can take in all the highlights, if not the small corners.

IF YOU HAVE 3 DAYS

See **Lucca** ④–⑪ and the Leaning Tower in **Pisa** ⑫, then head for 🏨 **San Gimignano** ⑭ to overnight. The next day, spend a few hours in **Siena** ⑮–⑳, then move on to 🏨 **Montepulciano** ㉔ for the night; the following day, see **Arezzo** ㉖ and head back to Florence, your starting point, via the A1.

IF YOU HAVE 5 DAYS

Florence makes a good starting point. From there, head for industrial **Prato** ① to see its striking medieval core; historic **Pistoia** ②, site of bitter Guelph–Ghibelline feuding; and **Montecatini** ③, one of Europe's most famous spas. Overnight in 🏨 **Lucca** ④–⑪ and spend part of the next day exploring this most elegant of cities, then head for **Pisa** ⑫; see the Leaning Tower and then move on to hilltop **Volterra** ⑬, a fortress town, and beautiful 🏨 **San Gimignano** ⑭ the archetypal Tuscan town and a good place to spend your second night. On the third day, while away the morning in **Siena** ⑮–⑳, perhaps Italy's loveliest medieval city, before heading for the **Abbey of Monte Oliveto Maggiore** ㉑, **Montalcino** ㉒ of wine-growing fame, the **Abbey of Sant'Antimo,** and then 🏨 **Montepulciano** ㉔, where you should overnight. Trace your road back on the morning of your fourth day for a tour of **Pienza** ㉓, designed for Pope Pius II to be the perfect Renaissance town. Move on to handsome but underappreciated **Arezzo** ㉖ and 🏨 **Cortona** ㉕, where there are galleries and lodging, visiting **Chiusi** and **Chianciano** along the way. Spend part of your fifth day in Cortona or Arezzo before returning to Florence.

IF YOU HAVE 7 DAYS

More time allows you to see more towns and more in those you visit. Be sure to rent a car if your goal is to soak up the essence of Tuscany—it's the only way to get to many of the vineyards and estates.

As you approach **Prato** ①, you'll have time to visit the Pecci Center of Contemporary Art. In **Montecatini Terme** ③ ride the funicular up to older Montecatini Alto. If you're an architecture buff, extend your visit to **Pisa** ⑫ beyond the main square to include the Renaissance buildings of the Piazza dei Cavalieri. To really see the Tuscan countryside, don't travel south to **Volterra** ⑬ when leaving Pisa; instead, continue toward Florence on the S67 and turn south on the meandering S222, which leads through a region that's perfect for leisurely exploration—for the best experience, always take winding smaller roads to and from the towns of interest. The S222 is also known as the Strada Chiantigiana because it runs through the heart of the Chianti wine-producing country; the most scenic section runs between Strada in Chianti, 16 kilometers (10 miles) south of Florence, and Greve in Chianti, 11 kilometers (7 miles) farther south, where rolling hillsides are planted with vineyards and olive groves. On your way, be sure to visit **Monteriggioni**, a hilltop hamlet encircled by formidable 13th-century walls.

Take time to make the lengthy detour around Colle Val d'Elsa's workaday lower town up to the ridge, where the medieval center remains practically intact. Break the drive to **Arezzo** ㉖ at prosperous-looking **Monte San Savino** and the tiny nearby fortified village of **Gargonza**. For more Tuscan countryside, don't return yet to Florence but instead detour through the Casentino, a mountainous region smothered in a huge forest that is a far cry from the pastoral images often associated with Tuscany. Return to Florence along the winding S67, known in Tuscany as the splendidly scenic Consuma, or "consumer," as it is a road wrought with hairpin turns and blind corners that require even the best driver to be alert.

When to Tour Tuscany

In summer, try to arrive in towns early in the morning. Italians are early risers, and most shops and museums open by 8:30. If you get up at cockcrow, you can avoid both the crowds and the often oppressive heat. In any case, Tuscany is not about late nights; most bars close their shutters at midnight.

If you plan to visit the frescoes in the Palazzo Pubblico in Siena at midday, be prepared to wait in line and, once inside, to be shuffled along by iron-willed guardians eager to see you in and out in the fastest time possible. If you want to photograph the towers of San Gimignano from a distance, do it in early morning, when the light is good and lines of neon-colored, diesel-spewing tour buses snaking up the hill will not ruin a perfect picture.

WESTERN TUSCANY

Tuscan Gateway: Prato, Pistoia, Lucca, and Pisa

Set in the shadows of the rugged coastal Alpi Apuane, where Michelangelo quarried his marble, this area isn't as lush as the south and lacks its vineyards and olive groves. The population centers here are real cities,

Tuscany

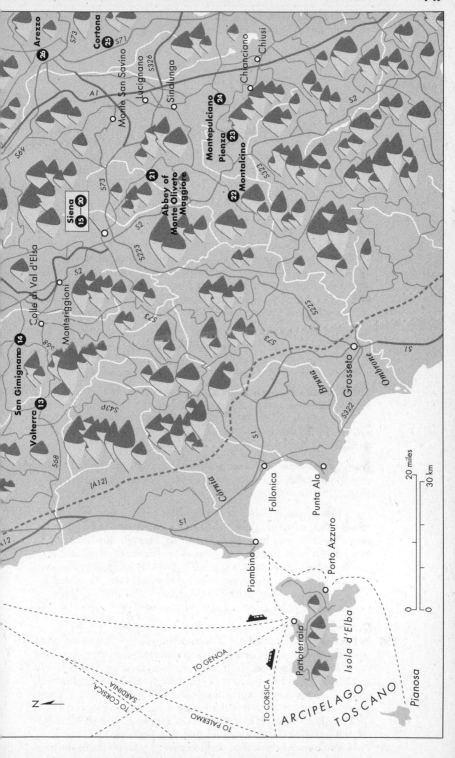

Arezzo **29**

Cortona **25** S71

Chianciano

Chiusi

S73

A1

Monte San Savino

Lucignano S326

Sinalunga

S64

S73

Montepulciano **24**

S2

Pienza **23**

Montalcino **22**

Abbey of Monte Oliveto Maggiore **21**

Siena **15 — 20**

S2

S223

S223

Colle di Val d'Elsa

S2

Monteriggioni

S68

San Gimignano **14**

S73

Volterra **13**

S68

S4,32

(A12)

A12

Cornia

S1

Bruna

S223

Ombrone

S1

Grosseto

S322

S1

Follonica

Punta Ala

Porto Azzuro

Piombino

Portoferraio

Isola d'Elba

ARCIPELAGO TOSCANO

Pianosa

TO GENOA

TO CORSICA/ SARDINIA

TO PALERMO

TO CORSICA

N

20 miles

30 km

with some rather unattractive suburbs in addition to their stunning medieval and Renaissance centers.

Numbers in the margin correspond to points of interest on the Tuscany map.

Prato

❶ *17 km (10.5 mi) northwest of Florence, 60 km (37 mi) east of Lucca.*

The wool industry in this city, one of the world's largest manufacturers of cloth, was known throughout Europe as early as the 13th century. It was further stimulated in the 14th century by a local cloth merchant, Francesco di Marco Datini, who built his business, according to one of his surviving ledgers, "in the name of God and of profit."

Prato's main attraction is its 11th-century **Duomo.** Romanesque in style, it is famous for its Chapel of the Holy Girdle (to the left of the entrance), which enshrines the sash of the Virgin; it is said that the girdle was given to the apostle Thomas by the Virgin herself, when she miraculously appeared after her Assumption. The Duomo also contains 16th-century frescoes by Prato's most famous son, the libertine monk Fra Filippo Lippi; the best known depict Herod's banquet and Salome's dance. ⊠ *Piazza del Duomo.* ☉ *Daily May–Oct. 6:30–noon and 4–7; Nov.–Apr. 6:30–noon, 3:30–6:30.*

Sculpture by Donatello that originally adorned the Duomo's exterior pulpit is now on display in the **Museo dell'Opera del Duomo.** ⊠ *Piazza del Duomo 49,* ☎ *0574/29339.* 🎟 *5,000 lire (includes Galleria Comunale).* ☉ *Mon., Wed.–Sat. 9:30–12:30, 3–6:30; Sun. 9:30–12:30.*

The **Galleria Comunale** contains a good collection of Tuscan and Sienese paintings, mainly from the 14th century. ⊠ *Palazzo Pretorio, Piazza del Comune,* ☎ *0574/452302.* 🎟 *5,000 lire (includes Museo dell'Opera del Duomo).* ☉ *Mon., Wed.–Sat. 9:30–12:30, 3–6:30; Sun. 9:30–12:30.*

Prato's **Pecci Center of Contemporary Art** has a burgeoning collection of works by Italian and other artists. ⊠ *Viale della Repubblica,* ☎ *0574/570620.* 🎟 *10,000 lire.* ☉ *Wed.–Sun. 10–7.*

For a look at gracious country living, Medici style, detour 7 kilometers (4 miles) south of Prato to the elegant **Villa Medici in Poggio a Caiano.** The villa was built by Giuliano da Sangallo for Lorenzo the Magnificent and lavished with frescoes by Andrea del Sarto and Pontormo, among others. 🎟 *4,000 lire.* ☉ *Apr.–May and Sept., Mon.–Sat. 9–5:30; June–Aug., Mon.–Sat. 9–6:30; Mar. and Oct., Mon.–Sat. 9–4:30; Nov.–Feb., Mon.–Sat. 9–3:30. Closed 2nd and 3rd Mon. of month. Ticket office closes 1 hr before closing time.*

Dining

$$$ ✕ **Piraña.** Oddly named for the cannibalistic fish swimming in an aquarium in full view of diners, this sophisticated restaurant, decorated in shades of blue with steely accents, is a local favorite. Seafood is the specialty and may take the form of *bavettine in cacciucco* (linguine with seafood) or *branzine in crosta di sale* (sea bass baked in salt). It's a bit out of the way for sightseers but handy if you have a car, as it's near the Prato Est autostrada exit. ⊠ *Via G. Valentini 110,* ☎ *0574/25746. AE, DC, MC, V. Closed Sun. and Aug. No lunch Sat.*

$$ ✕ **La Veranda.** A large antipasto buffet greets you just inside the door of this restaurant near Prato's 13th-century Castello dell'Imperatore. Although it's an elegant place with its pale pink walls, terra-cotta tiled floors, and Venetian glass chandeliers, the atmosphere is friendly and family oriented. The large menu offers several international dishes, including Spanish paella, but never ignores Tuscan specialties, such as *agnello alla cacciatora* (lamb with a tangy wine-vinegar sauce). ⊠ *Via dell'Arco 10,* ☎ *0574/38235. AE, DC, MC, V. Closed Sun. and Aug. No lunch Sat.*

Shopping
Prato makes hard almond cookies called *biscottini,* ideal for dunking in the beverage of one's choice. They're available at bakeries and food stores around town.

Pistoia

❷ *18 km (11mi) northwest of Prato, 36 km (20 mi) northwest of Florence, 40 km (25 mi) east of Lucca, 108 km (67 mi) north of Siena.*

The town saw the beginning of the bitter Guelph-Ghibelline conflict of the Middle Ages. Reconstructed after heavy bombing during World War II, it contains some fine Romanesque architecture.

The **Cathedral of San Zeno** in the main square (⊠ Piazza del Duomo) houses the *Dossale di San Jacopo,* a magnificent silver altarpiece. The two half-figures on its left side are by Filippo Brunelleschi (1377–1446), better known as the first Renaissance architect (and designer of Florence's magnificent Duomo dome). ☑ *Illumination of altarpiece: 2,000 lire.*

The 14th-century Palazzo del Comune houses the **Museo Civico,** containing medieval art. ⊠ *Museo Civico, Piazza del Duomo,* ☎ *0573/ 371275.* ☑ *5,000 lire; free Sat. 3–7.* ۞ *Tues.–Sat. 9–1 and 3–7, Sun. 9–12:30.*

Also in Pistoia are several other attractions. The **Ospedale del Ceppo** (⊠ Piazza Ospedale, a short way down Via Pacini from Piazza del Duomo), a hospital founded during the 14th century, has a superb early 16th-century terra-cotta frieze by Giovanni della Robbia. In the church of **Sant'Andrea** (⊠ Via Pappe to Via Sant'Andrea), the fine early 14th-century pulpit by Giovanni Pisano depicts the life of Christ.

۞ Just outside town is the **Giardino Zoologico,** especially laid out to accommodate the wiles of both animals and children. ⊠ *Via Pieve a Celle 160, Pistoia,* ☎ *0573/939219.* ☑ *13,000.* ۞ *Apr.–Sept., daily 9– 7; Oct.–Mar., daily 9–5.*

Dining
$$ ✕ **La Casa degli Amici.** The name means "the house of friends," and that's the atmosphere that the two industrious ladies who own it succeed in creating in this restaurant outside Pistoia's old walls, on the road toward the exit of the A11 autostrada. They offer homey specialties such as *ribollita* (a thick soup of white beans, bread, cabbage, and onions), pasta *e fagioli* (with beans), and some creative dishes, too. In summer, you can dine outdoors on the terrace. ⊠ *Via Bonellina 111,* ☎ *0573/ 380305. AE, DC, MC, V. Closed Tues. and Aug. No dinner Sun.*

$$ ✕ **Leon Rosso.** To find this small and usually crowded restaurant, walk straight down Via Roma off the Piazza del Duomo. You'll find Tuscan cuisine, starting with appetizing crostini and *fusilli all'orto* (corkscrew pasta with seasonal vegetables). For dessert try *panna cotta* (milk custard) with caramel sauce. ⊠ *Via Panciatichi 4,* ☎ *0573/29230. AE, DC, MC, V. Closed Sun. and Aug.*

$$ ✕ **Rafanelli.** *Maccheroni all'anatra* (pasta with duck sauce) and other game dishes, the specialties, have been served with careful attention to tradition and quality for more than half a century by the same family. The restaurant is just outside the old city walls in a garden setting that allows for alfresco dining during summer. ⊠ *Via Sant'Agostino*

47, ☎ 0573/532046. AE, DC, MC, V. Closed Mon. and Aug. No dinner Sun.

Montecatini Terme

❸ *16 km (10 mi) west of Pistoia, 48 km (30 mi) west of Florence, 55 km*
(34 mi) northeast of Pisa.

Immortalized in Fellini's 8½, Montecatini Terme is Italy's premier spa,
both for its reputed curative powers and, at least once upon a time,
for its great popularity with the wealthy. It is renowned for its mineral springs, which flow from five sources and are used to treat liver
and skin disorders. Those "taking the cure" report each morning to
one of the town's *stabilimenti termali* (thermal establishments) to
drink their prescribed cupful of water, whose curative effects became
known in the 1800s. The town's wealth of Art Nouveau buildings went
up during its most active period of development, at the beginning of
this century. Of these structures, the most attractive is the **Stabili-
mento Tettuccio,** a neoclassical edifice with colonnades. Here Montecatini's healthful water spouts from fountains set up on marble counters,
the walls are decorated with bucolic scenes depicted on painted ceramic
tiles, and an orchestra plays under a frescoed dome.

An older town of Montecatini, called **Montecatini Alto,** sits on top of
a hill near the spa town and is reached by a funicular.

Lucca

★ ❹ *27 km (17 mi) west of Montecatini Terme, 74 km (46 mi) southeast*
of La Spezia.

It was in this picturesque fortress town that Caesar, Pompey, and Cras-
sus agreed to rule Rome as a triumvirate in 56 BC; it was later the first
town in Tuscany to accept Christianity. Today it still has a mind of its
own, and when most of Tuscany was voting communist as a matter of
course, its citizens rarely followed suit. It is well worth exploring on foot.

Numbers in the margin correspond to points of interest on the Lucca
map.

★ ❺ The main attraction is the **Duomo** (⊠ Piazza del Duomo) on the southern side of town. Its round-arched facade is a fine example of the rigorously ordered Pisan Romanesque style, in this case happily enlivened
by an extremely disordered collection of carved columns. The decoration of the facade and of the porch below are worth a close look;
they make this one of the most entertaining church fronts in Tuscany.
The Gothic interior contains a moving Byzantine crucifix (called the
Volto Santo, or Holy Face), brought here in the 8th century, and the
masterpiece of the Sienese sculptor Jacopo della Quercia, the marble
Tomb of Ilaria del Caretto (1406).

❻ Slightly west of the center of town is the church of **San Michele** (⊠ Piazza San Michele), with a facade even more fanciful than the Duomo's;
it was heavily restored in the 19th century, however, and somewhat
jarringly displays busts of modern Italian patriots such as Garibaldi
and Cavour.

NEED A BREAK?	For dessert, try *buccellato*—a sweet, anise-flavored bread with raisins that is a specialty of Lucca, available at **Pasticceria Taddeucci** (⊠ Piazza San Michele 34)—or a coffee or ice cream at the venerable **Caffè di Simo** (⊠ Via Fillungo), a favorite of Giacomo Puccini, composer of some of the world's best-loved operas.

❼ The church of **San Frediano** (✉ Piazza San Frediano) is just inside the middle of the north town wall; it contains more works by Jacopo della Quercia, and, bizarrely, the lace-clad mummy of the patron saint of domestic servants, Santa Zita. To the southeast of the north town wall

❽ is **Piazza del Mercato,** where the **Anfiteatro Romano,** or Roman Amphitheater, once stood. The piazza takes its oval shape from the theater, but the tiers disappeared when medieval houses were built on top of them.

❾ Near the west walls of the old city, the **Pinacoteca Nazionale** is worth a visit to see the Mannerist, Baroque, and Rococo art on display. ✉ *Palazzo Mansi, Via Galli Tassi 43,* ☎ *0583/55570.* ✏ *8,000 lire.* ⊙ *Tues.–Sat. 9–7, Sun. 9–2.*

NEED A BREAK? For an inexpensive lunch in pleasant surroundings, try **Trattoria da Giulio** (✉ Via delle Conce 47, near Porta San Donato; closed Sun. and Mon.), which serves orzo and *porri* (leek) soups, roasted meats, and other simple Lucchese specialties.

❿ On the eastern end of the historic center, the **Museo Nazionale** houses an extensive collection of local Romanesque and Renaissance art. ✉ *Villa Guinigi, Via della Quarquonia,* ☎ *0583/46033.* ✏ *4,000 lire.* ⊙ *May–Sept., Tues.–Sun. 9–7; Oct.–Apr., Tues.–Sun. 9–2.*

⓫ Finally, the tower of the medieval **Palazzo Guinigi,** near the center of town, contains one of the city's most curious oddities: a grove of ilex trees has grown at the top of the tower, and its roots have grown into the room below. From the top, you will have a magnificent view of the city and the surrounding countryside. ✏ *4,500 lire.* ⊙ *10–sunset, 9–sunset in summer.*

OFF THE BEATEN PATH **MARLIA –** The Villa Reale is 8 kilometers (5 miles) north of Lucca in Marlia. Once the home of Napoléon's sister, Princess Elisa, and recently restored by the Counts Pecci-Blunt, this estate is celebrated for its spectacular gardens, laid out in the 18th and 19th centuries. Gardening buffs adore the legendary *teatro di verdura,* a theater carved out of hedges and topiaries; concerts are occasionally offered here. ✉ *Villa Reale,* ☎ *0583/30108.* ✏ *8,000 lire.* ⊙ *Guided tours, July–Sept., Tues.–Sun. 10, 11, 4, 5, 6; Oct.–Nov. and Mar.–June, Tues.–Sun., 10, 11, 3, 4, 5. Closed Dec.–Feb.*

FESTIVAL DI MARLIA – Held in July and August, this is one of the most popular among Tuscany's many summer music events.

Dining and Lodging

$$$ ✕ **Solferino.** About 6 kilometers (4 miles) outside town, on the road to Viareggio, this pleasant restaurant serves exquisite variations of regional favorites, such as *faraona cotta nella creta* (guinea hen baked in a clay oven, made with ingredients from the family farm. Ask for a piece of buccellato, Lucca's celebrated dessert bread. ✉ *San Macario in Piano,* ☎ *0583/59118. Reservations essential. AE, DC, MC, V. Closed Wed. and Jan. 7–15. No lunch Thurs.*

$$–$$$ ✕ **La Mora.** This former country inn 9 kilometers (6 miles) outside Lucca
★ is worth a detour. The menu offers a range of local specialties, from *minestra di farro* (wheat soup) with beans to *tacconi* (homemade pasta) with rabbit sauce and lamb from the nearby Garfagnana hills. You'll be tempted by the varied crostini and delicious desserts. ✉ *Via Sesto di Ponte a Moriano 1748,* ☎ *0583/406402. AE, DC, MC, V. Closed Wed. and Oct. 10–30.*

152

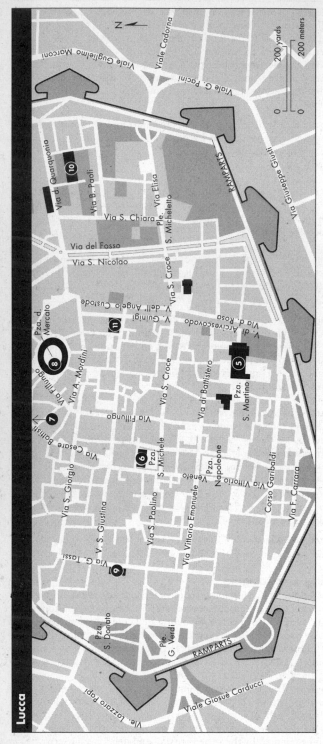

N

200 yards
200 meters

Via Guglielmo Marconi
Viale Cadorna
Viale G. Pacini
Via Giuseppe Giusti
RAMPARTS
Via di Quarquonia
Via B. Paoli
Via S. Chiara
Ple. Via Elisa
Via S. Micheletto
Via del Fosso
Via S. Nicolao
Pza. d. Mercato
Via A. Mordini
V. dell' Angelo Custode
V. Guinigi
V. S. Croce
V. di Arcivescovado
Via d. Rosa
Via Fillungo
Via S. Croce
Via di Battistero
Pza. S. Martino
Via Cesare Battisti
Via S. Giorgio
Via Fillungo
Pza. S. Michele
Via S. Michele
Pza. Napoleone
Pza. V. Veneto
Via Vittorio
Via Vittorio Emanuele
Corso Garibaldi
Via F. Carrara
Via S. Paolino
Via S. Giustina
Via V. S. Giustina
Via G. Tassi
Pza. S. Donato
Ple. G. Verdi
RAMPARTS
Viale Giosuè Carducci
Vle. Lazzaro Papi

5
6
7
8
9
10
11

Duomo, **5**
Museo Nazionale, **10**
Palazzo Guinigi, **11**
Piazza del Mercato, **8**
Pinacoteca
Nazionale, **9**
San Frediano, **7**
San Michele, **6**

$$ ✕ **Buca di Sant'Antonio.** The specialties at this rustic former inn near the church of San Michele are local dishes, some unfamiliar but well worth trying, such as ravioli *di ricotta alle zucchine* (cheese ravioli with zucchini) and roast *capretto* (kid) or agnello with savory herb seasoning. ✉ *Via della Cervia 3,* ☎ *0583/55881. AE, DC, MC, V. Closed Mon. and last 3 wks in July. No dinner Sun.*

$$ ✕ **Il Giglio.** Just off Piazza Napoleone, this restaurant has quiet, turn-of-the-century charm and classic cuisine. It's a place for all seasons, with a big fireplace and an outdoor terrace in summer. Among the local specialties are *farro garfagnino* (a thick soup made with grain and beans), and *coniglio con olive* (rabbit stew with olives). ✉ *Piazza del Giglio 3,* ☎ *0583/494508. AE, DC, MC, V. Closed Wed. No dinner Tues.*

$$$$ 🏨 **Principessa Elisa.** An intimate Relais et Châteaux hotel in a neoclassical villa, this deluxe spin-off of the adjacent Villa La Principessa (☞ *below*) is a notch higher on the scale of style and comfort. ✉ *Massa Pisana,* ☎ *0583/379737,* FAX *0583/379019. 10 suites with bath. Restaurant, bar, pool. AE, DC, MC, V. Closed Jan. 6–Feb. 6.*

$$$ 🏨 **Villa La Principessa.** Just outside Lucca, only 3 kilometers (2 miles) from town, this is an exquisitely decorated 19th-century country mansion. Some rooms have beamed ceilings, and doors are individually decorated; antique furniture and portraits give an aura of gracious living. The grounds are well manicured, the pool large and inviting. ✉ *Massa Pisana,* ☎ *0583/370037,* FAX *0583/379136. 40 rooms and suites with bath. Restaurant (closed Sun.), pool. AE, DC, MC, V. Closed Nov. 1–Mar. 31.*

$$ 🏨 **La Luna.** On a quiet, airy courtyard close to historic Piazza del Mercato, this family-run hotel occupies two freshly renovated wings of an old building. The desk and lounge look new, and the bathrooms are modern, but some of the rooms still have the atmosphere of Old Lucca. A parking lot for guests is a bonus. ✉ *Corte Compagni 12 (corner of Via Fillungo),* ☎ *0583/493634,* FAX *0583/490021. 30 rooms with bath. AE, DC, MC, V. Closed last 3 wks in Jan.*

$ 🏨 **Ilaria.** Rooms are small but fresh and functional in this family-run hotel beside a minuscule canal within easy walking distance of the main sights. ✉ *Via del Fosso 20,* ☎ *0583/47558. 17 rooms, 12 with bath. AE, DC, MC, V.*

Nightlife and the Arts

The **Estate Musicale Lucchese,** one of many music festivals throughout Tuscany, runs throughout the summer in Lucca.

Shopping

Lucca's olive oil, available throughout the city, is exported throughout the world; you'll find it at any food store. On the second Sunday of the month, there's a **flea market** in Piazza San Martino.

Numbers in the margin correspond to points of interest on the Tuscany map.

Pisa

⑫ *22 km (14 mi) southwest of Lucca, 75 km (46 mi) south of La Spezia, 22 km (14 mi) north of Livorno, 64 km (40 mi) northwest of Volterra, 77 km (48 mi) west of Florence.*

There is more to Pisa than its Leaning Tower—but not much more. The city offers surprisingly little temptation after the tower and its companion pieces: the Duomo, the Battistero (Baptistry) and the Camposanto. Nearby Lucca (☞ *above*) is more deserving of your attention.

Pisa's main attraction, situated at the northwestern edge of town, is the **Piazza del Duomo,** also known, appropriately, as the Campo dei Miracoli (Field of Miracles). On it stand the Duomo, the baptistery, and the famous Leaning Tower.

The **Leaning Tower** was begun in 1174, the last of the three structures to be built, and the lopsided settling began when construction reached the third story. The tower's architects attempted to compensate by making the remaining floors slightly taller on the leaning side, but the extra weight only made the problem worse. The settling has continued, and a few years ago it accelerated to a point that led many to fear it would simply topple over, despite all efforts to prop the structure up. Now it has been firmly anchored to the earth. Legend holds that Galileo conducted an experiment on the nature of gravity by dropping metal balls from the top of the 187-foot-high tower; historians say this legend has no basis in fact (which is not quite to say that it is false). ⊠ *Campo dei Miracoli. Closed for restoration.*

The **Duomo** was the first building to use the horizontal marble stripe motif (borrowed from Moorish architecture in the 11th century) so common to Tuscan cathedrals. It is famous for the Romanesque panels on the transept door facing the tower, which depict the life of Christ, and for its beautifully carved 13th-century pulpit, by Giovanni Pisano. The lovely Gothic **baptistery,** which stands across from the Duomo's facade, is best known for the pulpit carved by Giovanni's father, Nicola, in 1260. ⊠ *Campo du Miracoli.* 🏛 *Duomo: 2,000 lire, Nov.–Mar. free.* ☉ *Apr.–Oct., Mon.–Sat. 10–5, Sun. 1–5; Nov.–Mar. 10–12:30 and 3–5:30.* 🏛 *Baptistery: 10,000 lire for baptistery and 1 other attraction; 15,000 lire for baptistery and all 3 attractions (☞ below).* ☉ *Apr.–Oct., daily 8–7:30; Nov.–Mar., daily 10–12:30 and 3–5:30.*

The walled area on the northern side of the Campo dei Miracoli is the **Camposanto** (cemetery), which is filled, according to legend, with earth brought back from the Holy Land during the Crusades. Its galleries contain numerous frescoes, notably *The Drunkenness of Noah,* by Renaissance artist Benozzo Gozzoli, and the disturbing *Triumph of Death* (14th century), whose authorship is disputed, but whose subject matter shows what was on people's minds in a century that saw the ravages of the Black Death. ⊠ *Camposanto,* ☏ *050/560547.* 🏛 *10,000 lire.* ☉ *Apr.–Oct., daily 8–7:30; Nov.–Mar., daily 9–5:30.*

At the southeast corner of the Campo dei Miracoli, the **Museo dell'- Opera del Duomo** holds a wealth of medieval sculptures and the ancient Roman sarcophagi that inspired Nicola Pisano's figures. The well-arranged **Museo delle Sinopie** across the street, on the south side of the square, holds the *sinopie,* or preparatory drawings, for the Camposanto frescoes and is of limited interest to most tourists. ⊠ *Museo dell'Opera del Duomo: Via Arcivescovado,* ☏ *050/560547.* 🏛 *10,000 lire.* ☉ *Apr.–Oct., daily 9–7:30; Nov.–Mar., daily 9–5:30. Museo delle Sinopie:* ⊠ *Piazza del Duomo,* ☏ *050/560547.* 🏛 *10,000 lire.* ☉ *Apr.–Oct., daily 8–7:30; Nov.–Mar., daily 9–5:30.* 🏛 *Combined admission to baptistery, Camposanto, and museums: 10,000 lire for any 2 attractions, 15,000 lire for all 4.*

In the center of town, **Piazza dei Cavalieri** possesses some fine Renaissance buildings: the **Palazzo dei Cavalieri,** the **Palazzo dell'Orologio** and the church of **Santo Stefano dei Cavalieri.** The square was laid out by Giorgio Vasari in about 1560. Vasari was better known for the chronicles of the lives of Renaissance artists that made him the first art historian.

Along the northern side of the Arno, the **Museo di San Matteo** contains some incisive examples of local Romanesque and Gothic art. ⊠ *Lungarno Mediceo,* ☎ *050/541865.* ▦ *8,000 lire.* ☉ *Tues.–Sat. 9–7, Sun. 9–1.*

OFF THE BEATEN PATH

FORTE DEI MARMI – Tuscany's most exclusive beach resort is a favorite of moneyed Tuscans and Milanese, whose villas are neatly laid out in an extensive pine wood. It's 35 kilometers (22 miles) northwest of Lucca and 65 kilometers (30 miles) northwest of Florence. In summer, a beachcomber's bonanza takes place on Wednesday mornings, when everything from fake designer sunglasses to plastic sandals and terry-cloth towels goes on sale.

Forte dei Marmi is also near the marble-producing towns of **Carrara** (where Michelangelo quarried his stone), **Seravezza,** and **Pietrasanta.**

OFF THE BEATEN PATH

ELBA –The largest island in the Tuscan archipelago, Elba is an hour by ferry or a half hour by Hovercraft from Piombino, or a short hop by air from Pisa. Its main port is **Portoferraio,** fortified in the 16th century by the Medici Grand Duke Cosimo I. Victor Hugo spent his boyhood here, and Napoléon his famous exile in 1814–15, when he built (out of two windmills) the **Palazzina Napoleonica dei Mulini** and (a few miles outside town) the **Villa San Martino.**

The island's main attractions, however, are its rough landscape and pristine beaches offering a full array of sports. Portoferraio, the liveliest town and a transportation hub, is the best base for exploring the island. Good beaches can be found at Biodola, Procchio, and Marina di Campo. From Elba, private visits can be arranged to the other islands in the archipelago, including **Montecristo,** which inspired Alexander Dumas's 19th-century best-seller *The Count of Monte Cristo* and is now a wildlife refuge. Elba's restaurants offer excellent seafood, to be sampled with the local Moscato and Aleatico wines. ⊠ *Palazzina Napoleonica and Villa San Martino,* ☎ *0565/915846.* ▦ *6,000 lire for both if visited on same day.* ☉ *Tues.–Sat. 9–1:30, Sun. 9–1.*

Dining and Lodging

$$ ✕ **Bruno.** A pleasant restaurant, with beamed ceilings and the look of a country inn, Bruno is just outside the old city walls, a short walk from the bell tower and cathedral. Dine on classic Tuscan dishes, from *zuppa alla pisana* (a thick vegetable soup) to *baccalà* (cod) with leeks. ⊠ *Via Luigi Bianchi 12,* ☎ *050/560818. AE, DC, MC, V. Closed Tues. No dinner Mon.*

$$ ✕ **La Pergoletta.** In a medieval tower in the heart of the old town, on a street named for its "beautiful towers," this restaurant is small and simple and has a shady garden for outdoor dining. The signora who is the owner-cook offers traditional Tuscan minestra di farro and *grigliata* (grilled beef, veal, or lamb). ⊠ *Via delle Belle Torri 36,* ☎ *050/542458. Reservations advised. MC, V. Closed Tues. and Aug.*

$$ ✕ **Osteria dei Cavalieri.** Just off the beautiful old Piazza dei Cavalieri, this popular tavern and wine cellar in a centuries-old tower offers one-course lunch menus, as well as fixed-price menus, of either seafood, meat, or vegetarian dishes, including freshly made *tagliolini* (noodles) and *tagliata di manzo* (sliced beefsteak, usually served with mushrooms). ⊠ *Via San Frediano 16,* ☎ *050/580858. AE, DC, MC, V. Closed Sun. and Aug. No lunch Sat.*

$$$ ▣ **Cavalieri.** Opposite the railway station, in an unremarkable 1950s building, this Jolly Group hotel offers functional, modern comforts in completely soundproof and air-conditioned rooms, all with color TV and minibar. The restaurant specializes in homemade pasta and seafood and is open every day. ✉ *Piazza della Stazione 2,* ☎ *050/43290,* ℻ *050/502242. 100 rooms with bath or shower. Bar. AE, DC, MC, V.*

$$ ☷ **Royal Victoria.** In a pleasant palazzo facing the Arno, a 10-minute walk from the Campo dei Miracoli, this hotel is about as close as Pisa comes to Old World ambience. It's comfortably furnished, featuring antiques and reproductions in the lobby and in some rooms, whose style ranges from the 1800s, complete with frescoes, to the 1920s. ✉ *Lungarno Pacinotti 12,* ☎ *050/940111,* ℻ *050/940180. 48 rooms, 40 with bath. AE, DC, MC, V.*

TUSCAN HILL TOWNS
The Quintessential Tuscany

This area of rustic small cities and towns south of Florence has three distinct subdivisions. The first, directly south of Florence, is the Chianti district, Italy's most famous wine-producing area; its hill towns, olive groves, and vineyards comprise the quintessential Tuscany. Many British and northern Europeans have relocated here, drawn by the unhurried life, balmy climate, and picturesque villages; there are so many Britons, in fact, that the area has been nicknamed Chiantishire. Still, it remains strongly Tuscan in character and is sparsely populated. Marking the southernmost extremity of the Chianti region is the second subregion—Siena, a force unto itself; there's nowhere else in Italy where medieval strength and the elegance of the Renaissance are in such perfect balance. Farther south is the third area, where soft green olive groves give way to a blanket of oak and rich dark green cypress forests and reddish brown earth; here and there throughout this area are the vineyards that produce Brunello di Montalcino. Here, the towns are the size of the roads—small—and as old as the hills.

From Florence, there are two basic routes to Siena. The speedy modern S2 is good if you're making a day trip from Florence; to really experience the countryside, take the narrower and more meandering S222, known as the Strada Chiantigiana because it runs through the heart of the wine-producing region. Its most scenic section connects **Strada in Chianti,** 16 kilometers (10 miles) south of Florence, and **Greve in Chianti,** 11 kilometers (7 miles) farther south, whose triangular central piazza is surrounded by restaurants and vintners offering *degustazioni* (wine tastings).

Number in the margin correspond to points of interest on the Tuscany map.

Volterra

⑬ *64 km (40 mi) southwest of Pisa, 50 km (31 mi) west of Siena.*

D. H. Lawrence, in his *Etruscan Places,* sang the praises of Volterra, "standing somber and chilly alone on her rock." The town has long been known for its alabaster, which has been mined since Etruscan times; today the Volterrans use it to make ornaments and souvenirs sold all over town. **Piazza dei Priori,** where the 13th-century Palazzo dei Priori is emblazoned with heraldic emblems, is one of Tuscany's quintessential medieval squares.

A magnificent collection of small alabaster funerary urns that once held the ashes of deceased Etruscans (along with many other Etruscan artifacts) may be seen at the **Museo Etrusco Guarnacci** (✉ Via Don Minzoni). Later art can be found in the **Duomo,** at the **Pinacoteca** (✉ Palazzo Minucci-Solaini, Via dei Sarti 1), and at the **Museo di Arte Sacra** (✉ Via Roma; ☉ Daily 9–12:30). The town's best-known Renaissance works are the 15th-century frescoes in the Duomo by Benozzo Gozzoli and the 16th-century *Deposition* by Rosso Fiorentino in the Pinacoteca. 🖾 *Combined admission to Museo Etrusco Guarnacci, Pinacoteca, and Museo di Arte Sacra: 10,000 lire.* ☉ *Mar. 16–Oct. 14, daily 9:30–6:30 (Museo Etrusco Guarnacci closes 1–3); Oct. 15–Mar. 15, daily 9:30–1 (Museo Etrusco Guarnacci 9–2).*

The walls of Volterra also harbor one of the few pieces of Etruscan architecture that escaped Roman destruction: the **Arco Etrusco,** with its weatherworn Etruscan heads, at the Porta all'Arco.

Dining and Lodging

$$ ✕ **Etruria.** Turn-of-the-century frescoes on the walls and outdoor dining in the warm weather are among the attractions at this restaurant on the town's main square. An array of local game is used in such specialties as *pappardelle alla lepre* (broad noodles in hare sauce) and *cinghiale alla maremmana* (roast boar). ✉ *Piazza dei Priori 8,* ☎ *0588/86064. AE, DC, MC, V. Closed Thurs.*

$$ 🏨 **San Lino.** Located in a former convent, this hotel has modern comforts, a swimming pool, and its own regional restaurant. On top of that, it's within the town walls, 10 minutes' walk from the main piazza. ✉ *Via San Lino 26,* ☎ *0588/85250,* FAX *0588/80620. 43 rooms with bath. Restaurant, pool. AE, DC, MC, V.*

Shopping

SPECIALTY ITEMS

Volterra has a number of shops that sell boxes, jewelry, and other objects made of alabaster. For information and directions, contact **Cooperativa Artieri Alabastro** (✉ Piazza dei Priori 2, ☎ 0588/87590).

En Route Travel 88 kilometers (55 miles) northeast of Siena. (You may want to break the drive halfway with a rest stop at **Monte San Savino,** a prosperous-looking small town, with the tiny nearby fortified village of **Gargonza** that has been carefully restored into a vacation resort; (☞ Dining and Lodging, *below.*) Then proceed on to Arezzo.

San Gimignano

★ ⑭ *27 km (17 mi) east of Volterra, 57 km (35 mi) southwest of Florence, 31 km (20 mi) northwest of Siena.*

Time seems to have stood still since the Middle Ages in this most remarkable of all Tuscan hill towns, and it still lives up to its original name, San Gimignano-of-the-Beautiful-Towers. Its high walls and narrow streets are typical of Tuscan hill towns, but it is the surviving medieval "skyscrapers" that set the town apart from its neighbors and give the town a uniquely photogenic silhouette. Today 14 towers remain, but at the height of the Guelph-Ghibelline conflict, a forest of more than 70 such towers dominated the city. The towers were built partly for defensive purposes—they were a safe refuge and useful for pouring boiling oil on attacking enemies—and partly to bolster the egos of their owners, who competed with deadly seriousness to build the highest tower in town.

Many of the town's most important medieval buildings are clustered around the central **Piazza del Duomo.** They include the **Palazzo del Podestà,** with its imposing tower, the **Torre Grossa;** the **Palazzo del Popolo,** now the Museo Civico (municipal museum), displaying Sienese and Renaissance paintings; and the Romanesque **Collegiata**, containing fine 15th-century frescoes by Domenico Ghirlandaio in the **Chapel of Santa Fina.** 🖼 *A combined ticket (16,000 lire) is valid for all San Gimignano museums and the Chapel of Santa Fina. Museo Civico: 7,000 lire;* ○ *Apr.–Sept., Tues.–Sun. 9:30–7:30; Oct. and Mar., Tues.–Sun. 9:30–6; Nov.–Feb., Tues.–Sun. 9:30–1:30 and 2:30–4:30. Torre Grossa: 7,000 lire.* ○ *as Museo Civico (above); combined ticket for museum and tower (12,000) lire available only Apr.–Sept., Tues.–Sun. 12:30–3 and 6–7:30; Oct.–Mar., Tues.–Sun. 12:30–2:30. Chapel of Santa Fina:* 🖼 *3,000 lire.* ○ *Apr.–Sept., Tues.–Sun. 9–12:30 and 3–6; Oct.–Mar., Tues.–Sun. 9:30–12:30 and 3–5:30.*

Before leaving San Gimignano, be sure to see its most famous work of art, at the northern end of town, in the church of **Sant'Agostino**: Benozzo Gozzoli's utterly beautiful 15th-century fresco cycle depicting the life of St. Augustine. Also try a taste of Vernaccia, the local dry white wine.

Dining and Lodging

$$–$$$ ✕ **Bel Soggiorno.** On the top floor of a 100-year-old inn, this rustic restaurant has a wall of windows from which to view the landscape. Tuscan specialties include *zuppa del granduca* (a medieval soup of mushrooms, grain, and potatoes) and *sorpresa in crosta* (spicy rabbit stew with a bread crust). ⊠ *Via San Giovanni 91,* ☎ *0577/940375. AE, DC, MC, V. Closed Mon. and Jan. 7–Feb. 28.*

$$–$$$ ✕ **Le Terrazze.** This restaurant in a time-honored inn in the heart of San Gimignano has a charming view of rooftops and countryside and an ample menu featuring Tuscan dishes in seasonal variations. The specialties are served *alla sangimignanese* (baked in the oven). ⊠ *Piazza della Cisterna 23,* ☎ *0577/940328. AE, DC, MC, V. Closed Nov. 1–Mar. 9. No lunch Tues. and Wed.*

$$ ✕ **Stella.** At this rustic, upscale trattoria, between the main church and that of Sant Agostino, prices are more moderate than at places with a view. The owner prides himself on farm-fresh vegetables and his own olive oil. The specialty of the house is grilled meat, including beef, lamb, and pork. ⊠ *Via San Matteo 77,* ☎ *0577/940444. AE, DC, MC, V. Closed Wed. and Jan. 6–Feb. 15.*

$$ 🏠 **Pescille.** This is a rambling farmhouse 4 kilometers (2 ½ miles) outside San Gimignano that has been converted into a handsome hotel, in which restrained contemporary and country classic decors blend well. ⊠ *Località Pescille, Strada Castel San Gimignano,* ☎ *0577/940186,* 𝔽𝔸𝕏 *0577/943165. 40 rooms with bath. Pool, tennis court. AE, DC, MC, V. Closed Nov.–Feb.*

Monteriggioni

20 km (12 mi) southeast of San Gimignano, 93 km (58 mi) southeast of Pisa, 55 km (34 mi) south of Florence.

On your way north from Siena toward Colle Val d'Elsa, San Gimignano, and Volterra, be sure to visit this tiny hamlet, which sits on a rise within a circle of formidable 13th-century walls. Its 14 square towers, which Dante likened to giants, were Siena's northernmost defense against Florence. Take time to make the lengthy detour around Colle Val d'Elsa's workaday lower town up to the ridge, where the medieval center remains practically intact.

Dining

$$ ✕ **Il Pozzo.** On the village square, this rustic tavern serves hearty Tuscan country cooking, including *maltagliati al sugo di* agnello (with fresh pasta in a tomato sauce) and *cinghiale in dolce forte* (boar with a tangy sauce). The desserts are homemade. ⊠ *Piazza Roma 2,* ☎ *0577/304127. AE, DC, MC, V. Closed Mon., Jan., and 10 days in Aug. No dinner Sun.*

Siena

⑮ *15 km (9 mi) southeast of Montereggioni, 106 km (66 mi) southeast of Pisa, 68 km (42 mi) south of Florence.*

Italy's loveliest medieval city, Siena is the one trip you should make in Tuscany if you make no other. Florence's great historical rival was founded by Augustus around the time of the birth of Christ, although legend holds that it was founded much earlier by Remus, brother of Romulus, the legendary founder of Rome. During the late Middle Ages, the city was both wealthy and powerful (it saw the birth of the world's oldest bank, the Monte dei Paschi, still very much in business). It was bitterly envied by Florence, which in 1254 sent forces that besieged the city for over a year, reducing its population by half and laying waste to the countryside. The city was finally absorbed by the Grand Duchy of Tuscany, ruled by Florence, in 1559.

Numbers in the margin correspond to points of interest on the Siena map.

★ Unlike Renaissance Florence, Siena is a Gothic city, laid out over the slopes of three steep hills and practically unchanged since medieval times. Its main square, the **Piazza del Campo,** is one of the finest in Italy. Fan shaped, its nine sections of paving represent the 13th-century government of Nine Good Men, and, on the widest side, like an ornament, is the Fonte Gaia, so called because it was inaugurated to great jubilation. The bas-reliefs on it are reproductions of the originals by Jacopo della Quercia. Twice a year, on July 2 and August 16, the square explodes in a frenzy of local rivalries as the site of the famous **Palio,** a horse race in which the city's 17 neighborhoods compete to possess the cloth banner that gives the contest its name. Unlike many other such competitions in Italy, the Palio has a mystique in which the townspeople are deeply involved, and the rivalries it generates are taken very seriously.

★ **⑯** Dominating the Piazza del Campo is the **Palazzo Pubblico,** which has served as Siena's Town Hall since the 1300s. It now also contains the **Museo Civico,** its walls covered with pre-Renaissance frescoes, including Simone Martini's early 14th-century *Maestà* and *Portrait of Guidoriccio da Fogliano,* and Ambrogio Lorenzetti's famous *Allegory of Good and Bad Government,* painted from 1327 to 1329 to demonstrate the dangers of tyranny. The original bas-reliefs of the Jacopo della Quercia fountain, moved to protect them from the elements, are also on display. The climb up the palazzo's bell tower is long and steep, but the superb view makes it worth every step. ⊠ *Piazza del Campo,* ☎ *0577/292263.* ☞ *Bell tower: 5,000 lire.* ☉ *Mar. 15–Nov. 15, daily 10–1 hr before sunset; Nov. 16–Mar. 14, daily 10–1.* ☞ *Museo Civico: 6,000 lire.* ☉ *Mar. 15–Nov. 15, Mon.–Sat 9:30–7, Sun. 9–1:30; Nov. 16–Mar. 14, daily 9–1:30.*

NEED A BREAK? There are several *gelaterie* (ice-cream parlors) on Piazza del Campo, excellent for surveying the piazza while enjoying a refreshing ice cream. More substantial sustenance may be found nearby at **Ristorante Il Verrocchio** (⊠ Logge del Papa 2, closed Wed.), which serves inexpensive Sienese specialties and is a block east of the northern side of the campo.

★ **⑰** Siena's **Duomo,** several blocks west of Piazza del Campo, is beyond question one of the finest Gothic cathedrals in Italy. Its facade, with its multicolored marbles and painted decoration, is typical of the Italian approach to Gothic architecture, lighter and much less austere than the French. The cathedral, as it now stands, was completed in the 14th century, but at the time the Sienese had even bigger plans. They decided to enlarge the building, using the current church as the transepts of the new church, which would have a new nave running toward the southeast. The beginnings of construction of this new nave still stand and may be seen from the steps outside the Duomo's right transept. But in 1348 the Black Death decimated Siena's population, the city fell into decline, funds dried up, and the plans were never carried out.

The Duomo's interior is one of the most striking in Italy and possesses a fine coffered and gilded dome. It is most famous for its unique and magnificent marble floors, which took almost 200 years to complete (beginning around 1370); more than 40 artists contributed to the work, made up of 56 separate compositions depicting biblical scenes, allegories, religious symbols, and civic emblems. The Duomo's carousel pulpit, which is almost as famous as the floors, was carved by Nicola Pisano around 1265; the life of Christ is depicted on the rostrum frieze. In the **Biblioteca Piccolomini,** a room painted by Pinturicchio in 1509, frescoes depict events from the life of native son Aeneas Sylvius Piccolomini, who became Pope Pius II in 1458. The frescoes are in excellent condition and have a freshness rarely seen in work so old. ⊠ *Biblioteca Piccolomini,* ☎ *0577/283048.* ▨ *2,000 lire.* ⊘ *Mid-Mar.–Oct. 31, daily 9–7:30; Nov.–mid-Mar., daily 10–1, 2–5.*

⑱ Next to the Duomo is its museum, the **Museo dell'Opera del Duomo,** occupying part of the unfinished new cathedral's nave and containing a small collection of Sienese art and the cathedral treasury. Its masterpiece is unquestionably Duccio's *Maestà,* painted around 1310 and magnificently displayed in a room devoted entirely to Duccio's work. ⊠ *Piazza del Duomo,* ☎ *0577/283048.* ▨ *5,000 lire.* ⊘ *Mar. 12– Sept. 30, daily 9–7:30; Oct. 1–Oct. 31, daily 9–6:30; Nov. 1–Dec. 31, daily 9–1:30; Jan. 2–Mar. 11, daily 9–1:30.*

Steps between the cathedral and its museum lead to the **Battistero** (baptistery), with its 15th-century frescoes. Its large bronze baptismal font (also 15th century) was designed by Jacopo della Quercia and is adorned with bas-reliefs by various artists, including two by Renaissance masters: Lorenzo Ghiberti (*The Baptism of Christ*) and Donatello (*Herod Presented with the Head of St. John*).

⑲ Chief among Siena's other attractions is the **Pinacoteca Nazionale,** several blocks southeast of the entrance to the Duomo; it contains a superb collection of Sienese art, including Ambrogio Lorenzetti's 14th-century depiction of a castle that is generally considered the first nonreligious painting—the first pure landscape—of the Christian era. ⊠ *Via San Pietro 29,* ☎ *0577/281161.* ▨ *8,000 lire.* ⊘ *Apr.–Sept., Tues.–Sat. 8–6; Oct.–Mar., Tues.–Sat. 8:30–1:30, Sun. 8:30–1.*

⑳ Northwest of the Duomo is the church of **San Domenico;** its **Cappella di Santa Caterina** displays frescoes by Il Sodoma portraying scenes from the life of St. Catherine.

NEED A
BREAK?   Not far from the church of San Domenico, the **Enoteca Italica** is a fantastically stocked wine cellar in the bastions of the Medici fortress. Here you can taste wines from all over Italy and have a snack, too. ⊠ *Fortezza Medicea, Viale Maccari,* ☎ *0577/288497.* ⊘ *3 PM–midnight.*

Duomo, **17**

Museo
dell'Opera del
Duomo, **18**

Palazzo
Pubblico, **16**

Pinacoteca
Nazionale, **19**

San
Domenico, **20**

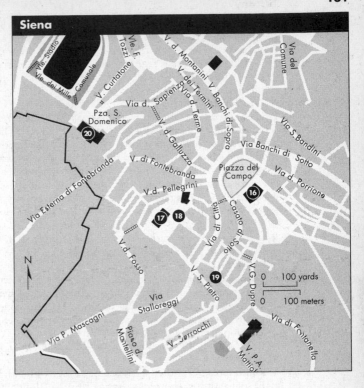

Dining and Lodging

$$ ✕ **Al Marsili.** Located between Piazza del Campo and the cathedral,
★ this 900-year-old wine cellar is an elegant place to dine, under broad,
brick-vaulted ceilings. The menu offers Tuscan and Italian specialties,
among them homemade pastas such as *tortelloni burro e salvia* (large
cheese-filled ravioli with butter and sage). Various meat dishes are cooked
in wine, and the wine list features the finest Tuscan and Italian labels,
including many from the nearby Chianti country. ✉ *Via del Castoro
3,* ☎ *0577/47154. AE, DC, MC, V. Closed Mon.*

$$ ✕ **Le Logge.** Near Piazza del Campo, this typically Sienese trattoria has
★ rustic dining rooms on two levels and tables outdoors from June to
October. The menu features Tuscan dishes, such as *malfatti all'osteria*
(ricotta and spinach dumplings in a cream sauce) and *coniglio con pig-
noli* (rabbit with pine nuts). ✉ *Via del Porrione 33,* ☎ *0577/48013.
MC, V. Closed Sun. and 2 wks in June and Nov.*

$$ ✕ **Tullio Tre Cristi.** This is a typical and historic neighborhood tratto-
ria, long ago discovered by tourists and still reliable. The paintings on
the walls are by famous local artists of the 1920s, but the culinary tra-
dition here goes back even further. Try spaghetti *alle briciole*, a poor-
man's dish of pasta with bread-crumbs, tomato, and garlic, or veal
escalopes (cutlets) subtly flavored with *dragoncello* (tarragon). You can
eat outdoors in summer. To find the restaurant, take Via dei Rossi from
Via Banchi di Sopra. ✕ *Vicolo di Provenzano 1,* ☎ *0577/280608. MC,
V. Closed Mon. and mid-Jan–mid-Feb. No dinner Sun.*

$$$$ 🏨 **Park.** Set among olive groves and gardens on a hillside just outside
the city walls, this hotel offers solid comfort and spacious rooms with

views of the grounds and countryside, which also includes a 6-hole practice golf course. A historic 16th-century villa, it has the easy elegance and antique charm of patrician Tuscan country life. The Olivo restaurant is known for fine regional cuisine. ⊠ *Via Marciano 18,* ☎ *0577/44803,* ℻ *0577/49020. 80 double rooms with bath or shower. Restaurant, bar, pool, 2 tennis courts. AE, DC, MC, V.*

$$$–$$$$ ✕⽥ **La Suvera.** This luxurious estate in the lovely valley of the River Elsa, 28 kilometers (17 miles) west of Siena and 56 kilometers (35 miles) south of Florence, was once owned by Pope Julius II. The papal villa and adjacent buildings have been restored to accommodate guests in rooms and suites that are magnificently furnished with antiques and appointed with the latest comforts. With drawing rooms, a library, Italian garden, park, pool, and the Oliviera restaurant (serving estate wines) to enjoy, guests find it hard to tear themselves away, though there is plenty to see in the vicinity. ⊠ *Pievescola (Casola d'Elsa), off S541,* ☎ *0577/960300,* ℻ *0577/960220. 19 rooms and 13 suites with bath. Restaurant, bar, pool, sauna, tennis court, horseback riding, meeting rooms, helipad. AE, DC, MC, V.* ☺ *Apr. 1–Oct. 31.*

$$$$ ⽥ **Certosa di Maggiano.** A former 14th-century monastery converted
★ into an exquisite country hotel, this haven of gracious living is a little more than a mile from the center of Siena. The atmosphere is that of an exclusive retreat in which a select number of guests enjoy the style and comfort of an aristocratic villa. ⊠ *Via Certosa 82,* ☎ *0577/288180,* ℻ *0577/288189. 18 rooms with bath. Restaurant, pool, tennis court. AE, DC, MC, V.*

$–$$ ⽥ **Antica Torre.** A restored 17th-century tower within the town walls in the southeast corner of Siena, Antica Torre is a 10-minute walk from Piazza del Campo. It is the work of a cordial couple who have created the atmosphere of a private home, furnished simply but in good taste and with only eight guest rooms. The old stone staircase, wooden beams, and original brick vaults here and there are reminders of the building's august age. ⊠ *Via Fieravecchia 7,* ☎ ℻ *0577/222255. 8 rooms with bath. AE, MC, V.*

$–$$ ⽥ **Chiusarelli.** A handy location—near the long-distance bus terminal and a parking area and only a 10-minute walk from the main sights— makes this hotel a good choice. In a well-kept neoclassic villa, built in the early 1900s complete with caryatids, it has functional rooms that are airy and reasonably quiet. There is a small garden and a downstairs restaurant that caters to tour groups. ⊠ *Viale Curtatone 9,* ☎ *0577/280562,* ℻ *0577/271177. 50 rooms with bath. MC, V.*

$–$$ ⽥ **Duomo.** Occupying the top floor of a 300-year-old building in the center of Siena, near Piazza del Campo, the hotel is quiet and is furnished in a neat contemporary style, with traces of the past showing in the artfully exposed brickwork in the breakfast room. Many bedrooms have superb views of the city's towers and the hilly countryside. Two rooms are endowed with balconies. ⊠ *Via Stalloreggi 38,* ☎ *0577/289088,* ℻ *0577/43043. 23 rooms with bath. AE, DC, MC, V.*

Nightlife and the Arts

In late July and August, Siena hosts the **Settimane Musicali Senesi,** a series of alfresco concerts of local and other music.

Shopping

The city is known for a variety of medieval desserts—*cavallucci, panforti,* and *ricciarelli*—as well as for ceramics.

Numbers in the margin correspond to points of interest on the Tuscany map.

Abbey of Monte Oliveto Maggiore

㉑ *37 km (23 mi) southeast of Siena.*

This **Benedictine abbey,** Tuscany's most visited, is an oasis of olive and cypress trees amid the harsh landscape of a zone known as the *crete*, where erosion has sculpted the hills starkly, laying open gashes of barren rock in lush farmland. Secluded amid thick woodlands in the deep-cut hills south of Siena, it is accessible by car but not easily by bus.

Olivetans, or "White Benedectines," founded it in 1313; this breakaway group sought to return to the simple ideals of the early Benedictines. The monastery's mellow brick buildings, restored in the last century and set in one of Tuscany's most striking landscapes, hold a treasure or two. Only the main cloister, the church, and portions of the park are open to the public. In the church, the wooden choir, with exquisite inlay designs, is an understated work of art that dates from 1503.

In the main cloister of the abbey, the frescoes by Luca Signorelli and Il Sodoma on the walls of the portico relate the life of St. Benedict with earthy realism, a quality that came naturally to Il Sodoma, described by Vasari as "a merry and licentious man . . . of scant chastity." ▧ *Free.* ⊙ *Daily 9:15–12, 3:15–5:45.*

Dining

$–$$ ✕ **La Torre.** This pleasant restaurant and café in the massive tower at the abbey's entrance provide more than adequate sustenance to visitors. The local specialties—served in a cozy dining room in winter or on an attractive terrace under tall cypresses in fair weather—include tagliatelle *ai funghi* (with mushroom sauce) or *zuppa di funghi* (mushroom soup). The wine list is excellent, and the tourist menu is a good value. ☎ *0577/707022. AE, MC, V. Closed Tues.*

Montalcino

㉒ *25 km (15.5 mi) south of the Abbey of Monte Oliveto Maggiore, 24 km (15 mi) west of Pienza, 41 km (25 mi) south of Siena.*

Another medieval hill town with a special claim to fame, Montalcino is home to Brunello di Montalcino, one of Italy's best red wines. You can sample it in wine cellars in town or visit a nearby winery for a free guided tour and tasting. One such winery is the Fattoria dei Barbi (☞ Dining, *below*).

Dining

$$$ ✕ **Poggio Antico.** One of Italy's renowned gourmet chefs, Roberto Minnetti, abandoned his highly successful restaurant in Rome a few years ago and moved to the country, about 2 miles outside Montalcino. Now he and his wife, Patrizia—who is also Poggio Antico's hostess—serve fine Tuscan cuisine, masterfully interpreted by Roberto, in a relaxed but elegant dining room replete with arches and beamed ceilings. Among the specialties are *paté di fegatini al moscadello* (liver paté flavored with wine) and *piccione ripieno in slasa d'agretto* (stuffed pigeon in a tangy sauce). ⊠ *Località I Poggi (2½ mi outside Montalcino on road to Grossetto). ☎ 0577/849200. AE, DC. Closed Mon. and 20 days in Jan.*

$$ ✕ **La Cucina di Edgardo.** This tiny restaurant on Montalcino's main street has three charming dining rooms in a former wine cellar with dark wooden beams, a fireplace, and terra-cotta floors. The specialties of the house, on a menu featuring creative versions of Tuscan food, are *ravioli di magro al basilico e noci* (cheese ravioli with basil and walnuts) and *brasato al Brunello* (beef braised in the local Brunello wine).

✉ *Via Soccorsi Saloni 21,* ☎ *0577/848232. MC, V. Closed Wed. and Jan. 8–Feb. 8.*

$$ ✕ **Taverna dei Barbi.** A meal at this delightful tavern, set among vine-
★   yards and mellow brick buildings on a wine-producing country es-
tate (Fattoria dei Barbi), may well be a highlight of your journey
through this part of Tuscany. The rustic dining room features a
beamed ceiling, huge stone fireplace, and arched windows. The es-
tate farm produces practically all the ingredients used in such tradi-
tional specialties as *scottiglia di pollo* (browned chicken served with
garlic bread) and a dessert called *ricotta montata* (farm-fresh ricotta
whipped with vin santo, sugar, and vanilla). The estate-produced
Brunello is excellent, and other wines with the Barbi label are avail-
able. ✉ *Fattoria dei Barbi,* ☎ *0577/849357. Reservations essential.
AE, DC, MC, V. Closed Wed., Jan. 15–31, and July 1–15. No din-
ner Tues.* ☉ *Winery (English-speaking guides) open weekdays 9–1
and 3–6, weekends 2:30–6.*

Abbey of Sant'Antimo

10 km (6 mi) south of Montalcino, 31 km (19 mi) south of Siena.

It's well worth your while to visit this **abbey,** a medieval gem of pale
stone set in the silvery green of an olive grove. The exterior and in-
terior sculpture is outstanding, particularly the nave capitals, a com-
bination of French, Lombard, and even Spanish influences. The
sacristy (rarely open) forms part of the primitive Carolingian church
(founded in 781 AD), its entrance flanked by 9th-century pilasters.
The small **vaulted crypt** dates from the same period. Above the nave
runs a *matroneum* (women's gallery), an unusual feature once used
to separate the congregation. Equally unusual is the ambulatory,
whose three radiating chapels (rare in Italian churches) were prob-
ably copied from the French model. ☉ *Daily 9–12 and 2–7 (winter
10–12 and 2–4).* ☒ *Free.*

Pienza

㉓ *10 km (6 mi) northeast of the Abbey of Sant' Antimo.*

Pienza owes its appearance to Pope Pius II, who had grand plans to
transform his home village of **Corsignano**—the town's former name—
into a model Renaissance town. The man entrusted with the trans-
formation was Bernardo Rossellini, a protegé of the great Renaissance
architectural theorist Leon Battista Alberti. His mandate was to cre-
ate a cathedral, a papal palace, and a town hall (plus miscellaneous
buildings) that adhered to the vainglorious pope's principles. Gothic
and Renaissance styles were fused, and the buildings were decorated
with Sienese and Florentine paintings. The net result was a project that
expressed Renaissance ideals of art, architecture, and civilized good
living in a single scheme: It stands as an exquisite example of the ar-
chitectural canons that Alberti formulated in the early Renaissance and
which were utilized by later architects, including Brunelleschi and
Michelangelo, in designing many of Italy's finest buildings and piaz-
zas. Today the cool grandeur of Pienza's center seems almost surreal
in this otherwise unpretentious village, known locally for *pienzino,* also
called *cacio,* a smooth sheep's-milk cheese.

Montepulciano

㉔ *12 km (7 mi) east of Pienza, 13 km (8 mi) west of the A1, 65 km (40
mi) south of Florence.*

Perched high on a hilltop, Montepulciano is made up of a pyramid of redbrick buildings set within a circle of cypress trees. At an altitude of almost 2,000 feet, it is cool in summer and chilled in winter by biting winds that sweep its spiraling streets. The town has an unusually harmonious look, the result of the work of three architects, Sangallo il Vecchio, Vignola, and Michelozzo, who endowed it with fine palaces and churches in an attempt to impose Renaissance architectural ideals on an ancient Tuscan hill-town. The town's showpiece is the beau-

★ tiful **Piazza Grande.** Montepulciano's many wine cellars and antiques dealers and a few trendy shops and cafés hint that this otherwise sleepy town gets its share of tourists, especially during an international arts festival in July and August. On the hillside below the town walls is the church of **San Biagio,** designed by Sangallo, a paragon of Renaissance architectural perfection that is considered his masterpiece.

Dining and Lodging

$$ 🍴 **Il Marzocco.** A 16th-century building within the town walls, it is furnished in 19th-century style, complete with dignified, old-fashioned parlors and a billiard room. Many bedrooms have large terraces overlooking the countryside, and many rooms are large enough to accommodate extra beds; they are furnished in heavy turn-of-the-century style or in spindly white wood. ⊠ *Piazza Savonarola 18,* ☎ *0578/757262,* ℻ *0578/757530. 18 rooms, 13 with bath or shower. Restaurant (closed Wed.). AE, DC, MC, V. Closed Nov. 20–Dec. 5*

$$$$ ✕🏨 **Locanda dell'Amorosa.** A medieval hamlet set in Tuscan farmland
★ has become a rustic retreat for jaded city folk, who reserve ahead for a meal or weekend in the country only a half hour by car from Siena or Arezzo and even less from Montepulciano, Cortona, and Monte Oliveto Maggiore. The stone and brick buildings have been tastefully adapted to their current use, and the restaurant serves regional dishes that seem to taste even better in such apt surroundings. You can take home estate-produced wines and preserves as a souvenir of your stay. ⊠ *Località Amorosa, Sinalunga, 10 km (6 mi) from the Valdichiana exit of A1,* ☎ *0577/679497,* ℻ *0577/632001. 17 rooms with bath. Restaurant, pool. AE, DC, MC, V. Restaurant closed Mon. and Tues. lunch and Jan. 8–Mar. 7).*

$ ✕🏨 **La Bandita.** This attractive old farmhouse has been converted into a hotel by the Fiorini family. It has great charm, with terra-cotta floors throughout, lace curtains and antiques in the bedrooms, and a fireplace and grandfather's 19th-century Tuscan provincial furniture in a large, brick-vaulted living room. Some rooms can accommodate an extra bed, there is a garden, and meals are available. ⊠ *Via Bandita 72, Bettolle, 1 km (.6 mi) from Valdichiana exit of A1 autostrada,* ☎ *0577/624649,* ℻ *0577/624649. 8 rooms with bath. Restaurant (closed Tues.).MC, V.*

Nightlife and the Arts

The **Cantiere Internazionale d'Arte,** held in July and August, is a multifaceted festival of figurative art, music, and theater, ending with a major theatrical production in Piazza Grande.

En Route The road leading to Chianciano climbs and dips, winding through woods of evergreens and oaks and affording glimpses of the vineyards that are the pride of this part of Tuscany. Two of Italy's best wines— Brunello di Montalcino and Vino Nobile di Montepulciano—originate here and bear the names of the towns where they are made.

Chianciano

9 km (5.5 mi) south of Montepulciano.

This small medieval town, surrounded by walls, has billboards pro-claiming that Chianciano's restorative waters are indispensable for a *fegato sano* (a healthy liver). It's a modern spa with neat parks and a host of hotels.

Chiusi

11 km (7 mi) east of Chianciano, 2.5 km (1.5 mi) east of the AI, 126 km (78 mi) south of Florence.

Known for the frescoed tombs that date from the 5th century BC in its necropolis, Chiusi was one of the most powerful of the 12 ancient cities in the Etruscan federation, and is a transportation hub accessi-ble from either the main north–south rail line or by car or bus from the A1 autostrada.

Cortona

 46 km (28.5 mi) northeast of Chiusi.

This is one of Tuscany's prettiest hill-towns. Magnificently situated, with olives and vineyards creeping up to its walls, it commands sweep-ing views over Lake Trasimeno and the plain of the Valdichiana. Its two fine galleries and scattering of churches are relatively unvisited, while its delightful medieval streets are a pleasure to wander for their own sake.

Cortona may be one of Italy's oldest towns—"Mother of Troy and Grandmother of Rome," in popular speech. Tradition claims that it was founded by Dardanus, the founder of Troy (after whom the Daradanelles are named). He was fighting a local tribe, so the story goes, when he lost his helmet (*corythos* in Greek) on Cortona's hill. In time a town grew up that took its name (Corito) from the missing headgear. By the 4th century BC the Etruscans had built the first set of town walls, whose cyclopedean traces can still be seen in the 2-mile sweep of the present fortifications. As a member of the Etruscans' 12-city Dodecapolis, it became one of the federation's leading northern cities. An important consular road, the Via Cassia, which passed the foot of its hill, maintained the town's importance under the Romans. Medieval fortunes waned, however, as the plain below reverted to marsh. After holding out against neighbors like Perugia, Arezzo, and Siena, the *comune* was captured by King Ladislas of Naples in 1409 and sold to the Florentines two years later.

The heart of Cortona is formed by **Piazza della Repubblica** and the adjacent **Piazza Signorelli.** Wander into the courtyard of the picturesque **Palazzo Pretorio,** and, if you want to see a representative collection of Etruscan bronzes, climb its centuries-old stone staircase to the **Museo dell'Accademia Etrusca** (Gallery of Etruscan Art). ✉ *Piazza Signorelli 9,* ☎ *0575/630415.* 🎫 *5,000 lire.* ☼ *Apr.–Sept., Tues.–Sun. 10–1, 4– 7; Oct.–Mar., Tues.–Sun. 9–1, 3–5.*

The **Museo Diocesano** (Diocesan Museum) houses an impressive num-ber of large and splendid paintings by native son Luca Signorelli, as well as a beautiful *Annunciation* by Fra Angelico, a delightful surprise to find in this small, eclectic town. ✉ *Piazza del Duomo 1,* ☎ *0575/ 62830.* 🎫 *5,000 lire.* ☼ *Apr.–Sept., Tues.–Sun. 9–1, 3–6:30; Oct.–Mar., Tues.–Sun. 9–1, 3–5.*

Dining and Lodging

$$ ✕ **La Loggetta.** Above Cortona's main medieval square, this attractive restaurant occupies a 16th-century wine cellar. In fair weather you can eat outdoors, overlooking the 13th-century town hall, dining on regional dishes and such specialties as cannelloni, here filled with spinach and ricotta, and tagliata. The owners pride themselves on their selection of Tuscan wines. ⊠ *Piazza Pescheria 3,* ☎ *0575/630575. AE, DC, MC, V. Closed Mon., Jan. 7–23, 2 wks in Mar.*

$$ ✕ **Tonino.** Deservedly well known and popular with locals and visitors alike, this large modern establishment can be noisy and crowded on holiday weekends. But it is very satisfactory indeed at all other times, when you can enjoy the view of the Chiana valley and feast on host Tonino's own *antipastissimo,* an incredible variety of delectables. This is the place to taste Chianina beefsteak. ⊠ *Piazza Garibaldi,* ☎ *0575/630500. AE, DC, MC, V. Closed Tues. No dinner Mon.*

$$$ ✕▣ **Il Falconiere.** A charming old villa less than 3½ kilometers (2 miles) outside Cortona, it once belonged to an early 19th-century poet and has been lovingly restored and impeccably furnished in the local style as an upscale inn. The winter garden and terrace have been transformed into a restaurant that features Tuscan dishes and seasonal specialties. ⊠ *Località San Martino,* ☎ *0575/612679,* ℻ *0575/612927. 12 rooms with bath. Restaurant, bar, pool. AE, DC, MC, V.*

Arezzo

㉖ *29 km (18 mi) north of Cortona, 81 km (50 mi) southeast of Florence.*

The birthplace of the poet Petrarch, of the Renaissance artist and art historian Giorgio Vasari, and of Guido d'Arezzo, the inventor of musical notation, is today best known for the magnificent, but very faint,
★ Piero della Francesca frescoes in the church of **San Francesco,** on Via Cavour in the center of town. Painted between 1452 and 1466, they depict *The Legend of the True Cross* on three walls of the choir. What Sir Kenneth Clark called "the most perfect morning light in all Renaissance painting" may be seen in the lowest section of the right wall, where the troops of the Emperor Maxentius flee before the sign of the cross. Unfortunately, part of the frescoes may be hidden from view while restoration work takes place.

With its irregular shape and sloping brick pavement, framed by buildings of assorted centuries, Arezzo's **Piazza Grande** echoes Siena's Piazza del Campo. Though not so grand, it is lively enough during the outdoor antiques fair every first Sunday of the month and when the **Joust of the Saracen,** featuring medieval costumes and competition, is held there on the first Sunday of September. The curving, tiered apse on Piazza Grande belongs to **Santa Maria della Pieve,** one of Tuscany's finest Romanesque churches. And Arezzo's medieval cathedral at the top of the hill harbors an eye-level fresco of a tender Magdalen by Piero della Francesca; look for it next to the large marble tomb near the organ.

There are several other attractions in Arezzo as well. The church of **San Domenico,** north of Piazza Grande at Piazza Fossombroni (just inside the walls) houses a 13th-century crucifix by Cimabue. The **Giorgio Vasari** house was designed and decorated by the region's leading Mannerist artist in 1540 for his own use. It's just west of San Domenico. The **Museo Archeologico** boasts a fine collection of Etruscan bronzes. ⊠ *Vasari house: Via XX Settembre 55,* ☎ *0575/300301.* ▣ *Free.* ☉ *Tues.–Sat. 9–7, Sun. 9–1.* ⊠ *Museo Archeologico: Via Margaritone 10,* ☎ *0575/20882.* ▣ *8,000 lire.* ☉ *Tues.–Sat. 9–2, Sun. 9–1.*

Dining and Lodging

$$ ✕ **Buca di San Francesco.** A frescoed cellar restaurant in a historic building next to the church of San Francesco, this "buca" (literally "hole," figuratively "cellar") has a medieval atmosphere and serves straightforward local specialties, including *ribollita*. Meat eaters will find the lean Chianina beef and the *saporita di Bonconte* (a selection of several meats) succulent treats. ✉ *Piazza San Francesco 1,* ☎ *0575/23271. AE, DC, MC, V. Closed Tues., and July. No dinner Mon.*

$$ ✕ **Tastevin.** Close to San Francesco and to the central Piazza Guido Monaco, Tastevin has introduced creative cooking styles in Arezzo but serves traditional dishes as well, in three attractive dining rooms, two in warm Tuscan provincial style, one in more sophisticated bistro style. At the small bar the talented owner plays and sings show tunes and Sinatra songs in the evening; there is a 15% cover charge for music. The restaurant's specialties are penne Tastevin (with cream of truffles) and seafood or meat carpaccio. ✉ *Via dei Cenci 9,* ☎ *0575/28304. AE, MC, V. Closed Mon. (Sun. in summer) and Aug. 1–25.*

$ ✕ **Spiedo d'Oro.** Cheery red-and-white tablecloths add a bright note to this large, reliable trattoria near the archeological museum. This is your chance to try authentic Tuscan home-style specialties, such as *zuppa di pane* (bread soup), *pappardelle all'ocio* (noodles with duck sauce), and osso buco *all'aretina* (sautéed veal shank). ✉ *Via Crispi 12,* ☎ *0575/22873. No credit cards. Closed Thurs. and July 1–18.*

$$ ✕🏠 **Castello di Gargonza.** A tiny 13th-century hamlet with a castle, church, and cobbled streets offers something unusual as hostelries go. All its houses—cottages and apartments, really—are for rent by the week, and rooms can be had by the night. This enchanting spot in the countryside between Siena and Arezzo, part of the fiefdom of the aristocratic Florentine Guicciardini family, was restored by the modern Count Roberto Guicciardini as a way to rescue a dying village. The houses have one to six rooms each, sleep two to seven people, and have as many as four baths. La Torre restaurant serves local specialties. ✉ *52048 Monte San Savino,* ☎ *0575/847021,* 𝖥𝖠𝖷 *0575/847054. 18 houses with bath. Restaurant (closed Tues.). AE, MC, V. Closed Jan. 10–Feb. 10.*

$$ 🏠 **Continental.** Centrally located near the train station and within walking distance of all major sights, the Continental has been a reliable and convenient place to stay since it opened in the 1950s. Recently refurbished, it now has bright white furnishings with yellow accents, gleaming new bathrooms complete with hair dryers, and a pleasant roof garden. Rates are at the low end of the $$ category. ✉ *Piazza Guido Monaco 7,* ☎ *0575/20251,* 𝖥𝖠𝖷 *0575/350485. 74 rooms with bath or shower. Restaurant (closed Mon., no dinner Sun.). AE, DC, MC, V.*

Outdoor Activities and Sports

A popular horseback riding site is **Rendola Riding** (✉ Rendola Valdarno, Arezzo, ☎ 0575/987045).

Shopping

Arezzo is known for its production of gold, as well as a burgeoning cottage knitwear industry. For sweaters, try **Maglierie** (✉ Piazza Grande).

The first Sunday of each month, a colorful **flea market** selling antiques and not-so-antiques takes place in the **Piazza Grande**.

TUSCANY A TO Z

Arriving and Departing

By Car
The Autostrada del Sole (A1), connects Florence with Bologna, 105 km (65 miles) north, and Rome, 277 kilometers (172 miles) south, and passes close to Arezzo.

By Plane·
The largest airports in the region are Pisa's **Galileo Galilei Airport** (☎ 050/500707) and Florence's **Peretola Airport** (☎ 055/373498).

By Train
The coastal line from Rome to Genoa passes through Pisa and all the beach resorts. The main line from Rome to Bologna passes through Arezzo, Florence, and Prato.

Getting Around

By Boat
Boat services link the islands of Tuscany's archipelago with the mainland; passenger and car ferries leave from Piombino for Elba: **Navarma Line** (✉ Via Pisacane 110, ☎ 0565/225211); **Elba Ferries** (✉ Piazzale Premuda, ☎ 0565/220956); **Toremar** (✉ Piazzale Premuda 13, ☎ 0565/31100). The ferry to Giglio leaves from Porto Santo Stefano on the Argentario peninsula (☞ Toremar, *above*).

By Bus
Tuscany is crisscrossed by bus lines that connect the smaller towns and cities on the autostrade and superhighways. They are a good choice for touring the hill towns around Siena, such as San Gimignano; you can then take a Tra-In or Lazzi bus from Siena to Arezzo and get back onto the main Rome-Florence train line. From Chiusi on the main train line you can get a bus to Montepulciano. Buses connect Florence and Siena with Volterra.

By Car
The best way to see Tuscany, making it possible to explore the tiny towns and country restaurants that are so much a part of the region's charm, is by car. A11 leads west from Florence and meets the coastal A12 between Viareggio and Livorno. The A1 autostrada links Florence with Arezzo and Chiusi (where you turn off for Montepulciano). A toll-free superstrada links Florence with Siena. Drivers should be prepared to navigate through bewildering suburban sprawls around Tuscan cities; to reach the historic sections where most of the sights are located, look for the CENTRO STORICO signs.

By Train
Italy's main rail line, which runs from Milan to Calabria, links Florence and Arezzo in Tuscany and runs past Chiusi and Cortona on its way south. Another main line extends through our Tuscan Gateway towns, connecting Florence with Pisa by way of Prato, Pistoia, and Lucca. There are a few other local lines.

Contacts and Resources

Car Rentals
Cars are for rent at the airports and in the larger cities in Tuscany; Alitalia may offer economical fly/drive packages with discounts on car rentals and hotels.

Avis has offices at Peretola Airport in Florence (☎ 055/372588), Arezzo (✉ Piazza della Repubblica 1/a, ☎ 0575/354232), Lucca (✉ Via Castracane 1217, ☎ 0583/490383), and Sinea (✉ Via Simone Martini, 36 ☎ 0577/270305). **Hertz** has offices at Galileo Galilei Airport in Pisa (☎ 050/49187), Prato (✉ c/o Autonoleggio Europa, Viale Vittorio Veneto 57, ☎ 0574/21055), and in Siena (✉ Via San Marco 96, ☎ 0577/41148).

Emergencies
Police, fire (☎ 113). **Ambulance** or medical emergency (☎ 118).

Fishing
For a license, contact the **Federazione Italiana della Pesca Sportiva** (✉ Via dei Neri 6, Firenze).

Guided Tours
From Florence, **American Express** (✉ Via Guicciardini 49/r, ☎ 055/288751) operates one-day excursions to Siena and San Gimignano and can arrange for cars, drivers, and guides for special-interest tours in Tuscany. **CIT** (✉ Via Cavour 56, ☎ 055/294306) has a three-day Carosello bus tour from Rome to Florence, Siena, and San Gimignano, as well as a five-day tour that also takes in Venice.

Horseback Riding
Rifugio Prategiano (✉ Montieri, Grosseto, ☎ 0566/997703), **Le Cannelle** (✉ Parco dell'Uccellina, Talamone, Grosseto, ☎ 0564/887020). For more information, contact the **Federazione Italiana Sport Equestre** (✉ Via Paoletti 54, Firenze, ☎ 055/480039).

Sailing
Charters in Tuscany are available through the **Centro Nautico Italiano** (✉ Piazza della Signoria 31/r, Firenze, ☎ 055/287045); **Mario Lorenzoni** (✉ Via degli Alfani 105/r, Firenze, ☎ 055/284790); and **Renato Lessi** (✉ Località Porto, Castiglione della Pescaia, Grosseto, ☎ 0564/922793). For more information, contact the **Federazione Italiana Vela** (✉ CP 49, Marina di Carrara, ☎ 0585/57323) or the **Federazione Italiana Motonautica** (✉ Via Goldora 16, 55044 Marina di Pietrasanta, ☎ 0584/20963).

Skiing
For information, contact the **Federazione Italiana Sport Invernali** (✉ Viale Matteotti 15, Firenze, ☎ 055/576987).

Travel Agencies
In Florence: **American Express** (✉ Via Guicciardini 49/r, ☎ 055/288751); **CIT** (✉ Via Cavour 56, ☎ 055/294306); or **Thomas Cook** (✉ c/o World Vision, Via Cavour 154/r, ☎ 055/579294).

Visitor Information
REGIONAL INFORMATION
Stop in **Florence** (✉ Via di Novoli, ☎ 055/439311).

LOCAL INFORMATION
There are tourist offices, generally open 9–12:30, 3:30–7:30, in **Arezzo** (✉ Piazza della Repubblica 28, ☎ 0575/377678); **Cortona** (✉ Via Nazionale 72, ☎ 0575/630352); **Lucca** (✉ Piazzale Verdi, ☎ 0583/419689); **Pisa** (✉ Piazza Duomo 8, ☎ 050/560464); **Pistoia** (✉ Palazzo dei Vescovi, ☎ 0573/21622); **Prato** (✉ Via Cairoli 48, ☎ 0574/24112); **San Gimignano** (✉ Piazza del Duomo, ☎ 0577/940008); **Siena** (✉ Via di Città 43, ☎ 0577/42209; ✉ Piazza del Campo 55, ☎ 0577/280551); **Volterra** (✉ Via Turazza 2, ☎ 0588/86150).

5 Venice

Canals, Palaces and Islands

It's easy to forgive Venice—thanks to its myriad canals—for its eternal preoccupation with its own beauty. All the picture books in the world won't prepare you for the city's exotic landmarks, such as the Basilica di San Marco and the Palazzo Ducale, which rise from the lagoons like mirages. With sumptuous palaces and romantic waterways, Venice is straight out of an 18th-century Canaletto masterpiece.

I**T IS CALLED LA SERENISSIMA.** The literal translation of this name is ungainly: "the most serene." The term "Serene Republic" more successfully suggests the monstrous power and majesty of this city that was for centuries the unrivaled mistress of trade between Europe and the Orient and the staunch bulwark of Christendom against the tides of Turkish expansion. It suggests, too, the extraordinary beauty of the city—and surely Venice is the most beautiful city in the world (although the Florentines would surely disagree)—and its lavishness and fantasy, the result not just of its remarkable buildings but of the very fact that Venice is a city built on water, a city created more than 1,000 years ago by men who dared defy the sea, implanting their splendid palaces and churches on mud banks in a swampy and treacherous lagoon.

Thanks to its myriad canals, Venice—most narcissistic of cities—is eternally preoccupied with the contemplation of its own loveliness. No matter how many times you have seen it in pictures or movies or TV commercials, the real thing is stranger and more dreamlike than you ever imagined. Its landmarks, the Basilica di San Marco and the Palazzo Ducale, seem hardly Italian: Delightfully idiosyncratic, they are exotic mélanges of Byzantine, Gothic, and Renaissance styles. Piazza San Marco is a true public gathering space, full of music and laughter and joy, yet only a minute's walk away are streets so quiet that your footsteps echo on the stone pavements and shuttered, crumbling facades. Sunlight shimmers here, and silvery mist softens every perspective. It is a city full of secrets, ineffably romantic, and—at times—given over entirely to pleasure.

You must walk everywhere in Venice—Venezia in Italian—and where you cannot walk, you go by water. Occasionally, from fall to spring, you have to walk *in* water, when extraordinarily high tides known as *acque alte* invade the lower parts of the city, flooding Piazza San Marco for a few hours. Unless you're lucky to find some makeshift *passarelle* (plank bridges) that appear from nowhere to keep certain busy routes open, you'll have to take off your socks and shoes, roll up your pant legs, and wade in with everyone else. The problem of protecting Venice and its lagoon from dangerously high tides has generated extravagant plans and so many committee reports that the city may sink as much under the weight of paper as under water. Progress is being made. For centuries Venice's canals were regularly dredged to keep them clean and navigable. After nearly 30 years' neglect, the dredging of canals was finally resumed in 1993. It is hoped that waterless and malodorous canals (caused by *acque basse*—exceptionally low tides) will soon be a thing of the past. Today, Venetians are being encouraged by state subsidies to renovate their homes, rather than leave the city to live and work on the mainland—a trend that over the last three decades has drastically reduced Venice's resident population.

In spite of these problems, Venetians have mastered the art of living well in their singular city. You'll see them going about their daily affairs in *vaporetti* (water buses), crowded aboard the *traghetti* (traditional gondola ferries) that ply between the banks of the Grand Canal, in the *campi* (squares), and along the *calli* (narrow Venetian streets). They are nothing if not skilled—and remarkably tolerant—in dealing with the veritable armies of tourists from all over the world that at peak times flow through the city, marching like regiments behind some improbable standard (multicolored umbrella, Day-Glo gas-filled balloon, silk scarf, or even pink teddy bear tied to a pole) born aloft by their leader, or clustered in bemused groups around guides straining to impart their knowledge in a competing babble of tongues. If you come during the most popular seasons, like the Venetians, you will have to adapt to the crowds, visiting the major sights at odd hours, when the tour groups are still at breakfast or have boarded buses on their return to the mainland (most of them are day-trippers). Get away from Piazza San Marco when it's crowded; you'll be surprised to find many areas of Venice practically deserted. Explore the districts of Cannaregio or Castello, quiet areas where you can find the time and space to sit and contemplate the watercolor pages of Venetian history.

Founded on the marshes by the Roman Veneti escaping from the barbarians, Venice rose from the waters to dominate the Adriatic and hold the gorgeous East in fee. Early in its history the city called in Byzantine artists to decorate its churches with brilliant mosaics, still glowing today. Then the influence of Lombard-Romanesque architecture from the 11th to 13th centuries gave rise to the characteristic type of palace for which Venice is famous the world over. Many of the sumptuous palaces along the Grand Canal were built at that time, strong reminders of Venice's control of the major trade routes to the East. Subsequently, Gothic styles from elsewhere in Europe were adapted to create a new kind of Venetian Gothic art and architecture.

Venice attained a peak of power and prosperity in the 15th and 16th centuries. It extended its domain inland to include all of what is now known as the Veneto region and even beyond. In the last half of the 15th century, the Renaissance arrived in Venice, and the city's greatest artists—Giovanni and Gentile Bellini and Carpaccio in the late 15th century; Giorgione, Titian, Veronese, and Tintoretto in the 16th century—played a decisive role in the development of Western art, and their work still covers walls and ceilings and altars all over the city today.

The decline of Venice came slowly. For 400 years the powerful maritime city-republic had held sway. After the 16th century the tide changed. The Ottoman Empire blocked Venice's Mediterranean trade routes, and newly emerging sea powers, such as Britain and the Netherlands, broke Venice's monopoly by opening oceanic trading routes. Like its steadily dwindling fortunes, Venice's art and culture began a prolonged decline, leaving only the splendid monuments to recall a fabled past, with the luminous paintings of Canaletto and the beautiful frescoes of Tiepolo striking a glorious swan song.

You can see the panoply of history by visiting only the major museums and churches, but if you want a fuller picture of the districts that keep this a living city, get off the beaten path as often as you can. You will almost certainly lose your way (everyone does), but Venetians are usually only too pleased to direct you if you ask; chances are, they will admire your initiative and put you back on the right track.

Pleasures and Pastimes

Carnival

" . . . All the world repaire to Venice to see the folly and madnesse of the Carnevall . . .'tis impossible to recount the universal madnesses of this place during this time of licence," commented traveler John Evelyn in 1646. Indeed, Carnevale (as it is known in Italian) was once a festival that was an excuse for all manner of carnal indulgence. In its 18th-century heyday, festivities began on December 26 and lasted two months; nowadays the festival has lost some of its more outlandish flavor and lasts only 10 days (the 10 days preceeding Ash Wednesday), but the event has become so vast—and so commercialized—that Venice frequently has to be "shut" during this time owing to the sheer weight of numbers.

Dining

The general standard of Venetian restaurants has suffered from the on-slaught of mass tourism, but it is still possible to eat well in Venice at moderate prices. Although seafood is a specialty here, the fact that the wholesale cost of fish is generally higher than meat is reflected in the prices, and you will find some fish dishes very expensive, especially those that are priced by weight (mainly baked or steamed fish). However, if you do want to eat fish, don't be shy about asking the cost. Under the auspices of the restaurant association, most of the city's restaurants offer special tourist menus, moderately priced according to the level of the restaurant and generally representing good value. It's always a good idea to reserve your table or have your hotel *portiere* (concierge) do it for you. Dining hours are short, starting at 12:30 or 1 for lunch and ending at 2:30 or 3, when restaurants close for the afternoon, open-ing up again to start serving at about 8 and closing again at 11 or mid-night. Most close one day a week and are also likely to close without notice for vacation or renovation. Few have signs on the outside, so when the metal blinds are shut tight, you can't tell a closed restaurant from a closed TV-repair shop. This makes them hard to spot as you explore the city. You may not find a *pane e coperto* (cover charge), but a service charge of 10%–15% will almost surely be on the check.

Venetian cuisine is based on seafood, with a few culinary excursions inland. Antipasto may take the form of a seafood salad, prosciutto *di San Daniele* (cured ham of the Veneto region), or pickled vegetables. As a first course Venetians favor risotto, a creamy rice dish that may be cooked with vegetables or shellfish. Pasta, too, is good with seafood sauces; Venice is *not* the place to order spaghetti with tomato sauce. *Pasticcio di pesce* is pasta baked with fish, usually *baccalà* (cod). A clas-sic first course is pasta *e fagioli* (thick bean soup with pasta). *Bigoli* is strictly a local pasta, made of whole wheat, usually served with a salty *tonno* (tuna) sauce. Polenta, made of cornmeal, is another pillar of re-gional cooking. It's often served as an accompaniment to *fegato alla veneziana* (liver with onions). Local seafood includes *granseola* (crab), *moeche* (small, soft-shelled crabs), and *seppie* or *seppioline* (cuttlefish).

The dessert specialty in Venice is *tiramisù*, a heavenly concoction of mascarpone (cream cheese), coffee, chocolate, and *savoirdi* (ladyfin-gers). The recipe originated on the mainland, but the Venetians have adopted it enthusiastically. Local wines are the dry white Tocai and Pinot from the Friuli region and bubbly white Prosecco, a naturally fermented sparkling wine that is a shade less dry. The best Prosecco comes from the Valdobbiadene; Cartizze, which is similar, is consid-ered superior by some but is expensive. Popular red wines include mer-lot, cabernet, Raboso, and Refosco. You can sample all of these and more in Venice's many *bacari* (old-style wine bars), where wine is served by the glass (known as an *ombra* in Venetian dialect) and ac-companied by *cicchetti* (assorted tidbits), often substantial enough for a light meal.

Lodging

Due to the city's great popularity, Venetian hotels can cater to all tastes and price ranges. Getting to your hotel is also the difference be-tween arriving in a water taxi or gondola direct to the front door, and wandering down curious alleys and side streets thinking to yourself, "Haven't we been here before?"

Most of Venice's hotels are in renovated palaces. The most exclusive of these are indeed palatial, although even they may have some small, dowdy "Cinderella"-type rooms. In lower categories, space is at a premium; some rooms may be cramped, and not all hotels have lounging areas. Because of preservation laws, some cannot install elevators. Air-conditioning can be essential for those who suffer in summer heat; some hotels charge a supplement for it. Although the city has no cars, it does have boats plying the canals and pedestrians chattering in the streets, even late at night, so ask for a quiet room if noise bothers you. And during the summer months, don't leave your room lights on at night *and* your window wide open: Mosquitoes can descend en masse.

EXPLORING VENICE

The church of San Marco is unquestionably the heart of Venice, but venturing even 50 yards from it can sometimes lead to confusion. Although the smaller canals (a canal is called a *rio*) are spanned by frequent bridges, the Grand Canal can only be crossed on foot at three points—near the train station, at the Rialto Bridge, and at the Accademia Bridge—which decidedly complicates matters. It's supremely maddening to find yourself on the wrong bank of a canal with no bridge in sight.

A street is called a *calle,* but a street that runs alongside a canal is called either a *riva* or a *fondamenta.* The closed-in streetscapes of Venice make it hard to see any reference point, such as the spire of the Campanile, above the rooftops, and the narrow backstreets often take unpredictable turns that foul up your sense of direction. Streets and canals may look deceptively familiar, only to make sudden dead ends. To get around Venice, travelers often use the vaporetti, those festive ferries that circulate through the city on set routes (this chapter uses the terms vaporetto and line interchangeably). A map of vaporetto routes is always helpful because the best way back to Piazza San Marco or your hotel may well be along one of these lines.

A scheme called *Dal Museo alla Città* (From Museum to City) was begun in 1995 to encourage visitors to seek out art not only in museums but also throughout the city proper—primarily in the churches and *scuole* (charitable confraternity halls) for which it was originally commissioned. As part of this, more than a dozen places selected for their artistic merit now have fixed visiting hours when tourists can be sure of finding the place open and of not intruding on church services. At these times (given in the itineraries below as "visiting hours") there should always be someone available to provide information, a free leaflet (available in English); there is also the opportunity to buy postcards and booklets about these important sights. New lighting systems have been installed, all of which take 500-lire coins. Although regular opening hours will continue (most likely 10–12 PM and 4–6 PM in winter or 5–7 PM in summer), visitors can now rely on confirmed admission during the new set schedule.

Great Itineraries

IF YOU HAVE 2 DAYS

Begin the first day with a look at Piazza San Marco and the surrounding buildings. Follow this with a cruise down the Grand Canal to see the more important palazzi. The second day, visit some of the prominent churches of Venice in the Merceria district and finish with a trip to the islands of Murano and Torcello.

IF YOU HAVE 4 DAYS

Spend your first day visiting the sights in and around that most famous of piazze, Piazza San Marco, including the Basilica and the Museo Correr. Dedicate the next day to cruising down the Grand Canal, stopping to visit the Accademia Gallery, a treasure-trove of Venetian painting, and the Ca' Rezzonico. Don't forget to walk over the Rialto Bridge to the surrounding markets. End your day with a visit to San Stae, a particularly characteristic neighborhood. On the third day, visit the Campo Santi Giovanni e Paolo and the the Campo dell'Arsenale, only a short walk from your next stop, the Museo Navale (Naval Museum). Return to Piazza San Marco and take the 52 or 82 line from San Zaccaria for a look at the impressive churches of San Giorgio Maggiore and Il Redentore, both of which are particularly beautiful sights at sunset. On your final day visit the islands of the lagoon: Be sure not to miss Murano and its glass museums, along with the islands of Burano and Torcello.

IF YOU HAVE 6 DAYS

Start at Piazza San Marco, where you should visit the Basilica, the Museo Correr, and the Palazzo Ducale, ending your day on the Ponte dei Sospiri (Bridge of Sighs). Dedicate the following day to cruising the Grand Canal, stopping at Santa Maria della Salute and the nearby Peggy Guggenheim Collection, before visiting the Accademia Gallery. Next visit the Ca' Rezzonico and take a walk over the Rialto Bridge to the surrounding markets. Spend the late afternoon walking through the neighborhood of San Stae. On the third day, visit Santa Maria dei Miracoli, Campo Santi Giovanni e Paolo, the Campo dell'Arsenale, and finally the Museo Navale (Naval Museum). If you have time, try to visit the island of San Pietro di Castello before returning to Piazza San Marco via the Scuola di San Giorgio degli Schiavoni, whose collection of Carpaccio's works is unparalleled anywhere in the world. On the fourth day, take the 52 or 82 line from San Zaccaria for a look at the impressive churches of San Giorgio Maggiore and Il Redentore, as well as the island of the Giudecca. Head directly across from the Giudecca to the Zattere, a lively promenade con Dorsoduro where you will find a number of pizzerias. Spend the fifth day exploring the area of Venice dedicated to Titian: Start in Campo Santo Stefano and then head for the Scuola dei Carmini and the church of San Sebastiano. A must is the Friari, home of some of Titian's best work. Next, visit the Scuola di San Rocco, where you will find some delightful paintings by Tintoretto. Devote your final day to exloring the islands of the lagoon. Be sure to visit Murano's glass museum and save time for stops on Burano and Torcello. If you can, squeeze in a visit to the cemetery island of San Michele.

Piazza San Marco, The Heart Of Venice

The most beautiful square in the world, Piazza San Marco (St. Mark's Square) is the heart of Venice, a vast open square enclosed by an orderly procession of arcades marching towards the fairy-tale cupolas and marble lacework of the Basilica di San Marco. Perpetually animated during the day when it's filled with people and crowds of fluttering pigeons, it can be magical at night, especially in the winter, when melancholy mists swirl around the lampposts and bell tower.

A Good Walk

Numbers in the text correspond to numbers in the margin and on the Venice map.

Start your day in the **Piazza San Marco** ① with a morning visit to the **Basilica di San Marco** ②, home of the **Pala d'Oro** and **St. Mark's Museum.** Move on to the smaller **Piazzetta San Marco** for a visit of the glorious **Palazzo Ducale** ④ and a look at the **Ponte dei Sospiri** at the east wing of the palace. Return to Piazza San Marco where directly opposite the facade of the basilica you will find the **Museo Correr** ⑤ in the **Ala Napoleonica** (Napoleonic Wing). End your exploring tour of San Marco with a bird's-eye of the piazza and the rest of the city from the **Campanile** ③.

TIMING

A full day is required to visit each sight thoroughly. If you have limited time, you will need to discipline yourself from straying too far from the Piazza San Marco; a half-day should be enough to see the essential sights, but do not miss the Pala d'Oro in the basilica, the Palazzo Ducale, and, of course, the piazza itself.

Sights to See

★ ❷ **Basilica di San Marco.** This is one of Europe's most beautiful churches. An opulent synthesis of Byzantine and Romanesque styles, it is laid out in a Greek cross topped off with five plump domes. The Basilica did not actually become the cathedral of Venice until as late as 1807, but its role as the church of the doge (the elected head of the Venetian republic) gave it immense power and wealth. It was begun in 1063, and inaugurated in 1094, to house the remains of St. Mark the Evangelist, which were filched from Alexandria two centuries earlier by two agents of the doge. The story goes that they stole the saint's remains and hid them in a barrel under layers of pickled pork to get them past the Muslim guards.

That escapade is illustrated in a mosaic in the lunette (semicircular decoration) over the farthest left of the front doors. This 13th-century mosaic is the earliest one on this heavily decorated facade; look at it closely and you can see a picture of the church as it appeared in the 13th century.

Over the years this church stood as a symbol of Venetian wealth and power, and it was endowed with all the riches the Republic's admirals and merchants could carry off from the Orient, earning it the nickname Chiesa D'Oro (Golden Church). The four bronze horses that prance and snort over the central doorway (copies only, but the originals are on view indoors in the Museo di San Marco, ☞ *below*) were classical sculptures that victorious Venetians took away from Constantinople in 1204, along with a lot of other loot that you can see inside. Just inside the central front doors in the church porch, look for a medallion of red porphyry set in the floor to mark the spot of another of Venice's political coups: the reconciliation between Barbarossa, the Holy Roman Emperor, and Pope Alexander III, brought about by Doge Sebastiano Ziani in 1177.

One of the innovations of this church was a roof of brick vaulting, rather than wood, enabling the ceiling to be decorated with mosaics. As you enter the basilica, you'll find it surprisingly dark inside, compared to the soaring light-filled Gothic cathedrals of northern Europe. This is because many of the original windows were filled in and covered with even more mosaics. In the mysterious dusk, candles flicker and the gold tiles of mosaics glitter softly, sensuously. (The tiles were laid on at slight angles to achieve precisely this effect.) The earliest mosaics are from the 11th and 12th centuries; later ones were done as late as the 16th century, such as the *Last Judgment* on the arch between the porch and the nave, said to be based on drawings by Tintoretto. The dim light, the galleries high above the naves—they served as the *matroneum,* the women's gallery—the massive altar screen, or iconostasis, the single massive Byzantine chandelier, even the Greek cross ground plan, give San Marco an exotic aspect quite unlike that of most Christian churches. The effect is remarkable. Here the pomp and mystery of Oriental magnificence are wedded to Christian belief, creating an intensely awesome impression.

Go into the **Zen Chapel** (to the right just off the porch, and named after a local cardinal rather than any form of Buddhism) to see some earlier (13th-century) mosaics, telling the story of the life of St. Mark. Next to it, the **baptistery** contains a bronze font cover by Jacopo

Sansovino and the tomb of Doge Andrea Dandolo (1307–54), a friend of Petrarch and a writer in his own right. Several of the earlier doges were buried here, while later ones were interred in the church of Santi Giovanni e Paolo (☞ *below*).

Two more chapels, both in the left transept, are worth a special look: the **Chapel of the Madonna of Nicopeia,** which holds a precious icon (part of the loot from Constantinople) that many consider Venice's most powerful protector; and next to it, on the left, a small chapel dedicated to the Virgin Mary with fine 15th-century mosaics depicting her life, possibly based on drawings by Andrea Mantegna.

If you stand in the central aisle facing the main altar, notice the polygonal pulpit to the right, at the intersection of the nave and right transept. After the coronation ceremony, each new doge stood here for the people to behold him in the glory of his new office.

The **Sanctuary** in the Basilica of San Marco charges an admission fee, but it's well worth it. The main altar, with its green marble canopy lifted high on carved alabaster columns, covers the tomb of St. Mark. Behind this is the real attraction: the **Pala d'Oro** (Golden Altarpiece), a dazzling gilded silver screen encrusted with 1,927 precious gems and 255 enameled panels. It was originally made in Constantinople in the 11th century, but was continually embellished over the next few centuries by Byzantine and Venetian master craftsmen, reaching its present state of extraordinary sumptuousness in the mid-14th century. It is well worth investing in the excellently produced color booklet on the Pala (3,000 lire at the card shop to the left of the atrium) so as not to miss its incredible artistic and narrative detail. The bronze door leading from the sanctuary back into the sacristy is another Sansovino work; check out the top left corner, where the artist included a self-portrait and, above that, a picture of his friend and fellow artist Titian. Tickets for the Sanctuary also include admission into the **Treasury,** which is entered from the right transept. It contains some exquisite pieces, many of them exotic treasures borne away from Constantinople and other vanquished places.

From the atrium, climb the steep stairway to the **Galleria** and the **Museo di San Marco** (St. Mark's Museum) for a look at the interior of the church from the organ gallery and a sweeping view of Piazza San Marco and the Piazzetta dei Leoncini from the outdoor gallery. The highlight of the museum is the close-up of the four magnificent gilded bronze horses that once stood outside on the gallery. The originals were probably cast in Imperial Rome, and later transported to the New Rome, Constantinople. Napoléon hauled them off to Paris after he conquered Venice in 1797, but they were returned after the fall of the French Empire.

Entrance to the church is free, but be warned: Guards at the door turn away any visitors, male or female, wearing shorts or inappropriate attire. If you want to take a free guided tour in English (offered Mon.–Sat. at 11 AM in summer, and with less certainty in winter, since the guides are volunteers), wait on the left in the porch for a group to form. ⊠ *Basilica of San Marco,* 🎫 *Free.* 🕐 *Mon.–Sat. 9:30–5, Sun. 2–5. Museum:* ☎ *041/522–5205.* 🎫 *3,000 lire.* 🕐 *Apr.–Sept., daily 9:30–5; Nov.–Mar., daily 10–4. Sanctuary:* ☎ *041/522–5697.* 🎫 *3,000 lire.* 🕐 *Apr.–Sep., Mon.–Sat. 9:30–5, Sun. 2–5; Oct.–Mar., Mon.–Sat. 10–4, Sun. 2–4 (hrs for Museum and Sanctuary may vary slightly at different times of the year).*

★ ❸ **Campanile.** The tall brick bell tower is a reconstruction of the original, which stood for 1,000 years before it collapsed one morning in

1912, practically without warning (miraculously none of the surrounding buildings suffered serious damage, and the only victim was a cat). In the 15th century, clerics found guilty of immoral behavior were suspended in wooden cages from the tower, sometimes to subsist on bread and water for as long as a year, sometimes to starve to death. The pretty marble loggia (covered gallery) at its base was built in the early 16th century by Jacopo Sansovino. It, too, has been carefully restored. The view from the tower on a clear day is worth the price of admission. You get an eagle's-eye view of the city, the Lido, the lagoon, and the mainland as far as the distant Alps. Oddly, you can't see the myriad canals that snake through the 117 islets on which Venice is built. ⊠ *Piazza San Marco,* ☎ *041/522–4064.* ▣ *5,000 lire.* ⊙ *Easter–Sept., daily 9:30–7; Oct., daily 10–6; Nov.–Easter, daily 10–4:30. Closed for maintenance most of Jan.*

⑤ Museo Correr. Inside this museum you will find a fascinating and varied collection of historical items and paintings by old masters. These works were once the private collection of the aristocrat Teodoro Correr, who donated them to the city in 1830. Exhibits range from the absurdly high-soled shoes worn by 16th-century Venetian ladies (who had to be supported by a servant on each side in order to walk on these precarious perches) to fine art by the talented Bellini family of Renaissance painters. ⊠ *Piazza San Marco, Ala Napoleonica,* ☎ *041/522–5625.* ▣ *8,000 lire.* ⊙ *Apr.–Oct., Wed.–Mon. 10–5; Nov.–Mar., Wed.–Mon. 10–4; last entry 1 hr before closing.*

★ ❹ Palazzo Ducale. This Gothic-Renaissance fantasia of pink-and-white marble, a majestic expression of the prosperity and power attained by Venice during its most glorious period, rises above Piazzetta San Marco. Its top-heavy design (the dense upper floors rest on the graceful ground-floor colonnade) has always confounded architectural purists, who insist that proper architecture be set out the other way around. The building was much more than just a palace. Rather it was a sort of combination White House, Senate, torture chamber, and prison rolled into one. Venice's government, set up sometime in the 7th century as a participatory democracy, provided for an elected ruler, the doge, to serve for life, but in practice he was simply a figurehead. Power really rested with the Great Council, originally an elected body but, from the 13th century on, an aristocratic stronghold, with members inheriting their seats from their noble ancestors. Laws were passed by the Senate, a group of 200 elected from the Great Council (which could have as many as 1,700 members); executive powers belonged to the College, a committee of 25 leaders. In the 14th century, the Council of Ten was formed to deal with emergency situations; this group's meetings were not open to the public, and the Council often proved more powerful than the Senate, though its members could only serve for limited terms before new members were elected.

A fortress for the doge existed on this spot in the early 9th century; the building you see today was a product of the 12th century, although, like the basilica next door, it was continually added to and transformed throughout the centuries. You enter the palace at the ornate Gothic **Porta della Carta** (Gate of the Paper, where official decrees were traditionally posted), which opens onto an immense courtyard. Ahead is the **Scala dei Giganti** (Stairway of the Giants), guarded by huge statues of Mars and Neptune by Jacopo Sansovino. Ordinary mortals do not get to climb these stairs, however; after paying your fee, walk along the arcade to reach the central interior staircase. Its upper flight is called the **Scala d'Oro** (Golden Staircase), also designed by Sansovino, with its lavish gilded decoration. Although it may seem odd that the gov-

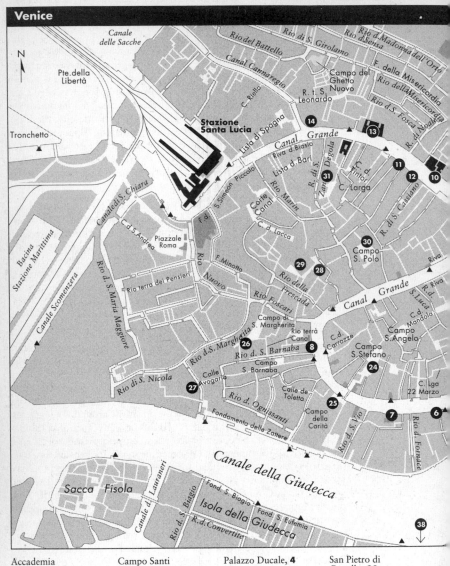

Sacca
della
Misericordia

Canale delle Navi

33 — 36

San
Michele

0   440 yards
0   400 meters

C. Pacchetta
Fondamente
Rio S. Caterina
32

Strada
Nuova
Rio d'Santi Apostoli
R.d. Gesuiti Nuova
Fondamente Nuove

Campo d.
Pescheria

C.d Testa
C.d. Squero
Rio della Panada
dei Mendicanti

Erberia
del Vin
9
Rio d. S. Marina
16
Campo Santi
Giovanni e Paolo
17   18
R. Barbaria   delle Tole

R.d S.
Guistina

del Carbon
Merceria
R.d Fava
Sol. d. S. Lio
C. d Bande
15
Ruga Giuffa
R.d. S. Severo
R.d S.Lorenzo
R.d S.
Francesco
19

Campo
Manin

Fabbri
R. d. Palazzo
SAN
ZACCARIA
5 1 3 2 4
Molo
Riva degli
Schiavoni

C. Lion
23
C. d.
Furlani
R.d Pietá
R. d.Greci
R. d Scudi
R.d Corpus

Canale
d. Galeazze

Darsena
Grande

Rio d. Vergini
Rio d. S. Daniele
di S. Pietro
22

Freezeria
S. Moise
R. d.
i
i
Piazza
San Marco

Rio della Tana
20
R.d Arsenale
21
V. Garibaldi
Riva dei Sette Martiri

Rio d.S. Anna
R. d. S. Giuseppe

Canale di S. Marco

37
Isola di
S. Giorgio
Maggiore

Fond.
delle Zitelle

Ci

Calle
Michelangelo

Riva dei Partigiani
Rio dei Giardini

KEY
i Tourist Information
▲ Boat stop

ernment's main council rooms and reception halls would be so far upstairs, imagine how effectively foreign emissaries must have been intimidated by this arduous climb.

Visitors must have also been overwhelmed by the sumptuous decoration of these apartments, their walls and ceilings covered with works by Venice's greatest artists. Among the grand rooms you can visit are the **Anticollegio** (a waiting room outside the College's chamber), which features two fine paintings, Tintoretto's *Bacchus and Ariadne Crowned by Venus* and Veronese's *Rape of Europa;* the **Sala del Collegio** (College Chamber), its ceiling magnificently painted by Veronese; and the **Sala del Senato** (Senate Chamber), with Tintoretto's *Triumph of Venice* on the ceiling. The huge *Paradise* on the end wall of the **Great Council Hall** is by Jacopo Tintoretto (1518–94): It is a dark, dynamic masterpiece. This is the world's largest oil painting (23 by 75 feet), a vast work commissioned for a vast hall. The massive carved and gilded ceiling is breathtaking, even dizzying, as you wheel around searching for the best vantage point from which to admire Veronese's majestic *Apotheosis of Venice* filling one of the center panels. Step onto the balcony of the Great Council Hall for a view of St. Mark's Basin, its waters churning with the wakes of countless boats. Look at the frieze of portraits of the first 76 doges around the upper part of the walls. One portrait is missing: A black painted curtain near the left-hand corner of the wall opposite Tintoretto's painting marks the spot where the portrait of doge Marin Falier should be. A Latin inscription bluntly explains that Falier was executed for treason in 1355. The Republic never forgave him.

At the ticket office of the Doge's Palace you can book a guided tour (unfortunately, only given in Italian) of the palace's secret rooms; it takes you to the doge's private apartments, up into the attic and Piombi prison, and through hidden passageways to the torture chambers, where prisoners were interrogated. The 18th-century writer and libertine, Casanova, a native of Venice, was imprisoned here in 1755, having somehow offended someone in power (the official accusation was of being a Freemason); he made a daring escape 15 months later and fled to France, where he continued his career of intrigue and scandal. From the east wing of the Doge's Palace, the enclosed marble **Ponte dei Sospiri** (Bridge of Sighs) arches over a narrow canal to the cramped, gloomy cell blocks of the so-called New Prison. During the age of Romanticism, the bridge's tragic and melancholic history made it one of the prize sights for 19th-century tourists. The bridge's name comes from the sighs of those being led to execution. Take a look out its windows to see the last earthly view many of these prisoners ever had. ⊠ *Palazzo Ducale, Piazzetta San Marco,* ☎ *041/522–4951.* 🎟 *10,000 lire.* ☉ *Apr.–Oct., daily 9–7; Nov.–Mar., daily 9–4 (last entry 1 hr before closing time). "Secret Itineraries" tour (in Italian only):* 🎟 *12,000 lire.* ☉ *Sept.–June, Thurs.–Tues. 10 AM and noon; July and Aug., Thurs.–Tues. 10 AM; reserve at least 1 day ahead.*

★ ❶ **Piazza San Marco.** Historically and geographically, St. Mark's Square is the logical place to start exploring the city. If you stand at the piazza's far end, facing the basilica, you'll notice that rather than being a strict rectangle it opens wider at the basilica end, enhancing the perspective and creating the illusion of being even larger than it is. On your left, the long arcaded building is the **Procuratie Vecchie,** built in the early 16th century as offices and residences for the powerful Procurators of San Marco, administrators of the basilica. Across the piazza, on your right hand, is the **Procuratie Nuove,** built half a century later in a more grandiose classical style. The Procuratie Nuove has impeccable architectural lineage: It was originally planned by perhaps Venice's greatest Renaissance architect, Jacopo Sansovino (1486–1570) of Florence, to carry on the look of his **Libreria Vecchia,** where the Marciana National Library is now housed (and where interesting special exhibitions are often held), though Sansovino died before the building was begun. The actual designer was Vincenzo Scamozzi (circa 1552–1616), a pupil of Palladio and a devout Neoclassicist; later sections were completed by Baldassare Longhena (1598–1682), Venice's other great architect, who belonged firmly to the Baroque tradition.

When Napoléon entered Venice with his troops in 1797, he called Piazza San Marco "the world's most beautiful drawing room"—and promptly gave orders to redecorate it. His architects demolished an old church that stood behind you, at the end of the square farthest from the basilica, and put up the **Ala Napoleonica** (Napoleonic Wing), or Fabbrica Nuova (New Building), to unite the two 16th-century buildings on either side.

Today the arcades of these three grand buildings shelter shops and cafés. Several of the cafés have their own small orchestras that play outdoors in fair weather; though patrons of the cafés must pay an additional charge for the entertainment, passersby in the piazza can enjoy it for free. On warm summer nights, the orchestras compete to see which can draw the biggest crowd, and the fun is infectious. To see the piazza at its most magical, however, get up at the crack of dawn. Only then is the piazza *senza popolo* (without people): In the absence of sunglasses, backpackers, and miniskirts you can't help but feel that you're wandering through a Canaletto painting.

NEED A BREAK?
On the Procuratie Vecchie side is the historic **Caffè Quadri** (closed Mon.), which was shunned by Venetians during the 19th century when the occupying Austrians made it their gathering place.

Caffè Florian (closed Wed.), on the Procuratie Nuove side, is where Casanova, Wagner, and Proust regularly visited. Like a gondola ride, eating and drinking at cafés may be a splurge, but it's a treat you shouldn't miss.

Snack Bar Carla (the colorful sign over the door actually reads PIETRO PANIZZOLO; closed Sun.) is ideal for superb sandwiches and hot dishes in an area where a good, cheap eating place is hard to find.

Piazzetta San Marco. This square leads from Piazza San Marco down to the waters of St. Mark's Basin. This landing stage, now crowded with excursion boats, was once the grand entrance to the Republic. Two tall columns rise here on the waterfront: One is topped by the winged lion, a traditional emblem of St. Mark that became by extension the symbol of Venice itself; the other bears aloft a statue of St. Theodore (the first patron saint of Venice) and his dragon.

Torre dell'Orologio. The Clock Tower was erected in 1496 and is endowed with an enameled timepiece and animated figures of Moors that strike the hour (HORAS NON NUMERO NISI SERENAS says the inscription on the tower—"Only happy hours"). During Ascension Week (40 days after Easter) and on Epiphany (Jan. 6), an angel and three wise men go in and out of the doors and bow to the Virgin. Unfortunately, it is currently closed for restoration.

ALONG THE GRAND CANAL

Venetians call it the Canalazzo, but to the rest of the world it's the Grand Canal, the city's main thoroughfare. A 2-mile-long ribbon of water it was, and to some extent still is, the Fifth Avenue of Venice. It was here that the city's richest families lived, building for themselves a series of magnificent palaces, remarkable even by the standards of this remarkable city. Any building is enhanced by the presence of water. Here, the combination of water and the most opulent, luxurious, and fantastic efforts of a people obsessed with opulence, luxury, and fantasy, has created a seemingly endless unfolding panorama of unique architectural richness. The sheer numbers of these buildings can produce a sort of cultural shell shock as you head up the canal. Accordingly, it makes sense to attempt little more at first than to sample, to breath in, the unparalleled magnificence of the Grand Canal, letting it wash over you (only metaphorically, of course; it may not be deep but it's very dirty). To begin your exploration, catch Line 1 at the San Marco landing stage. Don't forget to return for a gondola ride an hour or so before sunset; couples have long known that this is the most romantic way to see Venice. However, for an overall sightseeing tour of the canal, you get a better, more extensive view from a vaporetto—which is both higher in the water and much less expensive. Try to get one of the coveted seats in the prow, where you have a clear view. Once off the vaporetto, keep in mind the two-man traghetti that allow you, at many points along the Canalazzo, to ferry across from one bank to the other for only 500 lire.

The Grand Canal has an average depth of about 9 feet and varies from 40 to 76 yards in width. It winds like an inverted letter S through Venice, from the San Marco landing to the landing at the train station (Ferrovia), passing under three bridges and between 200 palaces dating from the 14th century to the 18th century, most of them in Venetian Gothic or Renaissance style.

Sights in "A Good Boat Trip," below, are in order as you come upon them working from Piazza San Marco down to the Railway Station.

A Good Boat Trip

As you leave Piazza San Marco on the vaporetto, **Santa Maria della Salute** ⑥, the huge, white, domed 17th-century Baroque church designed by Longhena, can be seen on the left. Not far from this stop is the **Peggy Guggenheim Collection** ⑦, which is well worth a visit. Across the canal you can see the imposing terraced front of the **Gritti Palace** hotel (☞ Lodging, *below*), which occupies the former Palazzo Pisani. A few minutes farther on, on the left bank at the Ca' Rezzonico stop, is Longhera's Baroque **Ca' Rezzonico** ⑧. Be sure to visit the Museo del Settecento Veneziano (Museum of 18th-Century Venice), housed here in gilded salons.

The canal narrows and boat traffic increases as you approach the **Rialto Bridge** ⑨, arched high over the canal. The Ca' d'Oro landing on the right, just beyond the Rialto, identifies the lovely Venetian Gothic palace of **Ca' d'Oro** ⑩. Across from the Ca' d'Oro, you'll see the classical facade, with loggias on two stories, of the **Palazzo Corner della Regina** ⑫. Just beyond the Corner della Regina you can't miss the imposing bulk of the grand Baroque **Ca' Pesaro** ⑪, designed by Longhena.

Not far beyond, on the left, another white church is adorned with Baroque statues; this is San Stae, and the landing here is a gateway to a part of Venice that most tourists never see, a neighborhood of narrow canals and airy squares. Back on the right bank, the Renaissance **Palazzo Vendramin-Calergi** ⑬ is now the winter home of Venice's glamorous Casino (☞ Nightlife and The Arts, *below*). Continue along the canal via the Strada Nuova in the direction of the railway station, cross the 16th-century Ponte delle Guglie, named for its spires, pausing for a look at the elegant facade of **Palazzo Labia** ⑭.

TIMING

All of this sights in this itinerary can be comfortably visited in one day. Jumping on and off the vaporetto is no problem, although you may be tempted just to take the ride and view the sights from the canal.

Sights to See

⑩ Ca' d'Oro. This lovely Venetian Gothic palace is adorned with marble traceries and ornaments that were once embellished with pure gold. Today it houses the **Franchetti Gallery,** a fine collection of tapestries, sculptures, and paintings. ⊠ *Calle della Ca' d'Oro,* ☎ *041/523–8790.* ☞ *4,000 lire.* ⊘ *Daily 9–2.*

⑪ Ca' Pesaro. Designed by Longhena, this palace is typical of the grand Baroque style. It's now home to two rather dull art collections, the **Galleria d'Arte Moderna** (Modern Art Gallery), containing mostly 19th-century and some 20th-century works, although the intention is also to display the gallery's large collection of contemporary art when restoration is completed, and the **Museo Orientale** (Oriental Art Museum). ⊠ *Galleria d'Arte Moderna:* ☎ *041/524–0695.* ☞ *5,000 lire.* ⊘ *Apr.–Oct., Tues.–Sun. 10–5; Nov.–Mar., Tues.–Sun. 10–4. Museo Orientale:* ☎ *041/524–1173.* ☞ *4,500 lire.* ⊘ *Tues.–Sun. 9–2.*

★ ⑧ Ca' Rezzonico. This huge Baroque mansion was begun by Longhena in the 1660s and completed by another architect, Giorgio Massari, in the 1740s. Here you'll find Venice's most magnificent ballroom—site of Venice's greatest costume balls (the last of which was held in the 1960s to honor Elizabeth Taylor and Richard Burton). This was the English poet Robert Browning's last home, where he died in 1889. Be sure to visit the **Museo del Settecento Veneziano** (Museum of 18th-Century Venice), housed here in gilded salons. Pictures by the 18th-century Venetian painters Francesco and Gianantonio Guardi and Pietro Longhi, and a fine series of frescoes by their younger contemporary Giandomenico Tiepolo at the back of the palace, really open a window onto that charming and delightfully frivolous social era. ⊠ *Fondamenta Rezzonico,* ☎ *041/522–4543.* ☞ *8,000 lire.* ⊘ *Apr.–Oct., Sat.–Thurs. 10–5; Nov.–Mar., Sat.–Thurs. 10–4.*

⑫ Palazzo Corner della Regina. This residence was built in 1724 and named after the *regina* (queen) of Cyprus, Caterina Cornaro, who was born in an older palace on this site. Head for the second floor *portego*—a hall running the length of a palace, a feature typical of Venetian palazzi—among the most beautiful to be seen in Venice (now housing the Biennale's library).

⑭ Palazzo Labia. Venice's showiest 18th-century family built this elegant palace on the Canal Cannaregio. Today the palace is the Venetian headquarters of RAI, the Italian radio and television giant. It is hard to imagine a broadcasting company in any other country establishing itself among such opulent splendor. The palazzo contains the final flowering of Venetian painting: the gorgeous ballroom decorated with Giambattista Tiepolo's illusionistic frescoes of Anthony and Cleopatra, teeming with dwarfs, Barbary pirates, and toy dogs. There is a sense here of a painter painting simply for the sheer pleasure it gave him. ⊠ *Campo San Geremia, Cannaregio,* ☎ *041/524–2821.* ☞ *Ballroom free, Wed., Thurs., Fri. 3–4; guided tour of ballroom and other rooms (available in English): 10,000 lire, by prior arrangement, weekdays 10–4.*

⑬ Palazzo Vendramin-Calergi. In 1883 the great German composer Wagner died in this renaissance palazzo designed by Coducci in 1509 in white stone with red marble medallions and an imposing carved frieze. It is now the winter home of Venice's glamorous **Casino** (☞ Nightlife and the Arts, *below*).

❼ Peggy Guggenheim Collection. The collection is well worth a visit (Apr. through Nov.) to admire the small but choice gallery of 20th-century painting and sculpture in the heiress's lavish former apartments in the Palazzo Venier dei Leoni. Guggenheim (1898–1979) used her wealth and social connections to become a serious patron of art—she was once married to the painter Max Ernst—and her holdings include several works by Picasso, Kandinsky, Ernst, Pollock, and Motherwell, among others. ✉ *Entrance on Calle San Cristoforo, Dorsoduro,* ☎ *041/520–6288.* 🎫 *10,000 lire.* ☉ *Sun., Mon., Wed.–Sat. 11–6.*

★ **❾ Rialto Bridge.** The canal narrows and boat traffic increases as you approach this bridge arched high over the canal. The windows in the arch belong to the shops inside; plan to return here on foot and walk across to admire fine views up and down the Grand Canal. This is a commercial hub of the city, with open-air vegetable, fruit, and fish markets on the left, and on the right, an upscale shopping district.

❻ The church of **Santa Maria della Salute** is a huge, white, domed 17th-century Baroque church designed by Longhena. ✉ *Punta della Dogana,* ☉ *Daily 10–noon and 4–6.*

The Arsenal and Beyond

A Good Walk

To explore the city's eastern districts and see some of its most beautiful churches, head out of Piazza San Marco under the clock tower into the Mercerie, one of Venice's busiest streets. It's actually a five-part series of streets (Merceria dell'Orologio, di San Zulian, del Capitello, di San Salvador, and 2 Aprile) leading more or less directly from Piazza San Marco to the Rialto bridge. At Campo San Zulian and the church of San Giuliano, turn right onto Calle Guerra and Calle delle Bande to reach the graceful white marble church of **Santa Maria Formosa** ⑮. It's on a lively square with a few sidewalk cafés and a small vegetable market on weekday mornings. Follow Calle Borgoloco into Campo San Marina, where you turn right, cross the little canal, and take Calle Castelli to the church of **Santa Maria dei Miracoli** ⑯. Behind the church, bear right to Calle Larga Giacinto Gallina, which leads to **Campo Santi Giovanni e Paolo** ⑰, site of the massive Dominican church of **Santi Giovanni e Paolo,** or San Zanipolo, as it's known in the slurred Venetian dialect. The powerful equestrian **monument of Bartolomeo Colleoni,** by Florentine sculptor Andrea del Verrocchio (1435–88), stands in the square.

Behind the east end of the Zanipolo church, on Barbaria del le Tole, is the church of **Santa Maria dei Derelitti,** with its over-the-top Baroque facade by Longhena. The attached **Ospedaletto** ⑱ (Little Hospital) was founded in the 16th century as one of Venice's Foundling Hospitals. Continue beyond the Ospedaletto to another large church, **San Francesco della Vigna** ⑲ built by Sansovino in 1534. Not many tourists find their way here, and local youngsters play ball in the square shadowed by the church's austere classical Palladian facade.

Go left as you leave the church to begin the 500-yard walk to the **Campo dell'Arsenale** ⑳ at the main entrance to the immense **Arsenal** dockyard. The **Museo Navale** ㉑ (Naval Museum) on nearby Campo San Biagio has four floors of scale boat models. If you still have time and energy, go east to the island and church of **San Pietro di Castello** ㉒ Two footbridges lead to this island. About midway between the Arsenal and Piazza San Marco, on your way back from the eastern district, is the **Scuola di San Giorgio degli Schiavoni** ㉓.

TIMING

The journey time around this neighborhood and as far east as the Island of San Pietro is approximately four to five hours. The focal points on the tour are visits to the church of San Zanipolo and the Ospedaletto, Santa Maria dei Miracoli, as well as the docks area and the Naval Museum with all its models. Try to avoid walking around this mostly open neighborhood during the hottest hours of the day if you plan to travel in summer. Spend time browsing through the Merceria district.

Sights to See

20 Campo dell'Arsenale. This is the main entrance to the **Arsenal,** is an immense dockyard that was founded in 1104 to build and equip the fleet of the Venetian republic and was augmented continually through the 16th century. For a republic founded on sea might, having a huge state-of-the-art shipyard was of paramount importance, and this one was renowned for its size and its employees' skill. All subsequent dockyards were named after it (the name comes from the Arabic *d'arsina,* meaning workshop). No wonder it has such a grandiose entrance, with four stone lions from ancient Greece guarding the great Renaissance gateway. ⊠ *Arsenale.*

★ **17 Campo Santi Giovanni e Paolo.** This large square has the massive Dominican church of **Santi Giovanni e Paolo** or San Zanipolo (visiting hrs Mon.–Sat. 9–noon, 3–6), as it's known in the slurred Venetian dialect, on one side, and the powerful equestrian **monument of Bartolomeo Colleoni** by Florentine sculptor Andrea del Verrocchio(1435–88) on the other. Colleoni had served Venice well as a *condottiere,* or mercenary commander (the Venetians preferred to pay others to fight for them on land and had the money to do it). When he died in 1475, he left his fortune to the city on the condition that a statue be erected in his honor "in the piazza before St. Mark's." The republic's shrewd administrators coveted Colleoni's ducats but had no intention of honoring anyone, no matter how valorous, with a statue in Piazza San Marco. So they commissioned the statue and put it up before the Scuola di San Marco, which is off to the side here and is the headquarters of a charitable confraternity that happened to have the right name, enabling them to collect the loot. San Zanipolo itself contains tombs of several doges, as well as a wealth of art. Don't miss the Rosary Chapel, off the left transept; with its Veronese ceiling paintings, it's a sumptuous study in decoration, built in the 16th century to commemorate the victory of Lepanto in western Greece in 1571, when Venice and a combined European fleet succeeded in destroying the Turkish navy.

21 The Museo Navale (Naval Museum), on Campo San Biagio, has four floors of scale boat models and an annex containing actual boats, from gondolas to doges' ceremonial boats, guaranteed to fascinate children—and boat lovers. ⊠ *Campo San Biagio, Castello,* ☏ *041/520–0276.* ☐ *2,000 lire.* ☉ *Mon.–Sat. 9–1.*

18 Ospedaletto. The Little Hospital (*ospedaletto* in Italian) was founded in the 16th century and was one of Venice's four Foundling Hospitals. The church of **Santa Maria dei Derelitti** ("of the Destitute") was also attached to the Ospedaletto. Each hospital had an orchestra and choir of little orphans (one of which was presided over by Antonio Vivaldi). Note the large gallery above the Derelitti's altar, built to accommodate the young musicians. The orphanage is now an old people's home, but the beautiful 18th-century **Sala della Musica** (Music Room), where rehearsals took place and patrons and honored guests were received—the only one of its kind to survive—has been magnificently restored and can be visited (enter through the church). On the Sala's end wall is a lovely fresco by Jacopo Guarana, depicting Apollo, the God of Music, surrounded by the orphan musicians conducted by their music master, Pasquale Anfossi. ⊠ *Calle Barbaria D. Tole.* ⌸ *Free, but donations to maintenance fund welcome. Church and Music Room* ⊘ *Thurs.–Sat. Apr.–Sep. 4–7; Oct.–Mar. 3–6.*

⑲ **San Francesco della Vigna.** This large classical church was built by Sansovino in 1534. A pretty cloister opens out from the severely simple gray-and-white interior. Not many tourists find their way here, and local youngsters play ball in the square shadowed by the church's austere classical Palladian facade. The interior is rather unadorned and it contains no major or particularly interesting works of art. ⊠ *Campo Di Confraternita.* ⌸ *Free.* ⊘ *Mon.–Sat. 9–12:30 and 3–6.*

㉒ **San Pietro di Castello.** This is an island church connected to the mainland by two footbridges. The church served as Venice's cathedral for centuries; now it presides over a picturesque workaday neighborhood, and its tipsy bell tower leans over a grassy square. ⊠ *Campo San Pietro Apostolo.* ⌸ *Free.* ⊘ *Mon.–Sat. 8:30–noon and 3–6.*

NEED A BREAK? If you're this far afield, you may need sustenance to get you back to the center of town. There are several moderately priced snack bars and trattorias on Via Garibaldi, midway between the Arsenal and the island of San Pietro. **Sottoprova** (closed Tues.) has tables outdoors.

⑯ **Santa Maria dei Miracoli.** Perfectly proportioned and sheathed in marble, this church is an early Renaissance gem, decorated inside with exquisite marble reliefs. Notice how the architect, Pietro Lombardo, made the church look bigger with various optical illusions: varying the color of the exterior marble to create the effect of distance; using extra pilasters to make the building's canal side look longer; slightly offsetting the arcade windows to make the arches look deeper. The church was built in the 1480s to house an image of the Virgin that is said to perform miracles—look for this icon on the high altar. ⊠ *Calle delle Erbe.* ⌸ *Free.* ⊘ *Daily 8–12 and 3–5.*

⑮ **Santa Maria Formosa.** This graceful white marble church was inspired by a vision of *una Madonna formosa* (a buxom Madonna) that appeared to Saint Magno in the 7th century. The matronly Madonna told him to follow a small white cloud and build a church wherever it settled. The present building, built by Mauro Coducci in 1492, was grafted on to the foundations of an earlier 11th-century church that replaced Magno's original. The church's interior is a unique architectural blend, merging a welter of Renaissance decoration with Coducci's ersatz collection of Byzantine cupolas, barrel vaults, and narrow-columned screens. Of interest are two fine paintings, Bartolomeo Vivarini's *Madonna of the Misericordia* and Palma Vecchio's *Santa Barbara.* Outside there is a lively square with a few sidewalk cafés and a small vegetable market on weekday mornings. ⊠ *Camp Santa Maria Formosa.* ⌸ *Free.* ⊘ *Daily 8:30–12:30 and 5–7.*

㉓ **Scuola di San Giorgio degli Schiavoni.** This is one of numerous *scuole* built during the time of the Republic. These weren't schools, as the present-day Italian word would imply, but confraternities devoted to charitable works. Many scuole were decorated lavishly, both in the private chapels and in the meeting halls where work was discussed. The Scuola di San Giorgio degli Schiavoni features works by Vittore Carpaccio (circa 1465–1525), a local artist who often filled his otherwise devotional paintings with acutely observed details of Venetian life. Study the exuberance of his *St. George* as he slays the dragon or the vivid colors and details in *The Funeral of St. Jerome* and *St. Augustine in*

His Study. ✉ *Calle dei Furlani,* ☎ *041/522–8828.* 🎫 *5,000 lire.* ◷
Tues.–Sat. 10–12:30, 3–6 (6:30 in summer); Sun. 10–12:30 (9:30–
12:30 in summer).

The Western and Northern Districts

If churches, further ramblings along dreamy canals, and masterpieces
by great Venetian artists (such as Titian and Tintoretto) continue to
interest you, head out of Piazza San Marco under the arcades of the
Fabbrica Nuova at the far end of the square.

A Good Walk

Leave Piazza San Marco via the Calle Bocca di Piazza. (If you want to
make a detour for an expensive drink at the fabled Harry's Bar, just
turn left down Calle Vallaresso, behind the Hotel Luna Baglioni.)
Then make for **Campo Santo Stefano** ㉔, which is dominated by the
14th-century church of Santo Stefano. Join the stream of pedestrians
crossing the Grand Canal on the Accademia Bridge to the district
called Dorsoduro (literally, "hard back") because of its strong clay foundation. The bridge leads you directly to the **Accademia Gallery** ㉕,
with its unparalleled collection of Venetian art.

Continue toward Campo Santa Margherita, passing Mondonovo, one
of Venice's best mask shops (☞ Shopping, *below*). At Campo Santa
Margherita, a busy neighborhood shopping square, stop in to see Giambattista Tiepolo's ceiling paintings in the **Scuola dei Carmini** ㉖.
Tiepolo was strongly influenced by Paolo Veronese, some of whose finest
works can be seen if you take a short and rewarding canal-side detour
along Fondamenta del Soccorso, making a sharp left turn along Fondamenta de San Sebastiano, and crossing the second bridge on the right,
which leads to the **church of San Sebastiano** ㉗.

Retracing your steps, continue from Campo Santa Margherita to the
Franciscan church of **I Frari** ㉘. Behind the Frari is the **Scuola di San
Rocco** ㉙, filled with dark, dramatic canvases by Tintoretto. The area
around San Rocco is well off the normal tourist trail, with narrow alleys and streets winding alongside small canals to little squares where
posters advertising political parties and sports events seem to be the
only signs of life. Head back past the Frari to **Campo San Polo** ㉚ one
of Venice's largest squares. From here you take Calle della Madonetta,
Calle dell'Olio, Rugheta del Ravano, and Ruga Vecchia San Giovanni
to the Rialto shopping district, where you can cross the Grand Canal
for the shortcut back to San Marco. Alternatively, you can go north
from Campo San Polo by way of Calle Bernardo, Calle dello Scaleter,
Rio Terrà Parrucchetta, and Calle del Tintor to **Campo San Giacomo
dell'Orio** ㉛, where the 13th-century church of San Giacomo stands on
a charming square that few tourists ever find. Here you're not far from
the San Stae vaporetto landing, so you can take the boat back along
the Grand Canal to the heart of the city.

TIMING
Not including time spent in the Accademia Gallery, walking this route
will take approximately three to four hours. There are fewer people
out and about in the early afternoon; this does make it easier to get
around, but keep in mind that many of the shops and some churches
are also closed at that time. Also remember: Only three bridges span
the Grand Canal, so be sure to be near one of them when you're ready
to call it a day. If you're not, you may have to backtrack.

Sights To See

★ ㉕ **Accademia Gallery.** Housed in this magnificent museum is unquestionably the most extraordinary collection of Venetian art in the world.

Highlights include Giovanni Bellini's altarpiece from the church of San Giobbe (notice how he carried the church's architectural details right into the frame of the painting) and his moving *Madonna with St. Catherine and the Magdalen;* a fine *St. George* by Andrea Mantegna, Bellini's brother-in-law from Padua; and Veronese's monumental canvas, *Feast in the House of Levi.* Here is the Venetian High Renaissance in all its richness, even glamour. The painting was commissioned as a Last Supper, but the Inquisition took issue with Veronese's inclusion of jesters and German soldiers in the painting. Veronese avoided the charge of profanity by changing the title, and the picture was then supposed to depict the bawdy, but still biblical, feast of Levi. A room preserved from the Scuola della Carità—which previously occupied the museum's site—holds on one wall its original masterpiece, Titian's *Presentation of the Virgin.* Don't miss the room containing various views of 15th- and 16th-century Venice by Vittore Carpaccio and Giovanni Bellini's brother Gentile—study them to see how little the city has changed since then. Room V holds one of the gallery's most famous paintings, the *Tempest,* by Giorgione (1477–1510), a work that has consistently baffled art historians as to its meaning, while charming all by its magical painterly qualities and exquisite landscape. The work is nothing if not ambiguous—what exactly is going on between this impassive young soldier and naked woman suckling a child?—but possesses a haunting melancholy and a distinct sense of threat created by the gathering summer storm in the background. Imagine how different the effect of this work would be with a sunny blue sky instead of the ominous grays and dark blues which fill the background. For the first time in art, the atmosphere of a painting became as important as the figures. In 1995, the top floor of the Accademia was reopened to show additional works previously in storage—including paintings by Cima di Conegliano, Veronese, and Mansueti—and to host special exhibitions. ⊠ *Campo della Carità,* ☎ *041/522-2247.* ☜ *12,000 lire.* ☉ *Fri.–Mon. 9–2, Tues.–Thurs. 9–7.*

NEED A   **Bar Belle Arti** (⊠ Accademia Gallery, Campo della Carità; closed Sun.)
BREAK?   is a coffee bar and sandwich shop with a variety of tasty sandwiches, quiches, and beer.

③ **Campo San Giacomo dell'Orio.** This is where the 13th-century **church of San Giacomo** stands on a charming square that few tourists ever find (and there are a number of reasonably priced pizzerias nearby).

㉚ **Campo San Polo.** One of Venice's largest squares and a favorite playground for neighborhood children, this *campo* has a church of the same name as well as an interesting palazzo, the Mocenigo.

㉔ **Campo Santo Stefano.** This is one of the nicest neighborhood squares in all of Venice. Until 1802 it was used for bullfights, during which bulls (or oxen) were tied to a stake and baited by dogs. For years the square was grassy, all except for a stone avenue known as the *liston.* This became such a popular place to stroll that it led to a Venetian expression, *andare al liston,* which means "go for a walk." The square is dominated by the 14th-century church of **Santo Stefano.** Check out the church's bell tower—the tipsiest in all Venice—and stop in to see the ship's-keel roof, a type found in several of Venice's older churches and the work of its master shipbuilders. ⊠ *Campo Santo Stefano.* ☜ *Free.* ☉ *Mon.–Sat. 9–noon.*

NEED A   **Caffè Paolin** (⊠ 4 Campo S. Angelo; closed Mon.), with tables occupy-
BREAK?   ing most of one end of the square, makes some of the best ice cream in Venice and is a pleasant place to sit and watch the passing parade.

★ ⓘ **I Frari.** This immense Gothic church, with its russet-color brick, was built in the 14th century for the Franciscans. The Frari (*frari* means friars) is deliberately austere and plain, befitting the simplicity of the Franciscans' lives, in which spirituality and poverty were key tenets. Paradoxically, however, the Frari also contains a number of the most sumptuous and brilliant pictures in any Venetian church. Chief among them are the magnificent **Titian altarpieces,** arguably the most dazzling works that the prolific artist produced. For its mellow luminosity, first check out Giovanni Bellini's *Madonna and Four Saints* in the sacristy, painted in 1488 for precisely this spot. The contrast with the heroic energy of Titian's large *Assumption* over the main altar—painted little more than 30 years later—is startling, and illustrates clearly the immense and rapid development of Venetian Renaissance painting. This altarpiece caused a sensation when it was unveiled in 1519 and was immediately acclaimed for its winning combination of Venetian color—especially the glowing reds—and Central Italian/classical Roman figure style. The *Pesaro Madonna* over the first altar on the left nave near the main altar is also by Titian; his wife, who died shortly afterward in childbirth, posed for the figure of Mary. The Madonna was radical for its time because the main figure was not placed squarely in the center of the painting, but look at how dynamic the picture is as a result. On the same side of the church, look at the spooky pyramid-shape monument to the sculptor Antonio Canova (1757–1822), containing his heart. Across the nave is a neoclassical 19th-century monument to Titian, executed by two of Canova's pupils. ⊠ *Campo dei Frari* 🎟 *1,000 lire.* ⊙ *Mon.–Sat. 2:30–6.*

㉗ **San Sebastiano.** Veronese established his reputation with the paintings he did at this church when still in his twenties, after leaving his native Verona (from which derives his name). He continued to embellish the interior for over a decade with amazing perspective and trompe-l'oeil scenes, and in 1588 he was finally buried here. ⊠ *Campo San Sebastiano.* ⊙ *Sun.–Fri. 2:30–5:30.*

㉖ **Scuola dei Carmini.** This *scuola* is home to Giambattista Tiepolo's ceiling paintings. The paintings, now displayed on the second floor, were commissioned to honor the Carmelite order by depicting prominent Carmelites in conversation with saints and angels. Of the three great Venetian painters whose names start with *T* (Titian, Tintoretto, and Tiepolo), Tiepolo came last chronologically (he painted in the 18th century, while the others were 16th-century artists) and achieved the greatest international fame in his own time, though an underlying melancholy in his ethereal, brightly colored paintings betrays a man of sober piety. Tiepolo's vivid techniques transformed some unpromising religious themes into flamboyant displays of color and movement. Mirrors are available on the benches to make it easier to see the ceiling without getting a sore neck. ⊠ *Campo dei Carmini,* ☎ *041/528-9420.* 🎟 *5,000 lire.* ⊙ *Mon.–Sat. 9–noon, 3–6.*

㉙ **Scuola di San Rocco.** This workshop is famed for its many dark, dramatic canvases by Tintoretto. Born some 30 years after Titian, Jacopo Robusti—called Tintoretto because his father was a dyer—was more mystical and devout than the sophisticated Titian. Though his colors are equally brilliant, he carried Titian's love of motion and odd composition to almost surreal effects, in the same Mannerist vein as El Greco (who was at one time a pupil of Titian's!). In 1564, Tintoretto beat other painters competing for the commission to decorate this building by submitting not a sketch but a finished work, which he additionally offered free of charge. The series of more than 50 paintings that he ultimately created took a total of 23 years to complete. These works, depicting Old and New Testament themes, were restored in the 1970s, and Tintoretto's inventive use of light has once more been revealed. ⊠ *Campo San Rocco*, ☎ *041/523–4864.* ☎ *8,000 lire.* ⊙ *Weekdays 9–5:30; weekends 10–4 in winter, 9–5:30 in summer.*

Islands of the Lagoon

The perfect vacation from your Venetian vacation is an escape to the magical islands of the city's lagoon—Murano, Burano, and Torcello—which can provide a welcome relief after the brooding, enclosed charms of Venice itself. Far from the madding crowd, Torcello is the actual birthplace of Venice, today visited for its haunting melancholy, its great Byzantine-era church, and that famous outpost of elegance, the Locanda Cipriani. (The island is also perfect for picnics, but bring food from Venice.) Burano is a toy town of little houses all painted in a riotous explosion of color—blue, yellow, pink, ocher, and dark red—and picked out in white trim; here, visitors love to shop for the best in Venetian lace. Murano is known the world over for its glass—but guided tours usually involve high-pressure attempts to make you buy, with little time left for anything else. It's more adventurous, and worth the extra effort, to make your own way around the islands, using the good vaporetto connections.

There are several options in getting to these islands: Line 12 to Murano, Burano, and Torcello from the landing stage at Fondamente Nove, almost due north of San Marco; and Line 52, which you can pick up in town (☞ Getting Around *in* Venice A to Z, *below*), to Fondamente Nuove, San Michele, and Murano, where you would then change to line 14 to continue to Torcello and Santa Maria Elisabetta on the Lido.

A Good Boat Trip

Numbers in the text correspond to numbers in the margin and on the Venetian Lagoon map.

Take Line 52 from Piazza San Marco to the Fondamente Nuove stop. There, in the Campo dei Gesuiti, is the church of **I Gesuiti** ㉜. It's only a five-minute ride from there to **San Michele** ㉝, the cemetery island that is home to the church of **San Michele in Isola.** Another five minutes on Line 52 takes you to **Murano** ㉞. Cross the Ponte Vivarini and turn right onto Fondamenta Cavour. Follow the Fondamenta around the corner to the Museo Vetrario (Glass Museum).

Make your way back along the same route to the landing stage, and take Line 12 to **Burano** ㉟, which is about 30 minutes from Murano. Of interest here is the Scuola di Merletti di Burano (Lace Museum), where there is traditional lace-making.

Line 12 continues from the Burano landing stage to the sleepy green island of **Torcello** ㊱, about 10 minutes farther. A brick-paved lane leads up from the landing stage and follows the curve of the canal toward the center of the island. You pass the Locanda Cipriani, an inn famous for its good food and the patronage of Ernest Hemingway. Just beyond is the grassy square that holds the only surviving monuments of the island's past splendor. Next to it is the cathedral of Santa Maria Assunta, also built in the 11th century.

TIMING

Boats leave every hour and the trip takes about 50 minutes each way. Stopping on every island and visiting the various sights will take a full day. If, however, you limit yourself to Torcello, Burano, and Murano, a full morning or a full afternoon will suffice.

Sights To See

★ ㉟ **Burano.** This small island is a fishing village with houses painted in cheerful colors and a raffishly raked bell tower on the main square, about 100 yards from the landing stage and clearly visible from there. Lace is to Burano what glass is to Murano, but be prepared to pay a lot for the real thing. Stalls line the way from the landing stage to Piazza Galuppi, the main square; the vendors, many of them fishermen's wives, are generally good-natured and unfamiliar with the techniques of the hard sell.

The **Scuola di Merletti di Burano** (Lace Museum) on Piazza Galuppi is the best place to learn the intricacies of the lace-making traditions of Burano. It is also useful for learning the nature of the skills involved in making the more expensive lace, in case you intend to buy some lace on your way back to the vaporetto. ⊠ *Piazza Galuppi.* ☎ *041/730034.* ☑ *3,000 lire.* ⊙ *Tues.–Sat. 9–6, Sun. 10–4.*

| NEED A BREAK? | Among the pleasant trattorie on Piazza Galuppi are **Ai Pescatori** (closed Mon.) and **Romano** (closed Tues.). Both serve seafood specialties à la carte, but keep your eye on the costs. |

㉜ **I Gesuiti.** This 18th-century church dominates the Campo dei Gesuiti. It is extravagantly baroque in style; the classical arches and straight lines of the Renaissance have been abandoned in favor of flowing, twisting forms. The marble of the gray-and-white interior is used like brocade, carved into swags and drapes. Titian's *Martyrdom of St. Lawrence,* over the first altar on the left, is a dramatic example of the great artist's feel for light and movement. ⊠ *Campo dei Gesuiti.* ☑ *Free.* ⊙ *Mon.–Sat. 8:30–noon, 4–6.*

★ ㉞ **Murano.** Like Venice, Murano is made up of a number of smaller islands linked by bridges. The island is known exclusively for its glassworks, which you can visit to see how glass is made. Many of these line the **Fondamenta dei Vetrai,** the canal-side walkway leading away from the Colonna landing stage. The houses along this walk are simpler than many of their Venetian counterparts; traditionally they were workmen's cottages. Just before the junction with Murano's Grand Canal—250 yards up from the landing stage—is the church of **San Pietro Martire.** This 16th-century reconstruction of an earlier Gothic church has several works by Venetian masters: notably, the *Madonna and Child* by Giovanni Bellini, and *St. Jerome* by Veronese.

The **Museo Vetrario** (Glass Museum) has a collection of Venetian glass that ranges from priceless antique to only slightly less expensive modern. The museum gives you a good idea of the history of Murano's glassworks, which were moved here from Venice in the 13th century because they were a fire risk. It's useful, too, to get a clear idea of authentic Venetian styles and patterns if you're planning to make some purchases later. ⊠ *Murano,* ☎ *041/739586.* ☑ *5,000 lire.* ⊙ *Apr.–Oct., Thurs.–Tues. 10–5; Nov.–Mar., Thurs.–Tues. 10–4.*

㉝ **San Michele.** Venice's cypress-lined cemetery island is home to the pretty Renaissance church of **San Michele in Isola,** designed by Coducci in 1478, and Venice's **cemetery.** It is a unique experience to walk among the gravestones with the sound of lapping water on all sides. The American poet Ezra Pound, the great Russian impresario and art critic Sergey Diaghilev, and the composer Igor Stravinsky are buried here. For most Venetians, however, the stay is short-lived here, as the cemetery has a policy of transferring those interred more than 10 years to another, less grandiose cemetery, making room for more recent burials.

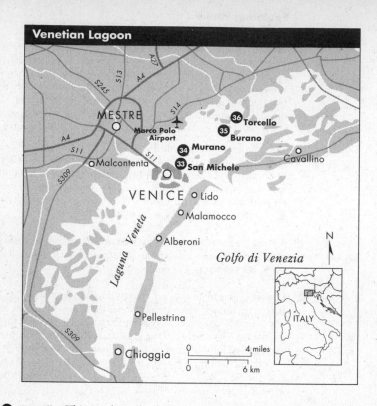

Venetian Lagoon

★ ㊱ **Torcello.** This is where the first Venetians landed in their flight from the barbarians 1,500 years ago. Even after many settlers left to found the city of Venice on the island of Rivo Alto (Rialto), Torcello continued to grow and prosper until its main source of income, wool manufacturing, was priced out of the marketplace. It's hard to believe now, looking at this almost deserted island, that in the 16th century it had 20,000 inhabitants and 10 churches.

Santa Maria Assunta is the island's cathedral. It dates from the 11th century. The ornate Byzantine mosaics are testimony to the importance and wealth of an island that could attract the best artists and craftsmen of its day. The vast mosaic on the inside of the facade depicts the Last Judgment as artists of the 11th and 12th centuries imagined it: Figures writhe in vividly depicted contortions of pain. Facing it, as if in mitigation, is the calm mosaic figure of the Madonna, alone in a field of gold above the staunch array of Apostles. ✉ *Torcello,* ☎ *041/730084.* 🎫 *1,500 lire.* ⊙ *Daily 10–12:30, 2–5 in winter, 2–6:30 in summer.*

NEED A BREAK?   **Locanda Cipriani** is an inn famous for its good food and the patronage of Ernest Hemingway, who often came to Torcello for the solitude. These days Locanda Cipriani is about the busiest spot on the island, as well-heeled customers arrive on high-speed powerboats for lunch. If you want to have lunch or dinner, count on at least 80,000 lire for a set menu. ✉ *Torcello,* ☎ *041/730150. Closed Tues. and Jan.–beginning of Carnival.*

San Giorgio Maggiore and the Giudecca

Beckoning all travelers across the Basin of San Marco like some sort of Venetian Bali Hai is the island of San Giorgio Maggiore, separated by a small channel from the Giudecca. A tall brick campanile on that distant bank perfectly complements the Campanile of San Marco. Behind it looms the stately dome of one of Venice's greatest churches, San Giorgio Maggiore. The island of Giudecca, a crescent cupped around the southern shore of Venice, is one of the most mysterious neighborhoods in all of Venice, with an obscure history and a sombre feel.

A Good Boat Trip

Take Line 82 from San Zaccaria near San Marco and head for the island of San Giorgio Maggiore, across the lagoon. Here you should visit Palladio's church of **San Giorgio Maggiore** ㊲. Return to the pier and proceed by vaporetto (still Line 82) to the island of Giudecca. Here, you should try to get a feel for the neighborhood and visit the church of **Il Redentore** ㊳, also by Palladio. If you have the time, continue on the vaporetto to the next stop, Zattere, which is opposite the Giudecca Bank. The promenade here is enchanting; you can eat in one of the many pizzerias that line the promenade and enjoy the lively atmosphere. Otherwise, you can return directly to San Marco.

TIMING

The journey takes only an hour, which should give you plenty of time to enjoy the sights. Allow at least an hour to visit each of the churches, and another hour to two hours to visit the Giudecca neighborhood and the Zattere promenade.

Sights to See

Numbers in the text correspond to numbers in the margin and on the Venice map.

㊳ **Island of Giudecca.** The Guidecca has always been seen as a place apart. Its name is something of a mystery. According to some, it derives from the possible settlement of Jews here in the 14th century, and according to others it was so called because in the 9th century nobles condemned to exile (*giudicato* means judged or sentenced) were sent here. It became a pleasure garden for wealthy Venetians during the long and luxurious decline of the Republic. Even today it has an atmosphere of its own, quite distinct from the heart of Venice. In one regard it is still the province of the wealthy, however: The exclusive Cipriani hotel (☞ Lodging, *below*) lies secluded on its eastern tip.

The main attraction here is the church of **Il Redentore** by Palladio. Its tranquil, stately facade is actually a series of superimposed temple fronts, topped by a dome and a pair of slim, almost minaretlike, bell towers. The interior, like San Giorgio Maggiore's (☞ *below*), is perfectly proportioned and airy, in contrast to the dusky mystery of the Basilica di San Marco. ✉ *Fondamenta San Giacomo, La Giudecca.* ⊙ *Mon.–Sat. 3–6.*

㊲ **San Giorgio Maggiore.** A church has been on this island since the late 8th century, with a Benedictine monastery added in the 10th century. The present church of San Giorgio Maggiore was begun in 1566 by the greatest architect of his time, Andrea Palladio, whose work is so evident throughout the Venetian Arc (☞ Chapter 6). Two of Palladio's hallmarks are mathematical harmony and architectural elements borrowed from classical antiquity, both of which are evident in this superbly proportioned neoclassical church of red brick and white marble. Inside, the church is refreshingly airy and simply decorated. Two important late Tintoretto paintings hang on either side of the chancel: *The Last Supper* and *The Gathering of Manna.* Over the first altar on the right-hand side of the nave is an *Adoration of the Shepherds* by Jacopo Bassano (1517–92), a painter from Bassano del Grappa on the mainland who possessed considerable originality and was especially adept at portraying nature and country life. The top of the campanile offers fine views of Venice and its harbor but, having been struck by a lightning bolt in 1993, it has been closed for repair and restoration. Although it was due to reopen in January, 1996, the campanile still remains closed to the public at press time.

The monastery of San Giorgio Maggiore, where the conclave that elected Pope Pius VII took place in 1800, later a barracks for the occupying Austrians, now houses an artistic and cultural foundation where conferences are often held, and is usually closed to the public. Palladio designed the monastery's first cloister, and Longhena was the architect for the grand baroque library. ⊠ *Isola di San Giorgio Maggiore,* ☎ *041/528–9900.* ⊡ *Free.* ☉ *Mon.–Sat., 9–6.*

DINING

CATEGORY	COST*
$$$$	over 120,000 lire
$$$	80,000–120,000 lire
$$	50,000–80,000 lire
$	under 50,000 lire

*per person, including three courses, wine, and service

$$$$ ✕ **Grand Canal.** The Grand Canal restaurant at the Monaco hotel is a
★ favorite with Venetians, who enjoy eating in summer on the lovely canalside terrace looking across the mouth of the Grand Canal to the island of San Giorgio Maggiore, and in the cozy dining room in winter. All the pasta is made fresh daily on the premises, and the smoked and marinated salmon are also home-produced. The traditional Venetian dishes are very well prepared, and the chef, Fulvio De Santa, also offers delicious meat and fish dishes such as scampi *alla Ca' d'Oro* (in a cognac sauce), served with rice. ⊠ *Hotel Monaco, Calle Vallaresso 1325, San Marco,* ☎ *041/520–0211. Jacket required. AE, DC, MC, V.*

$$$$ ✕ **Harry's Bar.** Turn the corner into Calle Valleresso and you'll find the humble door of this very unhumble watering place, legendary Venetian hangout of such notables as Hemingway, Maugham, and Onassis, not to mention Barbara Hutton, Peggy Guggenheim, and Orson Wells. Now rich tourists far outnumber the celebrities, but Harry's is still known for the best and driest martinis in town, the most heavenly Bellinis (fresh peach juice and champagne), and for a kitchen whose *cucina verita* (age-old recipes that call for produce in season, simple cooking methods, and short cooking times, to avoid destroying the freshness of the ingredients) is so fine that it's making Venetian cooking fashionable again. The decor is boring beige-on-beige, but the "pictures" on the walls upstairs—windows whose vistas look out on spectacular Santa Maria della Salute—easily compare with the finest Canaletto *vedute* (scenic paintings). ⊠ *Calle Vallaresso 1323,* ☎ *041/528–5777. Reservations essential. AE, DC, MC, V. Closed Jan. 4–Feb. 15.*

$$$$ ✕ **La Caravella.** Chateaubriand, bouillabaisse, and calves' kidneys' *au trois moutardes* (three mustards). You might think you had wandered into a temple of French haute cuisine here, but continue reading the very extensive menu to discover some of the best Venetian specialties in town, such as *taglierini alla granseola* (delicate pasta with crab sauce), scampi in port sauce, and fillets of locally caught sea bass and sole. The front room of this old favorite—long admired for its fine wine list and cordial, courteous service—is decorated like the dining saloon of an old Venetian sailing ship. Many prefer the pretty garden courtyard during summer. ⊠ *Calle Larga XXII Marzo 2397, San Marco,* ☎ *041/520–8901. Reservations essential. AE, DC, MC, V. Closed Wed. in winter.*

$$$$ ✕ **Quadri.** In the 19th century, princes, dukes, and countesses dined here, and you'll feel like one when you walk into the gilded salons of Venice's most beautiful restaurant. The decor is stunning—Quadri's second-floor aerie gives you a pigeon's-eye view of Piazza San Marco—and the four-star truffles-on-everything kitchen is also a major draw. Come September, when the Venice Film Festival is in session, the sequins-and-sunglasses set takes over. ⊠ *Piazza San Marco 120–124,* ☎ *041/528–9299. Reservations essential. AE, DC, MC, V. Closed Aug. 3–20.*

$$$ ✕ **Arturo.** Located on the Calle degli Assassini—a name common to several Venetian streets and a picturesque reminder of the centuries gone by when violence and betrayal were everyday occurrences—this tiny restaurant can offer a most peaceful and enjoyable evening. It has the distinction (in Venice) of not serving seafood. Instead there are varied and delicious fresh vegetable and salad dishes; tasty, tender, and generous meat courses, including the delicately pungent *braciola alla veneziana* (pork chop schnitzel with vinegar); and an authentic creamy homemade tiramisufor dessert. ⊠ *Calle degli Assassini 3656, San Marco,* ☎ *041/528–6974. Reservations essential. No credit cards. Closed Sun. and 3 wks in Aug.*

$$$ ✕ **Da Fiore.** Tucked away in a little calle off the top of Campo San Polo,
★ Da Fiore has long been a favorite with Venetians. Now that its fame has spread, it's imperative to reserve for a superlative seafood lunch or dinner, which might include delicate hors d'oeuvres of moeche, scallops, and tiny octopus, followed by a succulent risotto or *tagliolini con scampi e zucchine* (noodles with shrimp and zucchini), and a perfectly cooked main course of *rombo* (turbot) or *branzino* (sea bass). ⊠ *Calle del Scaleter 2202, San Polo,* ☎ *041/721308. Reservations essential. AE, DC, MC, V. Closed Sun., Mon., Aug. 10–early Sept., Dec. 25–Jan. 15.*

$$$ ✕ **Fiaschetteria Toscana.** Once a storehouse for a Tuscan wine and oil merchant, this spot lures visitors from terra firma—the mainland—and Venetians with its cheerful and courteous service and fine kitchen. Specialties include a delicate tagliolini *alla buranella* (with shrimp) and rombo with capers. In warm weather, the best tables are in the arbor on the square. ⊠ *Campo San Giovanni Crisostomo 5719, Cannaregio,* ☎ *041/528–5281. AE, DC, MC, V. Closed Tues. and July 1–15.*

$$ ✕ **Al Mondo Novo.** This restaurant is owned by a fish wholesaler in the Rialto market, who himself eats here every day, so you can be sure that everything is absolutely fresh. Specialties prepared by Signora Trevisan, the owner's wife, include *cape sante* (scallops) and *cape longhe* (razor clams), risottos and pasta dishes, and the best of the day's catch grilled on charcoal. Meat dishes are also available. ⊠ *Salizzada San Lio 5409, Castello,* ☎ *041/520–0698. AE, MC, V. Closed Wed. and Feb.–Mar.*

$$ ✕ **Cantinone Storico.** On a quiet canal near the Accademia, this comfortable, newly refurbished trattoria serves excellently prepared specialties such as risotto *terra mare* (with seafood, vegetables, and porcini mushrooms) and tagliolini alla granseola. There are good house wines. ⊠ *Fondamenta di Ca' Bragadin 660, Dorsoduro,* ☎ *041/523–9577. AE, DC, MC, V. Closed Sun., last wk July–1st wk Aug., and 3 wks before Carnival.*

$$ ✕ **Da Gigio.** A picturesque, friendly, family-run trattoria on the quay
★ side of a canal just off the Strada Nuova, Da Gigio is very popular with Venetians and visiting Italians, who appreciate the affable service; excellently cooked homemade pasta, fish and meat dishes; and imaginative and varied cellar and good-quality draft wine. It's good, too, for a cheap, simple lunch at tables in the barroom. ⊠ *Fondamenta de la Chiesa 3628/a, Cannaregio,* ☎ *041/528–5140. AE, DC, MC, V. Closed Mon., 2 wks in Jan. and 2 wks in Aug. No dinner Sun.*

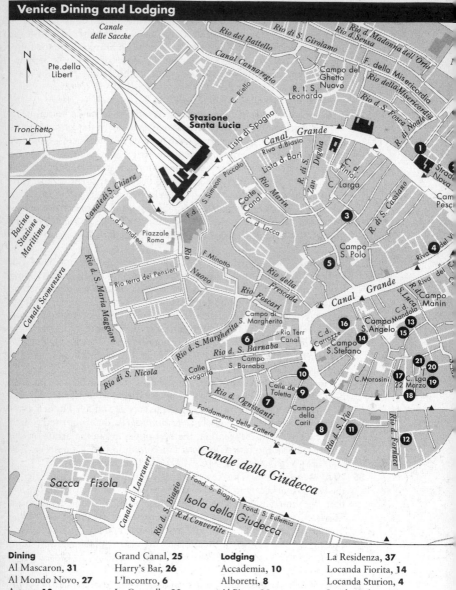

Venice Dining and Lodging

Canale delle Sacche

Pte. della Libert

N

Tronchetto

Canal Cannaregio

Rio del Battello

Rio di S. Girolamo

Rio d'. Sensa

Rio d Madonna dell'Ort

F. della Misericordia

Rio della Misericordia

Rio d. S. Fosca

R. di Noale

Campo del Ghetto Nuovo

R. I. S. Leonardo

Stazione Santa Lucia

Lista di Spagna

Canal Grande

Riva d'Biasio

Lista di Bari

R. di S. Zan Degola

C. d. Tintor

C. Larga

Strada Nova

R. di S. Cassiano

Cam Pesc

Riva d. del V.

Canale di S. Chiara

C. d S. Andrea

F. d S. Simeon Piccolo

Piazzale Roma

Corte Canal

Rio Marin

C. d. Lacca

Campo S. Polo

Riva d. del

Canal Grande

Campo Manin

S. Luca

Bacina Stazione Marittima

Canale Scomenzera

Rio d. S. Maria Maggiore

Rio terra dei Pensieri

Rio Nuovo

F. Minotto

Rio della Frescada

Rio Foscari

Campo di S. Margherita

Rio Terr Canal

C. d. Carrozze

S. Luca Mandola

Campo S. Angelo

Campo S. Stefano

Rio d. S. Margherita

Rio d. S. Barnaba

Campo S. Barnaba

Calle Avogaria

Rio di S. Nicola

Calle de Toletta

Campo della Carit

Calle de Ognissanti

Fondamenta delle Zattere

Rio d. S. Vio

Rio d. Fornace

C. Morosini

C. Lga 22 Marzo

Sacca Fisola

Canale d. Lauraneri

R. d. S. Biagio

Fond. S. Biagio

Fond. S. Eufemia

Isola della Giudecca

R. d. Convertite

Canale della Giudecca

Dining		Lodging	
Al Mascaron, **31**	Grand Canal, **25**	Accademia, **10**	La Residenza, **37**
Al Mondo Novo, **27**	Harry's Bar, **26**	Alboretti, **8**	Locanda Fiorita, **14**
Arturo, **13**	L'Incontro, **6**	Al Piave, **30**	Locanda Sturion, **4**
Cantinone Storico, **11**	La Caravella, **20**	Bernardi	Londra Palace, **34**
Da Fiore, **3**	Le Bistrot, **23**	Semenzato, **2**	Messner, **12**
Da Gigio, **1**	Locanda Montin, **7**	Bucintoro, **38**	Metropole, **35**
Da Ignazio, **5**	Metropole Buffet, **35**	Cipriani, **39**	Paganelli, **33**
Da Raffaele, **17**	Quadri, **24**	Concordia, **29**	Riva, **28**
Da Remigio, **36**	San Trovaso, **9**	Danieli, **32**	San Samuele, **16**
Fiaschetteria	Vino Vino, **15**	Flora, **19**	Saturnia
Toscana, **22**		Gritti Palace, **18**	Internazionale, **21**

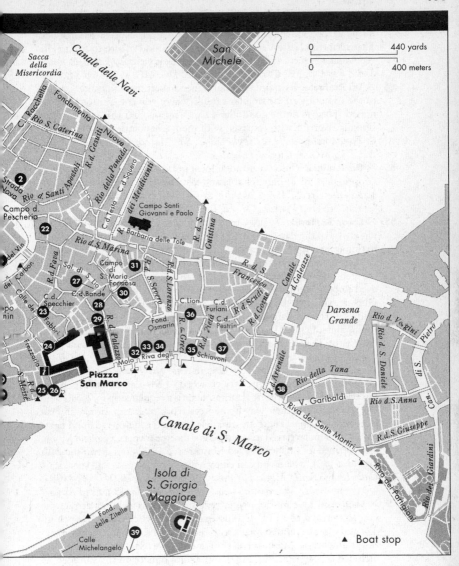

Sacca
della
Misericordia

Canale delle Navi

San
Michele

0 _____ 440 yards
0 _____ 400 meters

C. Racchetta
Fondamenta
Rio S. Caterina
R. d. Gesuiti
Nuove
Rio della Panade
C.d Squero
Rio dei Mendicanti

Stroda
Nova
2
Rio d'Santi Apostoli

Campo d.
Pescheria

22

C. Tesia

Campo Santi
Giovanni e Paolo

R. Barbaria delle Tole

R. d. S.
Giustina

del Vin

Rio d. S. Marina

R.d.Fava

Sol di S.Lio

Campo
di
S. Maria
Formosa

31

R.d S.Severo

R.d.S.Lorenzo

R. d. S.
Francesco

R. d. S.

del Corbon

Calle del

27

C.d.Bande

30

C.Lion

C.d
Furlani
C.d.
Pestrin

R. d. Scudi
R.d.Corna

Darsena
Grande

Rio d. V.gini

Rio d. S. Daniele

nin

23

C.d.
Specchier

28

29

Fond.
Osmarin

36

R. d. Greci

R. d. 2mda

di S. Pietro

Frezzaria

24

R. d. Palazzo

Molo

32 33 34

Riva degli

35

Schiavoni

37

R. d. Arsenale

Rio della Tana

Can.

S. Moise

i

Piazza
San Marco

25 26

38

V. Garibaldi

Rio d. S.Anna

Riva dei Sette Martiri

R. d. S.Giuseppe

Canale di S. Marco

Rio dei Giardini

Isola di
S. Giorgio
Maggiore

ci

Rio dei Partigiani

Fond.
delle Zitelle

Calle
Michelangelo

39

▲ Boat stop

$$ ✕ **Da Ignazio.** Smallish, pleasant, and near Campo San Polo, Ignazio is reliable for good food at reasonable prices, barring expensive fish dishes. The cuisine is classic Venetian here, from seafood risotto to fegato alla veneziana, but there are standard Italian items as well. ⊠ *Calle dei Saoneri 2749, San Polo,* ☎ *041/523–4852. AE, DC, MC, V. Closed Sat.*

$$ ✕ **Da Raffaele.** Its quintessential Venetian setting—quayside on one of the romantic *rii,* or smaller canals (where you can almost hear the muted splashes of the gondolier's oar)—means that this spot is occasionally overrun with tourists, with the kitchen suffering as a result. ⊠ *Fondamenta delle Ostreghe 2347, San Marco,* ☎ *041/523–2317. AE, DC, MC, V. Closed Thurs.*

$$ ✕ **Da Remigio.** This very popular local trattoria near the church of San Giorgio dei Greci offers reliable and tasty fish and meat dishes. ⊠ *Salizzada dei Greci 3416, Castello,* ☎ *041/523–0089. Reservations essential. No credit cards. Closed Tues. No dinner Mon.*

$$ ✕ **Locanda Montin.** Peggy Guggenheim used to take many of the leading artists of the day—including Jackson Pollock and Mark Rothko—to this archetypal Venetian inn, located not far from her Palazzo Venier dei Leoni, in the tranquil Dorsoduro section. While the walls are still covered with modern art, it's far from the haute bohemian hangout it used to be, except for the times when the Biennale crowd takes over. Outside, you can dine under an elongated arbor and enjoy such specialties as rigatoni *ai quattro formaggi* (with four cheeses) with mushrooms and tomatoes, spaghetti *Adriatica,* and antipasto *Montin* (seafood antipasto). Regulars let the waiters order for them. ⊠ *Fondamenta di Borgo 1147, Dorsoduro,* ☎ *041/522–7151. AE, DC, MC, V. Closed Wed., 15 days in Jan., and 15 days in Aug. No dinner Tues.*

$ ✕ **Al Mascaron.** The lively, very crowded Al Mascaron, with its paper tablecloths and very informal atmosphere, is a regular stop for locals who like to drop in on their way home from work to gossip, drink, and eat cicchetti at the bar. There are also delicious and generous seafood pasta dishes. So popular has Mascaron become that the owners, Gigi and Momi, have opened an offshoot called Mascareta a few doors down the calle (at No. 5183), where you can enjoy a glass of wine and cold snacks. ⊠ *Calle Lunga Santa Maria Formosa 5225, Castello,* ☎ *041/522–5995. No credit cards. Closed Sun., end Dec.–mid-Jan., last 2 wks in Aug.*

$ ✕ **Le Bistrot.** Live music, poetry readings, and art exhibits attract the younger crowd to this café-brasserie. Centrally located, it's open all day and offers a limited menu with the emphasis on pancakes and pizzas at lunchtime and in the evening until 1 AM. Service and cover are included in the prices, and there are tables outside in the summer. ⊠ *Calle dei Fabbri 4685, San Marco,* ☎ *041/523–6651. MC, V. Closed Tues. in winter.*

$ ✕ **L'Incontro.** This trattoria has a faithful clientele of Venetians and vis-
★   itors, attracted by flavorsome food, friendly service, and reasonable prices. Menu choices include freshly made Sardinian pastas, juicy steaks, wild duck, boar, and (with advance notice) roast suckling pig. It is between San Barnaba and Campo Santa Margherita. ⊠ *Rio Terrà Canal 3062/a, Dorsoduro,* ☎ *041/522–2404. MC, V. Closed Mon.*

$ ✕ **Metropole Buffet.** Here at the Hotel Metropole Buffet, in a charming and comfortable room overlooking the waterfront and the Pietà church, you can eat a substantial and tasty lunch or dinner (for a fixed price of around 50,000 lire), helping yourself from a varied selection of starters, soups, pastas, hot and cold dishes, and desserts. The price even includes a highly drinkable Bianco di Custoza (a light white wine from the Veneto region) on draft, but not mineral water or coffee. ⊠ *Hotel Metropole, Riva degli Schiavoni 4149, Castello,* ☎ *041/520–5044. AE, DC, MC, V.*

$ ✕ **San Trovaso.** A wide choice of Venetian dishes and pizzas, reliable house wines, and economical fixed-price menus make this busy tavern, conveniently near the Accademia Gallery, a good value. ✉ *Fondamenta Priuli 1016, Dorsoduro,* ☎ *041/520–3703. AE, DC, MC, V. Closed Mon.*

$ ✕ **Vino Vino.** The annex of the extremely expensive Antico Martini restaurant, this is a highly informal wine bar where you can sample Italian vintages and munch on a limited selection of (microwaved) dishes from the kitchens of its upscale big sister, next door. It's open 10 AM–midnight. ✉ *Calle delle Veste 2007/a, near Campo San Fantin, San Marco,* ☎ *041/523–7027. Reservations not accepted. AE, DC, MC, V. Closed Tues.*

★ ✕ **A Torcello Picnic.** No, this is not a restaurant, but for one of the dreamiest dining experiences in Venice, stock up before you take your vaporetto trip out to this historic lagoon island (☞ Exploring Venice, *above*): Get a bottle of Teroldego Rotaliano from a *vinatteria* (wine shop), chilled pâtés and a wedge of *taleggio* cheese from a *salumeria* (deli), a hunk of bread from a *panneteria* (bakery), a *semifreddo di fragoline* (liquor-drenched cake) from a *pasticerria* (pastry shop) and three gigantic Venetian peaches from one of the open-air markets, such as that on the Campo Santa Margherita. With the 11th-century campanile of the church of Santa Maria Assunta as backdrop, couples will quickly feel like reenacting the famous scene Katherine Hepburn and Rozzano Brazzi filmed here for *Summertime.*

LODGING

The busiest times for hotels are spring and autumn; December 20–January 2; and the two-week Carnival period leading up to Ash Wednesday, usually in February. Book well in advance. If you don't have reservations, you can almost always get a room in any category by going upon arrival to the **AVA** (Venetian Hoteliers Association) booths at the train station (☾ Apr.–Oct. 8 AM–10 PM, Nov.–Mar. 8 AM–9:30 PM); airport (☾ Apr.–Oct. 10 AM–9 PM, Nov.–Mar. 10:30 AM–6:30 PM); and at the municipal parking garage at Piazzale Roma (☾ Apr.–Oct. 9 AM–10 PM, Nov.–Mar. 9 AM–9 PM). The 15,000–60,000-lire deposit (depending on the category of the hotel) is refunded on your bill.

Most hotel rates include breakfast. Rates are generally comparable with Rome and Milan, but you can save considerably in the off-season. Also, remember that it is essential to know how to get to your hotel when you arrive in Venice.

CATEGORY	COST*
$$$$	over 450,000 lire
$$$	250,000–450,000 lire
$$	160,000–250,000 lire
$	100,000–160,000

All prices are for a standard double room for two, including taxes and service.

$$$$ ▥ **Cipriani.** It's impossible to feel stressed in this sybaritic oasis of stunningly decorated rooms and suites, some with garden patios. The Cipriani is on the Giudecca, across St. Mark's Basin from the heart of Venice, with views of San Giorgio and the lagoon. The hotel launch whisks you back and forth to San Marco at any hour of the day or night, but the Cipriani is not for anyone who wants to feel Venice's heartbeat. Cooking courses and fitness programs help to keep guests occupied. The newly restored Palazzo Vendramin annex (seven suites and three double rooms) is open all year. ✉ *Giudecca 10,* ☎ *041/520–7744,* FAX *041/520–3930. 104 rooms or suites with bath. Restaurant,*

bar, air-conditioning, pool, tennis courts. AE, DC, MC, V. Closed Dec.–mid-Mar.

$$$$ ⊞ **Danieli.** Venice's largest luxury hotel, the Danieli is a collage of newer buildings around a 15th-century palazzo built for the Doge Dandolo. You can feel like a doge staying at this palace, which is loaded with sumptuous Venetian decor and atmosphere. Some of the suites are positively palatial, but some of the less attractive rooms are overpriced. The four-story-high lobby is one of the sights of Venice, its salons and bar being chic places to relax and watch the celebrities go by. The rooftop terrace restaurant is justly famous for top-notch cuisine and its heavenly view of San Giorgio Maggiore and St. Mark's Basin which can also be seen from the best rooms. ⊠ *Riva degli Schiavoni 4196, Castello,* ☎ *041/522–6480,* 𝔉𝔄𝔛 *041/520–0208. 231 rooms or suites with bath. Restaurant, bar, air-conditioning. AE, DC, MC, V.*

$$$$ ⊞ **Gritti Palace.** Queen Elizabeth, Greta Garbo, and Winston Churchill
★ made this their Venetian address. The atmosphere of an aristocratic private home pervades this legendary hotel. Fresh flowers, fine antiques, sumptuous appointments, and Old World service give guests the feeling of being very special people. The dining terrace on the Grand Canal is best in the evening when the boat traffic dies down. ⊠ *Campo Santa Maria del Giglio 2467, San Marco,* ☎ *041/794611,* 𝔉𝔄𝔛 *041/520–0942. 88 rooms or suites with bath. Restaurant, bar, café, air-conditioning. AE, DC, MC, V.*

$$$ ⊞ **Concordia.** Twenty rooms in this centrally located, attractive, and attentively run hotel overlook the magnificent basilica of San Marco, as does the spacious breakfast room-cum-bar (a welcome haven, where light meals and snacks are also available all day). Guests like to dine in the romantic *mansarda*—a rooftop room with a panoramic view over the Piazza San Marco. The management makes a special effort to offer good price deals at off-peak times, so check when booking. ⊠ *Calle Larga San Marco 367, San Marco,* ☎ *041/520–6866,* 𝔉𝔄𝔛 *041/520–6775. 55 rooms with bath or shower. Air-conditioning. AE, DC, MC, V.*

$$$ ⊞ **Londra Palace.** This grand hotel commands a fine view of San Giorgio and St. Mark's Basin and has a distinguished ambience. The rooms are decorated in dark paisley prints, with sophisticated touches, and the rooftop suite is a honeymooner's dream. The Deux Lions restaurant offers fine Venetian and French cuisine, and the piano bar is open late. Guest perks include a complimentary Mercedes for one-day excursions and free entrance to the city casino. ⊠ *Riva degli Schiavoni 4171, Castello,* ☎ *041/520–0533,* 𝔉𝔄𝔛 *041/522–5032. 69 rooms and suites with bath. Restaurant, piano bar, air-conditioning. AE, DC, MC, V.*

$$$ ⊞ **Metropole.** This hotel is on a quieter part of the waterfront near the Pietà church, but still only a few minutes' stroll from Piazza San Marco. The spacious rooms and sitting areas are furnished with style and panache from the owner's impressive collection of antiques. Many rooms have a view of the lagoon, but the others overlooking a canal and peaceful gardens are also inviting. Special rates—including, in low season, the best rooms at the lowest price (if the hotel is not full)—are well worth checking out. You can step from your water taxi or gondola directly into the hotel lobby. ⊠ *Riva degli Schiavoni 4149, Castello,* ☎ *041/520–5044,* 𝔉𝔄𝔛 *041/522–3679. 73 rooms with bath. Restaurant, bar, air-conditioning. AE, DC, MC, V.*

$$$ ⊞ **Saturnia Internazionale.** There's lots of Old World charm in this historic palace, which is centrally located near Piazza San Marco but still manages to retain an air of peace and tranquility. Its beamed ceilings, damask-hung walls, and authentic Venetian decor impart real character to the solid comfort of its rooms and salons. Many rooms have been extensively redecorated and endowed with more glamorous—and much larger—bathrooms. ⊠ *Calle Larga XXII Marzo 2398, San*

Marco, ☎ *041/520–8377,* 𝖥𝖠𝖷 *041/520–7131. 95 rooms with bath. 2 restaurants, bar, air-conditioning. AE, DC, MC, V.*

$$
★ 🏠 **Accademia.** Probably the most enchanting hotel in Venice, the Accademia is also one of its most popular, so early reservations are a must. Just beyond an iron gate, a secret garden awaits, complete with mini Palladian-style villa, canal parterre, and verdant trees (all rarities in Venice). Lounges, bar, and a wood-paneled breakfast room are cheery, and breakfast outside on the garden terrace is a special treat. A note of alarm, however, is sounded by readers who report antique chairs with springs popping out of them, paint peeling, and other—perhaps quintessentially Venetian?—signs of neglect. ⊠ *Fondamenta Bollani 1058, Dorsoduro,* ☎ *041/521–0578 or 523–7846,* 𝖥𝖠𝖷 *041/523–9152. 27 rooms, 25 with bath or shower. Bar, air-conditioning. AE, DC, MC, V.*

$$ 🏠 **Bucintoro.** Whistler once stayed here and, today, the Bucintoro is still favored by artists who are drawn by the lagoon views outside each room. Off the tourist track, this friendly, family-run hotel on the waterfront by the Arsenal has clean, simple rooms and prices that are unbeatable for such a spectacular position. ⊠ *Riva San Biagio 2135, Castello,* ☎ *041/522–3240,* 𝖥𝖠𝖷 *041/523–5224. 28 rooms, 18 with bath. No credit cards. Closed Jan.–mid-Feb.*

$$ 🏠 **Flora.** This hotel has what many in this category lack: plenty of sitting rooms and a pretty courtyard with wrought-iron coffee tables. It's in a quiet, though central, location near San Moisè and Piazza San Marco. Rooms have Venetian period decor, which some might find a bit dark; some are rather small, with tiny bathrooms. When booking, ask about the availability of rooms with a view of the courtyard or the garden. ⊠ *Calle Bergamaschi 2283 (off Calle Larga XXII Marzo), San Marco,* ☎ *041/520–5844,* 𝖥𝖠𝖷 *041/522–8217. 44 rooms with bath or shower. Bar, air-conditioning. AE, DC, MC, V. Closed mid-Nov.–Jan.*

$$ 🏠 **La Residenza.** A little out of the way, this hotel in a Gothic palace may be worth the 10-minute walk from San Marco (or the vaporetto ride to the Arsenale stop). Breakfast is served in an authentic Venetian salon, and the rooms are well furnished. The atmosphere is subdued, almost staid—this is not the place to take children. ⊠ *Campo Bandiera e Moro 3608, Castello,* ☎ *041/528–5315,* 𝖥𝖠𝖷 *041/523–8859. 17 rooms, 14 with bath. AE, DC, MC, V. Closed 2nd wk Jan.–mid-Feb. and 2nd wk Nov.–1st wk Dec.*

$$ 🏠 **Locanda Sturion.** There was a hostelry here, by the Rialto Bridge, as long ago as the 13th century, and its sign, showing a *sturion* (sturgeon) to illustrate its name, appears in a 1494 Carpaccio painting in the Accademia. If you don't mind a longish walk upstairs, you'll find a friendly, pleasant hotel refurbished in the Venetian style. All rooms have baths, and two have views over the Grand Canal, as does a bright breakfast/day room. Extra beds for shared rooms are no problem, and prices in the off season can be as low as half those listed, so inquire when booking. ⊠ *Calle del Sturion 679, San Polo,* ☎ *041/523–6243,* 𝖥𝖠𝖷 *041/522–8378. 11 rooms with bath. Air-conditioning. AE, MC, V.*

$$ 🏠 **Paganelli.** The lagoon views here so impressed Henry James that he wrote the Paganelli up in the preface to his *Portrait of a Lady.* This charming, small hotel on the waterfront near Piazza San Marco, with an annex on the quiet square of Campo San Zaccaria (three rooms overlook the lagoon, six face the square), is tastefully decorated in the Venetian style. ⊠ *Riva degli Schiavoni 4182, Castello,* ☎ *041/522–4324,* 𝖥𝖠𝖷 *041/523–9267. 22 rooms, 19 with bath or shower. AE, DC, MC, V.*

$ 🏠 **Al Piave.** This small hotel, offering clean, basic accommodations is just off Campo Santa Maria Formosa, one of the city's most attractive squares. ⊠ *Ruga Giuffa 4840, Castello,* ☎ *041/528–5174,* 𝖥𝖠𝖷 *041/528–8512. 12 rooms without bath. AE, MC, V. Closed Jan. 6– Feb. 1.*

$ ⊞ **Bernardi Semenzato.** This is a particularly welcoming little hotel just
★   off Strada Nuova, and near the Rialto. All the rooms in the main hotel
were refurbished to a high standard in 1995, making the Bernardi better value than ever. Prices are even lower in the nearby annex (which
includes a big room with a lovely canal view). ⊠ *Calle dell'Oca 4366,
Cannaregio,* ☎ *041/522–7857,* ⨳ *031/522–2424. 18 rooms, 11 with
bath or shower; 7 rooms in annex, 2 with bath or shower. AE, MC,
V. Closed 1st 2 wks Dec.*

$ ⊞ **Locanda Fiorita.** This welcoming, small hotel is tucked away in a
★   sunny little square (where breakfast is served in the summer), just off
Campo Santo Stefano, near the Accademia Bridge, and is centrally located for sightseeing. The rooms have beamed ceilings and are simply
furnished. ⊠ *Campiello Novo 3457, San Marco,* ☎ *041/523–4754,*
⨳ *041/522–8043. 10 rooms, 7 with shower. AE, MC, V. Closed 2 wks
Nov.–Dec.*

$ ⊞ **Riva.** This small hotel, close to San Marco, is in a picturesque spot
at the junction of three canals much used by all manner of Venetian
watercraft. Although they are endlessly fascinating to watch, the boats
can seem a little noisy early in the morning. The Riva has been refurbished by its enthusiastic owner. ⊠ *Ponte dell'Angelo 5310, Castello,*
☎ *041/522–7034. 12 rooms, 10 with bath. No credit cards. Closed
mid-Nov.–Feb. 1, except 2 wks at Christmas.*

$ ⊞ **San Samuele.** Centrally located near the Grand Canal and Palazzo
Grassi, this friendly hotel, run by Signor Veronese (whose namesake
Paolo, the 16th-century painter, lived practically next door), has clean,
sunny rooms. ⊠ *Salizzada San Samuele 3358, San Marco,* ☎ *041/522–
8045. 10 rooms, 2 with bath. No credit cards.*

NIGHTLIFE AND THE ARTS

The Arts

You'll find a list of current and upcoming events in the "Guest in Venice"
booklet, free at your hotel, or available from the Assessorato al Turismo at Ca' Giustinian (2nd floor), Calle del Ridotto (close to Piazza
San Marco). Keep an eye out for posters announcing concerts and other
events. Venice hosts important temporary exhibitions in the Doge's
Palace, in Palazzo Grassi at San Samuele on the Grand Canal, and in
other venues. The **Biennale,** a cultural institution, organizes many
events throughout the year, including the film festival, beginning at the
end of August. The big Biennale international art exhibition, held
from the end of June to the end of September, has been held since 1993
in odd-numbered years.

Concerts

There are regular concerts at church of the Pietà, with an emphasis on
Vivaldi, and also at San Stae—though prices tend to be high and the
performance quality uneven. Concerts—sometimes free ones—are also
held in other churches by visiting choirs and musicians. For information on these often short-notice events, ask at the APT office and look
for posters on walls and in restaurants and shops. **Kele e Teo Agency**
(⊠ San Marco 4930, ☎ 041/520–8722) and **Box Office** (⊠ Calle
Loredan 4127, off Salizzada San Luca, ☎ 041/988369) handle tickets for many musical events.

Festivals

Carnevale (Carnival) takes place the ten days leading up to Ash Wednesday (Feb. 2–12 in 1997). During the festivities, the crowds of revelers
make the city almost impossible to visit, so unless you are intent on

joining in, stay away until it is over. For information on the carnival, check with the main APT office (☞ Contacts and Resources *in* Venice A to Z, *below*). On the third Sunday of July, the **Feasst of Il Redentore** (the Redeemer) is celebrated with the building of a pontoon bridge over the channel to the Giudecca, commemorating the doge's annual visit to this church to offer thanks for the end of a 16th-century plague. Traditionally, the Venetians take to the water in boats en masse, as midnight fireworks explode over the lagoon.

Opera and Ballet

Teatro La Fenice, on Campo San Fantin, is one of Italy's oldest opera houses, a pilgrimage shrine for opera lovers everywhere, and scene of many memorable operatic premieres, including, in 1853, the dismal first night flop of Verdi's *La Traviata*. Unfortunately this great opera house was very badly damaged by a fire in January 1996 and although plans are being made to restore the building, performances are not forecast to recommence until the year 2000.

Nightlife

Piazza San Marco in fair weather, when the cafés stay open late, is a meeting place for visitors and Venetians, though young Venetians tend to gravitate toward Campo San Luca and Campo San Salvador and Bartolomeo, near Rialto. There is far more nightlife in Venice than meets the eye. The best up-to-date guide to live music venues, discos, and late bars is "Fuori Orario: di Notte a Venezia e Mestre" (Out of Hours: By Night in Venice and Mestre), published by the Assessorato alla Gioventù (✉ City Youth Department, Corte Contarina 1529, 4th Floor, near Piazza San Marco), and available free at APT information offices. At present, the guide is only available in Italian, but with its useful maps and easy-to-follow notes it should be decipherable to any serious nighthawk.

Bars, Discos, and Nightclubs

The **Martini Scala Club** (✉ Calle delle Veste ☎ 041/522–4121. ☾ Wed.–Mon. 10 PM–3:30 AM) is an elegant piano bar with restaurant. One of the most popular nightspots for young Venetians is **Ai Canottieri** (✉ Fondamenta San Giobbe 690, Cannaregio, ☎ 041/715408, closed Sun. and in summer), which offers live music on Thursday and Saturday nights. **Devil's Forest Pub** (✉ Calle del Stagneri 5185, off Campo San Bartolomeo, ☎ 041/520–0623) is a popular spot with young Venetians. **Paradiso Perduto** (✉ Fondamenta Misericordia 2540, Cannaregio, ☎ 041/720581) serves good pizzas and other hot dishes at low prices (live music usually on the weekend, closed Wed. and 1st 2 wks Aug.). **Bar Salus,** just off Campo Santa Margherita (✉ Rio Terà Canal 3112, Dorsoduro, ☎ 041/528–5279, ☾ till 2 AM, closed Sun.) attracts a lively late-night crowd, particularly in summer. **Al Vapore** (✉ Via Fratelli Bandiera 8, Marghera, ☎ /FAX 041/930796) draws young Venetians out of the city to the mainland. **Dona Flor** (✉ Via Lissa 6, Mestre, ☎ 544–1310, closed July and Aug.) is a private club which you need proof of identity and 10,000 lire to join.

Casino

The city-operated gambling casino is open April–September in a modern building on the Lido (✉ Lungomare Marconi 4, ☎ 041/529–7111) and in the beautiful Palazzo Vendramin Calergi (same phone) on the Grand Canal during the other months. Both are open daily 3 PM–about 4:30 AM.

OUTDOOR ACTIVITIES AND SPORTS

Golf

The **Golf Club Lido di Venezia,** an 18-hole course, is on the Lido island (✉ Via del Forte, Alberoni, Lido, ☎ 041/731333).

Horseback Riding

Circolo Ippico Veneziano (☎ 041/526–5162) is at Ca' Bianca on the Lido. It is open all year.

Jogging

The best spot to jog is past the Giardini (public gardens) in the Castello district and over to the pine wood on Sant'Elena; you get a magnificent view of the city as you jog back toward the center.

Swimming

Many Venetians and visitors are happy to swim from the seaward-facing side of the Lido. There is free public access to the beach (look for the signs SPIAGGIA LIBERA) at either end of the Lido (Bus C, leaving every 20 minutes from the Santa Maria Elisabetta landing, goes all the way to Alberoni at one end, where there are usually fewer people, while Bus B goes to the beach at San Nicolò at the other end). The strand in between is sectioned off in the summer season into private beaches offering various facilities—changing rooms, bar, showers—for the use of guests of hotels on the Lido and of nonguests who are charged a fixed daily or weekly rate. However, considering the reputedly polluted state of the Adriatic, you may wish to swim in a pool. Venice's only public pool is the **Piscina Comunale** (☎ 041/528–5430), located on the island of Sacca Fisola, at the far end of Giudecca (take Line 82 to Sacca Fisola). The deluxe hotels **Excelsior** (☎ 041/526–0201) and **Hotel des Bains** (☎ 041/526–5921) are both on Lungomare Marconi on the Lido; their pools are open to nonguests for a fee.

Tennis

The **Hotel des Bains** (☞ Swimming, *above*) and the exclusive **Sea Gull Club** of the Cipriani hotel (☞ Lodging, *above*) will let nonguests play for a fee. There are several tennis clubs on the Lido, including **Lido Tennis Club** (☎ 041/526–0954) and **Club Ca' del Moro** (✉ Via F. Parri, ☎ 041/770965), which also has an outdoor swimming pool for summer use.

SHOPPING

Shopping in Venice is part of the fun of exploring the city, and you're sure to find plenty of interesting shops and boutiques as you explore. It's always a good idea to mark on your map the location of a shop that interests you; otherwise you may not be able to find it again in mazelike Venice. Shops are usually open 9–12:30 or 1 and 3:30 or 4–7:30 and are closed Sunday and on Monday morning. However, many tourist-oriented shops are open all day, every day. Food shops are closed Wednesday afternoon, except over the Christmas and New Year period, when they remain open. Some shops close for both a summer and a winter vacation.

Shopping Districts

The main shopping areas are the **Mercerie,** the succession of narrow and crowded streets winding from Piazza San Marco to the Rialto, and the area around Campo San Salvador, Calle del Teatro, Campo Manin, and Campo San Fantin. The **San Marco** area is full of shops and top-name boutiques such as Armani, Missoni, Valentino, Fendi, and Versace.

Food Markets

The open-air fruit and vegetable market at **Rialto** is colorful and animated throughout the morning. The adjacent fish market offers a vivid lesson in ichthyology, presenting some species you've probably never seen (⊙ Mornings Tues.–Sat.).

In the Castello district is **Via Garibaldi,** the scene of another lively food market on weekday mornings.

Supermarkets and Department Stores

Coin (⊠ Rialto Bridge), the only department-type store in Venice, features men's and women's fashions.

Mega (⊠ Western end of the Zattere) is a small but good supermarket.

The **Standa** stores (⊠ Strada Nuova and on the Lido) have supermarket sections.

Specialty Stores

EMBROIDERED FABRICS

Go to **Lorenzo Rubelli** (⊠ Campo San Gallo 1089, just off Piazza San Marco) for the same sumptuous brocades, damasks, and cut velvets used by the world's most prestigious decorators. Remember that much of the lace and embroidered linen sold in Venice and on Burano is made in China or Taiwan.

Venice's top name is **Jesurum** (⊠ Piazza San Marco 60-61). It is one of the few stores in Venice whose lace is made in and around the city.

Martinuzzi, Fabris, and **Tokatzian,** all on Piazza San Marco, have a good selection.

At **Norelene** (⊠ Calle de la Chiesa 727, near the Accademia) you'll find wonderful hand-printed fabrics.

Venetia Studium (⊠ Calle Larga XXII Marzo 2403, San Marco) has beautiful Fortuny-inspired lamps, furnishings, clothes, and accessories.

GLASSWARE

Glass, most of it made in **Murano** (☞ Islands of the Lagoon, *above*), is Venice's number-one product, and you'll be confronted by mind-boggling displays of traditional and contemporary glassware, often kitsch. Take your time and be selective. Should you buy glass in Venice's shops or in the showrooms of Murano's factories? You will probably find that prices are pretty much the same; showrooms in Venice that are outlets of Murano glassworks sell at the same prices as the factories. However, because of competition, shops in Venice stocking wares from various glassworks may charge slightly lower prices.

Galleria San Nicolò (⊠ Calle del Traghetto 2793, Dorsoduro, by the Ca' Rezzonico vaporetto stop) is owned by the American glass expert Louise Berndt. Opened in 1994, this shop shows the best of contemporary glass, including superb work by Yoichi Ohira, a Japanese designer long resident in Venice.

The **Domus** shop (⊠ Fondamenta dei Vetrai, Murano) has a selection of smaller objects and jewelry from the best glassworks.

For chic, contemporary glassware, **Carlo Moretti** is a good choice; his signature designs are on display at **L'Isola** (⊠ Campo San Moisè 1468, near Piazza San Marco).

Marina Barovier has an excellent selection of collectors' 20th-century glass at her gallery (⊠ Calle delle Botteghe 3172, San Marco, just off Campo Santo Stefano).

Go to Michel Paciello's **Paropàmiso** for stunning Venetian glass beads and traditional jewelry from all over the world (⊠ Frezzeria 1701, near Piazza San Marco).

Pauly (⊠ Piazza San Marco 73-77) is a centrally located store with a wide array of glassware.

In a category all his own is **Gianfranco Penzo** (⊠ Campo del Ghetto Nuovo 2895), who decorates Jewish ritual vessels in glass, makes commemorative plates, and takes special orders.

Salviati (⊠ Piazza San Marco 79B) is a reliable and respected firm.

Venini (⊠ Piazzetta dei Leoncini 314) has been an institution since the 1930s, attracting some of the foremost names in glass design.

Vetri d'Arte (⊠ Piazza San Marco 140) offers moderately priced glass jewelry.

MASKS

Emilio Massaro (⊠ Calle Vitturi 2934, San Marco) is a wholesaler whose prices tend to be cheaper than anywhere else; you can watch the masks being made.

Mondonovo (⊠ Rio Terrà Canal) is a cut above most other mask stores in the city.

Laboratorio Artigiano Maschere (⊠ Barbaria delle Tole, near Santi Giovanni e Paolo) is home to Giorgio Clanetti, the man credited with starting the current revival in mask-making.

PRINTS

Piazzesi. An old print of Venice makes a distinctive gift or souvenir. Hand-printed paper and desk accessories, memo pads, and address books abound at this well-known shop. ⊠ *Campiello della Feltrina, near Santa Maria del Giglio* ☉ *Daily 9–noon, 3–6.*

VENICE A TO Z

Arriving and Departing

By Bus

The bus terminal is at Piazzale Roma, near the vaporetto stop of that name. There are buses services to Mestre, the Brenta Riviera, Padua, and other destinations in the region.

By Car

If you bring a car to Venice, you will have to pay for a garage or parking space during your stay. Parking at Piazzale Roma (in the Autorimessa Comunale run by the city) costs between 15,000 and 25,000 lire, and at the private Garage San Marco (next door) between 30,000 and 45,000 lire per 24 hours, depending on the size of the car. To reach the privately run Tronchetto parking area, follow the signs to turn right before Piazzale Roma. Warning: Do not be waylaid by illegal touts—often wearing fake uniforms, and whose activities have in recent years become a scandal in a city generally remarkably free of con men and criminals—who may try to flag you down and offer to arrange parking and hotels, but continue on until you reach the automatic ticket machines. Parking here costs around 35,000 lire per 24 hours under cover and slightly less outside. (Do not leave valuables in the car. There is a left-luggage office, open daily 8 AM–8 PM, next to the Pullman Bar on the ground floor of the municipal garage at Piazzale Roma.) The Venetian Hoteliers Association (AVA) has arranged a discount of about 40% for hotel guests who use the official Tronchetto parking facility. Be sure to ask for a voucher on checking into your hotel; it will be issued when you settle the hotel bill. Present the voucher at Tronchetto when you pay the parking fee.

Line 82 runs from Tronchetto to Piazzale Roma and Piazza San Marco and also goes on to the Lido in summer. (When there is thick fog or extreme tides, a bus runs to Piazzale Roma instead.) Avoid private boats—they are a rip-off. You can take your car to the Lido, the long, narrow island shielding the Venetian lagoon; the car ferry (Line 17) leaves about every 50 minutes from a landing at Tronchetto, but in summer there can be long queues. The cost is from 12,000 to 30,000 lire, depending on the size of the car.

By Plane

Marco Polo airport at Tessera, about 10 kilometers (6 miles) north of the city on the mainland, is served by domestic and international flights, including connections from London, Amsterdam, Brussels, Frankfurt, Munich, Paris, Vienna, and Zurich. For information, call ☏ 041/2609260.

BETWEEN THE AIRPORT AND VENICE

By Boat. Depending on where your hotel is, this may be the best way to get to Venice from the airport. The most direct way is by the **Cooperativa San Marco** launch, with regular scheduled service throughout the day, until midnight; it takes about an hour to get to the landing just off Piazza San Marco, stopping at the Lido on the way, and the fare is 20,000 lire per person, including bags. A **water taxi** (a sleek, modern motorboat known as a *motoscafo*) from the airport costs about 100,000 lire, but it is always essential to agree on a water-taxi fare before boarding.

By Bus. Blue **ATVO** buses make the 25-minute nonstop trip from the airport to Piazzale Roma, which is where the road ends at the entrance to Venice; from Piazzale Roma you can get a water bus to the landing nearest your hotel. The ATVO fare is 5,000 lire. There are local **ACTV** buses from the airport, but you need a ticket (fare 1,200 lire) before boarding the bus, and there is no ticket office at the airport. You can buy a ticket at the tobacconist-newsstand in the airport, but this is not always open. Also, luggage can be a problem on the ACTV bus, which is usually crowded with local commuters.

By Taxi. A yellow taxi from the airport to Piazzale Roma costs about 60,000 lire.

By Train

Venice has rail connections with every major city in Italy and the rest of Europe.

Santa Lucia Station is on the Grand Canal in the northwest corner of the city. Some through trains do not terminate at Santa Lucia, stopping only at the Venezia-Mestre Station on the mainland. All trains traveling to and from Santa Lucia stop at Mestre, so to get from Venezia-Mestre to Santa Lucia, or vice versa (a 10-minute trip), take the first available train, remembering there is a *supplemento* (extra charge) for traveling on Intercity and Eurocity trains, and that if you do not pay it before boarding, you are liable for a hefty fine. For train information, call ☏ 041/715555 from 7:15 AM to 9:30 PM.

Getting Around

First-time visitors find that getting around Venice presents some unusual problems: The layout is complex; the waterborne transportation can be bewildering; the house-numbering system is baffling; many street names in the *sestieri* (six districts) of San Marco, Cannaregio, Castello, Dorsoduro, Santa Croce, and San Polo, are duplicated; and often you must walk, whether you want to or not. It's essential that you have a good map showing all street names and vaporetto routes; buy one at a newsstand. In the areas where you're most likely to wander, signs are posted on many corners pointing you in the right direction for the nearest major landmark—San Marco, Rialto, Accademia, etc.—but don't count on finding such signs once you're deep into residential neighborhoods.

By Gondola

No visit to Venice is complete without a gondola ride. But not many visitors know that the best time for one is in the late afternoon or early evening hours, when the Grand Canal isn't so heavily trafficked, or that it's best to start from a station on the Grand Canal because the lagoon is usually choppy. Make it clear that you want to see the smaller canals, and come to terms on the cost and duration of the ride before you start. Gondoliers are supposed to charge a fixed minimum of about 80,000 lire for up to five passengers for 50 minutes. After 8 PM the rate goes up. The official tariffs are quoted in the "Guest in Venice" booklet (☞ Nightlife and The Arts, *above*). Bargaining may get you a better price.

By Motoscafo

These stylish powerboat water taxis are extremely expensive, and the fare system is as complex as Venice's layout. A minimum fare of about 50,000 lire gets you nowhere, and you'll pay three times as much to get from one end of the Grand Canal to the other. Always agree on the fare before starting out.

By Traghetto

Few tourists know about the two-man gondolas that ferry people across the Grand Canal at various fixed points. They are the cheapest and shortest gondola ride in Venice and can save a lot of walking. The fare is 500 lire, which you hand to the gondolier when you get on. Look for traghetto signs.

By Vaporetto

ACTV vaporetti run the length of the Grand Canal and circle the city. There are about 20 lines, some of which connect Venice with the major and minor islands in the lagoon. Line 1 is the Grand Canal local, calling at every stop and continuing via San Marco to the Lido. (It takes about 45 minutes from the station to San Marco.)

There have been many changes to other routes in recent years, and more changes may yet occur. There are also some routes that only run in the summer. At press time (spring 1996), there are two VapLine 52 routes, one running from the railway station (Ferrovia) to San Zaccaria (at San Marco) via Zattere and the Giudecca Canal, and on to the Lido and vice versa; another going in the opposite direction round Venice, from the railway station, skirting the north of the city, via Fondamente Nove (where some boats leave for the islands of the northern lagoon) and Murano (you can cut out the Murano loop by changing boats at Fondamente Nove, using the same ticket) and continuing via the Arsenal to San Zaccaria and Zitelle on the island of Giudecca.

There are also two Line 82 routes, one of which runs from the Tronchetto, via Piazzale Roma, the railway station (Ferrovia), and Rialto, and continues, during the day, down the Grand Canal, with fewer stops than Line 1, to San Marco and, in the summer, on to the Lido (some 82 boats on this route only go as far as Rialto —check before you board if you need to travel farther). The other route goes from Tronchetto to San Zaccaria via the Giudecca Canal.

The fare is 3,500 lire on most lines. A 24-hour tourist ticket costs 14,000 lire, while a three-day tourist ticket costs 20,000; these are especially worthwhile if you are planning to visit the islands (☞ Islands of the Lagoon, *above*).

Timetables are posted at every landing stage, but there is not always a ticket booth operating. You may get on a boat without a ticket, but you will have to pay a higher fare. For this reason, it may be useful to buy *un blochetto* (a book of tickets) in advance. Landing stages are clearly marked with name and line number, but check before boarding, particularly with the 52 and 82, to make sure the boat is going in your direction.

Contacts and Resources

Consulates
U.K. Consulate ✉ (Campo della Carità 1051, Dorsoduro, ☎ 041/522–7207). There is no U.S. or Canadian consular service.

Doctors and Dentists
The British Consulate (☞ *above*) can recommend doctors and dentists. Your hotel or any pharmacy should also be able to offer advice.

Emergencies
Carabinieri, ☎ 112. English-speaking officers available 24-hours a day to deal with any kind of emergency.

Police, ☎ 113.

Ambulance (Venice Hospital), ☎ 041/523–0000.

Red Cross First Aid Station, (✉ 55 Piazza San Marco, near Caffè Florian, ☎ 041/528–6346. ☉ Mon.–Sat. 8:30–1).

English-Language Bookstores
Bookstores and newsstands throughout the city are well stocked with publications in English. **Fantoni,** on Salizzada San Luca, specializes in art books. Good general-interest bookstores include **Emiliana Editrice** (✉ Calle Goldoni), between Piazza San Marco and Campo San Luca; and **Studium** (✉ Calle de la Canonica), off Piazzetta dei Leoncini, to the left of the San Marco Basilica. **Libreria Editrici Filippi** (✉ on Casseleria, between Ponte de l'Anzolo, take the last left off Calle de la Canonica) has the best selection of books on every aspect of Venice and its history. Enrico Dori's newspaper shop, opposite the Milani bakery on the Frezzaria shopping street (✉ go to the right of the San Marco post office), has the best stock of English-language newspapers and magazines and is open from early in the morning until-late at night.

Guided Tours
EXCURSIONS
The Cooperativa San Marco organize tours of the islands of Murano, Burano, and Torcello (departing daily at 9:30 and 2:30 from the landing stage in front of the Giardini Reali near Piazza San Marco, lasting about 3½ hours, and costing about 25,000 lire per person). You can book directly with the Cooperativa at their booth on the waterfront where the boats depart, or through a travel agent. However, tours tend to be annoyingly commercial and emphasize glass-factory showrooms, pressuring you to buy, sometimes at higher prices than normal. You can visit these islands on your own, but it would take longer than the organized tour and you would probably want to stop off for a meal along the way (☞ Islands of the Lagoon, *above*).

American Express also offers a trip by car to the Venetian villas, Padua and Asolo, available all year round (about 140,000 lire per person). Bookings should be made the day before.

Excursions aboard the Burchiello motor launch, from Venice to Padua along the Brenta Canal, are expensive (about 150,000 lire) and not necessarily the best way to see the famous villas that line the canal, since so much time is spent on the boat. *Tours Apr.–Oct., Tues., Thurs., and Sat. Times vary per season; check locally.*

ORIENTATION TOURS

Two-hour walking tours of the San Marco area, taking in the basilica and the Doge's Palace, can be booked through **American Express** (☎ 041/520–0844) and other travel agencies. The American Express "Jewels of the Venetian Republic" tour (about 35,000 lire) ends with a glassblowing demonstration. From March 15 to November 15, American Express offers an afternoon walking tour that ends with a gondola ride (about 40,000 lire).

In recent years, Venice's municipal Youth Department has been running a special program to help young visitors: **"Rolling Venice,"** as it is somewhat oddly titled, is open to everyone aged 14–29, and costs 5,000 lire to join at Rolling Venice's offices behind the Piazza San Marco Post Office (✉ Assessorato alla Gioventù, Corte Contarini 1529, ☎ 041/2707650. ⊙ Weekdays 9:30–1, plus Tues. and Thurs. 3–5). Their office at the Santa Lucia railway station is open July–September. Benefits include handy guidebooks to the city and (sometimes substantial) discounts in hotels, restaurants, shops, and on ACTV vaporetto tickets. The Youth Department has also produced two useful leaflets, "Dormire Giovani" (Accommodations for Young People) and "Fuori Orario: di Notte a Venezia e Mestre" (Out of Hours: By Night in Venice and Mestre) (☞ Nightlife and The Arts, *above*).

PERSONAL GUIDES

American Express and other travel agencies can provide guides for walking or gondola tours of Venice, or cars with driver and guide for tours of the mainland. You can get a list of licensed guides and their rates from the main APT tourist office at the Palazzetto Selva off Piazza San Marco (☎ 041/522–6356) or contact the Guides' Association (✉ Calle San Antonio 5448/A, Castello, ☎ 041/523–9902, FAX 041/523–2012).

SPECIAL INTEREST TOURS

American Express and other operators offer group gondola rides with serenades, daily from May through October in the evening (about 40,000 lire), and other tours that go on to include dinner, followed by a cabaret entertainment of Venetian folk songs and a visit to the Casino (about 120,000 lire, drinks not included).

During the summer, free guided tours (some in English, including one at 11 AM) of the **Basilica di San Marco** are offered by the Patriarchate of Venice; information is available in the atrium of the church (☎ 041/520–0333; no tours Sun.).

Late-Night Pharmacies

Venetian pharmacies take turns opening late or on Sundays; the weekly list of late-night pharmacies is posted on the front of every pharmacy. Two with English-speaking staff are **Farmacia Italo-Inglese** (✉ Calle della Mandola 3717, in San Marco district, ☎ 041/522–4837) and **Farmacia Internazionale** (✉ Calle Larga XXII Marzo 2067, in San Marco district, ☎ 041/522–2311).

Travel Agencies

American Express (✉ Salizzada San Moisè 1471, ☎ 041/520–0844); **Sattis Viaggi** (✉ Calle Larga dell'Ascensione 1261, ☎ 041/528–5101/2/3); **Wagons-Lits/Turismo** (✉ Piazzetta dei Leoncini 289, ☎ 041/522–3405).

Visitor Information

The **APT** (tourist office) is at Palazzetto Selva, an elegant 19th-century coffeehouse, by the former Giardinetto Reale (Royal Garden) and the San Marco vaporetto stop, off Piazza San Marco (☎ 041/522–6356). There are information booths at the Santa Lucia train station (☎ 041/719078) and on the Lido (✉ Gran Viale S. Maria Elisabetta 6A, ☎ 041/526–5721).

6 The Venetian Arc

Verona, Padua, Vicenza and Palladio Country

The art and architecture of every city in the Venetian Arc—Verona, Vicenza, Padua, Treviso—echo in some way the graces and refinements of Venice. Here you'll find Asolo—the "City of a Hundred Horizons"; Padua, ennobled by Giotto's frescoes; Verona's romantic Romeo and Juliet settings; and the villas of Andrea Palladio, where 16th-century aristocrats led the privileged life.

AS ROME PRESIDES OVER THE LAZIO REGION, all of Venetia falls under the historical and spiritual influence of its namesake city. Take any city in the Venetian Arc and travelers will quickly note that all repeat, in one way or another, the grace and refinement of Venice. No lagoons, perhaps, but the region's architecture, paintings, and way of life all bask in the reflected splendor of La Serenissima.

Updated by
Giuliano
Davenport

Much of the pleasure of exploring this area comes from discovering the individual variations on the overall Venetian theme that confer special charm on each of the towns you'll visit. Some, such as Verona, Treviso, and Udine, have a solid medieval look; Asolo has an idyllic setting; Bassano combines a bit of both. If you are a confirmed or fledgling oenophile, you'll enjoy tasting local wines within view of the vineyards that produce some of the best-known Italian vintages—among them, Soave, Valpolicella, Bardolino, and Prosecco. But most of all, you'll find artistic jewels everywhere, from the great Venetian masters in Verona to Veronese's lighthearted frescoes in Villa Barbaro at Maser.

Pleasures and Pastimes

Dining

In the main cities of the Veneto region, restaurants are in the middle to upper ranges of each price category, but in smaller towns and in the countryside you can find some real bargains. At the eastern end of the Arc, in less trafficked Friuli–Venezia Giulia, prices are generally lower. Seafood is the specialty along the coast, of course, but inland the cuisine varies from the delicate risotto, radicchio, and asparagus of the Veneto to the more decisively flavored cooking of the Trieste area, heavily influenced by Austria. San Daniele del Friuli, near Udine, is famous for its delicious prosciutto *crudo* (cured). Polenta, made of cornmeal, is a staple throughout the area; it is served with thick, rich sauces or grilled as an accompaniment to meat dishes. Trieste's position near the Austrian and Slovenian borders has fostered a varied—and somewhat heavier—cuisine reflecting the tastes of those countries. The best local wines are Soave, Tocai, Prosecco, Riesling, and pinot—all white; and Bardolino, Valpolicella, merlot, cabernet, and pinot nero—reds. The Collio designation indicates wines from vineyards in the eastern part of Friuli, up against the Slovenian border. One of the best known and rarest wines produced here is the sauternelike Picolit, made in very limited quantities. Grappa is a locally distilled aquavit.

CATEGORY	COST*
$$$$	over 95,000 lire
$$$	70,000–95,000 lire
$$	35,000–70,000 lire
$	under 35,000 lire

per person, including house wine, service, and tax

Liqueurs

The Veneto and Friuli regions are renowned for their grappas (distilled wines). Justifiably popular are those made by the families Nardini, in Bassano, and Nonino, at Udine. Trieste is the home of the famous Stock liqueur.

Lodging

The area around Venice has been playing host to visitors for centuries, and the result is a range of comfortable accommodations at every price. As with dining, common sense should tell you that the slightly out-of-the-way small hotel will cost you less than its counterpart in a stylish Adriatic resort. Expect to pay more as you approach Venice, since many of the mainland towns absorb the overflow during the times when Venice becomes most crowded, such as Carnival (the two weeks preceding Lent) and throughout the summer.

CATEGORY	COST*
$$$$	over 250,000 lire
$$$	160,000–250,000 lire
$$	90,000–160,000 lire
$	under 90,000 lire

Prices are for a standard double room for two, including tax and service.

Concerts and Opera

The love of Italian culture need not stop at Venice; Verona, Trieste and Vicenza offer some of the most spectacular opportunities for indulging in the passions of open-air opera and concerts.

Trieste holds an open-air operetta festival each summer (July–Aug.), and an opera season in winter (Oct.–Apr.). For details of dates, times, and prices, contact the main tourist information office (☞ Contacts and Resources *in* Venetian Arc A to Z, *below*). Vicenza's Teatro Olimpico has a concert season in May–June, as well as a classical drama season in September. Even if your Italian is dismal, it's particularly thrilling to see a performance in Palladio's magnificent theater; this masterpiece was designed to be used, not just admired. For details, contact the Teatro Olimpico (☞ Vicenza, *below*).

Outdoor Activities and Sports

The Adriatic coastline and Alpine foothills provide many opportunities for you to burn off those pasta calories. Swimming is possible at most of the area's ports, but pollution has made the prospect risky at most beaches. Most towns of even moderate size have public swimming pools. Other sporting options are noted in the descriptions of the towns throughout the chapter. Note that tourist information offices should be able to provide comprehensive listings of local sports facilities, holidays, and events. The Veneto Regional Tourist Office (☞ Contacts and Resources *in* Venetian Arc A to Z, *below*) has information on golf courses in the area: It's best to write them well in advance.

Shopping

Many of the goods normally associated with Venice are actually produced in the surrounding areas of the Venetian Arc—which means that with a bit of diligence or luck you can pick up a bargain from the source. Mountain towns and villages—Bassano del Grappa is one—have the strongest handicraft tradition, and you can find a wide range of goods in artisans' shops on the side streets. The main towns on the coastal plain are often associated with one or two specialties, either because of traditional skills or because of ancient trading rights that set a pattern of importing specific items from other parts of the Mediterranean.

Villas and Palazzi

Local tourist offices may be able to provide some information on visiting the countless villas in the Venetian hinterland (☞ Contacts and Resources *in* Venetian Arc A to Z, *below*) Many of the villas are privately owned but are open to the public at certain times or by special request. These gracious country homes give insight into the way wealthy Venetians used to—and still do—vacation.

Exploring the Venetian Arc

This exploring section covers the broad Adriatic sweep of the Venetian Arc from west to east, beginning at Venice. Many of the first towns visited can be seen on one- or two-day excursions from Venice itself, although it is far better to give yourself time to appreciate the more remote spots by planning a few overnight stops en route.

The area known as the Venetian Arc comprises principally the coastal crescent and inland plain that stretches from the mouths of the Po and Adige rivers southwest of Venice. In addition the cities of Trieste and Udine lie east of Venice, and close to the Slovenian border. They bridge two Italian regions—the Veneto and Friuli–Venezia Giulia—a landscape of flat green farmland spotted with low hills that swells and rises steeply inland in a succession of plateaus and high meadows to the snow-tipped Alps.

Great Itineraries

Numbers in the text correspond to numbers in the margins and on the maps.

Hard as it may seem to leave the unique beauty of Venice behind, the Venetian Arc is the perfect last course to round off your stay. The towns are all beautiful, mixing grandiose architecture and medieval aristocracy in a flawless manner. One of these towns, Verona, also unknowingly produced the most tragic of all storie d'amore (love stories)—*Romeo and Juliet*. The sorrow that this tale inspires can be drowned in the delights of some of the best-known Italian wines.

A seven day trip will give you the time to savor the architecture, the history, and the culture of this beautiful region. A five day exploration will give you plenty to remember and even savor, but you will have to discipline yourself and move on to the next sight. A three day itinerary will exclude Trieste and restrict you to the other principal sights, but you can make up for it at night either by taking in a show or simply eating out to get a feel for the areas in general.

IF YOU HAVE 3 DAYS

Begin your drive at **Villa Pisani** ①, the most splendid of all Veneto villas. Move on to **Padua** ②, taking in the Capella Scrovegni. Continue toward 🏛 **Verona** ③–⑯, the city of *Romeo and Juliet*. The following day see some of Palladio's works in **Vicenza** ⑰ and head for **Marostica** ⑱, 🏛 **Bassano del Grappa** ⑲, and **Asolo**. ⑳ Save the last day for **Treviso** ㉒, **Conegliano** ㉓, and stop for a tour of **Udine** ㉔. Return to Venice along the A4, leaving out Trieste.

IF YOU HAVE 5 DAYS

Follow the itinerary described above until Asolo. Instead of moving on directly to Treviso, travel toward **Villa Barbaro** ㉑ in Maser and then on to **Treviso** ㉒. Visit **Conegliano** ㉓ and 🏛 **Udine** ㉔, where you can overnight. The next day head for **Cividale** ㉕ and down then to 🏛 **Trieste** ㉗. Spend a day in this border city and then move on to **Miramare Castle** ㉖ before taking the A4 back to Venice.

IF YOU HAVE 7 DAYS

Follow the itinerary described above, but in **Bassano del Grappa** ⑲ take in a visit to the famous Nardini distillery on the edge of town. From **Treviso** ㉒, head to Oderzo on the magnificent Red Wine Road, which wends through the cabernet and merlot country along the Piave River.

When to Tour the Venetian Arc

There are no particularly good or bad times to see the sights around the Venetian Arc. Most of the year, the area is free from very heavy traffic and congestion. If, however, you want to get the most out of your stay, come during the early summer months (May, June, July) or immediately after the end of August. Opera and theater buffs should come in the summer months, as most performances in this region are outdoors and are on only in spring and summer. It's a pleasure to walk in Verona, Vicenza, and Padua at the end of summer when temperatures aren't at their highest.

GREAT CITIES OF THE VENETO
Padua, Verona, and Vicenza

Foremost among the treasures of the Veneto region are the beautiful villas Andrea Palladio (1508–80) built to render la vita all the more dolce for 16th-century aristocrats. Other important sights include Giotto's 14th-century frescoes in Padua's Scrovegni Chapel and many of Donatello's greatest statues. Romeo and Juliet? In Verona, visitors are charged a small fee to see what is alleged to be the tomb of Juliet and not far away there is a 13th-century building in which the lovely Juliet Capuletti lived. Of Romeo, alas, the landmarks are vaguer.

Numbers in the margin correspond to points of interest on the Venetian Arc map.

Villa Pisani

❶ *10 km (6 mi) southeast of Padua.*

This extraordinary house in **Stra**, also called Villa Nazionale, is the most spectacular of all the Veneto villas. In the 16th to 18th centuries, wealthy Venetians sought to enjoy *villegiatura*—a vacation and escape from harried city life—by building stately residences on their country estates throughout Venetia. Many of them were constructed on the Brenta River, the main waterway Venetians would use to go inland. Villa Pisani is an imposing 18th-century edifice which that once belonged to Napoléon, who appreciated its similarities to Versailles. See the grandiose frescoes by Giambattista Tiepolo on the ceiling of the ballroom and explore the gorgeous park; also climb to the top of the little tower for a good look at the maze (open only in the summer). The maze should provide a good energy outlet for youngsters who are surfeited with old masters. It is about 7 kilometers (4¼ miles) east of Padua. ✉ *Stra,* ☎ *0423/923004.* 🎫 *8,000 lire.* ☉ *Apr.–Sept., Tues.–Sun., villa and grounds 9–6; Oct.–Mar., Tues.–Sun., villa 9–1, grounds 9–4.*

Padua

❷ *37 km (23 mi) west of Venice and 92 km (57 mi) east of Verona.*

Padua (Padova) is well worth a visit (although hotels in nearby Vicenza, in Bassano del Grappa, along the Brenta, and in Venice are better in terms of variety and quality than in Padua itself, which caters primarily to business travelers). It's a bustling city with a medieval nucleus, the seat of a famous university founded in 1222, but now surrounded by unattractive modern business districts. Pick up a map and brochures at the tourist office in the train station and head straight down **Corso del Popolo**, which changes its name to Corso Garibaldi about 400 yards on, when it crosses the Bacchiglione River.

★ The **Cappella degli Scrovegni** (Scrovegni Chapel) was erected by a wealthy Paduan, Enrico Scrovegni, to honor his deceased father in the 13th century near the site of an ancient Roman arena. Scrovegni called on Giotto to decorate its interior, a task that occupied the great artist

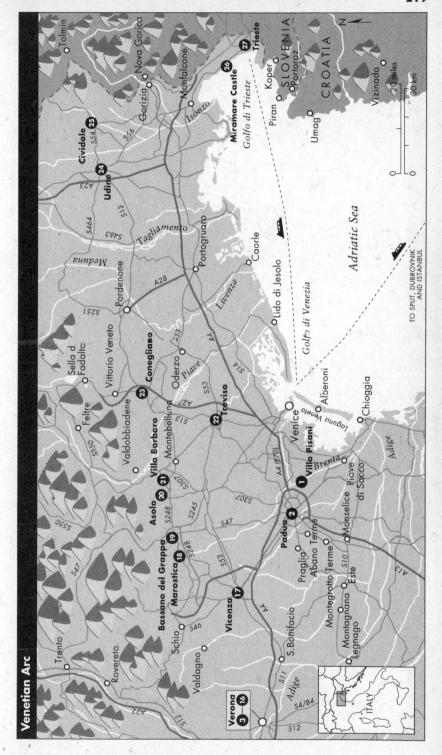

Tolmin

Nova Gorica

Montfalcone

Gorizia

26 Miramare Castle

27 Trieste

Golfo di Trieste

SLOVENIA

Koper

Portoroz

Piran

CROATIA

Umag

Vizinada

20 miles

30 km

25 Cividale

S54

S55

S56

24 Udine

A23

S464

S463

S13

Tagliamento

Portogruaro

Caorle

Lido di Jesolo

Adriatic Sea

Meduna

A28

Livenza

Pordenone

S251

Vittorio Veneto

Sella di Fadalto

23 Conegliano

Oderzo

Piave

S53

A27

S14

Golfo di Venezia

Alberoni

Chioggia

Feltre

S550

Valdobbiadene

21 Villa Barbaro

Montebelluna

S13

22 Treviso

Venice

Laguna Veneta

Adige

20 Asolo

S248

S307

A4 (E70)

1 Villa Pisani

Brenta

Piove di Sacco

19 Bassano del Grappa

18 Marostica

S248

S245

S47

S307

2 Padua

Praglia

Abano Terme

Monselice

S10

Este

A13

S47

S550

Schio

S46

Valdagno

17 Vicenza

A4

S53

S. Bonifacio

Montegrotto Terme

Montagnana

Legnago

Trento

Rovereto

A22

S12

S11

Adige

S4/B4

3 **16** Verona

S12

A22

TO SPLIT, DUBROVNIK AND ISTANBUL

ITALY

N

220

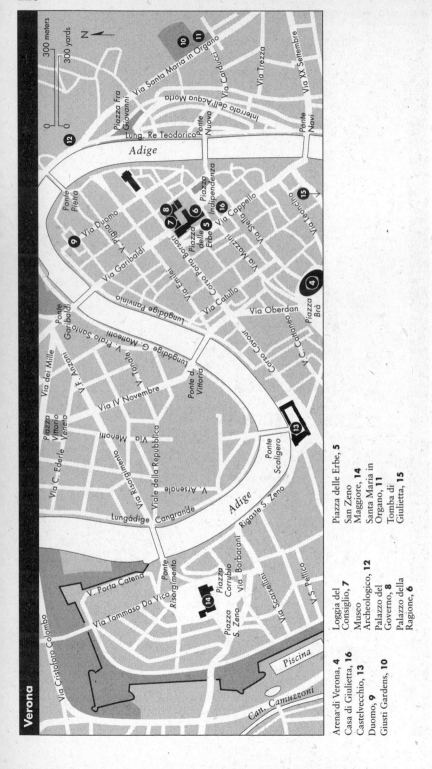

Verona

Arena di Verona, **4**
Casa di Giulietta, **16**
Castelvecchio, **13**
Duomo, **9**
Giusti Gardens, **10**

Loggia del
Consiglio, **7**
Museo
Archeologico, **12**
Palazzo del
Governo, **8**
Palazzo della
Ragione, **6**

Piazza delle Erbe, **5**
San Zeno
Maggiore, **14**
Santa Maria in
Organo, **11**
Tomba di
Giulietta, **15**

and his helpers from 1303 to 1305. They created a magnificent fresco cycle, arranged in typical medieval comic-strip fashion, illustrating the lives of Mary and Christ. The realism in these frescoes—which include the first blue skies in Western painting—was revolutionary. Visit Piazza Eremitani and the 13th-century **church of the Eremitani.** It contains some fragments of frescoes by Andrea Mantegna (1431–1506), the brilliant locally born artist, some of whose masterpieces are in nearby Mantua: Most of these frescoes, however, were destroyed in the Allied bombing of 1944. The **Museo Civico** (Civic Museum), housed in what used to be the monastery of the church, has its quota of works by Venetian masters. ⊠ *Corso Garibaldi,* ☎ *049/875–1153.* 🖼 *10,000 lire. Both open year-round Tues.–Sun. 9–6; chapel also open Mon. 9–6,* 🖼 *7,000 lire.*

NEED A BREAK?	**Caffè Pedrocchi** is a monumental 19th-century neoclassical coffeehouse that looks like a cross between a museum and a stage set—an impressive place for a cappuccino. The upstairs rooms, with their frescoed ceilings, often feature art shows. ⊠ *Corso Garibaldi,* ☎ *049/876-2576.*

The medieval-era **university** building incorporates a 16th-century facade. In the 15th century, this structure was known as the Osteria del Bo' (Ox Inn), a favorite student hangout; Padua University is still familiarly known as Il Bo'. This is worth a visit to see the exquisite and perfectly proportioned anatomy theater and a hall harboring a lectern used by Galileo. ⊠ *Via VIII Febbraio,* ☎ *049/820–9711.* 🖼 *5,000 lire. Guided visits only.* ⊙ *Call for tour times.*

Palazzo della Ragione (also called Il Salone), was built in the Middle Ages as the seat of Padua's parliament. Today its street-level arcades shelter shops and cafés. In the frescoed Great Hall on the upper level is an enormous wooden horse, a 15th-century replica of the bronze steed in Donatello's equestrian statue of Gattamelata. ⊠ *Piazza della Ragione.* 🖼 *7,000 lire.* ⊙ *Winter 9–6; summer 9–7. During special exhibitions, hours and admission price may vary.*

The huge basilica of **Sant'Antonio** is one of Padua's major attractions. A cluster of Byzantine domes and slender, minaret-like towers gives the church an Oriental look, reminiscent of San Marco in Venice. The interior is sumptuous, too, with marble reliefs by Tullio Lombardo, the greatest in a talented family of marble carvers who decorated many churches in the area—among them, Santa Maria dei Miracoli in Venice. The artistic highlights here, however, all bear Donatello's name; the 15th-century Florentine master did the remarkable series of bronze reliefs illustrating the life of St. Anthony—whose feast day, June 13, draws pilgrims from all over Europe—as well as the bronze statues of the Madonna and saints on the high altar. To mark the 800th anniversary of the birth of St. Anthony in 1195, a new museum, the **Museo Antoniano,** with 300 exhibits relating to the image of the saint and of the basilica, was opened in 1995 on the first floor of the church cloister building. Standing in front of the church is Donatello's powerful statue of the condottiere (mercenary general) Gattamelata, which was cast in bronze—a monumental technical achievement—in about 1450 and was to have an enormous influence on the development of Italian Renaissance sculpture. ⊠ *Via del Santo Basilica.* 🖼 *Free.* ⊙ *Summer 6:30 AM–7:45 PM; winter 6:30 AM–7 PM. Museum:* 🖼 *5,000 lire.* ⊙ *Daily 9–7.*

The **Orto Botanico** (Botanic Garden) was founded in 1545 by order of the Venetian Republic to supply the university with medicinal plants. The garden is in front of Sant'Antonio basilica. ⊠ *Via Donatello.* 🖼 *5,000 lire.* ⊙ *Summer, daily 9–12:30, 3–6; winter Mon.–Sat. 9–1.*

Piazza dei Signori has some fine examples of 15th- and 16th-century buildings and a cathedral just a few steps away.

Prato della Valle is an unusual and attractive piazza laid out in 1775, with a wooded oval park at the center, surrounded by a canal. (There is a Saturday market held here every week and a secondhand/antiques market on the third Sunday of every month.) At the southeast end of this immense square is the church of **Santa Giustina,** with finely inlaid choir stalls and Veronese's colossal altarpiece, *The Martyrdom of St. Justine.* ⊠ *Prato della Valle.* ⊙ *Mon.–Sat. 7:30–noon and 3:30–7:30, Sun. 7–1, 3:30–7:30.*

OFF THE
BEATEN PATH

ABANO TERME AND MONTEGROTTO TERME - These two spas, about 12 kilometers (7½ miles) south of Padua, are set in the dreamy landscape of the Euganean Hills. Colorful gardens and fresh summer breezes make them havens for those seeking a break from city life.

MONTAGNANA - This medieval city is 50 kilometers (30 miles) south-west of Padua. Its surrounding walls are remarkably well preserved, and there are 24 towers, a moat, and four city gates. Its former rivals, Este and Monselice, are only 20 kilometers (12 miles) east on the same road.

Dining and Lodging

$$$ ✕ **Belle Parti.** Related to the prestigious chain of El Toulà, Angelo Rasi's Belle Parti remains the best restaurant in town. The ambience is sophisticated, and the adventurous and seasonal cuisine has a Venetian accent. Specialties include risotto *al fior d'arancio con gamberi di fiume* (with oranges and river prawns) and *quaglia tartufata in crosta* (truffled quails in pastry). The wine list offers a fine selection of the area's best bottles. ⊠ *Via Belle Parti 11,* ☎ *049/875–1822. AE, DC, MC, V. Closed Sun. and first 3 wks in Aug. No lunch Mon.*

$$ ✕ **Cavalca.** A family-run establishment with a long tradition, Cavalca is just off Piazza dei Signori in the heart of Padua. Classic decor and simple but courteous service are hallmarks here. The specialties are pasta *e fagioli* (pasta and bean soup), roast *capretto* (kid), or a platter of *arrosti misti* (assorted roast meats). ⊠ *Via Manin 8,* ☎ *049/876–0061. Reservations essential. AE, DC, MC, V. Closed Wed., Jan. 12–22, and July 1–21. No dinner Tues.*

$ ✕ **Fagiano.** Located near the basilica of Sant'Antonio, Fagiano is a popular trattoria with locals and tourists. The specialties are hearty standbys: pasta e fagioli and *fagiano farcito* (stuffed pheasant). ⊠ *Via Locatelli 45,* ☎ *049/875–0073. MC, V. Closed Mon. and July 15– Aug. 15.*

$$$ ⊡ **Donatello.** Directly opposite the basilica of Sant'Antonio, the Donatello is central and popular with tourists. About half the rooms have a view of the square and church but can be noisy. The decor is contemporary; rooms have a minibar and color TV. ⊠ *Via del Santo 102,* ☎ *049/875– 0634,* ℻ *049/875–0829. 49 rooms, 42 with bath or shower. Restaurant, parking. AE, DC, MC, V. Closed mid-Dec.–mid-Jan.*

$$$ ⊡ **Villa Ducale.** Set in its own statued gardens, one of the country residences built along the Brenta River by Venetian noblemen has been turned into a stylish hotel with stuccoed walls and ceilings, Murano glass chandeliers and mirrors, and Venetian-style marble flooring. Recently restored and placed under new management, the Villa Ducale is in Dolo, which lies halfway between Venice and Padua, and is connected to both by a regular local train service. ⊠ *Riviera Martiri della Libertà 75, Dolo,* ☎ *and* ℻ *041/420094. 11 rooms with bath or shower. Restaurant, air-conditioning, parking. MC, V.*

Nightlife and the Arts

BARS

Caffè Pedrocchi in Padua is probably the best-known café in the Venetian Arc. Have your drink inside or out while you admire the uninhibited mixture of architectural styles.

DISCOS

The best bets in Padua are **Big Club** (⊠ Via Armistizio, ☎ 049/680934), **Wag** (⊠ Via Savonarola 149, ☎ 049/872–1530), and **Le Petit Palais** (⊠ Via Vecellio 1, ☎ 049/600134).

For those who like to play pool, **Limbo** (⊠ Via San Fermo 44, ☎ 049/656882) has a game room upstairs with live music downstairs.

JAZZ

Video Club Sisma (⊠ Via Chiesanuova 106, Padua, ☎ 049/871–6577).

Outdoor Activities and Sports

GOLF

Golf Club Padova (⊠ Via Noiera 57, Valsanzibio di Galzignano, 18 km/11 mi south of Padua, ☎ 049/913–0078, 🗷 049/913–1193).

HORSEBACK RIDING

Scuola Padovana Equitazione (⊠ Via Libia 20, Padua, ☎ 049/871–7244).

Shopping

Padua has a Saturday market featuring a wide range of goods in **Prato della Valle,** where an antiques market is held the third Sunday of every month.

En Route **Praglia,** a Benedictine monastery hidden in the hills, provides guided tours of its evocative 15th-century halls and cloisters. You can also buy wine and honey produced here by the monks. To get there head 12 kilometers (7 miles) southwest of Padua. ☎ 049/990–0010. ⊿ *Offerings appreciated.* ☉ *For tours Tues.–Sun. (except major religious holidays) Apr.–Oct. every ½ hr 3:30–5:30; Nov.–Mar. every ½ hr 2:30–4:30.*

Verona

❸ *89 km (53 mi) west of Padua, 60 km (37 mi) southwest of Vicenza.*

The attractive city of **Verona,** on the banks of the fast-flowing Adige River is, after Venice, the top attraction in the region and a rival to other Italian art cities. It has considerable charm; classical and medieval monuments; a picturesque town center where bright geraniums bloom in window boxes; and a romantic reputation, thanks to Shakespeare's *Romeo and Juliet,* which is set here. It is one of Italy's most alluring cities, despite extensive industrialization and urban development in its newer sections. Inevitably, with its lively Venetian air, proximity to Lake Garda, and renowned summer opera season, it attracts hordes of tourists, especially vacationing Germans and Austrians, who drive through the Brenner Pass just to the north.

Verona grew to power and prosperity within the Roman Empire as a result of its key commercial and military position in northern Italy. After the fall of the Empire, the city continued to flourish under the guidance of Barbarian kings such as Theodoric, Alboin, Pepin, and Berenger I, reaching its cultural and artistic peak in the 13th and 14th centuries, under the Della Scala dynasty. (You'll see the *scala,* or ladder, emblem all over town.) In 1404, however, Verona traded its independence for security and placed itself under the control of Venice. (The other recurring architectural motif is the lion of St. Mark, symbol of Venetian rule.) Verona remained under Venetian protection until 1797, when

Napoléon invaded. In 1814 the entire Veneto region was won by the Austrians, and it was finally united with the rest of Italy in 1866.

Numbers in the margin correspond to points of interest on the Verona map.

★ ☺ ❹ The obvious place to start your visit is at the **Arena di Verona,** in Piazza Brà, the vast and airy square at the center of the city. Built by the Romans in the 1st century AD, the arena is one of the largest and best-preserved Roman amphitheaters anywhere. Only four arches remain of the outer rings, but the main structure is so complete that it takes little imagination to picture it as the site of the cruel deaths of countless gladiators, wild beasts, and Christians. Today it hosts Verona's summer opera, famous for spectacular productions and audiences of as many as 22,000. The best operas to see here are the big splashy ones that demand huge choruses, Cinerama sets, lots of color and movement, and, if possible, camels, horses, and/or elephants. The music can be excellent, and the acoustics are fine, too. If you go, be sure to take or rent a cushion—four hours on 2,000-year-old marble can be an ordeal. ⊠ *Arena di Verona, Piazza Brà, 045/800–3204.* ☜ *6,000 lire; free 1st Sun. of month.* ☉ *Tues.–Sun. 8–6:30; Tues.–Sun. 8–1:30 during opera season in July and Aug.*

❺ **Piazza delle Erbe** (Vegetable Market Square) is the site of an ancient Roman forum and today a colorful market in the morning, when huge rectangular umbrellas are raised to shade the neat ranks of fruits and vegetables.

❻ The 12th-century **Palazzo della Ragione** has a somber courtyard, Gothic staircase, and medieval tower; it overlooks **Piazza dei Signori,** just off Piazza Brà, and is enclosed on all sides by stately public build-
❼ ings. The graceful **Loggia del Consiglio** was built in the 12th century
❽ to house city council meetings. At the end of the piazza is the **Palazzo del Governo,** the medieval stronghold from which the Della Scalas ruled Verona with an iron fist.

❾ The ornate Romanesque **Duomo** not only has some architectural characteristics typical of the Venetian style, but also some of those typical of the Byzantine. ⊠ *Via Duomo.* ☉ *Daily 7–12 and 4–7.*

❿ The **Giusti Gardens,** laid out on several levels around a 16th-century villa, are a symbol of things long past. There's a formal Italian garden and a fine view of the city from the terrace, from which Johann von Goethe, the German poet and dramatist, drew inspiration. At the southern end of the gardens is the Gothic church of **Sant'Anastasia** (☉ daily 7–noon and 4–7).⊠ *Via Giardino Giusti,* ☎ *045/803–4029.* ☜ *5,000 lire.* ☉ *Apr.–Sept. daily 9–8; Oct.–Mar. daily 9–sunset.*

NEED A   **Cacciatore,** in the Piazza Isolo section at this end of Ponte Nuovo, is one
BREAK?   of Verona's historic *osterie* (wineshops). The fine local wines are still a
             big draw for habitués, but some inexpensive dishes are also available.
             ⊠ *Via Seminario 4,* ☎ *045/594291. Closed Sun. and Aug.*

⓫ The medieval church of **Santa Maria in Organo** is worth a visit. The choir and sacristy are covered in inlaid-wood masterpieces of the 15th-century monk Fra Giovanni. A series of panels depicts varied scenes—local buildings, an idealized Renaissance town, wildlife, and fruit—that radiate a love of life and reveal the artist's eye for detail. ⊠ *Via Giardino Giusti,* ☎ *045/591440.* ☉ *Daily 7:30–11.*

⓬ The modest **Museo Archeologico** is in an old monastery above a Roman theater that was built in the same era as the Arena di Verona (☞ *above*).

The Roman theater is in the museum grounds and is sometimes used for dramatic productions. From here there are good views over the entire city. ✉ *Rigaste del Redentore,* ☎ *045/800–0360.* ☞ *5,000 lire; free on 1st Sun. of the month.* ⊙ *Tues.–Sun. 8–1.*

🖐 ⑬ **Castelvecchio** is a 14th-century castle built for Cangrande II Della Scala. A crenellated building in russet brick with massive walls, towers, turrets, and a vast courtyard, it looks like a fairy-tale castle that guards a bridge across the Adige. The whole street to which it belongs is lined with attractive old buildings and palaces of the old nobility. Inside, the **Museo di Castelvecchio** gives you a good look at the castle's vaulted halls and the treasures of Venetian painting and sculpture that they contain. ✉ *Corso Cavour,* ☎ *045/594734.* ☞ *5,000 lire; free on 1st Sun. of the month.* ⊙ *Tues.–Sun. 8–6:30; hrs and admission may change during special exhibitions.*

⑭ **San Zeno Maggiore** is possibly one of Italy's finest examples of a Romanesque church. It's set between two medieval bell towers and has a 13th-century rose window and 12th-century portal. The brick color scheme is typical of most Romanesque churches in Italy, but especially impressive here. Inside, look for Mantegna's *Madonna* over the main altar; there's a peaceful cloister off the left nave. ✉ *Piazza San Zeno,* ☎ *045/800–6120.* ⊙ *Daily 8–noon and 4–6:30.*

Romantic souls may want to see what the astute tourist office says is ⑬ **Tomba di Giulietta** (Juliet's Tomb). It's a pretty spot, though hardly a major attraction. Authentic or not, it is still popular with lovesick Italian teenagers, who leave notes for the tragic lover. ✉ *Via del Pontiere,* ☎ *800–0361.* ☞ *5,000 lire; free on 1st Sun. of month.* ⊙ *Tues.–Sun. 8–6:30.*

⑯ At **Casa di Giulietta** (Juliet's House), the balcony in the small courtyard will help to bring Shakespeare's play to life. Historians now believe that the couple had no real-life counterparts, but this hasn't discouraged anyone from imagining that they did. After all, historians are not as renowned for their storytelling as Shakespeare is. ✉ *Via Cappello 23,* ☞ *5,000 lire.* ⊙ *Tues.–Sun. 8–6:30.*

Dining and Lodging

$$$$ ✕ **Dodici Apostoli.** Vaulted ceilings, frescoed walls, and a medieval ambience make this an exceptional place to enjoy classic local and regional dishes. Near Piazza delle Erbe, it stands on the foundations of a Roman temple. Specialties include *zuppa scaligera* (soup of meat stock with vegetables and bread) and *vitello Lessinia* (veal with mushrooms, cheese, and truffles). ✉ *Corticella San Marco 3,* ☎ *045/596999. AE, DC, V. Closed Mon., Jan. 1–7, and June 15–July 7. No dinner Sun.*

$$$$ ✕ **Le Arche.** True to its name, this elegant restaurant is in a medieval building a step away from the Della Scala tombs. The dining room is furnished in art-nouveau style, featuring candlelight and flowers, and it has a turn-of-the-century air. Only seafood is served, absolutely fresh and superlatively prepared in the Venetian tradition. The specialties are ravioli *di branzino con vongole* (stuffed with sea bass with clam sauce) and *scorfano con olive nere* (baked sea scorpion with black olives). ✉ *Via Arche Scaligere 6,* ☎ *045/800–7415. AE, DC, MC, V. Closed Sun., first 2 wks of Jan., and July 1–21. No lunch Mon.*

$$–$$$ ✕ **Osteria All'Oste Scuro.** A trusty, family-run trattoria with a changing selection of traditional Veronese dishes (pasta e fagioli; polenta *con lardo,* with bacon; *pastisada de caval,* horse-meat stew), this friendly spot also offers, from September to May, once-or twice-weekly special fixed-price dinners featuring a regional menu—Piedmontese, Tuscan, Lombard, etc.—with each course accompanied by a glass of wine from the same region. These remarkably good-value gastronomic occasions, for which you need to book in advance, are very popular with the local clientele. ⊠ *Vicolo San Silvestro 10,* ☎ *045/592650. MC, V. Closed Sun. No dinner Sat.*

$$ ✕ **Al Calmiere.** This congenial trattoria on the lovely piazza in front of San Zeno Maggiore, one of the city's finest churches, is the ideal place to enjoy Veronese specialties of tagliatelle with *fegatini di pollo* (chicken-liver sauce), various types of pasta in *brodo* (broth), *bolito* (boiled) and roast meats, and local wines (there are some 20 different Valpolicellas alone available) at very reasonable prices. There is dining on the square in summer, and in a cozy inside room with an enormous open fireplace, used for cooking, in winter. ⊠ *Piazza San Zeno 10,* ☎ *045/803–0765. AE, DC, MC, V. Closed Thurs. and July. No dinner Wed.*

$$ ✕ **Antico Caffè Dante.** This historic coffeehouse has been taken over by Guido Morari, the proprietor of the upmarket Nuovo Marconi restaurant next door, and its stuccoed interior with portraits of Italian national heroes has been restored. It is now a brasserie-style café-restaurant where you can choose from a short but varied menu, including a delicious asparagus risotto (in season), fresh *papparedelle* (thick ribbons of pasta) with scampi, grilled lamb chops, and *stinco di maiale* (roast pork shin served with polenta) at lunch and dinner, or snack on tempting homemade cakes and pastries all day, while feasting your eyes on the pleasing view of the piazza. ⊠ *Piazza dei Signori 2,* ☎ *045/595249. AE, DC, MC, V. Closed Sun. in winter.*

$$ ✕ **La Greppia.** The classic decor with vaulted ceilings sets the tone in this popular restaurant off Via Mazzini between the Arena and Piazza delle Erbe. The kitchen produces fine versions of local and regional dishes, especially *tortelli di zucca* (pasta filled with squash) and *bolliti* (assorted boiled meats served with a choice of sauces). Service is courteous and efficient. ⊠ *Vicolo Samaritana 3,* ☎ *045/800–4577. AE, DC, V. Closed Mon., first wk of Jan., June 15–30.*

$ ✕ **Pizzeria Vesuvio.** Between Castelvecchio and San Zeno Maggiore, this authentic Neapolitan pizzeria has tables on the riverbank in summer, with a lovely breezy view of the Adige. ⊠ *Via Rigaste 41,* ☎ *045/595634. MC, V. Closed Mon.*

$$$$ ▥ **Colomba d'Oro.** This attractive four-star hotel right by the Arena occupies a building that dates from the 14th century. Repeatedly renovated over the past few years, it has retained a clubby atmosphere and European charm while providing up-to-date comfort. There is no restaurant. ⊠ *Via Cattaneo 10,* ☎ *045/595300,* ﬀ *045/594974. 49 rooms with bath or shower, 2 suites. Parking. AE, DC, MC, V.*

$$$$ ▥ **Gabbia d'Oro.** This historic building off Piazza delle Erbe in the ancient heart of Verona was fully and tastefully restored in 1990. Public rooms and individually furnished guest rooms have frescoes, beamed ceilings, and antique prints and furnishings. Guests can relax outdoors in the medieval courtyard or on the roof terrace. ⊠ *Corso Porta Borsari 4/a,* ☎ *045/800–3060,* ﬀ *045/590293. 27 rooms with bath. Restaurant, bar. AE, DC, MC, V.*

$$$$ ▥ **Villa del Quar.** This charming 16th-century villa surrounded by gar-
★ dens and vineyards in the Valpolicella country is only 7 kilometers (4½ miles) from the center of town (and easily reached by taxi). Architect Leopoldo Montresor and his wife Evelina, who live here with their young children, recently converted part of the villa into a stylish and sophisticated hotel. No expense has been spared: all rooms have marble bathrooms (some with Jacuzzi) and antique European furniture, and the outdoor swimming pool, restaurant, and breezy tranquillity make the Quar an ideal place for a stay around Verona. ⊠ *Via del Quar 12, Pede-*

monte, ☎ 045/680–0681, ⅎ𝔸𝕏 045/680–0604. *18 rooms and 4 suites. Restaurant, bar, air-conditioning, pool, parking. AE, DC, MC, V.*

$$
★ 🍽 **Torcolo.** The warm welcome extended by the owners, Signoras Diana and Silvia, the pleasant rooms decorated unfussily, and the central location on a peaceful street close to Piazza Brà and the Arena make the Torcolo outstanding value in its class. Breakfast is served outside on the terrace in front of the hotel in summer. ⊠ *Vicolo Listone 3,* ☎ *045/800–7512,* ⅎ𝔸𝕏 *045/800–4058. 19 rooms with bath or shower. MC, V.*

Nightlife and the Arts

DISCOS

Alter Ego (⊠ Via Torricelle 9, ☎ 045/915130) hosts a twentysomething crowd that might call itself alternative.

Berfi's (⊠ Via Lussemborgo 1, ☎ 045/508024) is a popular but expensive spot.

Excalibur (⊠ Via Provolo 24, ☎ 045/594295) attracts the youngest crowds

OPERA

Of all the venues for enjoying opera in the region, pride of place must go to the summer opera season in the **Arena di Verona.** The season runs from July through August, and the 22,000 in the audience sit on the original stone terraces which date from the time when gladiators fought to the death. The opera stage is huge and best suited to grand operas such as *Aïda,* but the experience is memorable no matter what is being performed. Sometimes, while sipping a drink in a café at **Piazza Brà,** you can overhear the opera being performed inside the adjacent arena. ⊠ *Contact: Ente Lirico Arena di Verona, Piazza Brà 28, 37121 Verona,* ☎ *045/590109/966/726,* ⅎ𝔸𝕏 *045/801–1566. Box office:* ⊠ *Via Dietro Anfiteatro 6B,* ☎ *045/800–5151,* ⅎ𝔸𝕏 *045/801–3287.* ☉ *Sept.–June weekdays 8:40–12:20 and 3–5:50; Sat. 8:40–12:20; July–Aug. Box office closed Mon.; open on days without performances 9:30–12:20, 3–6:20; and on days of performances 10–12:20 and 3:30–9:30. A 15% advance-sale fee is added to price of ticket for bookings made more than 24 hrs before performance.*

Outdoor Activities and Sports

GOLF

Golf Club Verona (⊠ Ca' del Sale 15, Sommacampagna, 16 km (10 mi) west of Verona or 2 km (1¼ mi) from the Sommacampagna exit on the A4 autoroute, ☎ 045/510060, ⅎ𝔸𝕏 045/510242).

TENNIS

There are public courts at **Via Col. Galliano** (☎ 045/566372).

Shopping

ANTIQUES

The area around the Gothic church of Sant'Anastasia is full of antiques shops, most of them catering to serious collectors; picnic on the Piazza dei Signori in the cool breeze after a strenuous day of antiques hunting.

FLEA MARKETS

Verona's **Piazza delle Erbe** market has a selection of food, wine, clothing, some antiques, and even pets. ☉ *Daily.*

Vicenza

17 *60 km (37 mi) east of Verona, 32 km (20 mi) west of Padua.*

Vicenza bears the distinctive signature of the 16th-century architect Andrea Palladio, and was designated by UNESCO in 1994 as a preeminent site of world cultural heritage. The architect, whose name is the basis of the term "Palladian," gracefully incorporated elements of classical architecture—columns, porticoes, and domes—into a style that reflected the Renaissance celebration of order and harmony. His elegant villas and palaces were influential in propagating classical architecture in Europe, especially Britain, and later in America—most notably, at Thomas Jefferson's Monticello.

In the mid-16th century Palladio was given the opportunity to rebuild much of Vicenza, which had suffered great damage during the bloody wars waged against Venice by the League of Cambrai, an alliance of the Papacy, France, the Holy Roman Empire, and several neighboring city-states. He imposed upon the city a number of his grand Roman-style buildings—rather an overstatement, considering the town's status. With the basilica, begun in 1549 in the very heart of Vicenza, he ensured his reputation and embarked on a series of lordly buildings, all of which proclaim the same rigorous classicism.

The Gothic **Duomo** contains a gleaming altarpiece by Lorenzo Veneziano, a 14th-century Venetian painter. The cathedral itself was partly destroyed in World War II, but nearly all the damaged areas have been restored. ⊠ *Piazza Duomo.* ⌦ *Free.* ⊙ *Daily 7–noon and 3:30–7.*

Corso Palladio is a memorable avenue, lined with a succession of imposing palaces and churches that run the gamut from Venetian Gothic to Baroque. Many of these palaces were designed by Palladio.

The church of **Santa Corona** holds an exceptionally fine *Baptism of Christ* (1500) by Giovanni Bellini over the altar on the left, just in front of the transept. ⊠ *Contrà S. Corona.* ⊙ *Daily 8:30–noon and 2:30–6.*

Palazzo Chiericati, on a square at the end of the Corso Palladio, is an exquisite and unmistakably Palladian building. The palace houses the city art gallery, with a representative collection of Venetian paintings. *Piazza Matteotti,* ☎ *0444/321348.* ⌦ *3,000 lire.* ⊙ *Tues.–Sat. 9:30–noon and 2:30–5, Sun. 9:30–noon.*

★ The **Teatro Olimpico** is Palladio's last, and perhaps, most exciting, work. Based closely on the model of the ancient Roman theater, it represents an important development in theater and stage design and is noteworthy for its acoustics and the cunningly devised false perspective of a classical street in the permanent backdrop. The anterooms are all frescoed with important figures in Venetian history. ⊠ *Piazza Matteotti,* ☎ *0444/323781.* ⌦ *5,000 lire.* ⊙ *Mar. 16–Oct. 15, Mon.–Sat. 9:30–12:20 and 3–5:30, Sun. 9:30–12:20; Oct. 16–Mar. 15, Mon.–Sat. 9:30–12:20 and 2–4:30, Sun. 9:30–12:20.*

Piazza dei Signori is the heart of Vicenza and is also the site of Palladio's "basilica," a confusing name, since it is not a church but a courthouse and public meeting hall, the **Palazzo della Ragione.** An early Palladian masterpiece, it was actually a medieval building that the architect modernized, and the skill with which he wedded the graceful two-story exterior loggias to the existing Gothic structure is remarkable. (Also note the Loggia del Capitaniato, opposite, which Palladio designed, but never completed.) ⊠ *Piazza dei Signori,* ☎ *0444/323681.* ⊙ *Tues.–Sat. 9:30–noon and 2:30–5, Sun. 9:30–noon.*

NEED A
BREAK?   **Gran Caffè Garibaldi** (⊠ Piazza dei Signori 5, ☎ 0444/544147) is a classic coffeehouse with a good restaurant upstairs. It looks out on the basilica. Or, just off the piazza, there's the cozier **Bar Firenze** in Piazzetta Palladio.

VILLA VALMARANA DEI NANI – This is an 18th-century country house decorated with a series of marvelous frescoes by Giambattista Tiepolo: These are fantastic visions of a mythological world, including one of his most stunning works, the *Sacrifice of Ighegenia*. The neighboring Foresteria, or guest house, holds more frescoes, showing vignettes of 18th-century Veneto life at its most charming, done by Tiepolo's son, Giandomenico. You can walk from Vicenza, but it is easier to take Bus 8 from Corso Palladio to the Via San Bastiano stop. From there you climb gently ⅓ kilometer (¼ mile) until you reach the villa. ✉ *Via San Bastiano 8,* ☎ *0444/321803.* 🎫 *8,000 lire.* ⊙ *Nov.–mid-Mar., Wed., Thurs., Sat, Sun. 10–noon; Mar.–Apr., Tues.–Sat. 2:30–5:30; May–Sept., Tues.–Sat. 3–6; Oct.–Nov., 2–5.*

★ **VILLA LA ROTONDA –** This is the most famous Palladian villa of all. In truth, it can hardly be called a villa, since Palladio was inspired by ancient Roman temples. Serene and symmetrical, it was the model for Jefferson's Monticello. Take the time to admire it from all sides, and you'll see that it was the inspiration not just for Monticello, but for nearly every state capitol in the United States. The interior is typical of Palladio's grand style, with a unique juxtaposition of solids and voids. It is within walking distance of the Villa Valmarani dei Nani. ✉ *Via della Rotonda 29,* ☎ *0444/321793.* 🎫 *To grounds, 5,000 lire; to interior and grounds, 10,000 lire.* ⊙ *Mar. 15–Nov. 4. Grounds open Tues.–Thurs. 10–noon, 3–6; interior open only Wed. 10–noon, 3–6.*

Dining and Lodging

$$ ✗ **Da Remo.** Located about a mile outside town, Da Remo is worth the taxi ride simply because it is one of Vicenza's best restaurants. In an attractive country house setting, with light, airy dining rooms and a garden terrace, you can enjoy a relaxing meal of Venetian specialties, among them *faraona* (guinea hen) with radicchio, and risotto with seasonal vegetables. ✉ *Via Ca'Impenta 14,* ☎ *0444/911007. AE, DC, MC, V. Closed Mon., last wk in July, first 3 wks in Aug., and Christmas holidays. No dinner Sun.*

$$ ✗ **Scudo di Francia.** A Gothic palace in the heart of town houses the ★ white vaulted dining rooms of Scudo di Francia. The regional cuisine features specialties such as *bignè caldi al prosciutto e tartufo* (hot pastry puffs with ham and truffles), pasta e fagioli, and *baccalà alla vicentina* (creamy cod). ✉ *Contrà Piancoli 4,* ☎ *0444/323322. AE, DC, MC, V. Closed Mon. and Aug. No dinner Sun.*

$–$$ ✗ **Al Paradiso.** This pizzeria–trattoria just off the Piazza dei Signori is one of a pair (the other is Vecchia Guardia, ☎ 0444/321231, closed Thurs.) right next door to each other, owned by two brothers. It's particularly attractive in summer, when you can sit at tables outside. The pizzas and other dishes are tasty and very reasonably priced. ✉ *Via Pescherie Vecchie 5,* ☎ *0444/322320. AE, DC, MC, V. Closed Mon.*

$$ ▦ **Due Mori.** In the heart of Vicenza just off Piazza dei Signori, this small hotel was recently refurbished and is a favorite with regular visitors. ✉ *Contra Do Rode 26,* ☎ *0444/321886,* ℻ *0444/326217. 28 rooms, 25 with bath or shower. MC, V.*

Shopping

Vicenza is one of Italy's leading centers for the production and sale of jewelry. Each year, in January and in June, it plays host to an international trade fair for goldsmiths. For details inquire at the local tourist office (☞ Contacts and Resources *in* Venetian Arc A to Z, *below*).

En Route From Villa Valmarana, continue along Via San Bastiano (which narrows to the size of a path) for a few hundred yards to reach Villa La Rotonda.

THE NORTHERN ARC
Villa Barbaro, Treviso and the Hillside Towns

In this area directly north of Venice, market towns towns cling to the steep foothills of the Alps and the Dolomites alongside streams that rage down from the mountains. Villa Barbaro, Palladio's most beautiful creation, is here, as are the arcaded streets of Treviso and the graceful Venetian Gothic styles of the smaller hill towns.

Marostica

⓲ *7 km (4¼ mi) west of Bassano del Grappa and 26 km (16 mi) northeast of Vicenza.*

In **Marostica,** there is a castle on the hillside overlooking the town. The main square is paved in checkerboard fashion, and a game of chess is acted out here by people in medieval costume on the second weekend in September in even-numbered years (for further information, ☎ 0424/7212, ℻ 0424/72800).

Bassano del Grappa

⓳ *7 km (4¼ mi) east of Marostica, 37 km (23 mi) north of Venice.*

Bassano del Grappa is a beautifully located town directly above the swift-flowing waters of the Brenta River at the foot of the Mt. Grappa massif (5,880 feet). Bassano's old streets are lined with low buildings sporting wooden balconies and eye-catching flowerpots. Bright ceramic wares produced here and in nearby Nove are displayed in shops along byways that curve uphill toward a centuries-old square, and, even higher, to a belvedere with a good view of Mt. Grappa and the beginning of the Valsugana Valley.

🦢 Bassano's most famous landmark is the **covered bridge** that has spanned the Brenta since the 13th century. Rebuilt countless times (floods are frequent), the present-day bridge is a postwar reconstruction using Andrea Palladio's 16th-century design. The great architect astutely chose to use wood as his medium, knowing that it could be replaced quickly and cheaply. Almost as famous is the characteristic **Nardini liquor shop** at one end of the bridge; it's redolent of the grappa that has been distilled here for more than a century. Stop in for a sniff or a snifter.

Dining and Lodging

$$ ✕ **Al Ponte–Da Renzo.** An ample family-run establishment on the Brenta River, this popular restaurant has big picture windows with a vista of the old town and the famed covered bridge. The tree-shaded garden for outdoor dining has the same view. The specialty of the house is seafood, with seafood antipasto and grilled fish fresh from the Adriatic featured on the menu, where you'll also find regional dishes according to the season. ⊠ *Via Volpato 60,* ☎ *0424/503055. V. Closed Tues. and Jan. No dinner Mon.*

$–$$ ✕ **Birreria Ottone.** This Old World restaurant in the center of town is a favorite with the locals, who appreciate the excellent cuisine, draft wine and beer, and the friendly atmosphere created by the Wipflinger family, headed by Otto, whose Austrian forebear founded this beer hall about 100 years ago. Equally good for a simple lunch or a more elaborate dinner, Ottone's specialties include a delicious goulash cooked with cumin. ⊠ *Via Matteoti 47/50,* ☎ *0424/522206. MC, V. Closed Tues. and first 3 wks in Aug. No dinner Mon.*

$$$–$$$$ ✕🏨 **Villa Palma.** This gracefully refurbished 18th-century country villa, only a short drive from Asolo (10 km/6 mi) and Bassano (5 km/3 mi), combines modern comforts and conveniences—including Jacuzzi baths or sauna showers, and fax and computer facilities—with rural calm and Old World style and charm—wooden beams, vaulted brick ceilings, tasteful furnishings, and an elegant restaurant, La Loggia. In summer meals are served on the terrace, overlooking the splendid garden. ⊠ *Via Chemin Palma 30, Mussolente,* ☎ *0424/577407,* FAX *0424/87687. 21 rooms and suites with bath or shower. Restaurant, air-conditioning, parking. AE, DC, MC, V.*

$$$ 🏨 **Belvedere.** This historic hotel has richly decorated public rooms with
★ period furnishings and Oriental rugs. A fireplace and piano music in the lounge and an excellent restaurant with a garden make for a very pleasant stay. The bedrooms are decorated in traditional Venetian or chic contemporary style. ⊠ *Piazzale G. Giardino 14,* ☎ *0424/529845,* FAX *0424/529849. 91 rooms with bath or shower. Restaurant, air-conditioning. AE, DC, MC, V.*

$$ 🏨 **Al Castello.** A central location in a recently restored town house at the foot of the medieval Civic Tower, and simply furnished but well-equipped rooms at very reasonable prices make the Castello—run by the Cattapan family—an extremely attractive proposition. There is a café-bar downstairs, with chairs out on the little sidewalk terrace in summer. ⊠ *Piazza Terraglio 19,* ☎ *0424/523462,* FAX *0424/228665. 9 rooms with shower. Bar, air-conditioning. AE, MC, V.*

Shopping

CERAMICS

Bassano del Grappa and nearby Nove are the best bets for ceramic items.

WROUGHT-IRON GOODS

A large number of shops in town feature wrought-iron and copper utensils, many of them made on the premises.

Asolo

★ ⓴ *18 km (11 mi) east of Marostica, 11 km (7 mi) east of Bassano and 33 km (20 mi) northwest of Treviso.*

Asolo is one of the most romantic and charming of the towns in the vicinity. This hillside hamlet was the consolation prize of an exiled queen. At the end of the 15th century, Venetian-born Caterina Cornaro was sent here by Venice's doges to keep her from interfering with their administration of her former kingdom of Cyprus, which she had inherited. To soothe the pain of exile, she established a lively and brilliant court in Asolo. Over the centuries, Venetian aristocrats continued to build gracious villas on the hillside, and in the 19th century Asolo once again became the idyllic haunt of musicians, poets, and painters. In the center of town you can explore Piazza Maggiore, with its Renaissance palaces and turn-of-the-century cafés, and then continue uphill, past Caterina's ruined castle and some Gothic-style houses, to the Roman fortress that stands on the summit. Other walks will take you past the villas once inhabited by Robert Browning and the actress Eleanora Duse. Be warned that Asolo's dreamy Old World atmosphere disappears on holiday weekends when the crowds pour in.

Dining and Lodging

$$ ✕ **Hosteria Ca'Derton.** The location is an attraction here: Ca'Derton is right on the main square. It has a pleasant, old-fashioned ambience, with early photos of Asolo on the walls and bouquets of dried flowers on each table. The friendly proprietor takes pride in the homemade pasta and desserts and in offering a good selection of both local and international dishes. Since a change of management in 1994 the food has, if anything, improved. ✉ *Piazza D'Annunzio 11,* ☎ *0423/952730. AE, DC, MC, V. Closed Tues., Feb. 15–28, and Aug. 17–31. No dinner Mon.*

Shopping

There are **antiques markets** in the center of Asolo on the second Sunday of the month (except July and Aug.).

Villa Barbaro

㉑ *7 km (4¼ mi) northeast of Asolo and 33 km (20½ mi) northwest of Treviso.*

Villa Barbaro is one of the most gracious Renaissance creations of Palladio. The fully furnished villa just outside the town of Maser is still inhabited by its owners, who make you slip heavy felt scuffs over your shoes to protect the highly polished floors. The elaborate stuccos and opulent frescoes by Paolo Veronese bring the 16th century to life. After La Rotonda, this is Palladio's greatest villa and is definitely worth going out of your way to see. ✉ *Via Cornuda 2,* ☎ *0423/923004.* 🎫 *8,000 lire.* ☉ *Apr.–Sept., Tues., weekends 3–6; Oct.–Mar., weekends 2:30–5.*

Dining and Lodging

$$ ✕ **Agnoletti.** In the town of Giavera del Montello near Maser, Agno-
★ letti is an 18th-century inn with Old World atmosphere and decor. The kitchen can produce an all-mushroom menu; but if you order something else, at least try the mushroom zuppa or *crostata* (tart). In the summer you eat in the garden. ✉ *Giavera del Montello, Via della Vittoria 191,* ☎ *0422/776009. No credit cards. Closed Mon., Tues., Jan. 1–20, and July 1–15.*

$$ ✕ **Da Bastian.** A good place to stop for lunch before visiting the Villa Barbaro, this establishment has a contemporary look, a pleasant garden for outdoor dining, and an interesting menu featuring a varied antipasto of pâtés, homemade vegetarian ravioli, and broiled meat with tasty sauces. ✉ *Via Cornuda,* ☎ *0423/565400. No credit cards. Closed Thurs. and Aug. No dinner Wed.*

$$$$ 🏨 **Villa Cipriani.** This historic old villa is set in a romantic garden on the hillside and surrounded by other gracious country homes. Tastefully furnished with 19th-century antiques, it offers Old World atmosphere, all creature comforts, and attentive service. The excellent restaurant has a terrace overlooking the garden. ✉ *Via Canova 298,* ☎ *0423/952166,* 🖷 *0423/952095. 31 rooms with bath or shower. Restaurant, parking. AE, DC, MC, V.*

Treviso

㉒ *30 km (19 mi) north of Venice.*

Treviso has arcaded streets, frescoed houses that were built in the 15th century, and channeled streams that run through the center of town. You can explore Treviso on foot in half a day; its restaurants are good places to stop for lunch.

The most important church in Treviso is **San Nicolò** an impressive Gothic building with an interesting vaulted ceiling. San Nicolò has frescoes of the saints by 14th-century artist Tommaso da Modena on the columns. But the best is the remarkable series of 40 portraits of Dominican friars by the same artist in the seminary next door. They are astoundingly realistic, considering that some were painted as early as 1352, and include one of the earliest-known portraits of someone wearing glasses. ⊠ *Capitolo dei Domenicani, Seminario Vescovile, Via San Nicolò,* ☎ *0422/3247.* ⊘ *Apr.–Sept., daily 8–12:30 and 3:30–7; Oct.–Mar., daily 8–12:30, 3–5:30. To enter, ring at custodian's desk at seminary entrance.*

Inside the **Duomo,** on the altar of one of the chapels to the right, is an *Annunciation* by Titian. ⊠ *Piazza Duomo* ⊘ *10:30–12:30.*

Piazza dei Signori is the heart of medieval Treviso and still the town's social center, with outdoor cafés and some impressive public buildings facing it. One of these, the Palazzo dei Trecento, has a small alley leading behind it. Follow the alley for about 200 yards to the **Pescheria** (fish market), on an island in one of the small rivers that flow through town.

Dining and Lodging

$$$ ✕ **El Toulà.** Clones of this, the original Toulà, have sprouted up in un-
★ likely places—even Japan. This is your chance to enjoy the art nou-
veau decor and classic international cuisine for which it became famous. There are regional dishes as well, among them risotto *con funghi* (with mushrooms) or asparagus in season. For cooking, ambience, and service, it's one of the region's best. ⊠ *Via Collalto 26,* ☎ *0422/540275. Jacket and tie. AE, DC, MC, V. Closed Mon. and July 25–Aug. 25. No dinner Sun.*

$$ ✕ **Beccherie.** In a town known for good eating, this rustic inn is a fa-
★ vorite. It's in the heart of old Treviso, behind the main square, and there are tables outside for fair-weather dining under the portico. Specialties vary with the season. In winter, look for *crespelle al* radicchio (crepes with radicchio) and faraona in *salsa peverada* (a peppery sauce); spring brings risotto with spring vegetables, stinco di *vitello* (veal), and *pasticcio di melanzane* (eggplant casserole). ⊠ *Piazza Ancilotto 10,* ☎ *0422/56601. AE, DC, MC, V. Closed Mon., and July 12–30. No dinner Sun.*

$$$$ 🏨 **Continental.** You'll find this hotel within the old city walls, between the train station and the sights. It is a traditional four-star hotel offering solid comfort. The rooms have a minibar, a color TV, and air-conditioning. Rich fabrics and Oriental rugs lend an air of opulence. ⊠ *Via Roma 16,* ☎ *0422/411216,* 𝔽𝔸𝕏 *0422/55054. 82 rooms with bath or shower. Air-conditioning, concierge. AE, DC, MC, V.*

$$ 🏨 **Al Fogher.** Located on the outskirts, Al Fogher is handy if you're traveling by car. It has a bright contemporary look, with lots of modern art on the walls and room decor about equally divided between classic and modern. All rooms are equipped with a minibar and a color TV, and all are air-conditioned. ⊠ *Viale della Repubblica 10,* ☎ *0422/432950,* 𝔽𝔸𝕏 *0422/430391. 54 rooms with bath or shower. Restaurant, parking. AE, DC, MC, V.*

Outdoor Activities and Sports

HORSEBACK RIDING
Lancenigo (⊠ 6 km/3½ mi north of Treviso, ☎ 0422/63357).

Shopping

Shops in Treviso feature wrought-iron and copper utensils.

Conegliano

㉓ *23 km (14 mi) north of Treviso and 71 km (44 mi) west of Udine.*

Conegliano is in the heart of wine-producing country. Conegliano it-self is attractive, with Venetian-style villas and frescoed houses, but the real attraction is the wine.

Dining and Lodging

$$ ✕ ⛨ **Canon d'Oro.** The town's oldest inn, the Canon d'Oro is in a 15th-century building in a central location near the train station. The restaurant's tranquil decor lets you concentrate on the good food, mainly regional specialties such as risotto, Canon d'Oro gnocchi, baccalà alla vicentina, and *fegato alla veneziana* (liver with onions). ✉ *Via XX Settembre 129,* ☎ *0438/34246,* ⛨ *0438/34246. 19 rooms with bath or shower. Restaurant. AE, MC, V.*

En Route Well marked and leading southeast from Conegliano, the **Strada del**
★ **Vino Rosso** (Red Wine Road) winds its way through cabernet and mer-lot country along the Piave River, and there are dozens of places to stop, sample, and buy the red—and some rosé—wines. The road ends at Oderzo.

THE EASTERN ARC
Udine and Trieste

Italy's northeastern corner is an ethnically jumbled cocktail of Italian, Slavic, and central European cultures. A potentially fascinating area, its peripheral position usually puts it beyond the range of most visi-tors. The old Hungarian port of Trieste—a symbol of Italian nation-alist aspirations for so long—and the medieval city of Udine are perfect bases for local excursions.

Numbers in the margin correspond to points of interest on the Vene-tian Arc map.

Udine

㉔ *71 km (44 mi) east of Conegliano, 64 km (40 mi) north of Trieste and 100 km (62 mi) east of Venice.*

Udine, in Italy's Friuli–Venezia Giulia region, commands a view of the surrounding plain and the Alpine foothills; according to legend, it stands on a mound erected by Attila the Hun so he could watch the burning of the important Roman center of Aquileia to the south. Udine flourished in the Middle Ages, thanks to its good location for trade and the rights it gained from the local patriarch to hold regular mar-kets. There is a distinct Venetian feel to the city, noticeable in the ar-chitecture of Piazza della Libertà, under the stern gaze of the lion of St. Mark, symbol of Venetian power.

The **Museo Archeologico Nazionale** is the best place to trace the his-tory of the area and the importance of Cividale and Udine in the for-mative period following the collapse of the Roman Empire. Among the interesting exhibits is a large collection of Lombard artifacts, including weapons, jewelry, and domestic wares from this warrior race, which swept into what is now Italy in the 6th century. ✉ *Piazza del Duomo,* ☎ *0432/700700.* 🎫 *4,000 lire.* ☉ *Mon.–Sat. 9–2, Sun. 9–1.*

NEED A   Stop for a moderately priced lunch of local dishes, especially mush-
BREAK?   rooms and game. **Al Fortino** is in an old castle with vaulted ceilings and

an open hearth. ⊠ *Via Carlo Alberto 46,* ☎ *0432/731217. Closed Mon. eve. and Tues., Jan. 1–15, Aug.*

Dining and Lodging

$$ ✕ **Alla Buona Vite.** This classic restaurant in the center of town specializes in seafood. *Tagliolini dello chef* (noodles with a creamy scampi sauce) and *rombo al limone e capperi* (turbot with lemon and capers) are among the many choices here. ⊠ *Via Treppo 10,* ☎ *0432/21053. AE, DC, MC, V. Closed Mon. and Aug. No dinner Sun.*

$$ ✕ **Antica Maddalena.** Just a few steps from Udine's pretty Piazza del-
★ l'Unità you'll find this elegant eating place, defined by its owner as a deluxe trattoria. Lots of warm wood tones, fresh flowers, and stained glass create a distinctive ambience to complement a menu of regional and Italian specialties, among them zuppa di funghi porcini, gnocchi *con zucca e ricotta* (with squash and ricotta cheese), and carpaccio *di salmone con rucola* (of chopped salmon with lemon and arugula). ⊠ *Via Pellicceria 4,* ☎ *0432/25111. AE, DC, MC, V. Closed Sun., Mon., 2 wks in Feb., and 2 wks in Aug. No lunch.*

$$ ✕ **Trattoria al Lepre.** A characteristic *focolare* (hearth) in one of the dining rooms is a symbol of traditional local cooking, and that's what you'll enjoy in this simple establishment. The specialties include tagliatelle con funghi and stinco di maiale. ⊠ *Via Poscolle 27,* ☎ *0432/295798. AE, DC, MC, V. Closed Sun. and 10 days in Aug.*

$$$ ▥ **Astoria Hotel Italia.** Centrally located, the Italia offers soundproofed, air-conditioned rooms furnished in traditional style, all with minibar and color TV. Public rooms feature Venetian glass chandeliers and comfortable armchairs. ⊠ *Piazza XX Settembre 24,* ☎ *0432/505091,* ⨐ *0432/509070. 80 rooms with bath or shower. Restaurant, parking. AE, DC, MC, V.*

En Route From Udine, the road eastward follows the coast under the shadow of the huge geological formation called the Carso, a large, barren expanse of limestone that forms a giant ledge, most of which is across the border in Slovenia. Italian territory goes only a few miles inland in this strip, and Italy's small Slovenian minority ekes out an agricultural existence in the region, which has changed hands countless times since the final days of Imperial Rome.

Cividale

㉕ *17 km (11 mi) east of Udine on S54.*

Cividale dates from the time of Julius Caesar. It is popularly supposed (particularly by locals) that it was built by Caesar when he was commander of Roman legions in the area. The city straddles the River Natisone and contains many examples of Venetian Gothic buildings, particularly the **Duomo** and the **Palazzo Comunale.** ⊠ *Piazza Duomo* ☎ *0432/731144.* ☉ *Summer: Mon.–Sat. 9:30–noon and 3–7, Sun. 3–6:45; winter: Mon.–Sat. 9:30–noon and 3–6, Sun. 3–5:45.*

Miramare Castle

★ ㉖ *7 km (4¼ mi) north of Trieste, 78 km (48 mi) South of Udine and 156 km (97 mi) east of Venice.*

This seafront castle is a 19th-century extravaganza in white stone, built for the Archduke Maximilian of Hapsburg (brother of Emperor Franz Josef). Maximilian spent a brief, happy time here until Napoléon III of France took Trieste from the Hapsburgs and sent the poor archduke packing. He was given the title of Emperor of Mexico in 1864 as a compensation, but met his death before a Mexican firing squad in 1867. You can visit the lush grounds and admire the memorable views over the Adriatic. ☜ *Grounds are free; guided tour of castle costs 8,000 lire.* ☉ *Grounds: daily, 9–1 hr before sunset. Castle: Mon.–Sat. 9–1, Sun. 9–12:30. For afternoon hrs in summer,* ☎ *040/224143.*

Trieste

 64 km (40 mi) southeast of Udine and 163 km (101 mi) east of Venice.

Surrounded by rugged countryside and beautiful coastline, Trieste is built on a hillside above what was once the chief port of the Austro-Hungarian Hapsburg Empire. Typical of Trieste are its turn-of-the-century cafés, much like Vienna's coffeehouses; these are social and cultural centers of the city, and much-beloved refuges from the city's prevailing northeast wind, the "bora."

The sidewalk cafés on the vast seaside **Piazza dell'Unità d'Italia** are popular meeting places in the summer months. The square is similar to Piazzetta San Marco in Venice; both are focal points of architectural interest that command the best views of the sea. The **Palazzo Comunale** (Town Hall) is at the end of the square, away from the sea; behind it, steps lead uphill, following the city's pattern of upward expansion from its roots as a coastal fishing port in Roman times.

Civico Museo Revoltella e Galleria d'Arte Moderna was founded in 1872 when the Venetian Baron Revoltella left the city his palazzo, library, and art collection. The gallery has one of the most important collections of 19th- and 20th-century art in Italy, with Italian artists particularly well represented. ⊠ *Via Diaz* ☎ *040/311361.* ☜ *2,000 lire.* ☉ *Mon., Wed.–Sat. 10–1 and 3–8, Sun. 10–1. Closed Tues.*

San Silvestro is a solid Romanesque construction dating from the 11th century; just beyond it is the Baroque extravagance of **Santa Maria Maggiore,** which backs onto a network of alleys (closed to traffic). ⊠ *Via S. Silvestro.* ☉ *Mon.–Sat. 10–1.*

Cattedrale di San Giusto is a 14th-century church that incorporates two much older churches, one dating from as far back as the 5th century. The exterior adds even more to the jumble of styles involved by using fragments of Roman tombs and temples: You can see these most clearly on the pillars of the main doorway. The highlights of the interior are the mosaics and frescoes dating from the 13th century. ⊠ *Piazza Cattedrale.* ☉ *Weekdays 9:30–4:30, Sun. mass.*

☖ **Castello di San Giusto** offers some of the best views from the hilltop. This 15th-century castle was built by the Venetians, who always had an eye for the best vantage point in the cities they conquered or controlled. The Hapsburgs, subsequent rulers of Trieste, enlarged it to its present size. The castle grounds are open daily until sunset. Some of the best exhibits in the **Castle Museum** are the displays of weaponry and armor. ⊠ *Piazza Cattedrale 3,* ☎ *040/313636.* ☜ *2,000 lire.* ☉ *Tues.–Sun. 9–1.*

NEED A BREAK?   **Bottega del Vino** is set inside two vaulted halls within the walls of Castello di San Giusto. It has a different entrance, so it keeps different hours from the rest of the castle, not opening until about 6 PM. For supper, try the gnocchi with porcini mushrooms while sitting on a terrace overlooking the bay. ⊠ *Piazza Cattedrale 3,* ☎ *040/309142.* ☉ *Closed Tues. and Jan.*

Piazza della Borsa is the square containing Trieste's original stock exchange, the **Borsa Vecchia**, a neoclassical building now serving as the chamber of commerce. The statue of Leopold I is at one end of the square.

Corso Italia is Trieste's busy shopping street and can be reached from Piazza della Borsa.

OFF THE
BEATEN PATH

GROTTA GIGANTE – This is the largest cave in the world open to tourists: It is more than 300 feet high, 900 feet long, and 200 feet wide, with spectacular stalactites and stalagmites. The tours take about 45 minutes. It is not far from Trieste, about 15 kilometers (9 miles) north of the city (take Tram 2 from Piazza Oberdan). ☎ 040/630464. ✉ Adults 10,000 lire. ☉ Apr.–Sept., tours every ½ hr 9–noon, 2–7; Oct. and Mar., tours every ½ hr 9–noon, 2–5; Nov.–Feb., tours every hr 10–noon, 2:30–4:30. Closed Mon.

Dining and Lodging

$$
★

✕ **Suban.** Despite its location in the hills on the edge of town, this historic trattoria is worth the taxi ride. The rustic decor is rich in dark wood, stone, and wrought iron, and you'll find typical regional fare with imaginative variations. You can eat under an arbor in fair weather. Among the specialties are *jota carsolina* (typical local minestrone made of cabbage, potatoes, and beans) and duck breast in Tokay sauce. ✉ *Via Emilio Comici 2,* ☎ 040/54368, AE, DC, MC, V. Closed Mon., Tues., and Aug. 1–20.

$$$–$$$$

🏨 **Duchi d'Aosta.** Located on the spacious Piazza dell'Unità d'Italia, this hotel is beautifully furnished in Venetian Renaissance-style and lavish with Old World atmosphere. Its restaurant, Harry's Grill, is one of the city's most elegant. ✉ *Piazza dell'Unità d'Italia 2,* ☎ 040/7351, FAX 040/366092. *52 rooms with bath or shower. Restaurant, bar.* AE, DC, MC, V.

$$–$$$

🏨 **Colombia.** Unpretentious but adequate, this small hotel caters mainly to a business clientele. There is no restaurant, but there's a typical beer cellar restaurant close by. ✉ *Via della Geppa 18,* ☎ 040/369333, FAX 040/369644. *40 rooms with bath or shower.* AE, DC, MC, V.

Nightlife and the Arts
Piazza dell'Unità d'Italia is a standout square surrounded by outdoor cafés.

Historic **Caffè San Marco** (✉ Via Battisti) is a shrine of Old World atmosphere.

Outdoor Activities and Sports
GOLF

Golf Club Trieste (✉ Padriciano 80, 6 km/4 mi from center of town, ☎ 040/226159).

Shopping
ANTIQUES

There are antiques markets in the streets of the city's old center on the third Sunday of summer months until November. Trieste has some 60 antiques dealers, jewelers, and secondhand shops, and a large antiques fair is held in the city in early November. Contact the tourist information office for details (☞ Contacts and Resources *in* Venetian Arc A to Z, *below*).

VENETIAN ARC A TO Z

Arriving and Departing

By Car

The main access roads to the Venetian Arc from southern Italy are both linked to the A1 (Autostrada del Sole) which connects Bologna, Florence and Rome. They are the A13, which culminates in Padua, and the A22, which passes through Verona in a north–south direction. The road linking the region from east to west is the A4, which is the primary route from Milan to as far as Trieste.

By Plane

The main airport serving the Venetian Arc is **Marco Polo** in Venice (☞ Venice A to Z *in* Chapter 5), which handles international and domestic flights to the region. A few European airlines have scheduled flights to **Villafranca Airport** (☎ 045/809–5666), 11 kilometers (7 miles) west of Verona, which is also served by a number of charter flights, as is **Treviso Airport** (☎ 0422/22667), about 32 kilometers (20 miles) north of Venice. A regular bus service connects Villafranca with Verona's Porta Nuova railway station. Flights to Treviso usually include transportation from the airport to Venice or other destinations; otherwise there is a local bus service to Treviso every half-hour during the day, or a taxi will come from Treviso, only 6 kilometers (4 miles) away, to pick you up. There are domestic flights to **Ronchi del Legionari Airport** (☎ 0481/773224), 35 kilometers (22 miles) north of Trieste, which is linked with Via Miramare in the center of town by a regular bus service.

By Train

The most important train routes arriving from the southern part of Italy will stop almost every hour in either Verona, Padua or Venezia. From northern Italy and the rest of Europe, trains usually enter via Milan to the west or through Porta Nuova station in Verona.

Getting Around

By Bus

There are interurban and interregional connections throughout the Veneto and Friuli. Local tourist offices may be able to provide details of timetables and routes; otherwise contact the local bus station, or in some cases the individual bus companies operating from the station.

Bassano (✉ Piazzale Trento, ☎ 0424/30850). **Padua** (✉ Piazzale Boschetti, ☎ 049/820–6811). **Treviso** (✉ Via Lungosile Mattei, ☎ 0422/412222). **Trieste** (✉ Piazza Liberta, ☎ 040/425001). **Venice** (✉ Piazzale Roma, ☎ 041/528–7886 for buses to Brenta Riviera, Padova and Treviso; ☎ 041/520–5530 for buses to Conegliano and Udine; ☎ 041/520–5530 for buses covering the Conegliano–Vittorio Veneto–Cortina route). **Verona** (✉ Porta Nuova, ☎ 045/800–4129). **Vicenza** (✉ Viale Milano 138, ☎ 0444/544333).

By Car

The main highway in the region is A4, which connects Verona, Padua, and Venice with Trieste. The distance from Verona, in the west, to Trieste is 263 kilometers (163 miles). Branches link A4 with Treviso (A27), Pordenone (A28), and Udine (A23).

By Train

To the west of Venice, on the main line running across the north of Italy, are Padua (20 min), Vicenza (1 hr), and Verona (1½ hrs); to the east is Trieste (2 hrs). Local trains link Venice to Bassano del Grappa (1 hr), Padova to Bassano del Grappa (1 hr), Vicenza to Treviso (1 hr) and Udine to Trieste (1 hr); Treviso and Udine both lie on the main line from Venice to Treviso, on which Eurocity trains continue to Vienna and Prague.

Contacts and Resources

Car Rentals

Avis. Padua (⊠ Piazza Stazione 1, ☎ 049/664198). **Trieste** (⊠ Piazza della Libertà, c/o Silos, ☎ 040/421521, and at the airport, ☎ 0481/777085). **Udine** (⊠ Viale Leopardi 5/A, ☎ 0432/501149). **Verona** (⊠ Stazione FS [train station], ☎ 045/26636). **Vicenza** (⊠ Viale Milano 88, ☎ 0444/321622).

Hertz. Padua (⊠ Piazza Stazione 5, ☎ 049/657877). **Trieste** (⊠ Piazza della Libertà, c/o Silos, ☎ 040/422122, and at the airport, ☎ 0481/777025). **Udine.** (⊠ Via Crispi 19, ☎ 0432/609160). **Verona** (⊠ Stazione FS, ☎ 045/25832). **Vicenza** (⊠ Viale Europa 50, ☎ 0444/321313).

Emergencies

Police, Ambulance, Fire (☎ 113). You can dial this number wherever you are and it will connect you to the nearest local police emergency service. For first aid, ask for *"pronto soccorso,"* and be prepared to give your address.

Doctors and Dentists (☎ 112). Or go to the **Ospedale Civile e Policlinico dell'Università** (⊠ Padua, ☎ 049/821–1111).

Late-Night Pharmacies. Pharmacies take turns staying open late and on Sunday. For information on which is open, call ☎ 192.

Guided Tours

Many of the best tours begin and end in Venice because so much of the region is accessible from there. (For Venice addresses of operators *see* Venice A to Z *in* Chapter 5.) The **Burchiello excursion boat** makes an all-day tour along the Brenta Canal, including lunch and visits to several villas, but the trip is expensive and not necessarily the best way to see the villas, since so much time is spent on the boat. For those who prefer to go it alone, American Express suggests itineraries that can be followed by rented car, with or without a hired driver (most cars need a driver), or it is possible to follow the Brenta quite easily by local train and bus.

Trieste and Vicenza offer special weekend package deals ("T for you" and "Vicenza Weekend") that include discounts in hotels and restaurants, free or reduced-price entrance to a selection of the cities' main tourist attractions, and some guided tours. For further details, contact the Trieste Tourist office and/or the Conzorsio di Promozione Turistica "Vicenza è" (☞ *below*).

Robe Vicentine offer tours around the Vicenza area, with guided visits to local villas, Renaissance-style lunches and dinners and other entertainments in Palladian villas. For information, ☎ FAX 0444/585168.

Should you wish to hire a guide, local tourist offices will be able to put you in contact with the Tourist Guides Association or provide you with a list of authorized guides, for whom there is an official tariff rate.

Travel Agencies

For agencies in Venice, *see* Venice A to Z *in* Chapter 5. Offices in the Venetian Arc include the following:

Padua (⊠ Tiarè Viaggi [American Express representative], Via Risorgimento 20, ☎ 049/666133).

Trieste (✉ Paterniti Viaggi [American Express representative], Corso Cavour 7, ☎ 040/366161, FAX 040/368888).

Verona (✉ Fabretto Viaggi [American Express representative], Corso Porta Nuova 11, ☎ 045/800–9040, FAX 045/800–9045).

Visitor Information

Veneto Regional Tourist Office (✉ Palazzo Sceriman, 168 Lista di Spagna, Cannaregio, 30121 Venice, ☎ 041/792644).

Padua (✉ Stazione Ferroviaria train station, ☎ 049/875–2077; ✉ Museo Civico Eremitani, ☎ 049/875–1153; ✉ Prato delle Valle, ☎ 049/875–3087). **Treviso** (✉ Via Toniolo 41, ☎ 0422/547632, FAX 0422/541397). **Trieste** (✉ Stazione Centrale, ☎ 040/420182). **Udine** (✉ Piazza Primo Maggio 7, ☎ 0432/295972). **Verona** (✉ Via Leoncino 61, ☎ 045/592828; ✉ Piazza delle Erbe 42, ☎ 045/803–0086; ✉ Railway station, ☎ 045/800–0861). **Vicenza** (✉ Piazza Matteotti 12, ☎ 0444/320854; ✉ Conzorsio di Promozione Turistica "Vicenza è," ☎ 0444/327141).

7 The Italian Riviera

Including Genoa, the Cinque Terre, and Portofino

It was the Italians who perfected il dolce far niente—*the sweet art of idleness—and all signs indicate they did it here, in the region called Liguria, better known to travelers as the Italian Riviera. To the west and east of Genoa, an art-filled city of understated splendor, the twin rivieras bask in the sun, dotted with seaside resorts and quaint villages. Like pearls in a string, the coastal towns of Rapallo, the Cinque Terre, and Portovenere glisten and glow—but everyone agrees Portofino wins the beauty contest.*

Updated by
Barbara Walsh
Angelillo

THE ITALIAN RIVIERA is just plain glamorous, an oxy-moronic statement, but how else can one encapsulate the cosmopolitan flavor of the area, its blend of provincial and smart-set, primitive and old-fashioned, luxurious and up-to-date?

Here, the eye is caught by the contours of a coastline that follows a serpentine arc from Ventimiglia to La Spezia; by the Ligurian Alps, which plunge sheerly or slope gradually to the sea; by the style and color of the resorts, the busy ports, and the stately yachts outlined against the horizon. For centuries, the region's charm has inspired scenic-hungry poets and artists; here is where Shelley praised the "soft blue Spezian bay"; here is where Lord Byron dared to swim from Portovenere to Lerici. Today, still, travelers searching to escape from the conceits of civilization head for the Italian Riviera for a cure. Mellowed by the balmy breezes blowing off the sea, they bask in the sun, then explore the tiny coastal towns where many things that are splendiferous haven't made it into the guidebooks yet.

Liguria's narrow strip of mountain-protected coastline varies considerably between the two rivieras. The Riviera di Ponente (western Riviera), which runs from the French border to Genoa, has protected bays and wide sandy beaches and is generally more developed and commercialized than its counterpart to the east, the Riviera di Levante. There, starting at Genoa, the coastline becomes steeper, rocky, and it's punctuated by minuscule bays and inlets.

If this coastline is a necklace, hung with jewels, the most scintillating pendant is the Portofino promontory. The mere sight of the village—it is the most photographed village in the world—is a pleasure in itself. If you pull up to the wharf by boat, chances are you'll shoot all your film before you disembark. Pastel houses frame the square, lending an air of festivity that becomes sheer enchantment at sunset when the houses are reflected in the dancing waters of the harbor. Other than the village square, several picturesque churches, and a castle, there aren't that many things to see in Portofino. The people here are the real attractions—it was, after all, Bogie and Bacall and Taylor and Burton who put the place on the map. Strolling around, you'll note expensive restaurants (forget the menu and order what you see other people eating) and even more expensive shops. The view, however, has no price tag.

Farther along the coast is a second peninsula; here the road weaves inland, leaving the visitor to hike or take a train or boat to explore the Cinque Terre, a collective community of five fishing villages perilously perched on bluffs above the sea. This area is the Italian Riviera at its unbuttoned best.

Set in the heart of the region is Genoa, Italy's largest port, which every American schoolchild knows as the birthplace of Christopher Columbus. That famous explorer was neither the first nor the last in the long line of seafaring Genoans. Today, most visitors come to Liguria less to see the art treasures of Genoa than for the region's mild climate, fine seafood, and coastal villages. But then relaxed Liguria is the sort of place where knowing the difference between scrub pine and cypress means more than knowing the difference between Rococo and Renaissance.

Pleasures and Pastimes

Dining

Liguria's cooking holds some surprises. It utilizes all sorts of seafood—especially anchovies, sea bass, squid, and octopus—but it makes even wider use of vegetables and the aromatic herbs that grow wild on the hillsides, together with liberal amounts of olive oil and garlic. Pesto is Liguria's classic pasta sauce; it's made from pine nuts, garlic, oil, cheese, and a type of basil that grows only along the coastal hills. You will also find *pansoti* (ravioli) and *trofie* (a chewy short pasta) with *salsa di noci,* a delicate sauce made of garlic, walnuts, and cream that, like pesto, is pounded in a mortar. *Vitello* (veal) is the most popular meat; *cima alla genovese,* breast of veal stuffed with a mixture of eggs and vegetables, is served as a cold cut. You should also try the succulent *agnello* (lamb) and fresh wild mushrooms picked from the hills.

When not snacking on pizza sold by the slice or by weight, the Genoese and other Ligurians eat *torta pasqualina* (vegetable pie), or *focaccia,* a salty, pizzalike bread that goes well with a glass of wine. Local vineyards tend to produce mainly light and refreshing whites, such as Pigato, Vermentino Ligure, and Cinque Terre. Rossese and Dolceacqua are good reds. Desserts are less rich than those in other Italian regions; *panna cotta,* a milk custard, and *gelato* (ice cream) are favorites.

CATEGORY	COST*
$$$$	over 85,000 lire
$$$	65,000–85,000 lire
$$	35,000–65,000 lire
$	under 35,000 lire

per person, including house wine, service, and tax.

Hiking and Walking

The hilly terrain makes walking strenuous but rewarding, with stunning views of the sea and little villages dotting the coast. Walking around Portofino is rewarding, whether you opt for the classic and relatively easy walk from Portofino to the Abbey of San Fruttuoso or the more challenging hike from Ruta to the top of Mount Portofino. You can walk from one to another of the five Cinque Terre fishing towns, thumbing your nose at the tourists on the sightseeing boats. Everywhere in Liguria, roads, mule paths, or footpaths lead into the hills, where you can discover the region at its unspoiled best.

Lodging

Depending on your interests, Liguria offers some good lodging options. If you want to delve into Genoa's artistic and historic treasures, stay in the city and make it your base for exploring the rest of the region on day-trips by train, bus, or car. If you want to take a more relaxed approach, settle into a resort and make your day-trips from there, including one to Genoa. When choosing your lodgings in Genoa you should be aware that this is ranked as one of Italy's noisiest cities; make sure your windows are double-glazed (*doppi vetri*). Because visitors generally prefer to stay in the towns and resorts along the coast, Genoa has relatively few hotels, and they tend to be geared more to the needs of business travelers than to tourists. Resort hotels are obviously the places to go for sea views, recreation facilities, and a vacation atmosphere. Reserve ahead: year-round for Genoa and during peak Easter and summer seasons for resorts. The best bargains and the warmest welcomes can be found in the less-visited inland areas: There are few hotels in this part of Liguria, but many of them are family-run and charming.

CATEGORY	COST*
$$$$	over 300,000 lire
$$$	170,000–300,000 lire
$$	110,000–170,000 lire
$	under 110,000 lire

*All prices are for a standard double room for two, including service and tax.

Sailing

With so much coastline (350 kilometers/217 miles) and so many pretty little harbors, it's no wonder that the Riviera attracts pleasure craft of all shapes and sizes, from rowboats to megayachts. San Remo, Rapallo, Santa Margherita Ligure, Chiavari, Finale Ligure, and Sestri Levante have large, well-equipped marinas. Every year in October, Genoa hosts a mammoth international boat show.

Exploring the Italian Riviera

All of Liguria's cities, towns, and resorts dot the elongated coastal strip stretching some 260 kilometers (161 miles) from Ventimiglia on the French border to La Spezia and Sarzana. At the center, Genoa separates the western (Ponente) from the eastern (Levante) Riviera, forming two distinct geographic areas to explore (three, including Genoa itself). The hilly and mountainous hinterland, very different in scenery and character from the Riviera, can be explored conveniently from towns along the coast. From the sea, a series of narrow valleys extend inland, giving access to the sparsely settled interior.

Great Itineraries

The Italian Riviera is a small and pretty package crammed with places to see and things to do, but to make the most of its easy-going atmosphere you should allow yourself some lazy hours of resort-style living. Fortunately, the region's main attractions are scenery, food, sports, and out-of-the-way villages. With the exception of Genoa, eclectic and opulent, the Riviera doesn't require much die-hard sightseeing. You can take in the scenery while getting from one place to another, and once you have arrived in one of the quaint towns or sophisticated resorts you can relax at a seaside café, enjoy the views, and stroll around, soaking up sun (usually) and atmosphere.

Genoa, the only city of note in the region, divides the Riviera in two. The focus of our first itinerary is the western side: Stretching from Ventimiglia near the French border to the small towns on Genoa's western side is the Riviera di Ponente, a narrow coastal strip punctuated by rocky outcrops jutting out between wide bays and sandy coves. Known as *La Superba* (The Proud), Genoa is not just the regional capital, but a maritime center and trading port the importance of which can be traced back to the 13th century. On the eastern side of the city, stretching down the coast to the Cinque Terre and La Spezia, is the Riviera di Levante, wilder and more rugged than the Riviera di Ponente, but with world-class resorts famous for their panache and easy elegance. This is the focus of our third itinerary.

Getting around the Riviera doesn't take much time, either. You could drive from one end of the Riviera to the other on the autostrada in less than three hours; a fast train takes less than two hours to cover the same route. This means that you can see a number of places in a relatively short time. The A10 and A12 autostrada on either side of Genoa skirt the coast, avoiding local traffic on the old Via Aurelia, laid out by the ancient Romans. The Via Aurelia, now known as national highway S1, connects practically all the towns along the coast. If you don't have a car, use local trains to get from one place to another along the coast and local buses to go inland. In seven days you can visit the prettiest resorts and fishing villages, spend a day or two in Genoa, and perhaps make an excursion inland. Five days would allow you to see the highlights, but you will probably want to see Genoa in a day so that you can visit more of the smaller towns. In three days you will be able to see Genoa and perhaps two major resorts and two or three of the smaller, more picturesque towns.

Numbers in the text correspond to numbers in the margin and on the Italian Riviera and Genoa maps.

IF YOU HAVE 3 DAYS

If you begin your tour of the region from the eastern side of the Riviera, devote your first day to exploring the picturesque villages and resorts that dot the coastline from Lerici to Genoa. As your time is limited, concentrate on select towns, namely the delightful fishing villages of **Portovenere** ㊴ and **Camogli** ㉛, detouring for a look at romantic **Portofino** ㉝, the jewel in the Riviera's crown. **Rapallo** ㉜ and **Santa Margherita Ligure,** one of the most unassuming resorts along the coast, will give you an idea of life on this part of the Riviera. Your second day should be spent in ⊞ **Genoa** ⑧–㉙, exploring the historic center and topping off your day's sightseeing with a stroll around the old harbor and a visit to the Aquarium, Europe's best. The western Riviera, which stretches from Genoa to the border with France, should be the focus of your third day's explorations; head for glitzy **San Remo** ④ or the more sedate resort of **Bordighera** ③, but allow about half a day along the way to visit the medieval centers of Albenga, Cervo, and Taggia. Naturally, you should follow this itinerary in the opposite direction if you are arriving in the region from the west.

IF YOU HAVE 5 DAYS

You can organize your itinerary to take you from one end of the Riviera to the other or you can start in Genoa and head east or west from there. If you make Genoa your base you can alternate excursions along the coast and into the interior with city sightseeing. On your first day explore ⊞ **Genoa** ⑧–㉙, taking in all of the sites mentioned below. If the day is a clear one, make sure to ride the **Granarolo funicular** ⑨ to the top for an aerial view of the city. On the second day head west by car or train and make a detour for Spotorno, proceeding from there to Noli, one of the best-preserved medieval towns on the entire Riviera. Then see the medieval delights of Cervo before going on to sophisticated ⊞ **San Remo** ④ and palm-studded ⊞ **Bordighera** ③, overnighting in either resort town. On the third day you could opt for a taste of *il dolce far niente*—remember, just being here is enough for most people—or you could venture inland, to the well-preserved medieval villages of Dolcedo and Valloria. On the fourth and fifth days explore the eastern Riviera, starting with stately **Nervi** ㉚, near Genoa. The Portofino promontory has multiple attractions, from the fishing village of **Camogli** ㉛ to superchic **Portofino** ㉝; don't miss the remarkable sea views from the hamlets of San Rocco, San Niccolò, and Punta Chiappa, accessible by foot from Camogli. Lodging options in the area abound: You can overnight in a stylish resort such as ⊞ **Santa Margherita Ligure** or ⊞ **Rapallo** ㉜; alternatively, you can go for lower-key ⊞ **Sestri Levante** ㉟, an industrial town with a charming medieval center, or the secluded town of ⊞ **Levanto** ㊱, closer to the Cinque Terre. If you have time on your fifth day, make an excursion by train or boat to the five rock-perched coastal villages of the **Cinque Terre** ㊲: Monterosso, Vernazza, Corniglia, Manarola, and Riomaggiore. All five are almost inaccessible but well worth the effort: medieval houses lean over narrow streets and elegant arcades; the last two villages sit on tiny harbors hemmed in by sheer cliffs. Proceed to ⊞ **Portovenere** ㊴, whose small, colorful houses date from as far back as the 12th century. Bypass industrialized La Spezia and wind up in **Lerici** ㊵, the pretty port village cherished for centuries by nature lovers, including the great Romantic poet Shelley.

IF YOU HAVE 7 DAYS

If you begin your visit of the region in ⊞ **Genoa** ⑧–㉙, two days will give you time to see the city's narrow alleys and medieval churches as well as one or two of its splendid but unsung museums, most of them housed in magnificent palaces that are themselves worth seeing. Take the **Granarolo funicular** ⑨, and take a boat tour of the port to see how the historic harbor wears the city like a crown. You will have time for an excursion to **Nervi** ㉚, studded with palatial mansions (some dating back to the 17th century) and gorgeous gardens, with a mile-long promenade cut into the rock overhanging the sea. On the third day head west from Genoa, either working your way gradually to Ventimiglia or going directly to Ventimiglia and then working your way back to Genoa. On the western Riviera, see the extraordinary cactus collection in the **Giardino Hanbury** ① near **Ventimiglia** ②, then turn inland to the medieval town of Dolceacqua, only 10 kilometers (6 miles) away, to photograph the romantic ruined castle. After stopping for tea in **Bordighera** ③, a genteel, palm-shaded resort favored by British travelers, you come to the much busier and more commercial resort of ⊞ **San Remo** ④, with a plethora of shops and ice cream parlors. The big fin de siècle casino and grand old hotels, which used to attract royalty, still give luster to the town. Climb the narrow streets through San Remo's old Pigna quarter to Piazza Castello for a good view. Stay overnight in San Remo or go on to Alassio—once famous in Europe, but now partially stripped of its charm by overdevelopment—or ⊞ **Finale Ligure** ⑤, two of the more attractive resorts along this stretch of coastline. On the fourth day, make an excursion to Noli: If you're driving, take the coast road (S1) from Finale Ligure to Noli and Spotorno. If you don't have a car, a bus from Spotorno takes you to Noli, where time has practically stood still since the Middle Ages. With the exception of Albisola Marina and Pegli, you can skip the industrialized coast between **Savona** ⑥ and Genoa.

On the fifth day, head east from Genoa on the A12 autostrada or on the slower S1 highway to the Riviera di Levante to see **Nervi**'s ㉚ well-manicured gardens and the offhand charm of **Camogli** ㉛. Take the turnoff for Santa Margherita Ligure and, if the traffic isn't heavy, head for ⊞ **Rapallo** ㉜ and ⊞ **Portofino** ㉝. At the height of the season you may want to take an excursion boat to Portofino from Camogli, Santa Margherita Ligure, or Rapallo to avoid the traffic jams on the narrow access road. You can overnight in either resort, but you may want to consider closing out your day by choosing accommodations in ⊞ **Chiavari** ㉞, a good hub for forays into the mountains on your sixth day, or even in ⊞ **Levanto** ㊱, where you can make a detour to the **Cinque Terre** ㊲. On the seventh day head east to **La Spezia** ㊳, an industrialized port where signs point you toward **Portovenere** ㊴. Alternatively, you can take a bus. Doubling back to La Spezia, take the coast road to charming **Lerici** ㊵. The La Spezia turnoff on the A12 and S1 highways is only about 15 kilometers (10 miles) from the border of Tuscany.

When to Tour the Italian Riviera

Your pace will be much more leisurely, in tune with the Riviera's carefree lifestyle. In order to fully appreciate the dolce far niente, however, a car is indispensable. Public transportation in the region is excellent, with every sight of interest reachable by train and/or bus, but having a car gives you greater freedom of movement.

Avoid driving through Ventimiglia on Friday, the busy market day. Though shops, cafés, clubs, and restaurants stay open late in resorts during high season (at Easter and during the summer), during the rest of the year they close early. Many hotels and restaurants in resort towns close from November through March.

THE RIVIERA DI PONENTE

The Riviera di Ponente stretches from Ventimiglia on the French border to Genoa. For the most part it is an unbroken chain of popular beach resorts sheltered from the north by the Ligurian and Maritime Alps, mountain walls which guarantee mild winters and a long growing season—resulting in its other nickname, the *Riviera dei Fiori* (Riviera of Flowers). Actually the name is prettier than the sight of once-verdant hillsides now swathed in plastic to form immense greenhouses. Many towns on the western Riviera have suffered from an epidemic of overbuilding, but most have preserved their historic cores, usually their most interesting features. In major resorts large new marinas cater to the pleasure-craft crowd. The Riviera di Ponente has both sandy and pebbly beaches with some quiet bays. Varazze, with a wide, sandy beach and many tall palm trees, is perhaps the last pleasant beach resort on the Riviera di Ponente before greater Genoa's industrial influence takes over. The towns and sights listed below are in geographical order, starting at the Giardino Hanbury in the west and ending at Genoa.

Numbers in the margin correspond to points of interest on the Italian Riviera map.

Giardino Hanbury

★ ❶ *6 km (4 mi) east of Ventimiglia, 165 km (102 mi) southwest of Genoa, 23 km (14 mi) west of San Remo.*

Mortola Inferiore, only 2 kilometers (1 mile) from the French border, is site of the world-famous **Giardino Hanbury** (Hanbury Garden), one of the largest botanical gardens in Italy. Planned and planted by a wealthy English merchant, Sir Thomas Hanbury, and his botanist brother, Daniel, in 1867, the terraced gardens contain a variety of species from five continents—including many palms and succulents (plants of the cactus group). There are panoramic views of the sea from the gardens, which descend right down to the beach. ✉ *Giardino Hanbury, Mortola Inferiore,* ☎ *0184/229507.* 🎟 *10,000 lire.* ☉ *June–Sept., daily 9–6; Oct.–May, Thurs.–Tues. 10–4.*

OFF THE BEATEN PATH

BALZI ROSSI CAVES – At the French border, 7 kilometers (4 miles) from Ventimiglia and 2 kilometers (1 mile) from the Giardino Hanbury, are the *Balzi Rossi* (Red Rocks), caves in the sheer rock in which prehistoric humans left traces of their lives and magic rites. You can visit the caves and a small museum containing some of the objects found there. ☎ *0184/38113.* 🎟 *4,000 lire.* ☉ *July–Aug., Tues.–Sun. 9–1 and 2:30–6:30; Sept.–June, 9–1 and 2:30–6.*

Ventimiglia

❷ *6 km (4 mi) east of Mortola Inferiore, 159 km (98 mi) southwest of Genoa, 17 km (10 mi) west of San Remo, 40 km (25 mi) northeast of Nice.*

Ventimiglia was once a pre-Roman settlement known as Albintimilium and contains some important archaeological remains, such as a

The Italian Rivieras

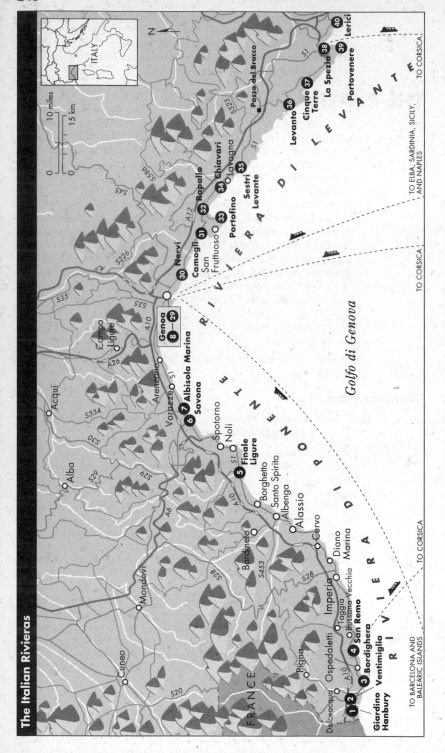

ITALY

N

10 miles

15 km

TO ELBA, SARDINIA, SICILY, AND NAPLES

TO CORSICA

TO CORSICA

TO CORSICA

TO BARCELONA AND BALEARIC ISLANDS

Golfo di Genova

R I V I E R A   D I   L E V A N T E

R I V I E R A   D I   P O N E N T E

R I V I E R A

FRANCE

Lerici **40**

39 Portovenere

La Spezia **38**

Cinque Terre **37**

36

Levanto

Passo del Bracco

Chiavari **34**

Lavagna

Rapallo **32**

Sestri Levante **35**

Portofino

Camogli **31**

San Fruttuoso **33**

Nervi **30**

Genoa **8 — 29**

Albisola Marina **7**

Savona **6**

Spotorno

Noli

Finale Ligure **5**

Borghetto

Santo Spirito

Albenga

Alassio

Cervo

Diano Marina

Imperia

Taggia

Bussana Vecchia

San Remo **4**

Bordighera **3**

Ventimiglia

Ospedaletti

Dolceacqua

Pigna

Giardino Hanbury **1 2**

Campo Ligure

Acqui

Alba

Mondovi

Cuneo

Arenzano

Varazze

2nd-century AD amphitheater. A vital trade center for hundreds of years, Ventimiglia declined in prestige as Genoa grew and is now little more than a frontier town that lives on tourism and the cultivation of flowers. The town is divided in two by the Roia River. The **Città Vecchia** (Old City), on the western side, is what you'll see first: It is a well-preserved and typical medieval town. The 11th-century **Duomo** (Cathedral) has a Gothic portal dating from 1222. Walk up Via del Capo to the ancient walls, which offer fine views of the coast. The large flower market is in the new part of town. Avoid Ventimiglia on Friday, a chaotic market day that draws crowds of bargain hunters from France, creating traffic gridlock.

NEED A BREAK?	While you're in the heart of the Città Vecchia, stop at the **Cuneo** (⊠ Via Aprosio 16, closed Tues. dinner, Wed., and June) for a lunch of fresh shellfish or pasta.

OFF THE BEATEN PATH	**DOLCEACQUA** – From Ventimiglia, a provincial road swings up the Nervia River valley to this lovely sounding medieval town, whose name translates as Sweetwater, with its ruined castle, and beyond to **Pigna,** another medieval village built in concentric circles on a hilltop.

Dining and Lodging

$$ ✕ **La Riserva.** Just 5 kilometers (3 miles) west of Ventimiglia, but more
★ than 1,100 feet above sea level, is the village of Castel d'Appio, where you'll find this innlike establishment. The staff is very helpful, providing, for example, regular lifts into town for those without cars. But there's no real need to leave La Riserva; apart from its excellent restaurant, it offers numerous activities and a lovely terrace for drinks or sunbathing. Full-board rates are a good value. Try for a room facing the sea. ⊠ *Castel d'Appio,* ☎ *0184/229533,* FAX *0184/229712. 29 rooms with bath or shower. Restaurant, bar, pool. AE, DC, MC, V. Closed Sept. 30– Easter (except Dec. 22–Jan. 6).*

Outdoor Activities and Sports

CYCLING

The Riviera's hilly terrain is a challenge for cyclists; to join them, contact the **Ventimiglia Cycling Club** (⊠ Corso Genoa 112, ☎ 00184/352879).

Bordighera

❸ *5 km (3 mi) east of Ventimiglia, 12 km (7.5 mi) west of San Remo, 115 km (71 mi) southwest of Genoa.*

Bordighera, on a large promontory with lush vegetation, wears its genteel past as a famous winter resort with unstudied ease. A large English colony, still very much in evidence, settled here in the second half of the 19th century, attracted by the mild climate. Bordighera is an elegant town with a fin de siècle atmosphere; expect to find people taking afternoon tea in the cafés. This garden spot was the first town in Europe to grow date palms, and its citizens still have the exclusive right to provide the Vatican with palm fronds for Easter celebrations. Walk along the **Lungomare Argentina,** the magnificent mile-long seafront promenade, beginning at the western end of the town, for a good view westward to the French Côte d'Azur. Thanks partly to its year-round English residents, Bordighera does not close down entirely in the winter like many Riviera resorts. With plenty of fine hotels and restaurants, it makes a good base for excursions and is quieter and less commercial than San Remo.

Dining and Lodging

$$–$$$ ✕ **La Reserve Restaurant.** This traditional and informal trattoria has access to the beach and excellent views of the sea from the dining room. There are even changing rooms for anyone who wants a post-lunch dip. Concentrate on the seafood here: Specialties are seafood ravioli *al finocchio selvatico* (with wild fennel) and a grilled seafood assortment. ⊠ *Via Arziglia 20,* ☎ *0184/261322. AE, DC, MC, V. Closed Mon. (except July and Aug.), and Oct. 15–Dec. 13.*

$$–$$$ ✕ **Le Chaudron.** The charming rustic interior, with ancient Roman arches, has the look of restaurants across the French border in Provence. Ligurian specialties are featured on the predominantly seafood menu of this centrally located restaurant: Try the *pansoti* (cheese ravioli with walnut sauce) and *branzino* (sea bass), served with artichokes or mushrooms. A café annex serves a daily lunch special (1$). ⊠ *Piazza Bengasi 2,* ☎ *0184/263592. Reservations essential. DC, MC, V. Closed Mon. and Jan. 15–Feb. 10.*

$$ ✕ **Piemontese.** Only a block from the seaside and five minutes from the train station, this simple restaurant features the typical cooking of the neighboring Piedmont region, including *risotto al Barolo* (rice with Barolo wine, sausage, and porcini mushrooms) and *bagna cauda* (raw vegetables with a garlic and oil sauce). Ligurian dishes and seafood are also on the menu. ⊠ *Via Roseto 8, off Via Vittorio Veneto,* ☎ *0184/261651. AE, DC, MC, V. Closed Tues. and Nov. 20–Dec. 20.*

$$$–$$$$ ⊞ **Grand Hotel del Mare.** At the top of a steep hill rising from the beach, this elegant hotel lives up to its name; the service and facilities are impeccable. The large rooms have panoramic views of the coastline; ask for one facing the water. One floor features beautiful antique furnishings. The hotel restaurant enjoys a fine reputation. ⊠ *Via Portico della Punta 34,* ☎ *0184/262201,* FAX *0184/262394. 115 rooms with bath. Restaurant, piano bar, saltwater pool, tennis courts, exercise room, beach. AE, DC, MC, V. Closed Nov. 1–Dec. 20.*

$$–$$$ ⊞ **Grand Hotel Capo Ampelio.** This hotel occupies a converted villa on a hill overlooking the town and the coastline; traditional architectural features in the reception rooms and staircases are enhanced by convenient modern features in the rooms, all with balconies. The hotel is somewhat outside the town center, so rooms are quiet; ask for one with a sea view. ⊠ *Via Virgilio 5,* ☎ *0184/264333,* FAX *0184/264244. 104 rooms with bath. Restaurant, bar, pool. AE, DC, MC, V. Closed Nov. 6–Dec. 22.*

San Remo

★ ❹   *12 km (7 mi) east of Bordighera, 146 km (90 mi) southwest of Genoa, 60 km (37 mi) east of Nice.*

The self-styled capital of the Riviera di Ponente is **San Remo,** also its largest resort. Renowned for its royal visitors, its famous casino (one of only four in Italy), and its romantic setting, San Remo still maintains some of the glamour of its heyday from the late 19th century to World War II. Among the rich and famous who flocked to San Remo, drawn by the mild climate and pleasant countryside, were Alfred Nobel, who built a summer house here, and Russian Empress Maria Alexandrovna, wife of Czar Alexander II. The Russian Orthodox church of **San Basilio,** with its onion domes, stands at one end of the Corso dell'Imperatrice and, like that imposing seafront promenade, is a legacy of the Empress. San Remo also has elegant world-class hotels, where you can stop to have a drink, and exotic gardens, in addition to its promenades.

San Remo is famous for the **Mercato dei Fiori,** Italy's most important wholesale flower market, held in a market hall between Piazza Colombo and Corso Garibaldi and open to dealers only. More than 20,000 tons of carnations, roses, mimosa, and innumerable other cut flowers are dispatched from here each year. The old part of San Remo, **La Pigna** (meaning pinecone), is a warren of alleyways worth exploring, climbing upward to Piazza Castello, with a splendid view of the town. The newer parts of San Remo suffer from the same epidemic of overbuilding that transformed so many towns on the western Riviera for the worse. And as center of northern Italy's flower-growing industry, the resort is surrounded by hills where once-verdant terraces are now blanketed with plastic to form immense greenhouses.

The **San Remo Casino** is one of only four in Italy. It is a sophisticated establishment reminiscent of the turn of the century, with a restaurant and nightclub. The view over the Ligurian coast is free, even if nothing else is. ⊠ *Corso Inglese, San Remo.* ۞ *Daily 2 PM–2 AM.*

OFF THE
BEATEN PATH
BUSSANA VECCHIA – About 8 kilometers (5 miles) by bus or car east of San Remo, in the hills where flowers are cultivated for export, is Bussana Vecchia, a self-consciously picturesque ghost town that was largely destroyed by an earthquake in 1877. The inhabitants packed up and left en masse after the quake, and for almost a century, the houses, church, and crumbling bell tower were empty shells, overgrown by weeds and wildflowers. Since the 1960s an artist's colony has grown up among the ruins. Painters, sculptors, artisans, and bric-a-brac dealers have restored dwellings for themselves and sell their wares to visitors.

Dining and Lodging

$$ ✕ **Nuovo Piccolo Mondo.** This small, centrally located trattoria has plenty
★ of charm and a homey atmosphere—the old wooden chairs date from the 1920s, when the place opened. Family-run, it has a faithful clientele, so get there early to grab a table and order Ligurian specialties such as spaghetti with artichokes and *polpo e patate* (stewed octopus with potatoes). ⊠ *Via Piave 7,* ☎ *0184/509012. No credit cards. Closed Sun. and 1st 3 wks in July.*

$$$$ ⌸ **Royal.** It would take a dedicated hedonist to determine whether this deluxe hotel or the Splendido in Portofino is the most luxurious in Liguria. One major difference is the location: Only a few paces from the Casino and the train station, the Royal is definitely part of San Remo, unlike the Splendido, which is set above Portofino. Try for a room facing the sea or one of the penthouse rooms and suites, with terrific views. The rooms have a mixture of modern appliances and antique furnishings, each with a unique feel. It is claimed that there is nearly always a member of European royalty in residence; the best place to find out is on the terrace, where there's music each night under the stars in season. ⊠ *Corso Imperatrice 80,* ☎ *0184/539145,* ⅢX *0184/661445. 146 rooms with bath. 3 restaurants, bar, pool, tennis courts. AE, DC, MC, V. Closed Oct. 6–Dec. 21.*

$$ ⌸ **Paradiso.** This small hotel is adjacent to a lush public park near the Royal, so it shares the advantages of its grander neighbor's central location. A quiet, palm-fringed garden gives it an air of seclusion, which is a plus in this sometimes hectic city. The rooms are modern and bright, and many have a little terrace. The hotel restaurant has a good fixed-price menu. ⊠ *Via Roccasterone 12,* ☎ *0184/571211,* ⅢX *0184/578176. 41 rooms with bath or shower. Restaurant, bar. AE, DC, MC, V.*

Outdoor Activities and Sports
GOLF

The 18-hole **San Remo Golf Club** (⊠ Via Campo Golf, ☎ 0184/557093) is 5 kilometers (3 miles) north of the town.

Taggia

10 km (6 mi) northeast of San Remo, 20 km (12 mi) west of Imperia.

The town of **Taggia** has a medieval core and one of the most imposing medieval stone bridges in the area. The church of **San Domenico,** on a rise south of Taggia, was part of a monastery that was founded in the 15th century and was a beacon of faith and learning in western Liguria for 300 years. An antiques market is held here on the fourth weekend of the month.

Imperia

23 km (14 mi) east of Taggia, 116 km (71 mi) southwest of Genoa.

Imperia actually consists of two towns: **Porto Maurizio,** a medieval town built on a promontory, and **Oneglia,** now an industrial center for oil refining and pharmaceuticals. Obviously, Oneglia can be skipped entirely. Porto Maurizio has a virtually intact medieval center, the Parasio quarter, an intricate spiral of narrow streets and stone portals, and some imposing 17th- and 18th-century palaces.

OFF THE BEATEN PATH

OLIVE MUSEUM – The story of the olive—its cultivation and the manufacture of olive oil—is the theme of this small museum in Imperia set up by the Carli olive oil company. Displays show farm implements, types of presses, and utensils used in making olive oil in many countries throughout history. ⊠ *Museo dell'Ulivo, Via Garessio 11, Imperia,* ☎ *0183/720000.* ☞ *Free.* ☉ *Mon. and Wed.–Sat. 9–noon and 3–6.*

Dining

$ ★ ⊞ **Candidollo.** This charming and good-value restaurant is worth a detour to the village of Diano Borello, on the valley road a couple of miles north of Diano Marina, 6 kilometers (4 miles) east of Imperia. It's a country inn, with checked tablecloths, worn terra-cotta floors, and antique utensils on the walls. Dining on the terrace of this out-of-the-way inn with a view of the sea and coast is what the Riviera is all about. Host Bruno Ardissone uses locally grown ingredients and traditional recipes that vary with the season. The menu usually includes *coniglio al timo* (rabbit with thyme and other herbs) and *lumache all'agliata* (grilled snails in piquant sauce). ⊠ *Diano Borello,* ☎ *0183/43025. No credit cards. Closed Tues. and Nov.–Mar. No lunch Mon.*

Cervo

10 km (6 mi) northeast of Imperia, 106 km (65 mi) southwest of Genoa, 35 km (22 mi) east of San Remo.

One of the most interesting towns on the entire western Riviera, **Cervo** is the quintessential Ligurian coastal village, nicely polished for the tourists who come to explore its narrow byways and street staircases. It is a remarkably well-preserved medieval town, crowned with a big Baroque church. In July and August the square in front of the church is the setting for chamber music concerts.

Albenga

> *23 km (14 mi) north of Cervo, 90 km (55 mi) southwest of Genoa, 57 km (35 mi) northeast of San Remo.*

Albenga has a medieval core, with narrow streets laid out by the ancient Romans. They form a network of alleys punctuated by centuries-old towers, surrounding the **cathedral** and baptistery dating back to the 5th century AD.

OFF THE BEATEN PATH
BARDINETO – For a look at some of the Riviera's mountain scenery, make an excursion by car to Bardineto. From Borghetto Santo Spirito (between Albenga and Finale Ligure), drive 25 kilometers (15 miles) inland to reach this attractive village in the middle of an area rich in mushrooms, chestnuts, and raspberries, as well as local cheese. A ruined castle stands high above the village.

Finale Ligure

> **⑤** *20 km (12 mi) northwest of Albenga, 72 km (44 mi) southwest of Genoa, 52 km (32 mi) northeast of Imperia.*

Finale Ligure is made up of three villages: Finalborgo, Finalmarina, and Finalpia. The last two have fine sandy beaches and modern resort amenities. The most attractive part of Finale Ligure, however, is the old village of **Finalborgo,** a medieval settlement planned to a rigid blueprint, with 15th-century walls. The village is crowned by the impressive ruins of the huge **Castel Gavone.** The Baroque church of **San Biagio** houses many works of art, and the 14th- to 15th-century Dominican convent of **Santa Caterina** can be visited for the shade of the courtyard or to see the museum of paleontology and natural history, which houses prehistoric remains found in the area. ✉ *Museo Civico,* ☎ *019/690020.* 🎫 *Free.* ☉ *May–Sept., Tues.–Fri. 10–noon and 3–6, weekends 9–noon; Oct.–Apr., Tues.–Fri. 9–noon and 2:30–4:30.*

OFF THE BEATEN PATH
NOLI – Nine kilometers (5½ miles) northeast of Finale Ligure, the picturesque ruins of a castle loom benevolently over the tiny town of Noli, a medieval gem. It is hard to believe that this charming village was, like Genoa, Venice, Pisa, and Amalfi, a prosperous maritime republic in the Middle Ages. If you don't have a car, you can get a bus for Noli at Spotorno, where local trains stop.

Dining

$$–$$$ ✗ **Ai Torchi.** Develop your taste for homemade pesto (pasta sauce made of basil and pine nuts) at this restaurant in the center of Finalborgo. ✉ *Via dell'Annunziata 12,* ☎ *019/690531. AE, DC, MC, V. Closed Tues. (except in Aug.) and Mon. (Oct.–May), and Jan. 7–mid-Feb.*

En Route The countryside around Finale Ligure is pierced by deep, narrow valleys and caves; the limestone outcroppings provide the warm pinkish stone found in many buildings in Genoa. Here there are rare reptiles and rare species of flora.

Savona

> **⑥** *11.5 km (7 mi) east of Spotorno, 48 km (29 mi) southwest of Genoa.*

Savona is the fifth largest seaport in Italy and handles vast oil and coal cargoes, as well as car and truck ferries. Much of the town is modern and not very interesting, although a small, austere older quarter near the harbor contains some fine homes of the town's merchant class. The large **Palazzo della Rovere,** on Via Pia, was designed for Pope Julius II by the Florentine Giuliano da Sangallo in 1495. There is also the 14th-century **Palazzo degli Anziani,** as well as three 12th-century towers. Every other year (next in 1998) on Good Friday, antique wooden carvings depicting the Passion of Christ are carried in procession. Watch for shops selling crystallized fruit, which is a local specialty.

Shopping

In **Millesimo,** a town 4 kilometers (2½ miles) west and 36 kilometers (18 miles) inland of Savona, little rum chocolates known as *millesimi* are produced. Look for bargains, too, in wrought-iron work, relief work on copper plate, and pieces in local sandstone.

Albisola Marina

❼ *4.5 km (3 mi) northwest of Savona, 43 km (26 mi) east of Genoa.*

Albisola Marina preserves its centuries-old tradition of ceramic making. Numerous shops here sell these distinctive wares, and a whole sidewalk, **Lungomare degli Artisti,** has been transformed by the colorful ceramic works of well-known artists. It runs along the beachfront. The 18th-century **Villa Faraggiana,** near the parish church on Via dell'Oratorio, has interesting antique ceramics and exhibits on the history of the craft. ✉ *Free.* ☉ *Apr.–Sept., Wed.–Mon. 3–7.*

Shopping

CERAMICS

Ceramiche San Giorgio (✉ Corso Matteotti 5, ☏ 019/482747) has been producing ceramics since the 17th century and is known for both classic and modern designs. **Mazzotti** (✉ Corso Matteotti 25, ☏ 019/481626) has an exclusive selection and a small in-house museum.

In Albisola Superiore, **Ernan** (✉ Corso Mazzini 77, ☏ 019/489916) features the classic blue-and-white Old Savona patterns typical of the 18th century.

Varazze

7 km (4 mi) northeast of Albisola, 36 km (22 mi) west of Genoa.

Varazze, known for its fine sandy beach, is good place to stop for some sea and sun. The town also has well-preserved ancient ramparts, with a 10th-century church facade built into one of the rampart walls.

Pegli

23 km (14 mi) northwest of Varazze, 13 km (8 mi) west of Genoa.

Once a popular summer home for many patrician Genoese families, **Pegli** still has museums, parks, and some elegant old villas with well-tended gardens. This residential suburb manages to maintain its dignity despite encroaching industry and the proximity of airport and port facilities. Two lovely villas make it worth an excursion (they're especially good for letting children work-off steam while romping in the gardens). Pegli can be reached conveniently by commuter train from Principe Station in Genoa.

Villa Doria, near the Pegli train station, has a large park. The villa itself, built in the 16th century by the Doria family, has been converted into a naval museum. ✉ *Villa Doria, Piazza Bonavino 7, Pegli,* ☏ *010/6969885.* ✉ *Villa: 6,000 lire; park: free.* ☉ *Villa: Tues.–Thurs. 9–1, Fri.–Sat. 9–7, Sun. 9:30–1; park: Daily 10–noon and 2–6.*

Villa Durazzo Pallavicini is set in 19th-century gardens featuring temples and artificial lakes. The villa has an archaeological museum. ⊠ *Via Pallavicini 11, Pegli.* 🎫 *6,000 lire.* ☉ *Tues.–Thurs. 9–7, Fri.–Sat. 9–1, 2nd and 4th Sun. of month 9–1.*

GENOA
Italy's Queen of the Seas

❽ *501 km (310 mi) northwest of Rome, 236 km (146 mi) northwest of Florence, 142 km (88 mi) south of Milan, 170 km (105 mi) southeast of Turin, and 194 km (120 mi) northeast of Nice.*

Busy, sprawling Genoa, which stretches for 20 kilometers (12 miles) along the coast, can offer a fascinating, rich, and colorful experience. Known as La Superba (The Proud), Genoa was from the 13th century a great maritime center that rivaled Venice and Pisa in power and splendor. In fact, Genoa has a proud history of trade and navigation that predates Columbus. Modern container ships unload at docks that centuries before served galleons and vessels bound for the spice routes. By the 3rd century BC, when the Romans conquered Liguria, Genoa was already an important trading station. The Middle Ages and the Renaissance saw the rise of Genoa as a great seaport and city. As a jumping-off place for the Crusaders, a commercial center of tremendous wealth and prestige, and a strategic bone of international contention, it was of key importance to Europe. Its bankers, merchants, and princes adorned the city with palaces and churches and amassed impressive art collections. By the 18th century, however, Genoa had declined as a sea power. Although it brims with historical curiosities and buildings (its lively medieval center is Europe's largest), it is also a thoroughly modern city struggling with problems of traffic, noise, and air pollution as well as a growing immigrant population. Its port is being equipped to keep up with new technologies; the city is also advanced in communications, electronics, and general commerce.

Europe's biggest boat show takes place here, as does the Euroflora flower show (held every five years—next in 2001). Classical dance and music are richly represented; the new Teatro Carlo Felice is a showcase (☞ Nightlife and the Arts, *below*), and the annual Niccolò Paganini Violin Contest, internationally renowned, also takes place in Genoa.

The historic harbor area was given a face-lift for the Columbus celebrations in 1992, and some of the fair installations, such as the Bigo elevator ride with harbor view, have become a permanent part of the city scene. The Acquario (Aquarium), the largest in Europe and second-largest in the world, is one of Genoa's more recent attractions.

Numbers in the margin correspond to points of interest on the Genoa map.

The best way to start your exploration of Genoa is to see it from above. ❾ The **Granarolo funicular,** actually a cog railway, takes you up the steeply rising terrain from the downtown area to one of the fortified gates in the 17th-century city walls. Dotted around the cirumference of the city are a number of huge fortresses, and this gate was part of the city's system of defenses. It takes 15 minutes to hoist you from Piazza del Principe, behind the Principe Station on Piazza Acquaverde, to **Porta Granarolo,** 1,000 feet above, where you can get a good sense of the size of Genoa. 🎫 *1,500 lire. Bus tickets are valid on this funicular. Leaves on the ¼ hr, 6 AM–11:45 PM.*

256

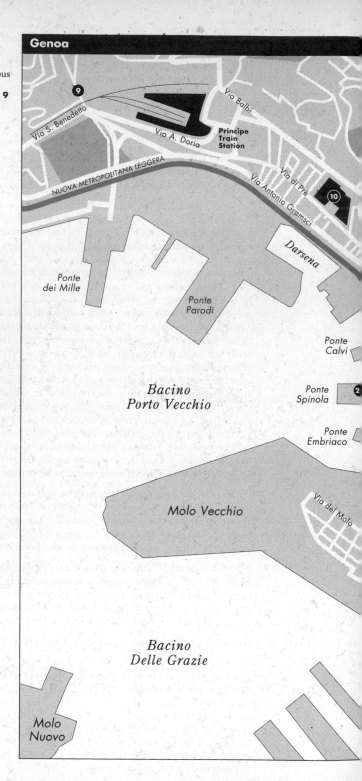

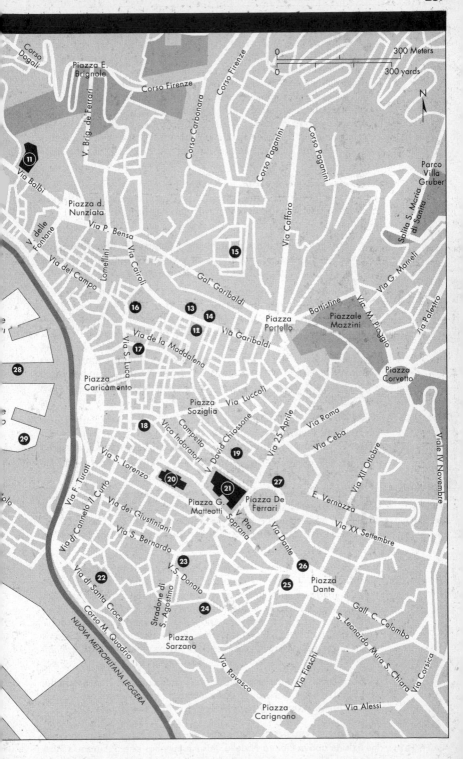

Corso Dogali

Piazza E. Brignole

Corso Firenze

Corso Firenze

Corso Carbonara

Corso Paganini

Corso Paganini

V. Brig. de Ferrari

11

Via Balbi

V. delle Fontane

Parco Villa Gruber

Piazza d. Nunziata

Via P. Bensa

Via Caffaro

Via del Campo

Lomellini

Via Cairoli

Salita S. Maria di Sanità

Via G. Maineli

15

Gal.ª Garibaldi

Battistine

Via M. Piaggio

Via Palestro

16

13

14

Piazza Portello

Piazzale Mazzini

12

Via Garibaldi

17

Via de la Maddalena

Via S. Luca

28

Piazza Caricamento

Piazza Corvetto

Piazza Soziglia

Via Luccoli

Via Roma

18

Campetto

V. David Chiossone

Via 25 Aprile

Via Ceba

Vico Indoratori

Via XII Ottobre

29

19

Via S. Lorenzo

Via F. Turati

20

27

Viale IV Novembre

21

E. Vernazza

Via d. Cannelo il Curto

Via dei Giustiniani

Piazza G. Matteotti

V. Pta.

V. Pta Soprana

Via Dante

Via XX Settembre

Via S. Bernardo

26

22

23

Piazza Dante

Via di Santa Croce

V. S. Donato

25

Gall. C. Colombo

Stradone di S. Agostino

24

S. Leonardo Mura S. Chiara

Corso M. Quadrio

Piazza Sarzano

Via Fieschi

Via Corsia

NUOVA METROPOLITANA LEGGERA

Via Ravasco

Via Alessi

Piazza Carignano

0 300 Meters

0 300 yards

N

★ ⑩ The **Palazzo Reale** is one of the most sumptuous in a city where conspicuous consumption was a game played by high society. Also known as **Palazzo Balbi Durazzo,** it was used as a royal palace by Italy's rulers. The palace, which dates from the 17th century, contains paintings, sculptures, tapestries, and Oriental ceramics. The building was bought by the Royal House of Savoy in the early 19th century and has some magnificent rooms decorated in the lavish and frivolous rococo style; the gallery of mirrors and the ballroom on the upper floor are particularly good examples. There are also works by Sir Anthony Van Dyck, who lived in Genoa for six years, from 1621, and painted many fine portraits of the Genoese nobility. ⊠ *Via Balbi 10,* ☎ *010/247–0640.* ☞ *8,000 lire.* ☉ *Sun.–Tues. 9–1:30, Wed.–Sat. 9–6:30.*

⑪ The **Palazzo dell'Università,** built in the 1630s as a Jesuit college, has been the site of Genoa's university since 1803. Climb the stairway flanked by lions to visit the elegant courtyard, with its portico of double Doric columns. ⊠ *Via Balbi 5.*

The 16th- to 17th-century church of the **Santissima Annunziata** has exuberantly frescoed vaults and is an excellent example of Genoese Baroque architecture. ⊠ *Piazza della Nunziata.*

★ **Via Garibaldi** was once known as the Via Aurea (Golden Street). Genoa's leading patrician families built their residences here from 1554 onward to escape the cramped conditions of the medieval section of town; 13 palaces were built along the street in just 10 years. Via Garibaldi is one of the most impressive streets in Italy, and its palace-museums house some of the finest art collections in the country. Most of the other palaces without museums on Via Garibaldi can be visited only by special application, but many have courtyards that are open to the public.

⑫ The 17th-century Baroque **Palazzo Rosso** (Red Palace) was named after the red stone used in its construction. It now contains, apart from a number of lavishly frescoed suites, works by Titian, Veronese, Caravaggio, Rubens, and Van Dyck. ⊠ *Via Garibaldi 18,* ☎ *010/282641.* ☞ *6,000 lire.* ☉ *Tues., Thurs., Fri., and Sun. 9–1; Wed. and Sat. 9–7.*

⑬ Originally white, as its name suggests, **Palazzo Bianco** has become considerably darkened from age and grime. It has a fine art collection, with the Dutch and Flemish schools well represented. ⊠ *Via Garibaldi 11,* ☎ *010/291803.* ☞ *6,000 lire.* ☉ *Tues., Thurs., Fri., and Sun. 9–1; Wed. and Sat. 9–7.*

⑭ **Palazzo Tursi** is Genoa's Town Hall, built in the 16th century by the wealthy Nicolò Grimaldi. The palace, also known as Palazzo Municipale, is made of pink stone quarried in the region. Visitors are welcome to view the richly decorated rooms and the famous Guarnerius violin that belonged to Paganini and is played once a year on Columbus Day (October 12). However, when the rooms are in use by Genoa's officials, as is often the case, they are closed to the public. ⊠ *Via Garibaldi 9,* ☎ *010/2098–2223.* ☞ *Free.* ☉ *Weekdays; call for hrs.*

⑮ One of Genoa's handy municipal elevators takes you from Piazza Portello, at the end of Via Garibaldi, to **Castelletto** for a good view of the old city. ☞ *600 lire one-way. Continuous service 6:40 AM–midnight.*

OFF THE   **MUSEO D'ARTE ORIENTALE CHIOSSONE** – In the Villetta di Negro park on
BEATEN PATH   the hillside above Piazza Portello, this museum has one of Europe's most extensive collections of Oriental art. The Japanese, Chinese, and Thai collections are noteworthy, and you can get a fine view of the city from the museum's terrace. ⊠ *Piazzale Mazzini (Piazza Corvetto),* ☎

010/542285. ☒ 6,000 lire. ⊙ Tues. and Thurs.–Sat. 9–1; 1st and 3rd Sun. of month, 9–1.

The winding, picturesque alleys—known as *caruggi*—that zigzag through the medieval city contain many medieval buildings (some decorated with typical Ligurian black-and-white facades); these buildings are on a more human scale than the grand, airy palaces of Via Garibaldi. But the caruggi district is also the city's most disreputable. Don't go there after dark, or on holidays, when shops are closed and the alleys deserted. In the heart of the medieval quarter, Via Soziglia is a street lined with shops selling handicrafts and tempting foods. South of Piazza Soziglia is the quarter where wealthy Genoese built their homes in the 16th century. Prosperous guilds, such as the goldsmiths, for whom Vico dei Indoratori and Via Orefici were named, also set up shop here.

NEED A BREAK? The **Klainguti Tearoom** (☎ 010/296502), in Piazza Soziglia, is an institution in Genoa. Try the excellent homemade cakes and ice creams.

🟢16 **San Siro,** Genoa's oldest church, served as the city's cathedral from the 4th to the 9th centuries; it was rebuilt in the 16th and 17th centuries. ⊠ *Via San Luca.*

🟢17 The **National Gallery** is housed in the richly adorned **Palazzo Spinola,** north of Piazza Soziglia. The collection contains, among other fine works, masterpieces by Luca Giordano (1634–1705) and Guido Reni (1575–1642). The *Ecce Homo,* by Antonello da Messina (1430–79), is a hauntingly beautiful painting and is also of historical interest because it was the Sicilian da Messina who first brought Flemish oil paints and techniques to Italy from his voyages in the Low Countries. ⊠ *Piazza Pellicceria 1,* ☎ 010/294661. ☒ 8,000 lire. ⊙ Mon. 9–1, Tues.–Sat. 9–7, Sun. 2–7.

Piazza San Matteo, south of Piazza Soziglia, is an excellently preserved medieval square, for 500 years the seat of the Doria family, who ruled Genoa and much of Liguria from the 16th to the 18th century and built fine palaces all over the city. The square is bounded by 13th- to 15th-century houses decorated with portals and loggias.

🟢18 You can buy a wide array of handicrafts and tempting foods at the **Loggia dei Mercanti** (covered market) in Piazza Banchi. The black-and-white
🟢19 church of **San Matteo** dates from the 12th century; its crypt contains the tomb of Andrea Doria, who framed a constitution for the city in 1529 and began his family's reign. Doria won his fame as an admiral, serving, in turn, the French and Spanish crowns, but managing to maintain the independence of his native city. ⊠ *Piazza San Matteo.*

🟢20 The cathedral of **San Lorenzo** stands at the heart of medieval Genoa's political and religious center. The cathedral is embellished inside and out with the contrasting black slate and white marble so common in Liguria. It was consecrated in 1118 to St. Lawrence, who passed through the city on his way to Rome in the 3rd century; the last campanile dates from the early 16th century. For hundreds of years the building was used for state, as well as religious, purposes: Civic elections, court rulings, and religious ceremonies and festivals all took place here. Note the lively 13th-century Gothic portal and the 15th- to 17th-
★ century frescoes inside. The **Museo del Tesoro di San Lorenzo** (San Lorenzo Treasury Museum), in the cathedral, contains some stunning medieval pieces. The art of goldsmiths and silversmiths, for which medieval Genoa was renowned, is particularly well represented here. Newly renovated, it reopened in the summer of 1996. Check locally for hours.

㉑ The **Palazzo Ducale** was built in the 16th century over a medieval hall, and its facade was rebuilt in the late 18th century. The building has
㉒ been restored and houses temporary exhibitions. **Santa Maria di Castello,** one of Genoa's greatest religious buildings, was an early Christian church. It was rebuilt in the 12th century and finally completed in 1513. You can visit the adjacent cloisters and see the fine artwork contained in the museum. ⊠ *Salita di Santa Maria di Castello 15,* ☎ *010/292986.* ⊠ *Free.* ☉ *Daily 9–noon and 3:30–6.*

㉓ The 12th-century Romanesque church of **San Donato,** with its original portal and octagonal campanile, stands almost directly in front of
㉔ Sant'Agostino. The 13th-century Gothic church of **Sant'Agostino** was damaged during World War II, but it still has a fine campanile and two well-preserved cloisters, which now house an excellent sculpture museum. ⊠ *Piazza Sarzano 35/r,* ☎ *010/201661.* ⊠ *6,000 lire.* ☉ *Tues.–Sat. 9–7, Sun. 9–12:30.*

At the southeastern end of the old city, the twin-towered, 12th-cen-
㉕ tury **Porta di Sant'Andrea,** or Porta Soprana, stands at the old gateway to the Roman road that led through Genoa. The ivy-covered ruins of a medieval house in the gardens adjacent to the Porta di Sant'An-
㉖ drea is the **childhood home of Christopher Columbus,** or so it's believed.
㉗ The **Teatro Carlo Felice,** the World War II–ravaged opera house in Genoa's modern center, **Piazza de Ferrari,** has finally been rebuilt, reopening in 1991 with a massive, much-criticized tower. It stands next to the **Academy of Fine Arts,** which contains a collection of Ligurian paintings from the 13th to the 19th century. ☎ *010/581957.* ⊠ *Free.* ☉ *Mon.–Sat. 9–1.*

㉘ Don't miss the **Acquario** (Aquarium), opened in 1992, with 50 tanks full of marine fauna and flora, reproducing saltwater and freshwater habitats. This is a must for children. ⊠ *Ponte Spinola,* ☎ *010/2481205.* ⊠ *14,000 lire.* ☉ *Tues., Wed., and Fri. 9:30–7 (ticket office closes 5:30 PM); Thurs. and weekends 9:30 AM–8:30 PM (ticket office closes 7 PM).*

㉙ Take the **Bigo elevator** up to the top of this mast erected as a symbol of the 1992 Columbus Quincentennial events. The view from the top takes in the harbor, the city, and the sea. ⊠ *4,000 lire.* ☉ *Mar.–Aug., Tues.–Sat. 11–1 and 3–6; Sun. 11–1 and 2:30–6:30. Sept.–Feb., Tues.–Sat. 11–12:30 and 2:30–4; Sun. 11–1 and 3–6.*

A boat tour gives you a good perspective on the **harbor,** the layout of which dates to Roman times. The Genoa inlet, the largest along the Italian Riviera, was also used by the Phoenicians and Greeks as a harbor and a vantage point from which they could penetrate inland to form settlements and to trade. The **Lanterna,** a lighthouse more than 360 feet high, was built in 1544 at the height of Andrea Doria's career; it is one of Italy's oldest lighthouses and a traditional emblem of Genoa.

Dining and Lodging

$$$–$$$$ ✕ **Gran Gotto.** Innovative versions of classic regional dishes are served in this elegant restaurant in spacious quarters decorated with contemporary paintings. Gran Gotto is near Brignole Station in the modern part of town. The service is quick and helpful; the waiter will proudly detail the ingredients of the day's specials. Try *filetti di triglia* (red mullet fillets with rosemary, celery, and balsamic vinegar) and the *antica torta di mele* (apple pie), one of the many excellent homemade desserts. ⊠ *Via Viale Brigata Bisagno 69/r,* ☎ *010/564344. Jacket and tie. AE, MC, V. Closed Sun. and Aug. 10–31. No lunch Sat.*

$$$–$$$$
★ ✕ **Zeffirino.** The five Belloni brothers share the chef's duties at this remarkable restaurant, which is full of odd combinations. The decor is a mixture of styles and materials, ranging from rustic wood to modern metallic. Try the *passutelli* (ravioli stuffed with ricotta cheese and fruit) or any of the homemade pasta dishes. ⊠ *Via XX Settembre 20,* ☎ *010/591990. Jacket and tie. AE, DC, MC, V. Closed Wed.*

$$–$$$ ✕ **Sette Nasi.** The historic Quarto dei Mille district is the setting for this large establishment, elegantly decorated with accents of gray slate and pink marble and proudly overseen by its chef, Fausto Nasi, who specializes in a wide range of Ligurian seafood dishes. Homemade desserts are also recommended. Summertime meals are served on the terrace, which has excellent sea views. Top off a lovely day spent at the annexed pool and beach club with a dinner of ravioli *di pesce* (seafood) or lasagna with pesto. ⊠ *Via Quarto 16,* ☎ *010/3731344. AE, DC, MC, V. Closed Tues., Nov.*

$$ ✕ **Da Genio.** On a byway in old Genoa, near Piazza Dante, this classic trattoria serves equally classic Genoese dishes, including *trenette al pesto* (pasta with pesto sauce) and minestrone, also laced with a dollop of pesto. ⊠ *Salita San Leonardo 61/r,* ☎ *010/588463. MC, V. Closed Sun. and Aug. 1–30.*

$$ ✕ **Marinella.** This restaurant is perched on seaside shoals in Nervi, 10 kilometers (6 miles) east of the center of Genoa. Competing for attention are an impressive wrought-iron chandelier and great sea views from windows and terrace. (There's an inexpensive hotel annex, too.) Try *zuppa di pesce* (fish stew); main dishes change from day to day, according to the fishermen's catch. ⊠ *Passeggiata Anita Garibaldi 18, Nervi,* ☎ *010/3728343. MC, V. Closed Mon. and Nov.*

$ ✕ **Trattoria Walter.** This family-run restaurant is in the heart of the city, near Palazzo Spinola and the Aquarium. Though unpretentious, it offers such extras as vaulted ceilings and classical music on the stereo. The owners pride themselves on courteous service and a menu featuring Genoese specialties such as *stoccafisso in umido co patate* (dried codfish stew with potatoes). To help you find this place among the narrow byways of Old Genoa, they encourage you to ask directions of neighboring shopkeepers. ⊠ *Vico Colalanza 2, corner of Via San Luca,* ☎ *010/290524. No credit cards. Closed Sun. and Thurs. evening, and Aug. 13–Sept. 3.*

$$$$ ▣ **Bristol Palace.** This grand hotel, on a fashionable downtown shopping street, was built in the last century and maintains the old-fashioned traditions of courtesy and discretion. The rooms are large, with high ceilings, and paintings decorate the large reception rooms. There's no restaurant, but the hotel is in the heart of the downtown area. ⊠ *Via XX Settembre 35,* ☎ *010/592541,* FAX *010/561756. 98 rooms with bath. Bar, café, snack bar. AE, DC, MC, V.*

$$$$ ▣ **President.** This member of the Starhotel chain of comfortable and reliable business hotels is also well located for tourists. The high-rise hotel opened in 1991 as part of a large new commercial and convention center near Brignole Station. The rooms have big windows and modern decor. ⊠ *Corte Lambruschini 4,* ☎ *010/5727,* FAX *010/553-1820. 193 rooms with bath or shower. Restaurant, bar, parking. AE, DC, MC, V.*

$$$ ▣ **Novotel.** Opened in 1994, this is a good choice for tourists who value modern comfort over atmosphere. It is in a semicentral location just beyond one end of the harbor; you can take a bus or taxi to the heart of town. ⊠ *Via Cantore 8/c,* ☎ *010/64841,* FAX *010/6484844. 223 rooms with bath. Restaurant, bar, pool, parking. AE, DC, MC, V.*

$$$ ⌂ **Villa Pagoda.** If you want to stay at a top-quality hotel outside the
★ center of Genoa, try this unusual establishment in Nervi, 10 kilometers (6 miles) east of Genoa. It occupies a 19th-century building designed to look like a pagoda, built at a time when Europe was fascinated by the exotic Orient. The interior was redecorated in 1995 and the restaurant totally refurbished along elegant lines. Most of the spacious rooms have gorgeous views of the sea, and the hotel is adjacent to a large, shady park. ⊠ *Via Capolungo 15, Nervi,* ☎ *010/3726161,* FAX *010/321218. 18 rooms with bath. Restaurant, bar, beach. AE, DC, MC, V.*

$$ ⌂ **Agnello d'Oro.** The central location in Genoa's old quarter, about
★ 100 yards from Principe Station, makes this hotel a good choice for budget travelers who want to be in the heart of things. There are simple modern furnishings in renovated rooms, a few of which have a balcony with a view. ⊠ *Vico delle Monachette 6,* ☎ *010/2462084,* FAX *010/2462327. 40 rooms with bath. Bar. AE, DC, MC, V.*

$$ ⌂ **Cairoli.** On a historic street near Principe Station and the Aquarium, this hotel's central location is a real plus. Happily, the rooms have been soundproofed so you'll get a good night's sleep—not always the easiest thing to do in this noisy city. Family-operated, it is neatly furnished and has a roof terrace. ⊠ *Via Cairoli 14,* ☎ *010/206531,* FAX *010/280041. 14 rooms, 12 with bath. Parking. AE, DC, MC, V.*

$$ ⌂ **Viale Sauli.** Conveniently located in the vicinity of Brignole Station, this hotel occupies several floors of an undistinguished modern building. It has a mainly business clientele. Here you can be sure of clean and functional accommodations in one of Genoa's more secure districts. ⊠ *Viale Sauli 5,* ☎ *010/561397,* FAX *010/590092. 56 rooms with bath. AE, DC, MC, V.*

Nightlife and the Arts

The **opera** season (October–May) at **Teatro Carlo Felice** (⊠ Passo al Teatro 4, ☎ 010/53811; box office ☎ 010/591697) attracts many lavish productions and occasionally sees the debut of a new work.

Shopping

Liguria is famous for its fine laces, its silver and gold filigree work, and its ceramics. Look also for bargains in velvet, macramé, olive wood, and marble. Genoa is the best spot to find all these specialties.

Codevilla (⊠ Via Orefici 53, ☎ 010/206567). This well-established shop is one of the best jewelers on a street devoted to goldsmiths.

Pescetto (⊠ Via Scurreria 8, ☎ 010/206633). You'll find designer clothes, perfumes, and gifts in this elegant shop near Codevilla.

Pietro Romanengo fu Stefano (⊠ Via Soziglia 74, ☎ 010/297869). Judge for yourself whether the handmade chocolates here are the best in Genoa (the management says they are).

Vinoteca Sola (⊠ Piazza Colombo 13, near Brignole station, ☎ 010/561329). The wine connoisseur will appreciate the selection of Italian and Ligurian wines on sale in this wineshop.

La Rinascente (⊠ Via Vernazza 5) and **Coin** (⊠ Via XII Ottobre 4) are Genoa's two major department stores.

Via XX Settembre and **Via Luccoli** are famous for their wide range of small, exclusive shops.

THE RIVIERA DI LEVANTE
On the Road to Portofino

Of the two Ligurian Rivieras, the Riviera di Levante, east of Genoa, is the wilder and more rugged, yet here you will also find towns world-famous for their panache and easy elegance, such as Portofino and Rapallo. Around every turn, the hills drop sharply to the sea and are pierced by compact bays and inlets. You may want to choose a base and take short day trips or explore the area by boat from the larger towns. For exercise, there are plenty of facilities for sailing, waterskiing, tennis and golf. Beaches on this coast are rocky, with many spectacular cliffs near the sea. There are small *ciazze* (coves) where you can anchor your boat in relatively calm water, and enjoy the enticing combination of sea and foliage. Portofino Promontory has one sandy beach, on the east side, at Paraggi. From Chiavari to Cavi di Lavagna, the coast becomes a bit gentler, with a few sandy areas. From Sestri Levante down to Portovenere, the coast is rugged; however, these areas are good for sailing.

Numbers in the margin correspond to points of interest on the Italian Riviera map.

Nervi

③⓪ *11 km (7 mi) east of Genoa, 97 km (60 mi) west of La Spezia*

Nervi is an elegant turn-of-the-century resort. It's famous for the mile-long Anita Garibaldi promenade, with its splendid sea views, and for palm-lined roads, and 300 acres of parks rich in orange trees and exotics.

The curious and eclectic collections in the **Museo di Villa Luxoro,** housed in a turn-of-the-century mansion, include 17th- and 18th-century Genoese furnishings, furniture, ceramics, and ornaments; Flemish and Genoese paintings and drawings; old silver and lace; and antique clocks. ✉ *Via Aurelia 29,* ☎ *010/322673.* 🎟 *6,000 lire.* ⊙ *Tues.–Sat. 9–1.*

An **International Festival of Ballet** is usually held in July in an amphitheater set up in the grounds of Villa Gropallo. The festival sometimes skips a year. For information contact City of Genoa Tourist Office (☎ 010/284091).

Camogli

★ ③① *10 km (6 mi) southwest of Nervi, 23 km (14 mi) northwest of Chiavari*

Camogli, at the edge of the large promontory and nature reserve known as the Portofino peninsula, has always been a town of sailors. By the 19th century this small village was leasing its ships throughout the Continent. The festival of San Fortunato, held on the second Sunday of May each year, is noteworthy for the Sagra del Pesce, a public—and free—feast of freshly caught fish cooked in pans 12 feet wide. The village has multicolored houses, a huge 17th-century sea wall in the harbor, and the Dragone Castle, built onto the sheer rock face by the harbor. Within the castle is the **Acquario,** with good displays of local marine life. The tanks are actually built into the ramparts. 🎟 *4,000 lire, 2,000 lire children under 10.* ⊙ *May–Sept., Mon.–Sun. 10–noon, 3–7; Oct.–Apr., Fri., Sat. and Sun. 10–noon and 2:30–6, Tues.–Thurs. 10–noon.*

SAN ROCCO, SAN NICOLÒ, AND PUNTA CHIAPPA – From Camogli you
can reach, by foot or boat, these hamlets with their remarkable sea
views. They lie along the western coast of the peninsula and are more
natural and less fashionable than those facing south on the eastern
coast. The small Romanesque church at San Nicolò was where sailors
who survived dangerous voyages came to offer thanks.

SAN FRUTTUOSO – On the sea at the foot of Mt. Portofino, 30 minutes by
boat from Camogli (20 minutes by boat from Portofino) the medieval
abbey of San Fruttuoso—built by the Benedictines of Monte Cassino—
protects a minuscule fishing village and can be reached only on foot or
by boat from Camogli, Portofino, Santa Margherita Ligure, or Rapallo.
The restored abbey is now property of a national conservation fund
(FAI). The church holds the tombs of some illustrious members of the
Doria family. The historic abbey and its grounds are a delightful place to
spend a few hours, perhaps lunching at one of the modest beach trattorias nearby. But boatloads of visitors can make it very crowded very
fast; it's best appreciated off-season. ☎ 0185/772703. ☜ 5,000 lire.
⊙ Tues.–Sun., Mar.–Apr. 10–1 and 2–4; May–Oct. 10–1 and 2–6;
Nov.–Jan. Sat., Sun. 10–1 and 2–4. Closed Feb.

Dining and Lodging

$$$ ✕ **Vento Ariel.** This tiny but friendly restaurant is right on the port,
and it has informal but elegant decor and place settings. It serves
seafood only and regularly runs out of items because it relies on the
day's catch. Try the spaghetti *alle vongole* (with clams) or the grilled
mixed fish, which differs according to the day's haul. ⊠ *Calata Porto,*
☎ *0185/771080. AE, DC, MC, V. Closed Wed. and Feb.*

$$$–$$$$ 🏨 **Cenobio dei Dogi.** Although this hilltop villa perched over the town
★ was once the summer home of Genoa's doges (medieval elected rulers),
it now has a modern look and was entirely renovated in 1995. The
rooms have TV and air-conditioning. Guests can relax in the well-kept
park gazing out on outstanding views of the Portofino peninsula, or
they can enjoy numerous sporting activities. Some of the rooms have
balconies with the same wonderul view. ⊠ *Via Cuneo 34,* ☎ *0185/7241,*
FAX *0185/772796. 107 rooms with bath. Restaurant, bar, pool, tennis
courts, private beach. AE, MC, V.*

Ruta

4 km (2½ mi) east of Camogli

This is a base for hikes on Mt. Portofino. The footpaths up to and around
the mountain cover terrain with a wide variety of plant species, as well
as excellent views of the Riviera di Levante.

Rapallo

③² *10 km (8 mi) east of Camogli, 37 km (23 mi) west of Genoa, 79 km
(49 mi) east of La Spezia.*

Rapallo was once one of Europe's most fashionable resorts, but it
passed its heyday before World War II and has suffered from the build-
ing boom brought on by tourism. Ezra Pound and D. H. Lawrence lived
here, and many other writers, poets, and artists have been drawn to it.
Today, the town's harbor is filled with yachts. A single-span bridge on
the eastern side of the bay is named after Hannibal, who is said to have
passed through the area after crossing the Alps. Two ancient buildings
are highlights in the center of town: The cathedral of Santi Gervasio

and Protasio, at the western end of Via Mazzini, was founded in the 6th century; across the road is the Leper House of San Lorenzo, which still retains parts of its original medieval frescoes on its exterior walls.

The **Museo Civico** has a collection of antique lace. Rapallo was famous for this type of handiwork. ✉ 4,000 lire. ⏲ Oct.–Aug., Tues.–Wed., Fri.–Sat. 3–6, Thurs, 10–11:30.

Dining and Lodging

$$ ✕ **Da Ardito.** This lively trattoria is in the village of San Pietro di Novella, which is just north of Rapallo. It's extremely popular with wine lovers, who appreciate the attention given to the wine list. For a change from seafood, try the *pansotti alla salsa di noci* (pasta served with creamy walnut sauce). ✉ *Via Canale 9, San Pietro di Novella,* ☎ *0185/51551. Reservations advised. MC, V. Closed Mon. and Feb.*

$$$$ ⊞ **Grand Hotel Bristol.** This large Victorian showcase has undergone total renovation, emerging as one of the most luxurious hotels on the Riviera. It is in an elevated position overlooking the sea outside Rapallo, and is set in lush gardens with a huge pool. Spacious rooms, many with balcony and sea view, are decorated in soft colors in a smart, contemporary style and have extra-large beds. The hotel has three restaurants, one of which is on a roof terrace. ✉ *Via Aurelia Orientale 369,* ☎ *0185/273313,* FAX *0185/55800. 90 rooms and suites with bath. 3 Restaurants, bar, pool, 18-hole golf course, tennis court, horseback riding, meeting rooms. AE, MC, V. Closed Jan.–Feb.*

$$$ ⊞ **Eurotel.** On the old coast road, but in an elevated position above the harbor, the Eurotel is a modern building set in a garden, with a large swimming pool. The decor is functional rather than charming, but rooms are bright, with balconies and sea views. ✉ *Via Aurelia Ponente 22,* ☎ *0185/60981,* FAX *0185/50635. 65 rooms with bath. Restaurant, bar, pool, free parking. AE, DC, MC, V.*

$$ ⊞ **Giulio Cesare.** Only a block from the sea, this old town house was transformed into a hotel that offers rooms with modern furnishings and sea views. Many rooms have balconies, but noise may be a problem, since the hotel is on a main street. ✉ *Corso Colombo 52,* ☎ *0185/50685,* FAX *0185/60896 . 33 rooms with bath. AE, MC, V. Closed Nov.–Dec. 15.*

Outdoor Activities and Sports

GOLF

The **Rapallo Golf Club** (☎ 0185/261777) has a lush 18-hole course about 2 kilometers (1 mile) northwest of the center of town.

HORSEBACK RIDING

The **Rapallo Riding Club** (✉ Via Santa Maria del Campo 196, ☎ 0185/50462) is near the golf club, about 2 km (1 mi) northwest of town.

Shopping

Zoagli. This attractive coastal village has been famous for silk velvet and damask ever since the Middle Ages. ✉ *On S1, 4 km (2½ mi) east of Rapallo.*

Chiavari. The traditional, light (they weigh only 3 pounds) *campanine* chairs made of olive wood or walnut are still produced here by a few craftsmen. Macramé lace also can be found here. ✉ *On S1, 12 km (7 mi) east of Rapallo.*

Santa Margherita Ligure

3 km (2 mi) south of Rapallo, 40 km (25 mi) southeast of Genoa, 82 km (51 mi) northwest of La Spezia.

A pretty resort favored by well-to-do Italians, **Santa Margherita Ligure** has everything a Riviera playground should have—plenty of palm trees and attractive hotels, cafés and a marina packed with yachts. There are even some of the trompe l'oeil frescoes typical of the old buildings on this part of the Riviera. It's a pleasant place to stay, and a good base for excursions by land and by sea.

Dining and Lodging

$$ ✕ **Da Baicin.** A very friendly family runs this bright trattoria. Outdoor tables afford a view of the seaside gardens in the center of Santa
★   Margherita. The specialties of the house are *zuppa di pesce* (fish stew) and *pansoti alla salsa di noci* (cheese ravioli with walnut sauce). ⊠ *Via Algeria 5,* ☎ *0185/286763. AE, DC, MC, V. Closed Mon. and Nov. 15–Dec. 1.*

$$ ✕ **Il Frantoio.** The large, hand-carved wooden screws that turned the olive press for which this rather elegant little restaurant is named stand at the entrance. And here you not only choose wine from a list; you can also consult the olive oil list for just the right condiment for your *bruschetta* (grilled bread with or without garlic). Quality is a keynote in the food, too, as in the traditional spaghetti with seafood sauce. The menu is varied enough to suit most tastes. ⊠ *Via del Giunchetto 23/a,* ☎ *0185/286667. AE, MC, V.*

$$$$ 🛏 **Grand Hotel Miramare.** Take the shore road south from town to reach this palatial turn-of-the-century hotel overlooking the bay. It has a lush garden and swimming pool, and a private swimming area on the sea. The bright and airy rooms are decorated in contemporary or late–19th-century style. The best have sea views, as do the hotel terraces. ⊠ *Lungomare Milite Ignoto 30,* ☎ *0185/287013,* 𝔽𝔸𝕏 *0185/284651. 83 rooms with bath. Restaurant, bar, pool, beach, waterskiing. AE, MC, V.*

$$$$ 🛏 **Imperial Palace.** Via Pagana climbs north out of Santa Margherita Ligure on its way toward Rapallo; just outside town it passes this Old World–style luxury hotel, which is set in an extensive park. The rooms are furnished with antiques; many overlook the shore drive to the sea. The reception rooms are elegantly decorated with tall windows, plush chairs, and potted plants. ⊠ *Via Pagana 19,* ☎ *0185/288991,* 𝔽𝔸𝕏 *0185/284223. 102 rooms with bath. Restaurant, bar, pool. AE, DC, MC, V. Closed Dec. 1–Mar. 1.*

$$$ 🛏 **Continental.** This resort hotel by the sea is a stately mansion with a columned portico, built in the early 1900s and set in a lush garden shaded by tall palms and pine trees. The decor is a blend of traditional furnishings, mostly in 19th-century style, with some more functional pieces. There is also a modern wing. The hotel's own cabanas and swimming area are at the bottom of the garden. Ask for a room with a sea view; many rooms have balconies, and the views are, indeed, superb. ⊠ *Via Pagana 8,* ☎ *0185/286512,* 𝔽𝔸𝕏 *0185/284463. 76 rooms with bath. Restaurant, bar, parking. AE, DC, MC, V. Closed Nov.*

$ 🛏 **Fasce.** An extremely good value, this small, modern hotel is cen-
★   trally located on one of the town's main thoroughfares, but from its pleasant roof garden you have views of the sea and surrounding hills. The Italian owner and his English wife take cordial interest in their guests' well-being and comfort. Rooms are attractively furnished and have satellite TV. ⊠ *Via Bozzo 3,* ☎ *0185/286435,* 𝔽𝔸𝕏 *0185/283580. 16 rooms with bath. Restaurant, parking. AE, DC, MC, V.*

Portofino

★ ㉝   *5 km (3 mi) south of Santa Margherita Ligure, 38 km (23 mi) southeast of Genoa, 87 km (54 mi) northwest of La Spezia.*

Portofino is one of the most picturesque villages along the coast. It is also precious, in the true sense of the word. Unless you are traveling on a deluxe level and can keep up with the Agnellis and Berlusconis, you will probably choose a hotel in Rapallo or Santa Margherita Ligure rather than one of Portofino's few and very expensive establishments. Tiny Portofino has an aura of romance and money. Some of Europe's wealthiest lay anchor here, but they stay out of sight during the day in their secluded villas or on their gorgeous yachts, appearing only in the evening after buses and boats have carried off the day-trippers. There's little to do in Portofino, other than stroll around the wee harbor, walk to Punta del Capo and a look at the pricey boutiques. Cafés and restaurants are pricey, too. If you have had to sit out a traffic jam to get there, you may wonder why you bothered. Trying to reach Portofino by bus or car on the single narrow road can be a nightmare in the summer and on holiday weekends. An alternative is to take a boat from Santa Margherita. If getting there was easy and you find the village relatively empty of tourists, you'll probably agree that it is a pretty place indeed.

From the harbor, follow the signs for the climb to the **Castello di San Giorgio,** with its medieval relics and excellent views. ⊠ *4,000 lire.* ☉ *Apr.–Sept., Wed.–Mon. 10–6; Oct.–Mar., Wed.–Mon. 10–4.*

Sitting on a ridge above the harbor is the church of **San Giorgio,** which is supposed to contain the saint's relics, brought back from the Holy Land by the Crusaders. Not surprisingly, Portofino enthusiastically celebrates St. George's day (April 23). Other excellent views can be seen from the lighthouse at Punta del Capo, a 15-minute walk along a marked path from the village.

If you have the stamina, you can hike to the Abbey of San Fruttuoso (☞ Camogli, *above*) from Portofino. It's a steep climb at first, and the walk takes about 2 1/2 hours one way. By boat, the trip takes about 20 minutes.

Dining and Lodging

$$$$ ✕ **Il Pitosforo.** A chic, tan clientele, many with luxury yachts in the harbor, gives this waterfront restaurant a glamorous atmosphere that is heightened by prices only the wealthy can afford. Spaghetti *ai frutti di mare* (with seafood) is recommended; adventurous diners might want to try *lo stocco accomodou* (dried cod in a savory sauce of tomatoes, raisins, and pine nuts). ⊠ *Molo Umberto I, 9,* ☏ *0185/269020. Reservations essential. AE, DC, MC, V. Closed Mon., Tues. and Jan.–Feb.15; June–Sept. dinner only.*

$$$$ ⌂ **Splendido.** Most people resort to superlatives when trying to describe ★ this luxury hotel, built in the '20s on a hill overlooking the sea. The abiding impression is one of color, from the coordinated fabrics and furnishings of the rooms to the fresh flowers in the reception rooms and on the large terrace. It's like a Jazz Age film set, and you almost expect to see a Bugatti or Daimler roll up the winding drive from Portofino below. A network of footpaths leads away from the wooded grounds. The Splendido's relatively small size means you get even more personal attention than at other luxury hotels. ⊠ *Viale Baratta 13,* ☏ *0185/269551,* FAX *0185/269614. 64 rooms with bath. Restaurant, 2 bars, pool, tennis court. AE, DC, MC, V. Closed Jan. –mid-Mar.*

Chiavari

③④ *22 km (13 mi) southeast of Portofino, 38 km (23 mi) southeast of Genoa, 69 km (43 mi) northwest of La Spezia*

Chiavari is a fishing town, rather than village, and it has considerable character, with narrow, twisting streets and a good harbor. Chiavari's citizens were energetic explorers, and many emigrated to South America in the 19th century. The town boomed, thanks to the wealth of the returning voyagers, but Chiavari still retains many medieval traces in its buildings.

There is an interesting **Museo Archeologico** (archaeological museum) in the center of town. Here you can see finds from an 8th-century BC necropolis, or city of the dead, excavated nearby. ⊠ *Palazzo Rocca, Piazza Matteotti.* ☜ *Free.* ☉ *Tues.–Thurs. 9–1, Fri.–Sun. 2–7.*

Outdoor Activities and Sports

HORSEBACK RIDING

Riding is a rewarding way to explore the wooded hills framing Chiavari. **Rivarola Carasco** (⊠ Via Veneto 212, ☎ 0185/382204) can provide mounts.

Sestri Levante

㉟ *8 km (5 mi) southeast of Chiavari, 50 km (311 mi) southeast of Genoa, 59 km (36 mi) northwest of La Spezia*

Though industrialized, with steelworks and shipyards, **Sestri Levante** has good views and an interesting **medieval district** surrounding what is known as the Baia del Silenzio (Bay of Silence), the small harbor just behind Piazza Matteotti. Walk up one of the alleyways to see some of the worked slate doorways of the older houses.

En Route   From Sestri, S1 turns inland past the spectacular Passo del Bracco and does not reach the coast again until the large port of La Spezia, more than 60 kilometers (40 miles) southeast.The Cinque Terre, five towns that lie on the less accessible coastal strip between Levanto and Portovenere (near La Spezia) were accessible only by boat until about 50 years ago.

Levanto

㊱ *25 km (15 mi) southeast of Sestri Levante, 32 km (20 mi) northwest of La Spezia, 83 km (51 mi) southwest of Genoa*

Levanto is a secluded town with good beaches and a few graceful buildings that date from the 13th century. Many of the buildings are adorned with clever trompe l'oeil paintings that give the impression that real town folk are looking at you from their windows.

Dining and Lodging

$$–$$$ ✕ **Araldo.** Arches and frescoes add to the atmosphere of this elegant little restaurant. Ambience, food, and service are outstanding; the menu, featuring creative Mediterranean cuisine, changes with the seasons and offers more than 100 wines. Try *pesce con patate alla ligure* (fillets of fish baked with potatoes in wine with olives and fres thyme). ⊠ *Via Jacopo 24,* ☎ *0187/807253. AE, DC, MC, V. Closed Tues. (except July–Aug.), Nov.*

$$$ ⊞ **Stella Maris.** Located in the center of Levanto and only a 10-minute
★   walk from the beach, this is a real find. It takes up one floor of a 19th-century palazzo (the ground floor houses a palatial bank). Seven rooms are decorated with original frescoes and 19th-century furniture, and seven are modern; the couple who run the hotel have an infectious enthusiasm for the building's history and decoration. A half-board plan is required, but that's no sacrifice because the home cooking features

Ligurian seafood specialties; you can have your homemade ice cream in the sunny garden. The room rate includes half board. ✉ *Via Marconi 4,* ☎ *0187/808258,* FAX *0187/807351. 15 rooms with shower. Restaurant. AE, DC, MC, V. Closed Nov.*

Cinque Terre

★ ③⑦ *Monterosso: 12 km (7 mi) east of Levanto; Vernazza: 3.5 km (2 mi) east of Monterosso; Corniglia: 3 km (2 mi) east of Vernazza; Manarola: 3 km (2 mi) east of Corniglia; Riomaggiore: 1.5 km (2 mi) east of Manarola, 10 km (6 mi) west of La Spezia.*

The aura of isolation that has surrounded five almost inaccessible coastal villages known as **Cinque Terre,** together with their dramatic coastal scenery, has made them one of the eastern Riviera's premier attractions, especially for those who visit them effortlessly, by excursion boat. Clinging haphazardly to steep cliffs, they are linked by footpaths, by train, and now by narrow, unasphalted and rather torturous roads, a fairly recent development. The local train on the Genoa-La Spezia line stops at each town beteween Levanto and Riomaggiore. Built against steep cliffs and linked by trails, the villages have long been a favorite destination for hikers. The classic, lower coastal trail is the Blue Trail (Trail 2), and the walk takes about five hours. You can catch a train back to your base. If you walk all or part of the way, wear sturdy shoes and a hat and carry a water bottle, as there is little shade. The westernmost village is Monterosso, but the easiest to reach by car is Riomaggiore, easternmost of the villages and closest to La Spezia and the A12 autostrada.

The largest of the five fishing towns is **Monterosso,** with a 12th-century church in the Ligurian style, lively markets, and small beaches. To the east is **Vernazza,** a charming village of narrow streets, small squares and arcades, and the remains of forts dating from the Middle Ages. **Corniglia,** the middle village, is perched on a hillside amid vineyards; it offers excellent views of the entire coastal strip. At the eastern end of the Cinque Terre the villages of **Manarola** and **Riomaggiore** huddle on tiny harbors hemmed in by sheer cliffs.

Dining and Lodging

$$ ✕ **Il Gigante.** A good introduction to Ligurian seafood is the *zuppa di pesce* (fish soup) served at this traditional trattoria in one of the fishing villages of the Cinque Terre. This soup is usually served as a first course, but is filling enough to be an entrée. The waiters are happy to advise you on the daily specials, which can include risotto *di frutti di mare* (with shellfish) and spaghetti with an octopus sauce. ✉ *Monterosso al Mare,* ☎ *0187/817401. AE, DC, MC, V. Closed Tues. and Oct. 15–Mar. 15.*

$$$ ▦ **Porto Roca.** In a panoramic position above the sea, Porta Roca is set ★ slightly apart, blessedly removed from the crowds who visit the village, especially on weekends. It has the look of a well-kept villa; its interiors have authentic antique pieces and there are ample terraces. The rooms are bright and airy, with sea breezes that visitors to the town below often miss, as well as air conditioning. Porto Roca is on a network of not-too-demanding hill walks and has a faithful U.S. clientele. ✉ *Via Corone 1,* ☎ *0187/817502,* FAX *0187/817692. 43 rooms with bath or shower. Restaurant, bar. AE, MC, V. Closed Nov. 4–Mar. 23.*

La Spezia

③⑧ *8 km (5 mi) north of Portovenere, 103 km (63 mi) southeast of Genoa, 144 km (89 mi) northwest of Florence.*

La Spezia is a large industrialized naval port on routes to the Cinque Terre and to Portovenere. La Spezia lacks the charm of the smaller towns, but it does have the remains of the massive 13th-century Castel San Giorgio.

Outdoor Activities and Sports

WATERSKIING

La Spezia Motorboat Club (✉ Via della Marina 224, ☎ 0187/50401) will put you on skis.

Portovenere

★ ㊴   *24 km (15 mi) east of Riomaggiore, 114 km (70 mi) southeast of Genoa.*

Portovenere's small colorful houses, some dating from the 12th century, were once all connected to the 12th- to 16th-century citadel, so that in times of attack the villagers could reach the safety of the battlements. The town has a strategic position at the end of a peninsula that extends southeast from the Cinque Terre and forms the western border of the Gulf of La Spezia. Lord Byron is said to have written *Childe Harold* here. The huge, strange grotto at the base of the sea-swept cliff is named after the poet, whose strength and courage were much admired after he swam across the gulf to the village of San Terenzo, near Lerici, to visit his friend Shelley. Above the grotto, on a formidable solid mass of rock, is San Pietro, a 13th-century Gothic church built on the site of an ancient pagan shrine. With its black-and-white-stripe exterior, it is a landmark recognizable from far out at sea.

Dining

$$ ✕ **Da Iseo.** Try to get one of the tables outside at this waterfront restaurant, which is decorated in the style of a bistro and has paintings of Portovenere on the walls. Seafood is the only choice: It's fresh and plentiful. Pasta courses are inventive; try spaghetti *alla Giuseppe* (with shellfish and fresh tomato) or spaghetti *alla Iseo* (with a seafood curry sauce). ✉ *Portovenere,* ☎ *0187/790610. AE, DC, MC, V. Closed Wed. and Jan.2–Feb.15*

$ ✕ **Antica Osteria del Carrugio.** Near the castle built to defend the coast from Pisan incursions, this is a 100-year-old tavern with maritime decor. The menu features seafood, which varies with the catch of the day. Specialties include trenette al pesto and focaccia. ✉ *Via Cappellini 66,* ☎ *0187/900617. Reservations not accepted. No credit cards. Closed Thurs., mid-Nov.–mid-Dec.*

$$$ ▥ **Royal Sporting.** Appearances are deceptive at this modern hotel,
★   which is on the beach about a 10-minute walk from the village. From the outside, the stone construction seems austere and unwelcoming, but the courtyards and interior are colorful and vibrant. There are fresh flowers and potted plants in the reception rooms and terraces, and the cool, airy rooms all have sea views. The sports facilities are among the best in the area. ✉ *Via dell'Olivo 345,* ☎ *0187/790326,* FAX *0187/529060. 62 rooms with bath. Restaurant, bar, pool, tennis court, beach. AE, DC, MC, V. Closed Oct. 15–Apr. (open Easter wk).*

$ ▥ **Locanda San Pietro.** This good-value inn occupies a castle at the edge of the village and is five minutes from the beach. The rooms, decorated in art-nouveau style, are quiet. Most have good views of the coastline around Portovenere. The restaurant features local cuisine and stresses seafood. ☎ *0187/900616. 31 rooms with bath or shower. Restaurant, bar. AE, MC. Closed Jan. 2–Mar. 14.*

Lerici

⑳ *11 km (7 mi) east of La Spezia, 65 km (40 mi) northeast of Pisa*

Lerici, which is near Liguria's border with Tuscany, is set on a magnificent coastline of gray cliffs and pine forests. The town once belonged to Tuscan Pisa, and the medieval castle that stands above the splendid bay, which has attracted lovers of nature for centuries, is 13th-century Pisan. Shelley was one of Lerici's best-known visitors and spent some of the happiest months of his life in the lovely white village of San Terenzo, 2 kilometers (1 mile) away. The Villa Magni, where he lived, has a collection devoted to him. After Shelley drowned at sea here in 1822, the bay was renamed Golfo dei Poeti, in honor of him and Byron.

LODGING

$$ ⚏ **Florida.** A seafront hotel, this family-run establishment has bright rooms with all the extras you would expect in a higher category: TV, fridge, bar, air-conditioning, soundproofing, and, best of all, a balcony with a sea view. For an even better view, loll in one of the deck chairs on the roof terrace. The Florida overlooks a small beach area and is close to tennis courts and a golf course. ✉ *Lungomare Biaggini 35,* ☎ *0187/967332,* FAX *0187/967344. 37 rooms with shower. AE, DC, MC, V. Closed Jan. 7–Mar. 15.*

ITALIAN RIVIERAS A TO Z

Arriving and Departing

By Boat

Genoa is Italy's largest port and can be reached from the United States as well as other parts of Liguria and Italy (Sardinia, La Spezia, and Savona). Ships berth in the heart of Genoa, including cruise ships of the Genoa-based **Costa Cruise Line** (✉ Via Gabriele D'Annunzio 2, ☎ 010/54831) and ferries to various ports around the Mediterranean, operated by **Tirrenia Navigazione** (✉ Stazione Marittima, ☎ 010/258041).

By Bus

Several bus lines, including STIE and PESCI, provide connections along the Ligurian coast and link Genoa with other parts of Italy, with the French Riviera, and with other cities in Europe. The main bus station is at Piazza Principe. Bus tickets, reservations, and information in Genoa are handled by these agencies: **PESCI** (✉ Piazza della Vittoria 94/r, Genoa, ☎ 010/564936), **Geotravels** (✉ Piazza della Vittoria 302/r, ☎ 010/587181), and **Guimar Tours** (✉ Via Balbi 192, ☎ 010/256337).

By Car

Autostrada A12 south from Genoa links up with the autostrada network for all southern destinations; Rome is a six-hour drive from Genoa. The 150-kilometer (90-mile) trip north to Milan on A7 takes two hours. Nice is 2½ hours west on A10.

By Plane

Cristoforo Colombo International Airport, at Sestri Ponente (☎ 010/2411), is only 6 kilometers (4 miles) from the center of Genoa. It has regular service to all main European cities. The nearest airports for U.S. flights are Nice, in France, about 2½ hours west of Genoa, and Milan, about 2 hours northeast. Volabus services (☎ 010/599–7414) from Cristoforo Colombo connect with Genoa's Brignole Station, stopping also at Piazza Acquaverde (Principe Station).

By Train

Frequent and fast train services connect Liguria with the rest of Italy. Genoa is 1½ hours from Milan and five hours from Rome. Many services from France (in particular, the French Riviera) pass along the Ligurian Coast on the way to all parts of Italy.

Getting Around

By Boat

This is the most pleasant (and, in some the cases, the only) way to get from place to place within Liguria. A busy network of local services connects many of the resorts. For general information about availability of services in Liguria, contact **Servizio Marittimo del Tigullio** (✉ Calata Zingari, Genoa, ☎ 010/265712) and **Alimar** (✉ Calata Zingari, Genoa, ☎ 010/255975). Or contact **Camogli–San Fruttuoso Maritime Services** (✉ Società Golfo Paradiso, Via Scalo 2, Camogli, ☎ 0185/772091), which runs between Camogli and San Fruttuoso (on the Portofino promontory), as well as between Recco and Punta Chiappa, two other towns close to Camogli. Summer excursions link both ports with the Cinque Terre and Portovenere.

By Bus

STIE and **PESCI** (☞ Arriving and Departing By Bus, *above*) buses run the length of the Ligurian Coast in both directions. Local buses serve the steep valleys that run to some of the towns along the western coast. Tickets may be bought at local bus stations, or at newsstands in the case of local buses. Buy your ticket before you board the bus.

By Car

Two good roads run parallel to each other along the coast of Liguria. Closer to shore and passing through all the towns and villages is S1, which has excellent views at almost every turn but which gets crowded in July and August. More direct and higher up than S1 is the autostrada, known as A10 west of Genoa and A12 to the east. This route saves a lot of time on weekends, in summer, and on days when festivals slow traffic in some resorts to a standstill.

By Train

Regular service, connecting all parts of Liguria, operates from Genoa's two stations, **Stazione Principe** (for points west) and **Stazione Brignole** (for the east). All the coastal resorts are on this line, and many international trains stop along the coast west of Genoa on their way from Paris to Milan or Rome.

Contacts and Resources

Car Rentals

Genoa. Avis (✉ Piazza Acquaverde, ☎ 010/255598, for reservations, ☎ 06/4780150); **Budget** (at the airport, ☎ 010/6503822); **Hertz** (✉ Via delle Casacce 3, ☎ 010/564412).

La Spezia. Avis (✉ Via Fratelli Rosselli 86/88, ☎ 0187/33345); **Hertz** (✉ Via Casaregis 76/r, ☎ 010/592101).

San Remo. Avis (✉ Corso Imperatrice 96, ☎ 0184/73897); **Hertz** (✉ Via XX Settembre 17, ☎ 0184/85618).

Emergencies

Police (☎ 113); Genoa municipal police (☎ 010/53631).

Ambulance (☎ 010/595951).

Doctors and Dentists

In case of an accident, call ☎ 113 or go to the public hospital in Genoa, **Ospedale Generale Regionale San Martino** (✉ Viale Benedetto XV, ☎ 010/516748).

Guided Tours

ORIENTATION

One of the joys of visiting even the tiniest of the Ligurian coastal resorts is the chance to take an informal **harbor cruise** or excursion to the next town along the coast. Some of these tours are scheduled and operated by the main ferry lines (☞ Getting Around by Boat, *above*), but you can have as much fun—if not more—negotiating a price with a boat owner at one of the smaller ports. You're likely to get someone whose English is rudimentary at best, but that shouldn't affect your appreciation of the rugged and colorful coastal scenery.

A three-hour **bus tour** of Genoa with an English-speaking guide is the best way to see the city and its panoramic upper reaches. A coach with multilingual guide aboard leaves every day at 9 AM from the **AMT** (municipal bus company) office at Piazza della Vittoria, stopping to pick up passengers at several points in the center of town; the last pick-up point is Piazza Acquaverde, at the Stazione Principe, at 9:25. Tickets (about 20,000 lire) can be purchased on the bus, but seats should be reserved at Cooptur Liguria (☎ 010/592658), or AMT (☎ 010/5997414). The tour includes an optional one-hour walking tour of the historic center and an optional 15-minute walk through the fishing enclave of Boccadasse.

You can also take a **boat tour** of the harbor in Genoa. The tour lasts about an hour and includes a visit to the breakwater outside the harbor, the Bacino delle Grazie, and the Molo Vecchio (Old Pier). You can see extensive views of the city throughout the tour. For information, contact the **Cooperativa Battellieri** (✉ Stazione Marittima, Ponte dei Mille, Genoa, ☎ 010/265712).

Late-Night Pharmacies

Europa (✉ Corso Europa 676, Genoa, ☎ 010/380239). **Ghersi** (✉ Corte Lambruschini [Tower A], Genoa, ☎ 010/541661).

Visitor Information

The main **APT** (tourist board) office for Genoa is in the center of town (✉ Via Roma 11, ☎ 010/541541, FAX 010/581408), just off Piazza De Ferrari. The helpful local tourist offices (☞ *below*) are known as **IAT.** There are two IAT information offices in Genoa: at Principe Station (☎ 010/2462633) and the airport (☎ 010/2415247). *APT office in Genoa* ☉ *Mon.–Fri. 8–1:30 and 2–5, Sat. 8–1:30; IAT Principe* ☉ *Mon.–Sat. 8 AM–8 PM; IAT Airport* ☉ *Mon.–Sat. 10–4:30.*

Alassio (✉ Palazzo Hanbury, Via Gibb 26, ☎ 0182/640346, FAX 0182/644690).

Albenga (✉ Via Martiri della Libertà, ☎ 0182/50475).

Bordighera (✉ Palazzo del Parco, ☎ 0184/262322, FAX 0184/264455).

Camogli (✉ Via XX Settembre 33r, ☎ 0185/771066).

Imperia (✉ Via Matteotti 54/a, ☎ 0183/24947, FAX 0183/24950).

La Spezia (✉ Via Mazzini 47, ☎ 0187/770900, FAX 0187/770908).

Lerici (✉ Via Gerini 40, ☎ 0187/967346).

Levanto (✉ Piazza Cavour 12, ☎ 0187/808125, FAX 0187/808125).

Rapallo (✉ Via A. Diaz 9, ☎ 0185/54573, FAX 0185/63051).

San Remo (✉ Corso Nuvoloni, ☎ 0184/571571, FAX 0184/507649).

Varazze (✉ Viale Nazioni Unite, ☎ 019/934609, FAX 019/97298).

Ventimiglia (✉ Via Cavour 61, ☎ 0184/351183).

8 Piedmont/Val d'Aosta

From Turin to the Alps and Across the Po Plain

Italy's windows on France and Switzerland, Piedmont and the magnificent Val d'Aosta come as delightful surprises even in a land of many natural splendors. Monte Bianco (Mont Blanc) and Monte Cervino (the Matterhorn) offer skiing at its best, while nearby Alpine valleys harbor storybook castles. Here, too, is the "Italian Detroit"—Turin, home of the Fiat empire, but also a gracious city with splendid piazzas and museums. The city's other well-known exports— Borsalino hats, vermouth, and Asti Spumante—mark it as a great cosmopolitan center.

Updated by
Barbara Walsh
Angelillo

FROM ALPINE VALLEYS hemming the highest mountains in Europe to the mist-shrouded lowlands skirting the Po River, from pulsating industrial centers turning out the best of Italian design to tiny stone villages isolated above the clouds, from hearty peasant cooking in farmhouse kitchens to French-flavored delicacies washed down by some of the finest wines in Italy, Piedmont and the spectacular Val d'Aosta offer the traveler a store of historical, cultural, and natural riches.

Piedmont's Italian Alps afford excellent skiing and climbing at renowned resort towns such as Courmayeur and Breuil-Cervinia. In the lowlands, Turin, the regional capital, is a historical center that today also serves as the heart of Italy's booming auto industry. Nearby are Alba, home of delectable Italian white truffles, seasonal delicacies that sell for more than $1,000 per pound; Asti, Barolo, and Barbaresco, the famous wine centers; and the modern business hubs Ivrea, Novara, and Alessandria.

Tucked away at the foot of the Pennine, Graian, Cottian, and Maritime Alps (the name Piemonte, in Italian, means "foot of the mountains"), Piedmont and the autonomous region of Val d'Aosta just north of it seem more akin to neighboring France and Switzerland. Well-dressed women in the elegant cafés of Turin are addressed more often as *madama* than *signora,* and French is often used in the more remote mountain hamlets.

Piedmont was originally inhabited by Celtic tribes who were absorbed by the Romans. As allies of Rome, the Celts held off Hannibal when he came down through the Alpine passes with his elephants but were eventually defeated, and their capital—Taurasia, the present Turin—was destroyed. The Romans rebuilt the city, giving its streets the grid pattern that survives today. Roman ruins can be found throughout both regions and are particularly conspicuous in the town of Aosta.

With the fall of the Roman empire, Piedmont suffered the fate of the rest of Italy and was successively occupied and ravaged by barbarians from the east and the north. In the 11th century, a feudal French family named Savoy ruled Turin briefly; toward the end of the 13th century they returned to the area, where they would remain, almost continuously, for 500 years. In 1798 the French Republican armies invaded Italy, but when Napoléon's empire fell, the House of Savoy returned to power.

Beginning in 1848, Piedmont was one of the principal centers of the Risorgimento, the movement for Italian unity. In 1861 the Chamber of Deputies of Turin declared Italy a united kingdom. Rome became the capital in 1870, marking the end of Piedmont's importance in the political sphere. Nevertheless, the architectural splendors of Turin, together with some unheralded but excellent museums, continue to draw travelers.

Piedmont became one of the first industrialized regions in Italy, and the automotive giant FIAT—the Fabbrica Italiana Automobili Torino—was established here in 1899. Today the region is the center of Italy's automobile, metalworking, chemical, and candy industries, having attracted thousands of workers from Italy's impoverished south.

The Val d'Aosta, to the north, is famous for its impressive fortified castles and splendid Alpine beauty. It was settled in the 3rd millennium BC by people from the Mediterranean and later by a Celtic tribe known as the Salassi, who eventually fell to the Romans. The Saracens were here in the 10th century; by the 12th century, the Savoy family had established itself, and the region's feudal nobles moved into the countryside, building the massive castles that still stand. Val d'Aosta enjoyed relative autonomy as part of the Savoy kingdom and was briefly ruled by the French four separate times. The region is still officially bilingual, speaking both Italian and French.

Pleasures and Pastimes

Dining

These two regions offer rustic specialties from farmhouse hearths and fine cuisine with a French accent—and everything in between. The favorite form of pasta is *agnolotti* (similar to ravioli), filled with meat, spinach, or cheese. Another regional specialty is *fonduta*—a local form of fondue, made with melted Fontina (a cheese from the Val d'Aosta), eggs, and sometimes grated truffles. Alba is the home of *tartufi bianchi* (white truffles), much rarer and more expensive than black ones and considered the tastiest by connoisseurs. They sell for at least $1,000 a pound wholesale. Another local dish is *bagna cauda,* a hot sauce (*bagna cauda* means hot bath) made from butter, oil, anchovies, cream, and shredded garlic. It is served with *cardi* (edible thistles) or other raw vegetables.

Turin is also known for delicate pastries and fine chocolates, especially for gianduiotti. Val d'Aosta is famous for a variety of schnappslike brandies made from fruits or herbs.

Piedmont is one of Italy's most important wine-producing regions. Most of the wines are full-bodied reds, such as Barolo, Nebbiolo, Freisa, Barbera, and Barbaresco. Asti Spumante, a sparkling wine, comes from the region, as does vermouth, which was developed in Piedmont by A. B. Carpano in 1786.

CATEGORY	COST*
$$$$	over 85,000 lire
$$$	60,000–85,000 lire
$$	35,000–60,000 lire
$	under 35,000 lire

per person, including house wine, service, and tax.

Lodging

There is a high standard of Old World opulence in Turin's better hotels, and it is translated into the Alpine idiom in the top resort hotels in the mountains. Less expensive hotels in cities and towns are generally geared to business travelers. You can usually count on a measure of charm at resorts and the Italian version of gemütlichkeit even in more modest hotels. Summer and winter occupancy rates and prices are usually quite high at resorts, with summer vacationers and skiers, respectively, monopolizing available accommodations. Hotels in mountain resorts may offer attractive half-board or off-season rates that can sometimes reduce the cost by a full price category. Many mountain resort hotels cater primarily to half- or full-board guests only, for stays of at least a week. It's better to take a package deal on a ski vacation; it may give you a break on the price of lift tickets.

CATEGORY	COST*
$$$$	over 300,000 lire
$$$	200,000–300,000 lire
$$	125,000–200,000 lire
$	under 125,000 lire

All prices are for a standard double room for two, including service and 9% tax (13% for luxury establishments).

Skiing

This is the major sport in both Piedmont and the Val d'Aosta. Resorts with excellent facilities abound near the highest mountains in Europe—Monte Bianco (Mont Blanc), Monte Rosa, Monte Cervino (the Matterhorn), and the Gran Paradiso.

BREUIL-CERVINIA

Because its slopes border the Cervino glacier, this resort at the foot of the Matterhorn offers year-round skiing.

CLAVIERE

A quaint village with slate-roof houses, Claviere is one of Italy's oldest ski resorts. Its slopes overlap with those of the French resort of Montgenevre.

COURMAYEUR

This famous spot for the well-heeled is well equipped and easy to reach, just outside the Italian end of the Mont Blanc tunnel. The skiing around Mont Blanc is particularly good, and the off-piste options are among the best in Europe.

SESTRIERE

At 6,670 feet, this resort was built in the late 1920s under the auspices of Turin's Agnelli clan. Although near the French border, it is just 50 kilometers (30 miles) west of Turin. The slopes get good snow from November until May.

Exploring Piedmont/Val d'Aosta

The vast Po Plain that stretches eastward in a wide swathe across the top of the Italian peninsula begins in Piedmont, where the River Po has its source in the Coolidge Glacier on 1,200-feet-high Monviso. But Piedmont is primarily a mountainous region. High Alpine crests rise to the north and west of the plain. The Maritime Alps lie to the south, and the rolling hills of the Monferrato and Langhe districts make folds in the landscape southeast of Turin. Nature has endowed Piedmont and the Val d'Aosta with some striking scenery. The itineraries below take you along rushing streams and into the highest reaches of the mountains, as well as through cities that have borne the imprint of humans for millennia.

Great Itineraries

With the exception of the mountain resorts, which may be packed at the height of the season, much of Piedmont and Val d'Aosta is off the beaten track for tourists. This part of Italy offers the pleasures of discovery: uncrowded, unhurried samplings of scenery, art, food, and some of Italy's finest wines.

We have divided the region into three distinct areas. The first is Turin, the regional capital and the area's largest city, and its environs, easily reached by car or public transportation from the city center. Don't be put off by Turin's industrial reputation; sure, it is the capital and headquarters of one of the world's major car manufacturers, but it is also home to beautiful churches, elegant piazzas, and interesting museums. Next, as you wind your way northeast into the Val d'Aosta, you are in the Italian Loire, where solid, imposing castles sit in the shadow of Europe's most impressive peaks, Mont Blanc and the Matterhorn. The ancient Roman city of Aosta itself is of great interest to the visitor. One of Italy's most popular winter playgrounds, it offers world-class skiing and accommodations. The third area of interest is the fertile Po Valley and its fortified cities, especially Asti, world-famous for its wine.

The amount of time you choose to spend here depends on your interests. If you want to admire the highest mountains in the Alps from the pistes or the deck of a chalet, sneak up on the chamoix in the Gran Paradiso National Park, and still have time to devote to Turin and the wine country, a total of nine days should be sufficient. Five days would give you a chance to visit Turin's attractions, make an excursion into the mountains, and discover some of the smaller cities. In three days you can see Turin and then head to Aosta for a look at some impressive Roman ruins and a quick trip into the mountains. If you budget your time carefully, you can spend half a day in Asti.

Numbers in the text correspond to numbers in the margin and on the Piedmont/Val d'Aosta and Turin maps.

IF YOU HAVE 3 DAYS

Visitors with limited time should concentrate first on ⚏ **Turin** ①–⑯ and its main sites, including the **Duomo** ②, where the famous shroud is housed; the 17th-century **Palazzo Reale** ③, former residence of the Savoy royal family; and the churches of **San Carlo** ⑥ and **Santa Cristina** ⑦, which flank the impressive **Piazza San Carlo** ⑧, considered by many to be Italy's finest square. Take time to enjoy one or more of the city's authentic Old World cafés and the view from the striking **Mole Antonelliana** ⑪, an odd structure that was once the world's tallest building. On the second day, head northeast along the A5 motorway to **Aosta** ㉖ to see its large and well-preserved Roman ruins before continuing on to ⚏ **Courmayeur** ㉗ for magnificent views of the **Monte Bianco** ㉘. You have several choices for the third day: You can stay in the mountains, heading for ⚏ **Breuil-Cervinia** ㉔ for a look at the Matterhorn, or you can double back from Aosta to ⚏ **Cogne** ㉙, where you can make a foray into the Gran Paradiso National Park. Another alternative is return to Turin and head southeast into the vineyard-blanketed hills around medieval **Asti** ㉚.

IF YOU HAVE 5 DAYS

Spend two days in ⚏ **Turin** ①–⑯, then head for the Roman city of **Aosta** ㉖, perhaps stopping on the way to see the fairy-tale castle of **Fénis** ㉕. On the third day, you can drink in the views of the **Monte Bianco** ㉘ from **Courmayeur** ㉗, see the Matterhorn from **Breuil-Cervinia** ㉔, or follow the trails from **Cogne** ㉙ into the Gran Paradiso National Park. On the fourth day double back to Turin and make an excursion to **Saluzzo** ㉒, an old town steeped in 15th-century atmosphere. On the fifth day continue southeast to **Asti** ㉚, exploring the rolling hills where great wines and good food make this a gourmet's paradise.

IF YOU HAVE 9 DAYS

Make ⚏ **Turin** ①–⑯ your base for three days, from which you can explore the city and the outlying towns, including **Saluzzo** ㉒, with its picturesque hilltop center and castles. Another excursion from Turin takes you to the castle at **Rivoli** ⑱, a sanctuary of contemporary art, and then over a pilgrim's route to two medieval abbeys, **Sant'Antonio di Ranverso** ⑲ and the **Sacra di San Michele** ㉑. Travel westward to Piedmont's high mountains and see the resorts of **Sestriere** and ⚏ **Bardonecchia,** close to the French border. On the fourth day head for the mountains of the Val d'Aosta; visit the castle at **Fénis** ㉕ on the way to ⚏ **Aosta** ㉖, which is a good base for excursions into the mountains that will keep you moving on the fifth and sixth days between **Courmayeur** ㉗, **Breuil-Cervinia** ㉔, and **Cogne** ㉙. Head south on the seventh day, doubling back to Turin and continuing southeast to **Asti** ㉚, a wine-growing center of international renown. Follow the provincial roads through the vineyards of the hilly Monferrato and Langhe districts of south-central Piedmont, delving into their culinary and enological delights. On the ninth day head east across the fertile Po Plain toward the rice-growing capital of **Vercelli** ㉜, making sure to take in the Duomo, the final resting place of several Savoy rulers, and the 13th-century Basilica di Sant'Andrea, an early example of Italian gothic architecture. The easternmost city of Piedmont is **Novara** ㉝, which is of little interest to the visitor except as a rest stop on the way to Milan, only 32 kilometers (20 miles) away.

When to Tour Piedmont/Val d'Aosta

Unless you are dead set on skiing, the region can be visited in either summer or winter. In winter, road conditions can be treacherous, especially higher up in the mountains, requiring the use of snow tires or chains. The ski resorts of the Val d'Aosta are popular with Italians and non-Italians alike, so book your accommodations in advance. If you intend to visit the region in summer, try to avoid the month of August, which is the holiday month for the vast majority of Italians, many of whom will come here for an Alpine holiday of walking, hiking, and relaxation.

TURIN AND ENVIRONS

❶ *176 km (105 mi) northwest of Genoa, 97 km (59 mi) southeast of Milan.*

Turin—in Italian, Torino—is roughly in the center of Piedmont/Val d'Aosta; it is on the Po River, on the edge of the Po plain that stretches eastward all the way to the Adriatic. Apart from its role as northwest Italy's major industrial, cultural, and administrative hub, Turin is a center of education, science, and the arts. It also has a reputation as Italy's capital of black magic and the supernatural. This distinction is enhanced by the presence of Turin's most controversial, fascinating, and unsettling relic, the Sacra Sindone (Holy Shroud), still believed by many Catholics to be the cloth in which Christ's body was wrapped when He was taken down from the cross.

Many of Turin's major sights are clustered around Piazza Castello, and others are on or just off the porticoed Via Roma, one of the city's main thoroughfares, which leads 1 kilometer (½ mile) from Piazza Castello south to Piazza Carlo Felice, a landscaped park with a fountain in front of the train station. First opened in 1615, Via Roma was largely rebuilt in the 1930s, during the time of Premier Benito Mussolini. From Piazza Carignano take the little road behind the palazzo to Via Po, turn right and take the fourth left (Via Montebello) to the Mole Antonelliana. Via Po leads to the large Piazza Vittorio Veneto, which slopes down to the Po River and the Ponte Vittorio Emanuele, the bridge leading to the church of Gran Madre di Dio. To reach the church of Santa Maria del Monte, follow Corso Moncalieri to the top of the hill. Then return to Corso Moncalieri and cross the next bridge downstream, Ponte Umberto I, to the Parco del Valentino.

❷ The most impressive feature of Turin's 15th-century **Duomo,** in the heart of town on Piazza San Giovanni, adjacent to the Royal Palace, is the shadowy, black marble–walled **Cappella della Sacra Sindone (Chapel of the Holy Shroud),** where the Holy Shroud is housed. The chapel was designed by the priest and architect Guarino Guarini (1604–83), a genius of the Baroque style who was official engineer and mathematician to the court of Duke Carlo Emanuele II of Savoy.

The **shroud** is a four-yard-long sheet of linen, unremarkable except for the fact that it contains an imprint of what the faithful claim is an image of the crucified Christ. It first made an appearance around the middle of the 15th century, when it was presented to Ludovico of Savoy in

Chambéry. In 1578 it was brought to Turin by another member of the Savoy royal family, Duke Emanuele Filiberto. It is only in the last few years that the Church has allowed rigorous scientific study of the shroud. The results have been double-edged. On the one hand, three separate university teams—in Italy, Britain, and the United States—have concluded, as a result of Carbon 14 dating, that the cloth is a forgery dating from between 1260 and 1390. On the other hand, they are unable to explain how the shroud's image, which is like a photographic negative, could have been created, and the shroud continues to be revered as a holy relic. While the Chapel remains closed for restorations, the urn containing the shroud is on the main altar of the cathedral.

❸ The 17th-century **Palazzo Reale** (Royal Palace) is the former Savoy royal residence. It is an imposing work of brick, stone, and marble that stands on the site of Turin's ancient Roman city gates. In contrast to its austere exterior, the palace's interior is characterized by luxurious, mostly Rococo, decor, including tapestries, gilded ceilings, and sumptuous 17th- to 19th-century furniture. ☎ *011/436–1455.* ☞ *8,000 lire.* ☉ *Tues.–Sun. 9–9.*

The **Armeria Reale (Royal Armory),** in a wing of the Royal Palace, holds one of Europe's most stunning collections of arms and armor. It is a must-see for connoisseurs. ✉ *Entrance on Piazza Castello,* ☎ *011/543889.* ☞ *8,000 lire.* ☉ *Tues. and Thurs. 2:30–7:30, Wed., Fri. (for groups only), and weekends 9–2.*

❹ **Palazzo Madama** occupies the center of Piazza Castello. It was named for the French queen Maria Cristina, who made it her home in the 17th century. The castle incorporates the remains of a Roman gate, as well as medieval and Renaissance additions. The architect Filippo Juvarra (1678–1736) designed the castle's elaborate Baroque facade in the early 18th century: He was intent on dispelling the idea that Italy's importance as a producer of contemporary art and architecture was in decline. Juvarra's bold use of the Baroque is also evident in the interior of the castle, where the huge marble staircase heralds his patron's wealth and prestige. The large assembly hall was the scene of the first Italian Senate meetings in the mid-19th century. Today the castle houses the **Museo Civico d'Arte Antica (Civic Museum of Ancient Art),** which has a rich collection of Gothic, Renaissance, and Rococo sculpture and paintings, as well as medieval illuminated manuscripts. This museum has been closed for some time for extensive restorations.

❺ The cupola and vividly painted interior of the church of **San Lorenzo** are standouts. Guarino Guarini was in his mid-60s when he began work on the church in 1668, but the sprightly collection of domes, columns, and florid Baroque features seems more the work of a younger architect cutting his teeth with a daring display of mathematical invention.

NEED A
BREAK?
Baratti e Milano, just to the east of Piazza Castello in the glass-roofed gallery between Via Lagrange and Via Po, is one of Turin's charming Old World cafés. It's famous for its chocolates, so you can indulge your sweet tooth here or buy some *gianduiotti* (hazelnut-flavored chocolates) or candied chestnuts to take home to friends.

❻
❼ The church of **San Carlo,** with its ornate Baroque facade, flanks the entrance to the southern end of Piazza San Carlo. The church of **Santa Cristina** is on the southeastern corner of Piazza San Carlo, opposite the church of San Carlo.

❽ **Piazza San Carlo,** a stately, formal expanse, is considered by many to be the grandest square in Italy. In the center stands a statue of Duke

Piedmont/Val d'Aosta

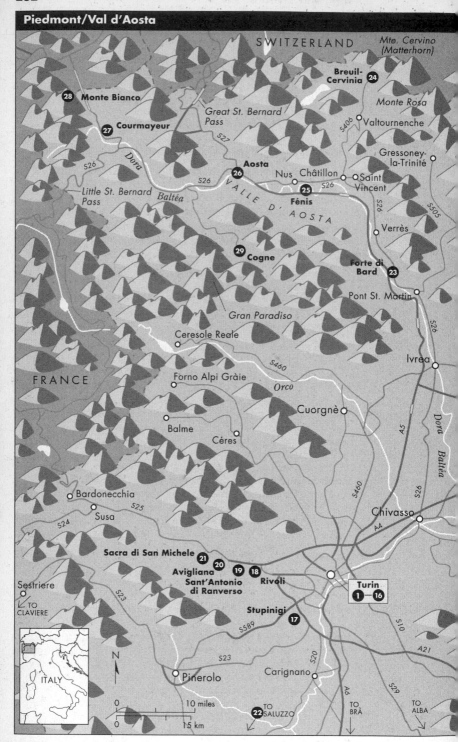

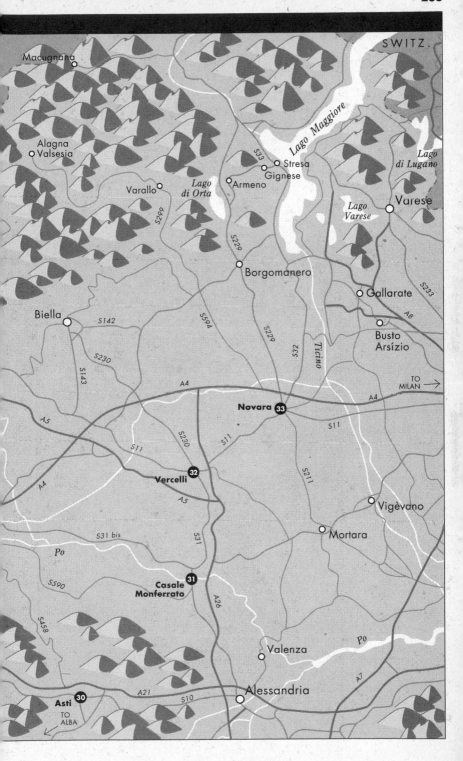

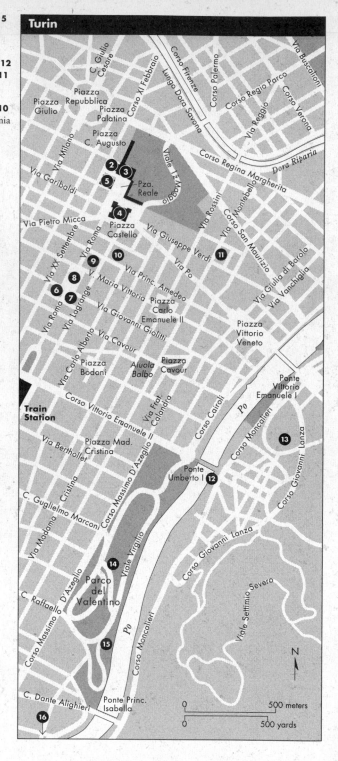

Turin

Emanuele Filiberto of Savoy, victor, in 1557, of the battle of San Quintino, which heralded the peaceful resurgence of Turin under the Savoys, after years of bloody dynastic fighting. The fine bronze statue, erected in the 19th century, is one of Turin's symbols.

NEED A
BREAK?

Café San Carlo, under the arcades running alongside the square, is another historic coffeehouse where locals love to stop for coffee and pastry at tiny marble-top tables under the huge crystal chandelier. On the opposite side of the square is **Stratta,** one of Turin's best-known chocolate shops.

9 Guarini's **Palazzo dell'Accademia delle Scienze** (Palace of the Academy of Sciences), a large Baroque building prefiguring the 18th century's preoccupation with logic and science, houses two of Turin's most famous museums, the Museo Egizio and the Galleria Sabauda.

The **Museo Egizio (Egyptian Museum)** is considered by many to be one of the finest outside Cairo. Its superb collection includes statues of pharaohs and mummies, and entire frescoes taken from royal tombs. Equally fascinating are the papyrus, art objects, and day-to-day utensils taken from the tombs of less noble ancient Egyptians. Look for the papyrus *Book of the Dead* and the 13th-century BC statue of Ramses II, which still glistens in its original colors. ⊠ *Via Accademia delle Scienze 6,* ☎ *011/5617776.* ⊠ *12,000 lire.* ☉ *Tues.–Sat. 9–7, Sun. 9–2.*

The **Galleria Sabauda** houses the collections of the house of Savoy. It is particularly rich in 16th- and 17th-century Dutch and Flemish paintings: Note Jan Van Eyck's *St. Francis with Stigmata,* with the saint receiving the marks of Christ's wounds while a companion cringes beside him as if feeling it all himself. Other Dutch masterpieces include paintings by Anthony Van Dyck and Rembrandt. Piero del Pollaiuolo's *Tobias and the Angel* is showcased, and other Italian artists featured include Fra Angelico, Andrea Mantegna, and Paolo Veronese. ⊠ *Via Accademia delle Scienze 6,* ☎ *011/547440.* ⊠ *8,000 lire.* ☉ *Tues.–Sun. 9–2.*

10 Another of Guarini's Baroque triumphs, the redbrick **Palazzo Carignano** was built from 1679 to 1685 and is one of Turin's and Italy's most historic buildings. Kings of Savoy, Carlo Alberto (1798–1849) and Vittorio Emanuele II (1820–78), were born within its walls; Italy's first parliament met here from 1860 to 1865. ⊠ *Piazza Carignano.*

★ **11** The striking **Mole Antonelliana** is a Turin landmark. Its unusual square dome and thin, elaborate spire tower above the city's rooftops. This odd structure, built between 1863 and 1897, was originally intended to be a synagogue, but costs escalated and eventually it was bought by the city of Turin. In its time it was the tallest building in the world. There is an excellent view of the city, the plain surrounding it, and the Alps beyond from a terrace at the top of the dome. Take the elevator to the top. ⊠ *Via Montebello 20,* ☎ *011/817–0496.* ⊠ *5,000 lire.* ☉ *Tues.–Fri. 10–4, weekends 9–7.*

12 The 19th-century church of **Gran Madre di Dio** (Great Mother of God), built in a neoclassical style based on the Pantheon in Rome, stands on the right bank of the Po, west of Piazza Castello.

13 On top of 150-foot Monte dei Cappuccini are the church and convent of **Santa Maria del Monte,** which date from 1583. Don't be surprised if you find yourself in the middle of a wedding party: Local couples often come here to have their pictures taken.

14 The **Castello del Valentino** stands on the left bank of the Po, in the pretty **Parco del Valentino,** laid out in 1856. The design of this 17th-century castle, built more for appearance than for defense, is based on models of 16th-century French châteaux. The interior is particularly elaborate, with frescoed walls and rich decoration, but the real attraction of the castle is its riverside setting amid the greenery of the park. The castle is closed for restoration.

⑮ The **Borgo Medioevale** (Medieval Village) is a forerunner of today's theme parks. The village, a faithful reproduction of medieval Piedmontese buildings, was created for the Turin Exposition of 1884. A visit here is like stepping back into the Middle Ages, with craftsmen's shops, houses, churches, and stores clustered along narrow streets and lanes. ⊠ *By the riverside at the southern edge of the Parco del Valentino,* ⊡ *Free.* ⊙ *Daily 8–8.*

No visit to car-manufacturing Turin would be complete without a pil-
⑯ grimage to the **Museo dell'Automobile** (Car Museum), with its perfectly conserved Bugattis, Ferraris, and Isotta Fraschinis. Here you'll get an idea of the importance of FIAT—and automobiles in general—to Turin's economy. There's a collection of antique cars dating from 1893, and displays show how the city has changed over the years as a result of its premier industry. ⊠ *Corso Unità d'Italia 40,* ☎ *011/677666.* ⊡ *9,000 lire.* ⊙ *Tues.–Sun. 10–6:30.*

Dining and Lodging

$$$$ ✕ **Vecchia Lanterna.** Sumptuously decorated with brocades, old paintings, and rich carpets, this elegant, intimate restaurant in the center of town serves classic food, made from antique regional recipes. For a first course, try *savarin di riso al Dogaressa* (a rice dish made with seafood). For a second course, *filetto di branzino al Barolo* is a surprising combination of fish and full-bodied red wine. A set menu of local fare is offered at a special price. ⊠ *Corso Re Umberto 21,* ☎ *011/537047. Reservations essential. Jacket and tie. AE, DC, MC, V. Closed Sun. and Aug. No lunch Sat.*

$$$–$$$$ ✕ **Cambio.** It's hard to match the setting and atmosphere of this restau-
★ rant in the heart of Turin, set in a palace that dates from 1757. It is probably one of the most beautiful and historic restaurants in Europe, with decorative moldings and mirrors and hanging lamps that look just as they did when Italian national hero Cavour dined here more than a century ago. The cuisine draws heavily on Piedmontese tradition and is served with a wide choice of fine Piedmontese wines. Recommended are pastas, such as the agnolotti in an *arrosto* (roast veal) sauce, and other traditional dishes, such as veal carbonada. ⊠ *Piazza Carignano 2,* ☎ *011/546690. Reservations essential. Jacket and tie. AE, DC, MC, V. Closed Sun. and Aug.*

$$$ ✕ **Due Lampioni.** Join the stylish clientele of this elegant Baroque-style restaurant in a 17th-century palace in the heart of the city. It serves fine classic cuisine and an excellent selection of French and Italian wines. Try the artichoke flan *Vecchio Piemonte* (with meat sauce) and *agnello ai funghi con marsala* (boned leg of lamb with mushrooms in a Marsala wine sauce). ⊠ *Via Carlo Alberto 45,* ☎ *011/8179380. Jacket and tie. AE, DC, MC, V. Closed Sun. and Aug.*

$$$ ✕ **La Smarrita.** Intimate and elegant, this restaurant is widely recog-
★ nized by critics as one of Turin's best. It is on the fringes of the Lingotto neighborhood, a short taxi ride from the city center. Host Moreno Grossi's light, innovative versions of Mediterranean dishes are very different from the usual Piedmontese fare. Try *tortelli di borragine* (fresh pasta filled with borage and served with fresh tomato sauce), or sea bass with artichokes, potatoes, and olives. And for dessert try the *gianduia* (chocolate) mousse. The wine cellar is excellent. ⊠ *Corso*

Unione Sovietica 244, ☎ *011/3179657. Reservations essential. Jacket and tie. AE, DC, MC, V. Closed Mon. and Aug.*

$$–$$$ ✕ **Taverna delle Rose.** The cooking of the Piedmont and Veneto regions, with some creative touches, dominates in this character-filled restaurant near the train station. One dining room has walls covered with paintings; the other is done in old bricks and candlelight. Specialties include faraona farcita *di carciofi* (stuffed with artichokes) and roast venison with raspberry sauce. From the Veneto comes *bigoli con ragù d'anatra* (whole-wheat pasta with duck sauce). ⊠ *Via Massena 24,* ☎ *011/538345. AE, DC, MC, V. Closed Sun. and Aug. No lunch Sat.*

$$ ✕ **Da Mauro.** Try the Tuscan dishes in this lively, popular family-run trattoria. Specialties include cannelloni alla Mirella (baked with mozzarella cheese, prosciutto, and tomato), *involtini di Gorganzola* (veal rolls with Gorgonzola cheese and a sauce of peppers and olives), and famous Florentine grilled beef. ⊠ *Via Maria Vittoria 21,* ☎ *011/8170604. Reservations not accepted. No credit cards. Closed Mon. and July.*

$$ ✕ **Ostu Bacu.** You'll find this small wood-paneled restaurant, in the same family for three generations, on the edge of town near the autostrada that goes to Milan. It specializes in regional Piedmontese dishes, such as agnolotti and *fritto misto di carne* (a typical Piedmontese specialty of fried mixed meats, vegetables, and sweet morsels). ⊠ *Corso Vercelli 226,* ☎ *011/2464579. AE, DC, MC, V. Closed Sun. and Aug.*

$$ ✕ **Tre Galline.** Only a few blocks northwest of Piazza Castello, this recently renovated trattoria has a long history of serving good Piedmontese cooking. The *insalata di gallina* (chicken salad) has the tang of mustard, and the *stinco di vitello* (veal shin) is redolent of thyme. ⊠ *Via Bellezia 37,* ☎ *011/4366553. AE, DC, MC, V. Closed Sun. No lunch Mon.*

$–$$ ✕ **Porto di Savona.** You have to look for this centuries-old tavern under the arcades of vast Piazza Vittorio Veneto, where it served as a terminal for the Turin-Savona stagecoach line. The small street-level and upstairs dining rooms have a decidedly old-fashioned air; the marble stairs are well-worn and period photos of Old Turin grace the walls. Customers sit at long wooden tables to eat home-style Piedmontese cooking, including gnocchi with a Gorgonzola cheese made by the owner and braised. The Barbera house wine is good. There are outdoor tables under the arcades. ⊠ *Piazza Vittorio Veneto 2,* ☎ *011/8173500. No credit cards. Closed Mon. and 2 weeks July–Aug. No lunch Tues.*

$$$$ ▥ **Principi di Piemonte.** The Principi is one of the best hotels in town, with over a half-century of experience. The rooms, elegantly furnished in antique style, are spacious and light, with high ceilings. It's conveniently located and popular with famous guests. ⊠ *Via Gobetti 15,* ☎ *011/562–9693,* ℻ *011/562–0270. 107 rooms with bath. Restaurant, bar. AE, DC, MC, V.*

$$$$ ▥ **Turin Palace.** You're right across from the train station at this century-old building in the center of town. Quiet, spacious, and well-furnished rooms have high ceilings and feature either leather-and-wood classic modern style or Imperial Louis XV furnishings. It's the classiest in town. ⊠ *Via Sacchi 8,* ☎ *011/562–5511,* ℻ *011/5612187. 123 rooms with bath. Restaurant, bar. AE, DC, MC, V.*

$$$ ▥ **Victoria.** Uncommon style and comfort are the hallmarks of this bou-
★ tique hotel, personally decorated and supervised by the caring management to create the atmosphere of a refined town house. The newer wing has a grand marble staircase and rooms individually decorated according to a theme, from romantic to clubby. The same attention to detail is given to the older rooms and to the attractive sitting room and break-

fast room overlooking a small park. ⊠ *Via Nino Costa 4,* ☎ *011/561–1909,* ℻ *011/5611806. 90 rooms with bath. Bar. AE, DC, MC, V.*

$$ 🏨 **Genio.** This 121-year-old building in the center of town has been decorated in a smart, modern style. The rooms are large and bright, with big, comfortable beds. There's no restaurant, but plenty are within easy walking distance. ⊠ *Corso Vittorio Emanuele 47,* ☎ *011/650–5771,* ℻ *011/6508264. 90 rooms with bath. Bar. AE, DC, MC, V.*

$$ 🏨 **Liberty.** Liberty is the Italian term for the Art Nouveau style, and this small, conveniently located hotel maintains that style in turn-of-the-century furnishings and an Old World atmosphere, enhanced by the Anfossi family's attentive courtesy. The hotel is a favorite of academics, artists, and others who appreciate its solid, old-fashioned comfort. ⊠ *Via Pietro Micca 15,* ☎ *011/5628801,* ℻ *011/5628163. 34 rooms with bath. AE, DC, MC, V.*

Nightlife and the Arts

A plush after-hours venue for Turin's smart set, **Hennessy** (⊠ Strada Traforo del Pino 23, ☎ 011/899–8522; closed Mon.) is in the upscale Superga residential district. The aptly named **Big Club** (⊠ Corso Brescia 28, ☎ 011/248–5656; closed Mon.) is a large disco that also hosts rock concerts. Hot Latin music, often live, is dished up with gusto for Turin's aficionados at **Sabor Latino** (⊠ Via Stradella 10, ☎ 011/852327; closed Mon.). **Pick Up** (⊠ Via Barge 8, ☎ 011/447–2204; closed Mon.) caters to a mixed crowd of young Turinese, university students, and visitors.

The **Teatro Regio** (☎ 011/8815241, ℻ 011/8815214), one of Italy's leading opera houses, begins its season in December. You can buy tickets for most performances (premieres are sold out well in advance) at the box office.

Classical music concerts are held in the famous **Conservatorio Giuseppe Verdi** (⊠ Via Mazzini 11) throughout the year, but mainly in the winter months. The September music festival also highlights classical music. Sacred music and some modern religious pieces are performed in the **Duomo** on Sunday evening; these are usually advertised in the vestibule or in the local edition of Turin's nationally distributed daily, *La Stampa.*

Outdoor Activities and Sports

BOATING

Turin makes good use of the Po's recreational potential for boating. The **Lega Navale di Torino** (⊠ Turin Boating League; Corso Unione Sovietica 316, ☎ 011/530979) organizes courses and special races throughout the summer.

GOLF

There are several courses in the Turin area. Three 18-hole courses are northwest of the city, one at **La Mandria,** 18 kilometers (11 miles) northwest (☎ 011/9235719), and two at **Fiano Torinese,** 20 kilometers (12 miles) northwest (☎ 011/9235440).

SOCCER

Turin's two professional soccer clubs, **Juventus** and **Torino,** play their games in the **Stadio delle Alpi,** a new stadium that was used during the World Cup of 1990. Juventus is Italy's most successful club (it is the holder of Europe's most prestigious cup, the Champions' Cup), and there is fierce rivalry between its supporters and those of visiting clubs. Home matches are usually played on Sunday afternoons during the season, which runs from late August to mid-May. The tourist office (☞ Piedmont/Val d'Aosta A to Z, *below*) can provide information on where to find tickets, which are difficult to come by.

Shopping

Piazza San Carlo, Via Po, and Via Maria Vittoria are lined with antiques shops, some—but not all—specializing in 18th-century furniture and domestic items.

BOUTIQUES

Most people know that Turin produces more than 75% of Italy's cars, but they don't realize that it is also a clothing manufacturing city. Top-quality boutiques stocking local, national, and international lines are clustered along Via Roma and Via Garibaldi.

FOOD AND FLEA MARKETS

Go to the famous **Balon Flea Market** (✉ Piazza Repubblica) on a Saturday morning for some excellent bargains in secondhand books and clothing and some stalls selling local specialties such as gianduiotti.

Stupinigi

⑰ *8 km (5 mi) southwest of Turin; bus 41 from Porta Nuova Station.*

The **Palazzina di Caccia** in the town of **Stupinigi** is an elaborate building was built by Juvarra in 1729 as a hunting lodge for the House of Savoy. It is more like a royal villa, with its many wings, landscaped gardens, and surrounding forests. This regal aspect was not lost on Napoléon, who lived here before claiming the crown of Italy. The castle interior is sumptuously decorated and today houses a collection of art and furniture in the appropriately named **Museo d'Arte e Ammobiliamento.** ☎ *011/358–1220.* ✆ *10,000 lire.* ☉ *Tues.–Sun. 9–11:50 and 2–4:20.*

Rivoli

⑱ *13 km (8 mi) east of Turin; Tram 1 from downtown Turin, then Bus 36.*

The Savoy court was based in **Rivoli** in the Middle Ages. The 14th- to 15th-century Casa del Conte Verde, right in the center of town, is a good example of medieval architecture of the transitional period, when its defensive function was giving way to the decorative.

The 18th-century Savoy castle, built in the Baroque style under the direction of Juvarra, now houses the **Museo d'Arte Moderna** (Modern Art Museum), which contains many examples of 20th-century Italian art. The Futurist movement is particularly well represented. ☎ *011/958–1547.* ✆ *10,000 lire.* ☉ *Tues.–Fri. 10–5, weekends 10–7, 1st and 3rd Thurs. of month 10–10.*

The Abbey of Sant'Antonio di Ranverso

⑲ *10 km (6 mi) west of Rivoli.*

The abbey of **Sant'Antonio di Ranverso** was originally an abbey hospital, founded in the 12th century by the Hospitalers of St. Anthony to care for victims of St. Anthony's Fire, a crippling disease contracted by eating contaminated grains. Pilgrims came here over the centuries for cures or, sometimes, to offer thanks for a miraculous recovery. The 15th-century fresco decorations, with their lifelike depictions of pilgrims and saints, retain the color of the originals. ☎ *011/936–7450.* ✆ *Donation requested.* ☉ *Tues.–Sun. 9–12:30, 2–5.*

Avigliana

② *6 km (4 mi) west of the Abbey of Sant'Antonio di Ranverso.*

The medieval town of **Avigliana** has an attractive lakeside setting. It was a favorite of the Savoys up until the mid-15th century, and medieval houses still line the twisting and narrow streets. **Casa della Porta Ferrata,** on the street of the same name, is a well-preserved example of Piedmont Gothic domestic architecture: Notice how the fascination with narrow pointed arches is carried through even to private houses.

Outdoor Activities and Sports

GOLF

Avigliana has a well-laid-out 18-hole golf course, **Le Fronde** (☎ 011/935083; closed Jan.–Feb.)

Sacra di San Michele

★ **②** *14 km (8.6 mi) west of Avigliana.*

A car is essential for an excursion to the **Sacra di San Michele** (Abbey of St. Michael). San Michele was built on Monte Pirchiriano in the 11th century to stand out: It is the most prominent location for miles around. When monks came to enlarge the abbey, they had to build part of the structure on supports more than 90 feet high—an engineering feat that was famous in medieval Europe. By the 12th century, this important abbey controlled 176 churches in Italy, France, and Spain, and one of the abbeys under its influence was Mont St-Michel in France. Because of the abbey's strategic position, it came under numerous attacks over the next five centuries, and it was eventually abandoned in 1622. It was restored in the late 19th and early 20th centuries.

From Porta dello Zodiaco, a splendid Romanesque doorway decorated with the signs of the zodiac, you climb 150 steps, past 12th-century sculptures, to reach the church. The interior has 16th-century frescoes on the walls: On the left are religious subjects representing New Testament themes, while on the right are stories depicting the founding of the church. Go down to the crypt to see the 9th- to 12th-century chapels. ✆ *Donation requested.* ☉ *Apr.–Sept., daily 9–noon and 3–7; Oct.–Mar., daily 9–noon and 2–dusk.*

Saluzzo

② *58 km (36 mi) southwest of Turin.*

The older and more interesting part of **Saluzzo** hugs a hilltop in the Po Valley and is crowned by a castle. This town of time-worn russet brick was a flourishing medieval center and was seat of a ducal court during the Renaissance. The narrow, winding streets and frescoed houses, the Gothic cathedral and the church of San Giovanni, and the 15th-century Casa Cavassa, a richly decorated palace that now houses a museum, take you back in time to the age of chivalry.

Knights and dames of old, heroes and heroines of an allegorical poem written by Marquis Tommaso III of Saluzzo, humanist lord of the castle, parade in full costume in the 15th-century frescoes in the **Baron's Hall** of the **Castle of Manta,** only 4 kilometers (2.4 miles) south of Saluzzo. The castle's exterior is austere, but the frescoes and other interior decorations, along with the surrounding park and good views, make it worth a visit. ✉ *Via al Castello, Manta,* ☎ *0175/87822.* ✆ *5,000 lire.* ☉ *Tues.–Sun. 10–1 and 2–6. Closed last wk in Dec. and first wk in Jan.*

Sestriere

93 km (58 mi) west of Turin, 32 km (20 mi) east of Briançon.

In the early 1930s, before skiing became a sport for everyone, the patriarch of the Fiat automobile dynasty had this resort built, with two distinctive tower hotels and ski facilities that have been developed into some of the best in the Alps. The resort lacks the charm of other, older Alpine centers, overbuilding has added some eyesores, and the mountains don't have the striking beauty of those in the Val d'Aosta. But skiers have an excellent choice of trails, some of them crossing the border into France. Sestriere's 18-hole **golf course** is open from mid-June to mid-September (☎ 0122/755444).

Lodging

$$$ ⌂ **Principi di Piemonte.** Large and elegant, this luxurious hotel is on the slopes above the town, near the lifts and golf course. Its secluded location heightens the sense of exclusivity, a quality appreciated by a very stylish clientele. There is a restaurant and a cozy bar for après-ski relaxation. ⊠ *Via Sauze,* ☎ *0122/7941,* FAX *0122/755411. 94 rooms with bath. Restaurant, bar. AE, DC, MC, V. Closed Easter–June, Sept.–Dec. 21.*

$$ ⌂ **Miramonti.** Nearly every room has a terrace at this pleasant, centrally located modern chalet. The ample, comfortable rooms are done in traditional mountain style, featuring lots of wood paneling and coordinated floral-print fabrics. ⊠ *Via Cesana 3,* ☎ *0122/755333,* FAX *0122/755375. 30 rooms with bath. Restaurant, bar. DC, MC, V. Closed May and mid-Sept.–mid-Nov.*

Bardonecchia

36 km (22 mi) northwest of Sestriere, 89 km (55 mi) west of Turin, 20 km (12 mi) south of Modane.

This is one of Italy's oldest winter resorts, attracting hardy sports enthusiasts from Turin ever since the 1920s. It is near the entrance to the Fréjus train and automobile tunnels. The town gets plenty of sun and is at the center of a vast ski area.

Lodging

$$ ⌂ **Asplenia.** Skiers love this small, modern version of a mountain
★ chalet, near the center of town and the ski lifts. The ample rooms are comfortably furnished, with a small entryway and a balcony affording beautiful views. ⊠ *Viale della Vittoria 31,* ☎ *0122/999870,* FAX *0122/96192. 25 rooms with bath. MC, V. Closed Easter–May and Sept.–Nov.*

$$ ⌂ **Des Geneys-Splendid.** One of the best hotels in the area, this establishment is in a private park near the center of town. Its 1930s style is evident in the arched windows on the ground floor, the stucco walls, and the long wrought-iron balconies. The public rooms are spacious and comfortable, and there's a playroom for children. ⊠ *Via Einaudi 21,* ☎ *0122/99001,* FAX *0122/999295. 57 rooms with bath. Restaurant, bar. DC, MC, V. Closed Apr. 15–June 15 and mid-Sept.–mid-Dec.*

$$ ⌂ **Riky.** This centrally located modern hotel has good service; comfortable, spacious rooms; a good restaurant; and pleasant public rooms, including a children's playroom equipped with video games. There's a solarium and a piano bar with a cozy fireplace, and almost all rooms have terraces with panoramic views. Catering mainly to longer stays at half-board rates, it offers excellent low-season rates (nearly half price) for people staying at least a week. ⊠ *Via della Vittoria 22,* ☎ *0122/9353.*

76 rooms with bath. Restaurant, bar. AE, DC, V. Closed Apr.–June, Sept.–Dec. 15.

MOUNTAIN MAGIC
The Val d'Aosta, the Matterhorn, and Mont Blanc

The highest peaks in the Alps, the unspoiled beauty of Italy's oldest national park, magnificent scenery, bracing mountain air, and warm hospitality are the attractions of the Val d'Aosta. The main Aosta Valley, largely on an east–west axis, is hemmed in by high mountains where glaciers have gouged out 14 tributary valleys, six to the north and eight to the south. Distances here are relative: short horizontally, as the crow flies, and much longer vertically, on steep slopes over tortuous roads.

Beyond Ivrea, the road takes you through countryside that becomes hillier and hillier, passing through steep ravines guarded by brooding, romantic castles. Another change that you may not notice from your car is the beginning of French-speaking territory, as you enter the Aosta region, about 18 kilometers (11 miles) north of Ivrea. Pont St. Martin is the first village of the region.

Forte di Bard

㉓ *3 km (1.6 mi) beyond Pont St. Martin.*

A few minutes beyond the French-speaking village of Pont St. Martin, you pass through the narrow Gorge de Bard and reach the **Forte di Bard** (closed to the public), a 19th-century reconstruction of a fort that stood for eight centuries, serving the Savoys for six of them. In 1800 Napoléon entered Italy through this valley and used the cover of darkness to get his artillery units past the castle unnoticed. Ten years later he remembered this inconvenience and had the fortress destroyed.

Saint Vincent

88 km (55 mi) north of Turin, 46 km (29 mi) north of Ivrea, 97 km (60 mi) northwest of Vercelli.

The town of **Saint Vincent** has been a popular spa resort since the late 18th century. Its main claim to fame these days is the **Casinò de la Vallée,** one of Europe's largest gambling casinos. Remember to pack your black tie—and a lot of lire.

Dining and Lodging

$$$$ ✕ **Batezar.** Although tiny, this restaurant is considered one of Italy's
★ best. Just steps from the casino, its eight well-spaced tables are always spoken for. The ambience is rustic yet elegant, with arches and beamed ceilings enhanced by local antiques and fine crystal and silver place settings. There's an extensive à la carte menu, changing with the season, but also recommended are the set menus: one of local specialties, the other of international gourmet treats. For a starter, try the *tazzarella* (a small pizza with porcini mushrooms, mozzarella, and truffles) or fettuccine with herbs, artichokes, and filet of rabbit. Book well in advance. ⊠ *Via Marconi 1,* ☎ *0166/513164. Reservations essential Jacket and tie. AE, DC, MC, V. Closed Wed., Dec. 25, June 1–20. No lunch weekdays.*

$$$$ ▥ **Billia.** A luxury Belle-Epoque hotel with pseudo-Gothic touches, the Billia is in a park in the middle of town and connected directly to the casino by a passageway. Half the rooms are done in modern and half in period decor, and all creature comforts are attended to. There's a bar, three restaurants (open-air dining in summer), and a nightclub with dancing and a midnight floor show. The hotel also offers a fully equipped conference center—not to mention a private fishing reserve on a nearby mountain stream. ⊠ *Viale Piemonte 72,* ☎ *0166/5231,* FAX *0166/523799. 250 rooms with bath. Pool, sauna, health club, tennis courts, billiards. AE, DC, MC, V.*

$–$$ 🏨 **Elena.** The central location is the selling point of this hotel near the casino. The spacious rooms, some with balconies and/or king-size beds, are decorated with color-coordinated fabrics in a comfortable modern style and have air-conditioning. ⊠ *Via Biavaz 2 (Piazza Zerbion),* ☎ *0166/512140,* FAX *0166/537459. 48 rooms with bath. Restaurant, bar. AE, DC, MC, V. Closed Nov.*

Breuil-Cervinia

㉔ *30 km (18 mi) north of Saint Vincent, 27 km (17 mi) north of Châtillon.*

Breuil-Cervinia is an Italian-Swiss village at the base of the Matterhorn (Monte Cervino, in Italian; Mont Cervin in French). Like the village, the famous peak straddles the border between Italy and Switzerland, and all sightseeing and skiing facilities are operated jointly. Serious climbers can make the ascent of the Matterhorn from Breuil-Cervinia (having registered with the local mountaineering officials at the tourist office), but this climb is for serious and experienced climbers only. You get splendid views of the peak from Plateau Rosa and the Cresta del Furggen, both of which can be reached by cable car from the center of Breuil-Cervinia. While many locals complain that the tourist facilities and the condominiums in the village have changed the face of their beloved Breuil, most would agree that the cable car has given them access to climbing and off-trail skiing in ridges that were once inaccessible.

Dining and Lodging

$$$$ ✕🏨 **Hermitage.** A marble relief of St. Theodolus at the entrance reminds
★ guests that this was the site of the saint's hermitage. But asceticism has given way to sybaritic comfort and elegance in what is now one of the most exclusive hotels in this part of the Alps, totally renovated in 1994 and one of the Relais and Châteaux group. It has the look and atmosphere of a relaxed but posh family chalet, with a fire always glowing on the enormous hearth and a romantic, candlelit dining room. The decor includes rustic antiques, petit-point upholstery, and the Neyroz family's collection of paintings of the Matterhorn. The bright bedrooms have balconies; suites have antique fireplaces and 18th-century furnishings. Even the indoor swimming pool has a view of the Matterhorn, and the ski lifts are within walking distance. ⊠ *Strada Cristallo,* ☎ *0166/948998,* FAX *0166/949032. 36 rooms with bath. Restaurant, bar, indoor pool, sauna. AE, DC, MC, V. Closed May–June, Sept. 10–Nov.*

$$$–$$$$ ✕🏨 **Cristallo.** An elegantly modern hotel high above town, the Cristallo has spectacular views. The two restaurants serve local specialties, such as fonduta and *bistecca alla* valdostana (chops cooked with cheese and ham). Facilities and decorations contribute to an overall feeling of pampering and comfort. 🏨 *Via Piolet 6,* ☎ *0166/943411,* FAX *0166/948377. 103 rooms with bath. 2 restaurants, bar, indoor-outdoor pools, tennis courts, exercise room. AE, DC, MC, V. Closed May–June, Sept.–Nov.*

$$–$$$ ✕🏨 **Neiges D'Antan.** In a pine wood at Perrères, just outside Cervinia,
★ this small, rustic family-run inn is quiet and cozy, with lots of wood decor, three big fireplaces, and a nice view of the Matterhorn. There

are no TVs in the rooms: "It disturbs the atmosphere," says one of the proprietors. There's an excellent restaurant serving local specialties, such as fonduta, *zuppa Valpellinentze* (a peasant soup of bread, cabbage, and Fontina cheese), and an opulent antipasto (local salami, country pâté, and tomino cheese). ✉ *Perrères, 3½ km (2 mi) outside Cervinia,* ☎ *0166/948775,* FAX *0166/948852. 28 rooms with bath. Restaurant, bar. V. Closed May 4–June 25, Sept. 15–Dec. 5.*

$$ ✕ 🛱 **Bucaneve.** This small, centrally located hotel is decorated in typical mountain style, with lots of wood paneling, flowers, and terraces. Some rooms have balconies. For après-ski activities, there's a restaurant and a cozy bar with a big fireplace, wood paneling, and a cozy atmosphere. The hotel caters to longer stays at half-board rates. ☎ *0166/949119,* FAX *0166/948308. 28 rooms with bath. Restaurant, bar, sauna. AE, MC, V. Closed May–July 10, Sept.–Oct.*

$$ ✕ 🛱 **Chalet Valdotain.** About a mile outside the town on the road from Châtillon, this Alpine chalet has wooden balconies and snug rooms with terrific views of the Matterhorn. It is known for good food and its friendly atmosphere. ✉ *Località Lago Bleu,* ☎ *0166/949428,* FAX *0166/948874. 35 rooms with bath. Restaurant, bar. AE, MC, V. Closed May, Oct.–Nov.*

Fénis Castle

★ **㉕** ⸱ *17 km (10.5 mi) west of Saint Vincent.*

The best-preserved fortress in the Val d'Aosta, the many-turreted castle of **Fénis** was built in the mid-14th century by Aimone di Challant, a member of a prolific family that was related to the Savoys. This castle is the sort imagined by schoolchildren, with pointed turrets, portcullises, and spiral staircases. The 15th-century courtyard has a stairway leading to a loggia (open walkway) with wooden balconies. Inside you can see the medieval kitchen, with much of the original cooking equipment, and a collection of weapons in the armory. If you have time to visit only one castle in the Val d'Aosta, this is it, even though parts of it may be closed for restoration. ☎ *0165/764263.* 🎟 *4,000 lire.* ☉ *Mar.–Oct., Wed.–Mon. 9–6:30 (group tour every ½ hr); Nov.–Feb., Wed.–Mon. 9:30–noon and 2–5 (group tour every hr).*

En Route   The highway continues climbing through the Val d'Aosta to the town of Aosta itself. The road at this point is heading almost due west, with rivulets from the Parco Nazionale del Gran Paradiso (a wilderness reserve) streaming down from the left to join the Dora Baltea River, one of the major tributaries of the Po. Be careful driving here in late spring, when melting snow can turn some of these streams into torrents.

Aosta

㉖ *12 km (7 mi) west of Fénis Castle, 30 km (18 mi) west of Saint Vincent.*

Aosta stands at the junction of two important trade routes from France to Italy—from the valleys of the Rhône and the Isère. Its significance as a trading post was recognized by the Romans, who built a garrison here in the 1st century BC. The present-day layout of streets in this small city, which is tucked away in the Alps more than 644 kilometers (400 miles) from Rome, is the clearest example of Roman street planning in Italy. Well-preserved Roman walls form a perfect rectangle around the center of Aosta, and the regular pattern of streets reflects its role as a military stronghold.

Start your visit to Aosta at the Arch of Augustus, then head west on Via Sant'Anselmo, making a right turn onto Via Sant'Orso to see the church. Continue down Via Sant'Anselmo (named for St. Anselm, who was born in Aosta and later became archbishop of Canterbury in England) to the Porta Pretoria and Teatro Romano. About 100 yards west of the Roman theater (down Via Monsignor de Sales) is the cathedral.

At the eastern entrance to town, in a square that commands a fine view over Aosta and the mountains, is the **Arco di Augusto** (Arch of Augustus), built in 25 BC to mark Rome's victory over the Celtic Salassi tribe.

The **Collegiata di Sant'Orso** (Collegiate Church of St. Orso) is the sort of church that has layers of history in its architecture. Originally there was a 6th-century chapel on this site, founded by the Archdeacon Orso, a local saint. Most of this structure was destroyed or hidden when an 11th-century church was erected over it. This church, in turn, was encrusted with Gothic, and later Baroque, features, leaving the church a jigsaw puzzle of styles, but—surprisingly—not a chaotic jumble. The 11th-century features are almost untouched in the crypt, and if you go up the stairs on the left from the main church you can see the 11th-century frescoes (ask the sacristan for entrance). These restored frescoes depict the life of Christ and the Apostles: Although only the tops are visible, you can see the expressions on the faces of the disciples. Take the doorway by the entrance to the crypt to see the crown-
★ ing glory of Sant'Orso—the 12th-century **cloister**. Beside the church, it is enclosed by some 40 stone columns with masterfully carved capitals representing Old and New Testament themes and scenes from the life of St. Orso.

The huge Roman **Porta Pretoria** is a remarkable relic of the Roman era. The area between the inner and outer gates was used as a mini-parade ground for the changing of the guard.

The 72-foot-high ruin of the facade of the **Teatro Romano** (Roman Theater) guards the ruins of the 1st-century BC amphitheater, which once held 20,000 spectators. Only seven of its original 60 arches remain, and these are built onto the facade of the adjacent convent of Santa Caterina. The convent usually allows visitors in to see these arches (ask at the entrance).

Aosta's **cathedral** dates from the 10th century, but all that remains from that period are the campaniles. The decoration inside is mainly Gothic, but the main attraction of the cathedral predates that era by 1,000 years: a carved ivory diptych (devotional work with two images) showing the Roman Emperor Honorius and dating from AD 406. *For admission to treasury, contact sacristan at Piccolo Seminario (⊠ 2 Piazza Giovanni XXIII, behind cathedral).*

Dining and Lodging

$$ ✕ **Piemonte.** A small restaurant in the center of town, the Piemonte
★ has a comfortable, rustic decor and offers *crespelle alla valdostana* (crepes with cheese) and *filetto alla provenzale* (beef fillet with porcini mushrooms). ⊠ *Via Porta Pretoria 13,* ☎ *0165/40111. MC, V. Closed Fri. and Nov.*

$$ ✕ **Vecchio Ristoro.** Local and Italian dishes predominate in this old mill, furnished with antiques, in the city center. Try the *trota affumicata* (smoked trout) or the *uova walzer* (eggs cooked with cream and cheese on a bed of crusty baked polenta seasoned with wild herbs). ⊠ *Via Tourneuve 4,* ☎ *0165/33238. AE, DC, MC, V. Closed Sun., July, and Feb. No lunch Mon.*

$ ✕ **La Brasserie du Commerce.** Small, lively, and informal, this place is in the heart of Aosta, near central Piazza Chanoux. On a sunny summer day try to get a table on the terrace. Typical valley dishes, such as fonduta, are on the menu, together with a wide range of vegetable dishes and salads. ⊠ *Via de Tillier 10,* ☎ *0165/35613. Reservations not accepted. MC, V. Closed Sun.*

$ ✕ **Taverna Nando.** A wine cellar with wooden floors and vaulted ceilings, this family-run tavern is in the center of Aosta, and it has a terrace for outdoor dining. The menu features regional specialties such as fonduta, *carbonada* (veal stew), and *cervo* (venison) with mushrooms. The wine list is impressive. ⊠ *Via de Tillier 41,* ☎ *0165/44455. AE, DC, MC, V. Closed Thurs. and June.*

$$$ ⊞ **Val D'Aosta.** You'll find this comfortable, modern four-star hotel with its pleasant garden on the outskirts of town. A few rooms on the fifth floor have balconies, but virtually all rooms have big windows and splendid views of the mountains. There are rooms equipped for people with disabilities. The restaurant ($$) is under separate management. ⊠ *Corso Ivrea 146,* ☎ *0165/41845,* 🆑 *0165/236660. 104 rooms with bath. Bar. AE, DC, MC, V. Closed late Nov.–late Dec.*

$$ ⊞ **Milleluci.** A small, cozy, family-run hotel, Milleluci is set in its own garden on the hillside overlooking Aosta, with good views of the city and mountains. A huge brick hearth and rustic wooden beams highlight the lounge. Bedrooms are bright, with prints *de Provence* and attractive wood fittings. The hotel provides breakfast only, leaving guests free to sample local restaurants. Rates are at the lower end of the $$ category. ⊠ *Località Roppoz,* ☎ *0165/235278,* 🆑 *0165/235284. 12 rooms with bath. Bar, tennis court. AE, MC, V.*

$$ ✕ **Rayon du Soleil.** Saraillon, a residential district in the hills above Aosta, is the setting for this traditional redbrick mountain hotel in a park. There are excellent views from the rooms, which are large, bright, and quiet. Furnishings in mellow oak are solid and comfortable. There are rooms equipped for people with disabilities. ⊠ *Saraillon 16,* ☎ *0165/262247,* 🆑 *0165/236085. 45 rooms with bath. Pool, parking. AE, DC, MC, V. Closed Oct.–Dec. 26, Jan. 7–mid-Mar.*

Nightlife and the Arts

Each summer there is a series of **concerts** held in different venues around the city. Organ recitals in July and August attract performers of world renown.

Shopping

Aosta and the surrounding countryside are famous for wood carvings and wrought-iron work. There is a permanent **crafts exhibition** in the arcades of Piazza Chanoux, in the heart of Aosta; it's a good place to pick up a bargain. Each year, on the last two days of January, the whole town turns out for the **Sant'Orso Fair,** when all sorts of handicrafts are on sale, including handmade lace from nearby Cogne, carved wood and stonework, and brightly colored woolens.D/rd

Courmayeur

★ ㉗ *35 km (21 mi) northwest of Aosta, 24 km (15 mi) from Chamonix.*

The main attraction of **Courmayeur** is a knock-'em-dead view of Europe's tallest peak, Mont Blanc. The jet-set celebrities who flock here, particularly in winter, are following a tradition that dates from the late 17th century, when Courmayeur's natural springs first began to draw visitors. The scenic spectacle of the Alps gradually surpassed the springs as the biggest drawing point (the Alpine letters of the English poet Shelley were almost advertisements for the region), but the biggest change in the history of Courmayeur came in 1965, when the Mont Blanc tunnel opened. Now Courmayeur stands on one of the main routes from

France into Italy, although the planners have managed to maintain some restrictions on wholesale development within the town.

Dining

$$ ✕ **Cadran Solaire.** This charming restaurant in the center of town, in what was the oldest tavern in Courmayeur, has been renovated by the Garin family, owners of the Maison de Filippo (☞ *below*), to highlight the 17th-century stone vault, old wooden floor, and huge fireplace. The menu offers seasonal specialties and innovative interpretations of regional dishes, such as *gnocchi gratinati* (potato and ricotta dumplings) and *filetto di trota alle nocciole* (fillet of trout with hazelnuts). ✉ *Via Roma 122,* ☎ *0165/844609. AE, MC, V. Closed Tues., May, and Oct.*

Monte Bianco (Mont Blanc)

㉘ *3 km (1.6 mi) north of Courmayer.*

At La Palud you can catch the cable car up to the **Monte Bianco.** The cable car crosses into France, so have your passport ready. Remember, too, that the cable car depends on the weather, and that can mean being stuck on the French side, sometimes overnight: Have French money with you, in case. You ride up to the viewing platform at **Punta Helbronner** (over 11,000 feet), which is also the border post with France. Mont Blanc's attraction is not so much its shape (much less distinctive than the Matterhorn) as its expanse and the vistas from the top. The next stage, as you pass into French territory, is particularly impressive: You dangle over a huge glacial snowfield (more than 2,000 feet below) and make your way slowly to the viewing station above Chamonix. From this point you're looking down into France, and if you change cable cars, you can make your way down to Chamonix itself. The return trip covers the same route, and the total time should be 90 minutes, weather permitting. ✉ *Funivie La Palud,* ☎ *0165/89925.* 🎫 *36,000 lire round-trip to Punta Helbronner; 43,000 lire from Punta Helbronner to Chamonix.*

Dining and Lodging

$$ ✕ **Maison de Filippo.** Here you'll find country-style home cooking in a character-filled mountain house furnished with antiques. Reserve in advance, for it's one of the most popular restaurants in the Val d'Aosta. In summer, you can eat outside, surrounded by stunning views. There is a set menu only, featuring a daily selection of specialties including a wide choice of *antipasti* (starters) and pasta dishes, such as agnolotti in various sauces and spaghetti *affumicata* (with salami and bacon). The inn provides ample parking. ✉ *Entreves,* ☎ *0165/869797,* 𝖥𝖠𝖷 *0165/869719. Reservations essential. V. Closed Tues. and June–July 6, Nov.–mid-Dec.*

$$$$ 🏨 **Royal.** A classic mountain hotel in the center of town, the Royal is decorated with terraces, flowers, and wood paneling. Informal but elegant, it has modern rooms, a restaurant, and an evening piano bar. The hotel caters to longer stays with half- or full-board service. ✉ *Via Roma 83,* ☎ *0165/846787,* 𝖥𝖠𝖷 *0165/842093. 85 rooms with bath. Restaurant, bar, grill, pool, sauna, health club. AE, DC, MC, V. Closed 1 wk after Easter–mid-June, mid-Sept.–mid-Dec.*

$$$ 🏨 **Palace Bron.** A posh, comfortable hotel, Palace Bron is set in a pinewood at Plan Gorret, above the town itself. There are beautiful views, and it's ideal for relaxing. The rooms are comfortably furnished with period pieces. The restaurant has a fireplace. ✉ *Plan Gorret,* ☎ *0165/846742,* 𝖥𝖠𝖷 *0165/844015. 27 rooms with bath. Restaurant, bar. AE, DC, MC, V. Closed May–June, Oct.–Nov.*

$$$ 🏨 **Pavillon.** This is a modern version of a rustic chalet, complete with wood paneling, nostalgic decoration, and friendly service. Some rooms have views of Mont Blanc. Near cableways, it attracts a lively crowd. The atmosphere and facilities are reminiscent of old-fashioned spas. The hotel offers money-saving full-board rates. ⊠ *Strada Regionale 62,* ☎ *0165/846120,* 🆇 *0165/846122. 50 rooms with bath. Restaurant, bar, indoor pool, sauna, health club. AE, DC, MC, V. Closed May–June 20, Oct. 3–Nov.*

$$ 🏨 **Cresta et Duc.** A bright, modern Alpine hotel in the center of town, the Cresta features plenty of wooden terraces, flowers, and wooden furnishings. For relaxation there's a good restaurant, bar, billiards room, and lounges. The rooms are large and warm, and the hotel offers good full- and half-board rates. ⊠ *Via Circonvallazione 7,* ☎ *0165/842585,* 🆇 *0165/842591. 39 rooms (no singles) with bath. Restaurant, bar. AE, DC, MC, V. Closed Easter–June, mid-Sept.–mid-Dec.*

$$ 🏨 **Croux.** This bright, comfortable hotel is near the town center on the road leading to Mont Blanc. Half the rooms have balconies, the other half have great views of Mont Blanc. There is no restaurant. ⊠ *Via Circonvallazione 94,* ☎ *0165/846735,* 🆇 *0165/845180. 33 rooms with bath. Bar. AE, DC, MC, V. Closed mid-Apr.–June, Sept. 25–Dec. 20.*

Cogne

㉙ *52 km (32 mi) southeast of Courmayeur, 27 km (17 mi) south of Aosta.*

Cogne is the gateway to the **Parco Nazionale del Gran Paradiso.** This huge park, once the domain of King Vittorio Emanuele II and bequeathed to the nation after World War I, is one of Europe's most rugged and unspoiled wilderness areas, with wildlife and many plant species protected by law. Try to visit in May, when spring flowers are in bloom and most of the meadows are clear of snow. This is one of the few places in Europe where you can see the ibex (a mountain goat with horns up to 3 feet long) or the chamois (a small antelope whose soft skin nearly drove it to extinction).

FORTIFIED CITIES OF THE PO PLAIN

Southeast of Turin, in the hilly wooded area around Asti known as the Monferrato and another, similar area around Alba known as the Langhe, further south, the rolling landscape is a patchwork of vineyards spotted with dark woods and dotted with little hill towns and castles. This is wine country, producing Italy's most famous reds and sparkling whites. And hidden away in the woods are the secret places where hunters and their dogs unearth the precious, aromatic truffles that are worth their weight in gold at Alba's truffle fair. To the north of these hills, across the Po, are the cities of the plain. Beyond them lies Lake Maggiore and eastward, across the Ticino River, is Milan.

Asti

㉚ *60 km (37 mi) southeast of Turin, 116 km (72 mi) northwest of Genoa, 127 km (78 mi) southwest of Milan.*

Asti is one of the main cities of the Monferrato. It is known to Americans mainly because of its wines (there are excellent reds as well as the famous sparkling white spumante), but its strategic position on trade routes between Turin, Milan, and Genoa has given it a broad economic base. In the 12th century, Asti began to develop as a republic, at a time when other Italian cities were also flexing their economic and military muscles. It flourished in the following century, when the inhabitants began erecting lofty towers for its defense. Some of these towers remain, giving the city a medieval look.

Corso Vittorio Alfieri is Asti's main thoroughfare, running west–east across the city. This road, known in medieval times as Contrada Maestra, was built by the Romans. At the western end of Corso Alfieri, the 18th-century church of Santa Caterina has incorporated one of the medieval towers, the **Torre Romana** (itself built on an ancient Roman base), as its bell tower.

The **Duomo** is an object lesson in the evolution of the Gothic style of architecture. The cathedral, built in the early 14th century, is decorated mainly in a Gothic style that emphasizes geometry and verticality: Pointed arches and narrow vaults are counterbalanced by the earlier, Romanesque, attention to balance and symmetry. The porch, on the south side of the cathedral, facing the square, was built in 1470 and represents Gothic at its most florid and excessive.

The center of Asti is studded with **medieval towers,** almong them the 13th-century **Torre Comentini** and the well-preserved **Torre Troyana,** a tall, slender tower attached to the Palazzo Troya, in Piazza Medici. The Gothic church of **San Secondo,** south of Corso Alfieri, is dedicated to Asti's patron saint, who is also patron of the city's favorite folklore/sporting event, the annual *palio,* the colorful medieval-style horse race held each year on the third Sunday of September in the vast Campo del Palio to the south of the church.

NEED A BREAK?	The **Enoteca** on Piazza Alfieri, a square adjacent to Campo del Palio, is a wine center and shop (⊘ Mon.–Sat. 9–4:30) where you can try the range of Asti vintages, buy some as souvenirs or picnic ingredients, or have a light snack.
OFF THE BEATEN PATH	**ALBA –** Thirty kilometers (18 miles) southwest of Asti, this small town has a compact core studded with medieval towers and Gothic buildings, and a gracious Old World atmosphere. The town is the wine and truffle capital of the area. Visit in October for the National Truffle Fair, the Cento Torri Joust, and the Palio degli Asini (donkey races).
	BAROLO – Some of Italy's finest wines are made within a radius of about 16 kilometers (10 miles) of Alba. The zone is dotted with castles, and every town has a wineshop where you can sample the local vintage. The **Castle of Barolo** houses a wineshop and a museum of wine making. ⊠ Barolo. ⊘ Fri.–Wed. 10–12:30 and 3–6:30. Closed Jan. and part of Feb.

Dining and Lodging

$$$$ ✕ **Gener Neuv.** Family-run and one of Italy's top restaurants, the
★ Gener Neuv offers a sumptuous menu of regional specialties in a warm, welcoming atmosphere of rustic-style elegance, highlighted by excellent service, fine linen, silver, and crystal. The location in a park on the bank of the Tanaro River is splendid, although it resulted in severe flood damage in 1994; the restaurant had to be rebuilt. Your choices may include agnolotti *ai tre stufati* (with a filling of ground rabbit, veal, and pork) and *faraona farcita al le erbe* (boned guinea hen with herbs). The prix-fixe menu is good value ($$$) but does not include beverages. ⊠ Lungo Tanaro 4, ☎ 0141/557270, ℻ 0141/436723. AE, MC, V. Closed Mon. and Aug. No dinner Sun.

$$$ ✕ **Falcon Vecchio.** There's been a restaurant in this ancient house in the historic center of Asti since the year 1670. Today, in intimate surroundings, the Falcon Vecchio serves rich local dishes that vary with

the season. In fall and winter there are mushroom, truffle, and game dishes. Otherwise, there's a big selection of antipasti; grilled vegetables; and *bollito misto* (a steaming tray heaped with seven types of boiled meat, served with various sauces). ⊠ *Via San Secondo 8,* ☎ *0141/ 593106. Reservations essential. MC, V. Closed Mon., 15 days in Aug., 10 days in Jan. No dinner Sun.*

$$$ 🏨 **Palio.** The hotel has the advantage of a central location in the historic heart of Asti and, though in an ultramodern building, it also has considerable character in individually decorated rooms featuring authentic antiques. Bathrooms in the minisuites are equipped with hot tubs. ⊠ *Via Cavour 106,* ☎ *0141/34371,* ℻ *0141/34373. 29 rooms with bath. AE, DC, MC, V. Closed Aug. 10–25 and Dec. 23– Jan 3.*

$–$$ 🏨 **Rainero.** An older hotel in the town center, near the station, Rainero has been under the same family management for three generations. It's been remodeled many times and is fitted with cheerful modern furnishings. There is no restaurant. ⊠ *Via Cavour 85,* ☎ *0141/353866,* ℻ *0141/594985. 54 rooms with bath. DC, MC, V. Closed Jan. 1–8.*

Nightlife and the Arts

September is a month of fairs and celebrations in this famous wine city, and the **Asti Competition** in the middle of the month brings musicians, who perform in churches and concert halls.

En Route From Alba double back to Asti to pick up the A21 autostrada. The road east from Asti to Alessandria is straight, skirting the southern edge of the Po plain, but for the first half of the drive you see to the south the green hillsides covered with vineyards. If you find yourself driving along this road during a thunderstorm (quite common on late summer afternoons) don't be surprised by the sound of explosions. Wine growers will often let off cannons loaded with blanks to force heavy clouds to rain, rather than build up and develop destructive hailstones.

Casale Monferrato

③¹ *42 km (26 mi) northeast of Asti, 31 km (19 mi) north of Alessandria, 75 km (46.5 mi) southwest of Milan.*

Casale Monferrato, strategically situated on the southern banks of the Po, was held by the Gonzagas, rulers of Mantua, before falling into the hands of the Savoys: The 16th-century **Torre Civica,** marking the heart of Casale Monferrato in Piazza Mazzini, commanded extensive views up and down the Po.

Casale's most enlightening sight is the **Museo Israelitico** (Jewish Museum) in the women's section of the synagogue on Via Alessandria. Inside is a collection of documents and sacred art of a community that was vital to the prosperity of this mercantile city. The synagogue dates from the late 16th century, and neighboring buildings on the same street formed the Jewish ghetto of that period. ☎ *0142/71807.* 🎟 *5,000 lire.* ⊙ *Aug.–June, Sun. 10–noon and 3:30–5:30; at other times, by appointment only, with an extra charge of 10,000 lire per person. Closed Sat. and Jewish holidays.*

Vercelli

③² *23 km (14 mi) north of Casale Monferrato, 80 km (50 mi) northeast of Turin, 74 km (46 mi) southwest of Milan.*

Vercelli is the rice capital of Italy and of Europe itself: Northern Italy's mainstay, risotto, owes its existence to the crop that was introduced to this fertile area in the late Middle Ages. **Piazza Cavour** is the heart of the medieval city and former market square. It was to this small square that merchants across northern Italy came in the 15th century to buy bags of the novelty grain from the East—rice. Rising above the low rooftops around the square is the **Torre dell'Angelo** (Tower of the Angel), whose forbidding military appearance reflects its origins as a watchtower.

The **Duomo,** a mainly late 16th-century construction on the site of what was a 5th-century church, contains tombs of several Savoy rulers in an octagonal chapel along the south (right) wall. The cathedral's *biblioteca* (chapter library—for entrance, see cathedral office) contains the "Gospel of St. Eusebius," a 4th-century document, and the *Codex Vercellensis,* an 11th-century book of Anglo-Saxon poetry.

The **Basilica di Sant'Andrea,** a Cistercian abbey church built in the early 13th century with funds from another Abbey of St. Andrew (in England), witnessed the growing influence of northern Europe on Italy. Sant'Andrea is one of Italy's earliest examples of Gothic architecture, which spread from the north but ran out of steam before getting much farther south than the Po plain. The church interior is a soaring flight of Gothic imagination, with slender columns rising up to the ribbed vaults of the high ceiling. Tombs along the side aisle continue the preoccupation with stylized decoration and relief work. The gardens on the north side (Corso De Gasperi side) of the basilica hold the remains of the abbey itself and some of the secondary buildings. It is only here that the unadulterated Gothic style is interrupted. The buildings surround a cloister in which you can see the pointed Gothic arches resting on the severe and more solid 12th-century Romanesque column bases.

The **Città Vecchia** is a collection of narrow streets and alleys. Many of the houses are five centuries old, and you can see partly hidden gardens and courtyards beyond the wrought-iron gates.

OFF THE BEATEN PATH **BORSA MERCI** – You can take an unusual guided tour of the rice exchange (✉ Via Zumaglini 4, ☎ 0161/5981), where the grain has been traded for centuries. Call first to check on tour times.

Novara

➌ *23 km (14 mi) northeast of Vercelli, 95 km (59 mi) northeast of Turin, 51 km (31 mi) west of Milan.*

Novara is the easternmost city in Piedmont, only about 10 kilometers (6 miles) west of the Ticino River, which forms the border with Lombardy. Milan is only 32 kilometers (20 miles) beyond the border, and over the centuries the opposing attractions of this neighboring giant and of the regional capital, Turin, have made Novara a bit schizophrenic. In the Middle Ages, Novara's pivotal position actually made it a battlefield. A major engagement took place as recently as 1849, when the Austrian forces from the east defeated the Piedmontese armies.

Much of the present city dates from the late 19th and early 20th centuries, although there are interesting buildings from earlier periods scattered around Novara. Novara's most famous landmark is the tall, slender cupola of **San Gaudenzio**. The church itself, built between 1577 and 1690, conforms to a Baroque design, with twisted columns and sumptuous statues. The main attraction for most people, though, is the cupola, which was built from 1840 to 1888 and soars to a height of just under 400 feet. This spire is visible from everywhere in the city and the surrounding countryside, and has become as much a symbol of Novara as the Mole Antonelliana is of Turin.

The **Broletto,** a cluster of well-preserved late-medieval buildings, is next to the **Duomo,** of medieval origins but reconstructed in neoclassical style. The **Battistero** (baptistery), which is just outside the entrance to the cathedral, shows its august age in a much more evident manner. This rotunda-shaped building dates from the 5th century, although it was substantially enlarged in the 10th and 11th centuries. Recent restoration work has uncovered pre-Romanesque frescoes, over 1,000 years old, decorating the inside walls. Their flat, two-dimensional style reflects the influence of Byzantine icons, and their restored colors add a frightening feel to the apocalyptic scenes depicted.

Lodging

$$ ▥ **Italia.** This modern hotel in the center of the city offers comfortable rooms and efficient service; the facilities cater mainly to businesspeople. There is a restaurant, and some rooms have extensive views of the town. ⊠ *Via Solaroli 8,* ☎ *0321/399316,* ℻ *0321/399310. 55 rooms with bath. Restaurant (closed Fri.), bar, sauna. AE, DC, MC, V.*

PIEDMONT/VAL D'AOSTA A TO Z

Arriving and Departing

By Bus

Two Turin-based lines, **SADEM** (⊠ Via della Repubblica 14, 10095 Grugliasco, Turin, ☎ 011/3111616) and **SAPAV** (⊠ Corso Torino 396, 10064 Pinerolo, Turin, ☎ 011/322032), offer services along the autostrada network to Genoa, Milan, and more distant destinations in Italy. **SITA** buses, part of the nationwide system, also connect Turin with the rest of Italy. The main bus station is on the corner of Corso Inghilterra and Corso Vittorio Emanuele.

By Car

Italy's autostrada network links the region with the rest of Italy and neighboring France. Aosta, Turin, and Alessandria all have autostrada connections, with the A4 heading east to Milan and the A6 heading south to the Ligurian coast and Genoa. If you drive in from France or Switzerland, you pass through either the Mt. Blanc or Grand St. Bernard tunnels: These are two of the most scenically dramatic entrances to Italy.

By Plane

The region's only international airport, **Aeroporto Caselle,** is 18 kilometers (11 miles) north of Turin. The airport is notoriously foggy in winter, and many flights are diverted to Genoa, on the coast, with bus connections provided to Turin. Buses from Caselle Airport to Turin arrive at the bus station on Corso Inghilterra in the center of the city. For airport information, call ☎ 011/567–6361.

By Train

Turin is on the main Paris–Rome express line and is also connected with Milan, only 90 minutes away on the fast train. The fastest trains cover the 667-kilometer (400-mile) trip to Rome in about six hours, but most take about nine.

Getting Around

By Bus

SADEM and **SAPAV** (☞ Arriving and Departing by Bus, *above*) are the specialists in bus transportation in Piedmont and the Val d'Aosta. **SAVDA** (✉ Strada Ponte Suaz 6, 11100 Aosta, ☎ 0165/361244) specializes in mountain service, providing frequent links between Aosta, Turin, and Courmayeur.

By Car

Turin is the hub of all the transportation systems in Piedmont, with autostrada connections to the north, south, and east. Well-paved secondary roads run through the rest of the region, following the course of mountain valleys in many places. Sudden winter storms can close off some of the mountain stretches: For information on road conditions, call ☎ 011/5711.

By Train

Services to the larger cities east of Turin are part of the extensive and reliable train network serving the Lombard Plain. West of the region's capital, however, the train services soon peter out in the steep mountain valleys. Continuing connections by bus serve these valleys, and information about train/bus mountain services can be obtained from train stations and tourist information offices.

Contacts and Resources

Car Rental

Avis (✉ Corso Turati 15, Turin, ☎ 011/500852; ✉ Caselle Airport, ☎ 011/470–1528). **Hertz** (✉ Corso Marconi 19, Turin, ☎ 011/650–4504; ✉ Caselle Airport, ☎ 011/470–1103).

Emergencies

General Emergencies (☎ 113). **Police** (☎ 112).

Guided Tours

Turin's guided tours are organized by the city's tourist office (✉ Via Roma 226, ☎ 011/535901). The range of tours is extensive, from group tours by bus to see the main sights of Turin and its surroundings, to specialist tours led by personal guides.

Alpine guides are not only recommended, they're essential if you're planning to traverse some of the dramatic ranges outside Saint Vincent, Courmayeur, or Breuil-Cervinia. Before embarking on an excursion (however short) into the mountains in these areas, contact the representative of the **CAI** (Club Alpinisti Italiani) about the risks involved and the availability of an experienced guide. The main regional office of the CAI is in Aosta (✉ Piazza Chanoux 8, ☎ 0165/40194, ☉ Tues. and Fri.); CAI information is also available at each tourist information office.

Late-Night Pharmacies

Pharmacies throughout the region take turns staying open late and on Sunday. Call (☎ 192) for the latest information, in Italian, on which are open.

Aosta. Farmacia Centrale (✉ Piazza E. Chanoux 35, ☎ 0165/262205).

Turin. Farmacia Internazionale (✉ Via Carlo Alberto 24, ☎ 011/535144).

Visitor Information

Alba (✉ Piazza Medford, ☎ 0173/35833). **Aosta** (✉ Piazza E. Chanoux 8, ☎ 0165/236627, FAX 0165/34657). **Asti** (✉ Piazza Alfieri 34, ☎ 0141/530357, FAX 0141/538200). **Bardonecchia** (✉ Viale Vittoria 44, ☎ 0122/99032, FAX 0122/980612). **Breuil-Cervinia** (✉ Via Carrel 29,

☎ 0166/949136, FAX 0166/949731). **Courmayeur** (✉ Piazzale Monte Bianco, ☎ 0165/842060, FAX 0165/842072). **Novara** (✉ Via Dominioni 4, ☎ 0321/623398, FAX 0321/393291). **Saluzzo** (✉ Via Griselda 6, ☎ 0175/46710, FAX 0175/46718). **Turin** (✉ Via Roma 226, ☎ 011/535901, FAX 011/530070; ✉ Porta Nuova train station, ☎ 011/531327). **Vercelli** (✉ Viale Garibaldi 90, ☎ 0161/58002, FAX 0161/257899).

In case you want to see the world.

At American Express, we're here to make your journey a smooth one. So we have over 1,700 travel service locations in over 120 countries ready to help. What else would you expect from the world's largest travel agency?

do more

AMERICAN EXPRESS

http://www.americanexpress.com/travel

Travel

In case you want to be welcomed there.

We're here to see that you're always welcomed at establishments everywhere. That's why millions of people carry the American Express® Card – for peace of mind, confidence, and security, around the world or just around the corner.

do more

Cards

In case you're running low.

We're here to help with more than 118,000 Express Cash locations around the world. In order to enroll, just call American Express before you start your vacation.

do more®

Express Cash

And just in case.

We're here with American Express® Travelers Cheques
and Cheques *for Two.*® They're the safest way to carry
money on your vacation and the surest way to get a
refund, practically anywhere, anytime.
Another way we help you...

do more

Travelers
Cheques

9 Milan, Lombardy, and the Lakes

From Ancient to Modern, from Nature to Renaissance

Old and new are often unexpectedly linked in Italy, and in Lombardy, they are married magnificently: Modern Milan is just a few hours from the 19th-century resort towns of Lake Como, Maggiore, and Garda. The lakes remain the perfect escape from Milan, a metropolis that is Italy's business center and crucible of chic. With their opulent villas, exotic gardens, and Alpine vistas, the Italian lakes are among the most achingly beautiful places in Europe.

Updated by
Giuliano
Davenport

ONE IS TEMPTED to describe Lombardy as a place with something for everyone—Milan, capital of all that is new in Italy; the great Renaissance cities of the plain, Pavia, Cremona, and Mantua, where even the height of summer can be comparatively peaceful; and the lakes, where glacial waters framed by the Alps have been praised as the closest thing to Paradise by writers as varied as Virgil, Tennyson, and Hemingway.

The truth, of course, is more complicated. Milan can be disappointingly modern—rather too like the place you have come here to escape—but it is also the perfect blend of old and new, with historic buildings and art collections rivaling those in Florence and Rome. The lakes, home to dozens of fashionable resorts, have preserved an astonishingly unspoiled beauty, often enhanced by sumptuous summer palaces and exotic formal gardens. Still, one cannot imagine Catullus returning to his "jewel" Sirmione, on Lake Garda, without being a little daunted by its development as a lively resort town. The great towns of the Lombardy plain are rich in history, but their art and architecture pale before the staggering wealth of Rome, Florence, and Venice.

More than 3,000 years ago—the date and the details are lost in the mysteries of Etruscan inscriptions—explorers from the highly civilized realm of Etruria in central Italy wandered northward beyond the River Po. The Etruscans extended their dominance into this region for hundreds of years but left little of their culture. They were succeeded by the Cenomanic Gauls, who, in turn, were conquered by the legions of Rome in the latter days of the Republic.

The region became known as Cisalpine Gaul, and under the rule of Augustus it became a Roman province. Its warlike, independent people became citizens of Rome. Virgil, Catullus, and both the Plinys were born in the region during this relatively tranquil era.

The decline of the Roman Empire was followed by the invasions of the Huns and the Goths. Attila and Theodoric, in turn, gave way to the Lombards, who ceded their iron crown to Charlemagne as the emblem of his vast but unstable empire.

Even before the fragile bonds that held this empire together had begun to snap, the cities of Lombardy were erecting walls in defense against the Hungarians and against each other. These communes did, however, form the Lombard League, which, in the 12th century, finally defeated Frederick Barbarossa.

Once the invaders had been defeated, new and even bloodier strife began. In each city the Guelphs (bourgeois supporters of the popes) and the Ghibellines (noble adherents to the so-called emperors) clashed with each other. The communes declined, and each fell under the yoke of powerful local rulers. The Republic of Venice dominated Brescia and Bergamo. Mantua was ruled by the Gonzaga, and the Visconti and Sforza families took over Como, Cremona, Milan, and Pavia.

The Battle of Pavia in 1525, when the generals of Charles V defeated the French (and gave Francis I the chance to coin the famous phrase "All is lost save honor"), brought on 200 years of Spanish occupation. The Spaniards were, on the whole, less cruel than the local tyrants and were hardly resisted by the Lombards.

The War of the Spanish Succession, in the early years of the 18th century, threw out the Spaniards and brought in, instead, the Austrians, whose dominion was "neither liked nor loathed" during the nearly 100 years of its existence.

Napoléon and his generals routed the Austrians. The Treaty of Campoformio resulted in the proclamation of the Cisalpine Republic, which quickly became the Republic of Italy and, just as rapidly, the Kingdom of Italy, which lasted only until Napoléon's defeat brought back the Austrians. But Milan, as the capital of Napoléon's republic and of the Kingdom of Italy, had had a taste of glory, and the city's inherently independent citizens, along with those of the other Lombardian cities, were not slow to resent and combat the loss of "national" pride.

From 1820 on, the Lombards joined the Piedmontese and the House of Savoy in a long struggle against the Hapsburgs and, in 1859, finally defeated Austria and brought about the re-creation of the Kingdom of Italy two years later.

Milan and other cities of Lombardy have not lost their independence and their hatred of domination. Nowhere in Italy was the partisan insurrection against Mussolini (to whom they first gave power) and the German regime better organized or more successful. Milan was liberated from the Germans by its own partisan organization before the entrance of Allied troops; escaping Allied prisoners could find sanctuary there when fighting was still going on far to the south.

Lombards are a forthright people. They are as much inclined to taciturnity as any Italian is ever apt to be, and, when they do talk, they mean exactly what they say. When they quote a price, there is little use haggling about it. A Milanese is inclined to be courteous, but probably has little time for pleasantries; his or her compatriot on the rice farm or in the mountains may be less talkative, but may take more interest in you as an individual.

Pleasures and Pastimes

Auto Racing

Though the fortunes of Italy's beloved Ferrari have waned in recent years, passion for the sport is undiminished here. A Formula 1 race is held in Monza, 15 kilometers (9 miles) from Milan, every September. The track was built in 1922 in the Parco di Monza, where there is also a hippodrome, golf course, and other facilities.

Dining

Unlike most Italian regions, Lombardy exhibits a northern European preference for butter rather than oil as its cooking medium, which imparts a rich and distinctive flavor to the cuisine. Lombardy is the home of *alla milanese*-style cooking, which means the food is usually dipped in egg and breadcrumbs mixed with grated Parmesan cheese, then fried in clarified butter. Among the most popular specialties is osso bucco alla milanese with risotto. Risotto alla milanese uses chicken broth and saffron, which gives the dish a rich yellow color. The lakes are a good source of fish, particularly trout and pike.

Gorgonzola, a rich veined cheese, and panettone, a yeast-leavened fluffy bread with raisins and candied fruit, both come from Milan and can be enjoyed throughout Lombardy. Although most of the wines in Lombardy are good accompaniments to the cuisine, try in particular to have the red Grumello or Sangue di Giuda (blood of Judas) wines or the delicious light sparkling whites from the Franciacorta area.

CATEGORY	MILAN*	OTHER AREAS*
$$$$	over 120,000 lire	over 90,000 lire
$$$	80,000–120,000 lire	60,000–90,000 lire
$$	45,000–80,000 lire	35,000–60,000 lire
$	under 45,000 lire	under 35,000 lire

per person, including first course, main course, dessert or fruit, and house wine

Golf

There are five courses near Milan and seven courses near Lake Como. For further details of courses in the area, contact local tourist offices, or the regional tourist offices.

Lodging

Lombardy is one of Italy's most prosperous regions, and hotels cater to a clientele that demands high standards and is willing to pay for extra comfort. Most of the famous lake resorts are expensive, although more basic—and reasonably priced—accommodations can be found in the smaller towns and villages. Milan may seem to have fewer tourists than other large Italian cities, but there is always competition for rooms, generated by the nearly year-round trade fairs and other business-related bookings. It is best—and almost essential in spring and summer—to make reservations.

Many Lombardy hotels are converted from beautiful old villas and have well-landscaped grounds. Try to visit one or two, even if they are out of your price range as accommodations.

CATEGORY	COST*
$$$$	over 400,000 lire
$$$	200,000–400,000 lire
$$	125,000–200,000 lire
$	under 125,000 lire

Prices are for standard double room for two, including tax and service.

Soccer

Like the rest of Italy, the region is soccer-mad, with most of the attention given to Milan's soccer teams, AC Milan and Inter Milan, which are two of the most successful in Europe. Matches are played on Sunday, with both teams sharing the San Siro soccer stadium in Milan for home matches. On match-day, close to 85,000 fans fill the San Siro to watch, cheer, and boo the performances of each team. For the rest of the week, Sunday's performance is debated and scrutinized in bars, cafés, and restaurants (not to mention the home, the workplace, the barber shop . . .). And then there's the following Sunday, when it all starts again. Match tickets are difficult but not impossible to obtain; information is available from the city tourist offices.

Water Sports

Schools for sailing, scuba diving, waterskiing and windsurfing are in Riva del Garda, on Lake Garda. Torbole, 5 kilometers (3 miles) east of Riva del Garda on S240, is a prime spot for windsurfing; At Lake Como, there are well-equipped sailing and windsurfing schools as well as waterskiing.

Exploring Milan, Lombardy and the Lakes

This area of northern Italy is dominated by the region of Lombardy and especially by Milan, which lies at its heart. From the north to the east of Milan lie all of the region's lakes. Some border Switzerland; others are at the foot of the Dolomites, Italy's foremost mountain range. Many of the region's most important cities are to the south and south-

east of Milan. These cities all have in common a flat geographical surrounding bordered by the Po river, hence they are categorized here as
cities of the plain.

"Nothing in the world," wrote Stendhal in 1817, "can be compared
to the fascination of those burning summer days passed on the Milanese
lakes, in the middle of those chestnut groves so green that they immerse
their branches in the waves . . ." Millions of travelers have since agreed
that, for sheer beauty, the lakes of Northern Italy—Como, Maggiore,
Garda, and Orta—have few equals. Where else can you find magnificent 18th- and 19th-century villas on the shores of lakes bordered by
toy villages and nestled under the foothills of mountains of almost Scan-
dinavian grandeur? From Pliny to d'Annunzio, visitors have found this
region—to quote Stendhal—"elegant, picturesque, and voluptuous."

"The lakes" actually denotes a vast region spread over the middle third
of the northern border region. Though our tour is limited to the main
four lakes, the best way to see the lake country is to rent a car in fall
or spring and thread a path, at as leisurely a pace as possible, along
the small mountain roads that link the lakes' least-spoiled northern tips.
This is splendid mountain-driving country, with some of the most
beautiful and challenging roads in the world. Without a car, however,
it is still possible to see many of the region's sights, thanks to extensive bus routes and the many vaporetti that ferry the lakes.

It is important to remember that the lakes are extremely popular seasonal resort areas. If your wish is not only to see the lakes but also to
stay at them, the throngs that descend in July and August (particularly
on weekends) make reservations absolutely essential—especially so at
Lake Como, the quintessential Italian lake resort.

Great Itineraries
*Numbers in the text correspond to numbers in the margin and on the
Milan and Lombardy and the Lakes maps.*

The roads that connect major cities in the region are excellent and are
supported by several major highways (Autostrada) as well as by secondary routes. Roads around the lakes, in particular Lake Garda and
Lago Maggiore, are scenic but windy. Give yourself time to travel
them at leisure. Traveling by car is usually the best way to get around
and fully appreciate the beauty of the landscape. There are plenty of
places to pull off for photographs or just a breath of fresh air.

A week is enough to see the area thoroughly, and although five days
will not exclude any sights, you have to keep on the move. Three days
will give you a taste of the major sights in the area, but time will be
precious and morning starts will have to be early. All itineraries begin
and end in Milan.

IF YOU HAVE 3 DAYS
Begin in **Milan** ①–⑪, taking in the city's major sights, before heading
south on the A7 autostrada to the cities of **Pavia** ⑫ and **Cremona** ⑬,
home to Stradivari, violin-maker extraordinaire. End your day in ☒
Mantua ⑮. The next day head north on the A22 as far as **Riva del Garda** ⑱ and make your way back through **Gargnano** ⑲, **Gardone Riviera** ⑳, and down into the jewel of Lake Garda's crown, **Sirmione** ㉑.
Overnight in ☒ **Bergamo** ㉓. The next day go as far as **Madonna del
Ghisallo** ㉔ and **Bellagio** ㉕ on Lake Como. Finally, move on to the Lago
Maggiore via **Cernobbio** ㉘, taking time out to cruise the lake on one
of the steamers. Return then to Milan.

IF YOU HAVE 5 DAYS

Travel south along the A7 to **Pavia** ⑫ and **Cremona** ⑬, and then move on to the elegant, star-shaped fortress-city of **Sabbioneta** ⑭, ending your day in 🖼 **Mantua** ⑮, where you can enjoy Mantegna's masterpieces. The next day head north to Lake Garda through the lakefront towns of **Punta di San Vigilio** ⑯, **Malcesine** ⑰, and, at the top of the lake, the pretty town of **Riva del Garda** ⑱. Head down the western side of the lake through **Gargnano** ⑲ and **Gardone Riviera** ⑳, where you should visit Gabriele d'Annunzio's former home, Il Vittoriale, before reaching 🖼 **Sirmione** ㉑. The next day pass through the wealthy city of **Brescia** ㉒ and on to **Bergamo** ㉓. From here head via **Madonna del Ghisallo** ㉔ to 🖼 **Bellagio** ㉕ on Lake Como, said to be the prettiest town in Europe. Take time in the afternoon to explore the lake towns of **Varenna** ㉖ and **Tremezzo** ㉗, where you will find the magnificent Villa Carlotta. If you can manage an early start the following morning, head for **Cernobbio** ㉘ and then west to **Orto San Giulio** ㉚ on Lake Orto. It's only a short hop to the Lago Maggiore. You can explore the area from here by steamer, traveling north to 🖼 **Stresa** ㉛ on the western side of the lake. From here it's a short excursion to the town of **Verbania Pallanza** ㉜, across the bay of the same name. The following day head for **Milan** ①–⑪ to see the main sights. Alternatively, you could visit Milan before setting off on your tour of the rest of the region.

IF YOU HAVE 7 DAYS

If you have the luxury of seven days to tour the area, make sure to linger in some of the lake towns, especially **Riva del Garda** ⑱ and **Sirmione** ㉑ on Lake Garda, **Bellagio** ㉕ on Lake Como, and **Verbania Pallanza** ㉜ on Lake Maggiore, where you can explore the magnificent botanical gardens of Villa Taranto. Take an extra day to visit **Milan** ①–⑪, which may appear to be yet another industrialized city at first glance but which has a plethora of artistic and architectural treasures.

When to Tour Milan, Lombardy, and the Lakes

In summer months, particularly July and August, lake roads can become congested, especially on evenings and weekends. Fewer people visit in fall, winter, and spring, so many of the lakeside towns are deserted and some restaurants as well as hotels close during these months. Note that many of the ferry and steamer boat services stop running in October and recommence in May. Early summer, late summer, and early fall are the best times to see the area, but October can be a tad chilly for swimming.

MILAN

❶ *93 km (60 mi) northwest of Cremona, 38 km (24 mi) north of Pavia.*

Milan's history as a capital city goes back at least 2,500 years. Its fortunes ever since, both as a great commercial trading center and as the object of regular conquest and occupation, are readily explained by its strategic position at the center of the Lombard plain. Directly south of the central passes across the Alps, Milan is bordered by three highly navigable rivers—the Po, the Ticino, and the Adda—which for centuries were the main arteries of an ingenious network of canals crisscrossing all Lombardy (and ultimately reaching most of northern Italy).

Virtually every invader in European history—Gaul, Roman, Goth, Longobard, and Frank—as well as every ruler of France, Spain, and Austria, has taken a turn at ruling the city and the region. Milan's glorious heyday of self-rule proved comparatively brief, from 1277 until 1500, which it was ruled by its two great family dynasties, the Visconti and subsequently the Sforza. These families were known, justly or not, for a peculiarly aristocratic mixture of refinement, classical learning, and cruelty, and much of the surviving grandeur of Gothic and Renaissance art and architecture is their doing. Be on the lookout in your wanderings for the Visconti family emblem—a viper, its jaws straining wide, devouring a child.

If you are wondering why so little seems to have survived from Milan's antiquity, the answer is simple—war. Three times in the city's history, partial or total destruction has followed conflict—in AD 539, 1157, and 1944.

Numbers in the margin correspond to points of interest on the Milan map.

★ ❷ The **Duomo** has been fascinating and exasperating visitors and conquerors alike since it was begun by Galeazzo Visconti III, first duke of Milan, in 1386. Consecrated in 1577, and not wholly completed until 1897, it is the third-largest church in the world and the largest Gothic building in Italy.

Whether you concur with travel writer H. V. Morton, writing 25 years ago, that the cathedral is "one of the mightiest Gothic buildings ever created," or regard it as a spiny pastiche of centuries, there is no denying that for sheer size and complexity it is unequaled. Its capacity—though it is hard to imagine the church filled—is reckoned to be 40,000. Usually it is empty, a perfect sanctuary from the frenetic pace of life outside and the perfect place for solitary contemplation. The poet Shelley swore by it—claiming it was the only place to read Dante.

The building is adorned with 135 marble spires and 2,245 marble statues. The oldest part is the **apse** (the end of the cruciform opposite the portals). Its three colossal bays of curving and counter-curved tracery, especially the bay adorning the exterior of the stained-glass windows, should not be missed.

Step inside and walk down the right aisle to the southern transept, to the **tomb of Gian Giacomo** Medici. The tomb owes something to Michelangelo, but is generally considered its sculptor's (Leone Leoni's) masterpiece; it dates from the 1560s.

Directly ahead is the Duomo's most famous sculpture, the rather gruesome but anatomically instructive figure of **St. Bartholomew**, whose glorious martyrdom consisted of being flayed alive. It is usually said the saint stands "holding" his skin, but this is not quite accurate. It would appear more that he is luxuriating in it, much as a 1950s matron might have shown off a new fur stole.

As you enter the apse to admire those splendid windows, glance at the sacristy doors to the right and left of the altar. The lunette on the right dates from 1393 and was decorated by Hans von Fernach. That on the left also dates from the 14th century and is ascribed jointly to Giacomo da Campione and Giovanni dei Grassi.

Don't miss the view from the Duomo's **roof:** Walk outside the left (north) transept to the stairs and elevator. Sad to say, late–20th-century air pollution has, on all but the rarest days, drastically reduced the view. But even in fog, the roof itself has a fairy-tale quality. As you stand among the forest of marble pinnacles, remember that virtually every inch of this gargantuan edifice, including the roof itself, is decorated with precious white marble. ✉ *Piazza del Duomo.* 🎫 *Stairs 5,000 lire, elevator 7,000 lire.*

Visit also the **Duomo Museum,** should you wish to learn more about the cathedral's history and see some of the treasures removed for safety

312

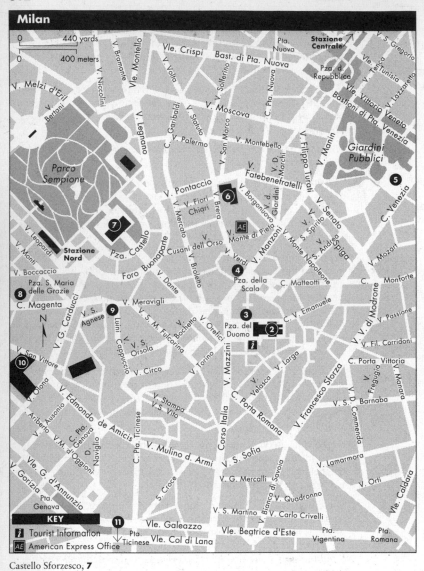

Milan

0 ─── 440 yards

0 ─── 400 meters

V. Melzi d'Eril
Bertani
V. Niccolini
V. Bramante
V. Montello
Vle. Crispi
V. Volta
V. Solferino
Bast. di Pta. Nuova
Pta. Nuova
C. Pta. Nuova
Pta. Nuova
Stazione Centrale
V. S. Gregorio
Vle. Tonale
V. Tunisia
V. Lazzaretto
V. Legnano
C. Garibaldi
V. Statuto
V. Palermo
V. San Marco
V. Moscova
V. Montebello
V. Filippo Turati
V. Manin
Pza. d. Repubblica
Vle. Vittoria Veneto
Bastioni di Pta. Venezia

Parco Sempione

Stazione Nord

V. Leopardi
V. Monti
V. Boccaccio
Pza. S. Maria delle Grazie
C. Magenta
N
V. G. Carducci
V. S. Agnese
Pza. Castello
Foro Buonaparte
V. Dante
V. Meravigli
V. S. M. Fulcorina
V. Luini
Cappuccio
V. S. Orsola
V. Circo

V. Pontaccio
V. Fiori Chiari
Brera
Mercato
Cusani dell'Orso
V. Broletto
V. Verdi
V. Borgonuovo
Giardini
V. D. Marchi
V. Fatebenefratelli
AE
Monte di Pietà
V. Manzoni
V. Spirito
V. S. Andrea
Monte Napoleone
V. Senato
V. Andrea
Spiga
C. Venezia
Giardini Pubblici
V. Mozart
Monforte
V. di Modrone
V. Passione
5

6
7
4
Pza. della Scala
C. Matteotti
3
Pza. del Duomo
2
i
C. V. Emanuele
V. Fil. Corridoni
C. Porta Vittoria
V. S. D. Barnaba
Manara
Freguglia

V. S. Vittore
V. Olona
Ariberto
Ausonio
V. Edmondo de Amicis
C. Pta. Genova
V. M. d'Oggiono
D. Naviglio
C. Pta. Ticinese
V. Stampa
V. S. Vito
V. Torino
Corso Italia
C. Porta Romana
V. Velasca
C. Larga
V. Francesco Sforza
V. S. Commenda
8
9
10

Pta. Genova
V. Gorizia
Vle. G. d'Annunzio
11
Pta. Ticinese
Vle. Galeazzo
Vle. Col di Lana
V. Mulino d. Armi
S. Croce
V. S. Sofia
V. S. Martino
V. Bianca di Savoia
V. Quadronno
V. Carlo Crivelli
Vle. Beatrice d'Este
V. G. Mercalli
V. Lamarmora
V. Orti
Vle. Caldara
Pta. Vigentina
Pta. Romana

KEY

i Tourist Information

AE American Express Office

Castello Sforzesco, **7**

Duomo, **2**

Galleria Vittorio Emanuele, **3**

La Scala, **4**

Museo Archeologico, **9**

Museo Civico di Storia Naturale, **5**

Museo Nazionale della Scienza e della Tecnica, **10**

Navigli district, **11**

Pinacoteca di Brera, **6**

The Last Supper, **8**

from the exterior. ⊠ *Museo del Duomo, Piazza del Duomo 14B,* ☎ *02/860358.* ▨ *7,000 lire.* ☉ *Tues.–Sun. 9:30–12:30 and 3–6.*

The **Baptistery,** a subterranean ruin dating from the 4th century, is beneath the Duomo's piazza. Although opinion remains divided, it is widely believed that this may have been where Ambrose (Milan's first bishop and patron saint) baptized Augustine. ⊠ *Battistero Paleocristiano, enter through cathedral.* ▨ *Free.* ☉ *Tues.–Sun. 10–noon and 3–5.*

NEED A BREAK? The best alternative to a conventional restaurant is **Peck** (⊠ Via Spadari 9, ☎ 02/860842), one of Italy's, if not the world's, most irresistible food emporiums. In the Duomo area, it is something better than a shop—it's six shops. Best for a quick stand-up lunch is **Bottega del Vino** (⊠ Via Victor Hugo 4, ☎ 02/861040), which offers almost 200 wines by the glass. **Peck Rosticceria** (⊠ Via Cantù 3, ☎ 02/869-3017) offers grilled takeout. The restaurant is closed Monday. For a relaxed lunch, try **Il Restaurant** (⊠ Via Victor Hugo 4, ☎ 02/876774). It's closed Sunday and two weeks in January. For do-it-yourself, try the **Delicatessen** (⊠ Via Spadari 9, ☎ 02/8646-1158).

★ ❸ The **Galleria Vittorio Emanuele** is a great glass-topped, barrel-vaulted tunnel. Anyone who has grown up on the periphery of a contemporary American city should recognize this spectacularly extravagant late–19th-century creation for what it is—one of the planet's earliest and most elegant shopping malls, rivaled perhaps only by GUM, off Red Square in Moscow, for sheer Belle Epoque splendor. Its architect, Giuseppe Mengoni, accidently lost his footing while on the roof and tumbled to his death on the floor of his own creation, just days before its opening.

Like its suburban American cousins, the Galleria fulfills a variety of social functions vastly more important than its ostensible commercial purpose. If you had only a half hour to spend in Milan, this would be the place to spend it. This is the city's heart, midway between the cathedral and La Scala opera house, and it is sometimes called *Il Salotto* (the Living Room). For all but a few hours of the week, it positively teems with life. If you're a bit weary from your exploration of the Duomo, stop here to enjoy that most delightful of spectator sports: people-watching. Pull up a chair at one of the strategically situated tables that spill from the Galleria's bars and restaurants, and prepare to enjoy one of those monstrously surcharged coffees that are the modest price for a front-row seat at one of the best shows in Italy.

Like the cathedral, the Galleria is cruciform in shape. The space at the crossing, however, forms an octagon. If this is where you're standing, don't be afraid to look up and gawk. Even in poor weather, the great glass dome makes a splendid sight. And the mosaics, usually unnoticed, are a vastly underrated source of pleasure, even if they are not to be taken too seriously. They represent Europe, Asia, Africa, and America; those at the entrance arch are devoted to science, industry, art, and agriculture.

Books, clothing, food, wine, pens, jewelry, and myriad other goods are all for sale in the Galleria, and one of Milan's most correct and traditional restaurants, Savini, is here. There is, in addition, one of those curious Italian institutions, an *albergo diurno* (daytime hotel), where you can take an hour's nap or a bath, get a haircut or a pedicure, and have your suit pressed or a button replaced. Most of its patrons are Italian, but it is hard to think of a better oasis for a vacationer who's worn out from sightseeing. ⊠ *Piazza del Duomo, beyond northern tip of cathedral's facade.*

❹ La Scala (Teatro alla Scala), where Verdi's fame was established and Maria Callas sang her way into opera lore, is one of the worlds most famous opera houses. It was completely renovated after its destruction by Allied bombs in 1943 and reopened at a performance led by the great Arturo Toscanini in 1946.

You need know nothing of opera to sense that, like Carnegie Hall, La Scala is something rather more than an auditorium. It looms as a symbol—both for the performer who dreams one day of singing here and for the buff who knows every note of *Rigoletto* by heart. For some, a visit to La Scala will be—even more than the Duomo—a solemn but pleasurable act of pilgrimage.

If you are lucky enough to be here during the opera season, which runs for approximately six months beginning each December 7, St. Ambrose Day, do whatever is necessary to attend—even if it requires perching among the rafters in one of the dreaded gallery seats. Hearing a Verdi or Puccini opera sung in Italian by Italians in Italy is a magical experience. For now, whet your appetite with a quick stroll through the theater's small museum, **Museo Teatrale alla Scala.** The visit allows you a peek at the gilded grandeur of the boxes. ⊠ *Piazza della Scala,* ☏ *02/805–3418.* 🎫 *5,000 lire.* ☉ *Mon.–Sat. 9–noon and 2–6; plus May–Oct., Sun. 9:30–noon and 2:30–6; closed occasionally during rehearsals.*

❺ The **Museo Civico di Storia Naturale,** facing Corso Venezia, offers exhibits that appeal to animal and nature lovers. Just behind the museum are the **Giardini Pubblici (Public Gardens),** which are good for young children. ⊠ *Corso Venezia 55,* ☏ *02/6208–5405.* 🎫 *Free.* ☉ *Tues.–Fri. 9:30–5:30, weekends 9:30–6:30.*

★ ❻ Pinacoteca di Brera. The picture collection in this art gallery is star studded, even by Italian standards. As everyone knows, the only way to "do" a large collection is to start with the best, while you're still fresh, eager, and observant, and leave the charming minor masterpieces for afterward. We suggest you begin by ignoring the 20th-century work displayed along the long entrance corridor and walk to the large, well-patrolled room (No. 22) with only two big paintings, both behind glass.

Note that Raphael painted *Betrothal of the Virgin* when he was 22, a time when many of us are still struggling with the question of what to do in life. The other painting, Piero della Francesca's *Madonna with Saints and Angels,* is just as lovely, much aided by its recent and skillful restoration and cleaning.

The gallery's best-known painting is probably the somber, beautiful, and moving *Dead Christ* by Mantegna, in Room 18. Though it is by far the smallest painting in the room, it dominates, with its sparse palette of gray and terra-cotta. Mantegna's shocking, almost surgical, precision—in the rendering of Christ's wounds, the face propped up on a pillow, the day's growth of beard—tells of an all-too-human agony. It is one of Renaissance painting's most quietly wondrous achievements, finding an unsuspected middle ground between the excesses of conventional gore and beauty in representing the Passion's saddest moment.

On your way out, pause a moment to view the fine paintings by Carlo Carrà (especially *La Musa Metafisica,* or *Metaphysical Muse*), suggesting Italy's confident and stylish response to the likes of Picasso and Max Ernst and to the schools of Cubism and Surrealism. ⊠ *Via Brera 28,* ☏ *02/862634.* 🎫 *8,000 lire.* ☉ *Tues.–Sat. 9–5:30, Sun. 9–12:45.*

OFF THE
BEATEN PATH **THE LATIN QUARTER** – Take time to wander around the lively quarter surrounding the Pinacoteca di Brera. The narrow streets, lined with boutiques, crafts shops, cafés, restaurants, and music clubs, comprise what
is often referred to as Milan's Greenwich Village. A longtime haunt of
artists and musicians, it has a number of clubs and cafés offering live
music until late at night.

❼ Castello Sforzesco. For the serious student of Renaissance military engineering, the imposing Castello must be something of a travesty, so
often has it been remodeled or rebuilt since it was begun in 1450 by
the condottiere (hired mercenary) who founded the city's second dynastic family, Francesco Sforza, fourth duke of Milan. As for the rest
of us children of all ages, it's clearly everything a storybook castle ought
to be—huge, for one.

Though today the word "mercenary" has a strongly pejorative ring,
during the Renaissance all Italy's great soldier-heroes were professionals hired by the cities and principalities that they served. Of them—
and there were thousands—Francesco Sforza is considered to have been
one of the greatest and most honest. It is said he could remember not
only the names of all his men, but of their horses, as well. And it is
with his era, and the building of the Castello, that we know we have
entered the enlightened age of the Renaissance. It took barely half a
century before it and the city were under foreign rule.

Today, the Castello houses municipal museums devoted variously to
Egyptian and other antiquities, musical instruments, paintings, and sculpture. Highlights are the **Salle delle Asse,** a frescoed room still sometimes attributed to Leonardo da Vinci, and Michelangelo's unfinished
Rondanini Pietà, believed to be his last work—an astounding achievement for a man nearly 90 and a moving coda to his life. ⊠ *Piazza
Castello,* ☎ *02/6208–3191.* ⊡ *Free.* ☉ *Tues.–Sun. 9:30–5:30.*

NEED A
BREAK? **Viel** (⊠ Largo Cairoli) just across the road from Castello Sforzesco, is
said to be the best *gelateria* (ice cream shop) in northern Italy.

★ ❽ Of **The Last Supper,** H. V. Morton noted that Milan might well be the
only city on earth where you could give a taxi driver the title of a painting as your destination. If this appeals to you, flag one down and say,
"*L'Ultima Cena,*" since this is how *The Last Supper* is known here.

The Last Supper has had an almost unbelievable history of bad luck
and neglect—its near destruction in an American bombing raid in August 1943 was only the latest chapter in a series of misadventures, including, if one 19th-century source is to be believed, being whitewashed
by the monks. Well-meant but disastrous attempts at restoration have
done little to rectify the problem of the work's placement: It is situated on a wall unusually vulnerable to climatic dampness. Yet the
artist chose to work slowly and patiently in oil pigments—which demand dry plaster—instead of proceeding hastily on wet plaster according
to the conventional fresco technique. Aldous Huxley called it "the saddest work of art in the world." After years beneath a scaffold, with restorers patiently shifting from one square centimeter to another,
Leonardo's famous masterpiece still is in a sad state, and studies in further methods to preserve this great fresco continue.

Despite Leonardo's carefully preserved preparatory sketches in which
the apostles are clearly labeled by name, there still remains some small
debate about a few identities in the final arrangement. But there can
be no mistaking Judas, small and dark, his hand calmly reaching for-
ward toward the bread, isolated from the terrible confusion that has

taken the hearts of the others. One critic, Professor Frederick Hartt, offers an elegantly terse explanation for why the composition works: It combines "dramatic confusion" with "mathematical order." Certainly, the amazingly skillful and unobtrusive repetition of threes, when first you see it—in the windows, in the grouping of the figures, and in their placement—adds a mystical aspect to what at first seems simply the perfect observation of spontaneous human gesture.

In the church and former Dominican monastery of **Santa Maria delle Grazie** is the **Cenacolo Vinciano,** which used to be the order's refectory. Take at least a moment to visit Santa Maria delle Grazie itself. It's a handsome church, with a fine dome by Bramante, which was added along with a cloister about the time that Leonardo was commissioned to paint *The Last Supper.* If you're wondering how two such giants came to be employed decorating and remodeling the refectory and church of a comparatively modest religious order, and not, say, the Duomo, the answer lies in the ambitious but largely unrealized plan to turn Santa Maria delle Grazie into a magnificent Sforza family mausoleum. Though Ludovico il Moro Sforza, seventh duke of Milan, was but one generation away from the founding of the Sforza dynasty, he was its last ruler. Two years after Leonardo finished *The Last Supper,* Ludovico was defeated and was imprisoned in a French dungeon for the remaining eight years of his life. ⊠ *Corso Magenta, Cenacolo Vinciano,* ☎ *02/ 498–7588.* ⊡ *6,000 lire.* ☉ *Tues.–Sun. 8–2, hours may vary.*

NEED A BREAK?	For those who don't scream for ice cream, a venerable neighborhood institution, the **Bar Magenta** (⊠ Via Carducci 13 at Corso Magenta) provides an excellent alternative en route. Luncheon, beer, or coffee provides only an excuse for coming here; the real attraction is its casual but civilized, quintessentially Milanese ambience.

❾ **Museo Archeologico.** Housed in a former monastery, there are some enlightening relics from Milan's Roman past here, from everyday utensils and jewelry to several fine examples of mosaic pavement. ⊠ *Corso Magenta 15,* ☎ *02/8645–0665.* ⊡ *Free.* ☉ *Tues.–Sun. 9:30–5.*

❿ The **Museo Nazionale della Scienza e della Tecnica** has models based on technical projects by Leonardo da Vinci and collections of locomotives, planes, and cars. ⊠ *Via San Vittore 21, near Sant'Ambrogio,* ☎ *02/4801–0040.* ⊡ *10,000 lire.* ☉ *Tues.–Sun. 9:30–5.*

⓫ Visit the picturesque **Navigli district** in the southern part of the city. In medieval times a network of navigable canals, called *navigli,* crisscrossed Milan. Almost all have been covered over, except for two long canals, Naviglio Grande and Naviglio Pavese, and part of a third, Darsena. The canals are lined with quaint shops, art galleries, cafés, pubs, restaurants, and clubs. Much of Milan's nightlife is centered here, and the neighborhood has a romantic, bohemian atmosphere. ⊠ *Corso Porta Ticinese.*

OFF THE BEATEN PATH	**MINITALIA PARK** – Between Milan and Bergamo, this theme park has a 1:500-scale relief model of Italy, with about 200 replicas of the country's most important monuments. ⊠ *A4 autostrada to Bergamo, 35 km (22 mi) from Milan, Capriate San Gervasio,* ☎ *02/909–1341.* ⊡ *17,000 lire.* ☉ *Mar.–Oct., daily 9–dusk.*
	PARCO DELLA PREISTORIA – Twenty-five kilometers (16 miles) east of Milan on the road to Brescia, kids will enjoy the 4-kilometer (2½-mile) path with 20 full-size replicas of prehistoric animals. Children will be delighted by the 70-foot-long brontosaurus and the fierce tyrannosaurus.

There is a picnic area and, for the adults, two bars. ⊠ *SS11 near Cassano d'Adda,* ☎ *0363/78184.* 🎟 *11,000 lire.* ☉ *Mar.–Nov., daily 9–dusk; ticket office closes at 6.*

Dining and Lodging

$$$$ ✕ **L'Antica Osteria del Ponte.** Make your way 20 kilometers (12 miles)
★ southwest of Milan to one of Italy's finest (and most expensive) restaurants, located in an attractive agricultural village. The Naviglio Grande (Grand Canal) flows nearby: It was built to carry the area's produce to Milan. Luckily, enough of this produce stays put to form the basis of a rich and imaginative menu that changes each season to follow the harvest cycle and sometimes the whim of chef Ezio Santin. The restaurant is set in a traditional country inn, and the inside is a cozy combination of wooden ceiling beams and a blazing fire. Inventive recipes include ravioli *di aragosta* (filled with lobster meat—summer only) and, in the fall, a range of specialties featuring porcini, the prized wild mushrooms. ⊠ *Cassinetta di Lugagnano; 3 km, or 2 mi, north of Abbiategrasso;* ☎ *02/942–0034. Reservations essential. Jacket and tie. AE, DC, MC, V. Closed Sun., Mon., Dec. 25–Jan. 15, and Aug.*

$$$$ ✕ **Savini.** Red carpets and glass chandeliers characterize the classy Savini, in the Galleria Vittorio Emanuele. It's a typical old-fashioned Milanese restaurant, with dining rooms on three floors, including a "winter garden," where you can watch the people strolling in the Galleria. This is a good place to try the Milanese specialty risotto *al salto* (cooked as a sort of pancake, flipped in the pan) or *costoletta di* vitello (veal cutlets). ⊠ *Galleria Vittorio Emanuele,* ☎ *02/720–03433. Jacket and tie. AE, DC, MC, V. Closed Aug. 10–20, Dec. 23–Jan. 3, and Sun.*

$$$$ ✕ **Scaletta.** The name means "little stairway" in Italian, and the steps leading up to the Scaletta restaurant are a little stairway to culinary paradise. This tiny restaurant could be the dining room of a gracious home, with cool pastel colors, book-lined walls, and a superb collection of blown glass. Host-sommelier Aldo Bellini and genius cook Mamma Pina in the kitchen treat their guests with cordiality and take time to discuss wines and menus with you, if you like. Pina's cooking is a light, personalized version of traditional Italian cuisine; menus change frequently. Reserve two weeks ahead. ⊠ *Piazzale Stazione Porta Genova 3,* ☎ *02/581–00290. Reservations essential. No credit cards Closed Sun., Mon., Easter, Aug., and Dec. 25.*

$$$–$$$$ ✕ **Boeucc.** This restaurant (pronounced "birch") is Milan's oldest. I
★ in the same square as novelist Alessandro Manzoni's house, not far f La Scala. Subtly lit, with cream-color fluted columns, chandel thick carpets, and a garden for warm-weather dining, it has co long way from the time when it was simply a basement "hole" (*bo* is old Milanese for *buco,* or hole). It serves not only typical Mil food, but also a wide range of other dishes, including penne *al bra e zucchine* (with sea bass and zucchini sauce) and gelato *di casta con zabaglione caldo* (chestnut ice cream with hot zabaglione). ⊠ *azza Belgioioso 2,* ☎ *02/760–20224. Reservations essential. AE. lunch Sun. Closed Sat., Aug., Easter, and Dec. 25.*

$$–$$$ ✕ **Antica Trattoria della Pesa.** Turn-of-the-century decor, dark wood paneling, and old-fashioned lamps re-create the atmosphere of this restaurant at its opening more than 100 years ago. This is authentic Old Milan, as the menu confirms, offering risotto, minestrone, and osso buco. ⊠ *Viale Pasubio 10,* ☎ *02/655–5741. AE, DC, MC, V. Closed Sun. and 2 weeks in Aug.*

$$ ✕ **Al Cantinone.** Operagoers still come here for an after-theater drink, just as they did a century ago. The decor is classic Milanese trattoria, the service is fast, and the food is homey and reliable. A bonus: homemade pasta. Try the *pappardelle* (noodles) or ravioli with meat sauce,

Tuscan style. There's a wide selection of grilled meats and a staggering choice of wines. ⊠ *Via Agnello 19, entrance on Via Ragazzi del 99,* ☎ *02/864–61338. AE, MC, V. No lunch Sat. Closed Sun., Aug., and 1 week at Christmas.*

$$ ✕ **La Capanna.** The signora cooks the food and her husband pours the wine and sees that everything goes smoothly in this popular trattoria near the Piola metro stop (and the university). The food is prevalently Tuscan—Tuscan salami, pappardelle, and steak—but some Milanese specialties are also on the menu. ⊠ *Via Donatello 9,* ☎ *02/2940–0884. AE, DC, MC, V. No dinner Mon. Closed Sat. and Aug.*

$$ ✕ **La Libera.** Although this establishment in the heart of Brera bills itself as a *birreria con cucina* (beer cellar with kitchen), its young clientele comes here as much for the excellent food and convivial atmosphere as for the draft beer. A soft current of jazz plays under the gentle ripple of conversation, and the decor is a restful dark green. Sample the imaginative cooking, including the insalata *esotica* (with avocado, chicken, rice, and papaya) or *rognone di vitello con broccoletti e gine-pro* (veal kidneys with broccoli and juniper berries). ⊠ *Via Palermo 21,* ☎ *02/805–3603. Reservations not accepted. No credit cards. No lunch Sun. Closed Sat., Aug., and Dec. 22–Jan. 1.*

$$ ✕ **Nabucco.** This is a smart restaurant in the Brera district, tastefully furnished, whose menu offers such delights as risotto con porcini, an excellent range of salads, and homemade pastries and desserts. Although moderately priced, the good fixed-price lunches take it into the lower category. ⊠ *Via Fiori Chiari 10,* ☎ *02/860663. AE, DC, MC, V. No lunch Mon. Closed Sun.*

$$ ✕ **Trattoria Milanese.** Situated between the Duomo and the Basilica of Sant'Ambrogio, this small, popular trattoria has been run by the same family for more than 80 years and is crowded with businesspeople at lunch and with regulars at dinner, when lingering is allowed. Food is classically regional, with risotto and *costoletta alla milanese* (breaded veal cutlet) good choices. ⊠ *Via Santa Marta 11,* ☎ *02/864–51991. AE, D, MC, V. Closed Tues., Aug., and Dec. 25.*

$–$$ ✕ **Bistrot di Gualtiero Marchese/Brunch.** Atop the Rinascente department store off Piazza del Duomo, this brunch eatery, bar, and bistro is supervised by the well-known chef Gualtiero Marchese and offers a variety of menus within a full range of prices. A bonus is a great view of the Duomo's spires. ⊠ *La Rinascente, Piazza Duomo,* ☎ *02/877120. AE, DC, MC, V. No dinner; no lunch Mon. Closed Sun.*

$–$$ ✕ **La Bruschetta.** You'll find this tiny, busy pizzeria off Corso Vittorio Emanuele, behind the Duomo; it is run by a partnership of Tuscans and Neapolitans. The wood stove is in full view, so you can see your pizza cooking in front of you, although there are plenty of nonpizza dishes available, too, such as spaghetti *alle cozze e vongole* (with clam and mussel sauce). ⊠ *Piazza Beccaria 12,* ☎ *02/869–2494. No credit cards. Closed Mon., Aug. 1–21, Dec. 24–28, and Good Fri.–Easter Mon.*

$ ✕ **La Giara.** In this Pugliese restaurant you eat tavern style, at wooden tables and benches in simple surroundings, often sharing a table with other diners. Yet the quality of the food from the limited menu is a revelation. Start with the antipasto *sott'olio* (eggplant, artichoke, mushroom, and tomato preserved in olive oil), and try one of the grilled-meat courses, cooked on a range at the front of the restaurant and eaten with nothing but the excellent Pugliese bread and olive oil provided. ⊠ *Viale Monza 10,* ☎ *02/261–43835. No credit cards. Closed Wed.*

$ ✕ **San Tomaso.** The atmosphere of an informal beer hall, a trendy young clientele, and a self-service counter add up to pleasant, easy eating. Very busy at lunch, it's usually quieter at night. ⊠ *Via San Tomaso 5,* ☎ *02/874510. No credit cards. Closed Sun.*

$ ✕ **Taverna Moriggi.** Near the stock exchange, it's a dusky, wood-paneled wine bar serving a fixed-price lunch for about 30,000 lire, or cold cuts and cheeses in the evening. ✉ *Via Moriggi 8,* ☎ *02/864–50880. D, MC, V. No lunch Sat. Closed Sun.*

$$$$ ⊞ **Duomo.** This is the obvious choice if a central location is your priority: You're only 20 yards from the cathedral itself, yet within a quiet pedestrian-only zone. Rooms on the second, fourth, and fifth floors look out onto the Gothic gargoyles and pinnacles of the Duomo. The hotel is spacious and modern, with air-conditioned rooms and duplex suites, snappily furnished in golds, creams, and browns. The guests' comfort is the important thing here: Celebrities have been turned away when it was thought they would attract noisy fans and paparazzi. ✉ *Via San Raffaele 1,* ☎ *02/8833,* FAX *02/864–62027. 160 rooms, 156 with bath. Restaurant, bar, air-conditioning, parking. AE, DC, MC, V. Closed Aug.*

$$$$ ⊞ **Four Seasons.** This elegant restoration of a 14th-century monastery is on an exclusive shopping street in the center of Milan and has produced a gem—a precious one, at the highest rates in the city. The hotel blends European class with American comfort. Individually decorated rooms have opulent marble bathrooms; most rooms face the quiet courtyard. Downstairs is the hotel's well-regarded Il Teatro restaurant. ✉ *Via Gesù 8,* ☎ *02/77088,* FAX *02/770–8500. 98 rooms with bath. Restaurant, bar, air-conditioning, business services, meeting rooms. AE, DC, MC, V.*

$$$$ ⊞ **Hotel de la Ville.** This modern hotel in the center of town is decorated in pleasingly subtle, pale colors with silk-hung walls in the guest rooms. Many of the rooms have small balconies, and some have a view of the spires of the Duomo. ✉ *Via Hoepli 6,* ☎ *02/867651,* FAX *02/866609. 105 rooms with bath. Bar, air-conditioning, meeting rooms. AE, DC, MC, V.*

$$$$ ⊞ **Pierre Milano.** No expense was spared to furnish each room of this luxury hotel in a different style with the most elegant color-coordinated fabrics and a variety of modern and antique furniture. Everything is electronic. You can open the curtains, turn off the lights, have personal messages from the front desk appear on your TV screen—all by pressing the buttons on your remote control. The Pierre is on the inner beltway, near the medieval church of Sant'Ambrogio. ✉ *Via De Amicis 32,* ☎ *02/720–00581,* FAX *02/805–2157. 47 rooms with bath or shower. Restaurant, bar, air-conditioning, parking. AE, DC, MC, V.*

$$$$ ⊞ **Principe di Savoia.** Of the three deluxe ITT-Sheraton Luxury Collection hotels in Milan, this is the most sumptuously elegant. Behind the neoclassical facade, the decor is in 19th-century Lombard style, with lavish mirrors, drapes, and carpets. Bedrooms have been enlarged and are more comfortable than ever. ✉ *Piazza della Repubblica 17,* ☎ *02/6230,* FAX *02/659–5838. 287 rooms with bath. Restaurant, bar, air-conditioning, health club. AE, DC, MC, V.*

$$$ ⊞ **Canada.** This friendly small hotel is close to Piazza del Duomo on the edge of a district full of shops and restaurants. It offers good value in rooms that are furnished in anonymous style but have TV, air-conditioning, and refrigerator-bar. ✉ *Via Santa Sofia 16,* ☎ *02/583–04844,* FAX *02/583–00282. 35 rooms with bath. Bar. AE, DC, MC, V.*

$$$ ⊞ **Carlton-Senato.** This is the ideal choice for visitors who intend to spend time shopping—or even window shopping—in the nearby high-fashion streets, Via della Spiga, Via Sant'Andrea, and Via Monte Napoleone. The hotel is very light and airy, with air-conditioning, double-thick windows, a garage with direct access to the hotel, and lots of little touches (such as free chocolates and liqueurs) to make up for the rather functional room furnishings. Some rooms have terraces large enough for a table, chair, and potted shrubs. ☒ *Via Senato 5,* ☎ *02/760–15535,* FAX *02/783300. 79 rooms with bath. Restaurant, bar, parking. AE, MC, V. Closed Aug.*

$$$ 🏠 **Casa Svizzera.** A faithful clientele considers this one of Milan's best small hotels in its price category, so it's advisable to make reservations early. The location, adjacent to the Duomo and a few yards from the Galleria, is central and handy to Metro and bus lines. The hotel has been renovated and soundproofed, and the air-conditioned rooms, with TV and refrigerator-bar, are decorated in a cheery floral-print fabric. ☒ *Via San Raffaele 3,* ☎ *02/8692246,* FAX *02/72004690. 45 rooms with bath or shower Bar. AE, DC, MC, V. Closed Aug.*

$$–$$$ 🏠 **Gritti.** The Picassos, Matisses, and Van Goghs in the lobby are originals—so the manager will tell you—except that they were painted quite recently "in the spirit." The Gritti is a bright hotel with a cheerful atmosphere, adequate rooms, and good views (from the inside upper floors) of tiled roofs and the gold Madonnina statue on top of the Duomo, only a few hundred yards away. ☒ *Piazza Santa Maria Beltrade 4, north end of Via Torino,* ☎ *02/801056,* FAX *02/89010999. 48 rooms with bath or shower. Restaurant, bar. AE, DC, MC, V.*

$–$$ 🏠 **London.** Close to the Duomo, the London has clean, spacious rooms
★   and an English-speaking staff. It has an arrangement with the Opera Prima restaurant in the same building, if you want to take your meals there at a discount (American Express, Discover, and MasterCard are accepted). ☒ *Via Rovello 3,* ☎ *02/720–20166,* FAX *02/805–7037. 29 rooms, 20 with shower. MC, V. Closed Dec. 25–Jan. 3 and Aug.*

$–$$ 🏠 **San Francisco.** Located near Metro stations on two lines (Loreto, Piola, or Pasteur stops) and not far from the Central Station, this modern hotel has a functional, flag-bedecked lobby, simply furnished rooms, and a small garden where guests can relax in fair weather. ☒ *Viale Lombardia 55,* ☎ *02/236–1009,* FAX *02/266–80377. 31 rooms with bath. AE, DC, MC, V.*

Nightlife and the Arts

BARS

El Brellin (☒ Vicolo Lavandai at Alzaia Naviglio Grande, ☎ 02/5810–1351) is one of the many bars in the Navigli district. It is closed Sunday.

In the Brera quarter, **Momus** (☒ Via Fiori Chiari 8, ☎ 02/805–6227) is upscale and intimate.

CONCERTS

La Scala opera house in Milan (☞ *above*) features a two-month season of **classical concerts** in October and November.

DISCOS

Lizard (☒ Largo La Foppa, ☎ 02/659–0890) is trendy, loud, and expensive—a formula that doesn't deter the young Milanese crowd. It's closed Monday and Tuesday and on Sunday evening.

Nepentha (☒ Piazza Diaz 1, ☎ 02/804837) is also a popular spot. It is closed Sunday.

GAY CLUBS

After Dark (☒ Via Certosa 134, ☎ 02/305585) is for men only. It's closed Tuesday. (Milan's so-called "Gay Street," with restaurants, bars, bookshops, etc., is Via Sammartini, just behind the Stazione Centrale.)

JAZZ

Le Scimmie (☒ Via Ascanio Sforza 49, ☎ 02/894–02874) is a good spot for cool jazz in a relaxed atmosphere. It's closed Tuesday.

NIGHTCLUBS

The following Milan clubs are good bets for an evening of dinner and dancing, but don't expect this entertainment to come cheap. **Stage** (✉ Galleria Manzoni off Via Monte Napoleone, ☎ 02/760–21071) serves dinner on Tuesday only and is closed Sunday. **Charly Max** (✉ Via Marconi 2, ☎ 02/871801) is closed Sunday.

OPERA

The season at Milan's famous **La Scala** opera house runs from December 7 (St. Ambrose Day) through May or later. Seats are usually sold out well in advance, but if you are prepared to pay the desk clerk at your hotel, you will probably be able to get hold of a pair of tickets. For information on schedules, ticket availability, and how to buy tickets, there is an Infotel Scala Service (with English-speaking staff) at the ticket office (✉ Teatro alla Scala, Ufficio Biglietteria, Via Filodrammatici 2, ☎ 02/720–03744), which is open daily 10–7. Telephone bookings are not accepted. From abroad you can book in advance, within a short specified period for each presentation (the dates are published at the beginning of the season; these tickets are allocated on a first-come, first-served basis), applying for a reservation by mail or fax (transmitted 9 6 local time, with time and date of transmission, and sender's fax number indicated on the fax, to FAX 02/877–996 or 02/805–1625), or at CIT or other travel agencies (at agencies, no more than 10 days before performance). Consult the listings in the informative monthly *Milano Mese,* free at APT (Italian Tourist Board) offices, or the weekly *Viva Milano.*

THEATER

Milan's **Piccolo Teatro** (✉ Via Rovello 2, ☎ 02/877663) and **Teatro Manzoni** (✉ Via Manzoni 40, ☎ 02/790543) are noted for their excellent productions, given in Italian, of course.

Outdoor Activities and Sports

GOLF

The **Parco di Monza,** 15 kilometers (9 miles) from Milan, contains 18- and nine-hole courses. Contact the **Golf Club Milano** (☎ 039/303081).

SPORTS CENTER

The best-equipped of Milan's many sport centers is the **Centro Saini** (✉ Via Corelli 136, ☎ 02/7380841), in the vast Parco Forlanini. Much like a municipal gym, it offers squash and volleyball facilities and weight rooms. It's outside the city center; take Bus 38.

Shopping

At the northern end of Piazza della Scala, Via Manzoni leads straight into the heart of Milan's most luxurious shopping district, perhaps the most luxurious shopping district in all of Italy. Right here, in a few small streets laid out like a game of hopscotch—**Via Monte Napoleone, Via Sant'Andrea, Via della Spiga**—lie the shops of the great Italian designers, such as Armani, Versace, and Gianfranco Ferre. Don't come here looking for affordable fashion—that has been relegated to the other side of the Duomo—but even though the prices are high, it costs nothing to stroll around and drink in the distinctive look and style that makes shopping in Milan special. Milan's fortissimo occurs twice a year, in March and October (for women) and June and January (for men), when the world's fashion elite descend upon the city for the famous ready-to-wear designer shows that invariably set next season's international styles.

Shops are usually open 9–1 (except Monday morning) and 4–7:30; many are closed in August.

CLOTHING

Benetton (⊠ Via Durini) is where Italian taste and styling can be found at more affordable prices. **Coin** (⊠ Piazza Loreto) is a smaller but stylish department store. **Emporio Armani** (⊠ Via Durini), for the more affordable Armani styles. **Gianfranco Ferre** (⊠ Via Sant'Andrea). **Gianni Versace** (⊠ Via Monte Napoleone). **Giorgio Armani** (⊠ Via Sant'Andrea). **La Rinascente** (⊠ Piazza del Duomo) is one of the bigger department stores in Milan. **Moschino** (⊠ Via Sant'Andrea) offers less conventional styles.

FLEA MARKETS

Flea markets are popular in Milan. Food and a vast array of items, new and old, are displayed in open-air stalls. In many markets, bargaining is no longer the custom. You can try to haggle, but if you fear getting ripped off, go to the stalls where prices are clearly marked. On Saturdays there is the huge **Mercato Papiniano,** on Viale Papiniano, and the Fiera di Senigallia, on Via Calatafimi, with old and new bargains. If you collect coins or stamps, go on Sunday morning to **Via Armorari,** near Piazza Cordusio, where there is a specialized market. The best antiques markets are held on the last Sunday of each month along the Navigli and the third Saturday of each month on **Via Fiori Chiari,** near Via Brera.

HOUSEWARES

L'Utile e il Dilettevole (⊠ Via della Spiga) sells enchanting Italian country-style items for the house.

LEATHER

Prada (⊠ Galleria Vittorio Emanuele, ☎ 02/876979) is a smart leather-goods store also famous for a series of turn-of-the-century murals on a travel theme (downstairs in the main sales area).

SHOES

Beltrami (⊠ Piazza San Babila 4/a). **Ferragamo** (⊠ Via Monte Napoleone 3). **Fratelli Rossetti** (⊠ Corso Matteotti). **Lario 1898** (⊠ Via Monte Napoleone 21).

SHOPPING DISTRICTS

Brera is a Milanese neighborhood with many unique shops. Walk along Via Brera, Via Solferino, Corso Garibaldi, and Via Paolo Sarpi.

Corso Buenos Aires is a wide avenue with a variety of shops, several offering moderately priced items.

Corso Vittorio Emanuele has clothing, leather goods, and shoe shops, some with items at reasonable prices.

Via Monte Napoleone has 10 top-notch jewelers and a profusion of antiques stores and designer fashion boutiques, as well.

CITIES OF THE PLAIN

Pavia, Cremona and Mantua

This section concentrates on some of the great Lombard cities of the Po River plain south of Milan: Pavia, celebrated for its Certosa, or charter house; Cremona, where history's great violin makers lived and worked; Sabbioneta, a diminutive utopian Renaissance city, the fruit of one man's lifelong obsession; and Mantua, home for almost 300 years of the fantastically wealthy Gonzaga dynasty.

Numbers in the margin correspond to points of interest on the Lombardy and the Lakes map.

Pavia

⑫ *38 km (24 mi) south of Milan (on E62), 57 km (35 mi) west of Cremona.*

Pavia was once Milan's chief local rival. The city dates at least from the Roman era and was the capital of the Lombard kings for two centuries (572–774). Pavia came to be known as "the city of a hundred towers" (of which only a handful have survived). Its prestigious university was founded in 1361 on the site of a 10th-century law school but has claims dating to antiquity.

The 14th-century **Castello Visconteo** now houses the local **Museo Civico** (Civic Museum), which has an interesting archaeological collection and a picture gallery featuring works by Correggio. ⊠ *Piazza Castello,* ☎ *0382/33853.* ▣ *5,000 lire.* ⊘ *Tues.–Sat. 9–1:30, Sun. 9–1.*

In the Romanesque church of **San Pietro in Ciel d'Oro,** you can visit the tomb of Christianity's most celebrated convert, St. Augustine, housed in a Gothic marble ark on the high altar. ⊠ *Via Matteotti.* ▣ *Free.* ⊘ *Mon.–Sat. 9–5, Sun. mass.*

The main reason for stopping in Pavia is to see the **Certosa** (the Carthusian monastery). Its facade is stupendous, anticipating by several hundred years, with much the same relish as the Duomo in Milan, the delightful first commandment of Victorian architecture: Always decorate the decoration.

The Certosa's extravagant grandeur was due, in part, to the plan to have it house the tombs of the family of the first duke of Milan, Galeazzo Visconti III (he died during a plague, at age 49, in 1402). And extravagant it was—almost unimaginably so in an age before modern roads and transport. Only the very best marble was used in construction, transported, undoubtedly by barge, from the legendary quarries of Carrara, roughly 240 kilometers (150 miles) away. Though the ground plan may be Gothic—a cruciform planned in a series of squares—the gorgeous fabric that rises above it is triumphantly Renaissance. On the facade, in the lower frieze, are medallions of Roman emperors and Eastern monarchs; above them are low reliefs of the life of Christ, as well as that of Galeazzo Visconti III.

The first duke was the only Visconti to be interred here, and then only some 75 years after his death, in a tomb designed by Gian Cristoforo Romano. Look for it in the right transept. In the left transept is a tomb of greater human appeal—that of a rather stern middle-aged man and a beautiful young woman. The man is Ludovico il Moro Sforza, seventh duke of Milan, who commissioned Leonardo da Vinci to paint *The Last Supper.* The woman is his wife, one of the most celebrated women of her day, Beatrice d'Este, the embodiment of brains, culture, birth, and beauty. Married when he was 40 and she was 16, they had enjoyed six happy years of marriage when she died suddenly, giving birth to a stillborn child. Ludovico commissioned the sculptor Cristoforo Solari to design a joint tomb for the high altar of Santa Maria delle Grazie in Milan. Originally much larger, the tomb for some years occupied the honored place in Santa Maria delle Grazie as planned. Then, for reasons that are still mysterious, the Dominican monks, who seemed to care no more for their former patron than they did for their faded Leonardo fresco, sold the tomb to their Carthusian brothers to the south. Sadly, part of the tomb, and its remains, were lost. ⊠ *Certosa; 8 km, or 5 mi, north of Pavia city center;* ☎ *0382/925613.* ▣ *Free; donation requested.* ⊘ *Nov.–Feb., Tues.–Sun. 9–11:30 and*

Lombardy and the Lakes

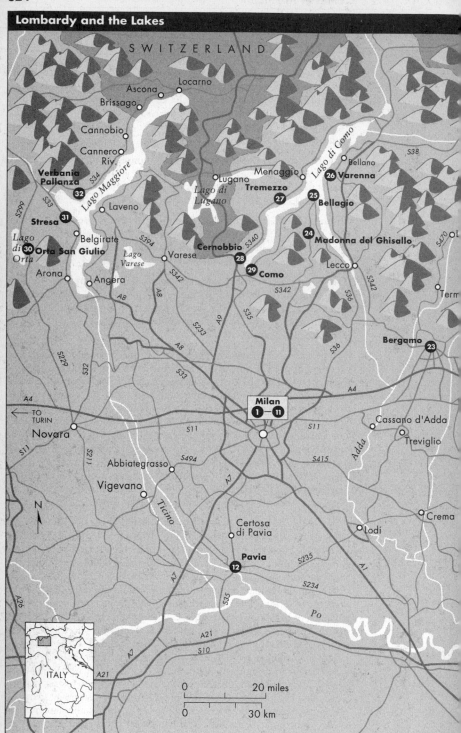

SWITZERLAND

Locarno
Ascona
Brissago
Cannobio
Cannero Riv.
Verbania Pallanza 32
Stresa 31
Lago Maggiore
S34
S33
S695
Lago di Orta
30 **Orta San Giulio**
Belgirate
Laveno
Arona
Angera
Lago Varese
Varese
S394
S342
A8
A8
S233
A9
S32
S229
A4
TO TURIN
Novara
S11
S11
S211
Abbiategrasso
S494
Vigevano
Ticino
A7

Lago di Lugano
Lugano
Menaggio
Tremezzo 27
Lago di Como
26 **Varenna**
Bellano
S38
25 **Bellagio**
24 **Madonna del Ghisallo**
Cernobbio 28
29 **Como**
Lecco
S340
S342
S36
S36
S35
S70
Term

Bergamo 23

Milan
1 — 11
S11
S11
Adda
Cassano d'Adda
Treviglio
A4
S415
A1
Crema
Lodi
Certosa di Pavia
Pavia 12
S235
S234
Po
A7
A26
A7
A21
S10
S35

N

ITALY
A21
A7

0   20 miles
0   30 km

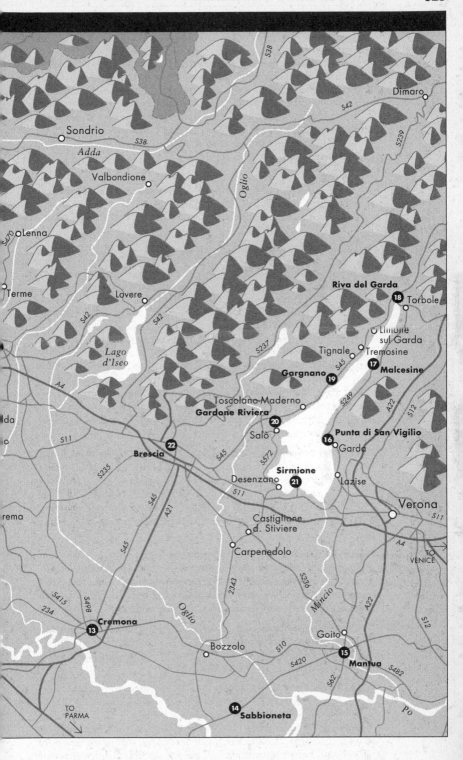

Dimaro

Sondrio

Adda

S38

Valbondione

Oglio

S42

S259

S38

S470

Lenna

Terme

Lovere

S42

S42

Riva del Garda

Torbole **18**

Limone
sul Garda

*Lago
d'Iseo*

S237

Tignale

Tremosine

17 **Malcesine**

Gargnano **19**

S45

A4

Toscolano-Maderno

S249

Gardone Riviera

Salò

20

A22

S12

S11

Brescia **22**

S45

S572

Punta di San Vigilio

16 Garda

S235

Desenzano

Sirmione

S45

S11

21

Lazise

S45

A21

Castiglione
d. Stiviere

Verona

S11

rema

Carpenedolo

A4

TO
VENICE

234

S415

S498

2343

S236

Oglio

Mincio

A22

S12

13 **Cremona**

Goito

Bozzolo

S10

15

S62

TO
PARMA

S420

Mantua

S482

14 **Sabbioneta**

Po

2:30–5; Mar.–Apr. and Sept.–Oct., Tues.–Sun. 9–11:30 and 2:30–5:30; May–Aug., Tues.–Sun. 9:30–11:30 and 2:30–6.

Dining

$$$ ✕ **Locanda Vecchia Pavia.** This attractive restaurant next to the cathe-
★ dral has art-nouveau decor and caters to sophisticated tastes. You'll
find creative versions of traditional regional cuisine, including *rane*
(frogs), the local specialty, in risotto or on a spit. *Casoncelli* (stuffed
pasta) and costoletta di vitello alla milanese are done with style, as are
more imaginative seafood dishes. ✉ *Via Cardinale Riboldi 2,* ☎
*0382/304132. Reservations essential. AE, DC, MC, V. No lunch Wed.
Closed Mon., Jan. 1–9, and Aug.*

Festivals

During the first half of September, Pavia's **Settembre Pavese** festival
presents street processions, displays, and concerts.

Cremona

⑬ *86 km (53 mi) east of Pavia, 67 km (42 mi) west of Mantua, 93 km
(60 mi) southeast of Milan.*

If there is only one place in Italy to buy a violin, it's Cremona—as true
today as when Andrea Amati (1510–80) opened up shop here in the
middle of the 16th century. Though cognoscenti continue to revere the
Amati name, it was the apprentice of Amati's nephew, Nicolo (1596–
1684), for whom the fates had reserved a wide and lasting international
fame. In a career that spanned an incredible 68 years, Antonio Stradi-
vari (1644–1737) made more than 1,200 instruments—including vi-
olas, cellos, harps, guitars, and mandolins, in addition to his fabled
violins. Labeled simply with a small printed slip, "Antonius Stradivarius
Cremonensis. Faciebat anno. . . ." (the date added in a neat italic
hand), they remain the best, most coveted, and most expensive stringed
instruments in the world.

Palazzo del Comune (City Hall). If you would like to see the original
Stradivarius instruments, go to the second floor of City Hall, where
five masterpieces by Cremonese *liutai* (violin makers), dating from the
16th to the 18th centuries, are on view. ✉ *Piazza del Comune,* ☎ *0372/
4071.* ▣ *5,000 lire, valid for all other Cremona museums, including
Museo Stradivariano (☞ below).* ⊘ *Tues.–Sat. 8:30–6, Sun. 9:15–12:15
and 3–6.*

Piazza del Comune has impressed visitors as one of Italy's loveliest:
The cathedral, campanile, baptistery, and City Hall are particularly dis-
tinctive and harmonious. The combination of old brick, rose- and
cream-colored marble, terra-cotta and old copper roofs brings Ro-
manesque, Gothic, and Renaissance together with unusual success.

Don't miss the **Torrazzo** (Big Tower), perhaps the tallest campanile in
the country, visible for a considerable distance across the Po plain. ✉
Piazza del Comune, ▣ *5,000 lire.* ⊘ *Apr.–Oct., Mon.–Sat. 10:30–noon
and 3–6:30, Sun. 10:30–12:30 and 3–7.*

Piazza Roma. Here, in this lovely square of gardens, trees, and lawns,
at No. 1, Antonio Stradivari lived, worked, and died. It is said that in
addition to knowing all there was to know about woods, varnish, and
the subtleties of assembling the 70-odd component parts that make up
a violin, Stradivari liked to keep each new instrument in his bedroom
for a month before varnishing it. This way, he claimed, by virtue of
some mysterious somnolent transmigration, he gave a soul to each of

his creations. In the center of the park is **Stradivari's grave,** marked by a simple tombstone.

The small **Museo Stradivariano** (Stradivarius Museum) has an informative display of Stradivari's plans and models, as well as violins made by Cremona's more modern masters. ⊠ *Via Palestro 17,* ☎ *0372/461886.* ≊ *5,000 lire* (☞ *Palazzo del Comune,* above). ⊙ *Tues.–Sat. 8:30–6, Sun. 9:15–12:15 and 3–6.*

Strolling about town, you may notice that violin making continues to flourish here. There are, in fact, more than 50 liutai, many of them graduates of the **Scuola Internazionale di Liuteria** (International School of Violin Making) who continue to work by traditional methods in small shops scattered throughout Cremona. Visitors are usually welcome to these ateliers, especially if contemplating the acquisition of their own ready-made or custom-built Cremonese violin. You can always drop in on any shop you may be passing, otherwise the local tourist office has a list of workshops and will arrange appointments.

Dining

$$$$
★
✕ **Ceresole.** This is Cremona's best—and most expensive—establishment. It offers a variety of international dishes but concentrates on local delights: *cotecchino* (a rich boiled sausage) and risottos, for example. ⊠ *Via Ceresole 4,* ☎ *0372/23322. No dinner Sun. Closed Mon.*

$$$
✕ **Aquila Nera.** One of the area's more formal restaurants, the Aquila Nera specializes in risotto and roast duck. ⊠ *Via Sicardo 3,* ☎ *0372/ 25646. No dinner Sun. Closed Mon.*

$$–$$$
★
✕ **Centrale.** Close to the cathedral, the Centrale, is a favorite among the locals for traditional Cremonese fare, such as cotecchino with *mostarda* (mustard-hot crystallized fruit), at moderate prices. ⊠ *Vicolo Petrusio 4,* ☎ *0372/28701. Closed Thurs. and July.*

Sabbioneta

⑭ *53 km (33 mi) southeast of Cremona, 34 km (21 mi) southwest of Mantua on S420.*

Vespasiano Gonzaga (1531–91), Sabbioneta's lord, founder, and chief architect, was not a particularly sympathetic man. The glory of his attainments in a life of public service is said to have been excelled only by the ignominy of his treatment of three wives and his only son. Upon retiring from military life at 47, he resolved to turn an old castle and a few squalid cottages into the Perfect City—a tiny, urbane metropolis where the most gifted artists and greatest writers would live in perfect harmony with a perfect patron. After some five years of planning and another five of work, the village was transformed into an elegant, star-shaped, walled fortress, with a rational grid of streets, two palaces, two squares, two churches, an exquisite theater (said to be the first in Europe with a roof) by Vincenzo Scamozzi, and a noble Gallery of Antiquities (a forerunner of today's art galleries). Gonzaga died four years later, survived only by the last of his wives.

When Aldous Huxley and his wife visited Sabbioneta in 1924, the town had reached an appalling state of neglect and decay. The Huxleys were given a tour (still the only way of seeing the interiors of most of Sabbioneta's buildings) much like the tour you take today.

In the **Palazzo Ducale** are four fine equestrian figures of Vespasiano and his Gonzaga forebears. They were led through what had once been the Cabinet of Diana, the ducal saloon, and other rooms, only to discover that the rooms had been converted to serve the structure's new function as the town hall. They were shown the little **theater** (an adaption of Palladio's, at Vicenza, by the man who helped him build it), but it lacked its stage, and its frescoes were covered with whitewash. Today you will find the theater restored and its frescoes uncovered. The third building on the tour, the **Palazzo del Giardino,** has a dusty but impressive gallery of antique sculptures. Tours begin whenever enough interested people have assembled. Apply at Bar Ducale (☎ 0375/52010) or at Ufficio Turistico (✉ Via Gonzaga 31, ☎ 0375/52039); the latter office is open daily 9:30–noon and 2:30–5:30. ✉ *Piazza Ducale,* ✆ *Tour 8,000.* ☉ *Apr.–Sept., Tues.–Sun. 9–noon and 2:30–7; Oct.–Mar., Tues.–Sat. 9–noon and 2:30–5, Sun. 9–noon and 2:30–5:30.*

The **synagogue** is a now shuttered and derelict building, the sole surviving trace of Sabbioneta's prosperous 16th-century Jewish community. You'll have to ask someone to point out the synagogue, as it no longer has an address. ✉ *Town center.*

Mantua (Mantova)

⑮ *67 km (42 mi) east of Cremona, 64 km (40 mi) south of Bardolino.*

Mantua is known as the seat of the Gonzagas, who, like the Viscontis and Sforzas of Milan (with whom they intermarried), lived with the regal pomp and circumstance befitting one of Italy's richest family dynasties. Their reign, first as marquesses, and later as dukes, was a long one—stretching from the first half of the 14th century into the beginning of the 18th.

Even if you've had enough of old palaces, you may still wish to come to Mantua. First, Virgil was born near here. Second, Mantegna (painter of the poignant *Dead Christ* in Milan's Brera) was the Gonzaga court painter for 50 years, and his best-known and only large surviving fresco cycle can be seen here. In addition, there are two fine churches by Leon Battista Alberti (1404–72). Both (much like Mantegna's work here) proved highly influential and were widely emulated by lesser architectural lights later in the Renaissance.

Palazzo Ducale (Ducal Palace). The 500-room complex that centuries of Gonzagas thought of, somehow, as home. This fortress and castle, a 500-room complex that centuries of Gonzagas thought of as home, gives one the sense that the palace took centuries to build. From a distance, the group of buildings dominates the skyline, and the effect is fascinating.

The **Appartamento dei Nani** (Dwarfs' Apartments) were literally that, dwarf collecting being one of the more amusing occupations of Renaissance princes. According to historians, the dwarfs were not mistreated but were considered to be something between members of the family and celebrity comics. The apartments were built both for the dwarfs' enjoyment and for that of the court.

The **Appartamento del Paradiso** is usually praised for its view but is somewhat more interesting for its decorator and first resident, Isabella d'Este. Not only was she married at 16, like her younger sister Beatrice (the beautiful young woman of the tomb in the Certosa at Pavia ☞ Pavia, *above*), she was apparently also Ludovico il Moro Sforza's first choice for a wife—until he learned she was already affianced to a Gonzaga rival. Isabella, too, is regarded as one of the great patrons of the Renaissance. She survived her sister by more than 40 years, and the archives of her correspondence, totaling more than 2,000 letters, are regarded as some of the most valuable records of the era.

The high point of all 500 rooms, if not of the city, is the **Camera degli Sposi** (literally, "Chamber of the Wedded Couple," because Duke Ludovico and his wife are the focus of attention; it was actually an audience chamber). It was painted by Mantegna over a nine-year period, when he was at the height of his power, and finished when he was 44. Here, Mantegna made a startling advance in painting by organizing the picture's plane of representation in a way that systematically mimics the experience of human vision. Even now, more than five centuries after the event, you can almost sense the excitement of a mature artist, fully aware of his painting's great importance, expressing his vision with a masterly, joyous confidence. The interiors of Mantua's Palazzo Ducale may be seen today only on a rigorous guided tour conducted in Italian by the municipality. ⊠ *Piazza Sordello,* ☎ *0376/320283.* ☜ *10,000 lire.* ☉ *Tues.–Sat. 9–1 and 2:30–6, Sun. and Mon. 9–2.*

Casa di Andrea Mantegna. The most serious Mantegna fancier will want to visit his house, designed by the artist himself and built around an intriguing circular courtyard, which is usually open to view (the interior can only be seen by appointment or when open for occasional art exhibitions). The artist's tomb is in the first chapel on the left in another church, **Sant'Andrea,** (1471, some sections earlier or later) a masterwork of the architect Alberti, which itself is considered Mantua's most important Renaissance creation. ⊠ *Casa di Andrea Mantegna, Via Acerbi 47,* ☎ *0376/360506;* ⊠ *Sant'Andrea, Piazza delle Erbe, south of Piazza Sordello.* ☜ *Free.* ☉ *Casa di Andrea Mantegna daily 9–12:30 and 3–6, Sant'Andrea daily 8–12:30 and 3–7.*

Palazzo Te is one of the greatest of all Renaissance palaces, built by Isabella d'Este's son, Federico II Gonzaga, between 1525 and 1535, for his mistress. Reopened in 1989 after restoration, it is the singular Mannerist creation of artist/architect Giulio Romano, decorated with mythological trompe l'oeil paintings that are not to every visitor's taste. Nevertheless, as the magnificently frescoed **Room of the Giants** proves, the palace does not skimp on pictorial drama. ⊠ *South of town walls,* ☎ *0376/365886.* ☜ *10,000 lire.* ☉ *Tues.–Sun. 10–6.*

Dining and Lodging

$$$$ ✕ **Al Bersagliere.** One of Lombardy's best restaurants can be found
★ in this rustic four-room inn, located in the tiny riverside hamlet of Goito, some 16 kilometers (10 miles) northwest of Mantua on Route 236 (the main Mantua–Brescia road). It has been run by a single family for more than 150 years. The fish in particular is excellent, as is the Mantuan classic, frog soup. ⊠ *Via Goitese 258, Goito,* ☎ *0376/60007. Reservations essential. AE, DC, MC, V. no lunch Tues. Closed Mon., 15 days in Jan., 15 days in Aug., and during Christmas.*

$$$ ✕ **L'Aquila Nigra.** Down a small side street opposite the Palazzo Ducale, this popular restaurant is set in a former medieval convent. Frescoes look down from the walls on diners making their way through local Mantuan dishes, such as frittata di zucchine and *faraona al pepe verde* (guinea fowl with green pepper). ⊠ *Vicolo Bonacolsi 4,* ☎ *0376/327180. Reservations essential. AE, DC, MC, V. Closed Sun., Mon., 3 weeks in Aug., and Dec. 24–Jan. 5.*

$$–$$$ ✕ **Trattoria dei Martini–Il Cigno.** With a romantic setting inside a 16th-century palazzo (and featuring some walls frescoed during that period), this restaurant scores well with atmosphere. The menu travels traditional Mantuan terrain, with local specialties such as *tortelli di zucca* (pasta stuffed with pumpkin), *insalata di cappone* (capon salad), and local variations on the Lombard favorite, risotto. ⊠ *Piazza Carlo d'Arco 1,* ☎ *0376/327101. Reservations essential. AE, DC, MC, V. Closed Mon., Tues., 1 week in Jan., 2 weeks in Aug.*

$–$$ ✕ **Cento Rampini.** Charmingly situated in a square in the heart of medieval Mantua, with outdoor tables in summer, this friendly, family-run trattoria is a favorite with the Mantuans themselves. Among the tasty traditional dishes are risottos, *agnoli* (meat-filled pasta dumplings), *luccio in salsa verde* (pike with herb sauce), *cotoletta d'agnello al timo* (lamb cutlets with thyme) and *punta di vitello arrosto* (roll of roast veal). ⊠ *Piazza Erbe 11,* ☎ *0376/366349. AE, DC, MC, V. No dinner Sun. Closed Mon., 1 week in late Jan., and first 15 days of Aug.*

$$$ ⌷ **San Lorenzo.** Mantua is a compact city, and the San Lorenzo is ideally placed in its center. The rooms are large and the decor is authentic early 19th century. Although there is no restaurant, you're within easy walking distance of the three listed above. Some people may find the rooms in the front a little noisy at night, when locals decide that the streets are empty enough of tourists to begin their own *passeggio,* or fashion-conscious constitutional stroll. The San Lorenzo has a rooftop terrace and exudes comfort and individual attention. ⊠ *Piazza Concordia 14,* ☎ *0376/220500,* ☏ *0376/327194. 41 rooms with bath or shower. Air-conditioning, minibar, parking. AE, DC, MC, V.*

Nightlife and the Arts

Each year on the feast of the Assumption (August 15), a **contest** is held in Mantua to determine who is the best *madonnaro* (street artist). Some of the painters can re-create masterpieces in a matter of minutes.

LAKE GARDA, BRESCIA AND BERGAMO

Of all the curious things to be noted about Lake Garda, one is its perennial attraction for writers. Even the 16th-century essayist Michel de Montaigne, whose 15 months of travel journals contain not a single other reference to nature, paused to admire the view down the lake from Torbole, which he called "boundless."

Lake Garda is 50 kilometers (31 miles) long, ranges from roughly 1–16 kilometers (½–10 miles) wide, and is as much as 1,135 feet deep. The terrain is flat at the lake's southern base, and mountainous at its northern tip. As a consequence, the standard descriptions of it vary from stormy inland sea to crystalline Nordic fjord. It is the biggest lake in the region and by most accounts the cleanest.

Punta di San Vigilio

⑯ *70 km (44 mi) north of Mantua, 6 km (4mi) north of Bardolino, 28 km (17 mi) south of Malcesine.*

Punta di San Vigilio, which just about everyone agrees is the prettiest spot on Garda's eastern shore, is full of cypresses from the gardens of the 15th-century **Villa Guarienti di Brenzone.** Expect more fine views of the lake.

Bardolino

64 km (40 mi) north of Mantua, 6 km (4 mi) south of Punta di San Vigilio, 34 km (21 mi) south of Malcesine.

Bardolino, which makes unremarkable but famous red wine, is one of the biggest summer resorts on the lake. It stands on the eastern shore at the widest end of the lake. Here there are two handsome Romanesque churches: **San Severo,** from the 11th century, and **San Zeno,** from the 9th. Both are in the center of the small town. Bardolino is a very lively spot at night, especially in relation to other towns on the lake.

Nightlife and the Arts

Bardolino is host to several festivals, but the best one is the **Grape Cure Festival,** a great excuse to indulge in some of the local wine, since the idea is that the more you drink the better the cure will be. Hold onto the aspirin, just in case.

Malcesine

⑰ *34 km (21 mi) north of Bardolino, 21 km (13 mi) south of Riva del Garda.*

Malcesine is one of the loveliest areas along the upper eastern shore of Lake Garda. It is principally known as a summer resort with sailing and windsurfing schools. The 13 campsites and tourist villages do tend to make the town a little crowded in summer. There are however, some nice walks from the town toward the mountains behind. Visit the 13th–14th-century **Castello Scaligero** built by the Della Scalas.

OFF THE BEATEN PATH

MONTE BALDO – You're in the Veneto now, and if you are fond of cable cars, take the 15-minute *funivia* (funicular) ride to the top of Monte Baldo (5,791 feet) for a great view of the whole lake in summer, or possibly a short ski run in winter.

Outdoor Activities and Sports

SKIING

Malcesine has a well-equipped resort with six lifts and more than 11 kilometers (7 miles) of runs of varying difficulty (☎ 045/7400044).

Riva del Garda

⑱ *21 km (13 mi) north of Malcesine, 29 km (18 mi) north of Gargnano.*

Riva del Garda is one of the biggest towns on the northern tip of the lake. It is large and prosperous, and if you're there in summer, you may want to lodge there if the towns farther south seem too crowded. Many of the town's public buildings date from the 15th century, when it was a strategic outpost of the Venetian Republic. The heart of town, the lakeside Piazza 3 Novembre, is surrounded by medieval palazzi. The **Torre Apponale,** predating the Venetian period by three centuries, looms above these houses: Its crenellations recall its defensive purpose. Standing in the piazza and looking out onto the lake, you can understand Riva del Garda's importance as a windsurfing center. Mountain air currents ensure good breezes on even the sultriest midsummer days.

NEED A BREAK?

Several hotels and cafés line Piazza 3 Novembre. **Hotel Centrale,** at the foot of the Torre Apponale, has tables outside, where you can have a cool drink while watching the boating and windsurfing activity offshore.

OFF THE BEATEN PATH

CASCATA DEL VARONE – This attractive waterfall, some 295 feet high, is 4 kilometers (2½ miles) north of town on the road to Tenno.

Outdoor Activities and Sports

WATER SPORTS

Contact **Circolo Surf Torbole** (✉ Colonia Pavese, ☎ 0464/505385) for news on windsurfing in the area.

En Route After passing the town of Limone (where it is said the first lemon trees in Europe were planted) take the fork to the right about 5 kilometers (3 miles) north of Gargnano and head to Tignale. The view from the **Madonna di Monte Castello** church, some 2,000 feet above the lake, is spectacular. Adventurous travelers will want to follow this pretty inland mountain road to Tremosine.

Gargnano

⑲ *29 km (18 mi) south of Riva del Garda, 12 km (7 mi) north of Gardone Riviera.*

This small port town was an important Franciscan center in the 13th century. One of the two houses owned and lived in by Mussolini is now a language school; the other, Villa Feltrinelli, has not yet been opened to the public, but plans are being made for a museum to open some time in 1998. An Austrian flotilla bombarded the town in 1866 and some of the houses still bear signs of cannon fire. The town comes alive in the summer months when mostly German tourists, many of whom have villas here, invade the small pebble beach.

Dining

$$$–$$$$ ✕ **La Tortuga.** La Tortuga is the best restaurant in this scenic village,
★   and one of the best on the lake itself. Specializing in local cuisine, it features soufflé *di verdura* (of greens) and the excellent *trota allo scalogno e tartufo* (trout with scallions and truffles). From the excellent—and extensive—wine list, try the local white Lugana, which is often served chilled. ✉ *Gargnano,* ☎ *0365/71251. AE, MC, V. No dinner Mon. Oct.–May. Closed Tues., Jan., and Feb.*

Outdoor Activities and Sports

HIKING

Tremosine, some 17 kilometers (11 miles) north of Gargnano, is known as the "Garda Terrace," and is a mountain forest area that is an ideal place for nature hikes. For more information, write or call the **Ufficio Comunale** (✉ Via Papa Giovanni XXIII, ☎ 0365/953185).

En Route   On the road from Gargnano to Gardone you pass the small town of **Toscolano-Maderno,** which has one of the oldest and biggest paper recycling factories in Italy. The town itself hails from Etruscan times but there are also remnants of Roman influence.

Gardone Riviera

⑳ *12 km (7 mi) south of Gargnano, 32 km (19 mi) north of Sirmione.*

Gardone Riviera is a once-fashionable turn-of-the-century resort, now delightfully faded, and the former home of the flamboyant Gabriele d'Annunzio (1863–1938), one of Italy's greatest modern poets. D'Annunzio's estate, **Il Vittoriale,** is an elaborate memorial to himself, clogged with souvenirs of conquests in art, love, and war (of which the largest is a ship's prow in the garden), and complete with a mausoleum. ✉ *Gardone Riviera,* ☎ *0365/20130.* 🎫 *15,000 lire, including tour of house.* ☉ *Winter, Tues.–Sun. 9–12:30 and 2–5:30; open later in summer.*

Dining and Lodging

$$$–$$$$ 🏠 **Villa del Sogno.** A small, winding road takes you from the village to
★   this imposing villa, which surveys the valley and the lake below it. The most popular rooms, inevitably, are those with this view, which can be savored from balconies. The large hotel terrace and the quiet surrounding grounds add to the feeling of getting away from it all, and you'll probably think twice about a busy sightseeing itinerary once you've settled into position in the sun, with a cool drink in hand. ✉ *Corso Zanardelli 107,* ☎ *0365/290181,* 🗎 *0365/290230. 34 rooms with bath or shower. Restaurant, pool, tennis court. AE, DC, MC, V. Closed Oct. 15–Easter.*

$$$ 🏨 **Grand Hotel Fasano.** A former 19th-century hunting lodge on the lakefront, the Fasano has matured into a seasonal hotel of a high standard. The staff is friendly, as are most of the guests, who seem to be keen to make the most use of the water sports at their disposal. It's worth paying a bit extra to get one of the larger rooms with a lake view and balcony. ✉ *Corso Zanardelli 160,* ☎ *0365/290220,* FAX *0365/290221. 75 rooms with bath or shower. Restaurant, bar, pool, beach. MC, V. Closed Nov.–May 15.*

$$$–$$$$ ✕🏨 **Villa Fiordaliso.** The pink-and-white lakeside Villa Fiordaliso—
★ once home to Claretta Petacci, given to her by her lover Benito Mussolini—is known as a high-quality restaurant, but it also has seven tastefully furnished rooms, some with their own balconies overlooking the lake. The menu is tied closely to the availability of fresh local produce, with seasonal treats such as zucchini flowers or porcini mushrooms used in salads or sauces. You can eat on the lakefront terrace in summer, and in the elegant art nouveau–style dining rooms in winter. ✉ *Via Zanardelli 132,* ☎ *0365/20158,* FAX *0365/290011. 7 rooms with bath. AE, DC, MC, V. Closed Mon., Jan., and Feb.*

Nightlife and the Arts

Il Vittoriale has a series of concerts in its outdoor theater during July and August. For information, call ☎ 0365/20347.

Sirmione

㉑ *32 km (20 mi) south of Gardone Riviera, 41 km (25 mi) east of Brescia.*

The ruins at this enchanting town on the southwestern shore of Lake Garda are a reminder that Garda has been a holiday resort for the pleasure-seeking well-to-do since the height of the Roman era. The locals will almost certainly tell you that the so-called **Grotte di Catullo** (Grottoes of Catullus) were once the site of the villa of Catullus, one of the greatest pleasure-seeking poets of all time. Present archaeological wisdom, however, does not concur, and there is some consensus that this was the site of two villas of slightly different periods, dating from about the 1st century AD. But never mind—the view through the cypresses and olive trees is lovely, and even if Catullus didn't have a villa here, he is closely associated with the area and undoubtedly did have a villa somewhere nearby. ☎ *030/916157. ☜ 6,000 lire. ☉ Apr.–Sept., Tues.–Sun. 9–6; Oct.–Mar., Tues.–Sun. 9–4.*

The **Rocca Scaligera** castle was built, along with almost all the other castles on the lake, by the Della Scala family. As hereditary rulers of Verona for more than a century before control of the city was seized by the Visconti in 1402, they counted Garda among their possessions. You may wish to go inside (particularly if you have children with you), since there is a nice view of the lake from the tower. Or you may want to go for a swim at the nearby beach before continuing on the brief clockwise circuit of Lake Garda's shore. The old part of town, in the shadow of the fortress, is still medieval in appearance. ☎ *030/ 916468. ☜ 6,000 lire. ☉ Sun. 9–1; June–Sept., Tues.–Sat. 9–6; Oct.–May, Tues.–Sat. 9–1.*

OFF THE **GARDALAND AMUSEMENT PARK –** This park has more than 40 different
BEATEN PATH rides and water slides and is one of Italy's biggest amusement parks. It is 16 kilometers (10 miles) east of Sirmione. ✉ *Castelnuovo del Garda,* ☎ *045/644-9777. ☜ 27,000 lire. ☉ July–mid-Sept., daily 9 AM–mid-*

night; Apr.–June, daily 9–6 (some days until 7 or 8); mid–late Mar. and Oct., weekends 9–6. Closed mid-Sept.–mid-Mar.

Dining and Lodging

$$$ ✕ **Vecchia Lugana.** At the base of the peninsula, this restaurant is con-
★ sidered one of Italy's best restaurants, and it specializes in fish from
the lake; grilled trout and fillet of perch with artichokes are especially
good. There's also an elegant garden. ✉ *Piazzale Vecchia Lugana 1,
Lugana di Sirmione,* ☎ *030/919012. AE, DC, MC, V. No dinner
Mon. Closed Tues. and Jan.*

$$ ✕ **Osteria del Pescatore.** The specialty of this simple and popular
restaurant is lake fish. The restaurant is in town, on the road that leads
to the Grotte di Catullo, and has a rustic look. Try grilled trout with
a bottle of local white wine. ✉ *Via Piana 20,* ☎ *030/916216. DC, MC,
V. Closed Jan., Feb., and Wed. Oct.–May.*

$$$$ 🏨 **Villa Cortine Palace.** An imposing former private villa set in a secluded
★ park and entered through large iron gates, Villa Cortine treads the fine
line between being ornately imposing and just plain ostentatious. It dominates a low hill, and the grounds—a colorful mixture of lawns, trees,
statues, and fountains—go down to the lake. The villa itself dates from
the early part of the 19th century, although a new wing (1952) has been
added: The trade-off is between the more charming Old World decor
in the older rooms and the better lake views from the newer ones. Either way you'll have the benefit of the extensive grounds and diverse
facilities, as well as the attention of the well-trained and friendly staff.
✉ *Via Grotte 6,* ☎ *030/916021,* ℻ *030/916390. 57 rooms with bath
or shower. Restaurant, bar, air-conditioning, pool, tennis court, beach.
AE, DC, MC, V. Closed Oct. 26–Mar.*

$$–$$$ 🏨 **Continental.** Conveniently located on the lakefront, right next to the
spa, the Continental operates on a half-pension basis only. This works
to keep the cost in check, and the hotel has the amenities and feel of
a much more expensive establishment. Most rooms have balconies, but
ask specifically for a lake view. ✉ *Via Punta Staffalo 7,* ☎ *030/990–
5711,* ℻ *030/916278. 53 rooms with bath or shower. Air-conditioning, pool, beach, parking. AE, DC, MC, V. Closed Dec.–Feb.*

$$ 🏨 **Hotel Sirmione.** Just inside the city walls, near the Castello, this charm-
ing hotel, which is also a spa, sits amid gardens and terraces beside the
lake. The guest rooms are decorated with comfortable Scandinavian
slat beds. Some have matching draperies and wall coverings in floral
prints, some have superbly executed, white, built-in furniture, and
many have balconies. The corner dining room overlooks the lake and
garden, and there is outdoor dining in fine weather. Many of the guests
have been coming for years, and there's a homelike feeling about the
place and the attentiveness of its staff. Full and half pension are of-
fered. ✉ *Piazza Castello 19,* ☎ *030/916331,* ℻ *030/916558. 76
rooms with bath. Restaurant, bar, air-conditioning, pool, spa, meet-
ing rooms, parking. AE, DC, MC, V.*

Brescia

22 *19 km (12 mi) west of Lake Garda, 49 km (30 mi) east of Bèrgamo.*

The ruins of the **Capitolino,** a Capitoline temple built by the Emperor
Vespasian in AD 73, testify to Brescia's Roman origin. Outstanding
among the sculptures in the adjoining **Museo Romano** is the famed
1st-century bronze *Winged Victory.* ✉ *Via dei Musei 57/a,* ☎
030/46031. 🎫 *5,000 lire.* ☉ *Tues.–Fri. 9–12:30 and 3–5, weekends
9–12:30 and 3–6.*

The **Pinacoteca Civica Tosio-Martinengo** accommodates—besides the works of the Brescia School—pictures by Raphael, Tintoretto, Tiepolo, and Clouet. ⊠ *Piazza Moretto,* ☎ *030/3774999.* ▭ *5,000 lire.* ☼ *Tues.–Fri. 9–12:30 and 3–5, weekends 9–12:30 and 3–6.*

Palazzo della Loggia. Palladio and Sansovino contributed to this splendid Lombard-Venetian palace of marble overlooking the Piazza della Loggia. The **Torre dell'Orologio** (Clock Tower) in Piazza della Loggia dates from the 16th-century and is modeled on the campanile in Venice's Piazza San Marco. In the church of **Madonna del Carmine** are a flight of stairs that climb to the ramparts of the Venetian **Castello,** high enough to give a panoramic view over the town and across the plain to the distant Alps. ⊠ *Piazza del Duomo.* ☼ *Closed Mon. and Wed.*

Dining and Lodging

$$$$ ✗ **L'Albereta.** Gualtiero Marchesi is never afraid to try something
★ new. Celebrated as the founder of *la cucina nuova* (nouvelle cuisine Italian-style), Italy's number-one chef first made his mark with impressive cookbooks, private-label products, and two restaurants in Milan. In September of 1993 he moved here, to a deluxe hotel villa near Brescia. The kitchen is celebrated for its spectacular flights of fantasy grounded with classic Lombardian finesse. Tiny lake fish are served within white paper folded origami-fashion, soups are garnished with caviar, and ravioli are served *aperto* (open and unsealed at the edges) or *fazzoletto,* handkerchief-style. You can easily become Romeo to Marchesi's dazzling Juliet—*a rombo in crosta di sale* (turbot in salt crust). The desserts—and prices—are heavenly. ⊠ *Via Vittorio Emanuele 11, Erbusco,* ☎ *030/776–05–62. Reservations essential. Jacket and tie. AE, DC, MC, V. Closed Sun. and Mon.*

$$$ ✗ **La Sosta.** Just south of Brescia's cathedral, La Sosta occupies a 17th-century building. The cuisine and service suggest a more expensive establishment, and the ambience is refined. A Brescian specialty is *casonsei* (large meat-filled ravioli). *Capretto alla bresciana* (roast kid with polenta) is an outstanding main course, but make sure you have room for it. ⊠ *Via San Martino della Battaglia 20,* ☎ *030/295603. AE, DC, MC, V. Closed Mon., Dec. 24–Jan. 7, and 3 weeks in Aug.*

$$$ ▦ **Vittoria.** Centrally located and set among 16th-century buildings, Vittoria has more than its share of atmosphere. Built in 1933, the hotel is in the Venetian style, with a hint of Byzantium and the Spice Routes in its pointed arches and windows. The rooms have been renovated and are decorated with antiques. ⊠ *Via delle X Giornate 20,* ☎ *030/280061,* FAX *030/280065. 65 rooms with bath or shower. Restaurant, bar, air-conditioning, meeting rooms. AE, DC, MC, V.*

Nightlife and the Arts

Brescia's **Teatro Grande** (☎ 030/375–0459) has a series of **classical music** concerts from November to May.

Bergamo

❷❸ *49 km (30 mi) west of Brescia, 58 km (36 mi) southeast of Bellagio.*

Bergamo is two cities—**Bergamo Bassa** (Lower Bergamo) and **Bergamo Alta** (Upper Bergamo), connected by a funicular railway. High up on the hillside, walled in by the ruins of ancient Venetian fortifications, surmounted by a fortress, is Bergamo Alta. The old city of Bergamo lies at the foot of the Bergamese Alps. It is one of northern Italy's most charming medieval centers.

The massive **Torre del Comune** offers a great view of the two cities, the lower and upper. Recent restoration has made the whole structure secure, and it is now open to the public. ⊠ *Piazza Vecchia,* ☎ *035/262566.* ☉ *Apr.–Sept, daily 10–noon and 2–6; Mar. and Oct., weekends 10– noon and 2–6; Nov.–Feb., weekends 10–noon and 2–4.*

The **Duomo** of Bergamo and **baptistery** are the most notable buildings in Piazza Vecchia. But the most impressive is the **Colleoni Chapel,** which has been cleaned, and its elaborate marble decoration is resplendent. ⊠ *Piazza Vecchia.* ☉ *Colleoni Chapel: Mar.–Oct., daily 9–noon and 2–6:30, and Nov.–Mar., Tues.–Sat. 9–noon and 2:30–4:30; baptistery by arrangement with parish priest of Duomo,* ☎ *035/217317.*

In the **Accademia Carrara** you will find one of Italy's greatest and most important art collections. Many of the Venetian masters are represented— Mantegna, Carpaccio, Tiepolo, Guardi, Canaletto—and there are some magnificent Bellinis and Botticellis as well. ⊠ *Bergamo Bassa, Piazza Carrara,* ☎ *035/399426.* 🎫 *3,000 lire, Sun. free.* ☉ *Wed.–Mon. 9:30– 12:15 and 2:30–5:30.*

Dining and Lodging

$$$$ ✕ **Dell'Angelo–Taverna del Colleoni.** Angelo Cornaro has closed the
★ celebrated Antico Ristorante Dell'Angelo to concentrate all his atten- tion on the Taverna del Colleoni, on the 15th-century Piazza Vecchia, right behind the Duomo, where he continues to serve a wide and imag- inative range of fish and meat dishes, all expertly prepared. There are tables outside in the summer. ⊠ *Piazza Vecchia 7,* ☎ FAX *035/232596. AE, DC, MC, V. Closed Mon., 1 week in Jan., and 2 weeks in Aug.*

$$ ✕ **Agnello d'Oro.** A 17th-century tavern on a main street in Upper Berg- amo, with wooden booths and walls hung with copper utensils and ceramic plates, Agnello d'Oro is a good place to imbibe the atmosphere as well as the good local wine. Specialties are typical Bergamasque risotto and varieties of polenta served with game and mushrooms. (The same establishment also has 20 modestly priced rooms with bath.) ⊠ *Via Gombito 22,* ☎ *035/249883. AE, DC, MC, V. Closed Mon. and mid- Jan.–mid-Feb.*

$$ ✕ **Da Ornella.** On the main street in the Upper Town, this trattoria is well known and popular, so reservations are a must. Vaulted ceilings, wooden beams, and antique ceramic ware on the walls enhance the Old World atmosphere. Ornella herself is in the kitchen, turning out casonsei in butter and sage and platters of assorted roast meats. ⊠ *Via Gombito 15,* ☎ *035/232736. AE, DC, MC, V. No lunch Fri. Closed Thurs., Christmas holidays, and July.*

$$ ✕ **La Trattoria del Teatro.** Traditional regional food tops the bill at this good-value restaurant in the Upper Town. Polenta makes an appear- ance as an accompaniment and as an alternative to pasta. Game is rec- ommended in season. Fettuccine *con funghi* (with mushrooms) is a deceptively simple but rich and memorable specialty. ⊠ *Piazza Mascheroni 3,* ☎ *035/238862. No credit cards. Closed Mon. and July 15–30.*

$–$$ ✕ **Bernabò.** From the funicular it's worth heading straight ahead, past Piazza Vecchia to the old military fortress and this corner trattoria. It has two simple rooms with vaulted ceilings, wrought-iron lamps, and wood-paneled walls. The clientele is a mix of locals and economy-minded tourists. All are treated cordially. Specialties are casonsei served with butter and sage, and veal scallopini or game with polenta. Pizza is also served. ⊠ *Via Colleoni 31,* ☎ *035/237692. MC, V. Closed Thurs. and July 15–Aug. 15.*

$$$ 🏨 **Cristallo Palace.** Located on the periphery of town, the Cristallo Palace offers the amenities of a modern, efficient hotel as well as the bonus of good parking and a convenient position on the *tangenziale* (the road

Your passport around the world.

- Worldwide access
- Operators who speak your language
- Monthly itemized billing

Use your MCI Card® and these access numbers for an easy way to call when traveling worldwide.

MCI — Calling Card

415 555 1234 2244
J.D. SMITH

Austria (CC) ♦†	022-903-012
Belarus	
From Gomel and Mogilev regions	8-10-800-103
From all other localities	8-800-103
Belgium (CC) ♦†	0800-10012
Bulgaria	00800-0001
Croatia (CC) ★	99-385-0112
Czech Republic (CC) ♦	00-42-000112
Denmark (CC) ♦†	8001-0022
Finland (CC) ♦†	9800-102-80
France (CC) ♦†	0800-99-0019
Germany (CC) †	0130-0012
Greece (CC) ♦†	00-800-1211
Hungary (CC) ♦	00▼800-01411
Iceland (CC) ♦†	800-9002
Ireland (CC) †	1-800-55-1001
Italy (CC) ♦†	172-1022
Kazakhstan (CC)	1-800-131-4321
Liechtenstein (CC) ♦	155-0222
Luxembourg†	0800-0112
Monaco (CC) ♦	800-90-19

Netherlands (CC) ♦†	06-022-91-22
Norway (CC) ♦†	800-19912
Poland (CC) ÷†	00-800-111-21-22
Portugal (CC) ÷†	05-017-1234
Romania (CC) ÷	01-800-1800
Russia (CC) ÷♦	747-3322
For a Russian-speaking operator	747-3320
San Marino (CC) ♦	172-1022
Slovak Republic (CC)	00-42-000112
Slovenia	080-8808
Spain (CC) †	900-99-0014
Sweden (CC) ♦†	020-795-922
Switzerland (CC) ♦†	155-0222
Turkey (CC) ♦†	00-8001-1177
Ukraine (CC) ÷	8▼10-013
United Kingdom (CC) †	
To call to the U.S. using BT ■	0800-89-0222
To call to the U.S. using Mercury ■	0500-89-0222
Vatican City (CC) †	172-1022

To sign up for the MCI Card, dial the access number of the country you are in and ask to speak with a customer service representative.

MCI

http://www.mci.com

It helps to be pushy in airports.

Introducing the revolutionary new TransPorter™ from American Tourister® It's the first suitcase you can push around without a fight. TransPorter's™ exclusive four-wheel design lets you push it in front of you with almost no effort–the wheels take the weight. Or pull it on two wheels if you choose. You can even stack on other bags and use it like a luggage cart.

Stable 4-wheel design.

TransPorter™ is designed like a dresser, with built-in shelves to organize your belongings. Or collapse the shelves and pack it like a traditional suitcase. Inside, there's a suiter feature to help keep suits and dresses from wrinkling. When push comes to shove, you can't beat a TransPorter™ For more information on how you can be this pushy, call 1-800-542-1300.

Shelves collapse on command.

that bypasses the center). The rooms are large and well equipped, the service is polished and prompt. The hotel's restaurant, L'Antica osa, is very good, and its prices are at the lower range of this catego ⊠ *Via Betty Ambiveri 35,* ☎ *035/311211,* FAX *035/312031. 90 room with bath or shower. Bar, air-conditioning, meeting rooms, parking AE, DC, MC, V.*

$$$ 🛏 **Excelsior San Marco.** The most comfortable hotel in the lower part of Bergamo, the Excelsior San Marco is only a short walk from the walls of the Upper Town. The rooms are surprisingly quiet, considering the central location of the hotel. Its restaurant, Tino Fontana, has a rooftop terrace. ⊠ *Piazza della Repubblica 6,* ☎ *035/366111,* FAX *035/223201. 176 rooms with bath or shower. Bar, air-conditioning, meeting rooms. MC, V.*

Nightlife and the Arts

An **International Piano Festival,** an event of more than 30 years' standing, is held in Bergamo's **Teatro Donizetti** (⊠ Piazza Cavour 14, ☎ 035/249631) in summer.

LAKE COMO

For those whose idea of heaven is palatial villas, rose-laden belvederes, operetta towns, hanging gardens of wisteria and bougainvillea, flicking lanterns casting a glow over lakeshore restaurants, and dreamy alpine vistas, heaven exists at Lake Como. Virgil liked Como at least as much as Garda, calling it simply our "greatest" lake. Stendhal described it as an "enchanting spot, unequaled on earth for loveliness," in his *Charterhouse of Parma.* Though summer crowds do their best to vanquish the lake's dreamy mystery and civilized, slightly faded, millionaire's-row gentility, they fail. Como remains a place of consummate partnership between the beauties of nature and those of humanity. Accordingly, our tour of the lake is of gardens and villas (of which a couple of the finest are now hotels). Like so many of Italy's most beautiful villa gardens, those of Como owe their beauty to the landscape architecture of two eras: Renaissance Italian, with its taste for order; and 19th-century English, with its fondness for illusions of natural wildness. The two are often framed by vast areas of the most picturesque farmland—notably olive groves, fruit trees, and vineyards.

Lake Como is some 47 kilometers (30 miles) long, measured north to south, and it is also Europe's deepest lake (almost 1,350 feet). Rarely out of sight to visitors, it looks like a burnished mirror—until a breeze ruffles its incandescence. Here, in the *centro di lago* (center region of the lake), travelers have long headed for Bellagio. This alluring town is known as the "punta di Bellagio" because it's at the point that divides Lake Como into three branches. It's an enchanting location, one that inspired Gabriel Faure to call Bellagio "a diamond contrasting brilliantly with the sapphires of the three lakes in which it is set." After just a few days on Lake Como, you'll understand why Verdi choose to compose *La Traviata* in Cadenabbia (across the lake from Bellagio). Today, for harried Milanese weekend-trippers, countless honeymooners, and visitors from around the world, going to Lake Como is not so much escape, as return; not getting so much away from it all, but returning to that *douceur de vie,* that sweetness of life, so rarely encountered anymore today.

If you're not going by car, you arrive at the lake by pulling into the railway station at Como, a leading textile center, famous for its silks. Most visitors hasten to the *vaporetti* (water taxis) waiting to take them to the centro di lago, the most beautiful part of the lake. Art lovers, however, should note that 15 or so blocks south of the station is one of the greatest Italian Romanesque churches, S. Abbondio—a detour they will consider well worth making once they've seen its awe-inspiring, gigantic nave interior. Although you can take a bus up either shore-line, most people take a ferry to Bellagio, the key town of the centro di lago; be sure to take an express ferry as the local vaporetti can turn a half-hour ride into a three-hour one. Once at Bellagio, vaporetti and car-ferries traverse the lake, making it easy for travelers to get to the other main towns, Cernobbio, Cadenabbia, and Varenna.

Madonna del Ghisallo

㉔ *48 km (30 mi) northwest of Bergamo, 18 km (11 mi) north of Cernobbio.*

The church of the **Madonna del Ghisallo** (the patroness of bicyclists), is not far from the shores of Lake Como arriving from Bergamo, and offers a fine view of the surrounding area. You will often see cyclists parked outside taking a breather after their uphill struggle, but many come just as a homage to this quite unique Madonna. From Bergamo you pass it on the road to Bellagio. ⊠ *Magreglio.* ☎ *Free.* ☉ *Mar.–Nov.*

Bellagio

㉕ *58 km (36 mi) northwest of Bergamo, 28 km (17 mi) north of Cernobbio.*

Sometimes called the prettiest town in Europe, **Bellagio** also has ferry services to most towns on the lake. Here, buildings always seem to be flag-bedecked, geraniums rustle from every window, and bougainvillea veils the staircases, or *montées,* that thread through the town. At dusk, Bellagio's nightspots—including the wharf where an orchestra serenades dancers under the stars—beckon vacationers to come and make merry.

Villa Serbelloni, a property of the Rockefeller Foundation, can also be visited for its celebrated gardens, on the site of Pliny the Elder's villa, overlooking Bellagio. As there are only two guided visits per day restricted to 30 people, and these tend to be commandeered by group bookings especially during May, you'd do well to book far in advance with the Bellagio tourist office (⊠ Piazza della Chiesa, ☎ 031/950204), which organizes the tours. ☎ *5,000 lire.* ☉ *Guided visits mid-Apr.–mid-Oct., Tues.–Sun. 10:30 and 4.*

The famous gardens of the **Villa Melzi** are open to the public and were once a favorite picnic spot for Franz Lizst. Although you can't get into the 19th-century villa, don't miss the lavish Empire-style family chapel. The Melzi were Napoléon's greatest allies in Italy (the family has passed down the name of Josephine to the present); directly across the lake is the Villa Carlotta, once residence of Count Sommariva, Napoléon's worst Italian enemy. ⊠ *3 km (2 mi) outside Bellagio,* ☎ *031/950318.* ☎ *5,000 lire.* ☉ *Late Mar.–early Nov., daily 9–6:30.*

OFF THE
BEATEN PATH

VILLA BALBIANELLO – This may be the most magical house in all of Italy. It sits on its own little promontory, Il Dosso d'Avedo—separating the bays of Venus and Diana—around the bend from the tiny fishing village of Ossuccio. Relentlessly picturesque, the villa is comprised of loggias, terraces, and *palazzetini* (tiny palaces), all of which spill down verdant slopes to the lakeshore where an old Franciscan church, magnificent stone staircase, and statue of San Carlo Borromeo blessing the waters welcome visitors (the only access to the villa is by launch, which leaves Ossuccio three times a week). Designed in 1596 by Pellegrino Pelligrini, it was enlarged by Count Lambertenghi (who insisted on calling all his guests "Count," but refused the title himself). In 1974 it was sold to Count

Monzino, who graciously willed it to the Fondo Ambiente Italiano, which has opened it to the public. Check with Bellagio tourist information (☎ 031/950204) for the hours of launch tours. ⊠ *Il Dosso d'Avedo.* 🎟 *5,500 lire.* ⊗ *Tues., Sat., and Sun. 10–12:30 and 4–6:30.*

Varenna

㉖ *10 km (6 mi) north of Bellagio.*

Using the ferry boat services in Bellagio, make your way to the town of **Varenna.** The principal sight here is the spellbindingly beautiful garden of the **Villa Monastero,** which, as its name suggests, was a monastery before it was a villa. Now it's an international science center. ⊠ *Varenna.* 🎟 *4,000 lire.* ⊗ *Apr.–Oct., daily 9–noon and 2–5.*

Tremezzo

㉗ *34 km (21 mi) north of Cernobbio.*

The only attraction of note in this small lakeside town is the magnificent **Villa Carlotta.** If you are lucky enough to visit in late spring or very early summer, you will find the villa a riotous blaze of color, with more than 14 acres of azaleas and dozens of varieties of rhododendron in full bloom. The range of the garden's collection is remarkable, particularly when you consider the difficulties of transporting delicate, exotic vegetation before the age of aircraft. Palms, banana trees, cactus, eucalyptus, a sequoia, orchids, and camellias are only the beginning of a list that includes more than 500 species. The villa itself, built between 1690 and 1743 for the luxury-loving Marquis Giorgio Clerici, is slightly newer than the Villa d'Este in Cernobbio (☞ Cernobbio, *below*).

According to local lore, one motive for the Villa Carlotta's magnificence was a keeping-up-with-the-Joneses sort of rivalry between the marquis's ambitious, self-made son-in-law, who inherited the estate, and the son-in-law's arch rival, who built *his* summer palace directly across the lake. Whenever either added to his villa and garden, it was tantamount to taunting the other in public. Eventually the son-in-law's insatiable taste for self-aggrandizement prevailed. The villa's last (and final) owners were Prussian royalty (including the "Carlotta" of the villa's name), and the property was confiscated during World War I.

The villa's interior is worth a visit, particularly if you have a taste for Antonio Canova's most romantic sculptures. The best known is his *Cupid and Psyche,* which depicts the lovers locked in an odd but graceful and passionate embrace, with the young god above and behind, his wings extended, while Psyche, her lips willing, waits for a kiss that will never come. Check with Bellagio tourist information (☎ 031/950204) for the hours of launch tours. ⊠ *Tremezzo,* ☎ *0344/40405.* 🎟 *Villa and gardens 8,000 lire.* ⊗ *Apr.–Sept., daily 9–6; mid–late Mar. and Oct.–early Nov., daily 9–11:30 and 2–4:30.*

Dining and Lodging

$$ ✕🏨 **Silvio.** At the edge of town, this family-owned trattoria with a terrace on the lakeshore is for those who love fresh lake fish. Served cooked or marinated, with risotto or as a ravioli stuffing, the fish is caught by Silvio's family. This is local cooking at its best. There are also 17 modestly priced rooms with bath. ⊠ *Lòppia di Bellagio, Via Carcano 12,* ☎ *031/950322. MC, V. Closed Jan.*

$–$$ ✕🏨 **La Pergola.** Located in Pescallo, about a kilometer (½ mile) from Bellagio, on the other side of the peninsula, La Pergola is a popular lakeside restaurant. Of course, try to reserve a table on the lakeside terrace and order the daily special of freshly caught lake fish. You can also stay in one of the inn's 13 rooms, all of which have baths. ⊠ *Pescallo,* ☎ *031/950263. AE, DC, MC, V. Closed Tues. and Nov.–Feb.*

$$$$ ⊞ **Grand Hotel Villa Serbelloni.** They used to say that those who drove Rolls-Royces stayed at the Villa d'Este hotel in Cernobbio and those who drove Bentleys came here. Once designed to cradle dukes and duchesses in high luxury, this hotel is now a comforting and refined haven for the discreetly wealthy. Just down the road from the punta di Bellagio, the hotel is set within a pretty park. Inside, the atmosphere is one of 19th-century luxury that has not so much faded as mellowed: The rooms are immaculate and plush. The public rooms are a riot of gilt, marble, and thick, colorful carpets. Service is discreet, and the staff is particularly good about arranging transportation across and around the lake. The best rooms—in which Churchill and Kennedy have stayed—face the lake and the Tremezzina, a group of towns on the shores opposite Bellagio. ⊠ *Lungolago Bellagio, Via Roma 1,* ☎ *031/950216,* ☎ *031/951529. 95 rooms with bath or shower. Restaurant, air-conditioning, pool, beauty salon, tennis court, health club. AE, DC, MC, V. Closed end Oct.–early Apr.*

$$ ⊞ **Du Lac.** In the center of Bellagio, by the Lake Como landing dock, Du Lac is a comfortable medium-size hotel owned by an Anglo-Italian family who create a relaxed and congenial atmosphere. Most rooms have views of the lake and mountains, and there is a rooftop terrace garden for drinks or just unwinding. ⊠ *Piazza Mazzini 32,* ☎ *031/950320,* ☎ *031/951624. 48 rooms with bath or shower. Restaurant, bar, air-conditioning. MC, V. Closed late Oct.–late Mar.*

$$ ⊞ **Excelsior-Splendide.** Chances are you'll be lulled to sleep at night here by the lilting sounds of an orchestra directly under your window— this hotel is opposite Bellagio's enchanting quay, where live music beckons one and all on summer nights. This hotel is perfectly serviceable, in the center of town, handy to restaurants, and just a five-minute walk from the stunning gardens of Villa Melzi. ⊠ *Lungo Lalio Mazzoni,* ☎ *031/950342,* ☎ *031/951224. 47 rooms with bath. Restaurant, pool. AE, DC, MC, V. Closed Oct. 21–May 1.*

Cernobbio

㉘   *28 km (17 mi) south of Bellagio, 34 km (21 mi) south of Tremezzo, 50 km (31 mi) east of Lago Maggiore.*

Cernobbio is the first town you come to as you head north from the town of Como. Although many of the villas of the southwest branch (the lake's most overbuilt district) remain private and closed to the public, they can be enjoyed from a boat.

If you're planning to say "budget be damned" in only one place, the **Grand Hotel Villa d'Este** could be it. If you can't stay at this legendary lakeside resort hotel, call ahead and ask to see the grounds or enjoy a wonderful meal in the hotel's restaurant (☞ Lodging, *below*).

Originally built for Cardinal Tolomeo Gallio (who began life humbly as a fisherman) over the course of approximately 45 years (it was completed in 1615), the Villa d'Este has had a colorful and somewhat checkered history, swinging wildly between extremes of grandeur and dereliction. Its tenants have included the Jesuits, two generals, a ballerina, the disgraced and estranged wife of a future king of England (Caroline of Brunswick and George IV, respectively), a family of ordinary Italian nobles, and, finally, a czarina of Russia. Its life as a private summer residence ended in 1873, when it was turned into the fashionable hotel it has remained ever since.

Though the gardens are not as grand as they are reputed to have been during the villa's best days as a private residence and though they have suffered some modification in the course of the hotel's building of tennis courts and swimming pools, they still possess an aura of stately, monumental dignity. The alley of cypresses is a fine example of a proudly repeated Italian garden theme. The fanciful pavilions, temples, miniature forts, and mock ruins make for an afternoon's walk of quietly whimsical surprises.

Lodging

$$$$ 🏨 **Grand Hotel Villa d'Este.** From Napoléon to the Duchess of Wind-
★ sor, this grand establishment has welcomed the rich and famous of several centuries. One of the most luxurious hotels in Italy (less cautious folk could extend that to Europe or even the whole world), Villa d'Este provides just about every conceivable comfort. The villa was built in the late 16th century, and the setting and decorations are enough to indulge the fantasies of a card-carrying hedonist. A broad veranda sweeps out to the lakefront, where a large swimming pool juts out above the water. Across the lake are blue, snowcapped mountains gradually blending into the deep green of the slopes that lead down to the shore. Inside, sparkling chandeliers cast their light on broad marble staircases, and the rooms are furnished in the discreet color-coordinated manner of wealthy Italians. The restaurant is on a par with every other aspect of Villa d'Este, and you can eat in the sumptuous grillroom or outside on the veranda. The jewel in the crown here is the extraordinary garden. ⊠ *Via Regina 40,* ☎ *031/511471,* 🖷 *031/512027. 158 rooms with bath. 2 restaurants, 2 bars, indoor and outdoor pool, sauna, 8 tennis courts, squash. AE, DC, MC, V. Closed Nov.–Mar.*

Como

㉙ *34 km (20 mi) south of Bellagio, 40 km (25 mi) south of Tremezzo, 56 km (33 mi) east of Lago Maggiore.*

Como, on the shores of Lake Como, is part elegant resort, part industrial town. Parks and bustling cafés line its lakefront promenade, all a stone's throw from the splendid 15th-century Renaissance–Gothic **Duomo.** Other fragments of old Como include **San Fedele** (once the town's cathedral), at the heart of the medieval quarter, and the **Porta Vittoria,** the late 12th-century gate. Brave the industrial quarter to see **Sant'Abbondio,** a beautiful 11th-century church.

OFF THE **CASTIGLIONE OLANA** – 18 kilometers (12 miles) west of Como is a
BEATEN PATH Gothic Collegiata and baptistry, with superlative frescos by Giotto's pupil Masolino da Panicale.

Dining and Lodging

$$$ ✕ **Da Angela.** Reservations are a must at this small and intimate restaurant serving Piedmontese specialties. The service is attentive, and the waiters will help you select from a menu that includes various homemade pasta dishes and tasty *coniglio alle olive e alloro* (rabbit with olives and bay leaves). ⊠ *Via Ugo Foscolo 16,* ☎ *031/304656. Reservations essential. AE, DC, MC, V. Closed Sun. and Aug.*

$$$ ✕ **La Locanda dell'Isola.** Isola Comacina, Lake Como's only island, five minutes by regular boat from Sala Comacina, is rustic and restful, but at times crowded. The same could be said for the Locanda, but in each case the visit is worth it. Forget any notions of choosing from a menu, because here the deal is a set price for a set meal, with drinks included in the price. The good news is that the food is delicious, the service friendly, and the setting (eating outdoors on a shady terrace) magnif-

icent. You'll have to pace yourself through a mixed antipasto, salmon trout, chicken, salad, cheese, coffee and dessert. ⌧ *Isola Comacina, Sala Comacina,* ☎ *0344/55083. No credit cards. Closed Nov.–Feb. and Tues. Sept.–May.*

$$$ ▦ **Barchetta Excelsior.** Despite its rather unprepossessing exterior, this
★   centrally located, modern hotel is comfortable, with many rooms look-
         ing directly across Piazza Cavour over to Lake Como. The rooms are
         airy and spacious, with those on the upper floors commanding the best
         views. Ask for a lake view because not all rooms have one. ⌧ *Piazza
         Cavour 1,* ☎ *031/3221,* ＦＡＸ *031/302622. 85 rooms with bath or
         shower. Restaurant, bar, air-conditioning, parking. AE, DC, MC, V.*

$$$ ▦ **Palace.** This well-run, completely refurbished 19th-century grand hotel
         on the waterfront has fine lake views and the advantage of being set
         back in its own gardens, where there is an outside bar in summer. ⌧
         16 Lungo Lago Trieste, ☎ *031/303303,* ＦＡＸ *031/303170. 99 rooms with
         bath. Restaurant, bar, air-conditioning, parking. AE, DC, MC, V.*

$$ ▦ **Tre Re.** Located only a block west of the central Piazza del Duomo,
         this clean, spacious, and welcoming hotel is just a few steps from the
         cathedral. Although the exterior gives away the age of this 16th-cen-
         tury former convent, the rooms inside are airy, comfortable, and mod-
         ernized. The moderately priced restaurant, which shares an ample
         terrace with the hotel, is popular with locals for Sunday lunch. ⌧ *Via
         Boldoni 20,* ☎ *031/265374,* ＦＡＸ *031/241349. 34 rooms, 30 with bath
         or shower. Restaurant, bar, parking. MC, V. Closed Dec. 10–Jan. 15.*

Outdoor Activities and Sports

SEAPLANES
Contact the **Seaplane Club Como** (⌧ Viale Masia 44, ☎ 031/574495).

SKIING
In the province of Como, fine snow skiing facilities abound: Val-
sassina, Val Lesina, Valvarrone, Valcavargna, and Val d'Intelvi (⌧
Provincial Tourist Board, Como, Via Borgovico 148, ☎ 031/230329
or 031/230111).

WATERSKIING
Numerous facilities for waterskiing and all water sports can be found
on the lake (⌧ Provincial Tourist Board, Como, Via Borgovico 148,
☎ 031/230329 or 031/230111).

LAKE MAGGIORE AND LAKE ORTA

Magnificently scenic, Lake Maggiore has its less mountainous eastern
shore in Lombardy, its higher western shore in Piedmont, and its north-
ern tip in Switzerland. Never more than 5 kilometers (3 miles) wide,
the lake is almost 50 kilometers (30 miles) long. The better-known re-
sorts are on the Piedmontese shore, particularly Stresa, a well-estab-
lished tourist town that partly provided the setting for Hemingway's
A Farewell to Arms.

A mountainous strip of land separates Lake Maggiore from Lake Orta,
its smaller neighbor to the west, in Piedmont. Orta attracts fewer vis-
itors than the three larger lakes, and consequently a tour around this
lake can be a pleasant alternative in the summer.

Stresa is the main town on Lake Maggiore, and Orta San Giulio is the
largest center on Lake Orta; all points of interest on the two lakes are
reached from these towns, respectively.

Orta San Giulio

③ *15 km (9 mi) west of Stresa, 76 km (47 mi) northwest of Milan.*

Orta San Giulio is at the end of a small peninsula that juts out into Lake Orta about a third of the way up its eastern shore. Intricate wrought-iron balustrades and balconies adorn the 18th-century buildings of this small and charming town. Small cafés and shops line the shady main square, which looks out across the lake to the small island of San Giulio. There are few more relaxing experiences than sipping a drink at one of these cafés and looking out at the languid waters being stirred by a mountain breeze, with sailboats busily making their way nowhere in particular.

OFF THE
BEATEN PATH

SACRO MONTE (SACRED MOUNTAIN) – Rising up behind Orta and looking down on the lake, this hill offers an enjoyable and interesting hike up from Orta. Pass the church of the Assumption, and just ahead you see a gateway marked SACRO MONTE. This leads to the path up the hill, a comfortable climb that takes about 40 minutes for the round-trip. As you approach the top, you pass no fewer than 20 17th-century chapels, all devoted to St. Francis of Assisi. They are decorated with frescoes and striking, life-size terra-cotta statue groups (a total of almost 400 figures) that illustrate incidents in the saint's life. You can climb the campanile of the last chapel for a panoramic view over the whole lake and the town, about 350 feet below.

The island of **San Giulio,** just offshore, is accessible by hiring the services of a boatman. The lake is no more than 2 kilometers (1¼ miles) wide, and most charge about 10,000 lire for up to four people to make the round-trip. The island takes its name from the 4th-century St. Julius, who—like St. Patrick in Ireland—is said to have banished snakes from the island. Julius is also said to have founded the **Basilica** in AD 390, although the present building shows more signs of its renovations in the 10th and 15th centuries. Inside, there is a black marble pulpit (12th century) with elaborate carvings, and downstairs you'll find the crypt containing relics of the saint. In the sacristy of the church is a large bone, which is said to be from one of the beasts destroyed by the saint, but which on closer examination seems to be a whalebone.

It only takes a few minutes to walk around the parts of the island that are open to the public: Much of the area is taken up by the grounds of private villas. The view back across the lake to Orta, with Sacro Monte behind it, is memorable, particularly in the late afternoon, when the light picks up the glint of the wrought-iron traceries.

Lodging

$$$ ⊡ **Hotel San Rocco.** A converted 17th-century convent in a lakeside garden on the edge of town, the San Rocco has undergone a major renovation in 1992. Half of the rooms have views of the lake, garden, and surrounding mountains. Many have balconies and are furnished in modern style. The restaurant features international cuisine and beautiful views of the lake. Among the specialties is *pesce persico* (perch). ⊠ *Via Gippini da Verona 11,* ☎ *0322/905632,* ℻ *0322/905635. 74 rooms with bath. Bar, pool, health club, parking. AE, DC, MC, V.*

En Route Follow the shore drive from Orta San Giulio north to Omegna, at the head of Lake Orta. A couple of kilometers west of Omegna, in the village of Quarna Sotto, there's a musical instrument factory that's worth a stop. The shore drive continues around the rest of the lake, and at the southern end you can pick up S229, which will take you back to the A4 autostrada.

Stresa

 70 km (43 mi) west of Cernobbio, 16 km (10 mi) east of Orta San Giulio.

Stresa, which has capitalized on its central lakeside position and its good connections to the Borromean Islands in Lake Maggiore, has to some extent become a victim of its own success. The luxurious elegance that distinguished it in its heyday has grown somewhat faded; the grand hotels are still grand but their surrounding parks and gardens are now encroached by traffic. Even the undeniable loveliness of the lakeshore drive has been threatened by the roar of diesel trucks and noisy BMWs. One way to escape is to head for the Borromean Islands just off Stresa (☞ *below*).

NEED A BREAK?   Have a drink or an ice cream in one of the several cafés in **Piazza Marconi.** You can sit back and relax, watching the Borromean Island steamers preparing to set off from the landing stage a few yards away.

Villa Pallavicino is a stately residence built on the hill rising from the lake with magnificent gardens. As you wander around the grounds, with their palms and semitropical shrubs, don't be surprised if you're followed by a peacock or even an ostrich: They're part of the zoological garden, and they are allowed to roam almost at will. From the top of the hill you can see the gentle hills of the Lombardy shore of Lake Maggiore and, nearer and to the left, the jewel-like Borromean Islands. As well as a bar and restaurant in the grounds, there are also picnicking spots. ⊠ *Off Corso Umberto I,* ☎ *0323/31533.* ☜ *8,000 lire.* ☺ *Mid-Mar.–Oct. 30, daily 9–6.*

Boats for the **Borromean Islands** leave every 15 minutes from Stresa. Although you can hire a boatman to take you to the islands, it's cheaper and just as convenient to use the regular service. Make sure to buy a ticket allowing you to visit all the islands—Bella, Dei Pescatori, and Madre.

The islands take their name from the Borromeo family, which has owned them since the 12th century. **Isola Bella** (Beautiful Island) is the most famous of the three, and the first that you'll visit. Its name is actually a shortened form of Isabella, wife of the 16th-century Count Carlo III Borromeo who built the palace and terraced gardens for her. Few wedding presents anywhere have been more romantic. Wander up the 10 terraces of the gardens, where peacocks roam among the scented shrubs, statues, and fountains. The view of the lake is splendid from the top terrace. Before Count Carlo began his project, the island was rocky and almost devoid of vegetation, and the soil for the garden had to be transported from the mainland. Visit the **palazzo** to see the rooms where famous guests—including Napoléon and Mussolini—stayed in 18th-century splendor. ☎ *0323/30556.* ☜ *Garden and palazzo 10,000 lire.* ☺ *Apr.–Oct., daily 9–noon and 1:30–5:30.*

Stop for a while at the tiny **Isola dei Pescatori** (Island of the Fishermen), which is less than 100 yards wide and only about ½ kilometer (¼ mile) long. Of the three islands, this is the one that has remained closest to the way they all were before the Borromeos began their building projects. The island's little lanes, strung with fishing nets and dotted with shrines to the Madonna, are so picturesque they practically drip off the canvas. Little wonder that this tiny fishing village is crowded with postcard stands in high season.

Isola Madre (Mother Island) is the largest of the three and, like Isola Bella, has a large botanical garden. Even dedicated nongardeners should stop to appreciate the profusion of exotic trees and shrubs running down to the shore in every direction. Two special times to visit are April (for the camellias) and May (when azaleas and rhododendrons are in bloom). Also on the island is a 16th-century palazzo, where an antique puppet theater is on display, complete with string puppets, prompt books, and elaborate scenery designed by Alessandro Sanquirico (1777–1849), who was a scenographer at La Scala in Milan. ⊠ *10,000 lire.* ⊙ *Apr.–Oct., daily 8:30–noon and 2–5:30.*

For more information about the islands and how to get there, contact the local tourist office (⊠ Via Principe Tomaso 70, Stresa, ☎ 0323/30150) or ask at the landing stages. ⊠ *Landing stage in Piazza Matteotti, look for* NAVIGAZIONE LAGO MAGGIORE *signs.* ⊙ *Mid-Mar.–Oct.*

NEED A BREAK?	Have lunch at one of several moderately priced restaurants on the islands: **Elvezia** (☎ 0323/30043) or **Delfino** (☎ 0323/30473) on Isola Bella. **Verbano** (☎ 0323/30408) or **Ristorante Italia** (☎ 0323/30456) on Isola dei Pescatori, or **La Pirateria** (☎ 0323/31171) on Isola Madre.

Verbania Pallanza

③② *16 km (10 mi) north of Stresa.*

Verbania Pallanza lies across the Gulf of Pallanza from Stresa. It's known for the **Villa Taranto,** which has magnificent botanical gardens containing some 20,000 species. Created by an enthusiastic Scotsman, Captain Neil McEachern, these gardens rank among Europe's finest. ⊠ *Verbania Pallanza,* ☎ FAX *0323/56667.* ⊠ *8,000 lire.* ⊙ *Apr.–Oct., daily 8:30–7:30.*

Dining and Lodging

$$ ✕ **Monferrato.** Centrally located, off Piazza Cadorna and close to the embarcadero, this hotel restaurant serves risotto *con filetti di persico* (with perch fillets) and typical Piedmontese meat dishes, such as beef braised in Barolo wine. ⊠ *Via Mazzini 14,* ☎ *0323/31386. AE, DC, MC, V. Closed Tues. and Nov.–late Feb.*

$$$–$$$$ ✕🏠 **Ristorante del Sole.** Chef Carlo Brovelli presides over this lakeside
★ inn on the southern, Lombardian shore of Lake Maggiore, with a cheerfulness that is infectious. You'll probably feel the same way if you get there early enough to snag one of the tables in the arbor and enjoy one of the best views of the lake, which figures in the menu, too, in the form of carpaccio made of fine slices of trout and perch. Pigeon is usually served caramelized in honey, while much of the menu changes with the season—artichokes, for example, in many forms in the spring, and eggplant in the summer. Take our advice on reservations to ensure the best table possible, because this restaurant is memorable. There are also nine sizeable apartments with bath. ⊠ *Piazza Venezia 5, Ranco, near Angera,* ☎ *0331/976507,* FAX *0331/976620. AE, DC, MC, V. No dinner Mon. Oct.–May. Restaurant closed Tues. and Jan.–Feb. 15.*

$$$$ 🏠 **Grand Hotel et des Iles Borromeès.** A palatial Old World hotel, this princely establishment has catered to a demanding European clientele since 1863. And though it still has the spacious salons and lavish decor of the turn of the century, it has also been discreetly modernized; rooms have luxurious bathrooms, and there is a fitness center, as well as convention facilities. ⊠ *Lungolago Umberto I 67,* ☎ *0323/30431,* FAX *0323/32405. 172 rooms with bath. Restaurant, bar, air-conditioning, pool, golf privileges, tennis courts, exercise room. AE, DC, MC, V.*

$–$$ ⊞ **Primavera.** In a plain 1950s building in the heart of Stresa, Primavera has balconies embellished with flower boxes. It has the advantage of a location in a quiet pedestrian zone only three minutes from the lake and embarcadero. Rooms are compact and simply furnished. ⊠ *Via Cavour 39,* ☎ *0323/31286,* FAX *0323/33458. 32 rooms with bath. Parking. AE, MC, V. Closed Jan., Feb., and mid-Nov.–mid-Dec.*

En Route   If you're going to Stresa from Lake Orta, take the twisting mountain road past Mottarone, the tallest peak between the lakes, to Gignese, where you'll be about 2,300 feet above sea level and can take in a last dramatic view of Maggiore. Follow the road up to Lake Orta, through the town of Armeno, shaded first by forests of evergreens, then oaks. In the late summer and early fall, you're likely to see whole families out in these woods, crouched down in their hunt for wild mushrooms, or—if they're particularly lucky—truffles.

MILAN, LOMBARDY, AND THE LAKES A TO Z

Arriving and Departing

By Bus

Italian bus service is best avoided on intercity routes, since it is neither faster, cheaper, nor more convenient than the railways. Most bus companies use Piazza Castello as a terminus, because Milan has no central bus terminal. For bus information, call **Autostradale** (☎ 02/801161) or **Zani Viaggi** (☎ 02/867131).

By Car

Two major autostrada routes cross at Milan: the A1, which leads south to Bologna, Florence, and Rome, and the A4, which runs west–east from Turin to Venice. A7 angles southwest down to Genoa from Milan. The city is ringed by a bypass road (the Tangenziale).

By Plane

Milan has two principal airports. **Malpensa,** about 50 kilometers (31 miles) northwest of the city, handles all intercontinental air traffic, and **Linate,** less than 10 kilometers (6 miles) east of the city, handles international and domestic air traffic. For air-traffic information for both airports and information on connections with Milan, call ☎ 02/7485–2200. Air Pullman (coaches) run twice daily in the morning between Malpensa and Linate airports. The fare is 20,000 lire, and the trip takes about 75 minutes.

BETWEEN THE AIRPORT AND DOWNTOWN

By Bus. There is bus service from **Malpensa** to Milan's Central Station. Buses usually leave every half hour in the morning and every hour in the evening. Cost is 12,000 lire. The trip takes about one hour. Buy your ticket inside before embarking. Alternatively, there is a bus-service link between the airport and an airport terminal at Lumpagnano (cost 10,000 lire; open winter, daily 7 AM–9 PM; summer, daily 7 AM–10 PM; journey time 35 minutes; check at airport for departure times, or call ☎ 02/380–11172). Lumpagnano is on the subway route to the city center. Buses leave **Linate** every 20 minutes for Milan's Central Station. The trip takes about 20 minutes; the cost is 4,000 lire. You can also take ATM municipal Bus 73 to Piazza San Babila (every 15 minutes); the cost is 1,400 lire.

By Car. From **Malpensa** take Route S336 east to the A8 autostrada southeast toward Milan. The drive takes about 40 minutes, depending on traffic and destination. From **Linate,** take what was once the Old Brescia Road west into the central downtown area.

By Taxi. A taxi stand is directly outside the arrivals building doors at **Malpensa.** Approximate fare is 120,000 lire. From **Linate,** the approximate fare is 30,000 lire. The duration of the journey is less than 20 minutes.

By Train

Although Milan claims a bewildering number of railway stations, only one is of concern, unless you travel on local routes at peculiar hours—in which case service can begin or terminate in suburban stations (most notably Milano Lambrate for Bergamo, and Stazione Nord for Como). **Milano Centrale** (a bombastic neo-Babylonian creation, from what is now politely termed the era of "rational" architecture) has, since opening in 1931, been Milan's main railway station. Premium international (EC) service and premium (IC) domestic service connect Milan with major European cities. The station is northeast of the historic center, about 5 kilometers (3 miles) from the Duomo and Galleria. Metro line 3 links it with Piazza de Duomo. For train information, call ☎ 02/67500.

Getting Around

By Bicycle

As part of its campaign to ban cars from Milan's center, the city government has begun to set up a network of one-way bicycle rental stations. At first, rentals were free; now there is a small charge. Though the bicycles are clearly intended for residents who would otherwise use cars, current opinion is that tourists may use them, too (although individual proprietors of stands may arbitrarily decide to disagree, especially if you are unable to explain your rights in Italian). Look for yellow stands filled with yellow bicycles.

By Boat

There is frequent daily ferry and hydrofoil service between towns on the lakes, and a range of round-trip excursions, with a dining service (optional) aboard. For all lakes call **Navigazione Laghi** (✉ Via Ariosto 21, Milan, ☎ 02/481–2086). Locally, call **Navigazione Lago di Garda** (☎ 030/914–1321) for Lake Garda, **Navigazione Lago di Como** (☎ 031/273324) for Lake Como, and **Navigazione Lago Maggiore** (☎ 0322/46651) for Lake Maggiore. In addition, lake tours can often be arranged by private launches at lakeside hotels.

By Bus

Trains are generally better than buses for getting around the cities of the plain. There is regular bus service between the small towns on the lakes, and it tends to be a cheaper way of getting around than ferry or hydrofoil service. The bus service around Lake Garda serves mostly towns on the western coast.

IN MILAN

Milan has an excellent system of public transport (for information, call ATM, 02/875495) consisting of trolley cars, buses, and a subway system, the **Metropolitana,** which runs on three lines. Tickets for each must be purchased before you board and must be canceled by machines at underground station entrances and mounted on poles inside trolleys and buses. Tickets cost 1,400 lire and can be purchased from news vendors, tobacconists, and machines at larger stops. Buy several at once—they remain valid until canceled. One ticket is valid for 75 minutes on all surface lines, or for one subway trip. A 24-hour ticket valid on all public transport lines costs 4,800 lire, and one ticket valid for 48 hours costs 8,000 lire; they are sold at **Duomo Metro** and **Stazione Centrale Metro** stations.

By Car

The A4 autostrada is the main east–west highway for this region. The A22 is a major north–south highway running just east of Lake Garda. Although these major highways will allow you to make good time between the cities of the plain, you'll have to follow secondary roads— often of great beauty—around the lakes. S572 goes along the southern and western shores of Lake Garda, S45bis along the northernmost section of the western shore, and S249 along the eastern shore. Around Lake Como, follow S340 along the western shore, S36 on the eastern coast, and S583 on the lower arms. S33 and S34 trace the western shore of Lake Maggiore.

IN MILAN

Serious pollution is responsible for a rigorously enforced effort to ban all unnecessary traffic from the city's center. Cars lacking a special resident's permit will be stopped and ticketed. Parked cars may be towed. For taxi service, call ☎ 02/6767, 02/8585, or 02/8388. For limousine service, call Autonoleggio Pini, (☎ 02/2940–0555, FAX 02/204748). If age or infirmity entitle you to special dispensation, ask your rental agency or hotel concierge about car permits for special cases.

By Taxi

Taxi fares in Milan seem expensive compared with those in American cities, but drivers are honest (to an extreme, compared with those in some cities). A short downtown hop averages 12,000 lire. Taxis wait at stands or can be called (☎ 02/6767, 02/8585, or 02/8388). It is not unknown to travel by taxi throughout the region, but the prices are prohibitive, making train or bus travel the better option.

By Train

From Milan, there is frequent direct service to Cremona, Bergamo, Pavia, Brescia, Mantua, Desenzano del Garda–Sirmione, and Como.

Contacts and Resources

Car Rentals

Car-rental agencies in Milan include **Avis** (☎ 02/668–00681), **Hertz** (☎ 02/20483), **Europcar** (☎ 1678/68088), or look under "Autonoleggio" in the Yellow Pages. The major international companies have offices at both airports.

Consulates

Most nations maintain consulates in Milan. **Australia** (⊠ Via Borgogna 2, ☎ 02/7601–3330), **Canada** (⊠ Via Pisani 19, ☎ 02/669–7451), **United Kingdom** (⊠ Via San Paolo 7, ☎ 02/723001), **United States** (⊠ Via Principe Amedeo 2, ☎ 02/290351).

Emergencies

There is now a nationwide network for all emergency calls. **Carabinieri** (☎ 112). English-speaking officers are available 24 hours a day to deal with every kind of emergency.

Police, Ambulance (☎ 113). You can dial this number wherever you are and it will connect you to the nearest local police emergency service. For first aid, ask for *"pronto soccorso,"* and be prepared to give your address.

English-Language Bookstores

In **Milan:** the **American Bookshop** (⊠ Largo Cairoli at Via Camperio, ☎ 02/7202–0030), the **English Bookshop** (⊠ Via Mascheroni 12,

☎ 02/469–4468), **Feltrinelli Bookstore** (✉ Via Manzoni 12, ☎ 02/7600–0386).

Health Spas
Off the Sirmione peninsula, in Lake Garda, is the Boiola thermal spring. Three Sirmione hotels offer thermal halls with various treatments: **Grand Hotel Terme** (☎ 030/916261), **Hotel Sirmione** (☎ 030/916331), and **Hotel Fonte Boiola** (☎ 030/916431).

Late-Night Pharmacies
There are a number of pharmacies open 24 hours a day, including one on the upper level of **Milan Central Station** (☎ 02/6690735) and **Cooperativa Farmaceutica** in Piazza Duomo (☎ 02/86460408). Others take turns staying open late and on weekends; for the location of the nearest one, check the roster outside any chemist, or the list published in the *Corriere della Sera*.

Travel Agencies
In **Milan: Compagnia Italiana Turismo** (✉ CIT, Galleria Vittorio Emanuele, ☎ 02/863701), **American Express Travel Agency** (✉ Via Brera 3, ☎ 02/809645), **Chiariva** (✉ Largo Domodossola 1, ☎ 02/481–8366).

Visitor Information
Bellagio (✉ Piazza della Chiesa 14, ☎ 031/950204). **Bergamo** (✉ Vicolo Aquila Nera at Piazza Vecchia, Upper Bergamo, ☎ 035/232730; ✉ Viale Papa Giovanni 106, Lower Bergamo, ☎ 035/242226). **Brescia** (✉ Corso Zanardelli 34, ☎ 030/43418). **Como** (✉ Piazza Cavour 16, ☎ 031/274064; ✉ Train station, ☎ 031/267214; ✉ Provincial Tourist Board, Via Borgovico 148, ☎ 031/230111). **Cremona** (✉ Piazza del Comune 8, ☎ 0372/23233). **Desenzano del Garda** (✉ Piazza Mattetotti 27, ☎ 030/914–1510). **Malcesine** (✉ Via Capitanato del Porto 6, ☎ 045/7400055). **Mantua** (✉ Piazza A. Mantegna 6, ☎ 0376/328253). **Milan** (✉ Via Marconi 1, ☎ 02/809662; ✉ Stazione Centrale, ☎ 02/669–0432; ✉ Municipal Information Office, Galleria Vittorio Emanuele, Piazza della Scala, ☎ 02/6208–3101 or 02/878363). **Pavia** (✉ Via Fabio Filzi 2, ☎ 0382/22156). **Riva del Garda** (✉ Giardini di Porta Orientale 8, ☎ 0464/554444). **Sabbioneta** (✉ Via Vespasiano Gonzaga 31, ☎ 0375/52039). **Sirmione** (✉ Viale Marconi 2, ☎ 030/916245). **Stresa** (✉ Via Principe Tomaso 70, ☎ 0323/30150).

10 The Dolomites

Bolzano, Trento, and Cortina d'Ampezzo

Little wonder Leonardo da Vinci depicted the Dolomites in the background of his Mona Lisa. Nature's skyscrapers, they are among the most extraordinary mountain ranges in Italy. Scenery-hungry tourists explore their meadows, crystal clear lakes, and stupefying cliffs. In summer, they marvel at the dramatic rose-color peaks which take on a purple hue near sunset, in winter, the lure is the charming town of Cortina d'Ampezzo—where skiing is almost as important as being seen.

UNLIKE OTHER FAMOUS ALPINE RANGES, this vast mountainous domain in northeast Italy has remained relatively undeveloped. The virginal landscape is the ultimate playground for the family or traveler on a quest for an original adventure. Ski fanatics travel across the world to dare some of the steep slopes that test even Olympic champions. Mountaineers risk the climb up sheer rock faces. For calmer souls there is the seduction of a landscape painted from a palette of extreme colors. The lowland valleys are laced with rivers spanned by awkward bridges and are dotted with secluded villages, picture-book castles, and unexpected historic sites.

The Dolomites, sprawling over the Trentino–Alto Adige region and into parts of Lombardy by the Swiss border and the Veneto along the Austrian border, became known to Americans as a winter sports center after Cortina d'Ampezzo catapulted to fame by hosting the Winter Olympics of 1956. Today, scores of funiculars, chairlifts, and ski lifts give access to 1,200 kilometers (750 miles) of ski runs, as well as ski jumps and bobsled runs.

Then there are the "untouchable" zones—inaccessible by means of chairlift or ski lift. These are the famous plateaus topping some of the highest mountains, from which you can see Italy on one side and Austria or Switzerland on the other. To enjoy such a rare spectacle, you must spend arduous hours climbing beyond where the lifts leave you, and when you reach the top, you will probably see cows casually grazing on the grass. It can make you dizzy just thinking of how they got there, but contradictions are common in the Dolomites.

This expansive land of rocks and valleys has long attracted Italians and other Europeans looking for a varied natural environment. What they—and you—find is a confusion of colors, architectural styles, and languages. At sunset, the colors of the rocks are highlighted by purples and pinks, with even the snowcapped peaks reflecting the pink glow. A meander through the valleys becomes a botanical escapade, with rare plant species abounding; high above you on the cliffs are castles, protected by their size and position. The serious climber will get a closer view of these remote fortresses. There, on the higher levels, are some rarely seen animals: bears, deer, mountain goats, and birds of prey. It's perhaps not surprising that Reinhold Messer, the first man to climb Everest without oxygen, lives in the Dolomites.

Straddling the Brenner Pass—the main access point to Italy from central Europe—the Dolomites play host to a mixture of cultures and languages. The people of the Alto Adige are predominantly German speaking, and their crafts and food have an Austrian accent (until World War I, the area was Austria's South Tyrol). The Trentino, on the other hand, is Italian speaking. Reflecting this diversity, the area, since 1948, has enjoyed special status as the Autonomous Region of Trentino–Alto Adige, made up of the independent provinces of Trento and Bolzano. But there is still another language to be heard in the area: Ladin, an offshoot of Latin still spoken by a small Ladin community, can credit centuries of isolation in mountain strongholds for its survival.

In this chapter, place-names are given in Italian, with German equivalents, where useful, in parentheses. Signs throughout much of the Dolomites are bilingual.

Pleasures and Pastimes

Dining

Encompassing the Germanic Alto Adige province and the Italian Trentino province, the Dolomites region combines Italian cuisine with local Tyrolean specialties, which are much like the dishes of Austria and central Europe. Local delicatessens teem with regional cheeses, pickles, salami, and smoked meats, while local bakeries present a wide selection of crusty dark rolls, caraway rye bread, and the like—perfect for picnics. Local dishes vary from one isolated mountain valley to the next. Don't miss speck, the local smoked ham. Other specialties include *canederli*, or *knoedel*, a type of dumpling with many variations, served either in broth or with a sauce; hot sauerkraut; ravioli made from rye flour, stuffed with spinach, and fried; and apple or pear strudel. And— as befits a wine-producing region—the local vintages (and fruit brandies) are delicious. In the fall in the South Tyrol, when autumn colors beautify the mountains, it's a tradition to make a tour of the cozy country wine taverns to drink the new wine and eat hot roast chestnuts.

CATEGORY	COST*
$$$$	over 85,000 lire
$$$	60,000 lire–85,000 lire
$$	30,000 lire–60,000 lire
$	under 30,000 lire

per person, including house wine, service, and tax

Folk Festivals

Essentially rural in character, the Dolomites offer a rich selection of folk festivals, harvest fairs, and religious celebrations. Chief among these is Trento's weeklong festival of San Vigilio (the last week of June), when marching bands and costumed choirs perform in the streets and squares of the heart of the city. The other major towns have similar festivals, but equally enjoyable are the more informal and low-key celebrations in the villages of the many valleys, sometimes amounting to nothing more than excuses for hardworking mountain farmers to get together for some local wine and song.

Lodging

Accommodations in the Dolomites range from refurbished castles to spick-and-span chalet guest houses, from stately 19th-century hotels to chic modern ski resorts. Even a small village may have scores of lodging places, many of them very inexpensive. Hotel information offices at train stations and tourist offices can help you avoid the language problem if you arrive without reservations: Bolzano train station has a 24-hour hotel service, and tourist offices will give you a list of all the hotels in the area, arranged by location and price. We've tried to mention here a few hotels in towns that make good bases for travel, as well as some notable hotels found along the road. Remember that many hotels in ski resorts cater primarily to longer stays at full or half board: It's wiser to book ski vacations as a package in advance. And a word of warning: Although spring and fall are wonderful times to travel in the region, many mountain hotels are closed for a month or two after Easter and for about six weeks before Christmas.

CATEGORY	COST*
$$$$	over 300,000 lire
$$$	140,000 lire–300,000 lire
$$	80,000 lire–140,000 lire
$	under 80,000 lire

All prices are for a standard double room for two, including tax and service.

Outdoor Activities and Sports

CROSS-COUNTRY SKIING

The Dolomites are an ideal place to learn or improve your *sci di fondo* (cross-country skiing). The major Alpine resorts, and even many out-of-the-way villages, have prepared trails (usually loops marked off by kilometers) catering to differing degrees of ability. Two of the best are at **Ortisei** and **Dobbiaco.** You can have a lot of fun blazing new trails across virgin snowfields; you can usually get permission by asking at the nearest farmhouse or by inquiring at local tourist offices.

DOWNHILL SKIING

The Dolomites offer some of the best skiing in Europe, with some centers also equipped for summer skiing. Generally the ski season runs from late November to April, by which time some people prefer to ski in shirt-sleeves. The most comprehensive centers are **Cortina d'Ampezzo,** in the heart of the Dolomites to the east of Bolzano, and **Madonna di Campiglio,** west of Trento. These resorts are unashamedly upscale, but for your money you get the extras you expect from world-class centers: miles of inter-connecting runs linked by cable cars and lifts, plus skating rinks, heated indoor pools, and lively après-ski activities.

For some of Cortina's charm, but at a fraction of the price, try the **Monte Rota** slopes, accessible from **Dobbiaco.**

Another comparatively inexpensive area is the **Badia Valley,** reached by heading south on S244 from Brunico.

Ortisei (St. Ulrich), just a few miles up the Val Gardena from the Adige Valley, is a popular skiing center, with lifts linking it to the Siusi range.

Stelvio is a year-round skiing center, with summer skiing on many of its runs.

HIKING AND WALKING

The Dolomites have a well-maintained network of trails for hiking and rock climbing, with *rifugi* (huts) on the most difficult ascents. It is important to follow safety procedures and have all the latest information on trails and conditions.

Shopping

Shopping is fun in the Dolomites, where larger towns, such as Bolzano, Bressanone, and Brunico have shops clustered in arcaded shopping streets designed to keep shoppers dry on rainy or snowy days. The ethnic mixture, with its strong Tyrolean influence, makes for local products and handicrafts that are quite different from those elsewhere in Italy. Tyrolean clothing—loden goods, lederhosen, dirndls, and linen suits with horn buttons—is a good buy and costs less than in neighboring Austria. Local handicrafts, such as embroidered goods, wood carvings, figures for nativity scenes, pottery, and handcrafted copper and iron objects, make good gifts.

Exploring the Dolomites

The best—and only—way to get around in this mountainous region is by following the course of the valleys that find their way to the heart of the massifs that compose the Dolomites. Two of the most important valleys are those formed by the Isarco and Adige rivers. The Isarco River begins at the Brenner Pass and runs due south to Bolzano where it joins the Adige River. The Adige itself originates near the Swiss border and also runs south through Bolzano. Italy's main road and rail connections to north central Europe follow the same rivers northward en route to the Brenner Pass.

Great Itineraries

Numbers in the text correspond to numbers in the margin and on the Dolomites and Bolzano maps.

The area of the Dolomites is a vast expanse of valleys, mountain roads and hillside towns. Unfortunately most roads, although of excellent quality, can be hazardous, especially during the winter months. Instead of rushing to get all the sights into your travels, try to be discerning and stick to the areas you would most like to see. A further note of caution involves the closure of some roads during the winter season, which can begin as early as November and continue until May, in particular the high mountain passes such as Passo di Gavia and Passo dello Stelvio in the east.

IF YOU HAVE 3 DAYS

Start in **Trento** ① and head south to **Rovereto** ② and **Riva** on the tip of Lake Garda, then on to the quaint towns of **Pinzolo** ③ and **Madonna di Campiglio** ④ for a birds-eye view of the Dolomites, ending your day via Dimaro in 🏨 **Bolzano** ⑨–⑯. The next day head for the lovely town of **Bressanone** ⑲ and on via **Brunico** ⑳ to the exclusive resort of 🏨 **Cortina d'Ampezzo** ㉒. The last day take the Great Dolomites road passing **Lake Carezza** ㉗ and return to Trento.

IF YOU HAVE 5 DAYS

Follow the itinerary described above as far as Dimaro, but instead of going directly to Bolzano, swing east and head for the dizzily high Passo di Gavia and down then to the small town of 🏨 **Bormio** ⑤. The next day proceed to the breathtaking **Passo dello Stelvio** ⑥ and on down to **Naturno** ⑦ before stopping in one of the pearls of the Alto Adige region, **Merano** ⑧. Continue on to 🏨 **Bolzano** ⑨–⑯, the principal city in this region. The next day head for **Cornedo** ⑰, **Chiusa** ⑱, and **Bressanone** ⑲. Move on to Brunico and 🏨 **Cortina d'Ampezzo** ㉒. The next day head to **Canazei** ㉓ via the breathtaking Passo di Sella and on down into **Ortisei** ㉔ in the heart of the Val Gardena. Return to Trento via **Fie** ㉕ and **Caldaro** ㉖.

IF YOU HAVE 8 DAYS

Follow the five-day itinerary as far as Brunico. The following day stroll through **Dobbiaco** ㉑ before moving on to 🏨 **Cortina d'Ampezzo** ㉒. From here follow the Great Dolomites Road through the Passo di Falzarego and slightly north through the Passo di Sella and into the Val Gardena and 🏨 **Ortisei** ㉔. On the last day, drive to **Fie** ㉕ and south on the A22. Just south of Cornedo, turn left onto the S241 to get to **Lake Carezza** ㉗. Continue along the road until you reach Vigo di Fassa, veering south onto the S48, passing through the small towns of Predazzo, Cavalese, and Ora, until you rejoin the A22 and continue south back to Trento.

When to Tour the Dolomites

If you are here for the skiing, most resorts open from mid-December to April. With the exception of the main bargain period known to Italians as *settimane bianche* (white weeks), usually running from January to February, the slopes are relatively crowd-free. Booking well in advance of your ski holiday is highly recommended, as lack of snow in the early part of the season can sometimes cause overcrowding later on. During the rest of the year accommodations are easier to find, but booking is still recommended. Note: Nearly all hotels and guest houses outside the main urban centers close from early November to mid- or late December.

WESTERN TRENTINO

The areas east and west of Trento are collectively known as the Trentino. The west side includes the peaks of the Brenta Massif, the Stelvio Pass and the Venosta Valley. Some of the passes in this region close during the winter months so if you are traveling during this period you will not be able to follow the entire itinerary. Towns are given in order as you come upon them by road.

Numbers in the margin correspond to points of interest on the Dolomites map.

Trento

❶ *51 km (32 mi) south of Bolzano, 24 km (15 mi) north of Rovereto.*

Trento, capital of the autonomous Trentino province, has somehow escaped the ravages of commercialization and retains its architectural charm, artistic attractions, and historic importance.

It was here, from 1545 to 1563, that the structure of the Catholic Church was redefined, at the famous Council of Trent. This was the starting point of the Counter-Reformation, which brought half of Europe back to Catholicism. Until 1803, Trento itself was ruled by prince-bishops. You'll see the word *consiglio* (council) everywhere in Trento—in hotel, restaurant, and street names, and even on wine labels.

Like most typical Italian towns, Trento has a square at its heart—**Piazza del Duomo.** In the center is a Baroque fountain of Neptune; the massive, low, Romanesque **Duomo** forms the southern edge of the square. Before entering the cathedral, pause to savor the view of the mountaintops ranged majestically around the city and visible above the rooftops in every direction. The mountain weather can change within minutes, and you can never be sure of the same visibility when you reemerge from the cathedral.

Step inside to see the unusual arcaded stone stairways on either side of the austere nave. Ahead of you is the *baldacchino* (altar canopy), a clear copy of Bernini's masterpiece in St. Peter's in Rome. In a small chapel to the right is a mournful 15th-century Crucifixion, with Mary and the Apostle John. This crucifix was a focal point of the Council of Trent: Each decree agreed on during the two decades of deliberations was solemnly read out in front of it. Outside, walk around to the back of the cathedral to see an exquisite display of 14th-century stonemasons' art, from the small porch to the intriguing knotted columns on the graceful apse. ✉ *Piazza Duomo* ☉ *weekdays 9:30–6, Sat. 9:30–noon, Sun. mass.*

The crenellated **Palazzo Pretorio,** which seems to be a wing of the cathedral, was built in the 13th century as the prudently fortified residence of the prince-bishops. Endowed with considerable power and autonomy, these clerics enjoyed a unique position in the medieval hierarchy. The Palazzo Pretorio now houses the **Museo Diocesano Tridentino,** where you can see paintings showing the seating plan of the prelates during the Council of Trent; early 16th-century tapestries by Pieter van Aelst, the Belgian artist who carried out Raphael's designs for the Vatican tapestries; carved wood altars and statues; and an 11th-century sacramentary, or book of services. These and other precious objects all come from the cathedral's treasury. ✉ *Piazza Duomo 18,* ☎ FAX *0461/234419.* 💶 *5,000 lire.* ☉ *Mid-Feb.–mid-Nov., Mon.–Sat. 9:30–12:30, 2:30–6.*

The Dolomites

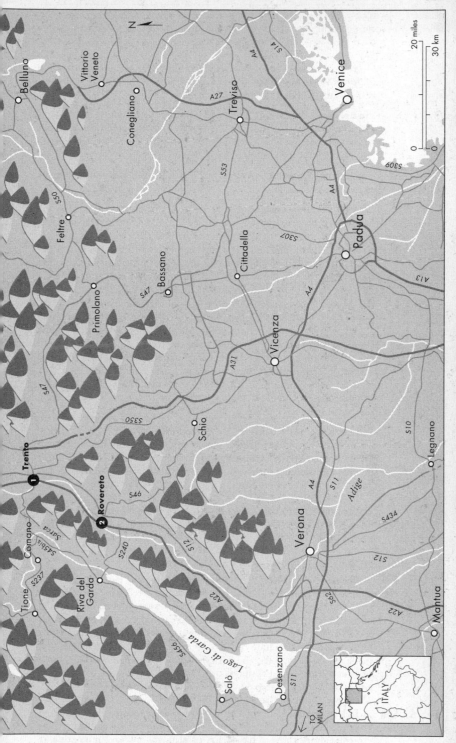

20 miles
30 km

Venice

Vittorio Veneto

Belluno

Conegliano

Treviso

A4

S14

A27

S53

Feltre

S50

Padua

A4

Cittadella

S307

Bassano

S47

Primolano

S47

A4

Vicenza

A13

A31

Schio

S350

Trento

S10

Legnano

S46

Rovereto

Adige

S11

A4

S434

Verona

S12

Comano

Sarca

S45bis

S237

S240

S12

Tione

Riva del Garda

A22

Mantua

A22

S62

Lago di Garda

S456

S11

Salò

Desenzano

TO MILAN

ITALY

NEED A
BREAK?
Locals love the ice cream and snacks at **Bertelli** (⊠ Via Oriola 29;
closed Mon.), an attractive café with tables outdoors on Piazza Lodron.
It's a short walk from the cathedral.

On the northwest side of Piazza del Duomo is the Renaissance church
of **Santa Maria Maggiore** (⊠ Via Cavour; closed Sat.) where many ses-
sions of the Council of Trent were held.

Via Belenzani is famous for its Renaissance palazzi, whose frescoed facades add a colorful note to the street. Locals sometimes call this
stretch of road Trento's outdoor gallery. It's an easy 50-yard walk up
the lane behind the church of Santa Maria Maggiore.

The street of **Via Manci** is a pleasant 200-yard climb past souvenir shops
and glassware outlets.

Castello del Buonconsiglio (Castle of Good Counsel), at the end of Via
Manci, is a huge castle and was the stronghold of the prince-bishops;
its position and size made it easier to defend than the Palazzo Pretorio. As you stand facing it, you can see the evolution of architectural
styles, starting with the medieval fortifications of the Castelvecchio section on the far left, down to the more decorative Renaissance Magno
Palazzo, built three centuries later in 1530. The Castello now houses
the **Museo Provinciale d'Arte** (Provincial Art Museum), where exhibits of art and archaeology are displayed in medieval halls or under
Renaissance coffered ceilings. The 13th-century **Torre dell'Aquila**
(Eagle's Tower) holds the highlight of the museum, a fresco cycle of
·the months of the year. It is full of charming and informatively detailed
scenes of 15th-century life in both court and countryside. ⊠ *Via B.
Clesio 5,* ☎ *0461/233770.* ▨ *6,500 lire.* ☉ *Oct.–Mar., Tues.–Sun. 9–
noon, 2–5; Apr.–Sept., 2–5:30. Admission and hrs vary when exhibitions are held.*

In Piazza Raffaello Sanzio is the **Torre Verde** (Green Tower), part of
Trento's 13th-century fortifications, which stands alongside other fragments of the city walls. **Torre Vanga,** in the street of the same name, is
another 13th-century fortification, this time guarding the medieval bridge
across the Adige, Ponte San Lorenzo.

OFF THE
BEATEN PATH
BELVEDERE DI SARDAGNA – Take the cable car from the station at the·
Ponte San Lorenzo bridge to the scenic spot, a vantage point 1,200 feet
above Trento.

Dining and Lodging

$$$ ✕ **Chiesa.** Near the castle in a building that dates from about 1400,
★   Chiesa is furnished with antiques and serves interesting dishes, some
from centuries-old recipes. The *taglieri di Bernardo Cles,* for example,
consists of coin-shape pasta in a sauce of veal and lettuce—but no toma-
toes: When the recipe was devised, tomatoes were not yet eaten in Italy.
Other specialties include risotto *alle mele,* a hearty minestrone soup
made of rice, vegetables, and barley, and the *tonco de Pontesel*—a stew
of mixed meat served with polenta, made according to a 15th-century
recipe. ⊠ *Via San Marco 64,* ☎ *0461/238766. Jacket and tie. DC, MC,
V. Closed Sun. and Aug. 15–31. No dinner Wed.*

$$–$$$ ✕ **Le Due Spade.** Near the Duomo, small and cozy, with wood panel-
ing and a beautiful antique stove providing warmth on chilly days, this
typical Tyrolean tavern has plenty of atmosphere. Given its popular-
ity with locals, reservations are a must. The cuisine is local, too, and
you can sample traditional *gnocchetti di* ricotta (ricotta cheese dumplings)
and polenta *con funghi* (with mushroom sauce). ⊠ *Via Don Rizzi 11,*

☎ *0461/234343. Reservations essential. AE, DC, MC, V. Closed Sun. No lunch Mon.*

$$ ✕ **Roma.** Centrally located, about halfway between the Duomo and Buonconsiglio castle, this restaurant is one of the busiest in Trento, especially at lunch, when businesspeople come for satisfying, well-prepared dishes in traditional style. On the menu are homemade canederli and *spezzatino trentino* (meat stew). ✉ *Via San Simonino 6,* ☎ *0461/984150. AE, DC, MC, V. Closed Sun. and Aug.*

$$$ ▣ **Accademia.** This friendly character-filled hotel occupies an ancient house in the historic center of Trento, close to Piazza del Duomo. The public rooms retain the ancient vaulting, but the bedrooms are modern and comfortably equipped. There's a good restaurant and a courtyard garden. ✉ *Vicolo Colico 4,* ☎ *0461/233600,* FAX *0461/230174. 43 rooms with bath. Restaurant, bar. AE, DC, MC, V.*

Nightlife and the Arts

From late June to late September a regional **"superfestival"** spotlights historic castles as venues for performances and evocations of fact and legend. Trains taking passengers on excursions to the castles are part of it, as are music, costumes, and banquets.

The Festivale di Musica Sacra (Sacred Music Festival)—a monthlong series of concerts held in the churches of Trento and the Trentino—is held in May–June (☎ 0471/972466 for information).

A summer bonus is the weeklong **San Vigilio Fair,** culminating on June 26, when townspeople don medieval clothing in honor of their patron saint.

Shopping

Antiquariato Corti (✉ Via Mantova 30), **Gasperetti** (✉ Via Torre Verde 52), and **Antichità** (✉ Piazza Santa Maria Maggiore 27) are the main antiques dealers.

Il Pozzo (✉ Piazza Pasi 14/L) is excellent for handcrafted wooden objects; **Il Laboratorio** (✉ Via Roma 12) specializes in terra-cotta pieces by local artists.

Piazza Lodron host a small morning market in the center of town.

Piazza d'Arogno has a flea market the third Sunday of every month; there is also a handicrafts market every Friday and Saturday, but the big shopping day is Thursday, when the weekly market spreads out around this piazza.

Rovereto

❷ *24 km (15 mi) south of Trento and 75 km (47 mi) south of Bolzano.*

Rovereto is a medieval town in the main north–south valley of the Adige. A 15th-century castle looks down on the town, but this district has more recent memories of warfare. Some of the fiercest fighting of World War I took place in the wooded hills around Rovereto, with Italian and Austrian troops bogged down in prolonged and costly conflict. Every night you're reminded of the thousands who fell: At nightfall the bells of the **Campana dei Caduti** (Bell of the Fallen) toll to commemorate war victims throughout the world.

En Route Traveling south from Rovereto, head west on S240, passing the lovely lakeside town of Riva del Garda, and then north on S45bis to Comano, a small but locally renowned spa. The road continues to Tione, a small farming community. From here head north on S239 to reach Pinzolo.

Pinzolo

❸ *75 km (47 mi) northwest of Rovereto, 14 km (9 mi) south of Madonna di Campiglio.*

In this quaint mountain village you can see a remarkable 16th-century fresco on the side of a small church. Follow the signs for the church of **San Vigilio,** which you'll come to after a short walk through the pines. On an exterior wall, a vivid fresco painted in 1539 by the artist Simone Baschenis describes the Dance of Death, with forty ghoulish figures offering a stern rebuke to potential sinners. Unfortunately, the church is usually closed to the public.

Madonna di Campiglio

★ **❹** *14 km (9 mi) north of Pinzolo, 92 km (57 mi) southeast of Bormio and 88 km (55 mi) southwest of Bolzano.*

Madonna di Campiglio is a chic winter resort with more than 130 kilometers (80 miles) of ski runs and 39 lifts. The resort itself is 5,000 feet up, but some of the runs (and summer hiking routes) approach the heights of the surrounding peaks, including Pietra Grande, at over 9,700 feet. An excursion to the Spinale peak by chairlift, (operational all year round) is highly recommended for a magnificent view of the Brenta Dolomites.

Lodging

$$$$ 🏨 **Golf.** You'll have to make your way up to Campo Carlo Magno,
★ the famous pass just north of town, to reach this grand hotel, which is the former summer residence of Hapsburg Emperor Franz Joseph. A modern wing has been added to the more-than-a-century-old original structure, but Old World charm remains: Rooms 114 and 214 are still decorated in the old imperial style. Other rooms are also elegantly maintained, and throughout are verandas, Persian rugs, and bay windows. The hotel is practically on the fairway of a golf course that draws a sophisticated summer crowd, and there is a shuttle bus into town. ✉ *Campo Carlo Magno,* ☎ *0465/41003,* ℻ *0465/40294. 120 rooms with bath, 4 suites. Restaurant, bar, golf course. AE, DC, MC, V. Closed mid-Apr.–June, mid-Sept.–Nov.*

$$$$ 🏨 **Savoia Palace.** A major renovation in 1988 strengthened the Savoia Palace's reputation as the premier hotel in the center of this fashionable ski resort. The owners knew enough not to tamper with the decor—mountain-style furnishings with lots of carved wood—or the intimate atmosphere of the reception rooms. Two fireplaces blaze away in the bar, where guests recall the day's exploits on the ski slopes. The elegant restaurant serves a mixture of local specialties and hearty dishes drawing on Italian and Austrian influences. Guests stay on full- or half-board terms only. ✉ *Via Dolomiti di Brenta,* ☎ *0465/41004,* ℻ *0465/40549. 55 rooms with bath. Restaurant, bar. AE, DC. Closed mid-Apr.–June, mid-Sept.–Nov.*

$$$ 🏨 **Grifone.** A comfortable hotel that catches the sun, the Grifone has distinctive wood paneling on the outside, flower-decorated balconies, and rooms with views of the forested slopes. The restaurant serves home cooking as well as international dishes. ✉ *Via Vallesinella 7,* ☎ *0465/42002,* ℻ *0465/40540. 40 rooms with bath. Restaurant, bar. AE, MC, V. Closed Apr. 15–June 30, Sept.–Nov.*

Nightlife and the Arts

Almost all the nightclubs and discos here are part of the many chic hotel complexes.

Outdoor Activities and Sports

GOLF

Campo Carlo Magno (☎ 0465/41003) is a nine-hole course set in the mountains near Madonna di Campiglio, open July 1–September 15.

SKIING

Madonna di Campiglio is one of the better known skiing resorts of the Dolomites with miles of interconnecting runs linked by cable cars and lifts.

En Route   Just a few kilometers north of Madonna di Campiglio is one of the highest points in the Dolomites, the **Carlo Magno Pass.** This is where Charlemagne is said to have stopped in AD 800 on his way to Rome to be crowned emperor. Stop to glance over the whole of northern Italy. Resume your descent with caution (in the space of a few miles, you descend more than 2,000 feet), getting steering practice on the hairpin turns and switchbacks. The strange, rocky pinnacles of the Dolomites, which jut straight up like chimneys and look at times more like Utah's Monument Valley than any European ranges, loom over scattered mountain lakes. Turn left at Dimaro, and continue 37 kilometers (23 miles) east to Ponte di Legno through another high pass, Passo del Tonale (5,600 feet). Here turn right on S300 and passing the so–called Black Lake on your left, head for Bormio, the famous Lombard skiing center, through the pass of Gavia.

Bormio

❺   *20 km (12 mi) south of Passo dello Stelvio, 100 km (60 mi) southwest of Merano.*

At the foot of the Stelvio Pass, in the Valtellina valley, **Bormio** is one of the most famous ski resorts on the western side of the Dolomites. It differs greatly from Madonna di Campiglio in that it is both a town in itself as well as a summer resort. Even Italians come here in the summer months to escape the humid conditions. With an altitude of close to 4,000 feet, the air is clean and fresh; popular activities in the region include hill walking, mountain climbing, as well as grass skiing (☞ Dolomites A to Z, *below*).

Bormio is small in size, and although there are few cultural sites to visit, there are plenty of shops, restaurants and hotels.

Lodging

$$$ 🏨 **Nazionale.** With its own private garden and bordering the Stelvio National Park, this centrally located hotel offers services for all the major winter and summer activities. Rooms are small but well equipped, with a TV and a safe. The exterior is, for the most part, wood, with balconies on nearly all floors (except the top floor) and shops on the ground level. There is a warm bar, two restaurants that serve local snacks and international dishes, a games room, and a sauna. The hotel also operates a shuttle bus to and from the cable cars. ⊠ *Via Stelvio,* ☎ *0342/903361,* ℻ *0342/905294. 54 rooms with shower. 2 restaurants, bar, sauna, recreation room. AE, MC, V. Closed Oct.–Dec.31.*

$$$ 🏨 **Larice Bianco.** This modern hotel in a quiet part of town, a five-minute walk from the center, is two minutes from hiking trails, ski lifts and other activities. The rooms are comfortable and adequately sized and all have private balconies. There is a piano bar for guests to show off their après-ski glow and if the sun fails to impress there is even a solarium. The hotel restaurant serves typical Valdisotto cuisine. ⊠ *Via Funivia 10,* ☎ *0342/904693,* ℻ *0342/904614. 45 rooms with bath. Restaurant, piano bar. AE, MC, V. Closed mid Sept.–Dec. 31.*

Passo dello Stelvio

★ **6** *20 km (12 mi) north of Bormio, 61 km (38 mi) west of Naturno, 80 km (48 mi) west of Merano.*

At just over 9,000 feet, **Passo dello Stelvio** (Stelvio Pass) is the second-highest pass in Europe. The view from the top is worth the effort because the pass connects the Venosta Valley with the Valtellina in neighboring Lombardy. Just to the right as you enter the pass is Switzerland. Stelvio is well known as a winter and summer skiing center.

NEED A BREAK?	You'll probably want a breather once you've made it to the top of the pass. A good place for a drink is the bar of the **Hotel Passo dello Stelvio** (☏ 0342/903162), where you can enjoy the view of two valleys.

En Route Between the Stelvio Pass and Spondigna is 30 kilometers (19 miles) of winding road, with 48 hairpin turns. This section of road can be a bit hair-raising for anyone who doesn't like mountain driving. Take your time and admire the mountainous landscape either side, or else shut your eyes, but only if you are not driving. In Spondigna keep to the right for the road to Naturno.

ALTO ADIGE AND CORTINA

Alto Adige (Sudtirol), the northern half of the region, was ceded to Italy at the end of World War I, hitherto having been part of the Austro-Hungarian Empire. As a result, everything here has more than a tinge of the Teutonic, which is none more apparent than in the fact that the majority of the inhabitants are German-speaking. Ethnic differences have led to inevitable tensions (including, alas, acts of terrorism), though a large measure of autonomy has, for the most part, kept the lid on nationalist ambitions. Towns are listed in order as you come upon them by road.

Numbers in the text correspond to numbers in the margin and on the Alto Adige and Cortina map.

Naturno

7 *61 km (38 mi) east of Passo dello Stelvio, 14 km (9 mi) west of Merano, 44 km (27 mi) northwest of Bolzano.*

Naturno is a large horticultural center, with streets lined with colorful houses that display painted murals on their walls. Lovers of art will also appreciate the church of **San Procolo,** which is frescoed inside and out, and has wall paintings that are the oldest in the German-speaking world, dating from the 8th century. Unfortunately, it is usually open only on Sundays.

Above the town, a short distance away, is the 13th-century Juval Castle, since 1983 the home of the South Tyrolese climber and polar adventurer Reinhold Messner—the first man to conquer Everest solo, and the first to scale all 14 of the world's highest peaks without oxygen. Since 1995 part of the castle has been a museum, showing Messner's collection of Tibetan art, mountaineering illustrations, and masks from around the world. ☏ FAX 0473/221852. ☞ 10,000 lire. ☉ Mid-April–June 30; Sept. 1–mid-Nov. 10–5:30.

NEED A BREAK?	Just below Juval Castle, Reinhold Messner has opened the **Juval Inn,** an old-style hostelry in a restored farmhouse, serving traditional local dishes and wines provisioned from his own farm. ✉ Schlosswirt-Juval, ☏ 0473/88238. ☉ Easter–end of Oct. Closed Wed.

Merano

★ ⑧ *24 km (15 mi) north of Bolzano, 100 km (62 mi) northeast of Bormio.*

Merano (Meran) is the second largest town in the Alto Adige, and has been famous as a spa town for 150 years due to its thermal waters which have natural radioactivity. It is also renowned for its "grape cure." Sheltered by mountains, Merano has an unusually mild climate, with summer temperatures rarely exceeding 80°F and winters that usually stay above freezing, despite the skiing that is within easy reach. (Chairlifts and cable cars connect Merano with the high Alpine slopes of Avelengo and San Vigilio.)

Along the narrow streets of Merano's old town, houses sport little towers and huge wooden doors, and the pointed arches of the Gothic cathedral sit with harmony next to neoclassical and art-nouveau buildings.

In the heart of the old town, **Piazza del Duomo,** is the 14th-century Gothic cathedral, with a crenellated facade and an ornate campanile. The **Cappella di Santa Barbara,** just behind the cathedral, is an octagonal church containing a 15th-century pietà.

Merano's main shopping street, the narrow, arcaded **Via dei Portici** (Laubengasse), runs west from the cathedral. A good place for souvenir shopping, it features most of the best regional products: wood carvings, Tyrolean-style clothes, embroidery, cheeses, salami, and fruit schnapps.

The **Terme** (Thermal Baths), is a huge complex and nerve center for spa facilities; although some hotels have their own, these are unique. Technicians are trained to treat you with mud packs, massages, and inhalation and sauna routines, or just with the thermal waters, which are said to be especially good for coronary and circulatory problems. Other cures include the famous grape cure at harvest time in the fall, when a two-week diet of fresh grapes has, since Roman times, been seen as a successful way to tone up digestive, liver, and urinary tract functions. ⊠ *Close to the Ponte del Teatro. For further information contact the local tourist office.*

Dining and Lodging

$$$$ ✕ **Andrea.** This elegant showcase for fine cuisine and service is just off Merano's main shopping street, Via dei Portici, and right by a cable-car station. In an atmosphere of relaxed modern elegance, enlivened by wood paneling and lots of green plants, you can dine on eye-pleasing specialties of both local and international cuisine, such as risotto *alle erbe* (with herbs), *filetto di vitello con salsa di alloro* (veal fillet with bay leaf sauce), or canederli *di ricotta su purea di frutta mista* (ricotta dumplings served with pureed fruit). A set menu (about 100,000 lire) offers a complete five-course dinner, including wines—and the wine cellar is also excellent. ⊠ *Via Galilei 44,* ☎ *0473/237400. Reservations essential. Jacket and tie. AE, DC, MC, V. Closed Mon. and 2 wks in Feb. No dinner Sun. in winter.*

$$$ ✕ **Flora.** There's room for only about 20 diners in this intimate candlelit restaurant under the historic arched arcades of Merano's ancient center. Chef Louis Oberstolz describes his imaginative cooking as "fresh, spontaneous, and natural, using only the finest ingredients." He offers a seven-course set menu. Among the specialties are *quaglia ripiena con fegato d'oca grasso* (boned quail stuffed with foie gras), and *schlutzkrapfen* (fresh pasta ravioli with various fillings). ⊠ *Via dei Portici 75,* ☎ *0473/231484. Reservations essential. AE, DC, MC, V. Closed Sun. and mid-Jan.–mid-Feb. No lunch Mon.*

$$$ ✕ **Tiffany Grill/Schloss Maur.** Stained-glass lamps and wood paneling
★ create a warm art-nouveau effect in these two restaurants of the Palace
Kurhotel. The main restaurant is the height of elegance, with huge mar-
ble columns, high ceilings, and crystal chandeliers. In the summer,
meals are served outdoors on the terrace overlooking the lovely park.
The emphasis is on Italian and international cuisine, such as house spe-
cialty spaghetti Schloss Maur (served with a sauce of zucchini, sage,
and green pepper) or roast saddle of lamb and lobster. The Tiffany Grill
(closed Sun.), which offers gourmet menus, is open only in the evening.
⊠ *Palace Kurhotel, Via Cavour 2/4,* ☎ *0473/211300. Reservations
essential. Jacket and tie. AE, DC, V.*

$–$$ ✕ **Terlaner Weinstübe Putz.** This local favorite is an old rustic stübe
under the arcades of Merano's old town. The wide menu focuses on
seasonal dishes and offers Tyrolean specialties. Try zuppa *al vino
bianco* (with white wine); crepes with radicchio; or the various risottos, including one made with asparagus in the spring, and with Barolo
wine later in the year. ⊠ *Via dei Portici 231,* ☎ *0473/235571. No credit
cards. Closed Wed. in Feb.–Mar., and July.*

$$$–$$$$ 🏨 **Palace Kurhotel.** Merano's grandest hotel is an opulent turn-of-the-
★ century establishment that provides top service and comfort. It is set
in an extensive garden with an indoor/outdoor pool, and all rooms on
the south side have balconies overlooking the park. The rooms are spa-
cious, decorated in a stately modern classic design in restful colors. The
public rooms are attractive and comfortable—there's a no-smoking
lounge—with art-nouveau touches, Tiffany glass, marble pillars, and
high ceilings. The hotel is equipped with an impressive spa, featuring
all sorts of baths, massages, mud treatments, and other cures. There
is a lovely fountain serving thermal Merano water. ⊠ *Via Cavour 2/4,*
☎ *0473/211300,* 🖷 *0473/234181. 124 rooms with bath. Restaurant,
bar, indoor-outdoor pool, spa. AE, DC, MC, V. Closed Jan.–Feb.,
mid-Nov.–mid-Dec.*

$$$ 🏨 **Castel Freiburg.** Set in a wooded valley about 7 kilometers (4 miles)
south of town, Castel Freiburg is a romantic hideaway where guests
feel pampered and welcome. A converted 14th-century castle, complete
with tower, it is surrounded by its own park, stretching up to the forest. Reception rooms are full of antiques, and the guest rooms are furnished with color-coordinated fabrics and decorations. Although only
some have terraces, all the rooms have good views of the mountains.
A combination of an excellent restaurant and extensive sports facilities means that many guests remain on the premises for days on end.
⊠ *Località Fragsburg, Via Labers,* ☎ *0473/244196,* 🖷 *0473/244488.
38 rooms with bath. Restaurant, bar, indoor-outdoor pools. AE, DC,
MC, V. Closed Nov.–mid-Apr.*

$$$ 🏨 **Castel Labers.** On a hilltop amid forested slopes about 3 kilome-
ters (2 miles) east of Merano's center, this hotel has a view of the town's
gabled roofs and gardens. Actually a castle set in its own well-kept
grounds, its red-tile gables, towers, and turrets give it an unmistakably
Tyrolean look, heightened on the interior by dark ceiling beams,
painted fresco decorations, and even crossed halberds on the walls. The
hospitable Stapf-Neubert family owns the hotel and takes an active part
in its management. In summer guests dine outdoors on the terrace and
can enjoy a game of tennis or a dip in the hotel pool. ⊠ *Via Labers
25,* ☎ *0473/234484,* 🖷 *473/234146. 32 rooms with bath. Restaurant,
pool, tennis court. AE, DC, MC, V. Closed Nov.–Mar.*

$$$ 🏨 **Schloss Rundegg.** A romantic, converted 12th-century castle with
an original tower, Schloss Rundegg is furnished with antiques and rich
fittings, such as Persian carpets. It's set in a park and functions as a
fully equipped thermal spa. The restaurant even provides special diets

for weight loss and other cures. Room 32, in the tower, has an interior staircase and 360-degree views. ⊠ *Via Scena 2,* ☎ *0473/234100,* FAX *0473/237200. 30 rooms with bath. Restaurant, bar, pool, sauna, spa. AE, DC, MC, V. Closed Jan. 6–31.*

$$–$$$ 🏨 **Minerva.** Recommended by locals as a good spot for budget travelers, this is another turn-of-the-century hotel, built in 1909 and furnished in traditional period style. Set in a garden, it's about 10 minutes by foot from the town center, near several of the luxury hotels. Almost all rooms have balconies with views of the mountains. Full-board rates are economical. ⊠ *Via Cavour 95,* ☎ *0473/236712,* FAX *0473/230460. 45 rooms with bath. Restaurant, pool. AE, DC. Closed Nov.–Mar., except for Dec. 24–Jan. 1.*

Nightlife and the Arts

Farmers test their horses in the highly charged **horse race** that is the highlight of Easter Monday.

The **Grape Festival** on the second Sunday of October has parades and wine tastings in Piazza del Duomo.

The **Bristol** hotel has a disco that's popular with locals as well as with visitors.

Outdoor Activities and Sports

TENNIS

Tennis Merano (⊠ Tennis Club Merano, Via Piave 46, ☎ 0473/236550).

Shopping

From the end of November until Christmas Eve, Merano holds a traditional **Christkindlmarkt** (Christmas market) in the main square.

Numbers in the text correspond to numbers in the margin and on the Bolzano map.

Bolzano

❾ *24 km (15 mi) south of Merano, 110 km (68 mi) west of Cortina d'Ampezzo, 70 km (43 mi) north of Trento.*

Bolzano (Bozen) is the capital of the autonomous province of Alto Adige. It is protected by the mountains to the north and the east and is on the main north–south artery between northern Europe and Italy. This quiet city at the confluence of the Isarco (Eisack) and Talvera rivers has retained a provincial appeal, but it contradicts its country image with commercial features acquired to cater to the needs of tourists. There are no high-rises, but McDonald's can be seen—housed, of course, in a more archaic building.

❿ Bolzano's heart is pedestrians-only **Piazza Walther,** named after the 12th-century German wandering minstrel Walther von der Vogelweide, whose songs lampooned the papacy and praised the Holy Roman Emperor. The square serves as an open-air living room where locals and tourists alike can be found at all hours sipping a drink (perhaps a glass of chilled Riesling) at the café tables.

NEED A BREAK? The bar at the **Hotel Grifone** (Grief), on Piazza Walther, is one of the best places for a view of the square. Tables are set up outside, but the cozy interior is enticing if the weather turns bad.

⓫ The city's Gothic **Duomo** was built between the 12th and 14th centuries. Its lacy spire looks down on the mosaiclike tiles covering its pitched roof. Inside the church are 14th- and 15th-century frescoes and an in-

Bolzano

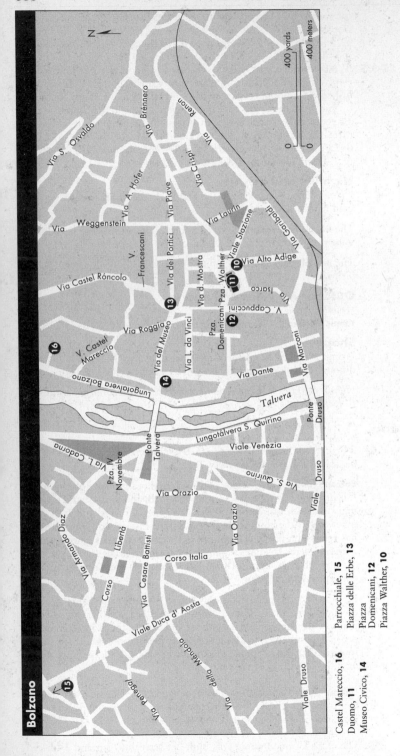

Castel Mareccio, **16**
Duomo, **11**
Museo Civico, **14**

Parrocchiale, **15**
Piazza delle Erbe, **13**
Piazza
Domenicani, **12**
Piazza Walther, **10**

tricately carved stone pulpit dating from 1514. ⊠ *Piazza Walther,* ⊘ *weekdays 9:30–6, Sat. 9:30–noon.*

⑫ **Piazza Domenicani,** with its 13th-century **Dominican church,** is renowned as Bolzano's main repository for paintings, especially frescoes. In the ★ adjoining **Cappella di San Giovanni** you can see frescoes of the Giotto school, one of which is the *Triumph of Death* (circa 1340). Despite its macabre title, this fresco shows the birth of a pre-Renaissance sense of depth and individuality. *Church and chapel:* ⊘ *Mon.–Sat. 9–6:30, Sun. mass.*

⑬ In **Piazza delle Erbe,** a bronze statue of Neptune presides over a bountiful fruit and vegetable market (open Mon.–Sat. 8–1). The stalls spill over with colorful displays of local produce; bakeries and grocery stores showcase hot breads, pastries, cheeses, and delicatessen meats— a complete range of picnic supplies. Try the speck and the Tyrolean-style apple strudel. The market is at the beginning of Bolzano's best known shopping street, **Via dei Portici (Laubengasse),** which is lined with long, narrow arcades. The shops specialize in Tyrolean handicrafts and clothing—lederhosen, loden goods, linen suits, and dirndls.

⑭ The **Museo Civico** (Civic Museum) houses a rich collection of traditional costumes, wood carvings, and archaeological exhibits. The mixture of styles is a reflection of the region's cultural cross-fertilization. ⊠ *Via del Museo 45,* ☎ *0471/974625.* ⊡ *2,000 lire.* ⊘ *Tues.–Sat. 9–12:30 and 2:30–5:30, Sun. 10–1.*

⑮ The **Parrocchiale** (parish church) of Gries, with its elaborately carved 15th-century wooden altar, is worth a visit. ⊠ *Corso Libertà,* ⊘ *Apr. 21–Oct. 30, weekdays 10–noon, 2–4, Sun. mass.*

Passeggiata del Guncina is an 8-kilometer (5-mile)-long botanical promenade, dating from 1892, that culminates in a panoramic view of Bolzano. (There are two other scenic promenades in Bolzano—ask in the local tourist office for details). ⊠ *Quartiere di Gries.*

⑯ **Castel Mareccio** (Schloss Maretsch) dates from the 13th-century and is nestled under the mountains and surrounded by vineyards. The castle is now a well-equipped conference center with a restaurant and bar, all open to the public. ⊠ *Lungotalvera Promenade,* ☎ *0471/976615. Closed Tues.*

OFF THE BEATEN PATH | **RENON (RITTEN) PLATEAU –** Just above Bolzano and reachable by the funicular to Soprabolzano, are the Earth Pyramids of Renon Plateau, a bizarre geological formation where erosion has left a forest of tall, thin, needlelike spires of rock, each topped with a boulder. Soprabolzano funicular leaves from Via Renon, about 300 yards left of Bolzano train station. At the top an electric train takes you to Collalbo, where Earth Pyramids are located.

Dining and Lodging

$$$ ★ ✕ **Grifone/Greif.** More than just a routine hotel restaurant, the Grifone is a continuing favorite in its own right, known for fine food and service. It's especially pleasant to eat outside at tables set up on Piazza Walther. The menu, which changes daily, includes various local specialties, such as *weinzuppe* (wine soup made with consommé, cream, white wine, and cinnamon), and *herrngröstl* (bite-size pieces of veal sautéed with potatoes and onions), served in the pan with cabbage salad. The grilled fish is also good. ✕ *Hotel Grifone/Greif. Piazza Walther,* ☎ *0471/977056. AE, DC, MC, V. Closed Sun.*

$$–$$$ ✕ **Abramo.** Although outside Bolzano's attractive old center, this restaurant is the best in town. Chef Abramo Pantezi offers an Italian variation of nouvelle cuisine in an attractive, elegantly modern setting designed to reflect Renaissance themes. Tables are set with crystal and silver. Specialties include fish dishes, such as *salmone allo* champagne (salmon in champagne sauce) and *tagliarini agli scampi* (thin noodles with shrimp). There's a vegetarian antipasto selection and a daily diet menu selected for calorie control. There's also an extensive wine cellar, which features even some top-quality California vintages. ⊠ *Piazza Gries 16,* ☎ *0471/280141. AE, DC, MC, V. Closed Sun. and Aug. 1–25.*

$$–$$$ ✕ **Belle Epoque.** This is the fashionable restaurant of Park Hotel Laurin. Its furnishings live up to its name and include potted palms and chandeliers. During the summer months, the restaurant expands to include a grill restaurant in the hotel's lush, extensive park. The menu includes Italian and international cuisine, as well as local specialties, and the kitchen prides itself on serving seasonal dishes. In spring, you can sample half a dozen asparagus dishes, for example, while in the fall the menu offers game, including hare and venison served in a variety of ways. ⊠ *Park Hotel Laurin. Via Laurino 4,* ☎ *0471/980500. Jacket and tie. AE, DC, MC, V. Closed Sun.*

$$ ✕ **Gostner Flora's Bistrot.** In a medieval tower on Bolzano's market square, this tiny place has been a tavern for centuries, and it has been lovingly restored. There is no menu; you choose from a limited number of typical homey Tyrolean specialties, different every day. They may include canederli or *schlutzkrapfen* (ravioli). The desserts are homemade, too. The young owner takes pride in a selection of good wines. ⊠ *Piazza delle Erbe 17,* ☎ *0471/974086. No credit cards. Closed Sun. No dinner Sat.*

$ ✕ **Batzenhausl.** A medieval building in the center of town houses this crowded *stübli* (Tyrolean-style drinking hall). It's a popular hangout for the local intellectual set, who hold long, animated conversations over glasses of local wine and tasty local South Tyrolean specialties, such as herrngröstl and apple pancakes with ice cream. Try the fried Camembert. ⊠ *Via Andreas Hofer 30,* ☎ *0471/976183. No credit cards. Closed Tues. and 2 wks in July. No lunch.*

$$$ ⊞ **Grifone/Greif.** For at least five centuries, there's been a hotel on this
★ spot, perfectly situated in the center of town on pedestrians-only Piazza Walther, looking across to the cathedral. You'll find a friendly atmosphere combined with old-fashioned elegance and a sense of history. The older wings have antique-style Tyrolean furnishings in some rooms, pleasant modern furnishings characterize the newer parts, and some back rooms have balconies looking past the hotel garden to the mountains. The hotel bar and restaurant set up tables and chairs right on Piazza Walther in the summer months. ⊠ *Piazza Walther,* ☎ *0471/977056,* FAX *471/980613. 130 rooms, 110 with bath. Restaurant, bar. AE, DC, MC, V.*

$$$ ⊞ **Park Hotel Laurin.** This big turn-of-the-century hotel, done in opulent art-nouveau style, is set in a large, shady park, in the middle of town. Most rooms have stunning views of the park and the mountains beyond. Some rooms carry through the Belle Epoque decor; others are furnished in a classic modern hotel style. The Belle Epoque restaurant (☞ above), with an outdoor buffet in the summer, serves local specialties. ⊠ *Via Laurino 4,* ☎ *0471/980500,* FAX *0471/970953. 96 rooms with bath. Restaurant, pool, parking. AE, DC, MC, V.*

$$$ ⊞ **Schloss Korb.** It's worth the 5-kilometer (3-mile) drive west from
★ Bolzano to reach this remarkable hotel. It's set in a romantic 13th-century castle with a crenellated roof and a massive central tower, perched in a park amid vine-covered hills. Much of the ancient decor is pre-

served, and the public rooms are filled with Tyrolean antiques, elaborate wood carvings, old paintings, and attractive plants. The rooms are comfortably furnished—some tower rooms have the old Romanesque arched windows. ⊠ *Missiano, Strada Castel d'Appiano 5,* ☎ *0471/636000,* FAX *471/636033. 56 rooms with bath. Indoor pool, pool, sauna, tennis courts. No credit cards. Closed Nov.–Easter.*

$$–$$$ 🏨 **Luna/Mondschein.** This central yet secluded hotel was built in 1798. Set in a lovely garden, it provides a tranquil, friendly atmosphere. The rooms are furnished in a comfortable, classic hotel style using wood paneling throughout. Some rooms overlooking the garden have balconies, but even the rooms overlooking the garage have good views of the mountains. The two restaurants include a typical Tyrolean weinstübe that serves inexpensive local specialties in a cozy, convivial setting. ⊠ *Via Piave 15,* ☎ *0471/975642,* FAX *0471/975577. 85 rooms with bath/shower. Restaurant, weinstübe. DC, MC, V.*

$$ 🏨 **Magdalenerhof.** Near the Renon cable-car station, this family-run hotel has the appearance of a Tyrolean inn and is set in a garden surrounded by vineyards. Comfort and service are up to meet the high local standards. ⊠ *Via Rencio 48/a,* ☎ *0471/978267,* FAX *0471/981076. 21 rooms with bath. Restaurant, pool. AE, DC, MC, V.*

Nightlife and the Arts

Spring is heralded each May with large flower markets and with spin-off events, including concerts and folklore and art exhibits.

On August 24 is the **Bartolomeo Horse Fair,** on Renon Mountain just northeast of the town. Hundreds of farmers converge for a day of serious trading and frivolous merriment.

For the **International Busoni Piano Competition** in late August, concerts and recitals are held in halls and churches. Internationally acclaimed performers usually head the panel of judges.

Outdoor Activities and Sports

HIKING

Club Alpino Italiano (⊠ Piazza delle Erbe 46, Bolzano, ☎ 0471/978172) is a helpful organization that provides information for hiking and rock climbing. It is important to follow safety procedures and to have all the latest information on trails and conditions.

TENNIS

Courts can be found in Bolzano at **Circolo Tennis Bolzano** (⊠ Via M. Koller 8, ☎ 0471/280587).

Shopping

The best store for locally made handicraft goods is **Artigiani Atesini** (⊠ Via Portici 39).

From the end of November until Christmas Eve there are traditional **Christkindlmarkt** in the main square of Bolzano with stalls selling all kinds of Christmas decorations and local handcrafted goods.

The outdoor fruit and vegetable market is held in the central **Piazza delle Erbe** every morning (8–1) except Sunday.

The big weekly flea market takes place Saturday morning in **Piazza della Vittoria.**

Numbers in the margin correspond to points of interest on the Dolomites map.

Cornedo

17 *6 km (4 mi) east of Bolzano and 24 km (15 mi) southwest of Chiusa.*

Cornedo, at the mouth of the Ega Valley (Eggental), is a place to savor the view of the Catinaccio Mountains. Their craggy peaks seem to be props for a lighting display, as pink and purple reflections dance over huge rocks. Their creation is the subject of a local German legend that tells of King Laurin, who lived in a vast palace on the Catinaccio, at a time when the mountain was covered with roses. King Laurin became infatuated with the daughter of a neighboring king, Similde, and kidnapped her, but Similde, searching for his daughter, recognized her place of imprisonment by the red roses that grew there. Laurin freed the girl and was made Similde's prisoner. When Laurin finally escaped he decreed that the roses that had betrayed him should be turned to rocks, so that they could be seen neither by day nor by night. Today, the spectacular pinkish-red display is at its best at dawn and at sunset.

Chiusa

⑱ *30 km (19 mi) northeast of Bolzano, 14 km (9 mi) south of Bressanone.*

Chiusa (Klausen) has beautiful narrow streets lined with houses built in the 15th and 16th centuries. Geraniums and begonias fill window boxes beneath the carved wooden shutters.

Above the town of Chiusa is the Benedictine monastery of **Sabiona** (Saeben), built as a castle in the 10th century but occupying a site that was fortified in Roman times. The monastery buildings date from the late Middle Ages and are a mixture of Romanesque and Gothic architecture, surrounded by walls and turrets. *Guided visits are organized by the Tourist Association in Chiusa. For information, contact the local tourist office,* ☎ *0472/847424,* ℻ *472/847244. Churches are open daily 9–5.*

Bressanone

⑲ *14 km (9 mi) north of Chiusa, 40 km (25 mi) northeast of Bolzano, 100 km (62 mi) northwest of Cortina d'Ampezzo.*

Bressanone (Brixen), is an important artistic center of the Alto Adige and for centuries was the seat of prince-bishops. Like their counterparts in Trento, these medieval administrators had the delicate problem of serving two opposing masters—the pope (the ultimate spiritual supervisor) and the Holy Roman Emperor (the civil and military leader). Since the papacy and the Holy Roman Empire were virtually at war throughout the Middle Ages, Bressanone's prince-bishops became experts at tact and diplomacy in order to survive. As you arrive from Brunico, you enter the town on Via Mercato Vecchio, a broad road leading to the imposing **Duomo.** It was built in the 13th century but acquired a Baroque facade 500 years later, and its 14th-century cloister is decorated with medieval frescoes.

★ The Bishop's Palace, which now houses the **Museo Diocesano** (Diocesan Museum), is a treasure-house of local medieval art, particularly Gothic wood carving. The wooden statues and liturgical objects were all collected from the cathedral treasury. During the Christmas season, the curators highlight displays of the museum's large collection of antique Nativity scenes: Look for the shepherds wearing Tyrolean hats. The palazzo is beside the Duomo. ⊠ *Palazzo Vescovile,* ☎ *0472/836401.* 🎫 *5,000 lire (2,000 lire for nativity scenes exhibition only).* ⊙ *Mar. 15–Oct., Mon.–Sat. 10–5; nativity scenes open Dec. 15–Feb. 10, Mon.–Sat. 2–5. Closed Dec. 24, 25.* 3

Dining and Lodging

$$ ✕ **Fink.** This popular restaurant, under the arcades in the pedestrians-
★ only center of town, has a friendly staff and features a good-value daily set menu. It has a rustic ambience upstairs with lots of wood panel-

ing, and serves international as well as hearty Tyrolean specialties. Try the *carré di maiale gratinato* (pork roasted with cheese and served with cabbage and potatoes) or the *castrato alla paesana* (a kind of lamb stew). ⊠ *Via Portici Minori 4,* ☎ *0472/834883. AE, DC, MC, V. Closed Wed. and July. No Tues. dinner Oct.–June.*

$$$ 🏨 **Dominik.** Well equipped and modern, this hotel is centrally located but has a quiet garden and dining terrace. Most doubles are spacious and modern, with comfortable armchairs, ample baths, and balconies. The superior restaurant features local trout (in season). ⊠ *Via Terzo di Sotto 13,* ☎ *0472/830144,* 𝔽𝔸𝕏 *472/836554. 29 rooms with bath. Indoor pool, sauna. AE, MC, V. Closed Nov. 4–Easter.*

$$–$$$ 🏨 **Elefante.** One of the best and most famous hotels in the region, this
★ cozy inn is in a historic 15th-century building: There's been a hotel on the site for more than 500 years. The hotel takes its name from an incident in 1550, when King John of Portugal stopped here for a few days while leading an elephant over the Alps as a present for Austria's Emperor Ferdinand. Each room is different, and many are decorated with antiques and paintings. The hotel is centrally located but is set in a large park with a swimming pool. Also in the park is the separate Villa Marzari, with 14 rooms. The hotel restaurant (closed Mon.) is known as one of the region's best. ⊠ *Via Rio Bianco 4,* ☎ *0472/832750,* 𝔽𝔸𝕏 *0472/836579. 44 rooms with bath. Restaurant, pool. DC, MC, V. Closed Nov. 15–Dec. 20, Jan. 10–Feb. 28.*

Outdoor Activities and Sports

Tennis can be played at **Club Bressanone** (⊠ Lungoisarco Sinistro, ☎ 0472/834792).

Shopping

From the end of November until Christmas Eve there are traditional *Christkindlmarkt* (Christmas markets) in the main square of Bressanone, with stalls selling all kinds of Christmas decorations and local handcrafted goods.

Brunico

★ ⑳ *33 km (20 mi) east of Bressanone, 65 km (40 mi) north of Cortina d'Ampezzo.*

Brunico (Bruneck), with its medieval quarter nestling below the 13th-century bishop's castle, is within the heart of the Pusteria Valley. This picturesque little town, often noted for its quiet and relaxing qualities, is divided by the Rienza river with the old quarter on one side and the modern quarter on the other.

The **Museo degli Usi e Costumi della Provincia di Bolzano** (Bolzano Province Customs and Costumes Museum, or Ethnographic Museum) is a re-creation of a typical local village, built around an authentic 300-year-old mansion. It reveals the functions and significance of traditional architecture. The wood-carving displays are particularly interesting. It's in the district of Teodone, just outside the town. ⊠ *Via Duca, Teodone 24,* ☎ *0474/32087,* 𝔽𝔸𝕏 *074/31764.* 🎫 *4,000 lire.* ☉ *Apr. 15–Oct., Tues.–Sat. 9:30–5:30, Sun. 2–6.*

Dining and Lodging

$–$$ ✕🏨 **Post.** The best choice for lodging in the center of town is this homey, old traditional hotel, recommended by locals, who also like its restaurant, café, and pastry shop. It has its own parking, which is important because of the pedestrians-only rules in effect throughout much of the central area. ⊠ *Via Bastioni 9,* ☎ *0474/555127,* [FAX] *474/31603. 60 rooms, 55 with bath. Restaurant, café. MC, V. Closed Nov.–mid-Dec.*

$–$$ ⌂ **Andreas Hofer.** There's a Tyrolean feel to this comfortable hotel set in a large garden outside the center of town. Traditional chalet-style balconies overlook the Pusteria Valley. The rooms have modern furnishings, and there are several rooms with special features for people with disabilities. The hotel restaurant is recommended. ⊠ *Via Campo Tures 1,* ☎ *0474/31469,* [FAX] *0474/31283. 54 rooms with bath. Restaurant, sauna. MC, V. Closed Apr.–May, mid-Nov.–mid-Dec.*

Special Event
January 22 sees a **dogsled race**; locals turn up with flasks of hot mulled wine to back their favorites.

Outdoor Activities and Sports
There are tennis courts along the river (⊠ Lungofiume San Giorgio, ☎ 0474/20444).

Dobbiaco

㉑ *25 km (16 mi) east of Brunico, 34 km (21 mi) north of Cortina d'Ampezzo.*

In **Dobbiaco** (Toblach), the influence of Austria, which is just 12 kilometers (7 miles) to the east along the Drau Valley, intensifies. Italian is spoken grudgingly here, Austrian money is accepted at most shops and restaurants, and the locals appear more blond and blue-eyed than the average Italian. It is not surprising that Gustav Mahler (1860–1911), the great Austrian composer, should have come here often for inspiration.

Lodging
$–$$ ⌂ **Alpino Monte Rota/Alpengasthof Ratsberg.** To reach this hotel,
★ you take the 10-minute cable-car ride to Monte Rota. It is in traditional style, with the timeless look of local chalets. Front rooms have stunning mountain views from balconies, while those in the back look out over the dense mountain forest. You needn't take the cable car back down for sustenance: The Alpino has a good restaurant (which even serves some low-calorie dishes), a bar, and a Tyrolean-style stübe. ⊠ *Monte Rota 10,* ☎ *0474/72213,* [FAX] *474/72916. 25 rooms with bath. Restaurant, bar, pool, sauna. MC, V. Closed mid-Apr.–May 30, mid-Oct.–mid-Dec.*

$–$$ ⌂ **Cristallo.** Wood beams and paneling lend an Old Tyrolean tone to this small hotel set in a garden just outside town. The architecture and furnishings reflect the local preference for combining traditional chalet design with functional, but comfortable, modern furniture. Most rooms enjoy a panoramic view of the valley; some of the best rooms have balconies. Guests relax in the cozy and informal stübe. ⊠ *Viale S. Giovanni 37,* ☎ *0474/72138,* [FAX] *0474/72755. 30 rooms with bath. Restaurant, bar, indoor pool. AE, MC, V. Closed mid Apr.–mid-May, mid-Oct.–mid-Dec.*

Outdoor Activities and Sports
SKIING
Prepared trails for cross-country skiing (usually loops marked off by kilometers) cater for differing degrees of ability. One of the best of this kind can be found at **Dobbiaco.** Inquire at the local tourist office. Downhill skiing can be found at **Monte Rota** slopes, accessible from Dobbiaco. These offer considerably lower rates than in many of the more exclusive resorts.

Cortina d'Ampezzo

★ ㉒ *65 km (40 mi) south of Brunico, 140 km (87 mi) east of Bolzano.*

Cortina d'Ampezzo, known as the "Pearl of the Dolomites," is set in a lush meadow 4,000 feet above sea level. Dense forests adjoin the town, and mountains encircle the whole valley. The town sprawls on the slopes along a fast-moving stream; a public park extends along one bank. Luxury hotels and the villas of the rich are conspicuously scattered over the slopes above the town—identifiable, ironically, by their attempts to hide behind stands of firs and spruces.

The bustling center of Cortina has little nostalgia for old-time atmosphere, despite its Alpine appearance. The tone is set by elegant shops and stylish cafés, as opulent as their well-dressed patrons, whose corduroy knickerbockers may well have been tailored by Armani. Cortina is the place to go for a whiff of the heady aroma of wealth and sophistication; if you want authentic Tyrolean gemütlichkeit, pass through Cortina and stop at one of the resorts later on the tour.

Dining and Lodging

$$$ ✕ **De la Poste.** The exclusive restaurants of the hotel on Cortina's main square have a casually chic clientele and a lively atmosphere. There's an elegant, high-ceilinged main dining room with three big chandeliers where you can dine on soufflés and nouvelle cuisine dishes (every Friday fresh fish is served). There's also a more informal grill room with wood paneling and the family pewter collection. In ski season it's always crowded. ✉ *Piazza Roma 14,* ☎ *0436/4271. Reservations essential. Jacket and tie. AE, DC.*

$$–$$$ ✕ **Tana della Volpe.** Near the Olympic ice skating rink, this popular restaurant has a bona fide Tyrolean ambience, with wood-paneled dining rooms and a local clientele. Here you can try Cortina specialties such as *zuppa di* porcini (wild mushroom soup), ravioli *di cervo* (stuffed with venison), and game. ✉ *Via dello Stadio 27/a,* ☎ *0436/867494. AE, DC, MC, V. Closed mid-June–mid July and November. Closed Wed., no lunch Thurs. May and Sept.*

$$ ✕ **Fanes.** This restaurant in the Hotel Fanes outside town serves homey food in rustic elegance. Game is a specialty, with dishes including *camoscio* (chamois) cooked several ways and *capriolo in salmì con* polenta (roe deer stewed in red wine and served with polenta). ✉ *Hotel Fanes, Via Roma 136,* ☎ *0436/3427. AE, MC, DC, V. Closed Mon.*

$$$$ ▥ **Europa.** This traditional mountain hotel, in the center of town, has the warm family-style atmosphere typical of a chalet. Antiques, including an antique wood stove, decorate the interior. A roaring fire enlivens the bar. There's also a nightclub, disco, and grill room. ✉ *Corso Italia 207,* ☎ *0436/3221,* 𝖥𝖠𝖷 *0436/868204. 52 rooms with bath. Restaurant, bar, parking. AE, DC, MC, V. Closed mid-Oct.–mid-Dec.*

$$$$ ▥ **Miramonti.** This imposing and luxurious hotel, nearly a century old, has a magnificent mountain valley location about a kilometer (½ mile) south of town. A touch of Old World formality accompanies the imperial Austrian design, and the interior decor carries the period style throughout. Most of the rooms have balconies and have been entirely redecorated. There's a restaurant, and in the cozy bar there's always a roaring fire in the hearth. ✉ *Località Peziè 103,* ☎ *0436/4201,* 𝖥𝖠𝖷 *0436/867019. 106 rooms with bath, 7 suites and 5 junior suites. Pool, sauna, golf course, tennis courts, exercise room. AE, DC, MC, V. Closed Easter–June 30, Sept. 15–Dec. 20.*

$$$ ▥ **De la Poste.** Skiers who want to be seen keep returning to this lively hotel on the main square in a pedestrian zone. It's been under the same family management since 1826, and the furnishings feature antiques in characteristic Dolomite style. Almost all rooms have wooden balconies. The hotel's main terrace bar, on the square, is always crowded and is one of Cortina's social centers. ⊠ *Piazza Roma 62,* ☎ *0436/4271,* ☒ *0436/868435. 83 rooms with bath. Restaurant, bar. AE, DC. Closed mid-Apr.–mid-June, mid-Oct.–mid-Dec.*

Nightlife and the Arts

At the **Europa** hotel (☞ Lodging, *above*) you can expect to mingle with the designer-clothing set at the VIP disco; nonguests are welcome, but don't expect to spend less than 50,000 lire.

Outdoor Activities and Sports

SKIING

Cortina d'Ampezzo is known as one of the most comprehensive centers for skiing enthusiasts.

TENNIS

Public courts can be found at Via Sopiazes (☎ 0436/2937).

En Route   As you enter the Crepa Tunnel along the S48, leaving Cortina d' Ampezzo behind, the ascent for the Passo di Falzarego begins. The **Passo Pordoi** will lead to the so–called "heart" of the Dolomites. The roads around this region of the Sella mountains are deemed to be among the most spectacular in Europe and many consider their rugged beauty to be unparalleled. A fork in the road farther ahead will lead left to Canazei and right into Val Garden.

THE HEART OF THE DOLOMITES

The area between Cortina d'Ampezzo and east to Bolzano is dominated by two major valleys, the Val di Fassa and the famous Val Gardena. Both share the spectacular panorama of the Sella mountain range, known because of its circular shape as the "Heart of the Dolomites". Val di Fassa is made up primarily of the Grande Strada delle Dolomiti (Great Dolomites Road), which runs from the mountain resort of Cortina d'Ampezzo as far as Bolzano. The route, opened in 1909, now comprises 110 kilometers (68 miles) of easy grades and smooth driving between the two cities.

With some of the best views of the Dolomites, Val Gardena is famous as a ski resort, dotted with well-equipped picturesque towns overlooked by the oblong Sasso Lungo (Long Rock), which is more than 10,000 feet above sea-level. It is also home of the Ladins, descendants of soldiers sent by the Roman Emperor Tiberius to conquer the Celtic population of the area in the 1st century AD. Forgotten in the narrow cul-de-sacs of isolated mountain valleys, the Ladins have developed their own folk traditions and speak an ancient dialect that is derived from Latin and is similar to Romansch, which is spoken in some high valleys in Switzerland.

Numbers in the text correspond to the numbers in the margin and to points of interest on the Dolomites map.

Canazei

❷❸   *60 km (37 mi) west of Cortina d'Ampezzo, 23 km (14 mi) east of Lake Carezza, 52 km (32 mi) east of Bolzano.*

Of the towns in the Fassa Valley, **Canazei** is the most popular ski resort as well as a summer haven. The area around this small town is full of mountain trails and ski slopes, surrounded by large pockets of conifers.

OFF THE
BEATEN PATH

COL RODELLA – An excursion from Campitello di Fassa to the vantage point of Col Rodella is a must. The cable car rises some 3,000 feet up the mountain to this most panoramic of viewpoints. From the balcony at the top you can see full circle around the region, including the Sasso Lungo and the rest of the Sella range.

Lodging

$$$ ⊞ **Alla Rosa.** This recently renovated hotel offers all modern facilities and a big family welcome. Centrally located, the hotel has a modest restaurant with a choice of either local or international cuisine, and a cozy bar. The three-story building has balconies in half of all rooms, and large reception areas. The bedrooms are well laid out with a pleasant rustic and modern mix, but the real attraction is the imposing view over the Dolomites. ⊠ *Via Dolomite 142,* ☎ *0462/601107. 37 rooms with bath. Restaurant, bar, recreation room. MC, V. Closed Oct.*

Ortisei

㉔ *80 km (50 mi) west of Cortina d'Ampezzo, 28 km (17 mi) north of Canazei, 35 km (22 mi) northeast of Bolzano.*

Ortisei (St. Ulrich), the jewel in the crown of Val Gardena's ski resorts, is a hub of activity both in summer and, especially, in winter. There are hundreds of miles of hiking trails as well as several hundred miles of accessible ski slopes, including the Siusi slopes to the south. Hotels are everywhere and facilities are excellent, with swimming pools, ice rinks, health spas, tennis courts and bowling. Most impressive of all is the location, a valley surrounded by imposing views in all directions. For further information on activities in Val Gardena contact the main Tourist Office (⊠ *Ortisei, Str. Rezia 1,* ☎ *0471/796328,* 𝔽𝔸𝕏 *0471/796749*).

For centuries Ortisei has also been famous for the expertise of its wood-carvers and there are still numerous workshops here. Apart from making religious sculptures—particularly the wayside Calvaries you come upon everywhere in the Dolomites—Ortisei's carvers were long famous for producing wooden dolls, horses, and other toys. As itinerant peddlers loading up their packs every spring, they traveled by foot as far as Paris, London, and St. Petersburg to sell their wares. Fine historic and contemporary examples of all kinds of locally carved wooden sculptures and artifacts can be seen at the **Museo della Val Gardena** at **Cesa di Ladins.** ⊠ *Via Rezia 83, Ortisei,* ☎ *0471/797554.* 🖭 *5,000 lire.* ☉ *July 1–Aug. 31, daily 10–noon, 3–7; Jun., Sept., Dec. 28–30, Jan. 4–7, and Feb. 8–Apr. 1, Tues.–Fri. 3–6:30.*

Lodging

$$$ ⊞ **Aquila/Adler.** Since 1810 there has always been a Hotel Aquila under the same family management in this popular Val Gardena sports center. Today it is regarded as one of the best in the valley. Set in a large park, the original building has been enlarged and renovated several times in the intervening 185 years, but it retains a lot of the old atmosphere, looking something like a turreted castle. The Tyrolean character is carried through in special Tyrolean parties held once a week for guests. The rooms are spacious, and many have balconies or little terraces; some are suitable for guests with disabilities. ⊠ *Via Rezia 7,* ☎ *0471/796203,* 𝔽𝔸𝕏 *0471/796210. 94 rooms, most with bath. Restaurant, bar, pool, beauty salon, sauna, tennis courts, health club. AE, DC, MC, V. Closed mid-Apr.–mid-May, mid-Oct.–mid-Dec.*

$$–$$$ ⊞ **Posta Cavallino Bianco.** In the center of town (but only five minutes' walk from the main ski facilities), this hotel looks more like a gigantic doll house, with delicate wooden balconies and an eye-catching wooden

gable. Inside, the decor is full of deep colors and ornate carpets and drapery. Wood is used lavishly throughout the interior, most notable in the cozy hotel bar with a large handcrafted fireplace. The rooms are a good size with all utilities, but not all have balconies. The hotel also has a restaurant, coffee shop, sun terrace and even a small disco. ⊠ *Via Rezia 22,* ☎ *0471/796392* FAX *0471/797517. 99 rooms with bath. Restaurant, bar. V, MC. Closed mid-Apr.–mid-May, mid-Oct.–mid-Dec.*

Special Event
The Val Gardena comes alive with a parade of horse-drawn sleighs on January 1.

Outdoor Activities and Sports
SKIING
With almost 600 kilometers (370 miles) of accessible downhill slopes, **Ortisei** is one of the most popular resorts in the Dolomites. Prices are good and facilities are amongst the most modern. There are more than 90 kilometers (56 miles) of cross-country skiing lanes.

TENNIS
Courts can be found in **Roncadizza** (☎ 0471/797275).

Fiè (Voels)

❷❺ *26 km (16 mi) southwest of Ortisei, 18 km (11 mi) east of Bolzano.*

Fiè (Voels) is set in a valley with the Renon mountains on one side and the Siusi on the other. The town is surrounded by acres of green coniferous forests. In the town is the parish church of **Santa Maria Assunta** in the late-Gothic style, built in the 16th century. The church, due to restoration is not open to the public.

Dining and Lodging
$$$ ✕⊡ **Turm.** The *turm* (tower) that houses this welcoming hotel on the
★   edge of the Sciliar National Park dates from the 13th century and has been used as a courthouse, prison, and tavern. Now owned and run by the Pramstrahler family, it's furnished with their charming collection of paintings and antiques. In addition, this picturesque hostelry also has an excellent restaurant. ⊠ *Piazza della Chiesa 9, Fiè allo Sciliar (Voels am Schlern),* ☎ *0471/725014,* FAX *0471/725474. 23 rooms with bath. Restaurant, indoor-outdoor pools, sauna, parking. AE, DC, MC, V. Closed early Nov.–Dec. 20.*

Special Event
The **Oswald von Wolkenstein Cavalcade,** named after the medieval South Tyrolese knight and troubadour, is held every year over the first or second weekend of June. After a colorful procession, teams of local horsemen and women compete in fast-paced events.

Caldaro

❷❻ *35 km (22 mi) west of Lake Carezza and 15 km (9 mi) south of Bolzano.*

Caldaro is a vineyard village with clear views of castles high up on the surrounding mountains, a backdrop that reflects the centuries of division that forged the unique character of the area. Caldaro architecture is famous for the way it blends Italian Renaissance elements of balance and harmony with the soaring windows and peaked arches of the local Gothic tradition. The church of **Santa Caterina,** on the main square, is a good example.

Close to the main square is the **South Tyrolean Museum of Wine** illustrating the history of wine-producing in this region. ⊠ *Via dell'Oro*

1, ☎ 0471/963168. ✉ 3,000 lire. ⊙ Easter–Oct., Tues.–Sat. 9:30–noon and 2–6, Sun. 10-noon.

★ *En Route* **Passo di Sella** is one of the most famous mountain passes in the Dolomites. It can be approached from the S48 and continues into Val Gardena among the most panoramic mountain scenery in Europe. The road descends to Ortisei, passing the small ski resort of Santa Cristina.

Lake Carezza

㉗ *23 km (14 mi) west of Canazei and 29 km (18 mi) east of Bolzano.*

A lake of icy cold glacial waters, **Lake Carezza** is some 5,000 feet above sea level. The azure blue of the waters can at times change to magical greens and purples, reflections of the surrounding forest and rosy peaks of the Dolomites.

THE DOLOMITES A TO Z

Arriving and Departing

By Car

The most important route in the region, A22, is the main north–south autostrada linking Italy with northern Europe via the Brenner Pass. It links Bressanone, Bolzano, Trento, Rovereto, and at Verona joins the A4, running east–west across northern Italy from Trieste to Turin.

By Plane

The nearest airports are Verona's Villafranca Airport in Italy and Munich Airport in Germany, both well connected by road and rail with the Dolomite area (☞ below).

By Train

The express train line that links the towns of Bolzano, Trento, and Rovereto connects with other main lines at Verona, just south of the region. Eurocity trains on the Dortmund-Venice and Munich-Rome routes also stop at these stations.

Getting Around

By Bus

Local buses connect the train stations at Trento, Bolzano, and Merano with the mountain resorts. The service is fairly frequent between most main towns during the day. Though some parts of the region remain out of the reach of public transportation, it is quite possible to visit even the remotest villages without a car if you are equipped with the local bus timetables, available from regional and local tourist offices.

By Car

Autostrada A22 connects Bressanone, Bolzano, Trento, and Rovereto. Roads in the broad mountain valleys are usually wide two-lane routes, but the roads up into the highest passes can be narrow and subject to sudden closure, even in the months when they are open to drivers. A Bolzano number (☎ 0471/993810 or 0471/978577) provides information on weather-related closures.

By Train

An express train line follows the course of the Adige Valley from the Brenner Pass southward past Bolzano, Trento, and Rovereto. Branch lines from Trento and Bolzano go to some of the smaller valleys, but most of the mountain attractions described in this chapter are beyond the reach of trains.

Contacts and Resources

Car Rentals
Avis (✉ Piazza Verdi 18, Bolzano, ☎ 0471/971467).

Emergencies
Carabinieri (☎ 112). English-speaking officers are available 24 hours a day to deal with any kind of emergency.

Police, Ambulance (☎ 113). For first aid, ask for "Pronto Soccorso," and be prepared to give your address.

Guided Tours
If you are without a car or if you don't care to drive over mountain roads, guided tours from Bolzano or Trento can show you the Dolomites the easy way. However, the sudden and frequent snowfalls mean that tours are offered in summer only.

In **Bolzano,** city sightseeing and local excursions are organized by the **SAD** bus company (✉ Via Conciapelli 60, near the train station, ☎ 0471/971259). In July and August, full-day mountain tours include a **Great Dolomites Tour** from Bolzano to Cortina and a tour of the **Venosta Valley** that climbs over the Stelvio Pass into Switzerland. A tour of the **Val Gardena** and the Siusi Alps is available from April to October.

In **Trento,** city sightseeing can be arranged through the city **APT** office (✉ Via Alfieri 4, ☎ 0461/983880). From June through September, the **Calderari e Moggioli** travel agency (✉ Via Manci 46, ☎ 0461/980275) offers a full-day guided bus tour of the **Brenta Dolomites** and the **Great Dolomites Tour,** a full-day drive over the Pordoi and Falzarego passes to Cortina d'Ampezzo and Lake Misurina. Also, from June through September, the Trentino regional **APT** (✉ Via Sighele 3, ☎ 0461/914444) organizes guided tours and excursions by train to castles in the region.

Hiking and Hill Walking
Two helpful organizations are the **Società degli Alpinisti Tridentini** (✉ Via Manci 57, Trento, ☎ 0461/986462) and **Club Alpino Italiano** (✉ Piazza delle Erbe 46, Bolzano, ☎ 0471/978172). Local tourist offices can provide information on less-demanding trails.

Late-Night Pharmacies
Pharmacies take turns staying open late or on Sundays; for the latest information, consult the current list posted on the front door of each pharmacy or ask at the local tourist office.

Visitor Information
The tourist board for the autonomous province of **Alto Adige** (✉ Piazza Parrocchia 11–12, Bolzano, ☎ 0471/993808, FAX 0471/975448). The **Trentino Tourist Board** (✉ Via Sighele 3, Trento, ☎ 0461/914444, FAX 0461/915978). The following are local tourist board offices: **Bolzano** (✉ Piazza Walther 8, ☎ 0471/975656, FAX 0471/980300). **Bormio** (✉ Via Stelvio, ☎ 0342/903300, FAX 0342/904696). **Bressanone** (✉ Via Stazione 9, ☎ 0472/36401, FAX 0472/36067). **Chiusa** (✉ Piazza Tinne 40, ☎ 0472/47424, FAX 0472/47244). **Cortina d'Ampezzo** (✉ Piazzetta San Francesco 8, ☎ 0436/3231, FAX 0436/3235). **Madonna di Campiglio** (✉ Via Pradalago 4, ☎ 0465/42000, FAX 0465/40404). **Merano** (✉ Corso della Libertà 45, ☎ 0473/35223, FAX 0473/35524). **Ortisei** (✉ Str. Rezia 1, ☎ 0471/796328 FAX 0471/796749).

11 Emilia-Romagna

Including Parma, Bologna, Rimini, and Ravenna

Gourmets the world over claim that Emilia-Romagna's greatest contribution to humankind has been gastronomic. Birthplace of fettuccine, tortellini, and lasagna, Bologna offers a bevy of great restaurants. But there are also many cultural riches here: Parma's Correggio paintings, Verdi's villa at Sant'Agata, the Renaissance splendors of Ferrara, and the Byzantine beauty of mosaic-rich Ravenna—glittering today as brightly as it did 1,500 years ago.

Updated by
Robert
Andrews

EMILIA-ROMAGNA owes its beginnings to a road. In 187 BC the Romans laid out the Via Aemelia, a long highway running straight from the Adriatic port of Rimini to the central garrison town of Piacenza, and it was along this central spine that the primary towns of the region developed. The old Roman road still exists (S9), and a modern superhighway (A1 and A14) runs parallel to it. Most of the exploring in this chapter will be along either the old road or its modern counterpart.

Despite the unifying factor of the Via Emilia, as the highway is now called, the region has had a fragmented history. The eastern portion of the region, roughly the area from the city of Faenza to the coast, known as Romagna, has looked first to the east and then to Rome for art, political power, and, some say, national character. The western portion, Emilia, from Bologna to Piacenza, had a more northern, rather dour sense of self-government and dissent. Italians say that in Romagna a stranger will be offered a glass of wine; in Emilia, a glass of water—if anything at all.

The principal city of the region is Bologna. It was founded by the Etruscans but eventually came under the influence of the Roman Empire. The Romans established a garrison there, renaming the old Etruscan settlement Bononia, the Bologna of today.

It was after the fall of Rome that the region began its fragmentation. Romagna, centered in Ravenna, was ruled from Constantinople. Ravenna eventually became capital of the empire in the West, in the 5th century, passing to papal rule in the 8th century. The city today, however, is still filled with reminders of two centuries of Byzantine rule.

The other cities of the region, from the Middle Ages on, became the fiefs of important noble families—the Este in Ferrara and Modena, the Pallavicini in Piacenza, the Bentivoglio in Bologna, and the Malatesta in Rimini. Today all these cities bear the marks of their noble patrons. When in the 16th century the papacy managed to exert its power over the entire region, some of these cities were divided among the families of the reigning popes—hence the stamp of the Farnese family on Parma, Piacenza, and Ferrara.

The region was one of the first to join the quest for a unified Italy in the 19th century, pledging itself to the king of Italy and the forces of Garibaldi in the 1840s. Loyalty to the crown did not last long, however. The Italian socialist movement was born in the region, and throughout Italy Emilia-Romagna has been known for rebellion and dissent. Benito Mussolini was born here, although in keeping with the political atmosphere of his home state, he was a firebrand socialist during the early part of his career. Despite being the birthplace of Il Duce, Emilia-Romagna did not take to fascism: it was in this region that the antifascist resistance was born, and during World War II the region suffered terribly at the hands of the Fascists and the Nazis.

Despite a long history of bloodletting, turmoil, and rebellion, the arts—both decorative and culinary—have always flourished in Emilia-Romagna. The great families financed painters, sculptors, and writers (Dante found a haven in Ravenna after being expelled from his native Florence). In modern times, Emilia-Romagna has given to the arts such famous sons as painter Giorgio Morandi, author Giorgio Bassani (author of *Garden of the Finzi-Continis*), filmmaker Federico Fellini, and tenor Luciano Pavarotti.

Gourmets the world over would argue that Emilia-Romagna's greatest contribution to humankind has been gastronomic. Bologna is the acknowledged leading city of Italian cuisine. It is home to two of the most famous Italian delicacies—foods that, sadly, have been poorly treated outside their native city. What the world calls "baloney" the Bolognese call *mortadella,* a robust pork sausage spiced with whole peppercorns (if there aren't peppercorns in it, then it isn't mortadella), which bears no resemblance to the stuff sliced at the typical U.S. deli counter. The other famous dish is spaghetti *al ragù,* known to the world as spaghetti *bolognese.* The spaghetti with meat sauce dished around the world is a far cry from the real thing. In Bologna a ragù sauce is made with onions, carrots, minced pork and veal, butter, and fresh tomatoes and is cooked for five or six hours in a special earthen pot. It is, in a word, exquisite. Few dining experiences in Italy can match the satisfaction of a properly cooked ragù.

Bologna is also the home of tortellini, lasagna, and *vitello* alla bolognese, a veal cutlet smothered with prosciutto and Parmesan cheese. The rest of the province has made substantial contributions to the kitchen. Parma is the home of Parma ham and the most famous of all Italian cheeses, Parmesan. Modena is the birthplace of *zampone* (stuffed pigs' feet, which tastes much better than it sounds) and *aceto balsamico*, the jet-black, fragrant herb vinegar that is now a must on the shelves of any self-respecting gourmet.

Pleasures and Pastimes

Dining

Bologna's reputation as the culinary capital of Italy is well deserved, but there is much fine dining to be had in the other cities of Emilia-Romagna as well. The inland part of the region takes its cue from Bologna, but each city has a traditional dish of its own. In Piacenza rice dishes predominate, particularly risotto in *padella* (with fresh herbs and tomatoes). Parma is most famous for its ham; Modena, for meat products and the delicious balsamic vinegar; Rimini, reflecting its position on the sea, is home to an elaborate fish stew called *brodetto;* Ferrara is famous for simple foods: pears, peaches, asparagus, and zucchini. Crumbly, fresh Parmesan cheese is produced throughout the region and can be picked up at bargain prices from the farms along the Via Emilia and other outlets.

The two most important pastas of the region are pasta al ragù, usually narrow egg noodles served with what is known the world over as Bolognese sauce, and the stuffed pasta called tortellini, which can be served with the ragù, in a cream sauce, or even in soups. Ravioli stuffed with ricotta cheese and spinach is a specialty of the area, as are the larger versions of the same thing: *agnolotti,* which can be stuffed with cheese but more frequently are filled with minced pork or beef, and *tortelli,* stuffed with squash.

The best-known wine of the region is Lambrusco, a sparkling red that has some admirers and many detractors. Some praise it for its tartness; others condemn it for the same quality. A lesser-known wine is Vino del Bosco, also a sparkling red, which comes from the region around Ferrara.

CATEGORY	COST*
$$$$	over 90,000 lire
$$$	60,000–90,000 lire
$$	30,000–60,000 lire
$	under 30,000 lire

*per person, including first course, main course, dessert or fruit, and house wine

Lodging

In Italy, the region of Emilia-Romagna has a reputation for an efficiency that outstrips that in most of the rest of the country. Consequently, even the smallest hotels are well run, with high levels of service and quality. Bologna is very much a businessperson's city, and most of the hotels cater to travelers of this type. There are, of course, smaller, more intimate hotels that cater to the tourist.

The business of Rimini is tourism. There are hundreds of hotels, grand ones with all sorts of luxury facilities and modest boarding houses with only a few rooms. Many offer full- or half-board plans—an economical alternative to eating in Rimini's many, but not particularly distinguished, restaurants. You should not go to Rimini during tourist season without confirmed hotel reservations: in July and August the city is filled to overflowing.

CATEGORY	COST*
$$$$	over 300,000 lire
$$$	160,000–300,000 lire
$$	100,000–160,000 lire
$	under 100,000 lire

*All prices are for a standard double room for two, including service and tax.

Exploring Emilia-Romagna

A tour through Emilia-Romagna has something for everyone: great art, stirring history, fabulous food—even a day at the beach at the seaside resort of Rimini. The best way to see the region is to begin your tour in the west, in Piacenza, and to proceed east along the Via Emilia to the sea. The major towns are either on that route or just off it, the longest detours being no more than 48 to 65 kilometers (30 or 40 miles) off the main road.

Great Itineraries

Although the region of Emilia-Romagna has a geographical logic—following the Via Emilia through the Po Valley and Romagna plain—it is not a compact area, making it hard to cover much of in a short time. If you are traveling straight through, then you will have to confine your stops to places along the main north–west artery. Alternatively, you could base yourself in the regional capital, Bologna, and make forays from this hub. From Bologna there are two choices of itineraries: head north to Ferrara and then east to Ravenna, or continue along the Via Emilia, stopping for short visits at some of the smaller towns en route to Rimini and the sea. More time will permit you to acquaint yourself at a deeper level with the varying moods of the places you visit on your travels. Bologna, in particular, has the most to offer and repays as much time as you can give it.

We have divided the region into two areas of discovery. The first, which extends along the main north–west artery from Piacenza to Savignano, near the Adriatic coastal resort of Rimini, includes the famed opera country between Piacenza and Parma. Birthplace and home of the great Romantic composer Giuseppe Verdi, this area is awash with memorials to the composer, including villas, palazzi, and a theater. Also not to be missed are the beautiful cities of Bologna, one of the most important historical, culinary, and cultural cities in Italy; Modena, famous as the birthplace of Ferrari sports cars and "the world's greatest tenor," Luciano Pavarotti; and Parma, a delightful, dignified town that has been ruled by most of the European powers throughout its history. The second area extends along the Adriatic coast from Rimini, the Italian equivalent of southern Spain's holiday resorts, to Ravenna, once the last capital of the Roman Empire, later part of the Byzantine Empire, and home to the finest mosaics in Western art. The Adriatic coast is also where you'll find Ferrara, a city of towers and turrets, historical palaces, and a mighty castle protected by a moat.

Numbers in the text correspond to numbers in the margin and on the Emilia-Romagna map.

IF YOU HAVE 3 DAYS

Given three days, you should set aside two nights' accommodation to see ⊞ **Bologna** ⑤–⑮ and its environs, including **Dozza** ⑯. The city itself has enough to fill much more than this, but while you are there, make a point of seeing the sights in and around Piazza Maggiore, including the **Basilica di San Petronio** ⑥, the **Palazzo Comunale** ⑦, with its art galleries, and the nearby two towers, which are the most distinguishing feature of the city's skyline. Agility and endurance will enable you to enjoy the view from the top, though no one will hold it against you if you decline! On your second day here, buy a train ticket or drive the short distance to ⊞ **Ferrara** ⑳, an unspoiled Renaissance city whose calm pace will provide a pleasant contrast to the regional capital. Set your sights here on the Castello Estense and the Duomo, leaving a couple of hours for one of the palazzi now containing galleries and museum collections. Where you spend your third day will depend on your route out of Emilia-Romagna. If you are going to Milan or Turin, make a stop after less than 100 kilometers (62 miles) from Bologna at **Parma** ③, where you could cover the major sights in two or three hours. If you are heading toward the Adriatic coast, ⊞ **Ravenna** ⑲ should be your priority stop. The great mosaic works here will probably be your most enduring memory of Emilia-Romagna. Of course, if you are heading north out of Bologna toward Venice, you should see Ferrara on this leg of the journey and take in Parma and Ravenna on the other days.

IF YOU HAVE 5 DAYS

Your itinerary will again depend on your route to and from Emilia-Romagna. Your extra freedom will allow you to spend longer in both ⊞ **Parma** ③ and ⊞ **Ravenna** ⑲, two essentials of any trip through the region. In Ravenna, make a point of seeing **Sant'Apollinare in Classe**, outside the city proper but well worth the excursion. More time in Parma will allow you to take full advantage of the outstanding cuisine available here, as well as sample some good accommodation choices. Fine food and wine should also be evaluated at every opportunity in **Modena** ④ and Bologna, two centers of the culinary culture in this region famed both for its produce and its flair for putting it to good effect. Consider a day and a night for Parma and Modena together. Leave two days for ⊞ **Bologna** ⑤–⑮ itself and one each for ⊞ **Ferrara** ⑳ and Ravenna.

IF YOU HAVE 7 DAYS

A week in the region will allow you to see all the places outlined in our exploring itineraries. If you want to spend time on the beach, spend a couple of days in ⊞ **Rimini** ⑱; in any case make sure you see the cathedral here, a building originally intended as a memorial to a great love affair. Rimini also has some good fish restaurants, but if its resort scene doesn't appeal, skip it altogether and spend more time in Ravenna or Bologna. On your way to (or from) Bologna, drop in on the ceramic center of **Faenza** ⑰, famed for its faience pottery. You can visit a factory here and find some unique souvenirs. Lodge two or three nights in 🔄 **Bologna** ⑤–⑮, depending on how you feel about large cities. It offers the region's widest range of cultural activities and would make a good place to catch up on some opera or theater. The pleasures of ambling the streets of 🔄 **Ferrara** ⑳ might tempt you to spend longer than one night here: you could see everything in a leisurely couple of days without feeling the time drag. Likewise, you might be tempted to while away a quiet couple of days in Parma, another good chance to acquaint yourself with the sophisticated ambience of the region's urban life. Northwest of Parma, make a slight detour from the autostrada or Via Emilia to see the cluster of places associated with the composer Verdi, centered on the village of **Busseto** ②. Still heading northwest, you could spend a pleasant morning or afternoon in the city of **Piacenza** ①, its elegance and harmony typical of Emilia-Romagna's centers of culture, and a fitting exit or entrance to the region. From here, it's a mere 66 kilometers (40 miles) to Milan.

When to Tour Emilia-Romagna

The climate of Emilia-Romagna has never been its most popular aspect. In this predominantly flat landscape, the winters are gray and cold, and summers are airless and hot, though the heat is lessened on the coast by sea breezes. If you are here in summer, rise early and do as much as you can in the morning. The afternoon should be left unplanned; the hours after five are best for sightseeing and traveling. In winter, make sure you are equipped for the humid, penetrating cold: if you are prepared for it, it won't depress you. Fog is common throughout the lowlying areas of the region and can be beautiful, though it can also be very hazardous when driving and restricting to say the least on the panoramic views. At all times, make sure you reserve ahead for your accommodation requirements: the cities are usually awash with commercial conventions and business conferences.

ON THE ROAD TO PARMA AND BOLOGNA

Three of Italy's most interesting cities lie along the main north–west artery: Piacenza, Parma, and Bologna. The area between Piacenza and Parma is opera country: In the quiet backwater towns north of the Via Emilia, the Italian opera composer Giuseppe Verdi lived and worked. The composer of *Aïda, Rigoletto, La Traviata,* and *Otello* was born in a very simple farmhouse in the hamlet of Roncole and built the grand villa of Sant'Agata in the town of Busseto after he became world famous.

Piacenza

❶ *66 km (41 mi) southeast of Milan, 182 km (114 mi) east of Turin, 40 km (25 mi) west of Cremona, 62 km (39 mi) northwest of Parma, 150 km (94 mi) northwest of Bologna.*

The city of **Piacenza** has always been associated with industry and commerce. Its position on the River Po has made it an important inland port since the earliest times—the Etruscans, then the Romans, had thriving settlements on this site. As you approach the city today, you could be forgiven for thinking that it holds little of interest. Piacenza is surrounded by ugly industrial suburbs (with particularly unlovely cement

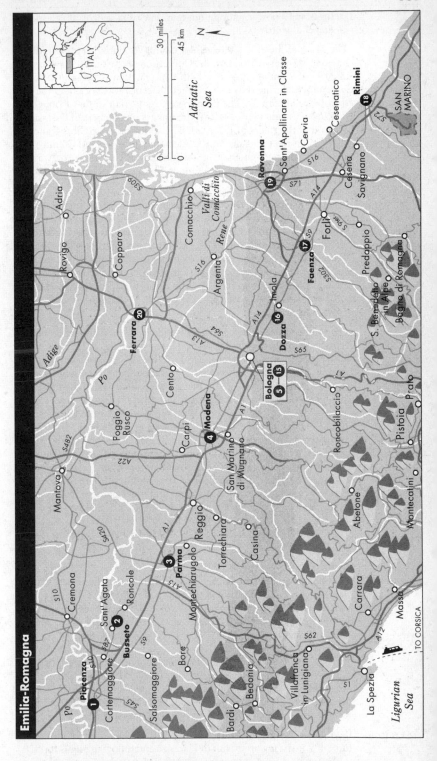

factories and a power station), but these enclose a delightfully unspoiled medieval downtown.

The heart of the city is **Piazza dei Cavalli** (Square of Horses), dominated by the massive Palazzo del Comune, a severe turreted and crenellated Gothic building of the 13th century. It was the seat of town government during those times when Piacenza was not under the iron fist of a ruling family. The flamboyant equestrian statues from which Piazza dei Cavalli takes its name are images of members of the last and greatest of the rulers of Piacenza. The statue on the right is Ranuccio Farnese; on the left is his father, Alessandro Farnese. Alessandro was a beloved ruler, enlightened and fair; Ranuccio, his successor, was less successful. Both statues are the work of Francesco Mochi, a master sculptor of the Baroque period.

Piacenza's impressive **Duomo** is from the mid-12th century. Attached to the massive bell tower is a *gabbia* (iron cage), where evildoers were exposed naked to the scorn (and missiles) of the crowd in the marketplace below. The interior of the cathedral is an odd mixture of Gothic and Baroque. Fine medieval stonework decorates the pillars and the crypt, and there are extravagant frescoes by 17th-century artist Guercino in the dome of the cupola. The Duomo can be reached by following Via XX Settembre down from Piazza dei Cavalli. ✉ *Piazza Duomo.* ☉ *Daily 7–noon, 4–7.*

The **Museo Civico** (Civic Museum), the city-owned collection of Piacenzan art and antiquities, is housed in the vast Palazzo Farnese, which was started by the ruling family in 1558 but never completed. The museum was closed for many years for restoration and the reordering of the collection, but it is again open to the public. The highlight of this rather eclectic exhibit is the *Etruscan Fegato di Piacenza*, a bronze tablet in the shape of a *fegato* (liver), with the symbols of the gods of good and ill fortune marked on it. By comparing this master "liver" with one taken from the body of a freshly slaughtered sacrifice, the priests could predict the future. On a more humanistic note, the collection also contains a painting by Botticelli, the *Madonna with St. John the Baptist,* and a series of Roman bronzes and mosaics. There is also a collection of carriages, arms and armor, and other paraphernalia owned by the Farnese, giving a good idea of the splendor of that powerful family. ✉ *Piazza Cittadella.* ▣ *4,500 lire.* ☉ *Tues., Wed., Fri. 9–12:30; Thurs. 9–12:30 and 3:30–5:30; Sat. 9–12:30 and 3–6; Sun. 9:30–noon and 3:30–6:30.*

Dining

$$$ ✕ **Antica Osteria del Teatro.** Set on a lovely piazza in the center of town,
★ this restaurant is generally held to be the best in Piacenza. Try the tortelli stuffed with ricotta, the roast duck, or the steamed sea bass. ✉ *Via Verdi 16,* ☏ *0523/323777. Reservations essential. AE, DC, MC, V. Closed Mon. and Aug. 1–25, Jan. 1–15. No dinner Sun.*

$ ✕ **Agnello.** Central (on the corner of Piazza Cavalli), simple, and cheap, Agnello is an excellent place to sit down and enjoy a lunchtime snack. Try the tortelli *alla Piacentina* (with ricotta and spinach in a butter and cheese sauce) or, for a meat dish, *coniglio alla Cacciatora* (rabbit in tomato sauce). ✉ *Via Calzolai 2,* ☏ *0523/20874 or 0523/320874. Reservations not accepted. No credit cards. Closed Mon.*

En Route If you are driving from Piacenza, take S10 northeast for Cremona, but turn off it just a few miles out of Piacenza and follow the signs for S587 to the town of Cortemaggiore. From Cortemaggiore, turn right onto a smaller rural road (not numbered) and follow the signs for Busseto, some 10 kilometers (6 miles) away. If you plan to visit all the area's

Verdi sights, invest in a 8,000-lire ticket valid for Villa Pallavicino, Palazzo Orlandi, Teatro Verdi, and Verdi's birthplace (but not Villa Sant'Agata).

Busseto

❷ *30 km (19 mi) southeast of Piacanza, 15 km (9½ mi) south of Cremona, 30 km (19 mi) northwest of Parma.*

Busseto's main attraction is the **Villa Pallavicino,** where Verdi worked and lived with his mistress (later wife), Giuseppina Strepponi. There is a small Verdi museum here that displays such relics of the maestro as his piano, scores, composition books, walking sticks, and other bits of memorabilia. ⊠ *3,000 lire.* ⊙ *Apr.–Sept., Tues.–Sun. 9:30–12:30 and 3–7; Oct.–Mar., 9:30–noon and 2:30–5.*

Palazzo Orlandi, owned for the past century by the Orlandi family, was Verdi's home for a few years from 1845. Only a few of its stately rooms are open to the public. ⊠ *3,000 lire.* ⊙ *Apr.–Sept., Tues.–Sun. 9:30–12:30 and 3–7; Oct.–Mar., Tues.–Sun. 9:30–noon and 2:30–5.*

In the center of Busseto is the lovely **Teatro Verdi,** dedicated, as one may expect, to the works of the hamlet's famous son. It is a well-preserved 19th-century-style theater, and it's worth a look to get a feel for a place where Verdi worked. (After lengthy restorations, the theater should have been reopened in September 1996, but check first.) ⊠ *4,000 lire.* ⊙ *Apr.–Sept., Tues.–Sun. 9:30–12:30 and 3–7; Oct.–Mar., Tues.–Sun. 9:30–noon and 2:30–5.*

OFF THE BEATEN PATH   **VILLA SANT'AGATA –** Five kilometers (3 miles) north of Busseto, Villa Sant'Agata is the grand country home Verdi built for himself in 1849, where some of his greatest works were composed. For Verdi lovers, Sant'Agata is a shrine. ⊠ 8,000 lire. ⊙ Apr. 1–Oct. 30, Tues.–Sun. 9–11:40 and 3–6:45.

RONCOLE – Giuseppe Verdi was born in a simple farmhouse on the edge of the town of **Roncole,** 3½ kilometers (2 miles) southeast of Busseto. Equally modest is the church in which he took some of his earliest steps in a musical career; he was the church organist here when still in his teens. ⊠ Verdi's birthplace 3,000 lire. ⊙ Apr.–Sept., Tues.–Sun. 9:30–12:30 and 3–7; Oct.–Mar., Tues.–Sun. 9:30–noon and 2:30–5.

Parma

❸ *28 km (17½ mi) southeast of Roncole along S588 and A1 or Via Emilia, 62 km (39 mi) southeast of Piacenza, 97 km (61 mi) northwest of Bologna.*

Parma is a delightful, dignified town that stands on the banks of a tributary of the River Po. Much of the historic center has been untouched by modern times, despite heavy damage during World War II, and thanks to the efforts being made by the city fathers to control traffic, strolling Parma's cobbled streets is a charming experience. The traffic regulations, although a boon to pedestrians, are a nightmare for motorists. Every obstacle is put in the way of motor traffic—one-way streets, no-turning zones, and the like—so it is best to leave your car outside the center and see the town on foot.

Almost every major European power has had a hand in ruling Parma at one time or another. The Romans founded the city—it was little more than a garrison on the Via Emilia—and then a succession of feudal lords held sway here. In the 16th century came the ever-avaricious Farnese family (who are still the dukes of Parma) and then, in fast succession, the Spanish, French, and Austrians, with the Austrians taking over following the upheavals in central Europe after the fall of Napoléon. The French influence is strong. The French novelist Stendhal lived in the city for several years and set his classic novel *The Charterhouse of Parma* here.

★ The **Piazza del Duomo**—site of the cathedral, the baptistery, the church of San Giovanni, and the palaces of the bishop and other notables—is the heart of the city. This square and its buildings make up one of the most harmonious, tranquil city centers in Italy.

The focal point of the piazza is the magnificent 12th-century **Duomo,** with its two vigilant stone lions standing guard beside the main door. The arch of the entrance is decorated with a delicate frieze of figures representing the months of the year, a motif repeated inside the baptistery on the right-hand side of the square.

Some of the original artwork still exists in the church, notably the *Descent from the Cross,* a carving in the right transept, by Benedetto Antelami (1150–1230), a sculptor and architect whose masterwork is this cathedral's baptistery (☞ *below*). You can still feel the emotion the artist wished to convey in the simple figures.

It is odd to turn from this austere work of the 12th century to the exuberant fresco in the dome, the *Assumption of the Virgin,* by the 16th-century painter Antonio Correggio. The fresco was not well received when it was unveiled in 1530. "A mess of frogs' legs," the bishop of Parma is said to have called it. In contrast to the rather dark, somber interior of the cathedral, though, the beauty and light of the painting in the dome are a welcome relief. Today, of course, Correggio is acclaimed as one of the leading masters of Baroque painting; his many works on view in Parma now constitute one of the greatest draws of the city. ✉ *Piazza Duomo.* ⏲ *Daily 7–noon and 3–7.*

The **Baptistery** is a solemn and simple Romanesque building on the exterior and an uplifting Gothic building within. The doors of the Baptistery are richly decorated with figures, animals, and flowers, and the interior is adorned with figures carved by Antelami, showing the months and seasons. It is to the side of the Duomo. 🎫 *4,000 lire.* ⏲ *Daily 9–12:30 and 3–6.*

San Giovanni Evangelista is a church with an elaborate Baroque facade and a Renaissance interior. Of the several works by Correggio in this church, it is his *St. John the Evangelist* (left transept) that is considered the finest. Also in this church (in the second and fourth chapels on the left) are works by Girolamo Parmigianino—a contemporary of Correggio's and the spearhead of the astonishing Mannerist art movement. Once seen, Parmigianino's anorexic and swan-necked Madonnas are never forgotten: They pose with all the precious élan of today's high-fashion models. ⏲ *Daily 6:30–noon and 3:30–8.*

Next door to the church, in the adjoining monastery, is a **pharmacy** where Benedictine monks used to mix medicines and herbals. The 16th-century decorations still survive, although the potions (the people of Parma swore they would cure almost every ill) are, alas, gone—the pharmacy stopped production in 1881. 🎫 *4,000 lire.* ⏲ *Daily 9–1:45.*

★ The **Galleria Nazionale** of Parma is the primary art gallery of the city, and it is housed in the vast, and rather grim-looking, **Palazzo della Pilotta,** on the banks of the river. The palace was built about 1600 and is so big that from the air it is Parma's most recognizable sight—hence, the destruction done to it when it was bombed by Allied forces in 1944. Much of the building has been restored, but not all. The palazzo takes its name from the ball game *pilotta*, a sort of handball played within the palace precincts in the 17th century.

★ To enter the art museum, which is on the ground floor of the palace, you pass through the magnificent and elaborately Baroque **Teatro Farnese,** built in 1628 and based on Palladio's theater in the northern Italian town of Vicenza. Built entirely of wood, the theater was burned badly during Allied bombing but has been faultlessly restored.

The art gallery itself is large and contains many examples of works by the two best-known painters of Parma—Correggio and Parmigianino. There are also works by Fra Angelico, Leonardo da Vinci, El Greco, and Il Bronzino. ▣ *12,000 lire.* ◷ *Daily 9–1:45.*

The **Camera del Correggio** is the former dining room of the abbess of the Convent of St. Paul. It was extensively frescoed by Correggio, and despite the religious character of the building, the decorations are entirely secular, with ravishingly beautiful (and very worldly) depictions of mythological scenes—the *Triumphs of the Goddess Diana,* the *Three Graces,* and the *Three Fates.* It is near the Palazzo della Pilotta, on Strada Garibaldi. ▣ *4,000 lire.* ◷ *Daily 9–1:45.*

NEED A BREAK?
Civilization in Parma is more than painting and architecture. To taste the delicacies that put Parma on the world culinary map, have a snack or buy the ingredients for a picnic at **Salumeria Melli** (✉ Via della Repubblica 68) or **Specialità di Parma** (✉ Via Farini 9/c).

Near the central Piazza Garibaldi is **Madonna della Steccata,** a delightful 16th-century domed church famous for a wonderful fresco cycle by Parmigianino. The painter took so long to complete it that his exasperated patrons imprisoned him briefly for breach of contract before releasing him to complete the work. ◷ *Daily 9–noon and 3–6.*

Dining and Lodging

$$ ✕ **Croce di Malta.** The historic premises once housed a convent, then an inn (there are still inexpensive rooms available here), before this attractive restaurant with turn-of-the-century decor opened in 1984. It's in the heart of Parma, and the food is traditional local fare. The homemade pasta is light and delicate; try tortelli with squash filling or tagliatelle in any fashion. Second courses are well prepared and filling versions of classic veal and cheese dishes. ✉ *Borgo Palmia 8,* ☎ *0521/235643. Reservations essential. AE, MC, V. Closed Sun. and 2 weeks in Aug.*

$$ ✕ **La Greppia.** Here, at the best and most elegant restaurant in the city,
★ *padella alla Greppia* (green tagliatelle in mushroom sauce) is excellent, as are the pâté in Marsala wine, the *torta di melanzane* (eggplant pie), and the fried porcini mushrooms. ✉ *Via Garibaldi 39A,* ☎ *0521/233686. Reservations essential. Jacket and tie. AE, DC, MC, V. Closed Mon., Tues., and July.*

$$ ✕ **Parma Rotta.** An old inn about 2 kilometers (1¼ miles) from down-
★ town Parma, the Parma Rotta remains an informal neighborhood trattoria serving hearty dishes like *pasta e fagioli* (bean and pasta soup), roast pork, and spit-roasted lamb. Take advantage of the garden here to eat outside in summer. ✉ *Via Langhirano 158,* ☎ *0521/581323. AE, DC, MC, V. Closed Sun. June–Aug., Mon. Sept.–May.*

$$ ✕ **Sant'Ambrogio.** This is an informal restaurant in the center of town. Duck and quail are the best bets, but try the *cotechino con crauti* (boiled pork sausage with pickled cabbage). ✉ *Vicolo Cinque Piaghe 1/a,* ☎ *0521/234482. AE, DC, MC, V. Closed Mon.*

$$$ 🏨 **Palace Hotel Maria Luigia.** A top-quality hotel convenient to old Parma and the train station, the Maria Luigia has large, well-furnished rooms and is popular with business travelers. ⊠ *Via Mentana 140,* ☎ *0521/281032,* FAX *0521/231126. 100 rooms with bath or shower. Restaurant, bar, meeting rooms. AE, DC, MC, V.*

$$$ 🏨 **Park Hotel Stendhal.** Completely renovated, the Stendhal is again one of the best hotels in Parma. It is on the edge of the historic center of town and convenient for the tourist and business traveler alike. Some rooms have views of the Palazzo della Pilotta. ⊠ *Via Bodoni 3,* ☎ *0521/208057,* FAX *0521/285655. 60 rooms with bath or shower. Restaurant, bar, meeting rooms. AE, DC, MC, V.*

$$ 🏨 **Torino.** A warm reception and pleasant surroundings are the best reasons for staying in this relaxed hotel. It's well run, comfortable—its modern, smallish rooms all with TV—and in a quiet pedestrian zone in the heart of town. ⊠ *Via Mazza 7,* ☎ *0521/281046,* FAX *0521/230725. 33 rooms with bath or shower. Bar, air-conditioning. AE, DC, MC, V. Closed Aug. 1–25.*

Nightlife and the Arts

Parma is the region's opera center, with performances held at the **Teatro Regio** (☎ 0521/218910) on Via Garibaldi. Opera here is taken just as seriously as in Milan, although tickets are a little easier to come by. Playwright Dario Fo helped found the **Teatro Due** (⊠ Viale Basetti 12, ☎ 0521/230242), a theater whose productions still maintain a mixture of comedy and politics—though your understanding of the themes will be limited without a knowledge of Italian.

Modena

❹ *56 km (35 mi) southeast of Parma along Route A1, 38 km (23 mi) northwest of Bologna.*

Modena is an old town that's famous today for three very modern names. The luxury high-performance cars Maserati and Ferrari come from Modena, and so does the world-famous opera star Luciano Pavarotti.

The modern town that encircles the historic center is extensive, and although the old quarter is small, it is filled with an Old World atmosphere, narrow medieval streets, and pleasant piazzas. Begin your exploration at the **Duomo** in the central Piazza Grande. The church is one of the finest examples of Romanesque architecture in the country and dates from the 12th century. As in Parma, the exterior is decorated with medieval sculptures showing scenes from the life of San Gemignano (patron saint of Modena) and fantastic beasts, as well as a realistic-looking scene of the sacking of a city by barbarian hordes, a reminder to the faithful to be ever vigilant in defense of the church. The bell tower is made of white marble and is known as *La Ghirlandina* (The Little Garland) because of its distinctive garland-shaped weather vane on the summit.

The interior of the church is very somber and is divided by an elaborately decorated gallery carved with scenes of the Passion of Christ. The carvings took 50 years to complete and are by an anonymous Modenese master of the 12th century. The tomb of San Gemignano is in the crypt. ⊠ *Piazza Grande.* ☉ *Daily 8–6.*

The principal museum of the town is housed in the **Palazzo dei Musei,** a short walk from the Duomo. (Follow Via Emilia—the old Roman road runs through the heart of the town—to Via di Sant'Agostino. The museum is in the piazza on the left). The collection was assembled in the mid-17th century by Francesco d'Este, Duke of Modena, and the gallery **Galleria Estense** is named in his honor. In the first room, there is a portrait bust of him by Bernini.

The duke was a man of many interests, as you can see from the galleries' collections of objets d'art—ivories, coins, medals, and bronzes, as well as works of art dating from the Renaissance to the Baroque. There are works here by Correggio, as well as by masters from other parts of Italy, such as the Venetians Tintoretto and Veronese, the Bolognese Reni and the Carracci brothers, and the Neapolitan Salvator Rosa.

The gallery also houses the duke's **library**, a huge collection of illuminated books, of which the best known is the beautifully illustrated bible of the 15th century, the *Bible of Borso d'Este*. A map, dated 1501, was one of the first in the world to show Columbus's discovery of America. ⊠ *Piazza Sant'Agostino.* ▣ *8,000 lire.* ☉ *Tues., Fri., Sat. 9–7; Wed., Thurs. 9–2; Sun. 9–1.*

In Piazza Roma (follow the curved Via Ramazzini away from the Palazzo dei Musei), you'll find the huge Baroque **palace** of the dukes of Modena. It is now a military academy; once the province of the dukes only, it is still off-limits, except to flocks of cadets in elaborate uniforms. Behind the academy are Modena's large public gardens.

Dining and Lodging

$$$ ✕ **Borso d'Este.** One of the city's most highly regarded restaurants—
★ particularly with the *crema* of the region's monied set—offers some delicious variations on old themes, like ravioli stuffed with game and Parmesan. Other specialties include *gnocchetti* (little dumplings) with melted cheese and radicchio, and a mushroom tart with truffle sauce. ⊠ *Piazza Roma 5,* ☎ *059/214114. Reservations essential. AE, DC, MC, V. Closed Sun. and Aug.*

$$$ ✕ **Fini.** A dining institution in Modena, Fini is widely held to be the best restaurant the city has to offer. It's Pavarotti's favorite—and you could easily gain a Pavarottiesque figure by making a habit of the *gran bollito misto,* a groaning board of boiled meats accented in a sauce *verde* (vegetable sauce). The decor is modern yet elegant. Round out your meal with excellent local wines and homemade desserts. ⊠ *Piazzale San Francesco,* ☎ *059/223314. Reservations essential. Jacket and tie. AE, DC, MC, V. Closed Mon., Tues., July 20–Aug. 20, last wk in Dec.*

$ ✕ **Papillon.** This cheerful, well-patronized trattoria on two floors makes no pretense of Old World character or sophistication, but you can still enjoy an excellent repast here. Along with some exotic Persian dishes on the menu, fish is the top choice: take your pick from a rich variety, such as *sogliola* (sole) or *triglie* (red mullet), according to season. Pizzas are also available. ⊠ *Piazza Matteotti 40,* ☎ *059/222610. Weekend reservations essential. AE, DC, MC, V. Closed Tues.*

$$$ ▥ **Canal Grande.** Once a ducal palace, the Canal Grande offers large, airy, well-equipped rooms with minibars. The hotel's restaurant, La Secchia Rapita, is rated highly. ⊠ *Corso Canalgrande 6,* ☎ *059/217160,* ℻ *059/221674. 75 rooms with bath or shower. Restaurant (closed Tues.), bar. AE, DC, MC, V.*

$ ▥ **La Torre.** Not a particularly exciting accommodation, La Torre is nonetheless the best choice in this price category, thanks to its location in the center of town, just off the Via Emilia. Rooms are functional, well equipped, and comfortable; there is also a good restaurant. ⊠ *Via Cervetta 5,* ☎ *059/222615,* ℻ *059/216316. 26 rooms, 19 with shower. Bar. AE, DC, MC, V.*

Bologna

⑤ *38 km (23 mi) southeast of Modena, 106 km (66 mi) north of Florence, 210 km (131 mi) southeast of Milan, 154 km (96 mi) southwest of Venice.*

Bologna is the principal city of Emilia-Romagna and one of the most important cities in Italy. Through its long history, first as an Etruscan city, then a Roman one, then as an independent city-state in the Middle Ages, Bologna has always been a power in the north of Italy. Through the centuries, the city has acquired a number of nicknames: Bologna the Learned, in honor of its ancient (the oldest in the world) university; Bologna the Turreted, recalling the forest of medieval towers that once rose from the city center (two remarkable examples still exist); and Bologna the Fat, a tribute to the preeminent position the city holds in the world of cuisine.

Wars, sackings, rebellions, and aerial bombing do not seem to have made much of an impression on the old center of the city: the narrow cobblestone streets are still there, as are the ancient churches, the massive palaces, the medieval towers, and the famous arcades that line many of the main thoroughfares of the town.

The streets are always bustling with students. The university was founded in the year 1050 and by the 13th century already had more than 10,000 students. It was a center for the teaching of law and theology, and it was ahead of its time in that many of the professors were women. Today the university has one of the most prominent business schools in Italy and has the finest faculty of medicine in the country. Marconi, the inventor of wireless telegraphy, first formulated his groundbreaking theories in the physics labs of the university.

The heart of the city is Piazza Maggiore and the adjacent Piazza del Nettuno. Grouped around these two squares are the imposing Basilica of San Petronio, the huge Palazzo Comunale, the Palazzo del Podestà, the Palazzo di Re Enzo, and the fountain of Neptune. It is one of the best groupings of public buildings in the entire country.

Numbers in the margin correspond to points of interest on the Bologna map.

❻ The **Basilica di San Petronio** was started in the 14th century, and work was still in progress on this vast building some 300 years later. It is still not finished, as you can see: the facade is only partially decorated, lacking most of the marble facing that the architects planned on several hundred years ago. The main doorway was carved by the great Sienese master of the Renaissance, Jacopo della Quercia. Above the center of the door is a Madonna and Child, flanked by Saints Ambrose and Petronius, patrons of the city.

The interior of the basilica is huge and echoing, 432 feet long and 185 feet wide. It is so vast that it's sobering to note that originally the Bolognans had planned an even bigger church (you can still see the columns erected to support the larger church outside the east end) but decided on this "toned-down" version in the interest of economy. The church museum contains models to show how the original church would have looked. The most important artworks in the church are in the left aisle, frescoes by Giovanni di Modena dating from the first years of the 1400s. Also in the left aisle, laid out in the pavement of the church, is a huge sundial, placed there in 1655, showing the time, date, and month. ⊠ *Piazza Maggiore.* ☉ *Basilica: summer, daily 7:30–6:30; winter, daily 7:30–5. Museo di San Petronio (inside church): Mon., Wed., Fri.–Sun. 10–12:30.*

❼ The **Palazzo Comunale** is a mixture of styles and buildings, dating from the 13th to 15th centuries. When Bologna was an independent commune, this huge palace was the seat of government, a function it serves today. Over the door is a giant statue of Pope Gregory XIII, Bologna-

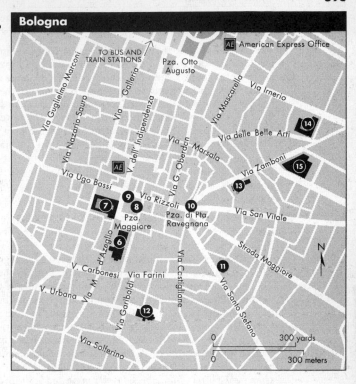

born and most famous for his reorganization of the calendar—the system in use today.

The Palazzo Comunale contains a picture gallery, the **Collezioni Comunali d'Arte,** which has paintings from the Middle Ages as well as some Renaissance works by Luca Signorelli and Tintoretto. On the same floor, a separate museum is dedicated to the 20th-century still-life paintings of **Giorgio Morandi,** complete with a re-creation of his studio and living space. Aside from this, however, the best reason to come is to get a look at the views of the piazza from the upper stories of the palace. ⊠ *Piazza Maggiore (on the right as you face the Basilica di San Petronio).* ▣ *Collezioni Comunali and the Museo Morandi: 5,000 lire each; 8,000 lire for both.* ☉ *Tues.–Sun. 10–6.*

❽ The **Palazzo del Podestà,** which faces the Basilica di San Petronio, was built in 1484, and attached to it is the soaring Torre dell'Arengo. The bells in this tower have rung since 1453, whenever the city has celebrated, mourned, or called its citizens to arms. ⊠ *Piazza Nettuno.* ,

❾ The medieval **Palazzo di Re Enzo** is the building in which King Enzo of Sardinia was imprisoned for 23 years (until his death in 1272). He had been unwise enough to wage war on Bologna and was captured after the fierce battle of Fossalta in 1249. The palace has other unhappy associations: common criminals received the last rites of the church in the tiny chapel in the courtyard before being taken out to be executed in Piazza Maggiore. It is next to the Palazzo del Podestà ⊠ *Piazza Nettuno.*

The elaborate Baroque **fountain** by the sculptor Giambologna in the Piazza Nettuno was sculpted in 1566 and is known by the nickname Il Gigante (The Giant), which certainly fits. Given Bologna's landlocked position, the choice of subject—the God of the Sea, Neptune, and his attendant dolphins and mermaids, the water spurting jauntily from their breasts—seems rather odd. It is next to the Palazzo di Re Enzo. ⊠ *Piazza Nettuno.*

The busy, chic Via Rizzoli runs from Piazza Nettuno directly into the medieval section of the city, passing Piazza di Porta Ravegnana. Here are two of Bologna's famous towers: the taller, the **Torre degli Asinelli,** is 320 feet high and leans an alarming 7½ feet out of the perpendicular; the other tower, the **Torre Garisenda,** was shortened for safety in the 1500s. It is 165 feet high and tilts 10 feet. The towers were built at the same time (1488) and are mentioned by Dante in *The Inferno.* They are the only two that remain of the more than 200 that once graced the city—every family of any importance had a tower as a symbol of its prestige and power. The Torre degli Asinelli can be climbed (500 steep stairs) and has a fine view of the city. ⊠ *Piazza di Porta Ravegnana.* ▣ *3,000 lire.* ⊙ *May–Sept., daily 9–6; Oct.–Apr., daily 9–5.*

The church of **Santo Stefano** is a remarkable building in that it is actually several churches contained in one building. The oldest, the church of Santi Vitale e Agricola, dates from the 8th century and contains a 14th-century nativity scene much loved by Bologna's children, who come at Christmastime to pay their respects to the baby Jesus. The church of San Sepolcro (12th century) contains the **Courtyard of Pontius Pilate,** so named for the basin in the center of the court that's said to be the basin Pilate washed his hands in after condemning Christ. Also in the building is a **museum** displaying various medieval religious works where you can buy sundry items made by the monks, such as honey, shampoo, and jam. ⊠ *Piazza Santo Stefano.* ⊙ *Daily summer, 9–noon, 3:30–6:30; winter, 9–noon and 3:30–5:30.* ▣ *Museum free.* ⊙ *Oct.–Mar., weekdays 9–noon and 3:30–6, Sun. 9–1 and 3:30–6:30; Apr.–Sept., daily 9–noon and 3:30–6:30.*

The church of **San Domenico,** a few blocks south of Via Farini, off Via Garibaldi, contains the tomb of Saint Dominic, who died here in 1221. The tomb of the saint, called the Arca di San Domenico, is in the sixth chapel on the right. Many artists contributed to the decoration, notably Niccolò di Bari, who was so proud of his work here that he changed his name to Niccolò dell'Arca to recall this famous work. The young Michelangelo carved the angel on the right. In the right transept of the church is a tablet marking the last resting place of the hapless King Enzo, whose prison you saw in Piazza Maggiore (☞ Palazzo di Re Enzo, *above*). In the square in front of San Domenico are two curious tombs raised above the ground on pillars, commemorating two famous 14th-century lawyers. ⊠ *Piazza San Domenico.* ⊙ *Daily 7–noon and 3:30–7.*

A few blocks up from Piazza di Porta Ravegnana, off the busy Via Zamboni, stop on the right to see the church of **San Giacomo Maggiore.** Inside is the burial chamber of the Bentivoglio family, the leading family in Bologna in the Middle Ages. The crypt is connected by underground passage to the Teatro Comunale, across the street—a rather odd feature, until you realize that the family palazzo of the Bentivoglio used to stand on that spot. The most notable tomb is that of Antonio Bentivoglio, carved by Jacopo della Quercia in 1435. We can tell his profession—lecturer in law—from the group of students carved on the base, all listening intently to their professor. ⊠ *Piazza Rossini.* ⊙ *Daily 6:30–noon and 3:30–6.*

The collection in Bologna's principal art gallery—also one of the most important in Italy—the **Pinacoteca Nazionale,** contains many works by the immortals of Italian painting, including Raphael's famous *Ecstasy of St. Cecilia.* There is also a beautiful multipaneled painting by Giotto and a Parmigianino *Madonna and Saints.* The centerpieces of the collection, however, are the many rooms devoted to the two most important Bolognese painters, Guido Reni and Annibale Carracci, both masters of the late 16th century. Some of the most interesting paintings, from a historical point of view, are by Giuseppe Crespi, a Bolognese painter of the 18th century who avoided grand religious or historical themes, preferring instead to paint scenes of daily life in his native city. These small canvases give you an excellent idea of the boisterous, earthy life of Old Bologna. ⊠ *Via delle Belle Arti 56,* ☎ *051/ 243222.* 🖃 *8,000 lire.* ⊙ *Tues.–Sat. 9–2, Sun. 9–1.*

⑮ The **university** district, which is bordered on one side by the Pinacoteca Nazionale (☞ *above*), is worth a walk through the adjoining streets to get a sense of what an Italian university is like. There is no campus, as such, but a jumble of buildings, some dating as far back as the 15th century, with the bulk of them from the 17th and 18th centuries. This neighborhood, like neighborhoods in most college towns, has lots of bookshops, coffee shops, and cheap snack bars and restaurants. None of them are particularly distinguished, but they all give a good idea of student life in the city. Political slogans and sentiments are scrawled on walls all around the university and tend, for the most part, to be ferociously leftist.

NEED A BREAK? For wonderful ice cream in the university district, try **Moline** (⊠ Via delle Moline 13; closed Tues.), which has simple but delicious *cioccolata con panna* (chocolate with heavy whipped cream) or a series of more adventurous flavors and delicate fruit ices.

Dining and Lodging

$$$$ ✕ **I Carracci.** For those who feel a good tasting meal can taste even better if the decor is delicious, this restaurant—Bologna's most *bellissimo*—is a must. Frescoed with scenes of the four seasons, the place is named after the family of 17th-century artists who made Europe go for Baroque. Critics are hoping the kitchen will come up to par with the decor. ⊠ *Grand Hotel Baglioni, Via dell'Indipendenza 8 (hotel guests) or Via Manzoni 2,* ☎ *051/225445. Reservations essential. Jacket and tie. AE, DC, MC, V. Closed Sun. and Aug.*

$$$ ✕ **Al Pappagallo.** Almost directly beneath Bologna's famous Asinelli and Garisenda towers, the Pappagallo was once synonymous with gourmet eating in the city. Though competition has shifted the spotlight from it in recent years, it retains enough of its reputation and quality cuisine to merit at least one slap-up feast, served in a stylish, semiformal atmosphere. The first-course specialty is lasagna *del Pappagallo,* made with veal, sirloin of pork, and wood mushrooms. For a main course, sample the *filetto di tacchino* (turkey stuffed with truffles, ham, and Parmesan). ⊠ *Piazza della Mercanzia 3/c,* ☎ *051/232807. Reservations essential. Jacket and tie. AE, DC, MC, V. Closed Sun. evening and Mon.*

$$$ ✕ **Notai.** Bologna's best—so say many residents of the gastronomic
★ capital of Italy. You'll hear the Angelus ring from the cathedral at this spot, just off beautiful Piazza Maggiore. The building is 14th-century, the decor is 19th-century, and the food can be sublime. For a true *boccadivino*—heavenly mouthful, that is—try the *piccoli* chateaubriand in béarnaise sauce. ⊠ *Via de'Pignattari 1,* ☎ *051/228694. Reservations essential. AE, DC, MC, V. Closed Sun.*

$$$ ✕ **Rosteria Luciano.** A changing list of daily specials augments what is already one of Bologna's most varied menus. Some of the best offerings are shrimp with pineapple, wild boar sausage, and excellent pork and veal roasts. Among the desserts is *ricottina al forno*—delicious, charcoal-flavored ricotta baked in the oven. ⊠ *Via Nazario Sauro 19,*

☎ 051/231249. *Reservations essential. AE, MC, V. Closed Wed., Aug., Dec. 23–Jan. 2.*

$$ ✕ **Bertino.** Popularity has not spoiled this traditional neighborhood trattoria. Meals are simple but prepared with care: Try the *paglia e fieno* (yellow and green pasta) with sausage, or choose from the steaming tray of bollito misto. ⊠ *Via delle Lame 55,* ☎ *051/522230. AE, DC, MC, V. Closed Sun., Dec. 25, Jan. 1, Aug. No dinner Mon.*

$$ ✕ **Da Carlo.** Dining on the medieval terrace in summer is a treat in this attractive restaurant, so be sure to reserve a table outside. Specialties include delicate game, such as braised pigeon with artichokes. ⊠ *Via Marchesana 6,* ☎ *051/233227. Reservations essential. AE, DC, MC, V. Closed Sun., Tues. and Jan. 1–22, Aug. 23–Sept. 3.*

$$ ✕ **Da Cesari.** Wine made by the owner's family, famous Bolognese dishes such as *gramigna alla salsiccia* (pasta with a sauce of sausage and tomato), and entrées such as duck with rosemary, make this one of the best restaurants in Bologna in its price category. ⊠ *Via de Carbonesi 8,* ☎ *051/237710. Reservations essential. AE, DC, MC, V. Closed Sun. and Aug.*

$$ ✕ **Osteria Du Madon.** American graduate students from the nearby Johns Hopkins institute and members of Bologna's championship basketball team are regulars at this family-run restaurant, located under the porticoes not far from the city's famous towers. Among the specialties on a menu of classic local dishes are freshly made pastas and gnocchi, and lamb chops dressed with balsamic vinegar. ⊠ *Via San Vitale 75,* ☎ *051/226221. Reservations essential. AE, DC, MC, V. Closed Sun. and first 3 wks in Aug. No lunch Sat.*

$$ ✕ **Rosteria Antico Brunetti.** Housed in a Romanesque tower steps away from Piazza Maggiore, this wood-paneled restaurant was founded in 1873 and is known as Bologna's oldest. Specialties here range from "Mama's tortellini" to veal smothered in white-wine sauce, but most diners opt for the pizzas or fabulous pastas with seafood sauces. Dining is on two floors, but even then the restaurant fills quickly. ⊠ *Via Caduti di Cefalonia 5,* ☎ *051/234441. AE, DC, MC, V. Closed Wed.*

$$ ✕ **Victoria.** It is not unusual for this unpretentious but tastefully decorated trattoria-pizzeria off Via dell'Indipendenza to have lines of people waiting for a table, so reserve ahead. Even if you can't, however, it's worth the wait. Although most people come for the wide choice of inexpensive pizzas, there is also a full menu of pasta, fish, and meat dishes. Beer, on tap or bottled, and wine are available. Try for a place in the room with the lovely 17th-century wooden ceiling. ⊠ *Via Augusto Righi 9c,* ☎ *051/233548. Reservations essential. AE, DC, MC, V. Closed Thurs.*

$$$$ ⛨ **Grand Hotel Baglioni.** Sixteenth-century frescoes by the Bolognese
★   Carracci brothers are rarely seen outside a museum or church, but here they provide the stunning backdrop for the public rooms and restaurant (☞ I Carracci, *above*) of one of Italy's most glamorous hotels. The rooms are warm and charming, and the staff is extremely attentive. The location is ideal, just a few steps from the central Piazza Maggiore. ⊠ *Via dell' Indipendenza 8,* ☎ *051/225445,* ℻ *051/234840. 125 rooms with bath or shower. Bar, meeting rooms. AE, DC, MC, V.*

$$$–$$$$ ⛨ **Corona d'Oro.** Once a medieval printing house, this centrally located
★   hotel has been in business for more than a century. The public space is a delight, with a lyrical art-nouveau decor, an atrium, and enough flowers for a wedding. The rooms are comfortable and air-conditioned. ⊠ *Via Oberdan 12,* ☎ *051/236456,* ℻ *051/262679. 35 rooms with shower. Bar, meeting room. Closed 2 wks in Aug. AE, DC, MC, V.*

$$$ ⛨ **Dei Commercianti.** Close to San Petronio and recently renovated, Dei Commercianti provides comfort and a good location at reasonable prices. Ask for one of the rooms with a terrace—those on the upper floors have wonderful views. ⊠ *Via dei Pignattari 11,* ☎ *051/233052,* FAX *051/224733. 31 rooms with shower. Bar. AE, DC, MC, V.*

$$$ ⚇ **Orologio.** Under the same management as the Dei Commercianti (☞ *above*), the Orologio is in a quiet pedestrian zone and has been recently renovated. Top-floor rooms have good views of San Petronio. ⊠ *Via IV Novembre 10,* ☎ *051/231253,* FAX *051/260552. 29 rooms with bath or shower. Bar. AE, DC, MC, V.*

$$ ⚇ **Accademia.** This small hotel is right in the middle of the university quarter, a comfortable base for exploring the area. The rooms are adequate, the staff friendly. ⊠ *Via delle Belle Arti 6,* ☎ FAX *051/263590 or 051/232318. 28 rooms, 24 with shower. No credit cards. Closed 10 days in Aug.*

$ ⚇ **San Vitale.** Modern furnishings and a garden distinguish this modest hostelry, which is a five-minute walk from the center of town. The service is courteous, and rooms are clean and bright. ⊠ *Via San Vitale 94,* ☎ *051/225966,* FAX *051/531346. 14 rooms with shower. No credit cards.*

Outdoor Activities and Sports

SWIMMING

There is a public swimming pool (⊠ Via Costa 174, ☎ 051/617–9022) open May–September, daily 9:30–7, and October–April, weekdays noon–3, Saturday 10:30–1, and Sunday 9–12:30 and 3–11:30 PM.

Nightlife and the Arts

The city hosts a wide selection of orchestral and chamber music concerts as well as an acclaimed opera season. The 18th-century **Teatro Comunale** presents concerts by Italian and international orchestras throughout the year, but opera dominates the theater's winter season. All events sell out quickly, so be sure to reserve seats well in advance (⊠ Largo Respighi 1, ☎ 051/529999). Operetta and musicals abound during the winter season at the modern **Teatro Sala Europa** (⊠ Piazza Costituzione, ☎ 051/372540). Theater and ballet can be enjoyed at the historic **Arena del Sole** (⊠ Via Indipendenza 44, ☎ 051/270790). **Teatro delle Moline** (⊠ Via delle Moline 1, ☎ 051/235288) is just one of the many small venues where contemporary drama, dance, and comedy productions are performed. Children learning Italian may enjoy the kids' productions at the **Teatro Testoni** (⊠ Via Matteotti 16, ☎ 051/377790). Check concert schedules for the **Sala Bossi** (⊠ Piazza Rossini 2, ☎ 051/225559) and the **Sala Mozart** in the Accademia Filarmonica, the principal music school of the city (⊠ Via Guerazzi 13, ☎ 051/222997).

Numbers in the margin correspond to points of interest on the Emilia-Romagna map.

Dozza

⑯   *31 km (19 mi) southeast of Bologna, 15 km (9 mi) west of Imola.*

As you head southeast out of Bologna, the first port of call is the little hamlet of **Dozza,** just off the Via Emilia (S9). It is a small village on a hill crowned with a splendid restored medieval castle. Artists from all over Italy flock to the town in September of odd years to take part in the mural competition—it seems that every square foot of the town has been painted with colorful scenes done with varying degrees of skill. The castle is home to the **Enoteca Regionale,** the wine "library" for the region. Here you can sample the different vintages that come from the surrounding countryside, particularly Dozza's own Albana, a white wine that comes dry or sweet. ☎ *0542/678089.* ▣ *4,000 lire.* ☉ *Apr.–Sept., Tues.–Sat. 10–noon and 3–6, Sun. 3–7; Oct.–Mar., Tues.–Sat. 10–noon and 2–5, Sun. 2–6.*

Dining

$$$$ ✕ **San Domenico.** Many gourmands venture out from Bologna—about
★   33 kilometers (20 miles) away—and even farther afield to this prize restaurant in the town of Imola. Ever since leading food critics discovered San Domenico it has been counted among the top 10 Italian restaurants—and there are those who say it might be number one. It is an expensive but worth-it place—tented ceilings, leather banquettes, Bucellattesque silver—and critics vow it's so well worth the trip that reservations must be made weeks in advance. Specialties of the house are the homemade pâté with white truffles, a delicious breast of duck in a sauce of black olives, and hand-stuffed—and, yes, therefore, more expensive—tortellini. ⊠ *Imola, Via Sacchi 1,* ☎ *054/229000. Reservations essential. Jacket and tie. AE, DC, MC, V. Closed Mon. and Aug. 1–20.*

Faenza

🄗   *49 km (30 mi) southeast of Bologna, 23 km (14 mi) southeast of Dozza, 15 km (9 mi) northwest of Forlì.*

Ceramics have been produced in **Faenza,** on the Via Emilia, since the 12th century—its faience pottery is known the world over. In the central **Piazza del Popolo** are dozens of shops selling the town's product. Faenza is also home to the **Museo delle Ceramiche,** one of the largest ceramics museums in the world, covering the potter's art in all phases of history and in all parts of the world. ⊠ *Viale Baccarini 19.* 🖼 *8,000 lire.* ☺ *Apr.–Oct., Tues.–Sat. 9–7, Sun. 9:30–1; Nov.–Mar., Tues.–Fri. 9:30–1:30, Sat. 9:30–1:30 and 3–6, Sun. 9:30–1.*

OFF THE   **PREDAPPIO** – From Faenza continue on S9 to the town of Forlì, 14 kilome-
BEATEN PATH   ters (9 miles) away, and turn off onto the rural Route 9ter (in Italian travel parlance, the abbreviation "ter" means a third, variant highway). This leads you through hilly country to the small town of Predappio, the birthplace of Benito Mussolini and Il Duce's final resting place. The cemetery on the outskirts of town contains the crypt of the Mussolini family, with the former dictator himself in the place of honor. A spotlit bust glowers at visitors, and glass cases contain some of his decorations and medals. It is a chilling place and has become the object of pilgrimage for followers of fascism (young and old), who write repugnant political slogans in the visitors' book. ⊠ *Cimitero Municipale.* ☺ *Daily 8 AM–sunset.*

SAVIGNANO – On S9 beyond Forlì, you pass through the modern towns of Forlimpopoli, Cesena, and Savignano. At this last town, there is a reminder that no matter how new the towns might look, you are still traveling in a place of great history—just outside the town is a small stream, the Rubicone. Cross it and you, too, have crossed the Rubicon, the river made famous by Julius Caesar when, in 49 BC, he defied the Senate of Rome by bringing his army across the river and plunging the country into civil war.

BYZANTINE SPLENDORS AND SIMPLE PLEASURES

Rimini, Ravenna, and Ferrara

From Savignano, the road leads on to the next three important destinations: Rimini, Ravenna, and Ferrara.

Rimini

● *121 km (76 mi) southeast of Bologna, 54 km (34 mi) southeast of Forlì, 52 km (32½ mi) southeast of Ravenna.*

Rimini is the principal summer resort on the Adriatic Coast and one of the most popular holiday destinations in Italy. Every summer, beginning in June, the city is flooded with vacationers, not just from Italy but from France, Austria, Germany, Scandinavia, and Great Britain, as well. The city is given over almost exclusively to tourism, with hundreds of hotels, grand and modest, and restaurants catering to virtually every national palate: You are just as likely to find a *bierkeller* (beer cellar) or an English tea shop as you are an Italian restaurant. The waterfront is lined with beach clubs that rent a patch of sand, a deck chair, and an umbrella by the day, week, month, or the entire season. Hotels along the beachfront have staked out their own private turf, so the chance of swimming (or even seeing the sea close up) without paying for the privilege is slim.

In the off-season, Rimini, in common with resorts the world over, is a ghost town. Some hotels and restaurants are open, but the majority are closed tight, hibernating until the return of the free-spending tourists. Summers are so crowded here that it is most unwise to go to Rimini without confirmed hotel reservations. For those who like sun by day, disco by night, and hordes of frolicking teenagers, Rimini is the town for you; those who prefer more sedate vacations are advised to stay away.

The new town has just about swallowed the old, but there are signs here and there that tell of Rimini's long and turbulent history. Rimini stands at the junction of two great Roman consular roads: the Via Aemilia, or Emilia as it is known now, and the Via Flaminia. In addition, in Roman times, it was an important port, making it a strategic and commercial center. From the 13th century onward, the city was controlled by the Malatesta family, an unpredictable group capable of grand gestures and savage deeds. The famous lovers in Dante's *Inferno,* Paolo and Francesca, were Malatestas. Paolo was the brother of Gianciotto Malatesta; Francesca, Gianciotto's wife. Gianciotto murdered them both for having betrayed him. Sigismondo Malatesta, lord of the city in the middle of the 15th century, was considered a learned man of great wit and culture. He also banished his first wife, strangled his second, and poisoned his third. He lived with his beautiful mistress, Isotta, until her death. He was so grief-stricken that he raised a mag-
★ nificent monument in her honor, the **Tempio Malatestiano.** It is the principal sight in the town.

Despite the irregular—from the church's point of view—nature of Sigismondo's relationship with Isotta, Sigismondo's memorial to his great love is today the **cathedral** of Rimini. The building was in fact originally a Franciscan church before Sigismondo took it over to make it into a monument to his beloved. The facade is a beautiful piece of Renaissance architecture by Leon Battista Alberti. It is in the shape of a Roman triumphal arch and is considered to be one of Alberti's masterpieces.

The interior is light and spacious and contains the tombs of both the lovers. The intertwined *I,* for Isotta, and the *S,* for Sigismondo, are dotted about everywhere and look rather like "$" signs. The carvings of elephants and roses recall the coat of arms of the Malatesta family. Sigismondo's tomb, on the right of the entrance door, is some distance from Isotta's in the second chapel. (Her tomb is on the left wall of the chapel; the original inscription in marble had a pagan twist and was covered with another in bronze.) On the right, in what is now the Tempio's book and gift shop, is a wonderful but badly damaged fresco by

Piero della Francesca showing Sigismondo paying homage to his patron saint. When the shop is closed, one of the cathedral's staff will be glad to unlock the room containing the fresco. Also on the right side of the church, look out for a crucifix attributed to Giotto, formerly over the main altar of the church. ⊠ *Via Quattro Novembre.* ⊙ *Daily 7–noon and 3:30–7.*

Rimini's oldest monument is the **Arco d'Augusto** (Arch of Augustus), now stranded in the middle of a square just inside the city ramparts. It was erected in 27 BC, making it the oldest Roman arch in existence, and it marks the meeting of the Via Aemilia and the Via Flaminia. To reach the Arch of Augustus from the Tempio Malatestiano, walk up Via Quattro Novembre to Piazza Tre Martiri (where, legend says, the mule carrying Saint Anthony suddenly stopped and knelt in honor of the Holy Sacrament that was being carried past at the time) and turn left onto Corso d'Augusto. The arch lies at the end of the street. ⊠ *Largo Giulio Cesare.*

Dining and Lodging

$$ ✕ **Picnic.** This restaurant, conveniently located near the historic Tempio Malatestiano, is a good lunchtime spot to savor some simple, well-cooked dishes in a modern setting. You can order—indoors or in a leafy garden—a selection from a daily-changing menu which might include such choices as *pappardelle al sugo di carciofi* (pasta with artichoke sauce), *faraona ripiena alla castagne* (guinea hen with chestnut stuffing), or just have a pizza (evenings only). ⊠ *Via Tempio Malatestiano 30,* ☎ *0541/21916. MC, V. Closed Mon.*

$$ ✕ **Zio.** Nothing but seafood is served here, and all of it is good value
★   for the money. The *zuppa dei crustacei* is a deliciously tangy shellfish broth; tortellini *al salmone* (stuffed pasta in a salmon sauce), and simple grilled sole are also recommended. ⊠ *Vicolo Santa Chiara 16,* ☎ *0541/786160. Reservations advised on weekends and July and Aug. AE, DC, MC, V. Closed Wed. and July–mid-Aug.*

$ ✕ **Rock Island.** Formerly a seafood restaurant, now a busy pub and *panineria* (sandwich bar), the Rock Island is at the end of a pier right on the sea. You can drink and snack here and take part in Rimini's raucous nightlife. Steamy, loud, and full of young people, it's not for the fainthearted. ⊠ *Porto Canale,* ☎ *0541/50178. No reservations. No credit cards. Closed weekdays in winter.*

$$$$ 🏨 **Grand Hotel.** Fellini paid homage to this grande dame of a hotel in
★   his *Amarcord.* The Grand is a turn-of-the-century extravaganza set in a quiet park, within easy reach of its own private beach. The rooms are large and airy, air-conditioned, and equipped with color TV and minibar. ⊠ *Via Ramusio 1,* ☎ *0541/56000,* FAX *0541/56866. 128 rooms with bath, 6 suites. 2 restaurants, 2 bars, 2 pools, beauty salon, sauna, private beach, 4 tennis courts, nightclub. AE, DC, MC, V.*

$$$ 🏨 **Club House Hotel.** Ultramodern and right on the sea, the Club House is a good hotel for summer vacations and is one of the few open during the off-season. All rooms have a balcony, minibar, and color TV. ⊠ *Viale Vespucci 52,* ☎ *0541/391460,* FAX *0541/391442. 28 rooms with bath. Restaurant, bar, private beach. AE, DC, MC, V.*

$ 🏨 **Annarita.** Set back in a leafy residential road leading off the main Viale Vespucci, this is small but comfortable, mainly frequented by a regular clientele (availability may consequently be limited). Facilities are rudimentary, rooms are basic (though all with TV), but the main benefits here are its closeness to the beach promenade and the friendly price. ⊠ *Viale Misurata 24,* ☎ *0541/391044. 16 rooms with shower. Restaurant, bar. No credit cards.*

En Route There are two routes from Rimini to Ravenna. The coast road, S16, hugs the shoreline as far as Cervia before edging inland. Although the distance, 52 kilometers (31 miles), is not great, the going along this route is slow. The coast north of Rimini is lined with dozens of small resort towns, only one having any charm, the seaport of Cesenatico; the others are mini-Riminis, and during summer the narrow road is hopelessly clogged with traffic. A faster route is to head inland on A14 and then turn off onto the inland S71, which leads directly into Ravenna. The distance is 64 kilometers (39 miles).

Ravenna

⑲ *76 km (47½ mi) east of Bologna, 52 km (32½ mi) northwest of Rimini, 74 km (46 mi) southeast of Ferrara.*

Ravenna is a stately old city, still living on the dreams of its faded glory. The high point in Ravenna's long history was 1,500 years ago, when the city became the capital of the Roman Empire, but by then the empire was in its period of irreversible decline. The city was taken by the barbarian Ostrogoths in the 5th century; then, in the 6th, it was conquered by the Byzantines, who ruled the city from Constantinople.

Because Ravenna spent much of its history looking to the East, its greatest art treasures show much Byzantine influence: above all, Ravenna is a city of mosaics, the finest in Western art. A single 9,000-lire ticket will admit you to six of Ravenna's most important monuments: the Tomb of Galla Placida, the church of San Vitale, the Neonian baptistery, and the church of Sant'Apollinare Nuovo, all described below, as well as the church of Spirito Santo and the Museo Arcivescovile e Cappella Sant'Andrea.

★ The **Tomb of Galla Placidia** and the church of **San Vitale** have the best-known, and most elaborate, mosaics in the city. The little tomb and the great church stand side by side, but the tomb predates the church by at least a hundred years. Galla Placidia was the sister of the last emperor of Rome, Honorius, the man who moved the imperial capital to Ravenna in AD 402. She is said to have been beautiful and strong-willed, taking an active part in the governing of the crumbling empire. She was also one of the most active Christians of her day, endowing churches and supporting priests and their congregations throughout the realm. This tomb, built for her in the mid-5th century, is her monument.

Outside, the tomb is a rather uninspired building of red brick; within, however, the color and clarity of the mosaics that decorate the ceiling are startling. The deep blue and gold catch the light and seem to glitter. The central dome has symbols of Christ and the evangelists, and over the door is a depiction of the Good Shepherd. The Apostles, in groups of two (there are only eight of them, for some reason), ring the inner part of the dome. Notice the small doves at their feet, drinking from the water of faith. In the tiny transepts are some delightful pairs of deer (which represent souls), drinking from the fountain of resurrection. There are three sarcophagi in the tomb, and, it is thought, not one contains the remains of Galla Placidia. She died in Rome in AD 450, and there is no record of her body having been transported back to the place where she wished to lie.

The mosaics of the Galla Placidia tomb are simple works that have not yet received the full impact of Byzantine influence. Quite the opposite is the case of the mosaics in the church of San Vitale, next door. The church was built in AD 547, after the Byzantines conquered the city, and it is decorated in an exclusively Byzantine style. In the area behind the altar are the most famous works in the church. These show accurate portraits of the emperor of the East, Justinian, attended by his court, and the bishop of Ravenna, Maximian. Facing him, across the chancel, is the emperor's wife, Theodora, with her entourage, holding a chalice containing the communion wine. From the elaborate headdresses and heavy cloaks of the emperor and empress, you can get a marvelous sense of the grandeur of the imperial court.

On the ceiling above the royal couple, ruling over all, is a mosaic of Christ the King. With him is the saint for whom the church is named, Vitale, and the founder of the church, Bishop Ecclesio, who holds a model of the building. *Tomb of Galla Placidia and Church of San Vitale.* ⊠ *Via San Vitale off Via Salara, near Piazza del Popolo.* 🎫 *5,000 lire (ticket valid for both), 4,000 lire for tickets bought at the adjacent Museo Nazionale.* ⊙ *Summer, daily 9–5:30; winter, daily 9–4:30.*

Next to the Church of San Vitale, the **Museo Nazionale** of Ravenna contains artifacts of ancient Rome, Byzantine fabrics and carvings, and other pieces of early Christian art. The collection is housed in a former monastery but is well displayed and artfully lit. ⊠ *Via Fiandrini.* 🎫 *8,000 lire.* ⊙ *Daily Tues.–Sun. 8:30–7:30.*

Next door to Ravenna's 18th-century cathedral, the **Neonian baptistery** is one of the town's most important mosaic sites. In keeping with the purpose of the building, the great mosaic in the dome shows the baptism of Christ, and beneath that scene are the apostles. The lowest band of mosaics contains Christian symbols, the Throne of God and the Cross. To reach the Neonian baptistery from the central Piazza del Popolo, walk along Via Rasponi toward Piazza John F. Kennedy. The baptistery is a few blocks along on the left. ⊠ *Via Battistero.* 🎫 *4,000 lire (includes Museo Arcivescovile and Cappella Sant'Andrea).* ⊙ *Summer, daily 9–5:30; winter, daily 9:30–4:30.*

The **tomb of Dante** is in a small neoclassical building next door to the large church of St. Francis. Exiled from his native Florence, the great poet, author of *The Divine Comedy,* died here in 1321. The Florentines have been trying to reclaim their famous son for hundreds of years, but the Ravennans refuse to give him up, arguing that Florence did not welcome Dante in life, so it doesn't deserve him in death. The site, a few blocks from the Neonian baptistery, contains a small museum. ⊠ *Via Ricci.* 🎫 *Dante's tomb free.* ⊙ *Summer, daily 9–7; winter, daily 9–noon, 2–5.* 🎫 *Museum 3,000 lire; free on Sun. and holidays.* ⊙ *Daily 9–noon.*

The last great mosaic site in the city proper is the church of **Sant'-Apollinare Nuovo.** Since the left side of the church was reserved for women, it is only fitting that the mosaic decoration on that side is a scene of 22 virgins offering crowns to the Virgin Mary. On the right wall are 26 men carrying the crowns of martyrdom. They are approaching Christ, who is surrounded by angels. The mosaics in Sant'-Apollinare Nuovo date from the early 6th century and are slightly older than the works in San Vitale. From the tomb of Dante, walk up Via Guaccimanni toward the busy Via Roma. The church stands at the intersection of the two streets, slightly to the left. ⊠ *Via Roma.* 🎫 *4,000 lire (includes church of Spirito Santo).* ⊙ *Summer, daily 9–7; winter, daily 9:30–4:30.*

OFF THE
BEATEN PATH

SANT'APOLLINARE IN CLASSE – This church, about 5 kilometers (3 miles) southeast of Ravenna, is landlocked now, but when it was built, it stood in the center of the busy shipping port of Classis. The arch above and the area around the high altar are rich in mosaics. Those on the arch, older than those behind it, are considered superior to the rest. They show Christ in judgment and the 12 lambs of Christianity leaving the cities of Jerusalem and Bethlehem. In the apse is the figure of Sant'Apollinare himself, a bishop of Ravenna, and above him is a magnificent Transfiguration decorated with flowers, trees, and little birds. ⊠ *Classe.* ☉ *Summer, daily 8:30–noon and 2–6; winter, daily 9–noon and 2–5.*

Dining and Lodging

$$–$$$ ✕ **Bella Venezia.** A refined classical decor sets the tone in this elegant
★ restaurant, which nonetheless manages to exude an intimate ambience. Dishes are carefully prepared and concentrate on local specialties. Try the risotto *Bazzani* (a buttery, cheesy concoction with ham, mushrooms, and peas) and, for the entrée, *bistecca all'ortolana* (veal with a slice of ham and zucchini bathed in a toothsome creamy sauce). ⊠ *Via IV Novembre 16,* ☎ *0544/212746. Weekend reservations advised. AE, DC, MC, V. Closed Mon.*

$ ✕ **Ca' de Ven.** A vaulted wine cellar in the heart of the old city, the Ca' de Ven is a wonderful place for a hearty lunch or dinner. You sit at long tables with the other diners and feast on platters of delicious cold cuts; *piadine* (flat Romagna bread); and cold, heady white wine. If you're here in chilly weather, try the wholesome pasta e fagioli. ⊠ *Via C. Ricci 24,* ☎ *0544/30163. No reservations. MC, V. Closed Mon.*

$ ✕ **Ristorante Scai.** Roast meat and game are what this restaurant does best, and a changing menu provides diners with pasta stuffed with roe deer, as well as main courses of venison, duck, pig's feet, or rabbit. ⊠ *Piazza Baracca 22 (near church of San Vitale, at end of Via Cavour),* ☎ *0544/212520. Reservations not accepted. AE, DC, MC, V. Closed Mon.*

$$ ⊞ **Hotel Centrale Byron.** In the heart of Ravenna's old town, this is an elegant, well-managed hotel, its rooms spacious and comfortably furnished. Because its location is in a pedestrian zone, tranquillity is assured, though you will have to leave your car in one of the nearby garages. ⊠ *Via IV Novembre 14,* ☎ *0544/33479. 54 rooms with bath or shower. Bar. AE, DC, MC, V.*

$ ⊞ **Al Guaciglio.** Halfway between the train station and the town center, this small pension offers neat and tidy rooms and a relaxed and friendly atmosphere. There are no frills here, but it is a perfectly adequate accommodation. ⊠ *Via Brancaleone 42,* ☎ *0544/39403. 16 rooms, 9 with shower. Restaurant, bar. MC, V.*

Ferrara

㉚ *47 km (29 mi) northeast of Bologna, 74 km (46 mi) northwest of Ravenna along S16.*

Ferrara is a city of turrets and towers, of a mighty castle protected by a deep moat, and of historic palaces of great grandeur. Although the site has been inhabited since before Christ and was once the possession of Ravenna, the history of Ferrara begins in the 13th century, with the coming of the Este family. From 1259 until 1598 the city was ruled by the dukes of the Este family, and in those 3½ centuries the city was stamped indelibly with their mark.

It was during the Renaissance that the court of the Este came into full flower. In keeping with their time, the dukes could be politically ruthless—brother killed brother, son fought father—but they were avid scholars and enthusiastic patrons of the arts. Duke Niccolò III murdered his wife and her lover but was a man of cultivation. The greatest of all the dukes, Ercole I, tried to poison his nephew, who laid claim to the duchy (and when that didn't work, Ercole I beheaded him), but it is to this pitiless man that Ferrara owes its great beauty. One of the most celebrated names in Italian history, Lucrezia Borgia, married into the Este family—and it seems that her infamous reputation is not at all deserved. She was beloved by the Ferrarese people and was mourned greatly when she died. She is buried in the church of Corpus Domini in the city.

★ Naturally enough, the building that was the seat of Este power dominates the town: it is the massive **Castello Estense,** placed square in the center of the city in Piazza della Repubblica. It is a suitable symbol for the Este family: cold and menacing on the outside, lavishly decorated within. The public rooms are grand, but deep in the bowels of the fortress are chilling dungeons where enemies of the state were held in wretched conditions—a function these quarters served as recently as 1943, when antifascist prisoners were detained there.

The castle was begun in 1385, but work was going on as late as the 16th century. The Sala dei Giochi (the Games Room) is extravagantly decorated with walls painted to show pagan athletic scenes, and the Sala dell'Aurora to show the times of the day. Oddly enough, the one chapel that is on view is not Catholic, but Protestant (one of the few to survive the Counter-Reformation), placed here for the use of the Protestant princess Renée of France, who married into the Este family in the 16th century. From the terraces of the castle and from the hanging garden, reserved for the private use of the duchesses, are fine views of the town and surrounding countryside. ⊠ *Piazza Castello.* 🖼 *6,000 lire.* ⊙ *Tues.–Sun. 9:30–5:30.*

A few steps from the castle is the magnificent Gothic **Duomo,** with its facade of three tiers of arches and beautiful carvings over the central door. It was begun in 1135 and took more than a hundred years to complete. The interior does not live up to the expectations fostered by the facade. It was completely remodeled in the 17th century, and none of the original decoration remain in place. ⊠ *Corso dei Martiri della Libertà.* ⊙ *Mon.–Sat. 7:30–noon and 3–6:30, Sun. 7:30–1 and 4–7:30.*

The treasures of Duomo's old interior are preserved in the **cathedral museum** above the church (entrance inside). Here are some of the lifelike carvings taken from one of the doors of the Duomo, dating from the 13th century and showing the months of the year. Also in the museum are a statue of the Madonna by the Sienese master Jacopo della Quercia and two masterpieces by the Ferrarese painter Cosimo Tura, an *Annunciation* and *St. George Slaying the Dragon.* ⊠ *Corso dei Martiri della Libertà.* 🖼 *Free, but donation accepted.* ⊙ *Summer, Mon.–Sat. 10–noon and 3:30–6; winter, Mon.–Sat. 10–noon and 4–6.*

The area behind the Duomo, the southern part of the city stretching between the Corso della Giovecca and the ramparts of the city above the river, is the oldest and most characteristic part of Ferrara. In this part of the old town various members of the Este family built themselves pleasure palaces, the most famous of which is the **Palazzo Schifanoia** (*schifanoia* means carefree—literally, "fleeing boredom"). Begun in the 14th century, the palace was remodeled in 1466 and is the first Renaissance palazzo in the city. The interior is lavishly decorated, particularly the **Salone dei Mesi,** with an extravagant series of frescoes showing the months of the year. The recently opened **Sala degli Stucchi** boasts a beautifully carved wooden ceiling from 1467, by Domenico di Paris, and an array of stuccos. The palazzo now houses the **Museo Civico** (City Museum), with its collection of coins, statuary, and paintings. ⊠ *Via Scandiana 23.* 🖼 *6,000 lire; free 2nd Sun. of each month.* ⊙ *Daily 9–7.*

Near the Palazzo Schifanoia, on Via XX Settembre, is the **Palazzo di Ludovico il Moro,** a magnificent 15th-century palace built for Ludovico Sforza, husband of Beatrice d'Este. The great but unfinished courtyard is the most interesting part of this luxurious palace, which also houses the region's **Museo Archeologico,** a repository of the relics of early man, the Etruscans, and Romans, found in the country surrounding the city. Unfortunately, the museum is closed indefinitely.

The courtyard of the peaceful palace called the **Palazzo del Paradiso** contains the tomb of the great writer Ariosto, author of the most popular work of literature of the Renaissance, the poem "Orlando Furioso." The building now houses the city library. ⊠ *Via Scienze.* 🎫 *Free.* ☉ *Weekdays 9–7:30, Sat. 9–1.*

The Estes were patrons of the poet Ariosto, and he passed a good deal of his life in Ferrara. **Ariosto's house** lies in the northern part of the city, at Via Ariosto 67. The interior has been converted into an office building and is not open to the public.

One of the best-preserved of the Renaissance palaces scattered along Ferrara's old streets is the charming **Casa Romei.** Downstairs there are rooms with 15th-century frescoes and several sculptures collected from churches that have been destroyed. The house lies not far from the Palazzo del Paradiso, in the area behind Ferrara's castello. ⊠ *Via Savonarola 30.* 🎫 *4,000 lire.* ☉ *Weekdays 8:30–2, weekends 8:30–7:30.*

On the busy Corso della Giovecca is the **Palazzina di Marfisa d'Este,** an elegant 16th-century home that belonged to Marfisa d'Este, a great patron of the arts. The house has painted ceilings, fine 16th-century furniture, and a garden containing a grotto and an outdoor theater. ⊠ *Corso della Giovecca 170.* 🎫 *3,000 lire; free 2nd Sun. of month.* ☉ *Summer, daily 9–12:30 and 3–6; winter, daily 9–12:30 and 2–5.*

NEED A BREAK? For a good cup of cappuccino, a piece of pastry, or rich ice cream, try **Gelateria Nazionale** (⊠ 28 Corso Martiri della Libertà 30, opposite the cathedral). It's closed Thursday and two weeks in August.

From the castle, cross the Corso della Giovecca and walk up the wide Corso Ercole d'Este. At the corner of Corso Porta Mare is the **Palazzo dei Diamanti** (Palace of Diamonds), so called for the 12,600 blocks of diamond-shape stone that stud the facade. The palace was built in the 15th and 16th centuries and today contains an extensive art gallery devoted primarily to the painters of Ferrara. ⊠ *Corso Ercole d'Este 21.* 🎫 *8,000 lire.* ☉ *Tues.–Sat. 9–2, Sun. 9–1.*

Dining and Lodging

$$–$$$ ✕ **La Provvidenza.** One of the best-known restaurants in Ferrara, ★ Provvidenza is a pleasant country-style inn with a lovely garden for summertime dining alfresco. The local specialties—fish grilled over charcoal (Thurs. and Fri. only) and the bollito misto (Sat. and Sun. in winter)—are the best. ⊠ *Corso Ercole d'Este 92,* ☎ *0532/205187. Reservations essential. AE, DC, MC, V. Closed Mon. and Aug. 10–20.*

$–$$ ✕ **Le Grazie.** In an atmospheric part of the old town, down a long cobbled street, this restaurant is a leading choice of pasta lovers. Try the tagliatelle *con cuori di carciofo e noci* (with artichoke hearts and nuts). Other dishes are local, as is the wine list. ⊠ *Via Vignatagliata 61,* ☎ *0532/761052. Reservations essential. MC, V. Closed Tues.*

$$$$ 🏨 **Duchessa Isabella.** On a quiet street near Piazza Ariostea, this converted 16th-century mansion is the place for those who relish period atmosphere—the staff wears Old World dress, and a horse-drawn landau is available to guests for sightseeing. Scrupulous attention to the details of decor is evident everywhere, from the painted wooden ceiling in the elegant dining room to the sumptuously draped and indi-

vidually named bedrooms and suites. Some may find the formality weary-
ing and the tone somewhat bogus; others will find a stay here to be
memorable. ✉ *Via Palestro 70,* ☎ *0532/202121,* FAX *0532/202638. 28
rooms with bath. Restaurant, bar, meeting rooms. AE, MC, V.*

\$\$\$ ⊞ **Ripagrande.** This hotel is in a meticulously restored 14th-century
★   palace in the heart of old Ferrara. Although the public rooms are in
authentic period style, most of the bedrooms are—unfortunately—modern: chrome-and-glass-decorated boxes with little appeal. The suites
are more tasteful, and the rooms on the top floor have a terrace,
beamed ceiling, and view of the city. The staff is very attentive, and
there is a recommended restaurant, with outdoor eating in summer.
✉ *Via Ripagrande 21,* ☎ *0532/765250,* FAX *0532/764377. 40 rooms
with bath or shower. Bar, meeting rooms. AE, DC, MC, V.*

\$\$ **Locanda Borgonuovo.** It calls itself a bed and breakfast, and its atmosphere is strongly reminiscent of the best kind of B&B, with individually named rooms of a comfortable size, all tastefully furnished with
good-quality antiques. What really sets this place apart, though, is the
attention to detail and the smiling, courteous attention of the hostess,
who also puts on a fine breakfast. The *locanda* is in a quiet lane in the
center of town. ✉ *Via Cairoli 29,* ☎ *0532/211100. 4 rooms with bath
or shower. MC, V.*

\$ ⊞ **San Paolo.** Now relocated to a quieter spot on the edge of the old
city, San Paolo is the best inexpensive choice in town. The 10-minute
walk from the heart of Ferrara's medieval quarter is effortless in a town
so amenable to strolling, and there are some good restaurants in the
vicinity. The rooms are outfitted in a modern style, and you'll hear the
Duomo's bells chiming on Sunday. ✉ *Via Baluardi 13,* ☎ *0532/762040,*
FAX *0532/762040. 20 rooms, 15 with shower. No credit cards.*

EMILIA-ROMAGNA A TO Z

Arriving and Departing

By Plane

Bologna is an important business and convention center and is therefore served by air routes that link it with other Italian cities, as well as
by direct flights to European capitals. The airport, **Guglielmo Marconi**
(✉ Borgo Panigale, ☎ 051/311578) is 7 kilometers (4 miles) from
town. Bus service connects it with a downtown air terminal at the central train station in Bologna proper.

By Train

Bologna is an important rail hub for the entire northern part of Italy
and has frequent, fast train service to Rome, Milan, Florence, and Venice.
For information about train departures call ☎ 051/246490.

Getting Around

By Bus

Private bus service links all the cities of Emilia-Romagna, with Bologna
being the central hub. The *autostazione* (bus terminal) is in Piazza XX
Settembre, at the top of Via dell'Indipendenza; for information call ☎
051/248374. City-run bus routes connect major towns with smaller
villages and hamlets in the district, but routes are roundabout, and schedules vary from place to place.

By Car

The Via Emilia (S9) runs through the heart of the region. It is a straight,
low-lying modern road, the length of which can be traveled in a few
hours. Ferrara and Ravenna are joined to it by good modern highways.

By Train

The railway follows the Via Emilia, and all the cities mentioned here can be reached by train.

Contacts and Resources

Emergencies

Police (☎ 112). **Ambulance** (☎ 113). **Doctors and Dentists** (☎ 113). **Late-Night Pharmacies** (☎ 051/192 for information).

Travel Agencies

Bologna (✉ Marconi Tours, Via Marconi 47, ☎ 051/235783).

Rimini (Urbinati, ✉ *Viale Vespucci 127, ☎ 0541/391660 or 390720*).

Visitor Information

Bologna (✉ Gugliemo Marconi airport, ☎ 051/647-2036; train station, ☎ 051/246541; ✉ Piazza Maggiore 6, *051/239–660*). **Ferrara** (✉ Corso Giovecca 21, ☎ 0532/209370 or 765728). **Modena** (✉ Piazza Grande 17, ☎ 059/206660). **Parma** (✉ Piazza Duomo 5, ☎ 0521/234735). **Piacenza** (✉ Piazzetta Mercanti 7, ☎ 0523/329324). **Ravenna** (✉ Via Salara 8, ☎ 0544/35404). **Rimini** (✉ Via Dante 86, in front of the train station, ☎ 0541/51331 or 0541/51480; ✉ Piazzale Fellini 3, waterfront, *0541/51101*). V110

12 Umbria and the Marches

Perugia, Assisi, Urbino, Spoleto, and Orvieto

Legends linger in this mystical, ethereal birthplace of the saints, a region where medieval enclaves wear their ancient histories lightly. Here, you'll find Gothic treasures—Giotto's frescoes at Assisi's Basilica di San Francesco and Orvieto's awe-inspiring cathedral—while more urbane pleasures await at Spoleto's Festival of Two Worlds. To the east lies the timeless city of Urbino. A visit there reveals more about the artistic energy of the Renaissance than dozens of history books.

By Robert
Andrews

BIRTHPLACE OF SAINTS AND CONDOTTIERI, Umbria has remained true to its name: "land of shadows." The hills, olive groves, and terraced vineyards of this mystic province are often wrapped in a bluish haze that gives its landscape an ethereal painted look—a landscape often recognized in the frescoes of its celebrated local artists, even when they were decorating churches far from their native soil. Blessed with steep, austere hills, deep valleys, and fast-flowing rivers, the region—roughly halfway between Florence and Rome—has not yet been swamped by tourism and has escaped the unplanned industrial expansion that afflicts much of central Italy. No town in Umbria boasts the extravagant wealth of art and architecture of Florence, Rome, or Venice, but this works in your favor. Cities can be experienced whole, rather than as a series of museums and churches, forced marches through 2,000 years of Western culture; in Umbria the visitor comes to know the towns as people live in them today.

This is not to suggest that the cultural cupboard is bare—far from it. Perugia, the capital of the region, and Assisi, Umbria's most famous city, are rich in art and architecture, as are Orvieto, Todi, and Spoleto. Virtually every small town in the region has a castle, church, or museum worth a stop.

The earliest inhabitants of Umbria, the Umbri, were thought by the Romans to be the most ancient inhabitants of Italy. Little is known about them, since with the coming of Etruscan culture, the tribe fled into the mountains in the eastern portion of the region. The Etruscans, who founded some of the great cities of Umbria, were in turn supplanted by the Romans. Unlike Tuscany and other regions of central Italy, Umbria had few powerful medieval families to exert control over the cities in the Middle Ages—its proximity to Rome ensured that Umbria would always be more or less under papal domination.

The relative political stability of the region did not mean that Umbria was left in peace. Located in the center of the country, it has for much of its history been a battlefield where armies from north and south clashed. Hannibal destroyed a Roman army on the shores of Lake Trasimeno, and the full and bloody course of the interminable Guelph-Ghibelline conflict of the Middle Ages was played out in Umbria. Dante considered it the most violent place in Italy. Trophies of war still decorate the facade of the Palazzo dei Priori in Perugia, and the little town of Gubbio continues a warlike rivalry begun in the Middle Ages—every year it challenges the Tuscan town of Sansepolcro to a crossbow tournament. Today, of course, the bowmen shoot at targets, but neither side has forgotten that 500 years ago its ancestors shot at each other.

In spite of—or perhaps because of—this bloodshed, Umbria has produced more than its share of Christian saints. The most famous is Saint Francis, the decidedly unmartial saint whose life shaped the Church and the history of his time. His great shrine at Assisi is visited by hundreds of thousands of pilgrims each year. Saint Clare, his devoted follower, was Umbria-born, as were Saint Benedict, Saint Rita of Cascia, and, ironically, the shadowy patron saint of lovers, Saint Valentine.

East of Umbria, the Marches—or Marche, in Italian—stretch between the hills of the southern Apennines down to the Adriatic sea. It is a scenic region of mountains and valleys, with great turreted castles standing on high peaks defending passes and roads—silent testament to the region's warlike past. The Marches have passed through numerous hands. First the Romans supplanted the native civilizations; then Charlemagne supplanted the Romans (and gave the region its name: it was divided into "marks," or provinces, under the rule of the Holy Roman Emperor); then began the seemingly never-ending struggle between popes and local lords. Cesare Borgia succeeded in wresting control of the Marches from the local suzerains, annexing the region to the papacy of his father, Alexander VI.

Despite all this martial tussling, it was in the lonely mountain town of Urbino that the Renaissance came to its fullest flower; that small town became a haven of culture and learning that rivaled the greater, richer, and more powerful city of Florence, and even Rome itself.

Pleasures and Pastimes

Dining

Umbria is mountainous, and the cuisine of the region is typical of mountain people everywhere. The food is hearty and straightforward, with a stick-to-the-ribs quality that sees hard-working farmers and artisans through a long day's work and helps them make the steep climb home at night. Italians are generally thought not to eat much meat, but this is untrue of Italy in general and of Umbria in particular. Novelist Anthony Burgess once observed that a beefsteak in Italy is never "*una bistecca*" but always "*una bella bistecca*"—a beautiful steak—and a simple steak in Umbria is almost always *bella*.

The region has made several important contributions to Italian cuisine. Particularly prized are black truffles from the area around Spoleto (signs warning against unlicensed truffle hunting are posted at the base of the grand Ponte delle Torri) and from the hills around the tiny town of Norcia. Norcia, in fact, exports truffles to France and hosts a truffle festival every year in November. Many regional dishes are given a grating of truffle before serving; unless the truffle is a really good one, however, its subtle taste may not come through. The local pasta specialty—thick, handmade spaghetti called *ciriole* or *strengozzi*—is good *al tartufo,* with a dressing of excellent local olive oil and truffles.

In addition, Norcia's pork products—especially sausages, salami, and *arista* (bone marrow of pig)—are so famous that pork butchers throughout Italy are called *norcini,* no matter where they hail from, and pork butcher shops are called *norcinerie.*

In the Marches, fish in various forms is the thing to look for. One of the characteristic dishes in Ancona is *brodetto,* a rich fish chowder containing as many as nine types of Adriatic saltwater fish. Ascoli Piceno, inland, is famous for two dishes: olives *ascolane* (stuffed, rolled in batter, and deep fried) and *vincisgrassi* (a local version of lasagna, far richer than you're likely to find elsewhere in Italy). Ascoli Piceno is also the home of the licorice-flavored liqueur anisette.

CATEGORY	COST*
$$$	60,000–85,000 lire
$$	25,000–60,000 lire
$	under 25,000 lire

per person, including first course, main course, dessert or fruit, and house wine

Lodging

Virtually every historic town in Umbria has some kind of hotel, no matter how small the place may be. In most cases a small city boasts one or two hotels in a high price category and a few smaller, basic hotels in the inexpensive-to-moderate ($–$$) range. The cheaper the hotel, the fewer the services. Most basic hotels offer breakfast, but few have restaurants or bars.

A recent and popular trend is the conversion of old villas and monasteries into first-class hotels. These tend to be outside the towns, in the countryside, and the splendor of the settings often outweighs the problem of getting into town. In all cases, these country hotels are comfortable, often luxurious, and offer a mixture of Old World charm and modern convenience.

Reservations at any hotel are recommended, and traveling in high season to Perugia, Assisi, Spoleto, Todi, or Orvieto without advance bookings is a chancy proposition.

CATEGORY	COST*
$$$$	over 300,000 lire
$$$	160,000–300,000 lire
$$	100,000–160,000 lire
$	under 100,000 lire

All prices are for a standard double room for two, including tax, service, and breakfast.

Hiking

Magnificent scenery makes Umbria fine hiking and mountaineering country. The area around Spoleto is particularly good, and the tourist office for the town (☞ Contacts and Resources *in* Umbria A to Z, *below*) will supply itineraries of walks and climbs to suit all ages and levels of ability.

Shopping

Pottery and wine are the two most famous Umbrian exports, and examples of both commodities are excellent and unique to the region. **Torgiano,** south of Perugia, is one of the best-known centers of wine making, where you can watch the process and buy the product; you can find some of the best ceramics at **Gubbio, Perugia,** and **Assisi.** Those with the most flair are found in **Deruta,** south of Torgiano on S3bis. The red glazes of Gubbio pottery have been famous since medieval times. The secret of the original glaze died with its inventor some 500 years ago, but there are contemporary potters who produce a fair facsimile.

Swimming

Lakes Trasimeno and Piediluco offer safe and clean bathing facilities. **Castiglione del Lago,** on Lake Trasimeno, has a public beach, with no strong undercurrents or hidden depths.

Exploring Umbria and the Marches

The steep hills and deep valleys that make Umbria and the Marches so picturesque also make them difficult to explore. Driving routes must be chosen carefully to avoid tortuous mountain roads; major towns are not necessarily linked to each other by train, bus, or highway. A convenient base for exploring the region might be Perugia, the largest city in Umbria, but to see the region properly you would still need to stay overnight in other towns along the way. Next we head east across the Apennines to the Marches region; we begin exploring it in the hilltop city of Urbino, travel down to the Adriatic coast to visit Ancona, and then climb back west into the hills to Loreto and Ascoli Piceno. Back in Umbria, we concentrate on two memorable towns: Spoleto, site of the famous arts festival, south of Perugia; and Assisi, St. Francis's hometown, just east of Perugia. The final tour centers on Orvieto, built on a huge rock outcropping in western Umbria, southwest of Perugia.

Great Itineraries

The region of Umbria is particularly suited to touring in a limited time. Basing yourself in Perugia, you can see all the major sights in the regional capital in the equivalent of a day, making easy excursions to the hill villages on your other days without feeling stressed out by constant travel.

Numbers in the text correspond to numbers in the margin and on the Umbria and the Marches, Perugia, and Assisi maps.

IF YOU HAVE 3 DAYS

In ⊞ **Perugia** ①–⑤, your main stops will be the refurbished Galleria Nazionale and the Collegio del Cambio, both contained in the atmospheric **Palazzo dei Priori** ③; much of the rest of your time will be spent alternately ambling along Corso Vannucci and toiling up and down the steep lanes on either side. Devote your second day to ⊞ **Assisi** ⑬–⑳, where the spiritual and the material are fused in a place that remains in essence a small medieval Umbrian town. The choice for a third excursion is a tough one, and you won't be disappointed by whichever place you opt for. Consider **Spoleto** ⑫: a tight-knit hill town whose narrow streets abound with evocative views and delightful surprises.

IF YOU HAVE 5 DAYS

Given five days, you will be able to spend a couple of them exploring the neighboring region of Marche. How you enter these rather inaccessible parts will depend on your mode of transport. In any case, start your tour in **Perugia** ①–⑤, and follow the schedule outlined above for your first two days. If you are traveling by public transport, spend your third night in ⊞ **Spoleto** ⑫, from which you can jump on a train bound for ⊞ **Ancona** ⑨, where you can board a bus or a train for Pésaro and **Urbino** ⑧. This hilltop gem retains its proud, self-contained character, almost untouched by ugly 20th-century construction. Looming over the town is the imposing Palazzo Ducale, which will occupy most of the sightseeing you'll want to do here. Calculate at least half a day for reaching Urbino from Spoleto, and it's not much shorter by car, crossing the Marches border from ⊞ **Gubbio** ⑦, where you might spend your third day as an alternative to Spoleto. Gubbio's charm is not hard to fathom, and you can enjoy a very pleasant day and night here, appreciating the views and shops as well as some choice accommodation and dining possibilities.

IF YOU HAVE 7 DAYS

Reserve four days for Umbria and three for the Marches. With greater flexibility you can choose how many nights you want to spend in Umbria's capital, **Perugia** ①–⑤, and how many in the region's smaller centers. More time in Perugia will allow you to explore the city thoroughly, including the archaeological museum, and you might take in the easy excursion to the wine village of **Torgiano** ⑥. ⊞ **Spoleto** ⑫ and ⊞ **Assisi** ⑬–⑳ are essential stops farther afield, where you might lodge for a night in each. Gubbio is also worth overnighting in, whereas **Orvieto** ㉑ can be seen on your way to or from Rome, from which it's only 90 minutes' travel time. The essential sight here is of course the cathedral, though there are also a couple of good museums, a plethora of fine restaurants and some cozy hotels. East of Perugia, the Marches invite leisurely exploring, though also some lengthy rides in between the main points of interest. ⊞ **Urbino** ⑧ is the premier attraction and is worth staying a night in; ⊞ **Ancona** ⑨ has little of interest though it is the biggest city in the region and has accordingly good facilities for eating and sleeping, not to mention banks, car hire agencies, and information offices. Sleep here if you must; otherwise head south for the infinitely preferable inland town of ⊞ **Ascoli Piceno** ⑪, with a small choice of hotels and a slow, enticing atmosphere. There is little in the way of galleries or sophisticated shops here, but the place oozes charm. On the way, or en route back, drop in at the holy sanctuary of **Loreto** ⑩, nestled in the mountains 15 miles south of Ancona. It is a curiosity, even for nonbelievers, attracting pilgrims from all over the world.

When to Tour Umbria and the Marches

Unlike many other regions of Italy, Umbria and the Marches are relatively free of the tourist hordes, even in summer, when you might welcome the lush greenness of these interior tracts. Indeed, in August, much of the population shifts to the Adriatic resorts of the Marches to enjoy their vacation—though there are more enticing places to resort to if you felt like doing the same. At the other end of the year, the predominantly hilly terrain of Umbria and the Marches means that winters can be bitterly cold, and snow is not uncommon. Since many of the places on our itinerary are hilltop towns, including Perugia itself, you should be prepared for harsh conditions if you're traveling at this time of year, and driving can be hazardous. From the point of view of the region's cuisine, however, winter is best: January–April is the season to sample the truffles for which the area around Norcia and Spoleto is famous (though of course truffles are dried and can be had at any time of year), whereas wild mushrooms are picked fresh in October–December. The forested hills of Umbria and the Marches also ensure beguiling colors in the fall and an explosion of greenery in spring, two seasons when the tourist count is especially low and the temperature usually comfortable.

From the practical point of view, unless you are specifically drawn to the festival scene, make a wide berth of Spoleto between June and July, when the *Due Mondi* and jazz festivals take place, and of Gubbio at the end of May, when the crossbow tournament usually entails a similar level of congestion. If you *are* planning to attend these crowd-pulling events, you will need to book accommodations months in advance.

Sightseers and pilgrims throng the streets of Assisi, the most visited city in Umbria, throughout the year, though the religious festivals of Christmas, Easter, and the feast of Saint Francis (October 4), as well as the town's Calendimaggio Festival (May 1), are particularly swarming. At other times, even weekends can be uncomfortable, so you would do well to schedule your visit to Assisi with care.

UMBRIAN HEIGHTS
Perugia to Gubbio

Perugia

❶ *180 km (112 mi) north of Rome, 153 km (96 mi) southeast of Florence, 455 km (284 mi) southeast of Milan.*

Perugia, the largest and richest of Umbria's cities, is an old and elegant place of great charm. Despite a rather grim crust of modern suburbs, Perugia's location on a series of hills high above the suburban plain has ensured that the medieval city remains almost completely intact. Perugia is the best-preserved hill town of its size, and few other places in Italy illustrate better the concept of the self-contained city-state that so shaped the course of Italian history.

The best approach to the city is by train—the station is in the unlovely suburbs, but there are frequent buses running directly to Piazza d'I-

Umbria and the Marches

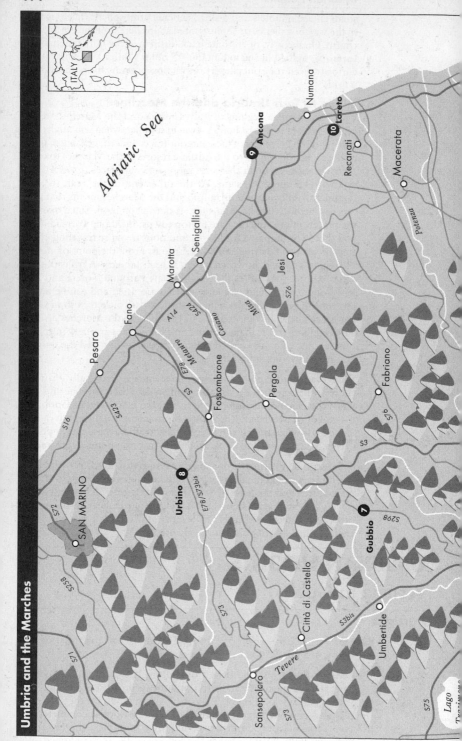

Adriatic Sea

Numana

9 Ancona

10 Loreto

Recanati

Macerata

Potenza

Senigallia

Marotta

Jesi

S76

Fano

A14

S424

Misa

Cesano

Pesaro

E78 Metauro

S3

Pergola

Fabriano

S76

Fossombrone

S16

S423

S3

San Marino

8 Urbino

S72

SAN MARINO

E78/S73bis

7 Gubbio

S298

S258

Città di Castello

S73

S3bis

Umbertide

S71

Tevere

Sansepolcro

S73

S75

Lago Trasimeno

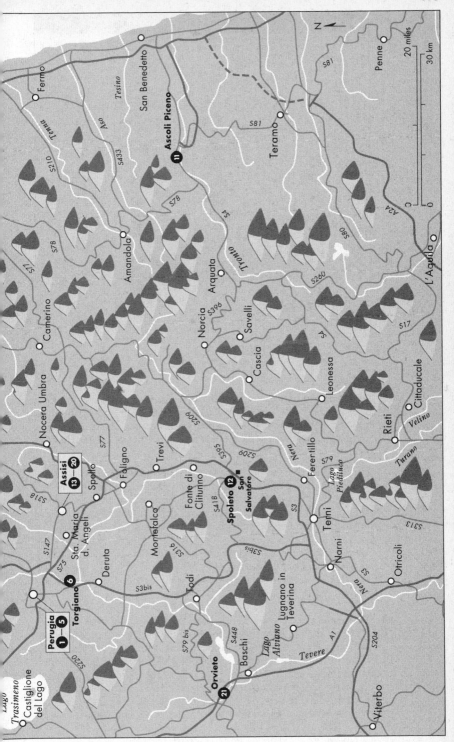

Z

20 miles
30 km

Penne

S81

Fermo

Tesino

San Benedetto

Aso

S210

S433

Ascoli Piceno **11**

S81

Teramo

S78

S5

Amandola

Arquata

Trontto

S260

L'Aquila

S80

Camerino

S78

S71

Norcia

S396

Savelli

Cascia

S4

S17

Cittaducale

Nocera Umbra

S77

Trevi

S208

S209

S260

Leonessa

Velino

Rieti

Turano

S318

Assisi **13**–**20**

Spello

Foligno

S395

S209

Nera

Ferentillo

S79

Lago
Piediluco

S313

Sta. Maria
d. Angeli

S147

S75

Montefalco

Fonte di
Clitunno

S418

Spoleto **12**

San=
Salvatore

S3

Terni

Perugia **1**–**5**

Torgiano **6**

Deruta

S3bis

S316

Todi

S3bis

Narni

Nera

S3

Otricoli

S220

S79 bis

Baschi

S448

Lago
Alviano

Lugnano in
Teverina

A1

S204

Orvieto **21**

Tevere

Viterbo

Lago
Trasimeno

Castiglione
del Lago

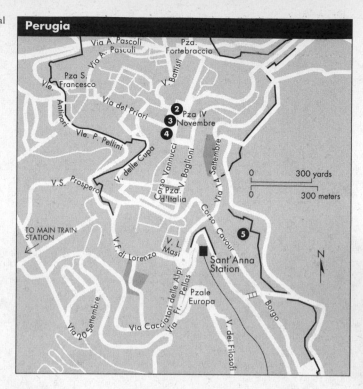

Perugia

talia, the heart of the old town. If you are driving to Perugia, it is best
to leave your car in one of the parking lots near the station and then
take the bus or the escalator (which passes through fascinating subterranean excavations of the Roman foundations of the city) to the center of town.

The nerve center of the city is the broad, stately **Corso Vannucci,** a pedestrian street that runs from Piazza d'Italia to Piazza IV Novembre. As
evening falls, Corso Vannucci is filled with Perugians out for their evening
passeggiata, a pleasant predinner stroll that may include a pause for
an aperitif at one of the many bars that line the street.

NEED A
BREAK?

You can enjoy the lively comings and goings on Corso Vannucci from
the vantage point of the **Bar Sandri** (⊠ Corso Vannucci 32). This fine old
bar is a 19th-century relic with wood-paneled walls and an elaborately
frescoed ceiling.

② The **Duomo** is a large and rather plain building dating from the Middle Ages but with many additions from the 15th and 16th centuries.
The interior is vast and echoing, with little in the way of decoration.
There are some elaborately carved choir stalls, executed by Giovanni
Battista Bastone in 1520. The great relic of the church—the wedding
ring of the Virgin Mary that the Perugians stole from the nearby town
of Chiusi—is kept in a chapel in the left aisle. The ring is the size of a
large bangle and is kept under lock (15 locks, actually) and key every
day of the year except July 30, when it is exposed to view. ⊠ *Piazza
IV Novembre.* ☉ *Daily 8–noon, 4–7:30.*

There is a large array of precious objects associated with the cathedral
in the **Museum of the Duomo,** including vestments, vessels, manuscripts,
and gold work, as well as one outstanding piece of artwork, an early

masterpiece by Luca Signorelli, the altarpiece showing the Madonna with Saint John the Baptist, Saint Onophrius, and Saint Lawrence (1484). ☒ *Piazza IV Novembre.* 🎟 *2,000 lire.* ⊘ *Wed.–Fri. 9–noon, Sat. 9–noon and 3:30–5:30, Sun. 3:30–5:30.*

★ ❸ The **Palazzo dei Priori** faces the Duomo across the piazza. It is an imposing building, begun in the 13th century, with an unusual staircase that fans out into the square. The facade is decorated with symbols of Perugia's pride and past power: the griffin is the symbol of the city; the lion denotes Perugia's allegiance to the Guelph (or papal) cause; and both figures support the heavy chains of the gates of Siena, which fell to Perugian forces in 1358.

The fourth floor of the Palazzo dei Priori contains the region's most comprehensive and absorbing art gallery, the **Galleria Nazionale d'Umbria,** recently reopened after a lengthy overhaul. Now enhanced by skillfully lit displays and computers allowing you to focus on details of the works and background information on them, the collection in 33 rooms includes work by native artists—most outstandingly Pinturicchio and Perugino—and others of the Umbrian and Tuscan schools, including Gentile da Fabriano, Duccio, Fra Angelico, Fiorenzo di Lorenzo, and Piero della Francesca. As well as paintings, the gallery has frescoes, sculptures, and some superb crucifixes from the 13th and 14th centuries; other rooms are dedicated to the city of Perugia itself, showing how the medieval city evolved. ☒ *Corso Vannucci 19,* 🎟 *8,000 lire.* ⊘ *Mon.–Sat. 9–7, Sun. 9–1. Closed 1st Mon. of each month.*

★ ❹ Attached to the Palazzo dei Priori, but entered from Corso Vannucci a few doors along from the Galleria Nazionale, is the **Collegio del Cambio,** a series of elaborate rooms that housed the meeting hall and chapel of the guild of bankers and money changers. The walls were frescoed from 1496 to 1500 by the most important Perugian painter of the Renaissance, Pietro Vannucci, better known as Perugino. The decorative program in the Collegio includes common religious themes, like the Nativity and the Transfiguration (on the end walls), but also figures intended to inspire the businessmen who congregated here. On the left wall are female figures representing the virtues, beneath them the heroes and sages of antiquity. On the right wall are the prophets and sibyls—said to have been painted in part by Perugino's most famous pupil, Raphael, whose hand, the experts say, is most apparent in the figure of Fortitude. On one of the pilasters is a remarkably honest self-portrait of Perugino, surmounted by a Latin inscription and contained in a faux frame. ☒ *Corso Vannucci 25.* 🎟 *5,000 lire.* ⊘ *Nov.–Feb., Tues.–Sat. 8–2, Sun. 9–12:30; Mar.–Oct., Mon.–Sat. 9–12:30 and 2:30–5:30, Sun. 9–12:30. During Christmas season (Dec. 20–Jan. 6) museum follows summer timetable.*

❺ A 10-minute walk south of the center along Corso Cavour leads to the **Archaeological Museum of Umbria,** which contains an excellent collection of Etruscan artifacts from throughout the region. Perugia was a flourishing Etruscan site long before it fell under Roman domination in 310 BC. (Other than this collection, little remains of Perugia's mysterious ancestors, although the Gate of Augustus, in Piazza Fortebraccio, the northern entrance to the city, is of Etruscan origin.) ☒ *Piazza Giordano Bruno.* 🎟 *4,000 lire.* ⊘ *Mon.–Sat. 9–1:30 and 2:30–7, Sun. 9–1.*

☺ Umbria's only attraction aimed directly at the younger set is **La Città della Domenica,** a Disney-style playground in the town of Montepulito, 8 kilometers (5 miles) west of Perugia on the secondary road that leads to Corciano. The 500 acres of parkland contain a variety of buildings based on familiar fairy-tale themes—Snow White's House, the Witches' Wood—as well as a reptile house, a medieval museum, an exhibit of shells from all over the world, game rooms, and a choice of restaurants. ⊠ *Località Montepulito.* ☎ *075/505–4941.* ☑ *15,900 lire (16,900 lire Sun. and public holidays).* ⊙ *Mid-Mar.–late-Sept., daily 9–7; late Sept.–Oct., weekends and holidays 9–7; Nov.–mid-Mar. (exhibitions only), Sat. 2–7, Sun. 10–7.*

Dining and Lodging

$$ ✕ **Il Falchetto.** Here you'll find exceptional food at reasonable prices, making this Perugia's best restaurant bargain. The service is smart but relaxed, and the two dining rooms are medieval, with the kitchen and chef on view. The house specialty is *falchetti* (homemade gnocchi with spinach and ricotta cheese). ⊠ *Via Bartolo 20,* ☎ *075/573–1775. Reservations essential. AE, DC, MC, V. Closed Mon.*

$$ ✕ **La Rosetta.** This restaurant, in the hotel of the same name, is a peaceful, elegant place. In the winter you dine inside under medieval vaults; in summer, in the cool courtyard. The cuisine is simple but reliable and flawlessly served. ⊠ *Piazza d'Italia 19,* ☎ *075/572–0841. Reservations essential. AE, DC, MC, V. Closed Mon.*

$$ ✕ **La Taverna.** Next to the Teatro Pavone, off Corso Vannucci, medieval steps lead to this rustic restaurant on two levels, where lots of wine bottles and artful clutter heighten the tavern atmosphere. The menu features regional specialties and better-known Italian dishes. Good choices include *chitarrini* (pasta), with either *funghi* (mushrooms) or *tartufi* (pricier truffles), and grilled meats. ⊠ *Via delle Streghe 8,* ☎ *075/572–4128. Dinner reservations essential. AE, DC, MC, V. Closed Mon.*

$$$$ 🏨 **Brufani Hotel.** The two hotels (this one and the Palace Hotel Bellavista; ☞ *below*) in this 19th-century palazzo were once one. The Brufani's public rooms and first-floor guest rooms have high ceilings and are done in the grand style of the Belle Epoque. The second-floor rooms are more modern, and many on both floors have a marvelous view of the Umbrian countryside or the city. ⊠ *Piazza d'Italia 12,* ☎ *075/573–2541,* 𝖥𝖠𝖷 *075/572–0210. 24 rooms with bath. Restaurant, bar, air-conditioning, meeting rooms. AE, DC, MC, V.*

$$$ 🏨 **Locanda della Posta.** This luxuriously decorated small hotel in the
★ center of Perugia's historic district is a delight to behold, from its fauxmarble moldings, paneled doors, and tile bouquets in the baths to the suede-upholstered elevator and fabric-covered walls. Architectural details of the 18th-century palazzo are beautiful, and views of city rooftops from windows and balconies are soothing. Breakfast is included here. ⊠ *Corso Vannucci 97,* ☎ *075/572–8925,* 𝖥𝖠𝖷 *075/572–2413. 40 rooms with bath or shower. Breakfast room, lobby lounge. AE, DC, MC, V.*

$$ 🏨 **Palace Hotel Bellavista.** The rooms in this hotel are decorated in splendid Belle Epoque grandeur, and many have a view over the hills. The hotel's entrance is unimpressive, but the public rooms are palatial. Weekly rates are available. ⊠ *Piazza d'Italia 12,* ☎ *075/572–0741,* 𝖥𝖠𝖷 *075/572–9092. 74 rooms with bath or shower. Bar, meeting rooms. AE, DC, MC, V.*

$$ 🏨 **Priori.** On an alley leading off the main Corso Vannucci, this unpretentious but elegant hotel has spacious and cheerful rooms with modern furnishings. There is a panoramic terrace where breakfast (included in the price) is served in summer. The hotel is difficult to find if you're driving, but a car is an encumbrance wherever you are in Perugia's historic center. ⊠ *Via Vermiglioli 3,* ☎ *075/572–3378,* 𝖥𝖠𝖷 *075/572–3213. 51 rooms with bath or shower. Bar. No credit cards.*

$ ⊞ **Rosalba.** This is a bright and friendly choice on the fringes of Perugia's historic center. Rooms—each equipped with telephone and television—are scrupulously clean, and the ones at the back enjoy a view. Although somewhat out of the way, the hotel is only a matter of minutes from Corso Vannucci by virtue of the nearby escalator stop, saving a good deal of legwork. Parking is easy, too. ⊠ *Via del Circo 7,* ☎ *075/572–8285. 11 rooms with shower. No credit cards.*

Nightlife and the Arts

Summer sees two music festivals in Perugia: the **Jazz Festival of Umbria** (July) and the **Festival of Sacred Music** (September). Event and ticket information for both festivals can be obtained, year-round, from the Perugia Tourist Office (⊠ Piazza IV Novembre 3, ☎ 075/572–3327).

A true devotee of Umbrian music should consider the lengthy trek to the **Chamber Music Festival of Umbria,** which is held every August and September in the town of Città di Castello, about 80 kilometers (49½ miles) north of Perugia on the S3bis. For information, contact the tourist office (⊠ Via R. di Cesare 2/b, ☎ 075/855–4817).

Shopping

Perugia is a well-to-do town, and judging by the array of expensive shops on **Corso Vannucci,** the Perugians are not afraid to part with their money. The main streets of the town are lined with clothing shops selling the best-known Italian designers, either in luxurious boutiques or shops—such as Gucci, Ferragamo, Armani, and Fendi—run by the design firms themselves.

The best and most typical thing to buy in Perugia is, of course, some of the famous and delicious **Perugina chocolate.** *Cioccolato al latte* (milk chocolate) and *fondente* (dark chocolate) are available in tiny jewel-like boxes or in giant gift boxes the size of serving trays. The most famous chocolates made by Perugina are the round chocolate- and nut-filled candies called Baci (kisses), which come wrapped in silver paper and, like fortune cookies, contain romantic sentiments or sayings.

Torgiano

⑥ *15 km (9 mi) southeast of Perugia.*

Wine lovers are certain to want to visit this home to the famous **Lungarotti winery,** best known for delicious Rubesco Lungarotti, San Giorgio, and chardonnay. The town is also home to a fascinating wine museum, which has a large collection of ancient wine vessels, presses, documents, and tools that tell the story of viticulture in Umbria and beyond. The museum traces the history of wine in all its uses—for drinking at the table, as medicine, and in mythology. You can also pick up one of the winery's award-winning reds and whites to take home. ⊠ *Corso Vittorio Emanuele 11.* ⊠ *5,000 lire.* ⊗ *Apr.–Sept., daily 9–noon and 3–7; Oct.–Mar., daily 9–1 and 3–6.*

Gubbio

⑦ *40 km (25 mi) northeast of Perugia.*

The trip from Perugia to **Gubbio** follows S298 through rugged, mountainous terrain. There is something otherworldly about this small jewel of a medieval town tucked away in a mountainous corner of Umbria. Even at the height of summer, the cool serenity and silence of Gubbio's streets remain intact. The town is perched on the slopes of Mt. Ingino, and the streets are dramatically steep.

Gubbio's relatively isolated position has kept it free of hordes of high-season visitors, but even during the busiest times of year the city lives up to its Italian nickname, the City of Silence. Parking in the central Piazza dei Quaranta Martiri (named for 40 hostages murdered by the Nazis in 1944) is easy and secure, and it is wise to leave your car there and explore the narrow streets on foot.

Walk up the main street of the town, Via della Repubblica (a steep climb) to Piazza della Signoria. This square is dominated by the magnificent **Palazzo dei Consoli,** a medieval building designed and built by a local architect known as Gattapone—a man still much admired by today's residents (every other hotel, restaurant, and bar has been named after him).

★

Although the Palazzo dei Consoli is impressive, it is the **piazza** itself that is most striking. When approached from the thicket of medieval streets, the wide and majestic square is an eye-opener. The piazza juts out from the hillside like an enormous terrace, giving wonderful views of the town and surrounding countryside.

The Palazzo dei Consoli houses a small museum, famous chiefly for the **Tavole Eugubine,** bronze tablets written in an ancient Umbrian language. Also in the museum are the **ceri,** three 16-foot-high poles crowned with statues of Saints Ubaldo, George, and Anthony. These heavy pillars are the focal point of the best-known event in Gubbio, the Festival of the Ceri (Candles), held every May 15. On that day, teams of Gubbio's young men, dressed in medieval costumes and carrying the ceri, race up the steep slopes of Mt. Ingino to the Monastery of Saint Ubaldo, high above the town. This festival, enacted faithfully every year since 1151, is a picturesque, if strenuous, way of thanking the patron saints of the town for their assistance in a miraculous Gubbian victory over a league of 11 other towns. ⊠ *Piazza della Signoria.* ⊠ *4,000 lire.* ☉ *Mid-Mar.–Sept., daily 9–12:30 and 3:30–6; Oct.–mid-Mar., daily 9–1 and 3–5.*

The **Duomo** and the Palazzo Ducale face each other across a narrow street on the highest tier of the town. The Duomo dates from the 13th century, with some Baroque additions—in particular, a lavishly decorated bishop's chapel. ⊠ *Via Ducale.* ☉ *Daily 9–12:30 and 3–5.*

The **Palazzo Ducale** is a scaled-down copy of the Palazzo Ducale in Urbino (Gubbio was once the possession of that city's ruling family, the Montefeltro). Gubbio's palazzo contains a small museum and a fine courtyard. There are magnificent views from some of the public rooms. *Palazzo Ducale.* ⊠ *Via Ducale.* ⊠ *4,000 lire.* ☉ *Mon.–Sat. 9–1:45, Sun. 9–1, also summer 3:30–6:30.*

NEED A BREAK?	Under the arches that support the Palazzo Ducale is the **Bar del Giardino Pubblico,** a bar set in the tiny public gardens, which seem to hang off the side of the mountain. It is a charming place for a cold drink and a rest after a tiring climb up to the Duomo and Palace. It's open May–September, daily 9–7.

♻ Among the region's historical pageants, Gubbio's costumed **crossbow tournament** is particularly exciting for young and old alike. The *Palio della Balestra* usually takes place on the last Sunday in May; contact the Gubbio tourist agency for details. ⊠ *Piazza Oderisi 6,* ☎ *075/ 922–0693.*

Dining and Lodging

$$ ✕ **Fornace di Mastro Giorgio.** This atmospheric restaurant is in the medieval workshop of a famous master potter, one of Gubbio's most famous sons. The food is lighter than typical Umbrian fare, with the

occasional southern dish, like *tiella barese* (a mixture of rice, mussels, and potatoes), added. ✉ *Via Mastro Giorgio 2,* ☎ *075/927–5740. Reservations essential in summer. AE, DC, MC, V. Closed Mon. Sept.–June and 2 wks in July. No dinner Sun.*

$$ ✕ **Grotta dell'Angelo.** This rustic trattoria is in the lower part of the Old Town, near the main square and tourist information office. The menu features simple local specialties, including *capocollo* (a type of salami), strengozzi pasta, and lasagna *tartufate* (with truffles). There are a few tables for outdoor dining. Inexpensive guest rooms are available here as well. ✉ *Via Gioia 47,* ☎ *075/927–3438. Reservations essential. AE, DC, MC, V. Closed Tues. and Jan. 7–Feb. 7.*

$$ ✕ **Taverna del Lupo.** It's one of the best restaurants in the city, as well as one of the largest—it seats 200 people and can get a bit hectic during the high season. Lasagna made in the Gubbian fashion, with ham and truffles, is the best pasta. You'll also find excellent desserts and an extensive wine cellar here. ✉ *Via G. Ansidei 21,* ☎ *075/927–4368. Reservations essential. AE, DC, MC, V. Closed Mon. Sept.–June and Jan.*

$$ ▦ **Hotel Bosone.** Occupying the old central Palazzo Raffaelli, the Hotel Bosone has many rooms decorated with frescoes from the former palace. The suites furnished with period detail are particularly lavish. ✉ *Via XX Settembre 22,* ☎ *075/922–0688,* ℻ *075/922–0552. 30 rooms with bath or shower. Restaurant, bar. AE, DC, MC, V.*

$ ▦ **Hotel Gattapone.** Right in the center of town is this hotel with wonderful views of the sea of rooftops. It is casual and family run, with good-size, modern, comfortable rooms, some with well-preserved timber-raftered ceilings. ✉ *Via Ansidei 6,* ☎ *075/927–2489,* ℻ *075/927–1269. 13 rooms with bath or shower. Closed Jan. AE, DC, MC, V.*

THE MARCHES
Mirror to the Renaissance

An excursion from Umbria into the region of the Marches is recommended for those who want to get off the beaten track and see a part of Italy rarely visited by foreigners. It must be admitted that traveling in the Marches is not as easy as in Umbria or Tuscany. Beyond the narrow coastal plain and away from major towns, the roads are steep and twisting. Train travel in the region is slow, and destinations are limited, although one can reach Ascoli Piceno by rail, and there's an efficient bus service from the coastal town of Pesaro to Urbino, the other principal tourist city of the region.

Urbino

❽ *170 km (106 mi) northeast of Perugia, 190 km (119 mi) east of Florence, 30 km (19 mi) southwest of Pésaro.*

Urbino is a majestic city, sitting atop a steep hill, with a skyline of towers and domes. It is something of a surprise to come upon it—the location is remote—and it is even stranger to reflect that this quiet country town was once a center of learning and culture almost without rival in western Europe. The town looks much as it did in the glory days of the 15th century, a cluster of warm brick and pale stone buildings, all topped with russet-colored tiled roofs. The focal point is the immense and beautiful Ducal Palace.

The tradition of learning in Urbino continues to this day. The city is the home of a small but prestigious Italian state university—one of the oldest in the world—and during term time the streets are filled with hordes of noisy students. It is very much a college town, with the usual array of bookshops, record stores, bars, and coffeehouses. During the summer, the Italian student population is replaced by foreigners who come to study Italian language and arts at several prestigious private fine-arts academies.

Urbino's fame rests on the reputation of three of its native sons: Duke Federico da Montefeltro, the enlightened warrior-patron who built the Ducal Palace; Raphael, one of the most influential painters in history and an embodiment of the spirit of the Renaissance; and the architect Donato Bramante, who translated the philosophy of the Renaissance into buildings of grace and beauty. Why three of the greatest men of the age should have been born within a generation of one another in this remote town has never been explained. Oddly enough, there is little work by either Bramante or Raphael in the city, but the duke's influence can still be felt strongly, even now, some 500 years after his death.

★ The **Ducal Palace** holds the place of honor in the city, and in no other palace of its era are the principles of the Renaissance stated quite so clearly. If the Renaissance was, in ideal form, a celebration of the nobility of man and his works, of the light and purity of the soul, then there is no place in Italy, the birthplace of the Renaissance, where these tenets are better illustrated. From the moment you enter the peaceful courtyard, you know that you are in a place of grace and beauty, the harmony of the building reflecting the high ideals of the men who built it.

Today the palace houses the **National Museum of the Marches,** with a superb collection of paintings, sculpture, and other objets d'art, well arranged and properly lit. It would be hard to mention all the great works in this collection—some originally the possessions of the Montefeltro family, others brought to the museum from churches and palaces throughout the region—but there are a few that must be singled out. Of these, perhaps the most famous is Piero della Francesca's enigmatic work, long known as *The Flagellation of Christ.* Much has been written about this painting, and few experts agree on its meaning. Legend had it that the three figures in the foreground represented a murdered member of the Montefeltro family (the barefoot young man) and his two murderers. Others claimed the painting was a heavily veiled criticism of certain parts of Christian Europe—the iconography is obscure and the history extremely complicated. Recently, however, Sir John Pope-Hennessy—the preeminent scholar of Italian Renaissance art—has proved that it represents the arcane subject of the Vision of Saint Lawrence. All the experts have always agreed that the painting is one of Piero della Francesca's masterpieces. Piero himself thought so. It is one of the few works he signed (on the lowest step supporting the throne).

Other masterworks in the collection are Paolo Uccello's *Profanation of the Host,* Piero della Francesca's *Madonna of Senigallia,* and Titian's *Resurrection* and *Last Supper.* Duke Federico's study is an astonishingly elaborate but tiny room decorated with inlaid wood, said to be the work of Botticelli. ⊠ *Piazza Duca Federico,* ☎ *0722/2760.* ☜ *8,000 lire.* ☉ *Aug.–Oct., Mon. 9–2, Tues.–Sun. 9–7; Nov.–July, daily 9–2.*

The **house of the painter Raphael** really is the house in which he was born and in which he took his first steps in painting (under the direction of his artist father). There is some debate about the fresco of the Madonna that adorns the house. Some say it is by Raphael, whereas others attribute it to the father—with Raphael's mother and the young painter himself standing in as models for the Madonna and Child. Either way, it's an interesting picture. ⊠ *Via Raffaello.* ☜ *5,000 lire.* ☉

Apr.–Sept., Tues.–Sat. 9–1 and 3–7, Sun. 9–1; Oct.–Mar., Thurs.–Sat. and Mon.–Tues. 9–2, Sun. 9–1.:

Dining and Lodging

$$ ✕ **La Vecchia Fornarina.** These two small rooms just down from Urbino's central Piazza della Repubblica are often filled to capacity. The trattoria specializes in meaty country fare, such as rabbit and *vitello alle noci* (veal cooked with nuts) or *ai porcini* (with mushrooms). There is also a good range of pasta dishes. ⊠ *Via Mazzini 14,* ☎ *0722/320007. Reservations essential. AE, DC, MC, V. Closed Wed.*

$ 🏨 **Hotel San Giovanni.** This hotel is in the Old Town and is housed in a renovated medieval building. The rooms are basic, clean, and comfortable—with a wonderful view from Nos. 18–21 and 24–31—and there is a handy restaurant–pizzeria below. ⊠ *Via Barocci 13,* ☎ *0722/2827. 33 rooms, 21 with shower. No credit cards. Closed July and Christmas wk.*

En Route To reach Ancona, on the Adriatic coast, from Urbino, take the E78 or S3 to the superhighway A14, which runs along the coast but inland by a kilometer (half mile) or so. The coast road, S16, is a congested two-lane highway with little to recommend it.

Ancona

⑨ *87 km (54 mi) southeast of Urbino, 60 km (37½ mi) southeast of Pésaro, 139 km (87 mi) northeast of Perugia, 262 km (164 mi) east of Florence, 286 km (179 mi) northeast of Rome.*

Ancona was probably once a lovely city. It is set on an elbow-shape bluff (hence its name; *ankon* is Greek for "elbow") that juts out into the Adriatic. But Ancona was the object of serious aerial bombing during World War II—it was, and is, an important port city—and was reduced to rubble. The city has been rebuilt in the unfortunate postwar poured-concrete style, practical and inexpensive but certainly not pleasing. Unless you are taking a ferry to Venice, there is little reason to visit the city—with a few exceptions. Once in a while there are glimpses of the old architecture, as in the Duomo San Ciriaco and the Loggia dei Mercanti. In addition, Ancona can be the base for an excursion to Loreto or to Ascoli Piceno, farther down the Adriatic coast.

Dining and Lodging

$$ ✕ **La Moretta.** This family-run trattoria is on the central Piazza del Plebiscito. In summer there is dining outside in the square, which has a fine view of the Baroque church of San Domenico. Among the specialties of La Moretta are tagliatelle *in salsa di ostriche* (in an oyster sauce) and the famous brodetto fish stew. ⊠ *Piazza del Plebiscito 52,* ☎ *071/202317. Reservations advised. AE, DC, MC, V. Closed Sun. and Dec. 25–Jan. 6.*

$$$ 🏨 **Grand Hotel Palace.** In the center of town, near the entrance to the port of Ancona, and widely held to be the best in town, this is an old-fashioned place well run by a courteous staff. ⊠ *Lungomare Vanvitelli 24,* ☎ *071/201813,* 𝖥𝖠𝖷 *071/207–4832. 41 rooms with bath. Bar. AE, DC, MC, V.*

$$ 🏨 **Hotel Roma e Pace.** The only two reasons to stay in this hotel are the location and price. The rooms are ugly and cramped, and those facing the street are noisy (choose inward-facing ones). A historical note: In 1907 a Russian named Josef Dzhugashvili applied for a job here and was refused. He later found better-paying employment as supreme head of the Soviet Union under the name Stalin. ⊠ *Via Leopardi 1,* ☎

071/202007, FAX 071/207–4736. 73 rooms with bath or shower. Restaurant, bar. AE, DC, MC, V.

Loreto

⑩ *24 km (24 mi) south of Ancona on A14.*

Loreto is famous for one of the best-loved shrines in the world, that of
★ the **house of the Virgin Mary.** The legend is that angels moved the house
from Nazareth, where the Virgin was living at the time of the Annunciation, to this hilltop in 1295. The reason for this sudden and divinely
inspired move was that Nazareth had fallen into the hands of Muslim
invaders, not suitable landlords, the angelic hosts felt. More recently,
following archaeological excavations made at the behest of the Church,
evidence has come to light proving that the house did once stand elsewhere and was brought to the hilltop by human means around the time
the angels are said to have done the job.

The house itself consists of three rough stone walls contained within
an elaborate marble tabernacle; built around this centerpiece is the giant
basilica of the Holy House, which dominates the town. Millions of visitors come to the site every year (particularly at Easter and on the Feast
of the Holy House, December 10), and the little town of Loreto can
become uncomfortably crowded with pilgrims. Many great Italian architects, including Bramante, Sangallo, and Sansovino, contributed to
the design of the basilica. Inside are a great many mediocre 19th- and
20th-century paintings but also some fine works by Renaissance masters such as Luca Signorelli and Melozzo da Forlì.

Nervous air travelers may take comfort in the fact that the Holy Virgin of Loreto is the patroness of air travelers and that Pope John Paul
II has composed a prayer for a safe flight—available in the church in
a half-dozen languages.

Ascoli Piceno

⑪ *105 km (65 mi) south of Ancona.*

Ascoli Piceno is not a hill town; rather, it sits in a valley ringed by steep
hills and cut by the fast-racing Tronto River. The town is almost unique
in Italy, in that it seems to have its traffic problems—in the historic
center, at any rate—pretty much under control; you can drive *around*
the picturesque part of the city, but driving *through* it is most difficult.
This feature makes Ascoli Piceno one of the most pleasant large towns
in the country for exploring on foot. True, there is traffic, but you are
not constantly assaulted by jams, noise, and exhaust fumes the way
you are in other Italian cities.

★ The heart of the town is the majestic **Piazza del Popolo,** dominated by
the Gothic church of San Francesco and the Palazzo del Popolo, a 13th-century town hall that contains a graceful Renaissance courtyard. The
square itself functions as the living room of the entire city. At dusk each
evening the piazza is packed with people standing in small groups, exchanging news and gossip as if at a cocktail party.

....
NEED A   Ascoli Piceno is indelibly associated with the Meletti distillery situated on
BREAK?   the outskirts of town. You can sample their famous aniseed spirits at the
              wood-paneled **Bar Centrale,** a small and cozy establishment that dates
              from the turn of the century, at Piazza del Popolo No. 9. For a light
              lunch or snack, pick up some delicious sandwiches and homemade pastries across the square at the **Pasticceria Angelini.**
....

  Ascoli Piceno's **Giostra della Quintana** takes place on the first Sunday in August. Children should love this medieval-style joust and the richly caparisoned processions that wind through the streets of the old town. Contact Ascoli's tourist office for details (✉ Piazza del Popolo, ☎ 0736/257288).

Dining and Lodging

$$ ✗ **Ristorante Tornasacco.** In this attractive family-run restaurant with
★ rustic decor and vaulted brick ceilings, you can sample Ascoli's specialties, like olives ascolane (here, stuffed with minced meat), as well as *maccheroncini alla contadina* (a homemade pasta in a thick meat sauce). ✉ *Piazza del Popolo 36,* ☎ *0736/254151. AE, DC, MC, V. Closed Fri. and June 15–30.*

$ ⬚ **Cantina dell'Arte.** This recently renovated hotel is one of the few lodgings in the center of the Old Town. Although the service can be sloppy, the rooms are clean and well equipped with TV and telephone, representing excellent value for the money. There is a boisterous and inexpensive restaurant run by the same management across the road. ✉ *Rua della Lupa 8,* ☎ *0736/255744. 11 rooms with shower. No credit cards.*

En Route   The 175-kilometer (108-mile) drive to Spoleto takes you out of the Marches and back into Umbria. The route—S4 southwest to Rieti, then S79 north to Terni, then S3 into Spoleto—is roundabout but vastly preferable to a series of winding mountain roads that connect Ascoli Piceno with Umbria.

SPOLETO AND ASSISI, BIRTHPLACE OF SAINT FRANCIS

  Spoleto and Assisi are two of the most popular towns in all of Italy, but for very different reasons. The delightful medieval town of Spoleto hosts Italy's most prestigious international arts festival, the *Festival dei Due Mondi* (Festival of Two Worlds), while Assisi is the birthplace of one of Christianity's most beloved saints, St. Francis.

Spoleto

★ ⑫   *50 kilometers (30 miles) south of Perugia, 35 kilometers (20 miles) south of Assisi.*

  Spoleto is an enchanting town perfectly situated in wooded countryside. "A little bit of heaven fallen to earth" it was once called, and it is not hard to understand the sentiment. "Quaint" may be an overused term, but it is the most appropriate word to describe this city, still enclosed by stout medieval walls. The chief pleasure of Spoleto is that the city itself is the sight. There is no long tramp through museums and churches in store for you here; rather, you can enjoy the simple treat of walking through the maze of twisting streets and up and down cobbled stairways, enjoying the beauty of the town and its wonderful peace and quiet.

  Quiet, that is, except when Spoleto is hosting the **Festival dei Due Mondi** (Festival of the Two Worlds), an arts festival, held every year from mid-June to mid-July. During those two months the sleepy town is swamped with visitors who come to see world-class plays and operas, to hear concerts, and to see extensive exhibitions of paintings and sculpture. Hotels in the city and countryside are filled to overflowing, and the streets are packed with visitors. It is unwise to arrive during this period without confirmed hotel reservations. Furthermore, experiencing the town itself, rather than the festival, is very difficult during these months. Those who don't care for crowds are advised to stay away during the festival.

Even in the off-season, parking in the Old City is difficult. If you are traveling by car, it is best to park outside the walls. There is usually ample parking available near Piazza della Vittoria.

Spoleto is dominated by a huge castle that was built in 1359–63 by the Gubbio-born architect Gattapone. It was until recently a high-security prison but has been undergoing restoration and is to become a museum. The castle was built to protect the town's most famous monument, the massive bridge known as the **Ponte delle Torri** (Bridge of the Towers), built by Gattapone on Roman foundations. This massive structure stands 262 feet above the gorge it spans and was built originally as an aqueduct. The bridge is open to pedestrians, and a walk over it affords marvelous views—looking down to the river below is the best way to appreciate the colossal dimensions of the bridge. The central span is actually higher than that of the dome of St. Peter's in Rome.

Spoleto's **Duomo** is set in a lovely sloping square at the bottom of a flight of steps below the castle. The church facade is dourly Romanesque but with the pleasant light addition of a Renaissance loggia and eight rose windows. The contrast between the heavy medieval work and the graceful later embellishments graphically demonstrates the difference, not only in style, but in philosophy, of the two eras. The earlier was strong but ungiving; the later, human and open-minded.

The Duomo's interior boasts the best of the city's art, notably the immaculately restored frescoes in the apse by the great Fra Filippo Lippi, showing the Annuciation, the Nativity, and the Death of Mary, with a marvelous Coronation of the Virgin adorning the dome; be ready with a 500-lire coin to illuminate the masterpiece. Another series of frescoes, including work by Pinturicchio, can be seen in the Eroli chapel off the right aisle. ⊠ *Piazza Duomo.* ☉ *Daily 8–1 and 4–6.*

From Piazza del Duomo make your way to **Piazza del Mercato,** site of the old Roman forum and today the main square of the Old Town.

NEED A BREAK?	Piazza del Mercato is lined with bars and delicatessens that serve good pastries and coffee. Parked in the square every day except Sunday is the van of a *porchetta* (suckling pig) vendor. These mobile snack bars are common to all central and northern Italy, and they serve only one product—roast pork. The whole pig is roasted on a spit, and slices are carved off to make delicious sandwiches on crusty rolls called *rosette*. The porchetta seller in Piazza del Mercato is particularly cheerful, and his portions are generous.

The **Arch of Drusus,** off the southern end of Piazza del Mercato, was built by the Senate of Spoleto to honor the Roman general Drusus, son of the emperor Tiberius.

Between Piazza del Duomo and Piazza del Mercato, on an extension of the picturesque Via Fontesecca, with its tempting shops selling local pottery and other handicrafts, is the church of **Sant'Eufemia** (in the courtyard of the archbishop's palace), an ancient, austere church built in the 11th century. Its most interesting feature is the gallery above the nave where female worshippers were required to sit—a holdover from the Eastern Church—one of the few such galleries in this part of Italy. ⊠ *Via Saffi.* ☉ *Summer, daily 8–8; winter, daily 8–6.*

At the southern end of Corso Mazzini is a small but well-preserved **Roman theater,** used in summer for performances of Spoleto's arts festival. The theater was the site of one of the town's most macabre incidents. During the Middle Ages, Spoleto took the side of the Holy Roman Emperor in the interminable struggle between Guelph (papal) and Ghibelline (imperial) factions over the question of who would control central and northern Italy. Four hundred of the pope's supporters were massacred in the theater, and their bodies were burned in an enormous pyre. It is not an episode of which Spoleto is proud, and, furthermore, the Guelphs were triumphant in the end. Spoleto was incorporated into the states of the Church in 1354. ☉ *Summer, Mon.–Sat. 9–1:30 and 3–7, Sun. 9–1; winter, Mon.–Sat. 9–1 and 3–5, Sun. 9–1.*

On the outskirts of the city, just off Via Flaminia (S3), is the lovely church of **San Salvatore.** You may already have seen a lot of old churches in Italy, but few are as old as this one. It needed renovation in the 9th century—by that time it was already 600 years old. It is nestled under cypresses and surrounded by Spoleto's cemetery and is quiet, cool, and peaceful. The church was built by Eastern monks in the 4th century, and little has been added (or removed) since its renovation. San Salvatore has an air of timelessness and antiquity rarely found in churches so close to major towns. ☒ *Via della Basilica di San Salvatore.* ☉ *Daily 8–1 and 4–6.*

Dining and Lodging

$$ ✕ **Il Pentagramma.** Just off the central Piazza della Libertà, this restaurant features such local dishes as *coda di bue alla spoletina* (oxtail) and lamb in a truffle sauce. ☒ *Via Martani 4,* ☏ *0743/223141. Reservations essential during the festival and on weekends. DC, MC, V. Closed Mon.*

$$ ✕ **Il Tartufo.** Spoleto's most famous restaurant has a smart modern dining room on the second floor and a rustic dining room downstairs—both of which incorporate the ruins of a Roman villa. The traditional cooking is spiced up in summer to appeal to the cosmopolitan crowd that is attending (or performing in) the Festival of Two Worlds. As its name indicates, the restaurant specializes in dishes prepared with truffles, though there is a second menu from which you can choose items not containing this expensive delicacy. ☒ *Piazza Garibaldi 24* ☏ *0743/40236. Reservations esential. AE, DC, MC, V. Closed Wed. and mid-July–1st wk in Aug.*

$$ ✕ **Trattoria Panciolle.** In the heart of Spoleto's medieval quarter, this restaurant has one of the most romantic settings you could wish for. Dining outside in summer is a delight in a small piazza filled with lime trees. Specialties include *strangozzi* (pasta) with mushroom sauce and *agnello scottadito* (grilled lamb chops). Seven guest rooms are also available here. ☒ *Via del Duomo 3,* ☏ *0743/45598. Reservations essential. AE, MC, V. Closed Wed.*

$$$ ⌂ **Dei Duchi.** This excellent, well-run hotel is in the center of the town, near the Roman amphitheater. It's a favorite with performers in the Festival of Two Worlds. Some rooms have fine views of the city. ☒ *Viale Matteotti 4,* ☏ *0743/44541,* FAX *0743/44543. 49 rooms with bath or shower. Restaurant, bar, meeting rooms, parking. AE, DC, MC, V.*

$$$ ⌂ **Hotel Gattapone.** The tiny four-star Hotel Gattapone is situated at the top of the Old Town, near the Ponte delle Torri, and has wonderful views of the ancient bridge and the wooded slopes of Monteluco. The rooms are well furnished and tastefully decorated. ☒ *Via del Ponte 6,* ☏ *0743/223447,* FAX *0743/223448. 14 rooms with bath. Bar. AE, DC, MC, V.*

$–$$ ⌂ **Nuovo Clitunno.** A renovated 18th-century building houses this pleasant hotel, a five-minute walk from the town center. Bedrooms and public rooms, some with lovely timber-beamed ceilings, have a mixture of period as well as less characterful modern furniture. ☒ *Piazza*

Sordini 6, ☎ 0743/223340, ℻ 0743/222663. 31 rooms with bath or shower. Restaurant, bar. AE, DC, MC, V.

Nightlife and the Arts

The **Festival of Two Worlds** in Spoleto (mid-June–mid-July) features star names in all branches of the arts—particularly music, opera, and theater—and draws thousands of visitors from all over the world. Tickets for all performances should be ordered in advance from the festival's box office, beginning at the end of April. ⊠ *Teatro Nuovo,* ☎ *0743/40265, closed Mon. Information available year-round from the Teatro Nuovo (☎ 0743/44097) or from the festival's Rome office (⊠ Via Beccaria 18, ☎ 06/321–0288).*

OFF THE
BEATEN PATH

VALNERINA – This is the name of the area east of Umbria, and it is the most beautiful of central Italy's many well-kept secrets. The roads that serve the rugged landscape are poor, but a drive through the region, even with all those time-consuming twists and turns, will be worth it to see forgotten medieval villages and dramatic mountain scenery. The first stop should be the **waterfalls at Marmore,** the highest falls in Europe. You'll find them a few miles east of Terni, on the road to Lake Piediluco and Rieti. The waters are diverted on weekdays to provide hydroelectric power for the town of Terni, so check with the tourist office (⊠ Viale C. Battisti 7/a, ☎ 0744/423048) in Terni before heading there. On summer evenings, when the falls are in full spate, the cascading water is floodlit—and a delightful sight.

Close to the picturesque town of Ferentillo (northeast of Terni on S209) is the outstanding 8th-century abbey of **San Pietro in Valle.** There are fine frescoes in the nave of the church, and the cloister is graceful and peaceful. As a bonus, one of the abbey outbuildings houses a fine restaurant with moderate prices.

Farther east are the towns of Norcia and Cascia; **Norcia** is the most famous town for Umbrian food specialties. It is also the birthplace of Saint Benedict. **Cascia** is the birthplace of the uncrowned patron saint of Italian women, Saint Rita.

Assisi

 47 km (30 mi) north and west of Spoleto on S3 and S75, 25 km (16 mi) east of Perugia.

The first sight of **Assisi** is memorable. The hill on which Assisi sits rises dramatically from the flat plain, and the town is dominated at the top of the mount by a medieval castle; on the lower slopes of the hill is the massive basilica of San Francesco, rising majestically on graceful arched supports. From a distance, Saint Francis's birthplace looks—to use an evocative phrase of travel essayist James Reynolds—"calm, white, pure as the fresh-washed wool from the Pascal Lamb."

Except in the depths of the off-season, Assisi, the most famous and most visited city in Umbria, is always thronged with sightseers and pilgrims. Somehow, though, despite the press of visitors, there is an unspoiled quality to the city—Assisi seems to be actually redolent of the sweet personality of its greatest citizen, Saint Francis, who is buried here in the huge 13th-century Basilica on the Hill of Paradise.

Saint Francis was born here in 1181, the son of a well-to-do merchant. He had, by his own account, a riotous youth but forsook the pleasures of the flesh quite early in life, adopting a life of austerity. His mystical approach to poverty, asceticism, and the beauty of man and nature struck a responsive chord in the medieval mind, and he quickly attracted a vast number of followers. He was a humble and unassuming man, and his compassion and humility brought him great love and veneration in his own lifetime. Without actively seeking power, as did many clerics of his day, he amassed great influence and political power, changing the history of the Catholic Church. He was the first person to receive the stigmata (wounds in his hands, feet, and side corresponding to the torments of Christ on the cross), injuries that caused him great pain and suffering, which he bore with characteristic patience. Nonetheless, Saint Francis welcomed the coming of "Sister Death," in 1226. Today the Franciscans are the largest of all the Catholic orders. And among the mass of clergy at Assisi, you can identify the saint's followers by their simple, coarse brown habits bound by sashes of knotted rope.

★ ⑭ The **Basilica of San Francesco** is one of Italy's foremost monuments and was begun shortly after the saint's death. What Saint Francis would have made of a church of such size, wealth, and grandeur—the opposite of all he preached and believed—is hard to imagine. His coffin, unearthed from its secret hiding place in 1818, is on display in the crypt below the lower church and is a place of piety. The basilica is not one church but two huge structures built one over the other. The lower church is dim and full of candlelit shadows, whereas the upper is bright and airy. Both are magnificently decorated artistic treasure houses, however, especially the upper church, where a fresco cycle by Giotto is a milestone in the history of Western art.

Visit the **lower church** first. The first chapel on the left of the nave was decorated by the Sienese master Simone Martini. Frescoed in 1322–26, the paintings show the life of Saint Martin—the sharing of his cloak with the poor man, the saint's knighthood, and his death.

There is some dispute about the paintings in the third chapel on the right. Experts have argued for years as to their authorship, with many saying that they were done by Giotto. The paintings depict the life of Saint Mary Magdalene. There is a similar dispute about the works above the high altar—some say they are by Giotto; others claim them for an anonymous pupil. They depict the marriage of Saint Francis to poverty, chastity, and obedience.

In the right transept are frescoes by Cimabue, a Madonna and saints, one of them Saint Francis himself. In the left transept are some of the best-known works of the Sienese painter Pietro Lorenzetti. They depict the Madonna with Saints John and Francis, a crucifixion, and a descent from the cross.

It is quite a contrast to climb the steps next to the altar and emerge into the bright sunlight and airy grace of the double-arched Renaissance cloister called the **Cloister of the Dead**. A door to the right leads to the treasury of the church and contains relics of Saint Francis and other holy objects associated with the order.

The **upper church** is dominated by Giotto's 28 frescoes, each portraying incidents in the life of Saint Francis. Although the artist was only in his twenties when he painted this cycle, the frescoes show that Giotto was the pivotal artist in the development of Western painting, breaking away from the stiff, unnatural styles of earlier generations and moving toward a realism and grace that reached their peak in the Renaissance. The paintings are viewed left to right, starting in the transept. The most beloved of all the scenes is probably *Saint Francis Preaching to the Birds,* a touching painting that seems to sum up the gentle spirit of the saint. It stands in marked contrast to the scene of the dream of Innocent III.

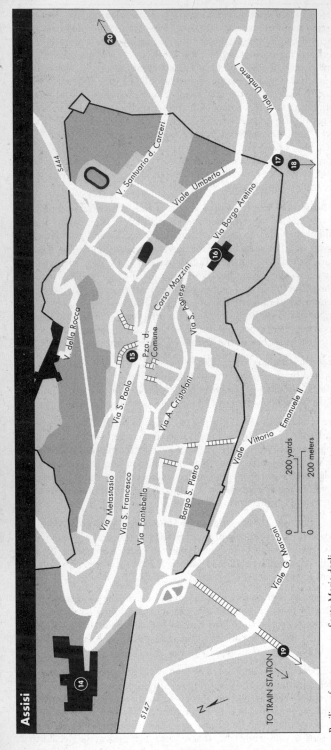

Assisi

Basilica of
San Francesco, **14**
Hermitage of the
Carceri, **20**
Porta Nuova, **17**
San Damiano, **18**
Santa Chiara, **16**

Santa Maria degli
Angeli, **19**
Temple of
Minerva, **15**

TO TRAIN STATION

200 yards

200 meters

The pope dreams of a humble monk who will steady the church. Sure enough, in the panel next to the sleeping pope, you see a strong Francis supporting a church that seems to be on the verge of tumbling down. ✉ *Piazza di San Francesco.* ⊙ *Upper and lower churches: Summer, Mon.–Sat. 7 AM–sunset, Sun. 2–sunset; winter, Mon.–Sat. 7–noon and 2–sunset, Sun. 2–sunset.*

The long, central square of the town, Piazza del Comune, holds the **15 Temple of Minerva.** It is made up of bits and pieces of a Roman temple that dates from the time of Augustus and was later converted into a church. The expectations raised by the perfect classical facade are not met by the interior, subjected to a thorough Baroque assault in the 17th century. ✉ *Piazza del Comune.* ⊙ *Daily 7–noon and 2:30–sunset.*

In the southeastern part of Assisi, near the Porta Nuova, the 13th-**16** century church of **Santa Chiara** is dedicated to Saint Clare, one of the earliest and most fervent of Saint Francis's followers and the founder of the order of the Poor Ladies, or Poor Clares, in imitation of the Franciscans. The church contains the body of the saint, and in the **Chapel of the Crucifix** (on the right) is the cross that spoke to Saint Francis and led him to a life of piety. A heavily veiled member of Saint Clare's order is stationed before the cross in perpetual adoration of the image. To get here from Piazza del Comune, walk down Corso Mazzini past the Pinacoteca. ✉ *Piazza Santa Chiara.* ⊙ *Daily 8–noon and 2:30–sunset.*

A little way beyond the church of Santa Chiara, along Via Borgo **17** Aretino, the walls of Assisi are cut through by the **Porta Nuova** gate. From the Porta Nuova, it is a walk of approximately 1 kilometer (½ **18** mile) to reach the church of **San Damiano.** It was here that the crucifix spoke to Saint Francis, saying *"Vade, Francisce, et repara domum meam"* ("Go, Francis, and repair my house"). It was also in this church, pleasantly situated in an olive grove, that Saint Francis brought Saint Clare into the religious life. The church became the first home of her order, and it and its convent, simple and austere, give a far better idea of Saint Francis and his movement than the great basilica. ✉ *Località San Damiano.* ⊙ *Daily 10–12:30 and 2:30–sunset.*

On the outskirts of the town, on the plain near the train station, is the **19** church of **Santa Maria degli Angeli.** It is a Baroque building constructed over the **Porziuncola,** a little chapel restored by Saint Francis. The shrine is much venerated because it was here, in the Transito chapel, then a humble cell, that Saint Francis died. ✉ *Località Santa Maria degli Angeli.* ⊙ *Daily 9–12:30 and 2:30–sunset.*

20 Four kilometers (2½ miles) east of Assisi is the **Hermitage of the Carceri,** a monastery set in dense woodlands on the side of Mt. Subasio. In the caves on the slope of the mountain, Francis and his followers established their first home, to which he returned often during his lifetime to pray and meditate. The church and monastery retain the tranquil contemplative air Saint Francis so prized. From a vantage point within the monastery visitors can take in one of the most beautiful vistas over the Umbrian countryside. True to their Franciscan heritage, the friars here are entirely dependent on alms from visitors. ✉ *Eremo degli Carceri.* ⊙ *Daily 8 AM–sunset.*

OFF THE
BEATEN PATH

CANNARA – A pleasant excursion from Assisi leads to this tiny town; a half-hour walk outside the town are the fields of Pian d'Arca, which legend identifies as the site of Saint Francis's sermon to the birds.

Dining and Lodging

$$ ✕ **Buca di San Francesco.** This central restaurant is Assisi's busiest and most popular. The setting is lovely no matter what the season. In summer you dine outside in a cool green garden; in winter, in the cozy cellars of the restaurant. The food is first-rate, and the *filetto al rubesco* (fillet steak cooked in a hearty red wine) is the specialty of the house. ⊠ *Via Brizi 1*, ☎ *075/812204. Reservations essential. AE, DC, MC, V. Closed Mon. and July.*

$$ ✕ **La Fortezza.** Parts of the walls of this modern restaurant were built by the Romans. The service is personable and the kitchen reliable. A particular standout is *anatra al finocchio selvatico* (duck cooked with wild fennel). La Fortezza also has seven simple but clean guest rooms available. ⊠ *Vicolo della Fortezza 19/b*, ☎ *075/812418. Reservations essential. AE, DC, MC, V. Closed Thurs. Oct.–July, Feb.*

$ ✕ **La Stalla.** A kilometer or two outside the town proper, this onetime stable has been turned into a simple and rustic restaurant. In summer, lunch and dinner are served outside under a delightful trellis shaded with vines and flowers. In keeping with the decor, the food is hearty country cooking. ⊠ *Via Eremo delle Carceri 8*, ☎ *075/812317. Reservations essential. No credit cards. Closed Mon.*

$$$ ⌂ **Hotel Subasio.** This hotel, close to the basilica of Saint Francis, has counted Marlene Dietrich and Charlie Chaplin among its guests. It is housed in a converted monastery and has plenty of atmosphere. Some of the rooms remain a little monastic, but the views, comfortable old-fashioned sitting rooms, flowered terraces, and lovely garden more than make up for the simplicity. Ask for a room with a view of the valley. ⊠ *Via Frate Elia 2*, ☎ *075/812206,* FAX *075/816691. 61 rooms with bath or shower. Restaurant, bar. AE, DC, MC, V.*

$$ ⌂ **Hotel Umbra.** A 16th-century town house is home to this hotel, which
★ is in a tranquil part of the city, an area closed to traffic, near Piazza del Comune. The rooms are arranged as small apartments, each with a tiny living room and terrace. ⊠ *Via degli Archi 6*, ☎ *075/812240,* FAX *075/813653. 32 rooms with bath or shower. Restaurant (closed Tues. and Wed. lunch), bar. Closed mid-Jan.–mid-Mar. and mid-Nov.–mid-Dec. AE, DC, MC, V.*

$$ ⌂ **San Francesco.** This is a centrally located hotel in a renovated 16th-century building. Some of the rooms have a view of the basilica or the valley. ⊠ *Via di San Francesco 48*, ☎ *075/812281,* FAX *075/816237. 44 rooms with bath or shower. Restaurant, bar. AE, DC, MC, V.*

En Route   The drive to Orvieto on S3bis ("bis" means alternative highway) is a pleasant one that cuts south through the center of the region and takes you through Todi, a lovely hill town. Todi has an extraordinary grouping of Gothic palaces and a medieval cathedral in its central Piazza del Popolo. At Todi, change to S448, which connects with the main north–south autostrada (A1).

Numbers in the margin correspond to points of interest on the Umbria and the Marches map.

Orvieto

㉑ *112 km (70 mi) southwest of Assisi, 86 km (53 mi) south of Perugia, 96 km (60 mi) northwest of Rome, 37 km (23 miles) west of Todi, off A1.*

Commanding a dramatic position on a great square rock, **Orvieto,** one of Umbria's greatest cities, is an amazing sight, dominating the countryside for miles in every direction. This natural fort was first settled by the Etruscans, but not even Orvieto's defenses could withstand the might of the Romans, who attacked, sacked, and destroyed the city in

283 BC. From that time, Orvieto has had close ties with Rome. It was solidly Guelph in the Middle Ages, and for several hundred years popes sought refuge in the city, at some times needing protection from their enemies, at times fleeing from the summer heat of Rome.

Orvieto's position on its rock has meant that little new building has ever been done here, giving the town an almost perfect medieval character. The jewel, the centerpiece of Orvieto, is its **Duomo,** set in the wide and airy Piazza del Duomo. The church, built to commemorate the Miracle of Bolsena, was started in 1290 and received the attention of some of the greatest architects and sculptors of the time. It was further embellished inside by great Renaissance artists. The facade is a prodigious work, covered with carvings and mosaics, the latter intricately ornamenting practically every pillar and post and also used in large representations of religious scenes (many of these were restored or redone in the 18th and 19th centuries). The bas-reliefs on the lower parts of the pillars were carved by Maitani, one of the original architects of the building, and show scenes from the Old Testament and some particularly gruesome renderings of the Last Judgment and Hell, as well as a more tranquil Paradise. (They have been covered with Plexiglas following some vandalizing in the 1960s.)

The vast interior of the cathedral is famous chiefly for the frescoes in the **Cappella Nuova** (the last chapel on the right, nearest the high altar). The earliest works here are above the altar and are by Fra Angelico. They show Christ in Glory and the prophets. The major works in the chapel, however, are by Luca Signorelli and show a very graphic Last Judgment. The walls seem to be filled with muscular, writhing figures, and most critics draw a direct connection between these figures and the later Last Judgment of Michelangelo on the wall of the Sistine Chapel. Leonardo da Vinci, however, was less than impressed. He said that the figures, with their rippling muscles, reminded him of sacks "stuffed full of nuts."

Across the nave of the cathedral from the Cappella Nuova is the **Cappella del Corporale.** It houses the relics of the Miracle of Bolsena, the raison d'être for the Duomo. A priest in the nearby town of Bolsena suddenly found himself assailed by doubts about the transubstantiation—he could not bring himself to believe that the body of Christ was contained in the consecrated communion host. His doubts were put to rest, however, when a wafer he had just blessed suddenly started to drip blood. Drops of blood fell onto the linen covering the altar, and this cloth and the host itself are the principal relics of the miracle. They are contained in a sumptuous gold-and-enamel reliquary on the altar of this chapel and are displayed on the Feast of Corpus Christi and at Easter. ⊠ *Piazza Duomo.* ☉ *Daily 7–1 and 3–sunset.*

To the right of the Duomo is the medieval **Palazzo dei Papi,** once the summer residence of popes, which contains the Archaeological Museum. ▨ *4,000 lire.* ☉ *May–Oct., Mon.–Sat. 9–1:30 and 3–7, Sun. 9–1; Nov.–Apr., Mon.–Sat. 9–1:30 and 2:30–6, Sun. 9–1.*

NEED A
BREAK?

Orvieto is known for its wines, particularly the whites. Some of the finest wines in Umbria are produced here (Signorelli, when painting the Duomo, asked that part of his contract be paid in wine), and the rock on which the town sits is honeycombed with caves used to ferment the Trebbiano grapes that are used in making Orvieto vintages. Taking a glass of wine, therefore, at the **wine cellar** at No. 2, Piazza del Duomo, is as much a cultural experience as a refreshment stop. You'll find a good selection of sandwiches and snacks there as well.

Dining and Lodging

$$ ✕ **Le Grotte del Funaro.** This restaurant has an extraordinary location,
★ deep in a series of caves within the volcanic rock beneath Orvieto. Once
you have negotiated the steep steps, typical Umbrian specialties, like
tagliatelle *al vino rosso* (with red wine sauce) and grilled beef with truf-
fles, await. Sample the fine Orvieto wines, either the whites or the lesser-
known reds. ✉ *Via Ripa Serancia 41,* ☎ *0763/43276. Reservations
essential. Sept.–May. AE, DC, MC, V. Closed Mon.*

$$ ✕ **Maurizio.** In the heart of Orvieto, just opposite the cathedral, this
★ warm and welcoming restaurant gets its share of tourists and has a local
clientele as well. The decor is unusual, with wood sculptures by Orvieto craftsman Michelangeli. The menu offers hearty soups and homemade pastas such as *tronchetti* (a pasta roll with spinach and ricotta
filling). ✉ *Via del Duomo 78,* ☎ *0763/41114. Reservations essential
in summer. AE, MC, V. Closed Tues. and 3 wks in Jan.*

$$$ 🏨 **Hotel La Badia.** This is one of the best-known country hotels in Um-
bria. The 700-year-old building, a former monastery, is set in rolling
parkland that provides wonderful views of the valley and the town of
Orvieto in the distance. Facilities include a swimming pool and sev-
eral tennis courts. The rooms are well appointed. ✉ *Località La Badia,
8.5 km (3½ mi) south of Orvieto,* ☎ *0763/90359,* ℻ *0763/92796. 26
rooms with bath or shower. Restaurant, bar, pool, tennis courts, meet-
ing rooms. Closed Jan.–Feb. AE, MC, V.*

$$$ 🏨 **Hotel Maitani.** The most deluxe hotel in the town of Orvieto itself,
the Hotel Maitani is also centrally located. It is set in a 17th-century
Baroque palazzo with a garden and a terrace with panoramic views
but no restaurant. The rooms are old-fashioned but comfortable. ✉
Via Maitani 5, ☎ *0763/42011,* ℻ *0763/42012. 40 rooms with bath
or shower. Bar, air-conditioning. AE, DC, MC, V.*

$$–$$$ 🏨 **Grand Hotel Reale.** The best feature of this hotel is its location in
the center of Orvieto, across a square that hosts a lively market. Facing the impressive Gothic-Romanesque Palazzo del Popolo, rooms are
spacious and adequately furnished, if somewhat old-fashioned. ✉ *Piazza del Popolo 25,* ☎ *0763/341247,* ℻ *0763/341247. 32 rooms
with bath or shower. Restaurant, bar. MC, V.*

$$–$$$ 🏨 **Villa Bellago.** This recently opened hotel lies outside the village of
Baschi, 12 kilometers (7½ miles) south of Orvieto. In a tranquil setting on a spit of land overlooking Lake Corbara, three farmhouses have
been completely overhauled to include well-lighted and spacious guest
rooms, a pool, a fully equipped gym, and a fine restaurant specializing in imaginatively prepared Umbrian and Tuscan dishes. Fresh fish
is always on the menu. ✉ *Baschi, 7½ km (4½ mi) south of Orvieto on
S448,* ☎ *0744/950521,* ℻ *0744/950524. 12 rooms with bath. Restaurant (closed Tues.), bar, tennis court. AE, DC, MC, V.*

$$ 🏨 **Virgilio.** The modest Hotel Virgilio is situated right in Piazza del
Duomo, and the rooms with views of the cathedral are wonderful. The
rooms are small but well furnished. ✉ *Piazza del Duomo 5,* ☎
0763/41882, ℻ *0763/43797. 13 rooms with bath or shower. Bar.
MC, V.*

Shopping

Orvieto is a center of **woodworking,** particularly fine inlays and ve-
neers. The Corso Cavour has a number of artisan shops specializing
in woodwork, the best known being the studio of the Michelangeli fam-
ily, which is crammed with a variety of imaginatively designed objects
ranging in size from a giant *armadio* (wardrobe) to a simple wooden
spoon.

Minor arts, such as **embroidery** and **lace making,** flourish in Orvieto as well. One of the best shops for *merletto* (lace) is Duranti (✉ Via del Duomo 10).

Excellent **Orvieto wines** are justly prized throughout Italy and in foreign countries. The whites are fruity, with a tart aftertaste, and are made from the region's Trebbiano grapes. Orvieto also produces its own version of the Tuscan dessert wine *vin santo*. It is darker than its Tuscan cousin and is aged five years before bottling.

En Route The countryside southeast of Orvieto, as you head toward the town of Narni, is rarely included in most travel itineraries—a pity, since the scenery and rustic charm of the small towns on the route make this one of the most pleasant parts of Umbria. It is also a manageable chunk of country that can be seen in a half day's touring by car.

UMBRIA A TO Z

Arriving and Departing

By Bus
Perugia and Orvieto are served by private bus services, leaving from Rome and Florence.

By Car
On the western edge of the region is the Umbrian section of the Autostrada del Sole (A1), the principal north–south highway in Italy. It links Florence and Rome with the important Umbrian town of Orvieto and passes near Todi and Terni. The S3 intersects with A1 and leads on to Assisi and Urbino. The Adriatica superhighway (A14) runs north–south along the coast, linking the Marches to Bologna and Venice.

By Train
The main rail line from Rome to Ancona passes through Narni, Terni, Spoleto, and Foligno. Travel time from Rome to Spoleto is a little less than 90 minutes on intercity trains. The main Rome–Florence line stops at Orvieto, and, with a change of trains at the small town of Terontola, one can travel by rail from Rome or Florence to Perugia and Assisi.

Getting Around

By Bus
There is good local bus service between all the major and minor towns of Umbria. Some of the routes in rural areas, especially in the Marches, are designed to serve as many destinations as possible and are, therefore, quite roundabout and slow. Schedules often change, so consult with local tourist offices before setting out.

By Car
Umbria has an excellent and modern road network. Central Umbria is served by a major highway, S75bis, which passes along the shore of Lake Trasimeno and ends in Perugia, the principal city of the region. Assisi, the most visited town in the region, is well served by the modern highway S75, which connects to S3 and 3bis, which cover the heart of the region. Major inland routes connect coastal A14 to large towns in the Marches, including Urbino, Jesi, Macerata, and Ascoli Piceno, but inland secondary roads in mountain areas can be tortuous and narrow.

By Train

Branch lines link the central rail hub, Ancona, with the inland towns of Fabriano and Ascoli Piceno. In Umbria, a small, privately owned railway runs from Città di Castello in the north to Terni in the south.

Contacts and Resources

Emergencies

Police: Perugia (✉ Piazza dei Partigiani, ☎ 113); **Assisi** (✉ Piazza Matteotti 3, ☎ 075/812239); **Spoleto** (✉ Viale Trento e Trieste, ☎ 0743/40324); **Orvieto** (✉ Piazza Cahen, ☎ 0763/342476).

Visitor Information

Ancona (✉ Via Thaon De Revel 4, ☎ 071/33249; railway station, Piazza Fratelli Rosselli, ☎ 071/41703). **Ascoli Piceno** (✉ Piazza del Popolo, ☎ 0736/257288). **Assisi** (✉ Piazza del Comune 12, ☎ 075/812534). **Gubbio** (✉ Piazza Oderisi 6, ☎ 075/922–0693). **Loreto** (✉ Via Solari 3, ☎ 071/977139). **Orvieto** (✉ Piazza del Duomo, ☎ 0763/341772). **Perugia:** Umbria's regional tourist office (✉ Corso Vannucci 30, ☎ 075/5041); Perugia's city tourist office (✉ Piazza IV Novembre 3, ☎ 075/572–3327). **Spoleto** (✉ Piazza della Libertà 7, ☎ 0743/220311). **Urbino** (✉ Piazza Duca Federico 35, ☎ 0722/2441).

13 Campania

Naples, Pompeii, and the Amalfi Drive

Emperors, kings, and artists have all
made Campania's sea-wreathed resorts
and starlit isles their abodes for more
than 2,000 years. And well they might,
for this region is a compressed realm of
undiluted beauty. Naples—the most
operatic of cities—rules over its
breathtaking bay. Nearby, ancient
Romans once led carefree lives at
Pompeii just as today's travelers now
soak up the 24-karat sun on Capri.
Beyond lie Sorrento, Positano, Amalfi,
and Ravello. The locals dare you to
find lovelier towns, even in your
imagination.

CAMPANIA IS A REGION OF NAMES to conjure with—
Capri, Sorrento, Pompeii, Paestum—names evok-
ing visions of cliff-shaded coves, sun-dappled waters,
and mighty ruins. And Naples, a tumultuous, animated city, the very
heart of Campania, stands guard over these treasures.

Updated by
Robert
Andrews

Campania stretches south in flat coastal plains and low mountains from
Baia Domizia, Capua, and Caserta to Naples and Pompeii on the mag-
nificent bay; past Capri and Ischia; along the rocky coast to Sorrento,
Amalfi, and Salerno; and farther still past the Cilento promontory to
Sapri and the Calabria border. Inland lie the bleak fringes of the Apen-
nines and the rolling countryside around Benevento.

On each side of Naples the earth fumes and grumbles, reminding natives and visitors alike that all this beauty was born of cataclysm. Toward Sorrento, Vesuvius smolders sleepily over the ruins of Herculaneum
and Pompeii, while north of Naples, beyond Posillipo, the craters of
the Solfatara spew steaming gases. And nearby are the dark, deep waters of Lake Averno, legendary entrance to Hades.

With these reminders of death and destruction so close at hand, it's no
wonder that the southerner in general, and the Neapolitan in particular, chooses to take no chances, plunging enthusiastically into the task
of living each moment to its fullest.

Campania was probably settled by the ancient Phoenicians, Cretans, and
Greeks. Traces of their presence here date from approximately 1000 BC,
some 300 years before the legendary founding of Rome. Herculaneum
is said to have been established by Hercules himself, and as excavation
of this once-great city—Greek and later Roman—progresses, further light
will be thrown on the history of the whole Campania region.

The origin of Naples, once called Parthenope and later Neapolis, pre-
sumably can be traced to what are now the ruins of Cumae nearby,
which legend tells us was already in existence in 800 BC. Here, in a dark
vaulted chamber, the Cumaean Sybil rendered her oracles. Greek civilization flourished for hundreds of years all along this coastline, but
there was nothing in the way of centralized government until centuries
later, when the Roman Empire, uniting all Italy for the first time,
surged southward and, with little opposition, absorbed the Greek
colonies. The Romans were quick to appreciate the sybaritic possibilities of such a lovely land, and it was in this region that the wealthy
of the empire built their palatial country residences. Generally, the peace
of Campania was undisturbed during these centuries of Roman rule.

Naples and Campania, with the rest of Italy, decayed with the Roman
Empire and collapsed into the abyss of the Middle Ages. Naples itself
regained some importance under the rule of the Angevins in the latter
part of the 13th century and continued its progress in the 1440s under
Aragonese rule. The nobles who served under the Spanish viceroys in
the 16th and 17th centuries, when their harsh rule made all Italy quail,
enjoyed their pleasures, and taverns and gaming houses thrived, even
as Spain milked the area with its taxes.

After a short-lived Austrian occupation, Naples—Napoli in Italian—
became the capital of the Kingdom of the Two Sicilies, which the Bourbon kings established in 1738. Their rule was generally benevolent, as
far as Campania was concerned, and their support of the papal authority
in Rome was an important factor in the development of the rest of Italy.
Their rule was important artistically, too, for not only did it contribute

greatly to the architectural beauty of the region, but it attracted great musicians, artists, and writers, who were only too willing to enjoy the easy life of court in such magnificent natural surroundings.

Finally, Giuseppe Garibaldi launched his famous expedition, and in 1860 Naples was united with the rest of Italy.

Times were relatively tranquil through the years that followed—with tourists of one nation or another thronging to Capri, to Sorrento, to Amalfi, and, of course, to Naples—until World War II. Allied bombings did considerable damage in Naples and the bay area. At the fall of the fascist government, the sorely tried Neapolitans rose up against Nazi occupation troops and in four days of street fighting drove them out of the city. A monument was raised to the *scugnizzo* (the typical Neapolitan street urchin) celebrating the youngsters who participated in the battle.

The war ended. Artists, tourists, writers, and ordinary lovers of beauty began to flow again into the Campania region that one ancient writer called "most blest by the Gods, most beloved by man." As the years have gone by, some parts gained increased attention from knowing visitors, while others lost the cachet they once had. The balance is maintained, with a steady trend toward more and more tourist development.

Pleasures and Pastimes

Beaches

The waters of the Bay of Naples are notoriously polluted. The waters around Capri and some, but not all, of Ischia's beaches, offer clean swimming. Pollution is intermittent along the Amalfi Coast, where the deep waters are generally clean. Beaches in the Salerno area are best avoided; the water gets cleaner the farther south you go.

Dining

Campania's cuisine is simple and relies heavily on the bounty of the region's fertile farmland. Its tomatoes are exported all over the world, but to try them here is a new experience. Even during the winter you can find tomato sauce made with small sun-dried tomatoes plucked from bright red strands that you can see hanging outdoors on kitchen balconies. Pasta is a staple here, and spaghetti *al pomodoro* (with tomato sauce) and spaghetti *alle vongole* (with clam sauce, either white or red, depending on the cook's whims) appear on most menus.

This is the homeland of pizza, served mainly in its simpler versions: *alla napoletana* (with anchovies); *alla margherita* (with tomato and mozzarella); and marinara (with tomato, garlic, and oregano). Locally produced mozzarella is used in many dishes; one of the most gratifying on a hot day is *insalata caprese* (with mozzarella, tomatoes, and basil). *Melanzane* (eggplant) and even zucchini are served parmigiana (fried and layered with tomato sauce and mozzarella). Meat may be served *alla pizzaiola* (cooked in a tomato-and-garlic sauce). Fish and seafood in general can be expensive, though fried calamari and *totani* (cuttlefish) are usually reasonably priced. Among the region's wines, Gragnano, Falerno, Lacrima Cristi, and Greco di Tufo are fine whites. Ischia and Ravello also produce good white wine. Campania's best-known reds are Aglianico, Taurasi, and the red version of Falerno.

Restaurant prices in the region are generally a little lower than in Rome and northern Italy, though Capri restaurants can be very expensive. On the islands, the Sorrento peninsula, and the Amalfi Coast, restaurants may be open every day of the week during the season, but may close for long periods in the winter.

CATEGORY	COST*
$$$$	over 85,000 lire
$$$	60,000–85,000 lire
$$	25,000–60,000 lire
$	under 25,000 lire

*per person, including house wine, service, and tax

Lodging

Although Capri, Ischia, Sorrento, and the Amalfi Coast offer generally fine accommodations in all categories, good accommodations in Naples are scarce, so reserve well in advance. High-season rates apply at all coastal resorts in July and August. These rates extend from April or May through September at Sorrento and Amalfi Coast resorts, where Christmas and Easter also draw crowds and command top rates. Whereas coastal resorts elsewhere close up tight from fall to spring, at least some hotels and restaurants are open in Sorrento and on the Amalfi Coast year-round. It's always a good idea to book ahead, and it's imperative in high season. Campania hotel rates are generally lower than those in major tourist cities to the north, but rates in Capri's top hotels are at premium levels for Italy. On the other hand, even in Capri and especially along the Amalfi Coast, you can find charming little hotels with attractive rooms and wonderful views at very reasonable rates; just don't expect to find vacancies in August. During the summer, hotels on the coast almost always require that you take half board if they serve meals. Local tourist information offices will help you find accommodations.

CATEGORY	COST*
$$$$	over 300,000 lire
$$$	160,000–300,000 lire
$$	100,000–160,000 lire
$	under 100,000 lire

*All prices are for a standard double room for two, including service and 9% tax (19% for luxury establishments).

Nightlife

In these parts, as elsewhere in southern Italy, nightlife usually takes the form of outdoor living in cafés and restaurants with views of the passing parade. Piazzas are lively until late in fair weather, especially in resort towns on the islands and on the Sorrento peninsula. Capri's Piazzetta is a classic example. Entertainment in the coastal resorts is mainly seasonal.

Most of the best bars have the attraction of a good location (overlooking the Bay of Naples, for example) or comfortable setting; there is sometimes music and dancing, but these establishments cannot truly be called nightclubs.

Exploring Campania

Most of the areas outlined in the following pages are clustered around the Bay of Naples—including the city itself and its satellite islands, Capri and Ischia, and the archaeological sites of Pompeii, Herculaneum and the Phlegrean Fields at the northern end of the Bay. At the southern end, Sorrento also lies within this charmed circle, and itself lies within easy distance of Positano, Amalfi and the pleasures of the Amalfi coast. Further distant, Paestum offers more classical marvels, while inland, Caserta and Benevento offer in turn a Bourbon palace and more majestic Roman remains.

Campania provides enough of both cultural stimulation and more basic relaxation to allow you a good deal of flexibility on choosing how to spend your time. Pace yourself, spend a little time planning, especially with only a limited number of days at your disposal, and even the brisk tempo of Naples is manageable, with peace and tranquility only a hydrofoil ride away on Ischia and Capri.

Great Itineraries

If art and antiquity are high on your list, and if you have only a few days to spend in the area, make Naples your base. Few fall in love with Naples at first sight, and many complain about its obvious flaws: urban decay and delinquency. But practically everyone who takes the time and trouble to discover its artistic riches and appreciate its vivacious atmosphere considers it worth the effort. Naples is near the most famous classical ruins, and you should dedicate at least a morning or afternoon to Pompeii or Herculaneum. And as the regional capital, it is connected by direct rail, road, and sea routes to nearly all the sights mentioned in this chapter.

With more time, or if you're looking for dramatic scenery and want to enjoy it at a relaxed pace, plan to spend time either in touristy Sorrento, on the islands of Capri and Ischia, or on the beautiful Amalfi Coast. Be warned, though: These areas become quite crowded in July and August, when throngs of vacationing Italians arrive.

Numbers in the text correspond to numbers in the margin and on the Campania, Naples, and Pompeii maps.

IF YOU HAVE 3 DAYS

In ☵ **Naples** ①–⑰ itself, a visit to the **Museo Archeologico** ⑧ is an essential preparation for an expedition to **Herculaneum** ㉑ and **Pompeii** ㉓–㊵, either of which is an indispensable sight for anyone visiting Campania. The museum could also be seen after your excursion, and apart from containing numerous finds from these sites holds plenty of other art treasures from the same era–spend at least half a day here. The islands of ☵ **Ischia** ㊸ and ☵ **Capri** ㊹ can also be approached from Naples, and make an ideal antidote to the city's noise. If you decide not to stay here, aim to spend a quiet day on one of the islands, perhaps returning to Naples after a stroll and/or meal in the evening. It is worth spending at least one night out of Naples, and a good alternative to the islands would be ☵ **Sorrento** ㊺ an easy hydrofoil ride away, and a good base to tour the nearby **Amalfi Coast,** ㊺–㊿, where you could visit three of the small towns —**Positano** ㊻, **Amalfi** ㊼, and **Vietri sul Mare** ㊾, for instance—on a third day's excursion.

IF YOU HAVE 5 DAYS

You could take in more than just one of the classical sights with more time, and a visit to the Greek temples of **Paestum** ㊶ is highly recommended for a glimpse at some of Magna Graecia's most stunning relics. You might also venture north to **Caserta** ㊶ where the Royal Palace will occupy a morning's wander around the apartments and an afternoon's stroll around the grounds, ideally with a meal at one of the town's trattorias sandwiched in between. Back in the Bay of Naples, spend your fourth and fifth days exploring ☵ **Ischia** ㊸ and ☵ **Sorrento** ㊺, both undemanding holiday resorts with plenty of natural beauty.

IF YOU HAVE 7 DAYS

A week in Campania will allow you to discover some of the more esoteric pleasures that Naples has to offer. Apart from the sheer vibrancy of its shopping streets and alleys, and the glorious views over the waterfront, **Naples** ①–⑰ has plenty of diversions within its tight mesh of streets, and you should make time for visiting some of its many famous churches—the **Duomo** ⑪, of course, but also **Santa Chiara** ⑩, **Santa Maria Donnaregina** ⑫, and the Cappella Sansevero, with its

Campania

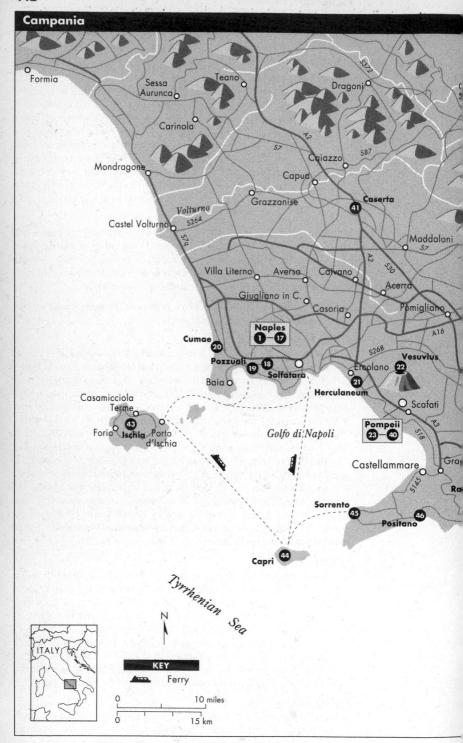

Formia

Sessa
Aurunca

Teano

Dragoni

Carinola

Mondragone

Caiazzo

Capua

Grazzanise

Caserta

Volturno

41

Castel Volturno

Maddaloni

Villa Literno

Aversa

Caivano

Acerra

Giugliano in C.

Casoria

Pomigliano

Naples
1 — 17

Cumae
20

Vesuvius
22

Pozzuoli
19 18

Ercolano

21

Solfatara

Baia

Herculaneum

Scafati

Casamicciola
Terme

Pompeii
23 — 40

Forio **Ischia** 43 Porto
d'Ischia

Golfo di Napoli

Castellammare

Sorrento
45

Ra

Positano
46

Capri 44

Tyrrhenian Sea

N

ITALY

KEY

Ferry

0 _____ 10 miles

0 _____ 15 km

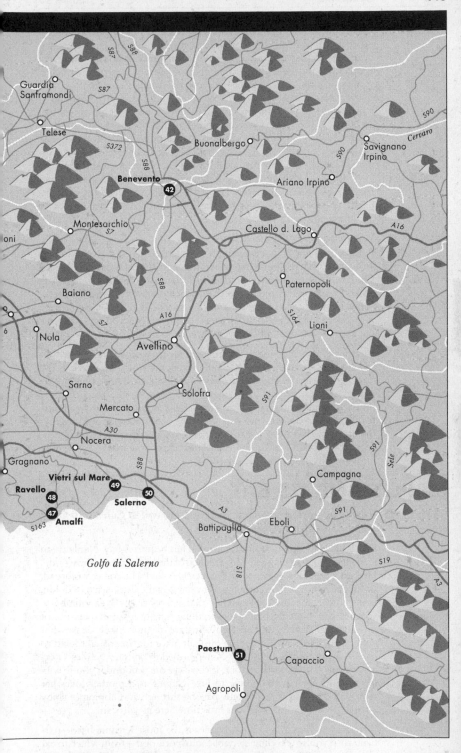

Golfo di Salerno

18th-century sculptures. Don't forget, either, some of the capital's secondary museums, the **Capodimonte** ⑭, for example, housed in another Bourbon royal palace with truly inspiring views. Outside town, head west to the volcanic region of the **Phlegrean Fields** ⑱–⑳, where Roman remains lie within a smoking, smoldering area rich with classical associations. Spend three nights on the Amalfi Coast, making sure to visit inland ☷ **Ravello** ㊽ and pass some time in pretty **Positano** ㊻ which defies any attempt to experience it on an overtight timetable. ☷ **Capri** ㊹, too, deserves a couple of nights to appreciate fully its beauty, easily eclipsing the island's more lurid tourist trappings. The island is rich with secluded coves and beaches, not to mention the famous Blue Grotto. The best walks inland are from Anacapri, and the best views are also out of town, from the Gardens of Augustus and Villa Jovis. You might pass a last day, perhaps en route out of Campania, in **Benevento** ㊷, which holds a well-preserved Roman theater and the renowned Arch of Trajan.

When to Tour Campania

Campania is not at its best in high summer: Naples is a sweltering inferno, the archaeological sites swarm, and the islands and Amalfi Coast resorts are similarly overrun with coaches and bad tempers. Any other time of year would be preferable, including winter, when the temperature rarely falls below the comfort threshold and rain is relatively rare. Swimming is possible all year round, though you will only see the hardiest bathers out between October and May.

Summer is also the worst time for ascents to Vesuvius: the best visibility occurs around spring and fall. Watch the clock, however, as the days get shorter: Excursions to Vesuvius, Pompeii, Ercolano, and the islands all require some traveling, and it's easy to get caught out by the dark. At most archaeological sites visitors are rounded up two hours before sunset, so the earlier you arrive the better. Remember, too, that the majority of hotels, restaurants, and other tourist facilities in Sorrento, the Amalfi Coast, and the islands close down from November until around Easter, drastically reducing choice.

NAPLES AND ITS BAY

❶ *8 km (5 mi) east of Solfatara, 16 km (10 mi) east of Cumae, 10 km (6 mi) north of Herculaneum.*

"Built like a great amphitheater around her beautiful bay, Naples is an eternally unfolding play acted by a million of the best actors in the world," Herbert Kubly observes in his *American in Italy.* "The comedy is broad, the tragedy violent. The curtain never rings down." Is it a sense of doom, living in the shadow of Vesuvius, that makes many Neapolitans so volatile, so seemingly blind to everything but the pain or pleasure of the moment? Poverty and overcrowding are the more likely causes, but whatever the reason, Naples is a difficult place for the casual tourist to like. The Committee of Ninety-Nine, formed to counter Naples's negative image, has its work cut out. If you have the time and if you're willing to work at it, you'll come to love Naples as a mother loves her reprobate son; but if you're only passing through and hoping to enjoy a hassle-free vacation, spend as little time here as you can.

Why visit Naples at all? First, Naples is the most sensible base—particularly if you're traveling by public transportation—from which to explore Pompeii, Herculaneum, Vesuvius, and the Phlegrean Fields. Second, it's the home of the Museo Archeologico Nazionale (National Archaeological Museum). The most important finds from Pompeii and Herculaneum are on display here—everything from sculpture to carbonized fruit—and seeing them will add to the pleasure of your trip to Pompeii and Herculaneum. Since the museum may be closed in the afternoon, depending on the time of year, spend the morning here and the afternoon visiting either the Phlegrean Fields or Herculaneum and Vesuvius. Spend the night back in Naples—perhaps at the world-famous San Carlo Opera House—and the following morning, set out for Pompeii.

To visit Naples, you need a good sense of humor and a firm grip on your pocketbook and camera. Better still, leave all your valuables, including passport, in the hotel safe. You'll probably be doing a lot of walking, for buses are crowded and taxis get stalled in traffic. If you come to Naples by car, park it in a garage as fast as you can, agree on the cost in advance, and then forget it for the duration of your stay (otherwise, window smashing and theft are constant risks). Take the Metropolitana (the city's subway system) to distant destinations and use the funiculars to get up and down the hills. (Bus or funicular fares are 1,200 lire, valid for 90 minutes; 4,000 lire buys a ticket for the whole day. Subway tickets cost 1,500 lire each.)

The sights on this tour that lie outside the city limits are easy to reach from Naples; they can be treated as outings on their own.

② A good place to start exploring is the **Castel Nuovo,** on Piazza Municipio, facing the harbor. Also known as the Maschio Angioino, this massive fortress was built by the Angevins (related to the French monarchy) in the 13th century and completely rebuilt by the Aragonese rulers (descendants of an illegitimate branch of Spain's ruling line) who succeeded them. The decorative marble triumphal arch that forms the entrance was erected during the Renaissance in honor of King Alfonso I of Aragón, and its rich bas-reliefs are credited to Francesco Laurana. Set incongruously into the castle's heavy stone walls, the arch is one of the finest works of its kind. Some rooms in the castle have recently been opened to the public and contain sculptures and frescoes from the 14th and 15th centuries. ⊠ *Castel Nuovo, Piazza Municipio.* ☎ *6,000 lire.* ☉ *Weekdays 9–7, Sat. 9–1:30.*

On the harbor behind the Castel Nuovo, the **Molo Beverello** pier is a hive of activity from which boats and hydrofoils leave for Sorrento and the islands.

OFF THE BEATEN PATH **SEAFRONT TOURS –** Evening boat tours take in the waterfront of Naples, from the port at Mergellina to Cape Posillipo, with a view of Castel dell'Ovo (☞ below) on the way back. ☎ *081/661434.* ☎ *10,000 lire.* ☉ July–Sept., daily 6, 7, and 8 PM.

---

③ The **Teatro San Carlo** is the focus for high culture in Naples. Lying between Piazza Municipio and the traffic-free Piazza Plebiscito, the large 18th-century theater was first built in 1737—40 years earlier than Milan's La Scala—though destroyed by fire and rebuilt in 1816. You can visit the impressive interior, decorated in the white-and-gilt stucco of the neoclassical era, as part of a guided group, and visitors are sometimes allowed in during morning rehearsals. ⊠ *Via San Carlo.*

NEED A BREAK? Across from the Teatro San Carlo towers the imposing entrance to the glass-roofed turn-of-the-century **Galleria Umberto,** a shopping arcade where you can sit at one of several cafés and watch the vivacious Neapolitans as they go about their business.

---

④ Dominating Piazza del Plebiscito, the huge **Palazzo Reale** (Royal Palace) dates from the early 1600s. It was renovated and redecorated by successive rulers, including Napoléon's sister Caroline and her ill-

Naples

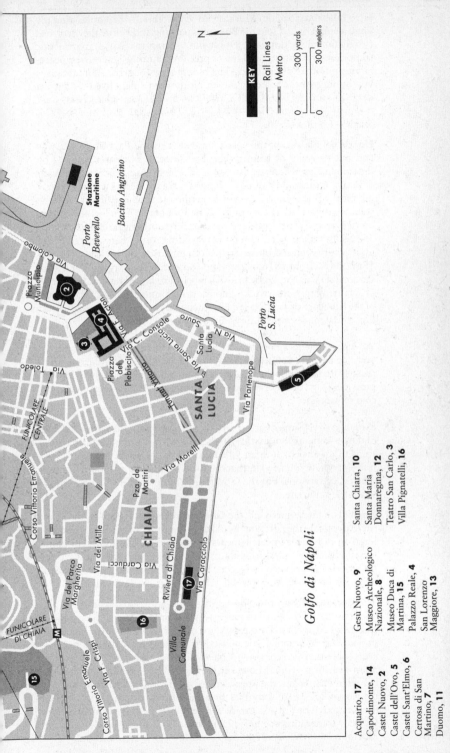

Golfo di Nápoli

Acquario, **17**
Capodimonte, **14**
Castel Nuovo, **2**
Castel dell'Ovo, **5**
Castel Sant'Elmo, **6**
Certosa di San
Martino, **7**
Duomo, **11**

Gesù Nuovo, **9**
Museo Archeologico
Nazionale, **8**
Museo Duca di
Martina, **15**
Palazzo Reale, **4**
San Lorenzo
Maggiore, **13**

Santa Chiara, **10**
Santa Maria
Donnaregina, **12**
Teatro San Carlo, **3**
Villa Pignatelli, **16**

KEY
—— Rail Lines
⎯⎯ Metro

0 ⊢⎯⎯⎯⊣ 300 yards
0 ⊢⎯⎯⎯⊣ 300 meters

fated husband, Joachim Murat, who reigned briefly in Naples after the French emperor had sent the Bourbons packing and before they returned to reclaim their kingdom. Don't miss seeing the royal apartments, sumptuously furnished and full of precious paintings, tapestries, porcelains, and other objets d'art. The monumental marble staircase gives you an idea of the scale on which Neapolitan rulers lived. ⊠ *Piazza del Plebiscito,* ☎ *081/413888.* ▣ *8,000 lire.* ☉ *Apr.–Oct., Tues.–Sun. 9–7:30; Nov.–Mar., Tues.–Wed. 9–2, Thurs.–Sat. 9–2 and 4–7:30, Sun. 9–1 and 4–7:30.*

Piazza del Plebiscito, the vast square next to the Palazzo Reale, was laid out by order of Murat, whose architect was clearly inspired by the colonnades of St. Peter's in Rome. The large church of San Francesco di Paola in the middle of the colonnades was added as a thanks offering for the Bourbon restoration by Ferdinand I, whose titles reflect the somewhat garbled history of the Kingdom of the Two Sicilies—made up of Naples (which included most of the southern Italian mainland) and Sicily, which were united in the Middle Ages, then separated and unofficially reunited under Spanish domination during the 16th and 17th centuries. In 1816, with Napoléon out of the way on St. Helena, Ferdinand IV of Naples, who also happened to be Ferdinand III of Sicily, officially merged the two kingdoms, proclaiming himself Ferdinand I of the Kingdom of Two Sicilies. His reactionary and repressive rule earned him a few more colorful titles among his rebellious subjects.

NEED A BREAK?	Walking up the fashionable Via Chiaia, behind Piazza del Plebiscito, you'll come upon **Caflisch** (⊠ Via Chiaia 144), a historic café that has recently transferred to these new premises, but continues its tradition of producing high-quality chocolates and pastries to nibble over a cappuccino or espresso.

⑤ Dangling over Naples harbor on a thin promontory, the **Castel dell'Ovo** makes a familiar landmark. This 12th-century fortress built over the ruins of an ancient Roman villa commands a view of the whole harbor—proof, if you need it, that the Romans knew a premium location when they saw one. For the same reason, some of the city's top hotels share the same site.

⑥ Perched on the Vómero hill, the **Castel Sant'Elmo** was built by the Spanish to dominate the port and the old city. The Spanish garrison was quartered in now-decaying tenements aligned in a tight-knit grid along incredibly narrow alleys; this notorious slum district is still known as the Quartieri. The area can be reached by way of the funicular from Piazza Montesanto up the Vomero Hill. ▣ *4,000 lire,* ☉ *Tues.–Sun. 9–2.*

♻ ⑦ The **Certosa di San Martino** enjoys a magnificent position on the Vómero hill. A Carthusian monastery restored in the 17th century in exuberant Neapolitan Baroque style, it now houses the **Museo Nazionale di San Martino,** an eclectic collection of ships' models, antique *presepi* (Christmas crèches), and Neapolitan landscape paintings. The main reason to come, however, is to see the splendidly decorated church and annexes, the pretty garden, and the view from the balcony off Room 25. There's another fine view from the square in front of the Certosa. The Certosa can be reached by way of the funicular from Piazza Montesanto up the Vómero hill. ⊠ *Museo Nazionale di San Martino,* ☎ *081/578–1769.* ▣ *8,000 lire.* ☉ *Tues.–Sun. 9–2.*

★ ♻ ⑧ The **Museo Archeologico Nazionale** (National Archeological Museum) is a major attraction for anyone interested in antiquity and for those planning to visit Pompeii or Herculaneum. The huge red building, a cavalry barracks in the 16th century, is dusty and unkempt, but it holds one of the world's great collections of Greek and Roman antiquities, including such extraordinary sculptures as the *Hercules Farnese,* an exquisite Aphrodite attributed to the 4th-century BC Greek sculptor Praxiteles, and an equestrian statue of Roman Emperor Nerva. Vividly colored mosaics and countless artistic and household objects from Pompeii and Herculaneum provide insight into the life and art of ancient Rome. The most recent addition to the treasures on permanent display is an entire fresco sequence—more than 300 feet wide—discovered in 1765 in perfect condition at the Temple of Isis in Pompeii. Invest in an up-to-date printed museum guide, because exhibits are poorly labeled. ⊠ *Piazza Museo,* ☎ *081/440166.* ☒ *12,000 lire.* ☉ *Aug.–Sept., Mon.–Sat. 9–7, Sun. 9–1; Oct.–July, Mon.–Sat. 9–2, Sun. 9–1.*

❾ The oddly faceted stone facade of the church of **Gesù Nuovo** was designed as part of a palace, but plans were changed as construction progressed, and it became the front of an elaborately decorated Baroque church. ⊠ *Piazza Gesù Nuovo.* ☒ *Free.* ☉ *Daily 7–noon and 4–7 (until 6 in winter).*

❿ The monastery church of **Santa Chiara** is a Neapolitan landmark and the subject of a famous old song. It was built in the 1300s in Provençal Gothic style, and it's best known for the quiet charm of its cloister garden, with columns and benches sheathed in 18th-century ceramic tiles painted with delicate floral motifs and vivid landscapes. The entrance is off the courtyard at the left of the church. ⊠ *Piazza Gesù Nuovo.* ☒ *Free.* ☉ *Daily 7–noon and 4–7 (until 6 in winter).*

Sooner or later you'll wind up at Via Toledo (also known as Via Roma), one of the busiest commercial arteries in this perennially congested city. However, don't avoid dipping into this parade of shops and coffee bars where plump pastries are temptingly arranged. Students from the nearby music conservatory hang out in **Piazza Dante,** the semicircular hub of an area rich in inexpensive trattorias and pizzerias.

Nowhere embodies the spirit of back-streets Naples better than the arrow-straight **Spaccanapoli,** a street divided into tracts bearing several names. It runs through the heart of the old city (*spacca* means "cut through") from west to east, beginning with Via Scura just west of Via Toledo and ending with Via Vicaria Vecchia just east of Via del Duomo, retracing one of the main arteries of the Greek, and later Roman, settlement. The tourist information office at **Piazza del Gesù** (☞ Contacts and Resources *in* Campania A to Z, *below*) can provide pamphlets with itineraries tracing the city's development in ancient, medieval, and modern times.

The section of Spaccanapoli known as **Via Benedetto Croce** was named in honor of the illustrious philosopher who was born here in 1866, in the building at No. 12. Continue past peeling palaces, dark workshops where artisans ply their trades, and many churches and street shrines. Where the street changes to **Via San Biagio dei Librai,** the shops stage a special fair of hand-carved crèche figures during the weeks before Christmas.

⓫ The **Duomo** was established in the 1200s, but the building you see was erected a century later and has since undergone radical changes, especially during the Baroque age. Inside the cathedral, 110 ancient columns salvaged from pagan buildings are set into the piers that support the 350-year-old wooden ceiling. Off the left aisle, you step down into the 4th-century church of Santa Restituta, which was incorporated into the cathedral; though it was redecorated in the late 1600s in the prevalent Baroque style, a few very old mosaics remain in the baptistery. The chapel also gives access to a series of paleochristian rooms dating from the Roman era. ☒ *Baptistery 1,500 lire, chapel 5,000 lire.*

⊙ *Baptistery and archaeological zone Mon.–Sat. 9–noon and 4:30–7, Sun. 9–noon and 5–7.*

On the right aisle of the cathedral, in the **chapel of San Gennaro,** are multicolored marbles and frescoes honoring St. Januarius, miracle-working patron saint of Naples, whose altar and relics are encased in silver. Twice a year—on September 19, his feast day, and on the first Sunday in May, which commemorates the transference of his relics to Naples—his dried blood, contained in two sealed vials, is believed to liquefy during rites in his honor. These dates see the arrival of large numbers of devout Neapolitans offering up prayers in his memory. ⊠ *Via del Duomo.* ⊞ *Free.* ⊙ *Daily 7–noon and 4–7.*

OFF THE
BEATEN PATH

MUSEO FILANGIERI – This Neapolitan museum contains a private collection of arms, armor, furniture, paintings, and fascinating memorabilia. It's housed in the Florentine-style Renaissance Palazzo Cuomo. ⊠ *Via Duomo 288,* ☎ *081/203175.* ⊞ *5,000 lire.* ⊙ *Tues.–Sat. 9–2, Sun. 9–1.*

⑫ One of the most interesting of the city's many churches, **Santa Maria Donnaregina,** lies about 100 yards ahead of the Duomo. It contains the towering Gothic funeral monument of Mary of Hungary, wife of Charles II of Anjou, who is said to have commissioned the frescoes in the church at a cost of 33 ounces of gold. ⊠ *Largo Donnaregina.*

⑬ It is unusual to find the Gothic style in Naples, but it has survived to great effect in the church of **San Lorenzo Maggiore.** Built in the Middle Ages and decorated with 14th-century frescoes, it is supposed to be where the poet Boccaccio first saw the model for his *Fiammetta.* ⊠ *Via Tribunali.*

★ ⑭ No one should leave Naples without having seen **Capodimonte,** the royal palace built by the Bourbons in the 18th century in a vast park that served as the royal hunting preserve and later as the site of the Capodimonte porcelain works that the family established. Allow plenty of time for your visit to the palace; it's packed with works of art. Capodimonte's greatest attraction is the excellent collection of paintings well displayed in the **Galleria Nazionale** on the palace's top floor. Included are works from the 13th to the 18th centuries, including many familiar masterpieces by Dutch and Spanish masters, as well as by the great Italians. At the coffee bar halfway through, be sure to climb the stairs to the roof terrace for a sweeping view of the bay. Then continue through halls hung with dramatic Mannerist works of the 17th and 18th centuries, among them some stunning works by Caravaggio (1573–1610), originally hung in the city's churches. Downstairs are 19th-century Italian paintings and the royal apartments, where numerous portraits provide a close-up of the unmistakable Bourbon features, a challenge to any court painter. You'll also find beautiful antique furniture, most of it on the splashy scale so dear to the Bourbons, and a staggering collection of porcelain and majolica from the various royal residences. ⊠ *Parco di Capodimonte,* ☎ *081/744–1307.* ⊞ *8,000 lire.* ⊙ *Apr.–Oct., Tues.–Sun. 9–7:30; Nov.–Mar., Tues.–Fri. 10–6, Sat. 10–9, Sun. 9–3.*

OFF THE
BEATEN PATH

CATACOMBS OF SAN GENNARO – Many of these catacombs in Naples predate the Christian era by two centuries. They are next to the huge Madre di Buon Consiglio church on Via Capodimonte. The church was inspired by St. Peter's in Rome. The niches and corridors of the catacombs are hung with early Christian paintings. ⊠ *Via Capodimonte.* ⊞ *5,000 lire.* ⊙ *Guided tours daily every 45 min. 9:30–11:45.*

15 The lushly shaded park and the view over Naples are two reasons to take the funicular of Chiaia from Via del Parco Margherita to the **Museo Duca di Martina.** Set on the slopes of the Vómero hill in a park known as Villa Floridiana, it houses a fine collection of European and Oriental porcelain and other objets d'art in a neoclassical residence built in the early 19th century by King Ferdinand I for his wife; their portraits greet you as you enter. Enjoy the view from the terrace behind the museum. ⊠ *Via Cimarosa 77,* ☎ *081/578–8418.* ✑ *4,000 lire.* ☉ *Tues.–Sat. 9–2, Sun. 9–1.*

16 The park of **Villa Pignatelli** holds a small, dignified museum near the lower station of the Chiaia funicular. The low-key exhibits are of limited interest to anyone who doesn't like 19th-century furniture, but there's a collection of antique coaches and carriages in a pavilion on the grounds that is worth a look. And a stroll in the park is a pleasant respite from the noisy city streets. ⊠ *Riviera di Chiaia 200,* ☎ *081/669675.* ✑ *4,000 lire, park free.* ☉ *Tues.–Sun. 9–2.*

☞ 17 For a change of pace, especially if you have children along, go to the **Acquario** (Aquarium) in the public gardens on Via Caracciolo. Founded by a German naturalist in the late 19th century, it's the oldest in Europe. About 200 species of fish and marine plants thrive in large tanks, undoubtedly better off here than in the highly polluted Bay of Naples, their natural habitat. ⊠ *Viale A. Dohrn,* ☎ *081/583–3111.* ✑ *3,000 lire.* ☉ *May–Sept., Tues.–Sat. 9–6, Sun. 10–6; Oct.–Apr., Tues.–Sat. 9–5, Sun. 9–2.*

OFF THE
BEATEN PATH

EDENLANDIA – This is the largest amusement park in Campania. It's in the Mostra d'Oltremare area of Naples, near San Paolo Stadium. ⊠ *Viale Kennedy,* ☎ *081/239-1182.* ✑ *Free, individual fares for rides.* ☉ *All year.*

MUSEO NAZIONALE FERROVIARIO – Children love to see the old-fashioned engines, cars, and railroad equipment on display in the restored railway works, founded by the Bourbon rulers of Naples in the last century. ⊠ *Corso San Giovanni a Teduccio,* ☎ *081/472003.* ✑ *Free.* ☉ *Mon.–Sat. 9–2.*

Dining and Lodging

$$$ ✕ **Casanova Grill.** Soft lights and a trendy art-deco look set the tone in the Casanova Grill, the Hotel Excelsior's restaurant. The seasonal specialties and antipasti arranged on the buffet will whet your appetite for such traditional Neapolitan dishes as the simple spaghetti al pomodoro and the classic *carne* (meat) alla pizzaiola. ⊠ *Hotel Excelsior, Via Partenope 48,* ☎ *081/764–0111. Jacket and tie. AE, DC, MC, V.*

$$$ ✕ **La Fazenda.** Overlooking the sea at Marechiaro, in one of the city's most picturesque spots, this restaurant is a favorite for leisurely dining and an invitingly informal atmosphere. The pastas, many with vegetable sauces, are particularly good. The specialty is seafood, but you can also find a good, honest *bistecca* (beefsteak) here. Desserts are homemade. Note that you must take a taxi to get to La Fazenda. ⊠ *Discesa Marechiaro 58,* ☎ *81/575-7420. AE, MC, V. Closed Mon. and Aug. 13–29.*

$$$ ✕ **La Sacrestia.** Popular with Neapolitans because of its location and
★ the quality of its food, La Sacrestia is set on the slopes of the Posillipo hill, with marvelous views of the city and bay. The specialties range from appetizing antipasti to linguine in *salsa di scorfano* (scorpion-fish sauce). Seafood has a place of honor on the menu, and there are interesting meat dishes as well. The setting in a patrician villa and the

ambience are definitely upscale. ⊠ *Via Orazio 116,* ☎ *081/761–1051. AE, DC, MC, V. Closed Mon. Sept.–June, Sun. July, and Aug.*

$$ ✕ **Ciro a Santa Brigida.** Centrally located off Via Toledo near the Castel Nuovo, Ciro is a straightforward restaurant popular with business travelers, artists, and journalists who are more interested in food than frills. In dining rooms on two levels, customers enjoy classic Neapolitan cuisine. The *scaloppe allà* Ciro (veal with prosciutto and mozzarella) is delicious. There's pizza, too. ⊠ *Via Santa Brigida 71,* ☎ *081/552–4072. AE, DC, MC, V. Closed Sun. and 2 weeks in Aug.*

$$ ✕ **Don Salvatore.** Head just west to the little port of Mergellina to find an unpretentious-looking place known for good local dishes and seafood. Linguine *cosa nostra* (with shellfish) and other pastas with seafood sauces are specialties, and the *fritto misto* (mixed fried fish) is as light as a feather. ⊠ *Via Mergellina 5,* ☎ *081/681817. AE, DC, MC, V. Closed Wed.*

$$ ✕ **La Bersagliera.** Most first-time visitors to Naples want to dine once on the Santa Lucia waterfront in the shadow of the medieval Castel dell'Ovo, and this is one of the best places to do so. It's touristy but fun, with an irresistible combination of spaghetti and mandolins. The menu offers uncomplicated classics, such as spaghetti *alla pescatora* (with seafood sauce) and melanzane alla parmigiana. ⊠ *Borgo Marinaro 10,* ☎ *081/764–6016. AE, DC, MC, V. Closed Tues.*

$$ ✕ **Mimì alla Ferrovia.** Near the central station, this bustling fish restaurant has scooped plenty of plaudits in recent years. The service is polite without being obsequious, the atmosphere relaxed, sometimes noisy. Try the *céfalo* (mullet) when it's in season, or the lobster at just about any time. Other dishes worth sampling are *peperoni ripieni* (stuffed peppers) and grilled mushrooms. ⊠ *Via Alfonso D'Aragona 21,* ☎ *081/553–8525. AE, DC, MC, V. Closed Sun. and Aug. 10–21.*

$$$$ 🏨 **Excelsior.** This ITT-Sheraton Luxury Collection hotel is on the shore drive, with views of the bay from the front rooms. The lobby and lounges are lavish, with Oriental carpets and gilt or glass chandeliers. Off the large semicircular lounge are a chic little bar and the Casanova restaurant. The rooms are decorated either in Empire style (with neoclassic furniture and brocades) or in more typically Neapolitan floral prints. ⊠ *Via Partenope 48,* ☎ *081/764–0111,* 🆅🆇 *081/764–9743. 102 rooms with bath or shower. Restaurant, bar, parking. AE, DC, MC, V.*

$$$ 🏨 **Jolly Ambassador.** This hotel occupies the top 14 floors of the only skyscraper on the downtown skyline (if you don't count the business center beyond the station), and the bedrooms and roof garden-restaurant command sweeping views of Naples and the bay. Decorated in the uninspired but functional style of the Jolly chain, with dark brown and white predominating, it promises comfort and efficiency in a city where these are scarce commodities. ⊠ *Via Medina 70,* ☎ *081/416000,* 🆅🆇 *081/551–8010. 251 rooms with bath or shower. Restaurant, bar, parking. AE, DC, MC, V.*

$$$ 🏨 **Paradiso.** Stay here if you want something special a step or two off
★   the beaten track. A modern air-conditioned building perched on the slopes of the hill above the port of Mergellina, the Paradiso is just a few minutes by taxi or funicular from downtown, and it has fabulous views from huge window walls in the lobby and all front rooms. The decor, in tones of blue and beige, is restful and attractive. Built-in furnishings of rosy wood with marble surfaces give the bedrooms a smart contemporary look. Though the rooms and bathrooms are smallish, they are well organized, with TV and minibar; about half have a balcony. Be sure to ask for a room with a view; there's no extra charge. There is a roof terrace for sitting, dining, and contemplating the entire bay as far as Vesuvius and beyond. ⊠ *Via Catullo 11,* ☎ *081/761–*

4161, FAX *081/761–3449. 74 rooms with bath or shower. Restaurant, bar, parking. AE, DC, MC, V.*

$$ ⌕ **Rex.** This hotel, which is at the higher end of its price category, has a fairly quiet location near the Santa Lucia waterfront. Situated on the first two floors of an art-nouveau building, it has no elevator; the decor ranges from 1950s modern to fake period pieces and even some folk art, haphazardly combined. Though it has no restaurant, there are many in the vicinity. ⊠ *Via Palepoli 12,* ☎ *081/764–9389,* FAX *081/764–9227. 37 rooms with bath or shower. Bar, parking. AE, DC, MC, V.*

Nightlife and the Arts

Classical Music
A classical music festival known as **International Music Weeks** takes place throughout May in Naples. Concerts are held at the Teatro San Carlo, the Teatro Mercadante, and in the neoclassic Villa Pignatelli. For information, contact the Teatro San Carlo box office. ⊠ *Via San Carlo 93/f,* ☎ *081/797–2111.*

Naples has a full **opera** season from fall through spring. The **Teatro San Carlo,** where the season runs from December to May, is one of Italy's top opera houses. ⊠ *Via San Carlo 93/f,* ☎ *081/797–2111.*

Nightclubs
Gabbiano (⊠ Via Partenope 26, ☎ 081/764–5717). Expect to be part of a sophisticated crowd at this fashionable watering hole; there is usually live music.

Papillon (⊠ Via Manzoni 207, Naples, ☎ 081/769–0800). This club caters to a young crowd.

Rosolino (⊠ Via Nazario Sauro 5–7, ☎ 081/764–0513). This addition to the Neapolitan entertainment scene also has a quiet piano bar and a restaurant with some moderately priced meals.

Shaker (⊠ Via Nazario Sauro 24, ☎ 081/416775). This disco, in the prime entertainment neighborhood of Naples, attracts a mixed crowd of locals and guests from the nearby hotels.

Outdoor Activities and Sports

Bowling
Bowling Oltremare (⊠ Viale Kennedy, ☎ 081/624444).

Fishing
For information on licenses and water quality, contact **Federazione Italiana Pesca Sportiva** (⊠ Piazza Santa Maria degli Angeli, Naples, ☎ 081/764–4921).

Golf
Minigolf Kennedy (⊠ Via Camillo Guerra 60, ☎ 081/587–1386) is in the suburb of Chiaiano, west of Naples.

Horseback Riding
For riding in Campania, contact the **Centro Ippico Agnano** (⊠ Via Circumvallazione, Agnano, between Naples and Pozzuoli, ☎ 081/570–2695).

Sailing
Nantic Coop (⊠ Piazza Amedeo 15, Naples, ☎ 081/415371).

Waterskiing
Sci Nautico Partenopeo (⊠ Lake Averno, Pozzuoli, ☎ 081/866–2214).

Shopping

Leather goods, coral, jewelry, and cameos are some of the best items to buy in Campania. In Naples, where many of the top leather and fashion houses have their factories, you'll find good buys in handbags, shoes, and clothing, but it's often wise to make purchases in shops rather than from street vendors.

The **Galleria Umberto** (☞ *above*) is a good introduction to shopping in Naples; a wide variety of retail outlets trade in the four glass-roofed arcades. Other areas and streets are more specialized: The area immediately around **Piazza dei Martiri** is the heart of luxury shopping, with perfume shops, fashion outlets, and antiques on display. **Via Toledo** and **Via Chiaia** are better bets for bargains.

THE PHLEGREAN FIELDS

The name—the fields of fire—was once given to the entire region west of Naples, including the island of Ischia. The whole area floats freely on a mass of molten lava very close to the surface. The fires are still smoldering. Greek and Roman notions of the Underworld were not the blind imaginings of a primitive people; they were the creations of poets and writers who stood on this very ground and wrote down what they saw.

Whether it's worth the half day it takes to tour these sights depends on your interests. If you've never seen volcanic activity, don't miss the Solfatara, the sunken crater of a volcano (it's quite safe if you stick to the path). The Amphitheater at Pozzuoli is fascinating because of its well-preserved underground passages and chambers, which give a good sense of how the wild animals were hoisted up into the arena. At Lake Avernus you'll be standing at the very spot that the ancients considered the entrance to Hades. The ruins at Baia, the resort town of the ancient Romans, won't mean too much unless you have more than a passing interest in antiquity. The Oracle at Cumae was as famous as the one at Delphi; if you've read *The Aeneid,* you'll want to enter the very cave described in Book VI, where Aeneas sought the Sibyl's aid for his journey to the Underworld.

Solfatara

18 *8 km (5 mi) west of Naples, 2 km (1¼ mi) east of Pozzuoli.*

Here at **Solfatara** you can experience at first hand the volcanic nature of this other-worldly terrain. In fact, the only eruption of this semiextinct volcano was in 1198, though according to one legend, every crater in the Phlegrean Fields is one of the mouths of a hundred-headed dragon named Typhon that Zeus hurled down the crater of Epomeo on the island of Ischia. According to another, the sulfurous springs of the Solfatara are poisonous discharges from the wounds the Titans received in their war with Zeus. Both legends, of course, are efforts to dramatize man's struggle to overcome the mysterious and dangerous forces of nature. The stark, scorched area exerts a strange fascination, slightly marred by the modern apartment blocks peering over the rim. ▦ *5,500 lire.* ☉ *Daily 8:30–1 hr before sunset.*

Pozzuoli

19 *8 km (5 mi) west of Naples, 2 km (1¼ mi) west of Solfatara.*

The **amphitheater** here (**Anfiteatro Flavio**) is the third-largest arena in Italy, after the Colosseum and Santa Maria Capua Vetere, and could accommodate 40,000 spectators, who were sometimes treated to mock naval battles when the arena was filled with water. ▦ *4,000 lire.* ☉ *Daily 9–1 hr before sunset.*

If you are visiting Pozzuoli's amphitheater, you may want to make a short side trip to the town's **harbor** and imagine St. Paul landing here in AD 61 en route to Rome. His own ship had been wrecked off Malta, and he was brought here on the *Castor and Pollux,* a grain ship from Alexandria that was carrying corn from Egypt to Italy only 18 years before the eruption at Vesuvius.

Baia

12 km (8 mi) west of Naples.

Now largely under the sea, this was once the most opulent and fashionable resort area of the Roman Empire, the place where Sulla, Pompey, Julius Caesar, Tiberius, Nero, and Cicero built their holiday villas. Petronius's *Satyricon* is a satire on the corruption and intrigue, the wonderful licentiousness of Roman life at **Baia.** (Petronius was hired to arrange parties and entertainments for Nero, so he was in a position to know.) It was here at Baia that Emperor Claudius built a great villa for his wife Messalina (who spent her nights indulging herself at public brothels); here that Agrippina poisoned her husband and was, in turn, murdered by her son Nero; here that Cleopatra was staying when Julius Caesar was murdered on the Ides of March. You can visit the excavations of the famous **baths.** The site lies 6 kilometers (4 miles) from Pozzuoli. ✉ *Via Fusaro 35,* ☎ *081/868–7592.* ▦ *4,000 lire.* ☉ *Daily 9–1 hr before sunset.*

En Route   Follow the loop around **Lake Miseno** (a volcanic crater believed by the ancients to be the Styx, across which Charon ferried the souls of the dead) and **Lake Fusaro.** You'll pass some fine views of Pozzuoli Bay.

Cumae

㉒ *16 km (10 mi) west of Naples.*

Perhaps the oldest Greek colony in Italy, **Cumae** overshadowed the Phlegrean Fields, including Naples, in the 6th and 7th centuries BC. The **Sibyl's Cave** (Antro della Sibilla) is here—one of the most venerated sites in antiquity. In the 5th or 6th century BC, the Greeks hollowed the cave from the rock beneath the present ruins of Cumae's acropolis. Visitors walk through a dark, massive stone tunnel that opens into a vaulted chamber where the Sibyl rendered her oracles. Standing here, the sense of mystery, of communication with the invisible, is overwhelming. "This is the most romantic classical site in Italy," wrote H. V. Morton. "I would rather come here than to Pompeii."

Virgil wrote the epic *The Aeneid,* the story of the Trojan prince Aeneas's wanderings, partly to give Rome the historical legitimacy that Homer had given the Greeks. On his journey, Aeneas had to descend to the Underworld to speak to his father, and to find his way in, he needed the guidance of the Cumaean Sibyl.

Virgil did not dream up the Sibyl's cave or the entrance to Hades—he must have stood both in her chamber and along the rim of Lake Avernus, as you yourself will stand. When he wrote, *"Facilis descensus Averno"*—"The way to hell is easy"—it was because he knew the way. In Book VI of *The Aeneid,* Virgil described how Aeneas, arriving at Cumae, sought Apollo's throne (remains of the **Temple of Apollo** can still be seen) and "the deep hidden abode of the dread Sibyl / An enormous cave . . .."

The Sibyl was not necessarily a charlatan; she was a medium, a prophetess, an old woman whom the ancients believed could communicate with the Other World. The three most famous Sibyls were at Erythrae, Delphi, and Cumae. Foreign governments consulted the Sibyls before mounting campaigns. Wealthy aristocrats came to consult with their dead relatives. Businessmen came to get their dreams interpreted or to seek favorable omens before entering into financial agreements or setting off on journeys. Farmers came to remove curses on their cows. Love potions were a profitable source of revenue; women from Baia lined up for potions to slip into the wine of handsome charioteers who drove up and down the street in their gold-plated four-horsepower chariots.

With the coming of the Olympian gods, the earlier gods of the soil were discredited or given new roles and names. Ancient rites, such as those surrounding the Cumaean Sibyl, were now carried out in secret and known as the Mysteries. The Romans—like the later Soviets—tried in vain to replace these Mysteries by deifying the state in the person of its rulers. Yet even the Caesars appealed to forces of the Other World. And until the 4th century AD, the Sibyl was consulted by the Christian bishop of Rome. ✉ *Via Acropoli.* ☎ *081/854–3060.* 🎫 *4,000 lire.* ⊙ *Daily 9–1 hr before sunset.*

Lake Avernus (Lago d'Averno)

11 km (7 mi) west of Naples.

The best time to visit the fabled Lago d'Averno is at sunset or when the moon is rising. There's a restaurant on the west side, where you can dine on the terrace. Forested hills rise on three sides; the menacing cone of Monte Nuovo rises on the fourth. The smell of sulfur hangs over this sad, lonely landscape seemingly at the very gates of hell. No place evokes Homer, Virgil, and the cult of the Other World better than this silent, mysterious setting. To reach the lake, drive west from Pozzuoli on S7 toward Cumae and then turn left (south) on the road to Baia. About a kilometer (½ mile) along, turn right and follow signs to Lake Avernus.

ANCIENT INSPIRATIONS
Herculaneum, Vesuvius, and Pompeii

Volcanic ash and mud preserved the Roman towns of Herculaneum and Pompeii almost exactly as they were on the day Mt. Vesuvius erupted in AD 79, leaving them not just archaeological ruins but testimonies of daily life in the ancient world. All three sights can be visited from either Naples or Sorrento, thanks to the Circumvesuviana (☞ Getting Around by Train *in* Campania A to Z, *below*), the suburban railway that provides fast, frequent, and economical service. If Naples is your base, your first stop is Herculaneum, at modern Ercolano, after which you will come across the mountain that caused the devastation, Vesuvius, one of the most notorious volcanoes in the world. Move on to the ancient Roman colony of Pompeii. From Sorrento you will explore these sights in reverse order.

Herculaneum

★ ㉑ *10 km (6 mi) south of Naples.*

Lying more than 60 feet below the town of Ercolano, the ruins of **Herculaneum** are set among the acres of greenhouses that make this area one of Europe's principal flower-growing centers. The entrance to the site is a short walk south from the Circumvesuviana station. Hercules himself is said to have founded the town, which became a famous weekend retreat for the Roman elite. It had about 5,000 inhabitants when it was destroyed; many of them were fishermen, craftsmen, and artists. A lucky few patricians owned villas overlooking the sea. Herculaneum was damaged by an earthquake in AD 63, and repairs were still being made 16 years later when the gigantic eruption of Vesuvius (which also destroyed Pompeii) sent a fiery cloud of gas and pumice hurtling onto the town, which was completely buried under a tide of volcanic mud. This semiliquid mass seeped into the crevices and niches of every building, covering household objects and enveloping textiles and wood—sealing all in a compact, airtight tomb.

Casual excavation—and haphazard looting—began in the 18th century, but systematic digs were not initiated until the 1920s. Today less than half of Herculaneum has been excavated; with present-day Ercolano and the unlovely Resina Quarter (famous among bargain hunters as the area's largest secondhand clothing market) sitting on top of the site, progress is limited. From the ramp leading down to Herculaneum's neatly laid out streets and well-preserved edifices, you get a good overall view of the site, as well as an idea of the amount of rock that had to be removed to bring it to light.

You could easily get lost in the streets of Pompeii, but not here. Most important buildings can be seen in about two hours. If you feel closer to the past at Herculaneum than at Pompeii, it's in part because there are fewer hawkers here. Also, though Herculaneum had only one-fourth the population of Pompeii and has only been partially excavated, what has been found is generally better preserved. In some cases, you can even see the original wooden beams, staircases, and furniture.

At the entrance you should pick up a map showing the gridlike layout of the dig. Decorations are especially delicate in the **House of the Mosaic Atrium,** with a pavement in a black-and-white checkerboard pattern, and in the **House of Neptune and Amphitrite,** named for the subjects of a still-bright mosaic on the wall of the nymphaeum (a recessed grotto with a fountain). Annexed to the latter house is a remarkably preserved wineshop, where amphorae still rest on carbonized wooden shelves. And in the **House of the Wooden Partition,** one of the best-preserved of all, there is a carbonized wooden partition with three doors. In the **baths,** where there were separate sections for men and women, you can see benches; basins; and the hot, warm, and cold rooms, embellished with mosaics. The **House of the Bicentenary** was a patrician residence with smaller rooms on the upper floor, which may have been rented out to artisan-tenants who were probably Christians because they left an emblem of the cross embedded in the wall. The palaestra and 2,500-seat theater, the sumptuously decorated suburban baths, and the House of the Stags, with an elegant garden open to the sea breezes, are all evocative relics of a lively and luxurious way of life.

Until a few years ago it was believed that most of Herculaneum's inhabitants had managed to escape by sea, since few skeletons were found in the city. Excavations at Porta Marina, the gate in the sea wall leading to the beach, have revealed instead that many perished there, a few steps from the only escape route open to them. ⊠ *Corso Ercolano,* ☎ *081/739–0963.* ⊡ *12,000 lire.* ☼ *Daily 9–1 hr before sunset, ticket office closes 2 hrs before sunset.*

Vesuvius

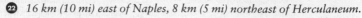 *16 km (10 mi) east of Naples, 8 km (5 mi) northeast of Herculaneum.*

You can visit **Vesuvius** either before or after Herculaneum. If possible, save the mountain till after you've toured the buried city and learned to appreciate the volcano's awesome power. The most important factor is whether the summit is lost in mist—when it is, you'll be lucky to see your hand in front of your face. The volcano is visible from Naples, and everywhere else along the Bay of Naples; the best advice is, when you see the summit clearing—it tends to be clearer in the afternoon—head for it. The view then is magnificent, with the curve of the coast and the tiny white houses among the orange and lemon blossoms.

Reaching the crater takes some effort. From the Ercolano stop of the Circumvesuviana, take scheduled buses (departures currently at 9:35, 10:35, 12:35, 1:35, and 3:35) or your own car to the Seggovia station, the lower terminal of the defunct chairlift. (Though there's talk of putting it back in working order, no one is optimistic about the possibility.) From here you must climb the soft, slippery cinder track on foot, a 30-minute ascent, and you must pay about 5,000 lire for compulsory guide service, though the guides don't do much more than tell you to stay away from the edge of the crater. If you're not in shape, you'll probably find the climb tiring. Wear nonskid shoes (not sandals).

Pompeii

★ ㉓ *24 km (15 mi) southeast of Naples, 11 km (7 mi) northeast of Herculaneum.*

Pompeii has its own stop (Pompeii–Villa Misteri) on the Circumvesuviana, close to the main entrance at the Porta Marina (there are other entrances to the excavations at the far end of the site, near the amphitheater). Ancient Pompeii was much larger than Herculaneum; a busy commercial center with a population of 10,000–20,000, it covered about 160 acres on the seaward end of the fertile Sarno Plain.

In 80 BC the Roman General Sulla turned Pompeii into a Roman colony, where wealthy patricians came to escape the turmoil of city life. The town was laid out in a grid pattern, with two main intersecting streets. The wealthiest took a whole block for themselves; those less fortunate built a house and rented out the front rooms, facing the street, as shops. The facades of these houses were relatively plain and seldom hinted at the care and attention lavished on the private rooms within.

When a visitor entered, he passed the shops and entered an open area (atrium). In the back was a receiving room. Behind was another open area, called the peristyle, with rows of columns and perhaps a garden with a fountain. Only good friends ever saw this private part of the house, which was surrounded by the bedrooms and the dining area.

Pompeiian houses were designed around an inner garden so that families could turn their backs on the world outside. Today we install picture windows that break down visual barriers between ourselves and our neighbors; the people in these Roman towns had few windows, preferring to get their light from the central courtyard—the light within. How pleasant it must have been to come home from the forum or the baths to one's own secluded kingdom, with no visual reminders of a life outside one's own.

Not that public life was so intolerable. There were wineshops on almost every corner, and frequent shows at the amphitheater. The public fountains and toilets were fed by huge cisterns, connected by lead pipes beneath the sidewalks. Since garbage and rainwater collected in the streets of Pompeii, the sidewalks were raised, and huge stepping stones were placed at crossings so pedestrians could keep their feet dry. Herculaneum had better drainage, with an underground sewer that led to the sea.

The ratio of freemen to slaves was about three to two. A small, prosperous family had two or three slaves. Since all manual labor was considered degrading, the slaves did all housework and cooking, including the cutting of meat, which the family ate with spoons or with their hands. Everyone loved grapes, and figs were popular, too. Venison, chicken, and pork were the main dishes. Oranges weren't known, but people ate quinces (a good source of vitamin C) to guard against scurvy. Bread was made from wheat and barley (rye and oats were unknown) and washed down with wine made from the grapes of the slopes of Vesuvius.

The government was considered a democracy, but women, children, gladiators, and Jews couldn't vote. They did, however, express their opinions on election day, as you'll see in campaign graffiti left on public walls.

Some 15,000 graffiti were found in Pompeii and Herculaneum. Many were political announcements—one person recommending another for office, for example, and spelling out his qualifications. Some were bills announcing upcoming events—a play at the theater, a fight among gladiators at the amphitheater. Others were public notices—that wine was on sale, that an apartment would be vacant on the Ides of March. A good many were personal, and give a human dimension to the disaster that not even the sights can equal. Here are a few:

At the Baths: "What is the use of having a Venus if she's made of marble?"

At a hotel: "I've wet my bed. My sin I bare. But why? you ask. No pot was anywhere."

At the entrance to the front lavatory at a private house: "May I always and everywhere be as potent with women as I was here."

㉔ Enter through **Porta Marina,** so called because it faces the sea. It is near the **Pompeii–Villa Misteri Circumvesuviana Station.** Past the **Temple**
㉕ **of Venus** is the **Basilica,** the law court and the economic center of the city. These oblong buildings ending in a semicircular projection (apse) were the model for early Christian churches, which had a nave (central aisle) and two side aisles separated by rows of columns. Standing in the Basilica, you can recognize the continuity between Roman and Christian architecture.

㉖ The Basilica opens onto the **Forum** (Foro), the public meeting place, surrounded by temples and public buildings. It was here that elections were held and speeches and official announcements made—a sort of Roman version of the village green. At the far (northern) end of the
㉗ forum is the **Temple of Jupiter** (Tempio di Giove). Walk around the right side of the temple, cross the street, and continue north on Via del Foro (Forum Street). There is a restaurant on your left.

㉘ The **House of the Faun** (Casa del Fauno), one of the most impressive examples of a luxurious private house, with wonderful mosaics (the originals are in the National Archaeological Museum in Naples).

㉙ The **Forum Baths,** on Via delle Terme, is smaller than the Stabian Baths
㉚ (☞ *below*) but with more delicate decoration. The **House of the Tragic Poet** (Casa del Poeta Tragico) is a typical middle-class house from the last days of Pompeii. On the floor is a mosaic of a chained dog and
㉛ the inscription CAVE CANEM ("Beware of the dog"). The beautiful **Porta Ercolano** (Gate of Herculaneum) at the end of Via Consolare was the

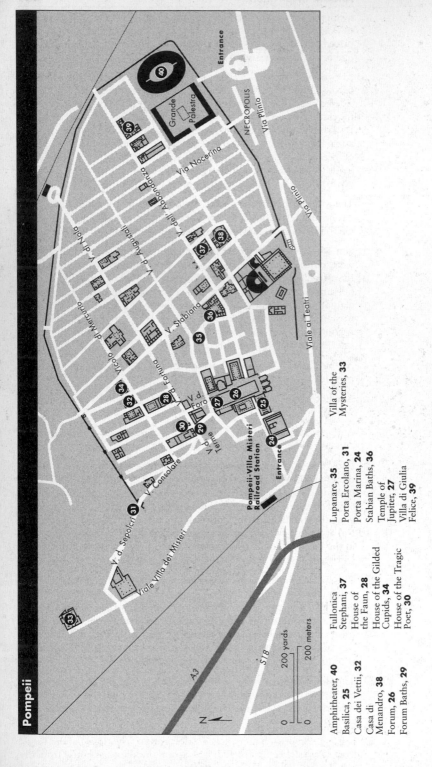

Pompeii

N

| 0 | 200 yards |
| 0 | 200 meters |

Ercolano (Gate of Herculaneum) at the end of Via Consolare was the main gate that led to Herculaneum and Naples.

32 The **Casa dei Vettii** (House of the Vetti), on Vicolo dei Vettii, is the best example of a rich middle-class merchant's house, faithfully restored with vivid murals.

33 The **Villa of the Mysteries** (Villa dei Misteri), outside Pompeii's walls, contains what some consider the greatest surviving group of paintings from the ancient world, telling the story of a young bride (Ariadne) being initiated into the mysteries of the cult of Dionysus. Bacchus (Dionysus), the god of wine, was popular in a town so devoted to the pleasures of the flesh. But he also represented the triumph of the irrational—of all those mysterious forces that no official state religion could fully suppress. The cult of Dionysus, like the cult of the Cumaean Sibyl, gave people a sense of control over fate, and in its focus on the Other World, helped pave the way for Christianity.

34 The **House of the Gilded Cupids** is an elegant, well-preserved home with original marble decorations in the garden. It is just off **Via Stabiana**, one of the two major intersecting streets of the town.

From the door of the house, turn right down Via Stabiana, go three blocks, and turn right onto Via Augustali. Your first left will take you **35** to the **Lupanare** (brothel) on Vicolo del Lupanare. On the walls are scenes of erotic games in which clients could engage.

Continue south on Vicolo del Lupanare, turning left onto Via dell'Abbondanza, the other main street of the old town. On your left are the **36** **Stabian Baths.** It was here that people came in the evening to drown the burdens of the day. The baths were heated by underground furnaces. The heat circulated among the stone pillars supporting the floor, rose through flues in the walls, and escaped through chimneys. The water temperature could be set for cold, lukewarm, or hot. Bathers took a lukewarm bath to prepare themselves for the hot room. A tepid bath came next, and then a plunge into cold water to tone up the skin. A vigorous massage with oil was followed by rest, reading, horseplay, and conversation.

37 The **Fullonica Stephani,** two blocks east of the baths on Via dell'Abbondanza, is a house converted into workshops for the cleaning of fabrics. All Roman citizens were required to wear togas, which weren't exactly easy to keep clean, in public. It's not hard to imagine why there were more toga cleaners (fullers) in Pompeii than anything else, except perhaps bakers. The cloth was dunked in a tub full of water and chalk and stamped upon like so many grapes. Washed, the material was stretched across a wicker cage and exposed to sulfur fumes. The fuller carded it with a long brush, then placed it under a press. The harder the pressing, the whiter and brighter it became. Behind the Fullonica Stephani **38** is the entrance to the **Casa di Menandro,** a patrician's villa with many **39** paintings and mosaics. The **Villa di Giulia Felice** (House of Julia Felix), ten blocks east of the Casa di Menandro on Via dell'Abbondanza, has a large garden with a lovely portico. The wealthy lady living here ran a public bathhouse annex and rented out ground-floor rooms as shops.

40 The games at the **Amphitheater** (Anfiteatro) were between animals, between gladiators, and between animals and gladiators. There were also Olympic games and chariot races. The crowds rushed in as soon as the gates opened—women and slaves to the bleachers. When the Emperor or some other important person was in attendance, exotic animals—lions and tigers, panthers, elephants, and rhinos—were released. At "half time," birds of prey were set against hares, or dogs against porcupines; the animals were tied to either end of a rope so neither could escape.

Most gladiators were slaves or prisoners, but a few were Germans or Syrians who enjoyed fighting. Teams of gladiators worked for impresarios, who hired them out to wealthy citizens, many of whom were running for office and hoping that the gory entertainment would buy them some votes. When a gladiator found himself at another's mercy, he extended a pleading hand to the president of the games. If the president turned his thumb up, the gladiator lived; if he turned his thumb down, the gladiator's throat was cut. The arena got pretty bloody after a night's entertainment and was sprinkled with red powder to camouflage the carnage. The victorious gladiator got money or a ribbon exempting him from further fights. If he was a slave, he was often set free. If the people of Pompeii had had trading cards, they would have collected portraits of gladiators; everyone had his favorite. Says one piece of graffiti: "Petronius Octavus fought thirty-four fights and then died, but Severus, a freedman, was victor in fifty-five fights and still lived; Nasica celebrates sixty victories." Pompeii had a gladiator school (Caserma dei Gladiatori), which you can visit on your way back to Porta Marina.

To get the most out of Pompeii, buy a detailed printed guide and map and allow plenty of time—at least three or four hours. You should have a pocketful of small change (500 lire coins) for tipping the guards who are on duty at the most important villas. They will unlock the gates for you, insist on explaining the attractions, show you some mild Pompeiian pornography if you ask for it, and expect a tip for their services. If you hire a guide, make sure he's registered and standing inside the gate. Agree beforehand on the length of the tour and the price. ✉ *Pompeii Scavi*, ☎ *081/861-0744.* 🎫 *12,000 lire.* ☉ *Daily 9–1 hr before sunset, ticket office closes 2 hrs before sunset.*

NEED A   You can have lunch at the restaurant and cafeteria near the **Forum,**
BREAK?   where there's a picnic area as well. There are also plenty of trattorias
           outside the entrances to the excavation.

Nightlife and the Arts

One of the most impressive theater seasons is Pompeii's late-summer festival of the performing arts, known as the **Panatenee Pompeiane.** This series of classical plays takes place in July and August. For information, contact one of the information offices in Naples or Pompeii (☞ Campania A to Z, *below*).

A NEAPOLITAN VERSAILLES

Caserta and Nearby Benevento

A northward excursion from Naples takes you to Caserta, the Italian version of Versailles, and if you proceed to Benevento, you'll view an almost perfectly preserved Roman arch. There's not much else of interest on this route with the exception of some mountain scenery and the museum in the small town of Capua, 11 kilometers northeast of Caserta. Benevento was badly damaged by World War II bombings, and you will have to content yourself here with picking out the medieval and even older relics that have survived in the oldest part of the city. Both Caserta and Benevento can be reached by train from Naples. Daily bus service from Naples is quite frequent to Caserta, 28 kilometers (17 miles) away, less so to Benevento, 62 kilometers (38 miles) away. If you go by car, make a brief detour to the medieval hamlet of Caserta Vecchia on the hillside, where there is a very old cathedral and one or two good restaurants.

Caserta

★ ④ *25 km (16 mi) southeast of Naples, 11 km (7 mi) northeast of Herculaneum.*

The **royal palace,** known as the Reggia, will show you how Bourbon royalty lived in the mid-18th century. Architect Luigi Vanvitelli devoted 20 years to its construction under Bourbon ruler Charles II, whose son, Charles III, moved in when it was completed in 1774. Both king and architect were inspired by Versailles, and the rectangular palace was conceived on a massive scale, with four interconnecting courtyards, 1,200 rooms, and a vast park. Though not as well maintained as its French counterpart, the main staircase puts the one at Versailles to shame, and the **royal apartments** are sumptuous. It was here, in what Eisenhower called "a castle near Naples," that the Allied High Command had its headquarters in World War II, and here German forces in Italy surrendered in April 1945. Most enjoyable are the gardens and parks, particularly the Cascades, where a life-size Diana and her maidens stand. The park is the Reggia's main attraction, with pools and fountains stretching for more than a mile, formal Italian gardens and a delightful English garden. Some of the fountains are splendid and may be playing at full force now that the aqueduct built by the Bourbons has been repaired. If you don't like walking, a minibus makes a circuit of the grounds. ⊠ *Piazza Carlo III,* ☎ *0823/321400.* ⊠ *Royal apartments 8,000 lire, park 4,000 lire, minibus 1,500 lire.* ☉ *Royal apartments: Summer, daily 9–6, and winter, Mon.–Sat. 9–1:30, Sun. 9–1, closed 2nd and 4th Mon. of each month and national holidays. Park: daily 9–1 hr before sunset.*

NEED A BREAK?

Ciacco (⊠ Via Maielli 37, ☎ 0823/327505) is an elegant restaurant in the center of town. There's good homemade pasta and fish at lunchtime, and a tempting selection of local wines. Ciacco is closed on Sunday and throughout August.

Dining

$$ ✕ **Antica Locanda.** This restaurant is worth the detour 2 kilometers outside Caserta's center, to the old silk-workers' district, San Leucio (signposted). The traditional *ambiente* is reflected in the cuisine, and you can sample such dishes as linguine *al cartoccio* (steamed with fresh tomatoes and shellfish) and *gazzerielli alla Borbone* (gnocchi with cheese and truffle sauce). ⊠ *Piazza della Seta, Frazione San Leucio,* ☎ *0823/305444. AE, DC, MC, V. Closed Mon. and Aug. 10–25.*

$$ ✕ **La Castellana.** Located in Casertavecchia, Caserta's medieval nucleus on the hillside overlooking the modern town, this tavern has atmosphere and hearty local specialties, such as *stringozzi alla Castellana* (homemade pasta with a piquant tomato sauce served in individual casseroles) and *agnello alla Castellana* (lamb sautéed in red wine). You dine inside or, in fair weather, under an arbor. ⊠ *Via Torre 4,* ☎ *0823/371230. Reservations essential. AE, DC, MC, V. Closed Dec. and Thurs. Oct.–June.*

Nightlife and the Arts

The festival **Settembre a Borgo** is held in the picturesque setting of Caserta Vecchia in September. For information, contact the Caserta tourist information office (☎ 0823/321137).

Capua

11 km (7 mi) northwest of Caserta, 33 km (20 mi) north of Naples.

Museo Campano. The nondescript town of Capua is home to this Provincial Museum, whose collection includes Le Madri (the Mothers), 200 eerily impressive stone votive statues representing highly stylized mother figures. They were found on the site of a sanctuary devoted to Matuta, the ancient goddess of childbirth, and date from the 7th to the 1st century BC. ⊠ *Via Roma*, ☎ *0823/961402*. 🎫 *8,000.* ⊙ *Tues.–Sat. 9–1:30, Sun. 9–1.*

Benevento

㊷ *60 km (37 mi) east of Naples, 35 km (22 mi) east of Caserta.*

Benevento owes its importance to its establishment as the capital of the Lombards, a northern tribe that invaded and settled what is now Lombardy when they were ousted by Charlemagne in the 8th century. Tough and resourceful, the Lombards moved south and set up a new duchy in Benevento, later moving its seat south to Salerno, where they saw the potential of the natural harbor. Under papal rule in the 13th century, Benevento built a fine cathedral and endowed it with bronze doors that were a pinnacle of Romanesque art. The cathedral, doors, and a large part of the town were blasted by World War II bombs, so there's little left to see; fortunately, the majestic **Arch of Trajan** survived unscathed. To reach it, follow Viale Principe di Napoli from the station and take the first left after the river. The arch is a fine 2nd-century AD work, decorated with reliefs exalting the many accomplishments of Roman emperor Trajan, who sorted out Rome's finances, brought parts of the Middle East into the empire, and extended the Appian Way through Benevento to the Adriatic. From the arch, take Via Traiano and turn right onto Corso Garibaldi to get to the **Duomo,** which has been rebuilt, with the remaining panels of the original bronze doors in the chapter library. Via Carlo, behind the cathedral, leads to the ruins of a **Roman theater** (Teatro Romano), with a seating capacity of 20,000. The theater is still in good enough shape to host a summer opera and theater season. ⊠ *Teatro Romano.* 🎫 *4,000 lire.* ⊙ *Daily 9–1 hr before sunset.*

SWEPT AWAY
The Islands of Ischia and Capri

History's hedonists have long luxuriated on Campania's famous islands. The Roman emperor Tiberius built a dozen villas on Capri to indulge his sexual whims. Later residents have included dancer Rudolf Nureyev and droves of artists and writers. These days day-trippers make up the bulk of the visitors, diminishing the islands' social cachet but unable to tarnish their incomparable beauty. Ischia, less pretty and less chic than Capri, is still a popular landing point on account of spas, beaches, and hot springs.

Ischia

㊸ *31 km (19 mi) west of Naples.*

While Capri wows you with its charm and beauty, **Ischia** takes time to cast its spell. In fact, an overnight stay is probably not long enough for the island to get into your blood. It does have its share of wine-growing villages beneath the lush volcanic slopes of Monte Epomeo and, unlike Capri, it enjoys a life of its own that survives when the tourists head home. But there are few signs of antiquity here, the architecture is unremarkable, the beaches are small and pebbly, there's little shopping beyond the high-trash gift shops that attract the German therapeutic trade, and most visitors are either German (off-season) or Italian (in-season). On the other hand, some of you will delight in discovering an island not yet overrun with tourists from the United States. Ischia also has some lovely hotel-resorts high in the mountains, offering therapeutic programs and rooms with breathtaking views. Should you want to plunk down in the sun for a few days and tune out the world, this is an ideal place to go; the mistake you shouldn't make is expecting Ischia to be an unspoiled, undiscovered Capri. When Augustus gave the Neapolitans Ischia for Capri, he knew what he was doing.

Unlike Capri, Ischia is volcanic in origin. From its hidden reservoir of seething molten matter come the thermal springs said to cure whatever ails you. As early as 1580, a doctor named Iasolino published a book about the mineral wells at Ischia. "If your eyebrows fall off," he wrote, "go and try the baths at Piaggia Romano. Are you unhappy about your complexion? You will find the cure in the waters of Santa Maria del Popolo. Are you deaf? Then go to Bagno d'Ulmitello. If you know anyone who is getting bald, anyone who suffers from elephantiasis, or another whose wife yearns for a child, take the three of them immediately to the Bagno di Vitara; they will bless you."

Today the island is covered with thermal baths surrounded by tropical gardens. Hydrofoils from Naples reach it in 45 minutes; the car ferry takes 90 minutes. The passenger-and-car ferry from Pozzuoli takes about 60 minutes. **Ischia Porto** is the largest town on the island and the usual point of debarkation. It's no workaday port, however, but a pretty resort with plenty of hotels and low flat-roofed houses arrayed on terraced hillsides above the water. Its narrow streets often become flights of steps that scale the hill, and its villas and gardens are framed by pines.

Most of the hotels are along the beach in the part of town called **Ischia Ponte,** which gets its name from the *ponte* (bridge) built by Alfonso of Aragón in 1438 to link the picturesque castle on a small islet offshore with the town and port. For a while, the castle was the home of Vittoria Colonna, poetess and platonic soul mate of Michelangelo, with whom she carried on a lengthy correspondence, and granddaughter of Renaissance Duke Federico da Montefeltro. If you choose to stay in Ischia Porto, you'll find a typical resort atmosphere; countless cafés, shops, and restaurants; and a half-mile stretch of fine sandy beach.

The **information office** is at the harbor. Remember that Ischia is off limits to visitors' cars from April through September; there's fairly good bus service, and you'll find plenty of taxis. One popular beach resort, just 5 kilometers (3 miles) west of Ischia Porto, is **Casamicciola.** Next is chic and upscale **Lacco Ameno,** distinguished by a mushroom-shaped rock offshore and some of the island's best hotels. Here, too, you can enjoy the benefits of Ischia's therapeutic waters.

The far western and southern coasts of the island are more rugged and attractive. **Forio,** at the extreme west, is an ideal stop for lunch or dinner. The sybaritic hot pools of the **Poseidon Gardens** spa establishment are on the Citara beach, south of Forio. You can sit like a Roman senator on a stone chair recessed in the rock and let the hot water cascade over you—all very campy, and fun. **Sant'Angelo,** on the southern coast, is a charming village; the road doesn't reach all the way into town, so it's free of traffic, and it's a five-minute boat ride from the beach of Maronti, at the foot of cliffs. The inland towns of **Serrara, Fontana,** and **Barano** are all high above the sea; Fontana, most elevated of the three, is the base for excursions to the top of **Mt. Epomeo,** the long-dormant volcano that dominates the island landscape. You can reach its 2,585-foot peak in less than 1½ hours of relatively easy walking.

A good 35-kilometer (22-mile) road makes a circuit of the island; the ride takes most of a day at a leisurely pace, if you're stopping along the way to enjoy the views and perhaps have lunch. You can book a **boat tour** (16,000 and 25,000 lire) around the island at the booths in various ports along the coast; there's a one-hour stop at Sant'Angelo.

Dining and Lodging

$$ ✕ **Gennaro.** This small family restaurant on the seafront at Ischia Porto serves excellent fish in a convivial atmosphere. Specialties include spaghetti alle vongole and linguine all'aragosta. ⊠ *Via Porto 66,* ☎ *081/992917. AE, DC, MC, V. Closed Nov.–mid-Mar. and Tues. in Mar., Apr., and Oct.*

$$$$ 🏨 **Grand Hotel Punta Molino.** Right in the town of Ischia Porto, but set in a quiet zone near the sea and framed with pine trees and gardens, is one of the best hotels on the island. The decor is bright and contemporary, with some luxury touches, and many rooms have sea views. There's a heated pool on one of the terraces. Half board is required. ⊠ *Lungomare Colombo,* ☎ *081/991544,* 𝔽𝔸𝕏 *081/991562. 82 rooms with bath or shower. Restaurant, bar, spa, beach, parking. AE, MC, DC, V. Closed Nov.–Apr. 24.*

$$$$ 🏨 **Regina Isabella.** Tucked away in an exclusive corner of the beach
★   in Lacco Ameno, Ischia's top luxury hotel has full resort facilities and pampers guests with spa treatments as well. The rooms are ample and decorated in warm Mediterranean colors. Most have terraces or balconies. Don't miss the fun of socializing with chic vacationers in the elegant bar or restaurant or at poolside. ⊠ *Piazza Santa Restituta, Lacco Ameno,* ☎ *081/994322,* 𝔽𝔸𝕏 *081/986043. 134 rooms with bath or shower. Indoor-outdoor pools, tennis court, beach. AE, DC, MC, V. Closed Oct. 16–Apr. 14.*

$$$–$$$$ 🏨 **Hotel San Montano.** This modern hotel overlooks the sea in a quiet location. San Montano is decorated with nautical motifs and ceramic-tile floors. The rooms have compact English-navy furnishings, color TV, and minibar. The San Montano has all resort facilities and provides spa treatments, too. ⊠ *Via Montevico 1, Lacco Ameno,* ☎ *081/994033,* 𝔽𝔸𝕏 *081/980242. 67 rooms with bath or shower. Restaurant, pool, tennis court, parking. AE, DC, MC, V. Closed Nov.–Mar.*

$$$ 🏨 **Villarosa.** You'll find this welcoming hotel in the heart of Ischia Porto
★   and only a short walk from the beach. It is a gracious family-run villa with bright and airy rooms. There's a thermally heated pool in the villa garden. In high season, half board is required, and you must reserve well in advance. Prices fall into the lower end of this category. ⊠ *Via Giacinto Gigante 3,* ☎ *081/991316,* 𝔽𝔸𝕏 *081/992425. 37 rooms with bath or shower. Restaurant. AE, MC, V. Closed Nov.–Easter.*

$ 🏨 **Del Postiglione.** This attractive, pink, Mediterranean-style edifice is smaller than it appears, with only 11 guest rooms. Its aura of understated luxury is created by marble floors, tropical plants adorning the outside, and generous balconies overlooking one of Ischia Porto's quiet back streets, a couple of minutes from the seafront. The rates are at the bottom of this category. Half board only is accepted in August. ⊠ *Via Giacinto Gigante 19,* ☎ *081/991579,* 𝔽𝔸𝕏 *081/991579. 11 rooms with bath or shower. Restaurant, bar, baby-sitting. No credit cards.*

Capri

④④   *31 km (19 mi) south of Naples.*

Erstwhile pleasure dome to Roman emperors, and now Italy's most glamorous seaside getaway, **Capri** (accent on the first syllable) is a craggy island at the southern approach to the Bay of Naples. It's easy to reach by boat or hydrofoil from Naples and Sorrento all year and from the Amalfi Coast or Ischia during the summer months. The boat from

Naples takes about 75 minutes; the hydrofoil, only about 40 minutes. In addition, there's direct helicopter service from Capodichino Airport in Naples (☞ Arriving and Departing by Plane *in* Campania A to Z, *below*). Note that from April 1 to October 31, no cars may be taken to the island.

The summer scene on Capri calls to mind the stampeding of bulls through the narrow streets of Pamplona: If you can visit in the spring or fall, do so. Yet even the crowds are not enough to destroy Capri's very special charm. The town is a Moorish opera set of shiny white houses, tiny squares, and narrow medieval alleyways hung with flowers. You can take a bus or the funicular to reach the town, which rests on top of rugged limestone cliffs, hundreds of feet above the sea, and on which huge herds of *capra* (goats) once used to roam (giving the name to the island).

The mood is modish but somehow unspoiled. The upper crust bakes in the sun in private villas; the secret is for you, too, to disappear while the day-trippers take over—offering yourself to the sun at your hotel pool or exploring the hidden corners of the island. Even in the height of summer, you can enjoy a degree of privacy on one of the many paved paths that wind around the island hundreds of feet above the sea. Unlike the other islands in the Bay of Naples, Capri is not of volcanic origin but is an integral part of the limestone chain of the Apennines, left above water when some subterranean cataclysm sank its connecting link with the mainland.

The Phoenicians were the earliest settlers of Capri. The Greeks arrived in the 4th century BC and were followed by the Romans, who made it their playground. Emperor Augustus vacationed here; Tiberius built 12 villas, scattered over the island, and here he spent the later years of his life, refusing to return to Rome even when he was near death. Capri was one of the strongholds of the 16th-century pirate Barbarossa, who first sacked it and then made a fortress of it. Moors and Greeks had previously established their citadels on its heights, and pirates from all corners of the world periodically raided it. In 1806 the British wanted to turn it into another Gibraltar and were beginning to build fortifications when the French took it away from them in 1808. However, the Roman influence has remained the strongest, reflecting a sybaritic way of life inherited from the Greek colonists on the mainland.

Capri has a reputation for being hideously expensive, and indeed some of its top-ranking hotels and restaurants are among the most costly in Italy. But plenty of moderately priced hotels and some inexpensive ones share the same fabulous views. There are also moderately priced trattorias off the beaten tourist track.

Thousands of legends concerning the lives and loves of mythological creatures, Roman emperors, Saracen invaders, and modern eccentrics combine to give Capri a voluptuous allure—sensuous and intoxicating—like the island's rare and delicious white wine. (Most of the wine passed off as "local" on Capri comes from the much more extensive vineyards of Ischia.) Certainly, there are fewer pleasures more gratifying than gazing out at the sea from the quiet of a sun-dappled arbor while enjoying a glass of chilled wine and flavorful insalata caprese.

All boats for Capri dock at **Marina Grande,** where you can board an excursion boat for the 90-minute tour to the **Blue Grotto.** If you're pressed for time, however, skip this sometimes frustrating and disappointing excursion. You board one boat to get to the grotto, and you have to transfer to another, smaller, one in order to get inside the grotto. If there's a backup of boats waiting to get in, you'll be given precious little time to enjoy the gorgeous color of the water and its silvery reflections. ✉ *About 22,000 lire, including 8,000-lire admission to grotto.* ☾ *Summer, daily 9:30–2 hrs before sunset; winter, 10–noon.*

OFF THE BEATEN PATH	**BOAT TRIP** – The approximately two-hour boat trip around the island is hassle-free and very enjoyable. These excursions start at **Marina Grande** and are run by the Grotta Azzurra company. The cost is 18,000 lire. Make either of these boat trips in the morning, when light and visibility are better.

One of the town's two tourist information offices is on the pier where the boats from the mainland dock; ask for a brochure map ("Piantina") showing the many walks you can take to get the best views and escape the crowds. You may have to wait in line for the cog railway (3,000 lire round-trip) to the town of **Capri.** If it's not operating, there's bus and taxi service. From the upper station, walk out into Piazza Umberto I, much better known as the **Piazzetta,** the island's social center, *the* place to see and be seen, deliberately commercial and self-consciously picturesque at the same time. You can window-shop in expensive boutiques and browse in souvenir shops along Via Vittorio Emanuele, which leads south toward the many-domed **Certosa di San Giacomo.** The church and cloister of this much-restored monastery can be visited, and you should also pause long enough to enjoy the breathtaking view of Punta Tragara and the Faraglioni, three towering shoals, from the viewing stand at the edge of the cliff. ✉ *Via Certosa.* ✉ *Free.* ☾ *Tues.–Sat. 9–2, Sun. 9–1.*

OFF THE BEATEN PATH	**BELVEDERE** – A short walk along Via Tragara leads to a belvedere overlooking the Faraglioni; another takes you out of town of on Via Matermania to the so-called Natural Arch, an unusual rock formation near a natural grotto that the Romans transformed into a shrine. The 20-minute walk from the Piazzetta along picturesque Via Madre Serafina and Via Castello to the belvedere at Punta Cannone gives you a panoramic view of the island.

Beyond the monastery of San Giacomo, Via Matteotti leads past bright shops and ice-cream stands to the **Giardini di Augusto** (Gardens of Augustus), a beautifully planted public garden with excellent views. From its terraces you can see the village of **Marina Piccola** below, where restaurants, cabanas, and swimming platforms huddle among the shoals. This is the best place on the island for swimming; you can reach it by bus or by following the steep and winding Via Krupp, actually a staircase cut into the rock, all the way down. (Friedrich Krupp, the German arms manufacturer, loved Capri and became one of the island's most generous benefactors.) Otherwise you swim off boats or take a hint from the family groups from Naples and Sorrento who swim off the unkempt but sandy beach at the end of Marina Grande past the cog railway station.

NEED A BREAK?	Just down Via Roma from the Piazzetta is **Verginiello** (☏ 081/837–0944), one of the island's best-value restaurants for lunch. Try the calamari.

OFF THE BEATEN PATH	**VILLA JOVIS** – From the town of Capri, the 45-minute hike east to Villa Jovis, the grandest of those built by Tiberius, is strenuous but rewarding. Follow the signs for Villa Jovis, taking Via Le Botteghe from the Piazzetta, then continuing along Via Croce and Via Tiberio. At the end of a lane that climbs the steep hill, with pretty views all the way, you come to the precipice over which the emperor reputedly disposed of the vic-

tims of his perverse attentions. From a natural terrace above, near a chapel, are spectacular views of the entire Bay of Naples and (on clear days) part of the Gulf of Salerno. Below are the ruins of Tiberius's palace. Allow 45 minutes each way for the walk alone. ⊠ *Via Tiberio.* 🎟 *4,000 lire.* ⊙ *Daily 9–1 hr before sunset.*

You can take a bus from Marina Grande (1,500 lire) or a taxi (about 15,000 lire one way; agree on the fare before starting out) up the tortuous road to **Anacapri,** the island's only other town. Here crowds are thickest around the square that is the starting point of the chair lift (6,000 lire) to the top of Mt. Solaro. Elsewhere, Anacapri is quiet and appealing. Look for the church of **San Michele,** where a climb to the choir loft rewards you with a perspective of the magnificent 18th-century majolica tile floor showing the Garden of Eden. From Piazza della Vittoria, picturesque Via Capodimonte leads to **Villa San Michele,** charming former home of Swedish scientist Axel Munthe, now a museum of his antiques and furniture. ⊠ *Via Axel Munthe.* 🎟 *6,000 lire.* ⊙ *Nov.–Feb., daily 10:30–3:30; Mar., daily 9:30–4:30; Apr. and Oct., daily 9:30–5; May–Sept., daily 9–6.*

Anacapri is also good for walks: Try the 40-minute walk (each way) to the Migliara belvedere and another walk of about an hour each way to the ruins of the Roman villa of Damecuta. If walking is not your idea of happiness, just join the other sybarites sitting in the Piazzetta and remember that Augustus called Capri Apragopolis (City of Sweet Idleness) or, as the Italians would say, dolce far niente.

Dining and Lodging

$$$ ✕ **La Pigna.** Ensconced in a glassed-in veranda and offering outdoor dining in a garden shaded by lemon trees, the Pigna is one of Capri's favorite restaurants. The specialties are a house-produced wine, *farfalle impuzzite* (bow-tie pasta with seafood and tomato), and *aragosta alla luna caprese* (lobster with mozzarella, tomato, and basil). The cordial host organizes party evenings with feasts of seasonal specialties and seafood. ⊠ *Via Lo Palazzo 30, Capri,* ☎ *081/837–0280. Reservations essential. AE, DC, MC, V. Closed Tues. and Nov.–Easter.*

$$–$$$ ✕ **La Capannina.** Known as one of Capri's best restaurants, La Capannina is only a few steps from the busy social hub of the Piazzetta. ★ It has a vine-draped veranda for dining outdoors by candlelight in a garden setting. The specialties, aside from an authentic Capri wine with the house label, are homemade ravioli alla caprese and regional dishes. ⊠ *Via Le Botteghe 14, Capri,* ☎ *081/837–0732. Reservations essential. AE, MC, V. Closed Nov. 10–Mar. 15 and Wed. Sept.–July.*

$$ ✕ **Al Grottino.** This small and friendly family-run restaurant, which is handy to the Piazzetta, has arched ceilings and lots of atmosphere; autographed photos of celebrity customers cover the walls. House specialties are gnocchi with tomato sauce and mozzarella, and linguine *ai gamberetti* (with shrimp and tomato sauce). ⊠ *Via Longano 27, Capri,* ☎ *081/837–0584. Reservations essential. AE, MC, V. Closed Tues. and Nov. 3–Mar. 20.*

$$$$ 🏨 **Europa Palace Hotel.** A modern resort atmosphere pervades this large Mediterranean-style hotel set in lovely gardens. Each of four junior suites has a private swimming pool and terrace. The bedrooms are tastefully decorated in contemporary style, with white predominating; marble is featured in the bathrooms, and many rooms have balconies. The only minus is being in Anacapri, a bus or cab ride from the restaurants and shops in the town of Capri. ⊠ *Via Capodimonte, Anacapri,* ☎ *081/837–3800,* 🖷 *081/837–3191. 93 rooms with bath or shower.*

Restaurant, bar, air-conditioning, pool, parking. AE, DC, MC, V. Closed Nov.–Mar.

$$$$ ⚜ **Quisisana.** Catering largely to Americans, this is the most luxurious and traditional hotel in the center of town. Spacious rooms are done in traditional or contemporary decor with some antique accents; many have arcaded balconies with views of the sea or the charming enclosed garden, in which there's a swimming pool. The bar and restaurant are casually elegant. ⊠ *Via Camerelle 2, Capri,* ☎ *081/837–0788,* FAX *081/837–6080. 143 rooms with bath or shower. Restaurant, bar, pool, sauna, tennis court. AE, DC, MC, V. Closed Nov.–mid-Mar.*

$$$$ ⚜ **Scalinatella.** The name means "little stairway," and that's how this
   ★   charming but modern small hotel is built, on terraces following the slope of the hill, overlooking the gardens, pool, and sea. The bedrooms are intimate, with alcoves and fresh, bright colors; the bathrooms feature Jacuzzis. The hotel has a small bar but no restaurant. ⊠ *Via Tragara 8, Capri,* ☎ *081/837–0633,* FAX *081/837–8291. 54 rooms with bath or shower. Bar, air-conditioning, pool, tennis court. AE, MC, V. Closed Nov.–Mar. 14.*

$$$ ⚜ **San Michele.** You'll find this large white villa-hotel next to Axel Munthe's Capri home. Surrounded by luxuriant gardens, the San Michele offers solid comfort and good value, along with spectacular views. The decor is contemporary, with some Neapolitan period pieces adding atmosphere. Most rooms have a terrace or balcony overlooking either the sea or island landscapes. ⊠ *Via G. Orlandi 5, Anacapri,* ☎ *081/837–1442,* FAX *081/837–1420. 56 rooms with bath or shower. 2 restaurants, pool. AE, DC, MC, V. Closed Nov.–Mar.*

$$$ ⚜ **Villa Brunella.** This quiet family-run gem nestles in a garden setting just below the lane leading to the Faraglioni. Comfortable and tastefully furnished, the hotel also has spectacular views, a swimming pool, and a terrace restaurant known for good food. ⊠ *Via Tragara 24, Capri,* ☎ *081/837–0122,* FAX *081/837–0430. 18 rooms with bath. Bar. AE, DC, MC, V. Closed Nov.–Mar.*

$$$ ⚜ **Villa Krupp.** Among the hotels that are open all year, this historic hostelry—onetime home of Maxim Gorky, whose guests included Lenin—occupies a quiet location overlooking the Gardens of Augustus. Rooms are plain but spacious, and some have a balcony. ⊠ *Via Matteotti 12, Capri,* ☎ *081/837–0362,* FAX *081/837–6489. 12 rooms with bath or shower. MC, V.*

$$$ ⚜ **Villa Sarah.** This whitewashed Mediterranean building has a homey look and bright, simply furnished rooms. It's close enough to the Piazzetta (a 10-minute walk) to give easy access to the goings-on there, while ensuring yet far enough away to ensure restful nights. There's a garden and a small bar, but no restaurant. ⊠ *Via Tiberio 3/a, Capri,* ☎ *081/837–7817,* FAX *081/837–7215. 20 rooms with bath. AE, MC, V. Closed Nov.–Mar.*

$$ ⚜ **Aida.** A 10-minute walk from the center of town in a tiny lane that borders the Gardens of Augustus, the Aida offers a tranquil haven from Capri's bustle and hard sell. The staff is sociable, and the rooms, which look onto a small garden, are spacious, comfortably furnished, and immaculately clean. The beach, at Marina Piccola, is only 20 minutes away. ⊠ *Via Birago, Capri,* ☎ *081/837–0366. 9 rooms, 5 with shower. No credit cards. Closed mid-Oct.–Apr.*

Special Events

Capri's **New Year's Eve** celebrations last all evening with dancing and music culminating in a magnificent fireworks display. On **New Year's Day** there are marching bands, pageants, and all the vigorous revelry you would expect on this exuberant island.

THE AMALFI DRIVE
Sorrento to Salerno

As travelers journey down the fabled Amalfi Drive, their route takes them past rocky cliffs plunging into the sea and small boats lying in sandy coves like so many brightly colored fish. Erosion has contorted the rocks into mythological shapes and hollowed out fairy grottoes where the air is turquoise and the water an icy blue. White villages, dripping with flowers, nestle in coves or climb like vines up the steep, terraced hills. The road must have a thousand turns, each with a different view, on its dizzying 69-kilometer (43-mile) journey from Sorrento to Salerno.

Sorrento

45 *50 km (31 mi) south of Naples.*

Sorrento is across the Bay of Naples, on autostrada A3 and S145; the Circumvesuviana railway, which stops at Herculaneum and Pompeii, provides another connection. The coast between Naples and Castellammare, where road and railway turn off onto the Sorrento peninsula, seems at times depressingly overbuilt and industrialized. Yet Vesuvius looms to the left, you can make out the 3,000-foot-high mass of Mt. Faito ahead, and on a clear day you can see Capri off the tip of the peninsula. The scenery improves considerably as you near Sorrento, where the coastal plain is carved into russet cliffs rising perpendicularly from the sea. This is the Sorrento (north) side of the peninsula; on the other side is the Amalfi Coast, more dramatically scenic and somewhat less overcome by tourists in summer. Many prefer the charming towns on the Amalfi Coast to the tourist haven of Sorrento, but Sorrento has at least two advantages: the Circumvesuviana railway terminal and a fairly flat terrain. (Positano, and to a lesser extent Amalfi and Ravello, clings to hillsides and requires some strenuous walking.)

Until the mid-20th century Sorrento was a small, genteel resort favored by central European princes, English aristocrats, and American literati. Now the town has grown and spread out along the crest of its famous cliffs, and apartments stand where citrus groves once bloomed. Tour groups arrive by the busload, and their ranks are swollen by Italian vacationers in the peak summer season. Like most resorts, Sorrento is best off-season, either in spring and early autumn or in winter, when Campania's mild climate can make a stay pleasant anywhere along the coast. Another reason to avoid the peninsula during peak season is the heavy traffic on the single coast road, where cars and buses may be backed up for miles. Highlights of a visit to Sorrento include a stroll around town, with views of the Bay of Naples from the **Villa Comunale** or from the terrace behind the **Museo Correale.** The museum features a collection of decorative antiques, from precious porcelain to furniture to landscape paintings of the Neapolitan school. ✉ *Via Correale.* 📷 *Museum and garden 8,000 lire, garden 2,000 lire.* ◷ *Apr.–Sept., Mon. and Wed.–Sat. 9–12:30 and 4–6, Sun. 9–12:30; Oct.–Dec., Feb., and Mar., Mon. and Wed.–Sat. 9–noon and 3–5, Sun. 9–noon.*

Around **Piazza Tasso** are a number of shops selling **embroidered goods** and **intarsia** (wood inlay) work. Along narrow Via San Cesareo, where the air is pungent with the perfumes of fruit and vegetable stands, there are more shops selling local and Italian handicrafts.

Just off Piazza Tasso is **Gigino** (✉ Via degli Archi 15), one of Sorrento's best-known inexpensive restaurants. Try the fixed-price menu at lunch. Gigino is closed Tuesday.

Explore the town's churches and narrow alleys and follow Via Marina Grande, which turns into a pedestrian lane and stairway, to Sorrento's only real beach, where the fishermen pull up their boats. You can take a bus or walk a mile or so to Capo Sorrento, then follow the signs to the **Villa of Pollio Felice,** the scattered seaside remains of an ancient Roman villa, where you can swim off the rocks or simply admire the setting.

Before you leave Sorrento, consider a side trip west along the road that skirts the tip of the peninsula; if you enjoy dramatic seascapes, this will be worth the extra time.

Dining and Lodging

$$ ✕ **Antica Trattoria.** An Old World dining room inside and garden tables in fair weather make this a pleasant place to enjoy the local cooking. The atmosphere is homey and hospitable. The menu (usefully translated into English) is voluminous and your choice will be difficult, but the specialties include spaghetti alle vongole and gamberetti Antica Trattoria (in tomato sauce). ✉ *Via Giuliani 33,* ☎ *081/807–1082. No credit cards. Closed Mon. and Jan. 10–Feb. 10.*

$$ ✕ **Parrucchiano.** Centrally located and popular, this is one of Sorrento's oldest and best restaurants. You walk up a few steps to glassed-in veranda dining rooms filled, like greenhouses, with vines and plants. The menu offers classic local specialties, among them *panzerotti* (pastry shells filled with tomato and mozzarella) and scaloppe *alla sorrentina* (with tomato and mozzarella). ✉ *Corso Italia 71,* ☎ *081/878–1321. MC, V. Closed Wed. Nov.–May.*

$$$$ 🏨 **Cocumella.** This hotel is set in a cliff-top garden in a quiet residen-
★   tial area on the edge of Sorrento (it's really in the adjacent town of Sant'Agnello). Occupying a historic old villa that was a monastery in the 17th century, it features a tasteful blend of antique and contemporary decor, with vaulted ceilings and archways, a dining veranda, and stunning tiled floors. It's exclusive and elegant without being stuffy. ✉ *Via Cocumella 7,* ☎ *081/878–2933,* 🗚 *081/878–3712. 61 rooms and suites with bath or shower. Restaurant, bar, pool, tennis court, parking. AE, DC, MC, V. Closed Jan. and Feb.*

$$$$ 🏨 **Excelsior Vittoria.** In the heart of Sorrento, but removed from the bustle of the main square, this historic hotel perches on the cliff. It has art-nouveau decor and some quite grand, though faded, furnishings. Tenor Enrico Caruso's bedroom is preserved as a relic; the guest bedrooms are slightly less elegant but spacious and comfortable. The views are wonderful. Winter prices are 10% lower than high-season rates. ✉ *Piazza Tasso 34,* ☎ *081/807–1044,* 🗚 *081/877–1206. 109 rooms and suites with bath. Restaurant, bar, pool. AE, DC, MC, V.*

$$$$ 🏨 **Imperial Hotel Tramontano.** The birthplace of the poet Torquato Tasso—the first of an impressive list of literary credentials—this palatial villa lies within a semitropical garden in the center of Sorrento. The sumptuous furnishings and Belle Epoque tone are set off by the spectacular views out to sea. ✉ *Via Veneto 1,* ☎ *081/878–2588,* 🗚 *081/807–2344. 120 rooms with bath or shower. Restaurant, bar, beach, meeting rooms, parking. AE, DC, MC, V. Closed Jan.–Mar.*

$$$ 🏨 **Eden.** In a quiet but central location, the Eden has a garden and bright, though undistinguished, bedrooms. The lounge and lobby have more character. It's an unpretentious but friendly hotel, although it can get crowded in high season. ✉ *Via Correale 25,* ☎ *081/878–1909,* 🗚

081/807–2016. 60 rooms with bath or shower. Restaurant, bar, pool, parking. AE, DC, MC, V. Closed Nov.–Feb.

$ ▣ **City.** The convenient location and excellent value for the money are the best reasons to stay in this modest establishment, close to the bus and train stations. Bedrooms are small and functional. The atmosphere is relaxed, and the management is always ready with information and advice. ⊠ *Corso Italia 221,* ☎ *081/877–2210,* 𝔽𝔸𝕏 *081/877–2210. 13 rooms with shower. MC, V.*

Nightlife and the Arts

BARS AND CAFÉS

Circolo dei Forestieri (⊠ Via de Maio 35, Sorrento, ☎ 081/807–4033). Here you'll get a memorable view of the Bay of Naples from the terrace. Drinks are moderately priced, and there is live music nightly in summer and every weekend the rest of the year.

Villa Pompeiana (⊠ Via Marina Grande 6, Sorrento, ☎ 081/877–2428). This bar, next to the Bellevue Syrene Hotel, has a garden terrace and an indoor tavern with an ancient-Roman setting. There's music in summer.

FILM

Each December, the **International Cinema Convention** in Sorrento draws an elite collection of producers, directors, and stars in a less frantic atmosphere than that of the festival in Cannes. While much of the activity revolves around deal making, a number of previews are screened, and the town sees the festival as a shot of energy in the middle of the quiet season. For details contact the Sorrento tourist office (☞ Contacts and Resources *in* Campania A to Z, *below*).

Shopping

This is the place to buy **embroidered table linens** and **crocheted lace.** Also, the wood-inlay art of **intarsia** is a centuries-old tradition here. Shops today offer everything from jewelry boxes to trays and coffee tables with intarsia decorations. **Ferdinando Corcione,** in his shop on Via San Francesco, gives demonstrations of his intarsia work, producing decorative plaques with classic or contemporary motifs.

Positano

★ ㊻ *14 km (9 mi) east of Sorrento, 40 km (25 mi) west of Salerno.*

The most popular town along the Amalfi drive, particularly among Americans, is **Positano,** a village of white Moorish-type houses clinging dramatically to slopes around a small sheltered bay. When John Steinbeck lived here in 1953, he wrote that it was difficult to consider tourism an industry because "there are not enough [tourists]." Alas, Positano has since been discovered. The artists came first, and, as happens wherever artists go, the wealthy followed and the artists fled. What Steinbeck wrote, however, still applies: "Positano bites deep. It is a dream place that isn't quite real when you are there and becomes beckoningly real after you have gone. Its houses climb a hill so steep it would be a cliff except that stairs are cut in it. I believe that whereas most house foundations are vertical, in Positano they are horizontal. The small curving bay of unbelievably blue and green water laps gently on a beach of small pebbles. There is only one narrow street and it does not come down to the water. Everything else is stairs, some of them as steep as ladders. You do not walk to visit a friend, you either climb or slide."

In the 10th century Positano was part of Amalfi's Maritime Republic, which rivaled Venice as an important mercantile power. Its heyday was in the 16th and 17th centuries, when its ships traded in the Near and

Middle East, carrying spices, silks, and precious woods. The coming of the steamship in the mid-19th century led to the town's decline, and some three-fourths of the town's 8,000 citizens emigrated to America, mostly to New York. One major task of Positano's mayor has been to find space in the overcrowded cemetery for New York Positanesi who want to spend eternity here.

What had been reduced to a forgotten fishing village is now the number-one attraction on the coast, with hotels for every budget, charming restaurants, and dozens of boutiques. From here, you can take hydrofoils to Capri during the summer, escorted bus rides to Ravello, and tours of the Grotta Smeralda (☞ *below*).

Positano may not have a castle, but it does have another attraction that's bringing the town considerable wealth: stylish summer clothes. From January to March, buyers from all over the world come to Positano to buy the trend-setting handmade clothes that are sold in more than 200 boutiques. One-size loose-fitting cotton dresses; full skirts, plain or covered with lace—some in light pastel colors with hand-printed designs, others in bold block colors: bright oranges, pinks, and yellows. The choice is endless, and the prices—well, you're on vacation, and the same dresses would cost twice as much in New York or Rome.

If you're staying in Positano, check whether your hotel has a parking area. If not, you will have to pay for space in a parking lot, which is almost impossible to find during the high season, from Easter to September. The best bet for day-trippers is to get to Positano early enough so that space is still available. No matter how much time you spend in Positano, make sure you have some comfortable walking shoes—no heels, please!—and that your back and legs are strong enough to negotiate steps.

Dining and Lodging

$$ ✕ **Buca di Bacco.** After an aperitif at the town's most famous and fashionable café downstairs, you dine on a veranda overlooking the beach. The specialties include spaghetti alle vongole and *grigliata* mista (mixed grilled seafood). ⊠ *Via Rampa Teglia 8,* ☎ *089/875699. AE, DC, MC, V. Closed Nov. 6–Mar.*

$$ ✕ **Capurale.** Among the popular restaurants on the beach promenade, this one just around the corner has the best food and lowest prices. Tables are set under vines on a breezy sidewalk in the summer, indoors and upstairs in winter. Spaghetti con melanzane and crepes *al formaggio* (with cheese) are among the specialties. ⊠ *Via Regina Giovanna 12,* ☎ *089/875374. AE, DC, MC, V. Closed Tues. Nov.–Mar. and 4 weeks in Jan. and Feb.*

$$$$ ▥ **Le Sirenuse.** A handsome 18th-century palazzo in the center of
★ town is the setting for this luxury hotel in which bright tiled floors, precious antiques, and tasteful furnishings are featured in ample and luminous salons. The bedrooms have the same sense of spaciousness and comfort; most have splendid views from balconies and terraces. The top-floor suites have huge bathrooms and Jacuzzis. One side of a large terrace has an inviting swimming pool; on the other is an excellent restaurant—both share the hotel's view of the town, beach, and sea. ⊠ *Via Cristoforo Colombo 30,* ☎ *089/875066,* ℻ *089/811798. 60 rooms with bath or shower. Bar, sauna, parking. AE, DC, MC, V.*

$$$$ ▥ **San Pietro.** Extraordinary is the word for this luxurious oasis for
★ the affluent international set. Located outside the town, set high above the sea with garden terraces, the San Pietro has sumptuous Neapolitan baroque decor and masses of flowers in the lounges, elegantly understated rooms (most with terraces), and marvelous views. There's a pool on an upper level, and an elevator whisks guests to the private

beach and beach bar. The proprietors organize boating excursions and parties and provide car and minibus service into town. ✉ *Via Laurito,* ☎ *089/875455,* FAX *089/811449. 60 rooms with bath or shower. Restaurant, 2 bars, outdoor pool, tennis court, beach, dock, parking. AE, DC, MC, V. Closed Nov.–Mar.*

$$$ 🏨 **Casa Albertina.** One of the few hotels here that is open all year, Casa Albertina is a pleasant place with a friendly owner-manager. The rooms are bright with color, some have views, and you can enjoy the panorama from the terrace, where you can have breakfast or drinks in fair weather. The main drawback is the stairs, which must be negotiated when leaving or returning to the hotel, though it's only a few steps up from one of the town's social hubs, the Bar De Martino, a good spot for an after-dinner drink. There's a restaurant and roof garden, and, except for the restaurant, rates are low in its category. ✉ *Via della Tavolozza 4,* ☎ *089/875143,* FAX *089/811540. 21 rooms with bath or shower. Bar, parking. AE, DC, MC, V.*

$$$ 🏨 **Palazzo Murat.** The location is perfect—in the heart of town, near the beachside promenade, but set in a quiet, walled garden. The old wing is a historic palazzo with tall windows and wrought-iron balconies; the new wing is a whitewashed Mediterranean building with arches and terraces. You can relax in antiques-accented lounges or in the charming vine-draped patio, and since there's no restaurant, you will avoid the half-board requirement applied in most hotels here in high season. ✉ *Via dei Mulini 23,* ☎ *089/875177,* FAX *089/811419. 28 rooms with bath and shower. Bar. AE, DC, MC, V. Closed Nov. 5–Mar.*

$$ 🏨 **Santa Caterina.** There is more to this hotel than meets the eye: Rooms descend on three levels down the steep slope. The owners have made the most of the exquisite view of the town and seashore, which can be relished from each of the rooms. On street level (the top floor), there is also a good fish restaurant. It's quite a hike to the beach—a good 15 minutes down the steps—but that's nothing new in Positano. ✉ *Via Pasitea 113.* ☎ *089/811513,* FAX *089/875019. 12 rooms with bath or shower. Restaurant, bar. AE, DC, MC, V. Closed Nov.–Mar.*

Nightlife

L'Africana (✉ Vettica Maggiore, Praiano, ☎ 089/874042). This is the premier nightclub on the Amalfi Coast and is built into a fantastic grotto above the sea. Praiano itself is only 3 kilometers (2 miles) east of Positano on the coast road.

Shopping

The picturesque streets of this coastal resort are lined with **boutiques** selling **casual fashions** and **beachwear** in splashy colors and extravagant fabrics.

Grotta Smeralda

13 km (8 mi) along the coastal road from Positano, 4 km (2½ mi) west of Amalfi.

A short distance outside Amalfi, you'll see signposts for the **Grotta Smeralda** (Emerald Grotto). You can park here and take an elevator down to the grotto, or you can drive on to Amalfi and return to the grotto by the more romantic route: via boat (boat tours leave from the Amalfi seafront approximately every two hours, according to demand; the charge is 10,000 lire per person). The grotto is named for its peculiar green light, which casts an eerie emerald glow over impressive formations of stalagmites and stalactites, many of them underwater. ☞ *5,000 lire.* ☉ *Summer, daily 9–5; winter, daily 10–3 (hours vary).*

Amalfi

47 *17 km (11 mi) east of Positano, 25 km (16 mi) west of Salerno.*

"The sun—the moon—the stars and—Amalfi," Amalfitans used to say. Today, the tourists have made it their own. Although **Amalfi** would seem to be a leading choice for a town to stay in along the drive, it would have to be a distant third—after Ravello and Positano—because of the congestion caused by tour buses, which make Amalfi the main stopping point on their excursions. The town is romantically situated at the mouth of a deep gorge and has some good-quality hotels and restaurants. It's also a convenient base for excursions to Capri and the Emerald Grotto.

During the Middle Ages, Amalfi was an independent maritime state—a little Republic of Venice—with a population of 50,000. The ship compass, trivia fans will be pleased to know, was invented here in 1302.

Amalfi's main historical attraction is its **Duomo** (Cathedral of St. Andrew), which shows an interesting mix of Moorish and early-Gothic influences. The interior is a 10th-century Romanesque skeleton in an 18th-century Baroque dress. The transept and the choir are 13th century. The handsome 12th-century campanile has identical Gothic domes at each corner. Don't miss the beautiful late–13th-century Moorish cloister, with its slender double columns. At least one critic has called the cathedral's facade the ugliest piece of serious architecture in Italy—decide for yourself. The same critic snickers at the tourists who fail to note the cathedral's greatest treasure, the 11th-century bronze doors from Constantinople. Turn right out of the doors for the **cloisters**, with whitewashed arches and palms, and a small museum in the adjoining crypt. ✉ *Duomo free, cloisters and crypt 3,000 lire.* ☉ *Duomo: Summer, daily 7:30 AM–9 PM, and winter, daily 7:30–noon and 4–6:30; cloisters and crypt: summer, daily 9–9, and winter, daily 10–1 and 2:30–5:30.*

The **parking problem** here is as bad as that in Positano. The small lot in the center of town fills quickly; if you can afford the steep prices, make a luncheon reservation at one of the hotel restaurants and have your car parked for you.

The main street leads back through town from the cathedral to the mountains, and passes a ceramic workshop and some water-driven paper mills where handcrafted paper is made and sold. Though it's not always open, there's a **paper museum** where you can see exactly how the mills work.

NEED A BREAK? — Stop in at the **Pansa** pastry shop on Piazza del Duomo for a giant *sfogliatella* (a multilayered pastry) or any of the other oven-fresh goodies.

Dining and Lodging

$$ ✕ **La Caravella.** You'll find this welcoming establishment tucked away ★ under some arches lining the coast road, next to the medieval Arsenal, where Amalfi's mighty fleet once was provisioned. La Caravella has a nondescript entrance but a pleasant interior decorated in a medley of colors and paintings of Old Amalfi. It's small and intimate; specialties include *scialatielli* (homemade pasta with shellfish sauce) and *pesce al limone* (fish with lemon sauce). ✉ *Via M. Camera 12,* ☎ *089/871029. AE, DC, MC, V. Closed Nov. 10–30 and Tues. Oct–June.*

$$$$ ▦ **Santa Caterina.** A large mansion perched above terraced and flow-★ ered hillsides on the coast road just outside Amalfi proper, the Santa Caterina is one of the best hotels on the entire coast, offering gracious living in a wonderfully scenic setting. The rooms are tastefully decorated; most have small terraces or balconies with great views. There are lovely lounges and terraces for relaxing, and an elevator whisks guests to the seaside saltwater pool, bar, and swimming area. On grounds lush with lemon and orange groves, there are two romantic villa annexes. ⊠ *Strada Amalfitana 9,* ☎ *089/871012,* 𝔽𝔸𝕏 *089/871351. 70 rooms with bath. Restaurant, bar, pool, parking. AE, DC, MC, V.*

$$$ 🏨 **Hotel Dei Cavalieri.** This terraced, white, Mediterranean-style hotel on the main road outside Amalfi has three villa annexes on grounds just across the road that extend all the way to a beach below. The bedrooms are air-conditioned and functionally furnished, with splashy majolica tile floors contributing a bright note throughout. An ample buffet breakfast is served, and, though half board is mandatory during high season, you can dine either at the hotel or at several restaurants in Amalfi by special arrangement. ⊠ *Via M. Comite 32,* ☎ *089/831333,* 𝔽𝔸𝕏 *089/831354. 60 rooms with bath. Restaurant, bar, parking. AE, DC, MC, V.*

$$$ 🏨 **Miramalfi.** A modern building perched above the sea, the Miramalfi has wonderful views, simple but attractive decor, terraces, swimming pool, and a sunning/swimming area on the sea, as well as a quiet location just below the coast road, only a kilometer (½ mile) from the center of town. Almost all rooms have balconies with sea views. ⊠ *Via Quasimodo 3,* ☎ *089/871588,* 𝔽𝔸𝕏 *089/871588. 48 rooms with bath or shower. Restaurant, beach, parking. AE, DC, MC, V.*

Ravello

★ ㊽ *5 km (3 mi) northeast of Amalfi, 25 km (16 mi) west of Salerno.*

Perched on a ridge high above Amalfi and the neighboring town of Atrani, the enchanting village of **Ravello** has stupendous views, quiet lanes, and two irresistibly romantic gardens—that of **Villa Rufolo,** where medieval ruins frame spectacular vistas, and **Villa Cimbrone,** a private estate open to the public (the villa itself is now a hotel) with spectacular views of the entire Bay of Salerno.

Because Ravello is a long, steep drive from the sea, tour buses are discouraged and crowds are less overwhelming than at Positano and Amalfi. By early afternoon, the day-trippers have departed, and the town becomes one of the most restful settings in the world. There's very little to do except walk through peaceful gardens, admire the view, and exist.

Dining and Lodging

$$ ✕ **Cumpa Cosimo.** This family-run restaurant a few steps from the cathe-
★ dral square offers a cordial welcome in three simple but attractive dining rooms. There's no view, but the food is excellent. Among the specialties are cheese crepes and roast lamb or kid. ⊠ *Via Roma 44,* ☎ *089/857156. AE, DC, MC, V. Closed Mon. Nov.–Mar.*

$$$$ 🏨 **Palumbo.** Occupying a 12th-century patrician palace furnished with antiques and endowed with modern comforts, this hotel has an elegant, warm atmosphere that gives you the feeling of being a guest in a lovely private home, under the personal care of courtly host Signor Vuilleumier. With lovely garden terraces, breathtaking views, and a sumptuous upstairs dining room, the hotel is a memorable one. ⊠ *Palazzo Confalone,* ☎ *089/857244,* 𝔽𝔸𝕏 *089/858133. 30 rooms with bath. Restaurant, bar. AE, DC, MC, V.*

$$$ 🏨 **Caruso Belvedere.** Charmingly old-fashioned, spacious, and com-
★ fortable, this rambling villa hotel has plenty of character and a full share of Ravello's spectacular views from its terraces and balconied rooms. Relax in the garden belvedere with its memorable vistas. The restaurant is known for fine food and locally produced house wine. ⊠ *Via*

Toro 52, ☎ 089/857111, ℻ 089/857372. *26 rooms with bath or shower. Bar. AE, DC, MC, V.*

$ ⛨ Villa Amore. A 10-minute walk from the main Piazza Duomo, this hotel is family-run, tidy, and comfortable, with a garden and an exhilarating view from most of its bedrooms. If you're looking for tranquillity, this is the place to find it, especially at dusk, when the valley is tinged with a glorious purple light. Furnishings are modest but modern. Full board is available here and may be required in the summer. Reserve ahead. ⊠ *Via Santa Chiara,* ☎ *089/857135,* ℻ *089/857135. 12 bedrooms with bath or shower. Restaurant, bar. MC, V.*

Vietri sul Mare

㊾ *6 km (4 mi) east of Salerno, 15 km (8 mi) west of Amalfi.*

This Amalfi Coast town is a major **ceramics** center, and its distinctive pottery, with sunny motifs and bright colors, is on sale in towns along the coast. Many small shops in Vietri sul Mare offer goods from local pottery workshops. You can pick over all kinds of dusty wares at the **Solimene** works.

Salerno

㊿ *42 km (26 mi) northwest of Paestum.*

Spread out along its bay, **Salerno** is a sad testimony to years of neglect and overdevelopment. An imposing Romanesque cathedral is the only sight most tourists consider worth seeing here. Built in 1085 and remodeled in the 18th century, it has Byzantine doors (1099) from Constantinople and an outstanding 12th-century pulpit. In the new Diocesan Museum behind it is a collection of astounding medieval carved tablets. Occupying two floors of the **monastery of San Benedetto,** the Provincial Museum holds a handsome bronze head of Apollo fished out of the bay in the 1930s. ⊠ *Via San Benedetto.* ⊙ *Daily 9–1.*

Paestum

★ **⑤** *42 km (26 mi) southeast of Salerno.*

One of Italy's most majestic sights lies on the edge of a flat coastal plain: the remarkably well-preserved Greek temples of **Paestum.** S18 from the north passes the train station (Stazione di Paestum), which is about 800 yards from the ruins, through the perfectly preserved **Porta Sirena archway.** The ruins stand on the site of the ancient city of Poseidonia, founded by Greek colonists in the 7th century BC. When the Romans took over the colony in 273 BC and called it Paestum, they enlarged the settlement, adding an amphitheater and a forum. Much of the archaeological material found on the site is displayed in the **museum,** and several rooms are devoted to the unique tomb paintings discovered in the area, rare examples of Greek and pre-Roman pictorial art. About 200 yards from the museum (in front of the main entrance), framed by banks of roses and oleanders, is the **Temple of Poseidon** (or Neptune), a magnificent Doric edifice, with 36 fluted columns and an extraordinarily well-preserved entablature (area above the capitals). Not even Greece itself possesses such a fine monument of Hellenic architecture. On the left of the temple is the so-called **Basilica,** the earliest of Paestum's standing edifices; it dates from very early in the 6th century BC. The name is an 18th-century misnomer, for the structure was in fact a temple sacred to Hera, the wife of Zeus. Behind it an ancient road leads to the **Forum** of the Roman era and the single column of the **Temple of Peace.** Beyond is the **Temple of Ceres.** Try to see the temples in the late afternoon, when the light enhances the deep gold of the stone and the air is sharp with the cries of the crows that nest high on the temples. ☒ *Museum and temple area 8,000 lire.* ☉ *Excavations daily 9–1 hr before sunset; museum daily 9–6:30, closed 1st and 3rd Mon. of each month.*

Dining and Lodging

$ ✕⊠ **Helios.** Directly across the road from the Porta della Giustizia and only a few steps from the temples, the Helios has cottage-type rooms, each with minibar, in a garden setting. Suites are also available. A pleasant restaurant serves local specialties and seafood: The home-produced ricotta and mozzarella are especially recommended. ⊠ *Zona Archeologica,* ☎ *0828/811451,* ☒ *0828/811600. 29 rooms with bath or shower. Restaurant, parking. AE, DC, MC, V.*

CAMPANIA A TO Z

Arriving and Departing

By Bus

Eurojet, a Rome-based line (☎ 06/474–2801) runs direct, air-conditioned buses from Rome to Pompeii, Sorrento, and Amalfi.

By Car

Italy's main north–south route, A2 (also known as the Autostrada del Sole), connects the capital with Naples and Campania. In good traffic the ride takes less than three hours.

By Plane

Capodichino Airport (☎ 081/789–6111), 8 kilometers (5 miles) north of Naples, serves the Campania region. It handles domestic and international flights, including several flights daily between Naples and Rome (flight time 45 minutes). Between May and September there is direct helicopter service (☎ 081/789–6273 or 081/584–4355) between Capodichino Airport and Capri or Ischia.

International travelers flying Alitalia to Rome's **Leonardo da Vinci Airport** can go directly from the airport to Naples' Mergellina train station via Alitalia's twice-daily airport train. Luggage is checked through to Naples, and meals are available on the train. Airport-train arrangements must be made when you buy your plane ticket. The service also operates in the other direction, returning from Naples to the da Vinci airport.

By Train

There are trains every hour between Rome and Naples. Intercity trains make the trip in less than two hours. Trains take either the inland route (through Cassino) or go along the coast (via Formia). Intercity and express trains to Naples stop at **Stazione Centrale** (Central Station) on Piazza Garibaldi (☎ 081/554–3188).

Getting Around

By Boat

Hydrofoil and passenger and car ferries connect the islands of Capri and Ischia with Naples and Pozzuoli. Boats and hydrofoils for these islands and for Sorrento leave from the **Molo Beverello,** Piazza Municipio, near the Castel Nuovo, or from Mergellina, about 1½ kilometers (1 mile) to the west.

Caremar (☎ 081/551–3882), **Lauro** (☎ 081/551–3236), and **Navigazione Libera del Golfo** (☎ 081/552–7209) have frequent passenger- and car-ferry services, as well as some hydrofoil services. **Alilauro** (☎

081/552–2838) and **SNAV** (☎ 081/761–2348) also provide hydrofoil services. In the summer, these lines have a residents-only policy for cars.

By Bus

There is an extensive network of local buses in Naples and throughout Campania. **ACTP** buses (☎ 081/700–5091) connect Naples with Caserta in one hour, leaving every 20 minutes from Piazza Garibaldi, every 40 minutes on Sundays. There are about six buses a day Monday–Saturday from Piazza Garibaldi to Benevento. The trip takes 90 minutes.

SITA buses (☎ 081/552–2176) for Salerno leave every 30 minutes on weekdays and every two hours on Sundays from the SITA terminal on Via Pisanelli, near Piazza Municipio. SITA buses also serve the Amalfi Coast, connecting Sorrento with Salerno.

By Car

Autostrada A3, a southern continuation of A2 from Rome, runs through Campania and into Calabria, to the south. It also connects with autostrada A16 to Bari, which passes Avellino and is linked with Benevento by expressway. Take S18 south from Naples for Ercolano (Herculaneum), Pompeii, and the Sorrento peninsula; for the Sorrento peninsula and the Amalfi Coast, exit at Castellammare di Stabia. To get to Paestum, take A3 to the Battipaglia exit and take the road to Capaccio Scalo/Paestum. All roads on the Sorrento peninsula and Amalfi Coast are narrow and tortuous, although they have outstanding views.

By Train

Frequent local trains connect Naples with Caserta and Salerno. Travel time between Naples and Sorrento on the Circumvesuviana line (☞ *below*) is one hour. Benevento is on the main line between Naples and Foggia.

A network of suburban trains connects Naples with several points of interest. The **Circumflegrea** (☎ 081/551–3328) runs from Piazza Montesanto Station in Naples to the archaeological zone of Cumae, with three departures in the morning. The **Ferrovia Cumana** (☎ 081/551–3328) runs from Piazza Montesanto Station to Pozzuoli and Baia. The line used most by visitors is the **Circumvesuviana** (☎ 081/779–2444), which runs from Corso Garibaldi Station and stops at Stazione Centrale before continuing to Ercolano (Herculaneum), Pompeii, and Sorrento.

Naples has a **Metropolitana** (subway system). Although rather old, it provides frequent service and can be the fastest way to get around the traffic-clogged city.

Contacts and Resources

Car Rental

Avis. Caserta (✉ Stazione FS, ☎ 0823/443756). **Naples** (✉ Stazione Centrale, ☎ 081/284041). **Sorrento** (✉ Viale Nizza 53, ☎ 081/878–2459).

Hertz. Caserta (✉ Reggia Palace Hotel, Viale Carlo III ☎ 0823/424090). **Naples** (✉ Piazza Garibaldi 91, ☎ 081/206228). **Sorrento** (✉ Garage Di Leva, Via degli Aranci 9, ☎ 081/807–1646).

Emergencies

Police (☎ 112).

Ambulance (☎ 081/752–0696 in Naples).

Doctors and Dentists (☎ 081/751–3177 in Naples).

LATE-NIGHT PHARMACIES

Farmacia Helvethia (✉ Piazza Garibaldi 11, opposite Stazione Centrale, Naples, ☎ 081/554–8894).

Guided Tours

A number of operators offer one-, two-, and three-day tours of Campania, starting in Rome. These tours use 60-passenger air-conditioned buses, transferring to boats for the islands. Shorter tours feature Pompeii or Capri; longer tours usually take in both. For up-to-date information and fares, contact these offices in Rome: **Appian Line** (☎ 06/488–4151) or **Carrani Tours** (☎ 06/488–0510 or 06/474–2501).

There is a wider choice of tours starting in Naples, all using English-speaking guides. These tours are either half- or full-day, and cover the archaeological sites of Pompeii and Paestum, as well as one or more of the islands. Contact **Tourcar** (✉ Piazza Matteotti 1, ☎ 081/552–3310), or **STS** (✉ Piazza Medaglie d'Oro 41, ☎ 081/578–9292).

Visitor Information

The main EPT (provincial tourist board) offices for Campania are in **Naples** (✉ Piazza dei Martiri 58, ☎ 081/405311; ✉ Stazione Centrale, ☎ 081/268779; ✉ Stazione Mergellina, ☎ 081/761–2102; ✉ Capodichino Airport, ☎ 081/780–5761).

Amalfi (✉ Corso Roma 19, ☎ 089/871107), **Benevento** (✉ Via Giustiniani 34, ☎ 0824/25424), **Capri** (✉ Marina Grande pier, ☎ 081/837–0634; ✉ Capri town, Piazza Umberto I, ☎ 081/837–0686), **Caserta** (✉ Piazza Dante, ☎ 0823/321137), **Naples** (✉ Piazza del Gesù, ☎ 081/552–3328), **Porto d'Ischia** (✉ Via Iasolino, Porto Salvo, ☎ 081/991146), **Ravello** (✉ Piazza Duomo, ☎ 089/857096), **Salerno** (✉ Piazza Amendola 8, ☎ 089/224744), **Sorrento** (✉ Circolo Forestieri, Via de Maio 35, ☎ 081/807–4033).

14 Apulia

*Bari, Brindisi, and
Gargano Peninsula*

*The gateway to Italy's south, Apulia is
steeped in ancient history and rich with
tantalizing sights that are only now
coming to the surface. The region
invites aimless exploration by intrepid
travelers who seek out its whitewashed
ports, imposing castles, and strange
igloo-shape dwellings, called* trulli. *The
cities of Brindisi, Bari, and Lecce hold
many fascinations, and the coastline is
full of seductions—unspoiled coves,
bougainvillea-draped vistas, and seas
that shimmer under a blazing sun.*

IT'S A PITY THAT all most tourists see of Apulia (called Puglia by the Italians—English-speakers are really using the Latin term) is the blur outside their car or train windows as they hurtle toward Bari or Brindisi for ferry connections to Greece.

This ancient land, the heel and spur of Italy's boot, contains some of the most unspoiled scenery, interesting artistic and historical sites, and finest beaches of the entire Italian peninsula. What's more, aside from the increasingly popular seaside resorts and a few major attractions, the region is still relatively free of tourists. Instead, your trip will take you through a sunbaked countryside where expanses of silvery olive trees and giant prickly-pear cacti fight their way through the rocky soil, as if in defiance of the relentless summer heat. Local buildings, too, do their best to dispel the effects of the sun: whitewashed ports stand coolly over the turquoise Mediterranean, and the landscape is studded with strange dwellings, called *trulli*—used as farmhouses and storage bins—which look like pointed igloos made of stone.

The trulli date to the Middle Ages, but Apulia had long before then been inhabited, conquered, and visited by travelers. The Greeks and later the Romans were quick to recognize the importance of this strategic peninsula, and among the nations later to raid or colonize Apulia were the Normans, Moors, and Spaniards, each leaving a mark. Some of the most impressive buildings are the Romanesque churches and the powerful castles built by 13th-century Holy Roman Emperor Frederick II of Swabia (part of present-day Bavaria), king of Sicily and Jerusalem. One of the outstanding personalities of the Middle Ages, he was dubbed Wonder of the World for his wide-ranging interests in literature, science, mathematics, and nature.

All these interests can still be pursued in present-day Apulia, but less intellectual attractions include the inexpensive and hearty cuisine, which uses local seafood and produce and picks the best from more than 2,000 years of foreign influences. Colorful local markets provide the chance to purchase local handicrafts, ranging from lace, wood carvings, and baskets to ceramic pots and painted clay whistles. Hundreds of miles of beaches and an extensive cave complex let you explore, exercise, or just cool off.

Pleasures and Pastimes

The Arts
In keeping with the general atmosphere of Apulia, the arts take on a folk flavor, with processions on religious occasions more prevalent than performing arts in theaters or opera houses. Still, there are some good festivals and pageants to help broaden your experience of life in Italy's deep south. The best newspaper for listings is the daily *Gazzetta del Mezzogiorno,* which covers the entire region.

Beaches
For the Italians and other tourists who return each summer, the sea is one of the major attractions of Apulia. The beaches along the Gargano Peninsula although no longer "undiscovered," offer safe swimming and sandy beaches. The whole coastline between Bari and Brindisi is well served with beach facilities. In even the smallest villages you'll find beaches where there are changing rooms and—essential in the blazing Apulian sun—beach umbrellas. If you don't mind venturing farther afield, try Gallipoli, on the south coast of the heel (take S101 from Lecce); the combination of historic town center and ample swimming and watersports facilities makes it a good choice for families.

Dining

Anyone who likes to eat will love traveling in Apulia. Southern cuisine is hearty and healthy, based on homemade pastas and cheeses, fresh vegetables, seafood, and local olive oil. Open-air markets and delicatessens burst with local fruits, vegetables, pastries, sausages, smoked meats, and cheeses.

Here you will find dishes unavailable elsewhere in Italy, such as *'ncapriata,* also called *favi e fogghi* (a delicious puree of fava beans served as a first course with a side dish of bitter chicory or other cooked vegetables). Focaccia *barese* (stuffed pizza) makes a great snack or lunch.

Apulia's pasta specialties include *orecchiette* (small, flat, oval pieces of pasta), *troccoli* (homemade noodles cut with a special ridged rolling pin), and *strascenate* (rectangles of pasta with one rough side and one smooth side). Among the many typical sauces is *salsa alla Sangiovanniello* (made with olive oil, capers, anchovies, parsley, and hot peppers), from Brindisi.

Don't miss the dairy products, such as ricotta and buttery *burrata* cheese, and remember that Apulia has a wealth of excellent local wines, ranging from the strong white wine of Martina Franca to the sweet red Aleatico di Puglia, and the sweet white Moscato di Trani to the rich, dry red Castel del Monte.

CATEGORY	COST*
$$$$	over 85,000 lire
$$$	60,000–85,000 lire
$$	25,000–60,000 lire
$	Under 25,000 lire

per person, including house wine, service, and tax

Lodging

There has been a rapid development of tourist facilities in some areas of Apulia, particularly along the miles of sandy beaches on the Gargano spur, now one of the most popular summer resorts for Italians. Here, and elsewhere on the coast, big white Mediterranean-style beach hotels have sprung up one after the other. Most are similar in design, price, and quality. In the busy season, many cater only to guests paying full board (lodging plus three meals per day at the hotel) or half board (lodging plus breakfast and one other meal per day at the hotel) on longer stays, and it is best to make your reservations through a travel agent.

Elsewhere in Apulia, particularly outside the big cities, hotel accommodations are still limited, and those available are generally modest—both in amenities and price—though this may be more than compensated for by friendly service. Some places, such as Bari during the annual Trade Fair in September, require reservations.

Many establishments, particularly the beach resorts, close during the winter months, so check for this also when choosing accommodations. And remember that in a region like this—blazing hot in summer and bitter cold in winter—air-conditioning and central heating are important.

CATEGORY	COST*
$$$$	over 300,000 lire
$$$	160,000–300,000 lire
$$	100,000–160,000 lire
$	under 100,000 lire

All prices are for a standard double room for two, including service and 9% tax (19% for deluxe hotels).

Nightlife

Apulia is one of Italy's most rural regions, and even the cities have a marked provincial air to them. This can be frustrating for someone who expects the glamour of nightclubs and discos of the sort Milan and Rome have to offer. On the other hand, in the cafés surrounding the squares of most towns, you can have a ringside seat for that most Mediterranean of pageants—the *passeggiata*. Local people of all ages dress in their most stylish clothing and stroll through the streets, starting around sunset. This is Italian life at its most relaxed and, at the same time, most structured. No one is in a hurry; there is an air of gaiety and conviviality; but young people will defer to their elders, and poorer people to those—the town doctor, lawyer, or monsignor—they consider to be their social superiors. And it's yours for the price of a cold drink at a sidewalk café.

Shopping

Apulia is rich in folk art, reflecting the influences of the many nations that have passed through the region or ruled it. Don't expect too many high-fashion boutiques of the sort you'd find in Rome, Milan, Florence, or Venice. Instead, look for handmade goods, such as pottery with traditional designs, and baskets, textiles, and carved wood figures. These are on sale in shops and in open markets, where some bargaining can enter into the purchase.

Exploring Apulia

Apulia's attractions are so varied and scattered that you may want to take a full week or more to explore it at a leisurely pace, selecting two or three bases in different parts of the region and taking day trips to nearby sights.

If you are mainly interested in spending time at the beach, the promontory of Gargano in the north offers some of Apulia's best coastline, although there are pleasant beach resorts within easy reach of most of the region's attractions. Convenient travel bases include Alberobello or Martina Franca in the trulli country (the region of dome-shape stone dwellings); Lecce, near the tip of the heel; and the small ports of Barletta, Molfetta, and Trani, up the coast from Bari.

We have split the province into four areas of exploration: The first concentrates on Bari, the regional capital, and its environs, including the small ports of Barletta, Molfetta, and Trani; next we go northwest up the Adriatic Coast past Barletta to the Gargano Peninsula, where whitewashed coastal villages and turquoise water contrast sharply with the dense forests and pilgrimage towns of the interior. The third itinerary takes you inland, toward the white villages of the Trulli District. Tourists come here to wonder at the igloo-shape houses made out of limestone that have given the area its name. The last itinerary crosses the heel and focuses on the southern tip of the peninsula, including the ports of Taranto, Brindisi, and the Baroque city of Lecce, close to the Salento shores.

Numbers in the text correspond to numbers in the margin and on the Apulia and Bari maps.

IF YOU HAVE 3 DAYS

With three days in Apulia, you will need to focus on one stop per day, starting in **Bari** ①–④, the regional capital. Here, a stroll around the old town will occupy a morning, taking in the Basilica di San Nicola and the cathedral, two glories of Apulian-Romanesque architecture, and the castle, containing a small collection of medieval art. After lunch, head south as far as ⌨ **Lecce** ㉓, where you should lodge a night. Spend a day in this graceful Baroque town, which is easy to explore on foot.

On the morning of the third day, retrace your route to **Brindisi** ㉒, stopping for a glance at the famous column marking the end of the Via Appia. Veer west along the Via Appia (the S7) and carry on to ⚑ **Taranto** ㉑ for your last night. Here, the Museo Nazionale is the essential sight, with the region's best collection of Greek and Roman art and artifacts. If you are heading back to Bari, drive through the **trulli district** ⑯–⑳ to gain an impression of these strange dwellings.

IF YOU HAVE 5 DAYS

Longer time at your disposal will give you the opportunity to explore the beautiful **Gargano Penisula** ⑨–⑮, northwest from **Bari** ①–④. A couple of days here should be enough to take the highlights of this forested promontory, which is fringed by some of Apulia's best beaches. A couple of hours in Bari should be sufficient to absorb the flavor and sights of the old center. Take the coastal road (S16) from the city northwest toward **Molfetta** ⑤, **Trani** ⑥, and **Barletta** ⑦, which have old ports reminiscent of Venetian ports such as Dubrovnik, across the Adriatic Sea in Croatia. **Manfredonia** ⑩, a lazy resort town on the southern lip of the promontory, was once a flourishing port ferrying crusaders across the Adriatic to Greece and beyond. The seaside fishing villages–cum–resorts of ⚑ **Vieste,** ⚑ **Peschici** ⑪, and ⚑ **Rodi Garganico** ⑫ offer the best choice of accommodation, although you can opt to overnight in ⚑ **Foggia** ⑨ or even use this city, which is on the main toll highway linking Apulia with the rest of the country, as a base to explore the Gargano. Aim to spend your fourth night in ⚑ **Alberobello** ⑯, the capital of trulli country—touristy but engaging—or in ⚑ **Ostuni** ⑲, a whitewashed, sleepy town whose picturesque views over the Adriatic can be magnificent. From Alberobello, it's a short run to **Taranto** ㉑, worth stopping in for only so long as it takes to whip around the archaeological museum. Break your journey for an hour or two in **Brindisi** ㉒, but save your last night for ⚑ **Lecce** ㉓, a treat that will generate some of your most abiding memories of Apulia.

IF YOU HAVE 7 DAYS

If your base is **Bari** ①–④, devote about a half-day to the city; after all, with so many days at your disposal, the temptation of spending more time in the **Gargano Peninsula** ⑨–⑮, either soaking up the sun and sea in one of the resort villages or venturing inland, may prove irresistible. A car is indispensable if you take the active option, since transport connections are tortuous and slow, but be prepared to abandon it for a half-day's ramble through the **Foresta Umbra** ⑬, for the most part visited only by pilgrims bound for the religious centers at **Monte Sant'Angelo** ⑭, dominated by a large Norman castle that was once host to Crusaders setting off for the East, and **San Giovanni Rotondo** ⑮, site of the tomb of Padre Pio, the pious monk reported to have received the stigmata, the sign of Christ's wounds. Make hops as you proceed down the Adriatic Coast back toward Bari, landing at the pretty fishing villages of **Barletta** ⑦, **Trani** ⑥, and **Molfetta** ⑤, and making an inland detour to view the fascinatingly geometrical **Castel del Monte** ⑧, where you can dine in pleasant surroundings. Then head southeast toward trulli country, spending a night in ⚑ **Alberobello** ⑯ or ⚑ **Martina Franca** ⑳, an elegant little town with a lot of Baroque character. At some point during your stay in this area, take a trip underground at the **Grotte di Castellana** ⑰, a soothing respite from the summer heat. The bustling cities of **Taranto** ㉑ and **Brindisi** ㉒ present a complete change of mood but are worth stopping in for their archaeological relics. Spend your last two nights in the heel of Italy, dividing your time beween the Baroque pleasures of **Lecce** ㉓ and the seaside village of ⚑ **Gallipoli** ㉔, a popular but still unspoiled resort with some alluring beaches. There is a good range of hotels here, and you might prefer to spend more time beach-lazing at this end of your tour than in the Gargano.

When to Tour Apulia

Summers are torrid this far south, and even the otherwise perfect villages of the interior are too dazzlingly white for comfort between the months of July and early September. So unless you are planning to be thoroughly idle—always a seductive prospect in Apulia—avoid the hot season. Of course, if you're in the Gargano Peninsula, which has Apulia's only elevation of any significance, you'll be able to appreciate all the more the forested interior. The Gargano littoral, however, is strictly a summer-holiday zone, with little happening outside the season and most hotels closing after September—also the case in the Gallipoli area, south of Lecce. Furthermore, you may want to avoid Taranto altogether, at least for the time being, as the archaeological museum—the city's main attraction—has closed for restoration; no date has been set for its reopening. Wintertime in Apulia can see heavy bursts of rain, often lasting several days at a time, which can ruin your holiday. The possibility should not altogether put you off, however, since the temperatures rarely fall into the chill zone. In the spring, the days are usually warm and the light crystal-clear; you can generally find water warm enough for comfortable bathing right into October. Apart from in Bari, Brindisi, and the resort areas, accommodation choices can be limited in Apulia, and the hotels there are often booked up with commercial travelers, so reserve well in advance. At Easter, rooms in the Alberobello area may be at a premium.

A word of warning is needed if you are driving in Bari or Brindisi. These cities are notorious for purse-snatchings, car thefts, and break-ins. Make sure you lock everything into the trunk, and find a guarded parking space if possible.

AROUND BARI

The coastal route in this itinerary has a strong flavor of the Norman presence in the south, embodied in the distinctive Apulian-Romanesque churches that were the most graceful contribution of the Normans. Bari is a busy, commercial port, whose charm resides in its compact and labyrinthine old quarter abutting the sea. Molfetta and Barletta are essentially fishing ports, their smaller scale inviting fleeting visits, with perhaps a lunch stop at Barletta, though the more attractive Trani is worth a longer stay, with a choice of accommodations and some decent places to eat. Inland, the imposing Castel del Monte is well worth an excursion, an enigmatic, octagonal structure built in the 13th century for reasons we may never know.

Bari

❶ *260 km (162 mi) southeast of Naples, 450 km (281 mi) southeast of Rome.*

Bari is a big, hectic, rough-and-tumble port and a transit point for travelers catching ferries across the Adriatic to Greece. Most of the city is set out in a logical 19th-century grid pattern, following the designs of Joachim Murat, Napoléon's brother-in-law and "King of the Two Sicilies." The heart of the modern town is Piazza della Libertà, but just beyond it, across Corso Vittorio Emanuele, is the *città vecchia* (old town), a maze of narrow, crooked streets on the promontory that juts out between Bari's old and new ports. Here, overlooking the sea and just off **❷** Via Venezia, is the **Basilica di San Nicola,** built in the 11th century to house the bones of Saint Nicholas, who is better known to us as Saint Nick, or Santa Claus. His remains are said to have been stolen by Bari

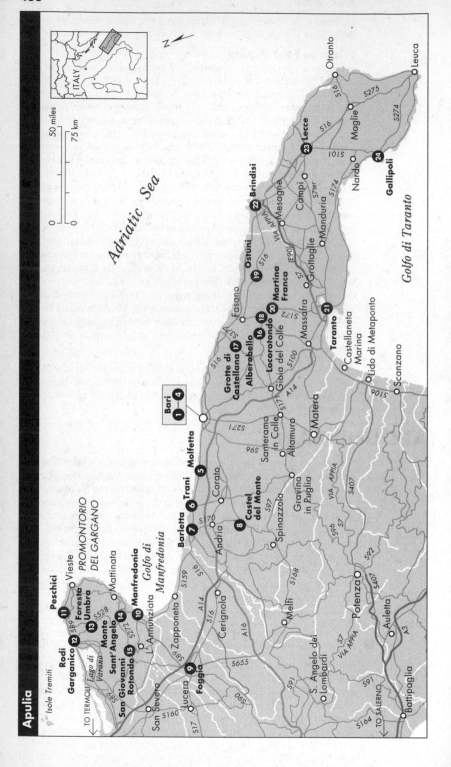

Apulia

ITALY

50 miles
75 km

Adriatic Sea

PROMONTORIO DEL GARGANO

Isole Tremiti

TO TERMOLI

Rodi Garganico 12
Peschici 11
Vieste
Foresta Umbra 13
Mattinata
Monte Sant'Angelo 14
San Giovanni Rotondo 15
Lago di Varano
Manfredonia 10
L'Annunziata
Golfo di Manfredonia
S. Angelo dei Lombardi
San Severo
Lucera
Foggia 9
Zapponeta
Cerignola
Melfi
Gravina in Puglia
Spinazzola
Andria
Castel del Monte 8
Corato
Barletta 7
Trani 6
Molfetta 5
Bari 1 – 4
Santeramo in Colle
Altamura
Matera
Gioia del Colle
Locorotondo 20
Alberobello 17
Grotte di Castellana 16
Fasano
Ostuni 19
18
Martina Franca 20
Massafra
Taranto 21
Castellaneta Marina
Lido di Metaponto
Scanzano
Golfo di Taranto
Brindisi 22
Mesagne
Campi
Grottaglie
Manduria
Lecce 23
Nardò
Gallipoli 24
Maglie
Otranto
Leuca

Potenza
Auletta
Battipaglia
TO SALERNO

Basilica di
San Nicola, **2**
Castello, **4**
Cattedrale, **3**

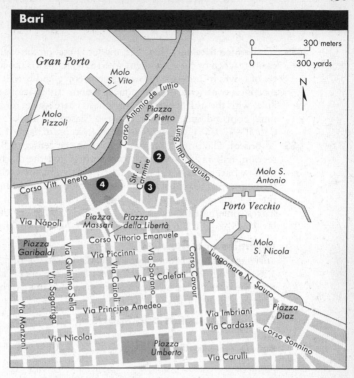

sailors from Myra, in what is now Turkey. The basilica, a solid and powerful construction, was the only building to survive the otherwise wholesale destruction of Bari by the Normans in 1152. ⊠ *Piazza S. Nicola.* ⊙ *Daily 9–noon and 5–7.*

❸ Follow the narrow Strada del Carmine from behind the basilica to reach the **Cattedrale** (cathedral), a century younger than the basilica. The seat of the local bishop, it was the scene of many significant political marriages between important families in the Middle Ages. Its solid architecture reflects the Romanesque style favored by the Normans of that period. ⊠ *Piazza dell'Odegitria.* ⊙ *Daily 9–noon and 5–7.*

❹ The huge **Castello** (castle) looms behind the cathedral. The current building dates from the time of Holy Roman Emperor Frederick II, who rebuilt an existing Norman-Byzantine castle to his own exacting specifications. Designed more for powerful effect than for beauty, it looks out beyond the cathedral to the Porto Vecchio (Old Port), Bari's small harbor. Inside is an interesting collection of medieval Apulian art. ⊠ *Piazza Federico II di Svevia.* ⊠ *4,000 lire.* ⊙ *Mon.–Sat. 9–1 and 3:30–7 (summer 4–7), Sun. 9–1.*

NEED A
BREAK? **Nuova Vecchia Bari** (⊠ Via Dante 47) is a good place for sampling the delights of Apulian cooking. Just take Via Sparano north one block from Piazza Umberto I, right behind the museum.

Dining and Lodging

$$ ✕ **Ristorante al Pescatore.** This is one of Bari's best fish restaurants, located in the old town opposite the castle and just around the corner from the cathedral. The cooking is done outside, where (in summer) you can sit amid a cheerful clamor of quaffing and dining. Try the *céfalo* (mullet) if it is available, accompanied by crisp salad and a carafe of invigorating local wine. ⊠ *Piazza Federico II di Svevia,* ☎ *080/523–7039. Reservations essential in high season. AE, DC, MC, V. Closed Mon.*

$$$$ ⌦ **Sheraton Nicolaus.** This large, modern hotel on the edge of the city is easily reached by car from Highway S16, which skirts the congested center of town. It caters mainly to businesspeople and is well equipped for meetings, conferences, and banquets. Rooms are spacious and comfortable, with the usual Sheraton amenities. There's even an indoor swimming pool and sauna. ⊠ *Via Agostino Ciasca 9,* ☎ *080/504–2626,* ᖴᴀX *080/504–2058. 175 rooms with bath. Restaurant, bar. AE, DC, MC, V.*

$$ ⌦ **Bristol.** The Bristol is a good choice in the center of Bari's modern section, halfway between the train station and the old town. One of the few Bari hotels not geared exclusively to a business clientele, it has well-equipped second-story rooms with modern furnishings. Although the mood is relaxed, the professionalism of the staff and management leaves something to be desired. ⊠ *Via Calefati 15,* ☎ *080/521–1503,* ᖴᴀX *080/521–1503. 6 rooms with shower. No credit cards.*

Nightlife and the Arts
Bari has the famous **Teatro Petruzzelli** (⊠ Corso Cavour, ☎ 080/524–1761), which features performances of drama, opera, and ballet. At the time of this writing, the theater was still being overhauled after a devastating fire in 1991.

Outdoor Activities and Sports
BIKING
Bari. G. S. De Bendictus (⊠ Via Nitti 23, ☎ 080/574–4345).

FISHING
For information on approved spots and license applications, contact **Federazione Italiana Pesca Sportiva** (⊠ Molo Pizzoli, Bari, ☎ 080/524–7070).

Molfetta

❺ *25 km (16 mi) northwest of Bari.*

Molfetta has an unusual 12th-century cathedral with distinct Byzantine features, such as the pyramid-shape covers to the three main domes. If you are in the area around Easter, don't miss Molfetta's colorful Holy Week processions, a surefire hit for young and old alike if you're traveling with kids.

Trani

❻ *18 km (11 mi) northwest of Molfetta, 43 km (27 mi) northwest of Bari.*

Trani is smaller than the other ports along this coast, Molfetta and Barletta. Its old town has polished stone streets and buildings, medieval churches, and a harbor filled with fishing boats. The 11th-century **cathedral,** considered one of the finest in Apulia, is built on a spit of land jutting into the sea. Trani had a flourishing Jewish community in medieval times, and there is still a Via Sinagoga (Synagogue Street) in the old town. Two of the four synagogues that existed here still survive, as the 13th-century churches of **Santa Anna,** where there is still a Hebrew inscription, and **Santa Maria Scolanova.**

Dining and Lodging
$$ ✕ **La Regia.** Just in front of the cathedral, on a spit of land jutting out
★   into the sea, La Regia has an antique flavor, with stonework, vaulted ceilings, and terra-cotta tile floors. There are also tables outside. Regional specialties are presented imaginatively: try the baked crepes (similar to cannelloni); risotto made with salmon, crab, and cream; lobster; or

grilled fish. ⊠ *Piazza Archivio 2,* ☎ *0883/586568. Reservations essential for Sun. lunch and dinner on summer weekends. MC, V. Closed Mon.*

$$–$$$ 🛏 **Royal.** This is an unpretentious and modern hotel near the train station. Furnishings are comfortable, and there is a piano bar by the restaurant. ⊠ *Via De Robertis 29,* ☎ *0883/588777,* FAX *0883/582224. 42 rooms with shower. AE, DC, MC, V.*

$ 🛏 **Hotel Duomo.** Situated above the La Regia restaurant (☞ *above*), and under the same ownership, this small hotel occupies a 17th-century palazzo. The rooms are comfortable and well proportioned, but the best feature is the superb location opposite Trani's cathedral. ⊠ *Piazza Duomo 2,* ☎ *0883/584527,* FAX *0883/553798. 9 rooms with shower. Restaurant, bar. Closed Nov. 1–17. MC, V.*

Barletta

❼   *13 km (8 mi) northwest of Trani, 56 km (35 mi) northwest of Bari.*

☖   In **Barletta,** don't miss the **Colossus,** a bronze statue more than 15 feet tall, thought to be of the Byzantine emperor Valentinian and dating from the 5th century AD. The 15-foot-tall Colossus should be especially popular with children. Part of Venice's booty after the sack of Byzantium's capital, Constantinople, in the 1200s, the Colossus was abandoned on the beach near Barletta when the ship carrying it to Venice foundered in a storm. It stands next to the church of San Sepolcro on Corso Vittorio Emanuele.

Dining

$$$$ ✕ **Bacco.** Here is a place where you can dine in style. Elegantly furnished and centrally located, the Bacco has silver cutlery, crystal, and flowers and candles on each table; there is a piano bar in the evening. It serves innovative regional dishes, such as *gamberi al basilico* (shrimp with basil), *spigola con fiori di zucchini profumato al Brandy* (sea bass with zucchino-flower and brandy sauce), and *capretto glassato al Moscato di Trani* (goat with wine sauce). ⊠ *Via Sipontina 10,* ☎ *0883/571000. Reservations advised. AE, DC, MC, V. Closed Mon. and Dec. 27–Jan. 5, Aug. No lunch Sun.*

$$ ✕ **La Casaccia.** Near a picturesque castle, this simple restaurant serves home cooking and local dishes, such as homemade orecchiette and penne *piccanti* (spicy). ⊠ *Corso Cavour 40,* ☎ *0883/533719. No reservations. No credit cards. Closed Mon.*

Nightlife and the Arts

The **Disfida a Barletta,** held on the last Sunday in August, is a reenactment of an event of the same name, which took place in 1503. The *disfida* (challenge) was issued by 13 Italian officers to 13 French officers, after one of the French insulted the Italians by stating that Italy would always be under foreign domination. The Italians taught the rash Frenchman and his compatriots a lesson. Every Italian child learns this story at school.

Outdoor Activities and Sports

SAILING

The local **sailing club** is at Via Cristoforo Colombo (☎ 0883/33354).

Castel del Monte

★ ❽   *30 km (19 mi) south of Barletta, 56 km (35 mi) west of Bari.*

One of Apulia's most impressive and mysterious monuments was built on an isolated hill in the first half of the 13th century by Frederick II.

☖   **Castel del Monte** is a huge, bare, octagonal castle with eight towers: it can be seen for miles around and commands a stunning view. Very lit-

tle is known about the structure, since virtually no records exist. It has
none of the usual defense features associated with medieval castles, so
it probably had little military significance. Some theories suggest it
might have been built as a hunting lodge or may have served as an astronomical observatory or a stop for pilgrims on their quest for the Holy
Grail. Today, children will be particularly impressed by the castle. To
get here from Barletta, take S170 south through the important market
town of Andria; then take the signposted minor road 18 kilometers (11
miles) farther south. ✏ *4,000 lire.* ☉ *Apr.–Sept., Mon.–Sat. 8:30–7,
Sun. 9–1; Oct.–Mar., Mon.–Sat. 8:30–1 and 2–sunset, Sun. 9–1.*

Dining

$$ ✕ **Ostello di Federico.** This large, beautifully positioned restaurant, at
the foot of the hill on which the celebrated Castel del Monte rises, has
a terrace overlooking splendid scenery, plus a bar, and a pizzeria with
a wood oven. The restaurant serves local dishes, including orecchiette
a rape (with greens), and local cheeses, such as ricotta and creamy bur-
rata. ⊠ *Castel del Monte,* ☎ *0883/569877. Reservations essential. AE,
DC, MC, V. Closed Mon., 1st 2 wks in Nov., last wk in Jan.*

Shopping

In Andria, **copper** objects and containers are made and sold.

THE GARGANO PENINSULA

The spur of Italy's boot is where the region's most attractive and pop-
ular beaches are found. Until a few years ago, this rocky peninsula of
whitewashed coastal towns, wide sandy beaches, and craggy lime-
stone cliffs topped by deep-green scrub pine was practically unknown:
some parts of the interior are still well off the usual tourist track. The
resort business here has boomed in the past decade, though, and
beaches can become crowded in midsummer. For the kids, the beaches
and forests of the Gargano Promontory are great places for letting off
steam, and many towns stage puppet shows in their public gardens.

Foggia

❾ *95 km (60 mi) west of Bari, 39 km (24 mi) southwest of Manfredonia.*

Foggia, the chief city in Apulia's northernmost province is not the most
inspiring destination, though it makes a useful overnight stop for vis-
itors to the Gargano. On the main line from Rome and Naples, and
easily accessible from the autostrada, Foggia has all the amenities one
might expect from a major commercial center, the venue for numer-
ous fairs and conventions throughout the year. This means that while
it enjoys a decent selection of lodgings and restaurants, you'll need to
reserve to make sure of accommodations. This is the place to attend
to money matters or rent a car for excursions to the Gargano.

Dining and Lodging

$$ ✕ **Mangiatoia.** This rustic-style restaurant, on the main road to Bari,
★ near the Foggia Agricultural Fairgrounds, has arches, white walls, and
wood-beamed ceilings—all reminding you that the building started life
as a farmhouse. Inside there's air-conditioning, but you can dine outdoors in a large garden, where tables made from wagon wheels surround an old well. Seafood is the specialty; fish and shellfish are
displayed live in tanks. The chef will supply recipes for dishes, such as
spaghetti *ai datteri di mare al cartoccio* (with razor clams in bags), orecchiette with sauce and grated ricotta *dura* (hard) cheese, and fettuccine in a creamy scampi sauce. ⊠ *Via Virgilio 2,* ☎ *0881/634457.
Reservations essential. MC, V. Closed Mon. and Fri. evening.*

$$$ ⊞ **Cicolella.** Near the station, this 1920s hotel has modern amenities and tastefully decorated rooms, a few of which have balconies. There are also some suites that are particularly recommended, though these fall into the $$$$ category. There is also a $$ restaurant (closed weekends), which specializes in international dishes as well as some well-prepared local dishes. ⊠ *Via Ventiquattro Maggio 60,* ☎ *0881/688890,* FAX *0881/678984. 106 rooms with bath. Parking. AE, DC, MC, V.*

Manfredonia

❿ *60 km (37 mi) northwest of Barletta, 39 km (24 mi) northeast of Foggia.*

Manfredonia, a resort town on the southern side of the Gargano, makes an excellent starting point for expeditions into the peninsula. There is a small museum in the Angevin castle located on the seafront, containing relics of the Daunian people who once inhabited the Gargano, but, apart from some adequate hotels and a buzzing evening passeggiata, there is little else to recommend spending much time here.

Lodging

$$ ⊞ **Gargano.** The functional, rather boxy rooms in this typical, white beach hotel are decorated in blue and white and have terraces. The public rooms are open-plan, the dining area overlooks the pool and the sea, and the dance club bar keeps the atmosphere lively on summer evenings. ⊠ *Viale Beccarini 2,* ☎ *0884/587621,* FAX *0884/586021. 46 rooms with bath or shower. Restaurant. MC, V.*

Outdoor Activities and Sports
BIKING
Bicycles can be rented from **G. S. Cicli Castriotta** (⊠ Viale Beccarini 7, ☎ 0884/583424).

En Route From Manfredonia, take the winding coastal road (S89), which threads through miles of silvery olive groves interspersed with almond trees and prickly-pear cacti. Along the way you'll come across many local craftsmen's stalls, selling homemade preserves, baskets, and carved olivewood bowls and utensils.

Mattinata

15 km (9 mi) northeast of Manfredonia.

Just inland of a fine sandy beach, where most of the campsites and hotels are located, this is a generally quiet village that comes into its own in the summer season.

Lodging

$$-$$$ ⊞ **Baia delle Zagare.** On the shore road around the Gargano Peninsula, north of Mattinata, Baia delle Zagare is a secluded, modern group of cottages overlooking an attractive inlet. An elevator takes you down to a private beach, and the hotel restaurant is good enough to keep you on the premises all day. (You're expected to take full board.) ⊠ *Strada Litoranea (17 km [10 mi] northeast),* ☎ *0884/4155,* FAX *0884/4884. 144 rooms with shower. Pool, tennis court. Closed Oct.–May. MC, V.*

$-$$ ⊞ **Alba del Gargano.** Although in the center of town, the Alba provides a restful atmosphere. Large balconies overlook a quiet courtyard garden, and a frequent (and free) bus service connects with a private beach, where you can use the hotel's beach chairs and umbrellas. The hotel is modern, the rooms are comfortably furnished, and there is a good restaurant. ⊠ *Corso Matino 102,* ☎ *0884/4771,* FAX *0884/4772. 43 rooms with shower, including 3 suites. Restaurant, bar. MC, V.*

Vieste

50 km (30 mi) northeast of Manfredonia.

This large town on the tip of the spur is the Gargano's main commercial center and an attractive place to wander around. Make for the castle, not open to the public but offering good views from its high position overlooking the beaches and town. The resort attracts legions of tourists in summer, some of them bound for the Tremiti Islands, connected to Vieste by regular ferries.

Lodging

$$$$ 🏨 **Pizzomunno.** Probably the most luxurious resort on the Gargano, ★   Pizzomunno is right on the beach and is surrounded by a large park. It is large, white, modern, air-conditioned, and well equipped. The rooms are ample and comfortable, and they all have terraces. There is a $$–$$$ restaurant specializing in fish, and there are many opportunities to unwind or try your hand at something a little more active, like tennis or archery. ✉ *Via Litoranea,* ☎ *0884/708741,* 🅵🅰🆇 *0884/707325. 183 rooms with bath. Restaurants, pool, sauna, health club, cinema, dance club, children's programs. Closed Nov.–Mar. AE, DC, MC, V.*

OFF THE   **TREMITI ISLANDS** – A ferry service from Termoli, north of the Gargano
BEATEN PATH   (1 hr, 40 min), and a hydrofoil service from Vieste, Peschici, Rodi
     Garganico, and Manfredonia (40 min to 1 hr, 40 min) connect the
     mainland with these three small islands north of the Gargano. Although
     somewhat crowded with Italian tourists in summer, they are famed for
     their sea caves, pine forests, and craggy limestone formations. There are
     also interesting medieval churches and fortifications on the islands.

Peschici

⑪   *22 km (14 mi) northwest of Vieste.*

You may want to make this pleasant resort on Gargano's north shore your base for spending a few days exploring the surrounding beaches and coast. Development has not wreaked too much damage on this whitewashed town, and the mazelike center retains its characteristic low houses topped with little domes.

Rodi Garganico

⑫   *20 km (12 mi) west of Peschici, 40 km (25 mi) west of Vieste.*

This fishing village squeezed between the hills and the sea takes its name from the island of Rhodes, recalling its former Greek population. Ringed by pine woods and citrus groves, Rodi is linked by hydrofoils with the Tremiti Islands, and things can get pretty hectic in high summer.

NEED A   **Gabbiano** (✉ Via Trieste 14) is a cheerful restaurant facing the sea in
BREAK?   Rodi Garganico. Admire the view here while having a lunch of locally
     caught seafood. It's closed Thursday.

Foresta Umbra

★ ⑬   *30 km (19 mi) southwest of Vieste, 25 km (16 mi) south of Rodi Garganico.*

In the middle of the peninsula is the majestic **Foresta Umbra** (Shady Forest), a dense growth of beech, maple, sycamore, and oak generally found in more northerly climates, thriving here because of the altitude—3,200 feet above sea level. Between the trees are occasional dramatic vistas opening out over the Gulf of Manfredonia. To reach here from the north coast, take S528 (midway between Peschici and Rodi Garganico) south to head through the interior of the Gargano, where you'll discover a different world.

Monte Sant'Angelo

★ ⑭ *60 km (19 mi) southwest of Vieste, 16 km (10 mi) north of Manfredonia.*

Perched amid olive groves on the rugged white limestone cliffs overlooking the gulf is the town of **Monte Sant'Angelo.** Pilgrims have flocked here for nearly 1,500 years—among them, Saint Francis of Assisi and the Crusaders setting off for the Holy Land from the then-flourishing port of Manfredonia. The town is centered on the **Sanctuary of San Michele,** built over the grotto where the archangel Michael is believed to have appeared before shepherds in the year 490. If you're here with kids, the supposed angelic visitation is guaranteed to capture young imaginations. Walk down a long series of steps to get to the grotto itself—on the walls you can see the hand tracings left by pilgrims as votive symbols. Steps lead left from the sanctuary down to the **Tomb of Rotari,** which is believed to have been a medieval baptistery, with some remarkable 12th-century reliefs. More steep steps lead up to the large, ruined Norman castle that dominates the town. Here you have the best chance to appreciate the intricate pattern of the streets and steps winding their way up the side of the valley. To the right, looking out from the castle, you can see the town's medieval quarter, the **Rione Junno,** a maze of little white houses squeezed into a corner of the narrow valley. To get there from the castle, take the steps down to Piazza Cappelletti and turn right.

NEED A
BREAK? Most shops in the Junno sell a local specialty called ***ostia piena*** (filled host), a pastry made with candied almonds and wafers of the type similar to communion hosts. The best place to munch them is at the southern end of the Junno, by the Villa Comunale, where you can also savor the view of the Gulf of Manfredonia. Sunset is the best time for this treat.

Lodging

$ 🏨 **Hotel Rotary.** This simple but welcoming modern hotel is set amid olive and almond groves just outside town. Most rooms have terraces with a good view of the Gulf of Manfredonia. ⊠ *Via per Pulsano,* ☎ *0884/562146,* FAX *0884/562146. 24 rooms with shower. Restaurant. AE, MC, V.*

Shopping

Local craftsmen make and sell **wooden utensils, furniture,** and **wrought-iron goods.** Shoemaker Domenico Palena displays his unique **leather sculptures** at his tiny shop in the Junno quarter.

San Giovanni Rotondo

⑮ *25 km (16 mi) west of Monte Sant'Angelo.*

The ancient village of **San Giovanni Rotondo,** on the winding S272, has gained importance in recent years as a center of religious pilgrimage. Devotees have flocked here to pay their respects to the shrine and tomb of Padre Pio (1887–1968), a monk revered for his pious life, for miraculous intercessions, and for his having received the stigmata, the signs of Christ's wounds. The **Casa Sollievo della Sofferenza** (Foundation for the Mitigation of Suffering), supported through contributions from around the world, is a testament to the enduring appeal of this holy man.

En Route   A short ride south on S273, and then east (left) at L'Annunziata, will take you back to Manfredonia, where you can link up with the coastal road to return to Bari.

THE TRULLI DISTRICT

The inland area to the southeast of Bari is one of Italy's oddest enclaves, a flat land devoted to olive cultivation and dotted with the idiosyncratic habitations that have lent their name to the district. The origins of the igloo-shape trulli go back to the 13th century and maybe further; the trulli are built of local limestone, without mortar, and with a hole in the top for escaping smoke. Some are painted with mystical or religious symbols; some are isolated, and others are joined together with roofs on various levels. The center of trulli country is Alberobello, holding the greatest concentration of the buildings, though you will spot scores of them all over this region, some in states of disrepair but always adding a quirky charm to the landscape. If you're traveling *en famille*, the igloolike dwellings are sure to intrigue children.

Alberobello

★ ☺ ⑯   *59 km (37 mi) southeast of Bari on S100 south and east on S172, 45 km (28 mi) north of Taranto.*

The **trulli** zone of **Alberobello,** where more than 1,000 trulli crowd together along steep, narrow streets, is a national monument. It is also one of the most popular tourist destinations in Apulia and a gold mine for people who enjoy shopping for souvenirs (☞ Shopping, *below*).

Dining and Lodging

$$–$$$ ✕ **Il Poeta Contadino.** Proprietor Marco Leonardo serves "creative regional cooking" in this rustic-style restaurant. Set in the heart of the attractive trulli zone, it features candlelit tables and a refined, understated ambience. Specialties to look for are fish platters and a house antipasto selection. ⊠ *Via Indipendenza 21,* ☎ *080/721917. Lunch reservations essential. AE, DC, MC, V. Closed Sun. evening, Mon., and Jan. 7–Feb. 20.*

$$ ✕ **Trullo d'Oro.** This welcoming restaurant occupies five trulli houses
★   and is decorated in the rustic style, with dark wood beams, whitewashed walls, and an open hearth. Local country cooking includes dishes using lamb and veal, vegetable and cheese antipasti, pasta dishes with crisp raw vegetables on the side, and almond pastries. Among the specialties are roast lamb with *lampasciuni* (a type of wild onion) and spaghetti *al trullo,* made with tomatoes, garlic, olive oil, *rughetta* (arugula, a bitter green), and four cheeses. ⊠ *Via F. Cavallotti 29,* ☎ *080/721820. Reservations essential. AE, DC, MC, V. Closed Mon. and Jan. 7–Feb. 6.*

$$$ 🏠 **Dei Trulli.** Trulli-style cottages in a pine wood near the trulli zone make this a pleasant hotel, decorated with rustic furnishings, including folk art rugs. There is a modestly priced restaurant serving local specialties. Guests are expected to take half or full board in high season. ⊠ *Via Cadore 28,* ☎ *080/932–3555,* 🖷 *080/932–3560. 33 rooms with bath or shower. Pool. AE, MC, V.*

Shopping

Rugs and **fabrics** are the best bets here, but because of the town's popularity with tourists, there is also a good deal of shoddy material. In the trulli zone, you'll find small shops selling hand-painted **clay figurines.**

Grotte di Castellana

🐚 **⑰** *20 km (12 mi) northwest of Alberobello.*

The **Grotte di Castellana** is a huge network of caves discovered in 1938. You can take one- or two-hour guided tours through the grottoes, which are filled with fantastically shaped stalagmites and stalactites: the grottoes constitute the largest network of caves on the Italian mainland. Children will love it. To get here from Alberobello, take S172 north, then S377 toward the coast. ☎ *080/896–5511.* 📧 *15,000 lire (1-hr tour) or 25,000 lire (2-hr tour).* ⊘ *Apr.–Oct., daily 8:30–12:30 and 2:30–6:30; Nov.–Mar., daily 8:30–12:30.*

Dining

$$ ✕ **Al Parco Chiancafredda.** The refined ambience and cuisine of this
★ restaurant, which is set apart from the tourist haunts in the area, make it pricier than its neighbors. But the food and service are worth the extra cost: try such regional dishes as *sformato di verdura* (a kind of vegetable stew) and *agnello alla castellanese* (local lamb). ✉ *Via Chiancafredda 12,* ☎ *080/896–8710. Reservations essential. MC, V. Closed Tues. and Nov.*

$$ ✕ **Taverna degli Artisti.** Located near the caves, this rustic tavern-style restaurant with a big garden specializes in local home cooking, such as roast lamb, homemade orecchiette, and dishes with fanciful names like *timballo fine del mondo* (end-of-the-world timbale) and *involtini al purgatorio* (purgatory roulades). ✉ *Via Vito Matarrese 27,* ☎ *080/896–8234. No reservations. No credit cards. Closed Dec. and Thurs. Oct.–June.*

Locorotondo

⑱ *9 km (5 mi) southeast of Alberobello on S172, 40 km (25 mi) north of Taranto.*

Still inside the trulli district, **Locorotondo** is an attractive hillside town in the Itria Valley. The *rotondo* in the town's name refers to the circular pattern of the houses, which is apparent from any vantage point at the top of the town.

Ostuni

⑲ *50 km (30 mi) west of Brindisi, 40 km (25 mi) northeast of Locorotondo.*

This sun-bleached, picturesque medieval town lies on three hills a short distance from the coast. The old center, on the highest of the hills, has steep cobbled lanes and stupendous views out over the coast and the surrounding plain.

Dining and Lodging

$$ ✕ **Chez Elio.** Enjoy local dishes and a memorable view of the coastline
★ from the terrace of this modern restaurant, set amid green hills outside town. Inside, white walls and table linens contrast with decorative plants and bright flowers, creating a light, fresh atmosphere. Specialties include orecchiette with tomato sauce and tagliatelle with

blueberries. ⊠ *Via dei Colli Selva 67,* ☎ *0831/302030. Reservations essential. AE, MC, V. Closed Mon.*

$$ 🏨 **Incanto.** A modest, modern hotel, it's outside the old town, which you can admire, along with the countryside and the sea in the distance, from many of its rooms. The decor and rooms are basic, but it's adequate as an overnight base for seeing the area. Prices fall at the very bottom of this category. ⊠ *Via dei Colli,* ☎ *0831/301781,* ℻ *0831/338302. 74 rooms with shower. Restaurant. AE, DC, MC, V.*

Martina Franca

② *6 km (4 mi) south of Locorotondo, 36 km (22 mi) north of Taranto.*

Martina Franca is a appealing town with a dazzling mixture of medieval and Baroque architecture in the light-colored local stone. Ornate balconies hang above the twisting, narrow streets, with little alleys leading off into the surrounding hills. Martina Franca was developed as a military stronghold in the 14th century, when a surrounding wall with 24 towers was built, but now all that remains of that role are the four gates that had been the only entrances to the town. Each July and August Martina Franca holds a music festival (☞ Nightlife and the Arts, *below*).

Dining and Lodging

$$ ✕ **Arcobaleno.** About 10 kilometers (6 miles) from Martina Franca,
★ halfway to Ostuni, this restaurant is one of the best in the area. The specialty is an antipasto that offers as many as 12 tasty items, ranging from freshly prepared vegetable tidbits to marinated meats in a variety of sauces. The unusual pasta dishes are favorites, too. ⊠ *Via Monte La Croce 105, Cisternino,* ☎ *080/718247. Reservations not accepted. AE, MC, V. Closed Tues. Sept.–June.*

$$$ 🏨 **Park Hotel San Michele.** This garden hotel makes a pleasant base for excursions in the warm months, when you can take a refreshing dip in the pool between jaunts. Rooms come in two categories with only a small price difference: opt for the slightly higher-priced ones. All are spacious, equipped with TV and telephone, and in some cases embellished by handsome furniture and bowls of fruit; many have views of the garden. It's favored by local businesspeople for meetings and dinners. ⊠ *Viale Carella 9,* ☎ *080/880–7053,* ℻ *080/880–8895. 86 rooms with bath or shower. Restaurant, bar. AE, DC, MC, V.*

Nightlife and the Arts

Martina Franca concentrates on music in its annual **Festival of the Itria Valley** each July and August.

ACROSS THE HEEL AND SOUTH TO LECCE

This far south, the mountains run out of steam and the land is uniformly flat although agriculturally quite important. The monotonous landscape, however, is redeemed by some of the region's best sandy coastline and a handful of alluring small towns. Not that the first two stops on this tour, Taranto and Brindisi, fit this description: both are big, bustly ports whose historical importance is obscured behind some unsightly heavy industry. Nonetheless, Taranto has its special attractions, not the least its archaeological museum; Brindisi's sights include the column marking the end of the Appian Way. Farther south, in the Salentine peninsula, Lecce is an unexpected oasis of grace and sophistication, whose swirling architecture will melt even the most un-compromising critic of the Baroque.

Taranto

㉑ *100 km (62 mi) southeast of Bari on the A14 and A7, 40 km (25 mi) south of Martina Franca on S172.*

Taranto—the stress is on the first syllable—was an important port even in Roman times. It occupies an excellent position toward the back of the instep of the Italian boot, on a broad bay, the Mare Grande, which is connected to a small internal basin, the Mare Piccolo, by two narrow channels, one artificial and one natural. The old town is on an island between the larger and smaller bodies of water; the modern city stretches inward along the mainland. Little remains of Taranto's past except the 14th-century church of San Domenico, at one end of the island, and the city's maritime heritage: Taranto is the home of a famous naval academy.

★ A shining beacon to shed light on the millennia of local history is the **Museo Nazionale,** whose large collection of prehistoric, Greek, and Roman artifacts came mainly from the immediate vicinity. The museum is just over the bridge from the old town on the promontory. Some of the prehistoric items from Apulian tombs date to before 1000 BC, but more plentiful are the examples of intricate craftsmanship in the Grecian jewelry dating from around 500 BC. The museum is a testament to the importance of this ancient port, which has always taken full advantage of its unique trading position at the end of the Italian peninsula. The museum closed for restoration in 1995, and no date has yet been set for its reopening. ⊠ *Corso Umberto 41,* ☎ *099/453–2112.* 🎫 *8,000 lire.* ☉ *Daily 9–2, in summer also Mon.–Sat. 3–7:30. Closed national holidays.*

NEED A BREAK? Overlooking the channel separating the old and new towns and just next to the bridge itself, **L'Approdo** (⊠ Via Matteotti 4) is a restaurant with a memorable view of the Castello Aragonese. It also has good seafood, pizza (at lunch), and pasta. It is closed on Friday.

Lodging

$$$ 🏨 **Grand Hotel Delfino.** A big, modern, well-equipped downtown hotel catering to business clients, the Grand Hotel Delfino has airy rooms with balconies. The restaurant serves regional specialties, especially seafood. ⊠ *Viale Virgilio,* ☎ *099/732–3232,* 📠 *099/732–3232. 198 rooms with bath or shower. Restaurant, minibars, pool. AE, DC, MC, V.*

$-$$ 🏨 **Villa Giusy.** About an hour's drive along the coast from Taranto,
★ modern amenities blend with an old-fashioned flavor in this little resort hotel in a pine wood only 300 yards from a wide, sandy beach. Most rooms have a balcony. There's an inexpensive restaurant serving local specialties; half or full board is required from July 20 to August 20, at reasonable rates. ⊠ *Via Sputnik 4, Castellaneta Marina,* ☎ *099/843–0031,* 📠 *099/843–0031. 24 rooms with bath. Bar, pool, playground. MC, V.*

Nightlife and the Arts

Taranto has Easter processions (Holy Thursday and Good Friday), called the **Procession of the Madonna Addolorata and of the Mysteries.**

Outdoor Activities and Sports

GOLF

Apulia's only 18-hole golf course is the **Riva dei Tessali** (⊠ Marina di Ginosa, 40 km [25 mi] west of Taranto along the coast road, ☎ 099/643–9007).

Sailors should contact the **Lega Navale** (⊠ Lungomare Vittorio Emanuele II, ☎ 099/459–3801).

Brindisi

㉒   *114 km (71 mi) southeast of Bari, 72 km (45 mi) east of Taranto.*

Occupying the head of a deep inlet on the eastern (Adriatic) coast, **Brindisi** (the first syllable, like that of Taranto, is stressed) has long been one of Italy's most important ports, and today most people think of the town only as a terminus for the ferry crossing that links Italy with Greece. Although this impression fails to give credit to the broader importance of the city (it has a population of nearly 100,000), it is a present-day reminder of the role Brindisi has always played as gateway to the eastern Mediterranean and beyond. The core of the city is at the head of a deep channel, which branches into two harbors with the city between them. Look for the steeple of the cathedral to get your bearings, but go beyond it and down the steps to the water's edge. Just to the left is a tall **Roman column** and the base of another one next to it. These

★   were built in the 2nd century AD and marked **the end of the Via Appia** (Appian Way), the Imperial Roman road that led from the capital to this important southern seaport. Brindisi has seen a constant flow of naval and mercantile traffic over the centuries, and in the Middle Ages it was an important departure point for several Crusades to the Holy Land. ⊠ *Viale Regina Margherita.*

A short walk from the column, the mosaic floor in the apse of the **Duomo** is worth stopping to have a look at; the floor dates from the 12th century, although much of the rest of the cathedral was rebuilt in the 18th. ⊠ *Piazza Duomo.*

The **Castello Svevo,** another of the defense fortifications built by the illustrious Frederick II in the 13th century, guards the larger of Brindisi's two inner harbors, though it is inaccessible by the public. From the far side (the harbor-front side) you can look back on the Roman column and the jutting old section of the city. ⊠ *Piazza Castello.*

Lodging

$$$ 🏨 **Majestic.** A modern hotel across from the train station and near the port, the Majestic is fully air-conditioned and furnished in comfortable, though uninspired, style. The hotel is somewhat overpriced for what it offers, but breakfast is included in the price. ⊠ *Corso Umberto 151,* ☎ *0831/222941,* 📠 *0831/524071. 68 rooms with bath or shower. Restaurant, parking. AE, DC, MC, V.*

$$$ 🏨 **Mediterraneo.** Comfort and a convenient central location are the advantages of this modern, air-conditioned hotel—though it is less accessible from the port than the Majestic. Most rooms have balconies, and there is a moderately priced restaurant. ⊠ *Viale Aldo Moro 70,* ☎ *0831/582811,* 📠 *0831/587858. 65 rooms with bath or shower. Free parking. AE, DC, MC, V.*

Nightlife and the Arts

The **City of Brindisi Festival** (July–September) is a citywide display of art and folklore.

Outdoor Activities and Sports

Yachters should contact Brindisi's **Lega Navale** (⊠ Via Vespucci, ☎ 0831/418824).

Lecce

② *40 km (25 mi) southeast of Brindisi on S16, 87 km (54 mi) east of Taranto.*

Although **Lecce,** the crowning jewel on the tour of Apulia, was founded before the time of the ancient Greeks, it is almost always associated with the term Lecce Baroque. This is because of a citywide impulse in the 17th century to redo the town in the Baroque fashion. But this was Baroque with a difference. Although Baroque architecture is often heavy and monumental, here it took on a lighter, more fanciful tone. Just look at the

★ **Basilica di Santa Croce,** with the **Palazzo della Prefettura** abutting it. Although every column, window, pediment, and balcony is given a curling Baroque touch—and then an extra one for good measure—the overall effect is lighthearted. This is partly because the scale of the buildings is unintimidating and partly because the local stone used is a glowing honey color: it couldn't look menacing if it tried. ✉ *Via Umberto I.*

In the middle of **Piazza Sant'Oronzo** is a **Roman column** of the same era and style as the one in Brindisi. Next to the column the shallow rows of seats in the **Roman amphitheater** suggest a small-scale version of the Roman Colosseum or Verona's arena. Coming out of the Basilica di Santa Croce, turn left for 100 yards until you reach Piazza Sant'Oronzo.

Dining and Lodging

$$ ✕ **Guido & Figli.** This is one of the busiest eateries in town, trading on its well-deserved reputation of quality food served in friendly surroundings. Located in spacious vaulted premises in the center of town (near the castle), the restaurant-pizzeria also offers an inexpensive self-service selection at lunchtime. In the evening, try such local dishes as orecchiette *alla Guido* (pasta in a rich meat and eggplant sauce) or linguine with scampi. There is a wide choice of fish and meat. The only drawback may be slow service on weekends. ✉ *Via Venticinque Luglio 14,* ☎ *0832/305868. Weekend reservations essential. AE, DC, MC, V. Closed Mon.*

$$ ✕ **Plaza.** Tucked away behind Lecce's castle, this is a high-quality restaurant that has been keeping the city's gourmets happy for 30 years. The focus here is on regional dishes given a personal touch, such as *tubettini alle cozze* (pasta with clams). The antipasti are worth dipping into. ✉ *Via 140 Fanteria 10,* ☎ *0832/305093. AE, MC, V. Closed Sun. and Aug.*

$$$ 🏨 **President.** Located in the business center of town, this large and modern first-class hotel has comfortable rooms and a restaurant. Conference rooms and function rooms cater to the business clientele, which finds the President convenient and efficient. ✉ *Via Salandra 6,* ☎ *0832/311881,* FAX *0832/372283. 154 rooms with bath. Restaurant, parking. AE, DC, MC, V.*

$$ 🏨 **Risorgimento.** An old-fashioned hotel in a converted palace in the heart of the Baroque old town, the Risorgimento combines historic charm and decor with modern comfort. There is a restaurant, cocktail lounge, and roof garden with a great view of the town. ✉ *Via Augusto Imperatore 19,* ☎ *0832/242125,* FAX *0832/245571. 57 rooms with bath or shower. Restaurant, meeting rooms. AE, DC, MC, V.*

$ 🏨 **Cappello.** This is a popular choice close to the train station but outside the old city walls, about a 10-minute walk from the center of town. Rooms are small but clean and comfortable, equipped with telephone and television. Reservations are advised. ✉ *Via Montegrappa 4,* ☎ *0832/308881,* FAX *0832/301535. 32 rooms with bath or shower. Bar. AE, DC, MC, V.*

Nightlife and the Arts

Lecce is a good place to visit in July, when the public gardens are used for productions of **drama** and, sometimes, **opera.**

Lecce features a festival of **Baroque music** in September, when churches throughout the city serve as venues.

Shopping

Wrought-iron work is the local specialty, but you should also look for works in **papier-mâché** (particularly nativity scenes). In **Maglie,** 28 kilometers (17 miles) south of Lecce, **fabrics** and **embroidery** are featured.

Gallipoli

㉔ *37 km (23 mi) south of Lecce on S101.*

The modern section of the town of **Gallipoli,** on the Gulf of Taranto, lies on the mainland; turn right on the main street at the end of the central square and cross a 17th-century bridge to the old town, crowded onto its own small island in the gulf. The Greeks called it Kallipolis, the Romans Anxa. Like the famous Turkish town of the same name on the Dardanelles, the Italian Gallipoli occupies a strategic location and thus was repeatedly attacked through the centuries—by the Normans in 1071, the Venetians in 1484, the British in 1809. The historic quarter, a mesh of narrow alleys and squares, is guarded by a formidable Aragonese **castello,** a massive fortification that grew out of an earlier Byzantine fortress that you can still see at the southeast corner. Other sights in town include the Baroque **Duomo** and the **church of La Purissima,** with a stuccoed interior as elaborate as a wedding cake (note especially the tiled floor). To return to Taranto, take S174 back up the coast 93 kilometers (58 miles).

Dining and Lodging

$$ ✕ **Marechiaro.** You have to cross a little bridge to this simple port-side
★ restaurant, which is actually not far from the town's historic center. It's built out onto the sea and decorated with wood paneling and flowers. Terraces right on the water provide panoramic views of the coast. Try the renowned *zuppa di pesce alla gallipolina* (fish stew made without tomatoes), succulent shellfish, and linguine with seafood. ✉ *Lungomare Marconi,* ☎ *0833/266143. Weekend reservations essential. AE, DC, MC, V. Closed Tues. Oct.–May.*

$$$ ⌂ **Costa Brada.** The rooms all have terraces with sea views at this mod-
★ ern white beach hotel of classic Mediterranean design. The interiors are comfortable and tastefully decorated; rooms 110, 111, 113, and 114 are particularly spacious and directly overlook the beach. There is a beach snack bar and a restaurant specializing in seafood. The hotel accepts only half-board or full-board guests in the high season. ✉ *At Baia Verde beach, Litoranea Santa Maria di Leuca,* ☎ *0833/202551,* ☏ *0833/202555. 80 rooms with bath. Indoor-outdoor pools, sauna, tennis court, exercise room. AE, DC, MC, V.*

$$ ⌂ **Le Sirenuse.** There is a private beach and pine forest at this gleaming white Mediterranean-style beach hotel complex. It is air-conditioned, with comfortable rooms whose terraces have good views of the coast. Half or full board is required in high season. ✉ *At Baia Verde beach,* ☎ *0833/202536,* ☏ *0833/202539. 125 rooms with bath. Pool, tennis court. Closed Nov.–Apr. MC, V.*

APULIA A TO Z

Arriving and Departing

By Plane
Alitalia flies regularly from other Italian cities to Bari and Brindisi. **Palese Airport** is 8 kilometers (5 miles) west of Bari; **Papola Casale Airport** is 5 kilometers (3 miles) north of Brindisi. Regular bus services connect both airports with the cities.

By Train
Bari is a transit point for train connections with northern Italy.

Getting Around

By Bus
Direct, if not always frequent, connections operate between most destinations in Apulia. In many cases the bus service is actually the backup to the train service (☞ *below*).

By Car
This is probably the best way to get around Apulia, and it is the only way to see some of the more remote sights. Apulia is linked with the Italian autostrada system, making it just a four- or five-hour drive from Rome to the Gargano Peninsula or Bari. Roads are good, and major cities are linked by fast autostrade. Secondary roads connect the whole region; more direct—but sometimes less scenic—routes provide a convenient link between Bari, Brindisi, and Lecce. Don't plan on any night driving in the countryside, because the roads can become confusing without the aid of landmarks or large towns.

By Train
Good train service, operated by **FS** (Italian State Railways), links Bari to Brindisi, Lecce, and Taranto, but smaller destinations can often be reached only by completing the trip on a connecting bus operated by the railroad. The private **Ferrovie Sud-Est** (FSE) line connects the trulli area and Martina Franca with Bari and Taranto, and the fishing port of Gallipoli with Lecce.

Contacts and Resources

Car Rental
Bari. Avis (✉ Via Zuppetta 5/a, ☎ 080/524–7154); **Hertz** (✉ Piazza Moro 47, ☎ 080/524–2250).

Brindisi. Avis (✉ Via del Mare 50, ☎ 0831/526407); **Hertz** (c/o Silver Travel, ✉ Corso Garibaldi 95, ☎ 0831/528333).

Foggia. Avis (train station, ☎ 0881/678912); **Hertz** (✉ Via Trinitapoli 2, ☎ 0881/608400).

Taranto. Avis (✉ Corso Umberto 61, ☎ 099/453–2278); **Hertz** (✉ Corso Umberto 49 (☎ 099/453–3763).

Emergencies
Police, Ambulance, Fire (☎ 113). This number will also put you in touch with the First Aid Service (Pronto Soccorso).

Late-Night Pharmacies. Pharmacies take turns remaining open late and on Sunday. A list of hours is posted on each *farmacia* (pharmacy).

Guided Tours
The **CIT** office in Bari (☞ *below*) is the best connection for guided tours in Apulia, which is otherwise poorly served by tour operators. The CIT

office can put you in touch with one of a number of local operators that offer everything from chauffeur-driven cars to inclusion in part of a longer excursion (such as southern Italy).

Travel Agencies

Bari. CIT (✉ Via Abate Gimma 150, ☎ 080/521–3552); **Wagon-Lits** (Thomas Cook, ✉ Via Cardassi 85, ☎ 080/554–0580).

Visitor Information

Bari (✉ Piazza Moro 32a, ☎ 080/524–2361 or 080/524–2244). **Brindisi** (✉ Piazza Dionisi, ☎ 0831/521944). **Lecce** (✉ Piazza Sant'Oronzo, ☎ 0832/304443). **Taranto** (✉ Corso Umberto 113, ☎ 099/453–2392). **Trani** (✉ Via Cavour 140, ☎ 0883/588830; kiosk in Piazza della Repubblica, ☎ 0883/43295). **Vieste (Gargano)** (✉ Piazza Kennedy, ☎ 0884/708806).

15 Sicily

On this fabled island, you may ski down a snow-muffled volcano, walk through palm and orange groves, and swim within sight of majestic ruins—all in the same day. Sicily's subtleties make it seem more like an offshoot of far-off kingdoms than of Italy. It has a stubborn personality: cynical yet passionate, languorous yet industrious. Marvels abound, including the panoramic perfection of Taormina, the Valley of the Temples, and the unforgettable sight of a rose-tinted moon rising over Mt. Etna.

Updated by
Robert
Andrews

ARRIVING IN SICILY for the first time, you may be surprised to see so many people with blond hair and blue eyes and to learn that two of the most popular boys' names are Ruggero (Roger) and Guglielmo (William), but that is what Sicily is all about. For 2,000 years it has been an island where unexpected contrasts somehow come together peacefully. Lying in a strategic position between Europe and Africa, Sicily at one time hosted two of the most advanced and enlightened capitals of Europe—a Greek one in Siracusa and an Arab-Norman one in Palermo. (The Normans are responsible for the blond-haired Rogers and blue-eyed Williams.) Sicily was one of the great melting pots of the ancient world and home to every great civilization that existed in the Mediterranean: Greek and Roman; then Arab and Norman; and, finally, French, Spanish, and Italian. Something of all of these peoples was absorbed into the island's artistic heritage, a rich tapestry of art and architecture that includes massive Romanesque cathedrals, two of the best-preserved Greek temples in the world, Roman amphitheaters, and delightful Baroque palaces and churches.

Modern Sicily is still a land of surprising contrasts. The traditional graciousness and nobility of the Sicilian people exist side by side with the atrocities and destructive influences of the Mafia, although recent events suggest that the Mafia's grip on the island is being slowly loosened. Alongside some of the most exquisite architecture in the world are the shabby products of some of the worst speculation imaginable. In recent years, Sicily, like much of the Mediterranean coast, has experienced a boom in tourism and a surge in condominium development that has only now begun to be checked. The chic boutiques purveying lace and linen in jet-set resort towns like Taormina give no clue to the poverty in which their wares are produced.

In Homer's *Odyssey*, Sicily represented the unknown end of the world, yet the region eventually became the center of the known world under the Normans, who recognized a paradise in its deep blue skies and temperate climate, its lush vegetation, and rich marine life. Much of this paradise does still exist today. Add to it Sicily's unique cuisine—another harmony of elements—which mingles Arab and Greek spices with Spanish and French dishes, using some of the world's tastiest seafood, and you can understand why those who arrived here were often reluctant to leave.

You do not have to be paranoid about safety in Sicily, but you do have to be careful: Do not flaunt your gold jewelry, and keep your handbag securely strapped across your chest. Leaving valuables visible in your car while you go sightseeing is inviting trouble. Be careful; then enjoy the company of the Sicilians. You will find them to be friendly and often willing to go out of their way to help tourists. It is not uncommon in small towns for visitors to receive invitations to a local's house for dinner. It doesn't matter if you don't speak Italian or speak only a little: They aren't usually offended if your pronunciation isn't perfect—as is sometimes the case elsewhere in Europe—and they will never submit you to a grammar lesson in the middle of the street. One of the reasons for this, no doubt, is the fact that many Sicilians or their close relatives have themselves been strangers in foreign lands, and empathy goes a long way.

Pleasures and Pastimes

Beaches

There is a surfeit of beaches in Sicily, but many of them are too rocky, too crowded, or too dirty to be enjoyed for long. Among the exceptions are Mondello, near Palermo, a popular sandy beach on a tiny peninsula jutting out into the Mediterranean; Sant'Alessio and Santa Teresa, north of Taormina (the beaches just below Taormina itself are disappointing); and Capo San Vito, on the northern coast, near Erice, a sandy beach on a promontory overlooking a bay in the Gulf of Castellammare.

Camping

Sicily has excellent camping facilities on both the main island and its satellite islands. The two best are El Bahira, in San Vito Lo Capo, and Bazia, in Furnari Marina, west of Milazzo. Both have restaurants and showers, as well as swimming pools, tennis courts, and discos.

Dining

Sicilian cooking reflects the different Mediterranean influences that have left their mark on the island. Fish, vegetables, and grains are used in imaginative combinations, sometimes served with Italian pastas and sometimes with Arab ingredients, such as couscous. Sweet and sour tastes are deftly mingled, and each cook has a distinctive touch, so that *caponata* (an antipasto of eggplant, capers, olives, and, in eastern Sicily, peppers) is different at each restaurant.

Sicily has always been one of Italy's poorest areas, so meat is seen rarely on menus. When it *is* featured, it is usually prepared *alla brace* (skewered) or in *falso magro* (a thin slice of meat rolled around sausage, onion, bacon, bits of egg, and cheese).

Seafood from Sicilian waters is the best and most varied in all Italy. *Tonno* (tuna) is a staple in many coastal areas, while *pesce spada* (swordfish) is equally common, if more expensive. Try *ricci* (sea urchins), which are a specialty of Mondello, near Palermo. Fish sauces for pasta are also noteworthy: Pasta *con le sarde* is made with fresh sardines, olive oil, anchovies, raisins, and pine nuts, and has the distinctive flavor of wild fennel. In Catania, spaghetti alla Norma, named for the heroine in the opera by local composer Vincenzo Bellini, has a sauce of tomatoes and fried eggplant. Desserts from Sicily are famous. *Cassata siciliana* is a rich combination of candied fruit, marzipan, and icing. Gelato is excellent and is usually homemade, sometimes in the form of lemon granita. Gooey cakes and very sweet desserts help raise the blood-sugar level, and the high priests of nouvelle cuisine would probably keel over if faced with a typical Sicilian dessert, like chestnut ice cream covered with hot zabaglione.

The sweet dessert wine, Marsala, is Sicily's most famous, but there is a range of other local wines, from the dark red Faro to the sparkling dry Regaleali, which is excellent with fish.

CATEGORY	COST*
$$$	60,000–85,000 lire
$$	25,000–60,000 lire
$	under 25,000 lire

per person, including house wine, service, and tax

Kids' Stuff

Almost every major city in Sicily has a theater giving performances of the world-famous Sicilian pupi. The most popular are in Palermo, Acireale, and Taormina. Stories center on heroes from the Norman fables, distressed damsels, and Saracen invaders. Even if you can't understand Italian, the action is fast and furious, so it's easy to figure out what's going on. Palermo has an International Museum dedicated to these and other types of marionettes (☞ Palermo, *below*). If you are in Sicily at Carnival time (about 45 days before Easter), Acireale, near Catania, has one of the best carnivals in Italy, with dozens of colorful torch-lit floats with papier-mâché characters aboard that are pulled through the streets by costumed revelers.

Lodging

Though Sicily is Italy's largest region, it has some of the most remote countryside and only a limited number of good-quality hotels. The major cities and resorts of Palermo, Taormina, and Agrigento are the only spots with a real range of accommodations. There are, of course, some superb establishments, such as converted villas with views over the sea or well-equipped modern hotels, but it is best not to expect to come across some charming spot in the middle of nowhere. If you want to get away from the major centers, make reservations well in advance.

Hotels in the $$$$ bracket provide comfort and services to match those in other Italian regions; they are usually the older, better established hotels. In the $$–$$$ range, you'll find newer hotels built to cater to the increased tourist trade of the past 20 years. Chains, such as Jolly Hotels, are predictable but reliable. Inexpensive establishments are usually family-run and offer a basic level of comfort: Although the bathroom will be clean, it will probably also be down the hall.

CATEGORY	COST*
$$$$	over 300,000 lire
$$$	160,000–300,000 lire
$$	100,000–160,000 lire
$	under 100,000 lire

All prices are for a standard double room for two, including service and 9% tax (19% for luxury establishments).

Scuba Diving

The island of Ustica, north of Palermo, is an international center for scuba diving and snorkeling. Its rugged coast is dotted with grottoes that are washed by crystal-clear waters and filled with an incredible variety of interesting marine life. In July Ustica hosts an International Meeting of Marine Fishing that attracts sportsmen as well as marine biologists from all over the world.

Shopping

Sicily is one of the leaders in the Italian ceramics industry, with important factories at Caltagirone, in the interior, and Santo Stefano di Camastra, along the northern coast between Messina and Cefalù. Colorful Sicilian folk pottery can still be bought at bargain prices.

Place mats, tablecloths, napkins, and clothing decorated with fine petit point are good buys in Cefalù, Taormina, and Erice, but they are not cheap. Make sure that any linen you buy is produced in Sicily and not on another continent.

Collectors have been combing Sicily for years for pieces of the colorful *carretti siciliani* (Sicilian carts). Before the automobile, these were the major form of transportation in Sicily, and they were decorated in bright primary colors and in primitive styles, with scenes from the Norman troubadour tales. The axles of these carts were ornamented with open filigree work, which was also brightly painted.

Skiing

Skiing is becoming a very popular sport in Sicily. Ski areas can be found on the slopes on the north side of Mt. Etna. The most popular is at

Linguaglossa, located in a magnificent pine forest about 45 kilometers (27 miles) from Catania. The other area for skiing in Sicily is in the Le Madonie mountains, south of Cefalù.

Exploring Sicily

Sicily is about 180 kilometers (112 miles) north to south and 270 kilometers (168 miles) across. For exploration purposes, the country can be divided into four distinct areas of interest. The first is centered on Palermo, the regional capital, and its environs. This historic city, warmly embracing a crescent-shape bay at the foot of Mount Pellegrino, offers much to the traveler in search of a unique experience, while sites such as the splendid cathedral at Monreale, just outside the city, and Cefalù, down the coast, are wonderful experiences in their own right. As you travel south from Palermo to Segesta, site of perhaps the most impressive Greek temple in the world and the your first stop in the land of temples, which stretches to Agrigento on the coast to the southeast, home to a cluster of temples on a hill that are the highlight of the area. Eastern Sicily, the focus of our next slice of the island, has an interior for the most part underpopulated and untrammeled (though the Roman villa at Casale, outside Piazza Armerina, attracts droves of tourists throughout the year), but the coastal cities you will encounter are bustling centers of activity which bear the positive (and not-so-positive) imprint of modern times. Siracusa is worth as much time as you can give it, a fascinating medley of ancient Greek, Renaissance, and Baroque architecture with some excellent museums; Catania is usually ignored by tourists (though it makes a good base for exploring Etna); and Messina has little to recommend it apart from its unparalleled position opposite the mountains of Calabria, and one of the island's best museum collections. Finally, we take you just off Sicily's northeast coast, where lies an archipelago of seven beautiful islands of volcanic origin. The Aeolian Islands were named after Aeolus, the Greek god of the winds, and they are a fascinating world of grottoes and clear-water caves carved by the waves through the centuries. They are ideal for snorkeling or scuba diving.

Great Itineraries

The following itineraries trace a loop around the island that begins in the capital city of Palermo, meeting point of Sicily's Arab and Norman cultures; moves west and south to the stunning Greek cities of Selinunte and Agrigento; dips inland to see the remarkable Roman mosaics at Piazza Armerina; continues southeast to Siracusa, once the rival of ancient Greece; skirts the base of volcanic Mt. Etna to the enchanting mountaintop town of Taormina; and ends in Messina, where ferryboats connect Sicily to the Italian mainland and the Aeolian Islands, seven islands of unparalleled tranquility and Mediterranean beauty.

Numbers in the text correspond to numbers in the margin and on the Sicily, Palermo, and Agrigento maps.

IF YOU HAVE 3 DAYS
A three-day sojourn on the island should not necessitate the use of a car if you base yourself in Sicily's capital, ⊡ **Palermo** ①–⑪. In this hub of Norman Sicily, the highlights include the **Palazzo dei Normanni** ② and the **Regional Archaeological Museum** ⑪, as well as a clutch of characteristic churches. Head out to **Monreale** ⑫ to admire the splendid cathedral, and compare it with the slightly earlier monument at **Cefalu** ⑬, similarly adorned with a spectacular array of mosaic work. Spend your last day exploring this seaside resort, 70 kilometers (42 miles) away, which also has good beaches and fine restaurants.

IF YOU HAVE 5 DAYS

A longer time on the island will allow you to venture beyond the Palermo area. In ⊞ **Palermo** ①–⑪, make sure you see the **International Museum of Marionettes** ⑩ as well as the sights mentioned above, and leave time for a wander through the various street markets which help to give the city its oriental flavor. Two days in the Sicilian capital should be enough to absorb its attractions and see nearby **Monreale** ⑫; do not, however, go inland just yet: Proceed westward along the north-western coast to ⊞ **Erice** ⑮, one of Sicily's loveliest and most panoramic places, and a good spot to overnight. Just up the road is **Trapani** ⑯, a port-city that has little to offer the visitor. Devote the rest of your visit to Sicily's classical heritage. Heading east through the interior, drop in on the imposing half-finished temple of **Segesta** ⑭, then swing south to the ruins of **Selinunte** ⑲, whose remarkable metopes you will have seen in Palermo's archaeological museum. Following the coast down, aim for ⊞ **Agrigento** ⑳–㉗, site of the most impressive group of Greek temples outside Greece itself. Allow a full day to explore this site, before heading north on the S189, back to Palermo.

IF YOU HAVE 9 DAYS

Spend your first two days in ⊞ **Palermo** ①–⑪, covering the major attractions as well as a visit to **Monreale** ⑫. On the morning of your third day, drive east along the coast to **Cefalu** ⑬, where you take the rest of the day to soak up the flavor of this delightful seaside town. Then, back in Palermo, set off westward, stopping en route at **Segesta** ⑭ until you reach ⊞ **Erice** ⑮ (you should overnight here instead of nearby **Trapani** ⑯). Now you have a choice: You could set aside a day and to go to **Pantelleria** ⑰, an evocative island near the Tunisian coast whose starkness may be considered unappealing by some (you may be wiser to save your excursion for a trip to the Aeolians); or continue down the coast to **Marsala** ⑱, home of the famous fortified wine, and carry on to **Selinunte** ⑲. Overnighting in ⊞ **Agrigento** ⑳–㉗, head inland toward **Enna** ㉘, worth a quick whirl around, then make a lunch-stop at **Piazza Armerina** ㉙ before viewing the exuberant mosaics of the Roman villa at **Casale** ㉚, for many the highlight of any Sicilian tour. If you have time, stop off to see the Ceramics Museum at **Caltagirone** ㉛ before continuing on the S124 to ⊞ **Siracusa** ㉜. You'll need a full day to absorb the many facets of this venerable city, though the chief interest lies in the extensive archaeological park, testifying to the city's former importance. Head north up the coast—a visit to **Catania** ㉝ is of limited interest—and carry straight on until you can see the silhouette of **Mt. Etna** ㉞ (a view best admired in the morning), an essential stop on any Sicilian tour. Spend the night in ⊞ **Taormina** ㉟, where you can enjoy the stylish dining scene. A couple of hours are enough for a drive up to the village of **Castelmola**, above Taormina; otherwise, go directly to **Messina** ㊱, which you should reach in time for lunch. If you can, see the Regional Museum here for your last blast of Sicilian art, before crossing the Straits to the seven islands of the Aeolian archipelago: **Lipari** ㊲ (the largest and best developed for tourism), **Vulcano** ㊳, **Salina** ㊴, **Panarea** ㊵, **Stromboli** ㊶, **Alicudi** ㊷, and **Filicudi** ㊸. Then, it's back to the mainland.

When to Tour Sicily

Sicily comes into its own in the spring, though this is common-enough knowledge to mean that you won't be alone. Taormina, especially, attracts a flood of visitors around Easter, as does Erice, on the other side of the island, and any visit scheduled for this time should be backed up by solid advance bookings. Other sites, such as inland Segesta, are also at their best in the clear spring light, and are far enough off the beaten track to ensure a fairly hassle-free time here. August, on the other hand, is hellish wherever you choose to roam, not just for the presence of fellow travelers, but for the extremely uncomfortable temperatures. The big cities, in particular, are sizzling in high season, and should be avoided. Don't think you'll find much respite on the beaches either, which can get pretty clogged with Italian and foreign vacationers. Come in September or October, and you'll find acres of beach-space. Cefalù, like Taormina a package-resort, sees year-round tourism, though some of the luxury hotels close down for the winter period. The traffic going in and out of town can be heavy: You may want to take the 50-minute train ride or 40-minute bus ride from Palermo instead of driving. As with Easter, Christmas and New Year see a lot of movement on the island, and reservations should always be made as early as possible. Other festivals, such as Agrigento's almond festival in February, can also mean a dearth of available accommodation: check first with the tourist office or any travel agency.

Sicily is so dense with places of interest that not even a week is sufficient to explore the island in depth, though with a car at your disposal you will be able to cover all the most important sites. The best way to visit it is to travel counterclockwise along the coast by car, bus, or train, making occasional detours inland. Plan to spend three nights in Palermo, one in Agrigento, two in Siracusa, and three at Taormina. If you can, add a few days to explore some inland towns, such as Caltagirone and Enna, and to visit the rugged Aeolian Islands off the northeast coast and the larger islands of Pantelleria in the southwest or Ustica in the northwest, which are paradises for swimming and skin-diving enthusiasts.

You needn't visit all seven of the Aeolian Islands individually. In summer, boats connect all seven, so you can stick to admiring most of them from the sea, getting off at Lipari, which the best-developed touristically, though all of the islands except Stromboli offer some kind of accommodation, from small, family-run guesthouses to beds in private homes.

PALERMO AND ENVIRONS

The Sicilian capital is a multilayered, vigorous metropolis, packed with interest, but also exhausting. Regulate your pace, don't attempt to see too much too quickly, and keep your head. If you have a car, install it in a garage as soon as you can, and don't take it out until you are ready to depart. As long as you approach the city in the right frame of mind, you'll find it an enriching and enjoyable place to explore, with a strong historical profile. The heritage of the past encompasses all ages, but Palermo's most unique aspect is its Arabo-Norman identity, an improbable marriage that, mixed in with Byzantine and Jewish elements, created some unforgettable and resplendent works of art. These are most notable in the churches, small jewels such as San Giovanni degli Eremiti or larger-scale works such as the cathedral. The Arab-Norman theme is continued in the cathedral at nearby Monreale (an easy bus ride from the center) and in Cefalù, 70 kilometers (42 miles) to the east, accessible on frequent trains. Here, along with the magnificent, mosaic-laden cathedral, you will find a pleasant beach-resort and a good selection of hotels, making it a viable alternative to staying in the capital itself.

Palermo

❶ *717 km (448 mi) south of Naples, 928 km (580 mi) south of Rome.*

Once the intellectual capital of southern Europe, **Palermo** has always been at the crossroads of civilization. Favorably located on a crescent-

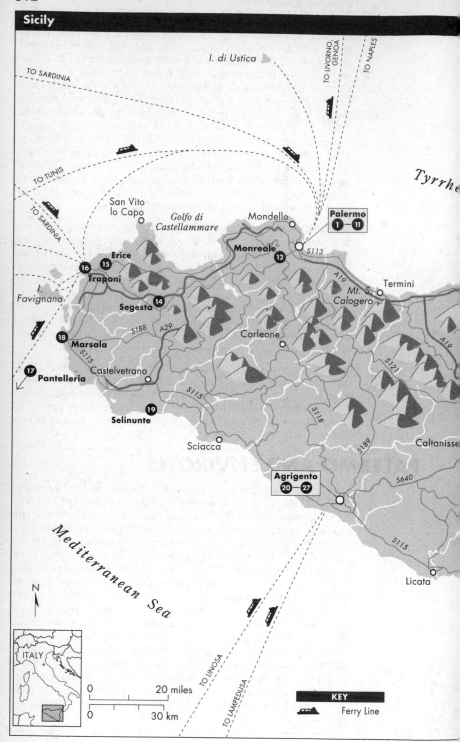

Tyrrhe

TO LIVORNO, GENOA

TO NAPLES

TO SARDINIA

I. di Ustica

Palermo ❶ — ⓫

Mondello

Golfo di Castellammare

San Vito lo Capo

TO TUNIS

Monreale ⓬ S113

TO SARDINIA

Erice ⑮

⑯ **Trapani**

I. Favignana

A19

Mt. S. Calogero

Termini

Segesta ⑭

S188 A29

Corleone

⑱ **Marsala**

S115

Castelvetrano

S115

S121

⑰ **Pantelleria**

S118

Selinunte ⑲

S189

Sciacca

Caltanisse

Agrigento ⑳ — ㉗

S640

Mediterranean Sea

S115

Licata

N

ITALY

TO LINOSA

TO LAMPEDUSA

0   20 miles

0   30 km

KEY

Ferry Line

Palermo

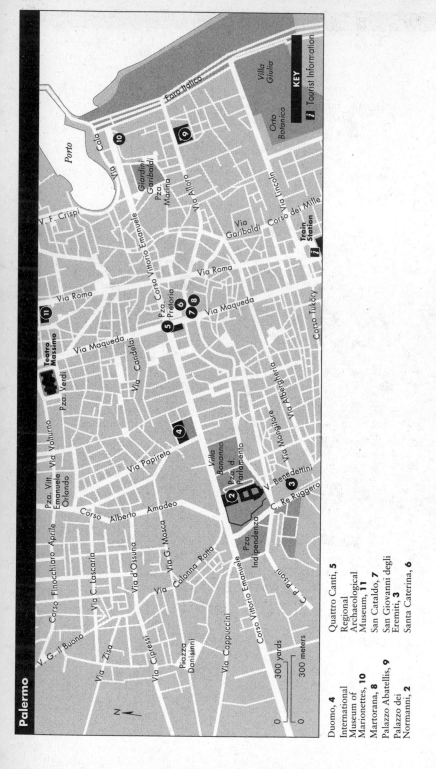

Duomo, **4**
International
Museum of
Marionettes, **10**
Martorana, **8**
Palazzo Abatellis, **9**
Palazzo dei
Normanni, **2**

Quattro Canti, **5**
Regional
Archaeological
Museum, **11**
San Cataldo, **7**
San Giovanni degli
Eremiti, **3**
Santa Caterina, **6**

shaped bay at the foot of Monte Pellegrino, it has attracted almost every people and culture touching the Mediterranean world. To Palermo's credit, it has absorbed these diverse cultures into a unique personality that is at once Arab and Christian, Byzantine and Roman, Norman and Italian.

Palermo was first colonized by Phoenician traders in the 6th century BC, but it was their descendants, the Carthaginians, who built the important fortress here that caught the covetous eye of the Romans. After the First Punic War, the Romans took control of the city, in the 3rd century BC. After several invasions by the Vandals, Sicily was settled by Arabs, who made the country an emirate and made Palermo a showpiece capital that rivaled both Cordoba and Cairo in Oriental splendor. Nestled in the fertile Conca d'Oro (Golden Conch) plain; full of orange, lemon, and carob groves; and enclosed by limestone hills, Palermo became a magical world of palaces and mosques, minarets and palm trees.

It was so attractive and sophisticated a city that the Norman ruler Roger de Hauteville decided to conquer it and make it his capital (1061). The Norman occupation of Sicily resulted in the Golden Age of Palermo (from 1072 to 1194), a remarkable period of enlightenment and learning in which the arts flourished. The city of Palermo, which in the 11th century counted more than 300,000 inhabitants, became the center of the Norman court in all Europe and one of the most important ports of trade between East and West.

Eventually the Normans were replaced by the Swabian ruler Frederick II, the Holy Roman Emperor, and incorporated into the Kingdom of the Two Sicilies. You will also see evidence in Palermo of the Baroque art and architecture of the Spanish viceroys, who came to power after the bloody Sicilian Vespers uprising of 1282, in which the French Angevin dynasty was overthrown. The Aragonese viceroys also brought the Inquisition to Palermo, which some historians believe helped foster the protective secret societies that eventually evolved into today's Mafia.

Palermo's main attractions are easily reached on foot, though you may choose to spend a morning taking a city bus tour to help you get oriented. The tourist attractions are scattered along three major streets: Corso Vittorio Emanuele, Via Maqueda, and Via Roma. The tourist information office in Piazza Castelnuovo will give you a map and a valuable handout that lists opening and closing times, which sometimes change with the seasons.

★ ❷ The **Palazzo dei Normanni** (Norman Royal Palace), at the far end of the Corso, away from the harbor, is now the seat of the Sicilian Parliament. The palace was, unfortunately, closed to the public for security reasons in 1992, but the **Cappella Palatina** (Palatine Chapel) inside, one of Italy's greatest art treasures, happily remains open. Built by Roger II in 1132, this is a dazzling example of the unique harmony of artistic elements that came together under the Normans. In it, the skill of French and Sicilian masons was brought to bear on the decorative purity of Arab ornamentation and the splendor of Greek Byzantine mosaics. The interior is covered with glittering mosaics and capped by a splendid Arab honeycomb stalactite wooden ceiling. Biblical stories blend happily with scenes of Arab life—look for one showing a picnic in a harem—and Norman court pageantry. Stylized Moorish palm branches run along the walls below the mosaics and recall the battlements on Norman castles—each one a different mosaic composition.

Upstairs are the royal apartments, including the **Sala di Ruggero** (King Roger's Hall), decorated with medieval murals of hunting scenes.

Tour guides escort you around these halls, which once hosted one of the most splendid courts in Europe. French, Latin, and Arabic were spoken here, and Arab astronomers and poets exchanged ideas with Latin and Greek scholars in what must have been one of the most unique marriages of culture in the Western world. *Cappella Palatina,* ✉ *Piazza Indipendenza.* 🎫 *Free.* 🕑 *Mon.–Fri. 9–12:30 and 3–5, Sat. 9– noon, Sun. 9–10 and noon–1. Closed during religious services and for weddings.*

❸ Distinguished by its five pink domes, **San Giovanni degli Eremiti** is one of the most picturesque of Palermo's churches. The 12th-century church was built by the Normans on the site of an earlier mosque— one of 200 that once stood in Palermo. The emirs ruled Palermo for almost two centuries and brought to it their passion for lush gardens and fountains. One is reminded of this while sitting in San Giovanni's delightful cloister of twin half-columns, surrounded by palm trees, jasmine, oleander, and citrus trees. You'll find the church to the left of the front of Palazzo dei Normanni. ✉ *Via dei Benedettini.* 🕑 *Daily 9–1, also Mon. and Thurs. 3–5.*

❹ Going east along Corso Vittorio Emanuele, you will soon see the **Duomo,** which is a prime example of Palermitan eclecticism. Its turrets, towers, dome, and arches come together in the kind of meeting of diverse elements that King Roger, whose tomb is inside along with that of Frederick II, fostered during his reign. Be sure to walk outside and look at the back of the apse, which is gracefully decorated with interlacing Arab arches, inlaid with limestone and black volcanic tufa. ✉ *Corso Vittorio Emanuele.* 🕑 *Mon.–Sat. 7–noon, 4–6:30; Sun. 4–7.*

❺ Bisecting Corso Vittorio Emanuele is **Quattro Canti** (Four Corners), actually the intersection with Via Maqueda. Here four rather traffic-blackened Baroque palaces from the Spanish rule meet at concave corners, each with its own fountain and representations of a Spanish ruler, patron saint, or one of the four seasons. As long as the spot remains one of the city's busiest junctions, you will have to exercise a great deal of imagination to appreciate the artistry.

Just off the Quattro Canti, **Piazza Pretoria** has as its centerpiece a lavishly decorated fountain, originally intended for a Florentine villa. Its abundance of nude figures so shocked some Palermitans when it was unveiled in 1575 that it got the nickname "the fountain of shame." It is even more of a sight at night, when it is illuminated.

Next to Quattro Canti and the fountains of Piazza Pretoria, Piazza Bellini holds a trio of eminent churches, among them the splendid Baroque ❻ church of **Santa Caterina** (1596). Its walls are covered in decorative 17th-century inlays of precious marble. ✉ *Piazza Bellini.*

Accessible by a staircase from Piazza Bellini, two churches stand next to each other forming a delightful Norman complex. The orange-red ❼ domes belong to **San Cataldo** (1160), whose spare but intense interior, punctuated by antique Greek columns, retains much of its original medieval simplicity. ✉ *Piazza Bellini.* 🕑 *Mon.–Sat. 8–1 and 3:30–7 (3:30–5 in winter).*

❽ Distinguished by an elegant campanile, the **Martorana** was erected in 1143 but had its interior altered considerably during the Baroque period. High along the western wall, however, is some of the oldest mosaic artwork of the Norman period. Near the entrance is an interesting mosaic of Roger being crowned by Christ. In it, Roger is dressed in a bejeweled Byzantine stole, reflecting the Norman court's penchant for all things Byzantine. Archangels along the ceiling wear the same stole, wrapped around their shoulders and arms. Like the archangels, the Norman monarchs liked to think of themselves as emissaries from heaven, engaged in defending Christianity by ridding the island of infidel invaders. ⊠ *Piazza Bellini.* ☉ *Mon.–Sat. 8–1 and 3:30–7 (3:30–5 in winter).*

9 Near the port, the **Palazzo Abatellis,** which houses the Regional Gallery of Sicily. Among its treasures is an Annunciation (1474) by Sicily's prominent Renaissance master, Antonello da Messina, and an arresting fresco by an unknown painter, titled *The Triumph of Death*, a macabre depiction of the plague years. ⊠ *Via Alloro 4,* ☎ *091/616–4317.* 🖾 *2,000 lire.* ☉ *Mon.–Sat. 9–1:30, also Tues. and Thurs. 3–7:30; Sun. 9–12:30.*

🐾 **10** The **International Museum of Marionettes** contains an impressive display of Sicilian and European puppets. The traditional Sicilian *pupi* (marionettes), with their glittering armor and fierce expressions, have become a symbol of Norman Sicily. Plots center on the chivalric legends of the troubadours, who, before the puppet theater, kept alive tales of Norman heroes in Sicily, such as Orlando Furioso and William the Bad. ⊠ *Via Butera 1,* ☎ *091/328060.* 🖾 *5,000 lire.* ☉ *Mon.–Sat. 9–1, also 4–7 in summer.*

Between Via Maqueda and Via Roma, and accessible from Corso Vittorio Emanuele, an outdoor market spreads out into a maze of side streets around Piazza Domenico. This is the **Vucciria**—a dialect word that means "voices" or "hubbub." It's easy to see why. Hawkers everywhere deliver their unceasing chants from behind stands brimming with mounds of olives, blood oranges, wild fennel, and long-stemmed artichokes. One of them goes at the trunk of a swordfish with a cleaver, while across the way another holds up a giant squid or dangles an octopus. All the time, the din continues. It may be Palermo, but this is really the Casbah.

NEED A BREAK? The **Vucciria** is full of stalls selling street food. Everything from *calzoni* (deep-fried meat- or cheese-filled pockets of dough) to *panelle* (chickpea-flour fritters). If you want to try something typically Palermitan that is a bit adventurous but delicious, look for a stall with a big cast-iron pot selling *guasteddi* (fresh buns filled with thin strips of calf's spleen, ricotta cheese, and a delicious hot sauce).

---

11 On Via Roma, the **Regional Archaeological Museum** has a small but excellent collection. Especially interesting are the examples of prehistoric cave drawings and a marvelously reconstructed Doric frieze from the Greek Temple at Selinunte that gives you a good idea of the high level of artistic culture attained by the Greek colonists in Sicily some 2,500 years ago. ⊠ *Piazza Olivella 4,* ☎ *091/662–0220.* 🖾 *2,000 lire.* ☉ *Mon.–Sat. 9–2, Sun. 9–1; also Tues. and Fri. 3–7.*

OFF THE BEATEN PATH **FLEA MARKET** – Behind Palermo's Duomo, on Via Papireto, is the flea market, a good place to hunt for antique marionettes of the Norman cavaliers or for brilliantly colored pieces from the carretti siciliani. This is also the antiques-store neighborhood, which spreads to the next street, Corso Amedeo.

Dining and Lodging

$$$ ✕ **Charleston.** You'll feel pampered by the discreet service and elegant
★ surroundings in this famous Palermo restaurant on a quiet square in the heart of the city. Impeccably dressed waiters coast effortlessly through the high-ceiling rooms, offering help with the extensive menu and wine list. Specialties run the gamut of Sicilian and international

dishes, with an emphasis on seafood, in keeping with the cuisine of the island. Try the spaghetti *all'aragosta*, with its delicious lobster sauce, or the pesce spada *arrosto* (roast swordfish), but leave room for the house dessert, *semifreddo alle mandorle*, a soft ice cream made with almonds. The whole restaurant operation moves 8 kilometers (5 miles) north to Mondello during the summer, where it sets up shop in a pavilion on the sea. ⊠ *Charleston: Piazza Ungheria 30,* ☎ *091/321366.* ⊙ *Oct.–May.* ⊠ *Charleston le Terrazze: Viale Regina Elena, Mondello,* ☎ *091/450171.* ⊙ *June–Sept. Reservations essential. Jacket and tie. AE, DC, MC, V. Closed Sun.*

$$$ ✕ **Da Renato.** There is an excellent view of the harbor from this top-
★   quality restaurant along the sea road toward Cefalù. It's enough out of the way to make it the insider's choice, and the clientele consists mainly of well-heeled locals who know their way around a good seafood menu. *Frutti di mare* (mixed seafood) makes a good antipasto, and the *zuppa di mare* (fish soup) is hearty enough to be a meal in itself. Grills are also recommended. ⊠ *Via Messina Marina 224,* ☎ *091/630–2881. AE, MC, V. Closed Sun. and Aug. 10–25.*

$$$ ✕ **Gourmand's.** A chic clientele frequents this modern restaurant, with its high-tech decor (lots of metal and primary colors) and nouvelle cuisine–influenced menu. Pesce spada *affumicato* (smoked swordfish) goes well with a bottle of local Regaleali. Gourmand's is in the northern end of Palermo, near Piazza Castelnuovo. ⊠ *Via della Libertà 37/e,* ☎ *091/323431. AE, DC, MC, V. Closed Sun. (except Nov.–Dec.) and Aug. 10–25.*

$$ ✕ **Lo Scudiero.** The antipasto and the *assaggini* (sample portions) of the various pastas give you a delicious introduction to Sicilian cuisine: The courteous waiters are also ambassadors for local cooking. Lo Scudiero has a subdued atmosphere, which will be appreciated in this noisy city. Try some of the nonseafood items on the menu—the meat dishes are excellent, especially the bistecca. The fritto misto contains meats and seasonal vegetables. ⊠ *Via Turati 7,* ☎ *091/581628. Reservations advised. AE, DC, MC, V. Closed Sun. evening and Mon. lunch, and Fri. evening–Mon. in Aug.*

$$ ✕ **Strascinu.** The specialty in this informal and busy restaurant is pasta con le sarde, the famous Arab-Sicilian blend of fresh sardines, wild fennel fronds, sultanas, and pine nuts. ⊠ *Viale Regione Sicil-iana 2286,* ☎ *091/401292. AE, DC, V. Closed 2 weeks in Aug.*

$ ✕ **Antica Focacceria San Francesco.** On the square in front of the church of San Francesco, off Corso Vittorio Emanuele in the heart of Palermo, this place is an institution, as you can see from the turn-of-the-century wooden cabinets and fixtures of what is still a neighborhood bakery. But it also bakes and fries the snacks that locals love—and from which you can well make an inexpensive meal. You can sit at marble-topped tables while you eat, or take food out if you wish. Beverages, including wine and beer, are available. ⊠ *Via Paternostro 58,* ☎ *091/320264. Reservations not accepted. No credit cards. Closed Mon.*

$ ✕ **Pizzeria Bellini.** The pizzas are good, the pastas are better, but the best reason to eat in this former theater is the location, overlooking the churches of San Cataldo and La Martorana in the heart of old Palermo. Get here early to make sure of a seat next to the window— or better still, in summer, eat alfresco in the square itself. Trade is brisk, and so is the service, which can be offhand. ⊠ *Piazza Bellini 6,* ☎ *091/616-5691. AE, DC, MC, V. Closed Wed.*

$ ✕ **Shangai.** There is nothing Chinese about this Palermo institution in the busy Vucciria market. It's on a terrace above the market (the source of all the ingredients): Look down and order your fish from the displays below, and it will be hoisted up in a wicker basket. The atmosphere is jovial and frantic, with lots of teasing and shouting. Calamari *al forno* (baked in the oven) is always a good bet. ⊠ *Vicolo Mez-zani 34,* ☎ *091/589702. No credit cards. Closed Sun.*

$$$$ 🏨 **Villa Igea.** A short taxi ride through some rough-looking districts
★ of Palermo takes you to this oasis of luxury and comfort, situated in
its own tropical garden at the edge of the bay. It's difficult to imagine
that you're so close to busy Palermo as you meander through the
grounds, which include an ancient Greek temple at the water's edge.
The large rooms (many with terraces overlooking the gardens and the
sea) are furnished individually, the most attractive with an Italian art-
nouveau flavor. Spacious lobbies and public rooms give onto a terrace
with its own restaurant. Sports facilities help make this elegant villa a
self-contained enclave in frenetic Palermo. ⊠ *Salita Belmonte 43,* ☎
091/543744, FAX *091/547654. 6 suites and 117 rooms with bath. Bar,
pool, tennis court. AE, DC, MC, V.*

$$$ 🏨 **Grande Albergo e delle Palme.** There is a faded charm about this
grande dame, whose public rooms suggest the elegant life of Palermo
society before World War I, when tea dances and balls were held here.
Guest rooms are uneven—some are charming period pieces stuffed with
antiques and heavy fabrics, others are dark and cramped. There is an
American-style cocktail bar and a rooftop terrace with good views of
Palermo. ⊠ *Via Roma 396,* ☎ *091/583933,* FAX *091/331545. 5 suites
and 187 rooms with bath or shower. Restaurant. AE, DC, MC, V.*

$$$ 🏨 **Mediterraneo.** An uninspiring hotel, it is nonetheless a useful, con-
veniently located base for exploring Palermo's sights. From the large
air-conditioned lobby furnished in 1970s style, elevators ascend five
stories to rather boxy rooms without much of a view, though well
equipped with TV and telephone. The bill includes breakfast. ⊠ *Via
Rosolino Pilo 43,* ☎ *091/581133,* FAX *091/586974. 106 rooms with
bath or shower. Restaurant, bar. AE, DC, MC, V.*

$$$ 🏨 **Mondello Palace.** The beach resort of Mondello is just north of
★ Palermo and is a perennial favorite because of its cleaner air and less
rushed atmosphere. The Mondello Palace is the leading hotel in the
resort, making the best use of its location near the beach. The private
beach has cabins and changing rooms for the use of Mondello Palace
guests, and most of the hotel rooms have a balcony with a view over
the sea. The rooms are well equipped and large, with bright fabrics
and large beds. In summer there's a choice of two popular restaurants—
one in the hotel and one on the nearby wharf. ⊠ *Viale Principe di Scalea,
Mondello Lido,* ☎ *091/450001,* FAX *091/450657. 9 suites and 83 rooms
with bath or shower. Bar, pool. AE, DC, MC, V.*

$ 🏨 **Principe di Belmonte.** This is a tasteful choice among Palermo's cheaper
hotels. It is family-run and friendly and centrally located—a convenient
walk both from the port and Piazza Castelnuovo—but is on a relatively
quiet street. Advance reservations are advised. En suite rooms have their
own TVs. ⊠ *Via Principe di Belmonte 25,* ☎ *091/331065,* FAX *091/611–
3424. 17 rooms, 14 with bath or shower. Bar. AE, DC, MC, V.*

Nightlife and the Arts

EVENTS
From July 11 to 15, Palermo stages a **street fair** in honor of its patron
saint, Santa Rosalia. There are fireworks displays in the evenings.

Epiphany (Jan. 6) is celebrated with Byzantine rites and a procession
of townspeople in local costume through the streets of **Piana degli Al-banesi,** near Palermo. The village, 24 kilometers (15 miles) south of
the island's capital, is named for the Albanian immigrants who first
settled there, bringing with them the Byzantine Catholic rites.

THEATER

Palermo's **Teatro Biondo** (☎ 091/582364) is Sicily's foremost theater, featuring a winter season of plays from November to May.

Shopping

De Simone (✉ Piazza Leoni 2) has a wide selection of ceramics decorated in a modern style that remind many of Picasso. They are very popular with visitors.

Modern "adaptations" of the **carretti siciliani,** an early version of the automobile, are available at the **flea market** (✉ Via Papireto, behind the Duomo).

Monreale

⑫ *10 km (6 mi) southwest of Palermo.*

There are several interesting day trips you can make from Palermo. Don't miss the splendid cathedral of **Monreale,** lavishly decorated with mosaics depicting events from the old and new testaments. Bring 500-lire coins to illuminate the mosaics. There are 130 pictures, covering 6,000 square yards. Be sure to see the rear exterior and the graceful Romanesque cloister to the left, laced with intricate arches, mosaic-inlaid twin columns, and capitals that represent one of the richest collections of Sicilian medieval sculpture. In a corner by the stylized palm-tree fountain, look for a capital showing William II offering the cathedral to the Virgin. *Cathedral: ✉ Piazza Duomo, ☎ 091/640–4413. ⊘ Daily 8–1, 3:30–6:30. Cloister: ☎ 091/640–4403. ⊑ 2,000 lire. ⊘ Mon.–Sat. 9–1, also Mon. and Thurs. 3–5 (3–6 in summer); Sun. 9–12:30.*

Dining

$$ ✕ **La Botte.** It's worth the short drive or inexpensive taxi fare to reach this good-value restaurant, which features local specialties. Dine alfresco on daily specials, such as *pennette agli odori* (with chopped tomato, garlic, and fresh herbs, including parsley, basil, mint, and origano), or regular favorites, such as stuffed involtini. Local wines are a good bet. ✉ *Contrada Lenzitti 416, S186,* ☎ *091/414051. AE, DC, MC, V. Closed Mon., weekday lunches in June, and July–Aug.*

Cefalù

★ ⑬ *70 km (42 mi) east of Palermo.*

Cefalù is a charming town built on a spur jutting out into the sea and dominated by a massive 12th-century Romanesque **Duomo** that is one of the finest Norman cathedrals in Italy. King Roger began it in 1131 as a thanks offering for having been saved here from a shipwreck. Its mosaics rival those of Monreale. Both cathedrals are dominated by colossal mosaic figures of the Byzantine Pantocratic Christ, high in the bowl of their apses. The Monreale figure is an austere and powerful image, emphasizing the divinity of Christ, while the Cefalù Christ, softer and more compassionate, seems to stress his humanity. *Cathedral, ✉ Piazza Duomo,* ☎ *0921/722021. ⊘ Daily 8–noon, 3–7. No shorts or beachwear.*

Dining and Lodging

$$ ✕ **Gabbiano.** The name, meaning "seagull," is appropriate for a harborside restaurant decorated with a nautical theme and specializing in seafood. The house specialties are *involtini di* pesce spada (swordfish rolls) and spaghetti marinara. ✉ *Via Lungomare Giardina 17,* ☎ *0921/21495. AE, DC, MC, V. Closed Wed.*

$$ ✕ **La Brace.** There is a lively atmosphere in this bistro-style restaurant near the cathedral in the center of town. Graceful ceiling arches and rustic walls lend an informal air that makes it popular with tourists. Stick to the excellent grills, and save room for the homemade desserts, such as cassata siciliana. ✉ *Via Venticinque Novembre 10,* ☎ *0921/23570. AE, DC, MC, V. Closed Mon. and mid-Dec.–mid-Jan.*

$$$ ⊡ **Baia del Capitano.** The peaceful district of Mazzaforno, about 5 kilo-
★ meters (3 miles) outside town, is the setting for this handsome hotel, which has a surprising number of extras, considering its size. The building is less than 30 years old, but it blends in with the traditional homes nearby. The colorful gardens, extending to the surrounding olive groves, are ideal for quiet reading or an afternoon siesta in the shade. A good sandy beach is an easy walk away, but many guests choose to stay by the pool and have drinks on the terrace. The rooms are large and quiet. ✉ *Contrada Mazzaforno, Mazzaforno,* ☎ *0921/20005,* 𝖥𝖠𝖷 *0921/20163. 39 rooms with bath or shower. Restaurant, bar, pool, tennis court. AE, MC, V.*

$$$ ⊡ **Kalura.** Caldura is the setting for this modern hotel, which shares the
★ advantages of Le Calette but is a bit harder to reach without a car. Taxis from Cefalù take only a few minutes, though. The Kalura is on a small promontory, making it something of a retreat. Sports facilities keep you from getting too sedentary, and the private beach is ideal for swimming. Most rooms have views of the sea, and the decor is bright and cheerful. ✉ *Contrada Caldura,* ☎ *0921/21354.* 𝖥𝖠𝖷 *0921/23122. 65 rooms with shower. Restaurant, bar, pool, tennis court. AE, DC, MC, V.*

$$ ⊡ **Le Calette.** This seaside hotel is popular with Scandinavians and Germans, who know a good place to sunbathe when they see one. The modern hotel is surrounded by gardens on the three sides that don't face the sea, and guests can use the private beach. The rooms are bright and airy; those facing the sea escape the hot Sicilian sun. The Caldura district, where Le Calette is located, is a little more than a kilometer (½ mile) from the center of town. ✉ *Contrada Caldura,* ☎ *0921/24144,* 𝖥𝖠𝖷 *0921/23688. 65 rooms with shower. Restaurant, bar, pool, dance club. AE, DC, MC, V. Closed Nov.–Mar.*

LAND OF TEMPLES
The Western Coast to Agrigento

Western Sicily has a remote air, less developed than the eastern coast, and redolent of the North African culture which for centuries exerted a strong influence on this end of the island. This quality is most tangible in the coastal towns of Trapani and Marsala, and the outlying island of Pantelleria, itself nearer to the Tunisian coast than the Sicilian. In contrast, the cobbled streets of the hilltop town of Erice, outside Trapani, retain a strong medieval complexion, giving the town the air of a last outpost gazing out over the Mediterranean. The Greek presence is still strong, however, in the splendidly isolated site of Segesta, and the cluster of ruined temples at Selinunte. But the crowning glory of this tour is the concentration of Greek temples at Agrigento, occupying a fabulous position on a height between the modern city and the sea.

Segesta

⓮ *85 km (53 mi) southwest of Palermo, 30 km (19 mi) east of Trapani.*

Segesta is where one of the most impressive **Greek temples** in the world is located—on the side of a windswept barren hill overlooking a valley of wild fennel. Virtually intact, the temple is considered by some

to be finer, in its proportions and setting, than any other Doric temple left standing. The Greeks started the temple in the 5th century BC
but never finished it. The walls and roof are missing, and the columns
were never fluted. Just over a kilometer (½ mile) away, near the top of
the hill, are the remains of a fine Greek theater, with impressive views,
especially at sunset, of nearby Monte Erice and the sea.

Erice

⑮   *35 km (22 mi) west of Segesta, 112 km (70 mi) west of Palermo.*

Erice perches 2,450 feet above sea level, an enchanting medieval mountaintop aerie of castles and palaces, fountains and cobblestone streets.
Erice was the ancient Eryx and was dedicated to a fertility goddess,
whom the Phoenicians called Astarte; the Greeks, Aphrodite; and the
Romans, Venus. According to Virgil, Aeneas built a temple to the goddess here, but it was destroyed when the Arabs took over and renamed
the place Mohammed's Mountain. When the Normans arrived, they
built a castle where today there is a public park with benches and belved-
eres, from which there are striking views of Trapani, the Egadi Islands,
and, on a *very* clear day, Cape Bon and the Tunisian coast.

NEED A   *Cassata di Erice*, a sponge cake filled with either ricotta cheese or al-
BREAK?   mond paste and chocolate cream, then covered with pistachio icing and
                elaborately decorated with candied fruit flowers, is a dignified version
                of the famous Sicilian dessert, which is of Arabic origin. Try a slice (a lit-
                tle goes a long way) at any of the pastry shops along Via Vittorio
                Emanuele or in Piazza Umberto I.

Dining and Lodging

$$ ✕ **La Taverna di Re Aceste.** This popular restaurant is named for Aces-
★   tus, the first king of Erice, and the house specialty, couscous Aceste (a
        spicy Arab-influenced couscous-and-seafood mixture) is in his honor, as
        are the murals along the walls. The chef also has a special pesto dish made
        with wild herbs. Try the grilled fish, but ask for the price, since you'll
        be paying by weight, not per order. The waiters are helpful and will guide
        you through the daily specials and the wine list. ⊠ *Viale Conte Pepoli,*
        ☎ *0923/869084. AE, DC, MC, V. Closed Tues. evening, Wed., and Nov.*

$$$ ⊡ **Moderno.** Local craft work and some antiques decorate the gracious
★   rooms of this intimate and well-run hotel on the cobblestone streets
        of the medieval town. Some rooms are in the modern annex. The main
        building, with a fire blazing in the lounge in winter, is one attraction;
        the restaurant, serving seafood pastas and homemade desserts, is an-
        other. Ask for a room facing the sea. ⊠ *Via Vittorio Emanuele 63,* ☎
        0923/869300, ℻ *0923/869139. 40 rooms with bath or shower. Bar.*
        AE, DC, MC, V.

$$ ⊡ **Ermione.** Spectacular views and cool breezes are the rewards of a
        visit to Erice, and this 1960s hotel overlooking the Tyrrhenian Sea is
        in a position to offer both. Nearly every room has a good view, although
        some would say that the terrace bar has the most panoramic vista. The
        hotel restaurant is popular locally, with fish couscous a standout. ⊠
        Via Pineta Comunale 43, ☎ *0923/869138,* ℻ *0923/869587. 46 rooms*
        with bath or shower. Bar, pool. AE, DC, MC, V.

Trapani

⑯   *30 km (18 mi) west of Segesta, 107 km (67 mi) west of Palermo.*

The modern town of **Trapani,** below Erice, is the departure point for
ferries to the Egadi Islands and the island of Pantelleria, near the

African coast. This rugged western end of Sicily is reminiscent of the terrain in American westerns—as it well should be, for many "spaghetti westerns" were filmed here. If you are familiar with North African couscous, Trapani is the place to try the Sicilian version, which is made with fish instead of meat. The result is a kind of fish stew with semolina, spiced with cinnamon, saffron, and black pepper.

Dining

$$ ✕ **P & G.** Couscous is a specialty of this small, popular restaurant on
★ a quiet street between the train station and the Villa Margherita public gardens. The couscous features fish in summer and meat in winter. A mixed grill of meats in a zesty orange sauce will revive any appetite suffering from fish fatigue. Wash it all down with a bottle of Donnafugata, a good white from the Rallo vineyards at Marsala. ✉ *Via Spalti 1,* ☎ *0923/547701. Reservations advised. AE, DC, V. Closed Sun. and Aug.*

Pantelleria

⑰ *100 km (62 mi) southwest of Sicily.*

Pantelleria, near the Tunisian coast, is one of Sicily's most evocative islands, although many find its starkness unappealing. Its volcanic formations, scant patches of forest, prehistoric tombs, and dramatic seascapes constitute an otherworldly landscape. From its grapes—the *zibibbo*—the locals make an amber-colored dessert wine and a strong, sweet wine called Tanit. Daily ferries and hydrofoils connect the island with Trapani.

Marsala

⑱ *30 km (18 mi) south of Trapani, 140 km (87 mi) southwest of Palermo.*

The quiet seaside town of **Marsala** is world famous for its rich-colored, sweet-tasting wine. In 1773 a British merchant named John Woodhouse happened upon Marsala and discovered that the wine there was as good as the port the British had long imported from Portugal. Two other wine merchants, Whitaker and Ingram, rushed in, and by 1800 Marsala was exporting its wine all over the British Empire.

Selinunte

⑲ *88 km (55 mi) southeast of Marsala, 15 km (9 mi) south of Castelvetrano.*

Near the town of Castelvetrano, an overwhelming array of ruined Greek temples is perched on a plateau overlooking the Mediterranean at **Selinunte.** The city was one of the most superb colonies of ancient Greece. The original complex held seven temples scattered over two sites separated by a harbor. Of the seven, only one—reconstructed in 1958—still stands. Founded in the 7th century BC, Selinunte became the rich and prosperous rival of Segesta, which in 409 BC turned to the Carthaginians for help. The Carthaginians sent an army commanded by Hannibal to raze the city. The temples were demolished, the city was laid flat, and 16,000 of Selinunte's inhabitants were slaughtered. The beautiful metopes preserved in Palermo's Regional Archaeological Museum (☞ Palermo, *above*) come from the frieze of Temple E here. There is also a small museum at the site that contains other excavated pieces. Selinunte is named after a local variety of wild celery that in spring still grows profusely among the ruined columns and overturned capitals. ▦ *To site and museum: 2,000 lire.* ◷ *Daily 9–1 hr before sunset.*

Agrigento

⑳ *100 km (60 mi) southeast of Selinunte, 126 km (79 mi) south of Palermo.*

Look out for the golden temples of **Agrigento** on a rise above the highway, a short distance inland from the sea. Agrigento, or Akragas as the Greeks called it, was settled by the Greeks in 580 BC and grew wealthy through trade with Carthage, just across the Mediterranean. Despite attacks from the Carthaginians at the end of the 5th century BC, the city survived through the Roman era, the Middle Ages (when it came under Arab and Norman rule), and into the modern age, and structures from all these eras sit side by side in Agrigento today. The birthplace of both the ancient Greek philosopher Empedocles and the modern Italian playwright Luigi Pirandello, Agrigento is a study in contrasts, but its chief attraction, the Valley of the Temples, remains one of the most impressive classical sites in all of Italy.

★ Coming upon the **Valley of the Temples** for the first time is a memorable moment—whether in the sunshine of spring, when they are surrounded by blossoming almond trees, or at night, when they are floodlit. Even in winter, when the vegetation is limited—perfectly limited—to agaves and gnarled gray olive trees, it is easy to understand why Pindar called Agrigento "the most beautiful city built by mortal men." Exiting from the highway, walk down from the parking lot on Via dei Templi and turn left. The first temple you encounter as you enter
㉑ the complex is the **Temple of Hercules**—eight pillars of the oldest temple in Agrigento, built during the 5th century BC. Up the hill from the
㉒ Temple of Hercules, is the **Temple of Concord,** one of the best-preserved Doric temples in the world and certainly the most impressive in Sicily. In the late afternoon, as the sun descends below the horizon, the temple's sandstone begins to change from honey-gold to pink russet, and the vertical lines of the fluted columns and their triangular pediment sharpen against the fading skyline. The columns were probably once covered by brightly painted stucco.

㉓ Follow up the Via Sacra to reach the **Temple of Juno,** which commands an exquisite view of the valley, especially at sunset. If you look carefully, you can see red fire marks on some of the columns—the result of the Carthaginian attack in 406 BC, which destroyed the city. From the parking lot in the Piazzale dei Templi (where there is a bar selling drinks and ice cream), cross to the opposite side of the road, where some of the most
㉔ impressive ruins lie. The **Temple of Jupiter** is the largest temple ever planned in Sicily. Though never completed, it was considered the eighth wonder of the world. The nearby sleeping giant is a copy of one of the 38 colossal Atlas figures, or telamones, that supported the temple's immense roof. Note that the Temple of Jupiter is generally closed at 5.

The four columns supporting part of an entablature of the much-pho-
㉕ tographed **Temple of Castor and Pollux,** have become a symbol of Agrigento, even though they were reconstructed in 1836, and probably from diverse buildings. At the end of Via dei Templi, where it turns
★ **㉖** left and becomes Via Petrarca, stands the **National Archaeological Museum,** which contains one of the original telamones, an impressive collection of Greek vases dating from the 7th century BC, and models of what the temples once looked like. ✉ *Contrada San Nicola,* ☎ *0922/401565. ▣ Free. ☺ Sat.–Tues. and Thurs. 8–12:30; Wed. and Fri. 8–5 (hrs can vary).*

On the opposite side of the road from the archaeological museum is
㉗ the **Hellenistic and Roman Quarter,** which consists of four parallel streets,

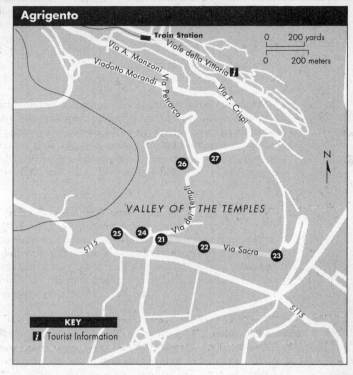

running north and south, that have been uncovered, along with the foundations of some houses from the Roman settlement (2nd century BC). Some of these streets still have their original mosaic pavements.

NEED A BREAK? There is little reason to go up the hill to the rather dreary modern city of Agrigento, where industrial speculation keeps threatening to encroach upon the Valley of the Temples below—except to ring the doorbell at the **convent of Santo Spirito** on the Salita di Santo Spirito off Via Porcello and try the *kus-kus* (sweet cake) made of pistachio nuts and chocolate, that the nuns there prepare.

OFF THE BEATEN PATH **PIRANDELLO HOUSE** – One of Agrigento's native sons was the distinguished dramatist Luigi Pirandello (1867–1936), whose plays, such as *Six Characters in Search of an Author,* express the fundamental ambiguity of life. Pirandello is buried under a pine tree behind the house where he was born, in Piazzale Caos, a few kilometers west of town. His house has been made into a museum of Pirandello memorabilia. Every year a festival of Pirandello's plays is held in Agrigento from late July to early August. ✉ *Free.* ◷ *Mon.–Sat. 9–1:30.*

Dining and Lodging

$$ ✕ **Caprice.** The specialty of this popular restaurant in the temple area is meat prepared alla brace, although there is also a good selection of seafood, particularly pesce spada. The waiters—when they are not rushed off their feet—are proud to explain some of the less-familiar entries on the wine list, which is relatively extensive. ✉ *Via Panoramica dei Templi 51,* ☎ *0922/26469. AE, DC, MC, V. Closed Fri. and July 1–15.*

$$ ✕ **Taverna Mosè.** This restaurant is popular with sightseers from nearby temples, so it can get busy in the early evening, when it becomes too dark for temple exploring. The atmosphere is bustling, with waiters shouting orders at each other and at the kitchen. The house specialties are homemade sausages and grilled fish, and the wine list is comprehensive. ⊠ *Contrada San Biagio,* ☎ *0922/26778. AE. Closed Mon. and Aug.*

$$ ✕ **Vigneto.** Unless you make reservations at this popular restaurant, it's best to arrive early to snag one of the good tables on the terrace, which has a memorable view of the temples. The menu changes, with daily specials reflecting whatever is in season or is freshest at the fish market. *Arrosti* (roast meats) are always a good bet. ⊠ *Via Cavaleri Magazzeni 11,* ☎ *0922/414319. AE, DC, MC, V. Closed Tues. and Nov. 1–30.*

$$$ ▣ **Jolly dei Templi.** Guests travel 8 kilometers (5 miles) southeast of town to Villagio Mosè to stay in this member of the Jolly hotel chain. Rooms are large, bright, and airy, and if there's a sense of having seen it all before, you probably have—in one of the other Jolly hotels or in any well-equipped U.S. motel. That is the price to pay for what are always comfortable, hassle-free accommodations. The Pirandello restaurant is excellent, so you won't have to head into Agrigento to dine. ⊠ *Parco Angeli, Villagio Mosè,* ☎ *0922/606144,* ℻ *0922/606685. 144 rooms with bath or shower. Bar, pool. AE, DC, MC, V.*

$$$ ▣ **Villa Athena.** There is much demand for this well-furnished former
★ villa, so make reservations as early as possible. Many rooms—they're all different—have terraces looking out on the large gardens and the swimming pool. The temple zone is an easy walk from the hotel, and there is a convivial atmosphere in the bar, where a multinational crowd swaps stories and advice. ⊠ *Via dei Templi 33,* ☎ *0922/596288,* ℻ *0922/402180. 40 rooms with bath or shower. Restaurant, bar, pool. AE, DC, MC, V.*

Nightlife and the Arts

On the first weekend in February, Agrigento hosts a **Festa delle Mandorle,** or Almond Blossom Festival, with international folk dances, a costumed parade, and the sale of marzipan and other sweets made from almonds.

EASTERN SICILY

On the Road to Taormina

This tour takes in a sizeable section of Sicily's interior, for the most part underpopulated and untrammeled, though the Roman villa at Casale, outside Piazza Armerina, attracts droves of tourists throughout the year. This complex—thought to be the lavish dwelling or hunting lodge of a Roman potentate—gives precious evidence of this historical epoch, from both the artistic and social points of view. Nearby Enna's commanding hilltop position is its best characteristic, and you could skip entering this rather dreary town, but don't miss Caltagirone, a ceramics center of renown. On the coast, Siracusa is worth as much time as you can give it, a fascinating medley of ancient Greek, Renaissance and Baroque architecture with some excellent museums. To the north, Catania is usually ignored by tourists, but has the vivacity of Palermo, if not the artistic wealth. The city makes a good base for exploring Etna, whose presence looms over the lava-built palazzi. Memorable views of the volcano can also be enjoyed from Taormina. On Sicily's northern tip, Messina has little to recommend it apart from its unparalleled position opposite the mountains of Calabria, and one of the island's best museum collections.

Enna

㉘ *105 km (63 mi) northeast of Agrigento, 136 km (85 mi) southeast of Palermo, 85 km (53 mi) west of Catania.*

Deep in Sicily's interior, the fortress city of **Enna** commands exceptional views of the rolling plains surrounding it, and, in the distance, Mt. Etna. The narrow winding streets are dominated at one end by the impressive castle built by Frederick II, easily visible as you approach the town.

Piazza Armerina

㉙ *40 km (25 mi) south of Enna, 110 km (69 mi) west of Catania.*

Reached through pine and eucalyptus woods and low farmland, **Piazza Armerina** is a tiny Baroque town visited mainly for the sumptuous Roman emperor's country house lying nearby.

Dining

$$ ✕ **Centrale da Totò.** At this reliable trattoria, the emphasis is on a family clientele, rather than intimate or expense-account dining, and the portions reflect this *mangia, mangia* outlook. Try the *pappardelle alla Centrale*, a rich, filling pasta dish made with tomato sauce and fresh vegetables. ✉ *Via Mazzini 29,* ☎ *0935/680153. AE, DC, MC, V. Closed Mon.*

Nightlife and the Arts

The **Palio dei Normanni,** a medieval tournament with participants dressed in 14th-century fashion, takes place on August 13.

Casale

㉚ *6 km (4 mi) southwest of Piazza Armerina.*

The exceptionally well-preserved **Imperial Roman Villa** here is thought to have been a hunting lodge of the Emperor Maximianus Heraclius (4th century AD). The excavations were not begun until 1950, and all the wall decorations and vaulting have been lost. However, some of the best mosaics of the Roman world cover more than 12,000 square feet under a shelter shaped to give an idea of the layout of the original buildings. The mosaics were probably made by Carthaginian artisans, because they are similar to those in the Tunis Bardo Museum. The entrance was through a triumphal arch that led into an atrium surrounded by a portico of columns. Through this, the *thermae,* or bathhouse, is reached. It is colorfully decorated with mosaic nymphs, a Neptune, and slaves massaging bathers. The Peristyle leads to the main villa, where in the Salone del Circo you look down on mosaics that illustrate Roman circus sports. Another apartment shows hunting scenes of tigers, elephants, and ostriches; the gym shows young girls exercising; the private apartments are covered with scenes from Greek and Roman mythology; and Room 38 even has a touch of eroticism. ✉ *Imperial Roman Villa, Casale,* ☎ *0935/680036.* ✉ *2,000 lire.* ☺ *Daily 9–1:30, 3:30–1 hr before sunset.*

Caltagirone

㉛ *30 km (18 mi) southeast of Piazza Armerina, 60 km (37 mi) southwest of Catania.*

Built over three hills, the charming Baroque town of **Caltagirone** is a leader in the Sicilian ceramics industry. Here you will find majolica balustrades, tile-decorated windowsills, and a monumental **tile staircase** of 142 steps—each decorated with a different pattern. On the feast of San Giacomo (July 24), the staircase is illuminated with candles that form a tapestry design over the steps. It is the result of months of work preparing the 4,000 *coppi*, or cylinders of colored paper that hold oil lamps. At 9:30 PM on July 24, a squad of hundreds of boys springs into action to light the lamps, so that the staircase flares up all at once. There is an interesting **Ceramics Museum** in the public gardens, which were designed by Basile, the master of Sicilian Art Nouveau. The exhibits in the museum trace the history of the craft from specimens excavated from the earliest settlements, through the influential Arab period, to the present. ⊠ *Museo Regionale della Ceramica, Giardino Pubblico,* ☎ *0933/21680.* ☞ *Free.* ☉ *Daily 9–6:30.*

Shopping
De Simone, whose Picasso-like faces on plates and pitchers are popular abroad, has an outlet here (⊠ Via Messina Marina 633).

Palazzolo Acreide

60 km (40 mi) east of Caltagirone, 40 km (25 mi) west of Trapani.

This small inland town is best known for its archaeological zone, the old Greek *Akrai,* containing the foundations of a temple dedicated to Aphrodite and a well-preserved theater.

Dining
$ ✕ **Da Alfredo.** This one-man show (Alfredo is the owner/chef) is on one of the most attractive streets of this Baroque town between Caltagirone and Siracusa. Specialties depend on the season, the availability of ingredients at the local markets, and the whims of Alfredo himself. Homemade pasta, such as tubular penne and cheese-filled ravioli, are specialties, and the sauces are hearty and spicy. During the summer, Alfredo transfers to Fontane Bianche, a seaside resort south of Siracusa. ⊠ *Via Duca d'Aosta 27,* ☎ *0931/883266. AE. Closed Wed. and June–Sept. 10.*

Siracusa

㉜ *100 km (60 mi) east of Caltagirone, 60 km (37 mi) south of Catania.*

Greek Sicily began along the Ionian coast, and some of the finest examples of Baroque art and architecture were also created here, particularly in **Siracusa.** The city was founded in 734 BC by Greek colonists from Corinth and soon grew to rival, and even surpass, Athens in splendor and power. Siracusa became the largest, wealthiest city-state in Magna Graecia and the bulwark of Greek civilization. Although it suffered from tyrannical rule, kings such as Dionysius filled their courts in the 5th century BC with Greeks of the highest artistic stature—among them, Pindar, Aeschylus, and Archimedes. The Athenians did not welcome the rise of Siracusa and sent a fleet to destroy the rival city, but the natives outsmarted them in what was one of the greatest naval battles of ancient history (413 BC). Siracusa continued to prosper until it was conquered two centuries later by the Romans.

There are essentially two areas to explore in Siracusa—the Archaeological Park, on the mainland, and the island of Ortygia, the ancient city first inhabited by the Greeks, which juts out into the Ionian sea and is connected to the mainland by two small bridges. The **Archaeological Park,** at the western edge of town, contains the ruins of a fine Roman amphitheater and the most complete Greek theater existing from antiquity. A comparison of these two structures reveals much about the differences between the Greek and Roman personalities. The Greek theater, in which the plays of Aeschylus premiered, was hewn out of the hillside rock in the 5th century BC. All the seats converge upon a single point—the stage—which had the natural scenery and the sky as its background. Drama as a kind of religious ritual was the intention here. In the Roman amphitheater, however, the emphasis was on the spectacle of combative sports and the circus. The arena is one of the largest of its kind and was built around the 2nd century AD. The corridor where gladiators and beasts entered the ring is still intact, and the seats, some of which still bear the occupants' names, were hauled in and constructed on the site from huge slabs of limestone. A crowd-pleasing show, and not the elevation of men's minds, was the intention here. Climb to the top of the seating area in the Greek theater, which could accommodate 15,000, for a fine view. In May and June of even-numbered years, performances of Greek tragedies are held here. If the Archaeological Park is closed, go up Viale G. Rizzo from Viale Teracati, to the belvedere overlooking the ruins, which are floodlit at night.

Near the entrance to the park is the gigantic altar of Hieron, which was once used by the Greeks for spectacular sacrifices involving hundreds of animals. Just beyond the ticket office you will come upon a lush tropical garden full of palm and citrus trees. This is the Latomie del Paradiso, a series of quarries that served as prisons for the defeated Athenians, who were enslaved; the quarries once rang with the sound of their chisels and hammers. At one end is the Orecchio di Dionisio, with an ear-shape entrance and unusual acoustics inside, as you'll discover if you clap your hands. The legend is that Dionysius used to listen in at the top of the quarry to hear what the slaves were plotting below. ⊠ *Viale Augusto,* ☎ *0931/66206.* ▨ *2,000 lire.* ☉ *Daily 9– 1 hr before sunset.*

Not far from the Archaeological Park, off Viale Teocrito, are the **catacombs** of San Giovanni, one of the earliest-known Christian sites in the city. Inside the crypt of San Marciano is an altar where St. Paul preached on his way through Sicily to Rome. The frescoes in this small chapel are still bright and fresh, though some date from the 4th century AD. ⊠ *Piazza San Giovanni.* ▨ *2,000 lire.* ☉ *Daily 9–1 and 4–6.*

Along Viale Teocrito, you'll soon come to the **papyrus studio** at No. 80, where you can see papyruses being prepared from reeds and then see the scrolls painted—an ancient tradition in Siracusa. Siracusa, it seems, has the only climate outside the Nile Valley in which the papyrus plant—from which we get our word "paper"—thrives. ⊠ *Viale Teocrito 80.*

The impressive collection contained in Siracusa's splendid **Archaeological Museum** is arranged by region around a central atrium and ranges from neolithic pottery to fine Greek statues and vases. You will want to compare the Landolina Venus—a headless, stout goddess of love who rises out of the sea in measured modesty (she is a 1st-century Roman copy of the Greek original)—with the much earlier (300 BC) elegant Greek statue of Hercules in Section C. Of a completely different type is a marvelous fanged Gorgon, its tongue sticking out, that once adorned the cornice of the temple of Athena in order to ward off evildoers. The pieces are generally well lit, and there are also several interesting, instructive exhibits. One depicts the Temple of Apollo, the oldest Doric temple in Sicily, on the island of Ortygia. ⊠ *Viale Teocrito,* ☎ *0931/464022.* ▨ *2,000 lire.* ☉ *Tues.–Sun. 9–1. Closed 1st and 3rd Sun. of every month.*

The central part of Siracusa is a modern city, with Corso Gelone its main shopping street. At its southern end, Corso Umberto leads to the **Ortygia Island** bridge, which crosses a pretty harbor lined with fish restaurants. In the piazza on the other side of the bridge, you'll find the ruins of the **Temple of Apollo** depicted in the Archaeological Museum. In fact, little of this noble Doric temple still remains today, except for some crumbled walls and shattered columns, along with a fragment (the window in the south wall) of a Norman church that was built much later on the same spot. ⊠ *Piazza Pancali.*

Apart from the Temple of Apollo, Ortygia is composed almost entirely of warm, restrained Baroque buildings. This uniformity is the result of an earthquake in 1693 that necessitated major rebuilding at a time when the Baroque was very popular. Wander into the backstreets—especially along Via della Maestranza or Via Veneto—and notice the bulbous wrought-iron balconies (said to have been invented to accommodate ladies' billowing skirts), the window-surrounds and cornices of buildings decorated with mermaids and gargoyles, and the stucco decoration on Palazzo Lantieri on Via Roma.

Ortygia has two main piazzas: Piazza Archimede and Piazza del Duomo. Piazza Archimede is easily recognized because of its Baroque fountain of fainting sea nymphs and dancing jets of water. The bars here are popular meeting and sitting places. **Piazza del Duomo,** one of the most
★ beautiful piazzas in Italy, holds Siracusa's **cathedral.** The building is an archive of island history, beginning with the bottommost excavations that have unearthed remnants of Sicily's distant past, when the Siculi inhabitants worshiped their deities here. During the 5th century BC, the Greeks built a temple to Athena over it, and in the 7th century, Siracusa's first Christian cathedral was built on top of the Greek structure. The elegant columns of the original temple were incorporated into the present structure and are clearly visible, embedded in the exterior wall along Via Minerva. The Greek columns were also used to dramatic advantage inside, where on one side they form chapels connected by elegant wrought-iron gates. The Baroque facade, added in 1700, displays a harmonious rhythm of concaves and convexes. The piazza in front is encircled by pink and white oleanders and surrounded by elegant buildings ornamented with filigree grillwork. In the right corner of Piazza del Duomo is the elegant **Palazzo Beneventano del Bosco,** with an impressive interior courtyard ending in a grand winding staircase. At one end of Piazza del Duomo stands the Baroque church of **Santa Lucia alla Badia,** with an engaging wrought-iron balcony and pleasing facade. The feast of the city's patroness, Santa Lucia (St. Lucy), is held on December 13, when a splendid silver statue of the saint is carried from the cathedral to the church on the site of her martyrdom, near the Catacombs of San Giovanni. A torchlight procession and band music accompany the bearers. ⊠ *Piazza del Duomo.*

Siracusa's **National Museum** is housed inside Palazzo Bellomo, a lovely Catalan-Gothic building with mullioned windows and an elegant exterior staircase. Among the select group of paintings and sculptures inside is a Santa Lucia by Caravaggio and a damaged, but still brilliant, Annunciation by Antonello da Messina. ⊠ *Via Capodieci 14,* ☎ *0931/69617.* ⌑ *2,000 lire.* ☉ *Tues.–Sun. 9–1.*

Just off the promenade along the harbor, you'll find the **Fountain of Arethusa,** a freshwater spring next to the sea. This anomaly is explained by a Greek legend that tells how the nymph Arethusa was changed into a fountain by the goddess Artemis (Diana) when she tried to escape the advances of the river god Alpheus. She fled from Greece, into the sea, with Alpheus in close pursuit, and emerged in Sicily at this spring.

Supposedly even today, if you throw a cup into the River Alpheus in Greece, it will emerge here at this fountain, which at present is home to a few tired ducks and some dull-colored carp—but no cups. Steps lead to the tree-lined promenade along the harbor front, where you can buy a drink and watch the ships come in. The southern tip of Ortygia island is occupied by the **Castello Maniace,** now an army barracks but once a castle of Frederick II, from which there are fine views of the sea.

North of the city, on the highlands that overlook the sea, Dionysius created, with the help of Archimedes, the fortress of **Euryalus,** as protection against the Carthaginians. This astonishing boat-shape structure once covered 15,000 square yards. Its intricate maze of tunnels is fascinating, and the view from the heights is superb. ⊠ *Belvedere, 8 km (5 mi) northwest of Siracusa.* ⊙ *9–1 hr before sunset.*

Dining and Lodging

$$–$$$ ✕ **Ionico.** Enjoy seaside dining in the coastal Santa Lucia district. The
★ Ionico boasts a terrace and veranda for alfresco meals, while the interior is plastered with diverse historical relics and has a cheerful open hearth for the winter. Chef/proprietor Roberto Giudice cooks meals to order or will suggest a specialty from a selection of market-fresh ingredients. Try the pasta *con acciughe e il pan grattato* (in an anchovy sauce). ⊠ *Riviera Dionisio il Grande 194,* ☎ *0931/65540. AE, DC, MC, V. Closed Tues.*

$$ ✕ **Archimede.** The antipasto misto should whet your appetite for the predominantly seafood menu of this small establishment in the Old Town. Risotto di mare and pesce spada are specialties, but the menu veers away from seafood when game is in season. Otherwise, sample the involtini *all'Archimede* (stuffed with cheese and ham, baked in bread crumbs). ⊠ *Via Gemmellaro 8,* ☎ *0931/69701. AE, DC, MC, V. Closed Sun. evening.*

$$ ✕ **Arlecchino.** A bustling bohemian atmosphere pervades this restaurant, which is midway between the archaeological zone and the Old Town. It's popular with artists and students, always a sign of good value. The Palermo-born proprietor serves specialties from his hometown, such as risotto *ai ricci* (with sea-urchins) and homemade cassata for dessert. ⊠ *Via dei Tolomei 5,* ☎ *0931/66386. AE, DC, MC, V. Closed Mon. and Aug.*

$$ ✕ **Minosse.** You'll find this small, old-fashioned restaurant in the heart of Siracusa's Città Vecchia. Fish is the specialty, and it comes broiled, baked, stuffed, and skewered. For an introduction to the local seafood, try the antipasto misto di frutti di mare. Ask for the daily special as your main course, or try the pesce spada alla brace. The zuppa di pesce is a local favorite. ⊠ *Via Mirabella 6,* ☎ *0931/66366. AE, DC, MC, V. Closed Mon. (may remain open daily in summer).*

$$$ ▥ **Forte Agip.** This standard motel, with modern comforts (color TV and minibar in all rooms) is across the street from the archaeological zone. The rooms are bright and clean, and the restaurant serves some local specialties as well as classic hotel food. ⊠ *Viale Teracati 30,* ☎ *0931/463232,* FAX *0931/67115. 87 rooms with shower. Restaurant, bar. AE, DC, MC, V.*

$$$ ▥ **Jolly Hotel.** The rooms are uniformly comfortable in this member of the Jolly hotel chain, Italy's answer to Holiday Inns. The big advantage, apart from knowing that the plugs work and the rooms are soundproofed, is the location. The hotel is half a kilometer (less than a quarter mile) from the train station and within easy walking distance of the archaeological zone. ⊠ *Corso Gelone 45,* ☎ *0931/461111,* FAX

0931/461126. 100 rooms with bath or shower. Restaurant, bar. AE, DC, MC, V.

Nightlife and the Arts
In May and June, Siracusa's impressive **Teatro Greco** (☎ 0931/67710) will be the setting for performances of classical drama and comedy; the festival is held in even-numbered years only.

Noto

32 km (20 mi) southwest of Siracusa.

Planned on a hierarchical plan following the destruction of the old town during the great earthquake of 1693, Noto presents a pleasing ensemble of honey-colored Baroque architecture, strikingly uniform in style, but never dull. Its centerpiece is the majestic Duomo, completed in 1776, atop a broad flight of steps.

Dining
$ ✕ **Il Giglio.** Seafood dishes with a Spanish touch are the specialty at this pleasant trattoria in the center of town run by Maria Luz Corruchaga and her husband, Corrado. Particularly recommended are pasta *al nero di seppia* (with cuttlefish) and *zuppa di vongole e cozze* (clam and mussel soup), though you won't find these on the good-value tourist menu. You'll also find paella. ✉ *Piazza Municipio*, ☎ *0931/838640. AE, MC, V.*

Catania

③③ *60 km (37 mi) north of Siracusa, 94 km (59 mi) south of Messina.*

The chief wonder of **Catania**, Sicily's second city, is that it is there at all. Its successive populations were deported by one Greek tyrant, sold into slavery by another, and driven out by the Carthaginians. Every time the city got back on its feet, it was struck by a new calamity: Plague decimated the population in the Middle Ages, a mile-wide stream of lava from Mt. Etna swallowed most of the city in 1663, and 25 years later a disastrous earthquake forced the Catanese to begin again. Today the city needs much renovation. Traffic flows in ever-increasing volume and adds to the smog from the industrial zone between Catania and Siracusa, but the views of Mt. Etna from Catania are superb. To Etna, Catania also owes a fertile surrounding plain and its site on nine successive layers of lava. Many of Catania's buildings are constructed from solidified lava, and the black lava stone has given the city a singular appearance. As a result, Catania is known as the city of lava and oranges. Catania's greatest native son is the composer Vincenzo Bellini, whose operas have thrilled audiences since their premieres about 170 years ago. His home, now the **Bellini Museum**, in Piazza San Francesco, preserves memorabilia of the man and his work. ✉ *Piazza San Francesco 3,* ☎ *095/715–0535.* ▣ *Free.* ◷ *Mon.–Sat. 9–1:30, Sun. 9–12:30.*

The **Villa Bellini**, Catania's public gardens, is to the north just off Via Etnea, and on clear days has lovely views of snowcapped Etna. The **Duomo,** at the bottom end of Via Etnea, is a fine work by Vaccarini (1736), as is the obelisk-balancing elephant carved out of lava stone in the piazza in front. Bellini is buried inside the cathedral. Also inside is the sumptuous chapel of St. Agatha, Catania's patron saint, who is credited with having held off, more than once, the fiery flows of lava that threatened the city. During the festival of her feast day (Feb. 3–5), huge 16-foot-tall, highly ornate carved wooden *cannelore* (large bundles of candles) are paraded through the streets at night.

NEED A
BREAK?

If you haven't had cannoli yet in Sicily, the pastry shops along Via Etnea are good places to try one of these wafer tubes filled with silky smooth ricotta cheese. If you're in need of something more substantial, duck into one of the trattorias along this street and order a dish of pasta *alla Norma*. It's named after one of Bellini's most famous operas and consists of short pasta with a rich eggplant-and-tomato sauce, garnished with basil leaves and grated ricotta cheese.

Dining and Lodging

$$$ ✕ **Costa Azzurra.** This seafood restaurant is in the Ognina district, just
★ north of the center and on the way to the Taormina road. Reserve a table on the veranda by the edge of the sea. There are good views of the harbor. The fritto misto can be ordered as an antipasto or a main course, and the pesce spada steak is a simple classic—served grilled with a large slice of lemon. ⊠ *Via De Cristofaro 4,* ☎ *095/494920. Jacket and tie. AE, DC, MC, V. Generally closed Mon. and Aug.*

$$ ✕ **Pagano.** This restaurant, behind the Hotel Excelsior, has been around a long time (since the 1950s) and remains a favorite with locals for genuine Catanese cooking. Seafood is the specialty, but it's the unpretentious kind that won't send the check into the stratosphere. Try *insalata di polipo* (octopus salad) as a starter and then sarde or *acciughe* (anchovies) in a variety of sauces. Like the sober, rather dated decor, the service is formal. ⊠ *Via De Roberto 37,* ☎ *095/537045. AE, DC, MC, V. Closed Sat. lunch and Aug. 15.*

$$$ 🏨 **Excelsior.** Ask for a room facing Piazza Verga, a neat tree-lined square in this quiet but central district of Catania. The Excelsior has air-conditioning and sound-insulating windows in all rooms. The rooftop garden is one of Catania's most chic meeting places, and the American Bar should provide solace to anyone pining for a Manhattan. ⊠ *Piazza Verga 39,* ☎ *095/537071,* 🅵🅰🆇 *095/537015. 167 rooms with bath or shower, most with bath. Restaurant, bar. AE, DC, MC, V.*

$$ 🏨 **Savona.** The Savona is an efficiently run and well-maintained hotel a stone's throw from Piazza del Duomo. The rooms are spacious and comfortable, solidly furnished, and equipped with TV and telephones. Prices include a Continental breakfast. Parking may be a problem. ⊠ *Via Vittorio Emanuele 210,* ☎ *095/326982,* 🅵🅰🆇 *095/715–8169. 25 rooms, 15 with shower. Bar. No credit cards.*

Nightlife and the Arts

Teatro Bellini (⊠ Piazza Bellini, Catania, ☎ 095/312020) hosts an opera season from October to mid-June, attracting top singers and productions to the birthplace of the great operatic composer Vincenzo Bellini.

Mt. Etna

★ ㉞ *30 km (19 mi) north of Catania, 60 km (37 mi) south of Messina.*

Catania is the departure point for excursions around—but not always to the top of—**Mt. Etna.** Buses leave from in front of the train station in early morning, or you can take the Circumetnea railroad around the volcano's base. Etna is one of the world's major active volcanoes and is the largest and highest in Europe. The cone of the crater rises to 10,958 feet above sea level. It has erupted 10 times in the past three decades, most spectacularly in 1971 and 1983, when rivers of molten lava destroyed the two highest stations of the cable car that rises from the town of Sapienza. Travel in the proximity of the crater depends at the moment on Etna's temperament, but you can walk up and down the enormous lava dunes and wander over its moonlike surface of dead craters.

The rings of vegetation change markedly as you rise, with vineyards and pine trees gradually giving way to growths of broom and lichen.

Taormina

★ ㉟ *43 km (27 mi) southwest of Messina, 50 km (31 mi) north of Catania.*

The natural beauty of the medieval mountaintop town of **Taormina** is so great that even the considerable overdevelopment that it has suffered in the past 50 years has not spoiled its grandeur. The view of the sea and Etna from its jagged cactus-covered cliffs is as close to perfection as a panorama can get, especially on clear days when the snowcapped volcano's white puffs of smoke are etched against the blue sky. Writers have extolled Taormina's beauty almost since its founding in the 6th century BC by Greeks from Naples. Goethe and D. H. Lawrence were among its enthusiasts. The Greeks put a high premium on finding impressive locations to stage their dramas, and Taormina's **Greek Theater** occupies one of the finest sites of any such theater. It was built during the 3rd century BC and rebuilt by the Romans during the 2nd century AD. Its acoustics are exceptional: Even today a stage whisper can be heard in the last rows. In summer, Taormina hosts an arts festival of music, cinema, and dance events, many of which are held in the Greek Theater. ⊠ *Via Teatro Greco.* ☜ *2,000 lire.* ☉ *Daily 9–2 hrs before sunset.*

The main street in town is **Corso Umberto,** which is lined with smart boutiques and antiques shops. There are also the inevitable, and all too numerous, shops selling cheap pottery and jewelry made from Etna's black lava stone, but Piazza 9 Aprile, along the Corso, commands wonderful views and is the perfect place to sit and have a cappuccino. The town's many 14th- and 15th-century palaces have been carefully preserved; especially beautiful is the **Palazzo Corvaja,** with characteristic black-lava and white-limestone inlays. Today, it houses the tourist office (☉ Mon.–Sat. 8–2, 4–7, also summer Sun. 9–1). The medieval **Castello Saraceno,** enticingly perched on an adjoining cliff above the town, can be reached by footpath or car. ☜ *Free.*

NEED A BREAK?	If you are a devotee of marzipan (almond paste), you should not leave Taormina without trying it at either the **Bar Mokambo** in Piazza 9 Aprile or at one of the pastry shops along the Corso. The marzipan is shaped like various fruits, including the ubiquitous *fico d'India* (prickly pear), which grows wild along the slopes of Taormina.

Dining and Lodging

$$–$$$ ✕ **Delfino.** This seaside restaurant is across the road from the cable-
★ car station in Mazzarò, to the east of Taormina proper. Seafood takes pride of place here, from hearty starters, such as the zuppa di pesce or risotto marinara, to main courses, such as *gamberetti* (shrimp) alla brace. Arrive early or reserve to get one of the best tables overlooking the sea. ⊠ *Via Nazionale, Mazzarò,* ☎ *0942/23004. AE, DC, MC, V. Closed Nov.–Easter.*

$$ ✕ **Luraleo.** You can dine indoors by candlelight or in the vine-covered garden in summer. It's touristy, but the food here is of a high standard, with the accent on fish—sample the risotto with salmon and pistachios, a specialty of the house. There is a rich selection of antipasti. A word of warning: Service can be extremely slow. ⊠ *Via Bagnoli Croci 27,* ☎ *0942/24279. MC, V. Closed Wed. Oct.–June.*

$$$$ ☷ **San Domenico Palace.** The panoramic views from this converted 15th-
★ century convent will stay in your mind long after you're gone. Luxury

and comfort are bywords in this deluxe hotel, which has managed to sneak a number of unobtrusive 20th-century comforts into its furnishings (such as wheelchair access and climate control). The essentially Renaissance flavor remains, however, from the cloisters to the chapel, which is now a bar. The rooms in the front of the hotel have sweeping views of the bay; those in back look out over the gardens, with Etna visible in the distance. The rooms are decorated with antiques and are brimming with fresh flowers. ⊠ *Piazza San Domenico 5,* ☎ *0942/23701,* FAX *0942/625506. 101 rooms with bath. 2 restaurants, 2 bars, pool. AE, DC, MC, V.*

$$$ 🏨 **Jolly Diodoro.** Located high on a cliff near the Greek amphitheater, this Jolly hotel shares the view with the much more expensive San Domenico Palace. Another departure from the sometimes functional Jolly format is the relaxing and colorful garden, where you can have a drink and watch the play of light over the sea. ⊠ *Via Bagnoli Croce 75,* ☎ *0942/23312,* FAX *0942/23391. 103 rooms with bath or shower. Restaurant, bar, pool. AE, DC, MC, V.*

$$ 🏨 **Villa Fiorita.** This converted private home near the Greek amphitheater has excellent views of the coast from nearly every room. The rooms vary in size and furnishings, but most are bright and colorful, with large windows that let in the sea breezes. Prices are reasonable for a hotel with a swimming pool and small garden. Note that the hotel is accessed by 65 steps, and there is no elevator. ⊠ *Via Pirandello 39,* ☎ *0942/24122,* FAX *0942/625967. 24 rooms with bath or shower. Pool, sauna. AE, MC, V.*

Nightlife and the Arts

CINEMA

Taormina hosts an international **film festival** each July in the grand setting of the Roman amphitheater. For information, call ☎ 0942/23220.

CONCERTS

The churches and theaters of Taormina are the venues for the summer festival of **classical music,** held each year from May to September. For information, call ☎ 0942/23751.

THEATER

Taormina's **Greco-Roman Theater** is the setting for regular theatrical performances from July to September. For information, call ☎ 0942/23220.

Shopping

Pieces of **carretti siciliani,** the island equivalent of the first automobile and a real find for collectors, sometimes appear at **Chez le Francais** (⊠ Piazza San Domenico 6).

Castelmola

5 km (3 mi) west of Taormina.

If your passion for heights hasn't been exhausted, visit **Castelmola,** the tiny town above Taormina, where the Bar Turrisi makes its own refreshing almond wine—the perfect complement to the spectacular 360-degree panorama.

Dining

$$ ✕ **Il Faro.** Castelmola is a small village above Taormina, and as you
★ dine in this family-run country restaurant, sitting under a grape arbor, you have an excellent view of the wild cliffs and sea. Meat dishes are recommended alla brace, particularly *pollo* (chicken) and *coniglio* (rabbit). Piera and Francesco, the owners, provide an antipasto with homegrown vegetables. Start your meal with *bruschetta all'ortolana* (country bread toasted with olive oil, topped with tomatoes and

onions). ✉ *Via Rotabile, Contrada Petralia,* ☎ *0942/28193. No credit cards. Closed Wed.*

En Route   The road between Taormina and Messina, about 50 kilometers (30 miles) north, is bordered by lush vegetation on one side and the sea on the other. The coast here has many inlets punctuated by gigantic odd-shape rocks. It was along this coast, legend says, that the giant one-eyed cyclopes hurled their boulders down on Ulysses and his terrified men as they fled to the sea and on to their next adventure in Homer's *Odyssey.*

Messina

 43 km (27 mi) northeast of Taormina, 94 km (59 mi) northeast of Catania.

Messina's ancient history is a series of disasters, but the city nevertheless managed to develop a fine university and a thriving cultural environment. But at 5 o'clock in the morning on December 28, 1908, Messina changed from a flourishing metropolis of 120,000 to a heap of rubble, shaken to pieces by an earthquake that turned into a tidal wave and left 80,000 dead and the city almost completely leveled. As you approach the sickle-shape bay, from which ferries connect Sicily with the mainland, you see nothing to alert you to the relatively recent disaster, except that the 3,000-year-old city looks modern. The somewhat flat look is a precaution of seismic planning: Tall buildings are not permitted. Messina's **cathedral** has been entirely rebuilt (it was originally constructed by the Norman King Roger II in 1197, and the reconstruction has maintained much of the original plan, including a handsome crown of Norman battlements, an enormous apse, and a splendid wood-beam ceiling). The adjoining bell tower—of a much later date—is one of the city's principal attractions. It contains one of the largest and most complex mechanical clocks in the world, constructed in 1933 with a host of gilded automatons—a roaring lion, a crowing rooster, and numerous biblical figures—that go into action every day at the stroke of noon. ✉ *Piazza del Duomo.*

Messina is the birthplace of the great Renaissance painter Antonello da Messina, whose *Polyptych of the Rosary* (1473) can be seen along with two large Caravaggios in the **Regional Museum,** located along the sea in the northern outskirts of the city. ✉ *Viale della Libertà,* ☎ *090/361292.* ✑ *2,000 lire.* ☉ *Mon., Wed., Fri., Sat. 9–1:30; Tues., Thurs., 9–1:30 and 3–5:30; Sun. and holidays 9–12:30.*

NEED A   **Bilé,** on the corner of Piazza Cairoli and Via Cannizzaro, is a good
BREAK?   place to visit for a lunchtime snack—if you don't mind standing up. At this bar, you can sample (or take away) such typical Sicilian snacks as *arancini* (deep-fried breaded rice balls filled with cheese or meat sauce), mozzarella in *carrozza* (deep-fried bread pockets), and *piddoni* (savory parcels of mozzarella or vegetables). If you *do* want to sit, similar fare can be found farther up Via Cannizzaro, where some of the snack bars have stools and counters.

OFF THE   **REGGIO DI CALABRIA** – From Messina, a hydrofoil will speed you across
BEATEN PATH   the strait to this city on the toe of the boot, where two larger-than-life-size 5th-century Greek bronze statues are exhibited in the excellent **National Museum of Magna Graecia.** The statues—known as the Riace bronzes—were found by accident by an amateur deep-sea diver off the coast of Calabria in 1972 and are worth going out of your way to see. ✉ *Corso Garibaldi, Piazza de Nava,* ☎ *0965/812255.* ✑ *8,000 lire.* ☉ *Summer, daily 9–7; winter, Sun.–Mon. 9–12:30, Tues.–Sat. 9–1, 3:30–7.*

Dining

$$$ ✕ **Alberto.** Recently transferred from the center of town to Mortelle,
★ Messina's seaside satellite 10 kilometers (6 miles) up the coast, this deluxe
restaurant still brings in plenty of business. If you're adventurous, and
not too worried about the cost, ask the waiter to order for you: You'll
get a succession of courses linked by a common theme of seafood. À
la carte items are also delicious, particularly the spaghetti *al cartoccio
con frutti di mare* (cooked in silver foil with seafood) and the invol-
tini di pesce spada. Have some vintage Marsala with one of the rich
homemade desserts. ✉ *Via Nazionale, Mortelle,* ☎ *090/321009. AE,
DC, MC, V. Closed Mon. and Jan.*

$$ ✕ **Pippo Nunnari.** Traditional Sicilian cooking is complemented by the
refined decor, with antiques and rich fabrics. A favorite Sicilian appe-
tizer is smoked salmon and pesce spada; you can also have the risotto
di mare (of the sea) whose ingredients change with each day's catch
of fish. Don't be embarrassed about ordering the *bistecca* (steak) here:
It's charcoal grilled and renowned locally. ✉ *Via Ugo Bassi 157,* ☎
090/293–8584. AE, MC, V. Closed Mon. and 2–3 wks in July–Aug.

Nightlife and the Arts

Messina stages a **folklore parade** of huge traditional effigies, called Giganti, each year on August 13 and 14.

THE AEOLIAN ISLANDS

Just off Sicily's northeast coast lies an archipelago of seven beautiful
islands of volcanic origin. The Aeolian Islands were named after Aeolus, the Greek god of the winds, who is said to keep all the Earth's
winds stuffed in a bag in his cave here. The islands are reachable by
hydrofoil from Messina, Palermo, and Milazzo. The latter also has a
ferryboat service to the islands, as do Palermo and Naples, but on a
less frequent schedule. In summer there are numerous boats and hydrofoil excursions connecting the individual islands. The Aeolians are
a fascinating world of grottoes and clear-water caves carved by the waves
through the centuries. They are ideal for snorkeling or scuba diving.
All Sicily's islands—and these seven in particular—are extremely popular in summer, and some of them are unpleasantly overcrowded in
July and August.

The bars in the Aeolian Islands, and especially those on Lipari, are known
for their *granite* (dishes of shaved ice made by freezing the juice and
pulp of fresh fruit). These are not snow cones doused with sickeningly
sweet syrups but fruit drinks made from fresh strawberries, melon,
peaches, and other fruits. Whenever the need arises for a real thirst-
quencher, order a lemon granita and keep adding water from the glass
or pitcher that usually accompanies your order. Many Sicilians begin
the hot summer days with a granita *di caffè* (a coffee ice topped with
whipped cream), into which they dunk their breakfast rolls. You can
have one any time of day.

Lipari

㊲ *37 km (23 mi) north of Milazzo.*

Lipari is the largest of the Aeolians and the one most developed for
tourism. Local buses circle the island and provide wonderful views of
Sicily and the other islands. Take a bus ride away from Lipari's distinctive pastel-colored houses and into its fields of spiky agaves to the
northernmost tip of the island, Aquacalda, where there are interesting
pumice and obsidian quarries. Or take a bus west to San Calogero,
where there are hot springs and mud baths. From the red lava base of

the island a plateau rises that is crowned with a 16th-century castle and a 17th-century **cathedral**. Next door is the **Archaeological Museum**, one of the best in Europe, with an intelligently arranged collection of prehistoric finds—some dating as far back as 4,000 BC—from various sites in the archipelago. ✉ *Via Castello,* ☎ *090/988–0174.* 🖾 *Free.* ☉ *Daily 9–2.*

Vulcano

38 *55 km (34 mi) northwest of Milazzo, 18 km (10 mi) northwest of Lipari.*

True to its name, **Vulcano** has plenty of fumaroles sending up jets of hot vapor, but the volcano here has long been dormant. You can ascend to the crater (1,266 feet above sea level) on muleback for a wonderful view, or take boat rides into the grottoes around the base. From Capo Grillo there is a view of all the Aeolians.

Salina

39 *15 km (10 mi) north of Lipari, 52 km (38 mi) northwest of Milazzo.*

The second-largest island, **Salina** is also the most fertile—which accounts for its good wine, the golden Malvasia. Excursions go up Mt. Fossa delle Felci, which rises to over 3,000 feet. It is also the highest of the islands, and the vineyards and fishing villages along its slopes add to its charm.

Panarea

40 *55 km (34 mi) north of Milazzo, 18 km (10 mi) north of Lipari.*

Panarea has some of the most dramatic scenery of the islands: wild caves carved out of the rock and dazzling flora. The exceptionally clear water and the richness of life on the seabed make Panarea especially suitable for underwater exploration. There is a small Bronze Age village at Capo Milazzese.

Stromboli

41 *63 km (40 mi) north of Milazzo, 40 km (25 mi) north of Lipari*

The island consists entirely of the cone of an active volcano. The view from the sea—especially at night, as an endless stream of glowing red-hot lava flows into the water—is unforgettable. **Stromboli** is in a constant state of mild dissatisfaction, and every now and then its anger flares up, so authorities insist that you climb to the top (about 3,031 feet above sea level) only with a guide. The climb takes about four hours.

Alicudi

42 *65 km (40 mi) west of Lipari, 102 km (68 mi) northwest of Milazzo.*

Alicudi is the farthest outpost of the Aeolians—it remains sparsely inhabited (although it does have a hotel), wild, and at peace.

Filicudi

43 *30 km (16 mi) west of Salina, 82 km (54 mi) northwest of Milazzo.*

Just a dot in the sea, **Filicudi** is famous for its unusual volcanic rock formations and the enchanting **Grotta del Bue Marino** (Grotto of the Sea Ox). At Capo Graziano there is a prehistoric village. The island has a hotel, and some local families put up guests.

SICILY A TO Z

Arriving and Departing

By Car and Ferry

Frequent **car ferries** cross the strait between Villa San Giovanni in Calabria and Messina on the island. The crossing usually takes about half an hour, but during the summer months there can be considerable delays. From Naples, overnight car ferries operate daily to Palermo and once a week to Catania and Siracusa; there is also an overnight ferry from Genoa to Palermo.

By Passenger Boat

Besides the ferries mentioned above (☞ *above*), **aliscafi** (hydrofoils), which carry passengers only, also cross the strait in about 30 minutes.

By Plane

Sicily can be reached from all major cities via Rome, Milan, or Naples. Planes land at **Punta Raisi Airport** (☎ 091/591698), 32 kilometers (20 miles) west of Palermo, or at Catania's **Fontanarossa Airport** (☎ 095/341900), 5 kilometers (3 miles) south of the city. At both, there is bus service into the center of town. During the high season, there are also direct charter flights to Sicily from New York, London, and Paris.

By Train

There are direct **express trains** from Milan and Rome to Palermo, Catania, and Siracusa. The Rome–Palermo journey takes at least 11 hours. After Naples, the run is mostly along the coast, so try to book a window seat on the right. At Villa San Giovanni, in Calabria, the train is separated and loaded onto a ferryboat to cross the strait to Messina.

Getting Around

By Bus

Air-conditioned coaches connect major and minor cities and are often faster and more convenient than local trains but slightly more expensive.

By Car

Renting a car is definitely the best way to travel in Sicily because the trains are unreliable and slow, and the buses, though faster and air-conditioned in summer, can be subject to delays and strikes. Modern highways circle and bisect the island, making all main cities easily reachable. Cars can be rented at airports and downtown locations in every major city.

By Train

Main lines connect Messina, Taormina, Siracusa, and Palermo. Secondary lines are generally very slow and unreliable. The Messina–Palermo run, along the northern coast, is especially scenic.

Contacts and Resources

Emergencies

Police, Ambulance, Fire (☎ 113). **Hospital** in Palermo (☎ 091/666–2207), in Catania (☎ 095/322216).

Guided Tours

City tours are provided by the Italian tour operator **CIT** in all major cities. CIT also arranges complete tours of Sicily, which range from seven-day tours of the island's major sights to a four-day minitour. Departures are once a week from Palermo in a comfortable air-conditioned coach with an English-speaking guide. The cost includes all meals and accommodations in three- or four-star hotels. CIT has offices in **Palermo**

(✉ Via della Libertà 12, ☎ 091/586333); **Catania** (✉ Via Mario San-giorgi 45, ☎ 095/538136); and **Taormina** (✉ Corso Umberto 101, ☎ 0942/23301).

Visitor Information

Aeolian Islands (✉ Corso Vittorio Emanuele 202, Lipari, ☎ 090/988–0095). **Agrigento** (✉ Viale della Vittoria 255, ☎ 0922/401352; Via Cesare Battisti 15, ☎ 0922/20454). **Caltagirone** (✉ Palazzo Libertini, ☎ 0933/53809). **Caltanisetta** (✉ Corso Vittorio Emanuele 109, ☎ 0934/584499). **Catania** (✉ Largo Paisiello 5, ☎ 095/730–6233; rail station, ☎ 095/730–6255; airport, ☎ 095/730–6266). **Cefalù** (✉ Corso Ruggero 77, ☎ 0921/21050 and 0921/21458). **Enna** (✉ Piazza Garibaldi 1, ☎ 0935/500901; Piazza Napoleone Colajanni 6, ☎ 0935/26119). **Erice** (✉ Via Conte Pepoli 11, ☎ 0923/869388). **Marsala** (✉ Via Garibaldi 45, ☎ 0923/714097). **Messina** (✉ Piazza Stazione, ☎ 090/672944; Via Calabria 301/b, ☎ 090/674236; Piazza Cairoli 45, ☎ 090/293–5292). **Monreale** (✉ Piazza Duomo, ☎ 091/656–4570). **Palermo** (✉ Piazza Castelnuovo 35, ☎ 091/583847; Stazione Marit-tima [port, summer only], ☎ 091/586830). **Piazza Armerina** (✉ Via Cavour 15, ☎ 0935/680201). **Siracusa** (✉ Via San Sebastiano 43, ☎ 0931/67710; Via Maestranza 33, ☎ 0931/464255; at the entrance to the Archaeological Park, ☎ 0931/60510). **Taormina** (✉ Largo Santa Caterina, Palazzo Corvaia, ☎ 0942/23243). **Trapani** (✉ Piazza Sat-urno, ☎ 0923/29000; Via Vito Sorba 15, ☎ 0923/27077).

16 Sardinia

An uncut jewel of an island, Sardinia remains unique and enigmatic. Too distant from Rome to be influenced by the character of the mainland, this island is as fascinating as its prehistoric stone structures, the nuraghi. *Modern luxury can also be found here: Just follow the high-fliers who sail their yachts to the Costa Smeralda. Severely beautiful, Sardinia is a prime destination for anyone seeking a getaway.*

THE SECOND-LARGEST ISLAND in the Mediterranean—
just smaller than Sicily—Sardinia is about 180 kilometers (112 miles) from mainland Italy and very
much off the beaten track. A Phoenician stronghold in ancient times
and later a Spanish dominion, Sardinia doesn't seem typically "Italian" in its color and flavor. It lies just a bit too far from the mainland—
from imperial and papal Rome and from the palaces of the Savoy
dynasty—to have been transformed by the events that forged a national
character. Yet Giuseppe Garibaldi, the charismatic national hero who
led his troops in fervid campaigns to unify Italy in the mid-19th century, chose to spend his last years in relative isolation on the small island of Caprera, just off the coast of Sardinia.

Although Sardinia (Sardegna) is now less than an hour by air and only
several hours by boat from mainland Italy, it is removed from the mainstream of tourism except for a brief two-month period in the summer,
when vacationing Italians take its beautiful coasts and clean waters by
storm. This is a good reason not to visit Sardinia in July or August.
May and October are the best touring months. In June and September the coasts are not too crowded, and ribbons of sandy beaches welcome sun worshipers. These are the best months if you want to combine
sightseeing with sunbathing. Winter in the north of the island is cold
and rainy, but is mild and generally sunny in the south. The interior is
never crowded; Italian tourists in Sardinia come for the sea, not for
the rugged and deserted mountain scenery.

Sardinia closely resembles Corsica, the French island across the 16-kilo-
meter (10-mile)-wide windswept Strait of Bonifacio to the north. A dense
bush, or *macchia,* barely penetrable in some districts, covers large
areas. The terrain is rough, like the short, sturdy shepherds you see in
the highlands—impassive figures engaged in one of the few gainful oc-
cupations that the stony land allows. Shaggy flocks of sheep and goats
are familiar features in the Sardinian landscape, just as their meat and
cheese are staples of the island's cuisine. Aside from the chic opulence
of the Costa Smeralda, there's little sophistication in Sardinia. The sprawling cities of Cagliari and Sassari have a distinctly provincial air. Newer
hotels may seem a little old-fashioned, and hotels—of any vintage—
are hard to find inland. There's little traffic on the roads, and trains,
buses, and people in general move at a gentle pace. There are hamlets
where women swathed in black shawls and long, full skirts look with
suspicion upon strangers passing through. Sardinians are courteous but
remote, perhaps because of their innate dignity.

Like mainland Italians, the Sardinians are of varied origin. On the northwest coast, fine traceries of ironwork around a balcony underscore the
Spanish influence. In the northeast, the inhabitants boast Genoese or
Pisan ancestry, and the headlands display the ruined fortresses of the
ancient duchy of Malaspina on the Italian mainland. As you explore
the southern coast, you'll come upon the physiognomies, customs, di-
alects, place-names, and holy buildings of the Turks, the Moors, the
Phoenicians, the Austrians, and the mainland Italians. If there are any
pure Sardinians—or Sards—left, perhaps they can be found in the
south-central mountains, south of Nuoro, under the 6,000-foot crests
of the Gennargentu Massif, in the rugged country still ironically called
Barbagia, "Land of Strangers."

People visit Sardinia for landscapes, rather than cathedrals or monuments; for easygoing excursions with plenty of detours, rather than a
highly organized itinerary; for a low-key entertainment scene that high-

lights folklore, rather than sophisticated or expensive nightlife. And, speaking of expense, the cost of living on Sardinia, as on most islands, is somewhat higher than on the mainland. On the other hand, if you're willing to rough it, you'll find low-cost lodgings at modest inns along your way.

Sardinia is not as large as some other regions, but its mountainous terrain makes some drives through deserted countrysides seem very long, indeed. The main highway linking Cagliari with Sassari was begun in 1820 by the Savoy ruler Carlo Felice; designated Highway 131, but still referred to as the Carlo Felice Highway by the islanders, it heads northwest through the fertile Campidano Plain for 216 kilometers (134 miles) to Sassari. The entire island is about 260 kilometers (162 miles) from north to south, and roughly 120 kilometers (75 miles) across. A fairly comprehensive tour taking in the coastline and interior can be accomplished in five to seven days.

Pleasures and Pastimes

The Arts

As one of Italy's most (perhaps *the* most) remote regions, Sardinia is not really a prime spot for sophisticated visual or performing arts. This same remoteness, however, can prove fruitful if you're interested in sampling some of the culture that has developed here, sometimes natively inspired, sometimes drawing on the influences of the traders and invaders who have left their mark on the islands over the millennia. Sardinia's own brand of Catholicism—occasionally bordering on the grotesque—can be witnessed in the local *feste*, or festivals. Ostensibly, the festivals celebrate a saintly or religious occasion, but often they are imbued with an almost pagan atmosphere.

Beaches

Sardinia's beaches are among the best in the Mediterranean; its waters are among the cleanest, with the exception of those in the immediate vicinity of Cagliari, Arbatax, and Porto Torres. The beach resorts of the Costa Smeralda are exclusive and expensive, but elsewhere on the island you can find a wide range of beaches.

Many agree that the most beautiful beaches on the island are those of Cala Luna and Cala Sisina, hidden among the rocky cliffs near Baunei and Dorgali, on the eastern coast; they can be reached only by boat from Cala Gonone or Arbatax, and can definitely be considered remote. For more accessible beaches with more amenities, go to Santa Margherita di Pula, near Cagliari, where there are several hotels; to Villasimius and the Costa Rei, on the southeastern coast; or to the sandy coves sheltered by wind-carved granite boulders on the northern coast in the Gallura district and the archipelago of La Maddalena. There are also beaches around Olbia, Alghero, and on the Costa Paradiso, near Castelsardo.

Dining

In the island's restaurants you'll find that Sardinian regional cuisine is basically Italian, with interesting local variations. Meat dishes are usually veal, lamb, or *porcheddu* (roast suckling pig). On the coast, seafood is king and is served in great variety. Langouste or *aragosta* (lobster) is a specialty of the northern coast; it can be expensive. Foreign conquerors left legacies of bouillabaisse (known here as *zimino*), couscous, and paella, but there are native pastas: *malloreddus* (small shells of bran pasta sometimes flavored with saffron), and *culingiones* (the Sardinian version of ravioli). Sharp cheese made of pecorino (sheep's milk), and thin crispy bread called *carta di musica* are typical island fare. Try the *sebadas* (fried cheese-filled ravioli doused with honey) for dessert. The red wines are sturdy and strong, with the whites tending to a light and delicate quality. Amber-colored Vernaccia is dry and heady.

CATEGORY	COST*
$$$$	over 85,000 lire
$$$	60,000–85,000 lire
$$	35,000–60,000 lire
$	under 35,000 lire

*per person, including house wine, service, and tax

Fishing

Check locally for regulations on deep-sea fishing. Underwater fishing is restricted to the daylight hours, and no more than 5 kilos (11 pounds) of fish and shellfish may be taken. No oxygen tanks or nets may be used for underwater fishing. Freshwater fishing is good along the Flumendosa, Tirso, Rio Mannu, and other rivers rising in the mountainous interior and in the artificial basins of Flumendosa and Omodeo.

Golf

Sardinia has two world-class golf courses, including the Pevero Golf Club on the Costa Smeralda, which was designed by Robert Trent Jones; and the Is Molas 18-hole course at Santa Margherita di Pula. Four more courses are planned for the Costa Smeralda.

Horseback Riding

Spaghetti westerns were once filmed in Sardinia, and it isn't easy to imagine why: The rugged, mountainous terrain of the inland is the perfect frontier setting for an adventure on horseback. On the barren hilltops of the Barbagio you may even catch a glimpse of the wild dwarf horse that is native to these parts, though numbers have dwindled over the years. If you prefer a more sedate way of seeing the island on horseback, you can stick to the coast, where the riding is easier but the scenery is still magnificent. *See* Sardinia A to Z, *below,* for details on group itineraries and horse rentals.

Kids' Stuff

Sardinia is a vast playground where children can roam, explore, and swim in season. There's nothing like a long hike along deserted beaches or through herb-scented hills to send them to bed early. Let them clamber over the nuraghi and poke into the countless *domus de janas* (witches' houses) and *tombe di giganti* (giants' tombs), fancifully named grottoes hewn in the rock by the island's prehistoric inhabitants. They served as burial places, but with a little imagination you can elaborate on their names and make up some good fairy tales. There are plenty around Sassari, at Anghelu Ruhu, and near Dorgali. Take the children to see the Elephant Rock near Castelsardo; hollowed out by primitive man to become a domus de janas, it resembles an elephant, trunk and all. Go to see the Wild West film-set village at San Salvatore near Oristano (☞ *below*). Visit the folk museum at Nuoro (☞ *below*).

Lodging

The island's most luxurious hotels are on the Costa Smeralda; they have magnificent resort facilities but close from fall to spring and are too out of the way to be good touring bases. Other, equally attractive coastal areas have seen a spate of resort hotels and villa colonies sprouting up, but they, too, close from October through April, which narrows the choice of hotels considerably during the other months. In the cities suggested as touring bases, you can expect to find standards of comfort slightly below those of the mainland; the best accommodations may be available at commercial hotels which means little atmosphere. Service is usually courteous and competent, with perhaps the exception of the seasonal resort hotels, where the staff is likely to change from year to year. In smaller towns throughout the island, you'll find modest hotels offering basic accommodations, restrained but genuine hospitality, and low rates.

CATEGORY	COST*
$$$$	over 300,000 lire
$$$	160,000–300,000 lire
$$	100,000–160,000 lire
$	under 100,000 lire

All prices are for a standard double room for two, including service and 9% tax (19% for luxury hotels).

Nightlife

Nightlife in much of Sardinia means a quiet drink before turning in early, tired out from the day's outdoor activity. But as if to make up for the sleepy atmosphere of most of the island, the Costa Smeralda sparkles most nights in the summer. Be prepared to part with a tidy sum if you visit the Costa, but if that doesn't deter you, go to the complex at the Cervo (☞ Porto Cervo, *below*) for a selection of high-class bars, restaurants, and discos.

Sailing

A popular sport in Sardinia, sailing is enjoyed all along the coast. The **Lega Navale Italiana** at Marina Piccola in Cagliari (☎ 070/303794) will furnish information on the island's facilities. The **Yacht Club Costa Smeralda** at Porto Cervo (☎ 0789/91332) offers temporary memberships.

Shopping

Sardinia is handicrafts heaven. Locally produced goods include bright woolen shawls and rugs, hand-carved wooden objects, gold filigree jewelry in traditional forms, coral jewelry, and, above all, handwoven baskets in all shapes and sizes. The best places to go for handicrafts are the various ISOLA centers in Cagliari, Olbia, Castelsardo, and Sant'Antioco. This government-sponsored exhibition of island handicrafts displays items which are also for sale. Larger towns have a complete range of Sardinian handicrafts, but elsewhere on the island the small towns and villages conform to the centuries-old tradition of specializing in one item.

Yachting

You can see the very rich engage in one of their favorite sports at the posh resorts of Costa Smeralda each August, when a number of regattas are held.

Exploring Sardinia

Driving is the only way to travel to and through the island's most interesting sights. Local transportation is not geared to the needs of tourists, so you can see more in less time if you have a car. If you don't, your best bet is to establish yourself in one of the larger towns and make excursions to as many attractions as time and schedules allow. We have divided the country into three exploring tours, each of which has at least one town large enough to act as a touring base.

Great Itineraries

Numbers in the text correpond to numbers in the margin and on the Sardinia and Cagliari maps.

IF YOU HAVE 3 DAYS

Three days in Sardinia will only give you enough time to see one corner of the island, and you would do well to confine your visit to ⌖ **Cagliari** ①–⑦ and its environs. This is where you will find Sardinia's best museum, the Museo Archeologico, with the fullest collection of nuraghic remains and other finds from antiquity. There are numerous other sights concentrated in the island's capital, as well as some of the best shops, and busiest *passeggiatas* (promenades). You can make easy day-excursions from Cagliari, and your priority should be the **Su Nuraxi** ⑫, the island's best preserved nuraghic monument, for which you need your own transport, or taxi. On your third day, head out to the small village of **Pula** ⑨, just outside of which the archaeological site of Nora encompasses Carthaginian and Roman remains. There are good beaches around here, though, again, your own transport is essential.

IF YOU HAVE 5 DAYS

With five days to spend here, you will be able to venture out to some of the attractions in the north of the island. Cut down your visit to 🏛 **Cagliari** ①–⑦ to two days—but still leaving enough time for a visit to **Pula** ⑨, just outside of the capital, and its Carthiginian and Roman remains. Spend your third night in 🏛 **Alghero** ⑰, an appealing walled town on the northwest coast of the island with a distinctly Spanish flavor, perhaps stopping for lunch en route at **Oristano** ⑭. Alghero has little specific in the way of sightseeing, barring the famous boat excursion to Neptune's Grotto, though there is ample pleasure to be had just wandering the Spanish-style streets of the historic center, and sampling the many fish restaurants. For your last two nights, you have a choice: You could spend them in the lap of luxury by checking into one of the top-class hotels in and outside of 🏛 **Porto Cervo** ㉒, on the Costa Smeralda. Here you can wander through the town and its fabled port packed with some of the world's most luxurious yachts, marveling at the magnificent villas of the international jet-set. However, if you are on a limited budget or prefer a more adventurous alternative, make 🏛 **Nuoro** ⑮ your base from which to explore the rugged interior of the island. Spend as little time as possible exploring the provincial capital before veering south into the mountainous **Barbagio** region, the island's most primitive district.

IF YOU HAVE 7 DAYS

If 🏛 **Cagliari** ①–⑦ is your point of arrival in Sardinia, spend your first two days exploring the capital, whose impressive Italianate architecture and churches in a variety of styles, as well as the extensive collection in the archaelogical museum, make Cagliari one of Italy's urban pleasures. On the third day, you could visit **Villasismus** ⑧, the only resort of interest on the southeastern tip of the island; despite its scenic value, it is nonetheless dotted with some drab, uninspiring industrial suburbs. Your best bet is to go southwest from Cagliari, taking in the remains of antiquity outside of **Pula** ⑨, before moving up along the western coast on the Carlo Felice highway as far as the sleepy village of **Sant'Antioco** ⑩. Here, you can catch a ferry over to the small island of **San Pietro** ⑪, a favorite weekend retreat of wealthy Cagliarans, whose picnic spots are delightful. Continue up toward Oristano, making a detour to the fascinating nuraghe of **Su Nuraxi** ⑫, off the main road outside the quiet town of Barumini. Wildlife enthusiasts may want to take another detour north of Barumini to the **Giara di Gesturi** ⑬, a basalt plateau that is home to some of the island's more exotic wildlife, including a species of wild dwarf horse. 🏛 **Oristano** ⑭ shone in the Middle Ages, but apart from some interesting Carthiginian ruins at Tharros, just outside the city, there is little else to recommend anything more than an overnight and a cursory walk through the town. Head northeast for **Nuoro** ⑮, a town of little interest to the traveler, and strike south into the **Barbagia** region: Torturous roads wind and loop their way over a wild and primitive terrain that seems impervious to the 20th century. If you prefer the coastal attractions to the inland ones, spend no more than half a day exploring the region and then head west from Nuoro on road 129 to Bosa, where you turn right into hilly and arid scrub country that eventually brings you to ☷ **Alghero** ⑰, on the northwest coast, where you should consider overnighting. Your itinerary now takes across the northern coast of the island, an area fringed with low cliffs, inlets, and small bays. Along the way, don't be distracted by **Sassari** ⑱, an important administrative and university town that is of little interest to the visitor, but appreciate the exquisite nature of the seaside resorts, including **Castelsardo** ⑲, a walled citadel that is a delight for basket lovers, and **Santa Teresa di Gallura** ⑳, a resort at the northern tip of the island that has not lost any of the relaxed and authentic ways of a real fishing village. You are now near the end of your itinerary, and what better way to relax after your adventure through such a rugged island than to pamper yourself on the sun-drenched beaches of one of Europe's premier holiday areas, the **Costa Smeralda**. Accommodations are expensive, exclusive, and extraordinary along this stretch of coast, especially in the area's most exclusive summer address, ☷ **Porto Cervo** ㉒.

When to Tour Sardinia

If you can help it, avoid Sardinia during the month of August, when not only is the island swamped by tourists from the mainland, but the Sards too take their annual break. The temperatures in high summer, in any case, can be unbearable, and the combination of this with crowded beaches, shortage of accommodation, and shuttered shops and offices, will be a fraying experience. September, on the other hand is much quieter, though still hot. Sudden storms can be a hazard, but these quickly blow over. The sea remains good for swimming until well into October. Winter is not the best time to be on the island: rain and cloud is not uncommon over high ground—and most of Sardinia is mountainous—and it snows most years in the Barbagia region. Lower down, the weather rarely turns cold, though neither is it particularly conducive to sitting on beaches. The mountainous interior is probably at its best in the spring, when the woods and valleys are alive with color and burgeoning growth. For the gradations of color, the fall is also a good time.

Above all, try to coincide your visit to Sardinia with one of the annual festivals for which the island is famous. The main ones are at Cagliari (beginning of May); Sassari (Ascension Day—the 40th day after Easter—and 14 Aug.), and Nuoro (penultimate Sunday in August). These are mega affairs, with accommodation and restaurant space at a premium, so plan well ahead. Apart from these, there are smaller festivals throughout the year, some of the best in the scattered mountain villages of the interior, such as the celebrations in local costume during the Feast of St. John, June 24, at Fonni, in the heart of the Barbagio; these festivities are not just expressions of religious devotion but also an explicit statement of of community identity.

CAGLIARI AND ENVIRONS

Cagliari

❶ *30 km (19 mi) northeast of Pula, 50 km (31 mi) west of Villasimius, 212 km (132 mi) south of Sassari.*

The island's capital, **Cagliari** has impressive Italianate architecture and churches in a variety of styles; it's clear that medieval Spanish conquerors from Aragon were here, as well as Austrians and Italians. Cagliari (the stress is on the first syllable) is Sardinia's largest city, characterized by a busy commercial center and waterfront with broad avenues, as well as by the typically narrow streets of the old town on a hill. From the city

Sardinia

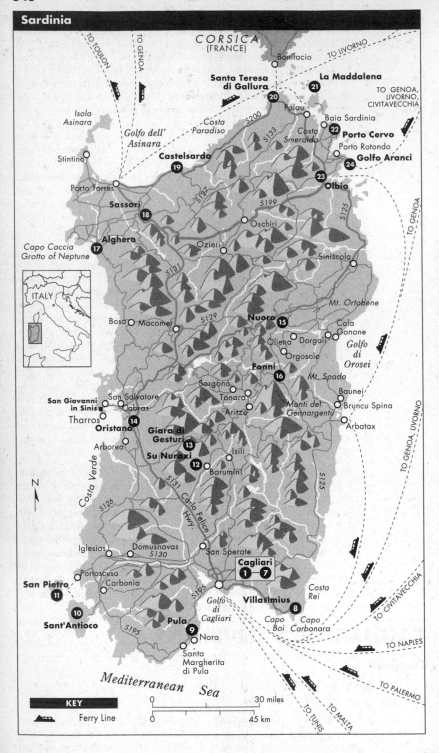

CORSICA
(FRANCE)

TO TOULON
TO GENOA
TO LIVORNO

Bonifacio

Santa Teresa
di Gallura

La Maddalena
21

20

Palau

Baia Sardinia
22 Porto Cervo

TO GENOA,
LIVORNO,
CIVITAVECCHIA

Costa
Paradiso

Costa
Smeralda

Porto Rotondo

Isola
Asinara

Golfo dell'
Asinara

S200

S133

24 Golfo Aranci

Castelsardo
19

23 Olbia

Stintino

Porto Torres

S127

Sassari
18

Oschiri

S199

S125

TO GENOA

Capo Caccia
Grotto of Neptune

Alghero
17

Ozieri

Siniscola

ITALY

S131

Mt. Ortobene

Bosa Macomer

S129

Nuoro
15

Cala
Gonone

Oliena Dorgali

Golfo
di
Orosei

Orgosolo

Fonni
16

Mt. Spada

San Giovanni
in Sinis
Tharros

San Salvatore

Cabras

Sorgono

Tonara

Baunei

Monti del
Gennargentu

Bruncu Spina

Oristano
14

Aritzo

Arbatax

Giara di
Gesturi
13

Arborea

Isili

TO GENOA, LIVORNO

Su Nuraxi
12

Barumini

S131

S125

Carlo Felice Hwy.

N

S126

Domusnovas
S130

Iglesias

San Sperate

Cagliari
1 — 7

Portoscuso

Carbonia

San Pietro
11

San Pedro

Sant'Antioco
10

S195

Pula
9

Villasimius
8

Costa
Rei

Costa Verde

Nora

Santa
Margherita
di Pula

Capo
Boi

Capo
Carbonara

Golfo
di
Cagliari

TO CIVITAVECCHIA

TO NAPLES

Mediterranean   Sea

TO PALERMO

TO TUNIS

TO MALTA

KEY

Ferry Line

0 _____ 30 miles
0 _____ 45 km

Cathedral, **5**
Museo
Archeologico, **2**
Roman
Amphitheater, **7**
Terrazza
Umberto I, **6**
Tower of the
Elephant, **4**
Tower of San
Pancrazio, **3**

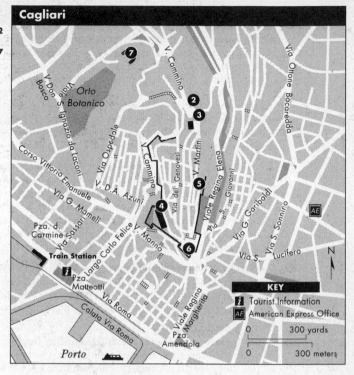

you can venture out to explore the surrounding area, including the ancient site of Nora, and the popular picnic islands of Sant'Antioco and San Pietro.

❷ Begin your visit at the **Museo Archeologico,** within the walls of the castle that the Pisans erected on the city's heights in the early 1300s to ward off attacks by the Aragonese and Catalans, from what is now Spain. The museum contains some intriguing pieces, especially bronze statuettes from the tombs and dwellings of Sardinia's earliest inhabitants, who remain a prehistorical enigma. These aboriginal people left scarcely a clue to their origins. Ancient writers called them the nuraghic people, from the name of their stone dwellings, the nuraghi, whose features are unique to Sardinia, just as the Aztec pyramids' are to Mexico. Archaeologists date the nuraghi from about 1300–1200 BC, a time when the ancient Israelites were establishing themselves in Canaan; when the Greeks were besieging Troy; when the Minoan civilization collapsed in Crete; when the Ramses pharaohs reigned in Egypt; and when many migrations were taking place along the shores and water routes of the Mediterranean. During the next 1,000 years, the nuraghic people gradually withdrew to the island's highland fastnesses to avoid more disciplined and better-armed invaders. (Their only weapons, say the chroniclers, were stones and boulders hurled down from the hilltops.) Their civilization eventually succumbed when the Romans, following on the heels of Carthaginian invaders, conquered the island in the 3rd century BC. Artifacts from Nuraghic, Carthaginian, and Roman times make up the museum's collections. ⊠ *Cittadella dei Musei, Piazza Arsenale,* ☎ *070/655911.* ⊠ *4,000 lire.* ☉ *Daily 9–7.*

❸ The medieval **Tower of San Pancrazio,** which was part of the imposing
❹ Pisan defenses, is just outside the archaeological museum. The **Tower of the Elephant,** twin to that of San Pancrazio, is at the seaward end of the bastions. **Piazza Palazzo,** at the top of Via Martini, is where you'll find
❺ the **cathedral,** which has been extensively rebuilt and restored. The tiers of columns on the facade echo those of medieval Pisan churches, but only the center portal is an authentic relic of that era. All around the church are the narrow streets of the Spanish quarter, where humble dwellings still open directly onto the sidewalk and the wash is hung out to dry on elaborate wrought-iron balconies. This is the most interesting part of the city, so take time to wander through it.

❻ The Bastion of St. Remy, better known as the **Terrazza Umberto I,** is a monumental neoclassic staircase and arcade was added in the 19th century to the bastion built by the Spaniards 400 years earlier. It offers a magnificent view over the city and port, the sandy beaches, and the lagoons shimmering in the sun that are characteristic of the landscape around Cagliari and Oristano. Sunset, viewed from the Terrazza Umberto I, can be a memorable sight. It is at the southern tip of the old city.

❼ Cagliari has a **Roman amphitheater** (below the Museo Archeologico), some very old churches, and a few good restaurants near the waterfront (☞ Dining and Lodging, *below*), but once you have seen the main attractions, you will probably be ready to explore the surrounding areas.

Dining and Lodging

$$$ ✕ **Dal Corsaro.** This popular restaurant just by the waterfront is one of the island's most commended eating places, so reservations are essential. The decor is informal, in tune with the cordial welcome. The menu features seafood and meat specialties, such as seafood antipasto and porcheddu, and the wine list is exceptional. ⊠ *Viale Regina Margherita 28,* ☎ *070/664318. AE, DC, MC, V. Closed Sun., Aug., and 1 week at Christmas.*

$$ ✕ **Il Gatto.** "The Cat," near the train station and the central Piazza del Carmine, is popular with locals. Follow their lead and make sure you have reservations because the restaurant can fill up quickly. It serves some of the best Sardinian seafood, such as the risotto with shellfish, but for a change of pace try the gnocchi *alla gorgonzola* (with gorgonzola cheese). ⊠ *Viale Trieste 15,* ☎ *070/663596. Reservations essential. AE, DC, MC, V. Closed Sat. lunch and Sun.*

$$$ 🏨 **Panorama.** Presenting an obtrusive and unprepossessing exterior, this useful hotel in downtown Cagliari is geared toward the business class. Rooms are functional, spacious, and comfortable: Try to reserve one on the upper of the nine floors and enjoy the view over the harbor and bay. Rates are low in the category. ⊠ *Viale Armando Diaz 231,* ☎ *070/307691, *FAX* 070/305413. 97 rooms with bath or shower. Restaurant, bar, pool, meeting rooms. AE, DC, MC, V.*

$$ 🏨 **Moderno.** A good overnight stop, the Moderno is convenient to the train station and the harbor, but don't expect atmosphere or more than adequate comfort. In compensation, rates are at the lower end of the category. ⊠ *Via Roma 159,* ☎ *070/660286, *FAX* 070/660260. 93 rooms with bath or shower. AE, DC, MC, V.*

Nightlife and the Arts

The **Feste del Mare** (Festivals of the Sea) is held each year on the first Sunday in April. The **Festa di Sant'Efisio** (May 1) offers a chance to take part in a festival of Sardinian folklore.

Cagliari's **university** (⊠ Via Università) has concerts throughout the academic year.

Outdoor Activities and Sports

For information on obtaining a fishing license, write to **Assessorato Regionale alla Difesa dell'Ambiente** (⊠ Via Biasi 7/9, 09100, Cagliari, ☎ 070/606–6620).

Shopping

The best place in Cagliari to get an idea of what's available is at **ISOLA** (⊠ Via Bacaredda 148, ☎ 070/400707), a government-sponsored exhibition of artisanal crafts where most of the work is for sale.

| OFF THE BEATEN PATH | **SAN SPERATE** – Practically every wall in this town outside of Cagliari has been brightened with *murales* (mural paintings) by local artists and some well-known Italian painters, transforming the entire town into an open-air art gallery. |

Villasimius

⑧ *50 km (31 mi) east of Cagliari.*

The eastern route takes you through some dismal industrial suburbs on the road that leads to the scenic coast and beaches of Capo Boi and Capo Carbonara; **Villasimius** ranks as the chief resort here.

Pula

⑨ *30 km (19 mi) south of Cagliari.*

The area southwest of the capital has its share of fine scenery and good beaches—resort villages sprawl along the coast, and the Is Molas championship golf course near **Pula** has won tributes from Tom Watson, Jack Nicklaus, and other professionals of the sport. On the marshy shoreline between Cagliari Airport and Pula, huge flocks of flamingos are a common sight.

★ The real attraction here is archaeological: On a narrow promontory less than 3 kilometers (2 miles) outside the town of Pula is **Nora,** the site of a Phoenician, then Carthaginian and, later, Roman settlement. Extensive excavations here have shed light on life in this ancient city from the 8th century BC onward. Many of the exhibits in Cagliari's archaeological museum were found here. An old Roman road passes the moss-covered ruins of temples, an amphitheater, and a small Roman theater. You can make out the channels through which hot air rose to warm the Roman baths; watch for the difference between the simple mosaic pavements laid by the Carthaginians and the more elaborate designs of the Romans. Taking in the views from Nora, you can see why the Phoenicians chose the site for settlement. They always scouted for locations with good harbors, cliffs to shelter their craft from the wind, and a position such as a promontory, from which they could defend themselves from attack. If the sea is calm, look under the clear waters along the shore for more ruins of the ancient city, submerged by earthquakes, rough seas, and erosion. ⊠ *Free.* ☉ *Excavations open daily 9–8 (9–6 in winter).*

While you are in the area, visit the small **archaeological museum,** with finds from the Nora site, in the nearby village of Pula. ⊠ *Corso Vittorio Emanuele 67, Pula,* ☎ *070/920–9610.* ⊠ *4,000 lire.* ☉ *Daily 9–8 (9–6 in winter).*

| NEED A BREAK? | Take advantage of the coastal location to have a seafood lunch at **Urru** (⊠ Via Tirso). Grilled fish specials depend on the day's catch. |

The hotels and beaches that cater to the summer hotel trade around Nora are concentrated a couple of miles south of the town, in a conglomeration of hotels that is the town of **Santa Marherita di Pula.** Guests at any of the hotels can avail of the international-standard Is Molas golf course here. Apart from this, little is open during the winter, and most of the best beaches are for the private use of hotel guests.

Lodging

$$$$ ⭐ 🏨 **Is Morus.** A luxurious enclave, the Is Morus is on a sandy cove and offers all the amenities of a fine beach resort, with low, attractive buildings shaded by pinewoods, plus the option (for guests taking half- or full-board) of golfing at the fine Is Molas course, about 11 kilometers (7 miles) away. ✉ *Santa Margherita,* ☎ *070/921171,* FAX *070/921596. 85 rooms with bath or shower. Restaurant, bar, pool, miniature golf, tennis court, beach. AE, DC, MC, V. Closed Nov.–Easter.*

$$$ 🏨 **Flamingo.** Also directly on the beach and in a shady setting, this resort hotel features a main building and several two-story cottages nestled among the eucalyptus trees. ✉ *Santa Margherita,* ☎ *070/920–8361,* FAX *070/920–8359. 134 rooms with bath or shower. Restaurant, piano bar, pool, tennis court, miniature golf, dance club, parking. AE. Closed Oct. 10–May.*

Outdoor Activities and Sports

Golfers can avail of the 18-hole **Is Molas** course (☎ 070/920–9165); the adjacent Is Molas Golf Hotel (☎ 070/924–1006) offers special golfing vacations.

OFF THE BEATEN PATH   **SANT'EFISIO –** The little Romanesque church of Sant'Efisio, at the base of the Nora promontory, plays a part in one of the island's most colorful annual events. Efisio, the patron saint of Sardinia, was a 3rd-century Roman soldier who converted to Christianity. A procession in early May accompanies a statue of the saint all the way from Cagliari and back again. The processional round-trip takes four days, with festive stops along the way, and culminates in a parade down Cagliari's main avenue that rivals the St. Patrick's Day parade in New York. If you're in Sardinia from May 1 to May 4, don't miss it.

Sant'Antioco

🔟 *92 km (57 mi) west of Cagliari.*

Off the southwest coast is **Sant'Antioco,** one of two islands that is a popular picnic spot with good beaches. You can drive over a causeway to get on the island, where the most hectic activity seems to be the silent repairing of nets by local fishermen who have already handled their daily catch.

Shopping

Visitors can stock up on local handicrafts at **ISOLA,** on Lungomare Vespucci.

OFF THE BEATEN PATH   **CARBONIA AND IGLESIAS –** Considering that all Sardinia is off the beaten track for most tourists, practically everything you do or see here comprises the unusual. But if your curiosity prods you to even more esoteric experiences, you could go just inland of Sant'Antioco to explore the rugged, once-booming mining country around Carbonia, a town built by Mussolini in 1938 to serve as an administrative center for the coal miners and their families. With its overpowering fascist architecture, it has been called an urban UFO set down in the Sardinian landscape. Nearby Iglesias is an authentic Sardinian town, with a medieval cathedral; traveling east past Domusnovas on the Cagliari-Iglesias high-way, you can detour and drive right through an immense cave, the **Grotta di San Giovanni.**

San Pietro

⑪ *5 km (3 mi) northwest of Sant'Antioco.*

A ferry at the small northern port of Calasetta connects Sant'Antioco with the smaller island of **San Pietro.** This is a favorite of wealthy Cagliarians, many of whom have built weekend cottages here.

THE BARE AND THE BEAUTIFUL
From Barumini to the Costa Smeralda

A more traditional—and wild—Sardinia awaits the traveler who ventures into the mountainous inland of the island. The Italian film directors, the Taviani brothers, made the hinterland of the Barbagia region, where traditional Sardinian customs are maintained in remote hilltop villages, the subject of an extraordinary portrait of rural life among the sheepherders of the area, *Padre Padrone.* Inland Sardinians are a hardy people, used to living in a climate that is as unforgiving in winter as it is intolerable in summer. Old traditions, including the vendetta, are firmly rooted in the social fabric of this mountainous land that is both barren and beautiful. Here, rare species of wildlife share the rocky uplands with sturdy medieval churches and mysterious nuraghi—ancient stone citadels left by prehistoric people. Oristano, the medieval center of Sardinian nationalism, is on the island's west coast and makes a good center for exploring this region.

As you move northward the timeless beauty of the landscape begins to show greater sign of 20th century development, such as the sunny resort of Alghero, the Spanish-influenced port on the west coast that is now a favorite retreat for wealthy Sardinians, and the Costa Smeralda, the luxury resort complex developed by the Aga Khan on the northeast corner of Sardinia, which, in the '60s and '70s was, along with the Côte d'Azur, *the* place to spend a summer and a sum. Although not as popular with the international jet set as it once was, it is nonetheless still one of Europe's premier vacation spots.

Su Nuraxi

★ **⑫** *60 km (37 mi) north of Cagliari.*

It is worth making a detour to the fascinating nuraghe of **Su Nuraxi,** off the main road outside the quiet little town of **Barumini.** You could spend hours clambering over this extraordinary structure of concentric rings of stone walls, chambers, passages, wells, and beehive tower; it's a good idea to take a flashlight along for peering into dark corners. This nuraghe is probably about half its original height, and some of the smaller towers around the main one have been reduced by pillaging and erosion to mere circles of stones on the ground. The nuraghi were fortified villages, prehistoric versions of medieval walled towns and the forts of the American West. Though this particular type of construction is unique to Sardinia, similar buildings dating from the same era are found in other parts of the Mediterranean, such as Cyprus and the Balearic islands off Spain. Of the 7,000 nuraghi on Sardinia, Su Nuraxi is the most impressive, with those of Sant'Antine and Losa, both

near Macomer, close runners-up. ⊠ *1 km (½ mi) west of Barumini.* 🖼
Free. ⊙ *Daily 9–1, 4–sunset.*

Giara di Gesturi

⓭ *8 km north of Barumini, 68 km (42 mi) north of Cagliari.*

The **Giara di Gesturi** is a basalt plateau that is home to some of the island's more exotic wildlife, including a species of wild dwarf horse. Another rare species to be found in the Giara is the mouflon, a wild sheep distinguishable from its domesticated counterpart by its long curving horns and skittishness when confronted by any human, however well intentioned. Long hunted for their decorative horns, the mouflon are now an endangered species, with only a few surviving on Sardinia and neighboring Corsica.

Oristano

⓮ *93 km (58 mi) northwest of Cagliari, 89 km (56 mi) southwest of Nuoro, 120 km (75 mi) south of Sassari.*

Oristano, on the west coast of the island, shone in the Middle Ages, when it was capital of the Giudicato of Arborea, an independent duchy led by Sardinia's own Joan-of-Arc-type heroine, Eleanora di Arborea. In the 14th century, Eleanora inherited the difficult task of defending the duchy's freedom, constantly undermined by the superior military might of the Spanish troops from Aragon. Although the duchy eventually reverted to Aragonese rule, Eleanora made a lasting contribution to Sardinia by implementing a code of law that was adopted throughout the island and remained in effect until Sardinia's unification with Italy in 1847. Now an important but slow-paced agricultural center, Oristano is the scene of livestock fairs and a rousing series of horse races, called Sa Sartiglia, marking the end of the Carnival season in February.

NEED A
BREAK?   Join the locals at the **Forchetta d'Oro** (⊠ Via Giovanni XXIII 8) for a
                 lunch of pasta with cuttlefish sauce.

Dining and Lodging

$$$ ✕ **Il Faro.** Locals and visiting gourmets consider this elegant restau-
★   rant to be one of the best in the area, as it offers authentic and well-
      prepared local dishes that change with the season. There's *capretto allo
      spiedo* (spit-roasted goat) in the winter and an aromatic *zuppa di fave*
      (fava bean soup with bacon and fennel) in the spring. Seafood is fea-
      tured throughout the year. ⊠ *Via Bellini 25,* ☎ *0783/70002. AE, DC,
      MC, V. Closed Sun. evening and Jan. 1–15, July 1–15.*

$$ ✕ **Salvatore.** In this classic seafood restaurant you can sample seafood
    from the tidal ponds of Cabras and Santa Giusta just outside Oristano.
    Specialties are spaghetti *alla bottarga* (with smoked fish roe) and grilled
    anguilla (eel). ⊠ *Via Carbonia 1,* ☎ *0783/357134. MC, V. Closed Sun.
    evening.*

$ 🏨 **Cama.** Located near the train station, the hotel is also within walk-
    ing distance of Oristano's interesting old town center. A parking lot
    and garage make it convenient for drivers. Another feature is air-con-
    ditioning, not always found in hotels of this category. ⊠ *Via Vittorio
    Veneto 119,* ☎ *0783/74374,* 🖷 *0783/74375. 54 rooms with shower.
    Restaurant, bar. MC, V.*

OFF THE BEATEN PATH   **CABRAS –** 10 kilometers (6 miles) west of Oristano, you can see the extensive marshlands where fishermen pole round-bottomed rush boats through shallow ponds teeming with eel and crayfish.

THARROS – The ruins of this Carthaginian city are along the road marked San Giovanni di Sinis; its position afforded it a strategic view over scenic Sinis peninsula. Like Nora to the south (☞ *above*), the site was chosen because it commanded the best views of the harbor and could provide an easy escape route if inland tribes threatened. It is 10 kilometers (6 miles) west of Cabras and 20 kilometers (12 miles) west of Oristano.

Nightlife and the Arts

The Sartiglia festival, on the last Sunday of Carnival season, includes rich costumes and a ritual joust. Each summer, the town holds an **arts-and-crafts** exhibition, with local foods and wines given prominence. Contact the tourist office (☞ Contacts and Resources *in* Sardinia A to Z, *below*) for information.

Shopping

Ceramics are featured in the small craft shops in Oristano.

En Route   On your way to Tharros, you'll pass the ghost town of **San Salvatore**, revived briefly in the 1960s as a location for spaghetti westerns and since abandoned. The saloon of the movie set still stands. Farther along, among the dunes, are large rush huts formerly used by fishermen and now much in demand as back-to-nature vacation homes. The 5th-century church of **San Giovanni di Sinis,** also on the peninsula, is the oldest Christian church in Sardinia.

Nuoro

⑮   *89 km (56 mi) northeast of Oristano, 181 km (113 mi) north of Cagliari.*

The provincial capital of **Nuoro** presents a somewhat shabby air, located on the edge of a gorge in the harsh mountainous area that culminates in **Gennargentu,** the island's highest massif (6,000 feet). The only things likely to interest you in Nuoro are the views from the park on Sant'Onofrio hill and the exhibits in the **Museo della Vita e delle Tradizioni Popolari Sarde** (Museum of Sardinian Life and Folklore), where you can see local costumes, domestic and agricultural implements, and traditional jewelry. ✉ *Via Mereu 56,* ☎ *0784/31426.* 🎫 *3,000 lire.* ⊙ *Daily 9–1 and 3–7.*

Make an excursion a few kilometers (two miles) east to **Mt. Ortobene** (2,900 feet), for some dizzying views over the gulch below Nuoro. Here you can also see up close the imposing statue of Christ the Redeemer that overlooks the city. Picnic tables make this a handy spot for an alfresco lunch stop.

OFF THE BEATEN PATH   **ORGOSOLO –** This old center of banditry halfway between Nuoro and Fonni is still a poor and largely depopulated village, but the houses have been daubed with *murales* (mural paintings) by local artists and some well-known Italian painters, transforming the entire town into an open-air art gallery.

Dining and Lodging

$$$ ✕🏨 **Su Gologone.** Despite attracting tourists in droves, this bustling coun-
★   try inn still manages to maintain a friendly atmosphere. If you don't want to stay here, the restaurant alone is worth a detour for an authentic Sardinian meal. The island specialties include *maccarones de busa* (thick homemade pasta), culingiones, porcheddu, and sebadas. Wash it all down with the local wine, Vernaccia. The hotel organizes riding and trekking

expeditions. ✉ *Località Su Gologone,* ☎ *0784/287512,* 🖷 *0784/287668.*
65 rooms with bath or shower. Restaurant, bar, pool, tennis court, mini-
golf. AE, DC, MC, V. Closed Nov.–Mar.

Nightlife and the Arts

The **Festa del Redentore** (Feast of the Redeemer) is held on the next-
to-last Sunday in August.

Wooden masks, made for local festivals, make unusual souvenirs.

Fonni

🔟 *30 km (19 mi) south of Nuoro.*

Fonni, in the heart of the **Barbagia** region, is the highest town on the
island and a good base for excursions by car to all sites of interest in
this mountainous district that is Sardinia's most primitive district, as
well as the Monte Spada and the Bruncu Spina refuge on the Gennargentu Massif. Life in some villages seems not to have changed much
since the Middle Ages. Here a rigidly patriarchal society perpetuates
the unrelenting practice of vendetta, and strangers are advised to mind
their own business. Tortuous roads wind and loop their way through
the landscape; towns are small and undistinguished, their social fabric seemingly impervious to the 20th century. On feast days elaborate
regional costumes are taken out of mothballs and worn as an explicit
statement of community identity.

You can see one of the most characteristic of the Barbagia's celebrations in local costume in Fonni on the Feast of St. John, June 24.

OFF THE
BEATEN PATH
ARBATAX – If you have the stamina, take the rickety old train that runs on
a single-gauge track between Cagliari and Arbatax, midway up the east
coast. If all goes well, it takes about nine hours to cover the approximately 250 kilometers (155 miles) of track, guaranteeing you a look at
a Sardinia few tourists ever see. The train rattles up into the Barbagia
district through some breathtaking mountain scenery, then eases down
into the desert landscape inland of Arbatax, where the trip ends on the
dock next to the fishing boats. The train is run by the Ferrovie Comple-
mentari, and the ticket costs less than 15,000 lire. For information, call
☎ 070/491304.

Shopping

Aritzo. This mountain village a couple of miles south of Fonni, high up
in the Barbagia, produces handcrafted wooden utensils and furniture.

Tonara. Special candies are made from honey and nougat and sold in
this hilltop town southwest of Fonni.

En Route Head west on road 129 from Nuoro to Bosa, where you turn right into
hilly and arid scrub country, with its abundance of cactus and juniper.
Pines and olive trees shelter low buildings from the steady winds that
make these parts ideal for sailing and unfit for agriculture. About the
only cash crop here is cork from the cork trees dotting the landscape.
Yet in the low valleys and along the riverbeds, masses of oleander bloom
in the summer, creating avenues of color.

Alghero

🔟 *34 km (21 mi) southwest of Sassari.*

Among the larger centers on the northwest coast is **Alghero,** which is
an appealing walled town with a distinctly Spanish flavor. It was built
and inhabited in the 14th century by the Aragonese and Catalans, who

constructed seaside ramparts and sturdy towers encompassing an inviting nucleus of narrow, winding streets. Rich, wrought-iron scrollwork decorates balconies and screens windows; Spanish motifs appear in stone portals and in bell towers. The dialect spoken here is a version of Catalan, not Italian: Locals would find it easier to converse in Barcelona than in Rome. Alghero is a popular resort, near broad sandy beaches and the spectacular heights of **Capo Caccia,** an imposing limestone headland to the west. At the base of the sheer cliff, the pounding sea has carved an entrance to the vast **Grotto of Neptune,** a fantastic cavern, which you must visit with a guide. By land, you reach the entrance at the base of the cliff by descending the more than 600 steps of the aptly named *escala del cabirol* (mountain goat's stairway), a dizzying enterprise—and the ascent is just as daunting. The excursion by sea is much less fatiguing, but is not possible when seas are rough. Boats leave the port of Alghero four times daily, or every hour or so in peak season, and the journey takes three hours. 🎫 *10,000 lire.* ⊙ *Daily June–Sept., 8–7; Oct., 10–5; Nov.–Mar., 8–2; Apr.–May, 9–5. Tours start on the hr. By Boat: Navisarda,* ☎ *079/975599. Fare: 14,000 lire;* 🎫 *to grotto: 3,000 lire. Daily Apr.–Oct.*

NEED A BREAK?   Hungry landlubbers need go only **Dieci Metri** (✉ Vicolo Adami 47, off Via Roma), from the center of Alghero for a nourishing meal of seafood and local wine.

Dining and Lodging

$$ ✕ **La Lepanto.** White stucco and wrought-iron grilles set a Spanish tone in Alghero's top seafood restaurant. The specialty is aragosta cooked in a variety of ways, including *alla catalana* (with tomato and onions). For starters, try risotto *nero di seppia* (with cuttlefish sauce). ✉ *Via Carlo Alberto 133,* ☎ *079/979116. AE, DC, MC, V. Closed Mon. Oct.–May.*

$ ✕ **Da Pietro.** On a narrow street in the picturesque old town near Largo San Francesco, this seafood restaurant has vaulted ceilings and a bustling atmosphere. The menu features *bucatini all'algherese* (pasta with a sauce of clams, capers, and tomatoes) and baked fish with white wine sauce; there are some meat dishes, too. ✉ *Via Ambrogio Machin 18,* ☎ *079/979645. AE, DC, MC, V. Closed Wed. Oct.–May and 2 wks at Christmas.*

$$$ 🏨 **Carlos V (Carlos Quinto).** Located on the shore boulevard about a kilometer (half mile) from the center of town, this hillside hotel is modern but attractive, with porticoes and terraces, one of which has a swimming pool. Smallish but bright rooms all have a balcony, many with a sea view. Low season rates are a bargain. ✉ *Lungomare Valencia 24,* ☎ *079/979501,* FAX *079/980298. 110 rooms with bath or shower. Restaurant, tennis courts. AE, MC, V.*

$$$ 🏨 **Villa Las Tronas.** The villa is a former royal mansion on a rocky bluff above the sea but still near the center of town. It has a turn-of-the-century atmosphere, modern comforts, and great views across the water to the old town. Rates are at the lower end of this category. ✉ *Lungomare Valencia 1,* ☎ *079/981818,* FAX *079/981044. 29 rooms in main building, all with bath or shower. Restaurant (summer only), pool, exercise room, private beach. AE, DC, MC, V.*

$ 🏨 **San Francesco.** Centrally located in Alghero's Spanish quarter, this hotel occupies the convent that was once attached to the church of San Francesco. The rooms are grouped around the 14th-century cloister and, though somewhat cramped, are modern and quiet. Breakfast is

included in the price. ✉ *Via Machin 2,* ☎ *079/980330,* FAX *079/980330.*
21 rooms with shower. Bar, meeting rooms. MC, V.

Shopping
Coral, still harvested in the bay, and **gold jewelry** are the traditional
handicrafts.

Sassari

⑱ *34 km (21 mi) northeast of Alghero, 212 km (132 mi) north of Cagliari.*

Inland **Sassari** is important as a university town and administrative center. It has little to interest a visitor other than an old and ornate cathedral and an archaeological museum. Sassari is the hub of several
highways and secondary roads leading to various scenic coastal resorts,
among them Stintino and Castelsardo (☞ *below*).

Castelsardo

⑲ *32 km (20 mi) northeast of Sassari.*

The walled seaside citadel of **Castelsardo** is a delight for basket lovers.
Roadside stands and shops in the old town sell tons of island handicrafts: rugs, wrought iron, and baskets—in myriad shapes and colors.

Shopping
There is an **ISOLA** workshop on Lungomare Colombo, where local handicrafts can be bought. The local specialty is a brightly colored basket
made of dwarf palms.

Santa Teresa di Gallura

⑳ *68 km (42 mi) northeast of Castelsardo, 65 km (41 mi) northwest of
Olbia.*

At the northern tip of Sardinia, **Santa Teresa di Gallura** has the relaxed,
carefree air of an authentic fishing-village-turned-resort.

Dining and Lodging
$$ ✕▥ **Canne al Vento.** This cheerful, family-run hotel and restaurant on
★ the edge of town is a popular choice. The restaurant specializes in au-
thentic island cuisine, for example zuppa *cuata* (bread, cheese, and
tomato soup), porcheddu, or seafood. The guest rooms, all equipped
with TV and telephone, fall into the $ category. ✉ *Via Nazionale 23,*
☎ *0789/754219,* FAX *0789/754948. 22 rooms with shower. MC, V.
Closed Mon. (except summer) and Oct.–Apr.*

$$$–$$$$ ▥ **Grand Hotel Corallaro.** Recently overhauled and enlarged, this hotel
offers comfortable, pleasing accommodations in a panoramic spot
overlooking the sea, not far from the center of town. ✉ *Via Nazionale
85,* ☎ *0789/755475,* FAX *0789/755431. 81 rooms with bath or shower.
Restaurant, pool, Turkish bath, exercise room. AE, DC, MC, V.*

La Maddalena

㉑ *30 km (19 mi) east of Santa Teresa di Gallura, 45 km (20 mi) north-
west of Olbia.*

From the port of Palau you can visit the archipelago of **La Maddalena,**
seven granite islands embellished with lush green scrub and wind-bent
pines. Pilgrims pay homage to Garibaldi's tomb on the grounds of his
hideaway on Caprera, one of the islands.

Porto Cervo

★ ㉒   *30 km (19 mi) north of Olbia.*

Sardinia's northeastern coast is fringed with low cliffs, inlets, and small bays. This landscape has become an upscale vacationland, with glossy resorts, such as Baia Sardinia and Porto Rotondo, just outside the confines of the famed Costa Smeralda, developed by the Aga Khan, who accidentally discovered its charms—and potential—in 1965, when his yacht took shelter here from a storm. The Costa Smeralda is still dominated by his personality; its attractions remain geared to those who can measure themselves by the yardstick of his fabled riches. Sardinia's most expensive hotels are here, and the world's most magnificent yachts anchor in the waters of **Porto Cervo.** The trend has been to keep this enclave of the really rich an exclusive haven, by encouraging more multimillionaires to build discreetly luxurious villas, and planning four more golf courses to be built for them.

All along the coast, carefully tended lush vegetation surrounds vacation villages and elaborate villa colonies that have sprung up over the past decade in a range of spurious architectural styles best described as bogus-Mediterranean.

Lodging

$$$$ 🏨 **Cala di Volpe.** Long a magnet for the jet set, this establishment was built to resemble an ancient Sardinian village. The hotel's decor is rustic-elegant, with beamed ceilings, Sardinian arts and crafts, and porticoes overlooking the sea. The presidential suite in the highest tower has a private pool. ⊠ *Cala di Volpe,* ☎ *0789/96083,* 𝙵𝙰𝚇 *0789/96442. 123 rooms and suites with bath or shower. Restaurant, bar, air-conditioning, pool, 3 tennis courts, private beach. AE, DC, MC, V. Closed Oct.–mid-May.*

$$$$ 🏨 **Cervo.** Low Mediterranean buildings surround a large swimming pool and garden in the heart of the Costa Smeralda's Porto Cervo. This complex is next to the marina and piazzetta (small piazza) and is popular with people who like to be seen. The rooms are large and most have a terrace. ⊠ *Porto Cervo,* ☎ *0789/92003,* 𝙵𝙰𝚇 *0789/92593. 90 rooms with bath or shower. Restaurant, piano bar, air-conditioning, pool, private beach. AE, DC, MC, V. Closed Oct.–Easter.*

$$$ 🏨 **Nibaru.** In a secluded inlet set in lush gardens, this hotel enjoys all the best features of the Costa Smeralda at comparatively low rates. Guests are just a few yards from the sea and some superb swimming spots and also within easy access to the Pevero Golf Club and the tennis courts of Porto Cervo. The buildings here are pinkish-red brick with tiled roofs. Each room has a balcony and view of the sea. ⊠ *Cala di Volpe,* ☎ *0789/96038,* 𝙵𝙰𝚇 *0789/96474. 45 rooms with bath. Restaurant, bar, pool. AE, DC, MC, V. Closed Oct.–May.*

Outdoor Activities and Sports

An 18-hole, world-class golf course designed by Robert Trent Jones is on the Bay of Pevero, near Porto Cervo (☎ 0789/96210).

Shopping

Contemporary **pottery** utilizing traditional motifs sells well, especially among the rich along the Costa Smeralda.

Olbia

㉓   *30 km (19 mi) south of Costa Smeralda, 106 km (66 mi) north of Nuoro.*

Set amid the resorts of Sardinia's northeastern coast, **Olbia** is a lively little seaport, not heavily industrialized, at the head of a long, wide bay.

Lodging

$$–$$$ 🏨 **De Plam.** Though aesthetically unimpressive, this seafront hotel can at least boast the best views in Olbia. The rooms are furnished in a motel style that is functional if not particularly memorable. The location is convenient to the port (though still a taxi ride away), and the town center is reached via a short walk. ⊠ *Via de Filippi 33,* ☎ *0789/ 25777,* FAX *0789/22648. 60 rooms with bath or shower. Restaurant, bar, air-conditioning, meeting rooms. AE, DC, MC, V.*

Shopping

ISOLA, the government-run artisana workshop with work for sale is at Corso Umberto 28.

Golfo Aranci

㉔ *19 km (12 mi) northeast of Oristano.*

At the mouth of the Gulf of Olbia, **Golfo Aranci** is a blossoming resort and debarkation point for FS ferries from the mainland.

SARDINIA A TO Z

Arriving and Departing

By Boat

Large modern ferries run by Tirrenia Lines, Navarma Lines, and the FS (Italian State Railways) connect the island with the mainland. **Tirrenia** (Rome, ☎ 06/474–2041 and 06/474–2242; Genoa, 010/258041; Naples, 081/761–3688) sails to several ports in Sardinia from Genoa, Civitavecchia, Naples, Palermo, and Trapani. **Navarma** (☎ 0565/9361) transports passengers and cars between Livorno and Olbia. **FS** ferries (☎ 0766/23273 on the mainland, or ☎ 0789/46800 in Golfo Aranci) carry trains as well as passengers and cars; they sail from Civitavecchia to Golfo Aranci, near Olbia. The Civitavecchia–Olbia/Golfo Aranci run takes about eight hours and there are overnight sailings. Depending on the season, the service is scheduled two or three times a week; reservations are essential in the summer.

By Plane

Alitalia and Alisarda connect Rome, Milan, Pisa, and other cities on the mainland and in southern Europe with Sardinia. Flying is by far the fastest and easiest way to get to the island. The Rome–Cagliari flight takes about an hour. Sardinia's major airports are at Cagliari and Alghero, with another, smaller one, at Olbia, providing access to the Costa Smeralda.

Cagliari Airport (☎ 070/240047) at Elmas is about 6 kilometers (4 miles) from the center of town, and there is a regular bus service from the airport to Piazza Matteotti, in front of the train station.

Alghero's **Fertilia Airport** (☎ 079/935124) is 13 kilometers (8 miles) from the city. A bus links the airport with the air terminal on Corso Vittorio Emanuele II.

Costa Smeralda Airport (☎ 0789/52600) is 4 kilometers (2½ miles) outside Olbia.

Getting Around

By Bus

Cagliari is linked with the other towns of Sardinia by a network of buses. Local destinations are served by **ARST** (☎ 070/40981), and the major cities, excluding Olbia, by **PANI** (☎ 070/652326). The heart of the Sardinian bus system is the **Stazione Autolinee** in Cagliari's Piazza Matteotti, across the square from the main tourist office. You can pick up a schedule and route map from either of these sources; if you can't find a convenient bus service, you can go to the west side of the square to the main train station. City buses in Cagliari and Sassari operate on the same system as those on the mainland: Buy your ticket first, at a tobacco shop or machine, and cancel it on the bus by slipping it into the machine until the ticket is punched. Fares are low for these local services, about 1,300 lire.

By Car
The best way to get around Sardinia is to drive. The roads are generally in good condition, but bear in mind that such roadside conveniences as gas stations and refreshment stands are infrequent on some routes, especially in the east. Cars may be taken on board most of the ferry lines connecting Sardinia with the mainland.

By Train
There are fairly good connections between Olbia, Cagliari, Sassari, and Oristano. You can reach Nuoro via Macomer; Alghero is reached via Sassari. Service on the few other local lines is infrequent and slow. The fastest train between Olbia and Cagliari takes more than four hours. A local train connects Golfo Aranci, the FS port for the train ferry, with Olbia and takes 20 minutes.

Contacts and Resources

Car Rental
Cagliari. Avis (⊠ train station, ☎ 070/668128; airport, ☎ 070/240081). **Hertz** (⊠ Piazza Matteotti 1, ☎ 070/668105; airport, ☎ 070/240037).

Olbia. Avis (⊠ Via Genova 67, ☎ 0789/22420; airport, ☎ 0789/69540). **Hertz** (⊠ Via Regina Elena 34, ☎ 0789/21733; airport, ☎ 0789/66024).

Sassari. Avis (⊠ Via Mazzini 2, ☎ 079/235547). **Hertz** (⊠ Corso Francesco Vico, ☎ 079/232184). **Maggiore** (⊠ Viale Italia 3, ☎ 079/235507).

Emergencies
Police (☎ 112, 113). **Hospital** (Cagliari, ☎ 070/543266). **Ambulance** (Cagliari, ☎ 070/539925).

Late-Night Pharmacies. On a rotating basis: Information on current schedules is pinned up on any pharmacy door or can be obtained by phoning (☎ 192).

Guided Tours
HORSEBACK RIDING
The **Associazione Nazionale di Turismo Equestre** (⊠ Via Carso 35a, Sassari, ☎ 079/299889) can provide information on renting mounts and joining riding parties with itineraries along the coast or into the heart of the island. The **Centro Vacanze Alabirdi** at Arborea, near Oristano (☎ 0783/800512) and the **Centro Vacanze Su Gologone** at Oliena (☎ 0784/287512) offer riding vacations.

ORIENTATION
The following guided tours are good introductions to Sardinia; all include travel from the Italian mainland, as well as travel and accommodations on Sardinia. They should be booked through a travel agent.

Chiariva offers two group tours of Sardinia by bus with guide. A nineday tour leaves from Genoa; an eight-day tour departs from Rome. Both operate from April to September.

Aviatour has a similar eight-day tour leaving from either Milan or Rome. The tour also runs from April to September only.

Appian Line can arrange a fly-drive package on the Costa Smeralda; transportation is by air, the rental car is picked up at the airport at Olbia. Accommodations are in good, but not outlandishly expensive, hotels on this famous coastline for the rich.

Travel Agency
Cagliari (✉ Viaggi Orru, ✉ *Via Roma 95*, ☎ *070/659858*).

Visitor Information
Alghero (✉ Piazza Porta Terra 9, ☎ 079/979054). **Cagliari** (✉ Piazza Matteotti, ☎ 070/669255; Piazza Deffenu 9, ☎ 070/651698 or 167/013153 [toll-free]; Elmas Airport, ☎ 070/240200). **Nuoro** (✉ Piazza Italia 19, ☎ 0784/30083). **Olbia** (✉ Via Catello Piro, ☎ 0789/21453; City Hall, Golfo Aranci, ☎ 0789/21672 [summer only]; Costa Smeralda Airport, ☎ 0789/21453). **Oristano** (✉ Via Cagliari 278, ☎ 0783/74191). **Sassari** (✉ Via Viale Umberto 72, ☎ 079/233534).

INDEX

NOTES

Escape to ancient cities and

journey to  *exotic islands with*

CNN Travel Guide, a wealth of valuable advice. Host

Valerie Voss will take you to

all of your favorite destinations,

including those off the beaten

path. Tune-in to your passport to the world.

CNN TRAVEL GUIDE
SATURDAY 12:30 PMET   SUNDAY 4:30 PMET

CNN ✈
Airport Network

Your
Window
To The
World
While You're
On The
Road

Keep in touch when you're traveling. Before you take off, tune in to CNN Airport Network. Now available in major airports across America, CNN Airport Network provides nonstop news, sports, business, weather and lifestyle programming. Both domestic and international. All piloted by the top-flight global resources of CNN. All up-to-the minute reporting. And just for travelers, CNN Airport Network features two daily Fodor's specials. "Travel Fact" provides enlightening, useful travel trivia, while "What's Happening" covers upcoming events in major cities worldwide. So why be bored waiting to board? **TIME FLIES WHEN YOU'RE WATCHING THE WORLD THROUGH THE WINDOW OF CNN AIRPORT NETWORK!**

WHEREVER YOU TRAVEL, *H*ELP IS NEVER FAR AWAY.

From planning your trip to providing travel assistance along the way, American Express® Travel Service Offices are always there to help.

Italy

Bigtours Travel Service (R)
Via Indipendenza 12
Bologna
51/224-923

American Express Company S.P.A.
Via Guicciardini 49/R
Florence
55/288-751

American Express Travel Service
Via Dante Alighieri 22R
Florence
55/509-81

Viatur SRL (R)
Piazza Fontane Marose 3
Genoa
10/561-241

American Express Travel Service
Via Brera 3
Milan
2/720-03-693

American Express Travel Service
Piazza Di Spagna 38
Rome
6/676-41

American Express Travel Service
1471 San Marco, San Moise
Venice
41/520-0844

Fabretto Viaggi E Turismo (R)
Corso Porta Nuova 11
Verona
45/800-9040

Travel

http://www.americanexpress.com/travel

American Express Travel Service Offices are found in central locations throughout Italy.